INTERNATIONAL COMMERCIAL ARBITRATION

A Transnational Perspective

Second Edition

By

Tibor Várady

*Professor of Law, Central European University, Budapest,
and Emory University School of Law*

John J. Barceló III

*William Nelson Cromwell Professor of International and
Comparative Law, Cornell Law School*

Arthur T. von Mehren

Story Professor of Law, Emeritus, Harvard Law School

AMERICAN CASEBOOK SERIES®

Mat #17790412

American Casebook Series and West Group are
registered trademarks used herein under license.

COPYRIGHT © 1999 WEST GROUP
COPYRIGHT © 2003 By WEST GROUP
            610 Opperman Drive
            P.O. Box 64526
            St. Paul, MN 55164–0526
            1–800–328–9352

ISBN 0–314–25235–5

TEXT IS PRINTED ON 10% POST
CONSUMER RECYCLED PAPER

*Dedicated to
Vera, Lucy, and Joan*

*

Preface to the First Edition

After several decades of accelerating change, enterprises the world over now conduct business on a dramatically more international scale. Producers contract with suppliers on several continents, and those producers, in turn, sell in global markets; service providers do business through branches and offshoot companies in several parts of the world; firms increasingly look abroad for merger partners and acquisition targets; distribution, franchise, and license networks readily span national borders. Because arbitration is frequently the dispute settlement method of choice for enterprises dealing with their counterparts in other countries—indeed, it has become the dominant method of settling international trade disputes—these changes have increased the importance of international commercial arbitration.

International commercial arbitration's increased importance in the modern world is only one of the reasons why the subject should become a regular part of law school curricula. It introduces students to matters of considerable importance and subtlety that are rarely—if ever—touched upon in other courses: the problems and potential of private dispute-resolution mechanisms that are not the creatures of any national law order but rather transnational or "anational" in character.

These materials draw upon legislation, court decisions, arbitral awards, and commentary from all parts of the world. Because of its truly transnational character, international commercial arbitration lends itself to this approach. The parties are from different countries; an arbitrator often has a different nationality from that of the other arbitrators and of the parties; the applicable law may be drawn from several legal systems; and once the award is rendered it is enforceable in any of the 116 parties [as of September, 2002, 132 parties] to the 1958 United Nations Convention on the Recognition and Enforcement of Foreign Arbitral Awards. Furthermore, the subject is becoming more and more "anational"; the arbitral tribunal is not created by and does not owe allegiance to any sovereign and is not bound—as a court would be—by the procedural or substantive law of the state in which it sits, or of any other state, unless the parties direct otherwise. Though contact with one or more national legal systems is inescapable, international commercial arbitration is never completely controlled by or contained within the confines of a single national system.

Our presentation of the subject follows in some respects a model that developed in American legal education during the twentieth century. In the early part of the century, many subjects—contracts, torts, civil procedure—were taught as regional or state-specific law. Technically, the law being studied and taught was generated by the legislature and courts of a single state of the United States. During the last two-thirds of the century, however, leading American law schools came to teach these courses as "national"—rather than state—subjects, despite the absence of truly national law in the technical sense. Course books in the United States now draw primary materials from all state systems and emphasize the subject's essential features, even though there may not be complete agreement among all 50 states of the United States. Examples of unique, important, or innovative solutions to special problems occurring in particular states are also introduced.

This basic model has guided us in developing these materials, but with a shift of focus, of course, from the "national" to the "transnational" level. For the approach to be successful there must be a considerable degree of global uniformity in the underlying legal concepts and solutions. Some variability among countries and legal systems, however, is tolerable, even enriching and enlightening. There is today considerable uniformity across national boundaries where international arbitration is concerned, largely because of the success of international agreements, among which the most important and the most prominent is the 1958 United Nations Convention on Recognition and Enforcement of Foreign Arbitral Awards. The work of the United Nations Commission on International Trade Law (UNCITRAL) in promulgating a model arbitration statute and model arbitration rules has also had a unifying effect.

Of course there are national differences, and these loom larger than the differences in tort or contract law that exist among the 50 states of the United States. Nevertheless, we believe the level of uniformity is quite sufficient to justify the transnational approach that we have taken. Moreover, arbitration's transnational and uniquely "anational" character give the subject a charm and fascination for students who usually think of legal problems as confined to a single legal system and only dimly sense the reality of the modern world of global markets and global transactions. The course should also be of highly practical value for students who in professional life may be called upon to draft an arbitration clause for an international contract, to represent a client in an international arbitration, to enforce (or resist enforcement of) a foreign arbitral award, or to advise an enterprise on the likely effectiveness and ramifications of using arbitration as a dispute resolution mechanism in this new transnational world.

Editing of Cases. Throughout the book we have used an ellipsis (* * *) to indicate when we have omitted something from a reproduced case or other material. To enhance readability, however, we have adopted one exception to this practice: we have frequently omitted citations of authority and many footnotes in the cases and have not marked these omissions with ellipses. We have numbered our own footnotes consecutively in each chapter, but we have retained the original numbering for footnotes appearing in the reproduced cases. Thus, in each chapter the numbering sequence of the authors' footnotes will be interrupted whenever a case appears containing footnotes, which are always numbered as in the original.

Acknowledgments. We owe deepest thanks to the many persons who have contributed greatly to this project. Zoltán Takács rendered invaluable assistance through research, assembling, and reproducing early versions of these materials. In the later stages of preparation of the manuscript and disks for publication, Darcy Bedore was incomparably dedicated to the work and rendered masterful help, without which the book would not have made its way into print. Before her, Ellen Zwingli single handedly typed very large sections of the manuscript and Jylanda Diles began the arduous task of formatting the longest chapter. Throughout this process we were aided by an outstanding group of student research assistants, who are listed here alphabetically: Sarah Buffett, Jason Casella, Tiffany Donovan, Amantha Holcomb, Colleen Kennedy, David Passey, and Paul Torchia. We want to express our very deepest appreciation and thanks to all of you.

TIBOR VÁRADY
JOHN BARCELÓ
ARTHUR VON MEHREN

Budapest, Hungary
Ithaca, New York
Cambridge, Massachusetts
September, 1998

*

Preface to the Second Edition

International commercial arbitration is a truly transnational (global) and transcultural process. It rarely begins and ends in the same country. Hence we have continued to stress—as we did in the first edition—a transnational approach to the subject, drawing on court decisions, arbitral awards, statutes, and procedural rules from all parts of the world. Parties, their legal counsel, and arbitrators may just as well be dealing with arbitration rules, procedures, concepts or statutes from China, or from Eastern Europe, or Russia, or India, or from France, Switzerland, Germany, Spain, Sweden or England, as from the United States. They may be arbitrating anywhere in the world, or seeking to enforce (or defend against) an award anywhere in the world—aspects that make the subject fascinating. At the same time, the New York Convention, the UNCITRAL Model Law, and other common concepts and practices bind all of these national approaches into a transnational system with a coherence that justifies studying it as a whole. This global perspective is increasingly the reality lawyers must cope with– at least those who aspire to practice in the field of international trade and international trade disputes.

Footnotes and Editing of Cases. As in the first edition, we have kept the original footnote numbers in all excerpts from cases, awards, and published works. We have numbered our own footnotes consecutively in each chapter, and to set them apart from the other footnotes, have enclosed them in brackets. We have also continued the practice, established in the first edition, of omitting citations of authority and inessential footnotes in reproduced cases, awards, and works, without indicating the omissions. We have used an ellipsis (* * *), however, to indicate the omission of text.

Acknowledgments. We want to express our gratitude to the following persons, whose work and assistance were indispensable to the preparation of the second edition. From the beginning to the end of this project, Ellen Zwingli was exceptionally dedicated to any and all tasks related to the book: to eliminating errors, getting proper copyright permissions, proofreading, tracking down materials, getting the right citation and all manner of other assistance. Darcy Bedore was outstanding in organizing and moving forward on the permissions process. We benefited enormously from the work of student research assistants. These included Anu Vabamae (LL.M.) and Zsofia Hermann (LL.M.), who did an excellent job in research and computer editing., Siddharth Wahi (LL.M.) who did the index singlehandedly, not to mention valuable research and proof-reading, and John Laplante (J.D.), who helped with research and permissions. To all of you we want to convey our warm and sincere gratitude.

TIBOR VÁRADY
JOHN BARCELÓ
ARTHUR VON MEHREN

Budapest, Hungary
Ithaca, New York
Cambridge, Massachusetts
October, 2002

Summary of Contents

Page

PREFACE TO THE 1ST EDITION v
PREFACE TO THE 2ND EDITION ix
TABLE OF CASES xxv

Chapter I. Introduction **1**
I.1. Approaches to Dispute Resolution 1
I.2. On the Evolution of the Standing of Arbitration Within the
     Legal System 41
I.3. On the Sources of Relevant Norms 62

Chapter II. On the Authority of Arbitration Tribunals **84**
II.1. The Arbitration Agreement as the Cornerstone of the Arbi-
     tration Process 84
II.2. Limits on Arbitrability 207

Chapter III. The Arbitrators **252**
III.1. The Arbitrators—Qualifications, Rights and Responsibilities .. 252
III.2. Appointment and Appointing Authorities 342
III.3. Challenges 379

Chapter IV. Focal Points in the Arbitration Process **411**
IV.1. Selected Elements of Procedure Before Arbitration Tribunals 411
IV.2. The Award 518
IV.3. Choice of Law Issues Before the Arbitrators 550

**Chapter V. The Effects and Limits of Awards Rendered in
International Commercial Arbitration** **606**
V.1. Confirmation, Merger Into Judgment, Concurrent and Con-
     secutive Proceedings 606
V.2. Judicial Control Over the Award: Setting Aside 643
V.3. Judicial Control Over the Award: Recognition and Enforce-
     ment 733

INDEX 843

Table of Contents

                                                                    Page

PREFACE TO THE 1ST EDITION -- v
PREFACE TO THE 2ND EDITION -- ix
TABLE OF CASES -- xxv

Chapter I. Introduction -- 1
I.1.   Approaches to Dispute Resolution -------------------------- 1
    I.1.a.   Note --- 1
    I.1.b.   Patterns of Problem–Solving ------------------------ 2
         Thomas M. Franck, The Structure of Impartiality: Examining the Riddle Of One Law in a Fragmented World 2
         Questions and Comments ------------------------------ 8
    I.1.c.   Arbitration and Mediation -------------------------- 8
         World Intellectual Property Organization Guide To WIPO Mediation -- 8
         Rules of Arbitration and Conciliation of the International Arbitral Center of The Federal Economic Chamber Vienna -- 16
         Zurich Chamber of Commerce, Rules of Procedure for the Zurich Mini–Trial ------------------------------------ 17
         Questions and Comments ------------------------------ 17
    I.1.d.   Technical Expertise -------------------------------- 18
         International Chamber of Commerce, Technical Expertise-- 18
         Questions and Comments ------------------------------ 18
    I.1.e.   Adaptation of Contracts ---------------------------- 18
         Frydman v. Cosmair, Inc. ---------------------------- 18
         Questions and Comments ------------------------------ 22
    I.1.f.   Arbitration and Litigation ------------------------- 23
         American Almond Products Co. v. Consolidated Pecan Sales Co,. Inc. ----------------------------------- 23
         James H. Carter, Dispute Resolution and International Agreements -- 24
         Christian Bühring-Uhle, Arbitration and Mediation in International Business: Designing Procedures for Effective Conflict Management ---------------------------- 26
         Questions and Comments ------------------------------ 26
    I.1.g.   Institutional and Ad Hoc Arbitration --------------- 27
         Gerald Aksen, Ad Hoc Versus Institutional Arbitration ------ 27
         Questions and Comments ------------------------------ 35
    I.1.h.   Fast–Track Arbitration ----------------------------- 36
         Hans Smit, Fast–Track Arbitration -------------------- 36
         Stockholm Rules for Expedited Arbitrations ------------ 40
         Questions and Comments ------------------------------ 40

Page

I.2.   On the Evolution of the Standing of Arbitration Within the
       Legal System 41
       I.2.a.   Note 41
                Tibor Varady, The Standing of Arbitration Within the
                Legal System 41
       I.2.b.   A Glimpse Back in History—A French Case 42
                L'Alliance v. Prunier 42
       I.2.c.   A Note on the Relevance of the International Dimen-
                sion 45
                Arthur von Mehren, International Commercial Arbitration:
                   The Contribution of The French Jurisprudence 45
                Questions and Comments 48
       I.2.d.   Another Glimpse Back in History—A U.S. Case 48
                Kulukundis Shipping Co., S.A. v. Amtorg Trading Corp. ... 48
                Questions and Comments 54
       I.2.e.   A Comparative Historical Survey on the Standing of
                   Arbitration Within the Legal System 54
                Arthur von Mehren, A General View of Contract 54
                Questions and Comments 61
I.3.   On the Sources of Relevant Norms 62
       I.3.a.   Note 62
       I.3.b.   Party Stipulation Versus Institutional Rules 68
                Preliminary Award Made in Case No. 2321 in 1974 (ICC) ... 68
                Questions and Comments 69
       I.3.c.   Party Stipulation Versus State Norms 71
                Al Haddad Bros. Enterprises, Inc. v. M/S Agapi 71
                Rederi Aktiebolaget Sally (Finland) v. S.R.L. Termarea
                   (Italy) 73
                Tarmarea S.R.L. (Italy) v. Rederiaktiebolaget Sally (Fin-
                   land) 76
                Albert Jan van den Berg, The New York Arbitration Con-
                   vention of 1958: Towards a Uniform Judicial Interpreta-
                   tion 80
                Questions and Comments 81

Chapter II.   On the Authority of Arbitration Tribunals 84
II.1. The Arbitration Agreement as the Cornerstone of the Arbi-
       tration Process 84
       II.1.a.   Note 84
                 II.1.a.i.   Variations of the arbitration agreement ... 84
                 II.1.a.ii.   "Referring the parties to arbitration ..." 84
                 II.1.a.iii. Existence and validity issues before courts
                                 and arbitrators 86
                 II.1.a.iv.   Formal requirements 88
                 II.1.a.v.   Scope 90
                 II.1.a.vi.   Further issues pertaining to the range and
                                 limits of the arbitration agreement ... 90
       II.1.b.   Compelling the Reluctant Party to Arbitrate:
                 Courses of Action and Waiver of the Right to
                 Compel 91
                 Tennessee Imports, Inc. v. P.P. Filippi & Prix Italia S.R.L. 91

Page

II.1.   The Arbitration Agreement as the Cornerstone of the Arbitration Process—Continued

Pepsico Inc. v. Oficina Central de Asesoria y Ayuda Tecnica, C.A. 99

Menorah Insurance Co., Ltd. v. INX Reinsurance Corp. 102

Questions and Comments 107

II.1.c.   Kompetenz–Kompetenz and Separability 109

Texaco Overseas Petroleum Co. & California Asiatic Oil Co. v. The Government of the Libyan Arab Republic 109

American Bureau of Shipping v. Jules Verne et al. 115

Questions and Comments 116

Sojuznefteexport (SNE) (USSR) v. Joc Oil, Ltd. (Bermuda) 118

Harbour Assurance Co. (UK), Ltd. v. Kansa General International Assurance Co., Ltd. 127

Questions and Comments 131

II.1.d.   The Form of the Arbitration Agreement 136

II.1.d.i.   "An Agreement in Writing" 136

Howard M. Holtzmann & Joseph E. Neuhaus, A Guide to the UNCITRAL Model Law on International Commercial Arbitration: Legislative History and Commentary 136

United Nations Convention on the Carriage of Goods by Sea 138

Neil Kaplan, Is the Need for Writing as Expressed in the New York Convention and the Model Law Out of Step With Commercial Practice? 139

Robobar Limited (UK) v. Finncold SAS (Italy) .. 141

Compagnie De Navigation et Transports SA (France) v. Mediterranean Shipping Co. SA (Switzerland) 143

Sphere Drake Insurance PLC v. Marine Towing, Inc. 147

Questions and Comments 149

II.1.d.ii.   Can a Battle of Forms Yield an Arbitration Agreement? 151

Nokia–Maillefer SA (Switzerland) v. Mazzer (Italy) 151

Questions and Comments 153

II.1.e.   Jurisdiction By Virtue of Tacit or Post–Agreement Submission or Estoppel 154

William Co. v. Guangzhov 154

Ocean Shipping Co. 155

Jiangxi Provincial Metal and Minerals Import and Export Corp. v. Sulanser Co., Ltd. 159

Claimant (Austria) v. Respondent (Germany) 161

Questions and Comments 163

UNCITRAL Working Group Draft Proposal to Amend Model Law Article 7 166

Questions and Comments 167

II.1.f.   Scope of the Arbitration Clause—Settlements and Renewals 168

Mediterranean Enterprises, Inc. v. Ssangyong Corp. 168

Ermenegildo Zegna Corp. v. Lanificio Mario Zegna S.P.A. .. 172

Page

II.1.   The Arbitration Agreement as the Cornerstone of the Arbitration Process—Continued
        Hart Enterprises International, Inc. v. Anhui Provincial
            Import & Export Corp. ------------------------------------ 177
        Becker Autoradio v. Becker Autoradiowerk ---------------- 180
        Questions and Comments ------------------------------------ 181
    II.1.g. The Position of the Parties Who Are Not Signatories
             of the Arbitration Agreement ------------------------- 183
        Cosmotek Mumessillik Ve Ticaret Limited Sirkketi v. Cosmotek USA, Inc. -- 183
        Questions and Comments ------------------------------------ 187
    II.1.h. Split Arbitration Clauses ------------------------------- 193
        Astra Footwear Industry v. Harwyn International, Inc. ------ 193
        Yugoslav Co. v. PDR Korea Co. ------------------------------ 197
        Questions and Comments ------------------------------------ 201
    II.1.i. Changed Circumstances ----------------------------------- 203
        Partial Decision of April 2, 1992 ------------------------- 203
        Questions and Comments ------------------------------------ 206
II.2.   Limits on Arbitrability -- 207
    II.2.a. Note -- 207
    II.2.b. Statutory Definitions of Arbitrability and Their Interpretation --- 210
        Fincantieri-Cantieri Navali Italiani SPA (Italy) v. Ministry
            of Defense, Armament and Supply Directorate of Iraq,
            Republic of Iraq -------------------------------------- 212
        Questions and Comments ------------------------------------ 217
    II.2.c. Arbitrability Tested in Court Practice ----------------- 221
        II.2.c.i.   Arbitrability of Antitrust Claims------------- 221
            Mitsubishi Motors Corporation v. Soler Chrysler–Plymouth, Inc. --------------------------- 221
            Questions and Comments ------------------------- 230
        II.2.c.ii. Arbitrability of Cargo Damage (COGSA)
                    Claims ------------------------------------ 235
            Vimar Seguros Y Reaseguros, S.A. v. M/V Sky
                Reefer------------------------------------- 236
            Questions and Comments ------------------------- 245
    II.2.d. Law Applicable to Arbitrability------------------------- 247
        M.S.A. (Belgium) v. Company M (Switzerland)--------------- 247
        Questions and Comments ------------------------------------ 249

Chapter III.   The Arbitrators-- 252
III.1. The Arbitrators—Qualifications, Rights and Responsibilities-- 252
    III.1.a. Note -- 252
    III.1.b. Oath and Fear of Gods as Safeguards of Impartiality 255
        M. Tod, International Arbitration Amongst the Greeks ------ 255
        Questions and Comments ------------------------------------ 256
    III.1.c. More Modern Considerations and Devices (Neutrality, Independence, Disclosure) ----------------------- 256
        Giorgio Bernini, Report on Neutrality, Impartiality, and
            Independence--- 256
        Andreas F. Lowenfeld, The Party–Appointed Arbitrator in
            International Controversies: Some Reflections------------- 263
        Questions and Comments ------------------------------------ 271

Page

III.1. The Arbitrators—Qualifications, Rights and Responsibilities 252
  III.1.d. How to Get (or Not to Get) the Right Arbitrator 273
    Lord David Hacking: Well, Did You Get the Right Arbitrator? 273
    Dr. K.V.S.K. Nathan: Well, Why Did You Not Get the Right Arbitrator? 278
    Questions and Comments 283
  III.1.e. Codes of Ethics 284
    AAA/ABA Code of Ethics for Arbitrators in Commercial Disputes (1977) 284
    The IBA Rules of Ethics for International Arbitrators 284
    Robert Coulson, An American Critique of the IBA's Ethics for International Arbitrators 285
    Robert Lutz E., Partisan Arbitrators and the Case Against Bias in International Arbitration 291
    Questions and Comments 292
  III.1.f. Rights and Responsibilities of the Arbitrators 294
    Philippe Fouchard, Relationships Between the Arbitrator and the Parties and the Arbitral Institution 294
    K/S Norjarl A/S v. Hyundai Heavy Industries Co., Ltd. 303
    Questions and Comments 315
  III.1.g. Rights and Responsibilities of the Arbitral Institution 317
    Cubic Defense Systems Inc. v. ICC 317
    Questions and Comments 325
  III.1.h. Can the Arbitrators Abandon Their Function? (Truncated Tribunals) 327
    Stephen M. Schwebel, The Validity of an Arbitral Award Rendered by a Truncated Tribunal 327
    Questions and Comments 339
III.2. Appointment and Appointing Authorities 342
  III.2.a. Note—Options in Appointment of Arbitrators 342
    Tibor Varady, On Appointing Authorities in International Commercial Arbitration 342
  III.2.b. Appointment by Courts 348
    Tibor Varady, On Appointing Authorities in International Commercial Arbitration 348
    Switzerland: Swiss Private International Law Act (1987).... 351
    Czech Republic: An Act of 1 November 1994 on Arbitral Proceedings and Enforcement of Arbitral Awards 352
    Questions and Comments 356
  III.2.c. Appointing Authorities Chosen by the Parties 358
    III.2.c.i. The Nature of the Decision of the Appointing Authority 358
      Sapphire International Petroleums Ltd. v. National Iranian Oil Company 358
      Elf Aquitaine Iran (France) v. National Iranian Oil Co. (Iran) 364
      Questions and Comments 365
    III.2.c.ii. An Appointing Authority Not Relied Upon 367
      Philips Hong Kong, Ltd. (Hong Kong) v. Hyundai Electronics Industries Co. Ltd. (Hong Kong) 367
      Questions and Comments 371

Page

III.2. Appointment and Appointing Authorities—Continued
    III.2.c.iii. An Appointing Authority That Ceased to
              Exist 372
              Gatoil International, Inc. (Panama) v. National
                 Iranian Oil Co. (Iran) 372
              Questions and Comments 376
    III.2.d. Multi–Party Arbitration and Selection of Arbitrators 376
        Siemens AG and BKMI Industrieanlangen GmbH v. Dutco
         Construction Co., Ltd. 377
        Questions and Comments 378
III.3. Challenges 379
    III.3.a. Introduction 379
        Albert Jan van den Berg, Report on the Challenge Proce-
         dure 379
        Questions and Comments 388
    III.3.b. Challenges and Court Control 389
        Refineries of Homs and Banias (Syria) v. International
         Chamber of Commerce 389
        State of Qatar v. Creighton Ltd (Cayman Islands) 390
        Questions and Comments 392
        Andros Compania Maritima v. Marc Rich & Co., A.G. 392
        Questions and Comments 402
        AT&T Corporation and Another v. Saudi Cable Company .. 402
        Questions and Comments 409

Chapter IV. Focal Points in the Arbitration Process 411
IV.1. Selected Elements of Procedure Before Arbitration Tribunals 411
    IV.1.a. Note 411
    IV.1.b. The Scope and the Relative Importance of the Lex
          Arbitri 412
        Union of India v. McDonnell Douglas Corporation 412
        Howard M. Holtzmann & Joseph E. Neuhaus, A Guide to
         the UNCITRAL Model Law on International Commercial
         Arbitration: Legislative History and Commentary 418
        Rules of the ICC International Court of Arbitration 422
        World Intellectual Property Organization Arbitration
         Rules 423
        Questions and Comments 423
    IV.1.c. Organizing Arbitral Proceedings 425
        UNCITRAL Notes on Organizing Arbitral Proceedings 425
        Questions and Comments 425
    IV.1.d. Party Discretion, Discretion of the Arbitrators, and
          Due Process 426
        Abati Legnami (Italy) v. Fritz Häupl 426
        Firm P (U.S.A.) v. Firm F (F.R.G.) 427
        Roger K. Ward, The Flexibility of Evidentiary Rules in
         International Trade Dispute Arbitration: Problems
         Posed to American–Trained Lawyers 428
        Questions and Comments 429
    IV.1.e. What Belongs to Arbitration Proceedings? 431
        Hebei Import & Export Corp. v. Polytek Engineering Co.
         Ltd. 432
        Court of Final Appeal Opinion, 1999 434
        Questions and Comments 436

Page

IV.1. Selected Elements of Procedure Before Arbitration Tribunals—Continued

IV.1.f. Terms of Reference.. 437
 ICC Rules of Arbitration (1998) 437
 ICC Rules of Arbitration (1988) 439
 J. Gillis Wetter, The Present Status of the International Court of Arbitration of the ICC: An Appraisal 440
 Stephen R. Bond, The Present Status of the International Court Of Arbitration of the ICC: A Comment on an Appraisal 441
 Carte Blanche (Singapore) Pte. Ltd. v. Carte Blanche International, Ltd. 443
 Questions and Comments 449
IV.1.g. Records and Minutes of the Hearing 450
 ICC Comparative Arbitration Practice and Public Policy in Arbitration 450
 Questions and Comments 454
IV.1.h. Presentation of the Case... 455
 IV.1.h.i. Problems With Discovery....................... 455
 In Re Application of Technostroyexport, A Foreign Economic Association Organized Under Laws of Russian Federation, Petitioner 455
 Elizabeth A. Fuerstman & Peter C. Thomas, The Implications of the Technostroy–Export Decision 460
 Questions and Comments 461
 IV.1.h.ii. Experts 462
 International Council for Commercial Arbitration, Comparative Arbitration Practice and Public Policy in Arbitration........................ 462
 Paklito Investment Ltd. v. Klöckner East Asia Ltd. 468
 Questions and Comments 477
 IV.1.h.iii. Language Issues 478
 Howard M. Holtzmann & Joseph E. Neuhaus, A Guide to the UNCITRAL Model Law on International Commercial Arbitration: Legislative History and Commentary 478
 N.Z. (No Nationality) v. I. (Romania) 481
 Seller (Denmark) v. Buyer (Germany) 482
 Questions and Comments 483
IV.1.i. Representation in the Proceedings; Is Local Counsel Required?... 486
 Michael Polkinghorne, The Right of Representation in a Foreign Venue 486
 Government of Malaysia v. Zublin–Muhibbah Joint Venture (Germany; Malaysia)... 490
 Questions and Comments 494
IV.1.j. Privacy and Confidentiality... 495
 Hassneh Insurance Co. of Israel and Others v. Stuart J. Mew 495
 Esso Australia Resources Ltd. & ORS v. The Honorable Sidney James Plowman (The Minister for Energy and Minerals) & ORS 501
 Bulgarian Foreign Trade Bank v. A.I. Trade Finance Inc. .. 504
 Questions and Comments 509

Page

IV.1. Selected Elements of Procedure Before Arbitration Tribu-
      nals—Continued
      IV.1.k. Time Limits for Accomplishing the Mission of the
              Arbitrators 513
              M. Tod, International Arbitration Amongst the Greeks 513
              England: Arbitration Act of 1996 514
              Peru: Decree Law No. 25935 515
              Romania: Book IV, Code of Civil Procedure, Arts. 340–370
                on Arbitration 515
              Thailand: Arbitration Act (1987) 516
              Rules of the ICC International Court of Arbitration 516
              Questions and Comments 517
IV.2. The Award 518
      IV.2.a. Form and Content of the Award 518
              IV.2.a.i. Statutory and Institutional Rules 518
                         Howard M. Holtzmann & Joseph E. Neuhaus,
                         A Guide to the UNCITRAL Model Law on
                         International Commercial Arbitration: Legis-
                         lative History and Commentary 518
                         The Netherlands: Arbitration Act (1986) 522
                         American Arbitration Association International
                         Arbitration Rules 524
                         China International Economic and Trade Arbi-
                         tration Commission [CIETAC] Arbitration
                         Rules 525
                         Questions and Comments 526
              IV.2.a.ii. An Award Written by Someone Else 528
                         Sacheri (Italy) v. Robotto (Italy) 528
                         Questions and Comments 529
      IV.2.b. Interventions After the Award Is Written 530
              IV.2.b.i. Institutional Scrutiny 530
                         Questions and Comments 531
              IV.2.b.ii. Correction, Interpretation, and Additional
                         Award 531
                         *Wintershall A.G. (F.R. Germany) et al v. Gov-
                         ernment of Qatar* 531
                         American Arbitration Association International
                         Arbitration Rules 538
                         China International Economic and Trade Arbi-
                         tration Commission (CIETAC) Arbitration
                         Rules 539
                         Questions and Comments 539
      IV.2.c. Deposit, Authentication, Certification 542
              Società Distillerie Meridionali (Italy) 545
              v. Schuurmans & Van Ginneken BV (The Netherlands) 546
              Appellant R. SA v. Appellee A. Ltd. 547
              Questions and Comments 549
IV.3. Choice of Law Issues Before the Arbitrators 550
      IV.3.a. Note 550
      IV.3.b. Applicable Substantive Law—The Prevailing Con-
              cept: Party Choice or Choice by the Arbitrators 553

Page

IV.3. Choice of Law Issues Before the Arbitrators—Continued
1961 European (Geneva) Convention On International
Commercial Arbitration, Article VII 553
Howard M. Holtzmann & Joseph E. Neuhaus, A Guide to
the UNCITRAL Model Law on International Commercial
Arbitration 554
Questions and Comments 561

IV.3.c. Interpreting Choice of Law Clauses and the Role of
the Lex Arbitri 562
Union of India v. McDonnell Douglas Corporation 562
*Claimant: Buyer (Mozambique) v. Defendant: Seller (The
Netherlands)* 562
A. von Mehren & E. Jiménez de Aréchaga, Final Report
on Arbitration Between States and Foreign Enterprises 571
Questions and Comments 573

IV.3.d. The Role of Lex Mercatoria 574
*Norsolor S.A. (France) v. Pabalk Ticaret Sirketi S.A. (Tur-
key)* 574
Questions and Comments 575

IV.3.e. Applicable Law in the Absence of Party Choice 577
Seller (Korea) v. Buyer (Jordan) 577
Questions and Comments 583

IV.3.f. The Problem of Mandatory Law 585
Principal (Italy) v. Distributor (Belgium) 585
Questions and Comments 590
Yves Derains, Public Policy and the Law Applicable to the
Dispute in International Arbitration 592
Ole Lando, Conflict–of–Laws Rules for Arbitrators, In Fest-
schrift für Konrad Zweigert 599
Questions and Comments 603

**Chapter V. The Effects and Limits of Awards Rendered in
International Commercial Arbitration** **606**

V.1. Confirmation, Merger Into Judgment, Concurrent and Con-
secutive Proceedings 606
V.1.a. Note 606
V.1.b. Confirmation, Leave to Enforce 607
V.1.c. Confirmation and Conversion 609
COSID, Inc. (U.S.) v. Steel Authority of India, Ltd. (India) 609
Fratelli Damiano (Italy) v. August Topfer & Co. (Germany) 612
*Seetransport Wiking Trader Schiffahrtsgesellschaft mbH &
Co. v. Navimpex Centrala Navala* 615
*Oriental Commercial & Shipping Co. (UK), Oriental Com-
mercial & Shipping Co. (Saudi Arabia), Abdul Hamid
Bokhari v. Rosseel, N.V.* 619
Questions and Comments 625
V.1.d. Concurrent and Consecutive Proceedings 627
V.1.e. Concurrent Proceedings 629
*Sumitomo Corporation, Oshima Shipbuilding Co. v. Parak-
opi Compania Maritima* 629
Renusagar Power Co. (India) v. General Electric Co. (U.S.) 634
Questions and Comments 637
V.1.f. Effects of a Partial Award 639
Mexican Construction Co. v. Belgian Co. 639

Page

V.1. Confirmation, Merger Into Judgment, Concurrent and Consecutive Proceedings—Continued
  Questions and Comments ---- 642
V.2. Judicial Control Over the Award: Setting Aside ---- 643
  V.2.a. Note—Judicial Control in the Country Where the Award Is Considered to Be Domestic ---- 643
  V.2.b. Domestic and Foreign Awards ---- 651
    International Standard Electric Corp. v. Bridas Sociedad Anonima Petrolera ---- 651
    Croatian Company v. Swiss Company ---- 656
    Oil & Natural Gas Commission v. Western Co. of North America ---- 657
    National Thermal Power Corporation v. The Singer Company ---- 663
    Jan Paulsson, Comment, The New York Convention's Misadventures In India ---- 669
    Questions and Comments ---- 674
  V.2.c. Public Policy, Fraud, and Evident Partiality as Grounds for Setting Aside ---- 678
    Spector v. Torenberg ---- 678
    European Gas Turbines SA (France) v. Westman International Ltd. (United Kingdom) ---- 684
    Questions and Comments ---- 692
  V.2.d. Standard of Review ---- 694
    V.2.d.i. Judicial Deference—or Lack Thereof—to Arbitrator Discretion ---- 694
      Transport En Handelsmaatschappij "Vekoma" B.V. (Netherlands) v. Maran Coal Corp. (U.S.A.) ---- 694
      Arab Republic of Egypt v. Southern Pacific Properties, Ltd & Southern Pacific Properties (Middle East), Ltd. ---- 698
      Questions and Comments ---- 704
    V.2.d.ii. Can the Parties Provide for Heightened Judicial Scrutiny of Arbitral Awards? 706
      Lapine Technology Corp. v. Kyocera Corporation ---- 706
      Questions and Comments ---- 713
  V.2.e. Due Process in Setting Aside as an Issue of Human Rights ---- 716
    Stran Greek Refineries & Stratis Andreadis v. Greece ---- 716
    Questions and Comments ---- 727
  V.2.f. Penalizing a Party for a Frivolous Challenge to an Award ---- 728
    Flexible Manufacturing Systems Pty. Ltd. v. Super Products Corporation ---- 728
    Questions and Comments ---- 733
V.3. Judicial Control Over the Award: Recognition and Enforcement ---- 733
  V.3.a. Awards Subject to the New York Convention ---- 733
    V.3.a.i. An Award Rendered in the State Where Recognition or Enforcement is Sought 734
      Sigval Bergesen v. Joseph Muller Corporation ---- 734

Page

V.3. Judicial Control Over the Award: Recognition and Enforcement—Continued

Questions and Comments 740

V.3.a.ii. Binding Awards and Awards Producing Only "Obligatory Effects" 741

Questions and Comments 743

V.3.a.iii. Partial Awards 745

Puerto Rico Maritime Shipping Authority v. Star Lines Ltd. 745

WTB (Germany) v. CREI (Italy) 747

Questions and Comments 749

V.3.b. Grounds Under the Convention for Refusing Recognition and Enforcement—An Introductory Case 750

Parsons and Whittemore Overseas Co. v. Societe Generale De L'Industrie du Papier (RAKTA) 750

Questions and Comments 758

V.3.c. Procedural Grounds Under the Convention for Refusing Recognition and Enforcement 759

V.3.c.i. Validity of the Agreement and Standard of Review 759

American Construction Machinery & Equipment Corp. Ltd. v. Mechanised Construction of Pakistan Ltd. 760

Southern Pacific Properties (Middle East) Ltd. v. Arab Republic of Egypt 763

Questions and Comments 766

SA X (Belgium) v. Mr. Y (Spain) 767

Questions and Comments 768

V.3.c.ii. Notice of Appointment of the Arbitrator and Waivability 769

Danish Buyer v. German Seller 769

Questions and Comments 773

V.3.c.iii. Scope of the Parties' Submission to Arbitration 773

Management & Technical Consultants S.A. v. Parsons–Jurden International 773

First Options of Chicago, Inc. v. Kaplan, et ux. and MK Investments, Inc. 777

Questions and Comments 782

V.3.c.iv. Improper Composition of Arbitral Authority or Improper Arbitral Procedure 783

China Nanhai Oil Joint Service Corporation, Shenzhen Branch v. Gee Tai Holdings 783

Questions and Comments 786

Compagnie des Bauxites de Guinee v. Hammermills, Inc. 786

Questions and Comments 793

V.3.c.v. An Award Set Aside in "the Country in Which, or Under the Law of Which, That Award Was Made" 795

Company A (Nationality Not Indicated) v. Company B (Slovenia) 795

Questions and Comments 797

Page

V.3. Judicial Control Over the Award: Recognition and Enforcement—Continued

        Pabalk Ticaret v. Norsolor 798

        Questions and Comments 803

        Chromalloy Aeroservices, A Division of Chromalloy Gas Turbine Corp. (U.S.) v. The Arab Republic of Egypt 803

        Questions and Comments 810

V.3.c.vi. The Limits of Deference—The Hilmarton Triangle and the Problem of Conflicting Awards 815

        Hilmarton Ltd. (U.K.) v. Omnium de Traitement et de Valorisation—OTV (France) 815

        Second Cour de Cassation Opinion 817

        Questions and Comments 818

V.3.d. Review of the Merits Under the Convention 821

V.3.d.i. Review of the Merits Under Article V(1) Standards 821

        Fertilizer Corp. of India v. IDI Management, Inc. 821

        Questions and Comments 825

        Pabalk Ticaret v. Norsolor 826

        Questions and Comments 826

V.3.d.ii. Review of the Merits for Manifest Disregard of the Law 826

        Brandeis Intsel Limited v. Calabrian Chemicals Corp. 826

        Questions and Comments 831

V.3.d.iii. Review of the Merits Under Article V(2)(b)—the Public Policy Standard 832

        Omnium de Traitement et de Valorisation SA v. Hilmarton Ltd. 832

        Questions and Comments 835

V.3.e. Estoppel 837

        China Nanhai Oil Joint Service Corporation Shenzhen Branch (PR China) v. Gee Tai Holdings Co. (Nationality Not Indicated) 837

        Questions and Comments 841

INDEX 843

Table of Cases

The principal cases are in bold type. Cases cited or discussed in the text
are roman type. References are to pages. Cases cited in principal
cases and within other quoted materials are not included.

Abati Legnami (Italy) v. Fritz Häupl, 426, 430
ABC v. C. Espanola SA, 544
Al Haddad Bros. Enterprises, Inc. v. M/S AGAPI, 71, 81, 82, 83
Ali Shipping Corp v. Shipyard Trogir, 509
American Almond Products Co. v. Consolidated Pecan Sales Co., 23
American Bureau of Shipping v. Jules Verne et al., 115, 118, 133
American Const. Machinery & Equipment Corp. Ltd. v. Mechanised Const. of Pakistan Ltd., 760, 766, 767
American Protein Corp. v. AB Volvo, 189
American Safety Equipment Corp. v. J.P. Maguire & Co., 228
Andros Compania Maritima, S.A. of Kissavos v. Marc Rich & Co. A.G., 392, 402
Appellant R. SA v. Appellee A. Ltd., 547
Application of (see name of party)
Arab Rebublic of Egypt v. Southern Pacific Properties, Ltd. & Southern Pacific Properties (Middle East), Ltd., 698, 705
Arbitration Between Keystone Shipping Co. and Texport Oil Co., Matter of, 188
Astra Footwear Industry v. Harwyn Intern., Inc., 193, 201, 202, 206
AT&T Corp. v. Saudi Cable Co., 402, 409, 410
Audi–NSU Auto Union A.G. v. S.A. Adelin Petit & Cie, 249

Baker Marine (Nig.) Ltd. v. Chevron (Nig.) Ltd., 814
Bancol Y Cia. S. En C. v. Bancolombia S.A., 424
BayWa Hungaria v. Gazdaszövetkezet Tóalmás, 85
Becker Autoradio U.S.A., Inc. v. Becker Autoradiowerk GmbH, 180, 182, 183

Bergesen v. Joseph Muller Corp., 734, 740, 741
Bowen v. Amoco Pipeline Co., 715
Brandeis Intsel Ltd. v. Calabrian Chemicals Corp., 811, 826, 831, 832
Brier v. Northstar Marine, Inc., 741
Bulgarian Foreign Trade Bank v. A.I. Trade Finance Inc., 504, 511, 512

Carte Blanche (Singapore) Pte. Ltd. v. Carte Blanche Intern., Ltd., 443, 449
Carte Blanche (Singapore) Pte., Ltd. v. Diners Club Intern., Inc., 189
Chimimportexport, 675, 676
China Nanhai Oil Joint Service Corporation, Shenzhen Branch v. Gee Tai Holdings, 783, 794, 837
Claimant (Austria) v. Respondent (Germany), 161, 165
Claimant: Buyer (Mozambique) v. Defendant: Seller (The Netherlands), 562
Commonwealth Coatings Corp. v. Continental Cas. Co., 410, 693
Compagnie de Navigation et Transports v. Mediterranean Shipping Company, 90
Compagnie de Navigation et Transports SA (France) v. Mediterranean Shipping Co. SA (Switzerland), 143, 150
Compagnie des Bauxites de Guinee v. Hammermills, Inc., 786, 793, 794
Company A (Nationality Not Indicated) v. Company B (Slovenia), 795, 812
Consultant (France) v. Egyptian Local Authority, 250, 251, 584
Continental U.K. Ltd. v. Anagel Confidence Compania Naviera, S.A., 188
COSID, Inc. (U.S.) v. Steel Authority of India, Ltd. (India), 609, 626
Cosmotek Mumessillik Ve Ticaret Ltd. Sirkketi v. Cosmotek USA, Inc., 183, 188, 191

Coveme SpA (Italy) v. Compagnie Francaise des Isolants SA (France), 219, 220, 221, 234

Croatian Company v. Swiss Company, 656

Cromalloy Aeroservices, a Div. of Chromalloy Gas Turbine Corp. and Arab Republic of Egypt, Matter of, 803, 810, 811, 812, 813, 814, 815, 818, 819, 820

Cubic Defense Systems Inc. v. ICC, 317, 325

Danish Buyer v. German Seller, 769, 773

Dean Witter Reynolds, Inc. v. Byrd, 638

Deloitte Noraudit A/S v. Deloitte Haskins & Sells, United States, 189

DuBois et Vanderwalle v. Boots Frites BV, 517

Eco Swiss China Time Ltd. v. Benetton International NV, 233, 234, 836

Elf Aquitaine Iran (France) v. National Iranian Oil Co. (Iran), 364, 367

EMAG AG v. Conceria G. De Maio, 82

Ermenegildo Zegna Corp. v. Lanificio Mario Zegna S.p.A., 172, 182

Esso Australia Resources Ltd. et al. v. Plowman et al., 501, 511

European Gas Turbines SA (France) v. Westman International Ltd. (United Kingdom), 684, 694

Fertilizer Corp. of India v. IDI Management, Inc., 821, 825

Fiat S.p.A. v. Ministry of Finance and Planning of Republic of Suriname, 117, 118, 133

Fidelitas Shipping Co. Ltd. v. V/O Exportchleb, 749

Filanto, S.p.A. v. Chilewich Intern. Corp., 85

Fincantieri–Cantieri Navali Italiani SPA (Italy) v. Ministry of Defense, Armament and Supply Directorate of Iraq, Republic of Iraq, 212, 217, 218, 219, 220, 221

Firm P (U.S.A.) v. Firm F (F.R.G.), 427

First Options of Chicago, Inc. v. Kaplan, 109, 777, 782

Flexible Mfg. Systems Pty. Ltd. v. Super Products Corp., 728

Fratelli Damiano (Italy) v. August Topfer & Co. (Germany), 612, 627

Frydman v. Cosmair, Inc., 18, 23

Gannet Shipping Ltd. v. Eastrade Commodities Inc., 540, 541

Gatoil International, Inc. (Panama) v. National Iranian Oil Co. (Iran), 372

Gemtel Partnership v. Société La Belle Créole, 485

Government of Guinea v. MINE (Maritime International Nominees Establishment from Liechtenstein), 526

Government of Malaysia v. Zublin–Muhibbah Joint Venture (Germany; Malaysia), 490, 494

Gutor Intern. AG v. Raymond Packer Co., Inc., 108

Gvozdenovic v. United Air Lines, Inc., 188

Halbout et société Matenac HG v. Epous Hanin, 576

Harbour Assurance Co. (UK) Ltd. v. Kansa General International Assurance Co. Ltd., 127, 132

Hart Enterprises Intern., Inc. v. Anhui Provincial Import & Export Corp., 177, 182

Hassneh Insurance Co. of Israel v. Stuart J. Mew, 495, 509

Hebei Import & Export Corporation v. Polytek Engineering Co. Ltd., 432, 437

Hilmarton Ltd. (U.K.) v. Omnium de Traitement et de Valorisation–OTV (France), 650, 813, **815,** 819, 820

Hiscox v. Outhwaite (No.1), 675, 676

Import Export Steel Corp. v. Mississippi Valley Barge Line Co., 188

Indussa Corp. v. S.S. Ranborg, 236, 242

In re (see name of party)

Interbras Cayman Co. v. Orient Victory Shipping Co., S.A., 188

International Standard Elec. Corp. v. Bridas Sociedad Anonima Petrolera, Indus. Y Comercial, 651

I.T.A.D. Associates, Inc. v. Podar Bros., 154

Jiangxi Provincial Metal and Minerals Import and Export Corp. v. Sulanser Co., Ltd., 159, 163, 164

J.J. Ryan & Sons, Inc. v. Rhone Poulenc Textile, S.A., 190

Katz v. Kar, 608

K/S Norjarl A/S v. Hyundai Heavy Industries Co. Ltd., 303, 313, 315, 316

Kulukundis Shipping Co., S/A, v. Amtorg Trading Corporation, 48, 54

L'Alliance v. Prunier, 42, 48

Lapine Technology Corp. v. Kyocera Corp., 2000 WL 765556, p. 714

Lapine Technology Corp. v. Kyocera Corp., 130 F.3d 884, pp. 650, **706,** 713, 714, 715, 716

Lapine Technology Corp. v. Kyocera Corp., 909 F.Supp. 697, p. 713

Malev Hungarian Airlines, Application of, 462

Management & Technical Consultants S.A. v. Parsons–Jurden Intern. Corp., 773, 782

Matter of (see name of party)

McBro Planning and Development Co. v. Triangle Elec. Const. Co., 190

Mediterranean Enterprises, Inc. v. Ssangyong Corp., 168, 182

Menicucci v. Mahieux, 48

Menorah Ins. Co., Ltd. v. INX Reinsurance Corp., 102, 108

Merrill Lynch, Pierce, Fenner & Smith, Inc. v. Bobker, 831

Mexican Construction Co. v. Belgian Co., 639, 642

Migout v. Arguad, 48

Ministry of Defense and Support for Armed Forces of Islamic Republic of Iran v. Cubic Defense Systems, Inc., 326

Mitsubishi Motors Corp. v. Soler Chrysler–Plymouth, Inc., 221, 230, 231, 232, 233, 234, 246, 836

M.S.A. (Belgium) v. Company M (Switzerland), 247, 249, 250, 251

National Thermal Power Corporation v. The Singer Company, 663, 676, 677, 678

Nokia–Maillefer SA (Switzerland) v. Mazzer (Italy), 151, 153, 154

Norsolor S.A. (France) v. Pabalk Ticaret Sirketi S.A. (Turkey), 574, 576

N.Z. (No Nationality) v. I. (Romania), 481

Oil & Natural Gas Commission v. Western Co. of North America, 657, 676, 677

Omnium de Traitement et de Valorisation SA v. Hilmarton Ltd., 832

O. Mustad & Sons v. Seawest Industries, Inc., In re, 108

Oriental Commercial & Shipping Co., (U.K.), Ltd. v. Rosseel, N.V., 619, 626, 627

Ospina v. Ribon, 48

Pabalk Ticaret v. Norsolor, 650, **798,** 803, 811, 812, 826

Paklito Investment Limited v. Klockner East Asia Limited, 468, 477, 478

Parsons & Whittemore Overseas Co., Inc. v. Societe Generale De L'Industrie Du Papier (RAKTA), 750, 758, 831, 837

PepsiCo Inc. v. Oficina Central De Asesoria y Ayuda Tecnica, C.A., 99, 107, 108

Petition of (see name of party)

Philips Hong Kong, Ltd. (Hong Kong) v. Hyundai Electronics Industries Co. Ltd. (Hong Kong), 367, 371

Pian del Sole s.p.a. v. s.r.l. Immobiliare La Fonte Cass. No. 6567, 744

Planting Machine for Potatoes, Bulbs or Similar Seed Crop (Seed Potatoes), 573, 574

Prima Paint Corp. v. Flood & Conklin Mfg. Co., 86, 87, 134, 135

Principal (Italy) v. Distributor (Belgium), 585

Protocom Devices, Inc. v. Figueroa, 608

Puerto Rico Maritime Shipping Authority v. Star Lines Ltd., 745, 749, 750

Qatar, State of v. Creighton Ltd. (Cayman Islands), 390

R. v Bow Street Metropolitan Stipendiary Magistrate Ex p. Pinochet Ugarte (No.2), 410

Rederi Aktiebolaget Sally (Finland) v. S.R.L. Termarea (Italy), 73

Refineries of Homs and Banias (Syria) v. International Chamber of Commerce, 389, 392

Renusager Power Co. (India) v. General Electric Co. (U.S.), 634, 638

Republic of Nicaragua v. Standard Fruit Co., 133, 134, 135

République de Guinée v. Chambre arbitrale de Paris, 727, 728

Rio Algom Ltd. v. Sammisteel Co., 88

Robobar Limited (UK) v. Finncold SAS (Italy), 141, 150

Sacheri (Italy) v. Robotto (Italy), 528, 529

Sandvik AB v. Advent Intern. Corp., 87, 133

Sapphire International Petroleums Ltd. v. National Iranian Oil Company, 358, 366, 367

SA X (Belgium) v. Mr. Y (Spain), 767

Scherk v. Alberto–Culver Co., 807

Schreter v. Gasmac Inc., 626

Seetransport Wiking Trader Schiffahrtsgesellschaft MBH & Co., Kommanditgesellschaft v. Navimpex Centrala Navala, 615, 625, 627

Seller (Denmark) v. Buyer (Germany), 482

Seller (Korea) v. Buyer (Jordan), 552, 577

Siemens AG and BKMI Industrieanlagen GmbH v. Dutco Construction Co., Ltd., 377

Smal v. Goldroyce, 149

Società Distillerie Meridionali (Italy) v. Schuurmans & Van Ginneken BV (The Netherlands), 546

Société Buzichelli v. Hennion et autre, 649

Société Corelf v. Société Worldwide, 646

Société de Diseno v. Société Mendes, 649, 714

Société Eurovia et autres v. SARL Grenobloise d'investissements, 576

Société La Moirette v. Société LTM France, 254

Société Van Hopplynus v. Société Coherent Inc., 182, 183

Sojuznefteexport (SNE) (USSR) v. Joc Oil, Ltd. (Bermuda), 118, 131

Somes v. de Saint–Rapt, 315

Southern Pacific Properties Ltd. and Southern Pacific Properties (Middle East) Ltd. v. Arab Republic of Egypt, 190

Southern Pacific Properties (Middle East) Ltd. v. Arab Republic of Egypt, 763, 766, 767

Spector v. Torenberg, 676, **678,** 693

Sphere Drake Ins. PLC v. Marine Towing, Inc., 147, 151

Spier v. Calzaturificio Tecnica S.p.A., 744

State of (see name of state)

Stran Greek Refineries & Stratis Andreadis v. Greece, 716, 728

Sumitomo Corp. v. Parakopi Compania Maritima, S.A., 629, 637

Sunkist Soft Drinks, Inc. v. Sunkist Growers, Inc., 189

Tai Ping Ins. Co., Ltd. v. M/V Warschau, 731 F.2d 1141, pp. 638, 639

Tai Ping Ins. Co., Ltd. v. M/V Warschau, 556 F.Supp. 187, p. 638

Tarmarea S.R.L. (Italy) v. Rederiaktiebolaget Sally (Finland), 76, 82, 83

Technostroyexport, Application of, 455, 461, 462

Temple Vihear, 165

Tennessee Imports, Inc. v. Filippi, 87, **91**

Texaco, Inc. v. American Trading Transp. Co., Inc., 638

Texaco Overseas Petroleum Co. & California Asiatic Oil Co. v. The Government of the Libyan Arab Republic, 109, 116, 118

Thomson–CSF, S.A. v. American Arbitration Ass'n, 188, 190

Tracomin S.A. v. Sudan Oil Seeds Company, 89

Transport en Handelsmaatschappij "Vekoma" B.V. (Netherlands) v. Maran Coal Corp. (U.S.A.), 694, 704, 705

Transrol Navegacao S.A., Petition of, 188

Union of India v. McDonnell Douglas Corp., 412, 424, 552, 562, 573, 574

Uzinexportimport v. Attock Cement, 88

Vimar Seguros y Reaseguros, S.A. v. M/V Sky Reefer, 221, **236,** 245, 246

Walter E. Heller & Co. v. Video Innovations, Inc., 189

Westland Helicopters Limited v. Arab Organization for Industrialization, 191

William Co. v. Guangzhov Ocean Shipping Co., 155, 163

Wintershall A.G. (F.R. Germany) et al. v. Government of Qatar, 531, 539

WTB (Germany) v. CREI (Italy), 747, 750

Yugoslav Co. v. PDR Korea Co., 197, 203

INTERNATIONAL COMMERCIAL ARBITRATION

A Transnational Perspective

Second Edition

*

Chapter I

INTRODUCTION

I.1. APPROACHES TO DISPUTE RESOLUTION

I.1.a. Note

Seen in a modern perspective, and in a cultural setting where courts represent the established tradition, arbitration can be regarded as an unorthodox and innovative method of settling disputes. In this context, arbitration is a response to questions that have been left unanswered within the judicial system, an innovative institution that meets specific needs that courts do not deal with satisfactorily.

From a wider historical and anthropological perspective, however, arbitration represents not a departure from established paths of litigation, but a variation within the spectrum of responses to the question: how should one resolve disputes? This question is still wide open. Compared with some other approaches to dispute resolution, arbitration and litigation appear to be at the same end of the spectrum; both involve third party adjudication. The discussion continues whether third party adjudication-that is to say, judicial or arbitral proceedings-is a better method than negotiation, mediation or conciliation for resolving controversies with international dimensions.

In section (b) of this subchapter I.1, an excerpt from Thomas Franck's "The Structure of Impartiality" discusses patterns of dispute resolution, focusing on one-and two-party approaches. The one-party approach means essentially the imposition of the will of one party (and thus the imposition of a solution by one of the two contestants). Two-party settlement is characterized not by force but by negotiation and compromise.

Section (c) shifts our focus to three-party approaches with examples of techniques akin to arbitration in the domain of international trade. Mediation, conciliation, and "med-arb" are hybrid two-three-party methods, in which a third party appears, yet the role of this third party boils down essentially to facilitation of a compromise, rather than decision-making.

1

Sections (d) and (e) focus on technical expertise and adaptation of contracts, which are, again, borderline areas between third party decision-making and facilitation of settlements.

Section (f) sets out pros and cons in the classic debate between arbitration and litigation.

Section (g) presents the option between the two basic forms of the arbitration process: institutional and ad hoc arbitration.

Section (h) concludes this subchapter on various approaches to dispute resolution by introducing "fast-track arbitration", a form which has come to the limelight within the last decade, but which has not yet been widely tested.

I.1.b.   *Patterns of Problem–Solving*

Thomas M. Franck, THE STRUCTURE OF IMPARTIALITY: EXAMINING THE RIDDLE OF ONE LAW IN A FRAGMENTED WORLD

11–19 (1968).*

In essence, there are three systems of problem-solving known to the law. They may operate independently, or successively, or they may be integrated in a single process.

The first system is distinguished by its *power* syndrome, and it operates where the community permits (or cannot prevent) the imposition, by force, of the will of one party on another. * * * You have taken my hat? Ordinarily, the law will allow me to snatch it back. Such illustrations should not, however, mislead the reader: American state and federal law, like that of all civilized states, recognizes both the dangers to peace, and the inequities, of one-party law-making. With only a restricted number of exceptions, therefore, we forbid the use of unilateral force, except by the state acting constitutionally on behalf of the entire community.

In relations between states, unfortunately, the unilateral use of power remains a much more common source of law. Military conquest, annexation, imposed treaties, economic boycott, "police actions," these have all been more-or-less tolerated by the international community as legitimate ways of making law. Such recognition is, of course, little more than a realistic acceptance by that community of the consequence of its weakness and lack of cohesion, and the equally indisputable phenomenon of *force* creating *order*, and of the will behind force justifying itself by reference to certain standards by which it is exercised and thus made "lawful."

In the United States we have examples of the use of power being *permitted* by law—the father is allowed to spank his child, and a man may hit back at an assailant or snatch back his stolen property—but force is not a *source* of law, as it is, still, in the more primitive international community. Primitiveness is, indeed, the style of one-party law-making. Aside from the fact that law made by unilateral exercise of power as often endangers as protects the peace, and that it invariably produces a law favoring the rich and powerful at the expense of the poor and weak, there is another even more serious defect in the power syndrome as a lawmaking device. It is that law made in this way frequently fails to produce substantive content.

The dispute, in 1962, between the United States, Russia, and Cuba over the placing of nuclear missiles in the Caribbean helps to illustrate this proposition. According to the United States, Russia's action in putting missiles on Cuban soil was an international wrong because it was done in secrecy and deceit, because it forcefully upset the world balance of power, and because it violated the integrity of the Western Hemisphere as declared in the Monroe Doctrine. Russia, on the other hand, contended that the United States could not have it both ways: either all overseas bases are wrongful, aggressive threats to the peace— in which case the United States should dismantle its bases in Western Europe, Turkey, the Philippines, Formosa, etc.—or else all bases are legal, in which case Russia was perfectly within its rights in setting up shop in Cuba.

By its "peaceful blockade," as we know, the United States persuaded Russia to withdraw its missiles from the Caribbean. Such an exercise in the use of unilateral force, accompanied by an extensive polemic, exchanges of notes, debates in the UN, and formal negotiations ought, presumably, to have had some lawmaking effect. But what law did it yield? Since Russia and the United States never agreed on what the dispute was about, there could not, of course, be agreement as to what the successful use of force actually decided. Those who side with the American view, for example, can assert that the emerging rule is that the Monroe Doctrine remains in effect and all foreign bases in the Western Hemisphere constitute aggression against the collective hemisphere. Those who side with the Russians can allege that the emerging rule is that all overseas nuclear missile bases are hostile, aggressive, illegal, and should therefore be dismantled; that America's continued refusal to apply this rule reciprocally to itself proves Washington's disdain for international law and equity. Still others, more cynically, see the entire polemic as nothing but propaganda window dressing, sound and fury signifying nothing, an exercise in *pure power*. The meaning of this term we will shortly examine. For the present, however, it is sufficient to note that when a problem is resolved by recourse to *power*, to one-party law-making, the solution one party imposes on another does not yield a clear-cut rule of law, when as often happens in a *power*-oriented solution, the various members of the international community and the parties, in particular, retain their different views of *what the issues were*, and therefore will continue to disagree as to *what was decided*. The world will only know *who won*, but not what *principle* the victory established, for they will not have a definitive statement of the issues on which it was decided. For the long-range prospects of peace it is less important to know who won than what principle was established. This is a hypothesis many will not share, but it marks the dividing line between an orderly community and the jungle. A system of decision-making which does not yield an agreed principle is like a rifle without a sight: lacking not in effect but in *predictable* effect. Without these principles of decision, there can be no prediction and thus, perhaps, no future.

Neither two-party law-making, employing the *compromise* syndrome, nor third-party law-making, employing the *impartiality* syndrome, suffers from this important defect. A court of law, for example, will attempt to have the parties agree as to the facts and issues on which the case is to be decided. But failing that, the court will itself decide which facts and what issues are relevant to its decision. In this way the judicial settlement of a dispute generally yields not only a *decision* but a *rule of law*.

The two-party system is marked by a *compromise* syndrome. This operates in disputes where the law sanctions the reconciliation of contending claims in a mutually acceptable agreement devised by the parties themselves. The parties, so to speak, write their own law. Our ordinary everyday business contracts are laws made by compromise, as are the wage agreements negotiated by conciliation boards. Most international agreements, treaties and their genus, are laws made by mutual accommodation and consent.

The system of compromise may simply involve two-party negotiation, or it may call for complex mechanical devices as well as reference to other systems of decision-making. Take, for example, the ingenious scheme for the consensual division of eighty-seven art treasures left "equally" to the Metropolitan Museum and the National Gallery by the will of the late Mrs. Timken of the ball-bearing fortune.

How can two museums, both steeped in the aesthetic prejudice we call "taste," agree to divide a collection of masterpieces "equally"? Had the two beneficiaries litigated the "equality" of every painting in relation to every other painting, the entire collection would probably have ended up being owned by the lawyers. A compromise was inevitable, and a particularly ingenious one was worked out. The directors of the two museums first grouped the items into a series of artistic categories, then divided each category into two sections of roughly equivalent value. Thereafter the directors wrote out, simultaneously, their first choice in each group. Each time both showed a preference for the same section of a particular category, a coin was flipped and the winner had first choice. The process was entirely successful in avoiding litigation. (It should be observed, however, that this procedure yielded not a principle of law but a principle of procedure.)

The *compromise* syndrome manifests two-party law. The parties to the dispute themselves may make law to suit their own needs by a process of negotiation. This is in contrast to the *power* syndrome, which manifests one-party law, and in which the stronger makes the law both for himself and for the weaker party.

Two-party law, unlike one-party law, continues to occupy an important role in the development of even sophisticated legal systems; especially in the continuing and ever-growing use of the adaptable idea of contract. It can also be located closer to the soul of our complex modern national societies, for it is readily apparent that *all* law can only operate within a general framework of applied consensus or compromise. Only when a community produces an expressed or implied agreement as to *how* its law is to be made, as it did with * * * historic genius in the "contract" that is the United States Constitution, can the members of that community begin to distinguish the sheep of legal order from the goats of personal and political expediency. And only when a community has an agreed measure for making that distinction can it be said to have reached its socio-political *take-off* point. This fundamental community consensus, which Professor H.L.A. Hart of Oxford calls a "rule of recognition," generally originates in a confluence of popular opinion or will, although it may also be the product of revolutionary charisma. It is frequently a complex pattern woven of multiple strands of two-party law-although it may also, of course, be imposed unilaterally by a dictator or a revolutionary class, thereby becoming a manifestation of one-party law-making. Without either an imposed or agreed basic norm or group of such norms, however, and in the absence of a new socially conditioned breed of men who act invariably and voluntarily according to harmonious social principles that are natural to them, law would remain in a state of opinion where each man, and therefore *no* man, is king.

Professors Charles Manning and Lon L. Fuller have demonstrated by reference to *games* that communities of children and adults tend to develop imaginatively within their community those agreed guidelines necessary to allow their chosen activity to proceed. Underlying these guidelines of the game is a remarkably seldom-challenged common assumption or set of assumptions which may be unenunciated, but of which the "rules of the game" are symptomatic. Manning has called this human flair for games "an association on the basis of make-believe" and this may, indeed, also be both a happier and more accurate definition of the phenomenon underlying law than is "social contract." It must be remembered here, however, that "make-believe" is used to denote not sham, for the phenomenon of the game-in-progress, or of the community, is real enough. Rather it means an exercise of the creative imagination by which a disordered group calls itself into being as a working society made possible by the belief that certain rules of its own creation are superior even to those who were its originators.

One of the agreed "rules of the game," in particular, merits further attention, for it is basic to the third category of decision-making, which operates by using the *impartiality* syndrome, as well as to law-making that uses the *power* and *compromise* syndromes. If this rule is ignored, neither the *power* nor the *impartiality* syndrome can yield what is generally acceptable to the community as law. This agreed rule of the game is thus obviously one of great importance. It may be described as the rule of philosophical consistency, linear reasoning, or logical deduction, * * *. Plato's dialogues are its fountainhead, and its impact on the West has never diminished in 2,300 years, despite repeated efforts by the early Christian dogmatists to turn it upside down by substitution of the illogical paradox (life through death, joy through suffering, wisdom through simpleness, and even conception through virginity), or the effort of Hegel and Marx to substitute "thesis-antithesis-synthesis" as a way of thinking. Philosophical consistency is the triumph of the intellect, of "pure" reason, and it provides the bridge between arbitrary, selfish, and isolated decision-making and promotes the emergence of a set of knowable and predictable rules for the exercise (and restraint) of authority: In other words, it facilitates *law*. It is not the sole component of good law for which there must also be mercy, feeling-perception, and an awareness of public policy, but it is the indispensable prerequisite to the existence of a legal system.

Suppose the caveman, Ug, has begun his autumnal hunt by killing a dinosaur. Having left his lethal flint-axe in its heart, he continues on his hunt, intending later to return with his family to gather the carcass. Two days afterward, his neighbor, Og, stumbles across the dead animal. With the aid of his wife and ten children and the expenditure of two days work, Og succeeds in dragging the cadaver to his cave. Once Ug has returned from his hunt, he traces the missing carcass to Og's cave and demands its return.

Depending upon the degree of sophistication Ug and Og have achieved, this story can have various climaxes:

(1) Ug and Og could simply clout each other with the jaw bones of asses in that familiarly primitive manner of problem-solving and decision-making first attributed to Abel and Cain or Romulus and Remus. Such a contest involves no thought for either past or future conduct. The parties are concerned neither with laying down principles for solving future disputes nor with applying to a present dispute the lessons of comparable disputes in the past. They are concerned only with one immediate-and no doubt to them vital-question: Who gets the dinosaur? This, then, is the use of *pure* power to reach a decision, and it yields no law, unless some future disputants, by benevolent induction, read a reasonable principle into Ug and Og's seemingly mindless contest of strength and apply it to solve their own predicament. It is just conceivable that the battle between Ug and Og might in this way gradually come to be accepted as a law stating that dinosaurs killed and left behind on autumnal hunts may be taken by any person strong enough to defend his title. That such a rule of law sanctioning and regulating a contest of pure or mindless power is not entirely fanciful will be seen by recalling the extensive role of trial by combat and its refinement, the duel, in medieval European and also Oriental systems. The role of the law in associating itself with a contest of pure power in order to impart to it a

trace of its grace and order is like that of the Church in blessing dictators, senselessly warring armies, and the shrines of pagan cults.

(2) On the other hand, Ug might reason: "This dinosaur is mine because I killed it and impressed on it my mark of conquest. To allow you, Og, to take this carcass from me merely because I left it to continue my hunt would be to admit a principle that would make the whole business of organized autumnal hunts impossible." In reply Og might contend that the abandonment of carcasses during a hunt is a socially undesirable, wasteful practice, that it leaves them exposed to the ravages of other beasts, that oft-times carcasses go unclaimed for weeks while they rot in the sun, that moreover, by dragging the carcass home, Og did far more than Ug of the actual work necessary to reduce it to a commodity capable of ownership and use. After that, Ug and Og, if they are deadlocked, may still rely on asses jawbones to club each other to a violent verdict. *But in this case, the outcome would yield a solution based on power as a law-making device.* The difference is a simple one. Suppose Ug is the winner. Suppose that, the following autumn, the same events recur but with the roles reversed. It would be difficult for Ug now to contend that a newly killed dinosaur, temporarily abandoned during a hunt, becomes the property of a finder who drags it home. His sense of honor and consistency would probably shame him into obeying the "law" he made by force of arms only a year earlier. If it does not, Og's neighbors, outraged by Ug's shameless inconsistency, would probably rally to his aid. Ug and Og would have discovered that not only judges and lawyers but the public as a whole, even in primitive societies, have an extraordinary, seemingly innate preference for action that is consistent, and at a more sophisticated state, can be *seen and expressed* to be consistent with what has gone before. This preference, which appears as a universal social instinct, is an essential ingredient in the emergence of a rule of law, and it means little more than that men do not simply do whatever they feel like doing, or whatever they think they can get away with, but only that which they can "justify." Power relationships, as we have noticed, often fail to yield such neutral principles, but sometimes, fortunately, they do–either because the contest of power took place between champions of two explicit principles, or because historical forces conspire to pretend that it did.

(3) Ug and Og might not fight at all. Instead, they might haggle in the presence of flowing jugs of clover wine. They might, in a soggy euphoria of good fellowship, together set out to kill another dinosaur so the needs of each might be satisfied. Or they might, to the same end, pillage the larder of Hugh, the arch enemy of Ug, taking from it sufficient booty that the needs of both are sated. Or they and their kinfolk might tug and pull at the carcass until it came apart near the middle, whereupon they might simply resign themselves each to their portion and stalk away. Or Og might take one of Ug's ugly daughters as wife, whereupon the grateful father of the bride might bestow the dinosaur upon the groom as dowry. *All of these solutions represent the triumph of pure compromise.* As between Ug and Og they may be *ad hoc*

"political" solutions, but they yield no, or very little, law unless others, later, choose to adopt this purely "one-shot" procedure as a model or principle applicable to themselves in a similar dispute, or again, unless historical forces conspire to "find" a logical principle where, in fact, there had been none.

(4) Ug and Og might themselves decide to emulate prior conduct. They might sit down to their clover wine and remember that a similar incident once arose between two fellow villagers, T'Bo and Hun, who could reveal that the earlier quarrel had been happily resolved by an agreement of the parties to divide the carcass: the bulk of it going to the hunter, but the prime hindquarter fittingly being bestowed upon the one who provided the transportation. This would be a solution by reference to the law-making compromise syndrome. Rational principles are here set out, applied, and reapplied to obtain solutions, which, as to both form and substance, are philosophically consistent with each other and generate a tendency toward logical progression and analogy in problem-solving.

Questions and Comments

1. In international transactions do the parties ever resort to one-party, or two-party, dispute settlement? Can you think of examples?

Why are parties reluctant to submit to third party decision-making?

2. In the words of Ihering, "The end of law is peace; but the means to this end is war". Does this observation apply to dispute settlement in international disputes?

3. A characteristic of both one-party and of two-party decision-making is that both arose before law, and can work outside the framework of legal procedure. (Of course, once law has arisen, society endeavors to bring one-party and two-party decision-making within its legal framework.)

Three-party decision-making assumes that a third party (judge, arbitrator, village elder, the king, a much respected kinsman of Ug and Og) may proclaim a solution that one—or even all—of the parties may not desire. If the third party is chosen by the two contestants, and derives his powers from the mandate given by them, we have arbitration. Can arbitration exist outside the framework of a legal system?

I.1.c. Arbitration and Mediation

WORLD INTELLECTUAL PROPERTY ORGANIZATION GUIDE TO WIPO MEDIATION

6–13 (1996).*

* * *

* Reprinted by permission of World Intel-   to WIPO Mediation (1996).
lectual Property Organization from Guide

What Is Mediation?

Mediation is first and foremost a *non-binding* procedure. This means that, even though parties have agreed to submit a dispute to mediation, they are not obliged to continue with the mediation process after the first meeting. In this sense, the parties remain always in control of a mediation. The continuation of the process depends on their continuing acceptance of it.

The non-binding nature of mediation means also that a decision cannot be imposed on the parties. In order for any settlement to be concluded, the parties must voluntarily agree to accept it.

Unlike a judge or an arbitrator, therefore, the *mediator* is not a decision-maker. The role of the mediator is rather to assist the parties in reaching their own decision on a settlement of the dispute.

There are two main ways in which mediators assist parties in reaching their own decision, which correspond to two types or models of mediation practiced throughout the world. Under the first model, *facilitative mediation*, the mediator endeavors to facilitate communication between the parties and to help each side to understand the other's perspective, position and interests in relation to the dispute. Under the second model, *evaluative mediation*, the mediator provides a non-binding assessment or evaluation of the dispute, which the parties are then free to accept or reject as the settlement of the dispute. It is up to the parties to decide which of these two models of mediation they wish to follow. The WIPO Arbitration and Mediation Center ("the Center") will assist them in identifying a mediator appropriate for the model that they wish to adopt.

Mediation is a *confidential* procedure. Confidentiality serves to encourage frankness and openness in the process by assuring the parties that any admissions, proposals or offers for settlement will not have any consequences beyond the mediation process. They cannot, as a general rule, be used in subsequent litigation or arbitration. The WIPO Mediation Rules contain detailed provisions directed also at preserving confidentiality in relation to the existence and outcome of the mediation.

How Does Mediation Differ From Arbitration?

The differences between mediation and arbitration all stem from the fact that, in a mediation, the parties retain responsibility for and control over the dispute and do not transfer decision-making power to the mediator. In concrete terms, this means two things principally:

1. In an arbitration, the outcome is determined in accordance with an objective standard, the applicable law. In a mediation, any outcome is determined by the will of the parties. Thus, in deciding upon an outcome, the parties can take into account a broader range of standards, most notably their respective business interests. Thus, it is often said that mediation is an interest-based procedure, whereas arbitration is a rights-based procedure. Taking into account business

interests also means that the parties can decide the outcome by reference to their future relationship, rather than the result being determined only by reference to their past conduct.

2. In an arbitration, a party's task is to convince the arbitral tribunal of its case. It addresses its arguments to the tribunal and not to the other side. In a mediation, since the outcome must be accepted by both parties and is not decided by the mediator, a party's task is to convince, or to negotiate with, the other side. It addresses the other side and not the mediator, even though the mediator may be the conduit for communications from one side to the other.

Naturally, in view of these differences, mediation is a more informal procedure than arbitration.

For Which Disputes Is Mediation Appropriate And What Are Its Advantages?

Mediation is not a suitable procedure for settling disputes in all cases. Where deliberate, bad-faith counterfeiting or piracy is involved, mediation, which requires the cooperation of both sides, is unlikely to be appropriate. Similarly, where a party is certain that it has a clear-cut case, or where the objective of the parties or one of them is to obtain a neutral opinion on a question of genuine difference, to establish a precedent or to be vindicated publicly on an issue in dispute, mediation may not be the appropriate procedure.

On the other hand, mediation is an attractive alternative where any of the following are important priorities of either or both of the parties:

— minimizing the cost-exposure entailed in settling the dispute;

— the maintenance of control over the dispute-settlement process;

— a speedy settlement;

— the maintenance of confidentiality concerning the dispute; or the preservation or development of an underlying business relationship between the parties to the dispute.

The last-mentioned priority, in particular, makes mediation especially suitable where the dispute occurs between parties to a continuing contractual relationship, such as a license, distribution agreement or joint research and development (R & D) contract, since, as mentioned above, mediation provides an opportunity for finding a solution by reference also to business interests and not just to the strict legal rights and obligations of the parties.

At Which Stages of a Dispute Can Mediation Be Used?

Mediation can be used at any stage of a dispute. Thus, it can be chosen as the first step towards seeking a resolution of the dispute after any negotiations conducted by the parties alone have failed. Mediation can also be used at any time during litigation or arbitration where the parties wish to interrupt the litigation or arbitration to explore the possibility of settlement.

Another common use of mediation is more akin to dispute prevention than dispute resolution. Parties may seek the assistance of a mediator in the course of negotiations for an agreement where the negotiations have reached an impasse, but where the parties consider it to be clearly in their economic interests to conclude the agreement (for example, negotiations on the royalty rate to apply on the renewal of a license).

What Types of Dispute Can Be Mediated At WIPO?

The Center offers specialized services for mediation of intellectual property disputes, that is, disputes concerning intellectual property or commercial transactions and relationships involving the exploitation of intellectual property. Common examples of such commercial transactions and relationships are patent, know how and trademark licenses, franchises, computer contracts, multimedia contracts, distribution contracts, joint ventures, R & D contracts, technology-sensitive employment contracts, mergers and acquisitions where intellectual property assets assume importance, and publishing, music and film contracts.

It should be noted, however, that there is no limitation on the competence of mediators appointed under the WIPO Mediation Rules to deal with different classes of subject matter. A mediator appointed under the WIPO Mediation Rules is competent to deal with all aspects of any dispute. It is up to the parties to decide whether they consider the subject matter suitable for WIPO mediation.

How It Works: The Principal Stages in a WIPO Mediation

There are few formalities associated with a mediation. The structure that a mediation follows is decided by the parties with the mediator, who together work out, and agree upon, the procedure that is to be followed.

As mentioned above, the somewhat unstructured nature of a mediation can be disconcerting to those who may be entertaining the idea of submitting a dispute to mediation, but who may not be sure what to expect. For such persons, some guidance is set out in the following paragraphs, which outline the main steps in the conduct of a WIPO mediation. The procedure outlined should, however, be understood as being for guidance only, since the parties may always decide to modify the procedure and to proceed in a different way.

Getting to the Table: The Agreement to Mediate

The starting point of a mediation is the agreement of the parties to submit a dispute to mediation. Such an agreement may be contained either in a contract governing a business relationship between the parties, such as a license, in which the parties provide that any disputes occurring under the contract will be submitted to mediation; or it may be specially drawn up in relation to a particular dispute after the dispute has occurred.

The last section of this Guide contains recommended clauses for both situations, which provide a choice between agreeing to mediation alone or agreeing to mediation followed, in the event that a settlement is not reached through the mediation, by arbitration.

Starting the Mediation

Once a dispute has occurred and the parties have agreed to submit it to mediation, the process is commenced by one of the parties sending to the Center a *Request for Mediation*. This Request should set out summary details concerning the dispute, including the names and communication references of the parties and their representatives, a copy of the agreement to mediate and a brief description of the dispute. These details are not intended to perform the legal function of defining arguments and issues and limiting the requesting party's case. They are intended simply to supply the Center with sufficient details to enable it to proceed to set up the mediation process. Thus, the Center will need to know who is involved and what the subject matter of the dispute is in order to be able to assist the parties in selecting a mediator appropriate for the dispute.

The Appointment of the Mediator

Following receipt of the Request for Mediation, the Center will contact the parties (or their representative) to commence discussions on the appointment of the mediator (unless the parties have already decided who the mediator will be). The mediator must enjoy the confidence of both parties and it is crucial, therefore, that both parties be in full agreement with the appointment of the person proposed as mediator.

Typically, the Center would discuss the various matters described in the box opposite in order to be in a position to propose the names of suitable candidates for the consideration of the parties.

Following these discussions (which may take place by telephone or in person), the Center will usually propose several names of prospective mediators, together with the biographical details of those prospective mediators, to the parties for their consideration. If necessary, further names can be proposed until such time as the parties agree upon the appointment of a mediator.

At this stage also, the Center will commence discussions with the parties concerning the physical arrangements for the mediation; where it is to take place (which will usually have been specified in the agreement to mediate) a meeting room and any other support facilities needed.

The Center will also fix, in consultation with the mediator and the parties, the fees of the mediator at the stage of the appointment of the mediator.

Selecting the Mediator

Perhaps the most important step in the whole process is the selection of the mediator. What should the parties consider?

One of the principal functions of the WIPO Arbitration and Mediation Center is to assist the parties in identifying and agreeing upon the mediator. The Center does this through consultation with the parties and by supplying them with the names and biographical details of potential candidates for their consideration.

The parties should consider at least the following matters in deciding whom to appoint as mediator:

- what *role* do they want the mediator to play; do they want the mediator to provide a *neutral evaluation* of their dispute, or do they want the mediator to act as *facilitator of their negotiations* by assisting them in identifying the issues, exploring their respective underlying interests and developing and evaluating possible options for settlement?

- do they want a mediator with substantial training and experience in the subject matter of their dispute, or do they want a mediator more particularly skilled in the process of mediation? This will depend in part on whether they wish the mediator to play an evaluative or a facilitative role.

- do they want a single mediator or more than one mediator? In particularly complex disputes involving very specialized and highly technical subject matter, the parties may wish to consider having both a subject-matter and a process specialist as co-mediators. Similarly, where the parties have very different cultural and linguistic backgrounds, they may wish to envisage two co-mediators.

- what nationally should the mediator have (or what nationalities should the mediator not have)?

- are the candidates independent, that is, are they free of any past or present business, financial or other disqualifying connections with either of the parties to the dispute or with the particular subject matter of the dispute?

> • **what are the professional qualifications and experience, training and areas of specialization of the candidates?**

Initial Contacts Between the Mediator and the Parties

Following appointment, the mediator will conduct a series of initial discussions with the parties, which typically will take place by telephone. The purpose of these initial contacts will be to set a schedule for the subsequent process. The mediator will indicate what documentation, if any, he or she considers should be provided by the parties prior to their first meeting and set the timetable for the supply of any such documentation and the holding of the first meeting.

The First Meeting Between the Mediator and the Parties

At the first meeting, the mediator will establish with the parties the ground rules that are to be followed in the process. In particular, the mediator will

— discuss with, and obtain the agreement of the parties on, the question whether all meetings between the mediator and the parties will take place with both parties present, or whether the mediator may, at various times, hold separate meetings (caucuses) with each party alone; and

— ensure that the parties understand the rules on confidentiality set out in the WIPO Mediation Rules.

At the first meeting, the mediator will also discuss with the parties what additional documentation it would be desirable for each to provide and the need for any assistance by way of experts, if these matters have not already been dealt with in the initial contacts between the mediator and the parties.

Subsequent Meetings

Depending on the issues involved in the dispute and their complexity, as well as on the economic importance of the dispute and the distance that separates the parties' respective positions in relation to the dispute, the mediation may involve meetings held on only one day, across several days or over a longer period of time. The stages involved in the meetings held after the first meeting between the mediator and the parties would, where the mediator is playing a facilitative role, normally involve the following steps:

(i) the gathering of information concerning the dispute and the identification of the issues involved;

(ii) the exploration of the respective interests of the parties underlying the positions that they maintain in respect of the dispute;

(iii) the development of options that might satisfy the respective interests of the parties;

(iv) the evaluation of the options that exist for settling the dispute in the light of the parties' respective interests and each party's alternatives to settlement in accordance with one of the options; and

(v) the conclusion of a settlement and the recording of the settlement in an agreement.

Naturally, not all mediations result in a settlement. However, a settlement should be achieved where each party considers that an option for settlement exists which better serves its interests than any alternative option for settlement by way of litigation, arbitration or other means.

Parties' Private Consultations

Throughout the process of the mediation, naturally each party will wish to undertake, at various stages, private consultations with its advisors and experts for the purposes of discussing various aspects of the mediation or of evaluating options. It goes without saying that such private consultations may occur during the mediation process.

The Role of the WIPO Arbitration And Mediation Center

The Center performs the following functions as administering authority of a mediation:

— it assists the parties in selecting and appointing the mediator, as described above;

— it fixes, in consultation with parties and the mediator, the fees of the mediator;

— it administers the financial aspects of the mediation by obtaining a deposit from each party of the estimated costs of the mediation and paying out of the deposit the fees of the mediator and any other support services or facilities, such as fees for interpreters, where they are required;

— where the mediation takes place at WIPO in Geneva, it provides a meeting room and party retiring rooms free of charge; where the mediation takes place outside Geneva, it assists the parties in organizing appropriate meeting rooms;

— it assists the parties in organizing any other support services that may be needed, such as translation, interpretation or secretarial services.

* * *

The Main Steps in a Mediation

The Agreement to Mediate

↓

Commencement:
Request for Mediation

↓

Appointment of the Mediator

↓

Initial Contacts Between the Mediator and the Parties

* setting up the first meeting

* agreeing any preliminary exchange of documents

↓

First and Subsequent Meetings

* agreeing the ground rules of the process

* gathering information and identifying issues
* exploring the interests of the parties

* developing options for settlement

* evaluating options

↓

Concluding

RULES OF ARBITRATION AND CONCILIATION OF THE INTERNATIONAL ARBITRAL CENTER OF THE FEDERAL ECONOMIC CHAMBER VIENNA

(Vienna Rules)

Adopted by the Board of the Federal Economic Chamber on 30 November 2000, with effect from 1 January 2001

* * *

Conciliation Rules

[See Documents Supplement]

ZURICH CHAMBER OF COMMERCE, RULES OF PROCEDURE FOR THE ZURICH MINI–TRIAL

11 Yearbk. Comm. Arb'n 241 (1986).

[See Documents Supplement]

Questions and Comments

1. What are the main differences between arbitration on one hand and related forms of dispute settlement (mini trial, med-arb, conciliation, etc.) on the other hand?

2. What is the goal of mediation and how should a mediator go about reaching that goal? What does a mediator actually do?

3. Are there any mediator methods that an arbitrator should not use? Which ones and why not?

(How active should an arbitrator be in trying to encourage settlement? By revealing to the parties a tentative position on the issues, an arbitrator may encourage settlement, but may compromise the ability to change his or her mind on the final award. Would the parties be prepared to reveal any willingness to compromise to an arbitrator, who has the power to impose a "settlement" in a binding award? Would willingness to compromise be seen by an arbitrator as an admission of weakness in one's case? By a mediator?)

4. The WIPO Guide makes a distinction between facilitative mediation and evaluative mediation. If you needed mediation which form would you choose?

(Which would you choose if you were a mediator?)

5. The UNCITRAL Conciliation Rules (adopted by the UN General Assembly by Resolution 35/52 on 4 December 1980) provide in Article 7(4): "The conciliator may, at any stage of the conciliation proceedings, make proposals for a settlement of the dispute." * * * Article 12 of the same Rules adds: "Each party may, on his own initiative or at the invitation of the conciliator, submit to the conciliator suggestions for the settlement of the dispute."

What benefits and what risks do you see in these provisions?

6. By virtue of Articles 4 and 5 of the Vienna Conciliation Rules, a conciliator may continue as an arbitrator only if a settlement is reached. What is the logic of this rule?

7. According to Article 7 of the LCIA (London Court of International Arbitration) Mediation Procedure (effective 1 October 1999):

"If terms are agreed in settlement of the dispute, the parties, with the assistance of the mediator if the parties so request, shall draw up and sign a settlement agreement, setting out such terms.

By signing the settlement agreement, the parties agree to be bound by its terms."

Compare this "settlement agreement" with the outcome(s) contemplated in Article 4 of the Vienna Conciliation Rules. What differences do you see?

I.1.d. Technical Expertise

INTERNATIONAL CHAMBER OF COMMERCE, TECHNICAL EXPERTISE

(1993).

[See Documents Supplement]

Questions and Comments

1. Suppose the parties have a quality dispute. Buyer is reluctant to pay, because he believes that the quality of the goods was inadequate. Seller asserts that the quality fully conformed to the contract requirements. The parties choose to rely on the ICC Technical Expertise Procedure to find out who is right regarding the quality of the goods. After scrutinizing the matter, the ICC appointed expert comes up with the following finding: "The quality of the goods delivered was in conformity with the specifications set out in the Contract."

Where do you go from this point? Does this decision oblige Buyer to pay?

2. Suppose that in the above case the parties agreed that within the meaning of Article 8.3, the findings of the expert shall be binding. How could a successful party utilize the expert's determination?

I.1.e. Adaptation of Contracts

FRYDMAN v. COSMAIR, INC.

United States District Court, Southern District of New York, 1995.
1995 WL 404841.

MEMORANDUM AND ORDER

PRESKA, DISTRICT JUDGE.

On February 2, 1994, plaintiffs filed this action in the Supreme Court of New York, New York County, alleging fraudulent conversion, conspiracy to defraud and aiding and abetting fraud. Defendants removed the action to this Court pursuant to Sections 203 and 205 of the [law implementing the] Convention on the Recognition and Enforcement of Foreign Arbitral Awards ("the Convention"). See 9 U.S.C. §§ 201–208. Plaintiffs now move to remand, arguing that this action does not relate to an arbitration falling under the Convention. Upon reviewing the parties' submissions, I find plaintiffs' arguments persuasive and order this action remanded to the Supreme Court of the State of New York, County of New York.

*

B. *An Article 1592 [of the French Civil Code] Price Arbitration*[a] *is not an Arbitration Falling Under the Convention.*

Where, as in this case, there is a dispute as to whether the parties agreed to arbitrate, the court must look to the state law which governed the contract formation. See Progressive Casualty Co. v. C.A. Reaseguradora Nacional De Venezuela, 991 F.2d 42, 45–46 (2d Cir.1993) ("[W]e apply state law in determining whether the parties have agreed to arbitrate") (relying on Perry v. Thomas, 482 U.S. 483 (1987)).[7] Since the contract in dispute here was formed in France between French citizens, French law applies in the determination of whether it constitutes an agreement to arbitrate. Both parties have submitted translations of various French court decisions and documents, together with sworn affidavits by experts in French law.

The parties agree that plaintiffs and defendant L'Oreal entered into an agreement to arbitrate the value of plaintiffs' Paravision shares in December 1989. They also agree that in June 1990, the parties entered into a contract whereby L'Oreal agreed to buy plaintiffs' Paravision holdings at a price to be determined by the same person who had been appointed for the arbitration. The parties disagree, however, as to whether the final decision constituted an arbitral award or merely a price fixation conducted as part of a contract formation.

An examination of the record indicates that, under French law, the differences between general arbitrations and Article 1592 price arbitrations are more than merely "technical." In fact, as both parties' experts have noted, general arbitrations and Article 1592 price arbitrations are "two different institutions." It is true, as defendants note, that the plain language of Article 1592 of the French Civil Code refers to an "arbitration by a third party arbitrator." It is equally true, however, that an Article 1592 price appraisal-unlike an arbitral award-does not carry the status of a judgment, nor must an appraisal be conducted in the same manner as an arbitration. Furthermore, Article 1592 falls within the section of the French Civil Code relating to sales contracts, not within the section pertaining to arbitrations. Although neither party points to any French ruling that states definitively whether 1592 proceedings generally constitute arbitrations within the meaning of the Convention,[9]

---

a. Authors' note: Under French law a sale is not complete until the parties have agreed upon the object and the price. Concerning the price, the French Code Civil provides as follows:

Article 1591. The price of the sale must be determined by the parties.

Article 1592. It may nevertheless be left to the arbitration [*l'arbitrage*] of a third person: if such third person will not or cannot make an estimate, there is no sale.

7. By contrast, where there is no question as to the existence of an arbitration agreement, but there exists a dispute as to whether a particular issue is covered by that arbitral agreement, federal law governs. See Cook Chocolate Co. v. Salomon, Inc., 684 F. Supp. 1177 (S.D.N.Y.1988) (While state law governs the determination of whether an arbitral agreement exists, "once an agreement is found to exist, federal substantive law ... governs the scope and interpretation of the agreement").

9. Note, however, that the Paris Tribunal de Grande Instance has determined that the June 11, 1990 agreement, accepted by Mayoux on June 12, was "not an arbi-

plaintiffs have demonstrated that, in this case, the 1592 proceeding was merely a price appraisal and not an arbitration falling under the Convention.

Plaintiffs' experts, Professors Sauveur Vaisse and Geraud de Geouffre de la Pradelle, argue that although the language of Article 1592 refers to a "third party arbitration," such a proceeding does not constitute "real arbitration" within the meaning of the Convention.[10] In fact, several important distinctions exist between actual arbitrations and price valuations under 1592. Arbitrators, for instance, must hold "full adversarial hearings" and their awards "must be supported by detailed reasoning." Furthermore, since an arbitral award has the status of a judgment, "an action lodged against [it] . . . comes within the jurisdiction of the Court of Appeal." On the other hand, a third party designated under Article 1592 is required neither to hold hearings nor to support the decision with detailed reasoning. * * * [B]ecause the decision does not have the status of a judgment, an action against it must be instituted in a trial-level court. Plaintiffs note that, in fact, they brought an action against Mayoux's Israeli rights arbitral award in the Paris Court of Appeals, where it was canceled. They brought an action against the 1592 price valuation, on the other hand, in the Paris TGI [Tribunal de grande instance], a trial-level court, where the valuation was quashed.[11] Under French law, plaintiffs argue, the TGI would not have had the jurisdiction to quash the price decision if the decision were truly an arbitral award. Moreover, the French court specifically found that the proceeding under Article 1592 was not an arbitration. In the July 2, 1990 decision denying plaintiffs' "summons to summary proceedings," the TGI stated that:

> [T]he agreement of June 11, 1990, accepted by Jacques MAYOUX on June 12, in which he is granted the power to fix sales price pursuant to Article 1592 of the Code of Civil Law . . . is not an arbitration agreement but only a mandate granted by the parties the sole object of which was to estimate and evaluate the thing being sold.

* * * The French court proceedings and the July 1990 holding by the TGI provide significant insight into how an Article 1592 price fixation is perceived by French courts. There is little doubt that, under French law, the price fixation performed by Mayoux was not an arbitration falling under the Convention.

Even if federal law applied to this question, as defendants argue, the agreement in issue would not constitute an arbitration agreement. There are two major distinctions between arbitrations and Article 1592 price

---

tration agreement." (Arkin Reply Aff., Exh. A).

10. Nomenclature, in this case, cannot be determinative, especially in light of the foreign nature of the statute at hand. The court in McDonnell Douglas Finance Corp. v. Pennsylvania Power and Light Co., 858 F.2d 825, 830 (2d Cir.1988), held that "[i]t is irrelevant . . . [that] the contract language in question does not employ the word

'arbitration'." It follows that the mere fact that a foreign statute employs the word "arbitration" does not necessarily result in a true arbitration falling under the Convention.

11. Again, we have the benefit of knowing how the French courts would view the two separate proceedings; we need not guess.

appraisals. First, while general arbitrations are conducted as a means of resolving disputes, Article 1592 price arbitrations are conducted as a means of providing the price term for contracting parties. Second, and more importantly, a general arbitral award, under normal circumstances, takes on the status of a judgment; the same is never true for an Article 1592 price appraisal. It is for these two primary reasons that an Article 1592 appraisal cannot be recognized as falling under the Convention.

Defendants argue that to qualify as an arbitration agreement under the Convention, "all that is required is an agreement to submit a question or issue to a third party for binding resolution." (Def. Mem. at 17.) In support of this argument, defendants point to McDonnell Douglas Finance Corp. v. Pennsylvania Power and Light Co., 858 F.2d 825, 830 (2d Cir.1988) ("[W]hat is important is that the parties clearly intended to submit some disputes to their 'chosen instrument for the definitive settlement of [certain] grievances under the Agreement)'" (quoting International Longshoremen's Ass'n v. Hellenic Lines, Ltd., 549 F. Supp. 435 (S.D.N.Y.1982)). By using the phrase "question or issue," defendants mischaracterize the McDonnell Douglas Finance court's holding, which specifically refers to "disputes" and "grievances."[12] In fact, plaintiffs and L'Oreal, by June 1990, had reached an agreement whereby L'Oreal would purchase plaintiffs' Paravision shares at a price to be determined by Mayoux. The Article 1592 proceeding was conducted as part of a contract formation and not for the purpose of resolving a dispute. The court in City of Omaha v. Omaha Water Co., 218 U.S. 180 (1910) held that when

> the parties had agreed that one should sell and the other buy a specific thing, and the price should be a valuation by persons agreed upon, it cannot be said that there was any dispute or difference. Such an arrangement precludes or prevents difference, and is not intended to settle any which has arisen. This seems to be the distinction between an arbitration and an appraisement, though the first term is often used when the other is more appropriate.[13]

* * * In their June 11, 1990 letter to Mayoux, plaintiffs and defendant L'Oreal informed Mayoux that his "decision [would] form the parties' will concerning the price of the FRYDMAN Group's stake." (emphasis added) That is hardly the language of dispute. It is precisely because plaintiffs and defendant L'Oreal had come to an agreement and no longer had a dispute making an arbitration necessary that they terminated the arbitration as to the Paravision shares and replaced it with the Article 1592 price appraisal.

12. The other cases relied upon by defendants in support of their argument also refer to "disputes," and not to mere price fixations. CAE Indus. Ltd. v. Aerospace Holdings Co., 741 F. Supp. 388 (S.D.N.Y. 1989); Campeau Corp. v. May Dep't Stores Co., 723 F. Supp. 224 (S.D.N.Y.1989).

13. The City of Omaha holding is reflected in the words of Professor Corbin: "Where two parties make an agreement of purchase and sale, providing that the price shall be determined by a named third party, we have an appraisal but not an arbitration." 6A Corbin on Contracts § 1442 at 430–31 (1962).

Finally, and most importantly, even under federal law, because a 1592 price appraisal could never attain the status of a judgment, it cannot be considered an arbitration falling under the Convention. Parties are encouraged to arbitrate their disputes in order to avoid lengthy trial proceedings. In Brener v. Becker Paribas, Inc., 628 F. Supp. 442, 448 (S.D.N.Y.1985), for example, the court noted that "[a]rbitration provides a prompt and efficient method of resolving disputes, without the expense, delays or complications that are inherent in litigation." The result of an arbitration is a binding, enforceable judgment. See Whirlpool Corp. v. Philips Electronics, N.V., 848 F. Supp. 474 (S.D.N.Y.1994) ("The confirmation of an arbitration award is generally a summary proceeding that converts a final arbitration award into a judgment of the Court.") Similarly, in France, arbitral awards generally obtain "exequatur," making them enforceable as judgments of the court. The enforceability of arbitral awards as judgments of the court provides a powerful incentive for parties to arbitrate their disputes. A price fixation pursuant to Article 1592, however, never obtains the status of a judgment and therefore lacks an important and necessary arbitral function. It is not clear why the parties terminated the original arbitration, but the fact that the parties chose to fix the price pursuant to Article 1592 rather than by an arbitration is dispositive.

As plaintiffs note, a price appraisal pursuant to Article 1592 merely supplies the price term for a contract of sale; one party's refusal to comply with that term would constitute nothing more than a breach of contract. Such breach would not constitute a failure to comply with a court judgment. For example, if, after Mayoux set the share price, L'Oreal had simply refused to pay that amount, plaintiffs could not have come to this Court to seek enforcement. This Court would lack jurisdiction because, since the price decision is simply a contract term, it is not an arbitral "award" capable of being enforced under the Convention.

CONCLUSION

Because this action does not relate to an arbitration falling under the Convention, and because no other basis for federal subject matter jurisdiction has been alleged, this Court lacks subject matter jurisdiction. Accordingly, plaintiffs' motion to remand this case to the Supreme Court of the State of New York, County of New York, is granted. The Clerk of the Court shall mark this matter closed.

SO ORDERED.

Questions and Comments

1. There have been attempts to design special procedures for adaptation of contracts. For example, the ICC set up a "Standing Committee for the Regulation of Contractual Relations" and adopted "Rules for Adaptation of Contracts". The undertaking was not a success and the Rules have been abrogated. The need still exists, however, and arbitration experts have continued to try to find an appropriate legal framework for adaptation of contracts by arbitrators. One of the key questions is that of the legal

nature—and thus the consequence—of any adaptation. Article 11.3 of the ICC Rules for Adaptation of Contracts, provided that: "When the third person takes a decision, that decision is binding on the parties to the same extent as the contract in which it is deemed to be incorporated." This means that the resulting adaptation is not an award but becomes a provision of the contract that is binding to the extent other contractual provisions are. Could the adaptation made by a third person be challenged as unconscionable?

2. In what circumstances would you consider seeking adaptation of your contract?

3. Article 1020 of the Dutch 1986 Arbitration Act (Book IV of the Code of Civil Procedure) states:

> Parties may also agree to submit the following matters to arbitration:
>
> > (a) the determination only of the quality or condition of the goods;
> >
> > (b) the determination only of the quantum of damages or a monetary debt;
> >
> > (c) the filling of gaps in, or modification of, the legal relationship between the parties referred to in paragraph (1).

This (uncommon) provision considers these matters as possible subjects of arbitration. Does this mean that the result of such arbitration is a binding and enforceable award?

4. In *Frydman v. Cosmair* the court held that a price fixed pursuant to Article 1592 of the French Code Civil "never obtains the status of a judgment and therefore lacks an important and necessary" characteristic of an arbitral award. What do you see as the differences between a price-fixation and an arbitral proceeding? How would you define each of these proceedings?

5. What would a "real" arbitral award say in a dispute of the kind involved in *Frydman v. Cosmair*?

I.1.f. Arbitration and Litigation

AMERICAN ALMOND PRODUCTS CO.
v. CONSOLIDATED PECAN
SALES CO,. INC.

United States Court of Appeals, Second Circuit, 1944.
144 F.2d 448, 450.

LEARNED HAND, CIRCUIT JUDGE.

* * *

Arbitration may or may not be a desirable substitute for trials in courts; as to that the parties must decide in each instance. But when they have adopted it, they must be content with its informalities; they may not hedge it about with those procedural limitations which it is precisely its purpose to avoid. They must content themselves with looser approximations to the enforcement of their rights than those that the law accords them, when they resort to its machinery.

James H. Carter, DISPUTE RESOLUTION AND INTERNATIONAL AGREEMENTS

International Commercial Agreements 435–45 (1995).*
(Commercial Law and Practice Course Handbook Series, No. A726, 439).

Chair

Michael Gruson

DISPUTE RESOLUTION AND INTERNATIONAL AGREEMENTS

1. ARBITRATION OR LITIGATION?
    A. Why is arbitration so prevalent as a dispute settlement mechanism in international agreements?
        1. *Predictability*: the dispute will be resolved in one place and not by a race to judgment in the courts of two nations.
        2. *Competence*: at least in theory, the arbitrators will have applicable specialized commercial and legal expertise.
        3. *Party participation*: the procedures often are shaped by the parties as well as the arbitrators, rather than dictated by detailed rules as in litigation.
        4. *Finality*: the resulting award will be subject to relatively little risk of being set aside or altered by a court. This is particularly true of U.S. courts, which frankly espouse a pro-arbitration bias.
        5. *Enforceability*: the U.S. and most other nations are parties to the U.N. Convention on Recognition and Enforcement of Arbitral Awards (the "New York Convention"), making a foreign arbitral award typically easier to enforce than a foreign judgment.
        6. *Costs (to some extent)*: There usually are no costly depositions in arbitration, reducing costs somewhat; but since arbitrators must be paid, the cost may be ultimately as high as litigation (or even higher).
        7. *Privacy (up to a point)*: There are no open hearings or filings, but the proceeding still may become known publicly due to ancillary litigation or required regulatory filings.
    B. However, there are drawbacks.
        1. In arbitration, a panel must be selected before anything substantive can happen. Therefore, speedy relief is unlikely.
            a. Not all courts will provide provisional remedies in aid of arbitration. In New York for instance, attachment or a preliminary injunction in aid of arbitration under CPLR § 7502(c) is available when "the award to which the applicant may be entitled may be rendered ineffectual" without provisional relief. However, *no* provisional remedy is available from a New York state court in an *international* arbitration situation unless expressly pro-

---

* Reprinted by permission of James H. Carter, Partner, Sullivan & Cromwell.

vided. Compare *Drexel Burnham Lambert, Inc.* v. *Ruebsamen*, 139 A.D.2d 323 (1st Dep't 1988) with *Remy Amerique, Inc.* v. *Touzet Distribution, S.A.R.L.*, 816 F. Supp. 213 (S.D.N.Y.1993).

    b. Courts that do provide provisional remedies in international arbitration matters, which include the majority of Federal courts (*e.g.*, *Borden, Inc.* v. *Meiji Milk Products Co., Ltd.*, 919 F.2d 822 (2d Cir.1990), typically are reluctant to go beyond the barest maintenance of the *status quo* and want to avoid intruding on matters that might more appropriately be dealt with by the arbitrators.

  2. In a bitter dispute, there may be not only the specified arbitration but also litigation resulting from attempts to avoid the arbitration.

  3. Some consider that arbitration tends toward splitting the difference rather than deciding either side is totally right or totally wrong.

C. Litigation may be preferable because one party will not agree to arbitrate in a place or under terms the other will accept.

  1. Arbitration might be unwieldy, too, if the transaction involves several participants or if related arbitrations cannot be consolidated, *see United Kingdom* v. *Boeing Co.*, 998 F.2d 68 (2d Cir.1993). Litigation techniques for dealing with multiple parties are more advanced.

  2. Although it is hard to predict in advance, one side may need access to broader judicial discovery (particularly the broader discovery available as to non-parties).

D. Since arbitration or other forum clauses usually are inserted before the nature of a dispute can be predicted, factors such as whether broad discovery is necessary often cannot be anticipated. At bottom, the desire for predictability and avoidance of a potentially hostile foreign court is the largest incentive for choice of arbitration.

E. Forum selection clauses for litigation * * *, if they can be accepted by both sides, at least limit the risk of multiple litigation in competing fora. But if no judicial forum can be agreed on, arbitration may be preferable as the only predictable alternative.

F. Mediation, mini-trials and other alternative dispute resolution techniques are available and are beginning to make some headway in international dispute resolution, but use of them remains relatively infrequent.

G. Factors to consider in selecting a dispute resolution mechanism.

  1. What are the sorts of disputes most likely to arise?

    a. Who is the likely claimant?

    b. Who will be holding the money or goods?

    c. Who will be holding the records and other evidence?

  2. Will there be other leverage at the time of a dispute, such as dependence by one party on another for spare parts or service?

  3. Where are the parties' assets?

  4. Is there security in the form of guarantees or letters of credit?

  5. In what language will the parties be dealing?

6. What will be the governing law of the contract?
7. Does either party have a substantial base of operations in a third country and familiarity with its legal system?

Christian Bühring-Uhle, ARBITRATION AND MEDIATION IN INTERNATIONAL BUSINESS: DESIGNING PROCEDURES FOR EFFECTIVE CONFLICT MANAGEMENT

395–96 (1996).*

APPENDIX 1: RESULTS OF SURVEY ON ARBITRATION AND SETTLEMENT IN INTERNATIONAL BUSINESS DISPUTES (ALL RESPONDENTS)

I. ADVANTAGES OF ARBITRATION

Below is a list of the most commonly cited advantages of international commercial arbitration over litigation. Do these advantages really exist and if so, what is their relevance in deciding whether to choose arbitration? ("HR" = highly relevant (3), "S" = significant (2), "OF" = one factor among many (1), "NR" = not relevant (O), "NE" = advantage does not exist (–1)):

		resp.	"HR"	"S"	"OF"	"NR"	"NE"	avg.
a.	forum is neutral	57	41 (72%)	6 (11%)	6 (11%)	1 (2%)	3 (5%)	2.4
b.	forum has expertise	58	21 (36%)	16 (28%)	8 (14%)	2 (3%)	1 (19%)	1.6
c.	the results are more predictable	60	2 (3%)	5 (8%)	5 (8%)	3 (5%)	45 (75%)	– 0.4
d.	greater degree of voluntary compliance with results	57	4 (7%)	19 (33%)	5 (9%)	2 (4%)	27 (47%)	0.5
e.	treaties ensure enforcement of results abroad	55	35 (64%)	15 (27%)	2 (4%)	0 (0%)	3 (5%)	2.4
f.	confidential procedure	56	18 (32%)	18 (32%)	15 (27%)	1 (2%)	4 (7%)	1.8
g.	limited discovery	57	13 (23%)	20 (35%)	9 (16%)	3 (5%)	12 (21%)	1.3
h.	no appeal	57	21 (37%)	13 (23%)	10 (18%)	0 (0%)	13 (23%)	1.5
i.	procedure is less costly	53	4 (8%)	7 (13%)	11 (21%)	4 (8%)	27 (51%)	0.2
j.	less time consuming	54	6 (11%)	13 (24%)	13 (24%)	2 (4%)	20 (37%)	0.7
k.	more amicable	54	6 (11%)	17 (31%)	6 (11%)	3 (6%)	22 (41%)	0.7

Questions and Comments

1. In the contemporary world, is litigation best characterized as:

* Reprinted with permission from Kluwer Law International.

(a) A search for truth?

(b) A striving for victory in a fair battle?

(c) Something else?

2. Two values are central to the decision-making process: impartiality (neutrality) and balance (equal procedural chances offered to both sides). In what ways are these values expressed in litigation, arbitration, and related forms of dispute settlement?

3. What are, generally speaking, some of the major differences between arbitration and litigation as forms of dispute settlement? In terms of the authority of the third-party decision maker?

4. The survey on Arbitration and Settlement in International Business Disputes was directed to specialists, arbitrators with many years of experience, law professors, and attorneys who have had a significant number of arbitration cases. Parties referring their disputes to arbitration may have a somewhat different picture. Points as to which different views could well emerge are speed, costs, and the "amicable character" of arbitration. Regarding these issues, parties typically expect more comparative advantages from arbitration than the specialists do.

5. Although arbitration has clearly established itself as the dominant method of settling international trade disputes, in a relatively large number of cases in which the contract contains an arbitration clause, one party insists on arbitration while the other party opposes arbitration. How do you explain this phenomenon?

6. If you accept the view that arbitration offers considerable advantages, do you prefer arbitration only as opposed to litigation in a foreign court, or to litigation in general?

I.1.g. Institutional and Ad Hoc Arbitration

Gerald Aksen,[b] AD HOC VERSUS INSTITUTIONAL ARBITRATION

2 ICC ICArb. Bull. 8–14 (1991)*

I—INTRODUCTION

International commercial arbitration has become the generally acceptable method of resolving disputes between transnational contracting parties. Business people tend to avoid the perceived uncertainty and unpredictability of foreign courts. Fear of foreign laws, lawyers and language together with loss of confidentiality, considerable expense and lengthy court proceedings have undoubtedly convinced foreign traders and international business to utilize an alternative dispute resolution

b. Partner, Reid & Priest.

* ICC International Court of Arbitration Bulletin; Vol. 2/No. 1CISSN 1017–284X; Published in its official English version by the International Chamber of Commerce. Copyright © 1991—ICC International Court of Arbitration. Available from: ICC Publishing SA, 38 cours Albert 1er, 75008 Paris, France. (*www.iccbooks.com*) Reprinted with permission from ICC.

mechanism. Fortified by a modern treaty[1] that enforces international arbitration agreements and awards, as well as modern sets of laws and rules, it's clear that international commercial arbitration has arrived.

One of the more interesting issues that does remain, however, is whether to arbitrate under the rules of an Arbitral Institution or to use an ad hoc procedure. The choice has been made more difficult since the promulgation in 1976 of the UNCITRAL Arbitration Rules-an ad hoc set of rules. In order to make an intelligent choice of institutional or ad hoc arbitration, one must appreciate the advantages and disadvantages of each.

II—Definitions

Institutional arbitration means that the proceedings are administered by an organization, usually in accordance with its own rules of arbitration. Readers of this Bulletin, for example, will immediately recognize the International Chamber of Commerce (ICC) as an institution with an International Court of Arbitration that administers cases pursuant to the ICC Rules of Arbitration.[4]

Ad hoc arbitration means that there is no formal administration by any established arbitral agency; instead the parties have opted to create their own procedures for a given arbitration. This can be accomplished, for example, either by drafting a set of ad hoc procedures in a contract, or by reference to the UNCITRAL Arbitration Rules, or by allowing the arbitration tribunal to fashion its own procedures after the dispute has arisen.

III—Advantages of Ad Hoc Arbitration

Ad hoc arbitration can have several advantages over institutional arbitration. The first is flexibility. An ad hoc procedure can be "shaped to meet the wishes of the parties and the facts of the particular dispute."[5] To accomplish this goal, however, requires the complete cooperation of the disputants and their legal representatives. As D.A. Redfern, an eminent English lawyer and author, notes, "if such cooperation is forthcoming, the difference between an ad hoc arbitration and an institutional arbitration is like the difference between a tailor made suit and one which is bought off the peg."[6]

---

1. United Nations Convention on the Recognition and Enforcement of Foreign Arbitral Awards, June 10, 1958, 21 U.S.T. 2517, T.I.A.S. N° 6997, 330 U.N.T.S. 38.

4. Other leading organizations that administer international arbitrations include the American Arbitration Association (AAA), the London Court of International Arbitration (LCIA), the Stockholm Chamber of Commerce (SCC), the Arbitral Centre of the Federal Economic Chamber in Vienna, the Vancouver (British Columbia) Cen-

tre for Commercial Disputes, the Quebec Arbitration Centre, the Korean Commercial Arbitration Board, the Japan Commercial Arbitration Association and the Hong Kong International Arbitration Centre.

5. D.A. Redfern, *Why arbitrate transnational disputes? Should institutional or ad hoc arbitration be provided?* The Institute for Transnational Arbitration (unpublished remarks).

6. *Id.*

Other stated advantages are cost and speed. Since most arbitral institutions charge fees for their administrative services, the parties save the administration fees when they opt for ad hoc arbitration. Similarly, avoiding the various institutions' sometimes cumbersome internal procedures and time periods for, among other things, selecting arbitrators, filing documents, and (in the case of the ICC) Terms of Reference and Award review procedures may minimize delays.

The most significant boost for ad hoc arbitration came from the United Nations Commission on International Trade Law in 1976 when it promulgated the UNCITRAL Arbitration Rules. Prior to the fashioning of this relatively complete set of rules, parties to ad hoc proceedings either had to draft their own set of procedures whether in the initial contract or after a dispute had arisen, or leave the issuance of procedures to the arbitrators. Reference in the parties' contract to the UNCITRAL Rules will immediately incorporate a full blown set of arbitration procedures. Thus, the UNCITRAL Arbitration Rules are in this respect a substitute for the rules of arbitral institutions.

Further, since UNCITRAL does not in any way act as an administrator or furnish a secretariat to the parties, UNCITRAL has no fees. There is therefore a cost savings. In theory the UNCITRAL Rules offer a low cost and speedy, flexible alternative to institutional arbitration.

The advantages of ad hoc arbitration presume an essential caveat—that the disputing parties, their counsel and the arbitrators work together to make the process work without need to resort to administrative or judicial oversight. Without this cooperation, the theoretical advantages of ad hoc arbitration have, in my own experience, proven sadly illusory.

Finally, it is important not to exaggerate the benefits of ad hoc arbitration. The costs saved by the UNCITRAL Arbitration Rules, for example, are those of an administering agency itself, but not the usually far larger legal and arbitrators' fees. Moreover, since most international institutions are now facing substantial competition from other arbitral bodies, transnational businesses are enjoying the benefit of lower and more reasonable fees. The ICC, for example, now has a maximum fee of $50,500 or $25,250 per party for all cases of $50 million dollars or more.[c] These capped fees can be well worth the price. There are many real and not often recognized advantages of institutional, and particularly ICC, administration.

IV—Advantages of Institutional Arbitration

1—Drafting the Arbitration Agreement

A principal advantage of institutional arbitration is the ease of incorporating by reference the institution's rules in an international contract. Instead of trying to reinvent the wheel, the parties can take comfort in the time tested rules and procedures drafted by professionals

---

c. Authors' note: As of July 1, 2001 the ICC's maximum administrative fee is $75,800 for all cases where the sum in dispute is $80 million or more.

in the institutional commercial arena. The ICC Rules, for example, are almost 70 years old and are updated when necessary to meet the ever changing climate of dispute settlement.

Use of the ICC Rules and its recommended broad arbitration clause has proven to be valuable in preventing parties, after a dispute arises, from successfully asserting in national courts that the claims are non-arbitrable. In one recent instance, a U.S. federal appeals court expressly recognized the broad nature of the ICC's recommended clause in denying a party's claims that certain disputes fell outside the scope of the arbitration agreement:

"The International Chamber of Commerce's recommended clause which provides for arbitration of" (a)ll disputes arising in connection with the present contract "must be construed to encompass a broad scope of arbitrable issues. The recommended clause does not limit arbitration to the literal interpretation or performance of the contract. It embraces every dispute between the parties having a significant relationship to the contract regardless of the label attached to the dispute."[7]

Another particularly helpful feature of the ICC Rules is that they are available in seven major languages—English, French, German, Italian, Spanish, Arabic and Japanese. I have found it very useful to show a negotiating party a copy of the ICC Rules in its own language when discussing the terms of the arbitration clause.

2—Arbitrator Selection

Selecting arbitrators is unquestionably the most important service an administering agency can perform. A successful arbitration usually depends upon the intelligence and management skills of the arbitrators. Choosing good arbitrators is, therefore, of utmost importance.

In this area, the institutions generally excel. I have been involved in arbitrator appointments in cases before the ICC, AAA, LCIA, SCC, Federal Economic Chamber in Vienna and the Romanian Chamber of Commerce. In most cases the institutions' appointments have been well qualified to resolve the dispute at hand.

Where the ICC appoints a sole arbitrator, or a chairman, or all three arbitrators, the Secretariat will ensure the selection of arbitrators with legal training, and usually with prior arbitral experience, to hear the case. To aid in the arbitrator selection process the ICC takes advantage of its National Committees in almost sixty countries around the world to nominate candidates. The ICC Court then reviews the nominees and appoints only those persons deemed qualified and experienced to hear the case.

During the past decade of my arbitral experience, ICC arbitrators have been leading professors of international law from France, Germany,

---

7. *J.J. Ryan & Sons, Inc. v. Rhone Pou-*   Cir.1988).
lenc Textile, S.A., 863 F.2d 315, 321 (4th

the Netherlands, Switzerland and the United Kingdom or retired judges or private practitioners with years of practical experience from the same countries, as well as from Canada, Egypt, Italy, Ireland, Japan, Sweden and the U.S. The arbitrators have always been fluent in the language to be used in the proceeding and more often than not have a background in international law and practice and trade customs.

It is equally possible for parties to ad hoc arbitrations to select these very same persons as arbitrators without benefit of an arbitral institution. However, in many instances it's difficult for disputing parties to agree on arbitrator selection, particularly since the dispute itself has heightened tensions and disrupted relations so that mutual distrust hinders a smooth arbitrator selection process. Then, too, the choice of a foreign neutral may be difficult to make because of plain lack of familiarity with good candidates. Therefore, a neutral agency with the authority to appoint an independent arbitrator eases the process of tribunal formation. For this reason many parties to ad hoc arbitration will engage the services of an Arbitral Institution as an appointing authority in lieu of judicial appointment by a national court.

Of equal importance is the institution's role in engaging the arbitrator's services. The parties are spared the burden of negotiating a fee for services with their adjudicator. Since, in most countries, parties and their counsel never have to concern themselves with how judges are compensated for their services, there is little experience with negotiating arbitrators' fees. As a result, parties to ad hoc international arbitrations have found themselves in difficult or embarrassing situations.

Two recent international cases demonstrate some examples of the fee practices that have either delayed or derailed ad hoc arbitral proceedings. In Israel, an arbitral proceeding was terminated and a legal malpractice suit ensued because one had paid an advance "booking fee" to its party appointed arbitrator.[8] In England, a court criticized the arbitrators for seeking commitment fees after they had accepted appointment with no such condition.[9] Neither of these instances would have occurred under ICC practices where the fees of all three arbitrators are set by the institution and the arbitrators have little or no voice in determining their charges. Further, the ICC fee schedule for arbitrators is on balance fair and reasonable.

Institutional arbitration also provides an administrative referee to ensure that all arbitrators, including party-appointed arbitrators, are truly independent. Disclosure and challenge procedures are provided for the institution to remove and replace any arbitrator nominees whose independence is challenged by a party. In ad hoc proceedings, when an arbitrator refuses to disqualify himself, it usually requires court assistance to obtain his removal.

---

8. *Wolcott v. Ginsburg,* 746 F. Supp. 1113 (D.D.C.1990).

9. *Norjarl A/S v. Hyundai Heavy Industries Co., Ltd.,* The Independent, Feb. 22, 1991.

3—Professional Administration

A third advantage of institutional arbitration is the professional staff available to guide disputants through the arbitration process. At the ICC, for example, the Secretariat maintains a secretary general, a general counsel, five teams of lawyers (soon to be six) trained in diverse legal systems, and assistants to administer the case from the initial filing of the Request for Arbitration to the rendering of the final Award. The Secretariat performs a multitude of tasks that cannot truly be matched in ad hoc arbitration. The mere fact that they are there to answer basic questions in seven major languages is helpful and reassuring to parties filing cases.

Institutional administration provides a variety of routine services. The most common services involve acknowledging and serving arbitration requests and answering documents, fixing and processing fees, prodding the parties to observe the various response times, selecting arbitrators, ruling on challenges to arbitrators, replacing arbitrators, locating the place of arbitration, and, generally following-up to ensure the expeditious and formal completion of the proceedings.

It is the professional help on unusual requests that has generally impressed me with ICC services. Once it was necessary to obtain documentary proof in Spanish to convince a court in Central America that the ICC Rules permitted provisional remedies in aid of arbitration. The prompt delivery of the documents with properly authenticated papers from the local Embassy office in Paris enabled my client to obtain an injunction.

In addition, truly helpful service can be obtained when a losing party fails to honor an award. The ICC has written letters to recalcitrant parties pointing out the importance of honoring their obligations and encouraging the prompt payment of the award. Correspondence to foreign governmental entities has proven successful in some instances.

4—Judicial Deference to Institutional Arbitration

A fourth benefit is derived from the fact that arbitral institutions have received the increasingly favorable recognition of national courts. In this respect, several institutions have enjoyed notable success due to their long and proven track records. England has accepted the reference to ICC Rules as evidencing an intent to opt out of appeals to the national courts of that country.[10] The U.S. Supreme Court permitted the ICC and the AAA to file amicus curiae briefs as friends of the court on the procedures of international arbitration in the most important international arbitration case decided in the U.S. in the last decade.[11] Indeed, the Supreme Court in that case cited to the ICC's brief in expanding the range of issues resolvable in international arbitration.[12]

10. *Arab African Energy Corp. Ltd. v. Olieprodukten Nederland B.V.*, (1983) 2 Lloyd's Rep. 419.

11. *Mitsubishi Motors Corp. v. Soler Chrysler–Plymouth, Inc.*, 469 U.S. 1102 (1985). [Reproduced infra, chapter II.2.c.i.]

12. *Mitsubishi Motors Corp. v. Soler Chrysler–Plymouth, Inc.*, 473 U.S. 614, 634 n. 18, 637 n. 19 (1985).

Judicial respect for the integrity of arbitral awards is most important to a party which must seek enforcement of an award in national courts. In general, national courts are much more comfortable in confirming commercial awards where there is some assurance that a neutral body, such as an arbitral institution, has fairly referred both the procedural and substantive controversies which invariably arise during the course of arbitration proceedings. Ad hoc arbitration does not usually provide the same level of comfort.

* * *

U.S. judicial respect for the ICC was recently dramatized when a federal appeals court refused to second guess the ICC Court's review of an award which the losing disputant sought to nullify:

"Furthermore, the final damages award was approved by the Court of the ICC in accordance with Article 21 of the Rules. . . . As the district court pointed out, '(t)he ICC Court is the best judge of whether its procedural rules have been satisfied, and when it certified the award as final, it certified that the procedural rules had been complied [with] to its satisfaction.' "[13]

Similarly, another federal appeals court turned down a party's claim that it should review the ICC Court's determination under ICC Rules 8(3) that a prima facie agreement to arbitrate existed:

"Ordinarily, (a party) would be entitled to have these issues resolved by a court. By contracting to have all disputes resolved according to the Rules of the ICC, however, (the party) agreed to be bound by Articles 8.3 and 8.4. These provisions unmistakably allow the arbitrator to determine her own jurisdiction when, as here, there exists a prima facie agreement to arbitrate whose continued existence and validity is being questioned."[14]

As previously mentioned, there are a host of prominent arbitral institutions in many countries of the world that administer international disputes. Most, however, suffer from being identified with a particular country. In the United States of America, the American Arbitration Association (AAA) is a prime example. It has perhaps the largest caseload in the world of domestic arbitrations but its international cases are a small portion of its activities. Indeed, it has just promulgated a new set of "International Arbitration Rules" in an effort to accord greater recognition to its international capabilities. In the United Kingdom the London Court of International Arbitration (LCIA) is a preeminent arbitral institution with a growing caseload. In Sweden, the Stockholm Chamber of Commerce (SCC) has been made famous because of its key

13. *Carte Blanche (Singapore) Pte., Ltd. v. Carte Blanche International, Ltd.*, 888 F.2d 260 (2d Cir.1989) (quoting 683 F.Supp. 945, 957 (S.D.N.Y.1988)).

14. *Apollo Computer, Inc. v. Berg*, 886 F.2d 469, 473 (1st Cir.1989) (citations omitted). *See also the Daiei, Inc. v. United States Shoe Corp.*, 755 F. Supp. 299, 303 (D.Haw. 1991) (party's claim concerning ICC selection of sole arbitrator is itself arbitrable pursuant to party's arbitration agreement incorporating ICC Rules).

role in resolving East–West disputes, particularly under the Optional U.S.—U.S.S.R. arbitration procedures. The Arbitral Centre of the Federal Economic Chamber in Vienna wants to encourage dispute settlement in the developing economies of Eastern Europe. Similarly, the arbitral institutions in Canada, Hong Kong, Japan and Korea have made significant strides by increasing their international, practical, legal and geographical advantages. Mention should also be made of the International Centre for the Settlement of Investment Disputes (ICSID) since it also has no ties to any national state. However, its usefulness is limited because its activities are designed for contracts between private parties and States.

5—Default Award

A seldom used but very helpful feature of institutional arbitration is the ability to proceed in the absence of a defaulting party. Most institutions have rules like Article 15(2) of the ICC Rules, which provides:

> "If one of the parties, although duly summoned, fails to appear, the arbitrator, if he is satisfied that the summons was duly received and the party is absent without valid excuse, shall have power to proceed with the arbitration, and such proceedings shall be deemed to have been conducted in the presence of all parties."

In ad hoc arbitrations it may be more difficult to enforce a default award. The enforcing court doesn't have the same degree of assurance that due process was accorded the defaulting party. This is especially true when the defaulting party is a foreign government or other state-controlled organization. At the ICC the notice and summons procedure is done by and supervised by the ICC Secretariat so that the arbitrator can feel assured that the defaulting party had notice of the arbitration and for whatever reason, elected not to appear. I know from personal experience that enforcing courts have given due recognition to default ICC awards against foreign government entities.[15]

* * *

CONCLUSION

Ad hoc and institutional arbitration will always have their own respective adherents. Whether one is really superior to the other is an unanswerable question in the abstract. Ad hoc enthusiasts now have the benefit of an international set of rules from UNCITRAL that have received relatively little criticism in the 15 years of their existence. If the parties are able to select experienced arbitrators promptly and there is reasonable cooperation between counsel and the proceedings progress quickly, the use of ad hoc international arbitration can certainly be an attractive option.

15. *See American Construction Machinery & Equipment Corporation Ltd. (ACME) v. Mechanised Construction of Pakistan Ltd. (MCP)*, 659 F. Supp. 426 (S.D.N.Y.), *aff'd.* 828 F.2d 117 (2d Cir.1987), *cert. denied*, 108 S. Ct. 1024 (1988) (U.S. courts enforced ICC default award against Pakistani state instrumentality).

If, at any stage of the proceedings matters go awry through party obstruction or circumstance, then the hoped for ad hoc arbitration benefits of speed, economy and flexibility can easily be dissipated. Since one never knows when the contract is being drafted whether there will be a cooperative attitude at the time of arbitration, the prudent advice is to opt for institutional arbitration. The added benefits will certainly aid the neophyte in international arbitration proceedings. The savvy practitioner and client will benefit from the experienced administration and from the name recognition afforded institutional awards by national courts.

Questions and Comments

1.   The choice between institutional and ad hoc arbitration is a delicate one. Incomplete or inconsistent arbitration agreements are more likely to be filled out appropriately when within an institutional framework. (A safety net—though perhaps one less complete—is available for ad hoc arbitration if the parties adopt a pre-established set of procedural regulations such as the UNCITRAL rules.)

To draft a good ad hoc clause one needs to understand the arbitration process thoroughly when the contract containing the arbitration agreement is being drafted. (Of course, lack of understanding of arbitration can lead to fatal mistakes even if the parties choose institutional arbitration.[1])

Institutions seek to protect their own standing, reputation, and interests. They establish administrative and arbitrators' fee scales and some, for example in Article 28(1) of the 1998 ICC Rules, also provide that the award shall not be notified to the parties until the fees are fully paid. (The ICC administrative fees, now capped at $75,800, are at the higher end of the spectrum of administrative costs.)

The arbitrators' fees are more predictable in institutional than in ad hoc arbitrations. In the latter, they must be negotiated between the arbitrators and the parties. The parties should agree on this delicate matter with the prospective ad hoc arbitrators before the latter are appointed, if possible. (There is some evidence that ad hoc arbitrators' fees are increasingly being set by reference to an appropriate institutional fee schedule.) Other features of institutional arbitration aimed at preserving the integrity of the institution may be viewed by some as a mixed blessing. The ICC, for example, has the unique rule (Article 27 of the 1998 Rules) that it must scrutinize the award-in principle, only on procedural and technical issues-before it is released by the tribunal to the parties. This may yield more uniformity and eliminate errors; however it may also limit to some degree the freedom of the arbitrators and is certainly not a time-saving device.

Having considered these arguments and any others that may occur to you, can you identify situations in which you would prefer ad hoc instead of institutional arbitration, or vice versa?

[1]. On the consequences of imperfec-   infra Chapter II.1.
tions in various arbitration agreements, see

I.1.h. Fast–Track Arbitration

Hans Smit,[d] FAST–TRACK ARBITRATION*

2 Am. Rev. Int'l Arb'n 138 (1991).

I. INTRODUCTION

There is a new product on the international arbitration market. It is called fast-track arbitration. Although it was provided for in contracts between international business enterprises, the creative efforts of the ICC International Court of Arbitration in Paris have made it a reality. If left to its own devices, it would most probably have died a natural death. But through the joint efforts of the ICC International Court of Arbitration, the tribunal, and the parties, it was brought into the world alive and kicking. It is likely to have a very promising life.

In the case in which it was born, long-term contracts provided for renegotiation and arbitration within a sixty-day period of certain components of the price of a commodity, composed of various elements. The contract spelled out in adequate detail the steps to be taken in the renegotiating process. The party initiating the process had to serve written notice of its proposals on the other party at least sixty days before the new contract year. The other party had to serve its written response within fifteen days thereafter. If no agreement could be reached within 15 days before the beginning of the new contract year, either party could, within the next ten days, elect arbitration under the ICC Rules. The tribunal had to render its award sixty days after the commencement of the new contract year, which was November 1.

However, no provision was made as to how this arbitration was to be conducted. The only things the contract provided were that the tribunal, composed of three members, was to render its award within 60 days after the beginning of the new contract year and that it could decide only the issues contractually specified for this fast-track treatment. It was left to the ICC International Court of Arbitration and the tribunal to determine whether and how this could be done.

The following is a description of the steps taken to achieve this end and the problems encountered and resolved.

II. THE PROBLEMS FACING THE ICC COURT

The request for arbitration was filed on October 21, only 10 days before the beginning of the new contract year. The award had to be rendered by December 30. This left some seventy days to D-day. However, the opposing party significantly decelerated the pace by taking the full thirty days allotted by article 4(1) of the ICC Rules to file its answer. This brought the case down to forty days.

---

d. Stanley H. Fuld Professor of Law and Director of the Parker School of Foreign and Comparative Law, Columbia University.

* Reprinted by permission of Hans Smit and the American Review of International Arbitration.

A further complication then arose; the respondent objected to the arbitrator proposed by the claimant. The moment the non-confirmation request was made, the ICC Secretariat moved with lightning speed. Benefitting from the fact that article 2.7 of the ICC Rules prescribes no fixed time limit for processing a request for non-confirmation, it managed to rule on the request within a very short period. However, since the Secretariat upheld the challenge, the claimant had to propose a new arbitrator. The Court gave it twenty-four hours for this purpose. In the meantime, since the parties had not agreed upon the chairman, the Court had to take the necessary steps to have a chairman appointed. This required going through the National Committee of the neutral country selected, which, of course, also had to act with all possible speed.

By December 20, the tribunal was in place, and the file transmitted to its members. Under the contract, the tribunal had until December 30 to render its award. Furthermore, all of its members, including the chairman and the arbitrator newly selected by the claimant, were still subject to challenge by the parties within 30 days after their appointment in the period between December 18 and 20, 1991. Fortunately, the ICC Court had managed to persuade the parties to give the tribunal a little more breathing space by stipulating January 8 as the date by which the award was to be rendered. All other problems were left for the tribunal to resolve. Among these problems were the fact that the tribunal had been appointed in two separate proceedings, which raised the same issues but which the parties had refused to consolidate, the still open possibility of challenge of the arbitrators, and, most important of all, how the actual arbitration was to be conducted.

III.   THE TRIBUNAL'S RESOLUTION OF THESE PROBLEMS

When the tribunal started functioning on December 20, the first items of business to be taken care of were drafting the terms of reference and setting a schedule for the actual arbitration. Under article 13 of the ICC Rules, a tribunal may not proceed with the preparation of the case until the terms of reference have been submitted to, and-if not signed by all parties and the members of the tribunal-approved by, the Court. The drafting of the terms of reference therefore became a matter of first concern. However, it was clear that the tribunal could not remain inactive until the terms of reference had been submitted to, or approved by, the Court. The tribunal therefore proceeded on two fronts. It submitted to the parties proposed terms of reference and it set a schedule for briefing and hearing the case. Both sides were directed to submit all their papers, including argument, documentary proof, written statement of witnesses, and any other material, by the close of business on December 30. The hearing was set for January 2, with each side allowed three hours for argument, examination or cross-examination of witnesses or any other purpose. No information could be introduced at the hearing that had not been previously disclosed in the papers submitted or otherwise, except for good cause shown.

This procedure appears to have worked well. The requirement of simultaneous submission, coupled with the prohibition against introducing at the hearing information not disclosed earlier, precluded withholding information and promoted voluntary disclosure. And the requirement that all documentary and testimonial evidence be introduced at the submission of papers stage virtually eliminated the need to spend any time for that purpose at the hearing. Indeed, although the parties were free to use their allotted time at the hearing for examination and cross-examination of witnesses, they largely forewent that opportunity. The tribunal had directed that all witnesses be available at the hearing, but, to the extent they were heard at all, they mostly responded to questions put to them by members of the tribunal.

After the schedule had been set, the tribunal sought to complete the terms of reference. A big step forward was achieved when the parties, responding to some prompting by the tribunal, agreed to consolidation. However, it was also most desirable that agreement be reached on all aspects; otherwise, under article 13(2) of the ICC Rules, the ICC Court would have to become involved and set a time limit for signature by the party refusing to sign. This time limit would most likely have been very short, but, of course, would have consumed additional valuable time.

Another potential problem was resolved when the parties accepted the tribunal and forewent any possible challenges. This eliminated the possibility that an arbitrator would be challenged while the tribunal was hearing the case and formulating its award or, possibly, even after that. Getting the signatures of everyone concerned on the same document posed a technical problem that was overcome by having each person sign a separate copy and having a duplicate copy bearing all signatures executed at the hearing.

Immediately upon the conclusion of the hearing, the tribunal deliberated and completed the thirty-odd page award, which was sent to the ICC Court on January 4. The Court scrutinized, and, pursuant to article 21 of the ICC Rules, approved, the draft on January 7, 1992 and communicated it to the parties on the same day, one day before the expiration of the deadline.

IV. LESSONS FOR THE FUTURE

Speed of adjudication has long been touted as one of the great advantages of arbitration. However, whether arbitration achieves it depends, under presently prevailing rules, in large measure on the tribunal. A provision such as that of article 14(1) of the ICC Rules, which prescribes that the arbitrator shall proceed within as short a time as possible to establish the facts of the case, although mandatory in form, is often only exhortatory in practice. Contractual provision for fast-track treatment changes this. It seems clear, however, that adjustments of the institutional rules would be most useful if fast-track arbitration is to work.

The parties may seek to provide in their contract for their details of the procedure to be followed. But their provisions would be likely to conflict with the institutional rules if these were not adjusted. In the case discussed here, the tribunal largely managed to avoid such conflicts, but in the next case this may not be possible. Furthermore, the parties, if left to their own devices, might well come up with rules that do not work well in practice and that vary from case to case.

It is far preferable for the institutions to provide an appropriate regime for fast-track treatment. If made sufficiently flexible, such a regime would appear to have excellent prospects. The regime to be created should have the following features:

(a) It should be set forth in separate rules, dealing only with fast-track arbitration, the application of which the parties could trigger by specific reference to these rules in the arbitration clause.

(b) The fast-track rules should significantly shorten the time limits for filing answers, challenges, and the like. Even if specific time limits are set, the institution or the tribunal should be given authority to modify them.

(c) The rules should probably set out the procedure to be followed for submissions and hearings, but should also give the tribunal authority to modify it as the circumstances may warrant.

(d) Provision should be made for extension of the contractual time limit for rendition of the award by the institution or the tribunal. Depending on the peculiarities of the particular case, it may be impossible to meet the deadline and accord due process to the parties. Rather than suffer an attack on the award, the institution or tribunal should therefore have authority to extend the deadline. To provide a check, the authority may be given to the tribunal, subject to approval by the institution.

(e) Since, as in the case here described, fast-track treatment may be reserved for a limited number of issues, the rules should make adequate provisions to grant the tribunal authority to deal with issues that are improperly tendered in the fast-track mode. In the case at hand, the tribunal ruled that certain issues tendered for decision in the fast-track mode did not qualify for fast-track treatment and provided for their determination in a sequel to the fast-track proceeding under a general arbitration clause contained in the contract. One of the parties objected to the tribunal's adjudicating these additional issues on the ground that the tribunal's authority was limited to adjudication in the fast-track mode. The case was settled before the tribunal could issue its award on this question to the parties.[1]

---

1. The question of whether the tribunal had the authority to deal with issues not prescribed by the contract for fast-track treatment was raised by Respondent in both the fast-track segment and the slower-track segment. The tribunal avoided ruling on this question in an interim award, because it wished to preclude an attack in court, which would have frustrated the whole arbitration process at an intermediate stage of the proceedings.

(f) The tribunal should perhaps be granted general authority to modify the rules for processing the case when justice so requires. After all, there may be cases in which, even though fast-track treatment is selected, some measure of discovery is fair and reasonable. It is probably not desirable to alert parties to this possibility, but it may be that, in particular cases, the tribunal should have the authority to direct appropriate discovery.

It would appear most probably that the ICC International Court of Arbitration, having pioneered fast-track arbitration, will, in the near future, take appropriate steps to provide institutional rules for an accelerated form of arbitration. Even if it does not do so, other institutions may make provisions for this novel procedure. In any event, there is no doubt that many lawyers, and especially their clients, will be most interested in this novel form of expedited dispute settlement.

STOCKHOLM RULES FOR EXPEDITED ARBITRATIONS

Adopted by the Stockholm Chamber of Commerce and in force as of 1 April 1999

[See Documents Supplement]

Questions and Comments

1.   Where would you place fast-track arbitration within the spectrum of various methods of alternative dispute-settlement?

2.   The Smit article stresses that fast-track rules should significantly shorten time limits, but adds that, "Even if specific time limits are set, the institution or the tribunal should be given authority to modify them." Do you agree? (In responding, you may consider the rules set out in paragraphs 7, 16, and 21 of the Stockholm Rules for Expedited Arbitrations.)

3.   In the introductory explanations to the Stockholm Rules it is stated that "Expedited arbitration is primarily recommended for **minor disputes** (emphasis added) where the parties desire a speedy and inexpensive procedure." Please comment.

4.   According to Article 21 of the Stockholm Rules for Expedited Arbitrations, an oral hearing will only take place "if a party so requests, and if the arbitrator deems it necessary." In his short comment on the Stockholm Rules, Akerman considers this rule to be one of the key features that brings about a rapid and inexpensive procedure.[2] (Akerman commented on the 1995 Rules, but his comment remains pertinent because the provision on oral hearings did not change in the 1999 Rules—it just became Article 21 instead of Article 16.) Would this feature encourage you to submit your dispute to Stockholm expedited arbitration?

5.   In negotiating an international transaction (before knowing whether a dispute will emerge, and if one should, whether it will be a "minor" or "major" one), would you recommend that a client accept fast-track arbitration? (The Stockholm experience has been rather encouraging. From 1995

[2].   R. Akerman, *Rules for Expedited Arbitration Procedure*, 6 Amer. Rev. Int'l Arb'n 301 (1995).

through April 2001, 72 requests for expedited arbitration were filed. Out of these 72 cases 32 ended with an award; 23 cases terminated for some other reason (settlement, lack of jurisdiction, or because fees were not paid); 17 cases were still pending in April 2001. /See A. Magnusson, "Fast Track Arbitration—The SCC Experience" www.chamber.se/arbitration.shared_files/fasttrack.html)

6. An arbitration proceeding moves through several stages, from filing a claim requesting arbitration, to choosing the arbitration panel, to holding hearings, to deliberating on an award, to drafting an award opinion. Which stage in the arbitration process do you think is generally the most time consuming? Does fast-track arbitration speed up all stages of the process?

I.2. ON THE EVOLUTION OF THE STANDING OF ARBITRATION WITHIN THE LEGAL SYSTEM

I.2.a. Note

Tibor Varady, THE STANDING OF ARBITRATION WITHIN THE LEGAL SYSTEM

Law & Reality: Essays on National and International Procedural Law 351–52
(Mathilde Sumampouw et al. eds. 1995)*

1. INTRODUCTION

Arbitration is an institution which preceded courts; yet shortly after the appearance of the latter, arbitration assumed the position of the younger (and weaker) brother. In the course of history, this predicament has only been confirmed and aggravated. Courts of justice have become the representatives of the "normal" settlement of disputes, their legitimacy has been beyond doubt. Arbitration has been reduced to an exception, the limits and the functioning of which have been firmly controlled by courts. There have been revolts against this plight, yet there is practically only one area in which such revolts have really been successful. This is in the domain of international trade. Today, it is an uncontested fact that arbitration is the dominant method of settling international trade disputes; and at the same time, international commercial arbitration has become an almost completely self-sufficient institution. While gaining ground and strength, international commercial arbitration has also gained self-confidence. It has been stressed with increasing frequency (and determination) that the self-reliance of international commercial arbitration is a virtue, and that it advances broader common causes. In the opening sentence of his article on court intervention in arbitral proceedings, Delaume stresses: "It is generally recognized that, in order to be fully effective, transnational arbitration must be freed from judicial interference."[1]

---

* Reprinted by permission of T.M.C. Asser Institute.

1. G.R. Delaume, "Court Intervention in Arbitral Proceedings", in Th.E. Carbonneau, ed., *Resolving Transnational Disputes Through International Arbitration* (1984) p. 195 at p. 195.

In its struggle for self-reliance (and domination) the main allies of arbitration have been the parties. Arbitration has been justified and marketed with emphasis on its ability to be structured, and restructured, to meet the needs of businessmen. Time and again, it has been pointed out that—unlike courts which are tied to procedure and substantive law which have not been tailored to the needs of the international business community-arbitration may follow a much more simple, flexible, and speedy procedure, and it may apply the "new *lex mercatoria*" as well. Arbitration may be shaped to meet the wishes of the parties, and it also gives more room for maneuver in the search for a mutually acceptable compromise. In their book on international commercial arbitration in New York, dealing with the question "Why arbitrate?", McClendon and Goodman state unequivocally: "The most obvious advantage is party autonomy resulting from the fact that arbitration is the creature of a contract between the parties."[2] Arbitration owes its justification to its adaptability to party needs, but it also owes its very existence in each dispute to the will of the parties-and party autonomy has been the crucial tool in removing obstacles hampering the constitution and the functioning of arbitral tribunals. As was stated most clearly by Schmitthoff, "The first and foremost principle of law in commercial arbitration is that it is founded on the autonomy of the parties' will."[3]

One has to add that party autonomy has not remained the *only* mainstay of international commercial arbitration. Over the past decades a network of international instruments pertaining to international commercial arbitration has emerged,[4] as a result of which arbitration agreements have become reliable, while arbitration awards have become more efficient (more readily enforceable) than court decisions on the international scene. An important role in stabilizing the position of arbitration may also be ascribed to its institutionalization, assisted by model-rules. Courts have also become much more supportive of arbitration.

I.2.b. A Glimpse Back in History—A French Case

L'ALLIANCE v. PRUNIER

Cour de cassation, Chambre civile, 10 July 1843.

The Court:—Whereas the jurisdiction (*compétence*) of the courts is a matter of general law (*droit commun*); As the only exception to this

---

2. J.S. McClendon and R.E. Goodman, *International Commercial Arbitration in New York* (1986) at p. 3.

3. C. Schmitthoff, "Defective Arbitration Clauses", in Chia–Jui Cheng, ed., *Clive M. Schmitthoff's Select Essays on International Trade Law*, p. 608.

4. Most importantly, the 1958 New York Convention on the Recognition and Enforcement of Foreign Arbitral Awards (with 84 Member States by January 1992); the 1961 European Convention on International Commercial Arbitration (with 21 Member States by January 1992) with the 1962 Agreement Relating to Application of the European Convention on International Commercial Arbitration (entered into between the Member States of the Council of Europe); and the 1965 Washington Convention on the Settlement of Investment Disputes between States and National of Other States (ICSID Convention, with 97 Member States by January 1992).

mandatory principle (*d'ordre public*), is for commercial companies, and only in the case of voluntary arbitration;

Whereas the insurance policy dated 28 September 1837, signed by the company *l'Alliance* and by Prunier, did not establish a commercial association and, accordingly, article 51 of the Code de Commerce, relative to compulsory arbitration, cannot be applied;

Whereas article 332 of the same Code, which authorizes the parties to submit to arbitrators, in case of a dispute, does not apply to this case because the article only applies to maritime insurance. . . .

Whereas voluntary arbitrations are regulated by a single title of Book 3 of the Code de procédure civile;

Whereas, by article 15 of the policy dated September 28, the company *l'Alliance* and Prunier have, it is true, stipulated that all disputes with respect to the damage resulting from a fire, to the work and evaluation of experts, and to the performance of the policy, would be adjudicated, in final instance, at Paris, by three arbitrators; but as the arbitrators were not named, as article 1006 of the Code de Procédure civile prescribes;

Whereas article 1003 of this Code, which authorizes all persons to arbitrate their rights, must not be taken in isolation and as proclaiming a general principle not subject to any qualification;—As, on the contrary, it is necessary to combine this article with those that immediately follow it, in particular with article 1006, from which it results that one does not conclude a valid compromise or, what amounts to the same thing, does not validly compromise, when one does not set out the object of the controversy and the names of the arbitrators;—As the distinction between a compromise agreement and a compromise is not established by any provision of law and could not be recognized without ignoring the true spirit of the procedural Code's title on an arbitration;—As one invokes in vain article 1134 of the Civil Code in order to validate for civil matters the so-called arbitration clause because agreements replace the law for those who have entered into them only when the agreements are legally formed and as an agreement is not legally formed when it lacks the provisions expressly required by the legislators;

Whereas the practice of inserting in fire insurance policies a stipulation identical to that contained in article 15 of the policy dated September 28, 1837 cannot prevail over article 1006 of the Code de procédure civile, and a failure to observe its provision results in nullity.

* * *

Whereas, if the simple arbitration agreement or compromise clause were validated for fire insurance contracts, it would be necessary to recognize and consecrate the clause's validity in all contracts when it was agreed that, in case of failure to perform or of difficulties in performing, the matter would be submitted to arbitrators as yet unnamed;—As this provision would become commonplace (*banal*) and a matter of style and as one would be deprived of the guaranties that the courts provide;

Whereas the requirement that the arbitrators be named at the time of the compromise is designed to avoid disputes and litigation respecting the composition of an arbitral tribunal and, basically, to put citizens on guard against their own failure to reflect which leads them to agree too quickly and without foresight to future arbitrations without being certain to have, as voluntary judges, capable persons worthy of their confidence;—As, in the actual case, the importance and the necessity of the provisions of article 1006 appear clearly from the position in which the insurer wishes to place their insureds with respect to the adjudication of all their disagreements;—As, in effect, the company *l'Alliance*, whose principal office is in Paris, and which does business throughout France, wants, by article 15 of the policy, to force the insureds, regardless of how large or small may be the loss, to constitute at Paris-where most of the insureds do not have any business connection, and even do not know anybody—, far from the place where the fire occurred and where the losses caused can be verified and evaluated, an arbitral tribunal that would judge finally;

Whereas it follows from the aforesaid that in declaring void the arbitration clause in the policy of September 18, 1837, because the names of the arbitrators were not given, the challenged decision not only did not violate any law but correctly interpreted article 1131 of the Code civil and made a correct application of articles 1003 and 1006 of the Code de procédure civile; . . .

Reject.

Devill, Note to *L'Alliance* v. Prunier, S.1843.I.561: This decision will produce a great sensation from both the doctrinal and the practical point of view. Everyone knows that the provision called the *clause compromissoire*, by which the contracting parties in advance submit themselves to arbitrators, named or unnamed, for all the disagreements not foreseen and impossible to foresee, that may arise under their contracts, has become general in many types of contracts . . . Until now, such a clause has generally been considered valid, not, of course, as a *compromis*, in the sense of article 1006 of the Code de procédure civile, but as a promise to arbitrate, a promise which no provision of law appeared to prohibit or to render ineffective. . . .

I.2.c. *A Note on the Relevance of the International Dimension*

Arthur von Mehren, INTERNATIONAL COMMERCIAL ARBITRATION: THE CONTRIBUTION OF THE FRENCH JURISPRUDENCE

46 La. L. Rev. 1045, 1048–51 (1986)*

Paradoxically, in France not only were the courts to be the prime agents of change, but development of an acceptable regime for international commercial arbitration long preceded a comparable accomplishment for internal commercial arbitration. The consequences of the *Prunier* rule nullifying arbitration clauses proved to be so harmful to international commercial relations[10] that by the end of the nineteenth century French courts had begun to create a distinct and special legal regime for arbitration in matters of international commerce. In this regime rules respecting the recognition and enforcement of foreign awards were only one element—and by no means the most important— among many.

II

The first step in developing for French law a special regime for international commercial arbitration could only be overturning the *Prunier* rule. As early as 1865 in *Migout v. Arguad*,[11] the Court of Appeal of Paris was prepared to hold that, where a French party had agreed that the contract containing an arbitration clause was subject to a law which considered such clauses valid, article 1006 of the French Code of Civil Procedure did not apply. This approach to the *Prunier* rule relies on choice-of-law mechanisms. Accordingly, when French law was applicable the arbitration clause was void.[12] Moreover, until near the end of the century, the *Cour de cassation* had not spoken authoritatively on the issue and most courts held all arbitration clauses invalid, regardless of the applicable law and "whether they were agreed to in France or abroad, by Frenchmen or by foreigners...."[13]

The *ordre public* objection to the *Migout* result remained an obstacle to relaxing the *Prunier* rule by recourse to choice of law until 1899, when the *Chambre des requêtes* of the *Cour de cassation* decided *Ospina v. Ribon*.[14] A contract, containing an arbitration clause, concluded in France and there registered by three foreigners residing in Paris, was

---

* Reprinted by permission of the Louisiana Law Review, Louisiana State University, Baton Rouge, LA.

10. See J. Rubellin–Devichi, supra note 3, at 21.

11. Cour d'appel de Paris, 11 Jan. 1865, D.1865.11.188, S.1866.11.147.

12. E.g., Chemins de fer autrichiens v. Perier, Cour d'appel de Paris, 8 Nov. 1865; D.1867.11.21 at 23, S.1866.11.117 at 118.

13. J. Hamel, La clause compromissoire dans les rapports de commerce internationaux, 18 Revue de droit international privé 721, 723 (1922–23).

14. Cass. req., 17 July 1899, D.1904.1.225 (note Pic).

held by the Court of Appeal of Paris to be subject to the law of Colombia. The clause provided for arbitration either in Colombia or in France. The *Chambre des requêtes*, addressing the *ordre public* issue directly, concluded that "such an agreement contains nothing contrary to the *ordre public*."[15] In 1904, the *Chambre des requêtes* again took the position— this time in a matter involving enforcement of an award rendered in Belgium against a Frenchman—that article 1006 did not involve the "*ordre public*."[16]

These inroads on the *Prunier* rule all depended on a choice-of-law analysis; accordingly, they all involved, in some sense at least, international transactions. Thus, a separate and distinct legal regime for international arbitration began to emerge in French law. Inevitably, the question arose of where the line lies between national and international arbitrations. *Mardelé v. Muller*,[17] decided in 1930, illustrates the willingness of the *Cour de cassation* to give a very inclusive meaning to international transactions by bringing within that category situations in which no true choice of law issue arises.

In *Mardelé*, a French merchant had bought from a French firm 100 tons of Chilean wheat, c.i.f. Le Havre. The contract was subject to the conditions of the London Corn Trade Association which provided for arbitration in London. The law of 30 December 1925, which had set aside the *Prunier* rule for commercial contracts—domestic as well as international—, did not apply to the cause, the decision in first instance having been rendered prior to the law's effective date. The Court of Appeals of Rennes considered the situation as one in which—there being no significant non-French contacts-the parties could not stipulate a foreign law.[18] Accordingly, article 1006 of the Code of Civil Procedure rendered the clause void.

The appeal court's decision was quashed by the *Chambre civile* of the *Cour de cassation*. The high Court no longer relied centrally on a choice-of-law analysis to escape the *Prunier* rule; it is enough that the situation "involves the interests of international commerce." Where such is the case,

> the nullity of the arbitration clause provided for by article 1006 of the Code of Civil Procedure not being of the *ordre public* in France, even if both parties are French they can validly derogate in a contract, whether concluded abroad or in France, from the provi-

---

15. Id. at 229. Pic's Note in Dalloz to the decision (id. at 225) remarks that the *Chambre des requêtes* "had already admitted [in 1892] without great difficulty, that a French court seized of a demand for *exequatur* of an arbitral award rendered abroad must determine its regularity under the foreign law ... Today the court goes much further since it allows French judges to determine the regularity, under the national law of the parties, of an award rendered between foreigners but on French soil...." Id. at 288.

16. George Bernard v. Société la General Mercantile Company, Cass. req., 21 June 1904, D.1906.1.395, S.1906.1.22.

17. Cass. civ., 19 Feb. 1930, S.1933.1.41 (note Niboyet).

18. Société Muller v. Mardelé, Cour d'appel de Rennes, 26 July 1926, 22 Revue de droit international privé 523, 526–527 (note Niboyet).

sions of this text and refer to a foreign law, such as English law, which considers such clauses valid....[19]

The *Mardelé* case effectively frees international commercial arbitration from the shackles of the *Prunier* rule. If the case law from *Migout v. Arguad* to *Mardelé* had only this significance, the episode—though of historical importance—would be of relatively little contemporary interest. After all, article 631 of the *Code de commerce* had been amended in 1925 to provide that "parties may, when they contract, agree to submit to arbitration" the following classes of controversies "when they arise": disputes respecting engagements and transactions between traders, merchants, and bankers; disputes between partners respecting a commercial partnership; and all disputes between partners respecting commercial acts (*actes de commerce*) regardless whether domestic or international commerce be in question.[20]

But the *jurisprudence* that culminated in *Mardelé* also implied ideas and techniques that were to continue to shape the French law's handling and understanding of international commercial arbitration. In particular, this case law strongly suggests that various aspects of the legal regime applicable to domestic arbitrations do not apply to arbitrations which involve the interests of international commerce. The *jurisprudence* further intimates that certain of the rules and principles governing the regime applicable to international commercial arbitrations need not flow from rules and principles found in a national law. Particular rules and principles of a non-national character can be developed to take into account the special qualities and requirements of international commercial arbitration as a dispute-resolution process.

The position that article 1006 of the Code of Civil Procedure does not implicate the *"ordre public"* clearly involves the first of these two propositions. Both before and after article 1006 was moderated by amending article 631 of the Commercial Code, party agreement could not set aside the article in domestic arbitrations. The article's rule was mandatory. Of course, this mandatory character need not prevent a party stipulation for a foreign law that accepts arbitration clauses; the forum's *"ordre public international"* can well differ from its domestic *ordre public*. The analysis depends, however, on the proposition that in the circumstances the forum allows, as a matter of choice of law, stipulation for a foreign law. But does the *Mardelé* case involve a situation in which party stipulation for a foreign law is permitted? Is the case not better understood as allowing parties, in view of the importance of arbitration for contracts involving the interests of international commerce, to derogate from the mandatory domestic rule contained in article 1006 regardless whether, for other aspects of the transaction, the parties could escape the application of mandatory domestic rules?

---

19. S.1933.1.41.

20. Amendment of article 631 was triggered by France's signature of the Geneva Protocol on Arbitration Clauses of 24 Sept. 1923. See I.J. Hamel & P. Lagarde, Traité de droit commercial no. 70 (1954).

The second proposition-that the rules that apply to international commerce need not be contained in any national law—was relied upon in 1975 by the Court of Appeal of Paris in yet another decision[21] involving the validity of an arbitration clause. There the court held that "in view of the autonomy in an international contract (*contrat international*) of a clause providing for arbitration, the clause is valid independent of a reference to any national law (*valable indépendamment de la référence à toute loi étatique*)."[22]

Questions and Comments

1. In *L'Alliance v. Prunier*, the Cour de cassation particularly emphasizes the requirement "that the arbitrators be named at the time the compromise (agreement to arbitrate disputes)" was signed. It was explained that this requirement puts citizens:

> on guard against their own failure to reflect which leads them to agree too quickly and without foresight to future arbitrations without being certain to have, as voluntary judges, capable persons worthy of their confidence.

Was the court's concern on this score justified? Did the court suggest a more serious concern?

Today, parties typically do not include names of given arbitrators in their agreements to arbitrate future disputes. Why not?

2. The *Prunier* case is a good, articulate example of mistrust of arbitration. Can you identify rational (or irrational) grounds for this mistrust?

3. The *Migout* case and later *Ospina v. Ribon*, both discussed in the von Mehren excerpt, display more deference towards arbitration agreements, assuming such treatment is permitted by the (other-than-French) applicable law.

In *Menicucci v. Mahieux* (1975), cited in footnote 21 of the von Mehren excerpt, the Paris Cour d'appel took another big leap (presumably forward), stating that in international contracts, an arbitration clause is valid "independent of a reference to any national law."

Can you imagine an effective arbitration agreement, and an effective arbitration process, outside the framework of any national law?

I.2.d. Another Glimpse Back in History—A U.S. Case

KULUKUNDIS SHIPPING CO., S.A. v. AMTORG TRADING CORP.

United States Court of Appeals, Second Circuit, 1942.
126 F.2d 978.

FRANK, J.

* * *

Appellant admits—as it must—that the district court had jurisdiction to determine whether the parties had made an agreement to

---

21. Menicucci v. Mahieux, Cour d'appel de Paris, 13 Dec. 1975, 65 Revue critique de droit international privé 507 (note Opettit) (1976).

22. Id. at 509.

arbitrate.[3] Appellant contends, however, that, once the court determined in this suit that there was such an arbitration agreement, the court lost all power over the suit beyond that of staying further proceedings until there had been an arbitration as agreed to;[4] in that arbitration, argues appellant, the arbitrators will have jurisdiction to determine all issues except the existence of the arbitration clause. This jurisdiction, it is urged, is broad enough to permit an independent determination, by the arbitrator, that the contract itself is not valid or binding. Appellee asserts that the defendant had repudiated the charter-party, and that, therefore, the arbitration clause must be wholly disregarded.

In considering these contentions in the light of the precedents, it is necessary to take into account the history of the judicial attitude towards arbitration: The English courts, while giving full effect to agreements to submit controversies to arbitration after they had ripened into arbitrators' awards, would-over a long period beginning at the end of the 17th century-do little or nothing to prevent or make irksome the breach of such agreements when they were still executory.[5] Prior to 1687, such a breach could be made costly: a penal bond given to abide the result of an arbitration had a real bite, since a breach of the bond's condition led to a judgment for the amount of the penalty. It was so held in 1609 in Vynior's Case, 8 Coke Rep. 81b. To be sure, Coke there, in a dictum, citing precedents, dilated on the inherent revocability of the authority given to an arbitrator;[6] such a revocation was not too important, however, if it resulted in a stiff judgment on a penal bond. But the Statute of Fines and Penalties (8 & 9 Wm.III c. 11, s. 8), enacted in 1687, provided

3. Under Section 3 of the Act, the court cannot grant a stay until it is "satisfied that the issue involved in such suit . . . is referable to arbitration under" an "agreement in writing for . . . arbitration." Clearly the court cannot be thus "satisfied" without a determination that the parties made such an agreement to arbitrate.

4. Or, if plaintiff had so requested, then under Section 4, directing the parties to proceed with the arbitration.

5. The early English history of enforcement of executory arbitration agreements is not too clear. Arbitration was used by the medieval guilds and in early maritime transactions. Some persons trace an influence back to Roman law, doubtless itself affected by Greek law; others discern the influence of ecclesiastical law. See Sayre, Development of Commercial Arbitration Law, 37 Yale L.J. (1927) 595, 597; Jones, Development of Commercial Arbitration, 21 Minn.L.Rev. (1927) 240, 243–244; Baum and Pressman, The enforcement of Commercial Arbitration, 8 N.Y.U.L.Q.Rev.

(1930) 238, 239–249; Red Cross Line v. Atlantic Fruit Co., 1924, 264 U.S. 109, 121, 44 S.Ct. 274, 68 L.Ed. 582; Cohen, Commercial Arbitration and The Law (1918); Aristotle, Rhetoric, Bk. I, Ch. 13, 1374b; Vinogradoff, 2 Historical Jurisprudence (1922) 50, 146, and Aristotle and Legal Redress, 14 Col. L.Rev. (1914) 548, 559; Buckland, Textbook of Roman Law (1921) 527–528; Radin, Handbook of Roman Law (1927) 308.

6. Cohen, loc. cit., 104ff, criticizes Coke's use of the precedents; Sayre, loc. cit., is on Coke's side. Cf. Peterson, J., dissenting in Park Const. Co. v. Independent School Dist., 1941, 209 Minn. 182, 296 N.W. 475, 478ff, 135 A.L.R. 59.

That Coke was not always an honest or careful reporter of precedents, see authorities cited, United States v. Forness, 2 Cir., 125 F.2d 928 notes 32 and 33; Hume v. Moore–McCormack Lines, 2 Cir., 121 F.2d 336, 344 notes 24 and 29; Veeder, The English Reports 1537–1895, in 2 Select Essays in Anglo–American Legal History, 131–

that, in an action on any bond given for performance of agreements, while judgment would be entered for the penalty, execution should issue only for the damages actually sustained.[7] Coke's dictum as to revocability, uttered seventy-eight years earlier, now took on a new significance, as it was now held that for breach of an undertaking to arbitrate the damages were only nominal.[8] Recognizing the effect of the impact of this statute on executory arbitration agreements, Parliament, eleven years later, enacted a statute, 9 Wm.III c. 15 (1698), designed to remedy the situation by providing that, if an agreement to arbitrate so provided, it could be made a "rule of court" (i.e., a court order), in which event it became irrevocable, and one who revoked it would be subject to punishment for contempt of court; but the submission was revocable until such a rule of court had been obtained. This statute, limited in scope, was narrowly construed and was of little help.[9] The ordinary executory arbitration agreement thus lost all real efficacy since it was not specifically enforceable in equity, and was held not to constitute the basis of a plea in bar in, or a stay of, a suit on the original cause of action.[10] In admiralty, the rulings were much the same.

It has been well said that "the legal mind must assign some reason in order to decide anything with spiritual quiet."[11] And so, by way of rationalization, it became fashionable in the middle of the 18th century to say that such agreements were against public policy because they "oust the jurisdiction" of the courts.[12] But that was a quaint explanation,

132; Bolland Manual of Year Book Studies (1925) 85–86; 22 Halsbury, Laws of England (1st ed., 1912) 128, 152; Boulton v. Bull, 2 H–l. 463, 491 (1795), 126 Eng.Rep. 651, 665.

7. 9 C.J. pp. 128, 129; 11 C.J.S., Bonds 130; 12, Holdsworth, History of English Law (1938) 519–520.

8. See Sayre, loc. cit. at 604.

9. See Sayre, loc. cit. at 606; Annotation, 47 L.R.A., N.S. 436; Chaffee & Simpson, 1 Cases on Equity. (1934) 552–553. In 1833, a statute (3 & 4 Wm IV, c. 42) was passed which was intended to reinforce the 1680 statute, but it still left a submission revocable until an action was brought in connection with an arbitration proceeding.

An act of 1854 (17 & 19 Vict. c. 125) provided that any arbitration agreement could be made the basis of a stay and irrevocable except by leave of court, granted in the exercise of the court's discretion.

The arbitration act of 1889 (52 & 53 Vict. c. 49) provided that any such agreement, unless a contrary intention is expressed therein, shall be irrevocable, except by leave of court, and shall have the same effect as if

it had been made an order of court; it provided adequate court review of questions of law raised in the arbitration hearing. See Sayre, loc. cit., 606–607; 47 L.R.A., N.S., 436ff; Chaffee & Simpson, loc. cit.

10. See 1 Chaffee & Simpson, loc. cit. 520ff; Tobey v. County of Bristol, 23 Fed. Cas.page 1313, No. 14,065, 3 Story 800; 2 Story, Equity Jurisprudence, Section 670.

11. Hough, J., in United States Asphalt R. Co. v. Trinidad Lake P. Co., D.C. 1915, 222 F. 1006, 1008. He discusses and shows the "worthlessness" of the several "causes advanced for refusing to compel men to abide by their arbitration contracts."

12. This phrase seems to have been coined in Kill v. Hollister, 1 Wils. 129 (1746). Some judges justified it by referring to Coke on Littleton, 53b; "If a man make a lease for life, and by deed grant that if any waste or destruction be done, that it shall be redressed by neighbors, and not by suit or plea," nevertheless an "action of waste shall lye, for the place wasted cannot be recovered without a plea." See critical comments by Creswell and Campbell in Scott v. Avery, 5 H.C.L. 811, 837, 853 (1855). Campbell, here as elsewhere, was distinctly not Coke-eyed.

inasmuch as an award, under an arbitration agreement, enforced both at law and in equity, was no less an ouster; and the same was true of releases and covenants not to sue, which were given full effect. Moreover, the agreement to arbitrate was not illegal, since suit could be maintained for its breach. Here was a clear instance of what Holmes called a "right" to break a contract and to substitute payment of damages for non-performance;[13] as, in this type of case, the damages were only nominal, that "right" was indeed meaningful.

An effort has been made to justify this judicial hostility to the executory arbitration agreement on the ground that arbitrations, if unsupervised by the courts, are undesirable, and that legislation was needed to make possible such supervision.[14] But if that was the reason for unfriendliness to such executory agreements, then the courts should also have refused to aid arbitrations when they ripened into awards. And what the English courts, especially the equity courts, did in other contexts, shows that, if they had had the will, they could have devised means of protecting parties to arbitrations. Instead, they restrictively interpreted successive statutes intended to give effect to executory arbitrations.[15] No similar hostility was displayed by the Scotch courts.[16] Lord Campbell explained the English attitude as due to the desire of the judges, at a time when their salaries came largely from fees, to avoid loss of income.[17] Indignation has been voiced at this suggestion;[18] perhaps it is unjustified.[19] Perhaps the true explanation is the hypnotic power of the

13. Holmes, The Path of The Law, 10 Harv.L.Rev. (1897) 457, reprinted Holmes, Collected Legal Papers (1920) 167, 175. Cf. Globe Refining Co. v. Landa Cotton Oil Co., 190 U.S. 540, 543, 23 S.Ct. 754, 47 L.Ed. 1171; 1 Holmes–Pollock Letters (1941) 80, 119 note, 120, 177 and note; Holland, Jurisprudence (4th ed.) 212–213.

14. Sayre, loc. cit.; Peterson, J., dissenting in Park Const. Co. v. Independent School Dist., supra. Sayre argues that if the courts had really been unfriendly to arbitrations they would not have enforced arbitrators' awards. The real truth, however, seems to be that they were unfriendly but did not carry out their hostility to its logical conclusion.

15. See the statutes cited in note 8, and Annotation, 47 L.R.A., N.S., 436; Chaffee & Simpson, loc. cit.

16. Cases cited later in this opinion. The Scotch attitude may well have been due to Roman law influences. As to such influences on Scotch law generally, see Radin, Book Review, 45 Yale L.J. (1935) 380, reviewing Mackintosh, Roman Law in Modern Practice (1933).

17. "The doctrine," he said, "had its origin in the interests of the judges. There was no disguising the fact that, as formerly, the emoluments of the Judges depended

mainly, or almost entirely, upon fees, and as they had no fixed salaries, there was great competition to get as much as possible of litigation into Westminster Hall for the division of the spoil ... And they had great jealousy of arbitrations whereby Westminster Hall was robbed of those cases which came not into Kings Bench, nor the Common Pleas, nor the Exchequer. Therefore they said that the courts ought not to be ousted of their jurisdiction, and that it was contrary to the policy of the law to do so. That really grew up only subsequently to the time of Lord Coke, and a saying of his was the foundation of the doctrine." Scott v. Avery, 25 L.J.Ex. 308, 313; the report of his remarks in 5 H.C.L. 811 is more meager.

18. See Sayre, loc. cit.; dissenting opinion of Peterson in Park Const. Co. v. Independent School Dist., supra.

19. Yet able historians have stressed this pecuniary motive as an important factor in the struggles for jurisdiction between the several English courts; see Goebel, Cases and Materials in Development of Legal Institutions (1937) 90, 120, 206, 221; 1 Holdsworth, History of English Law (3d ed. 1922) 254, 255, 259, 261; 2 ibid. (3d ed. 1923) 591; Usher, Rise and Fall of The High Commission (1913) 55; cf. Adam Smith,

phrase, "oust the jurisdiction."[20] Give a bad dogma a good name and its bite may become as bad as its bark.

In 1855, in Scott v. Avery, 5 H.C.L. 811, the tide seemed to have turned. There it was held that if a policy made an award of damages by arbitrators a condition precedent to a suit on the policy, a failure to submit to arbitration would preclude such a suit, even if the policy left to the arbitrators the consideration of all the elements of liability. But, despite later legislation, the hostility of the English courts to executory arbitrations resumed somewhat after *Scott v. Avery*, and seems never to have been entirely dissipated.

That English attitude was largely taken over in the 19th century by most courts in this country. Indeed, in general, they would not go as far as *Scott v. Avery*, supra,[21] and continued to use the "ouster of jurisdiction" concept:[22] An executory agreement to arbitrate would not be given specific performance or furnish the basis of a stay of proceedings on the original cause of action. Nor would it be given effect as a plea in bar, except in limited instances, i.e., in the case of an agreement expressly or impliedly making it a condition precedent to litigation that there be an award determining some preliminary question of subsidiary fact upon which any liability was to be contingent. Hamilton v. Liverpool, 1890, etc., Ins. Co., 136 U.S. 242, 255, 10 S.Ct. 945, 34 L.Ed. 419. In the case of broader executory agreements, no more than nominal damages would be given for a breach.[23]

* * *

Generally speaking, then, the courts of this country were unfriendly to executory arbitration agreements. The lower federal courts, feeling bound to comply with the precedents, nevertheless became critical of this judicial hostility.[24] There were intimations in the Supreme Court that perhaps the old view might be abandoned, but in the cases hinting at that newer attitude the issue was not raised.[25] Effective state arbitration

Wealth of Nations (Modern Library ed. 1937) Bk. V, Pt. II, 679; 6 Wigmore on Evidence (3d Ed., 1940) § 1845, note 6. And as to the effect of this same factor in the fight between the common law courts and Chancery; see Taylor v. Carryl, 20 How. 583, 612–617, 15 L.Ed. 1028; Fischer v. Carey, 173 Cal. 185, 189, 159 P. 577, L.R.A. 1917A, 1100; 2 Campbell, Lives of The Chancellors, 184–185.

20. Words sometimes have such potency. For an excellent 18th century American essay on "semantics" along these lines, see Mr. Justice Wilson's opinion in Chisholm v. Georgia, 1793, 2 Dall. 419, 454ff, 1 L.Ed. 440; Cf. United States v. Forness, 2 Cir., January 20, 1942, 125 F.2d 928, 934, and note 9.

21. See, e.g., Whitney v. National Masonic Accident Ass'n, 52 Minn. 378, 54 N.W. 184; Annotation, 47 L.R.A., N.S., at page 448.

22. E.g., Insurance Co. v. Morse, 1874, 20 Wall. 445, 451, 22 L.Ed. 365.

23. See Williston, 6 Contracts (rev. ed. 1938), Section 1927A (p. 5392, note 9); Munson v. Straits of Dover S.S. Co., 2 Cir., 102 F. 926; but cf. McCullough v. Clinch–Mitchell Const. Co., 8 Cir., 71 F.2d 17; Annotation, 47 L.R.A., N.S., 409, 410.

24. See, e.g., the sarcastic remarks of Hough, J., in United States Asphalt Refining Co. v. Trinidad Petroleum Co., D.C. 1915, 222 F. 1006; Mack, J., in Atlantic Fruit Co. v. Red Cross Line, D.C. 1921, 276 F. 319; Atlantic Fruit Co. v. Red Cross Line, 2 Cir., 1924, 5 F.2d 218.

25. The Atlanten, 1920, 252 U.S. 313, 315, 40 S.Ct. 332, 64 L.Ed. 586; Red Cross Line v. Atlantic Fruit Co., 1924, 264 U.S. 109, 123, 124, 44 S.Ct. 274, 68 L.Ed. 582.

statutes were enacted beginning with the New York Statute of 1920.[26]

The United States Arbitration Act of 1925 was sustained as constitutional, in its application to cases arising in admiralty. Marine Transit Corp. v. Dreyfus, 1932, 284 U.S. 263, 52 S.Ct. 166, 76 L.Ed. 282. The purpose of that Act was deliberately to alter the judicial atmosphere previously existing. The report of the House Committee[27] stated, in part: "Arbitration agreements are purely matters of contract, and the effect of the bill is simply to make the contracting party live up to his agreement. He can no longer refuse to perform his contract when it becomes disadvantageous to him. An arbitration agreement is placed upon the same footing as other contracts, where it belongs. * * * The need for the law arises from an anachronism of our American law. Some centuries ago, because of the jealousy of the English courts for their own jurisdiction, they refused to enforce specific agreements to arbitrate upon the ground that the courts were thereby ousted from their jurisdiction. This jealousy survived for so long a period that the principle became firmly embedded in the English common law and was adopted with it by the American courts. The courts have felt that the precedent was too strongly fixed to be overturned without legislative enactment, although they have frequently criticized the rule and recognized its illogical nature and the injustice which results from it. The bill declares simply that such agreements for arbitration shall be enforced, and provides a procedure in the Federal courts for their enforcement. * * * It is particularly appropriate that the action should be taken at this time when there is so much agitation against the costliness and delays of litigation. These matters can be largely eliminated by agreements for arbitration, if arbitration agreements are made valid and enforceable."

In the light of the clear intention of Congress,[28] it is our obligation to shake off the old judicial hostility to arbitration. Accordingly, in a case like this, involving the federal Act, we should not follow English or other decisions which have narrowly construed the terms of arbitration agreements or arbitration statutes.

* * *

26. For a discussion of the earlier American state legislation, see Chaffee and Simpson, 1 Cases on Equity (1934) 552–553; Sturges, Commercial Arbitration (1930) Sections 1–6.

27. 68 Cong., 1st Sess., House of Rep. Report No. 96.

28. The United States Arbitration Act of 1925 was not the first evidence that Congress was not in sympathy with judicial hostility to arbitration. In 1860, foreign service officers were assigned the duty of encouraging the settlement of disputes by arbitration. These officers were, and still are, authorized to prepare submissions, accept acknowledgments, and indorse such awards. See 22 U.S.C.A. § 161. The Bankruptcy Act of 1898 authorized the submission to arbitration of disputes arising in the settlement of estates. The provision is Sec. 26 of the present Act, 11 U.S.C.A. 49. There is an arbitration provision in the Suits in Admiralty Act of 1920, 46 U.S.C.A. 786. Since 1909 it has been a criminal offense for an arbitrator acting under a federal act to accept a bribe. 18 U.S.C.A. 239. This trend toward encouraging arbitration has not waned. An arbitration provision was included in the Federal Prison Industries Act of 1930, 18 U.S.C.A. § 744g, and the Norris–LaGuardia Act bars injunctive relief to a complainant who has failed to make a reasonable effort to settle a labor dispute by arbitration. 29 U.S.C.A. § 108. There are also elaborate provisions for arbitration in the Railway Labor Act of 1926, 45 U.S.C.A. §§ 157–159.

Questions and Comments

1. Before the enactment of special arbitration statutes in the early twentieth century, what was the normal remedy for breach of an agreement to settle disputes by arbitration? Was specific performance available? How could a judge enforce specific performance of a contract to arbitrate?

Prior to the Federal Arbitration Act of 1925, in American practice, a judge would not issue an injunction ordering a party to proceed with arbitration and appoint an arbitrator or arbitrators in good faith, on penalty of being found in contempt of court. The Act was passed specifically to make injunctive relief possible. Is any technique, other than imposing a penalty for contempt of court, conceivable by which a recalcitrant party could be compelled to arbitrate?

2. If damages were available, what would be their measure?

The 1992 Arbitration Act of Peru (Decree Law No. 25935, in force since December 10, 1992) provides in Article 4(3):

> The agreement may provide sanctions for the party that fails to comply with an act that is required for the effectiveness of the agreement, establish guarantees to ensure compliance with the award and grant special powers to the arbitrators for the execution of the award in case of default by the obligor.

Compare this provision of Peruvian law with the use of penal bonds in 17th century England to render executory arbitration clauses enforceable. See Kulukundis, supra.

3. In the *Kulukundis* decision, the court stated that:

> [s]ome centuries ago, because of the jealousy of the English courts for their own jurisdiction, they refused to enforce specific agreements to arbitrate upon the ground that courts were thereby ousted from their jurisdiction.

Is jealousy the only plausible reason behind this attitude?

Are judges today less jealous?

I.2.e. A Comparative Historical Survey on the Standing of Arbitration Within the Legal System

Arthur von Mehren, A GENERAL VIEW OF CONTRACT

7 International Encyclopedia of Comparative Law ch. 1, pp. 52–56 (1982).*

* * *

57. *Historical background.*—Before discussing the contemporary handling of arbitration from several perspectives that throw light on these problems, a brief glance at history is suggestive. The struggle that many legal orders went through to establish a monopoly of the administration of justice in the central political authority[316] has left a residual

---

* Reprinted by permission of Mohr Siebeck, Germany.

316. For FRANCE and GERMANY, see *von Mehren and Gordley 13–14.*

government antagonism towards—and a related tendency to suspect—private tribunals. On the other hand, where the procedures followed in the official tribunals are very intricate, slow, and costly, and where the substantive law is obscure, complex, or out of touch with contemporary needs and realities, a body of opinion favoring arbitration emerges.

Presumably these latter considerations, together with the epoch's optimistic rationalism, explain the euphoria with which the FRENCH legislator viewed arbitration in the period immediately following the Revolution. In 1790, the Constituent Assembly characterized arbitration as "the most reasonable method for terminating disputes between citizens".[317] Enthusiasm for arbitration declined somewhat in the next decade[318] but the *Loi sur l'organisation des tribunaux* of 1800[319] art. 3 states that the "right of citizens to have their controversies judged by arbitrators of their choice is in no way restricted: the decision of these arbitrators will not be subject to any review unless the contrary is expressly provided." The Code of Civil Procedure of 1806, perhaps surprisingly in view of this background, does not deal with arbitration clauses but merely regulates compromises of existing disputes in art. 1003–1028. However, it appears that in the early decades of the nineteenth century, both FRENCH theory and practice provided generous scope for arbitration clauses.[320]

During this period arbitration was at a low point in GERMANY.[321] The very validity of arbitration clauses was disputed.[322] Where enforceable, they could not exclude review by the regular courts and the arbitrator was in principle bound to follow the law.[323] Arbitration, instead of simplifying and expediting the handling of controversies, came to have the opposite effect.

In the early part of the nineteenth century, doubtless due in considerable measure to the prestige and power of the judicial establishment, the COMMON LAW's position respecting arbitration was the most restrictive of all. Arbitration clauses were in principle void; one could not oust the jurisdiction of the official courts.[324] It is interesting to speculate why the COMMON LAW took at this period such a restrictive attitude towards arbitration—one that still obtains, though in a modified form, in ENGLAND and in some of the states of the UNITED STATES—while FRANCE and GERMANY were somewhat more receptive to private tribunals. Perhaps the traditional COMMON LAW position is normal for

---

317. Quoted by *Hello* in his conclusions to Cass.civ. 10 July 1843, S. 1843.1.561 at 566.

318. See *idem.*

319. Bulletin de Lois de la République no. 103, 15 (27 ventôse an VIII (1800)).

320. Note *Devill* to Cass.civ. 10 July 1843, S. 1843.1. 561, 562; see also *Johnson*, The Clause Compromissoire. Its Validity in Quebec (Montreal 1945) 1–60.

321. See *Krause* 88.

322. *Idem* 76.

323. *Idem* 78–81, 89; cf. PRUSSIAN *Allgemeine Gerichtsordnung* of 1793 Iz § 171 (the arbitrator must follow the "essential" provisions of state legislation).

324. See *Cheshire, Fifoot* (-*Furmston*) 353–355. The ENGLISH courts did accept, though with some reluctance, clauses making arbitration a precondition to bringing an action under a contract; *Scott v. Avery* (1856), 10 E.R. 1121 (H.L.).

a society in which, unlike FRANCE and GERMANY, the official courts were able to establish their supremacy relatively early and thereafter provided, at least by contemporary standards, a tolerably efficient administration of justice. Certainly the popularity of arbitration for those who led the French Revolution was due in part to the past failure of the official courts to provide a centralized and modestly efficient brand of justice. In addition, COMMON LAW courts were articulating and adapting their society's law in a fashion that went far beyond CONTINENTAL EUROPEAN theory or practice. Such a law making function both reinforces a court's sense of its own importance and provides an additional reason—the undesirability of impoverishing the body of experience in terms of which the community's law is fashioned—for considering problematical the ousting of official tribunals in favor of private adjudicators. Finally, of course, in the nineteenth century in ENGLAND and in the UNITED STATES judges, rather than legislators as in FRANCE and GERMANY, determined the basic limits within which private tribunals could be established. Courts are jealous of their jurisdiction; legislators show less sensitivity on the issue and—especially when their thinking is formed by the optimistic rationalism that characterizes the late eighteenth and early nineteenth century in FRANCE—tend to see in privately constituted tribunals the virtues of expeditiousness and simplicity.

Against this background, the developments in the latter part of the nineteenth century and the present posture of the several systems under discussion are not without surprises. The broadest scope for private autonomy in constituting private tribunals is today accorded in certain states of the UNITED STATES and in GERMANY; on the other hand, FRANCE and ENGLAND, although their laws have shown significant movement in the direction of according greater scope to arbitration, still impose here not unimportant restrictions on private autonomy.[325]

58. *French law.*—In FRANCE the recent history of arbitration clauses has two turning points. The first is the decision in 1843 of the *Cour de cassation* in *Comp. l'Alliance v. Prunier.*[326] There the highest court, reasoning by analogy from CCProc. art. 1006 which was to the effect that "an agreement of compromise that does not specify the matters in dispute and the names of the arbitrators is void," held arbitration clauses unenforceable except as specifically authorized by law. The court observed that, if arbitration clauses were enforced, they might well be adopted quite generally and individuals "would be deprived of the guarantees that the courts afford".[327] After the *Prunier*

325. The discussion that follows is limited to domestic arbitrations. In both ENGLAND and FRANCE, significantly greater scope is accorded to private autonomy where nondomestic arbitrations are concerned; see Arbitration Act 1979 (c. 42) esp. s. 3 and 4; *Goldman*, Règles de conflit, règles d'applicaton immédiate et règles matérielles dans l'arbitrage commercial international: Trav.com.fr.d.i.p. 1966/69, 119–148; *von Mehren*, Special Substantive Rules

for Multistate Problems—Their Role and Significance in Contemporary Choice of Law Methodology: 88 Harv.L.Rev. 347–371, 362–363 (1974).

326. Cass.civ. 10 July 1843, D. 1843.1.343; S. 1843.1.561, concl. *Hello, supra* n. 317 and note *Devill, supra* n. 320.

327. D. 1843.1.343 (344), S. 1843.1.562 (568). It is interesting to note that the BELGIAN courts enforced arbitration

decision, arbitration clauses remained unenforceable in FRANCE until Comm.C art. 631 was amended in 1925 to provide that "parties may, when they contract, agree to submit to arbitration when they arise" the following classes of controversies: disputes respecting engagements and transactions between traders, merchants, and bankers; disputes between partners respecting a commercial partnership; and all disputes respecting commercial acts (*actes de commerce*).[328]

The principal arguments advanced to support arbitration clauses were that arbitration was more expeditious and less costly than court proceedings and had the further advantage of confidentiality.[329] A substantial current of opinion believed that arbitration clauses should be enforceable in civil as well as commercial transactions. The more inclusive proposals were rejected because, in non-commercial situations, "standard clauses [providing for arbitration] and imprudent surrenders of the guarantees provided by regular courts are to be feared."[330] In the post-Word War II period, CCProc. art. 1009 under which the parties can allow arbitrators to depart from most procedural arrangements and rules applicable in judicial proceedings, and CCProc. art. 1019, under which arbitrators can, subject to some exceptions, be authorized to depart from substantive rules of law, have permitted a rapid development of arbitration practice in commercial matters.[331]

59. *German law.*—While FRANCE, which at the start of the nineteenth century had accorded such wide latitude for the constitution of private tribunals by agreement, subsequently saw a radical rejection, followed later by a resurgence, of arbitration, GERMANY moved in the same period from a restrictive approach to a position affording very wide scope to private autonomy. Arbitration is regulated in the Tenth Book (§ 1025 through 1048) of the Code of Civil Procedure of 1877.[332] CCProc. § 1025 provides that "An agreement to the effect that one or more arbitrators shall decide a legal controversy is legally effective insofar as the parties had the right to conclude a compromise with respect to the matter in dispute." However, if one party took advantage of his dominant economic or social position to procure the other party's agreement to arbitration or to obtain, with respect to possible proceedings, a superior position (*Übergewicht*), especially in the selection of arbitrators,

---

clauses although the BELGIAN Code of Civil Procedure contained the same provisions on compromise agreements as were found in the FRENCH Code; see *Morel* 487.

328. Amendment of Comm.C art. 631 was triggered by FRANCE's signature of the Geneva Protocol On Arbitration Clauses of 24 Sept. 1923; see *Hamel and Lagarde*, Traité de droit commercial 1 (Paris 1954) no. 70. The Protocol recognizes in art. 1 the validity of arbitration clauses in contracts between parties "subject respectively to the jurisdiction of different Contracting States". A contracting state has the option to restrict the Protocol's effects to contracts

that are considered commercial under its national law.

329. See *Morel* 488–489.

330. *Colin*, Rapport sur l'admission dans notre législation de la clause compromissoire: Bull.soc.études lég. 17 (1921) 315–321, 318.

331. See *Robert* 201 no. 160–161; he remarks (p. 2) that today in FRANCE arbitration "enjoys a success without precedent".

332. See *Glossner* 60.

the agreement is unenforceable.[333] CCProc. § 1026 is to the effect that "An arbitration agreement with respect to future legal controversies has no legal effect unless it refers to a specific legal relationship and the legal controversies arising therefrom." Under CCProc. § 1027a, a party can challenge a court's jurisdiction on the basis of a valid arbitration clause. The Tenth Book of the Code of Civil Procedure as administered by the GERMAN courts has resulted in the GERMAN law today being "among the legal orders most favorably disposed towards arbitration".[334]

60. *English law.*—The COMMON LAW world has, especially in the past, also disagreed respecting the extent to which party agreements establishing private tribunals should be given effect. In ENGLAND, legislation dating back to 1889 recognizes arbitration but still maintains significant judicial control over the arbitral decision.[335] The special case procedure, through which this control was exercised, was criticized on the grounds of cost and delay.[336] Until 1979, the Arbitration Act, 1950[337] s. 21, which derived originally from the Arbitration Act, 1889 s. 19[338], ensured ultimate judicial control by providing that,

(1) An arbitrator or umpire may, and shall if so directed by the High Court, state—

(a) any question of law arising in the course of the reference; or (b) an award or any part of an award, in the form of a special case for the decision of the High Court.[339]

A court would direct that a case be stated if,

"The point of law should be real and substantial and such as to be open to serious argument and appropriate for decision by a court of law ... The point of law should be clear cut and capable of being accurately stated as a point of law-as distinct from the dressing up of a matter of fact as if it were a point of law ... The point of law should be of such importance that the resolution of it is necessary for the proper determination of the case ..."[340]

The Arbitration Act 1979 (c. 59) repeals s. 21 of the 1950 Act and abrogates as well the common law jurisdiction of the High Court to set

---

333. CCProc. § 1025 par. 2.

334. *Schwab*, The Legal Foundations and Limitations of Arbitration Procedures in the U.S. and Germany: *Sanders* (ed.), Arbitration 301–312, 303.

335. It has been observed that, "in no other legal system of the world is the judicial element as strongly emphasized as in England, as is shown by the development of the so-called supervisory jurisdiction of the English courts": *Schmitthoff*, The Supervisory Jurisdiction of the English Courts: *Sanders* (ed.), Arbitration 289–300, 289.

336. See *Schmitthoff*, The Reform of the English Law of Arbitration: 1977 J.B.L. 305–311, 306.

337. 14 & 15 Geo. 6, c. 27.

338. 52 & 53 Vict., c. 49.

339. See also s. 22 (court order remitting an award in whole or in part to the arbitrator for reconsideration) and s. 23 (court order setting aside an arbitral award where an arbitrator has "misconducted himself or the proceedings"); see generally *Russell* (-*Walton*), Russell on the Law of Arbitration (ed. 19 London 1979) 420–451 and Supplement. It can also be noted that, under the 1950 Act (*supra* n. 337) s. 4, for "sufficient reason" an ENGLISH court could in effect break an arbitration clause; see *Schmitthoff* (*supra* n. 335) 291.

340. *The Lysland*, [1973] 1 Lloyd's Rep. 296, 306 (C.A.). It is said that a request by a party for a case to be stated was virtually never refused; see *Marshall* 241.

aside or remit an award on the ground of errors of fact or law appearing on the face of the award (s. 1). Judicial review remains available, but in a more restricted form than under the 1950 Act. The Act of 1979 s. 1 permits appeal against an award if all the parties consent to the reference or the High Court gives leave.[341] Leave will not be granted unless the court considers that determination of the issue of law in question could substantially affect the rights of a party; moreover, leave can be conditioned, e.g. on the applicant's furnishing security for the amount of the award. It is believed that these new procedures will reduce significantly the number of cases brought to the High Court for review on points of law.[342]

The Act of 1950 s. 21 was not subject to displacement by provisions of an arbitration clause,[343] but the Act of 1979 now permits certain exclusion agreements in s. 3 and 4. So far as domestic arbitrations are concerned, such agreements are effective only if they are entered into after the arbitration has commenced.[344]

The Act of 1950 s. 4(1) remains in effect and gives the judge power at his discretion to stay a judicial proceeding if there is a valid arbitration clause covering the controversy.[345]

61. *American law.*—The courts in the UNITED STATES took in the nineteenth century the position that arbitration agreements, though not illegal, were generally unenforceable although an agreement that an action would not be brought until arbitrators had given an award on a

---

341. In addition, the Act of 1979 s. 2 provides for determinations of preliminary points of law by the High Court in certain cases. A party can apply to the High Court with the consent of the arbitrator or of all the other parties. The High Court, before considering the reference, must satisfy itself both that the question of law could substantially affect the rights of a party and that deciding on the application might produce substantial savings in costs to the parties.

342. See *Marshall* 243.

343. See *idem* 243–244; *cf., Czarnikow v. Roth, Schmidt & Co.,* [1922] 2 K.B. 478 (C.A.): contract provision to the effect that a special case was not to be stated in connection with the arbitration held "contrary to public policy and so unenforceable" in view of the need to maintain judicial control over arbitrations and of the Arbitration Act, 1889 (*supra* n. 338) s. 7 and 19 which provide for the stating of a special case for judicial decision.

344. See s. 3(6). Exclusion agreements are allowed much greater scope in non-domestic arbitrations; see s. 3 and 4. A "domestic arbitration agreement" is one that "does not provide, expressly or by implication, for arbitration in a State other

than the United Kingdom and to which neither—"

(a) an individual who is a national of, or habitually resident in, any State other than the United Kingdom, nor

(b) a body corporate which is incorporated in, or whose central management and control is exercised in, any State other than the United Kingdom, is a party at the time the arbitration agreement is entered into (s. 3 (7)). "In order to secure the economic advantage of such arbitration business some measure more radical than the mere substitution of a new judicial review procedure for the case-stated procedure was seen to be both essential and urgent. What was wanted was freedom to contract out of judicial review, and if that freedom were withheld London would be used less and less as an arbitration centre in the future . . .:" *Marshall* 244.

345. The UNITED KINGDOM has ratified the New York Convention on the Recognition and Enforcement of Foreign Arbitral Awards; see Arbitration Act 1975, c. 3. Accordingly, under the Convention art. 1, the judge must stay judicial proceedings where a case with an "international element" presents a valid arbitration clause.

limited, clearly specified issue was usually given effect.[346] Rules more favorable to arbitration were first introduced by statutes providing, *inter alia*, for specific enforcement of arbitration agreements and for the enforcement of awards.[347] By the third quarter of this century, the cumulative effect of these statutes was such that "it seems likely that even in the ... states [that have not enacted such legislation], there has been a change in the former judicial attitude of hostility toward agreements to arbitrate future disputes ..."[348]

The Uniform Arbitration Act, approved in 1955 by the *National Conference of Commissioners on Uniform States Laws* and the *American Bar Association*, can serve as a model of contemporary AMERICAN legislation favorable to arbitration.[349] Section I provides broadly that "a provision in a written contract to submit to arbitration any controversy thereafter arising between the parties is valid, enforceable and irrevocable, save upon such grounds as exist at law or in equity for the revocation of any contract." An award can be vacated by court order under § 12 where the "award was procured by corruption, fraud or other undue means"; an arbitrator appointed as a neutral showed "evident partiality" or there was "corruption in any of the arbitrators or misconduct prejudicing the rights of any party"; the "arbitrators exceeded their powers"; the hearing was not conducted as provided in § 5 of the Act and, in consequence, the rights of a party were substantially prejudiced; there "was no arbitration agreement and the issue was not adversely determined in proceedings under Section 2 and the party did not participate in the arbitration hearing without raising the objection".[350]

The federal Arbitration Act of 1947[351] applies to "maritime transactions" and to "commerce", in particular "commerce among the several

---

346. *Corbin* VIA § 1431. The Restatement of Contracts (1932) § 550 states that "a bargain to arbitrate either an existing or a possible future dispute is not illegal, unless the agreed terms of arbitration are unfair, but will not be specifically enforced, and only nominal damages are recoverable for its breach. Nor is any bargain to arbitrate a bar to an action on the claim to which the bargain relates." *Sturges*, A Treatise on Commercial Arbitrations and Awards (Kansas City, Mo. 1930) § 15 p. 45, wrote in 1930 that "It is an elementary proposition of the common law cases, and is almost universally accepted by the American courts, that future disputes clauses and provisions for arbitration are revocable." Restatement of Contracts 2d (1979) not only found it unnecessary to include a section analogous to § 0 but considered arbitration clauses enforceable in principle and irrevocable: see Restatement of Contracts 2d (1979) Introductory Note to ch. 8.

347. See *Corbin* VIA § 1431.

348. See Restatement of Contracts 2d (1979), *supra* n. 346.

349. The Uniform Act followed "the pattern of the arbitration statutes of New York and of some fifteen other states": Uniform Laws Annotated VII (St. Paul, Minn. 1978) 2. By 1979, the Act had been adopted by 23 states. *Ibidem*, Cumulative Annual Pocket Part (St. Paul, Minn. 1980) 1.

350. An award can be modified or corrected under § 13 where: "(1) There was an evident miscalculation of figures or an evident mistake in the description of any person, thing or property referred to in the award; (2) The arbitrators have awarded upon a matter not submitted to them and the award may be corrected without affecting the merits of the decision upon the issues submitted; or (3) The award is imperfect in a matter of form, not affecting the merits of the controversy."

351. Act of 30 July 1947 (61 Stat. 669) § 1 codifying and enacting title 9 U.S.C., "Arbitration".

States or with foreign nations . . .[352] and resembles in many respects the Uniform Act." Under § 2a "written provision . . . to settle by arbitration a controversy thereafter arising out of such contract or transaction . . . shall be valid, irrevocable, and enforceable, save upon such grounds as exist at law or in equity for the revocation of any contract." § 10, providing for vacating of awards, is similar to the Uniform Act § 12; § 11, dealing with modification and correction of awards, parallels the Uniform Act § 13.

POSTSCRIPT:

The trend towards acceptance and facilitation of arbitration as an essentially party-designed and controlled dispute resolution process, in full flood as the 1980s began, has continued unabated. In May 1981, Book IV, Arbitration (arts. 1442–1507 of the New [French] Code of Civil Procedure) entered into force. Titles 5 and 6 strengthened the position of international arbitrations conducted in France by providing that French-court review of such awards was to be no stricter than that given foreign awards whose recognition in France was sought under the 1958 United Nations Convention on the Recognition and Enforcement of Foreign Arbitral Awards.

In 1985, the United Nations Commission on International Trade Law (UNCITRAL) adopted a Model Law on International Commercial Arbitration. That law's progressive, modern arbitration regime has had considerable influence on state arbitration laws both through direct adoption or, as in the new German Arbitration Act of 1998, more indirectly.

The most significant development in national legislation during these two decades was the enactment by the United Kingdom of a new Arbitration Act in 1996. This law went well beyond the 1979 Act to ensure that international commercial arbitration could be conducted in the United Kingdom without unwanted judicial intrusion.

The UNCITRAL Model Law, Book IV of the New [French] Code of Civil Procedure, the United Kingdom Arbitration Act of 1996, and the German Arbitration Act of 1998 are set out in the Documents Supplement. All are considered in various connections in this book.

Questions and Comments

1. The examples of France, Germany, England and the U.S. show that the lines of development were very much parallel. Agreements providing for arbitration of an already existing specific dispute received earlier recognition than agreements submitting to arbitration possible future disputes; likewise, state (court) control has been declining, while at the same time, the readiness of courts to enforce arbitration agreements has increased.

Can you explain the reasons for these changes in the standing of arbitration (and of international commercial arbitration in particular) within the legal system? Pressure from the community of merchants? Overcrowded

---

352. "Maritime transactions" and "commerce" are defined in § 1.

court-dockets? Change of philosophy? (What philosophy?) Growing importance of international trade? Something else?

I.3. ON THE SOURCES OF RELEVANT NORMS

I.3.a. Note

Arbitration—and international commercial arbitration in particular-has generally been regarded as a creation of the parties. This "creation" can only function, however, within the framework of a legal system. Without a foothold in some legal system, arbitration would depend entirely on the cooperation of the parties, and this would seriously jeopardize the efficiency of the arbitration process. Arbitration tends to strive for the best in both worlds. It endeavors, relying on party autonomy, to set the decision-making process free of municipal law and formal procedure; yet at the same time it relies on court assistance when party cooperation is lacking, and hence, the party-driven process faces a road-block.

What norms then ultimately control the unique process of international commercial arbitration, and what is the hierarchical relationship among them? This issue will emerge in various guises in practically all chapters of these materials; here we offer a brief preliminary survey of the pertinent norms.

(a) Party autonomy

Party autonomy is certainly the *differentia specifica* of the arbitration process. The crucial difference between arbitration and courts lies in the fact that the basis of the jurisdiction of an arbitral tribunal is the will of the parties, while courts owe their competence to procedural norms of a state or of an international convention.

Not only its right to proceed, but the composition of the arbitral tribunal depends on party agreement, just as do the site, rules of proceeding, and language—in other words, the whole pattern of decision-making.

The freedom of the parties to shape the arbitral tribunal and the arbitral process though not unlimited, is certainly very wide. Some limits are posed in mandatory procedural norms of particular countries and in a number of international agreements.

(b) Institutional rules of other than state origin

Parties rarely take full advantage of the opportunity of shaping a complete decision-making process according to their own design. To do so would of course be a formidable task, requiring more time than the parties can possibly spend, and asking for more expertise than they have available. One must not forget that the main focus of an international contract is on the transaction itself, rather than on the dispute settling methodology. For these reasons, prefabricated patterns and models are widely relied upon. In response to a rather pronounced need, institutional arbitration has been developed, offering a pre-established set of procedural rules and providing solutions for various typical problem-patterns, such as the designation of the second arbitrator in case of obstruction by a party, or of a third arbitrator in case the two arbitrators (or the two parties), who are supposed to choose this arbitrator by common consent, cannot reach agreement. Institutional rules also step in where disagreement exists respecting such important issues as the site or language of the proceedings.

These institutional norms are usually rules of an organization offering services in arbitration, such as the International Chamber of Commerce's International Court of Arbitration in Paris, the London Court of International Arbitration, the American Arbitration Association, the Arbitration Institute of the Stockholm Chamber of Commerce, the Arbitration Center of the Federal Economic Chamber in Vienna, the Court of Arbitration at the Hungarian Chamber of Commerce in Budapest, the Cairo Regional Center for International Commercial Arbitration, the China International and Economic Trade Arbitration Commission in Beijing (with subcommissions in Shenzen and Shanghai), the Foreign Trade Court of Arbitration at the Russian Federation Chamber of Commerce and Industry in Moscow, and many other institutions established for the same purposes. Recent versions of the rules of these institutions—as well as of other well known arbitration centers—have shown a rather pronounced tendency to converge, guided to some extent by the concepts and rules elaborated under the auspices of the UNCITRAL (United Nations Commission on International Trade Law). Of course, institutional rules only apply if the parties choose them or designate the institution that administers the rules.

If instead the parties choose themselves to establish a tribunal for their dispute (an ad hoc tribunal), they will have more maneuvering room but also larger responsibilities; if they miss an issue, no previously agreed backup solution will be at hand. Even within the framework of ad hoc arbitration, however, pre-established sets of solutions may play an important role. There have been several endeavors to draft rules which the parties may adopt as their own instead of relying either on a particular institution or themselves assuming the task of structuring a detailed procedural framework. The best known (and the most successful) of these is the UNCITRAL Arbitration Rules adopted by the UN General Assembly on December 15, 1976.[3] The Resolution of the General Assembly, in adopting these Rules, emphasized that: "the establishment of rules for *ad hoc* arbitration that are acceptable in countries with different legal, social and economic systems would significantly contribute to the development of harmonious international economic relations."

The UNCITRAL Rules undertook to harmonize the approaches of various legal systems and are being relied upon with increasing frequency world-wide. Some arbitral institutions have decided to adopt the UNCITRAL Rules as their own;[4] others allow the parties to choose

---

[3]. Resolution 31/98.

[4]. See, e.g., Article 12 of the Statute of the Cairo Regional Center for International

between the institution's own rules and the UNCITRAL Rules.[5] The (indirect) success of the UNCITRAL Rules is also evidenced by the adoption by the Inter–American Commercial Arbitration Commission of rules that almost duplicate the UNCITRAL Rules. By virtue of Article 3 of the Inter–American Convention, the Inter–American rules will not only apply when expressly chosen by the parties, but also "in the absence of an express agreement of the parties" respecting the applicable procedural rules.

Parties may, in principle, also combine pre-established institutional rules with solutions designed by themselves. Problems may, however, emerge should the procedural mechanism conceived by the parties contradict particular solutions contained in the institutional rules or even the rules' basic concept. For example, a party stipulation that would oblige the arbitrators to hear all witnesses proposed by the parties, or even worse, to hear all witnesses proposed by one of the parties, could seriously undermine the functioning and even the fairness of the institutionally designed decision-making process. In such a case, since the authority of the arbitrators is derived from the agreement of the parties, the arbitral tribunal could not disregard explicit requirements stated in the arbitration clause; it could only refuse to arbitrate under the given conditions.

A related, but somewhat different, issue arises when the party stipulation, though compatible with the principles established by the institution's rules, is inapplicable in the given circumstances. For example, the parties submit their dispute to ICC arbitration, but designate a separate appointing authority that is to replace the ICC International Court of Arbitration (which acts as the appointing authority under the ICC Rules). These arrangements may be compatible, but what happens if the appointing authority chosen by the parties fails to make an appointment?[6]

(c) Municipal procedural rules

International commercial arbitration has become essentially a self-contained and self-reliant decision-making structure, yet it has not entirely escaped from the control-albeit very limited-of municipal procedural rules. The relationship between party arrangements and mandatory municipal rules is well illustrated by Article 182 of Chapter 12 of the 1987 Swiss Private International Law Act, which provides a solution in principle:

Commercial Arbitration, established by the Asian–African Legal Consultative Committee on January 23, 1978.

[5]. See, e.g., Article 45 of the October 1997 Rules of the Foreign Trade Court of Arbitration at the Economic Chamber of Yugoslavia in Belgrade.

[6]. For a case presenting this problem-pattern, see the Preliminary Award Made in ICC Case No. 2321 (1974), reported 1 Yearbk. Comm. Arb'n 133 (1976), infra subsection I.3.b.

"1. The parties may, directly or by reference to arbitration rules, determine the arbitral procedure; they may also submit it to a procedural law of their choice.

2. Where the parties have not determined the procedure, the arbitral tribunal shall determine it to the extent necessary, either directly or by reference to a law or to arbitration rules.

3. Whatever procedure is chosen, the arbitral tribunal shall assure equal treatment of the parties and the right of the parties to be heard in an adversarial procedure."

In other words, arbitration tribunals may freely follow procedural rules drafted (or chosen) by the parties, as long as they observe basic requirements of due process.

In addition to furnishing a very general orientation regarding the proceedings before an arbitration tribunal, municipal rules may also become relevant with respect to such issues as referring the parties to arbitration, constituting the arbitral tribunal, challenging arbitrators, and other related matters. The local procedural framework also becomes important when recognition of foreign awards is sought.

The question of which municipal law governs in particular situations also arises. This complex conflict of laws issue has many ramifications and nuances. In this introductory section, only the most basic solutions are mentioned: where recognition of an award is sought, the laws of the recognizing country (or international agreements ratified by that country) apply; on the other hand, the law governing the arbitration proceedings (*lex arbitri*, sometimes called curial law) is generally that of the country in which the arbitration tribunal has its seat.

Municipal procedural rules pertaining to international commercial arbitration are normally contained in legislation, with the bulk of the rules typically concentrated in acts on civil procedure,[7] on private international law,[8] or on arbitration.[9]

Another UNCITRAL effort to harmonize the rules on international commercial arbitration must also be mentioned: the Model Law on International Commercial Arbitration (hereinafter ML).[10] The aim was to provide a set of rules which would be acceptable world-wide, and which could be progressively adopted by national legislators. A Model

---

[7]. In the 1981 French Code of Civil Procedure, Book IV is devoted to arbitration, titles V and VI of Book IV to international arbitration. In the Italian Code of Civil Procedure, as amended in 1994, arbitration is covered in Book IV, Title VIII; in the 1983 version of the Austrian Code of Civil Procedure, in Chapter IV; in the 1986 version of the Dutch Code of Civil Procedure, in Book IV.

[8]. E.g., the 1987 Swiss Act on Private International Law (Chapter 12); the 1982 Yugoslav Private International Law Act (Chapter IV) in combination with the rele-

vant provisions of the 1976 Code of Civil Procedure (Chapter XXXI).

[9]. E.g., the United States Arbitration Act (Title 9, U.S. Code para 1–14, first enacted in 1925, most recently amended in 1990); the 1996 Arbitration Act of England, Wales and Northern Ireland; the 1988 Spanish Act on Arbitration; the 1996 Indian Arbitration and Conciliation Ordinance; the 1994 Hungarian Arbitration Act; the 1999 Swedish Arbitration Act.

[10]. Adopted by UNCITRAL on June 21, 1985.

Law cannot, of course, yield complete uniformity, and it may even be debatable how close a national enactment should be to the ML in order to qualify that country as an ML country.[11] According to an August 8 2002 UNCITRAL update, legislation based on the ML has been enacted in 38 jurisdictions.[12] Alongside these jurisdictions are those that adopted legislative acts "under the influence" of the ML. Classification is not easy. The UNCITRAL document does not list Romania as a "Model Law country," but it has been argued that the Model Law has strongly influenced the Romanian rules.[13] The 1996 Arbitration Act of England, Wales, and Northern Ireland has adopted many Model Law solutions, but also has a fair number of different norms. Scotland has a different act, and belongs to the "Model Law countries." After the adoption of the 1998 version of Chapter X of the *Zivilprozessordnung* (Code of Civil Procedure), Germany has been listed as a "Model Law country," since the enacted changes have brought the Code closer to the Model Law. In any event, it is undeniable that the ML is a most ambitious undertaking, and after the first decade, one may speak of a considerable success. It is also important that countries that have adopted the ML are fairly evenly spread around the globe[14].

The ML has also been adopted in a number of federal units, including all the provinces of Canada, and eight states of the United States: California, Connecticut, Florida, Georgia, North Carolina, Ohio, Oregon, and Texas. The adoption in Connecticut has been the most complete; the ML was enacted in its full text, without changes except for the addition of a 37th article, which states: "This Act may be cited as the UNCITRAL Model Law on International Commercial Arbitration."[15]

The number of ML countries is growing, and one might say that the ML has brought about a worldwide trend towards convergence in the domain of international commercial arbitration.

(d) International agreements

International commercial arbitration cannot be a success without some international framework which provides for recognition of the arbitration process and of its result (the award) beyond the boundaries of a particular country. Numerous efforts have been made to provide such a framework, and the results achieved have lived up to the original

[11]. See P. Sanders, Unity and Diversity in the Adoption of the Model Law, 11 Arbt'n Intl'l 1 (1995).

[12]. UNCITRAL, Status of Conventions and Model Laws, last updated August 8, 2002

(Website: *www.uncitral.org/en-index.htm*)

[13]. See the assessment of a well known Romanian author: Capatina, L'Application en Roumanie de la Loi-type et du Réglement d'arbitrage de la CNUDCI, in Hague Yearbook of International Law, M. Nijhoff, 1996, 11.

[14]. That this would be the case seemed clear from the very outset. The first countries which adopted ML-based legislation were Canada (1986), Cyprus (1987), Bulgaria and Nigeria (1988), Australia and Hong Kong (1989), Scotland (1990), Peru, Bermuda, the Russian Federation, Mexico, and Tunisia (1993).

[15]. Publ. Act No 89–179, 1989, Conn. Legis. Serv. (West) approved June 1, 1989, in force since October 1, 1991.

expectations: Today, international commercial arbitration is backed and guided by a unique network of international conventions which makes possible an almost worldwide recognition of arbitral awards. These conventions have also had a positive impact on attitudes on the domestic scene towards arbitration. In a number of countries, the acceptance of international conventions led to new and improved standards in municipal procedural rules as well. We should also stress that two highly important global international conventions devoted to commercial arbitration have enjoyed great success. The 1958 New York Convention and the 1965 Washington Convention have been adopted by more than 100 countries from all parts of the world.

The conventions which represent today the mainstay of the international standing of commercial arbitration, are the following:

— the 1958 New York Convention on the Recognition and Enforcement of Foreign Arbitral Awards (concluded under the auspices of the United Nations);[16]

— the 1961 (Geneva) European Convention on International Commercial Arbitration, with the 1962 (Paris) Agreement Relating to the Application of the European Convention on International Commercial Arbitration;[17]

— the 1965 Washington Convention on the Settlement of Investment Disputes between States and Nationals of Other States (ICSID Convention);[18]

— the 1975 (Panama) Inter–American Convention on International Commercial Arbitration.[19]

Mention must also be made of two Geneva agreements concluded under the auspices of the League of Nations, still in force, which have lost most of their practical relevance because of the success of the New York Convention: the 1923 Geneva Protocol on Arbitration Clauses, and the 1927 Geneva Convention on the Execution of Foreign Arbitral Awards.

In addition to multilateral agreements, bilateral agreements have also contributed to the worldwide standing of international commercial arbitration.

[16]. In force in 132 states according to an August 8, 2002 UNCITRAL survey (see footnote 12).

Another source (Yearbook Commercial Arbitration) adds to the list extensions, like the extension made by the United States to American Samoa, or the extension to Bermuda made by the United Kingdom. With these extensions, the count is 153. (26 Yearbk Comm. Arb'n, 716 (2001)).

[17]. In force in 28 countries as of October 1, 2001 (26 Yearbk. Comm. Arb'n 1133 (2001)).

[18]. In force in 152 countries, as of August 7, 2001 (26 Yearbk. Comm. Arb'n 1151 (2001)).

[19]. See Organization of American States, Treaty Series no. 42 (Appendix C at U.S.C.A. Para 301), ratified by Argentina, Bolivia, Brazil, Chile, Colombia, Costa Rica, Dominican Republic, Ecuador, El Salvador, Guatemala, Honduras, Mexico, Nicaragua, Panama, Paraguay, Peru, the United States, Uruguay, and Venezuela.

I.3.b. ***Party Stipulation Versus Institutional Rules***

PRELIMINARY AWARD MADE IN CASE NO. 2321 IN 1974 (ICC)

1 Yearbk. Comm. Arb'n 133 (1976).*

APPOINTMENT OF ARBITRATOR—PLEA OF STATE IMMUNITY

The arbitrator was sitting in Sweden in a dispute between two enterprises as claimants and, as defendants a State other than their own and a public authority of this latter state. The action against the State was based on the fact that it had in the contract guaranteed the commercial transaction entered into by the public authority. Before going into the merits of the case, the arbitrator was called upon to decide two points of a procedural nature raised by the defendants.

A.   *Appointment of the arbitrator*

The defendants first of all contested the regularity of the nomination of the arbitrator by the Court of Arbitration of the I.C.C., which, according to them had not been done in conformity with the contractual provisions.

The general conditions of the contract (the General Conditions drawn up by the Fédération Internationale des Ingénieurs–Conseils—F.I.D.I.C.) provided for an arbitration according to the I.C.C. Rules by one or more arbitrators appointed in accordance with the said Rules. An annex to the contract provided however that the appointment of the arbitrator should be made by an authority other than the Court of Arbitration of the I.C.C. (this other authority is referred to in the extract given hereafter as "the Chairman"). When this other authority was called upon to appoint an arbitrator, he refused, and the Court of Arbitration of the I.C.C. considered that in these conditions it was up to it to proceed to the nomination of the arbitrator, applying the usual provisions of its Rules. It was this decision which had led to the appointment of the arbitrator which the defendants considered to have been ineffective.

The arbitrator held that he had validly been appointed by the Court of Arbitration itself giving the following reasoning:

> I agree so far with the defendants that an arbitration clause may have, as to its scope, to be interpreted strictly. Such maxim, however, may not have the same bearing when it comes to the appreciation of the validity or the effectiveness of an arbitration clause. On the contrary when inserting an arbitration clause in their contract the intention of the parties must be presumed to have been willing to establish an effective machinery for the settlement of disputes covered by the arbitration clause.

* Reprinted with permission of Yearbook Commercial Arbitration, International Council for Commercial Arbitration.

The basic agreement on arbitration in this case is to be found in Clause 67 of the General Conditions where it is clearly provided that all disputes shall be finally settled under the Rules of I.C.C. "by one or more arbitrators appointed in accordance with the said Rules" ... Generally the Court appoints the single or third arbitrator. However, the Rules foresee in Art. 7.1 the possibility that the parties stipulate otherwise. In the case before me the parties have exercised such option by inserting in an Appendix to the Contract the provision that the said chairman should be the Appointer of the Arbitrator.

The chairman which was requested by the claimants to appoint an arbitrator, did not expressly appoint the Court to make the ultimate appointment. He just refused to appoint an arbitrator saying that he considered that the Court should appoint the arbitrator in accordance with the Rules as provided for in Clause 67 of the General Conditions.

The Rules, which as aforesaid the parties have incorporated into and made a part of the Contract, provide in Art. 7.2 that, failing agreement between the parties (on the nomination of a sole arbitrator) within a period of thirty days from the notification of the request for arbitration to the opposite party, the arbitrator shall be appointed by the Court. Although the parties, as said above, have agreed upon a method of appointing the sole arbitrator, they nevertheless—when this method later proved to be ineffective because of the refusal of the chairman to appoint an arbitrator—must be said to have failed to nominate an arbitrator by common agreement. Then, according to Art. 7.2 of the Rules, the arbitrator shall be appointed by the Court.

Questions and Comments

1. The 1974 ICC Preliminary Award was based on an earlier (1955) version of the ICC Rules. Article 7(1) of those rules included the principle that the parties may provide for another means of appointing arbitrators:

The Court of Arbitration does not itself settle disputes. Except when otherwise stipulated, it appoints or confirms the nomination of arbitrators in accordance with the following provisions.

The relevant subsection on default appointment of a sole arbitrator (Article 7(2)) provided:

If the parties have agreed to the settlement of a dispute by a sole arbitrator, they may nominate him by common agreement for confirmation by the Court.

Failing agreement between the parties within a period of thirty days from the notification of the request for arbitration to the opposite party, the arbitrator shall be appointed by the Court.

As the arbitrator in this case, would you have found your appointment valid?

Assuming you would not have, would there have been an alternative procedure for appointing an arbitrator or should the arbitration agreement have been found ineffective and the parties directed to litigate their dispute in court?

2. With appointment made by the ICC Court of Arbitration, did the parties get what they envisaged (or should have envisaged) as a fall-back solution, or did they wind up with the very solution they explicitly tried to avoid?

3. Suppose the arbitration had been ad hoc instead of institutional, and the parties' agreed method for choosing arbitrators failed to work as here. What outcome?

4. Can a possible solution for the case be inferred from Article 1493 of the French Code of Civil Procedure?

5. In the 1998 ICC Rules, Article 7(6) gives party autonomy priority over institutional appointment, and Article 8(3) deals with substitute appointment of sole arbitrators by the Court. Read articles 7(6) and 8(3), in particular, and compare them with Article 7 of the 1955 Rules, and consider whether the same result would be reached in the 1998 setting as was reached in 1974.

6. Suppose that the appointment problem emerges in connection with appointing the third arbitrator. Suppose further that the parties have agreed on arbitration in accordance with the 1998 ICC Rules, but that they have also specified that the third arbitrator shall be appointed by, let us say, the Chairman of the Ithaca Chamber of Commerce. Can this arrangement co-exist with Article 8(4) of the 1998 ICC Rules? What would you do as an arbitrator if faced with such an arrangement?

7. In another ICC arbitration clause[20] (which can hardly be qualified as a masterpiece) the parties agreed on three arbitrators. It was stipulated that each side should select one arbitrator, the two arbitrators were to select the third, and in case they could not agree, the third arbitrator would be selected by the President of the International Court of Justice in The Hague. At the same time, however, the arbitration clause stated that "the constitution of the arbitral tribunal as well as the applicable procedure" shall be governed by the ICC Rules. To make things even more complicated, the parties chose Buenos Aires as the site of arbitration, and—adding one more source of authority—stated that the federal tribunals of the Argentinean Republic were competent to decide the constitution of the arbitral tribunal. When a dispute arose, claimants (E.T.P.M. and Ecofisa) decided to take a shortcut, and, without much ado, asked the ICC Court of Arbitration to constitute the tribunal. The Court, again without much ado, applied its institutional rules and nominated all three arbitrators. The arbitrators confirmed their jurisdiction, and decided on the merits. The Paris Cour d'appel refused to recognize the award rendered in Argentina, upholding the objections of the Respondent, and stating that the agreement of the parties

[20]. The clause was scrutinized by the French Cour de cassation in Société E.T.P.M. and Ecofisa v. Société Gas del Estado, Decision of December 4, 1990, Reported in 1991 Revue de l'arbitrage 81.

regarding the constitution of the arbitral tribunal was not respected. The Cour de cassation agreed with the Cour d'appel.

Do you agree?

I.3.c. *Party Stipulation Versus State Norms*

AL HADDAD BROS. ENTERPRISES, INC. v. M/S AGAPI

United States District Court, District of Delaware, 1986.
635 F.Supp. 205.

OPINION

CALEB M. WRIGHT, SENIOR DISTRICT JUDGE.

Plaintiff Al Haddad Brothers Enterprises ("Al Haddad") brought this action to recover for damages to a cargo of salt and detergent carried from Wilmington to Turkey on board the vessel, the Agapi, owned and operated by defendant Diakan Love, S.A. ("Diakan"). Currently before the Court is the motion of Diakan for summary judgment on a counterclaim seeking recognition and enforcement of a London arbitration award in favor of Diakan against Al Haddad. * * *

I. BACKGROUND

Al Haddad filed suit in February 1982 against Diakan * * * to recover for damage done to Al Haddad's cargo during its transport in February—March, 1981. In answer, Diakan raised as an affirmative defense the existence of an arbitration provision in the charter party between Al Haddad and Diakan. The clause states:

> 51. Any dispute arising under the Charter to be referred to Arbitration in London, one Arbitrator is to be nominated by the Owners and the other by the Charterers, and in case the Arbitrators shall not agree, then to the decision of an Umpire to be appointed by them, the award of the Arbitrators or the Umpire to be final and binding upon both parties. The Arbitrators and Umpire, if any, to be members of the London Arbitrators Association.

Diakan moved to stay proceedings until the merits of Al Haddad's claim had been decided in London pursuant to the provision in the charter party. * * * The Court granted Diakan's motion and stayed the case * * * . * * *

* * * Diakan in October 1981 initiated an arbitration proceeding in London against Al Haddad for unpaid charter hire. Diakan appointed its arbitrator, Bruce Harris, and gave notice of that fact to Al Haddad on November 3, 1981. When Al Haddad did not nominate an arbitrator by December 23, 1981, Diakan asked Harris to serve as sole arbitrator. Notice of this appointment was sent to Al Haddad on December 31, 1981. At one point, Al Haddad retained solicitors in relation to the arbitration, but it later discharged them and did not provide any defense in the proceeding or otherwise participate in it. Harris entered an award

of \$143,712.04 plus interest and costs in favor of Diakan against Al Haddad on July 12, 1983.

[Seeking to ignore the arbitration award, Al Haddad filed a motion to re-open the litigation in the U.S. district court in Delaware. In response, Diakan filed a counterclaim seeking to enforce the London arbitration award and moved for summary judgment on this counterclaim.]

II. DISCUSSION

Al Haddad * * * argues that the Court should not enforce the arbitration award because the arbitration authority which rendered the award was not composed in accordance with the alleged agreement.

* * *

b. Enforcement of the London Award

Under the Convention on the Recognition and Enforcement of Foreign Arbitral Awards (hereinafter "Convention"), a United States court can recognize a foreign arbitral award if the party seeking recognition has met two requirements. He must present the duly authenticated original award or a certified copy, and the original arbitration agreement or a certified copy. Id. art. IV(1). The party opposing recognition then may attempt to prove one or more of the defenses permitted by the Convention. Id. art. V(1) (listing defenses). If the party objecting to recognition does not meet his burden of proof, the court will convert the award into a judgment.

Al Haddad makes two arguments why this Court should refuse to enforce the London award. It argues first that Diakan has not met one of the requisites for recognition of the foreign award, because Diakan has not submitted the original arbitration agreement between the parties or a certified copy. Diakan instead has appended to its Supplemental Answer an unverified document which it asserts is the parties' agreement.

Secondly, Al Haddad invokes the defense that "[t]he composition of the arbitral authority or the arbitral procedure was not in accordance with the agreement of the parties, or, failing such agreement, was not in accordance with the law of the country where the arbitration took place." Id. art. V(1)(d). In particular, the arbitration provision in the Agapi charter party called for an arbitration panel composed of one arbitrator appointed by each party and, if the two arbitrators did not agree, an umpire appointed by the two arbitrators would render the decision. Al Haddad points out that a sole arbitrator appointed by Diakan made the award here.

The Court rejects Al Haddad's first argument and finds that it is unnecessary for Diakan to submit a certified copy of the parties' arbitration agreement in this situation. The purpose for requiring submission of the original agreement or a certified copy is to prove the existence of an agreement to arbitrate. Such proof already exists in this case because the

Court has determined on several prior instances that the charter party between Al Haddad and Diakan contained a London arbitration provision. Those rulings form sufficient verification of the existence of an arbitration agreement to allow enforcement of the award here.

The arbitration award Diakan seeks to enforce admittedly was not rendered in accordance with the parties' agreement, but that fact is not fatal to its validity. The Convention allows recognition of an award which, although not in accord with the parties' agreement, complied with the laws of the country where the arbitration occurred. Convention, art. V(1)(d). Under the British arbitration statute, a sole arbitrator appointed by one of the parties may decide a dispute when the other party fails to appoint an arbitrator under the agreement, after being called upon to do so. Arbitration Act, 14 Geo. 6, ch. 27, § 7(b) (1950). However, the party who has appointed an arbitrator initially must wait seven clear days after notifying the opposing party of the initial appointment before appointing its arbitrator to act as sole arbitrator. Id.

Diakan followed this procedure. Diakan's solicitors sent notice to Al Haddad on November 3, 1981, that they had appointed Bruce Harris as arbitrator. Having received no response from Al Haddad, Diakan's solicitors appointed Harris as sole arbitrator on December 23, 1981, and sent notice to Al Haddad on December 31, 1981. Al Haddad does not argue that it failed to receive notice of Diakan's actions. The London award therefore is entitled to recognition and enforcement under the Convention.

* * *

REDERI AKTIEBOLAGET SALLY (FINLAND) v. S.R.L. TERMAREA (ITALY)

Italy, Corte di Appello di Firenze [Court of Appeal of Florence], 1978.
4 Yearbk. Comm. Arb'n 294 (1979).*

[Authors' note: In this decision of the Court of Appeal of Florence and in the English case that follows, sections 8 and 9 of the English Arbitration Act of 1950 are of crucial importance. We set out here relevant excerpts from those sections for easy reference.

Section 8 **Umpires**

(1) Unless a contrary intention is expressed therein, every arbitration agreement shall, where the reference is to two arbitrators, be deemed to include a provision that the two arbitrators shall appoint an umpire at any time after they are themselves appointed.

(2) Unless a contrary intention is expressed therein, every arbitration agreement shall, where such a provision is applicable to the reference, be deemed to include a provision that if the arbitrators have delivered to any party to the arbitration agreement, or to

* Reprinted with permission of Yearbook Commercial Arbitration, International   Council for Commercial Arbitration.

the umpire, a notice in writing stating that they cannot agree, the umpire may forthwith enter on the reference in lieu of the arbitrators.

* * *

Section 9 **Majority award of three arbitrators**

(1) Where an arbitration agreement provides that the reference shall be to three arbitrators, one to be appointed by each party and the third to be appointed by the two appointed by the parties, the agreement shall have effect as if it provided for the appointment of an umpire, and not for the appointment of a third arbitrator, by the two arbitrators appointed by the parties.

* * *]

FACTS

By a charter party of March 11, 1975 on an "EXXONVOY 1969" form Sally chartered to Termarea a vessel. Clause 24 of the charter party provided for the following:

"ARBITRATION. Any and all differences and disputes of whatsoever nature 'arising out of this Charter shall be put to arbitration in the City of New York or in the City of London, whichever place is specified in Part I of this Charter pursuant to the laws relating to arbitration there in force, before a board of three persons, consisting of one arbitrator to be appointed by the Owner, one by the Charterer, and one by the two so chosen.' The decision of any two of the three on any point or points shall be final. Either party hereto may call for such arbitration by service upon any officer of the other, wherever he may be found, of a written notice specifying the name and address of the arbitrator chosen by the first moving party and a brief description of the disputes or differences which such party desires to put to arbitration. If the other party shall not, by notice served upon an officer of the first moving party within twenty days of the service of such notice, appoint its arbitrator to arbitrate the dispute or differences specified, then the first moving party shall have the right without further notice to appoint a second arbitrator, who shall be a disinterested person with precisely the same force and effect as if the said second arbitrator has been appointed by the other party. In the event that the two arbitrators fail to appoint a third arbitrator within twenty days of the appointment of the second arbitrator, either arbitrator may apply to a Judge of any court of maritime jurisdiction in the city abovementioned for the appointment of a third arbitrator, and the appointment of such arbitrator by such Judge on such application shall have precisely the same force and effect as if such arbitrator had been appointed by the two arbitrators. (...)".

Part I of the charter party specified London as place of arbitration.

Sally began arbitration pursuant to the abovementioned clause, claiming demurrage payable in the sum of appr. US $41,000 from Termarea in respect of excess time at the loading and discharging ports.

Sally and Termarea each appointed an arbitrator.[e] The two arbitrators thus chosen did not appoint the third arbitrator. In the award of September 30, 1976, the arbitrators explained this as follows:

> "Clause 24 of the said charter party required arbitration before a board of three persons, the third arbitrator to be appointed by the two chosen by the parties. The Arbitration Act 1950 Sect 9, para. 1, states that any such provision shall take effect as if it provided for the appointment of an Umpire. As the two arbitrators were minded to agree, an Umpire was not required and if so appointed would not have entered into the Reference".

The two arbitrators held Termarea liable to Sally in the amount of appr. US $24,000, plus interest of 8.5% per annum from June 1, 1975.

When Termarea was unwilling to pay, Sally sought enforcement of the award in Italy. The Court of Appeal of Florence, however, refused enforcement for the following reasons.

Extract

"According to Art. V, para. 1 under *d*, of the New York Convention, implemented in Italy by Law No. 62 of January 10, 1968 (the applicability of the above Convention to the present case is self-evident), the recognition of a foreign arbitration award is to be refused where 'the composition of the arbitral authority or the arbitral procedure was not in accordance with the agreement of the parties, or, failing such agreement, was not in accordance with the law of the country where the arbitration took place'. From the arbitral award which is the subject of the present suit it results that same was issued on the basis of clause 24 of a charter party stipulated between the parties on March 11, 1975. Said clause provided for the arbitral award to be issued by three persons, two of them respectively appointed by the parties, and the third to be appointed by the other two. From same award it also results that, on the contrary, it was issued only by the two arbitrators appointed by the parties. As a consequence, in accordance with the above mentioned provision, the award cannot be declared enforceable, since the arbitral tribunal was not in conformity with the one provided for by clause 24 of the charter party. In this connection the claimant invokes Sect. 9 para. 1, of the English Arbitration Act 1950, which, according to the wording quoted by him, provides as follows:

> "Where an arbitration agreement provides that the reference shall be to three arbitrators, one to be appointed by each party and the third to be appointed by the two appointed by the parties, the agreement shall have effect as if it provided for the appointment of

---

e. Authors' note: In the English case that follows, dealing with the same dispute, Mocatta J. says that the shipowner, Sally, appointed an arbitrator for the charterer, Termarea.

an umpire, and not for the appointment of a third arbitrator, by the two arbitrators appointed by the parties".[1]

"However, even if we should accept as proven said provision of the English law, same is insufficient to make enforceable in Italy the arbitral award which is the subject of the present suit. In the first place, in fact, we must bear in mind that, in accordance with the above quoted Article of the New York Convention, the conformity of the composition of the arbitral tribunal with the law of the country where the arbitration takes place (England, in this case) must be observed for the enforcement of the award only if the parties have not provided for a different composition of the arbitral tribunal. In this case, the charter party provided that the arbitral tribunal was to be made up of three arbitrators."

* * *

TARMAREA S.R.L. (ITALY) v. REDERIAKTIEBOLAGET SALLY (FINLAND)

Queen's Bench Division (English Court), 1979.
Wkly. L. Rep. November 16, 1979.*

* * *

February 7. MOCATTA J. read the following judgment. This is an originating summons taken out by the plaintiffs, who were charterers of a Finnish vessel, the *Dalny*, owned by the defendants, to set aside an order of mine made ex parte on September 21, 1978, that the owners have leave to enforce the award of Mr. J. L. Potter and Mr. Donald Davies, dated September 30, 1976, in the same manner as a judgment or order to the same effect, pursuant to section 26 of the Arbitration Act 1950. By the award, in favour of the owners, the two arbitrators found the charterers liable to the owners in the sum of U.S. $24,190.65 plus interest and costs.

Four grounds for setting aside the ex parte order [for enforcement] were contained in the summons, the only two of relevance in view of the arguments of counsel being (i) that the award was bad in that the

---

1. *Note—Gen. Ed. Russell on Arbitration* (1970) states on p. 98 that 'Sect. 9, para. 1 is mandatory; it provides that where there is an apparent reference to three arbitrators the third of them is to be treated as though he were an umpire, and the provision that "The decision of any two of the three on any point or points shall be final" must be overridden by Sect. 9'.

The *Commercial Court Committee* in its Report on Arbitration of July 1978 (Cmnd. 7284) observes in this connection in para. 59 (p. 15) that Sect. 9, para. 1 is "unpopular with those sections of the commercial community which favour three-arbitrator agreements. They point out, not unreasonably, that if they had wanted an umpire, they would have so provided in their agreement. Instead they wanted a third arbitrator who would be seized of their dispute *ab initio*. Parliament, for reasons which are wholly unexplained, has frustrated their intentions. This complaint is unanswerable and should be remedied by amending the Section".

* * *

* Reprinted by permission of The Weekly Law Reports, The Incorporated Counsel of Law Reporting.

arbitrators lacked jurisdiction, and (ii) that the arbitrators failed to appoint an umpire thus contravening both section 8 of the Arbitration Act 1950 and clause 24 of the relevant charterparty dated March 11, 1975.

Under that charterparty, the vessel was to proceed to Tartour in Syria to load a part cargo of fuel oil and carry the same to one safe port in Italy, which was nominated as Leghorn. The owners claimed that demurrage had been incurred at both loading and discharging ports.

Clause 24 of the charterparty was a lengthy clause dealing with arbitration, of which it is only necessary to set out the first two sentences, which were as follows:

> "Any and all differences and disputes of whatsoever nature arising out of the charter shall be put to arbitration in the city of New York or in the city of London, whichever place is specified in Part I of this charter pursuant to the laws relating to arbitration there in force, before a board of three persons, consisting of one arbitrator to be appointed by the owners, one by the charterer, and one by the two so chosen. The decision of any two of the three on any point or points shall be final."

The charter, on an Exxonvoy form, provided for arbitration proceedings to be in London.

What happened prior to the award was that the owners appointed Mr. J. L. Potter as their arbitrator, and then, through Messrs. Sinclair, Roche & Temperley, notified the charterers by telex of that fact on November 5, 1975, requiring the latter to appoint their arbitrator within 20 days. This accorded with later provisions of clause 24 that I have not set out.

The answer from the charterers to the owners' agents in Finland was that they did not wish to enter into any legal action and relied upon force majeure. In consequence the owners, pursuant to further provisions of 24, appointed Mr. Donald Davies as the charterers' arbitrator and the charterers were notified of this. Messrs. Sinclair, Roche & Temperley informed Mr. Potter of Mr. Davies' appointment and suggested that pursuant to clause 24 a third person had to be appointed. Mr. Potter, however, answered that he did not think it was necessary to make this third appointment at that time.

On June 29, after the two arbitrators had been supplied with documents constituting the owners' case, Mr. Davies wrote to the charterers enclosing a copy of the owners' submissions and requesting that the charterers would deliver submissions and supporting documents to him by August 3. He added:

> "My co-arbitrator and I have fixed 11 a.m. on September 7, 1976, at the Baltic Exchange, London, E.C.3, for the hearing of this case and it is our intention to proceed to an award on the documentation then before us."

Subsequently the charterers provided Mr. Davies with various letters and documents to support their case, and on September 30, 1976, the two arbitrators made their award in favour of the owners as previously mentioned. At no time was a third arbitrator or umpire appointed.

As regards the point argued for the charterers that Mr. Potter and Mr. Davies had no jurisdiction, the argument advanced by Mr. Speed was that the arbitration clause in the charter provided for a board of three persons and that as no third person had been appointed, the only two arbitrators who were appointed had no jurisdiction.

Mr. Speed sought support for this argument in the decision of the Court of Appeal in *British Metal Corporation Ltd.* v. *Ludlow Bros. (1913) Ltd.* [1938] 1 All. E.R. 135. There a dispute arose between two parties who had made a contract subject to the rules and regulations of the London Metal Exchange. Those rules provided inter alia that if a dispute arose it should be referred to two arbitrators, one to be chosen by each party in difference, the said arbitrators having power to appoint a third arbitrator in case they should deem that necessary. The two arbitrators had a full hearing of the case and then appointed a third arbitrator. The case was not re-argued before the three, but they all signed an agreed award. This was set aside on the ground of improper conduct because the third arbitrator had not heard the full argument as had the other two. It was sought to defend the award by what now appears in section 9 (1) of the Arbitration Act 1950, namely:

> "Where an arbitration agreement provides that the reference *shall be* to three arbitrators,"—the italics are mine—"one to be appointed by each party and the third to be appointed by the two appointed by the parties, the agreement shall have effect as if it provided for the appointment of an umpire, and not for the appointment of a third arbitrator, by the two arbitrators appointed by the parties."

The Court of Appeal held that this subsection had no application because it was only relevant where the tribunal was necessarily and compulsorily a tribunal of three.

In the present case the special arbitration clause in the charter that I have quoted from does provide that there shall be a tribunal of three arbitrators. It therefore differs from the position in British Metal Corporation Ltd. v. Ludlow Bros. (1913) Ltd. [1938] 1 All E.R. 135 and, since the arbitration was to be held in accordance with English law, section 9 (1) of the Act applied, depriving the parties of their right to a tribunal of three arbitrators. This view is supported, if further authority be necessary, by the decision of Megaw J. in Marinos & Frangos Ltd. v. Dulien Steel Products Inc. [1961] 2 Lloyd's Rep. 192. There the arbitration agreement in clause 35 of the charter was in the same terms, so far as this point goes, as clause 24 in the present charter, and effect was given to the provisions of section 9(1).

It seems to me to follow that pursuant to section 8(1) of the Act of 1950 Mr. Potter and Mr. Davies should have appointed an umpire immediately after they themselves were appointed. But this, in my view, did not deprive them of jurisdiction in view of the provisions of section 8(2) that the umpire may forthwith enter on the reference in lieu of the arbitrators once the two latter have given him notice in writing that they cannot agree. It follows from this that if the two arbitrators do agree, as here, they have jurisdiction to make an award without calling in the umpire. In view of the provisions and application of section 9(1), I do not think any reliance can be placed on the words "unless a contrary intention is expressed therein" in section 8(2), because section 9(1) has substituted an umpire for a third arbitrator.

I would add that whilst it is understandable that Mr. Potter and Mr. Davies did not appoint an umpire, money and time is often saved by such an appointment, as I think there should have been here, since the umpire can then sit in with the arbitrators and hear the arguments and evidence and there will then be no need for these to be repeated if the arbitrators disagree.

I therefore, for the above reasons, consider the two arbitrators had jurisdiction and there is therefore no justification for setting aside my ex parte order under section 26 of the Act on that ground.

As regards the failure of the two arbitrators to appoint an umpire, as I think they should have done, this was at the most a "procedural mishap" without any consequential effect upon the award: see G.K.N. Centrax Gears Ltd. v. Matbro Ltd. [1976] 2 Lloyd's Rep. 555, 581–582, *per* Bridge L.J. Apart from this, had the charterers wished to attempt to set aside the award on this ground as amounting to technical misconduct, their proper procedure was to have moved within six weeks of publication to have set aside the award. It is well established that proceedings under section 26 of the Act to enforce an award as a judgment are not appropriate for raising the issue of misconduct: see Scrimaglio v. Thornett & Fehr (1924) 18 Lloyd's Rep. 148. Indeed towards the end of the argument Mr. Speed admitted that his case depended upon lack of jurisdiction.

* * *

It follows that the summons must be dismissed and that the order I gave ex parte under section 26 of the Arbitration Act on September 21, 1978, stands.

Summons dismissed.

Albert Jan van den Berg, THE NEW YORK
ARBITRATION CONVENTION OF 1958: TOWARDS
A UNIFORM JUDICIAL INTERPRETATION

328–80 (1981).*

* * *

The Court of Appeal of Florence, before which the enforcement of
the award was sought by the Finnish * * * [shipowner] against the
Italian * * * [charterer], refused to grant the enforcement on account of
Article V(1)(d) of the [New York] Convention, considering that the
composition of the arbitral tribunal was not in accordance with the
agreement of the parties. The Court overruled the applicability of
Section 9(1) of the English Arbitration Act of 1950 arguing that according to Article V(1)(d) the agreement of the parties prevails over the law
of the country where the arbitration took place.

The decision of the Court of Appeal makes it clear that even in the
case of an express agreement of the parties on the law governing the
composition of the arbitral tribunal—the arbitral clause read: "...
pursuant to the laws relating to arbitration there in force ..."—that law
is not to be taken into account under Article V(1)(d) in the case of an
agreement of the parties on the composition of the arbitral tribunal and
the arbitral procedure.

One may argue that it is not entirely satisfying that the agreement
in question was not construed under English arbitration law. In that
case the validity of the composition of the arbitral tribunal would
certainly have been upheld. But if that would have been done, the
purpose of Article V(1)(d) to restrict the role of the law of the country
where the arbitration took place would be defeated because, as noted, in
most cases that law is implicitly or expressly agreed upon. It would mean
that in most cases the law of the place of arbitration, including all its
particularities and its public policy, has to be taken into account under
Article V(1)(d). On the other hand, it may also be pointed out that the
Finnish and Italian party probably had not expected that their agreement on three arbitrators would mean an agreement on two arbitrators
and an umpire under English arbitration law. Moreover, this unusual
case of a deviation of the agreement of the parties from the law of the
country where the arbitration takes place will no longer occur in England as the arbitration law has changed in the meantime.[257]

* Reprinted by permission of T.M.C. Asser Institute.

257. Sect. 9(1) has been changed by
Sect. 6(2) of the Arbitration Act of 1979 as
follows:

"Unless the contrary intention is expressed in the arbitration agreement, in
any case where there is a reference to
three arbitrators, the award of any two of
the arbitrators shall be binding."

This change was prompted by the Commercial Court Committee which observed in its
Report on Arbitration of July 1978 (Command Report 7284) in para. 59 at p. 15 that
Sect. 9(1) is

"unpopular with those sections of the
commercial community which favour
three-arbitrator agreements. They point
out, not unreasonably, that if they wanted an umpire, they would have so provid-

The moral is that parties should be very careful in drafting the arbitral clause. At the time of concluding the charter party, the arbitral clause in EXXONVOY 1969 was not a well drafted clause: depending on the place of arbitration specified in Part I, the arbitral tribunal would have consisted of two arbitrators and eventually an umpire in the case London was specified, and of a tribunal of three ordinary arbitrators in case New York was specified, in which jurisdiction the former particularity of English arbitration law does not exist.

The decision of the Court of Appeal of Florence shows, however, that the desire of the drafters of the Convention to degrade the law of the country where the arbitration took place may create a Scylla and Charybdis situation in the exceptional case that the agreement of the parties on the composition of the arbitral tribunal and the arbitral procedure deviates from the mandatory provisions of the law of the country where the arbitration is to take place. The Scylla is that if the two arbitrators, as they did, followed English arbitration law in disregard of the letter of the agreement of the parties, the award was valid in England, but the enforcement was to be refused under Article V(1)(d) of the Convention in Italy. The Charybdis is that if the arbitrators had followed the agreement of the parties and appointed a third arbitrator in disregard of mandatory English arbitration law, the award would have been enforceable under the Convention in Italy. However, in the latter case the Italian party could have instituted setting aside procedures before the High Court in London. If the Court in London had set aside the award for the reason that the composition of the arbitral tribunal was in violation of mandatory English arbitration law, the enforcement of the award could have been resisted in Italy on the ground contained in Article V(1)(e) of the Convention that the award "has been set aside ... by a competent authority of the country in which ... that award was made". This "side-effect" of Article V(1)(d) is unfortunate but apparently inevitable.

* * *

Questions and Comments

1. Judge Wright says in the *Haddad* case: "The Convention allows recognition of an award which, although not in accord with the parties' agreement, complied with the laws of the country where the arbitration occurred. Convention, art. V(1)(d)." Do you agree with this interpretation of the Convention? Are there other possible interpretations? What did the parties' arbitration agreement say about how the arbitration panel was to be formed?

2. Was the panel formed according to the agreement?

ed in their agreement. Instead they wanted a third arbitrator who would be seized of their dispute *ab initio*. Parliament, for reasons which are wholly unexplained, has frustrated their intentions. This complaint is unanswerable and should be remedied by amending the Section."

3. Does the N.Y. Convention Article V(1)(d) provide a good ground for refusing to recognize the award? According to Article V(1)(d), the law of the country where arbitration took place shall apply "failing such agreement," i.e. agreement of the parties. Can one say that in the *Haddad* case such an agreement was failing?

4. Suppose the arbitration clause reads as follows: "In the event of a dispute all questions arising from or related to this transaction shall be submitted to arbitration in Berlin, Germany under the rules of the International Chamber of Commerce. Prior to the first formal hearing the parties shall be allowed full discovery known to American law, including depositions (examinations before the hearing) of the parties and all witnesses, including written interrogatories." Suppose under German law such discovery is not provided for, and accordingly, to avoid delay, the arbitrators sitting in Germany refuse to allow it. Is the award enforceable under the New York Convention?

5. In the *Termarea* case (spelled *Tarmarea* in the English case), the facts, as stated by the English and Italian courts, differed in some respects. According to the English court, both arbitrators were nominated by the owner (one immediately and one upon default by the charterers), while the Italian court assumed that each party nominated one arbitrator. Is this relevant?

6. Is the result reached by the Italian court in the *Termarea* case consistent with the *Haddad* result? With Judge Wright's reasoning in *Haddad*? Should it be consistent?

7. According to A. van den Berg, the purpose of Article V(1)(d) is to restrict the role of the law of the country where arbitration took place, and this purpose would have been defeated, had the validity of the composition of the arbitral tribunal in *Termarea* been upheld. Do you agree?

8. Van den Berg thinks that the conflict between party agreement and the English *lex arbitri* requires navigation between Scylla and Charybdis. Do you see a way out?

One way is, of course, to change the English legislation, or to rephrase party agreements if English law is likely to become the *lex arbitri*. As a matter of fact, the English law has changed. Relevant changes were already made in the 1979 Arbitration Act. The 1996 English Arbitration Act[21] goes even further; in Section 16, it treats the two arbitrators plus umpire variation on an equal footing with the solution of having two party-appointed arbitrators plus a presiding arbitrator. Section 15, dealing with agreements on two arbitrators, tilts the balance in favor of the third arbitrator as presiding arbitrator, and states that "an agreement that the number of arbitrators shall be two or any other even number shall be understood as requiring the appointment of an additional arbitrator as chairman of the tribunal."

9. In a 1995 Italian case[22] dealing again with the 1950 English Arbitration Act, claimant appointed an arbitrator, and respondent failed to

---

[21]. Arbitration Act of June 17, 1996, applicable in England, Wales, and Northern Ireland—not applicable in Scotland.

[22]. *EMAG AG v. Conceria G. De Maio*, Supreme Court of Italy, decided on January 20, 1995, Reported in 21 Yearbk. Comm.Arb'n. 602 (1996).

do so. However, the remedy was not the one applied in the *Haddad* case. Claimant's arbitrator was not appointed as sole arbitrator by virtue of Section 7(b) of the 1950 Arbitration Act; instead, the arbitral institution appointed a second arbitrator, and the two rendered an award. Here, the issue was not that of inconsistency between party agreement and the *lex arbitri*, because the arbitration clause merely stated "Place of arbitration London," and, for the rest, referred to the International Hide and Skins Contract No. 2.[23] The question posed was whether appointing the first arbitrator to act as sole arbitrator was the only fall-back solution permitted by the *lex arbitri*.[24] The Italian court held that the solution laid down in Section 7(b):

> is a mere faculty of the said party, as evidenced by the use of the verb "may". It can also be deduced from its effects that [this faculty] is, among the possible mechanisms by which to obtain the constitution of the arbitral tribunal when one of the appointing parties does not act, the most radical remedy, which derogates most from the provisions aiming at guaranteeing the impartiality of the arbitral tribunal, as it goes so far as to entrust one party alone with the appointment of the person who will decide the dispute. Where the party does not make use of this faculty, appointment by a third party, as the arbitral institution referred to, is a greater protection for the inactive party.[25]

Could this line of reasoning have helped in either the *Haddad* or in the *Termarea* case?

[23]. Id. at 603.
[24]. Id. at 606.

[25]. Id.

Chapter II

ON THE AUTHORITY
OF ARBITRATION
TRIBUNALS

II.1. THE ARBITRATION AGREEMENT AS THE CORNER-STONE OF THE ARBITRATION PROCESS

II.1.a. Note

II.1.a.i. Variations of the arbitration agreement

The authority of arbitration tribunals rests on an agreement between the parties executed in accordance with law. Such agreements can take two forms: one that submits to arbitration already existing disputes and one that covers disputes that may arise in the future. The former is traditionally called a *compromis*, the latter a *clause compromissoire*. The term "arbitration agreement" is currently used to refer to either or both of these forms. The *clause compromissoire* is much more frequent in practice. An agreement to arbitrate is easier to reach when lawsuits are a not-too-likely theoretical possibility. When a dispute already exists, tensions and mistrust make agreement much more difficult. Also, it is easier to stipulate details such as the site of arbitration or the applicable substantive law, when the solution reached cannot be seen as favoring a particular claim since there are as yet no claims. Though considerably less frequent, the role of a *compromis* is not negligible; where a dispute has arisen, the parties may agree to arbitrate because they have a common interest in finding a (relatively) speedy, less adversarial, and less public way of resolving the dispute.

II.1.a.ii. "Referring the parties to arbitration ..."

The New York Convention, the Model Law, and other modern arbitration statutes not only accept arbitral decision making, they also provide a mechanism for compelling arbitration where a valid arbitration agreement has been concluded. A key provision of the New York Convention, Article II(3), states:

The court of a Contracting State, when seized of an action in a matter in respect of which the parties have made an agreement within the meaning of this article, shall at the request of one of the parties, refer the parties to arbitration, unless it finds that the said agreement is null and void, inoperative or incapable of being performed.

There are basically two situations in which courts refer cases to arbitration; the way in which the reference is accomplished depends on whether the underlying controversy is "independent" or "embedded". In Filanto v. Chilewich Int'l Corp.[1] the U.S. Court of Appeals defines independent suits as those in which:

> the plaintiff seeks an order compelling or prohibiting arbitration or a declaration that a dispute is arbitrable or not arbitrable, and no party seeks any other relief * * * ; "while the suit is embedded if" a party has sought some relief other than an order requiring or prohibiting arbitration (typically some relief concerning the merits of the allegedly arbitrable dispute), * * *.[2]

In simple terms, if there are doubts about the validity of the arbitration agreement, one of the parties may wish to clarify this before seeking another form of dispute settlement. (This will yield an "independent suit".) An "embedded suit" occurs when the moving party seeks damages from a court (in spite of an arbitration clause), and the respondent, relying on the arbitration agreement, contests the jurisdiction of the court. States party to the New York Convention undertake a clear commitment to refer the case to arbitration "at the request of one of the parties", unless the arbitration agreement relied upon is "null and void, inoperative, or incapable of being performed". Some national statutes go even further, and mandate a referral to arbitration ex officio. In other words, if upon scrutinizing the documents submitted, the court finds that the parties are bound by an arbitration agreement, it must refer the case to arbitration even without party request. An example of this approach is Section 8(1) of the 1994 Hungarian Act on Arbitration:

> A court before which an action is brought in a matter which is the subject of an arbitration agreement—with the exception of the action in accordance with Section 54[3]—shall reject the statement of claim without issuing summons, or shall non-suit the action upon request of any of the parties, unless it finds the arbitration agreement null and void, inoperative or incapable of being performed.

(Accordingly, if the documents submitted with the statement of claim contain a valid arbitration agreement,[4] the court must reject the statement of claim without even sending notice to the defendant.)

[1]. 984 F.2d 58 (2d Cir.1993).

[2]. Ibid., 59.

[3]. Section 54 speaks of setting aside.

[4]. See Decision No 5.G.40.074/1996/2 of the District Court of the Pest District in BayWa Hungaria v. Gazdaszövetkezet Tóal-

más of April 30, 1996. In this case the Pest District Court dismissed the claim of Bay-Wa Hungaria without issuing summons, after it found that Article VII of the contract submitted with the claim contained a valid arbitration clause conferring jurisdiction on

II.1.a.iii.   Existence and validity issues before courts and arbitrators

The issue of the existence and the validity of an arbitration agreement may be discussed by both arbitrators and courts. Today it is clear that arbitrators have competence to decide upon their own competence (the *Kompetenz-Kompetenz* principle); it is also clear that the conclusion of the arbitrators on this issue can be reviewed by courts in recognition or setting-aside proceedings. The final word on the issue of arbitral competence belongs to the courts. Dilemmas persist, however, regarding the degree of deference, if any, courts shall give to an arbitral tribunal's decision respecting its competence.

A related dilemma arises when a court has before it the issue of the existence or validity of the arbitration agreement. In such situations, the question arises whether the court should resolve the issue or allow it to be decided in arbitration. The New York Convention takes no position on this question, leaving it to the discretion of national legal systems.

Even a very pro-arbitration national legal system will draw back from automatically referring **all** existence and validity questions to arbitrators. If the legitimacy of arbitration is based on consent—as it is—how can a court refer a party to arbitration—especially concerning the method of dispute settlement—unless it first determines for itself that the party has entered a valid arbitration agreement? On the other hand, if every existence or validity question is retained for full court scrutiny, opportunities for obstructing the arbitration process will abound. A party bent on delay or obstruction will raise issue after issue for court determination. There are two particularly noteworthy approaches to this dilemma, one American and the other French.

The U.S. Approach. In the U.S. the basic compromise focuses on whether the party resisting arbitration targets its complaint on the larger contract, which contains the arbitration clause, or on the arbitration clause itself. If the challenging party alleges that the larger "container" contract is invalid—for example, because of fraudulent misrepresentation affecting the entire transaction—and that the arbitration clause is therefore derivatively invalid (it stands or falls with the rest of the contract), then U.S. courts will send this "container-contract" question to the arbitrators. It is only if the alleged invalidating defect goes specifically to the arbitration clause itself—for example, a claim that the clause was included in the contract by fraudulent misrepresentation—that the court would retain jurisdiction to decide the question. This is clearly a pro-arbitration result, because it is usually easier for a party seeking delay or obstruction to conjure up invalidating complaints about the container contract as a whole, than about the arbitration clause specifically.

The well-known Supreme Court decision in Prima Paint v. Flood & Conklin, 388 U.S. 395, 404 (1967), is often cited as the most authoritative statement of this American approach. Note the reference to the

the Court of Arbitration at the Hungarian   Chamber of Commerce.

Prima Paint rule in the *Tennesee Imports* case included in the materials below.

If the challenge to arbitration alleges that the container contract never came into existence–as opposed to alleging that an existing contract is invalid—the *Prima Paint* rule is still basically applicable. The chief difference, however, is that a defect in the formation of the container contract—for example, the absence of a proper offer or acceptance–would, if true, generally undermine the separate arbitration clause (directly, not derivatively) just as much as it would the container contract. Hence an American court will generally decide such existence questions for itself before referring the parties to arbitration.[5]

The French Approach. In France the division of competence between judge and arbitrator is regulated in the French New Code of Civil Procedure, Article 1458, whose provisions have been extended to international arbitration by judicial decision.[6] French law takes a deferential attitude toward arbitration—in fact, one that seems even more deferential than the *Prima Paint* rule. The French approach turns on two basic considerations. First, if an arbitration tribunal has already been seised of the matter, a French court will refuse jurisdiction and leave validity and existence questions to the arbitrators. (Of course judicial review will be available in post-award set aside or enforcement proceedings.) If an arbitration tribunal has not been seised, then the second concept comes into play. The court will undertake a limited scrutiny of validity and existence questions and will retain jurisdiction only if the arbitration agreement is **manifestly** null. If the answer to these existence and validity questions is not manifestly in the negative, the court will refer the parties to arbitration.

These two elements of the French approach are captured in the French New Code of Civil Procedure, Article 1458:

> Whenever a dispute submitted to an arbitral tribunal by virtue of an arbitration agreement is brought before the court of the state, such court shall decline jurisdiction.

> If the arbitral tribunal has not yet been seised of the matter, the court should also decline jurisdiction unless the arbitration agreement is manifestly null.

> In neither case may the court determine its lack of jurisdiction on its own motion.

An Ontario court took a somewhat similar position in interpretation of articles 8 and 16 of the UNCITRAL Model Law—at least with respect

---

[5]. See Sandvik AB v. Advent International Corp., 220 F.3d 99 (3d Cir.2000) (Party seeking stay of court action in favor of arbitration claimed container contract did not come into existence because its purported signatory did not have authority. It nevertheless sought to rely on the arbitration clause in the container contract. The Third Circuit Court of Appeals refused to apply the separability concept and ruled that a court decision on the existence of the contract was a prerequisite to sending the parties to arbitration.)

[6]. See Fouchard, Gaillard ,Goldman, On International Commercial Arbitration at para. 672 (E. Gaillard, J. Savage, eds, 1999).

to the first element of the French test. Article 16 sets out the principle that an arbitral tribunal may rule on its own jurisdiction; article 8 states that "A court before which an action is brought in a matter which is the subject of the arbitration agreement shall * * * refer the parties to arbitration, unless it finds that the agreement is null and void, inoperative or incapable of being performed". In Rio Algom Ltd. v. Sammisteel Co.[7] the Ontario Court of Justice concluded that court scrutiny under Article 8 only applies if arbitration has not yet started. The Ontario court went on, however, to explain that court scrutiny was only postponed:

> It is important to note that where the arbitrator decides a question of jurisdiction or scope of authority raised in the arbitration proceedings, the jurisdiction of the courts is not ousted; once the arbitrator has made a preliminary ruling or a final decision on the merits a party may move the court to set it aside (Article 16(3) and Article 34).[8]

Judicial Review of Decisions Declining Jurisdiction. Different national approaches also exist concerning the finality of a decision by arbitrators declining jurisdiction. The Model Law does not provide for a court remedy against such decisions.[9] In a number of jurisdictions that have not accepted the Model Law, a plea against a decision by arbitrators declining jurisdiction is not allowed.[10] In some countries, however, courts may overrule an arbitral decision refusing jurisdiction.[11]

II.1.a.iv. Formal requirements

Legal restraints and requirements applicable to the arbitration agreement are relatively scarce, and there is a rather powerful trend to harmonize the requirements imposed in various countries. A widely established requirement is that there be a written agreement. During the last decades, however, the accepted notion of what constitutes a written agreement has become more and more flexible. A general understanding has emerged that the arbitration agreement meets this formal condition if it is concluded by an exchange of letters, telexes, telegrams, or by reference in the contract to a document containing an arbitration clause.[12]

[7]. Ontario Judgments: O.J. No. 268 (1991), Action No. 43610/89. Decision of March 1, 1991, Reported in Model Arb'n Law Quarterly Reports 1992, 33.

[8]. Model Arb'n Law Quarterly Reports, 1992, 37.

[9]. Article 16(3) of the Model Law only provides for a court remedy against arbitral rulings that accept jurisdiction.

[10]. See e.g., Article 23(2) of the 1988 Spanish Arbitration Act and Article 1052 (5) of the 1986 Dutch Arbitration Act.

[11]. In the absence of an explicit rule, French courts scrutinize arbitral decisions denying jurisdiction. See Uzinexportimport v. Attock Cement, Cour d'appel de Paris,

decision of July 7, 1994, 1995 Revue de l'arbitrage 107 (comment by S. Jarvin). The Swiss Private International Law Act makes it clear in Article 190(2)(b) that Swiss courts may set aside the decision of an arbitral tribunal that, in the court's view, wrongly declared itself to have, or not to have, jurisdiction. The draft new Swedish Arbitration Act provides explicitly for an appeal against the decision of arbitrators declining jurisdiction (Ny lag om Skiljeförfarande, SOU 1994, p. 25 and 42).

[12]. With some variations, this approach finds expression in practically all international documents that set the contemporary standards in these matters: e.g.,

Because arbitration has now clearly established itself as a viable and trustworthy method of dispute settlement, it is understandable that the sentry at its frontier has become less vigilant. Yet the threshold is still important. Differences between arbitration and litigation have remained significant, and—which is also important—the institutional structure of arbitration is malleable; it can be molded by the parties (or possibly by one of them, if they are unequal in respective bargaining power or understanding of the arbitration process). Consequently, the maintenance of some border controls is still seen as prudent. It always was— and still is—very important to allow and to facilitate arbitration when the parties really want it; and to disallow arbitration, when one of the parties never really wanted it, when the expressed intention of the parties did not reach a minimum coherence, or when the parties did not really establish an operative structure for decision making. Approving the trend towards flexibility does not mean that preventing welshing is the only guiding principle for deciding whether arbitration should proceed.

In this context, it is understandable why the degree of flexibility that is desirable has become one of the most topical arbitration issues. To achieve a better understanding of the present range, scope of, and limits on arbitration agreements, we shall explore problems that test the formal requirements of an agreement: the relevance of acceptance by conduct of a written (but not signed) contract, the battle of forms pertaining to the arbitration clause, and the position of parties closely connected with the transaction but not signatories of the arbitration agreement.

As previously mentioned, significant efforts have been made to obtain international agreement on the conditions that must be satisfied for an arbitration agreement to be formally valid. The most widely accepted are those set out in Article II of the New York Convention. Article II(2) obliges each Contracting State to recognize "an agreement in writing," and explains that: "The term 'agreement in writing' shall include an arbitral clause in a contract or an arbitration agreement, signed by the parties or contained in an exchange of letters or telegrams." Obviously, Contracting States must recognize arbitration agreements which comply with the formal requirements of Article II(2). The open question is whether Article II has set (for the Contracting States) a minimum international standard. In other words, may a Contracting State recognize an agreement that does not meet the requirements of Article II(2)? In *Tracomin S.A. v. Sudan Oil Seeds Company* the Swiss Supreme Court held that:

> By requiring the written form, Art. II of the New York Convention means to exclude arbitration agreements concluded orally or tacitly. This provision of the Convention is actually strict in comparison

the 1958 New York Convention on Recognition and Enforcement of Foreign Arbitral Awards (Article II(2)), the 1961 European Convention on International Commercial Arbitration (Article I(2)(a)), and the 1985 UNCITRAL Model Law on International Commercial Arbitration (Article 7(2)).

with several foreign legal systems. Article II sets not only a maximum, but also a minimum requirement. Obviously, a Contracting State may not impose stricter requirements as to form, nor can it accept less far reaching formal requirements.[13]

This clear-cut position taken in 1985, was qualified ten years later in Compagnie de Navigation et Transports v. Mediterranean Shipping Company[14] (see infra section II.1.d.i.). The Austrian Supreme Court has also ruled that the formal requirements for the arbitration agreement are not controlled by national law but exclusively by Article II(2) of the New York Convention.[15] German courts have taken a completely different approach. The Bundesgerichtshof has held that if resorting to arbitration is a trade usage within a particular branch of trade, a signed arbitration agreement may not be necessary. The Court stated: "Since Buyer did not explicitly exclude an arbitration agreement, then—in the presence of an appropriate trade usage—its declaration may be deemed to include a tacit arbitration agreement."[16] This ruling rests partly on the assumption that Article II: "allows reliance upon an arbitration agreement concluded informally according to municipal law."[17]

II.1.a.v. Scope

Another important issue is the scope of the arbitration agreement. Since arbitration is not presumed as the method of settling disputes, the arbitration agreement determines not only whether there will be arbitration but also what issues will be submitted to arbitration. Determining the range of disputes which the parties intend to arbitrate (rather than to litigate) is one of the critical issues that must be faced in drafting arbitration clauses. One important consideration is to avoid splitting related claims between arbitration and litigation, since the power of courts or of arbitration tribunals to consolidate court and arbitration proceedings is at best questionable when some of the claims were properly referred to arbitration while others were not.

The scope of the arbitration agreement relating to subject matter and to temporal reach is especially problematic when the parties reach a settlement without disposing of all issues, or when they renew the contract without explicitly adopting its arbitration clause.

II.1.a.vi. Further issues pertaining to the range and limits of the arbitration agreement

A discussion of the arbitration agreement as the source of the arbitral tribunal's authority, raises a number of further issues that are

---

[13]. Reported in 12 Yearbk. Comm. Arb'n. 511, 513 (1987).

[14]. 121 Decision of January 16, 1995, 121 Arrêts du Tribunal Fédéral 38–46 (1995); Reported in 21 Yearbk. Comm. Arb'n. 690 (1996).

[15]. Oberster Gerichtshof, Decision of November 17, 1971; Reported in English in 1 Yearbk. Comm. Arb'n. 183 (1976).

[16]. Decision of December 3, 1992 of the Bundesgerichtshof; Reported in 20 Yearbk. Comm. Arb'n. 666, 670 (1995).

[17]. Ibid. at 668. The Bundesgerichtshof cites Schwab, Schiedsgerichtsbarkeit (4th edition, Chapter 44, issue 12), as authority supporting this position. (Arguments for the alternative relevance of municipal law can be derived from Article VII of the New York Convention.)

of particular importance in both theory and practice. One key question is whether arbitrators themselves have the right to decide upon their proper competence (the *Kompetenz–Kompetenz* problem), another is the issue of autonomy (or separability) of the arbitration clause: does the arbitration clause have its own destiny, can it be regarded as valid (or invalid) notwithstanding the invalidity (or validity) of the main contract?

Serious problems also arise in connection with imperfections in the arbitration agreement and the consequences of flawed party stipulations. Difficulties are especially likely when the parties opt for a split arbitration clause which confers jurisdiction on more than one tribunal according to an allocation criterion.

Difficulties arise quite independently of the quality of the party stipulation when the agreed arbitral institution is transformed (it changes its name, its rules, or ceases to function) or when political changes, such as the ones in the former Yugoslavia or the former Soviet Union, convert the contemplated environment from domestic to foreign—and possibly from friendly to hostile.

If a party addresses an arbitration tribunal without an arbitration agreement, the other party can easily object by drawing attention to the absence of this essential element. But what happens if the respondent does not object? Can the tribunal proceed on the basis of tacit submission? The New York Convention does not recognize implicit submission as a way of establishing arbitral jurisdiction. On the other hand, The UNCITRAL Model Law, Article 7(2), equates with an agreement in writing the: "exchange of statements of claim and defence in which the existence of an [arbitration] agreement is alleged by one party and not denied by another."

This list of issues is by no means exhaustive. In practice, moreover, these problems are most often intertwined, although they can be analytically separated. The following pages endeavor to identify and illustrate some of the most important questions in connection with the role and potential of the arbitration agreement and thus offer a starting point for analysis.

II.1.b. *Compelling the Reluctant Party to Arbitrate: Courses of Action and Waiver of the Right to Compel*

TENNESSEE IMPORTS, INC. v. P.P. FILIPPI & PRIX ITALIA S.R.L.

United States District Court, Middle District of Tennessee, 1990.
745 F.Supp. 1314.

JOHN T. NIXON, DISTRICT JUDGE.

[In 1985, Prix, an Italian corporation that manufactured sequential pricing and labeling machines, appointed Tennessee Imports, a Tennessee corporation, its exclusive distributor of the machines for the U.S., Canada, and Mexico. In August, 1989, Prix gave the required notice to terminate the exclusive contract, but Tennessee Imports alleges it remained in effect until August 1, 1990. Tennessee Imports further alleges that in May, 1989, while the exclusive distribution contract was still in effect and before the termination notice had been given, the export manager of Prix, Paulo Filippi, traveled to New York City and Miami and "made false, misleading, and intentionally incorrect statements by advising individuals at the meeting that Prix had no relationship with Tennessee Imports … [and] that Prix would not in the future sell any of its products to Tennessee Imports." Tennessee Imports alleges that Mr. Filippi told these individuals that they were free to import and resell the Prix machines that were then the subject of Prix's exclusive contract with Tennessee Imports. Tennessee Imports alleges that these and other actions by Mr. Filippi were "grossly negligent", that they destroyed "the valuable dealer network, advertising, and other exclusive trade developed by Tennessee Imports", and that they "induced and procured a breach of the contract between Prix and Tennessee Imports." Based on these allegations, Tennessee Imports brought an action against Prix and Mr. Filippi in a U.S. federal district court in Tennessee for breach of contract and tortious interference with contract.]

* * *

In response to the plaintiff's complaint, the defendants moved to dismiss for lack of proper venue or, alternatively, for lack of subject matter jurisdiction. In support of their motion, the defendants point to Article 8 of the contract between Prix and Tennessee Imports which provides:

> Should any dispute arise between the contractual parties or in connection with the relations stipulated by this contract and no settlement can be achieved, then both parties agree to the competence of [the] Arbitration Court of [the] Chamber of Commerce in Venice (Italy).

The defendants claim that this forum selection clause renders venue in this Court improper and thus that this action should be dismissed.

Tennessee Imports filed a memorandum in opposition to Defendants' Motion to Dismiss ("Plaintiff's Memo") making the following arguments:

> 1) That Article 8 of the contract is not a forum selection clause because the Arbitration Court of the Chamber of Commerce in Venice is not a "judicial institution" listed in the Martindale–Hubble [sic] Italy Law Digest and therefore is a "non-judicial and possibly non-existent forum";

> 2) That enforcement of Article 8 would result in substantial inconvenience to Tennessee Imports and would deny Tennessee Imports effective relief;

> 3) That, because the sequential machines manufactured by Prix are a unique product and unavailable from other free-world sources, the bargaining position of the two parties was unequal. Thus,

Tennessee Imports argues, Prix used its economic power to obtain Tennessee Imports' agreement to Article 8 without negotiation and, as such, Article 8 is adhesive and unconscionable;

4) That Mr. Filippi's conduct in inducing and procuring Prix's breach of contract was tortious and, therefore, that its claim against Mr. Filippi is not within the scope of the forum selection clause found in Article 8 of the contract; and

5) That the public policy of the State of Tennessee and the State's interest in protecting its citizens and in providing them with an equitable forum warrant the Court's retention of this action.

Darrell Johnson, CEO of Tennessee Imports, attests that, after inquiry by Tennessee Imports regarding the "availability of [Prix's] machines for import and distribution into the State of Tennessee," Prix drew up the contract at issue and forwarded it to Tennessee Imports; that "there was no bargaining at all concerning the forum selection clause;" that the sequential machines manufactured by Prix were unavailable from any other source in the free world; and that upon receiving the contract from Prix, Mr. Johnson executed it. Mr. Johnson also attests that "all of the evidence and witnesses except [Mr.] Filippi ... are found in the United States."

The defendants have responded to the plaintiff's arguments as follows:

1) That the Arbitration Court referred to in Article 8 is the Arbitration Court of the International Chamber of Commerce (the "ICC Arbitration Court"), a well-recognized and competent arbitral body which may conduct proceedings at the Venice location specified in the contract. The defendants maintain that the ICC Arbitration Court is "specifically tailored to handle international disputes" such as that between Prix and Tennessee Imports and will afford Tennessee Imports an effective forum in which to seek relief;

2) That Tennessee Imports has failed to show that arbitration in Italy would cause Tennessee Imports sufficient inconvenience to justify a refusal by this Court to enforce Article 8 of the contract;

3) That the contract between Prix and Tennessee Imports was the result of "arms length negotiations by experienced and sophisticated business entities;"

4) That Tennessee Imports' claim of tortious interference falls within the scope of Article 8 and thus should be resolved through arbitration; and

5) That, because of the expansion of American trade and commerce in world markets, public policy now supports upholding forum selection clauses such as Article 8 of the contract.

In support, Prix has submitted the affidavit of Deborah Enix–Ross, the Manager of Legal Affairs for the United States Council for International Business (the United States Affiliate of the ICC) attesting to the expertise of the ICC Arbitration Court in settling international commercial disputes and to the availability of ICC arbitration in Venice. The defendants have also submitted the sworn declaration of Mr. Filippi stating that although Tennessee Imports did not bargain about Article 8, neither did it raise any objections to its inclusion in the contract. * * *

* * *

C. Tennessee Imports' Claims Against Prix Italia

1. Claims at Law

The contract between Tennessee Imports and Prix clearly evidences a commercial relationship between the parties: the sale and purchase of goods by corporate entities. This transaction is also an international one. Prix manufactures sequential machines in Italy. Tennessee Imports purchased them for sale in the United States, Canada, and Mexico. Each of the two parties is incorporated and has its principal place of business in a different signatory country; Tennessee Imports in the United States and Prix in Italy. Article 8 of the sales contract contains an express agreement to arbitrate and provides for arbitration in Italy, a signatory to the Convention. Clearly, the arbitration agreement between Tennessee Imports and Prix is the type of agreement contemplated by the Convention. Thus, if the disputes between these parties fall within the scope of their arbitration agreement, this Court must enforce that agreement unless the Court finds that it falls within the meaning of the "null and void" clause of the Convention.

In Article 8, the parties agree to arbitrate *"any dispute aris[ing] between the contractual parties or in connection with the relations stipulated* by the contract [for which] no settlement can be achieved ..." (emphasis added). The emphasized language gives this clause a very broad scope. Indeed, the Second Circuit has observed that "[i]t is difficult to imagine broader general language than contained in the ... arbitration clause, 'any dispute' ..." Caribbean Steamship Co. v. Sonmez Denizcilik Ve Ticaret, 598 F.2d 1264, 1266 (2d Cir.1979); accord Sedco, 767 F.2d at 1145. When the language of an arbitration clause is broad, the court should "focus on the factual allegations in the complaint rather than the legal causes asserted. If the allegations underlying the claims 'touch matters' covered by the parties' [contract], then those claims must be arbitrated, whatever the legal labels attached to them." Genesco, 815 F.2d at 847 (citing Mitsubishi Motors, 473 U.S. at 622 n. 9, 624 n. 13, 105 S.Ct. at 3352 n. 9, 3353 n. 13); accord J.J. Ryan & Sons, 863 F.2d at 319.

Tennessee Imports has made no claims at law against Prix which do not touch in some way upon the exclusive agreement between the parties. First, Tennessee Imports claims a breach of contract. There can be no doubt that this claim falls within the scope of Article 8. Tennessee Imports' claim of inducing and procuring breach cannot be directed at Prix. "A party cannot tortiously induce a breach of its own contract." Nashville Marketplace Company v. First Capital Institutional Real Estate, Ltd., slip copy, 1990 WL 33373 at 9 (Tenn.App.1990). Although Tennessee Imports has alleged some facts which might give rise to other tort claims (misrepresentation of bad faith, e.g.), Tennessee Imports cannot escape arbitration merely by characterizing these claims as sounding in tort. Courts have consistently held that broad arbitration clauses encompass contract-based tort claims. See, e.g., J.J. Ryan & Sons, 863 F.2d 315 (unfair trade practices, tortious interference, conversion, libel, and defamation are all arbitrable issues); Genesco, 815 F.2d 840 (fraud, unfair competition, unjust enrichment, and tortious interference). The Court finds no basis for any claims against Prix that fall outside the scope of Article 8 which encompasses virtually any dispute which touches upon the parties' contractual relationship. Thus, all of Tennessee Imports' claims against Prix are arbitrable ones, and only if the Court finds, in accordance with Article II(3) of the Convention, that the arbitration clause is "null and void, inoperative, or incapable of being performed" may it refuse to refer the parties to arbitration.

Here, Tennessee Imports has made several relevant arguments. First, Tennessee Imports argues that Article 8 is not a forum selection clause because the Arbitration Court of the Chamber of Commerce in Venice is not a "judicial institution" listed in the Martindale–Hubble [sic] Italy Law Digest and therefore is a "non-judicial and possibly non-existent forum." Considering this argument in light of the Arbitration Act, the Court takes this as an argument that the clause is "incapable of being performed."

Tennessee Imports' argument that the Arbitration Court of the Chamber of Commerce in Venice is a non-judicial forum completely ignores the quasi-judicial nature of arbitral bodies. The omission of an arbitral body from the Martindale–Hubble [sic] listing of Italy's judicial institutions provides no support at all for Tennessee Imports' half-hearted contention that the Arbitration Court is a "*possibly* non-existent forum." (emphasis added). There is no reason for a quasi-judicial body to be listed among judicial institutions, and such an omission is neither surprising nor dispositive in any way.

Furthermore, Tennessee Imports has offered no reply to the defendants' assertion that Article 8 refers to the ICC arbitration court. The ICC Arbitration Court is, as the affidavit of Ms. Enix–Ross attests, a well-recognized and highly-regarded arbitral institution specializing in the field of international commercial disputes. There is little doubt that the ICC Arbitration Court can offer Tennessee Imports an effective forum. Even absent the defendants' assertion, however, Tennessee Imports has offered this Court no substantive evidence that enforcement of Article 8 would in fact deprive it of a forum in which to seek redress for its grievances.

Tennessee Imports' argument that enforcing Article 8 would cause it substantial inconvenience, presumably by forcing it to transport witnesses and to incur the expense and risk of seeking redress in a distant and foreign forum, is equally without merit. As the Second Circuit has observed, the:

> inability to produce one's witnesses before an arbitral tribunal is a risk inherent in an agreement to submit to arbitration. By agreeing to submit disputes to arbitration, a party relinquishes his courtroom rights—including that to subpoena witnesses—in favor of arbitration "with all of its well know advantages and drawbacks."

Parsons & Whittemore Overseas Co., Inc. v. Societe Generale de L'Industrie du Papier, 508 F.2d 969, 975 (2d Cir.1974) (quoting Washington–Baltimore Newspaper Guild, Local 35 v. The Washington Post Co.), 442 F.2d 1234, 1238 (D.C.Cir.1971).

The frequency with which depositions and affidavits are used in international litigation and arbitration further detracts from the Tennessee Imports argument. See M/S Bremen v. Zapata Off–Shore Co., 407 U.S. 1, 19, 92 S.Ct. 1907, 1918, 32 L.Ed.2d 513 (1972) (noting that "[i]t is not unusual for important issues in international admiralty cases to be dealt with by deposition"). The Court agrees with the defendants that Tennessee Imports has failed to demonstrate that it will be inconvenienced and prejudiced so significantly as to overcome the strong presumption in favor of arbitration mandated by the Arbitration Act and the Convention.

In *Mitsubishi Motors*, the Supreme Court observed that, while honoring this strong presumption in favor of arbitrability, courts must still "remain attuned to well-supported claims that the agreement to arbitrate resulted from the sort of fraud or overwhelming economic power that would provide grounds for 'the revocation of any contract.'" 473 U.S. at 627, 105 S.Ct. at 3354 (emphasis added). In the case of a broad arbitration clause, the court's inquiry is limited to whether the arbitration clause itself, as opposed to the entire contract, was obtained through such means. See Pierson v. Dean, Witter, Reynolds, Inc., 742 F.2d 334, 338 (7th Cir.1984) (citing cases).

Mr. Johnson attests that he "would not have executed the contract ... [had he] known that [the defendants] would take the action which is described in the Complaint." Mr. Johnson maintains that the defendants' failure "to reveal in advance that they would take such action ... was false and misleading." Certainly, not every breach of contract rises to the level of fraud or misrepresentation. Nevertheless, assuming arguendo that Prix entered into or renewed its contract with Tennessee Imports intending to breach that contract, such actions would call into question the formation of and obligations arising under the entire contract, not simply the arbitration agreement. Such claims would fall within the broad scope of the parties' arbitration agreement.

Tennessee Imports also makes allegations which specifically attack the validity of Article 8. Tennessee Imports argues that Prix used its superior economic power to obtain Tennessee Imports' assent to Article 8 without negotiation and, as such, Article 8 is adhesive and unconscionable. The Uniform Commercial Code[6] addresses the subject of unconscionability in § 2–302. Comment 1 states that:

> [t]he basic test [of unconscionability] is whether, in the light of the general commercial background and the commercial needs of the particular trade or case, the clauses involved are so one-sided as to be unconscionable under the circumstances existing at the time of the making of the contract.... The principal [sic] is one of the prevention of oppression and unfair surprise and not of disturbance of allocation of risks because of superior bargaining power (citations omitted).

U.C.C. § 2–302, Comment 1 (1989).

Although, by this definition, unconscionability may fall short of outright duress or fraud, the language of comment 1 suggests that unconscionability does encompass a sort of quasi-duress ("oppression") and quasi-fraud ("unfair surprise"). As such, unconscionability is sufficiently related to duress and fraud that a finding that Prix obtained Tennessee Imports' agreement to Article 8 by an unconscionable means could serve to negate the validity of that agreement.

Tennessee Imports argues that because "the sequential machines are not available through any other source in the free world, ... Tennessee Imports was in no position to bargain" and that it "agreed to [the arbitration clause] in order to become the United States distributor of the unique product." Plaintiff's Memo, 9. Nevertheless, as comment 1 suggests, superior bargaining power on the part of one of the parties is, in and of itself, insufficient to support a claim of unconscionability. Pierson, 742 F.2d at 339. Otherwise, virtually every distributor of a "unique product" would be subject to unconscionability claims.

Tennessee Imports has made no allegation that it attempted unsuccessfully to negotiate over the inclusion of Article 8 in the contract or that it voiced any objection to it. Even assuming, as Tennessee Imports maintains, that the inclusion of Article 8 was non-negotiable, the plaintiff's own argument indicates that it considered Article 8 the price of becoming the exclusive distributor of Prix's "unique product." If that price was too dear, Tennessee Imports was free to walk away. Instead, Tennessee Imports choose to execute the contract as submitted by Prix.

Neither has Tennessee Imports made any allegations which might support a claim that it was unfairly surprised by the presence of the arbitration clause in its contract with Prix. Article 8 is not hidden in the small print boilerplate of a standard form contract. It is not the product of a battle of forms. It is not buried among the provisions of a lengthy and complex sales agreement. On its face, the contract appears to be one specifically drawn to define the relationship between these two parties. Article 8 is the final provision of the contract and appears on the same

---

6. In the absence of well-established principles of federal contract law, the Court seeks guidance from the Uniform Commercial Code in evaluating Tennessee Imports' claims of unconscionability. *See Spring Hope Rockwool, Inc. v. Industrial Clean Air, Inc.*, 504 F.Supp. 1385, 1388 (E.D.N.C. 1981).

page as the parties signatures. Tennessee Imports appears to have had ample opportunity to examine the contract before executing it.

In short, Tennessee Imports has alleged no facts nor made any arguments which convince this Court that it was the victim of the type of oppression or unfair surprise contemplated by the doctrine of unconscionability. As White and Summers have observed, "the courts have not generally been receptive to pleas of unconscionability by one merchant against another. Presumably, few businessmen ... are victims of the kinds of gross advantage taking that usually calls forth § 2–302." White & Summers, Uniform Commercial Code § 4–2 at 149 (2d ed. 1980). It may well be true that Tennessee Imports had no choice other than to take or leave the contract as presented by Prix, including an unwanted arbitration clause. Nevertheless, Tennessee Imports chose to take it, a choice made in anticipation of enjoying the profits of an exclusive distributorship. Having made its choice, Tennessee Imports must now abide by it.

Finally, Tennessee Imports argues that public policy dictates against enforcement of Article 8. Tennessee Imports argues that innocent parties should not be forced to seek redress in distant, foreign forums. Whether or not Tennessee Imports is in fact an innocent party, this argument demonstrates the type of parochialism which the Arbitration Act and the Convention have sought to overcome. The Act, the Convention, and the case law interpreting them clearly establish a strong federal policy favoring arbitration. "The utility of the Convention in promoting the process of international commercial arbitration depends upon the willingness of national courts to let go of matters they normally would think of as their own." Mitsubishi Motors, 473 U.S. at 639, n. 21, 105 S.Ct. at 3360, n. 21. Absent any reason to except Tennessee Imports from this policy, this Court has no choice but to refer Tennessee Imports' claims against Prix to arbitration.

* * *

[The court concluded that the claim against Paulo Filippi should not be dismissed; Filippi, as an individual, was not a party to the agreement and therefore not a party to the arbitration agreement. The claim against Filippi, however, was closely related to, and in part dependent upon, the claim against Prix. To succeed against Filippi, for example, Tennessee Imports would have to show that Prix did in fact breach the contract, and any such breach would, in all likelihood, involve the actions of Filippi as agent for Prix. Also to prevent double recovery, any damages collected against Prix would have to be subtracted from the claim against Filippi. For these reasons the court stayed the action against Filippi to await the result of the arbitration.]

III. Summary

In summary, as to Prix Italia, S.R.L., the Court GRANTS the defendants' motion to dismiss. The parties are hereby referred to arbitration. As to Pier Paulo Filippi, the Court DENIES the defendants' motion to dismiss, but the Court ORDERS that further proceedings against Pier Paulo Filippi be STAYED and placed on the Retired Docket pending the completion of arbitration between Tennessee Imports and Prix Italia, S.R.L.

* * *

PEPSICO INC. v. OFICINA CENTRAL DE ASESORIA Y AYUDA TECNICA, C.A.

United States District Court, Southern District of New York, 1996.
945 F.Supp. 69.

* * *

MEMORANDUM ORDER

RAKOFF, DISTRICT JUDGE.

By order to show cause, petitioners move for immediate determination of a Petition filed October 16, 1996 that seeks to compel arbitration of respondents' contractual disputes with petitioners and to enjoin respondents from further litigating those disputes in the courts of Venezuela. Respondents, in turn, ask the Court to decline jurisdiction as a matter of international comity. After full consideration of the parties' written submissions and oral arguments, the Court denies the motion for immediate relief but retains jurisdiction of the underlying Petition, subject to a 60–day stay of proceedings to allow the Venezuelan court to determine, if it chooses, a threshold question of Venezuelan law.

The essential facts may be stated briefly. Petitioner PepsiCo Inc., a North Carolina corporation with its principal place of business in Purchase, New York, wholly owns co-petitioner Pepsi–Cola Panamericana, S.A., a Venezuelan corporation with general offices in Caracas, Venezuela. Respondent Oficina Central De Asesoria y Ayuda Tecnica, C.A. ("OCAAT") is a Venezuelan corporation that represents, manages and controls the co-respondent bottling companies (the "Cisneros bottling companies"), which are Venezuelan companies owned by Diego Cisneros, a Venezuelan citizen. As of January 1, 1988, petitioners, by written contract, granted each Cisneros bottling company the exclusive right to bottle Pepsi–Cola in its respective area of Venezuela for a term of 15 years.

Paragraph 23 of each bottling contract provides that any party prematurely terminating the contract must pay specified liquidated damages to the other party. Paragraph 30 of each contract states in pertinent part that: "This Agreement shall be governed by the laws of the Republic of Venezuela. Any controversy or claim arising out of or relating to this contract, or the breach thereof, . . . shall be finally settled by arbitration in accordance with the rules of conciliation and arbitration of the International Chamber of Commerce. . . . The arbitration, including the rendering of an award, shall take place in New York, New

York, United States of America.... The arbitrators shall apply the substantive law of the State of New York, United States of America ..."

By letter dated August 16, 1996, an authorized representative of the Cisneros bottling companies terminated each of these contracts, explaining that the bottling companies were defecting to Coca Cola. Petitioners responded on August 22, 1996 by demanding payment within 60 days of 56,240,446,386 bolivars (approximately $118,400,940) in liquidated damages, pursuant to paragraph 23 of the contracts. Before the sixty days expired, the bottling companies, on October 1, 1996, petitioned a civil court in Caracas, Venezuela for a declaration that the amount of liquidated damages actually due petitioners was a much smaller sum. In support of the petition, the bottling companies alleged, inter alia, that the arbitration provision of paragraph 30 of the bottling contracts was "inoperative" because of its "obscurity and ambiguity" and because it was, in any event, "not applicable to the present case." Petitioners responded on October 11, 1996 by filing a formal request for arbitration with the International Chamber of Commerce, and then, on October 16, 1996, by filing the Petition now before this Court.

Respondents expressly concede this Court's subject matter jurisdiction and power to compel arbitration in this case.[1] They nonetheless urge the Court to decline jurisdiction in favor of the Venezuelan court. In this regard, Article II.3 of the United Nations Convention On The Recognition And Enforcement Of Foreign Arbitral Awards, to which both the United States and Venezuela are signatories, provides that "The court of a Contracting State, when seized of an action in a matter in respect of which the parties have made an agreement [to arbitrate] * * * shall, at the request of one of the parties, refer the parties to arbitration, unless it finds that the said agreement is null and void, inoperative or incapable of being performed." As noted, respondents, in their papers previously filed in the Venezuelan court, contend that the arbitration agreement set forth in paragraph 30 of the bottling contracts is either entirely "inoperative" or else "not applicable" to a dispute over the calculation of liquidated damages. Whether or not this is so is plainly a matter of Venezuelan law, for paragraph 30 flatly states that the contracts are governed by the laws of Venezuela.[3]

While the Court is not blind to the facially flimsy aspect of the objections to arbitrability raised in the papers respondents have filed in the Venezuelan court, respondents have submitted some authority to support their contention that the objections have arguable merit. See

---

1. Personal jurisdiction over every respondent except possibly OCAAT is also clear. See Victory Transport Inc. v. Comisaria General de Abastecimientos y Transportes, 336 F.2d 354, 363 (2d Cir.1964).

3. By contrast, New York law comes into play under paragraph 30 only after a contractual dispute is referred to arbitration. Put another way, the language of paragraph 30 clearly contemplates that matters subject to determination by a court, such as threshold disputes over arbitrability (see First Options of Chicago, Inc. v. Kaplan, 514 U.S. 938, ___, 115 S.Ct. 1920, 1923, 131 L.Ed.2d 985 (1995); Progressive Casualty Ins. Co. v. C.A. Reaseguradora Nacional De Venezuela, 991 F.2d 42, 45 (2d Cir. 1993)) will be governed by Venezuelan law, while matters to be determined by arbitrators will be governed by New York law.

Iberian Tankers Co. v. Terminales Maracaibo, C.A., 322 F.Supp. 73, 75 (S.D.N.Y.1971). In any event, in the absence of any challenge to the adequacy of the Venezuelan legal process (see Tr., 10/21/96, at 26–27; see also Blanco v. Banco Industrial de Venezuela, S.A., 997 F.2d 974, 981 (2d Cir.1993)) the Venezuelan court that already has the issue of arbitrability before it ought to be afforded the initial opportunity to determine this threshold question of Venezuelan law before a non-Venezuelan court is called upon to do so.[4]

It makes obvious good sense, as well as offering a considerable savings of judicial time and resources, for this Court to have the benefit of a Venezuelan court's speedy determination of a threshold question of Venezuelan law that must be resolved before this or any other court can compel arbitration in this case. Nor will any material delay be occasioned thereby, for respondents have represented, through the sworn declaration of their Venezuelan law expert, that the Venezuelan court is required to decide such jurisdictional issues within five working days of the November 21, 1996 date when petitioners are required to file their answering papers in the Venezuelan action. See Declaration of Oscar E. Ochoa dated Oct. 21, 1996 at ¶ 10. In addition to considerations of legal economy and international comity, such deference is also consistent with the parties' reasonable expectations: for when they expressly agreed that these contracts, involving largely Venezuelan activities by mostly Venezuelan parties, would be governed by Venezuelan law except as to disputes submitted to arbitration, they plainly anticipated that such disputes as a court might have to decide (such as arbitrability) would quite likely be submitted to a Venezuelan court.

Accordingly, the motion for immediate determination of the Petition is denied. At the same time, this Court is mindful not only of the strong policy favoring prompt arbitration expressed in the U.N. Convention, but also of the many facial indications that respondents are utilizing dubious strategems [sic] to try to evade their plain contractual obligations. A thimblerig is still a scam even if the thimbles be courts of separate sovereigns. To entirely eschew oversight of this controversy in such circumstances would be a derogation of duty and an invitation to fraud. See Caspian Investments, Ltd. v. Vicom Holdings, Ltd., 770 F.Supp. 880, 887 (S.D.N.Y.1991). Accordingly, notwithstanding the pendency of the Venezuelan action, this Court will retain jurisdiction of the underlying Petition in this case, but stay further proceedings for a period of 60 days (i.e., through December 27, 1996), in order to afford the Venezuelan court the opportunity to determine, if it chooses, the threshold question of arbitrability under Venezuelan law.

SO ORDERED.

4. While petitioners question whether respondents' petition in the Venezuelan court has formally placed this threshold issue of arbitrability before that court, they do not contest that the answer to that petition that they must file by November 21, 1996 will challenge the jurisdiction of the Venezuelan court on the ground that the underlying dispute is required to be arbitrated.

MENORAH INSURANCE CO., LTD.
v. INX REINSURANCE CORP.

United States Court of Appeals, First Circuit, 1995.
72 F.3d 218.

LYNCH, CIRCUIT JUDGE.

After unsuccessfully attempting to invoke arbitration under international business contracts, Menorah Insurance Company obtained an $812,907 default judgment in an Israeli court against INX Reinsurance Corporation and then sought to enforce the judgment in a Puerto Rican court. After waiting a year, and on the eve of having an exequatur judgment entered against it, INX removed the action to the U.S. District Court for Puerto Rico under the Convention on the Recognition and Enforcement of Foreign Arbitral Awards, implemented in 9 U.S.C. § 201 et seq. (1994). The federal court found that INX had waived arbitration and remanded. We affirm because INX has both explicitly and implicitly waived arbitration.

Under seven reinsurance treaties between them, Menorah, an Israeli company, and INX, a Puerto Rican corporation, agreed that "all disputes" between them would be arbitrated and should be settled "in an equitable rather than in a strictly legal manner."[2] The locus of arbitration was to be Tel Aviv, Israel. Each side was to appoint an arbitrator and should the two arbitrators disagree, then an "Umpire," previously designated by the two arbitrators, would decide. There was a default provision of sorts: "In the event of either party failing to appoint an umpire within two months after arbitration has been supplied [sic] for under the question in dispute, then in either such case the arbitrators and/or umpire shall be appointed by the chairman for the time being of the Israeli Fire Insurance Association."

Menorah made a claim to INX for over $750,000 under the reinsurance treaties, to which INX replied that it owed no more than $178,000 and intimated that fraud accounted for the $500,000 difference. After unsuccessful negotiations, Menorah, on July 1, 1992, informed INX by letter that it would seek arbitration, asked INX to assent to arbitration and appoint its arbitrator, said if INX failed to appoint an arbitrator, Menorah would ask that one be appointed for INX, and that if INX failed to assent, then Menorah would feel "free to pursue all other legal and

---

2. The arbitration clause presented by INX as being representative provides that:

All disputes which may arise between the two contracting parties with reference to the Interpretation or the carrying out of this Agreement or to any matter originating therefrom or in any way connected with the same, and whether arising before or after the termination of notice under this agreement shall be entitled [sic] in an equitable rather than a strictly

legal manner and in such cases the parties agree to submit to the decision of arbitrator[s], one to be chosen by the Company and the other by the Reinsurer and in the event of disagreement between these two, then an Umpire, who shall have been chosen by the said two arbitrators previous to their entering upon the reference, the arbitrators and/or umpire shall be managers or chief officials of fire Insurance and/or reinsurance companies.

judicial measures available." INX responded promptly that it would not arbitrate, that its financial condition was precarious, and that even if ordered to arbitrate, its financial condition would preclude it from doing so.

On September 10, 1992, Menorah filed suit in Tel Aviv against INX. Although actually served, INX chose not to respond or contest, and default judgment was entered against it for $812,907, interest at an annual rate of 11%, costs and attorneys' fees. INX did not pay nor did it seek to remove the default.

On September 2, 1993, Menorah filed an exequatur[3] action in the Superior Court in San Juan to enforce the judgment. INX moved to dismiss, claiming for the first time that the controversies between the parties had to be arbitrated. On August 8, 1994, the court denied the motion, finding that INX had waived arbitration and that the Israeli judgment was valid, and ordered INX to answer. INX answered, again claiming arbitration, and counterclaimed that Menorah's failure to submit the exequatur action to arbitration was in breach of its contractual duty of good faith. On October 14, 1994, the Superior Court issued an order to show cause why the petition for exequatur should not be granted. In response, INX removed the action to the federal court under 9 U.S.C. § 205.[4]

The federal court remanded the case on March 15, 1995, finding that INX had waived arbitration and the remaining claims were not subject to the federal arbitration scheme. Now, over three years after Menorah's original request for arbitration was refused and after the travel of this matter internationally through three different courts, INX asks us to reverse the district court and send the matter to arbitration.

* * *

Against * * * [the] backdrop of a strong United States policy favoring arbitration, INX essentially makes two arguments. The district court erred, it says, in deciding that it waived arbitration in the events of 1992. In any event, INX says, it now has the right to have the question of the enforceability of the Israeli judgment, including INX's counterclaim, determined by an arbitrator.

3. "Exequatur" refers to an action to execute a judgment from another jurisdiction. See Seetransport Wiking Trader Schiffahrtsgesellschaft MBH & Co. v. Navimpex Centrala Navala, 29 F.3d 79, 81–82 (2d Cir.1994).

4. Section 205 provides:

Where the subject matter of an action or proceeding pending in a State court relates to an arbitration agreement or award falling under the Convention, the defendant or the defendants may, at any time before the trial thereof, remove such action or proceeding to the district court of the United States for the district and division embracing the place where the action or proceeding is pending. The procedure for removal of causes otherwise provided by law shall apply, except that the ground for removal provided in this section need not appear on the face of the complaint but may be shown in the petition for removal. For the purposes of Chapter 1 of this title any action or proceeding removed under this section shall be deemed to have been brought in the district court to which it is removed.

The district court did not err on either the facts or the law. The explicit waiver came when INX was invited to arbitrate in July 1992. INX expressly declined. It is not saved from that declination by the fact that Menorah had offered in the July 1, 1992 letter to have an arbitrator appointed for INX. That offer too was declined and INX said it was both unwilling and unable to participate in the arbitration.[5]

The implicit waiver came from INX's entire course of conduct. This court has repeatedly held that "parties may waive their right to arbitration and present their dispute to a court." Caribbean Insurance Services, Inc. v. American Bankers Life Assurance Co., 715 F.2d 17, 19 (1st Cir.1983). In Caribbean, we found waiver where the party claiming arbitration delayed doing so until six months after it was sued and it had entered a stipulation for a speedy trial in exchange for a "reprieve from a likely contempt finding." Id. at 20. In Jones Motor Co. v. Chauffeurs, Teamsters and Helpers Local Union No. 633, 671 F.2d 38, 43 (1st Cir.), cert. denied, 459 U.S. 943, 103 S.Ct. 257, 74 L.Ed.2d 200 (1982), we found waiver where eleven months of litigation occurred before arbitration was first raised, saying:

> [T]o require that parties go to arbitration despite their having advanced so far in court proceedings before seeking arbitration would often be unfair, for it would effectively allow a party sensing an adverse court decision a second chance in another forum.

That sentiment applies here. In Gutor Int'l AG v. Raymond Packer Co., 493 F.2d 938, 945 (1st Cir.1974), we found waiver where a party unconditionally submitted part of an arbitrable matter to the courts, but later attempted to take advantage of the arbitration clause when the opposing party counterclaimed. Cf. Raytheon Co. v. Automated Business Systems, Inc., 882 F.2d 6, 8 (1st Cir.1989) (defendant waived issue of whether it consented to issue of punitive damages being submitted to arbitration by delaying and then raising it in desultory manner on first day of arbitration and not pursuing it).

It has been the rule in this Circuit that in order for plaintiffs to prevail on "their claim of waiver, they must show prejudice." Sevinor v. Merrill Lynch, Pierce, Fenner & Smith, Inc., 807 F.2d 16, 18 (1st Cir.1986) (finding no prejudice where defendants explicitly and promptly raised arbitration as a defense to a suit); accord Commercial Union, 992 F.2d at 390. Because there was ample prejudice here, as the district court found, we have no reason to reconsider whether to apply the litmus test of a showing of prejudice to establish waiver or to apply a totality of circumstances test, as other circuits have done. See Metz v. Merrill Lynch, Pierce, Fenner & Smith, Inc., 39 F.3d 1482, 1489 (10th Cir.1994) (applying a "totality of the circumstances" test for the determination of waiver, where prejudice was but one factor); S+L+H S.p.A. v. Miller–St. Nazianz, Inc., 988 F.2d 1518, 1527 (7th Cir.1993).

5. INX claims the agreement required an arbitrator be appointed for it if it declined to do so. The language, hardly a model of clarity, does not so directly provide, and easily could have done so were that the intent.

Ignoring its failure to appear in the Israeli action,[6] INX characterizes its delay of over a year in seeking arbitration as insufficient to show prejudice. There is no per se rule that a one year delay is or is not sufficient to support waiver. Cf. J & S Constr. Co., Inc. v. Travelers Indem. Co., 520 F.2d 809 (1st Cir.1975) (thirteen month delay and participation in discovery was [sic] not enough to constitute a showing of prejudice). The period of delay here was not one in which information useful to the ultimate resolution of the dispute was being procured through discovery. Cf. Cabinetree of Wis., Inc. v. Kraftmaid Cabinetry, Inc., 50 F.3d 388, 391 (7th Cir.1995) (explaining that delay alone is not automatically a source of prejudice and that on occasion it can comprise time the parties spend in determining information they would need in arbitration anyway). INX chose not to invoke arbitration from July 1992 until October 1993 and Menorah bore the costs of proceeding to try to obtain the sums it thought owed. See Van Ness Townhouses v. Mar Indus. Corp., 862 F.2d 754, 759 (9th Cir.1988) (waiver found where party made conscious decision to delay demand for arbitration while continuing to seek judicial determination of arbitrable claims). There was no error in the district court's finding that Menorah incurred expenses as a direct result of INX's dilatory behavior and that that was prejudice enough.

INX suggests that the question of arbitrability should be decided in the first instance by the arbitrator. As to that and to INX's argument that the issue of the enforceability of the Israeli judgment must itself be arbitrated, we are guided by First Options of Chicago, Inc. v. Kaplan, 514 U.S. 938, 115 S.Ct. 1920, 131 L.Ed.2d 985 (1995).[a] There, the court was faced with the question of who has the primary power to decide whether parties agreed to arbitrate the merits of their dispute. Id. at ___, 115 S.Ct. at 1923. Here, we face a variant of that question—who has the primary power to decide whether the parties agreed to arbitrate the issue of enforceability of a default judgment following failure to arbitrate under an arbitration clause. That question is appropriate because it is conceivable that parties could decide that such enforceability disputes are subject to arbitration. "[A]rbitration is simply a matter of contract between the parties; it is a way to resolve those disputes—but only those disputes—that the parties have agreed to submit to arbitration."[7] Id. at ___, 115 S.Ct. at 1924.

6. INX asserts that its inaction during the proceedings in Israel was justified by its desire to preserve its right to challenge the jurisdiction of the Israeli court. But INX voluntarily entered into reinsurance agreements with an Israeli corporation that specified Tel Aviv as the site for any arbitration proceedings. In the commercial context a forum selection clause, even one for arbitration, confers personal jurisdiction on the courts of the chosen forum. See Unionmutual Stock Life Ins. Co. of Am. v. Beneficial Life Ins. Co., 774 F.2d 524, 527 (1st Cir. 1985).

a. [Authors' note: *First Options* is included in chapter V at V.3.c.iii.]

7. There is precedent that, as a matter of law, actions to enforce foreign money judgments, even those confirming arbitration awards, are not preempted by the Convention. See Island Territory of Curacao v. Solitron Devices, Inc., 489 F.2d 1313, 1319 (2d Cir.1973), cert. denied, 416 U.S. 986, 94 S.Ct. 2389, 40 L.Ed.2d 763 (1974). We think, however, the better rule here is to follow First Options. See also Mastrobuono v. Shearson Lehman Hutton, Inc., 514 U.S.

So we apply the First Options rule: "Courts should not assume that the parties agreed to arbitrate arbitrability unless there is 'clear and unmistakable' evidence that they did so." Id. (citations omitted). There is nothing in the agreement between INX and Menorah clearly stating that the question of arbitrability of judgments should be decided by an arbitrator. The question is one for resolution by the court.

We also agree with the district court that arbitration of the enforceability of the Israeli judgment is not required. "[G]iven the principle that a party can be forced to arbitrate only those issues it specifically has agreed to submit to arbitration," id. at ___, 115 S.Ct. at 1925, we do not interpret the silence of the agreement on this point to create a right of arbitration. And if the agreement could be read for such an implication, INX has nevertheless waived its right to arbitrate enforceability of the judgment.

The law does not lend itself to INX's claims and ultimately, the strong policy reasons favoring arbitration and underlying the adoption of the Convention would be undercut, not served, by acceptance of INX's position. Arbitration clauses were not meant to be another weapon in the arsenal for imposing delay and costs in the dispute resolution process. * * *

In the context of international contracts, the opportunities for increasing the cost, time and complexity of resolving disputes are magnified by the presence of multiple possible fora, each with its own different substantive rules, procedural schematas, and legal cultures. This is fertile ground for manipulation and mischief, and acceptance of INX's arguments would lead to the very problems the Convention sought to avoid. Cf. Elizabeth Warren, Bankruptcy Policymaking in an Imperfect World, 92 Mich.L.Rev. 336, 348–49 (1993) (Differences among legal systems provide incentives for "nonproductive strategic behavior" as debtors attempt to take advantage of opportunities presented in ways that are wasteful and drive up costs.). "The intention behind such [arbitration] clauses, and the reason for judicial enforcement of them, are not to allow or encourage parties to proceed, either simultaneously or sequentially in multiple forums." Cabinetree, 50 F.3d at 390.

Neither efficiency nor economy are served by adopting INX's arguments. The scenario here—in which a party knowingly opts out of the arbitration for which it has contracted (even if driven by looming insolvency),[8] sits on its hands while a default judgment is entered against it after service, refuses to pay, requires an enforcement action be filed against it, and only then cries "arbitration"—undermines both the

---

52, 56, 115 S.Ct. 1212, 1216, 131 L.Ed.2d 76 (1995) (issue of whether arbitrator may award punitive damages "comes down to what the contract has to say about the arbitrability of petitioners' claim for punitive damages").

8. Ordinarily in a dispute between ongoing commercial players "reputational"

costs serve to soften inclinations to obtain an advantage in a single dispute. But where a party is in financial distress, these reputational checks become far less effective. Cf. Ronald J. Gilson, Value Creation by Business Lawyers: Legal Skills and Asset Pricing, 94 Yale L.J. 239, 289–90 (1984).

certainty and predictability which arbitration agreements are meant to foster. * * *

* * *

The district court's order remanding the case to the Superior Court of Puerto Rico, so that the exequatur action may proceed, is affirmed. Double costs are awarded to Menorah.

Questions and Comments

1. Opposing arbitration, Tennessee Imports raised five arguments. Some of these are not particularly convincing (e.g., the argument that the chosen arbitral institution is not a judicial institution, because it is not listed in the Martindale–Hubbell Directory). Which arguments were the most serious ones in your opinion?

2. Are all of Tennessee Imports' claims against Prix and against Mr Filippi within the scope of the arbitration clause?

3. What happens to any claims not within the scope of the arbitration clause?

4. Note that Prix defended its position by stating that "the Arbitration Court referred to in Article 8 is the Arbitration Court of the International Chamber of Commerce". Is this what the arbitration clause says? If not, what consequences might follow?

It is clear that institutional arbitration under the rules and auspices of the International Chamber of Commerce Court of Arbitration in Paris can take place in any country. Is this what the parties stipulated?

As counsel for Tennessee Imports what arguments would you raise comparing the arbitration clause with Prix's pleading referred to above?

5. In *PepsiCo v. Oficina Central* the same arbitration clause was relied upon in both an "embedded" and an "independent" suit. In Venezuela the bottling companies sought a declaratory judgment regarding the amount of liquidated damages, and *PepsiCo* asserted in its defense that the issue should be arbitrated rather than litigated. Before the U.S. District Court, *PepsiCo* was the moving party, seeking the same relief (referral to arbitration) in an independent action. In addition, a third forum—the International Chamber of Commerce—was also seised and asked to decide the issue of the validity of the arbitration clause.

Do you agree with the (qualified) deferral in favor of the Venezuelan court?

Suppose the Venezuelan court holds the arbitration agreement inoperative. Would this holding bind the U.S. court?

Suppose that, with the helping wind of the policy favoring arbitration, both the U.S. court and the court in Venezuela come to the conclusion that the arbitration agreement is valid and operative, but the ICC arbitrators find the clause inoperative. What would be the result? (As a matter of fact, in the *PepsiCo* case you do not really need much of a helping wind to uphold the arbitration clause, yet there are more and more cases in which the courts refer the parties to arbitration relying on an arbitration clause of questionable coherence.)

Can the arbitrators refuse jurisdiction after the court has referred the case to arbitration?

6. In *PepsiCo* would the outcome have been the same had the parties not chosen Venezuelan law to govern the arbitration agreement?

7. The parties can agree to arbitrate arbitrable issues. Thereby, they create a right of each of them to insist on arbitration, even if the other party is not faithful to the arbitration agreement. This right can also be waived. *Menorah v. INX* is an example of a waiver. Do you agree with the decision, and if so, do you also agree that INX's argument "undermines both the certainty and the predictability which arbitration agreements are meant to foster"?

8. Suppose that all other circumstances remain unchanged, and that *Menorah* seeks exequatur of the Israeli judgment in a country where reciprocity is one of the conditions for granting exequatur, and that there is no reciprocity between Israel and the country where exequatur is sought. Could *Menorah* return to arbitration? Or could *Menorah* be held to have waived its right to arbitrate?

9. The *Menorah* court refers to Gutor Int'l AG v. Raymond Packer,[18] where it was held that the party waived its right to arbitrate after it unconditionally submitted part of an arbitrable matter to courts, but later attempted to take advantage of the arbitration clause when the opposing party counterclaimed. In a similar case involving counterclaims (O. Mustad & Sons v. Seawest Industries, Inc.[19]) Seawest filed a petition for relief under Chapter 11 of the Bankruptcy Code, and Mustad filed proof of a claim in these proceedings. The bankruptcy court converted Mustad's claim and Seawest's affirmative defense into an adversarial proceeding. Until this point, Mustad had not mentioned the arbitration clause, or arbitration in Norway. Thereafter, Seawest moved for an order allowing joinder of its counterclaims against Mustad. Mustad then moved for leave to withdraw its claim from the bankruptcy proceedings and for a stay of Seawest's counterclaim pending arbitration. The bankruptcy court denied Mustad's motion, concluding that Mustad had waived its right to arbitration. The District Court used the following three prong test to determine when a party waives its right to arbitration: "(1) a party was aware of its right to arbitration, (2) acted in a manner inconsistent with the exercise of that right, (3) prejudiced the opposing party as a result."[20]

Using this test, the District Court came to the conclusion that Mustad did not waive its right to arbitrate, because only the first test was satisfied (Mustad was aware of its right to arbitrate). The Court adopted the following reasoning:

> There is nothing inconsistent about Mustad's actions—in fact, they were quite logical. As long as Mustad faced only disallowance of its claim it was happy to remain in bankruptcy court. When Seawest turned the tables and demanded additional recompense from Mustad in the form of lost profits, cost of repair, litigation costs and attorney's fees, Mustad

[18]. 493 F.2d 938, 945 (1st Cir.1974).   [20]. *Id.* at 948.
[19]. 73 B.R. 946, 947 (W.D.Wash. 1987).

was thrown on the defensive. Facing possible liability for the first time, Mustad immediately asserted its right to compel arbitration. This is not behavior that can be defined as inconsistent with the exercise of Mustad's right to demand arbitration of Seawest's counterclaims. The bankruptcy court found that prejudice would result to Seawest if the arbitration clause was enforced. Certainly all parties will be forced to expend time and resources if this dispute is arbitrated in Norway. However, if Seawest had asserted its counterclaims in July 1986, rather than waiting until December 1986, immediately prior to trial, such prejudice could have been avoided. Thus it cannot be concluded as a matter of law that Mustad waived its contractual right to request arbitration.[21]

Where do you stand regarding the assertion of the right to arbitrate only after a counterclaim has been lodged?

10. The 1988 Spanish Arbitration Act offers an explicit legislative definition of waiver. According to Article 11(2):

The parties may waive by agreement their right to arbitration, leaving open the judicial channels. A party shall be deemed to have waived its right to arbitrate when, after the filing of the statement of claim by another party, the first party undertakes any procedural activity other than a timely and proper plea as to the existence of the arbitration agreement.

As a legislator would you adopt this provision?

If the norm of Article 11(2) were applicable, what would be the outcome regarding a waiver by INX, a waiver by Menorah (in the above hypothetical question No. 8), and a waiver by Mustad?

11. INX wanted to arbitrate exequatur. It is questionable at best, whether this is an arbitrable issue. INX argued that the arbitrators should decide this arbitrability question. The First Circuit Court cites the *First Options*[22] rule: "Courts should not assume that the parties agreed to arbitrate arbitrability, unless there is a 'clear and unmistakable' evidence that they did so." Suppose there was such a "clear and unmistakable" evidence in the wording of the arbitration clause. Could exequatur (recognition and enforcement) of a judgment be decided by arbitrators rather than by courts? Is the same true for recognition and enforcement of an arbitral award?

II.1.c.   *Kompetenz–Kompetenz and Separability*

TEXACO OVERSEAS PETROLEUM CO. & CALIFORNIA ASIATIC OIL CO. v. THE GOVERNMENT OF THE LIBYAN ARAB REPUBLIC

53 Int'l L. Rep. 389–409 (1979).
Preliminary Award, 27 *November* 1975.*

Dupuy, Sole Arbitrator

* * *

---

[21]. *Id.*
[22]. For the U.S. Supreme Court's *First Options* decision, see infra section V.3.c.iii.

* Reprinted by permission of International Law Reports, Cambridge University Press.

II.   The Arbitral Proceedings

6.   The present arbitral proceedings have been instituted under the following conditions:

— By two separate letters dated 2 September 1973, Texaco Overseas Petroleum Company and California Asiatic Oil Company made it known to the Government of the Libyan Arab Republic that they intended, in conformity with Article 20, Paragraph 1, of the Petroleum Law of 1955 and Clause 28 of the Deeds of Concession, to submit to arbitration their dispute with the said Government; the two Companies also notified the Libyan Government that they designated as their arbitrator a member of the New York bar, Mr. Fowler Hamilton;

— During the time limit accorded to the Government of the Libyan Arab Republic pursuant to Clause 28 of the Deeds of Concession (which time limit expired on 1 December 1973), the Government abstained from designating its arbitrator and, by means of a circular letter dated 8 December 1973, the Government declared that it rejected the demand for arbitration;

— The abstention of the Libyan Government and its refusal to designate an arbitrator have led the Companies to avail themselves of Clause 28 of the Deeds of Concession which, under the conditions which will be analyzed at greater length hereinafter, permits concession holders to request the President of the International Court of Justice to designate a Sole Arbitrator: such was the intent of the joint letter which the two Companies addressed to the President of the International Court of Justice on 3 April 1974;

* * *

III.   The Question of the Jurisdiction of the Sole Arbitrator

8.   The text giving rise to the appointment of the Sole Arbitrator by the President of the International Court of Justice obviously should be recalled. That text, Clause 28 of the Deeds of Concession which binds the Plaintiff Companies and the Government of the Libyan Arab Republic, is worded as follows:

(1) If at any time during or after the currency of this Concession any difference or dispute shall arise between the Government and the Company concerning the interpretation or performance hereof, or anything herein contained or in connection herewith, or the rights and liabilities of either of such parties hereunder and if such parties should fail to settle such difference or dispute by agreement, the same shall, failing any agreement to settle it any other way, be referred to two Arbitrators, one of whom shall be appointed by each such party, and an Umpire who shall be appointed by the Arbitrators immediately after they are themselves appointed.

In the event of the Arbitrators failing to agree upon an Umpire within 60 days from the date of the appointment of the second Arbitrator, either of such parties may request the President or, if the President is a national of Libya or of the Country where the Company was incorporated, the Vice–President, of the International Court of Justice to appoint the Umpire.

(2) The institution of Arbitration proceedings shall take place upon the receipt by one of such parties of a written request of Arbitration from the other which request shall specify the matter in respect of which Arbitration is required and name the Arbitrator appointed by the party requiring Arbitration.

(3) The party receiving the request shall within 90 days of such receipt appoint its Arbitrator and notify this appointment to the other of such parties failing which such other party may request the President, or in the case referred to in paragraph (1) above, the Vice–President, of the International Court of Justice to appoint a Sole Arbitrator and the decision of a Sole Arbitrator so appointed shall be binding upon both such parties.

(4) If the Arbitrators appointed by such parties fail to agree upon a decision within 6 months of the institution of Arbitration proceedings or any such Arbitrator becomes unable or unwilling to perform his functions at any time within such period, the Umpire shall then enter upon the Arbitration. The decision of the Arbitrators, or in case of a difference of opinion between them the decision of the Umpire, shall be final. If the Umpire or the Sole Arbitrator, as the case may be, is unable or unwilling to enter upon or complete the Arbitration, then, unless such parties otherwise agree, a substitute will be appointed at the request of either such party by the President or, in the case referred to in paragraph (1) above, the Vice–President, of the International Court of Justice.

(5) The Umpire however appointed or the Sole Arbitrator shall not be either a national of Libya or of the country in which the Company or any Company which directly or indirectly controls it was incorporated nor shall he be or have been in the employ of either of such parties or of the Government of Libya or of any such Country as aforesaid.

The Arbitrators or, in the event they fail to agree within 60 days from the date of appointment of the second Arbitrator, then the Umpire, or, in the event a Sole Arbitrator is appointed, then the Sole Arbitrator, shall determine the applicability of this Clause and the procedure to be followed in the Arbitration.

In giving a decision the Arbitrators, the Umpire or the Sole Arbitrator, as the case may be, shall specify an adequate period of time during which the party to the difference or dispute against whom the decision is given shall conform to the decision, and such party shall not be in default if that party has conformed to the decision prior to the expiry of that period.

* * *

9.   It is for the Sole Arbitrator, and for him alone, to render a decision on his own jurisdiction by virtue of a traditional rule followed by international case law and unanimously recognized by the writings of legal scholars.

International case law has continuously confirmed that arbitrators are necessarily the judges of their own jurisdiction, since Lord Chancellor Loughborough[2] in the *Betsey* case decided to adopt that rule. That same rule has been expressly confirmed in the contemporary era by several decisions of the International Court of Justice, notably by the judgment in the *Nottebohm*[3] case and by the judgment relating to the *Case concerning the Arbitral Award Made by the King of Spain on December 23, 1906.*[4] It has been formally adopted in a great number of International instruments.[5]

10.   As for the authors, their opinions can be summarized in saying as Professor David[6] did that "the writings of legal scholars unanimously recognize that arbitrators may decide their own jurisdiction".

11.   This solution, which is justified by its necessity, is, moreover, in harmony with the dual nature of arbitration: with respect to the jurisdictional nature ("nature juridictionnelle"), by its function in the sense that the arbitrator is vested with the duty of stating the law and in so doing resolving the dispute which has been submitted to him, but also with respect to the contractual nature ("nature conventionnelle") if one considers the origin of the arbitrator's duty which is found directly or indirectly in the agreement of parties. One comes to the conclusion that the Sole Arbitrator is competent to decide his own jurisdiction, no matter which of these two aspects one envisions in this case.

12.   If one looks at arbitration from its jurisdictional aspect, one is evidently bound to apply to the arbitrator the rule according to which

---

2.   J. B. Moore, 4 International Adjudications, Ancient and Modern, History and Documents (1931), at 81 and 179 *et seq.*

3.   [1953] I.C.J. 111 *et seq., especially page 119*; 20 I.L.R. 567.

4.   [1960] I.C.J. 192 *et seq.*, especially page 206; 30 I.L.R. *457.*

5.   In particular, Art. 36(4) of the Statute of the Permanent Court of International Justice and Art. 36(6) of the Statute of the International Court of Justice, and also Art. 41(1) of the Washington Convention of 18 March 1965 on the Settlement of Investment Disputes between States and Nationals of Other States, Art. 5(3) of the 1961 European Convention on International Commercial Arbitration, as well as Art. 13(3) of the Rules of Conciliation and Arbitration of the International Chamber of Commerce of 1955 which provisions were reaffirmed by Art. 8(3) of the 1975 Rules which became effective on 1 June 1975. Finally, it is confirmed by the Rules of Arbitration and Conciliation of the Permanent Court of Arbitration for the Settlement of International Disputes between Two Parties of which Only One is a State, of which Art. 4 is worded as follows: "The arbitral Tribunal, which shall be the judge of its own competence, shall have the power to interpret the instruments on which that competence is based".

6.   R. David, L'Arbitrage Commercial International en Droit Comparé, Cours de Doctorat 1968–1969, at 313 and the writers referred to therein.

any tribunal and any judge is, in the first place, judge of its own jurisdiction. As Messrs. Cornu and Foyer[7] write:

> "When a judge is entrusted with the duty of deciding a dispute, he necessarily becomes, by this very fact, the judge of certain questions which are directly related to his mission and to his activities and it would be practically inconceivable to submit these questions to another judge. This rule is without exception.
>
> Every judge is judge of his own jurisdiction.—Jurisdiction to decide jurisdiction is one of the illustrations of this natural necessity. Even in the absence of a text of law in this sense, it is generally recognized that every judge is judge of his jurisdiction.
>
> For a judge, whoever he may be, the question of his jurisdiction is never a question of an interlocutory character...."

Thus, if we take into account the jurisdictional character of arbitration, we have here a first reason why we should apply to the Sole Arbitrator the rule which is applicable to "any judge whoever he may be" to the effect that every judge is judge of his own jurisdiction.

13.   But, if one looks at the contractual nature of the Arbitration, we would arrive at the same conclusion: this conclusion obviously flows from the letter (reference: 57.029), dated 18 December 1974, sent by the Registry of the International Court of Justice to the Libyan Government to explain to it the reasons which led the President of the International Court of Justice to exercise his power of appointment in the present case. According to the terms of that letter,

> The provisions of Clause 28 of the Deeds of Concession reveal that the parties anticipated not only the possibility of differences concerning the interpretation or performance of the Concession Deeds, but also the possibility of a failure to agree as to the applicability of the clause, and that they agreed that that latter issue should be for determination by any Sole Arbitrator appointed by the President of the Court. In these circumstances, having regard to the jurisdiction conferred by the clause on the Sole Arbitrator with regard to questions concerning the applicability of the clause, the President feels that it would not be proper for him to enter upon such considerations, inasmuch as to rule upon such a question would amount to a judicial act, pre-judging one of the very questions which it has been agreed should be for determination by the Arbitrator.

The passage of this letter, which has just been quoted, properly draws attention to the rule expressed in paragraph 5, Section 2, of Clause 28 of the Deeds of Concession according to the terms of which

> ... the Sole Arbitrator, shall determine the applicability of this Clause and the procedure to be followed in the Arbitration.

7. G. Cornu and J. Foyer, Procédure   Civile 138 (1958).

For the parties to have provided, as they have, in this Clause 28 that the Arbitrator shall determine the applicability of the arbitral clause is necessarily tantamount to their deciding that it rests with the Arbitrator—and with him alone—to determine the question as to whether he has jurisdiction.

Consequently, not only a customary rule, which has the character of necessity, derived from the jurisdictional nature of the arbitration, confirmed by case law more than 100 years old and recognized unanimously by the writings of legal scholars, but also the terms themselves of the clause by virtue of which the Sole Arbitrator has been appointed, require that the Sole Arbitrator should be competent to decide his own jurisdiction.

14.   As for the solution of the problem which creates the question of the jurisdiction of the Sole Arbitrator in the present case, that solution is linked to the answer to be given to the two following questions:

A.   Supposing that the measures of nationalization could have had the effect of voiding the Deeds of Concession themselves, can this effect extend to the provisions of these Deeds relating to arbitration and, more specifically, to Clause 28?

15.   Before examining the argument on this first point, it would be appropriate to emphasize the fact that the premise assumed therein is purely and simply a hypothesis designed merely to make it possible to pursue the argument: it does not prejudge in any way the question of the validity or the effects of the measures of nationalization, which relates solely to the merits of the dispute. It is under the reservation of this essential and preliminary observation that one asks the question if—assuming the measures of nationalization could have the effect indicated above—would this effect extend to the provisions of the Deeds of Concession relating to arbitration?

16.   The principle to which it is appropriate to refer in this matter is that of the autonomy or the independence of the arbitration clause. This principle, which has the consequence of permitting the arbitration clause to escape the fate of the contract which contains it, has been upheld by several decisions of international case law. More particularly, in this connection, two decisions should be cited:

— On the one hand, the award given in the *Lena Goldfields* case[9] in which the Arbitral Tribunal, after stating that the company would have never signed the Deed of Concession if it did not contain an arbitration clause, went on to rule that:

> ... Although the Government has thus refused its assistance to the Court, it still remains bound by its obligations under the concession agreement, and in particular by the terms of article 90, of the arbitration clause of the contract.

9. 5 Annual Digest of International Law Cases Nos. 1 and 258 (1929–1930), at 38 and 426, respectively. See also Nussbaum, "The Arbitration between the Lena Goldfields, Ltd. and the Soviet Government", 36 Cornell L.Q. 31 (1950).

— On the other hand, the award in the *Losinger* case[10] is, if possible, even more to the point because of the circumstances in which it was given: the dispute involved a Swiss company and the Government of Yugoslavia and resulted in an arbitral award. While the arbitration proceeding was under way, the Yugoslav Government unilaterally took the initiative of cancelling the contract, which led the Losinger Company to submit the case a second time to the Arbitral Tribunal as provided for in the contract: on that occasion, the Yugoslav Government claimed that the arbitration clause had lapsed following the cancellation of the contract. To this argument, the Umpire gave his answer in the following terms:

If it [the Yugoslav claim] were well-founded, it would have permitted one party to escape from the jurisdiction of the arbitral tribunal simply by enacting a unilateral measure in a dispute precisely for which the arbitration has been provided—it is well-established in case law that the unilateral cancellation of a contract can have no effect on the arbitration clause which continues to be operative, at least until a legal pronouncement is made on the motives of the cancellation as well as on the consequences of an unjustified cancellation. (p. 110)

* * *

19. With respect to all the preceding considerations, it is appropriate to add another one drawn from the wording of the arbitration clause in the present case. In fact, in its very first phrase, Clause 28 of the Deeds of Concession refers to a difference or dispute which might arise: "If, at any time during or after the currency of this Concession any difference or dispute shall arise...." The parties to the Deeds of Concession themselves have expressly provided that, whatever the fate of the Deeds may be, in case a dispute arises recourse must be had to arbitration; thus, a hypothetical termination of the Deeds of Concession would be of no consequence. Such an event would not deprive the arbitrator of jurisdiction.

* * *

AMERICAN BUREAU OF SHIPPING
v. JULES VERNE ET AL.

Cour de cassation (Supreme Court of France) (1st Civil Chamber) June 26, 2001.
Translation in 17 Mealey's Int'l Arb. Rep. 30 (Jan. 2002).*

The Court,

— *On the first plea*:

In view of the principle that an arbitrator is entitled to rule on his own competence;

---

10. [1936] P.C.I.J., Ser. C., No. 78, at 105.

* Mealey's International Arbitration Report. Reprinted with the permission of

LexisNexis, a division of Reed Elsevier Inc.

WHEREAS to declare the Paris Commercial Court competent to hear the dispute between the shipping company Jules Vernes, owner of the ship "Tag Hauer," and the insurers of said ship, concerning compensation for damage resulting from an accident to said ship, the Court of Appeal notes that the arbitration agreement invoked by the company ABS, and stipulated in the contract of classification, is not applicable to the plaintiffs;

WHEREAS in so determining, and without raising the manifest nullity of the arbitration agreement, the only * * * [finding that could pose an exception] to the aforementioned principle that establishes priority of arbitral competence to rule on the existence, the validity and the scope of the arbitration agreement, the Court of Appeal did not give a legal basis for its decision;

FOR THESE REASONS, and without cause to rule on the other pleas:

Quashes and annuls in full, in all its provisions, the judgment delivered on May 19, 1999, between the parties, by the Paris Court of Appeal; and as a consequence returns the parties to their status prior to said judgment; and sends the dispute back to the Paris Court of Appeal, before different judges, for resolution; * * *

Questions and Comments

1. The *Texaco v. Libya* case offers a restatement of the by now classic arguments in favor of the right of arbitrators to rule on their own jurisdiction. The arguments also mirror a theoretical debate which was unavoidable a few decades ago: the controversy between proponents of the "jurisdictional," the "contractual," and the "mixed" character of arbitration. Today, the debate has subsided. The reason is not that proponents of one or the other theory have conceded victory. (Such concessions are practically unknown on the battlefields of legal scholarship.) A more practical reason explaining the fading of the debate on the legal nature of arbitration is the impressive expansion of both national and international regulation. Today, answers to specific questions are typically derived from interpretation of applicable rules, rather than from the conceived legal nature of arbitration.

2. In *Texaco*, Sole Arbitrator Dupuy found it important that the arbitration agreement contained the following wording: "the Sole Arbitrator, shall determine the applicability of this Clause and the procedure to be followed in the Arbitration." Suppose the drafters had omitted the words "the applicability of this Clause and". Would this undermine the competence of Sole Arbitrator Dupuy to rule on his own competence?

3. The 1996 English Arbitration Act, which applies in England, Wales and Northern Ireland, adopted the following wording in Section 30(1) (regulating *"Kompetenz–Kompetenz"*): "Unless otherwise agreed by the parties, the arbitral tribunal may rule on its own jurisdiction, that is, as to:

(a) whether there is a valid arbitration agreement;

(b) whether the tribunal is properly constituted; and

(c) what matters have been submitted to arbitration in accordance with the arbitration agreement."

Would arbitrator Dupuy have competence to rule on his own competence if the 1996 English Act were applicable, but the arbitration clause did not state that the arbitrator "shall determine the applicability of this Clause?"

4.   According to Article 16(1) of the Model Law:

The arbitral tribunal may rule on its own jurisdiction, including any objections with respect to the existence or validity of the arbitration agreement. For that purpose, an arbitration clause which forms part of a contract shall be treated as an agreement independent of the other terms of the contract. A decision by the arbitral tribunal that the contract is null and void shall not entail *ipso jure* the invalidity of the arbitration clause.

Do you see any material differences between the provisions of the English Act and of the Model Law (apart from the fact that the Model Law deals within the same subsection with separability as well as with *Kompetenz–Kompetenz*)?

5.   Today it is well established that arbitrators are indeed entitled to pass judgment on their own competence. This means that arbitrators need not desist and wait for a court decision in case one of the parties contests the jurisdiction of the arbitral tribunal.[23] It is, thus, quite plain that contesting jurisdiction will not yield an interruption of the ongoing arbitral process. If the arbitral process is to be efficient, the arbitral tribunal must be able to rule on whether the controversy presented to it falls within its adjudicatory authority.

The consequences of the *Kompetenz–Kompetenz* principle are less clear if the debate takes place before a court. Arbitrators are competent to rule on their own jurisdiction, but so are courts. If one party seeks relief from a court while the other party asserts arbitral jurisdiction, two approaches are possible. On one hand, a broad understanding of the *Kompetenz–Kompetenz* idea suggests that the court should let the arbitrators first decide whether they have competence. On the other hand, one can argue that the court is obliged first to establish its own competence or incompetence. In the latter case—assuming the court would be competent in the absence of the arbitration agreement—the court will only refer the case to arbitration after it establishes that there is a valid and operative arbitration agreement, because only valid and operative arbitration agreements "oust" the jurisdiction of courts.

6.   In FIAT S.p.A v. The Ministry of Finance and Planning of the Republic of Suriname,[24] the American Arbitration Association rendered an award in favor of Suriname, against ONYX Development Corporation and FIAT. FIAT moved to vacate the award, on the ground that it was not a party to the arbitration agreement.[25] Suriname argued that arbitral jurisdiction over FIAT was well established, because ONYX and FIAT were partners and joint venturers, and they were represented by the same person.[26] The U.S. District Court noted that there was no clear evidence showing that the arbitration clause was binding on FIAT, and held:

[23].   The finding of the arbitrators does not escape all court scrutiny, because courts may revisit the finding of the arbitrators in setting aside or recognition proceedings.

[24].   1989 WL 122891, *1 (S.D.N.Y.).

[25].   Id. at *3.

[26].   Ibid.

In this case, the arbitration proceeding was not the proper forum for deciding whether an arbitrator may afford relief against a non-signatory who is not covered by an arbitration agreement. * * * The proper forum would have been before the Court on a motion to compel arbitration. This Court vacates the award as against FIAT because the determination as to whether to afford relief against FIAT, a non-party to the arbitration clause, was not the arbitrator's to make.[27]

Do you agree with this line of reasoning?

7.   In the *Jules Verne* case the Cour de cassation expressed itself with classic terseness in the French style. The issue is similar to that raised in *FIAT*, supra in question 6, but it arose before French courts before an arbitral tribunal had been seised of the case. The Cour de cassation remanded the case to the Paris Court of Appeal (before different judges). Must the Paris Court of Appeal refer the parties to arbitration, or could it reach a different result? Is the issue one of "existence" or "validity" of the arbitration agreement? Does it make a difference?

8.   In a short comment on the *Jules Verne* case, Professor E. Gaillard, describes the "positive effect" of the *Kompetenz–Kompetenz* principle as recognizing that arbitrators have jurisdiction to decide their own competence—one of the issues in the *Texaco v. Libya* case. Gaillard notes that the *Jules Verne* case captures the "negative effect" of *Kompetenz–Kompetenz*. Can you explain why the "negative effect" might be said to derive from the "positive effect"? See E. Gaillard, "The Negative Effect of Competence–Competence" in 17 Mealey's Internat'l Arb. Report 27 (2002).

In French law the negative effect reflected in *Jules Verne* is codified in Article 1458 of the French New Code of Civil Procedure: "If the arbitral tribunal has not yet been seised of the matter, the court should also decline jurisdiction unless the arbitration agreement is *manifestly null*" (emphasis added). How would a U.S. court have dealt with the *Jules Verne* case?

SOJUZNEFTEEXPORT (SNE) (USSR) v. JOC OIL, LTD. (BERMUDA)

Court of Appeal of Bermuda, 1989.
15 Yearbk. Comm. Arb'n 384 (1990).*

[The following summary of facts is based on the Bermuda Court of Appeal opinion.

Sojuznefteexport (SNE)is a Foreign Trade Organization of the former Soviet Union. It was a legal entity under Soviet law with capacity to enter binding contracts; its chairman was Mr. V.E. Merkulov. SNE sold oil for export from the Soviet Union.

Joc Oil is a company incorporated in Bermuda with its registered office there. It bought and resold oil and gas in the global market; its president was Mr. Johannes Deuss.

---

[27].   Id. at *5.

* Reprinted with permission of Yearbook Commercial Arbitration, International Council for Commercial Arbitration.

In November, 1976 SNE and Joc Oil entered a long-term sale and purchase contract for oil and oil products. The contract was signed in Paris, on behalf of Joc Oil by Mr. J. Deuss and on behalf of SNE by Mr. V. Merkulov. The contract contained SNE's standard contract terms and the following arbitration clause:

> "All disputes or differences which may arise out of this contract or in connection with it are to be settled, without recourse to the general Courts of Law, in the arbitration order by the Foreign Trade Arbitration Commission of the USSR Chamber of Commerce and Industry in Moscow, in conformity with the rules of procedure of the above commission."

The contract also contained a clause providing that: "The USSR is regarded as the place of conclusion and fulfillment of the contract."

Between January and June, 1977 SNE made 39 shipments of oil and oil products to Joc Oil. The parties fell into dispute over their respective performances, Joc Oil fell behind on its payments, and on May 24, 1980 SNE began proceedings against Joc Oil at the Foreign Trade Arbitration Commission of the USSR Chamber of Commerce and Industry (FTAC). Among other defenses and counterclaims, Joc Oil contended that the November 1976 sale contract was invalid because it was not signed by the two requisite signatories under certain provisions of Soviet legislation and that consequently FTAC lacked jurisdiction to render an award in this arbitration.

Pursuant to Rule 1(3) of the FTAC Rules of Procedure, which authorizes the arbitrators to decide on their own competence,[5] the FTAC ruled that it had good jurisdiction, stating that it would give reasons for the ruling in the final award. Two days thereafter the FTAC also ruled, as Joc Oil had contended, that the sale contract was invalid for want of the requisite two signatures on behalf of SNE.

The Bermuda Court of Appeal explained this ruling as follows:

> " * * * In the USSR foreign trade is centrally planned and is conducted as a state monopoly. This, however, does not entail the consequence that the USSR in its sovereign capacity, negotiates, signs and performs foreign trade contracts. Rather, the main business of contracting, exporting and importing is done by a network of Foreign Trade organizations, of which SNE is a typical example. They are legal entities juridically separate from the state, and conclude contracts and commercial transactions as principals. The State accepts no liability for the obligations of a Foreign Trade Organization, which must accept responsibility for the satisfaction of its obligations. The State, however, ensures control in the realm of foreign trade by demanding strict compliance with its legislative controls.

---

5. Rule 1(3) of the 1975 FTAC Rules of Procedure reads:

"The question of the competence of the Foreign Trade Arbitration Commission in a particular case shall be decided by the tribunal considering the case."

"Thus Art. 125(2) of the 1961 Fundamentals of Civil Legislation of the USSR (Art. 565 of the 1964 RSFSR Civil Code) states:

> "The form of foreign trade transactions entered into by Soviet organizations and the method for their signature, are laid down by the legislation of the USSR irrespective of the place of transaction."

"At the time material to the dispute herein, the relevant provisions of USSR legislation governing the signature of foreign trade contracts by Soviet Foreign Trade organizations were contained in the Decree of the Central Executive Committee and Council of Peoples' Commissars of the USSR dated 26 December 1935 ("the 1935 Decree"). Art. 2(2) of the Decree states as follows:

> "In case of the need to conclude foreign trade transactions or the grant of Bills of Exchange or other monetary obligations outside of Moscow by the said Foreign Trade Organization (both within the USSR and abroad) such transactions and monetary obligations must be signed by two persons who have received a Power of Attorney to sign from the Chairman of the organization."

"Further, a note to Art. 2 of the 1935 Decree reads:

> "The first names and surnames of persons who have received the right of signature of foreign trade transactions and monetary obligations in foreign trade must be published in the official organ of the Peoples' Commissariat of Foreign Trade. Such persons shall acquire their right of signature not earlier than their publication in the said organ of the Peoples' Commissariat of Foreign Trade."

* * *

> "Art. 14, para. 4 of the Fundamental Principles of Civil Legislation provides the sanction for non-compliance. It reads in part:

> "... the failure to observe the form of foreign trade transactions and the procedure for signing them (Art. 125 of the present Fundamental Principles) shall entail the invalidity of the legal transactions." (Art. 45 of the RSFSR Civil Code contains a corresponding provision)."

Since the 1976 SNE–Joc Oil sale contract contained only Mr. Merkulov's signature and he was not even one of the two authorized signatories, the FTAC ruled that the sale contract was invalid. In its final award issued July 9, 1984, the FTAC nevertheless decided that Joc Oil should pay SNE a substantial sum. The FTAC reached this outcome by applying rules of Soviet law (found in the RSFSR Civil Code) equivalent to doctrines of restitution and unjust enrichment.

The total award was for US$199,255,719.55. It included the sum of US$101,341,443.70 as the value of 33 shipments of oil products for which Joc Oil had not paid, a value that was in fact equivalent to the sale price at the time of delivery of the oil. To that amount the tribunal added US$96,922,893.42 as profits that Joc Oil obtained or should have obtained on the unpaid oil shipments and the sum of US$991,402.43 as costs of the arbitration.

Joc Oil refused to pay, and SNE began proceedings against Joc Oil in Bermuda seeking to enforce the award. The Bermuda Court of Appeal summarized several important findings and conclusions of the Bermuda trial court as follows:

* * *

(ii) "Despite what may appear to be the intransigence of Joc, I have no doubt that the parties here intended, and did so agree that Soviet law should govern their relations under this purported contract. (. . .)

* * *

(iv) "Looking at all the evidence tendered in this regard and taking the most generous view of it, I cannot say that it satisfies me that SNE has established, on a balance of probabilities, that there has been a consistent practice of FTAC that autonomy of the arbitration clause is a part of Soviet law. Nor indeed has any practice at all to this effect been established.

"All in all I am not satisfied that the doctrine of separability or autonomy or whatever it is called was, at the relevant time of this contract, or even now is part of Soviet law. (. . .)

(v) "The Tribunal having held that the contract was invalid for the reason that Mr. Merkulov, who alone signed on behalf of SNE, lacked the necessary capacity to bind SNE to the contract, it follows that the arbitration clause contained in it was also invalid ab initio . . . There being no arbitration clause, the Tribunal, in my view, had no jurisdiction to proceed.

* * *

(vi) "Even if he were wrong and there was some degree of separability in Soviet law, any such separability would not assist SNE in the case of voidness ab initio of the underlying contract. * * *

(vii) "Without attempting to set out the bases for these various arguments, I accept those of SNE's experts and that of Professor Joffe in preference to that of Professor Berman and would hold that it would not be necessary to have two authorized signatures in order to create a valid arbitration clause. * * * "

The Court of Appeal noted that a number of issues litigated below had been dropped and listed the main issues for consideration in the appeal as follows:

"1. Does the 1935 Signature Decree apply to the arbitration clause?

"2. Is there a doctrine of separability in Soviet law? And if so what is its ambit?

"3. Was the main contract non-existent or only invalid ab initio?"

With one judge dissenting, the Court of Appeal reversed the lower court's decision. Excerpts from the Court of Appeal's decision addressing the three main issues follow.]

* * *

"V. *Separability of the Arbitration Clause*

* * *

[33] "The doctrine of separability is at the heart of the case. It has loomed large at all stages because it goes to the issue of the validity of the arbitration agreement. i.e., it relates to the defence under Sect. 5(2)(b) of the 1976 Act [of Bermuda implementing the New York Convention]. Joc Oil's argument throughout has been that the arbitration agreement is invalid because the contract in which it is imbedded is invalid under Soviet law. In short, the invalidity of the main agreement taints the arbitration clause.

* * *

[The Court of appeal here rejects Joc Oil's argument that because separability is a procedural issue Bermuda law should apply. It held that Soviet law governed the contract and the separability question.]

* * *

(b) *The Validity of the Arbitration Clause*

[39] "It would appear that logically the question of whether the arbitration clause is itself a 'transaction in foreign trade' within the meaning of the 1935 Signature Decree (as Joc Oil contends) so as to require the signatures of two authorized persons should be considered before one embarks upon an examination of the doctrine of separability, for if Joc Oil is right in their contention, and there is no valid arbitration agreement and that is an end of the matter and the question of the existence of the doctrine of separability in Soviet law would become an academic issue. The FTAC Arbitrators held that the 1935 Signature Decree had no application.

* * *

[40] "Having considered the arguments advanced by both SNE and Joc Oil, I can see no reason to doubt the correctness of the conclusion reached by three of the experts on Soviet law, by the FTAC Arbitrators and by the learned Judge, that the 1935 Signature Decree has no application to an arbitration clause.

* * *

(d) *What is Separability*

* * *

[42] "It is common ground that the question of the validity of the arbitration clause depends on whether the doctrine of separability is part of Soviet law. The doctrine of separability of the arbitral clause is referred to as 'severability' in the United States and 'autonomy' in France and the Federal Republic of Germany, each connoting the fact that the doctrine has as its main effect that the invalidity of the main contract does not, in principle, entail the invalidity of the arbitral clause. . . .

[43] "There is no difference between the experts as to what the doctrine of autonomy entails. Professor Joffe's definition in his second expert opinion is accepted by SNE and was quoted by the learned Judge in his judgment. It states:

> "The concept of separability means that the validity of the arbitration clause does not depend upon the validity of the remaining parts of the contract in which it is contained. This allows an arbitration tribunal to declare a contract invalid and yet retain its jurisdiction to decide a dispute as to the consequences of such invalidity provided that the arbitration clause is valid as a separate entity and is sufficiently broad in its wording so as to cover non-contractual disputes."

* * *

[44] "One of the foundations forming the rationale of the doctrine has been graphically formulated by Judge Schwebel as follows:

> ". . . when the parties to an agreement containing an arbitration clause enter into that agreement they conclude not one but two agreements, the arbitral twin of which survives any birth defect or acquired disability of the principal agreement." [See International Arbitration, Three Salient Problems by Stephen M. Schwebel, p. 5].

[45] "The concept of separability must be distinguished from competence-competence. The concept of competence-competence denotes a tribunal's power to adopt an initial ruling on its own competence. It concerns, as Mr. Broches pointed out, in his report 'the degree (if any) to which an arbitral tribunal may rule on its own jurisdiction as defined by the arbitration clause'. It is in essence a rule of convenience which obviates the necessity for halting proceedings in limine merely because one of the parties challenges the jurisdiction of the arbitral tribunal. It permits the tribunal to consider and rule upon its own jurisdiction and competence in the first instance. Its application in English law was explained by Devlin J. in *Christopher Brown v. Genossenschaft Oesterreichischer Waldbesitzer* . . . (1984) 1 Q.B. 8, 12. Its application however carries with it an inherent logical difficulty, i.e., for the purpose of making its decision the tribunal has to assume its competence or

jurisdiction. The concept however, it is argued, is a necessary adjunct to the realization of the objectives of commercial arbitration.

[46] "Its primary relevance to separability is explained by Mr. Broches in his evidence as follows:

'So it certainly goes without saying that separability has an effect not on the concept of competence-competence, but on the practice of competence-competence. If separability is accepted, an arbitral tribunal will in fewer instances be found compelled to deny its own jurisdiction on the ground that the main agreement is invalid....'

[47] "There are two qualifications on the doctrine of separability which are generally accepted. The first is succinctly stated by Pieter Sanders, Emeritus Professor of Law at Erasmus University, Rotterdam, as follows:

"There is, however, one important exception to this principle. This is the case where the existence of the contract itself is contested. If the question arises whether the parties have indeed concluded a contract containing an arbitration clause, the jurisdiction of the arbitrator is put in question. If there is no contract at all, the legal basis of the arbitrator's powers which reside in the arbitration clause found in the contract 'is also missing'." (Pieter Sanders, Hommage à Frédéric Eisemann Liber Amicorum (1979) p. 34, cited by Mr. Broches. * * *

[48] "This exception recognizes that there is a distinction between the nullity of a contract and its never having existed at all. However, where prima facie evidence is presented showing that the parties have entered into a contract, the burden of demonstrating that there never was a contract will be a heavy one, particularly if at any stage the parties acted as if there were a contract between them.

[49] "The second qualification arises when the attack is not upon the principal agreement but upon the validity of the arbitration clause itself—whether, for instance, it conformed to the requirements for conclusion of a valid arbitration agreement under the proper law of the agreement or whether it is, for example, itself vitiated by fraud. Here, while the arbitral tribunal is competent to pass upon that question, it is, as a rule not competent to pass upon it with definitive effect.

* * *

(h) *Assessment and Conclusion*

* * *

[75] "One can stress too the final observation of Judge Schwebel:

'Thus the principle of the severability of the arbitration agreement which is supported by the weight of international arbitral codification and cases is substantially supported as well by the national arbitral jurisprudence of leading centres of national and international commercial arbitration. While not the rule in all countries or at all times, it clearly enjoys the predominant and expanding position.' (Schwebel ubi sup. p. 59.)

[76] "Other writers are prepared to go further; as for example, Professor Pieter Sanders, a former President of the International Council for Commercial Arbitration and a recognized authority on the subject, who concluded that:

'Separability has become, like the competence of the arbitrator to rule upon his competence, a truly international rule of law.' (Sanders, 'L'autonomie de la clause compromissoire' at p. 42; cited Schwebel, ubi sup. p. 60).

[77] "The answer to any question of illogicality must surely be that the life of the law is not logic but experience, and experience 'has entrenched and established the doctrine of separability'.

[78] "In my judgment the evidence in this case does establish the existence of the doctrine of separability in Soviet law. * * * [The learned Judge] found otherwise. But, with respect, the learned Judge's failure to analyse the Award critically or at all, his initial error in acceding to Joc Oil's contention that the burden was on SNE to prove a valid Convention award, led to another fundamental error on the part of the learned Judge on this issue. He held that SNE had not satisfied him that the doctrine of separability exists in Soviet law. However, under the 1976 Act, implementing the New York Convention that burden was not imposed on SNE. It was for Joc Oil to establish that the doctrine of separability was not part of Soviet law, because the legal burden was on Joc Oil to prove the existence of a ground for refusing enforcement of the Award under Sect. 5(2) of the 1976 Act.

* * *

(b) *Was the 1976 Contract Invalid or Non-existent?*

[96] "It is stated by all writers (and accepted by SNE) that the doctrine of separability does not, in any event, apply to a non-existent contract. They assert that there is a clear distinction in principle between a contract that is void ab initio and one that is non-existent.

* * *

[97] "An analysis of the problem must begin by asking why in some countries (e.g., France, Germany and the US) which recognize the doctrine of autonomy that doctrine has been held to have no application to a non-existent contract. The answer is that it is outside that doctrine because it entails the non-existence of the arbitration clause itself. If no contract ever came into existence, no arbitration agreement could have come into existence either.

[98] "The defence of lack of authority is normally one that is raised by a defendant who denies that he entered into any contract at all. A few examples from the cases referred to during the hearing of this appeal will suffice to illustrate the point.

[99] "In *Arab Republic of Egypt v. Southern Pacific Properties Ltd.* (Journal du Droit International 1985 p. 129),[20] the Paris Appeal Court held that 'the Egyptian Government is not described as one of the bodies which are parties to the contract and are therefore not bound by contract'. As the Egyptian Government was not a party to the agreement there consequently could be no question of assent to an arbitration agreement. This was a case of a non-existent contract.

[100] "In *Centrala Cooperativa de Import si Export v. Murel et Cie* ATF 651 19, (1939) a Swiss federal tribunal held that the contract was not signed by 'a person with the capacity to incur an obligation'. In the *Centrala Cooperativa* case the person purporting to sign on behalf of the respondent company had no authority to do so. In the present case there is no question but that Mr. Merkulov, as Chairman of SNE had power to sign an arbitration agreement.

[101] "In the US case of *Interocean Shipping Co. v. National Shipping & Trading Corp.* 462 F.2d 673 (1972) the charterers denied the very existence of the contract which allegedly embodied the arbitration agreement. The US Court of Appeals held that that issue had first to be resolved by the courts before any question of arbitration could arise.

[102] "As observed above, a defence of lack of authority is always raised by a defendant. A question of authority is never raised by a plaintiff for the obvious reason that, by the very act of suing or initiating arbitration proceedings, the plaintiff ipso facto adopts and ratifies the contract. The impediment to this course being adopted in this case was not the want of authority but the lack of the requisite signatures, (the 1935 Signature Decree) coupled with the effect of Art. 45 of the RSFSR Civil Code.

[103] "If a contract purportedly entered into by a company is ultra vires it is trite law that such a contract cannot be adopted or ratified by the company because it is outside the objects of the company. On the other hand, where there is only a failure to comply with the formal rules, such as who is entitled to sign for the company under its Articles, such an irregularity does not render the contract void. It merely renders the contract voidable at the suit of the company, because the company can itself regularize and adopt the contract.

* * *

[104] "In my judgment therefore this was not a case of a non-existent contract but one of invalidity by reason of breach of the 1935 Signature Decree with the consequence prescribed by Art. 45 of the RSFSR Civil Code. If the arbitrators were right (and the judge held that they were) that an arbitration agreement does not require two signatures then Mr. Merkulov was fully authorized to put his signature to the document.

20. Reported in Yearbook X (1985) pp. 113–122. [Authors' note: the *Southern Pa-* *cific* case is included in the materials below in Chapter V at V.2.d.i.]

[105] "In conclusion, on this issue, one may, by adopting the language (mutatis mutandis) and the reasoning of Diplock LJ., as he then was, in *Mackender v. Feldia* (1967) 2 Q.B. 590, at p. 602, put the matter thus: a claim that a contract is invalid for lack of the required two authorized signatures does not raise any issue as to whether or not the parties agreed to the terms of the contract. It concedes that they did, but asserts that their agreement gave rise to no enforceable contractual rights or duties. It raises no issue about the consensus ad idem of the parties.

[106] "Put briefly SNE and Joc Oil had entered into a contract which turned out to be an invalid transaction solely for lack of two authorized signatures by one of the parties."

* * *

[While an appeal from the Bermuda Court of Appeal to the Privy Council was pending, the parties reached a settlement.]

HARBOUR ASSURANCE CO. (UK), LTD. v. KANSA GENERAL INTERNATIONAL ASSURANCE CO., LTD.*

United Kingdom, Court of Appeal (Civil Division), 1993.
1 Lloyd's Law Rep. 455 (1993).[1]

LORD JUSTICE RALPH GIBSON: This is an appeal, brought with the leave of Steyn J, by the first, third, fourth and fifth defendants against his order of 16 July 1991 in an action brought by Harbour Assurance Co (UK) Ltd. By that order Steyn J [1992] 1 Lloyd's Rep 81 dismissed the application by the defendants for a stay of the action under section 1 of the Arbitration Act 1975.

This case raises the question whether in English law, under the principle of the separability or autonomy of the agreement expressed in an arbitration clause, which clause is contained in a written contract, the clause can give jurisdiction to the arbitrators under that clause to determine a dispute over the initial validity or invalidity of the written contract, upon the assumptions that upon its true construction the

---

* [Authors' Note: In this decision the Court of Appeal overruled a line of prior decisions that Steyn J. in the lower court felt obliged to follow. Harbour Assurance, a British insurance and reinsurance company had initiated the action against Kansa and other Finnish insurance and reinsurance companies to declare illegal and void various reinsurance contracts under which Harbour had agreed to re-insure the defendants. Harbour Assurance's theory, on which it succeeded in the lower court, was that the Finnish defendants were not authorized to engage in the insurance business in the U.K. and therefore the reinsur-

ance as well as the underlying insurance contracts were illegal and void. The defendants sought to stay the action by relying on the arbitration clause in the reinsurance contracts, but Steyn J. concluded he was bound by the "void ab initio" doctrine then prevailing in U.K. law. Harbour Assurance Co. (UK), Ltd. v. Kansa General International Co., Ltd., [1992] Lloyd's Law Rep. 81 (Queen's Bench Div., Comm. Ct., 1991). The Court of Appeal decision overruled the "void ab initio" doctrine.]

1. Reprinted by permission of Lloyd's Law Reports, LLP Limited.

arbitration clause covers such a dispute and that the nature of the invalidity alleged does not attack the validity of the agreement expressed in the arbitration clause itself.

The orthodox view in English law has always been, it has been said for the plaintiffs, that if the contract in which the arbitration clause is contained is void *ab initio*, and therefore nothing, so also must be the arbitration clause in the contract. That is the proposition that nothing can come of nothing: *ex nihil nil fit*. It has also been called in this case the argument of logic.

* * *

As a result of agreement between the parties the only issues considered by him were whether, as the defendants alleged, the arbitration clause was wide enough to cover the illegality issue, and whether there was no impediment in law to giving effect to the arbitration agreement.

For the reasons set out in his judgment, Steyn, J. concluded that he was compelled by authority to hold that the principle of separability could not extend so as to enable the arbitrator to determine whether or not the contract, in which the arbitration clause is contained, is in fact void *ab initio* for illegality. He therefore dismissed the application for a stay of proceedings in which the plaintiffs seek to establish that illegality.

The appeal by the defendants was directed only to the last passages of the judgment by the judge, by which he held that he was required by authority to hold as he did. In all other respects the defendants adopted and supported the conclusions and reasoning of the judge.

* * *

In brief summary, the judge held as follows.

(i) The principle of the separability of the arbitration clause or agreement from the contract in which it is contained exists in English law; and, provided that the arbitration clause itself is not directly impeached, the arbitration agreement is, as a matter of principled legal theory, capable of surviving the invalidity of the contract so that the arbitrators could have jurisdiction under the clause to determine the initial validity of the contract. Further, it would be consistent to hold that an issue as to the initial illegality of the contract is also capable of being referred to arbitration, provided that any initial illegality does not directly impeach the arbitration clause.

(ii) The illegality alleged in this case does not impeach the arbitration clause.

(iii) The arbitration clause on its proper construction is wide enough to cover a dispute as to the initial illegality of the contract.

(iv) To his evident regret, however, Steyn, J. was driven to hold that the principle of separability could not apply when the alleged ground of invalidity of the contract was initial illegality.

The contentions of the plaintiffs, in their respondents' notice, included:

(i) The judge was wrong not to hold that the non-arbitrability of an issue of initial illegality was established by the reasoning of the majority in Heyman v. Darwins Ltd [1942] AC 356.

(ii) English law has adopted the principle of separability only so far as to leave disputes as to initial validity or legality outside the jurisdiction of arbitrators.

(iii) The logical ground for excluding the arbitrator's jurisdiction in cases of initial invalidity and initial illegality is *ex nihil nihil fit,* and it would be contrary to logic and principle to differentiate between cases of "direct" and "indirect" invalidity of the arbitration clause.

(iv) Disputes as to the legality of the contract do impeach the arbitration clause contained in the contract either directly or sufficiently directly to exclude the arbitrator's jurisdiction.

(v) Lastly, this arbitration clause is not wide enough to cover disputes as to the initial validity of the retrocession agreement, or disputes as to illegality.

* * *

The policy consideration which is of greatest weight, in my judgment, is what the judge called the imperative of giving effect to the wishes of the parties unless there are compelling reasons of principle why it is not possible to do so.

The first argument for the plaintiffs, that is, the orthodox view to which we are invited to adhere, is based on the logic of the proposition that nothing can come from nothing.

* * *

The reference to an extraordinary arbitration clause as possibly outside the logical proposition is in effect an argument that, for the principle of separability to be applied so as to save the clause from voidness by reason of the voidness of the containing contract, special words are needed. I do not accept this argument. An arbitration clause, in ordinary terms—that is to say, without special words to ensure survival—is usually, and has been held to be, a self-contained contract collateral to the containing contract. As with any other contract, it must be construed according to its terms in and with regard to the relevant factual situation. I see no reason to establish a principle of this nature which would require special words to be inserted in order to secure that which the parties would probably suppose was covered by the ordinary words.

* * *

Mr. Longmore pointed out that a party to a contract the making of which he says was induced by fraud, would be surprised to be told that he is bound to have the issue tried by an arbitrator appointed under a clause in that contract. He also pointed out that when such a party alleges that the contract is void for illegality, he might well be astonished to be told that the issue of that illegality is to be determined by an arbitrator appointed under it.

There is, I think, force in these comments, but I add that in my view they are no more than forceful comments. Steyn, J. said that the question of fraud or initial illegality was *capable* of being referred to arbitration. He did not qualify the clearly stated principle that if the validity of the arbitration clause itself is attacked, the issue cannot be decided by the arbitrator. His reference to direct impeachment was, as I understand his judgment, to distinguish an attack upon the clause otherwise than by the logical proposition that the clause falls with the containing contract. When it is said that the contract was induced by fraud it may well be clear that, if it was, the making of the independent arbitration clause was also induced by the fraud. * * *

Next, as to illegality, the question whether the particular form of illegality will, if proved, render void both the contract and the arbitration clause must depend upon the nature of the illegality and, as Hoffmann, L.J. pointed out in the course of argument, when it is said to consist of acts prohibited by statute, upon the construction of the relevant provisions of the statute.

* * *

In my judgment, Steyn, J. was right to hold that, as a matter of construction of the contract, the present clause covers the issue of illegality, and his conclusion does not conflict with the judgment of Nourse, L.J. in the *Fillite* case with which Hollings, J. there agreed.

In agreeing that "all disputes or differences arising out of this agreement shall be submitted to the decision of two arbitrators," the parties were indeed presupposing that "the agreement" had some relevant existence. For this purpose I think "this agreement" means the act of the parties recorded in the document which contains the mutual promises which they have made. The meaning and effect of those promises with references to their subsequent acts would be determined according to law and, if necessary, under the proviso for arbitration. The words must be construed by reference to any relevant facts (see Prenn v. Simmonds [1971] 1 WLR 1381) but there has been no reliance on any particular circumstances for this purpose other than those evident from the making of the contract itself. The question whether all the promises contained in the agreement were rendered invalid and void at the time when the parties signed the documents by the illegality of the agreement, is, in my judgment, a dispute arising out of the agreement.

There was much material put before the court to which I have not referred. The material was provided to us before the hearing so that we were able to read it before the argument commenced. We are indeed grateful for this assistance. I have not referred to the authorities copied, to the extracts from textbooks and articles, and to the reports of decisions in the courts of the United States, Australia, Germany and Bermuda. In a case of this nature it was, I think, of importance that we be shown this material so that we should be instructed as to the development in this part of the law in other jurisdictions. The parties were not at one as to the precise direction and extent of such development. It is sufficient in my judgment to say that I have read much that has encouraged me to reach the conclusion expressed in this judgment, and nothing to suggest that in doing so I would be ignoring any substantial matter of policy or departing from any principle which should form part of the development of the common law.

I would allow this appeal.

Questions and Comments

1.   In the *Joc Oil* case the separability concept was relied upon to give the arbitration clause a chance to survive. If the arbitration clause shares the destiny of the main contract, it is doomed, because the main contract is clearly invalid without the second signature. However, divorcing the arbitration clause does not yield a final victory. Although the arbitration clause is allowed to have an independent destiny, its validity may still be challenged. The question is whether the two signatures requirement of Article 2(2) of the 1935 Decree, quoted in the summary of the facts, applies to arbitration agreements. The FTAC [Foreign Trade Arbitration Commission of the USSR Chamber of Commerce and Industry] arbitrators found it did not. Can you think of sound policy reasons for such a distinction, or does it seem to you to be arbitrary (and hence perhaps incorrect)?

2.   The FTAC arbitrators awarded SNE, the Soviet Foreign Trade Organization, approximately $200 million. The arbitration agreement was found in a clause of the larger sales agreement, sometimes called the "container contract." After finding the sales contract invalid, on what basis did the arbitrators make the award?

3.   The Bermuda judges cite Judge Schwebel who states that, "when the parties to an agreement containing an arbitration clause enter into that agreement they conclude not one but two agreements, the arbitral twin of which survives any birth defect or acquired disability of the principal agreement."

It is true that the fate of the twins is not necessarily identical, but it is by no means certain that in case only one of the twins survives, it has to be the "arbitration twin." Separability simply means separate scrutinies, and possibly different rules under which each scrutiny is conducted. Results may vary. As we shall see in the next subchapter's discussion of formal requirements for the validity of the arbitration agreement, one may very well imagine a rule which would impose more stringent formal requirements on the arbitration clause than apply to the underlying contract.

4.   On the issue of what law governs the separability question, the Bermuda judges opted for Soviet (Russian) law. Do you agree?

The Bermuda trial court, following the British tradition that foreign law must be proved as a fact, concluded that SNE had failed to prove that separability was a part of Soviet (Russian) law. The Bermuda Court of

Appeal concluded that this was an incorrect allocation of the burden of proof. Can you explain why? See New York Convention Art. V(1) (first paragraph).

5. Among other scholarly authorities, the Bermuda judges also rely on P. Sanders, who explains that the doctrine of separability reaches its limits when the existence of the contract itself is contested. In the words of Sanders,

[I]f the question arises whether the parties have indeed concluded a contract containing an arbitration clause, the jurisdiction of the arbitrator is put in question.

In a similar vein, Lord Justice Hoffmann of the Court of Appeal states in *Harbour v. Kansa* (in a part of the opinion not reproduced above):

There will obviously be cases in which a claim that no contract came into existence necessarily entails a denial that there was any agreement to arbitrate.

Is there a distinction between a contract that is "void ab initio" and one that is non-existent? What does the Bermuda court decide on this point?

6. In *Harbour v. Kansa*, a distinction is drawn between direct attack on the validity of the arbitration clause itself, and indirect impeachment of the arbitration agreement by challenging the contract (by force of "the logical proposition that the clause falls with the containing contract"). Is this a valid distinction?

(Consider in this connection the following point made by Judge Schwebel:

if one party could deny arbitration to the other party by the allegation that the agreement lacked initial or continuing validity, if by such allegation it could deprive an arbitral tribunal of the competence to rule upon that allegation, upon its constitution and jurisdiction and upon the merits of the dispute, then it would always be open to a party to an agreement containing an arbitration clause to vitiate its arbitral obligation by the simple expedient of declaring the agreement void.[28])

7. If you do make a distinction between direct and implied challenges to the arbitration clause, would you require the arbitrators to desist in face of a direct challenge to the arbitration clause proper?

8. In an unpublished case, the contract between two motion picture companies ("A" and "M") contained a rather straightforward arbitration clause. Problems emerged, however, with the last clause of the contract, which read: "No provision of this contract will take effect before 'A' makes a down payment of 100,000 German Marks." The down payment was never made, and "M" submitted a claim to the arbitral institution agreed upon in the contract. "A" responded by challenging the jurisdiction of the arbitration tribunal, stating that no provision of the contract came into force. Claimant "M" asserted that the doctrine of separability allows the arbitrators to assume jurisdiction. Does it?

What if the critical clause read: "This contract will not take effect before 'A' makes a down payment of 100,000 German Marks"?

[28]. S. Schwebel, International Arbitration: Three Salient Problems 4 (1987).

Suppose these same issues arise in a proceeding before a court. Should the court decide them or refer the parties to arbitration?

9. Suppose Prosperity, Inc. enters into a joint venture (JV) agreement (containing an arbitration clause) with Deadbeat, Inc. Deadbeat reneges on its obligations under the JV agreement claiming the person who signed had no authority to bind Deadbeat. Prosperity brings a court action against Deadbeat for damages, and Deadbeat asks the court to refer the parties to arbitration? What result? Would the separability doctrine operate to support Deadbeat's position? (Is the result the same under the U.S. and French approaches? If not, which do you prefer?) Can Deadbeat claim that at least now there is an agreement to arbitrate because it is ratifying the prior purported agreement? See Sandvik AB v. Advent International Corp., 220 F.3d 99 (3d Cir.2000), discussed supra in text at II.1.a.iii, fn. 5.

10. The *Kompetenz–Kompetenz* and separability doctrines were developed by courts to facilitate arbitration and make it more efficient and effective. The *FIAT* case in question and comment 6, supra, following the *Jules Verne* case, suggests there are limits to a court's willingness to privilege arbitration and defer to arbitrators' decisions. Do some courts occasionally go beyond reasonable limits? How do you assess the following case.

REPUBLIC OF NICARAGUA V. STANDARD FRUIT CO., 937 F.2d 469 (9th Cir.1991). After preliminary negotiations, Standard Fruit and Nicaragua executed a "Memorandum of Intent" that envisioned renegotiation and replacement of four operating contracts, and established essential elements of a fruit purchase agreement. It was contested whether this document represented a binding contract, or only an agreement to agree.[29] Paragraph IV of the Memorandum included the following clause:

Any and all disputes arising under the arrangements contemplated hereunder * * * will be referred to mutually agreed mechanisms or procedures of international arbitration, such as the rules of the London Arbitration Association.[30]

Nicaragua admitted that the "London Arbitration Association" does not exist. The Standard Fruit lawyer who principally drafted the Memorandum, Robert Moore, sent Nicaragua's representative a letter three weeks after the negotiations. The letter described "the deep sense of urgency on both sides" and the "exceedingly tight time schedule." The letter said that in the negotiations neither party could remember the name of the arbitration body in London, and stated: "[w]hat resulted was *an agreement providing for arbitration* but without finally fixing the forum or an automatic method of transmitting disputes."[31] The letter went on to suggest: "we would be better off agreeing in advance that Paragraph IV was to be read and interpreted to provide for arbitration by [a certain] agency," and concluded "I am sure you will agree that it is best done *in the infancy of the agreement and at a time that negotiations of the implementing agreements are being worked out.*"[32]

---

[29]. 937 F.2d at 471.

[30]. Id. at 473.

[31]. Id.

[32]. Ibid. (Emphasis in original.)

Claiming breach of contract, Nicaragua began an action in federal district court against Standard Fruit and, relying on Paragraph IV, moved to compel arbitration. The district court granted summary judgment denying this motion on the basis of its preliminary factual conclusion that the Memorandum as a whole "was not a binding contract" and that the arbitration provision was not an actual agreement to submit to arbitration, but merely "a provision declaring the expectations of the parties that contracts to be negotiated later would include agreements to arbitrate."[33] The district court apparently drew upon the language of the Memorandum and testimony given by Robert Moore. (Recall that summary judgment is proper only if there is no evidence or offer of proof inconsistent with the preliminary factual finding, so that no trial is needed to establish the facts.) The Ninth Circuit reversed, holding that the district court erred in considering the contract as a whole to determine the threshold question of whether Nicaragua may enforce the arbitration agreement contained in the Memorandum. Nicaragua's motion to compel arbitration was granted, leaving to the arbitrators to decide whether a valid arbitration agreement existed.

The Ninth Circuit relied on *Prima Paint*,[34] where the Supreme Court held that the arbitration clause was severable in spite of the fact that Prima Paint may have been fraudulently induced to enter into the contract as a whole, because fraud did not go to the making of the arbitration clause itself.

It is rather clear that some causes of invalidity need not affect directly the arbitration clause, and therefore the arbitration agreement need not share the destiny of the container contract. If someone fraudulently introduces himself as an experienced salesman of musical instruments (although he is actually a janitor in a music shop), the contract concluded upon this representation may very well be voidable for fraud. This deceitful representation need not amount in itself, however, to a fraudulent inducement to include an arbitration clause into the agency contract. Thus the arbitration clause may survive the voidness of the agency contract. On the other hand, if the ground of nullity is, let us say, lack of capacity (e.g., one of the contracting parties is a minor) the destiny of the arbitration clause is hardly divorceable from the fortune of the container agreement. Admitting that the destinies of the arbitration clause and of the container contract are separable in principle, does not mean that they should actually be divorced in each case.

Are the circumstances in *Prima Paint* distinguishable from the circumstances in the *Republic of Nicaragua* case? (Is the destiny of the arbitration clause divorceable from the validity of the Memorandum of Intent? Could an agreement to agree contain a valid arbitration clause?)

The Ninth Circuit referred Nicaragua and Standard Fruit to arbitration. To what arbitral tribunal should Claimant go, according to the given arbitration clause?

Suppose Claimant found a court to appoint an arbitrator, and you are that arbitrator. Would you find that a valid arbitration agreement exists?

[33]. Id. at 474.

[34]. Prima Paint v. Flood & Conklin, 388 U.S. 395, 404 (1967).

Who has the burden of proof? Or is there a presumption favoring arbitration?

11.   In the *Republic of Nicaragua* case, the Ninth Circuit justified its ruling in part as follows:

In the instant case, the district court made a preliminary "Factual Conclusion" that the Memorandum "was not intended as a binding contract," in direct opposition to the *Prima Paint* rule. In addition to providing the basis for granting summary judgment on the merits, this conclusion is also the basis for the alternative [holding] that no agreement to arbitrate existed, * * *. However, as Nicaragua correctly points out, Moore's testimony [the Standard Fruit lawyer who principally drafted the Memorandum] directly conflicts with contemporary documents in the record [the Moore letter], which should have precluded any summary judgment. As a matter of law, the key language in Paragraph IV seems highly ambiguous, since it refers to "the arrangements contemplated hereunder," and thus requires extensive inquiry into just what arrangements are being referred to. * * *[35]

* * *

The district court also found that the clause's "lack of specificity" mitigated against its enforcement. However, the clear weight of authority holds that the most minimal indication of the parties' intent to arbitrate must be given full effect, especially in international disputes.... Under this analysis, Paragraph IV here was not too vague to be given effect, especially when considered in light of Robert Moore's letter explaining the ambiguity. The scope of the clause must also be interpreted liberally: as a matter of federal law, any doubts concerning the scope of arbitrable issues should be resolved in favor of arbitration, whether the problem at hand is the construction of the contract language itself or an allegation of waiver, delay, or a like defense to arbitrability.

* * *

* * * [W]e hold that Paragraph IV's commitment to arbitrate "any and all disputes arising under the arrangements contemplated hereunder" is arguably susceptible of an interpretation that the parties agreed to arbitrate this claim. As we must resolve all doubts in favor of arbitration, we hold that this dispute must be referred to the arbitrators.[36]

* * *

In the end the Ninth Circuit ordered the parties to arbitration. Should it have done so, or should it have remanded the case to the District Court for further fact finding? There is a difference between the *scope* of an arbitration clause (an inquiry into which disputes are included in the agreement to arbitrate) and the *existence* of an agreement to arbitrate. Which issue is involved in the *Nicaragua* case? Should both issues be governed by the principle of resolving ambiguities in favor of arbitration? The Ninth Circuit seems to say: send the parties to arbitration if their dispute "is arguably susceptible of an interpretation that the parties agreed to arbitrate * * * ." Do you agree with this approach? What result under French law?

[35].   937 F.2d at 476.   [36].   Id. at 478–479.

II.1.d. *The Form of the Arbitration Agreement*

II.1.d.i. "An Agreement in Writing"

Howard M. Holtzmann & Joseph E. Neuhaus, A GUIDE TO THE UNCITRAL MODEL LAW ON INTERNATIONAL COMMERCIAL ARBITRATION: LEGISLATIVE HISTORY AND COMMENTARY

258–62 (1989).*

ARTICLE 7. DEFINITION AND FORM OF ARBITRATION AGREEMENT

* * *

(2) The arbitration agreement shall be in writing. An agreement is in writing if it is contained in a document signed by the parties or in an exchange of letters, telex, telegrams or other means of telecommunication which provide a record of the agreement, or in an exchange of statements of claim and defence in which the existence of an agreement is alleged by one party and not denied by another. The reference in a contract to a document containing an arbitration clause constitutes an arbitration agreement provided that the contract is in writing and the reference is such as to make that clause part of the contract.

* * *

Paragraph 2. Paragraph 2 of Article 7 requires that an arbitration agreement be in writing. This is not merely a requirement that there be written *evidence* of an agreement; the agreement itself must be in writing. One reason for this requirement is that it was agreed at the outset that the Model Law should not conflict with the New York Convention, and in fact, as noted, Article 7 was modeled on that text. In addition, a survey of national laws undertaken by the Secretariat revealed that most legal systems require a writing. Furthermore, even in those States that permit oral agreements it was found that this form is rarely used or difficult to rely upon because of strict standards of proof. The Working Group was agreed that the requirement of a writing applied to all purported arbitration agreements within the scope of the Model Law (i.e., international commercial arbitration). Thus, oral agreements are not a matter left to national rules outside the Model Law, but rather are enforceable only to the extent that the Model Law provides for a waiver of the requirement (see below).

The basic test for a written agreement is that each party have declared in writing its consent to arbitration. Thus, a common example of an impermissible nonwritten arbitration agreement is one in which there is a written offer and an oral (or otherwise nonwritten) acceptance,

---

*Reprinted with kind permission from Kluwer Law International.

or an oral offer and a written confirmation.[15] Considerable concern was expressed in the Commission about arbitration agreements in bills of lading, which often are not signed by the shipper and therefore are probably not written agreements for the purposes of the Model Law. Two amendments were considered by the Commission that would bring such bills of lading clearly within the ambit of the Model Law. Neither was adopted, however, primarily, it appears, because it was not considered possible to stretch the New York Convention's requirement of a writing that far. Nevertheless, two factors mitigate to some extent the difficulties of this result. First, some bill-of-lading problems may ultimately be covered by treaty, particularly the United Nations Convention on the Carriage of Goods by Sea (Hamburg 1978).[18] Second, any objections to an oral agreement may be waived by failure to raise them early in the arbitral proceedings. See Articles 7(2) (discussed further below) and 16(2).[19]

The writing requirement extends to any agreement to submit a dispute to arbitration. Thus, it probably extends to amendments to the original agreement by which additional disputes are submitted to the arbitral tribunal, even if this is done, as is sometimes the case, during the arbitral proceedings. Again, however, the provisions of Article 7(2) and 16(2) might validate an otherwise oral agreement in this situation. A more difficult question is whether separate agreements on procedural questions concerning the arbitration must be in writing. There is nothing in Article 7 that suggests this, since it does not require that the parties describe every feature of the future arbitration in their arbitration agreement. Article 4, however, provides for a waiver by a failure to object in certain circumstances to requirements contained in the "arbitration agreement." As a result, the consequences of a written agreement on procedure may be different from those of such an agreement made orally. This point is discussed in the commentary on Article. 4.

Prior to the start of work on the Model Law, the Secretariat completed a study of the application and interpretation of the New York Convention by courts in a variety of countries. That study noted a

---

15. The Commission Report notes that such agreements are common in certain kinds of commodities and reinsurance trades. Id.

18. * * *Article 22 of this convention addresses arbitration. Article 1(1) of the Model Law provides that the Law is "subject to any agreement in force between this State and any other State or States."

19. Furthermore, one representative suggested an interpretation of the last sentence of paragraph 2 that would bring many bills of lading within the scope of the writing requirement. That sentence states that the reference in a contract to a document containing an arbitration clause constitutes an arbitration agreement if the contract is in writing and the reference makes the clause part of the contract. The representative noted that this sentence does not require that the "contract" be signed, only that it be in writing. * * * While bills of lading are frequently unsigned, they often incorporate the terms and conditions of related charter-parties, which include arbitration clauses. Thus, under this interpretation such bills of lading could be said to meet the requirements of Article 7 even though they are unsigned because they are "contracts" that incorporate other documents containing arbitration clauses. Some resistance was expressed to this view in the Commission. * * * It would seem odd to allow parties to avoid the requirement of a written assent by each party merely by placing the arbitration agreement in a separate document.

number of points of uncertainty in the interpretation of the writing requirement for arbitration agreements under the New York Convention. The Working Group decided to clarify two of these points: whether the writing requirement is satisfied by use of modern means of telecommunications, and whether it is met by references in contracts to general conditions in separate documents. In addition, the Commission sought to clarify that a written arbitration agreement could be created by an exchange of statements of claim and defence in which one party alleged and the other did not deny the existence of an arbitration agreement. This was intended to encompass the situation in which the parties submitted to and participated in the arbitration despite formal flaws in their arbitration agreement. The Commission was of the view that these modifications to the wording of the New York Convention were merely elaborations of that wording and that any award that satisfied the requirements of Article 7 would be enforceable under the Convention.[25]

* * *

UNITED NATIONS CONVENTION ON THE CARRIAGE OF GOODS BY SEA

(The Hamburg Rules).
Hamburg, 30 March 1978.

* * *

Article 22—Arbitration

1.   Subject to the provisions of this Article, parties may provide by agreement evidenced in writing that any dispute that may arise relating to carriage of goods under this Convention shall be referred to arbitration.

2.   Where a charter-party contains a provision that disputes arising thereunder shall be referred to arbitration and a bill of lading issued pursuant to the charter-party does not contain a special annotation

---

25.   * * *Article II(2) of the New York Convention states:

The term "agreement in writing" shall include an arbitral clause in a contract or an arbitration agreement, signed by the parties or contained in an exchange of letters or telegrams.

During the Commission's deliberations, it was noted that the English text of this provision appears to provide a nonexhaustive list of what constitutes an "agreement in writing," because it uses the term "shall include." * * * There are five equally authentic texts of the Convention: Chinese, English, French, Russian, and Spanish. It was also noted that the French text—which uses the phrase "[o]n entend par 'convention écrite' "—as well as an unofficial German translation, have a more mandatory and exhaustive meaning. * * *. The official Spanish and Chinese texts use the terms "denotará", and "wei," respectively, both of which convey the same suggestion as the French text. The Russian text, on the other hand, uses the term "vklyuchact," which is closer to the English meaning. Van den Berg concludes, primarily from the wording of the French and Spanish texts, as well as an examination of the sparse drafting history, that the definition is intended to be exhaustive, and that other forms of written arbitration agreements are not included. A.J. van den Berg, The New York Arbitration Convention: Towards a Uniform Judicial Interpretation *178–80 (1981)*.

providing that such provision shall be binding upon the holder of the bill of lading, the carrier may not invoke such provision as against a holder having acquired the bill of lading in good faith.

3. The arbitration proceedings shall, at the option of the claimant, be instituted at one of the following places:

(a) A place in a State within whose territory is situated:
    (i)   The principal place of business of the defendant or, in the absence thereof, the habitual residence of the defendant; or
    (ii) The place where the contract was made, provided that the defendant has there a place of business, branch or agency through which the contract was made; or
    (iii) The port of loading or the port of discharge; or

(b) Any place designated for that purpose in the arbitration clause or agreement.

4. The arbitrator or arbitration tribunal shall apply the rules of this Convention.

5. The provisions of paragraph 3 and 4 of this Article are deemed to be part of every arbitration clause or agreement, and any term of such clause or agreement which is inconsistent therewith is null and void.

6. Nothing in this Article affects the validity of an agreement relating to arbitration made by the parties after the claim under the contract of carriage by sea has arisen.

* * *

Neil Kaplan, IS THE NEED FOR WRITING AS EXPRESSED IN THE NEW YORK CONVENTION AND THE MODEL LAW OUT OF STEP WITH COMMERCIAL PRACTICE?

12 Arb'n Int'l 27, 29–30 (1996)*

* * *

I.   The Writing Requirement

Why I have chosen the writing requirement as the main focus of this lecture? The simple reason is that after nearly five years of applying the Model Law in Hong Kong in my former judicial capacity, I found that problems arising from the application of Article 7(2) of the Model Law were the most difficult and frustrating which came before me. A more fundamental reason is because it is at the stage of recognition or denial of an effective agreement to arbitrate that tensions can still be seen between the courts and the arbitral process.

As Holtzmann and Neuhaus put it in relation to Article 7(2) of the Model Law.[4]

* Reprinted with permission from Kluwer Law International.

4. See Holtzmann and Neuhaus, *Guide to the UNCITRAL Model Law*, Kluwer 1989 at p. 258.

Any effort at unifying law has its greatest potential effect not in the court or hearing room but at the point where it meets the everyday transactions of life. For arbitration statutes, that point is the rule that sets down the requirements for drafting a valid arbitration agreement, for it is that law that will influence most directly the ease with which business people and their lawyers are able to use arbitration as a system for resolving international commercial disputes. Thus, Article 7 of the Model Law, which defines the term 'arbitration agreement,' is as a practical matter one of the most important parts of UNCITRAL's attempts to unify national arbitration statutes. It is here that states should resist most strongly any temptation to impose more onerous or peculiarly local requirements.

Another reason is that the New York Convention is coming up for its 40th birthday and the time is ripe to examine whether Article II(2) meets the needs of modern business practices. Article 7 of the Model Law is slightly more extensive than Article II(2) of the Convention, but in my judgment both fail to provide a satisfactory solution to problems that arise in practice and, as I will shortly point out, these practical difficulties were well-known to at least some of the delegates at the discussions which led to the New York Convention.

At this point it may be helpful to ask why there is a requirement of writing at all? We already know that substantial contracts are made and enforced only on oral terms. I can see the argument that parties should not be deprived of access to national courts unless they have actually agreed on arbitration. I can see the argument that allowing oral agreements would lead to uncertainty and litigation. But what I have difficulty in seeing is why if one party is sent a contract which includes an arbitration clause and that party acts on that contract and thus adopts it without any qualification, that party should be allowed to wash his hands of the arbitration clause but at the same time maintain an action for the price of the goods delivered or conversely sue for breach. Some might say that this is the price we have to pay for the doctrine of separability!

Before looking at the history of Article II(2) upon which Article 7(2) of the Model Law was based, I would like to refer to a case decided in Hong Kong the facts of which were simple and common place.

In *Smal v. Goldroyce*[5] A agreed to buy from B a quantity of goods on certain terms and conditions which were set out in writing and sent to B with a request that he sign and return the order. The Order contained an arbitration clause. B did not sign the order form or send any document in response to the order. However B did manufacture the goods and deliver them in accordance with the contract to A who paid for them in accordance with the contractual terms. In due course a quality dispute arose and B offered some compensation to A which was rejected. A then applied to the court for the appointment of an arbitrator on

5.   [1994] 2 HKC 526.

behalf of B who had refused to appoint one. Pausing here, this was a domestic arbitration but the definition of "Arbitration Agreement" contained in the Model Law applies to domestic cases in Hong Kong as well as to international ones.

B opposed the appointment of an arbitrator on the grounds that there was no compliance with Article 7(2) of the Model Law. The court adjourned the application to give A an opportunity of placing before the court some document emanating from B upon which an argument for compliance with Article 7(2) could be based. No such document was forthcoming. The court therefore reluctantly ruled that Article 7(2) had not been complied with and refused to appoint an arbitrator thus forcing the parties to litigation. Although a decision on Article 7(2) the same result would have been achieved if compliance with Article II(2) had been in issue.

I venture to suggest that this decision, even if technically correct, produces an absurd result which is inconsistent with commercial reality. There was no doubt that the parties entered into a contract which was contained in or evidenced by the written order and B's conduct. Why on earth should the arbitration clause in the contract [be] require[d] to be established by any higher degree of proof than [that needed to establish] the basic contractual terms themselves? I hasten to add that I am not advocating the bringing within the New York Convention of oral agreements to arbitrate. All I am suggesting is that on the facts of the case under discussion there are sufficient legal theories available which could lead to a form of words which would bring the case not only within the Model Law but also the New York Convention.

* * *

ROBOBAR LIMITED (UK) v. FINNCOLD SAS (ITALY)

Corte di Cassazione [Supreme Court of Italy], 1993.
20 Yearbk. Comm. Arb'n 739 (1995).*

FACTS

In the years 1989–1991, Finncold supplied refrigerating units to Robobar for the manufacture of refrigerators for European and US hotels. The purchase confirmations sent by Robobar contained a clause reading (Italian original): "Any dispute arising out of this order shall be exclusively referred to arbitration by a person to be appointed by the President of the Law Society".

In 1991, Robobar suspended payment alleging that the units delivered by Finncold were defective and of a poor quality and were the cause of the complaints made by several customers concerning the Robobar refrigerators. Robobar actually mentioned the faulty performance of the Finncold units when answering these complaints.

Finncold initiated proceedings before the Court of First Instance of Casale Monferrato, Italy, seeking payment of the purchase price (68 million lire) and 1 billion lire in punitive damages for loss of its good reputation.

Robobar requested a preliminary ruling on jurisdiction by the Supreme Court, which held that the Italian court had jurisdiction over the case as the arbitration agreement was not valid.

EXCERPT

[1]   "Robobar—an English company—seeks a declaration that Italian courts lack jurisdiction over the above case, concerning a supply of refrigerating units by Finncold, which has been contested by Robobar for defects and poor quality. The purchase confirmations sent by Robobar contain the following clause: 'Any dispute arising out of this order shall be exclusively referred to arbitration by a person to be appointed by the President of the Law Society". [Robobar alleges] that there can be no doubt as to the validity of the arbitration clause, since it falls within the field of application of the New York Convention.

[2]   "This ground is unfounded. Art. II of the [New York Convention] recognizes as valid an arbitral clause for foreign arbitration contained in a document signed by the parties or in an exchange of letters or telegrams. There is no doubt that none of these formalities has been met in this case, since the clause is only contained in Robobar's confirmations, upon which Finncold does not seem to have agreed by letter or telegram.

[3]   "Petitioner has presented several arguments in its statement and pleadings in order to overcome this formal defect, which results in the clause being inoperative (see, for all, Supreme Court no. 12268/92);[1] none of them, however, can be accepted.

[4]   "The argument that [Finncold] agreed to the clause ex. Art. 1327 CC,[2] by performing under the contract provided in writing by [Robobar], does not take into account two insurmountable obstacles: (a) that Art. 1327 cannot apply where the written form is required (*see* Supreme Court 2 November 1959 no. 3234); (b) that all argument linking the form of the arbitral clause to the form of the contract in which it is contained is at odds with the principle of the autonomy of the

---

1. The Supreme Court referred to its own decision of 16 November 1992, no. 12268, *ILET—Industria Legnami Trentina srl v. Ditta Holzindustrie Schweighofer srl and Co. sas*, reported in Yearbook XIX (1994) pp. 694–696 (Italy no. 128).

2. Art. 1327 of the Italian Civil Code reads:

"When, at the request of the offeror or by the nature of the transaction or according to usage, the performance should take place without a prior reply, the contract is concluded at the time and place in which performance begins.

The acceptor must promptly give notice of the beginning of performance to the other party and, if he does not, is liable for damages."

arbitration agreement in respect to the contract in which it is contained. According to this principle, the agreement to arbitrate contained in an arbitral clause in a contract is an independent agreement; its validity and efficacy must be ascertained independently of the validity and efficacy of the contract. Petitioner's argument that it would be contrary to good faith to contest the validity of the arbitral clause after having performed under the contract in which that clause is contained must be denied, since the formal requirement cannot be derogated from.

[5] "We must also reject petitioner's argument based on [the Brussels Convention of 1968] ('form which accords with practices in that trade or commerce of which the parties are or ought to have been aware' [Art. 17(1)]), since it can only concern the [Brussels Convention] and thus the jurisdiction of State courts, arbitration being *explicitly* excluded by the Convention (Art. 1(2) (no. 4))."

[6] The Supreme Court concluded that there was no valid arbitral clause between the parties under the New York Convention and went on to establish that the Italian courts had jurisdiction over the case.

COMPAGNIE DE NAVIGATION ET TRANSPORTS SA (FRANCE) v. MEDITERRANEAN SHIPPING CO. SA (SWITZERLAND)

Tribunal Fédéral [Swiss Supreme Court], 1995.
21 Yearbk. Comm. Arb'n 690 (1996).[b][*]

FACTS

By a bill of lading of 21 December 1991, Somatrans ZAE, a French company, concluded a maritime carriage contract with MSC—Mediterranean Shipping Company SA (MSC) for transporting two sealed containers from Marseille to Île de la Réunion. The consignee was Somatrans, Île de la Réunion (Somatrans Réunion).

General conditions were printed on the back of the bill of lading; Art. 2 read:

LAW AND JURISDICTION. Claims and disputes arising under or in connection with this B/L shall be referred to arbitration in London or such other place as the Carrier [MSC] in his sole discretion shall designate, one arbitrator to be nominated by the Carrier, a second by the Merchant [Somatrans ZAE] and the third by the two so chosen. The arbitrators to be commercial men engaged in shipping. English law shall be applied, unless some other law is compulsorily applicable, except the claims and disputes relating to cargo carried to or from the United States shall be subject to the sole jurisdiction of the US in the US District Court, Southern District of New York, and US law shall be applied.

b. 121 Arrêts du Tribunal Federal 38 (1995).

* Reprinted with permission of Yearbook Commercial Arbitration, International Council for Commercial Arbitration.

The original bill of lading was signed by MSC—Mediterranean Shipping Company France SA (MSC France) as agent and representative of MSC; it was not signed by Somatrans ZAE. Upon arrival of the containers, Somatrans Réunion, the consignee, signed a copy of the bill of lading on the side of the general conditions, adding the hand-written mention: "conform to the original". Somatrans Réunion also signed the original bill of lading on the side where the general conditions were printed.

When it was discovered that the containers had been forced open, fifty-six packages were missing and two had been damaged, Somatrans ZAE filed a request for indemnification with the insurer, Compagnie de Navigation et Transports SA (CNT), and received FF 72,206.93.

On 19 January 1993, CNT commenced proceedings against MSC before the Court of First Instance of Geneva, seeking reimbursement of the indemnification. MSC objected that the State court lacked jurisdiction because of the arbitration clause in the bill of lading. On 7 September 1993, the Court of First Instance dismissed the objection and found that it had jurisdiction over the dispute.

On appeal by MSC, the Court of Appeal of the Canton Geneva reversed the judgment on 18 March 1994.

The Supreme Court affirmed the appellate decision, finding that a valid arbitration clause had been concluded between the parties although the shipper had not signed the bill of lading. The Court reasoned that, due to the development of modern means of communication, the distinction between signed and unsigned documents is to be approached in a less strict manner and that in the specific case the parties were experienced traders which entertained regular business relationships since several years, always making use of the general conditions which were also printed on the back of the bill of lading at issue.

EXCERPT

[1] "Both France and Switzerland, the States in which the parties to the proceedings have their seat, as well as Great Britain, the State of the chosen seat of the arbitral tribunal according to the general conditions in the bill of lading at issue, are Parties to the [New York Convention]. It is undisputed that the Convention applies to the present case.

* * *

[2] "In the present case, we must first determine whether the carrier [MSC] and the shipper, Somatrans ZAE, are bound by a valid arbitration clause. It is not disputed that, if so, the arbitration clause at issue would bind claimant, which substitutes for the shipper.

[3] "Defendant does not allege that the arbitral tribunal instituted by Art. 2 of the general conditions of the bill of lading has its seat in

Switzerland. Hence, Art. 178 PILA[1] * * * is not applicable and it is not necessary to discuss the relationship between this provision and Art. II of the New York Convention as to the required form of the arbitration agreement (Art. 176(1) PILA;[2] Handelsgericht Zürich in ZR 91/1992 no. 23 consid. 3.2; on the conflict of laws see Volken, IPRG–Kommentar, note 12 to Art. 7 and note 9 to Art. 178 PILA; Lalive/Poudret/Reymond, *Le droit de l'arbitrage interne et international en Suisse*, note 3 to Art. 7 and note 6 et seq. to Art. 178 PILA).

* * *

[8] "The arbitration agreement on which defendant relies is valid only if it meets the requirement of the written form of Art. II(2) of the New York Convention. On this subject we must observe that the requirement in the [Convention] is both more liberal than Art. 6 *Concordat*,[9] which must be understood by analogous application of Art. 13 CO,[10] and stricter than Art. 178 PILA, which merely requires a means of communication allowing for a written proof of the arbitration agreement (Lalive/Poudret/Reymond, *op. cit.*, note 5 to Art. 178 PILA). Art. II(2) of the New York Convention requires that the arbitration agreement be signed by the parties or contained in an exchange of letters or telegrams. The Supreme Court has indeed * * * [equated] telexes to telegrams, but it is in any case necessary that the parties have expressed their intention to submit to arbitration in writing (ATF 111 Ib 253; in the same sense Van den Berg, *The New York Arbitration Convention of 1958*, p. 204).

[9] "According to a majority opinion, the said provision must be interpreted in the light of the [UNCITRAL Model Law], the authors of which wished to adapt the regime of the New York Convention to modern needs without modifying it (Bucher, *op. cit.*, p. 49 note 123;

---

1. Art. 178 of the Swiss Private International Law Act (PILA) reads:

1. As regards its form, the arbitration agreement shall be valid if made in writing, by telegram, telex, telecopier or any other means of communication which permits it to be evidenced by a text.

2. As regards its substance, the arbitration agreement shall be valid if it conforms either to the law chosen by the parties, or to the law governing the subject matter of the dispute, in particular the law governing the main contract, or if it conforms to Swiss law.

3. The validity of an arbitration agreement cannot be contested on the ground that the main contract is not valid or that the arbitration agreement concerns a dispute which has not yet arisen.

2. Art. 176(1) of the Swiss Private International Law Act reads:

The provisions of this Chapter shall apply to all arbitrations if the seat of the arbitral tribunal is situated in Switzerland and if, at the time when the arbitration agreement was concluded, at least one of the parties had neither its domicile nor its habitual residence in Switzerland.

9. Art. 6 of the Intercantonal Arbitration Convention reads:

Form. The arbitration agreement shall be in writing.

It may take the form of a written declaration whereby the parties agree to adhere by the statutes of a body corporate provided that the declaration expressly refers to the arbitration clause contained in the statutes or rules made under them.

10. Art. 13 of the Swiss Code of Obligations reads:

A contract which by law must be in written form (Art. 12) must bear the signatures of all persons who are to be bound by it.

Where the law contains no provision to the contrary, a letter or a telegram is deemed to be in writing, provided that the letter or the telegram form bears the signatures of the persons binding themselves.

Volken, *op. cit.*, note 12 to Art. 7 PILA; Schlosser, *op. cit.*, p. 267 et seq. note 368 et seq.). Art. 7(2) of the Model Law provides at the beginning (see Husslein–Stich, Das UNCITRAL–Modellgesetz über die internationale Handelsschiedsgerichtsbarkeit, p. 38 et seq. and p. 238):

> The arbitration agreement shall be in writing. An agreement is in writing if it is contained in a document signed by the parties or in an exchange of letters, telex, telegrams or other means of telecommunication which provide a record of the agreement. * * *

Art. 178 PILA is clearly inspired by this text, which takes into account the development of modern means of communication. It thus must equally serve the interpretation of Art. II(2) of the New York Convention. It follows herefrom that the formal requirements of the international treaty can actually be reconciled with those of Art. 178 PILA (Volken, *op. cit.*, note 12 to Art. 7 PILA). Hence, it is in the light of these criteria and with a free power of examination in law that we must ascertain whether the arbitration clause invoked by defendant has been concluded by the shipper and the carrier according to the required forms.

[10] "The Court of Appeal has established, in a way which is binding on the Supreme Court, that the MSC group companies and shipper Somatrans ZAE are specialized in international maritime transport, that they have [had] business relationships * * * [extending over] several years and regularly use for this purpose the bills of lading printed on MSC's stationery. Hence, the shipper is in any case perfectly aware of the general conditions appearing on the back of these documents. The cantonal court has further found that the shipper itself filled in the bill of lading of 21 December 1991, and concludes that Somatrans ZAE has expressed in writing both its acceptance of the bill of lading and its adhesion to the arbitration clause printed on the document, so that the written form requirement of the New York Convention is met even if only MSC, through its agent, has signed the bill of lading. After all, continues the cantonal court, the consignee [Somatrans Réunion], a company of the Somatrans group, has signed a copy of the bill of lading and endorsed the original document when receiving the goods. According to claimant, the arbitration clause is not valid as the signature of the shipper does not appear on the bill of lading.

[11] "In ATF 110 II 54, the Supreme Court has recognized that in the case of two commercial companies experienced in the business, the reference to the conditions of a charter party (*Frachtvertrag*)—deemed to be known by the parties and containing an arbitration clause—which reference was contained in a bill of lading signed by the carrier and the shipper on behalf of a company belonging to the same group as the charterer, was a valid arbitration clause (approved by Lalive/Poudret/Reymond, *op. cit.*, note 13 to Art. 178 PILA). The present case differs however from the circumstances underlying that decision: the arbitration clause at issue appears on the bill of lading itself and not in a document to which the bill of lading refers; the shipper did not sign the bill of lading of 21 December 1991 and has not referred to it otherwise in

a signed document. The question of the validity of the arbitration agreement thus arises, taking into consideration the fact that no document concerning the voyage at issue is signed by Somatrans ZAE.

[12] "According to the formal requirements applicable *in casu*, arbitration clauses are valid which are either contained in a signed contract or in an exchange of letters, telegrams, telexes and other means of communication. In other words, a distinction should be made between agreements resulting from a document, which must in principle be signed, and agreements resulting from an exchange of written declarations, which are not necessarily signed (Schlosser, *op. cit.*, p. 270 et seq.; Van den Berg, *op. cit.*, p. 192 et seq.). If we apply this distinction strictly, the validity of the arbitration clause should be denied, unless we admit that the signature by Somatrans Réunion, both on the original and the copy of the bill of lading, binds the shipper. However, we should not forget that, with the development of modern means of communication, unsigned written documents have an increasing importance and diffusion, that the need for a signature inevitably diminishes, especially in international commerce, and that the different treatment reserved to signed and unsigned documents is under discussion.

[13] "We must add that, in particular situations, a certain behaviour can replace compliance with a formal requirement according to the rules of good faith (Schlosser, *op. cit.*, p. 272 note 374). This is exactly the case here. The parties, which have a long standing business relationship, base it in fact on general conditions containing, at Art. 2, the arbitration clause at issue. Further, the shipper itself has filled in the bill of lading before returning it to the carrier, which signed it. Leaving aside the fact that this procedure is not different from an exchange of declarations by telex or similar documents, the carrier had the right to believe in good faith that the shipper, its business partner since several years, approved of the contractual documents which it had filled in itself, including the general conditions on the back, among which the arbitration clause (see Schlosser, *op. cit.*, p. 272 et seq. note 374).

[14] "Thus, the Court of Appeal did not violate federal law by declaring the said arbitration clause valid, considering the whole of the circumstances of the case."

SPHERE DRAKE INSURANCE PLC v. MARINE TOWING, INC.

United States Court of Appeals, Fifth Circuit, 1994.
16 F.3d 666.

DUHE, CIRCUIT JUDGE:

Sphere Drake Insurance PLC sued Marine Towing, Inc. to stay litigation and compel arbitration of certain claims under a protection and indemnity policy. Defendant–Appellant Marine Towing, Inc. moved to dismiss for lack of jurisdiction. The district court denied Marine Towing's motion and ordered arbitration. Marine Towing appeals. Sphere

Drake challenges our appellate jurisdiction, arguing that the district court order is not final. We find both appellate and district court jurisdiction and affirm.

I. FACTS

Marine Towing contacted Schade & Co. to acquire protection and indemnity insurance for its vessels. Schade eventually secured a policy from Sphere Drake, a London marine insurer. Before Schade delivered the policy to Marine Towing, but during the policy period, an insured vessel sank. Upon receiving the policy, Marine Towing discovered a provision requiring arbitration of coverage disputes in London.

Marine Towing nevertheless sued Sphere Drake and Schade in state court for a declaration of rights under the policy and coverage. Sphere Drake removed the case to federal court and moved to compel arbitration and stay the litigation pending arbitration. Marine Towing moved to remand, and the district court eventually remanded the case because Sphere Drake had not joined all defendants in the notice of removal. After remanding, the court dismissed the motions regarding arbitration as moot.

Before the remand of the removed case, Sphere Drake filed this case, a separate action, to stay litigation and to compel arbitration under the Convention on the Recognition and Enforcement of Foreign Arbitral Awards, June 10, 1958, 21 U.S.T. 2517, 330 U.N.T.S. 38, reprinted in 9 U.S.C.A. § 201 note (West Supp.1993) [hereinafter "the Convention"]. Marine Towing moved to dismiss this case, arguing that the court lacked jurisdiction both because of the remand of the removed case and because Marine Towing never agreed to arbitrate under the Convention. The court denied Marine Towing's motion, ordered arbitration, and stayed all litigation between the parties. From these orders, Marine Towing appeals.

* * *

B. Jurisdiction under the Convention

Marine Towing next argues that the district court lacked jurisdiction under the Convention[4] because Marine Towing and Sphere Drake had no "agreement in writing" to arbitrate.[5] The Convention provides that the phrase " 'agreement in writing' shall include an arbitral clause in a contract or an arbitration agreement, signed by the parties or contained in an exchange of letters or telegrams."[6]

Marine Towing contends that, because it did not sign the insurance contract, the policy cannot provide the agreement in writing. Marine Towing would define an "agreement in writing" only as 1) a contract or

---

4. A proceeding "falling under the Convention shall be deemed to arise under the laws and treaties of the United States," and original jurisdiction is in the district courts. 9 U.S.C.A. § 203 (West Supp.1993).

5. The Convention applies if there is "an agreement in writing" in which the parties undertake to submit their differences to arbitration. Convention, art. II § 1.

6. *Id.* § 2.

other written agreement signed by the parties or 2) an exchange of correspondence between the parties demonstrating consent to arbitrate. We disagree with this interpretation of the Convention. We would outline the Convention definition of "agreement in writing" to include either

(1) an arbitral clause in a contract or

(2) an arbitration agreement,

    (a) signed by the parties or

    (b) contained in an exchange of letters or telegrams.

The insurance contract indisputably contains an arbitral clause. Because what is at issue here is an arbitral clause in a contract, the qualifications applicable to arbitration agreements do not apply. A signature is therefore not required.[7] But see Sen Mar, Inc. v. Tiger Petroleum Corp., 774 F. Supp. 879, 882 (S.D.N.Y.1991) (requiring that arbitration clause be found in a signed writing or an exchange of letters to be enforceable). The district court properly did not require that the contract containing an arbitral provision be signed to constitute an agreement in writing under the Convention.

    IV. COMPELLING ARBITRATION

The final question is whether the district court properly compelled the parties to arbitrate. Of the requirements for referring a dispute to arbitration under the Convention, only one is at issue: whether there is an agreement in writing to arbitrate. This question having been answered in the affirmative in resolving Marine Towing's jurisdictional challenge, the district court properly compelled arbitration.

Affirmed.

Questions and Comments

1. Disturbed by the outcome in *Smal v. Goldroyce*, N. Kaplan asks: "Why on earth should the arbitration clause in the contract [be] require[d] to be established by any higher degree of proof than [that needed to establish] the basic contractual terms themselves?" Can you give an answer?

In his book *Arbitration in International Trade*, under the subtitle "Necessity for strict rules," R. David makes the following observation:

> Arbitration agreements are agreements of a peculiar kind. Parties submit themselves in advance to the decision of a third person, who will determine how their contract shall be modelled, or how their dispute has to be settled. Such agreements may be recognized and sanctioned by the law, but severe conditions ought to be required to this purpose, making sure that the parties have unequivocally assented to such an agreement and stated with enough precision which difference was submitted by them to arbitration and how the arbitration should be organized. The

---

7. Additionally, we do not reach the agency arguments pertaining to whether an   exchange of correspondence occurred.

decision of the arbitrator must have at its basis an agreement which is clear and undisputable.[37]

Is this the answer?

(Note that in their commentary Holtzmann and Neuhaus state that an agreement in which there is a written offer and an oral (otherwise non-written) acceptance, or an oral offer and a written confirmation is "a common example of an impermissible non-written arbitration agreement".)

2.   In *Robobar v. Finncold* the Supreme Court of Italy (Corte di Cassazione) made no effort to construe acceptance of a written arbitration agreement by conduct as being compatible with Article II(2) of the New York Convention. Is this just old fashioned, or is it the correct decision under the Convention in light of the "agreement in writing" requirement?

3.   In *CNT v. MSC* the Swiss Supreme Court clearly made efforts to sustain the validity of the arbitration agreement, but it did not simply apply Article 178 of the Swiss Private International Law Act (which contains a more flexible formulation than the one in Article II(2) of the New York Convention). Why was Article 178 not applicable?

4.   The Swiss Supreme court tried to build a bridge between Article II(2) of the New York Convention, Article 7(2) of the Model Law, and Article 178 of the Swiss Private International law Act. (It stated that through the relevant provision of the Model Law, the authors wished to adapt the regime of the New York Convention to modern needs without modifying it; and that Article 178 of the Swiss Act is clearly inspired by Article 7(2) of the Model Law, and thus it "must equally serve the interpretation of Article II(2) of the New York Convention".) Compare the three relevant provisions. Can the differences really be bridged by interpretation?

5.   The Swiss Supreme Court offers a number of arguments in favor of sustaining the arbitration clause:

— shipper itself filled in the bill of lading;

— the bill of lading was signed by the consignee, who is a member of the Somatrans group (to which the shipper also belongs);

— shipper acknowledged and accepted the content of the bill of lading by conduct;

— during their long standing business relationship, both parties had been well acquainted with the general conditions containing an arbitration clause.

Which argument is the most convincing? Which comes closest to meeting the requirements of Article II(2) of the New York Convention?

6.   Which arbitration clause is more difficult to qualify as satisfying the "agreement in writing" requirement: the one presented to the Swiss Supreme Court, or the one submitted to the Corte di Cassazione in *Robobar*?

7.   Suppose that in *CNT v. MSC* the Swiss Supreme Court measured the circumstances of the case against the standard set in Article 22 of the 1978 UN Convention on the Carriage of Goods by Sea. What result?

[37]. R. David, *Arbitration in Interna-   tional Trade* 195–196 (1985).

8. In *Sphere Drake Insurance v. Marine Towing*, the Court of Appeals of the Fifth Circuit is suggesting a possible interpretation of Article II(2) that was left out of consideration by both the Swiss and the Italian Supreme Court. Is this a creative interpretation, or does the court simply misread Article II(2)? Under the Fifth Circuit's interpretation would an oral agreement between two parties referring to and incorporating a standard form contract containing an arbitration clause satisfy the writing requirement?

9. It is important to note that the relevance of the formal requisite of Article II(2) is reinforced by Article IV (1)(b) of the same Convention which states that the party seeking recognition and enforcement has to present to the court "the original agreement referred to in Article II or a duly certified copy thereof." That such a requirement must be satisfied if recognition is sought adds a consideration bearing on the range and possible interpretations of the "agreement in writing" requirement.

10. Note also that the Hong Kong Arbitration (Amendment) Ordinance, promulgated on October 4, 1996, and in effect from June 27, 1997, accepts arbitration agreements that are in writing, but not signed by both parties.

II.1.d.ii. *Can a Battle of Forms Yield an Arbitration Agreement?*

NOKIA–MAILLEFER SA (SWITZERLAND) v. MAZZER (ITALY)

[Tribunal Cantonal (Vaud)], 1993.
21 Yearbk. Comm. Arb'n 681 (1996).*

FACTS

On 30 March 1988, Nokia–Maillefer SA (Nokia), in reply to an order from Mr. Mazzer, sent him a confirmation of order; the confirmation referred to Nokia's enclosed general conditions of sale, providing for a Swiss forum.

On 31 March 1988, Leasindustria, an Italian financing company, replied to Nokia by sending a purchase order to which general conditions of purchase were annexed. Art. 10 of the general conditions provided for a Milan forum. Two months later, Nokia returned the purchase order, replacing the word "Milan" in Art. 10 with "International Chamber of Commerce, Paris". By a telex to Leasindustria, Mr. Mazzer accepted the modification.

When a dispute arose, the Italian buyer commenced court proceedings before the *Cour Civile* [Court of First Instance] of Canton Vaud, at the seat of the Swiss supplier. Nokia requested the Court to refer the dispute to arbitration according to the contractual agreement.

The Court of First Instance dismissed the objection, holding that no formally valid arbitration clause had been concluded under the Intercan-

* Reprinted with permission of Yearbook Commercial Arbitration, International Council for Commercial Arbitration.

tonal Arbitration Act (*Concordat*), and that no tacit acceptance is possible under Art. II(2) of the New York Convention and Art. 6(1) of the *Concordat*,[1] as Mr. Mazzer had agreed to the ICC clause by an unsigned telex to Leasindustria.

Upon appeal by Nokia, the Court of Appeal affirmed the lower court's decision. Without referring to the New York Convention, the Court found that the common intent of the parties to refer their dispute to arbitration was not evinced by their exchange of ambiguous indications as to the settlement of disputes.

EXCERPT:

[1] "The dispute is whether Art. 10 of the purchase order, as modified, is a valid arbitration clause. The autonomy of the arbitration clause as to the contract in which it is contained or to which it refers is unanimously recognized. Hence, to the exception of cases where a ground for nullity of the contract also affects the clause, the validity of the arbitration clause must be examined separately (Lalive, Poudret and Reymond, *Le droit de l'arbitrage interne et international en Suisse*, note 3 to Art. 4 *Concordat*, p. 49; Journal des Tribunaux 1990 I 563, especially p. 566).

[2] "An arbitration clause can only be validly concluded where there is a common intention of the parties to refer a possible dispute to arbitration. The existence of such an agreement must be ascertained according to the general principles of the Code of Obligations, in particular Art. 2 CO.[2] Considering the important consequences of an arbitration agreement, the court shall beware of finding too easily that such an agreement has been concluded (Journal des Tribunaux 1990 I 563, especially p. 565).

[3] "In the present case, the arbitration clause at issue takes the place of an arbitration agreement, and does not appear in a general agreement to arbitrate.

[4] "The question of the authority having jurisdiction to decide on a possible dispute has been dealt with in different stages in two different documents, one of which has been modified by one party. In the annex to the confirmation of order ... which it sent on 30 March 1988 to Giacomo Ezio Mazzer, Nokia enclosed the general conditions of sale

---

1. Art. 6 of the Intercantonal Arbitration Convention reads:

The arbitration agreement shall be in writing.

It may be the form of a written declaration whereby the parties agree to adhere by the statutes of a body corporate provided that the declaration expressly refers to the arbitration clause contained in the statutes or rules made under them.

2. Art. 2 of the Swiss Code of Obligations reads:

"When the parties have agreed with regard to all essential points, it is presumed that a reservation of ancillary points is not meant to affect the binding nature of the contract. Where agreement with regard to such ancillary points so reserved is not reached, the judge shall determine them in accordance with the nature of the transaction.

The foregoing shall not affect the provisions regarding the form of contracts (Arts. 9–16)."

which, at no. 17.1, provided that the forum be at the seat of the supplier. Subsequently, the general conditions of purchase annexed to the purchase order sent on 31 March 1988 by Leasindustria initially provided that the parties agreed to accept the jurisdiction of the Milan courts over all possible disputes. Lastly, Milan was replaced by 'International Chamber of Commerce, Paris'. Thus, the question of the authority having jurisdiction to decide on a possible dispute has not been provided for straight away in a clear and indisputable manner.

[5] "In this evolutionary and uncertain context, there is no common intent on arbitration unless the 'final' arbitration clause, that is, Art. 10 as modified, has a manifest and certain meaning. It is at least necessary that a common intent of the parties can be deduced from their expressions.

[6] "Considering the clause, it is not possible to ascertain the common intent of the parties, in particular as to the arbitration agreement. Initially, the clause at issue provides under 'forum' for the jurisdiction of the (State) courts of Milan. Only the term 'Milan' has been replaced by 'International Chamber of Commerce, Paris', with no mention of the fact that the jurisdiction of the courts is excluded and replaced by private arbitration.

[7] "The jurisdiction of the International Chamber of Commerce of Paris cannot be deemed to be tantamount to the appointment of an arbitrator, as the word arbitrator or arbitration does not appear and the International Chamber of Commerce itself does not act as arbitrator. Only physical persons may be arbitrators, to the exclusion of legal entities or *collectivités*; in particular, a Chamber of Commerce cannot be appointed as arbitrator (Jolidon, *Commentaire du Concordat suisse sur l'arbitrage*, p. 201).

[8] "Appellant must bear the consequences of the ambiguity and obscurity of the alleged clause, which it modified with the intention of transforming a *prorogatio fori* into an arbitration clause functioning also as arbitration agreement. Appellee's agreement as to the modifications does not clear away the uncertainty as to the meaning of the clause and, consequently, of the agreement.

[9] "In a context in which it should not be held too easily that an agreement has been concluded, we cannot accept an unclear clause as proof of an agreement having an uncertain subject matter. Hence, we must hold that the parties did not conclude a valid arbitration agreement nor an arbitral clause. For this single reason, the request for referral had to be denied. Consequently, the appeal must be denied as well."

Questions and Comments

1. The "battle of forms" often includes a battle of various forum selection clauses. In *Nokia v. Mazzer* some of the clauses pertaining to

dispute settlement referred to various courts, one formulation referred to the ICC.

In your opinion, was the main shortcoming of this exchange of messages that in the phrase "jurisdiction of the Milan courts," the word "Milan" was simply replaced by "International Chamber of Commerce Paris," without mentioning arbitration? That Mazzer accepted the modification, including the reference to ICC, in an "unsigned telex?" That this telex was sent to Leaseindustria, rather than to Nokia? Or the messiness of the whole situation?

We do not know whether Leaseindustria forwarded Mr. Mazzer's telex to Nokia. If it had, would this change the outcome?

2. I.T.A.D. Associates, Inc. v. Podar Brothers[38] is a battle of forms case with a different outcome. There, I.T.A.D., a New York company, placed purchase orders, which were then confirmed by contracts issued by Podar, a partnership with its primary place of business in Bombay, India. Both the purchase orders submitted by I.T.A.D. and the contracts issued by Podar contained arbitration clauses; however, the purchase orders referred to arbitration in New York City, while the contracts specified Bombay as the place of arbitration. When a dispute arose, I.T.A.D. sued in a U.S. court, while Podar moved to compel arbitration. Two arguments were advanced against compelling arbitration: I.T.A.D. asserted both that the declarations of the parties pertaining to arbitration were inconsistent, and that Podar's actions and conduct had waived the arbitration agreement. The U.S. District Court for the District of South Carolina at Charleston upheld the objection pertaining to waiver. On appeal, the Fourth Circuit Court of Appeals held that both objections were unfounded, and remanded the case to the District Court. According to the decision of the Court of Appeals, "the purchase orders and contracts submitted by the parties are in conflict regarding the place of arbitration; this conflict is remanded to the district court for resolution."[39]

It appears that the Fourth Circuit assumed that an arbitration agreement exists even though the parties remained at odds concerning the site of arbitration. (The site was, incidentally, the only element of the arbitration process specified.) An agreement was construed from the converging elements of two different declarations. Relying on the policy favoring arbitration, the court accorded paramount importance to the fact that both parties wanted arbitration.

Do you agree with the approach of the Fourth Circuit? Can a declaration opting for arbitration in Bombay (or New York) be interpreted as a willingness to arbitrate at a site to be determined by a court?

Can you distinguish *I.T.A.D. v. Podar* from *Nokia v. Mazzer*?

[38].   636 F.2d 75 (4th Cir.1981).   **[39].**   *Id.* at 77.

II.1.e. Jurisdiction By Virtue of Tacit or Post–Agreement Submission or Estoppel

WILLIAM CO. v. GUANGZHOV OCEAN SHIPPING CO.ᶜ

High Court of Hong Kong, 1993.
[1993] Hong Kong Law Digest 137.*

[Plaintiff, a cargo owner, brought an action in the High Court of Hong Kong against the defendant ship owner for damage to cargo. The claim was based on a bill of lading issued by the defendant in Hong Kong. The plaintiff claimed that under Hong Kong law the Hague–Visby Rules applied because the bill of lading was issued in Hong Kong. These Rules—and the earlier Hague Rules that they replaced—are based on a widely adopted international agreement (the 1924 Brussels Convention) regulating the liability of carriers for damage to cargo. The Rules provide that any provision of a bill of lading is invalid if it lessens the carrier's liability below a certain minimum amount for certain kinds of carrier negligence. The bill of lading contained the following clause:

> "3. All disputes arising out or in connection with this Bill of Lading shall, in accordance with Chinese Law, be resolved in the courts of the People's Republic of China or be arbitrated in the People's Republic of China."

The defendant sought to have the Hong Kong court refer the parties to arbitration in China. The plaintiff argued against such an order on two grounds: first, that the clause was unenforceable because too uncertain, given that it did not choose either arbitration or litigation to the exclusion of the other; and second, that the arbitration clause was not formally valid. This latter argument arose because the defendant had signed the bill of lading but the plaintiff had not. The formal validity issue was governed by the UNCITRAL Model Law, because Hong Kong had adopted the Model Law before the bill of lading was issued. Based on the provisions of Model Law Article 7(2), the clause was valid only if a positive answer could be given to one of two sub-issues: (1) whether there was an exchange of letters that provided a record of the agreement or (2) whether there had been an exchange of statements of claim and defense in which the existence of an agreement was alleged by one party and not denied by the other. The following correspondence was central to the analysis of these issues. By letter dated 27 November 1992, the defendant's solicitors wrote to the plaintiff's solicitors and stated:

> "Upon perusal of the relevant documents, we note that Clause 3 of the bill of lading * * * provides that 'all disputes arising from or related to this bill of lading should, in accordance with Chinese Law, be resolved in PRC Courts or by arbitration in PRC'.
>
> In the circumstances, we are of the view that the Hong Kong Court has no jurisdiction and the present proceedings should be dismissed."

c. The case excerpt reproduced after the summary of facts comes from N. Kaplan, J. Spruce, and M. Moser, eds., Hong Kong and China Arbitration Cases and Materials 209 (1994).

* Reprinted by permission of Sweet & Maxwell Asia, formerly FT Law & Tax Asia Pacific.

The next day the plaintiff's solicitors wrote back that, because of the operation of the Hague–Visby Rules, Clause 3 was invalid. They explained that those rules nullified any clause in the contract of carriage that lessened the carrier's liability below that provided for in the rules. They set out the clauses in the bill of lading that either excluded or lessened the carrier's liability and asserted that a People's Republic of China court would give effect to those terms in the bill of lading and not to the Hague–Visby Rules.

After the defendant's solicitors wrote on December 1 disagreeing with the plaintiff's solicitors' argument, the plaintiff's solicitors replied on December 14 and said:

> "It remains our view that Hong Kong is the proper and appropriate forum in which to determine our client's claim notwithstanding the express choice of law and jurisdiction clause contained in the bill of lading."

Affidavits were submitted by both parties. The plaintiff's affidavit stated as follows:

> "While the said Bill of Lading contains a choice of law/jurisdiction clause. I would ask this court to declare the said clause null, void and of no effect by reason of art III Rule 8 of the Hague–Visby Rules since the effect of the clause is to lessen and/or exclude the first defendant's liability, otherwise than would be the case pursuant to the Hague–Visby Rules. This fact has repeatedly been made to the first defendant's lawyers in correspondence * * *."

The defendant's solicitors argued that the correspondence between solicitors was an exchange of letters that provided a record of the agreement. They stressed that both parties had referred to the same bill of lading and to the same clause in which it was agreed that arbitration or litigation under Chinese law in China should be the method of dispute settlement. They also argued that the phrase "provide a record of the agreement" was broad enough to include correspondence that post-dated the arbitration agreement.

The defendant's solicitors also argued in the alternative that the correspondence itself was an exchange of statements of claim and defense in which the existence of an agreement was alleged by one side and not denied by the other. They pointed out that plaintiff's argument was that the clause was null and void because of the operation of the Hague–Visby Rules and not that the plaintiff had never agreed to any such clause. They argued further that although the words "statement of claim and defence" in Model Rule Art. 7(2) were originally intended to refer to submissions in an arbitration proceeding, the same rationale would support applying the phrase to court pleadings and other documents in which the parties set out their respective cases. The court ruled in favor of the defendant.][d]

* * *

d. Having decided that there was a formally valid arbitration agreement, the Hong Kong court stayed the proceedings in favor of arbitration. It left to the arbitrators

Held:

(1) The dispute resolution clause is not void for uncertainty. It is a clause in a commercial document and the court must strive to give it meaning within the context of the commercial relationship of the parties.

> In my judgment, this clause should be construed in the following manner. The parties have agreed on arbitration or litigation in China. When a dispute arises, the claimant has a choice. He can either seek arbitration or litigation in China. Once he has made the choice that is the end of the matter and the defendant will have no say. Once arbitration or litigation in China is chosen that creates a binding choice to which the court will usually give effect.

> However, in this case, the plaintiff opted for a method of dispute resolution not agreed upon in the contract, namely, litigation in Hong Kong. Thus it is open to the defendants to exercise their choice in the matter. By applying for a stay under art 8 of the Model Law, they have opted for arbitration in China. On this basis, the plaintiff's choice is invalid as it does not come within the range of options agreed upon. Subject to all other points, I conclude that, prima facie, the defendants are entitled to a stay in favour of arbitration in China because they have made a valid choice from one of the two permissible methods of dispute resolution contained in the bill of lading.

(2) The defendants have established that the bill of lading complies with art 7(2) of the Model Law.

> The purpose behind art 7(2) is to ensure that parties do not get forced into arbitration unless it is clear beyond doubt that they have agreed to it. This can either be proved by an agreement in writing or by an exchange of letters which provide a record of the agreement or an exchange of statements of claim and defence in which the existence of an agreement is alleged by one side and not denied by the other.

> On the facts of the present case art 7(2) has been complied with.

> If I were wrong there is a very strong case for further consideration of art 7 so as to bring within its ambit cases such as the present which are commonplace in a trading centre like Hong Kong [at p 16 of the judgment].

(3) The phrase "provide a record of the agreement" in art 7(2) is wide enough to include correspondence which post-dates the arbitration agreement.

> Take the reductio ad absurdum. If after a dispute arises, one party writes to the others and says "There is a clause in this bill of lading which provides for arbitration in China—do you agree?" Assume then that the other party replies "Yes, we agree that there is such a clause but we do not want arbitration in China and are going to institute court proceedings in Hong Kong and will resist vigorously

the issue of whether the Hague–Visby Rules
or Chinese law should apply on the merits.

any application you take out for a stay of such proceedings." Would it not be strange to say that there was no record of the agreement to arbitrate in China because the record came into being after the agreement was entered into and acted upon, albeit that it was not signed by one party?"

* * *

I have also considered the commentary to art 7 contained in Holtzman and Neuhaus' *Guide to The Uncitral Model Law* at p 263 where they say:

'The requirement of a "record" is to ensure that there is some writing involved.... It should be noted that the "exchange" of letters, telexes, etc. does not require that both mention the arbitration agreement, or even that one or both letters be signed. What is sought is a written form of assent from each party.' [at pp. 13, 14 of the judgment]

* * * It is clear that an agreement to arbitrate cannot be oral and then later be evidenced in writing. In this case the agreement is in writing and the plaintiff's assent to it is contained in the material to which the court referred.

I would only add that such assent can be given by either party's agent, in this case his solicitor, whose authority to act has never been withdrawn and whom I am entitled to assume obtained instructions before instituting these proceedings for damages based on this very bill of lading. [at p 14 of the judgment]

(4) There is a valid arbitration agreement within art 7(2).

Each case has to be considered on its own facts. In the present case, the material which I have set out above shows quite conclusively, in my judgment, that the parties did agree on arbitration or litigation in China and that such material contains a record of that agreement. I would further hold on the basis of the above material that the existence of the agreement to arbitrate or litigate in China is recorded in documents which can, without violence to the language, be described as statements of case and defence. I note that there is no definition of these terms in the Model Law and that they are not referred to with capital letters.

At the end of the day, the court has to be satisfied that these parties agreed on arbitration or litigation in China. It seems to me clear beyond doubt on this material that such agreement is recorded in the manner I have set out. I respectfully differ from Mayo J in concluding that material which post-dates the agreement to arbitrate can provide a record of the agreement to arbitrate. To decide otherwise, would seem to me to place an unnecessarily narrow construction on art 7(2) which does not do justice to the language used and which would produce a result which conflicts with the commercial reality of the situation. [at p. 15 of the judgment]

(5) As art. 7 of the Model Law has been complied with, there is no discretion other than to apply art. 8 of the Model Law and to stay these proceedings in favour of arbitration in China.

> I have to apply art 8 because I do not find that the agreement, namely, the arbitration agreement is null and void, inoperative or incapable of being performed. [at p 30 of the judgment]

(6) These proceedings are stayed under art 8 of the Model Law as sought by the defendants.

* * *

JIANGXI PROVINCIAL METAL AND MINERALS IMPORT AND EXPORT CORP. v. SULANSER CO., LTD.

Supreme Court of Hong Kong, 1995.
21 Yearbk. Comm. Arb'n 546 (1996).*

FACTS

Jiangxi Provincial Metal and Minerals Import and Export Corp. (Jiangxi or the plaintiff) and Sulanser Company Limited (Sulanser or the defendant) entered into a contract for the sale by Jiangxi of cement to Sulanser (the Agreement). The Agreement contained, *inter alia*, a dispute settlement clause providing for arbitration at the China International Economic Trade Arbitration Commission (CIETAC). The terms of the Agreement were reduced into writing, but were not signed by the parties.

Jiangxi delivered the cement by sea. There was a delay and Jiangxi had to pay demurrage for the vessel it had chartered. Jiangxi considered the delay to be due to a default by Sulanser and commenced legal proceedings against Sulanser at the Wuhan Admiralty Court, claiming compensation for the demurrage. Sulanser contested the claim and the jurisdiction of the court, invoking the arbitration clause in the Agreement. In view of Sulanser's argument, Jiangxi submitted a request for arbitration to CIETAC. The Wuhan Admiralty Court subsequently declined jurisdiction and referred the parties to arbitration.

After both parties had appointed arbitrators, Sulanser challenged the jurisdiction of the arbitrators because of the absence of a signed written agreement between the parties and, consequently, in its view, the absence of any arbitration agreement. The arbitrators rendered an interim award declaring to have jurisdiction over the dispute. They held there was an agreement between the parties which had been performed and that Sulanser had confirmed in writing that there was a binding arbitration clause, by its written defence invoking arbitration submitted to the Wuhan Maritime Court. Following that, Sulanser submitted a

* Reprinted with permission of Yearbook Commercial Arbitration, International Council for Commercial Arbitration.

substantive defence and made submissions to the arbitral tribunal. The arbitral tribunal rendered a final award in favour of Jiangxi.

Jiangxi applied for enforcement of the award and the Supreme Court of Hong Kong, High Court, *per* D.J. Leonard, J., issued an order granting leave to enforce the arbitration award. Sulanser applied for the setting aside of the order and of the judgment entered on the order, alleging, *inter alia*, that there was no arbitration agreement as a basis for arbitrators' jurisdiction. * * *

EXCERPT

* * *

[8] "If one looks at Art. II of the New York Convention as set out in the 3rd Schedule to the Arbitration Ordinance, one sees at paragraph 2 the following words: 'The term "agreement in writing" shall include an arbitral clause in a contract or an arbitration agreement, signed by the parties or contained in an exchange of letters or telegrams.' That definition is not exclusive and is not a bar to the application of Art. 7(2), which does not exclude any arbitration agreement covered by Art. II of the New York Convention.

[9] "The defendant has expressly alleged the existence of the arbitration agreement. In addition to the defendant's letter to the Maritime Court, there was a letter by way of defence sent to that Court by a firm of Hong Kong Solicitors acting for the defendant in that matter. It is dated 2 August 1991 and paragraph 6 is in the following terms:

'6. Finally, according to the sales contract, any contract disputes should be submitted to arbitration by the Foreign Trade Arbitration Commission of the China Council for the promotion of International Trade in Beijing. Also, in accordance with "foreign economic contract" (Article 38) only if a contract does not contain any arbitration clause, can the contracting parties commence court proceedings. Therefore, this matter should now be referred to arbitration by the Foreign Trade Arbitration Commission in Beijing.'

[10] "By those letters the defendant affirmed the existence of the contract, including the arbitration agreement and claimed that the matter should go to arbitration. The plaintiff accepted the allegation and produced the written record to the Wuhan Court. The matter did go to arbitration, and after a preliminary argument as to jurisdiction, the defendant submitted to the jurisdiction of CIETAC and proceeded to contest the plaintiff's claim on its merits. I find that the production [to] this court of the written terms of the contract, which include an arbitration clause, taken together with the defendant's letter and defence submitted to the Wuhan Maritime Court satisfy the requirements of Sect. 43 of the Ordinance.[e]

e. Authors' note: This section of the Hong Kong Ordinance implements Model Law Article 35, which itself tracks the language of New York Convention Article IV.

[11] "The defendant has argued that if there is to be reliance upon an exchange of letters, these must have been exchanged between the plaintiff and defendant. Accordingly, the defendant says that a letter sent by the defendant to the Wuhan Maritime Court does not satisfy the requirement of an exchange of letters. Art. 7(2) of the UNCITRAL Model Law does not specify an exchange directly between the parties. It simply specifies an exchange, as does Art. 2(2) of the Convention. It is clear that copies of documents submitted by each party to the Wuhan Court and to CIETAC were received by the other. Sect. 44(1) of the Ordinance provides that 'enforcement of a Convention award shall not be refused except in the cases mentioned in this Section'.

[12] "It has been suggested on the part of the defendant that the Arbitration Agreement was not valid under Chinese Law. One of the grounds for refusing enforcement is set out in Sect. 44(2)(b) as follows:

> "That the arbitration agreement was not valid under the law to which the parties subjected it or, failing any indication thereon, under the law of the country where the award was made;"[f]

The defendant wanted to call evidence as to Chinese Law in order to show that the arbitration agreement was invalid. I ruled that the defendant was estopped from claiming in this Court that the arbitration agreement was invalid.

* * *

CLAIMANT (AUSTRIA) v. RESPONDENT (GERMANY)

International Arbitral Tribunal of the Federal Economic Chamber, Vienna, 1994.
2 UNILEX, E. 1994–14, p. 331, No. SCH–4366.[g]

* * *

1. By the request of arbitration of 30 March 1993, the claimant [a company with place of business in Austria] applied for an award against the respondent [a company with place of business in Germany] for payment of a total of US$[. . .] DM [. . .]. It submitted that the respondent had not fulfilled its obligations on the basis of two contracts for the delivery of cold-rolled sheet concluded with the claimant, since it had either not taken delivery of or had not paid for part of the goods purchased.

* * *

3. The competence of Arbitral Centre is founded on the last paragraphs of the two contracts concluded between the parties. According

f. Authors' note: This section of the Hong Kong ordinance implements Model Law Article 36(1)(a)(i), which itself tracks the language of New York Convention Article V(1)(a).

g. Authors' note: UNILEX is a looseleaf service edited by Professor Michael Joachim

Bonnell and fully cited as 2 UNILEX, International Case Law & Bibliography on the UN Convention on Contracts for the International Sale of Goods (Tansnat'l Pub., Inc.).

thereto, all disputes that cannot be settled amicably should be finally decided according to the Arbitral Rules of the Austrian Federal Economic Chamber by one or more arbitrators appointed in accordance with those rules.

3.1   It is true that the contracts—and thus the aforesaid arbitration clause—exist only in the acknowledgment of order sent by the claimant to the respondent, which the latter never countersigned. However, there can be no doubt of the validity of the arbitration clause. The fact that Article II, paragraph 1 of the Convention on the Recognition and Enforcement of Foreign Arbitral Awards (The New York Convention), which applies in this case, provides that the agreement must be [in] writing, does not mean that the arbitration clause must be contained in a contractual document signed by both parties. According to article II, paragraph 2 of the New York Convention, an "arbitral clause in a contract or an arbitration agreement, signed by the parties or contained in an exchange of letters or telegrams" is sufficient. The predominant view in international legal writings is that the requirement is therefore also met if the addressee replies in writing to the acknowledgment of an order in such a way that need only conclusively show that he accepts the acknowledgment of the order together with the arbitration clause mentioned therein, for example, if he expressly refers in subsequent letters or invoices to the contractual document in question (see inter alia A.J. van den BERG, the New York Arbitration Convention of 1958, 1981, 198 ff.; P. SCHLOSSER, *Das Recht der internationalen privaten Schiedsgerichtsbarkeit*. 2. Aufl. 1989, 280; App. Firenze, 8.1.1977, Yearbook Commercial Arbitration IV (1979) 289).

3.2   That is exactly what happened in the present case. Though initially the respondent only tacitly accepted the two acknowledgments of the order by the claimant, it subsequently—to be precise in a letter to the claimant of 19 January 1993—expressly referred to the relevant contracts No. 19038 and No. 19101 and thus satisfied the requirement as to the written form of the arbitration clause contained therein.

3.3   Furthermore, in the present case, on the basis of the general legal principle of good faith, the respondent would be precluded from relying on the absence of an arbitration clause in writing for the purpose of negating the competence of the arbitral centre. Within a little less than three months, the respondent concluded three contracts with the claimant with essentially identical wording but never countersigned the acknowledgment of the orders together with the arbitration clause contained therein that were sent to it by the claimant. That did not prevent the respondent from relying on that specific arbitration clause and from entrusting the Arbitral centre of the Federal Economic Chamber of Austria specified therein with the settlement of a dispute concerning the second of the three contracts. To rely on one occasion on the arbitration clause signed only by the opposing party in order to assert one's own claims and, on a second occasion, when the opposing party goes to law, to dispute the validity of an arbitration clause agreed upon in exactly the same form, would not be compatible with the requirement of the observance of good faith and fair business dealings, which is also fully valid within the scope of the New York Convention (see also A.J. van den BERG, loc, cit, 182 ff.).

Questions and Comments

1. There have been arbitral awards rendered without a proper arbitration agreement, after one party referred the case to arbitration, and the other party did not contest the jurisdiction of the arbitral tribunal. When the award is not contested, the tacit submission of the dispute may yield an efficient settlement. If it is contested, the requirements of the New York Convention will create difficulties. It will be hard to reconcile tacit submission with the "agreement in writing" requirement of Article II(2) and with the Article IV(1) duty to submit "the original agreement referred to in Article II or a duly certified copy thereof."

Article 7(2) of the Model Law seeks to help by stretching the notion of "agreement in writing" to encompass: "an exchange of statements of claim and defence in which the existence of an agreement is alleged by one party and not denied by another." This provision normally assumes an exchange of statements of claim and defense **before the arbitral tribunal**. *William v. Guanghzov* seems to suggest that such an exchange may also take place before courts. Do you agree?

2. In *William v. Guanghzov*, it is difficult to consider the behavior of the parties as a tacit or post agreement submission to arbitration. The plaintiff in the court proceedings clearly opposed arbitration; it did not contest the existence of an arbitration agreement, presumably because it considered the ground on which it contested arbitration sufficient. (It is true, of course, that the bill of lading did contain an arbitration clause; however, it was not signed by both parties.) Is this decision in accordance with the Model Law? Is the award recognizable under the New York Convention? Is the result fair?

3. In *Jiangxi v. Sulanser* two arguments were advanced to support the jurisdiction of the CIETAC: (1) an exchange of written communications providing a record of the arbitration agreement, and (2) estoppel. Which argument do you find more persuasive?

Could one argue that an arbitration agreement was created in this case through an exchange of statements of claim and defense?

Was there a tacit submission in this case?

4. Suppose Claimant addresses an arbitration tribunal without alleging the existence of an arbitration agreement (without mentioning the issue of jurisdiction), and Respondent in its statement of defense pleads only issues pertaining to the merits without contesting (or mentioning) jurisdiction. Would an arbitration agreement have been created under Article 7(2) of the Model Law?

5. In *Jiangxi v. Sulanser* the Hong Kong court applied Hong Kong's version of the UNCITRAL Model Law to decide whether to enforce the award. Section 43 of the Hong Kong Ordinance implements Article 35 of the Model Law, which itself tracks the language of New York Convention Article IV. Do you agree that the arbitration agreement meets the requirements of

Article IV of the Convention—and by reference back under the terms of Article IV(1)(b), those of Article II of the Convention?

6.   To support its view that the Model Law Art. 7(2) definition of "agreement in writing" is consistent with Art. II(2) of the New York Convention, the Hong Kong court stressed: "That definition [in Art. II(2) of the New York Convention] is not exclusive and is not a bar to the application of Art. 7(2), which does not exclude any arbitration agreement covered by Art. II of the New York Convention." The relevant language of Article II(2) of the Convention is: "The term 'agreement in writing' shall *include* * * *." (emphasis added) Do you agree that the Article II(2) definition—at least in English—is not exclusive?

Article XVI of the New York Convention says: "the Chinese, English, French, Russian and Spanish texts shall be equally authentic." The following are the relevant portions of Article II(2) in French, Spanish, and Russian, all official languages, and also German, an unofficial language:

French: "2. *On entend par* 'convention écrite' * * * ['agreement in writing' *means* * * *]" (emphasis added)

Spanish: "2. La expresión 'acuerdo por escrito' *denotará* * * * [The expression 'agreement in writing' *denotes* [or *means*] * * *]" (emphasis added)

Russian: "2. Termin 'pis'mennoe soglashenie' *vklyuchaet* * * * [The term 'agreement in writing' *includes* * * *]" (emphasis added)

German: "2. Unter einer 'schriftlichen Vereinbarung' *ist* eine Schiedsklausel in einem Vertrag oder eine Schiedsabrede *zu verstehen*, * * * ['agreement in writing' *means* * * *]" (emphasis added)

Do these language differences affect your view of how to interpret Article II(2) of the New York Convention? Is Article II(2) exclusive or not?

7.   The defendant in *Jiangxi v. Sulanser* raised a second invalidity claim, based on Section 44(2)(b) of the Hong Kong Ordinance, implementing Article 36(1)(a)(i) of the Model Law, which itself tracks the language of New York Convention Article V(1)(a). The court found the defendant estopped from raising this claim. Had there been no estoppel, would this have been a good defense? If an arbitration agreement satisfies the requirements of Article IV of the Convention (and hence those of Article II), could it at the same time fail to meet the requirements of Article V(1)(a)? Is Article V(1)(a) limited to "material invalidity" claims, or does it also encompass "formal invalidity" arguments? We focus on Article V grounds for refusing enforcement of an award in Chapter V infra.

8.   The estoppel principle is not unique to common law legal systems. In Germany the principle finds support in the general obligation of performance in good faith (*Treu und Glauben*) contained in Article 242 of the German Civil Code. The maxim *non concedit venire contra factum proprium* has also wide application in civil law countries. Moreover, it has been suggested that the prohibition against contradicting oneself to the detriment

of others is a general principle of international commercial law.[40] The same idea has a strong foothold in the sphere of Public International Law as well: the International Court of Justice held in the *Temple Vihear* case that "one state should not be permitted to rely on its own inconsistency to the detriment of another state."[41]

Those who want arbitration and whose only hope is estoppel do not lack resources, but they do not have certainty. Arguing on the ground of general principles is more difficult than arguing on the basis of explicit rules.

9.   According to Article 16(3) of the Commercial Arbitration and Mediation Center for the Americas (CAMCA) Mediation and Arbitration Rules[42]

[o]bjections to the arbitrability of the claim must be raised no later than thirty (30) days after notice to the parties of the commencement of the arbitration by CAMCA and, in respect to a counterclaim, not later than thirty (30) days after filing the counterclaim.

If claimant sues on the ground of an unsigned contract containing an arbitration clause and respondent does not oppose arbitration within 30 days, do we have a valid arbitration agreement? (If your answer is yes, what is the legal ground of jurisdiction. Is there a ground in the CAMCA Rules? Do these Rules apply without a preexisting valid arbitration agreement? Can you find a ground in the Model Law? Is this an estoppel situation?)

10.   Like the CAMCA provision (and other institutional norms), Article 21(3) of the UNCITRAL Rules states:

"A plea that the arbitral tribunal does not have jurisdiction shall be raised not later than in the statement of defence, or with respect to counter-claim, in the reply to the counter-claim."

Does this formulation allow variants of tacit submission which are not encompassed by Article 7(2) of the Model Law?

Can the jurisdiction of the arbitration tribunal ever be established when, in the face of an unsigned arbitration agreement, the Respondent simply says nothing?

11.   In *Claimant (Austria) v. Respondent (Germany)*, the Vienna arbitrators identified two alternative bases for their jurisdiction.

The first argument takes us back to the issue of written form. In evaluating this argument (outlined in subsections 3.1 and 3.2 of the Award), one would like to know the exact words in the Respondent's letter to Claimant of January 19, 1993 referring to the relevant contracts. Suppose Respondent wrote, "I expect our next contract to be drafted along the same lines as your order acknowledgment No. . . . ". Would this satisfy Article II(2) of the New York Convention? Or suppose the relevant part of the letter read: "Next time we shall order only one half of the amount of cold-rolled sheet stated in your order acknowledgment No. . . . "

[40].   See E. Gaillard, L'interdiction de se contredire au détriment d'autrui comme principe général du droit du commerce international, Revue de l'Arbitrage 241 (1984).

[41].   International Court of Justice Reports 1962, 6 and 63; See also Bin Cheng, General Principles of Law as Applied by International Tribunals 143 (1954).

[42].   Effective March 15, 1996, 35 Int'l Legal Materials 1541, 1554 (1996).

12. The second argument advanced by the Vienna arbitrators is based on good faith. Do you agree with the conclusion reached by the arbitrators?

As we have seen, estoppel and good faith doctrines do not countenance contradictions and inconsistencies in a party's actions. The estoppel doctrine protects an opposing party who relies on one of these inconsistent actions; the good faith doctrine is broader and does not require reliance. In the Vienna case, Respondent clearly did contradict himself, but not within the same lawsuit. The Vienna arbitrators did not find this to be critical. Would you?

Does the good faith argument of the Vienna arbitrators have any support in the provisions of either Article II of the New York Convention or Article 7 of the Model Law?

UNCITRAL WORKING GROUP DRAFT PROPOSAL TO AMEND MODEL LAW ARTICLE 7

United Nations General Assembly Document A/CN.9/WG.II/Wp.118 (Feb. 6, 2002) (as agreed to be amended by the Working Group on Arbitration, U.N. General Assembly Document A/CN.9/508 (April 12, 2002))

Article 7. Definition and form of arbitration agreement

(1) "Arbitration agreement" is an agreement by the parties to submit to arbitration all or certain disputes which have arisen or which may arise between them in respect of a defined legal relationship, whether contractual or not. An arbitration agreement may be in the form of an arbitration clause in a contract or in the form of a separate agreement.

(2) The arbitration agreement shall be in writing. "Writing" means any form, including without limitation a data message, that provides a record of the agreement or is otherwise accessible so as to be usable for subsequent reference.

(3) "Data message" means information generated, sent, received or stored by electronic, optical or similar means including, but not limited to, electronic data interchange (EDI), electronic mail, telegram, telex or telecopy.

(4) Furthermore, an arbitration agreement is in writing if it is contained in an exchange of statements of claim and defence in which the existence of an agreement is alleged by one party and not denied by the other.

(5) For the avoidance of doubt, the reference in a contract or a separate arbitration agreement to a writing containing an arbitration clause constitutes an arbitration agreement in writing provided that the reference is such as to make that clause part of the contract or the separate arbitration agreement, notwithstanding that the contract or the separate arbitration agreement has been concluded orally, by conduct or by other means not in writing. In such a case, the writing containing the

arbitration clause constitutes the arbitration agreement for purposes of article 35.

Questions and Comments

1. What are the major differences between this proposed amendment and the current version of Model Law Article 7?

How would each of the following examples be treated under the proposed amendment and under the existing Model Law Article 7?

(a) A maritime salvage contract concluded orally through radio with a reference to a pre-existing standard contract form containing an arbitration agreement, such as Lloyd's Open Form.

(b) A contract concluded by performance or by conduct with reference to a standard form containing an arbitration clause, such as documents established by the Grain and Food Trade Association (GAFTA).

(c) A contract concluded orally but subsequently confirmed in writing or otherwise linked to a written document containing an arbitration clause, such as the general sale or purchase conditions established unilaterally by a party and communicated to the other.

(d) A purely oral contract.

2. Would you favor UNCITRAL's adopting this amendment? With or without modifications?

3. The UNCITRAL Working Group on Arbitration is also considering a proposal that UNCITRAL adopt an interpretive declaration, which would not have binding force, containing the following (or similar) language:

"Declaration regarding interpretation of article II(2) of the Convention on the Recognition and Enforcement of Foreign Arbitral Awards, done at New York, 10 June 1958

"The United Nations Commission on International Trade Law,

* * *

"[7] *Concerned about* differing interpretations of article II(2) of the Convention that result in part from differences of expression as between the five equally authentic texts of the Convention,

"[8] *Desirous of* promoting uniform interpretation of the Convention in the light of the development of new communication technologies and of electronic commerce,

"[9] *Convinced* that uniformity in the interpretation of the term "agreement in writing" is necessary for enhancing certainty in international commercial transactions,

"[10] *Considering* that in interpreting the Convention regard is to be had to its international origin and to the need to promote uniformity in its application,

"[11] *Taking into account* subsequent international legal instruments, such as the UNCITRAL Model Law on International Commercial Arbitration and the UNCITRAL Model Law on Electronic Commerce,

"[12] [*Recommends*] [*Declares*] that the definition of 'agreement in writing' contained in article II(2) of the Convention should be interpreted to include [wording inspired from the revised text of article 7 of the UNCITRAL Model Law on International Commercial Arbitration]".

See "Report of the Working Group on Arbitration" on the work of its thirty-sixth session (New York, 4–8 March 2002), U.N. Gen'l Assembly Document A/CN.9/508 (12 April 2002) subsection II(B).

Would you favor UNCITRAL's adopting such a declaration? Or, would you prefer instead that UNCITRAL draft and promote for adoption a Protocol to the New York Convention amending Article II(2)? (A protocol is an international treaty binding only those countries that adopt it.) What would be the advantages and disadvantages of each of these approaches—an interpretive declaration, on one hand, and a protocol amending the New York Convention, on the other?

If you favor an amending protocol, what should it say? How should it differ from the current Article II(2)?

4. Read Section 1031 of the 1998 German arbitration statute (German Code of Civil Procedure, Chapter 10) in the Documents Supplement. Is it consistent with New York Convention Article II(2)?

New York Convention Article VII (1) contains a provision sometimes characterized as a "more-favorable-right" concept. For those countries that prefer a less strict approach to the writing requirement (would Germany be an example?), is Article VII a workable solution to the writing requirement? Would it apply to enforcing an arbitration agreement?

II.1.f. Scope of the Arbitration Clause—Settlements and Renewals

MEDITERRANEAN ENTERPRISES, INC. v. SSANGYONG CORP.

United States Court of Appeals, Ninth Circuit, 1983.
708 F.2d 1458.

NELSON, CIRCUIT JUDGE:

Defendant-appellant Ssangyong Construction Co. (Ssangyong) appeals the district court's interlocutory order staying the action and sending to arbitration certain issues raised in a complaint filed by plaintiff-appellee Mediterranean Enterprises, Inc. (MEI). Ssangyong contends that the district court improperly interpreted the scope of the arbitration clause in a contract between the parties. We affirm the district court's order.

FACTUAL AND PROCEDURAL BACKGROUND

MEI, a California corporation, provides engineering services for modular housing projects in developing countries. In May, 1978, MEI was invited by the Saudi Arabian Royal Commission to bid on certain construction projects in Saudi Arabia. In connection with this invitation, MEI contacted Ssangyong, a Korean contractor.

On September 9, 1978, in Los Angeles, MEI and Ssangyong signed a "Preliminary Agreement for Formation of a Joint Venture" (Agreement). The arbitration clause in the Agreement provides as follows:

> Any disputes arising hereunder or following the formation of joint venture shall be settled through binding arbitration pursuant to the Korean–U.S. Arbitration Agreement, with arbitration to take place in Seoul, Korea.

Subsequently, MEI and Ssangyong entered into an Agency Agreement dated October 21, 1978, with Trac Enterprises, providing that Trac would serve as the agent of the joint venture in Saudi Arabia.

The contemplated MEI—Ssangyong joint venture was never actually formed. In its complaint, MEI alleges that Ssangyong used the Agreement merely to gain access to the Saudi projects, and wrongfully commenced the projects in association with Trac (named as a defendant below) rather than with MEI. Ssangyong claims that no breach occurred, and that its non-performance of the Agreement was due to its inability to obtain certain Korean government approvals required by paragraph 20 of the Agreement.[1]

On November 5, 1980, MEI commenced this action in district court. The complaint contains six counts against Ssangyong: breach of contract and breach of fiduciary duty (counts 1, 2 and 4), inducing and conspiracy to induce breach of contract [the Trac Agency Agreement] (count 7), quantum meruit (count 8), and conversion (count 9).[2]

On November 9, 1981, the district court rejected MEI's contention that Ssangyong had fraudulently inserted the words "arising hereunder or" in the arbitration clause, and ordered Ssangyong to prepare findings of fact and conclusions of law on all of the issues relating to its motion to stay the proceedings pending arbitration. Ssangyong submitted its proposed findings and conclusions, which the court signed shortly thereafter. On December 1, 1981, the court held a hearing on the scope of the arbitration clause and took the matter under submission.

On July 19, 1982, the court entered its order amending one earlier conclusion of law, stating:

> The issues raised by Counts 1, 2 and 4 of Mediterranean Enterprises, Inc.'s Complaint against Ssangyong Construction Co., Ltd. are found to be arbitrable and are ordered to arbitration between said parties pursuant to paragraph 16 of the Preliminary Agreement of September 9, 1978 between Mediterranean Enterprises, Inc. and Ssangyong Construction Co., Ltd.

The order also provides that "the action is stayed pending receipt by this court of the results of the arbitration between [MEI] and [Ssangyong]." It is from this order that Ssangyong appeals.

* * *

---

1. On February 16, 1981, Ssangyong filed a Request for Arbitration in Korea with the Korean Commercial Arbitration Board.

2. Counts 3, 5 and 6 of the complaint, which involve only defendants Trac Enterprises and its president, are not involved in this appeal.

The parties cite strong policies in support of their respective positions. Ssangyong argues that federal policy favors the enforcement of arbitration agreements, especially in international business transactions, citing *Scherk v. Alberto–Culver Co.*, 417 U.S. 506, 516–17, 94 S.Ct. 2449, 2455–56, 41 L.Ed.2d 270, 279–80 (1974). MEI does not dispute the existence of such a federal policy, but counters by arguing that "arbitration is a matter of contract and a party cannot be required to submit to arbitration any dispute which he has not agreed to submit," quoting *United Steelworkers v. Warrior & Gulf Navigation Co.*, 363 U.S. 574, 582, 80 S.Ct. 1347, 1353, 4 L.Ed.2d 1409, 1417 (1960). Both statements are sound, and are not at all unreconcilable. Ultimately, the issue of arbitrability "is to be determined by the contract entered into by the parties." * * * The task before this court remains one of contractual interpretation.

C. Scope of "arising hereunder"

Ssangyong argues that the arbitration clause "was designed to cover 'any' disputes between the parties." MEI argues that the phrase "arising hereunder" means "arising under the contract itself" and was not intended to cover "matters or claims independent of the contract or collateral thereto." Neither side points to, and additional research has not uncovered, cases in this circuit which define "arising hereunder" in the context of an arbitration agreement. However, we are persuaded by a line of cases from the Second Circuit that MEI's interpretation is the more reasonable one.[5]

We interpret "arising hereunder" as synonymous with "arising under the Agreement." The phrase "arising under" has been called "relatively narrow as arbitration clauses go." *Sinva, Inc. v. Merrill, Lynch, Pierce, Fenner & Smith, Inc.*, 253 F.Supp. 359, 364 (S.D.N.Y. 1966). In *In re Kinoshita & Co.*, 287 F.2d 951, 953 (2d Cir.1961), Judge Medina concluded that when an arbitration clause "refers to disputes or controversies 'under' or 'arising out of' the contract," arbitration is restricted to "disputes and controversies relating to the interpretation of the contract and matters of performance." Judge Medina reasoned that

5. The cases cited by Ssangyong in support of its broad interpretation are unpersuasive. Most cited cases involve arbitration clauses which were drafted in broader terms and intended to cover a broader spectrum of disputes than the clause involved here. *See, e.g., Griffin v. Semperit of America, Inc.*, 414 F.Supp. 1384, 1387 (S.D.Tex. 1976) (clause read, "[a]ny controversy or claim arising out of or relating to this agreement"); *Acevedo Maldonado v. PPG Indus., Inc.*, 514 F.2d 614, 616 (1st Cir. 1975) (same); *Altshul Stern & Co., Inc. v. Mitsui Bussan Kaisha, Ltd.*, 385 F.2d 158, 159 (2d Cir.1967) (clause read, "any dispute . . . arising out of or relating to this contract or the breach thereof"). Most of the cases cited by Ssangyong also involve disputes more clearly arising under the contract than those involved here. *See, e.g., Haig Berberian, Inc. v. Cannery Warehousemen*, 535 F.2d 496, 499 (9th Cir.1976) (holding arbitrable a claim which itself purported to be based on an interpretation of the contract); *Georgia Power Co. v. Cimarron Coal Corp.*, 526 F.2d 101, 106 (6th Cir.1975), *cert. denied*, 425 U.S. 952, 96 S.Ct. 1727, 48 L.Ed.2d 195 (1976) (holding that, under an arbitration clause which read, "any controversy . . . arising under this Agreement," no "provision of the contract [was] wholly outside of the arbitration provision").

the phrase "arising under" is narrower in scope than the phrase "arising out of or relating to," the standard language recommended by the American Arbitration Association. *Id.*

In a recent case, a district court amplified Judge Medina's reasoning. In *Michele Amoruso E Figli v. Fisheries Development Corp.*, 499 F.Supp. 1074, 1080 (S.D.N.Y.1980), the court discussed the Supreme Court's interpretation of an arbitration clause, noting that "arising out of or relating to this agreement" had been labelled a "broad arbitration clause." *Id.* (quoting *Prima Paint Corp. v. Flood & Conklin Mfg. Co.*, 388 U.S. 395, 398, 87 S.Ct. 1801, 1803, 18 L.Ed.2d 1270, 1274 (1967)). The court went on to say that in the case before it, "the clause is limited to differences or disputes 'arising out of this Agreement'; notably, it omits reference to disputes 'relating to' the agreements. The omission is significant in the Second Circuit." *Michele Amoruso E Figli*, 499 F.Supp. at 1080.

The omission should be significant in this circuit as well. The standard clause suggested in the U.S.–Korean Commercial Arbitration Agreement contains the phrase, "out of or in relation to or in connection with this contract, or for the breach thereof." We have no difficulty finding that "arising hereunder" is intended to cover a much narrower scope of disputes, i.e., only those relating to the interpretation and performance of the contract itself.

D. *Arbitrability of claims*

In light of our interpretation of the arbitration clause in the Agreement, we must next decide whether the district court properly sent "the issues raised by" counts 1, 2 and 4 to arbitration. This entails examining MEI's complaint to determine the extent to which the counts against Ssangyong refer to disputes or controversies relating to the interpretation and performance of the contract itself.

Counts 1, 2 and 4, alleging breach of the Agreement and breach of the fiduciary duty created by the Agreement, clearly fall within the scope of the arbitration clause and are thus proper subjects for arbitration. However, counts 7, 8 and 9 appear to raise issues that are either primarily or wholly outside the scope of the arbitration clause.

Count 7 alleges that Ssangyong induced and conspired to induce breach of the Trac Agency Agreement, a separate and distinct contract. Ssangyong's alleged conduct appears to relate only peripherally to the MEI–Ssangyong Agreement, and could have been accomplished even if the Agreement did not exist. Count 7 therefore alleges activity and raises issues which are predominantly unrelated to the central conflict over the interpretation and performance of the Agreement.

Count 8 sets forth a claim in quantum meruit, which by its own terms rests on the theory that services were performed and accepted pursuant to an implied contract or "quasi-contract." An action does not lie on an implied contract where there exists between the parties a valid express contract which covers the identical subject matter. *Swanson v.*

Levy, 509 F.2d 859, 861 (9th Cir.1975). Thus, by definition, count 8 does not directly relate to the interpretation and performance of the Agreement itself.

Count 9 alleges that Ssangyong converted to its own use and benefit certain prequalification documents delivered by MEI. The Agreement provides only that each of the parties would bear his own costs at the prequalification stage. MEI's claim that Ssangyong misappropriated these documents appears to raise issues largely distinct from the central conflict over the interpretation and performance of the Agreement itself.

By sending "the issues raised by" counts 1, 2 and 4 to arbitration, the district court authorized the arbitrator, in accordance with the expressed intention of the parties, to decide those issues relating to the interpretation and performance of the Agreement. Counts 1, 2 and 4 appear to be completely arbitrable. By deciding those issues necessary to resolve counts 1, 2 and 4, the arbitrator might well decide issues which bear in some way on the court's ultimate disposition of counts 7, 8 and 9. Nothing in the district court's order, or in this opinion, would bar such a result. The arbitrator's award, if it clearly exceeds the scope of his authority by deciding a matter not within the ambit of the arbitration clause, will not be given effect by the court. *See Los Angeles Paper Bag Co. v. Printing Specialities and Paper Products Union*, 345 F.2d 757, 760 (9th Cir.1965); *Lundgren v. Freeman*, 307 F.2d 104, 109–10 (9th Cir. 1962). *See also Davis v. Chevy Chase Financial Ltd.*, 667 F.2d 160, 165 (D.C.Cir.1981). After the district court receives the results of the arbitration, it should proceed to adjudicate those issues which fall outside the scope of the arbitration clause.

CONCLUSION

We find the district court's order staying the action and sending to arbitration certain issues raised by MEI's complaint proper in all respects.

Accordingly, the order is

AFFIRMED.

ERMENEGILDO ZEGNA CORP. v. LANIFICIO MARIO ZEGNA S.P.A.

United States District Court, Southern District of New York, 1996.
1996 WL 721079.

OPINION AND ORDER

LEISURE, DISTRICT JUDGE:

This action arises out of a Stipulation and Agreement and Order so ordered by this Court on April 9, 1987 (the "Agreement"). Plaintiff, Ermenegildo Zegna Corporation, and its parent corporation, Lanificio Ermenegildo Zegna, S.p.A. ("LEZ"), entered into the Agreement with defendant, Lanificio Mario Zegna S.P.A. ("LMZ"), to resolve an international trademark dispute regarding the use of the ZEGNA trademark. The Agreement includes a no-contest clause and an arbitration provision. Following a recent change in Italian trademark law, defendant served a Petition for Arbitration against EZC and LEZ in Italy seeking an equitable modification of the Agreement in light of the change in the law. Plaintiff contends that this arbitration constitutes a violation of the Agreement's no-contest clause. Plaintiff moves, by way of order to show cause, for an order of civil contempt against defendant, and for summary enforcement of the Agreement by way of permanent injunction. Defendant moves for an order staying this action and compelling plaintiff to submit to arbitration in Milan, Italy. For the reasons set forth below, plaintiff's motion is denied and defendant's motion is granted.

BACKGROUND

Plaintiff is a New York corporation engaged in the business of wholesaling and retailing high fashion men's clothing throughout the United States and Canada. Plaintiff's parent corporation, LEZ, is an Italian corporation engaged in the business of designing, manufacturing, selling and distributing high fashion clothing and fine fabric throughout the world. Plaintiff owns several U.S. trademark registrations incorporating the name ZEGNA. Defendant is an Italian corporation engaged in the business of weaving and selling fine woolen fabrics. Plaintiff and defendant originated from the same Italian family which began to manufacture woolen fabrics in 1915. By 1941, the family business had divided into two separate companies. To avoid disputes over the ZEGNA name, the two companies entered into an agreement on December 30, 1949, regulating the use of the ZEGNA name in Italy and elsewhere.

This agreement lasted for over thirty-five years, until plaintiff initiated an action before this Court for trademark infringement and unfair competition based on defendant's use of the name Mario Zegna in the United States. The parties were able to negotiate a settlement embodied in the Agreement so ordered by this Court on April 9, 1987. The Agreement purported to resolve all disputes over the ZEGNA mark and dictated the precise manner in which defendant could use the name Mario Zegna in the future. Two provisions contained in the Agreement are key in the present action. The first is an arbitration clause which states:

> Should there be any dispute arising between the parties with respect to the interpretation of this Agreement and Stipulation or with respect to the rights, duties and obligations undertaken by the parties herein, or arising herefrom, * * * [i]f such dispute arises in the Republic of Italy, it shall be submitted for arbitration in Milan, Italy under Section 806 et. seq. of the Italian Code of Civil Proceedings.

The second is a no-contest clause which provides:

> The parties agree that they will not contest the validity of this Agreement and Stipulation or seek to set it aside in any proceeding.

If any portion or provision, hereof, is found to be invalid, the balance of the Agreement ... will continue to be in full force and effect as among the parties.

A change in Italian trademark law liberalizing the treatment of co-existing trademarks using the same surnames prompted defendant to commence the arbitration on or about July 19, 1996. Defendant claims that the change in the law raises considerations regarding the fairness of the Agreement as it affects the parties in Italy.

* * *

The resolution of this action turns upon the interplay between the Agreement's arbitration and no-contest provisions. The defendant claims that the underlying dispute is within the scope of the arbitration provision. The plaintiff argues that the no-contest clause excludes the underlying dispute from arbitration. The Court will address these contentions in order.

A. *The Arbitration Clause*

The arbitration clause provides for the arbitration of two types of disputes: (1) disputes regarding an interpretation of the Agreement; and (2) disputes regarding the rights, duties and obligations undertaken by the parties. Defendant first argues that the underlying dispute involves an interpretation of the Agreement. This argument is without merit. Webster's Third New International Dictionary 1182 (1981), defines the word "interpretation" as, "1: the act or the result of interpreting: as a: explanation of what is not immediately plain or explicit ... or unmistak-able...." Defendant does not claim that the terms of the Agreement are unclear or ambiguous; rather, it claims that the terms of the Agreement are unfair in light of the recent change in Italian law. Defendant, through the arbitration, does not seek an explanation of provisions contained in the Agreement; rather, it seeks to eliminate or modify certain provisions. Defendant's argument that the arbitration seeks an interpretation of the Agreement is inconsistent with the plain meaning of the word interpretation. The first clause of the arbitration clause is not susceptible of an interpretation that covers the underlying dispute.

Defendant next argues that the underlying dispute concerns the rights, duties and obligations of the parties and therefore falls within the second clause of the arbitration provision. The dispute underlying the Milan arbitration arose because of a change in Italian trademark law liberalizing the treatment of co-existing trademarks using the same surnames. Defendant claims that the liberalization raises equitable considerations regarding the Agreement as it applies in Italy. In light of this change in the law, defendant seeks to modify or eliminate certain rights, duties and obligations of the parties in Italy. Plaintiff vigorously opposes these proposed modifications to the rights, duties and obligations. The Court cannot say with positive assurance that this dispute falls outside the scope of the arbitration clause. To the contrary, it is quite possible that this dispute is one regarding the rights, duties and obligations of the parties.

Plaintiff argues that the second part of the arbitration provision only applies to disputes of implementation. In other words, plaintiff contends that the clause refers to situations where one party is not performing its rights, duties or obligations under the Agreement. This reading is more narrow than the plain language of the provision. Paragraph 12(a) broadly states that "any dispute ... with respect to the rights, duties and obligations" of the parties shall be submitted to arbitration. If the parties intended to limit the scope of arbitration provision to disputes of implementation, they would not have used the word "any." They would have used language similar to that used in the arbitration provision at issue in Washburn v. Societe Commerciale de Reassurance, 831 F.2d 149 (7th Cir.1987). The provision in that case stated, "Should any difference of opinion arise between the [parties] which cannot be resolved in the normal course of business with respect to the interpretation of this Agreement or the performance of the respective obligations of the parties under this Agreement, the difference shall be submitted to arbitration." Although plaintiff's reading of the arbitration provision is plausible, it does not comport with the well-settled principle that "any doubts concerning the scope of arbitrable issues should be resolved in favor of arbitration." Mitsubishi Motors Corp., 473 U.S. at 626 (quoting Moses H. Cone Mem'l Hosp., 460 U.S. at 24–25) (internal quotation marks omitted). Accordingly, the Court finds that the arbitration clause is susceptible of an interpretation that covers the underlying dispute. See Oneida Indian Nation, 90 F.3d at 61; Spear, Leeds & Kellogg, 85 F.3d at 28; Leadertex, Inc., 67 F.3d at 27.

B. The No–Contest Clause

Although the underlying dispute appears to be arbitrable when considering paragraph 12(a) in isolation, the Court must consider the Agreement in its entirety. See Oneida Indian Nation, 90 F.3d at 63 (emphasizing "the cardinal principle of contract construction that all provisions of a contract should be given effect if possible)" (citing Mastrobuono v. Shearson Lehman Hutton, Inc., 115 S. Ct. 1212, 1219 (1995)). Thus, the Court must still determine whether the no-contest clause operates to exclude this type of dispute from arbitration in light of the principle that provisions which purport to exclude certain disputes from arbitration must be "clear and unambiguous." Genesco, 815 F.2d at 847 (quoting S.A. Mineracao Da Trindade–Samitri, 745 F.2d at 194) (internal quotation marks omitted); see Oneida Indian Nation, 90 F.3d at 62.

The Court's analysis begins with the language of the no-contest clause, which states that the parties shall not "contest the validity of th[e] Agreement and Stipulation or seek to set it aside in any proceeding." The clear and unambiguous language of the clause prohibits the parties from contesting the Agreement in its entirety but does not prohibit the parties from contesting certain provisions contained in the

Agreement. It does not state that the parties shall not contest the validity of any provision of the Agreement or seek to set aside any provision of the Agreement. The parties involved in this case are sophisticated. If they intended to preclude challenges to specific provisions of the Agreement, they could have clearly expressed such an intent. Furthermore, the no-contest clause contains a severability provision which states that "[i]f any portion or provision, hereof, however, is found to be invalid, the balance of the Agreement . . . will continue to be in full force and effect as among the parties." Id. This language contemplates that certain provisions of the Agreement may be eliminated without doing violence to the whole. Based on the language of the Agreement, the Court finds that the no-contest clause only precludes challenges to the Agreement in its entirety. Therefore, the Milan arbitration does not constitute a violation of the no-contest provision unless it seeks to "contest the validity of" the entire Agreement or "seek[s] to set it aside" in its entirety.

The Milan arbitration seeks an equitable modification of paragraphs five, seven, and nine of the Agreement. The arbitration does not seek to eliminate or modify any of the other eighteen paragraphs contained in the Agreement. At oral argument, plaintiff conceded that the defendant does not, by the Milan arbitration, seek to set aside the Agreement in its entirety. However, plaintiff argued that the paragraphs that the Arbitration seeks to eliminate or modify are so central to the Agreement, that a challenge to them is, in effect, a challenge to the entire Agreement. The Court recognizes that at some point, a challenge to certain provisions of the Agreement would be equivalent to a challenge to the Agreement as a whole. If, for example, the arbitration sought to eliminate every provision in the Agreement except for the no-contest clause, the arbitration would certainly be improper. The Court need not decide at what specific point a challenge to particular provisions would violate the no-contest clause because that point has not been reached in the present case. Furthermore, although paragraphs five, seven, and nine contain important restrictions on the future use of the ZEGNA name, the arbitration only seeks to modify those paragraphs as they apply in Italy. Regardless of the outcome of the Milan arbitration, those paragraphs will remain in effect in every country throughout the world except for Italy.[2] The Milan arbitration does not violate the no-contest clause because it does not seek to invalidate or set aside the Agreement in its entirety.

In sum, the Court cannot say with positive assurance that the underlying dispute does not involve the rights, duties and obligations of the parties. Furthermore, the no-contest clause which prohibits chal-

---

2. The Court notes that if the terms of the Agreement are modified in Italy, it will be difficult to contain the effects of the modification within the Italian borders. Inevitably, items manufactured in Italy, that violate the terms of the Agreement as it stands outside of Italy, will enter the stream of commerce and cross the Italian border. This spillover will lead to future litigation over whether such items violate the terms of the Agreement. Although this issue is of concern to the Court, it goes to the merits of the dispute and not to whether the dispute is arbitrable. Thus, the Italian arbitration panel, and not this Court, must address the spillover problem.

lenges to the Agreement in its entirety does not clearly and unambiguously exclude the underlying dispute from the scope of the arbitration clause. Interpreting the arbitration and no-contest provisions in light of the "strong federal policy favoring arbitration as an alternative means of dispute resolution," Oneida Indian Nation, 90 F.3d at 61, the Court finds that the underlying dispute should be submitted to arbitration. Accordingly, the Court must stay the proceedings and order the parties to submit to arbitration. See Dean Witter Reynolds, Inc., 470 U.S. at 218; Progressive Casualty Ins. Co., 991 F.2d at 45.

CONCLUSION

For the reasons stated above, plaintiff's motion for civil contempt and summary enforcement of the Court's prior order by way of permanent injunction is DENIED. Defendant's cross-motion for an order staying these proceedings and compelling plaintiff to submit to arbitration in Milan, Italy is GRANTED. Plaintiff is HEREBY ORDERED to submit to arbitration, and the action is HEREBY STAYED.

SO ORDERED.

HART ENTERPRISES INTERNATIONAL, INC. v. ANHUI PROVINCIAL IMPORT & EXPORT CORP.

United States District Court, Southern District of New York, 1995.
888 F.Supp. 587.

AMENDED MEMORANDUM OPINION

KAPLAN, DISTRICT JUDGE.

This is an action by a New York textile purchaser against a Chinese supplier for damages for alleged quality deficiencies in the goods and for breach and rescission of a settlement agreement between the parties. The defendant moves to stay the action pending arbitration in the People's Republic of China pursuant to arbitration clauses contained in the confirmations of the sales by defendant to plaintiff. The motion is granted.

FACTS

From August 1991 to April 30, 1992, defendant Anhui Provincial Import & Export Corp. ("Anhui") entered into * * * [twelve] contracts to sell ramie/cotton dyed and polyester/viscose dyed yarn. * * * [The] contracts, all of which were headed "Sales Confirmation," were with Hart Enterprises International, Inc. ("Hart") and signed by Hart's Mr. Haroutiounian. All * * * contained an arbitration clause which stated:

Arbitration: All disputes arising from the execution of, or in connection with the S/C, shall be settled amicably through friendly negotiation. In case no settlement can be reached through negotiation, the case shall then be submitted to The Foreign Trade Arbitration Commission of the China Council For the Promotion of International Trade, Peking, for arbitration in accordance with its provisional rules of procedure. The arbitral award is final and binding upon both parties. The fees for arbitration shall be borne by the losing party unless otherwise awarded.

Disputes arose between Anhui and Hart. On September 2, 1993, they entered into a settlement agreement concerning all * * * [twelve] contracts that called for Hart to make a series of scheduled payments, which represented a reduction of the amount claimed by Anhui. The agreement further provided that:

> It is clearly understood by both parties that the new prices for the above mentioned invoices are special deduction [sic] subject to party B's [Hart's] settlement on above mentioned schedule, and if party B [Hart] fails in fully performing the agreement or in case of partially performed [sic], party A [Anhui] is entilted [sic] to claims by law all its losses such as interst [sic], price difference in selling the goods according to the original contracts.

Hart failed to make the payments required under the settlement agreement. On May 5, 1994, Anhui applied to the China International Economic and Trade Arbitration Commission in Beijing for commencement of arbitration against Hart for breach of contract. The Commission confirmed the application on July 20, 1994 and sent notice of the arbitration to Hart, requesting Hart to appoint an arbitrator and forward its statement of the case. Hart did not respond, so the Commission appointed an arbitrator on Hart's behalf and confirmed that the tribunal had been constituted.

In November 1994, Hart commenced this action against Anhui in the State court, and the case was removed. Also in November 1994, the Commission scheduled an arbitration hearing for February 20, 1995 in Beijing and Hart was so notified. Hart did not respond or otherwise appear. The hearing was adjourned and a new date has not yet been set.

DISCUSSION

Hart resists arbitration on a number of grounds, all of which lack merit.

1.   Hart maintains that a condition precedent to its obligation to arbitrate has not been met in that the arbitration clause states that arbitration is required only "[i]n case no settlement can be reached through negotiation ..." It argues that the dispute was settled by the September 2, 1994 agreement. The argument is rejected.

To begin with, the only rational reading of the clause is that the parties were obliged to attempt in good faith to resolve any disputes before resorting to arbitration. That they did. Although those efforts appeared, as of September 2, 1994, to have been successful, the appearance of success proved short-lived. The dispute unmistakably has not been settled and the parties, having pursued a negotiated resolution unsuccessfully, now are free to resort to their arbitration remedies.

Indeed, any other construction would permit a party to frustrate the arbitration provision by entering into a sham "settlement," without any intention to perform, and then to avoid arbitration by asserting that the matter had been "settled."

Second, the September 2 agreement, in the second passage quoted above, makes it abundantly clear that the settlement was contingent upon Hart's making the scheduled payments, failing which Anhui is entitled to pursue its remedies under the original contracts. That certainly included arbitration.

Finally, even if Hart's construction were colorable, arbitration nonetheless would be required. "Arbitration should be compelled unless it may be said with positive assurance that the arbitration clause is not susceptible of an interpretation that covers the asserted dispute." United Steelworkers of America v. Warrior and Gulf Navigation Co., 363 U.S. 574, 582–83* * *.

2. Hart argues next that the September 2 settlement agreement is a contract separate and distinct from the original contracts and that it is not obliged to arbitrate because the dispute concerns alleged breach of the settlement agreement. It is mistaken.

While in some circumstances a party to two separate and distinct contracts, one containing an arbitration clause and the other not, may not be obliged to arbitrate a claim arising under the latter,[1] that principle does not apply here. The claims relating to the settlement agreement, not to mention the settlement agreement itself, are inextricably interrelated to the sales contracts that contain the arbitration clauses. Moreover, it is worth noting that the principal claim asserted in Hart's complaint is for breach of the sales contracts themselves. In consequence, all of Hart's claims are arbitrable.

First Options of Chicago, Inc. v. Kaplan, 514 U.S. 938, 941–47, 115 S.Ct. 1920, 1923–26, 131 L.Ed.2d 985 (1995), is not to the contrary. The Supreme Court there held that a party cannot be forced to arbitrate an issue unless the party clearly agreed to submit the dispute to arbitration, even where a contract related to the dispute between the parties contained an arbitration clause. In First Options, however, the disputes concerned an agreement that was embodied in four separate but related documents. Only one of the four documents contained an arbitration clause. The Kaplans, the parties disputing that their disagreement with First Options was arbitrable, did not sign the one document containing the arbitration clause. The Court held there was insufficient evidence of a clear agreement to arbitrate on the part of the Kaplans despite the related agreement containing the arbitration clause. Here, in contrast, Hart signed sales confirmations containing the arbitration clauses, thus leaving no doubt as to its intention to arbitrate.

* * *

1. See Necchi S.p.A. v. Necchi Sewing Machine Sales Corp., 348 F.2d 693 (2d Cir. 1965), cert. denied, 383 U.S. 909, 86 S.Ct. 892, 15 L.Ed.2d 664 (1966).

4. Hart finally argues that remitting it to arbitration in Beijing would subject it to undue hardship. The short answer to the assertion is that Hart should have thought of that before it signed contracts specifying arbitration in Beijing in the event of a dispute.

Remedy

Although the parties have not briefed the issue of remedy, the Court notes that there is some debate as to whether the appropriate disposition in these circumstances is a stay pending arbitration or a final judgment containing a direction to proceed to arbitration. E.g., Filanto, 789 F.Supp. at 1241–42. In view of the fact that no useful purpose would be served by a stay, the Court will enter a final judgment containing an appropriate injunction directing the parties to arbitrate in Beijing in accordance with the Convention and the contracts.

Settle judgment on five days notice.

SO ORDERED.

BECKER AUTORADIO v. BECKER AUTORADIOWERK

United States Court of Appeals, Third Circuit, 1978.
585 F.2d 39.

[Becker Autoradio, a Pennsylvania corporation, entered on July 1, 1974 into an Exclusive Distribution Agreement with Becker Autoradiowerk, a West German corporation. By its terms, the Agreement terminated on June 30, 1976. The Agreement provided that, should an extension be desired, negotiations to that effect should be initiated at least six months prior to the termination date. Becker USA and BAW entered into renewal negotiations but a renewal agreement was never signed. Early in 1977, alleging an oral promise, made prior to June 30, 1976, to renew the 1974 Agreement for a five-year term provided that Becker USA fulfilled certain conditions, Becker USA brought the instant action against BAW. Becker USA asserted that the relevant conditions had been satisfied and sought relief for BAW's breach of contract. The district court denied BAW's motion to stay judicial proceeding and compel arbitration. The Court of Appeals reversed and directed the district court to order arbitration and to stay the judicial proceeding.

The 1974 Agreement's arbitration clause provided for arbitration of "all disputes arising out of and about this agreement." Becker USA argued that the dispute did not involve a breach of the 1974 Agreement or of any right or obligation stemming from that Agreement which terminated on June 30, 1976.

In reaching its conclusions, the court distinguished cases, in which the disputed transaction occurred prior to the expiration of the contract whose arbitration clause was invoked, from cases in which the transaction occurred *after* expiration. In the former type of case, at least where essentially the entire original agreement would be carried forward were there a renewal, the dispute as to termination and renewal "arises out of" or is "about" the agreement that contains the arbitration clause. The court concluded, therefore, that the issues raised in the judicial action " 'arise out' of the 1974 Agreement in that they all arose in the course of and during the on-going relationship between Becker USA and BAW, which relationship was created and governed by the 1974 Agreement."]

GARTH, CIRCUIT JUDGE.

* * *

The controversy in this case centers on whether BAW agreed to extend the 1974 Agreement beyond its 1976 expiration date. This purported extension promise was made while the 1974 Agreement was in effect, and was allegedly conditioned on the performance of various tasks, all but one of which related to the subject matter of the 1974 Agreement (i.e., the distribution in the United States of Becker radios). The extension was alleged to have been on the same terms as the 1974 Agreement. Indeed, accepting Becker U.S.A.'s version of the existence and terms of the oral agreement, it would appear that the only change required in the 1974 Agreement would be the substitution of the expiration date in article 11(1). As we understand Becker U.S.A.'s position, the alleged oral agreement would substitute the date of June 30, 1981, for the expiration date of June 30, 1976. All other terms of the 1974 Agreement would be carried forward and would continue in effect until 1981, including, we surmise, the arbitration clause itself. In this context, where the entire original agreement would be included "lock, stock and barrel" in the extended agreement, we find it difficult to understand how a dispute concerning the termination and renewal clause of that agreement (See article 11, paragraphs 1, 2 and 5 of the 1974 Agreement) did not "arise out of" or is not "about" the 1974 Agreement.

* * *

[Moreover, the applicable federal standard requires] " * * * that doubts are to be resolved in favor of arbitration unless * * * [one] can state with 'positive assurance' that arbitration of the dispute was not intended by the parties. * * * "

Questions and Comments

1. Arbitrators have jurisdiction if the parties have given them adjudicatory power, and that power extends only to the issues the parties have entrusted to them. Therefore, it is important not only to establish whether the parties agreed to arbitrate, but also to know exactly which issues the parties submitted to arbitration. Threshold questions are not limited to those pertaining to the existence and the validity of the agreement to arbitrate; they also arise with respect to the scope of the arbitration agreement.

In *Mediterranean Enterprises*, the court found that some of the contested issues were within, while others were beyond, the scope of the arbitration clause. The result was split litigation. The 9th Circuit attempted to coordinate matters by staying court proceedings until the arbitrator decided the issues within the scope of the arbitration clause. The outcome is not a coherent and efficient dispute settling mechanism. Was there a better option?

2. Suppose that one of the contested issues was the formal validity of the "Preliminary Agreement" between MEI and Ssangyong. Would this issue be within the scope of the given arbitration clause?

3. The key words in the *MEI v. Ssangyong* arbitration clause were "arising hereunder," but the clause contained another scope provision that could have become important: "Any disputes ... following the formation of joint venture." This language became irrelevant, however, because no joint venture was formed. How would you describe the potential scope of the expression, "following the formation of joint venture".

4. How would you have worded the arbitration clause?

5. In *Ermenegildo Zegna* the interpretation of the arbitration clause is combined with—some would say complicated by—a no-contest clause. In court proceedings in most countries, a no-contest clause could pose a barrier, but most probably not one jurisdictional in nature. Courts would assume jurisdiction, if a valid basis were present, and then decide not to grant a remedy on the merits because of the no-contest clause. Is there a reason to proceed differently in arbitration?

6. Assuming that a no-contest clause can affect the jurisdiction of an arbitral tribunal, could one argue that the disputed issue pertains to the interpretation of the no-contest clause, and is therefore within the scope of the arbitration agreement?

7. What issues would be arbitrable had MEI and Ssangyong adopted the wording of the *Zegna* arbitration clause: "Should there be any dispute between the parties with respect to the interpretation of this Agreement and Stipulation or with respect to the rights, duties and obligations undertaken by the parties herein, or arising herefrom * * * ."

8. In *Hart v. Anhui* the court held that only an actual settlement (rather than a settlement agreement) bars arbitration. Do you agree?

Assume that a dispute arose regarding the interpretation of a settlement agreement (that did not itself contain an arbitration clause). Would the dispute be a matter for Beijing arbitration or for courts?

9. In *Becker* the court faced a situation where the contract containing an arbitration clause is followed by a promise or other transaction, not itself containing an arbitration clause, potentially implying renewal of the original contract. The Belgian case of Société Van Hopplynus v. Société Coherent Inc.[43] raised similar issues. In *Van Hopplynus*, the Brussels Commercial Court (Tribunal de commerce de Bruxelles), rejecting the argument that an arbitration agreement can only be renewed in a written form, held that a

---

[43]. Tribunal de commerce de Bruxelles, Decision of October 5, 1994, reported in Revue de l'arbitrage 1995, 311, with comments by Hanotiau.

tacit renewal of the contract containing an arbitration clause entails, as well, a valid renewal of the arbitration clause. In *Becker*, the parties failed to sign a renewal agreement, and the contract did not have a clause providing for tacit renewal. Becker U.S.A. brought an action alleging that the defendant had made an oral promise to renew. The defendant (BAW) asked the court to refer the case to arbitration under the arbitration clause in the expired contract providing for ICC arbitration in Germany. In *Van Hopplynus* arbitral jurisdiction was based on the assumption that the arbitration clause was renewed together with the contract that contained it. In *Becker*, on the other hand, the contract was not renewed; the plaintiff simply alleged that BAW's failure to renew constituted a breach of an oral agreement to do so. Can you justify the decision of the Third Circuit?

10. Is it critical that BAW allegedly made its promise to renew before June 30, 1976, the date of expiration of the Distribution Agreement containing an arbitration clause?

11. Do you agree with the Third Circuit that this is "a dispute concerning the termination and renewal clause" of the 1974 Agreement?

12. Suppose the arbitration clause in the Distribution Agreement had omitted two words: "and about". What result?

13. In the circumstances of the *Becker* case, suppose there were a written renewal not containing an arbitration clause. Would a claim based on breach of this renewed agreement be subject to arbitration?

II.1.g. *The Position of the Parties Who Are Not Signatories of the Arbitration Agreement*

COSMOTEK MUMESSILLIK VE TICARET LIMITED SIRKKETI v. COSMOTEK USA, INC.

United States District Court, District of Connecticut, 1996.
942 F.Supp. 757.

DORSEY, CHIEF JUDGE.

Defendants move to stay this proceeding pursuant to the Federal Arbitration Act (FAA) 9 U.S.C. § 3. Defendants claim that their contract requires the parties to arbitrate. Plaintiff opposes, asserting that Advanced Power Systems International, Inc. (APSI) cannot be compelled to arbitrate because it was not a party to the contract.

I. BACKGROUND

Cosmotek USA (USA), and Cosmotek Mumessillik ve Ticaret Limited Sirkketi (Turkey), entered into an agreement (contract) whereby Turkey became USA's distributor and sales representative for the sale of Fitch Catalyst units (units). The units were manufactured by APSI who was neither a signatory nor a party to the contract.

The contract provides that it shall be construed in accordance with the laws of New York and any dispute arising under the contract shall be resolved by final and binding arbitration.

II. Discussion

A. Federal Arbitration Act

Defendants assert that the FAA governs enforceability of the arbitration clause. Plaintiff argues that APSI's presence, as non-party to the contract, mandates deference to the choice of state law provision.

Enforceability of an arbitration agreement is determined pursuant to the FAA if "(1) the parties have entered into a written arbitration agreement,[1] (2) there exists an independent basis for federal jurisdiction, and (3) the underlying transaction involves interstate commerce."[2] In re Chung, 943 F.2d 225, 229 (2d Cir.1991); General Textile Printing v. Expromtorg Int'l Corp., 891 F.Supp. 946, 954 (S.D.N.Y.1995). A contract choice of law clause defines the rights and duties of the parties in accordance with the chosen state law. However, the arbitration clause subjects the duty to arbitrate to the FAA.

The FAA governs enforcement of the arbitration clause as to USA as the conditions precedent to FAA applicability are all present.

Plaintiff argues that its claims are against both defendants and should be heard together, in federal court, notwithstanding the applicability of the FAA to its claims against USA, because APSI cannot be forced to arbitrate.

Arbitration agreements are "valid, irrevocable, and enforceable" absent any grounds for revocation. 9 U.S.C. § 2. District courts have no discretion to excuse a party from arbitration regarding issues covered by a written arbitration agreement. Dean Witter Reynolds, Inc. v. Byrd, 470 U.S. 213, 218, 105 S.Ct. 1238, 1241, 84 L.Ed.2d 158 (1985). An arbitration agreement must be enforced "notwithstanding the presence of other persons who are parties to the underlying dispute but not to the arbitration agreement." Moses H. Cone Memorial Hosp. v. Mercury Constr., 460 U.S. 1, 20, 103 S.Ct. 927, 939, 74 L.Ed.2d 765 (1983). Plaintiffs cannot avoid the arbitration for which they had contracted simply by adding a nonsignatory defendant, lest the efficacy of contracts and the federal policy favoring arbitration be defeated. Lawson Fabrics, Inc. v. Akzona, Inc., 355 F.Supp. 1146, 1151 (S.D.N.Y.1973) (quoting Hilti, Inc. v. Oldach, 392 F.2d 368, 369 n. 2 (1st Cir.1968)). Defendants' motion to stay is granted as to USA.

APSI, on the other hand, is not a party to the contract and is mentioned in it only as the manufacturer. The failure to satisfy the first prong of the Chung test precludes application of the FAA to plaintiff's claims against APSI.

---

1. The FAA defines a written arbitration agreement as "[a] written provision in any ... contract evidencing a transaction involving commerce to settle by arbitration a controversy thereafter arising out of such contract or transaction...." 9 U.S.C. § 2 (1994).

2. The FAA defines "commerce" as "commerce ... with foreign nations...." 9 U.S.C. § 1 (1994).

B. *Binding a Nonsignatory to an Arbitration Agreement*

While a party cannot be forced to arbitrate a dispute, absent an agreement to do so, five circumstances have been delineated in which a nonsignatory may be bound to an arbitration agreement: incorporation by reference, assumption, veil-piercing, alter ego, estoppel, and agency. Thomson–CSF, S.A. v. American Arbitration Ass'n, 64 F.3d 773, 776 (2d Cir.1995). Neither [party] alleged facts nor presented evidence to support the first four.[3]

However, plaintiff asserts that USA contracted as APSI's agent holding itself out as APSI's fully disclosed agent. Defendants neither concede this assertion, nor do they expressly contest it. There is no mention in the contract of any agency relationship between USA and APSI, and USA executed the contract in its own name with no indication it was acting as APSI's agent. In fact, APSI is not mentioned in the contract other than being identified as the manufacturer/marketer of the Units.

A nonsignatory to an arbitration agreement may be bound by an agreement under principles of agency law. Thomson–CSF, S.A., 64 F.3d at 777. An agent who signs a contract on behalf of a disclosed principal will not be individually bound absent explicit evidence of the agent's intention to bind himself instead of or as well as the principal. Lerner v. Amalgamated Clothing & Textile Workers Union, 938 F.2d 2, 5 (2d Cir.1991). When an agent signs a contract and does not indicate in the contract that he is signing on behalf of a disclosed principal, as its agent, "the agent is deemed to be acting on his own behalf." Beck v. Suro Textiles, Ltd., 612 F.Supp. 1193, 1194 (S.D.N.Y.1985) (citing Unger v. Travel Arrangements, Inc., 25 A.D.2d 40, 266 N.Y.S.2d 715 (1966); Special Sections, Inc. v. Rappaport Co., 25 A.D.2d 896, 269 N.Y.S.2d 319 (1966)). Additionally, "an agent whose agency is not disclosed in the instrument cannot introduce evidence to show that he is not a party [to the instrument], except for the purpose of reformation." Restatement (Second) of Agency § 155, comment d (1958).

C. *APSI's Motion to Stay*

Since APSI is not bound by the arbitration agreement, its requested stay does not fall within the purview of the FAA. It is governed by the court's inherent power to "control the disposition of the causes on its docket." Landis v. North American Co., 299 U.S. 248, 254, 57 S.Ct. 163, 165–66, 81 L.Ed. 153 (1936); Sierra Rutile Ltd. v. Katz, 937 F.2d 743, 750 (2d Cir.1991). Such a decision is left to the court's discretion. Moses H. Cone Memorial Hosp., 460 U.S. at 19–21, 103 S.Ct. at 939. A stay may be appropriate where issues involved may be determined in arbitration. Id. (quoting Nederlandse Erts–Tankersmaatschappij, N.V. v. Isbrandtsen Co., 339 F.2d 440, 441 (2d Cir.1964)).

---

3. Plaintiff argues that a nonsignatory may be bound to an arbitration agreement based on interrelatedness of the issues. The Second Circuit has expressly rejected this "hybrid" approach, characterizing it as an improper extension of the law of this Circuit. Id. at 776, 780.

Accordingly, the primary questions are (1) whether there are common issues in the arbitration and the court proceeding, and (2) if so, whether those issues will be finally determined by the arbitration. American Shipping Line v. Massan Shipping Indus., 885 F.Supp. 499, 502 (S.D.N.Y.1995). If the answer to both questions is in the affirmative, the movant must then bear the heavy burden of showing that "the nonarbitrating party will not hinder the arbitration, that the arbitration will be resolved within a reasonable time, and that such delay that may occur will not cause undue hardship to the parties." American Shipping Line, 885 F.Supp. at 502 (citing Sierra Rutile Ltd., 937 F.2d at 750); Nederlandse, 339 F.2d at 442. A stay may not be granted, despite the existence of compelling reasons to grant it, if defendants have not shown that plaintiff would not undergo undue hardship from the resultant delay.[4] See Sierra Rutile Ltd., 937 F.2d at 750; American Shipping Line, 885 F.Supp. at 503.

Plaintiff's complaint alleges breach of purchase order, breach of express warranty, and breach of implied warranty against both defendants. There will undoubtedly be multiple common issues in the arbitration and the court proceedings. Pursuant to paragraph 11 of the Contract, the decision of the arbitrator "shall be final and binding" on Turkey and USA. The arbitration will inevitably determine whether defective Units were delivered and no replacements proffered, and "thus will at least partially determine the issues which form the basis of the claim" against APSI. See Lawson Fabrics, Inc., 355 F.Supp. at 1151.

The heavy burden on defendants to show the necessity for the stay, Sierra Rutile Ltd. v. Katz, 937 F.2d 743, 750 (2d Cir.1991), has not clearly been met. Though the deficiency would normally result in the denial of a stay, it would appear that hindrance of the arbitration is unlikely and no undue, prejudicial delay will be caused plaintiff.

It is noted that APSI has moved for the stay for the purpose of permitting the dispute to be resolved by arbitration. It has thus put its imprimatur on arbitration and assuming its good faith in the promotion of arbitration as the resolving forum, it is also assumed that APSI is committed to the expeditious resolution of the matter as intended by arbitration. Additionally, APSI is represented by the same attorney who represents the party to the contract, thus a unified approach to the resolution of the plaintiff's claims appears to be the case. In fact the quality of the product is the crux of the dispute and plaintiff has claims against two parties based on essentially the same product deficiency. Thus it would not appear that plaintiff would suffer any hindrance or obstruction in an expeditious determination of its claims by a stay and relegation, at first blush, to arbitration.

---

4. Such hardship may include the danger that evidence supporting the nonarbitrable claim may grow stale, become unavailable, or be lost, particularly when the dispute is of an international nature. Chang v. Lin, 824 F.2d 219, 222 (2d Cir.1987); American Shipping Line, 885 F.Supp. at 503.

One forum for the resolution would advance finalization of plaintiff's claims as it would foster cooperation and coordination of the resolution by the two parties from which plaintiff seeks to recover. It would be to plaintiff's advantage to have the matter in one forum as any disputes between the two targets of the claims can be resolved there as opposed to the need for plaintiff to litigate the claims twice, or be delayed while the two targets resolve any disputes between them as to the ultimate responsibility. By putting the two targets in one forum, their costs can be reduced, which would permit more resources to be applied to settling the claims with plaintiff. No delay would result to plaintiff. Indeed if counsel are conscientious, a faster resolution can be achieved in arbitration than would be the case in court in view of the present interval between filing and trial in court. From the nature of the case, there is nothing to suggest that plaintiff would otherwise be compromised such as by loss of evidence or witnesses.

To insure against the adverse risks to which plaintiff should not be subjected by a stay, a reporting schedule will be imposed to * * * [assure] the court that the early hearing and decision which are the hallmark of arbitration are in fact afforded to plaintiff. Further, plaintiff is assured that should any of the factors required for a stay prove not to be the case, such as hindrance/obstruction by APSI or delay in obtaining a hearing/decision in arbitration, a request to vacate the stay can always be presented to the court and the matter revisited to insure plaintiff's untrammeled rights to a prompt resolution of its claims.

Accordingly the motion for a stay on behalf of APSI is granted, subject to the reporting as to the status of the matter, its progress in arbitration, the absence of any delay or hindrance/obstruction to its resolution in arbitration and an estimate of the time of its determination in arbitration on November 1, 1996 and each three months thereafter. Further plaintiff may, by motion, seek a revisiting of the propriety of the stay at any time in the face of hindrance/obstruction or prejudicial delay in an expeditious decision on its claims.

III. CONCLUSION

Defendants' motion for a stay pending arbitration (doc. #6) is granted in accordance with this ruling.

SO ORDERED.

Questions and Comments

1.   The U.S. District Court (District of Connecticut) rejected the agency theory on the ground that the agent-principal relationship was not disclosed in the contract. In some countries, other hurdles might also emerge. For example, in Italy, Article 1392 of the Code of Civil Procedure ties the validity of the arbitration agreement to an uninterrupted chain of written declarations, which means that in addition to the contract between the agent and the third party, the authorization given by the principal to the agent also has to be executed in a written form. Do you agree with the logic of this provision?

2. The *Cosmotek* decision relies on Thomson–CSF, S.A. v. American Arbitration Association,[44] which delineated five common law theories under which non-signatories may be bound to the arbitration agreement of others. The decision gives a rare (and important) judicial summary of the problem:

"I. *Traditional Bases For Binding Nonsignatories*

This Court has recognized a number of theories under which nonsignatories may be bound to the arbitration agreements of others. Those theories arise out of common law principles of contract and agency law. Accordingly, we have recognized five theories for binding nonsignatories to arbitration agreements: 1) incorporation by reference; 2) assumption; 3) agency; 4) veil-piercing/alter ego; and 5) estoppel. * * *

A. Incorporation by Reference

[4] A nonsignatory may compel arbitration against a party to an arbitration agreement when that party has entered into a separate contractual relationship with the nonsignatory which incorporates the existing arbitration clause. See Import Export Steel Corp. v. Mississippi Valley Barge Line Co., 351 F.2d 503, 505–506 (2d Cir.1965) (separate agreement with nonsignatory expressly "assum[ing] all the obligations and privileges of [signatory party] under the . . . subcharter" constitutes grounds for enforcement of arbitration clause by nonsignatory); Matter of Arbitration Between Keystone Shipping Co. and Texport Oil Co., 782 F.Supp. 28, 31 (S.D.N.Y. 1992); Continental U.K. Ltd. v. Anagel Confidence Compania Naviera, S.A., 658 F.Supp. 809, 813 (S.D.N.Y.1987) (if a "party's arbitration clause is expressly incorporated into a bill of lading, nonsignatories . . . who are linked to that bill through general principles of contract law or agency law may be bound"). * * *

B. Assumption

[5], [6] In the absence of a signature, a party may be bound by an arbitration clause if its subsequent conduct indicates that it is assuming the obligation to arbitrate. See Gvozdenovic v. United Air Lines, Inc., 933 F.2d 1100, 1105 (2d Cir.) (flight attendants manifested a clear intention to arbitrate by sending a representative to act on their behalf in arbitration process), *cert. denied*, 502 U.S. 910, 112 S.Ct. 305, 116 L.Ed.2d 248 (1991); *Keystone Shipping*, 782 F.Supp. at 31; *In re Transrol Navegacao S.A.*, 782 F.Supp. 848, 851 (S.D.N.Y.1991). * * *

C. Agency

[7] Traditional principles of agency law may bind a nonsignatory to an arbitration agreement. See Interbras Cayman Co. v. Orient Victory Shipping Co., S.A., 663 F.2d 4, 6–7 (2d Cir.1981); *A/S Custodia*, 503 F.2d at 320; *Fisser*, 282 F.2d at 233–38; *Keystone Shipping*, 782 F.Supp. at 31–32. * * *

D. Veil Piercing/Alter Ego

[8], [9], [10] In some instances, the corporate relationship between a parent and its subsidiary are [sic] sufficiently close as to justify piercing the corporate veil and holding one corporation legally accountable for the actions

[44]. 64 F.3d 773, 776–780 (2d Cir. 1995).

of the other. As a general matter, however, a corporate relationship alone is not sufficient to bind a nonsignatory to an arbitration agreement. *See Keystone Shipping*, 782 F.Supp. at 30–31. Nonetheless, the courts will pierce the corporate veil "in two broad situations: to prevent fraud or other wrong, or where a parent dominates and controls a subsidiary." Carte Blanche (Singapore) Pte., Ltd. v. Diners Club Int'l, Inc., 2 F.3d 24, 26 (2d Cir.1993); * * *.

[11] Veil piercing determinations are fact specific and "differ[] with the circumstances of each case." American Protein Corp. v. AB Volvo, 844 F.2d 56, 60 (2d Cir.), *cert. denied*, 488 U.S. 852, 109 S.Ct. 136, 102 L.Ed.2d 109 (1988). This Court has determined that a parent corporation and its subsidiary lose their distinct corporate identities when their conduct demonstrates a virtual abandonment of separateness. *See Carte Blanche*, 2 F.3d at 29 ("No bank accounts, offices, stationery, transactions, or any other activities were maintained or carried on in the name of [the subsidiary]."); *Wm. Passalacqua*, 933 F.2d at 139 (corporate veil is pierced where, among other things, parent and subsidiary 1) share common office and staff; 2) are run by common officers; 3) intermingle funds; 4) do not deal at arms length with each other; and 5) are not treated as separate profit centers); see also Walter E. Heller & Co. v. Video Innovations, Inc., 730 F.2d 50, 53 (2d Cir.1984) (absence of corporate formalities relevant factor in piercing corporate veil). "[T]he factors that determine the question of control and domination are less subjective than 'good faith'; they relate to how the corporation was actually operated." *Carte Blanche*, 2 F.3d at 28–29.

* * *

E. Estoppel

[12] This Court has also bound nonsignatories to arbitration agreements under an estoppel theory. In Deloitte Noraudit A/S v. Deloitte Haskins & Sells, U.S., 9 F.3d 1060, 1064 (2d Cir.1993), a foreign accounting firm received a settlement agreement concerning the use of the trade name "Deloitte" in association with accounting practices. Under the agreement— containing an arbitration clause—local affiliates of the international accounting association Deloitte Haskins & Sells International were entitled to use the trade name "Deloitte" in exchange for compliance with the dictates of the agreement. A Norwegian accounting firm received the agreement, made no objection to the terms of the agreement, and proceeded to utilize the trade name. This Court held that by knowingly exploiting the agreement, the accounting firm was estopped from avoiding arbitration despite having never signed the agreement. See 9 F.3d at 1064 ("Noraudit failed to object to the Agreement when it received it.... In addition, Noraudit knowingly accepted the benefits of the Agreement.... Thus, Noraudit is estopped from denying its obligation to arbitrate under the 1990 Agreement."). * * *

* * *

Several courts of appeal have recognized an alternative estoppel theory requiring arbitration between a signatory and nonsignatory. See Sunkist Soft Drinks, Inc. v. Sunkist Growers, Inc., 10 F.3d 753, 757–58 (11th

Cir.1993), *cert. denied*,513 U.S. 869, 115 S.Ct. 190, 130 L.Ed.2d 123 (1994); J.J. Ryan & Sons, Inc. v. Rhone Poulenc Textile, S.A., 863 F.2d 315, 320–21 (4th Cir.1988); McBro Planning & Dev. Co. v. Triangle Elec. Constr. Co., 741 F.2d 342, 344 (11th Cir.1984). In these cases, a signatory was bound to arbitrate with a nonsignatory at the nonsignatory's insistence because of "the close relationship between the entities involved, as well as the relationship of the alleged wrongs to the nonsignatory's obligations and duties in the contract . . . and [the fact that] the claims were 'intimately founded in and intertwined with the underlying contract obligations.'" *Sunkist*, 10 F.3d at 757 (quoting *McBro Planning*, 741 F.2d at 344). * * *

Authors' Note: The court in the discussion of incorporation by reference set out above does not distinguish between a signatory's effort to join a nonsignatory as a party in an arbitration and a nonsignatory's effort to intervene in an arbitration against the objection of one or both parties. In practice, the first situation is far more common than the second. The policy considerations involved being quite different—see 64 F.3d at 779–80—results reached in one situation are not decisive for the other.

In *Thomson* the District Court, using what the Court of Appeals characterized as a hybrid approach, had held the arbitration clause enforceable against a nonsignatory. Thompson's "conduct in 'voluntarily bec[oming] * * * an affiliate,' * * * the degree of control Thompson exercises over [Rediffusion], and * * * the interrelatedness of the issues * * *" (id. at 780), taken together, justified bringing the company into the arbitration despite its objections. The Court of Appeals saw the decision as an impermissible dilution of "the protections afforded nonsignatories by the 'ordinary principles of contract and agency.' * * * A nonsignatory may not be bound to arbitrate except as dictated by some accepted theory under agency or contract law. * * * Anything short of requiring a full showing of some accepted theory * * * imperils a vast number of parent corporations. * * *" Id. at 780.

3. Are these theories compatible with the "agreement in writing" requirement of Article II(2) of the New York Convention, and Article 7(2) of the Model Law?

4. Not infrequently, persons who are the real debtors, or without whom litigation would be fragmented and possibly inefficient, tend to remain behind the scene. Since willingness is not a condition to become a party in court proceedings, courts have clearly had more success (than arbitration tribunals) in asserting adjudicatory authority over persons who cautiously avoided formal commitments. As arbitration has become the dominant form of settlement of international trade disputes, the temptation has grown to reach for the real *personae dramatis*, disregarding inherent limitations.

In (Southern Pacific Properties Ltd. and Southern Pacific Properties (Middle East) Ltd. v. Arab Republic of Egypt,[45] an I.C.C. tribunal endeavored to assume jurisdiction over Egypt in addition to the party who signed the arbitration agreement, on the grounds that the Egyptian Minister of Tourism approved the contract and that Egypt signed the terms of reference

[45]. 22 International Legal Materials V.2.d.i.]
752 (1983). [Authors' note: see infra section

although the terms of reference contained a clear statement by Egypt contesting the existence of an arbitration agreement). The award was set aside, however, by the Paris Court of Appeals, on the ground that there was no arbitration agreement binding Egypt.[46] Another I.C.C. tribunal asserted jurisdiction over four states (United Arab Emirates, Saudi Arabia, Qatar, and Egypt) when the party signing the arbitration agreement was an organization created by these states.[47] This award was likewise set aside by the Court of Justice of Geneva; on appeal, the decision of the Geneva court was confirmed by the Swiss Federal Tribunal.[48] Earlier, the Swiss Federal Tribunal corrected another overextension of arbitral authority, holding that Libya was not bound by an arbitration clause concluded between the Libyan National Oil Company and a foreign corporation.[49]

The temptation is clearly great. Non-signatories may very well be the real parties, and it appears to be both expedient and fair to reach for them. At the same time, the most basic principle of arbitration is dependence on party agreement. Arbitration is a creation of the parties. In the absence of a submission by both parties, litigation is still available as a possible avenue of justice.

In this conflict between two sets of values, which should win out in your view?

5. Note that, given the international setting, a policy of allowing arbitration to proceed between persons or entities that are not parties to the arbitration agreement might conceivably represent a mixed blessing, and in some cases might indeed hinder, rather than advance efficient dispute settlement. If arbitration is ordered in a country where arbitration is favored even beyond the limitations of the arbitration clause, yet this arbitration has to proceed—or enforcement of the award must ultimately be sought—in a country with different views, the moving party might wind up without relief from either courts or arbitration.

Returning to the *Cosmotek* pattern, suppose the court had referred the case to arbitration regarding both defendants (the sales representative bound by a valid arbitration clause, and the manufacturer who did not sign the arbitration agreement). Suppose further that the arbitrators refuse jurisdiction with respect to the manufacturer. What happens then?

Another, perhaps more difficult, variation of this situation is where the arbitrators accept jurisdiction, Cosmotek Turkey seeks recognition and en-

[46]. Decision of July 12, 1984, 23 International Legal Materials 1048, 1054 (1984). [Reproduced infra p. 678.] Regarding the argument with respect to the terms of reference, the French court stated: "it would not be possible to explain how the terms of reference, in which the A.R.E. claims immunity from jurisdiction and maintains, before any arguments on the merits, that there was no arbitration agreement, could replace such an agreement."

[47]. Westland Helicopters Limited v. Arab Organization for Industrialization, United Arab Emirates, Kingdom of Saudi Arabia, State of Qatar, Arab Republic of Egypt, and Arab British Helicopter Compa-

ny, I.C.C. Case No. 3879, Interim award of March 5, 1984, 23 International Legal Materials 1071 (1984).

[48]. The Swiss courts found that there was no arbitration agreement between Westland Helicopters and the four states, yet the award was annulled only in regard to Egypt, in absence of challenge by the other three states. 28 International Legal Materials 687 (1989).

[49]. Federal Tribunal, Decision of November 14, 1979, in *Arab Republic of Libya v. Wetco*, 102 Semaine Judiciaire 443 (1980).

forcement against APSI (the manufacturer), but this is denied on the ground of Article V(1)(a) of the New York Convention, because the court finds that there is no valid arbitration agreement. As advisor to Cosmotek Turkey, what course of action would you suggest?

REVIEW PROBLEM (Sale of Lumber)

A. Before a Court

Suppose Bois et Meubles, a French company, brings a claim in the Tribunal de Grande Instance of Paris (trial court) against Lumber Mills of Budapest, a Hungarian company. Bois et Meubles seeks return of the partial payment of the purchase price and damages for an allegedly nonconforming shipment of lumber made by Lumber Mills in fulfillment of a sale agreement with Bois et Meubles entered on September 23, 2002. Lumber Mills asks the French court to stay the action and refer the parties to arbitration before the Court of Arbitration attached to the Hungarian Chamber of Commerce and Industry in Budapest. Lumber Mills admits that the sale agreement did not contain an arbitration clause, but claims that the parties had entered a "framework agreement" in February, 2002 that contemplated lumber sales and provided for arbitration. Lumber Mills submitted the following written contract:

Mutual Agreement

February 21, 2002   Budapest, Hungary

Subject Matter: Execution of commercial activities

Field of Activities: Trade in timber, manufacturing furniture, and other commercial activities

Duration: Five Years

This agreement is made by Mr. Herve Bucheron, on behalf of _____ , on one hand, and by Mr. Janos Kossuth and Mr. Gabor Szasz, on the other hand. The parties hereby declare and acknowledge, that Mr Janos Kossuth and Mr Gabor Szasz will act as sole commercial partners in Hungary for Mr Herve Bucheron. The parties herewith undertake, that they're not going to arrange any commercial deal between Hungary and France through other individuals or companies, independently that the above mentioned individuals would conduct such an activity as private enterpreneures or companies.

In case of controversial matters the parties determine the selected court, which operates next to the Chamber of Commerce in Budapest.

The written pleadings establish without disagreement that Mr. Bucheron is the owner and CEO of Bois et Meubles and that Janos Kossuth and Gabor Szasz are joint owners of Lumber Mills of Hungary. The agreement was originally drafted in Hungarian by Mr. Kossuth and Mr. Szasz. The designation "selected court which operates next to the Chamber of Commerce in Budapest" is a literal translation. The Hungarian term "választott-bíróság" means arbitration, but its literal translation is "selected court". Kossuth and Szasz also argue in their pleadings that "Chamber of Commerce in Budapest" can only mean the Hungarian Chamber of Commerce and Industry, since in Hungary no other chamber of commerce has a court of arbitration.

How should the French court rule?

B.   Before Arbitrators

Suppose the French court stays the action to await arbitration and Mr. Kossuth and Mr. Szasz, on behalf of Lumber Mills, initiate arbitration against Bois et Meubles before the Court of Arbitration attached to the Hungarian Chamber of Commerce and Industry claiming for the unpaid portion of the sales price. Although the Hungarian Court of Arbitration informs Bois et Meubles of the proceeding, Bois et Muebles refuses to participate or to respond in any way. Lumber Mills appoints its arbitrator, the Hungarian Court of Arbitration appoints an arbitrator for Bois et Muebles, and the two choose a presiding arbitrator. To explain why the Hungarian Court of Arbitration has jurisdiction to hear the case, Mr. Kossuth and Mr. Szasz, acting for Lumber Mills, submitted the Mutual Agreement (above) to the arbitrators and explained that it was a framework agreement under which the parties contemplated that they would enter sales agreements of the kind that was now in dispute.

Should the arbitrators accept jurisdiction to hear the case?

II.1.h.   *Split Arbitration Clauses*

ASTRA FOOTWEAR INDUSTRY v. HARWYN INTERNATIONAL, INC.

United States District Court, Southern District of New York, 1978.
442 F.Supp. 907.

MEMORANDUM OPINION AND ORDER

PIERCE, DISTRICT JUDGE.

Petitioner Astra Footwear brings this action to compel arbitration to resolve a contract dispute which has arisen between the parties. Petitioner is a footwear manufacturer located in Zagreb, Yugoslavia; respondent is a footwear distributor with offices in New York.

In May, 1975 the parties entered into an agreement under which petitioner agreed to sell and deliver and respondent agreed to purchase 13,400 pairs of shoes. Petitioner alleges that it has shipped footwear pursuant to the agreement, but that respondent has refused to pay for invoices totalling $115,820.00 covering said shipments.

Petitioner seeks to compel arbitration before the International Chamber of Commerce, a body which exists for the purpose of settling international business disputes. In so requesting, petitioner relies on paragraph 12 of the contract, which provides:

> "12. *Disputes*: For all claims of disputes arising out of this agreement which could not be amicably settled between the parties, is competent the arbitrage for export trade at the Federal Chamber of Commerce in Beograd. (sic) In the case that the buyer is accused, the Chamber of Commerce in New York is competent."

It is petitioner's position that in designating the "Chamber of Commerce in New York," the parties were referring to the International Chamber of Commerce (ICC), which is based in Paris and has offices in New York.[2]

Petitioner further indicates that should the Court determine that the ICC was not agreed to, it stands ready to arbitrate before any arbitrator appointed by the Court, including the American Arbitration Association.

In reply, respondent maintains that the agreement refers to and the parties intended the New York Chamber of Commerce (NYCC) to arbitrate disputes arising thereunder. In support of its position, respondent asserts that prior to entering into this agreement it had never before done business with a Communist concern, and therefore was careful to choose an arbitration body—NYCC—that would best protect its interests.

It appears that the New York Chamber of Commerce ceased to arbitrate disputes in April, 1973 when it merged to become the New York Chamber of Commerce & Industry (NYCCI). It is respondent's position that the naming of NYCC was "an integral part of the substantive rights bargained for by Harwyn," and that in light of NYCCI's inability to hear the dispute, the agreement to arbitrate has been vitiated and the petition must be dismissed.

Respondent argues that the question of whether the agreement was to arbitrate in general or was to arbitrate before a particular organization is an issue mandating a jury trial under 9 U.S.C. § 4 (1970) of the Federal Arbitration Act.[3] To support this position, respondent cites a New York case,[4] *Laboratorios Grossman, S.A. v. Forest Laboratories, Inc.*, 31 A.D.2d 628, 295 N.Y.S.2d 756 (1st Dep't 1968) which dealt with a closely analogous fact situation. There the parties agreed to arbitrate "in accordance with the rules and procedures of the Pan–American Arbitration Association", an organization which had never in fact existed. A petition was brought to stay arbitration. The Court, in ordering a hearing to determine the parties' intent, stated: "the issue to be decided is whether the dominant purpose of the agreement was to settle disputes by arbitration, rather than the instrumentality through which arbitration should be effected." *Id.*, 295 N.Y.S.2d at 757. * * *

---

2. Petitioner in fact approached the International Chamber of Commerce in January 1977 and requested arbitration before that body. ICC denied petitioner's request since it was not the organization specified in the agreement and respondent refused to consent to ICC jurisdiction.

3. 9 U.S.C. § 4 (1970) provides in pertinent part: "If the making of the arbitration agreement or the failure, neglect, or refusal to perform the same be in issue, the court shall proceed summarily to the trial thereof.... Where such an issue is raised, the party alleged to be in default may ... demand a jury trial of such issue."

4. The New York statutes relevant to this inquiry are N.Y.C.P.L.R. §§ 7503 & 7504 (McKinney 1963). They are similar to the Federal Arbitration Act, 9 U.S.C. § 1, et seq. (1970) in providing for a trial where there is a question regarding the making of an agreement to arbitrate and in providing for Court appointment of a substitute arbitrator. However, the federal statute, 9 U.S.C. § 4, provides for trial by jury if one is demanded.

Petitioner, on the other hand, has cited the case of *Delma Engineering Corp. v. K & L Construction Co.*, 6 A.D.2d 710, 174 N.Y.S.2d 620 (2d Dep't 1958), *aff'd*, 5 N.Y.2d 852, 181 N.Y.S.2d 794, 155 N.E.2d 675 (1958), which has a factual situation bearing greater resemblance to the present case than does Laboratorios. The contract in Delma provided for arbitration before the New York Building Congress which refused to take the case because it had discontinued arbitration procedures and neither disputant was a member of the Building Congress. The Appellate Division rejected the argument that since the provisions for arbitration had failed, the parties were relegated to their remedies in court. Instead, the court held that there was a dominant intent to arbitrate and not merely to arbitrate before particular arbitrators. Without requiring a trial on the question of intent, the appellate court directed the lower court to appoint three arbitrators of its own selection, pursuant to the New York statute.[5]

The Court of Appeals for this Circuit has stated that what a party must show in order to place the making of an arbitration agreement in issue or to make a genuine issue entitling a party to a trial by jury is "an unequivocal denial that the agreement had been made ... and some evidence should have been produced to substantiate the denial." *Interocean Shipping Co. v. National Shipping & Trading Corp.*, 462 F.2d 673, 676 (2d Cir.1972), quoting *Almacenes Fernandez, S.A. v. Golodetz*, 148 F.2d 625, 628 (2d Cir.1945). In Interocean, the party opposing arbitration denied the very existence of the contract that contained the arbitration clause. In the present case, respondent's main objection to arbitration appears to be fear that the arbitrator would not support American business interests.[6] Respondent has not unequivocally denied that an arbitration agreement was made in the present case. From the language of the contract and the position of the parties, the Court finds that an arbitration agreement was made and that the making of such agreement is not in issue here.

The Court further finds that by the terms "Chamber of Commerce in New York" the parties intended the New York Chamber of Commerce, and not the International Chamber of Commerce which has an office in New York. Respondent has pointed out that even the petitioner

---

5. Although the Court of Appeals for this Circuit has consistently held that federal rather than state law controls in determining the validity of a contract to arbitrate, *Coenen v. R. W. Pressprich & Co.*, 453 F.2d 1209 (2d Cir.), *cert. denied*, 406 U.S. 949, 92 S.Ct. 2045, 32 L.Ed.2d 337 (1972); *Robert Lawrence Co. v. Devonshire Fabrics, Inc.*, 271 F.2d 402 (2d Cir.), *app. dismissed*, 364 U.S. 801, 81 S.Ct. 27, 5 L.Ed.2d 37 (1960), state law is particularly helpful in this situation where the state and federal arbitration statutes are fairly similar and there is no apparent federal precedent. Cf. *Lea Tai Textile Co. v. Manning Fabrics, Inc.*, 411 F.Supp. 1404 (S.D.N.Y.1975)

(Court looked to Uniform Commercial Code in determining the question of existence of contract to arbitrate.)

6. Respondent apparently feels that the International Chamber of Commerce would not be as protective of the interests of American businesses as would the New York Chamber of Commerce. However, although preferring the International Chamber of Commerce, petitioner is willing to appear before any arbitrator including the American Arbitration Association, which apparently should alleviate respondent's fears of the arbitrator being prejudiced against American businesses.

when seeking arbitration applied first to the New York Chamber of Commerce and Industry. In addition, the International Chamber of Commerce when approached as an arbitrator also suggested that the parties try the New York Chamber of Commerce.

Since the New York Chamber of Commerce no longer arbitrates and the International Chamber of Commerce was not specified in the agreement, petitioner next requested that the Court appoint an arbitrator pursuant to 9 U.S.C. § 5 (1970) which provides:

> "If in the agreement provision be made for a method of naming or appointing an arbitrator or arbitrators or an umpire, such method shall be followed; but if no method be provided therein, or if a method be provided and any party thereto shall fail to avail himself of such method, or if for any other reason there shall be a lapse in the naming of an arbitrator or arbitrators or umpire, or in filling a vacancy, then upon the application of either party to the controversy the court shall designate and appoint an arbitrator or arbitrators or umpire, as the case may require, who shall act under the said agreement with the same force and effect as if he or they had been specifically named therein; and unless otherwise provided in the agreement the arbitration shall be by a single arbitrator." (Emphasis supplied.)

However, respondent contends that "(w)hile there is a strong policy favoring arbitration ... it remains a creature of contract. (The Court should) not impose its will on parties whose intentions are in clear conflict on this important issue." *Lea Tai Textile Co. v. Manning Fabrics, Inc.*, 411 F.Supp. 1404, 1407 (S.D.N.Y.1975). But respondent's reliance on Lea Tai is misplaced. In that case, Judge Duffy held that there was no agreement to arbitrate since buyer and seller had exchanged forms with "hopelessly" inconsistent arbitration terms. In the present case, as has been noted, it is undisputed that the parties did agree to arbitrate albeit before the "Chamber of Commerce in New York."

The Court finds that 9 U.S.C. § 5 was drafted to provide a solution to the problem caused when the arbitrator selected by the parties cannot or will not perform. In view of the federal policy to construe liberally arbitration clauses and to resolve doubts in favor of arbitration, *Coenen v. R. W. Pressprich & Co.*, 453 F.2d 1209 (2d Cir.), *cert. denied*, 406 U.S. 949, 92 S.Ct. 2045, 32 L.Ed.2d 337 (1972), the Court concludes that it cannot ignore the plain language of 9 U.S.C. § 5, nor do the equities of the case[7] warrant doing so. The Court thus agrees to appoint an arbitrator pursuant to 9 U.S.C. § 5.

7. But *cf. CIA De Navegacion Omsil, S.A. v. Hugo Neu Corp.*, 359 F.Supp. 898 (S.D.N.Y.1973) (Court did not appoint arbitrator when one arbitrator on three person panel died, but instead ordered parties to select a new panel. The Court noted that it would not be fair for the appointed arbitrator "respondent's arbitrator" to join in the deliberations after a series of hearings and meetings had transpired without him. "The two remaining arbitrators, 'petitioner's' and the neutral, have worked together and been exposed to each other's influence. The results of that may have been good, bad, or

Accordingly, petitioner's motion to arbitrate is hereby granted. The only matter remaining is the appointment of a substitute arbitrator. The parties are invited to submit in writing to the Court by January 26, 1978 the names of possible alternate arbitrators. Should the parties fail together in agreeing upon one arbitrator, the Court will designate one.

SO ORDERED.

YUGOSLAV CO. v. PDR KOREA CO.

Arbitration Court attached to the Chamber for Foreign Trade of the GDR[h], 1982.
8 Yearbk. Comm. Arb'n 129 (1983).*

FACTS

In January 1978, the parties concluded a contract for the delivery of frozen arctic fish. The Yugoslav buyer complained about the quality of the goods and derived claims therefrom which the seller has so far neither recognized nor satisfied.

The contract contains the following arbitration clause "12th Clause: In the case any problems arise in the course of our business, they should be settled by mutual consent. If no mutual consent is reached the arbitration of the People's Republic of China, the People's Republic of Poland and the GDR will be adopted."

Basing himself on this clause the Plaintiff filed on July 7, 1981, a petition with the Arbitration Court attached to the Chamber for Foreign Trade of the GDR, claiming for damages. In the writ the Plaintiff states, among other things, that he had, on May 15, 1979, filed the same petition with the *Colegium Arbitrow*, Warsaw, and that the Polish Arbitration Court had, after the Defendant had challenged its competence, declared itself incompetent and that for that reason the petition had been rejected.

The Defendant has, by telex of November 7, 1981, confirmed to the Berlin Arbitration Court the receipt of the statement of claim. By telex of December 10, 1981, he commented on the competence of the Arbitration Court and the case before the court. As to competence he states:

> "It was not indicated to choose a court at one's will in the contract.... If one court of arbitration among the countries which are indicated in the contract will hope to treat an affair, they must have the Defendant's opinion. The right of choice of a court of arbitration can be granted to one party only by agreement between both parties. Therefore we insist, that any court cannot treat his affair without agreement between both parties for choice of court".

nil for respondent.... It is not fair or fitting to impose the risk, which respondent never agreed to accept, by judicial command." *Id. at 899*).

    h. Authors' note: German Democratic Republic (East Germany).

The Defendant did not comply with the invitation to nominate an arbitrator. Upon request of the Claimant the Vice-president of the Arbitration Court acting as an appointing authority nominated ... an arbitrator with effect for the Defendant.

The arbitration committee fixed a date for an oral hearing in order to find, by negotiations between the two parties, a way to solve the contested issue of competence, but only the Plaintiff made an appearance at that hearing. He moved for the issue of an interim award concerning the competence of the Arbitration Court.

EXTRACT

The Arbitration Court attached to the Chamber for Foreign Trade of the GDR decides, according to Art. 1, para. 1 of its Arbitration Rules on disputes arising from international commercial and scientific-technical relations between judicial persons from different countries, as far as its competence is established.

The competence of this Arbitration Court is substantiated, if *either* a written arbitration agreement is presented *or* the Defendant, without challenging the competence of the arbitration court joins issues on the matter itself *or* if the parties are, by dint of legal provisions, obliged to file their litigations with the arbitration court for the sake of a decision.

There is no doubt that no internationally binding agreements exist between Yugoslavia and the People's Democratic Republic of Korea which compulsorily prescribe dispute settlement by arbitration for companies taking part in bilateral trade.

Furthermore: The Defendant did not deny the competence of this Berlin Arbitration Court, but pointed out that the arbitration clause requires a further agreement to be effective.

It was necessary therefore to examine whether the above-mentioned clause of the contract may be regarded as an effective arbitration agreement and thereby regarded as a basis for the competence of the Arbitration Court.

The arbiters in every arbitration proceeding must carefully examine their competence. Usually, however, no special decision is issued on the matter of competence. This competence is mentioned in the final award on the matter itself and, if need be, substantiated in more detail.

Since in this case the competence of the arbiters already presents a contested issue, the settlement of which will determine for the plaintiff the further handling of the matter, the Arbitration Court decided to render an interim award.

* * *

The arbitrators have from the clause and the pleadings of the parties decided that both parties desire a settlement of disputes outside state jurisdiction. That wish, expressed by both parties, has essentially determined the attitude of the arbitrators vis-à-vis the clause inserted into the contract. They felt an obligation to help the parties realize such a wish.

The arbitrators cannot help expressing the critical remark that the clause has not been well formulated. In order to be able to apply it, there is need for interpretation. The arbitrators, however, state that such an imperfection is not a particularity of that clause. The whole written contract had been set up in the very same unsatisfactory manner, in a way which corresponds neither to the international character of the commercial transaction nor the rather considerable value of the contract. It is essential therefore for the assessment of the clause that its style, way of expression and language is in complete accord with the other text of the contract.

The arbitrators interpret the clause as an optional one which allows the Plaintiff the choice of applying to any arbitration court of the three mentioned countries. Obviously the parties did have in mind, regarding the (central) chambers of foreign trade of the three countries, the permanent arbitration courts existing there, i.e.,

— The Arbitration Court attached to the Chamber of Foreign Trade of the GDR,

— Arbitration Court *(Kolegium Arbitrow)* attached to the Polish Chamber of Foreign Trade in Warsaw and

— the Foreign Economic and Foreign Trade Arbitration Commission of the China Council for the Promotion of International Trade (CCPIT) in Peking.

The clause does not divulge anything about the setting up of an ad hoc arbitration in those countries, nor is the idea of a combined arbitration tribunal possible for practical reasons: the clause itself gives no hint either of any sort of co-operation between the three permanent arbitration courts for the sake of a combined tribunal.

The agreement on a optional clause is, from the point of view of the Berlin Arbitration Court, nothing unusual. Thus, e.g., clauses occur rather frequently which permit the Plaintiff to choose between a certain arbitration court and the state court with competence for the residence of the defendant. Precondition for the recognition of such a clause is, in every case, that either party is entitled to avail himself of that option. Since that option was granted to the Plaintiff who, however, had not at all been certain at the time of the signing of the contact, the fact can, in this concrete case, be established that neither party may benefit in an unjustified manner from such an option.

The arbitrators had to deal with the objection raised by the Defendant that the clause merely represented a sort of preliminary agreement *(pactum de contrahendo)* which binds the parties to agree, in case of a dispute, on the actual arbitration clause. Such a two-stage procedure in agreements on settling disputes by means of arbitration still exists in some countries. In GDR law such a two-stage arrangement has never existed, nor in the legislation of other socialist countries. Thereby these legal systems are in agreement with the well-known international conventions in the field of arbitration, e.g., the New York Convention of 1958 on the Recognition and Enforcement of Foreign Arbitral Awards and the European Convention of 1961 on International Commercial Arbitration. These conventions provide for the single-stage arbitration agreement on disputes which have already originated or may originate in future. Even those countries, which in their arbitration legislation or in their civil procedural laws still provide a two-stage agreement on arbitration, adhere, in actual practice, in cases of international commercial transactions with extensive approval by their courts, to the single-stage agreement. The arbitrators follow that international trend, particularly as the arbitration law of the GDR, which applied according to Art. 1 of the above-mentioned Decree to any arbitration held in the GDR, provides only for a single-stage arbitration agreement.

The arbitrators proceed from the idea that the application of the arbitration laws of the GDR to such a procedure does not cause any injustice to the parties concerned. Although its transaction has no relation at all to the GDR and its legislation, the parties themselves have established such a relationship between themselves by their agreement including a clause referring among other things, to the arbitration administered through the permanent Arbitration Court attached to the Chamber of Foreign Trade of the GDR. It cannot, therefore, come as a surprise to the parties when the arbiters make use of the arbitration legislation of the venue of the proceedings for deciding on procedural issues.

Drawing a conclusion from all that, the arbitrators regard the clause "12th Clause", which is contained in the contract and signed by both parties, as being valid and effective. They understand it as an optional clause which leaves it to the Plaintiff to submit his claim to an arbitration whose proceedings are administered by a permanent arbitration court in Peking, Berlin [or] Warsaw.

The arbiters felt themselves under the obligation to examine to what extent the petition, which had been filed in 1979 with the Warsaw Arbitration Court and rejected there due to lack of competence, impairs the effectiveness of the clause and the filing of the petition in Berlin.

The rejection of the statement of claim by the Warsaw Arbitration Court members was based exclusively on their concept of the incompetence of the local arbitration court. The case itself had not been dealt with in Warsaw. That leads the arbitrators of the Arbitration Court attached to the Chamber of Foreign Trade of the GDR to the conclusion that the arbitration clause has not been consummated.

Furthermore, the fact has to be taken into consideration that the Arbitration Courts in Warsaw and Berlin are two independent institutions without any connection. Decisions taken by either arbitration court do not bind the other arbitration court. This applies to decisions on the merits as well as on procedure. Accordingly the arbiters have taken interested cognizance of the decision on lack of competence taken by the

Warsaw Arbitration Court, but such a decision has not influenced this interim award on the competence of the Berlin Arbitration Court.

The arbitrators decided that the competence of this Arbitration Court for arbitration arising from the contract between the parties dated January 1978 regarding the delivery of frozen fish is established.

Questions and Comments

1. Split arbitration clauses were normally used in the CMEA (COMECON) General Conditions of Delivery.[50] Each member country of the CMEA having had one institutional tribunal of general competence,[51] under the General Conditions of Delivery, disputes were to be settled by arbitration and the competent arbitral institution was, in principle, the one in the respondent's country. The General Conditions are no longer in effect, nor is arbitration in the country of the respondent mandatory. However, businessmen from these states often endeavor to provide for arbitration in the respondent's country.

Outside the CMEA (or former CMEA) split arbitration clauses are less frequent, but they are by no means unheard of either.

The allocation criterion in split arbitration clauses is typically the position of the parties in the lawsuit (claimant or respondent) or the nature of the dispute (e.g. some clauses refer "technical disputes" to one arbitral body, and "legal" or "non-technical" disputes to another). Other distinguishing criteria are also used.

One of the main problems with split arbitration clauses is the inherent difficulty in drawing the dividing line. It may be relatively easy to distinguish between claimants and respondents (and thus it is easy to know which arbitral institution is that of the country of the respondent), but it is less clear to which forum this criterion would direct a counterclaim. Distinctions between technical and non-technical issues or between issues pertaining to the responsibility of the contractor and issues relating to the liability of the investor may also be very difficult to administer.

2. In *Astra Footwear v. Harwyn*, the parties struggled to escape the predicament that resulted from an imperfect and split arbitration clause. Astra resorted to a rather strained argument, stating that in designating the "Chamber of Commerce in New York," the parties were actually referring to the International Chamber of Commerce which is based in Paris but has offices in New York. In turn, respondent asserted, as stated in the decision, that "prior to entering into this agreement it had never before done business with a Communist concern, and therefore was careful to choose the arbitra-

[50]. Article 104 and 105 of the 1968/1988 General Conditions of Delivery (then) accepted by all countries of the Council of Mutual Economic Assistance. (Membership in the CMEA largely coincided with membership in the Warsaw Pact.)

See a German text (in addition to a Hungarian and Russian text) published by the Hungarian Chamber of Commerce in *Külk-* *ereskedelmi Jogi Dokumentáció, 16. füzet, Budapest 1989* "Allgemeine Bedingungen für die Warenlieferungen zwischen den Organisationen der Mitgliedslander des RGW 1968/1988."

[51]. Some countries, like the USSR and Poland, had a maritime arbitral institution as well.

tion body—the NYCC—that would best protect its interests.''[52] (If this was really a careful choice spurred by ideological precautions, one may wonder what considerations led the New York firm to agree on Belgrade arbitration if it were the plaintiff, and to agree on a non-existing arbitral institution were it to appear in the role of respondent.)

The court did not appreciate certain "refinements" proposed by the parties. The proposition that arbitration at the Chamber of Commerce in New York actually means I.C.C. arbitration was rejected; nor was the defendant's argument accepted. Instead the court ordered arbitration before an ad hoc tribunal. The U.S. District Court relied on 9 U.S.C. para. 5 (1970) which provides for court assistance when the arbitrator selected by the parties cannot or will not perform. This rule was extended to a situation in which the institution selected by the parties cannot perform arbitral functions.

Was the extension appropriate?

3.   If Harwyn counterclaims against Astra, would arbitration in Belgrade result?

4.   Staying with Yugoslavian examples, in a dispute between a German lessor and a Yugoslav lessee, the parties' contract contained the following arbitration clause:

"Lessor and Lessee shall take all measures to settle by negotiation all disputes and differences arising out of this contract.

a) if Lessor is liable, the dispute shall be settled through the competent court in Heidelberg, in accordance with the arbitration rules of the said court,

b) if Lessee is liable the Foreign Trade Court of Arbitration at the Economic Chamber of Yugoslavia in Belgrade shall have competence, in accordance with the rules applicable here.

The decision of the Arbitration is final and binding on both parties.

Counterclaims shall be considered by the arbitration which is competent for the primary claim."

This split arbitration clause certainly has, at least, the merit of dealing explicitly with the issue of counterclaims. (Other merits are not so easy to find.) A claim was brought before the Belgrade court of arbitration against the Yugoslav lessee, by an Austrian agent of the German lessor suing (erroneously) in its own name. Respondent (the lessee) argued against the jurisdiction of the Belgrade arbitral tribunal on two grounds. First it asserted that the Austrian claimant had no standing; second, it stressed that the arbitration clause was "inoperative and incapable of being performed" within the meaning of Article II of the New York Convention, because no one could know which party is liable before the dispute was settled, and therefore, liability of one or the other party cannot serve as a distinguishing criterion. Thus there was no way of establishing which of the two institutions had jurisdiction.

[52].   442 F.Supp. 907, 908 (1978).

On February 25, 1997, the Enlarged Panel of the Belgrade Court of Arbitration refused jurisdiction[53] on the ground of lack of standing, without reaching the other ground asserted by respondent.

What result would follow if the second issue is faced? Is this split arbitration clause beyond repair—inoperative or incapable of being performed—or can a benevolent interpretation be found to rescue this arbitration?

5. In the cases referred to above, the core of the problem was the imperfection of the criterion of division. The GDR arbitration tribunal in *Yugoslav Co. v. PDR Korea Co.*, supra, faced another (pathological) variant of split arbitration clauses: lack of any criterion of division.

Is this clause an agreement to agree (stipulation requiring a further agreement in order to be effective)?

6. Do you agree with the decision of the GDR arbitrators? If you do, what reasons would you advance? (If you disagree, what are your arguments?)

7. Assuming that you accept the position of the Respondent that clause 12 was not an operative arbitration agreement, but merely an agreement to agree, could all three arbitral institutions refuse jurisdiction in the absence of a "further agreement"?

II.1.i. Changed Circumstances

PARTIAL DECISION OF APRIL 2, 1992[i]

Landgericht [District Court] Kassel.
Recht der Internationalen Wirtschaft [RIW], 239 (1993).*

THE FACTS:

The claimant is claiming from the defendant the remaining payment. As the defendant was not prepared to voluntarily fulfill his payment obligations, the claimant approached the court for remedy. The claimant did not claim at the Foreign Trade Arbitration Tribunal of the Chamber of Commerce of the Socialist Federal Republic of Yugoslavia (SFRY) in Belgrade, as agreed upon in Art. XII of the Contract dated February 27, 1985, because of the break up of the SFRY and the war turmoil following such break up, by which events all post and other telecommunication links between Ljubljana, the capital of the now independent state of Slovenia, and Belgrade/Serbia have been interrupt-

---

[53]. Case No T–15/96—unpublished.

i. Authors' translation. Abbreviations in text:

BGB: Bürgerliches Gesetzbuch—Civil Code;

BGH: Bundesgerichtshof—Federal Court of Germany;

EGBGB: Einführungsgesetz zum Bürgerlichen Gesetzbuch—Introductory Provisions to the Civil Code;

GG: Grundgesetz—Basic Law (Constitution);

NJW: Neue Juristische Wochenschrift (New Legal Weekly);

ZPO: Zivilprozessordnung (Code of Civil Procedure).

* Reprinted by permission of Recht der Internationalen Wirtschaft, Verlag Recht und Wirtschaft GmbH.

ed and direct journeys between these two cities became impossible. At the same time the claimant gave notice to the defendant to terminate, as a precaution, the arbitration agreement for cause. The claimant argues that the Chamber of Commerce of the SFRY is an institution of the Yugoslavian Central Government, and * * * [on this basis] the agreed upon competent arbitration tribunal, * * * [is] no longer * * * active for an enterprise domiciled in Slovenia (proof: information from the Ministry of Foreign Affairs of the Federal Republic of Germany). Further, the claimant argues that it is unreasonable to expect him to call upon a tribunal situated in an (indisputably) enemy country. The defendant argues that according to Art. XII of the Contract the claim is invalid. In consideration of the actual negotiations between the European Community and the Government of Belgrade, a status similar to peace is expected to be reached in the near future, and on this basis the arbitration tribunal could become active. The claim led to judgment against the defendant.

THE REASONS:

"The claim is admissible and—as far as it is ripe for decision—it is sustainable.

(1) § 1027a ZPO is not in contradiction to the material decision made by the court called upon: as according to this provision possible clauses of an arbitration agreement only prevent a claim being made to a state court provided a party is not deprived by such agreement of reasonable legal protection.

Arbitration agreements should by their content, purpose and aim only transfer the decision making process of a certain dispute from a state court to a private (arbitration) court, it should not have a lasting effect to * * * exclude a state court completely. Should therefore such an arbitration agreement become—for whatever reason—practically unfulfillable, each party shall have the right to terminate it for cause. According to the principles of good faith (§ 242 BGB) applicable on ground of a valid choice of German law, the termination of arbitration agreements for cause is, in principle, admissible (cf. Palandt, BGB 50. ed., Art. 27 EGBGB, notice 2e) just as * * * in other durable contractual relations (BGH NJW 1964, 1129; BGH NJW 1969, 277; cf. also Raeschke–Kessler NJW 1988, 3040). Because of the importance of the legal protection the substance of the right to terminate such an agreement does not depend, as a general rule, on the fact whether an arbitration proceeding has already been introduced or not or whether the party seeking termination of such agreement is responsible for carrying out of the proceeding. Although by concluding an arbitration agreement a party renounces to a large extent * * * the legally guaranteed judge and by this * * * [as well] an important basic right according to Art. 102 I 2 GG, this does not yield, however, a renunciation of legal protection of state courts even if an arbitration becomes impossible to carry out. On the contrary, such an event justifies the right to extraordinary termination of such an agreement as stated in § 242 BGB as a general rule to be filled out by the principle of a state founded on the rule of law according to which such state cannot accept that its citizens find themselves in an area totally without law (BGH NJW 1980, 2136/2137).

From the principle of a state founded on the rule of law as stated in the Constitution a guarantee of an effective legal protection also for civil litigation can be deduced which, as a general rule, has to make possible the full legal examination of the facts as well as a binding decision by a judge. An effective legal protection necessarily also includes that such protection can be obtained within a reasonable period; otherwise the rights of individuals recognized by the legal order would have only a minor practical importance. This legal protection can only be altered even by agreement of the parties at the most in some concrete provisions because of its essential importance for the continued existence of the legal order; however, it cannot be deprived of its substance (BGH NJW 1989, 1477). Being that every arbitration proceeding aims to re-establish the legal peace between the parties by an arbitral award, termination of the arbitration agreement has to be possible at least when cases occur in which an effective legal protection can no longer be expected (BGH NJW 1986, 2765 (2766); cf. BGH NJW 1988, 1215).

Such a situation can be presumed according to the presentation of the parties; for since the conclusion of the Contract on February 27, 1985 such important upheavals took place that the claimant cannot be obliged to follow the way foreseen for resolution of a dispute contemplated in the above mentioned Contract. By stating this it can even be * * * [necessary] to examine whether the Foreign Trade Arbitration Tribunal of the Chamber of Commerce of SFRY in Belgrade is able to function as such at all; even if * * * [such] would be the case, in principle, * * * [the Chamber] would not be accessible to the claimant in a fair way. It is so far undisputed between the parties that for the time being all post and other telecommunication links between Ljubljana and the place of the arbitration tribunal are interrupted and journeys from Slovenia to Serbia are only possible by detour via Hungary. It is furthermore undisputed between the parties that the separated territorial parts of ex-SFRY are practically in a state of war among themselves and no serious evidence can be found to sustain the allegation of the defendant that 'in the near future' 'a status similar to peace' will return nor could such a development be observed otherwise. Taking into consideration that the originally foreseen arbitration tribunal is actually situated, contrary to the situation at the conclusion of the Contract and from the point of view of the claimant, in a foreign enemy country in which an orderly proceeding can not really be reached, one would transgress in a lasting way the borders drawn by the principle of the observance of the Contract in a good faith (cf. Palandt cit. § 242, note 6Bc) if one would nevertheless adhere to the arbitration agreement concluded under totally different circumstances.''

Questions and Comments

1.   Arbitration tribunals are—in principle—neutral in every sense. They are not part of a state or of state institutions. Still, if an institutional tribunal becomes an institution within another state (because of change of borders), the issue of changed circumstances (*rebus sic stantibus*) arises.

One of the authors of this book can confirm that telephone and postal communications between Slovenia and Serbia were indeed interrupted in April 1992, and travel was only possible via neighboring Hungary (a detour of up to 100 kilometers). The Belgrade Court of Arbitration was legally not "an institution of the Yugoslavian Central Government," nor did it ever decline to entertain cases of Slovenian partners—but no such cases were arbitrated in Belgrade in 1992. There was no war in Slovenia in 1992, nor was there war in Belgrade or Serbia. However, Yugoslavia (Serbia and Montenegro) was involved in the ongoing armed conflicts in Croatia and Bosnia–Herzegovina.

Towards what decision would these facts lead you?

2.   Suppose the dispute between the Slovenian and German parties were to emerge now, when hostilities have ceased. Relations between the successor states of the former Yugoslavia are less than harmonious, but "a status at least more similar to peace" has certainly been reached. Ambassadors have been exchanged, and the persisting animosities may not be greater than the resentment between certain other countries and nations that were not recently at war. The fact remains that, for a Slovenian, Belgrade is not the same environment that it was before the breakup of Yugoslavia. It is no longer home ground. Is this critical?

3.   A similar problem might have emerged in *Astra v. Harwyn* under the split arbitration clause. If Harwyn had been the claimant and had begun proceedings in Belgrade, could Astra have successfully resisted arbitration in Belgrade on the ground that this is now the capital of a foreign country, not the one to which Astra belongs? (Astra is a Zagreb company; Zagreb is the capital of Croatia.)

4.   The issue is not restricted to the breakup of Yugoslavia.[54] For example, similar problems emerge regarding arbitration clauses providing for the competence of the Moscow Foreign Trade Court of Arbitration. Moscow is still the capital of Russia, but is no longer the capital of the USSR. Could a party from Vilnius, Lithuania refuse to arbitrate in Moscow because, although home ground at the time the contract was executed, circumstances (and boundaries) have changed, and arbitrating in Moscow is a different matter from what it was when the arbitration agreement was concluded?

5.   Consider the following facts. The Belgrade Court of Arbitration had a list of arbitrators, which included persons from Slovenia and Croatia. These persons are no longer on the list. Since 1997 foreigners can be included on the list. According to Article 5 of the Rules of the Belgrade Court

---

[54].   *See* A. Uzelac, Succession of Arbi-   Yearbook 71–89 (1996).
tral Institutions, 3 Croatian Arbitration

of Arbitration,[55] foreigners from outside the list may also be nominated as arbitrators by the foreign party. Thus, a Croatian or Slovenian party could still nominate a Croatian or Slovenian arbitrator. However, the chairman of the arbitration panel can only be chosen from the list and has to be a Yugoslav citizen.

Does this information help you in taking a position?

6.   The Rules of the International Commercial Arbitration Court of the Chamber of Commerce and Industry of the Russian Federation[56] provide for a list of arbitrators. The rules contain no limitations regarding the nationality of arbitrators put on the list. According to Paragraph 2(3) "Persons not included in the List of Arbitrators may also act as arbitrators unless otherwise envisaged by the present Rules." Paragraph 20(3) provides that the chairman of an arbitration panel can only be chosen from the List.

7.   Suppose a change occurs in a less dramatic way than via change of borders. The arbitral institution may change its site. For example, let us presume that the International Chamber of Commerce moves its headquarters from Paris to Amsterdam. Would this influence the validity of an arbitration clause submitting disputes to "Arbitration of the International Chamber of Commerce in Paris?"

8.   On July 6, 1994, another German court (Oberlandesgericht [Court of Appeal] Hamm[57]) was also faced with the impact of the breakup of Yugoslavia on arbitration. The Belgrade Tribunal rendered an arbitral award in favor of a Croatian claimant against the German respondent. The award was rendered after the breakup of Yugoslavia. The claimant sought recognition and enforcement in Germany. Respondent argued that the arbitration agreement lost its validity after Croatia became a separate state. The German court did not accept this argument. It held that the arbitration agreement is a private contract which is not affected by changes of sovereignty.

Is this decision compatible with the holding of the Landgericht Kassel?

9.   After July 1, 1997, Hong Kong became a part of the P.R. of China. According to the Basic Law of the Hong Kong Special Administrative Region of the P.R. of China, adopted in April 1990 by the P.R. of China National Congress (in force July 1, 1997) "the capitalist system and way of life" will remain unchanged in Hong Kong for fifty more years. Most of Hong Kong's legislation (the Arbitration Ordinance included) will also remain unchanged. Still, there is a change of sovereignty. Are the changes that have occurred in Hong Kong's legal status and environment such as to draw in question the continued validity of arbitration clauses providing for arbitration in Hong Kong? What of the future?

II.2.   LIMITS ON ARBITRABILITY

II.2.a.   Note

Arbitration is a private (non-state) process, with a large degree of autonomy and self-sufficiency. Courts—or other authorities entrusted

---

[55].   Rules of October 15, 1997.
[56].   In force since May 1, 1995.

[57].   Reported in 3 Croatian Arbitration Yearbook 242 (1996).

with the protection of the public interest—have only very limited rights of interference. Courts still maintain a rather significant role when it comes to enforcing arbitral awards. The refusal of the courts of one country to enforce an award does not, however, render the award worthless; courts in another country may decide to enforce it.

For these and other reasons countries have traditionally been reluctant to allow arbitration in spheres where there is a strong public interest at stake. Even after the early hostility towards arbitration was reversed, countries continued to distinguish between domains in which public interest and public control are relatively weak, and areas in which society (the state) has strong vested interests and policies. Disputes belonging to the first domain are arbitrable; lawsuits falling into the latter area are reserved for courts and other state authorities. The issue of arbitrability is thus one of the most important threshold questions in the arbitration process.

National decision-makers (legislatures or courts) have essentially been left to their own discretion in defining the disputes that can be settled by arbitration. The New York Convention, for example, impliedly and expressly acknowledges that nonarbitrability may defeat an arbitration agreement or prevent enforcement of an award, but it does not attempt to define the concept, as one sees from the following provisions:

> Article II(1): Each Contracting State shall recognize an agreement in writing [to submit disputes to arbitration] * * * *concerning a subject matter capable of settlement by arbitration.* [Emphasis added.]

> Article II(3): The court of a Contracting State, * * *, shall, * * *, refer the parties to arbitration, *unless it finds that the said agreement* [to submit disputes to arbitration] *is null and void, inoperative or incapable of being performed.* [Emphasis added.]

> Article V(2): Recognition and enforcement of an arbitral award may also be refused if the competent authority in the country where recognition and enforcement is sought finds that:

> (a) *The subject matter of the difference is not capable of settlement by arbitration under the law of that country*; * * * [Emphasis added.]

The same is true of the UNCITRAL Model Law, which while advancing numerous uniform solutions in other areas, did not propose a definition of arbitrability.

Countries following the civil-law tradition have often turned to legislation to mark the borderline between what is—and is not—arbitrable. The touchstone in this legislation is often the distinction between claims that are, and those that are not, within the free disposition of the parties; or, in other words, between cases in which society's (the state's) interest in achieving a certain result is such that the rules established to advance this purpose cannot be overridden by an agreement between the parties (cases regulated by mandatory law), and those in which the state does not impose mandatory rules. Trying to identify disputes that may be submitted to arbitration, the French Code Civil speaks of "rights of which one can dispose freely"; the Japanese Code of Civil Procedure refers to disputes that "the parties are entitled to settle"; the Portuguese Act on Voluntary Arbitration mentions "disposable rights"; whereas the Swiss Private International Law Act treats as arbitrable "any dispute involving an economic interest". Excerpts from these legislative provisions are included in the materials below.

As one might expect, common-law jurisdictions rely largely on caselaw to delimit arbitrability. The materials below include two leading cases from the United States, cases which reflect the modern trend toward expanding the boundaries of arbitrability.

In both civil-law and common-law courts disputes in the following areas have sometimes been found nonarbitrable: antitrust, securities law, intellectual property, damage from unilateral termination of exclusive distributorship agreements, political embargoes, damage to cargo carried under a bill of lading (COGSA claims), bankruptcy, and administrative contracts. These areas are generally regulated by mandatory rules of law designed to protect important public interests. Sometimes that public interest has sweeping implications for society as a whole, as in the case of antitrust whose rules aim to ensure an efficient allocation of society's productive resources through the workings of competitive markets. Sometimes the public interest is narrower, for example to protect investors from fraud, shippers from uncompensated damage to their cargo, or exclusive distributors from uncompensated termination of distribution agreements. In these latter cases, the public policy concern over unequal bargaining power is evident, for otherwise the injured party could be expected to bargain for appropriate protection in the governing contract.

A nonarbitrability doctrine generally reflects distrust in the capacity of arbitrators or the institution of arbitration to resolve appropriately disputes in these areas. One could justify such distrust on several grounds: that arbitrators need not be trained lawyers; arbitration generally does not provide for appellate review to correct mistakes (except where one of the limited grounds for setting aside exists); compulsory process is generally lacking; and, most significantly, arbitrators are beholden to the parties and derive their authority from the arbitration agreement. This last point means that one can expect arbitrators to be heavily influenced by the parties' agreement in areas where mandatory law and concerns about unequal bargaining power would lead courts to give less—or no—deference to agreements that do not respect the public policy underlying mandatory law.

Despite the coherence of these reasons for nonarbitrability, the trend in most legal systems is in the direction of sharply limiting the doctrine, at least with respect to international arbitration and in disputes over enforcement of the arbitration agreement. The arbitrability issue can arise at four points in the life of an arbitrated dispute: before a national court deliberating whether to enforce an arbitration agreement;

before the arbitrators themselves as they try to decide the scope of their competence; before a court, generally in the country where the arbitration has taken place, in an action to set aside the award; and, finally, before a court asked to recognize and enforce the award. The materials below address the arbitrability issue primarily at the first juncture, when a court is trying to decide whether to enforce an arbitration agreement. In that context, and especially for international cases, the trend is to break down the barriers prohibiting arbitration. A lingering question is whether this trend is fully justified.

First we explore the attempt in some legal systems to regulate the arbitrability issue by legislative provisions. We then turn to important court decisions in two representative areas, antitrust and COGSA claims, to demonstrate the trend—and the analysis supporting it—in favor of expanding the kinds of disputes that can be arbitrated. Thereafter the problem of what law should decide the question of arbitrability is addressed.

II.2.b. *Statutory Definitions of Arbitrability and Their Interpretation*

France (Code Civil, 1804)

Article 2059. One can arbitrate [*compromettre* (accept arbitration)] with respect to all rights of which one can dispose freely.

Article 2060. One cannot submit to arbitration questions of status and capacity of persons, questions relative to divorce and separation, or questions respecting controversies that concern public entities or public establishments and more generally any matter that concerns the public order.

However, public establishments of an industrial or commercial character can by decree be authorized to arbitrate.

Italy (1990 Italian Code of Civil Procedure)

Article 806. *Submission to arbitration.* The parties may have arbitrators settle the disputes arising between them, excepting those * * * regarding issues of personal status and marital separation and those others that cannot be the subject of a compromise.[j]

Japan (1890 Code of Civil Procedure)

Article 786 (of Book VIII). An agreement to refer a dispute to one or more arbitrators for determination is valid only insofar as the parties are entitled to settle the matter in dispute.

---

j. This article was not modified by the 1994 reform of Italian arbitration law.

The Netherlands (1986 version of the Code of Civil Procedure)

Article 1020

1. Parties may agree to submit to arbitration disputes which have arisen or may arise between them out of a defined legal relationship, whether contractual or not.

2. The arbitration agreement mentioned in paragraph 1 includes both a submission by which the parties bind themselves to submit to arbitration an existing dispute between them and an arbitration clause under which the parties bind themselves to submit to arbitration disputes which may arise in the future between them.

3. The arbitration agreement shall not serve to determine legal consequences of which the parties cannot freely dispose.

4. Parties may also agree to submit the following matters to arbitration:

(a) the determination only of the quality of the goods;

(b) the determination only of the quantum of damages or a monetary debt;

(c) the filling of gaps in, or modification of, the legal relationship between the parties referred to in paragraph 1.

5. The term "arbitration agreement" includes an arbitration clause which is contained in articles of association or rules which bind the parties.

6. Arbitration rules referred to in an arbitration agreement shall be deemed to form part of that agreement.

Portugal (1986 Act on Voluntary Arbitration)

Article 1. Arbitration agreement

1. Any dispute relating to disposable rights, which has not been exclusively submitted by a special [legislative] act to a court or to compulsory arbitration, may be submitted by the parties to decision by arbitrators.

* * *

4. The State or any other public legal entities may conclude arbitration agreements if they are authorized to do so by a special act or if the subject matters of the arbitration agreement are disputes regarding [a] private law relationship.

Switzerland (Chapter 12 of the 1987 Private International Law Act)

Article 177

1. Any dispute involving an economic interest[k] may be the subject-matter of arbitration.

2. A state, an enterprise owned, or an organization controlled by, a state which is a party to the arbitration agreement cannot rely on its

---

k. In French: "de nature patrimoniale"; in German: "vermögensrechtliche An-   spruch"; in Italian: "qualsiasi pretesa patrimoniale".

own law in order to contest its capacity to be a party to an arbitration or the arbitrability of a dispute covered by the arbitration agreement.

FINCANTIERI-CANTIERI NAVALI ITALIANI SPA (ITALY) v. MINISTRY OF DEFENSE, ARMAMENT AND SUPPLY DIRECTORATE OF IRAQ, REPUBLIC OF IRAQ

Italy, Corte di Appello [Court of Appeal] of Genoa, 1994.
21 Yearbk. Comm. Arb'n 594 (1996).*

FACTS

Through the Armament and Supply Directorate of its Ministry of Defence, the Republic of Iraq (the Iraqi parties) entered into a certain number of contracts with shipbuilders Fincantieri–Cantieri Navali Italiani SpA and Oto Melara SpA (the Italian parties) for the supply of corvettes for the Iraqi Navy. * * * [All contracts contained an arbitration clause.]

An embargo against Iraq was declared by the UN Security Council in August 1990, following the invasion of Kuwait; embargo legislation was issued shortly thereafter by the European Union and Italy. At that time, most of the corvettes had not yet been built or delivered.

The Italian parties commenced proceedings against Iraq in the Court of First Instance of Genoa, alleging frustration of contract and seeking termination and damages. The Iraqi parties objected to the Court's jurisdiction and maintained that the dispute should have been referred to arbitration as provided for in the contracts. The Italian parties replied that only arbitrable matters may be referred to arbitration and that in the case at hand the dispute concerned matters which would have been arbitrable before the embargo legislation was issued but were no more so. They maintained that arbitrability must be ascertained under Italian law and relied on Art. 806 CCP[1], according to which only disputes concerning rights of which the parties may freely dispose ("be the subject of a compromise") may be referred to arbitration. They alleged that, due to the embargo legislation, the parties could no more freely dispose of the contractual rights at issue.

On 9 December 1992, the Court of First Instance of Genoa granted the Iraqi parties' objection and found that it had no jurisdiction over the case. It held that arbitration is excluded under Art. 806 CCP only when it directly affects *diritti indisponibili* (rights of which the parties may not freely dispose) by bringing about a result which is forbidden by the law, in casu, delivery of the corvettes. It found that in the present case the dispute did not directly affect such rights, as the claimants were only seeking termination of the contracts and damages.

* Reprinted with permission of Yearbook Commercial Arbitration, International Council for Commercial Arbitration.

1. See supra page 222.

The Italian parties appealed from this decision to the Court of Appeal of Genoa * * *.

* * *

EXCERPT

[1] "Each of the contracts at issue contains a clause, according to which 'any dispute which may arise under the present contract ... shall be finally settled according to the Conciliation and Arbitration Rules of the Paris Chamber of Commerce by three arbitrators appointed according to the said Rules'. The validity of this clause must be ascertained according to the [New York Convention].

. . .

[3] "Counsel for [the Italian parties] maintains that the dispute falls outside the scope of the arbitration clause because of its subject matter, that is, because the parties may not freely dispose of it.

[4] "We may first mention that Art. II(3) of the New York Convention provides that, if the arbitral clause is null and void or incapable of being performed, the State court has jurisdiction to decide the dispute. It is almost superfluous to mention that in Italian law: 1) according to Art. 806 CCP, the parties may by a 'submission to arbitration' have arbitrators settle 'the disputes arising between them', with the exception of those disputes expressly excluded in the same Article and 'those others that cannot be the subject of a compromise';

. . .

[5] "It is beyond doubt that the rights deriving from the contracts between [the parties] could be freely disposed of at the time when the arbitral clause was stipulated. It is equally beyond doubt that they could not when this action was commenced, as a consequence of the international measures sanctioning Iraq's aggression of Kuwait and of the legislative measures implementing them in our country.

(. . . .)

[6] "The Court of First Instance of Genoa did not deny that according to the law applicable to the merits [these rights] could not be freely disposed of, in the sense of and for the reasons mentioned above: it denied that this could be an obstacle for referring the dispute to arbitration. The Court started from the assumption that an arbitral clause relating to *diritti indisponibili* [rights of which the parties may not freely dispose] is null and void on two conditions: that the [underlying] contract affects these rights by disposing of them in violation of the law; and that the disputes arising under that contract, when arbitrated, may affect them. . . . The Court held that 'in the present case, the first condition is undeniably met, as the contracts containing the arbitral clause provide that goods be sold and delivered to the MOD [Ministry of Defence]: this is clearly at odds with [Italian embargo legislation]'. However, 'on the other hand the second condition is not met, as

claimants ... essentially seek a declaration that the supply contracts are frustrated as a result of the lack of performance by the MOD and the Republic of Iraq, as well as damages; both requests do not affect the prohibition to dispose of the rights as provided for in the said legislation'.

[7] "We do not agree with the lower court's reasoning that 'any dispute on the validity or termination of the contract, which does not lead to a decision on *diritti indisponibili*, cannot be deemed to fall outside the jurisdiction of the arbitrators'. The Court of First Instance bases this principle almost literally on the Supreme Court decision of 19 May 1989, no. 2406, which reads:

> 'For an arbitral clause concerning disputes on *diritti indisponibili* to be null and void ..., it is necessary that the contract containing the clause (which clause remains autonomous) affects such rights by transferring, renouncing them etc. in violation of the law. It is also necessary that the disputes arising from that contract, if negotiated by the parties or settled by arbitrators, affect *diritti indisponibili*, i.e., that the agreement of the parties or the arbitral decision disposes of them in violation of the law. * * * [Given that any dispute on the validity of the contract that does not involve a decision on *diritti indisponibili* falls within the arbitrators' jurisdiction,[m] the arbitrators retain that jurisdiction even if the parties raise issues involving *diritti indisponibili* in the course of the proceedings. In such cases should the arbitrators render an award in violation of mandatory law (*diritti indisponibili*) that award would be null and void, but this would not mean that the arbitration clause itself was invalid.']

[8] "The decision of the Supreme Court * * * concerns the autonomy of the arbitral clause from the underlying contract and its independence from the latter's defects. Consequently, it concerns the role played in national arbitration by *indisponibili* contractual rights, both as a ground for the objection that the arbitral clause is null and void and as a ground for setting aside the award under Art. 829(1)(1) CCP.[4] This does not affect the role which the *diritti indisponibili* may otherwise play with respect to the arbitrators' failure to observe the rules of law, which may be censured according to Art. 829(2) CCP.[5] However, in the present

---

m. Authors' note: In another part of the opinion the Italian Supreme Court (Corte di Cassazione) explained that an arbitration clause that specifically referred questions of *diritti indisponibili* to arbitration would be null and void, but not one that used general, nonspecific language in referring issues to arbitration. In the latter case the arbitrators could decide the dispute without transferring or affecting *diritti indisponibili*, and thus they would have good jurisdiction.

4. Art. 829 of the Italian Code of Civil Procedure reads in relevant part:

"One may institute proceedings on the ground of nullity, notwithstanding any waiver, in the following cases:

(1) if the submission is void;

(. . . .)"

This part of Art. 829 has not been modified by the 1994 reform of Italian arbitration law.

5. Art. 829(2) of the Italian Code of Civil Procedure reads:

"One may also make recourse on the ground of nullity where the arbitrators,

case there is no question of nullity, since the original validity of the arbitral clause is neither challenged nor seriously challengeable: at the time of the clauses' conclusion all formal and substantial conditions were met and the parties could freely dispose of their contractual rights. As we have seen, this situation came to an end later on.

[9] "In order to deal with this problem, we must first adequately and exhaustively consider the said [New York Convention] and in particular its Art. II(1), which provides that: 'Each Contracting State shall recognize an agreement in writing under which the parties undertake to submit to arbitration all or any differences which have arisen or which may arise between them in respect of a defined legal relationship, whether contractual or not, concerning a subject matter capable of settlement by arbitration'; and its Art. II(3), which provides that: 'The court of a Contracting State, when seized of an action in a matter in respect of which the parties have made an agreement within the meaning of this Article, shall, at the request of one of the parties, refer the parties to arbitration, unless it finds that the said agreement is null and void, inoperative or incapable of being performed'.

. . .

[12] "There is no doubt that, although the Convention's language is subjectively and objectively very broad, the derogation from court jurisdiction must be interpreted in the light of the other provisions of the Convention and in particular of the fundamental provision of Art. I. According to Art. I, derogation is possible only when the arbitration proceedings aim at a decision which is enforceable under the Convention, particularly as to the requirement that the dispute be arbitrable. If the dispute cannot be settled by arbitration, a derogation is not possible and State courts . . . again have jurisdiction. Art. V(2)(a) of the Convention, which denies recognition and enforcement to those arbitral awards which, according to the law of the State where recognition or enforcement is sought, concern a non-arbitrable dispute, leads to the same conclusion.

[13] "For the present purpose it is sufficient to answer the question whether, at the time of commencing this action . . ., the arbitral clause in the contracts was 'null and void, inoperative or incapable of being performed'. The answer must be sought in Italian law, according to the jurisprudential principle that, when an objection for foreign arbitration is raised in court proceedings concerning a contractual dispute, the arbitrability of the dispute must be ascertained according to Italian law as this question directly affects jurisdiction, and the court seized of the action can only deny jurisdiction on the basis of its own legal system. This also corresponds to the principles expressed in Arts. II and V of the [New York Convention]. Hence, the answer to the question

when making their decision, have not observed the rules of law, unless the parties have authorized them to decide according to equity or unless they have declared that

there may be no recourse against the award."

This paragraph has not been modified by the 1994 reform.

[of arbitrability] can only be that the dispute was not arbitrable due to [Italian embargo legislation].

. . .

[15] "This solution finds no obstacle in the fact that claimants' main claim aimed at terminating the contracts, not at obtaining performance under them. Also in this case, referral of the dispute to the arbitrators could have affected ... rights which international and national embargo legislation had made *indisponibili*. Indeed, if the claim had been accepted and the contracts terminated, a restitution ... would have been effected which was prohibited under the above legislation. Further, as a set-off had been claimed, in case termination were granted, between the Iraqi parties' credits for advance payments made and their allegedly higher debts, the arbitration could have led to meeting [Iraqi requests] in violation of the said supranational legislation. Also, an hypothetical arbitral award against the claimants, denying termination of the contract, would have recognized the continuing validity of the contracts, thereby affecting, in a contrary but similar manner, *diritti indisponibili*.

[16] "The Court of First Instance of Genoa apparently missed this point and held the arbitral clause (which we hold to be null and void) to be valid. It reasoned that the Italian claimants' claim that the contract was frustrated due to the Iraqi parties' behaviour, and their connected request for damages, if and when granted by award, would not affect *diritti indisponibili* as there would be no actual transfer of property nor delivery of the contractual goods to the Iraqi parties. The Court further ignored the possibility that the arbitrators would reach the opposite solution, which would be as capable of (otherwise) affecting *diritti indisponibili*.

[17] "In its reasoning on the issue of jurisdiction the Court of First Instance apparently anticipated its own evaluation, incidentally but unequivocally made when dealing with the merits, that 'performance under the main contract (has) become impossible not due to the suppliers but solely to the embargo legislation caused by Iraq's aggression of Kuwait' and that 'there exists sure proof that non-performance under the contracts was due to force majeure independent of [the Iraqi parties]'. It is difficult to say whether this has been the psychological reason for what formally appears as a lacuna in the reasoning and an incongruity in the *ratio decidendi*. In any case, it cannot justify the fact that [the Court] did not consider the effect of the request for termination on the *diritti indisponibili* at issue; otherwise, the logical and juridical order of preliminary questions of jurisdiction and questions on the merits would be unacceptably subverted: when dealing with the issue of jurisdiction, the court must consider it *in abstracto* and in the light of all potential outcomes of the examination of the merits, and this latter must be logically subsequent and totally independent.

[18] "Also, the Court of First Instance should not have distinguished (as it implicitly did, although this was possibly not the psycho-

logical reason underlying its decision) the delivery of warfare goods from the mere regulation of monetary aspects of the same relationship through a money transfer from the Italian to the Iraqi party as activities capable of causing a situation not allowed under the embargo legislation. Such distinction is at odds with the supranational legislation issued in the historical situation at hand, which legislation is very far-reaching as it not only prohibits the supply of weapons and accessories to Iraq: it also juridically and commercially isolates that State, held responsible of a particularly severe violation of the right of the peoples, that is, an attempt to erase neighbouring Kuwait from the number of sovereign States member of the international community."

Questions and Comments

1. Note that the *Fincantieri* court applied Italian law to decide the question of arbitrability. Were there other possibilities? Do you agree with the court's reasoning on this point? We explore the choice-of-law question more fully below in section II.2.d.

2. Under the *Fincantieri* court's interpretation of Article 806 of the Italian Code of Civil Procedure, should an Italian court ever refer to arbitration a dispute that could plausibly involve a question of mandatory law? (Should it send all issues except mandatory issues to arbitration?) Are other interpretations of Article 806 available? Would one of these be preferable to the *Fincantieri* interpretation? Note that most of the other statutes reproduced above define arbitrability in language very similar to that of Article 806. Do these statutes impose appropriate restraints on arbitral competence or are they too restrictive? Do they give helpful guidance on the question of arbitrability? What would be the outcome in *Fincantieri* under the Swiss statute?

3. The Italian embargo legislation is contained in two executive decrees (August 6, 1990 and August 23, 1990) later converted into laws by acts of the Italian parliament. Relevant portions of the laws read as follows:[58]

Decreto legge 220 of August 6, 1990

Art. 1.1

Any act of disposal and all transactions, for whatever purpose, concerning moveable goods including intangible goods, immoveable goods, firms and other legal entities, securities or shares having a financial or monetary nature, however named or described, are forbidden, if those goods, securities or shares belong to, even if through intermediaries, the Republic of Iraq or any other person, agency, entity or organization directed or controlled by the Republic of Iraq, or in which the Republic of Iraq participates.

(Published in Gazzetta Ufficiale n. 182 of Aug. 6; converted into legge n. 278 of October 5, 1990.)

Decreto legge 247 of August 23, 1990

[58]. Translated by Michele Angelo Lu-   gna Faculty of Law.
poi, Dottore di ricerca, University of Bolo-

Art. 1.1

Italian citizens anywhere in the world, and foreign citizens resident, domiciled or temporarily resident in Italy are prohibited from performing any activity meant to promote, favor, accomplish, even indirectly, sales or supply contracts, involving export or transport of goods of whatever kind to Kuwait and Iraq, or coming from those States.

Art. 1.2

The persons referred to in Art. 1.1 are also forbidden from performing transfers of funds destined to, even if indirectly, entities or persons in Kuwait and Iraq.

Art. 1.3

Prohibitions under art. 1 * * * of decreto-legge n. 220 of August 6, 1990, apply, as concerns Italian citizens, even if the activities mentioned therein are performed in a foreign territory.

* * *

(Published in Gazzetta Ufficiale n. 196–bis of August 23; converted into legge n. 298 of October 19, 1990, modified by art. 1, legge 224 of July 19, 1991.)

The *Fincantieri* court seems to interpret this embargo legislation as prohibiting even an award that would recognize Iraqi legal claims by way of set off against the claimant's larger damage claims or that would refuse to rescind the contract. This may be a controversial interpretation of the legislation. (Would the mere rendering of an award outside Italy violate the Italian law?)[59] Taking it as correct, however, the arbitrators could still have applied the embargo legislation correctly and given damages to the Italian plaintiff without allowing a set off for Iraq's claims. Does the *Fincantieri* decision mean that Article 806 of the Italian Code of Civil Procedure invalidates any arbitration clause under which arbitrators *might* reach a result inconsistent with Italian mandatory law?

4.   Is there good reason to be concerned about turning over this dispute to an arbitral tribunal? Suppose the dispute had been arbitrated and the arbitrators awarded damages to Fincantieri, but in a significantly reduced amount because of Iraq's set off claim. Enforcement of such an award would not have honored the embargo legislation (under the *Fincantieri* court's

---

[59].   The Council of the European Communities also imposed an embargo, less sweeping than the Italian law, in Council Regulation (EEC) No. 2340/90 of 8 August 1990; 1990 OJ L213:

Article 2

* * * [T]he following shall be prohibited in the territory of the Community or by means of aircraft and vessels flying the flag of a Member State, and when carried out by any Council national:

1.   all activities or commercial transactions, including all operations connected with transactions which have already been concluded or partially carried out, the object or effect of which is to promote the export of any commodity or product originating in, or coming from, Iraq or Kuwait;

2.   the sale or supply of any commodity or product wherever it originates or comes from:

— to any natural or legal person in Iraq or Kuwait

— to any other natural or legal person for the purposes of any commercial activity carried out in or from the territory of Iraq or Kuwait;

3.   any activity the object or effect of which is to promote such sales or supplies.

interpretation). Would Fincantieri have had any other remedy? What if the arbitrators had found the contract valid and ordered specific performance? Would that have violated the embargo legislation? Could such an award have been enforced in Italy? Elsewhere? Suppose the arbitrators had upheld the contract and rendered a monetary award in Iraq's favor, would that have violated the embargo law? Could such an award be enforced in Italy? Elsewhere?

5. In a decision seemingly at odds with *Fincantieri*, the Court of Appeal of Bologna has decided that antitrust matters are arbitrable. Coveme SpA (Italy) v. Compagnie Française des Isolants SA (France), Corte di Appello [Court of Appeal], Bologna, 1991, 18 Yearbk.Comm.Arb'n 422 (1993). In *Coveme* an exclusive distribution contract barred the distributor in Italy from selling similar products for a period of two years after termination of the contract. It also provided for ICC arbitration in Paris under French substantive law.

After termination of the distribution contract, the Italian distributor sued before the Court of First Instance in Bologna to have the non-competition clause declared invalid. The distributor claimed that the clause violated European Community antitrust law, namely Article 85(1)[60] of the EC Treaty, and that by operation of Article 85(2)[61] the clause was invalid and unenforceable. The French manufacturer challenged the Italian court's jurisdiction by invoking the arbitration clause. The Court of First Instance applied Italian law to the question of arbitrability (following a *lex fori* principle), noted that EC antitrust law is mandatory, and found that Article 806 of the Italian Code of Civil Procedure barred arbitration. The court's reasoning was similar to that in *Fincantieri*. See Coveme SpA (Italy) v. Compagnie Française des Isolants SA (France), Tribunale [Court of First Instance], Bologna, 1987, 17 Yearbk.Comm.Arb'n 534 (1992). On appeal the Court of Appeal of Bologna reversed and referred the parties to arbitration. It applied Italian law (Article 806), not based on a *lex fori* principle but because the French party had not shown that French law differed from Italian law. Excerpts from the opinion follow.

[6] For the arbitral clause concerning disputes on *diritti indisponibili* to be null and void—and consequently for the contract to be null and void, since the parties' intent was invalid—it is necessary, according to a recent and very accurate Supreme Court decision, that the contract containing the arbitral clause affect the *diritti indisponibili* by transferring, waiving them, etc., thereby disposing of them in violation of the law. Or, that settlement of the disputes arising under the contract, or their referral to arbitration, should also affect *diritti indisponibili*.

---

[60]. EC Treaty Art. 85(1) reads:

The following shall be prohibited as incompatible with the common market; all agreements between undertakings, * * * which may affect trade between Member States and which have as their object or effect the prevention, restriction or distortion of competition within the common market, * * *.

[Authors' note: The numbering of EC Treaty articles has been changed; Art. 85(1) is now Art. 81(1).]

[61]. EC Treaty Art. 85(2) reads:

Any agreement * * * prohibited pursuant to this Article shall be automatically void.

[Authors' note: The numbering of EC Treaty articles has been changed; Art. 85(2) is now Art. 81(2).]

[7]   It ensues from the aforesaid, in the Supreme Court's opinion, that "all other disputes, included [sic] those disputes concerning the validity of a contract having as its object *diritti indisponibili*, are arbitrable—just as are arbitrable all other disputes concerning the contract's validity—insofar as they do not affect *diritti indisponibili* [as described in para. 6] * * * ".

* * *

[9]   In the present case, since the arbitral clause in the contract between CFI and Coveme generically refers to arbitration, we hold that the parties thereby meant all disputes concerning the contract, that is, also disputes concerning the contract's validity.

[10]   Since the arbitral clause is autonomous with respect to the contract—so that the nullity of the latter does not automatically affect the former—we hold that disputes concerning the contract's validity are arbitrable.

* * *

[13]   The issue of the invalidity of the non-competition agreement, which has been raised by Coveme, is only one of the possible and innumerable disputes for which settlement by arbitration has been provided. Hence, independently from the fact that it is possible to imagine that the parties' *diritti indisponibili* might be affected by the referral of the dispute to arbitrators, we hold that the arbitral clause is valid. Id. at 424–25.

What explains the difference in the *Coveme* and *Fincantieri* approaches to Article 806 of the Italian Code of Civil Procedure? Which approach is the better interpretation of the statutory language?

6.   The *Coveme* and *Fincantieri* opinions each discuss the Italian Supreme Court decision of 19 May, 1989 (no. 2406). That 1989 decision involved scrutiny of an arbitral award. Epargne had agreed to sell its business to Quaker, including know-how and an important trademark. In return, Quaker had agreed to pay royalties to Epargne. Under Italian mandatory law, it is forbidden to sell a trademark without also selling the firm (or branch of the firm) that makes the product to which the trademark attaches.

The agreement was not carried out, and the parties went to arbitration over the resulting dispute. Epargne asked for execution of the agreement and payment of royalties; Quaker sought to avoid performance under the agreement, but without challenging the agreement's original validity. The arbitrators, considering the validity of the agreement not in question, rendered an award in favor of Epargne and ordered the payment of royalties. Quaker sought to set aside the award on the ground that the arbitration agreement was invalid.

When the case reached the Italian Supreme Court, it ruled as follows. First, the arbitration clause would be invalid, if two conditions were met: (i) the container contract, in which it was found, actually transferred rights that the law prohibited to be transferred (*diritti indisponibili*) and (ii) any party settlement or arbitral award concerning the contract actually transferred a non-disposable right (*diritto indisponibile*). Second, the arbitration clause would be invalid if it *expressly* authorized the arbitrators to decide whether the container contract transferred a non-disposable right (*diritto indisponbile*) and hence was invalid. Because the award merely ordered the payment of royalties and because the arbitration clause was of a generic, non-specific nature, the court found the arbitration agreement valid. The court also noted that if arbitration proceeds under a valid, general arbitration clause and in that proceeding a party raises a claim of invalidity because a non-disposable right has been transferred, then the award will be annulled if the arbitrators do not apply the mandatory law correctly. In this case, however, the court found that neither party raised an invalidity claim before the arbitrators. Quaker raised the *diritti indisponibili* problem for the first time in the set aside proceedings. The award was therefore not set aside. (The court indicated, without deciding the point, that the Italian mandatory trademark law had probably not been violated.) Which Court of Appeal decision, *Coveme* or *Fincantieri* seems more consistent with 1989 Italian Supreme Court ruling?

7.   The UNCITRAL Model Law Article 8(1) provides for enforcing an arbitration agreement unless the court "finds that the agreement is null and void, inoperative or incapable of being performed." Article 34(2)(b) provides that an award may be set aside if "the court finds that: (i) the subject-matter of the dispute is not capable of settlement by arbitration under the law of this State; * * * ." Article 36(1)(b) provides that an award may be refused recognition and enforcement "if the court finds that: (i) the subject-matter of the dispute is not capable of settlement by arbitration under the law of this State; * * * ." Nowhere in the Model Law, however, is there a definition of arbitrability. Do you think there should be? If so, would you prefer the Italian definition, the Swiss, or some other? Return to this question after considering the materials in the next subsection on arbitrability of antitrust and cargo damage claims.

II.2.c.   *Arbitrability Tested in Court Practice*

Common-law jurisdictions have generally relied on court decisions to set the standard of arbitrability. The *Mitsubishi* case that follows is the leading United States decision on arbitrability. After it we turn to *Sky Reefer*, a more recent U. S. Supreme Court decision, in which inequality of bargaining power was the main public policy concern.

II.2.c.i.   *Arbitrability of Antitrust Claims*

MITSUBISHI MOTORS CORPORATION v. SOLER CHRYSLER–PLYMOUTH, INC.

United States Supreme Court, 1985.
473 U.S. 614.

JUSTICE BLACKMUN delivered the opinion of the Court.

The principal question presented by these cases is the arbitrability, pursuant to the Federal Arbitration Act and the [New York] Convention on the Recognition and Enforcement of Foreign Arbitral Awards (Convention), of claims arising under the Sherman Act and encompassed within a valid arbitration clause in an agreement embodying an international commercial transaction.

I

Petitioner-cross-respondent Mitsubishi Motors Corporation (Mitsubishi) is a Japanese corporation which manufactures automobiles and has its principal place of business in Tokyo, Japan. Mitsubishi is the product of a joint venture between, on the one hand, Chrysler International, S.A. (CISA), a Swiss corporation registered in Geneva and wholly owned by Chrysler Corporation, and, on the other, Mitsubishi Heavy Industries, Inc., a Japanese corporation. The aim of the joint venture was the distribution through Chrysler dealers outside the continental United States of vehicles manufactured by Mitsubishi and bearing Chrysler and Mitsubishi trademarks. Respondent-cross-petitioner Soler Chrysler–Plymouth, Inc. (Soler), is a Puerto Rico corporation with its principal place of business in Pueblo Viejo, Guaynabo, Puerto Rico.

On October 31, 1979, Soler entered into a Distributor Agreement with CISA which provided for the sale by Soler of Mitsubishi-manufactured vehicles within a designated area, including metropolitan San Juan. On the same date, CISA, Soler, and Mitsubishi entered into a Sales Procedure Agreement (Sales Agreement) which, referring to the Distributor Agreement, provided for the direct sale of Mitsubishi products to Soler and governed the terms and conditions of such sales. Paragraph VI of the Sales Agreement, labeled "Arbitration of Certain Matters," provides:

> "All disputes, controversies or differences which may arise between [Mitsubishi] and [Soler] out of or in relation to Articles I–B through V of this Agreement or for the breach thereof, shall be finally settled by arbitration in Japan in accordance with the rules and regulations of the Japan Commercial Arbitration Association."

Initially, Soler did a brisk business in Mitsubishi-manufactured vehicles. As a result of its strong performance, its minimum sales volume, specified by Mitsubishi and CISA, and agreed to by Soler, for the 1981 model year was substantially increased. In early 1981, however, the new-car market slackened. Soler ran into serious difficulties in meeting the expected sales volume, and by the spring of 1981 it felt itself compelled to request that Mitsubishi delay or cancel shipment of several orders. About the same time, Soler attempted to arrange for the transshipment of a quantity of its vehicles for sale in the continental United States and Latin America. Mitsubishi and CISA, however, refused permission for any such diversion, citing a variety of reasons, and no vehicles were transshipped. Attempts to work out these difficulties failed. Mitsubishi eventually withheld shipment of 966 vehicles, apparently representing orders placed for May, June, and July 1981 production, responsibility for which Soler disclaimed in February 1982.

The following month, Mitsubishi brought an action against Soler in the United States District Court for the District of Puerto Rico under the Federal Arbitration Act and the Convention.[2] Mitsubishi sought an

---

2. The complaint alleged that Soler had   failed to pay for 966 ordered vehicles; that

order, * * * to compel arbitration in accord with ¶ VI of the Sales Agreement. Shortly after filing the complaint, Mitsubishi filed a request for arbitration before the Japan Commercial Arbitration Association.

Soler denied the allegations and counterclaimed against both Mitsubishi and CISA. It alleged numerous breaches by Mitsubishi of the Sales Agreement,[5] * * * and asserted causes of action under the Sherman Act, * * *. In the counterclaim premised on the Sherman Act, Soler alleged that Mitsubishi and CISA had conspired to divide markets in restraint of trade. To effectuate the plan, according to Soler, Mitsubishi had refused to permit Soler to resell to buyers in North, Central, or South America vehicles it had obligated itself to purchase from Mitsubishi; had refused to ship ordered vehicles or the parts, such as heaters and defoggers, that would be necessary to permit Soler to make its vehicles suitable for resale outside Puerto Rico; and had coercively attempted to replace Soler and its other Puerto Rico distributors with a wholly owned subsidiary which would serve as the exclusive Mitsubishi distributor in Puerto Rico.

[The District Court ordered Mitsubishi and Soler to arbitrate the issues raised in the complaint and the antitrust counterclaims. The First Circuit Court of Appeals affirmed as to the issues in the complaint but reversed as to the antitrust counterclaims, holding them nonarbitrable.]

II

[The Court here addressed and rejected Soler's contention that the arbitration clause could not be read to encompass the statutory antitrust claims stated in its answer to the complaint.]

III

We now turn to consider whether Soler's antitrust claims are nonarbitrable even though it has agreed to arbitrate them. In holding that they are not, the Court of Appeals followed the decision of the Second Circuit in *American Safety Equipment Corp. v. J.P. Maguire & Co.*. Notwithstanding the absence of any explicit support for such an exception in either the Sherman Act or the Federal Arbitration Act, the Second Circuit there reasoned that "the pervasive public interest in enforcement of the antitrust laws, and the nature of the claims that arise in such cases, combine to make ... antitrust claims ... inappropriate for arbitration." We find it unnecessary to assess the legitimacy of the American Safety doctrine as applied to agreements to arbitrate arising from domestic transactions. As in *Scherk v. Alberto–Culver Co.*, 417 U.S.

---

it had failed to pay contractual "distress unit penalties," intended to reimburse Mitsubishi for storage costs and interest charges incurred because of Soler's failure to take shipment of ordered vehicles; that Soler's failure to fulfill warranty obligations threatened Mitsubishi's reputation and goodwill; that Soler had failed to obtain required financing; and that the Distributor and Sales Agreements had expired by their terms or, alternatively, that Soler had surrendered its rights under the Sales Agreement.

5. The alleged breaches included wrongful refusal to ship ordered vehicles and necessary parts, failure to make payment for warranty work and authorized rebates, and bad faith in establishing minimum-sales volumes.

506, 94 S.Ct. 2449, 41 L.Ed.2d 270 (1974), we conclude that concerns of international comity, respect for the capacities of foreign and transnational tribunals, and sensitivity to the need of the international commercial system for predictability in the resolution of disputes require that we enforce the parties' agreement, even assuming that a contrary result would be forthcoming in a domestic context.

[Here the Court emphasized the importance of predictability and orderliness in international transactions: "agreeing in advance on a forum acceptable to both parties is an indispensable element in international trade, commerce, and contracting," * * *.]

* * * And at least since this Nation's accession in 1970 to the [New York] Convention, and the implementation of the Convention in the same year by amendment of the Federal Arbitration Act, that federal policy applies with special force in the field of international commerce. Thus, we must weigh the concerns of American Safety against a strong belief in the efficacy of arbitral procedures for the resolution of international commercial disputes and an equal commitment to the enforcement of freely negotiated choice-of-forum clauses.

At the outset, we confess to some skepticism of certain aspects of the American Safety doctrine. As distilled by the First Circuit, the doctrine comprises four ingredients. First, private parties play a pivotal role in aiding governmental enforcement of the antitrust laws by means of the private action for treble damages. Second, "the strong possibility that contracts which generate antitrust disputes may be contracts of adhesion militates against automatic forum determination by contract." Third, antitrust issues, prone to complication, require sophisticated legal and economic analysis, and thus are "ill-adapted to strengths of the arbitral process, i.e., expedition, minimal requirements of written rationale, simplicity, resort to basic concepts of common sense and simple equity." Finally, just as "issues of war and peace are too important to be vested in the generals, . . . decisions as to antitrust regulation of business are too important to be lodged in arbitrators chosen from the business community—particularly those from a foreign community that has had no experience with or exposure to our law and values."

Initially, we find the second concern unjustified. The mere appearance of an antitrust dispute does not alone warrant invalidation of the selected forum on the undemonstrated assumption that the arbitration clause is tainted. A party resisting arbitration of course may attack directly the validity of the agreement to arbitrate. Moreover, the party may attempt to make a showing that would warrant setting aside the forum-selection clause—that the agreement was "[a]ffected by fraud, undue influence, or overweening bargaining power"; that "enforcement would be unreasonable and unjust"; or that proceedings "in the contractual forum will be so gravely difficult and inconvenient that [the resisting party] will for all practical purposes be deprived of his day in court."

The Bremen, 407 U.S., at 12, 15, 18. But absent such a showing—and none was attempted here—there is no basis for assuming the forum inadequate or its selection unfair.

Next, potential complexity should not suffice to ward off arbitration. We might well have some doubt that even the courts following American Safety subscribe fully to the view that antitrust matters are inherently insusceptible to resolution by arbitration, as these same courts have agreed that an undertaking to arbitrate antitrust claims entered into after the dispute arises is acceptable. And the vertical restraints which most frequently give birth to antitrust claims covered by an arbitration agreement will not often occasion the monstrous proceedings that have given antitrust litigation an image of intractability. In any event, adaptability and access to expertise are hallmarks of arbitration. The anticipated subject matter of the dispute may be taken into account when the arbitrators are appointed, and arbitral rules typically provide for the participation of experts either employed by the parties or appointed by the tribunal. Moreover, it is often a judgment that streamlined proceedings and expeditious results will best serve their needs that causes parties to agree to arbitrate their disputes; it is typically a desire to keep the effort and expense required to resolve a dispute within manageable bounds that prompts them mutually to forgo access to judicial remedies. In sum, the factor of potential complexity alone does not persuade us that an arbitral tribunal could not properly handle an antitrust matter.

For similar reasons, we also reject the proposition that an arbitration panel will pose too great a danger of innate hostility to the constraints on business conduct that antitrust law imposes. International arbitrators frequently are drawn from the legal as well as the business community; where the dispute has an important legal component, the parties and the arbitral body with whose assistance they have agreed to settle their dispute can be expected to select arbitrators accordingly.[18] We decline to indulge the presumption that the parties and arbitral body conducting a proceeding will be unable or unwilling to retain competent, conscientious, and impartial arbitrators.

We are left, then, with the core of the American Safety doctrine— the fundamental importance to American democratic capitalism of the regime of the antitrust laws. Without doubt, the private cause of action plays a central role in enforcing this regime. As the Court of Appeals pointed out:

> " 'A claim under the antitrust laws is not merely a private matter. The Sherman Act is designed to promote the national interest in a competitive economy; thus, the plaintiff asserting his rights under

---

18. * * *

We are advised by Mitsubishi and amicus International Chamber of Commerce, without contradiction by Soler, that the arbitration panel selected to hear the parties' claims here is composed of three Japanese lawyers, one a former law school dean, another a former judge, and the third a practicing attorney with American legal training who has written on Japanese antitrust law.

* * *

the Act has been likened to a private attorney-general who protects the public's interest.' "

The treble-damages provision wielded by the private litigant is a chief tool in the antitrust enforcement scheme, posing a crucial deterrent to potential violators. * * *

* * *

There is no reason to assume at the outset of the dispute that international arbitration will not provide an adequate mechanism. To be sure, the international arbitral tribunal owes no prior allegiance to the legal norms of particular states; hence, it has no direct obligation to vindicate their statutory dictates. The tribunal, however, is bound to effectuate the intentions of the parties. Where the parties have agreed that the arbitral body is to decide a defined set of claims which includes, as in these cases, those arising from the application of American antitrust law, the tribunal therefore should be bound to decide that dispute in accord with the national law giving rise to the claim.[19] And so long as the prospective litigant effectively may vindicate its statutory cause of action in the arbitral forum, the statute will continue to serve both its remedial and deterrent function.

Having permitted the arbitration to go forward, the national courts of the United States will have the opportunity at the award-enforcement stage to ensure that the legitimate interest in the enforcement of the antitrust laws has been addressed. The Convention reserves to each signatory country the right to refuse enforcement of an award where the "recognition or enforcement of the award would be contrary to the public policy of that country." Art. V(2)(b). While the efficacy of the arbitral process requires that substantive review at the award-enforcement stage remain minimal, it would not require intrusive inquiry to

---

19. In addition to the clause providing for arbitration before the Japan Commercial Arbitration Association, the Sales Agreement includes a choice-of-law clause which reads: "This Agreement is made in, and will be governed by and construed in all respects according to the laws of the Swiss Confederation as if entirely performed therein." The United States raises the possibility that the arbitral panel will read this provision not simply to govern interpretation of the contract terms, but wholly to displace American law even where it otherwise would apply. The International Chamber of Commerce opines that it is "[c]onceivabl[e], although we believe it unlikely, [that] the arbitrators could consider Soler's affirmative claim of anticompetitive conduct by CISA and Mitsubishi to fall within the purview of this choice-of-law provision, with the result that it would be decided under Swiss law rather than the U.S. Sherman Act." At oral argument, however, counsel for Mitsubishi conceded that American law

applied to the antitrust claims and represented that the claims had been submitted to the arbitration panel in Japan on that basis. The record confirms that before the decision of the Court of Appeals the arbitral panel had taken these claims under submission.

We therefore have no occasion to speculate on this matter at this stage in the proceedings, when Mitsubishi seeks to enforce the agreement to arbitrate, not to enforce an award. Nor need we consider now the effect of an arbitral tribunal's failure to take cognizance of the statutory cause of action on the claimant's capacity to reinitiate suit in federal court. We merely note that in the event the choice-of-forum and choice-of-law clauses operated in tandem as a prospective waiver of a party's right to pursue statutory remedies for antitrust violations, we would have little hesitation in condemning the agreement as against public policy.

ascertain that the tribunal took cognizance of the antitrust claims and actually decided them.[20]

As international trade has expanded in recent decades, so too has the use of international arbitration to resolve disputes arising in the course of that trade. * * * If * * * [arbitral tribunals] are to take a central place in the international legal order, national courts will need to "shake off the old judicial hostility to arbitration," *Kulukundis Shipping Co. v. Amtorg Trading Corp.*, 126 F.2d 978, 985 (C.A.2 1942), and also their customary and understandable unwillingness to cede jurisdiction of a claim arising under domestic law to a foreign or transnational tribunal. To this extent, at least, it will be necessary for national courts to subordinate domestic notions of arbitrability to the international policy favoring commercial arbitration.[21]

Accordingly, we "require this representative of the American business community to honor its bargain," *Alberto–Culver Co. v. Scherk*, 484 F.2d 611, 620 (C.A.7 1973) (Stevens, J., dissenting), by holding this agreement to arbitrate "enforce[able] . . . in accord with the explicit provisions of the Arbitration Act."

The judgment of the Court of Appeals is affirmed in part and reversed in part, and the cases are remanded for further proceedings consistent with this opinion.

It is so ordered.

Justice Powell took no part in the decision of these cases.

Justice Stevens, with whom Justice Brennan joins, and with whom Justice Marshall joins except as to Part II, dissenting.

[Justice Stevens first argued in Part II that the arbitration clause should not be construed to include antitrust claims. In Part III he stressed the importance of antitrust policy. ("Antitrust laws in general, and the Sherman Act in particular, are the magna carta of free enterprise. They are as important to the preservation of economic freedom

20. See n. 19, *supra*. We note, for example, that the rules of the Japan Commercial Arbitration Association provide for the taking of a "summary record" of each hearing, Rule 28.1; for the stenographic recording of the proceedings where the tribunal so orders or a party requests one, Rule 28.2; and for a statement of reasons for the award unless the parties agree otherwise, Rule 36.1(4).

Needless to say, we intimate no views on the merits of Soler's antitrust claims.

21. We do not quarrel with the Court of Appeals' conclusion that Art. II(1) of the Convention, which requires the recognition of agreements to arbitrate that involve "subject matter capable of settlement by arbitration," contemplates exceptions to arbitrability grounded in domestic law.* * *

* * * [Nevertheless, the] utility of the Convention in promoting the process of international commercial arbitration depends upon the willingness of national courts to let go of matters they normally would think of as their own. Doubtless, Congress may specify categories of claims it wishes to reserve for decision by our own courts without contravening this Nation's obligations under the Convention. But we decline to subvert the spirit of the United States' accession to the Convention by recognizing subject-matter exceptions where Congress has not expressly directed the courts to do so.

and our free-enterprise system as the Bill of Rights is to the protection of our fundamental personal freedoms.'') He stressed also that the mandatory treble damages provisions of United States antitrust law signal the importance Congress attached to the private-attorney-general role of private litigants who in pursuing private antitrust claims are at the same time protecting the broad public interest in the proper functioning of the free market. The opinion continues with the following quote from the Second Circuit opinion in *American Safety.*]

" * * * Antitrust violations can affect hundreds of thousands—perhaps millions—of people and inflict staggering economic damage. * * * We do not believe that Congress intended such claims to be resolved elsewhere than in the courts. * * * [I]t is also proper to ask whether contracts of adhesion between alleged monopolists and their customers should determine the forum for trying antitrust violations." *American Safety Equipment Corp. v. J.P. Maguire & Co.*, 391 F.2d 821, 826–827 (2d Cir.1968) (footnote omitted).

* * *

Arbitration awards are only reviewable for manifest disregard of the law, 9 U.S.C. §§ 10, 207, and the rudimentary procedures which make arbitration so desirable in the context of a private dispute often mean that the record is so inadequate that the arbitrator's decision is virtually unreviewable.[31] Despotic decision making of this kind is fine for parties who are willing to agree in advance to settle for a best approximation of the correct result in order to resolve quickly and inexpensively any contractual dispute that may arise in an ongoing commercial relationship. Such informality, however, is simply unacceptable when every error may have devastating consequences for important businesses in our national economy and may undermine their ability to compete in world markets.[32] Instead of "muffling a grievance in the cloakroom of arbitration," the public interest in free competitive markets would be better served by having the issues resolved "in the light of impartial public court adjudication."[33]

31. The arbitration procedure in this case does not provide any right to evidentiary discovery or a written decision, and requires that all proceedings be closed to the public. Moreover, Japanese arbitrators do not have the power of compulsory process to secure witnesses and documents, nor do witnesses who are available testify under oath. Cf. 9 U.S.C. § 7 (arbitrators may summon witnesses to attend proceedings and seek enforcement in a district court).

32. The greatest risk, of course, is that the arbitrator will condemn business practices under the antitrust laws that are efficient in a free competitive market. In the absence of a reviewable record, a reviewing district court would not be able to undo the damage wrought. Even a Government suit or an action by a private party might not be available to set aside the award.

33. The Court notes that some courts which have held that agreements to arbitrate antitrust claims generally are unenforceable have nevertheless enforced arbitration agreements to settle an existing antitrust claim. These settlement agreements, made after the parties have had every opportunity to evaluate the strength of their position, are obviously less destructive of the private treble-damages remedy that Congress provided. Thus, it may well be that arbitration as a means of settling existing disputes is permissible.

IV

[Justice Stevens here stressed that the New York Convention would allow the United States to refuse to order arbitration of antitrust claims on the ground of nonarbitrability, citing Articles II(1) and II(3).]

* * * The courts of other nations * * * have applied the exception provided in the Convention, and refused to enforce agreements to arbitrate specific subject matters of concern to them.[35]

It may be that the subject-matter exception to the Convention ought to be reserved—as a matter of domestic law—for matters of the greatest public interest which involve concerns that are shared by other nations. The Sherman Act's commitment to free competitive markets is among our most important civil policies. This commitment, shared by other nations which are signatory to the Convention, is hardly the sort of parochial concern that we should decline to enforce in the interest of international comity. * * *

[Justice Stevens here distinguished the *Scherk* case as involving international conflict-of-laws problems because the many contacts with Europe in that case raised serious doubts about the applicability of United States securities law. He found no such doubts in this case about the applicability of U.S. antitrust law: "I consider it perfectly clear that the rules of American antitrust law must govern the claim of an American automobile dealer that he has been injured by an international conspiracy to restrain trade in the American automobile market."]

* * *

V

* * *

In my opinion, the elected representatives of the American people would not have us dispatch an American citizen to a foreign land in search of an uncertain remedy for the violation of a public right that is protected by the Sherman Act. This is especially so when there has been no genuine bargaining over the terms of the submission, and the arbitration remedy provided has not even the most elementary guarantees of fair process. Consideration of a fully developed record by a jury, instructed in the law by a federal judge, and subject to appellate review, is a surer guide to the competitive character of a commercial practice than the practically unreviewable judgment of a private arbitrator.

35. For example, the Cour de Cassation in Belgium has held that disputes arising under a Belgian statute limiting the unilateral termination of exclusive distributorships are not arbitrable under the Convention in that country, *Audi–NSU Auto Union A.G. v. S.A. Adelin Petit & Cie.* (1979), in 5 Yearbook Commercial Arbitration 257, 259 (1980), and the Corte di Cassazione in Italy has held that labor disputes are not arbitrable under the Convention in that country, *Compagnia Generale Construzioni v. Piersanti,* [1980] Foro Italiano I 190, in 6 Yearbook Commercial Arbitration 229, 230 (1981).

Unlike the Congress that enacted the Sherman Act in 1890, the Court today does not seem to appreciate the value of economic freedom. I respectfully dissent.

Questions and Comments

1. The argument against allowing antitrust claims to be arbitrated stems from the importance of antitrust law's public policy goals and suspicion that arbitrators will see themselves as beholden to the parties and the parties' agreement, rather than to the goals of public policy. If the arbitrators either fail to apply the relevant antitrust law or misapply it, those goals could be compromised. The goals reach beyond the immediate private interests of the parties. The U.S. antitrust law provides that successful claimants are to receive three times their proven damages. This rule encourages claims and causes private claimants to function as "private attorneys general" in bringing about greater compliance with antitrust law. In the *Mitsubishi* context, what is the potential threat to the public welfare deriving from the parties' contractual arrangements?

In U.S. antitrust law the validity of territorial restrictions in exclusive distribution agreements is governed by what is called the "rule of reason" (as opposed to the "per se" doctrine, applicable, for example, to price-fixing). Under the rule of reason, a court must weigh the anticompetitive tendencies of a given agreement against the pro-competitive and other welfare-enhancing aspects of the transaction. Antitrust law is violated only if on balance the anticompetitive aspects predominate. In the context of the *Mitsubishi* case, what are the anticompetitive tendencies of the parties' contractual arrangements? What are the procompetitive and other welfare-enhancing aspects? What would you need to know to decide the predominant tendency? Are you confident that arbitrators will be able to understand and apply this body of law correctly? How important is it that they do so?

2. In the United States, private attorneys general are not the only enforcers of antitrust law. The Antitrust Division of the Justice Department can seek both civil relief and criminal penalties and employs a large staff of lawyers for those purposes. The Federal Trade Commission also has authority to enforce the antitrust laws and also employs a large staff of lawyers. Does the existence of these two administrative enforcers of antitrust law argue for or against the *Mitsubishi* outcome?

3. Jacques Werner, a Swiss lawyer practicing in Geneva, published a critical comment not long after the *Mitsubishi* decision was handed down. He stressed that the choice-of-law clause in the relevant agreement expressly provided for the application of the "laws of the Swiss Confederation". He also noted that Swiss antitrust law differs from that of the United States. He then quoted footnote 19 of the *Mitsubishi* Court's opinion (supra), and continued:

On this, two comments:

A. The International Chamber of Commerce's statement contained in its *Amicus Curiae* brief whereby it would be unlikely that the arbitrators would consider Soler's claim of anticompetitive conduct to be decided under the Swiss law rather than under U.S. law, came as a bad surprise to many long-time users of ICC arbitration, both counsel and arbitrators. Here is a major arbitral institution whose own rules of arbitration provide that "The parties shall be free to determine the law to be applied by the arbitrator to the merits of the dispute" (Article 13.3)[62] but which, inexplicably, comes to forget the very basics of arbitration which it preached for so many years, namely that arbitration and arbitrators do exist only by the clear agreement of the parties to that effect, and within the limits set by such agreement. As ICC should very well know, what is indeed very unlikely, to say the least, is that arbitrators would accept to apply U.S. antitrust law to claims to be ruled, according to the parties' clear will, by Swiss law! And this irrespective of all the present day talk on arbitration and public policy, which tend to be used in an increasingly dangerous way for conferring to arbitrators powers which parties never wanted them to have.

B.　Buried at the end of footnote 19 is probably the main message delivered by the Supreme Court in this decision: it is perfectly permissible to arbitrate foreign antitrust claims so long as the arbitrators will, no matter what the law chosen by the parties for governing their dispute says, apply U.S. laws to such claims. Otherwise enforcement of the award might well be denied. I do not want to discuss here the rather strange views of the Supreme Court of the grounds on which enforcement of an award could be refused in the United States, a country which is a party to and bound by the 1958 New York Convention. I would like merely to notice that we have here a magnificent example of an attempt to export U.S. substantive laws where they had no place up to now; in international arbitration proceedings held outside the United States under an arbitration agreement providing for a non-U.S. law as law governing the dispute. If the price for *Mitsubishi* is this dilution of parties' freedom and extension of U.S. substantive laws operated in tandem, I doubt that users of international arbitration can afford to pay it.[63]

Do you agree with Werner's claim that arbitrators would not be inclined to apply U.S. antitrust law when the parties' choice-of-law clause expressly opts for the substantive law of a different country? Does this suggest *Mitsubishi* is unsound?

4.　In response to Mr. Werner, Sigvard Jarvin, then General Counsel of the I.C.C. Court of Arbitration, stressed that the ICC *amicus* brief was merely predicting what was likely to happen in practice and not what it thought should happen or what its own rules required. Mr. Jarvin drew attention to the following excerpt from the ICC brief:

* * * When [an antitrust] claim is raised as it is in this case, U.S. antitrust policy will, of course, be vindicated when an arbitrator applies the law of the United States to resolve the claim. Whether the arbitrator will apply U.S. law in a particular case depends upon several considerations. The most important factors are the terms and scope of the choice of law provision in the contract and, absent such a provision, upon a proper application of the appropriate principles of conflict of laws, (37)

[62]. Authors' note: Essentially the same provision is included in the 1998 ICC Rules, Article 17(1).

[63]. 3 J. Int'l. Arb'n. 81 (1986).

but a further factor that international arbitrators increasingly consider is the significance of the relationship between the United States and the facts of the underlying claim of anticompetitive conduct (38).

(37) In accordance with the principle of "party autonomy", the ICC Rules, for example, provide that the parties are "free to determine the law to be applied by the arbitrator to the merits of the dispute," and in the absence of such a determination the arbitrator "shall apply the law designated as the proper law by the rule of conflict which he deems appropriate." ICC Rules 13(3). In practice, this latter provision means that, absent party choice, the ICC arbitrator usually makes his choice of substantive law based on a consideration of the conflicts principles applied by each of the jurisdictions having a relation to the dispute. * * *

(38) According to leading German and French authorities, there is a growing tendency of international arbitrators to take into account the antitrust laws and other mandatory legal rules expressing public policy enacted by a state that has a significant relationship to the facts of the case, even though that state's law does not govern the contract by virtue of the parties' choice or applicable conflicts rules. * * *

Nevertheless, the possibility remains that an arbitrator might not apply U.S. antitrust law in deciding a party's affirmative claim for damages based on the other party's anticompetitive conduct. In the instant case, for example, CISA, Mitsubishi, and Soler provided that their Sales Promotion Agreement would be "governed by" the laws of Switzerland "in all respects . . . as if entirely performed therein." * * * Conceivably, although we believe it unlikely, the arbitrators could consider Soler's affirmative claim of anticompetitive conduct by CISA and Mitsubishi to fall within the purview of this choice-of-law provision, with the result that it would be decided under Swiss law rather than the U.S. Sherman Act.

Mr. Jarvin went on to say: "When making its forecast the ICC expressed what seemed likely to happen. It did not express an opinion of what it wished the arbitrators to do. And the ICC could hardly express any such wish since the arbitration was to be carried out under other rules than those of the ICC. * * * " If the parties had chosen arbitration under ICC Rules, what do you think the ICC should wish the arbitrators to do? If the parties choose ICC arbitration and a substantive law to govern their agreement other than that of the United States, should U.S. courts enforce the arbitration clause?

5.   After *Mitsubishi* was decided, Hans Smit observed: "[I]t is likely that litigants in international arbitrations will be tempted by the Court's reference to the possible invalidation of awards that improperly resolve antitrust claims to raise antitrust claims and defenses with the intention of using them in later attacks upon the award." H. Smit, *Mitsubishi: It Is Not What It Seems To Be*, 4 J. Int'l. Arb'n 7, 14 (1987). He argued further: "The perceived advantages of the arbitrability of antitrust claims simply pale into insignificance when compared with the substantial disadvantage of creating an additional ground for setting aside, or denying enforcement to, arbitral

awards." Id. at 10. Do you agree that *Mitsubishi* is actually a significant setback for international arbitration?

What would have happened to the antitrust issues had *Mitsubishi* been decided the other way?

Would the arbitration have gone forward on all other issues?

6. Would it be necessary for parties to raise antitrust issues in arbitration in order to establish a ground for attacking the award? In Eco Swiss China Time Ltd v Benetton International NV, Case C–126/97, 1998 ECR I–4493 (June 01, 1999), the Court of Justice of the European Communities (ECJ) held that a Dutch court, called upon to annul an arbitral award made in the Netherlands, was required to do so if the award was based on a licensing agreement that was void for violation of European Union antitrust law (Article 85 (now 81) of the EC Treaty). In the *Benetton* case, neither the parties nor the arbitrators had raised antitrust issues during the arbitration proceedings. In his opinion in the Benetton case, Advocate General Saggio[64] specifically mentioned the risk to antitrust enforcement that would otherwise arise if the parties' failure to raise antitrust issues in the arbitration would immunize the award from antitrust attack. Were that the rule, parties to an illegal agreement could deliberately invoke arbitration, fail to raise antitrust issues, and obtain an award confirming the validity of the agreement, which award would then bar, on the ground of res judicata, any later challenge to the agreement's validity.

In *Benetton* the ECJ held that a Dutch court was required to annul an award (and in a relevant case to refuse to recognize or enforce such an award) where it violated European Union antitrust law, even though under Dutch law an award's inconsistency with Dutch antitrust law would not have risen to the level of public policy needed to annul an award. The *Benetton* case thus expresses the great importance placed by the ECJ on observance of EU antitrust law, which must be enforced in all European Union member states. Excerpts from the Court's opinion follow:

> "32 It is to be noted * * * that, where questions of Community law are raised in an arbitration resorted to by agreement, the ordinary courts [of the member states] may have to examine those questions, in particular during review of the arbitration award, which may be more or less extensive depending on the circumstances and which they are obliged to carry out in the event of an appeal, for setting aside, for leave to enforce an award or upon any other form of action or review available under the relevant national legislation * * *.

* * *

[64]. Following the French procedural model, an Advocate General is a judicial official having the rank of a judge, but who does not participate in the deliberations or vote of the actual judges assigned to the case. Instead, before the case is given to the judges for decision, the Advocate General renders his or her own written opinion on how the case should be decided. The judges usually begin their deliberations with the Advocate General's opinion before them. ECJ opinions are typically deductive and non-discursive in nature. They generally do not go into policy considerations and issues underlying the interpretative issues in the case. The Advocate General's opinion, on the other hand, often does discuss such questions and thus can be very helpful in explaining the Court's judgment, which in most cases agrees in result with that of the Advocate General.

"35 Next, it is in the interest of efficient arbitration proceedings that review of arbitration awards should be limited in scope and that annulment of or refusal to recognise an award should be possible only in exceptional circumstances.

"36 However, according to Article 3(g) of the EC Treaty (now, after amendment, Article 3(1)(g) EC), Article 85 of the Treaty constitutes a fundamental provision which is essential for the accomplishment of the tasks entrusted to the Community and, in particular, for the functioning of the internal market. The importance of such a provision led the framers of the Treaty to provide expressly, in Article 85(2) of the Treaty, that any agreements or decisions prohibited pursuant to that article are to be automatically void.

"37 It follows that where its domestic rules of procedure require a national court to grant an application for annulment of an arbitration award where such an application is founded on failure to observe national rules of public policy, it must also grant such an application where it is founded on failure to comply with the prohibition laid down in Article 85(1) of the Treaty.

"38 That conclusion is not affected by the fact that the New York Convention of 10 June 1958 on the Recognition and Enforcement of Foreign Arbitral Awards, which has been ratified by all the Member States, provides that recognition and enforcement of an arbitration award may be refused only on certain specific grounds, namely where the award does not fall within the terms of the submission to arbitration or goes beyond its scope, where the award is not binding on the parties or where recognition or enforcement of the award would be contrary to the public policy of the country where such recognition and enforcement are sought (Article V(1)(c) and (e) and (2)(b) of the New York Convention).

"39 For the reasons stated in paragraph 36 above, the provisions of Article 85 of the Treaty may be regarded as a matter of public policy within the meaning of the New York Convention."

Is the ECJ's attitude toward antitrust enforcement different from that of the U.S. Supreme Court in *Mitsubishi*? Does *Benetton* cut for or against an approach in Europe similar to that of *Mitsubishi* (e.g., the *Coveme* decision in Italy)? Or is it entirely irrelevant to the issue of non-arbitrability?

7. Suppose a U.S. company and an Italian company produce widgets and each markets its widgets in the other company's home market as well as its own. Suppose these two companies agree to a friendly merger and they include a clause in the agreement providing for arbitration of all claims before the I.C.C. in Paris. Before the merger is effected, the board of directors of the U.S. company changes and the new board resists the merger on the ground that it violates both U.S. and European Union antitrust law (applicable in Italy). The U.S. company seeks arbitration of the validity of the merger before the I.C.C. in Paris. Should a U.S. court refer the parties to arbitration? An Italian court? What do you think is the preferable outcome?

8. Suppose a U. S. company agrees to sell gidgets (from its U.S. plant) to a company in Tunisia. The parties agree to arbitrate all disputes arising

out of or in connection with the contract before the International Chamber of Commerce in Paris. After the contract is signed by both parties, the U.S. imposes a partial boycott of shipments from the U.S. to Tunisia and requires all such shipments to be authorized by a special license. The U.S. company applies for a license, but the U.S. Office of Export Control refuses to grant one. The seller so informs the buyer. The buyer begins arbitration before the I.C.C. in Paris and submits two questions for inclusion in the terms of reference: i) Is the seller liable to the buyer for failing to ship the gidgets according to the contract of sale? and ii) Was the seller entitled to an export license? Are both issues arbitrable? Why or why not?

II.2.c.ii.   *Arbitrability of Cargo Damage (COGSA) Claims*

Whereas doubts about the arbitrability of antitrust claims arise because of the importance of antitrust law for the general public welfare, questions concerning the arbitrability of cargo damage claims arise largely because of the adhesion contract nature of bills of lading. To understand these issues it is helpful to have some background in the history and content of national regulations concerning carrier liability for damage to sea-transported cargo.

Goods are transported by sea in two basic forms, private carriage and common carriage. In private carriage the vessel owner ("carrier") leases the entire vessel under a lease contract known as a "charter party". The carriage contract is normally the charter party, not a bill of lading, and the cargo owner (also known as the "shipper") usually ships a vessel-load quantity of goods. Private carriage is negotiated by parties of relatively equal bargaining power and has not been subjected to mandatory rules imposed by national statutes. The parties are free to strike any bargain they choose and to subject their disputes to arbitration.

Common carriage is different. In common carriage a vessel owner leases space in a single vessel to a large number of different cargo owners. The contract of carriage is contained in the bill of lading, issued by the carrier to each shipper of goods. Carriers normally use a standard-form contract for the bill of lading, most of whose terms are thus completely non-negotiable. Maritime legislation in most countries of the world regulates the content of bills of lading to protect cargo owners from unfair terms carriers might otherwise impose. Prior to this legislation, for example, carriers had frequently included clauses exonerating themselves from all liability for damage to cargo—even when caused by their own negligence. These clauses were enforced in some countries and rejected in others, giving rise to considerable confusion and uncertainty.

Countries party to the 1924 Brussels Convention[65] sought predictability and uniformity in the regulation of the shipper-carrier relationship through adoption of the "Hague Rules". Under these rules—applicable only to carriage governed by a bill of lading (common carriage)—the carrier is not allowed to contract out of liability for damage

---

[65]. International Convention for the Unification of Certain Rules of Law Relat- ing to Bills of Lading. 120 U.N.T.S. 155 (signed in Brussels, Aug. 25, 1924).

to cargo arising from the carrier's (i) negligence in handling the cargo or (ii) negligence in failing to provide a seaworthy vessel at the beginning of the voyage. On the other hand, the carrier is absolved of liability for negligence in navigation and in managing the vessel. Even where the carrier is liable for cargo damage, that liability is limited to $500 per package or customary freight unit.

Most of the commercial nations of the world are parties to the Brussels Convention and hence enforce the Hague Rules—or an amended version, the Hague–Visby Rules. The United States is a party to the original convention and has implemented the Hague Rules through the 1936 Carriage of Goods by Sea Act (COGSA).[66] That act contains a mandatory choice of law section applying the U.S. COGSA to all shipments *to or from a U.S. port*. 46 U.S.C. § 1312. Section 1303(8) of COGSA also provides that a carrier may not lessen its liability below the mandatory COGSA requirements through provisions in the bill of lading contract:

> "Any clause ... in a contract of carriage relieving the carrier or the ship from liability for loss or damage to or in connection with the goods, arising from negligence, fault or failure in the duties and obligations provided in this section, or lessening such liability otherwise than as provided in this chapter, shall be null and void and of no effect." 46 U.S.C. § 1303(8).

Hence choice-of-law, and even choice-of-forum, clauses in bills of lading have been held invalid by U.S. courts. See Indussa Corporation v. S.S. Ranborg, 377 F.2d 200 (2d. Cir.1967). What about an arbitration clause in a bill of lading? Are COGSA issues arbitrable? Consider the following case.

VIMAR SEGUROS Y REASEGUROS, S.A. v. M/V SKY REEFER

United States Supreme Court, 1995.
515 U.S. 528.

JUSTICE KENNEDY delivered the opinion of the Court.

This case requires us to interpret the Carriage of Goods by Sea Act (COGSA), as it relates to a contract containing a clause requiring arbitration in a foreign country. The question is whether a foreign arbitration clause in a bill of lading is invalid under COGSA because it lessens liability in the sense that COGSA prohibits. Our holding that COGSA does not forbid selection of the foreign forum makes it unnecessary to resolve the further question whether the Federal Arbitration Act

---

[66]. Provisions very similar to those of COGSA are also included in the 1893 Harter Act, 46 U.S.C. §§ 190–195, which applies to shipments to or from a U.S. port at both ends of the carriage operation—from the time the cargo is in the carrier's possession until it is loaded on board and from the time it is off-loaded at the point of destination until it is delivered to the consignee. COGSA applies to the period in between; but by contract the parties may supplant the Harter Act by extending COGSA's coverage to the pre-loading and post off-loading periods.

(FAA), would override COGSA were it interpreted otherwise. In our view, the relevant provisions of COGSA and the FAA are in accord, not in conflict.

I

The contract at issue in this case is a standard form bill of lading to evidence the purchase of a shipload of Moroccan oranges and lemons. The purchaser was Bacchus Associates (Bacchus), a New York partnership that distributes fruit at wholesale throughout the Northeastern United States. Bacchus dealt with Galaxie Negoce, S.A. (Galaxie), a Moroccan fruit supplier. Bacchus contracted with Galaxie to purchase the shipload of fruit and chartered a ship to transport it from Morocco to Massachusetts. The ship was the M/V Sky Reefer, a refrigerated cargo ship owned by M.H. Maritima, S.A., a Panamanian company, and time-chartered to Nichiro Gyogyo Kaisha, Ltd., a Japanese company. Steve-dores hired by Galaxie loaded and stowed the cargo. As is customary in these types of transactions, when it received the cargo from Galaxie, Nichiro as carrier issued a form bill of lading to Galaxie as shipper and consignee. Once the ship set sail from Morocco, Galaxie tendered the bill of lading to Bacchus according to the terms of a letter of credit posted in Galaxie's favor.

Among the rights and responsibilities set out in the bill of lading were arbitration and choice-of-law clauses. Clause 3, entitled "Governing Law and Arbitration," provided:

"(1) The contract evidenced by or contained in this Bill of Lading shall be governed by the Japanese law.

"(2) Any dispute arising from this Bill of Lading shall be referred to arbitration in Tokyo by the Tokyo Maritime Arbitration Commission (TOMAC) of The Japan Shipping Exchange, Inc., in accordance with the rules of TOMAC and any amendment thereto, and the award given by the arbitrators shall be final and binding on both parties."

When the vessel's hatches were opened for discharge in Massachusetts, Bacchus discovered that thousands of boxes of oranges had shifted in the cargo holds, resulting in over $1 million damage. Bacchus received $733,442.90 compensation from petitioner Vimar Seguros y Reaseguros (Vimar Seguros), Bacchus' marine cargo insurer that became subrogated pro tanto to Bacchus' rights. Petitioner and Bacchus then brought suit against Maritima in personam and M/V Sky Reefer in rem in the District Court for the District of Massachusetts under the bill of lading. These defendants, respondents here, moved to stay the action and compel arbitration in Tokyo under clause 3 of the bill of lading and § 3 of the FAA, which requires courts to stay proceedings and enforce arbitration agreements covered by the Act. Petitioner and Bacchus opposed the motion, arguing the arbitration clause was unenforceable under the FAA both because it was a contract of adhesion and because it violated COGSA § 3(8). The premise of the latter argument was that the inconvenience and costs of proceeding in Japan would "lesse[n] ... liability" as those terms are used in COGSA.

[The District Court ruled for the ship owner and referred the parties to arbitration, retaining jurisdiction pending arbitration. The First Circuit affirmed. It assumed that the foreign arbitration clause lessened the ship owner's liability and hence violated COGSA, but it resolved the conflict between the statutes in favor of the FAA, which it considered to be the later enacted and more specific statute.]

II

The parties devote much of their argument to the question whether COGSA or the FAA has priority. * * * There is no conflict unless COGSA by its own terms nullifies a foreign arbitration clause, and we choose to address that issue rather than assume nullification arguendo, as the Court of Appeals did. We consider the two arguments made by petitioner. The first is that a foreign arbitration clause lessens COGSA liability by increasing the transaction costs of obtaining relief. The second is that there is a risk foreign arbitrators will not apply COGSA.

A

The leading case for invalidation of a foreign forum selection clause is the opinion of the Court of Appeals for the Second Circuit in *Indussa Corp. v. S.S. Ranborg*, 377 F.2d 200 (1967) (en banc). The court there found that COGSA invalidated a clause designating a foreign judicial forum because it "puts 'a high hurdle' in the way of enforcing liability, and thus is an effective means for carriers to secure settlements lower than if cargo [owners] could sue in a convenient forum,". The court observed "there could be no assurance that [the foreign court] would apply [COGSA] in the same way as would an U.S. tribunal subject to the uniform control of the Supreme Court". Following Indussa, the Courts of Appeals without exception have invalidated foreign forum selection clauses under § 3(8). As foreign arbitration clauses are but a subset of foreign forum selection clauses in general, the Indussa holding has been extended to foreign arbitration clauses as well. The logic of that extension would be quite defensible, but we cannot endorse the reasoning or the conclusion of the Indussa rule itself.

The determinative provision in COGSA, examined with care, does not support the arguments advanced first in Indussa and now by the petitioner. Section 3(8) of COGSA provides as follows:

> "Any clause, covenant, or agreement in a contract of carriage relieving the carrier or the ship from liability for loss or damage to or in connection with the goods, arising from negligence, fault, or failure in the duties or obligations provided in this section, or lessening such liability otherwise than as provided in this chapter, shall be null and void and of no effect."

The liability that may not be lessened is "liability for loss or damage ... arising from negligence, fault, or failure in the duties or obligations provided in this section." The statute thus addresses the lessening of the specific liability imposed by the Act, without addressing the separate question of the means and costs of enforcing that liability. The difference is that between explicit statutory guarantees and the procedure for enforcing them, between applicable liability principles and the forum in which they are to be vindicated.

The liability imposed on carriers under COGSA § 3 is defined by explicit standards of conduct, and it is designed to correct specific abuses by carriers. In the 19th century it was a prevalent practice for common carriers to insert clauses in bills of lading exempting themselves from liability for damage or loss, limiting the period in which plaintiffs had to present their notice of claim or bring suit, and capping any damages awards per package. Thus, § 3, entitled "Responsibilities and liabilities of carrier and ship," requires that the carrier "exercise due diligence to . . . [m]ake the ship seaworthy" and "[p]roperly man, equip, and supply the ship" before and at the beginning of the voyage, § 3(1), "properly and carefully load, handle, stow, carry, keep, care for, and discharge the goods carried," § 3(2), and issue a bill of lading with specified contents, § 3(3). Section 3(6) allows the cargo owner to provide notice of loss or damage within three days and to bring suit within one year. These are the substantive obligations and particular procedures that § 3(8) prohibits a carrier from altering to its advantage in a bill of lading. Nothing in this section, however, suggests that the statute prevents the parties from agreeing to enforce these obligations in a particular forum. By its terms, it establishes certain duties and obligations, separate and apart from the mechanisms for their enforcement.

If the question whether a provision lessens liability were answered by reference to the costs and inconvenience to the cargo owner, there would be no principled basis for distinguishing national from foreign arbitration clauses. Even if it were reasonable to read § 3(8) to make a distinction based on travel time, airfare, and hotels bills, these factors are not susceptible of a simple and enforceable distinction between domestic and foreign forums. Requiring a Seattle cargo owner to arbitrate in New York likely imposes more costs and burdens than a foreign arbitration clause requiring it to arbitrate in Vancouver. It would be unwieldy and unsupported by the terms or policy of the statute to require courts to proceed case by case to tally the costs and burdens to particular plaintiffs in light of their means, the size of their claims, and the relative burden on the carrier.

Our reading of "lessening such liability" to exclude increases in the transaction costs of litigation also finds support in the goals of the Brussels Convention for the Unification of Certain Rules Relating to Bills of Lading, (Hague Rules), on which COGSA is modeled. Sixty-six countries, including the United States and Japan, are now parties to the Convention, and it appears that none has interpreted its enactment of § 3(8) of the Hague Rules to prohibit foreign forum selection clauses.

And other countries that do not recognize foreign forum selection clauses rely on specific provisions to that effect in their domestic versions of the Hague Rules, see, e.g., Sea–Carriage of Goods Act 1924, § 9(2) (Australia); Carriage of Goods by Sea Act, No. 1 of 1986, § 3 (South Africa). In light of the fact that COGSA is the culmination of a multilateral effort "to establish uniform ocean bills of lading to govern the rights and liabilities of carriers and shippers inter se in international trade," we decline to interpret our version of the Hague Rules in a manner contrary to every other nation to have addressed this issue. * * * .

* * * Petitioner's skepticism over the ability of foreign arbitrators to apply COGSA or the Hague Rules, and its reliance on this aspect of Indussa, must give way to contemporary principles of international comity and commercial practice. * * *

That the forum here is arbitration only heightens the irony of petitioner's argument, for the FAA is also based in part on an international convention, [the New York Convention], intended "to encourage the recognition and enforcement of commercial arbitration agreements in international contracts and to unify the standards by which agreements to arbitrate are observed and arbitral awards are enforced in the signatory countries." The FAA requires enforcement of arbitration agreements in contracts that involve interstate commerce, and in maritime transactions, including bills of lading, * * *. If the United States is to be able to gain the benefits of international accords and have a role as a trusted partner in multilateral endeavors, its courts should be most cautious before interpreting its domestic legislation in such manner as to violate international agreements. That concern counsels against construing COGSA to nullify foreign arbitration clauses because of inconvenience to the plaintiff or insular distrust of the ability of foreign arbitrators to apply the law.

B

Petitioner's second argument against enforcement of the Japanese arbitration clause is that there is no guarantee foreign arbitrators will apply COGSA. This objection raises a concern of substance. The central guarantee of § 3(8) is that the terms of a bill of landing may not relieve the carrier of the obligations or diminish the legal duties specified by the Act. The relevant question, therefore, is whether the substantive law to be applied will reduce the carrier's obligations to the cargo owner below what COGSA guarantees.

Petitioner argues that the arbitrators will follow the Japanese Hague Rules, which, petitioner contends, lessen respondents' liability in at least one significant respect. The Japanese version of the Hague Rules, it is said, provides the carrier with a defense based on the acts or omissions of the stevedores hired by the shipper, Galaxie, (carrier liable "when he or the persons employed by him" fail to take due care), while COGSA, according to petitioner, makes nondelegable the carrier's obligation to "properly and carefully ... stow ... the goods carried,"

COGSA § 3(2). But see COGSA § 4(2)(i), 46 U.S.C. § 1304(2)(i) ("[N]either the carrier nor the ship shall be responsible for loss or damage arising or resulting from . . . [a]ct or omission of the shipper or owner of the goods, his agent or representative") * * *.

Whatever the merits of petitioner's comparative reading of COGSA and its Japanese counterpart, its claim is premature. At this interlocutory stage it is not established what law the arbitrators will apply to petitioner's claims or that petitioner will receive diminished protection as a result. The arbitrators may conclude that COGSA applies of its own force or that Japanese law does not apply so that, under another clause of the bill of lading, COGSA controls. Respondents seek only to enforce the arbitration agreement. The district court has retained jurisdiction over the case and "will have the opportunity at the award-enforcement stage to ensure that the legitimate interest in the enforcement of the . . . laws has been addressed." *Mitsubishi Motors*. Were there no subsequent opportunity for review and were we persuaded that "the choice-of-forum and choice-of-law clauses operated in tandem as a prospective waiver of a party's right to pursue statutory remedies . . ., we would have little hesitation in condemning the agreement as against public policy." *Mitsubishi Motors*. Cf. *Knott v. Botany Worsted Mills*, 179 U.S. 69, 21 S.Ct. 30, 45 L.Ed. 90 (1900) (nullifying choice-of-law provision under the Harter Act, the statutory precursor to COGSA, where British law would give effect to provision in bill of lading that purported to exempt carrier from liability for damage to goods caused by carrier's negligence in loading and stowage of cargo). Under the circumstances of this case, however, the First Circuit was correct to reserve judgment on the choice-of-law question, as it must be decided in the first instance by the arbitrator. As the District Court has retained jurisdiction, mere speculation that the foreign arbitrators might apply Japanese law which, depending on the proper construction of COGSA, might reduce respondents' legal obligations, does not in and of itself lessen liability under COGSA § 3(8).

Because we hold that foreign arbitration clauses in bills of lading are not invalid under COGSA in all circumstances, both the FAA and COGSA may be given full effect. The judgment of the Court of Appeals is affirmed, and the case is remanded for further proceedings consistent with this opinion.

It is so ordered.

JUSTICE BREYER took no part in the consideration or decision of this case.

JUSTICE O'CONNOR, concurring in the judgment.

I agree with what I understand to be the two basic points made in the Court's opinion. First, I agree that the language of the Carriage of Goods by Sea Act (COGSA) and our decision in Carnival Cruise Lines, Inc. v. Shute preclude a holding that the increased cost of litigating in a distant forum, without more, can lessen liability within the meaning of COGSA § 3(8). Second, I agree that, because the District Court has retained jurisdiction over this case while the arbitration proceeds, any claim of lessening of liability that might arise out of the arbitrators' interpretation of the bill of lading's choice of law clause, or out of their application of COGSA, is premature. Those two points suffice to affirm the decision below.

Because the Court's opinion appears to do more, however, I concur only in the judgment. Foreign arbitration clauses of the kind presented here do not divest domestic courts of jurisdiction, unlike true foreign forum selection clauses such as that considered in *Indussa Corp. v. S.S. Ranborg*. That difference is an important one—it is, after all, what leads the Court to dismiss much of petitioner's argument as premature—and we need not decide today whether Indussa, insofar as it relied on considerations other than the increased cost of litigating in a distant forum, retains any vitality in the context of true foreign forum selection clauses. Accordingly, I would not, without qualification, reject "the reasoning [and] the conclusion of the Indussa rule itself," * * *. As the Court notes, "[f]ollowing Indussa, the Court of Appeals without exception have invalidated foreign forum selection clauses under § 3(8)." I would prefer to disturb that unbroken line of authority only to the extent necessary to decide this case.

JUSTICE STEVENS, dissenting.

[Justice Stevens noted that COGSA, by its terms, applies to bills of lading issued by ocean carriers transporting cargo into or from U.S. ports and that it provides for mandatory carrier liability in certain circumstances to override the adhesion-contract nature of bills of lading that traditionally had included various exculpatory clauses. ("Because a bill of lading was (and is) a contract of adhesion, which a shipper must accept or else find another means to transport his goods, shippers were in no position to bargain around these no liability clauses.") He then turned to consistent lower court holdings, and in particular to the Second Circuit's en banc opinion (written by Judge Friendly) in *Indussa* holding invalid under COGSA both a choice of foreign forum clause and a choice of foreign law clause in a bill of lading.]

* * * In Indussa, the bill of lading contained a provision requiring disputes to be resolved in Norway under Norwegian law. Judge Friendly first remarked on the harsh consequence of "requiring an American consignee claiming damages in the modest sum of $2600 to journey some 4200 miles to a court having a different legal system and employing another language." The decision, however, rested not only on the impact of the provision on a relatively small claim, but also on a fair reading of the broad language in COGSA. Judge Friendly explained:

> "[Section] 3(8) of COGSA says that 'any clause, covenant, or agreement in a contract of carriage * * * lessening [the carrier's liability for negligence, fault, or dereliction of statutory duties] otherwise than as provided in this Act, shall be null and void and of no effect.' From a practical standpoint, to require an American plaintiff to assert his claim only in a distant court lessens the liability of the carrier quite substantially, particularly when the claim is small.

Such a clause puts 'a high hurdle' in the way of enforcing liability, Gilmore & Black, supra, 125 n. 23, and thus is an effective means for carriers to secure settlements lower than if cargo could sue in a convenient forum. A clause making a claim triable only in a foreign court would almost certainly lessen liability if the law which the court would apply was neither the Carriage of Goods by Sea Act nor the Hague Rules. Even when the foreign court would apply one or the other of these regimes, requiring trial abroad might lessen the carrier's liability since there could be no assurance that it would apply them in the same way as would an American tribunal subject to the uniform control of the Supreme Court, and § 3(8) can well be read as covering a potential and not simply a demonstrable lessening of liability."

* * *

Thus, * * * the federal courts' consistent interpretation of COGSA, buttressed by scholarly recognition of the commercial interest in uniformity, demonstrate that the clauses in the Japanese carrier's bill of lading purporting to require arbitration in Tokyo pursuant to Japanese law both would have been held invalid under COGSA prior to today.[7]

The foreign arbitration clause imposes potentially prohibitive costs on the shipper, who must travel—and bring his lawyers, witnesses and exhibits—to a distant country in order to seek redress. The shipper will therefore be inclined either to settle the claim at a discount or to forgo bringing the claim at all. The foreign-law clause leaves the shipper who does pursue his claim open to the application of unfamiliar and potentially disadvantageous legal standards, until he can obtain review (perhaps years later) in a domestic forum under the high standard applicable to vacation of arbitration awards.[8] Accordingly, courts have always held that such clauses "lessen" or "relieve" the carrier's liability, * * *.

* * *

II

The Court assumes that the words "lessening such liability" must be narrowly construed to refer only to the substantive rules that define the carrier's legal obligations. * * *

---

7. Of course, the objectionable feature in the instant bill of lading is a foreign arbitration clause, not a foreign forum selection clause. But this distinction is of little importance; in relevant respects, there is no difference between the two. Both impose substantial costs on shippers, and both should be held to lessen liability under COGSA. * * *

8. I am assuming that the majority would not actually uphold the application of disadvantageous legal standards—these, even under the narrowest reading of COGSA, surely lessen liability. Nonetheless, the majority is apparently willing to allow arbi-

tration to proceed under foreign law, and to determine afterwards whether application of that law has actually lessened the carrier's formal liability. As I have discussed above, this regime creates serious problems of delay and uncertainty. Because the majority's holding in this case is limited to the enforceability of the foreign arbitration clause—it does not actually pass upon the validity of the foreign law clause—I will not discuss the foreign law clause further except to say that it is an unenforceable lessening of liability to the extent it gives an advantage to the carrier at the expense of the shipper.

In my opinion, this view is flatly inconsistent with the purpose of COGSA § 3(8). That section responds to the inequality of bargaining power inherent in bills of lading and to carriers' historic tendency to exploit that inequality whenever possible to immunize themselves from liability for their own fault. A bill of lading is a form document prepared by the carrier, who presents it to the shipper on a take-it-or-leave-it basis. Characteristically, there is no arms-length negotiation over the bill's terms; the shipper must agree to the carrier's standard-form language, or else refrain from using the carrier's services. * * *

When one reads the statutory language in light of the policies behind COGSA's enactment, it is perfectly clear that a foreign forum selection or arbitration clause "relieves" or "lessens" the carrier's liability. The transaction costs associated with an arbitration in Japan will obviously exceed the potential recovery in a great many cargo disputes. As a practical matter, therefore, in such a case no matter how clear the carrier's formal legal liability may be, it would make no sense for the consignee or its subrogee to enforce that liability. * * *

Even if the value of the shipper's claim is large enough to justify litigation in Asia, contractual provisions that impose unnecessary and unreasonable costs on the consignee will inevitably lessen its net recovery. If, as under the Court's reasoning, such provisions do not affect the carrier's legal liability, it would appear to be permissible to require the consignee to pay the costs of the arbitration, or perhaps the travel expenses and fees of the expert witnesses, interpreters, and lawyers employed by both parties. * * *.

More is at stake here than the allocation of rights and duties between shippers and carriers. A bill of lading, besides being a contract of carriage, is a negotiable instrument that controls possession of the goods being shipped. Accordingly, the bill of lading can be sold, traded, or used to obtain credit as though the bill were the cargo itself. Disuniformity in the interpretation of bills of lading will impair their negotiability. Thus, if the security interests in some bills of lading are enforceable only through the courts of Japan, while others may be enforceable only in Liechtenstein, the negotiability of bills of lading will suffer from the uncertainty. COGSA recognizes that this negotiability depends in part upon the financial community's capacity to rely on the enforceability, in an accessible forum, of the bills' terms. Today's decision destroys that capacity.

* * *

III

[Here Justice Stevens argued that his position would not bring COGSA into conflict with the FAA. Although the latter requires arbitration agreements in international commerce to be enforced: "Like any other contractual clause, * * * an arbitration clause may be invalid without violating the FAA if, for example, it is procured through fraud or forgery; there is mutual mistake or impossibility; the provision is unconscionable; or, as in this case, the terms of the clause are illegal under a separate federal statute which does not evidence a hostility to arbitration.'']

* * *

I respectfully dissent.

Questions and Comments

1. The *Sky Reefer* Court rejects the argument that increased costs accompanying foreign arbitration would violate COGSA § 3(8). Is it clear that arbitration abroad would in most cases be more expensive than litigation in the United States? Do you think uncertainty on this point influenced the Court?

2. In arbitration the winning party can claim as part of the award in its favor reasonable attorney's fees and the other costs of the arbitration. Does this support or undercut the *Sky Reefer* decision?

3. Suppose the arbitration clause provides that all costs of arbitration of both parties, including attorneys' fees, must be borne by the cargo owner irrespective of the outcome of the arbitration. Would that provision be enforceable? If not, on what ground would it not be? Would it invalidate the entire clause?

4. In *Sky Reefer* the claimant argued that arbitrators would apply Japanese law and that under that law the carrier would have a defense not available under U.S. COGSA law:

> The Japanese version of the Hague Rules, it is said, provides the carrier with a defense based on the acts or omissions of the stevedores hired by the shipper, Galaxie, (carrier liable "when he or the persons employed by him" fail to take due care), while COGSA, according to petitioner, makes nondelegable the carrier's obligation to "properly and carefully ... stow ... the goods carried," COGSA § 3(2). But see COGSA § 4(2)(i), 46 U.S.C. § 1304(2)(i) ("[N]either the carrier nor the ship shall be responsible for loss or damage arising or resulting from ... [a]ct or omission of the shipper or owner of the goods, his agent or representative") * * *.

Does it seem to you from this excerpt that the Japanese and U.S. versions of the Hague Rules differ? Does the existence of some uncertainty on this point argue for or against referring the parties to arbitration? Does it influence your decision that Congress expressly provided that the U.S. COGSA would apply on all shipments into and from U.S. ports?

5. Suppose the bill of lading chose arbitration in Maritima and Maritima law to govern the parties' rights and obligations under the carriage contract. Suppose further that Maritima law does not incorporate the Hague Rules and allows carriers to contract out of all liability for cargo damage. Should a U.S. court refer the parties to arbitration?

6.   The *Sky Reefer* Court's response to the mandatory law problem is the same as that invoked in *Mitsubishi*. It has come to be called the "second look" doctrine. The Court notes that U.S. courts will have an opportunity at the award-enforcement stage to ensure that mandatory U.S. law has been respected. If it has not been, U.S. courts will be able to invoke public policy as a ground for refusing to recognize or enforce the award. If the carrier wins a victory in arbitration, however, there will be no occasion to enforce the award in the United States. So how will the "second look" occur? Is this the issue Justice O'Connor has in mind in stressing that the District Court retained jurisdiction even after it referred the parties to arbitration? Why is that significant? Would the situation have been different had the parties included a choice-of-foreign-forum—instead of a foreign-arbitration—clause?

7.   Is it a full answer to the issues raised in questions 4 and 5 above to note that the cargo claimant could always reinstitute its claim in the District Court? What if the carrier had no assets in the United States? Except for the time delay, would the cargo claimant's position be any weaker (in seeking to enforce a U.S. court judgment abroad) because the District Court had referred the parties to arbitration? Does the second look doctrine provide full protection to cargo claimants? If the cost of arbitrating in a foreign forum is by itself not enough to constitute "lessening a carrier's liability", would the added costs associated with delay and further litigation tip the balance against arbitration? Should it do so if the carrier appears to have employed choice-of-law and choice-of-arbitration clauses to evade the application of COGSA (for example, as in question 5)?

8.   Bills of lading are often negotiable in order to permit the original shipper to deal in the goods before they are available for physical delivery. This is accomplished by transferring (negotiating) the bill of lading to the seller, who then has legal control of the goods. Justice Stevens claims that the *Sky Reefer* decision will undercut the value of bills of lading in commerce into and from U.S. ports. Do you agree? If you were a dealer in oranges accustomed to buying shipments for resale in the United States, would the *Sky Reefer* decision affect the way you did business? Does this influence your assessment of the decision's soundness?

9.   Justice Kennedy for the majority in *Sky Reefer* argues: "If the United States is to be able to gain the benefits of international accords and have a role as a trusted partner in multilateral endeavors, its courts should be most cautious before interpreting its domestic legislation in such manner as to violate international agreements." In context, however, Kennedy seems to be referring to the New York Convention. Do you agree that an opposite outcome in *Sky Reefer* would have violated the New York Convention? Could the United States, consistent with the New York Convention, enforce agreements to arbitrate in the United States but reject agreements to arbitrate in foreign countries? Are Australia and South Africa in violation of the New York Convention because they have adopted statutes refusing to recognize foreign forum selection clauses in their domestic versions of the Hague Rules?

II.2.d. *Law Applicable to Arbitrability*

M.S.A. (BELGIUM) v. COMPANY M (SWITZERLAND)

Cour d'Appel [Court of Appeal] of Brussels 1985.
14 Yearbk. Comm. Arb'n 618 (1989).*[n]

FACTS

On 23 March 1974 the parties signed an exclusive distributorship agreement having its effects, inter alia, in Belgium. The agreement contained an arbitration clause and explicitly stated that Swiss law applied.

When a dispute arose, the Belgian party started court proceedings before the *Tribunal de Commerce* [Court of First Instance] of Brussels. The Swiss party objected to the Court's jurisdiction on the basis of the arbitration clause in the agreement.

The *Tribunal de Commerce* found that the arbitration clause was invalid under Art. II(1) of the New York Convention, since it concerned a subject matter not capable of settlement by arbitration under Belgian law. Hence, it recognized its jurisdiction to hear the case.

The Swiss party resorted to the Court of Appeal, which reversed the lower court's decision for the following reasons.

EXCERPT

[1]   The [*Tribunal's*] decision is in particular based on the consideration that "a coherent interpretation of the Convention requires that Art. II(1) and Art. II(3)—the latter being invoked by the Swiss party and providing that the court of a Contracting State must refer the parties to arbitration at the request of one of them, unless it finds that the said agreement is null and void, inoperative or incapable of being performed"—is to be read in conjunction with Art. V(2)(a) which provides that the authority of the country where recognition and enforcement are sought may refuse it, if it finds that "the subject matter of the difference is not capable of settlement by arbitration under the law of that country". This opinion of the lower court cannot be shared.

[2]   In fact, the arbitrability of a dispute must be ascertained according to different criteria, depending on whether the question arises when deciding on the validity of the arbitration agreement or when deciding on the recognition and enforcement of the arbitral award.

[3]   In the first case, the arbitrability is ascertained according to the law which applies to the validity of the arbitration agreement and, more in particular, to its object. It is therefore the law of autonomy which provides the solution to the issue of arbitrability.

* Reprinted with permission of Yearbook Commercial Arbitration, International Council for Commercial Arbitration.

n.   105 Journal des Tribunaux 93 (1986). 64 Revue de Droit International et de Droit Comparé 296 (1987).

[4]   An arbitrator or court faced with this issue must first determine which law applies to the arbitration agreement and then ascertain whether, according to this law, the specific dispute is capable of settlement by arbitration (M. Huys and G. Keutgen, *L'arbitrage en droit belge et international* ...).

[5]   In other words, when the arbitrability of the dispute is considered only from the point of view of the validity of the arbitration agreement, i.e., when the issue arises before the arbitrator (who must examine whether he is competent to hear the case by ascertaining the validity of the arbitration agreement on which his jurisdiction is founded) or before a court requested to decide only on this issue (hence, independently from any enforcement proceedings concerning the award itself), it will be sufficient—for the arbitrator or the court—to ascertain whether the law of autonomy authorizes the submission of the dispute to arbitration (Ph. Fouchard, *L'arbitrage commercial international*....)

[6]   Within the framework of the New York Convention, the expression "concerning a subject matter capable of settlement by arbitration" (Art. II(1)) does not affect the applicability of the law designated by the uniform solution of conflict of laws for deciding on the arbitrability of the dispute at the level of the arbitration agreement (B. Goldman, 'Arbitrage (droit international privé)', in *Encyclopédie Dalloz, Rép. dr. intern.* ...).

[7]   According to the New York Convention, the arbitrability of the dispute under the law of the forum must be taken into consideration only at the stage of recognition and enforcement of the award and not when examining the validity of the arbitration agreement. This rule can be explained by the consideration that the arbitral award will, in the majority of cases, be executed without the intervention of an enforcement court—either spontaneously or under the pressure of moral or professional sanctions....

[8]   The preceding considerations lead to the result that in the present case the arbitrability of the dispute between the parties must be ascertained, at the actual stage of the procedure, according to the law of autonomy.

[9]   It is not contested that the parties have agreed that their contractual relations will be governed by Swiss law (Art. 12 of the Contract).

[10]   Furthermore, it is not contested either, and it also results from the documentary evidence submitted by the appellant, that according to Swiss law the dispute between the parties is capable of settlement by arbitration.

[11]   Hence, the lower court was wrong in holding that it could not recognize the arbitration agreement between the parties according to Art. II(1) of the New York Convention.

[12]   For these reasons, the court reverses the judgment under appeal; holds that the *Tribunal de Commerce* of Brussels had no jurisdic-

tion to hear the case submitted by the appellee; and, as a consequence, it refers the parties to arbitration as agreed upon in the contract of 23 March 1974.

Questions and Comments

1. The competing Belgian law that the *Company M* court refused to apply is found in a statute, the Law of July 27, 1961 on the Unilateral Termination of Concessions for Exclusive Distributorship of an Indefinite Time. The statute applies to "concessions of sale" (exclusive distributorships) and provides for a reasonable notice period before unilateral termination by the manufacturer and for compensation to be paid to the exclusive distributor in certain circumstances.

Article 4 of the statute provides:

"1. Upon the termination of a concession of sale which concerns wholly or partially the Belgian territory, the aggrieved concessionnaire can cite in all cases the grantor of the concession in Belgium, whether before the court of his own domicile, or before the court of the domicile or seat of the grantor of the concession.

"2. In the case that the dispute is brought before a Belgian court, the latter shall apply exclusively Belgian law."

Article 6 of the statute provides:

"The provisions of this Law are applicable notwithstanding agreements to the contrary which are concluded before the end of the contract under which the concession is granted."

In a 1979 case with facts similar to those in *Company M*, a German manufacturer sought recognition of a Swiss arbitral award to bar a Belgian distributor's court action in Belgium based on the statute. The Belgian Cour de cassation (Supreme Court) relied on New York Convention Article V(2)(a) to refuse to recognize the Swiss award on the ground that under Belgian law the subject matter of the difference was not capable of settlement by arbitration. The Cour de cassation reasoned that the 1961 Belgian statute was a mandatory law that guaranteed both the right of a court action in Belgium and the substantive statutory protections, unless the distributor gave up those rights *after* the contract came to an end. Audi–NSU Auto Union A.G. v. S.A. Adelin Petit & Cie, Cour de cassation (1979), 5 Yearbk. Comm. Arb'n 257 (1980).[67] If the Belgian distributor can agree to give up its statutory rights *after* the contract comes to an end, why not *before*, by agreeing to an arbitration clause?

2. What is the purpose of the Belgian law? If it is to protect the party in the weaker bargaining position, the distributor, does the *Company M* result defeat that purpose by enforcing a choice-of-law clause? Would the Belgian party be bound by the arbitral award, or could it sue in Belgian courts after the award is rendered? If an action before Belgian courts would still be available, why force the parties to the trouble and expense of arbitration in the first place?

[67]. Major provisions of the Belgian statute are quoted in English translation and discussed in Audi–NSU Auto Union A.G. v. S.A. Adelin Petit & Cie, Cour d'appel de Liege, 4 Yearbk. Comm. Arb'n 254, 255–56, nn. 2, 3 and 7 (1979).

3. In his commentary on the New York Convention Albert Jan van den Berg, discusses the law applicable to the question of arbitrability as follows:

"For the enforcement of the arbitral award, the Convention refers in Article V(2)(a) to the law of the country where the enforcement is sought, i.e., the *lex fori*. For the enforcement of the arbitration agreement the Convention is silent on this point; Article II(1) merely states that the agreement must concern a 'subject matter capable of settlement by arbitration'. Notwithstanding this silence, it must be presumed that for the enforcement of the arbitration agreement also the *lex fori* governs the question of arbitrability. Internal consistency of the Convention requires such an analogous interpretation. Also the main effect of an arbitration agreement is the exclusion of the competence of the courts in favour of arbitration. As a court derives its competence as a rule from its own law, it should inquire under its own law whether the competence has lawfully been excluded in favour of arbitration." Albert Jan van den Berg, THE NEW YORK ARBITRATION CONVENTION OF 1958, 152 (1981).

Do you agree with the *Company M* court or with van den Berg? The New York Convention Article V(2)(a) does not use the term "lex fori". It merely applies the law of the state where recognition and enforcement of the award is sought. In an action to enforce the agreement to arbitrate the state where the award might be enforced is not known. Does that mean that it is impossible to construe Article II(1) and V(2)(a) in harmony, or that one can do so, as van den Berg does, by understanding Article V(2)(a) to be applying a *lex fori* rule?

4. Suppose the arbitration is to take place in a country other than the country where the enforcement of the arbitration agreement is sought. Should the court before which the arbitration agreement is being challenged apply its own law and also judge the dispute's arbitrability under the law of the place of arbitration? If it does not do so, would not the award be subject to being set aside at the place of arbitration? See Albert Jan van den Berg, THE NEW YORK ARBITRATION CONVENTION OF 1958, 153 (1981) (reporting that in all cases he consulted, courts applied their own law on arbitrability and not the law of the place of arbitration). Would it promote uniformity if all courts, including those where the arbitration takes place, followed the *Company M* approach?

5. In Consultant (France) v. Egyptian Local Authority, 17 Yearbk. Comm.Arb'n 153 (1992) (ICC Arbitral Award, Geneva, Switzerland, 1990), the parties entered a contract, under which the consultant (Claimant) was to make technical and financial studies and prepare the book of tender for a construction project in Egypt. The contract provided for arbitration in Geneva under the ICC Rules and in a different clause said: "Egyptian laws will be applicable". The Egyptian Local Authority (Respondent) argued that under Egyptian law the contract was an "administrative contract" and that as such the administrative courts of Egypt were exclusively competent; hence the dispute was non-arbitrable. Without deciding whether the parties' agreement was, or was not, an administrative contract, the arbitrator concluded that because the seat of the arbitration was Geneva: "It is therefore necessary to determine to which extent the Swiss rules governing

international arbitration apply to decide on the issue of arbitrability and enable an arbitral tribunal to refuse to apply foreign legal provisions according to which the dispute would not be arbitrable." The arbitrator then relied on Article 177(2) of Chapter 12 of the 1987 Swiss Private International Law Act[68] (see Documents Supplement) to conclude that the Egyptian Local Authority could not invoke Egyptian law to contest the arbitrability of the dispute. Is the arbitrator's approach consistent with that of the Belgian court in the *Company M* case? Which approach do you favor and why? Is the Swiss rule designed to encourage arbitration in Switzerland? Do you think the arbitrator in *Egyptian Local Authority* was motivated to enforce the parties' intent as expressed in the contract, advance the policy underlying the Swiss law, or legitimate the tribunal's authority to decide the case? Would the award in this proceeding be enforceable in Egypt?

[68]. The 1987 Swiss Act came into effect on January 1, 1989. Because the arbitration began before that date, the parties disputed the temporal applicability of Article 177 of the 1987 Swiss Act. The arbitrator avoided this difficulty by concluding that the rule expressed in Article 177(2) was a part of Swiss law before January 1, 1989 (and implicitly at the time the arbitration began).

Chapter III

THE ARBITRATORS

III.1. THE ARBITRATORS—QUALIFICATIONS, RIGHTS AND RESPONSIBILITIES

III.1.a. Note

One of the crucial comparative advantages of international commercial arbitration lies in the possibility of entrusting the dispute to a forum which is essentially equidistant from both parties.

International litigation usually proceeds on the home ground for one of the litigants.[1] Such a home court grants a number of privileges and conveniences, even without assuming any bias. These are: familiarity with the language, with the procedure, indeed with the whole legal environment, little or no travel related problems and expenses, and easier access to local counsel. Further, it is not easy to dispel expectations of bias, or fear of bias, if the case is litigated before the courts of one of the parties.

Arbitration can provide a truly neutral ground for the settlement of a dispute. One of the most important elements of this neutrality or equidistance, is the arbitrators. The arbitration framework allows each party to choose an arbitrator from its own country or from a third state. In doing so, the parties may combine or choose between the two main types of fairness in third party decision-making: impartiality or balance.

Neutrality is not synonymous with impartiality. Rather, it is an exterior sign or an indication of likely impartiality; neutrality is easier to recognize, and easier to translate into standards.

What neutrality entails is often discussed in two dimensions: personal (direct) and general (indirect). On a personal level, neutrality supposes essentially the absence of family and business ties. On the general plane, consideration is also given to group affiliation, such as nationality, religion, ethnic background, etc. Parties are usually rather sensitive to

---

[1]. Litigation before the court of a third country either on the basis of the plaintiff's choice among available forums or of a *prorogatio fori* is possible, but relatively rare, and is not supported by a worldwide scheme of international arrangements, such as is in place for arbitration.

both dimensions of the problem. Arbitral institutions are also aware of these issues and work to address concerns by establishing practical guidelines, rather than by spelling out rules. While the definition of neutrality on a personal level may be difficult, to exclude individual members of a group and to conceptualize group-biases opens a Pandora's box.

Legislators have generally refrained from posing requirements based on group-affiliation. After lengthy consideration, the drafters of the UNCITRAL Model Law decided on the following formulation regarding nationality of the arbitrators: "[n]o person shall be precluded by reason of his nationality from acting as an arbitrator, unless otherwise agreed by the parties." (Article 11(1)). Institutional rules have shown more sensitivity to appearance of bias on the ground of nationality. The UNCITRAL Rules took a hesitant step towards using nationality as a criterion, stating that the appointing authority: "shall take into account as well the advisability of appointing an arbitrator of a nationality other than the nationalities of the parties." (Article 6(4)) (concerning appointment of a sole arbitrator). The 1998 ICC Rules (Article 9(5)), like the 1998 Rules of the London Court of International Arbitration (Article 6(1)), include a clear rule stating that the sole arbitrator, or the third arbitrator, shall be chosen from a country other than those of which the parties are nationals.[2]

Thus, the rules on standards of neutrality are usually scarce. In the words of Fouchard, the rules of the French New Code of Civil Procedure: "remain most discreet on the person, the mission, rights and obligations of the arbitrator."[3] General guidelines on the direct (personal) level may be found in the applicable *lex arbitri* or in institutional rules, but to a critical extent, the parties themselves have been left to translate their trust and mistrust into criteria of selection. Potential arbitrators are expected to help the parties in their choice, by disclosing any circumstances which may give rise to justifiable doubts as to their impartiality.

In addition to considerations of neutrality and impartiality, the choice of arbitrators is certainly influenced by professional reputation, command of languages and other qualities. It is self-evident that only natural persons can act as arbitrators.

In some countries (e.g., Spain[4]) if the dispute is of a legal nature (**de jure** arbitration), only lawyers can be appointed as arbitrators.

A frequent dilemma concerns the number of arbitrators. In the vast majority of cases the parties choose either a sole arbitrator or three arbitrators. The relative merits of these two options are still debated.

---

[2]. ICC Rules Article 9(5) provides an exception to the nationality rule if neither party objects.

[3]. Ph. Fouchard, Le statut juridique de l'arbitre dans la jurisprudence française, 1996 Revue de l'arbitrage 325, 326.

[4]. See Article 12(2) of the Law 36/1988 on Arbitration of December 5, 1988.

The 1998 ICC Rules (Article 8(2)) have given a certain priority to the sole arbitrator, stating:

> "Where the parties have not agreed upon the number of arbitrators, the Court shall appoint a sole arbitrator, save where it appears to the Court that the dispute is such as to warrant the appointment of three arbitrators."

A contrary solution was adopted by Article 5 of the UNCITRAL Rules:

> "[i]f the parties have not previously agreed on the number of arbitrators (i.e., one or three), and if within fifteen days after the receipt by the respondent of the notice of arbitration the parties have not agreed that there shall be only one arbitrator, three arbitrators shall be appointed."

> In the opinion of Redfern and Hunter, "International commercial arbitrations (other than those involving issues or sums of money that are not significant) are usually most effective when an arbitral tribunal of three arbitrators is appointed. This is more expensive than an arbitration conducted by a sole arbitrator; and it will also generally take longer to obtain an award. However, an arbitral tribunal of three arbitrators is likely to prove more satisfactory to the parties, and the ultimate award is more likely to be acceptable to them."[5]

In the majority of countries (England being one of the important exceptions) the number of arbitrators must be uneven. The implications of this requirement are illustrated in a case in which a French court scrutinized an arrangement of the parties to submit their dispute to two arbitrators and to engage a third arbitrator (an umpire) only in the event that the two arbitrators could not agree (an arrangement quite common in English law and practice). The Paris Cour d'Appel held that this party agreement was contrary to French mandatory norms; the arbitration clause was, therefore, null and void.[6]

Once selected, the arbitrators enjoy rather wide powers, which are not limited by appellate level scrutiny. Under many national laws—the New York Convention does not govern vacation—an award can only rarely and with difficulty be vacated on the ground of improper or unskilled behavior of the arbitrators. In ancient Greece, the major device for containing and checking the power and the behavior of arbitrators was fear of the gods. Before starting their deliberations, arbitrators took an oath, which spelled out in great detail the horrible consequences awaiting dishonest arbitrators, and the name of the specific gods who would administer these consequences. Today, such instruments are lacking. The safeguards are: scrutiny before choice, challenge procedure, and a limited number of grounds for setting aside or refusing recognition of the award.

[5]. A. Redfern and M. Hunter, Law and Practice of International Commercial Arbitration, 3rd ed., 194 (1999).

[6]. *Société La Moirette v. Société LTM France*, Cour d'appel de Paris, September 13, 1995; reported in 1995 Revue de l'arbitrage 631.

The issues of neutrality and impartiality are closely linked to the standards of expected behavior, as well as the rights and responsibilities of the arbitrators. Some questions emerging in this context have an answer in the applicable *lex arbitri*, while others border on—or are beyond the range of—legal norms; codes of ethics also play a role in standardizing arbitrator behavior.

III.1.b. *Oath and Fear of Gods as Safeguards of Impartiality*

M. Tod, INTERNATIONAL ARBITRATION AMONGST THE GREEKS
115–16 (1913).*

[CHAPTER] IV—THE PROCEDURE OF THE TRIBUNAL

* * *

The inquiry was frequently conducted * * * in a sanctuary, and the members of the court took an oath, as was the universal practice in Greek courts of law. Sometimes this oath preceded the hearing of the evidence: this was certainly the case at Magnesia, * * *

* * * [T]he same custom seems to have been followed at Cnidus and in the arbitral trial between Sparta and the Acheans. But in one case the tenor of the narrative leaves no doubt that the oath was taken after the hearing of the evidence and immediately preceded the giving of votes, * * *. The exact formula of this oath is preserved in a decree passed by the Cnidians:

> 'By Zeus and Lycian Apollo and Earth, I will judge the case to which the contesting parties have sworn in accordance with the justest judgement, and I will not judge according to a witness if he does not seem to be bearing true witness; nor have I received gifts from any one on account of this trial, neither I myself nor any one else, man or woman, on my behalf, in any way or under any pretext whatsoever. If I swear truly, may it be well with me, if falsely the reverse.'

Similarly the oath taken by the Delphian Amphictiones before deciding a number of questions, of which one involved international relations, is preserved almost entire and runs as follows:

> 'Every question in the judgement relating to the moneys and boundaries of Apollo I will decide as is true to the best of my belief, nor will I in any wise give false judgements for the sake of favour or friendship or enmity; and the sentence passed in accordance with the judgement I will enforce to the best of my power with all possible speed, and I will make just restoration to the god. Nor will I receive gifts, neither I myself nor any one else on my behalf, nor will I give aught of the common moneys to any one nor receive it myself.

* Marcus Niebuhr Tod, International Arbitration Amongst the Greeks 115–116 (1913). Reprinted by permission of Oxford University Press.

These things I will thus do. And if I swear truly may I have many blessings, but if I swear falsely may Themis and Pythian Apollo and Leto and Artemis and Hestia and eternal fire and all gods and goddesses take from me salvation by a most dreadful doom, may they permit me myself and my race to enjoy neither children nor crops nor fruits nor property, and may they cast me forth in my lifetime from the possessions which now I have, if I shall swear falsely.'

So important was this oath considered that the official record, deposited at Megalopolis, of an award between Sparta and Megalopolis contained not only the formula of the oath, but also the names of those Spartan envoys who were present when it was administered to the judges.

Questions and Comments

1. The Tod book reports that in Magnesia and some other places, the oath was taken before hearing the evidence. In other places, however, it was taken after the hearing of the evidence, and before voting. Is the timing of the oath significant?

2. The text of the pledges given to Zeus and Apollo endeavors to cover a wide ground. Fear of gods as a safeguard did not rely solely on a vague distinction between acting honestly and acting in bad faith. What are the possible patterns of bias that the two Greek oaths recognize?

III.1.c. More Modern Considerations and Devices (Neutrality, Independence, Disclosure)

Giorgio Bernini,[a] REPORT ON NEUTRALITY, IMPARTIALITY, AND INDEPENDENCE

The Arbitral Process and the Independence of Arbitrators 31–37 (ICC ed., 1991)*

Summary

1. Introduction

2. Neutrality, impartiality and independence: definitions, overlappings and diversities.

3. Should the requirements of neutrality, impartiality and independence also be referred to party-appointed arbitrators?

4. Standards of behaviour to be applied by the arbitrators to maintain independence.

5. Duties of the arbitrator: further examples touching on independence.

6. When independence is carried too far.

7. Neutrality, impartiality and independence in the relations among arbitrators.

a. *Honorary President, International Council for Commercial Arbitration (ICCA).*
*ICC Publication No. 472—ISBN 92.842.0093.8 (EF). Published in its official

English version by the International Chamber of Commerce. Copyright 8 1991—International Chamber of Commerce (ICC), Paris. Reprinted with permission from ICC.

8. The impact of experience.

9. Neutral versus non-neutral arbitrators.

* * *

2. Neutrality, Impartiality and Independence: Definitions, Overlappings and Diversities

2.1. The theme of our discussion is focussed upon the independence of the arbitrators, which is deemed a pillar of the arbitral system, and on the standards of behaviour by which the arbitrators are most likely to preserve it. Independence is a situation to be verified "in vivo", i.e., in terms of actual fact. Independence is the result of two basic features, traditionally referred to the arbitrators, which are not univocally appraised in different arbitral environments: neutrality and impartiality.

2.2. In the framework of arbitration the notions of neutrality and impartiality differ from the corresponding notions as traditionally interpreted when viewed in the ambit of the judiciary system, wherein neutrality and impartiality are institutional features of the organ (monocratic or collegiate) entrusted with exercising the jurisdictional function. In arbitration neutrality and impartiality, as prerequisites to independence, are to be tested in each individual case. The arbitrators' jurisdiction, resting on a merely contractual basis, is indeed binding only "inter partes".

2.3. Neutrality and impartiality cannot be equated as regards their intrinsic nature. At the risk of oversimplification neutrality may be defined as an objective status, i.e. the likelihood for the arbitrator to be, and remain, wholly equidistant in thought and action throughout the arbitral proceedings. Impartiality, on the contrary, partakes more of a subjective status to be actually tested in the context of the concrete relations existing between the arbitrator(s) and each individual party. It follows that one can be impartial without being neutral; conversely no arbitrator may be deemed neutral, if he/she is behaving partially.

2.4. A further distinction touches upon the definition of the parties' state of mind when analyzed in terms of neutrality as opposed to impartiality. A person may lack neutrality in perfectly good faith, whereas if he/she is not impartial this can only happen as the outcome of some conduct carried out either in bad faith, i.e. when guided by a malicious intent (dolus), or induced by a lack of diligence or care regarding the arbitrator's most elementary duties (culpa).

* * *

3. Should the Requirements of Neutrality, Impartiality and Independence Also Be Referred to Party-appointed Arbitrators?

3.1. As regards impartiality, a preliminary caveat should be put forward. My remarks are based on the assumption that impartiality is to be expected from both the party-appointed arbitrator as well as the third arbitrator. I am aware that in many a circumstance the parties do not expect their appointee to act neutrally and impartially. If this is their wish, they should hasten to make the proper disclosure beforehand; otherwise, it is dutiful to assume that also the party-appointed arbitrator(s) should be neutral and act impartially.

3.2. This is a delicate subject often complicated by terminological uncertainties which may conceal true (and dangerous) misunderstandings. To dissipate any doubts, and in harmony with the definitions adopted hereinabove, I readily concede, also in the light of existing practices, a margin of discretion in allowing departure from the basic canon of neutrality. As regards impartiality, however, the acceptance of possible deviations must be reduced to the barest minimum.

3.3. It has been said that the arbitrator may be partial but not dishonest. I understand this statement as an ethical justification only if partiality is the result of some bona fide (i.e. justifiably negligent) conduct. However, if one relinquishes the ethical outlook, an arbitrator who is innocently partial cannot be accepted in the framework of fair and orderly proceedings. This would allow tolerance of a lack of independence which, though morally admissible, would betray the arbitral function at its very roots.

3.4. A slightly different conclusion may be reached with reference to neutrality. It is acceptable that one party seek, in terms of legal and cultural extraction, greater intellectual propinquity with its appointed arbitrator. This, however, does not adversely affect "per se" the independence of the arbitrator. Non-neutral arbitrators, therefore, do not necessarily antagonize the nature of arbitration, as traditionally envisaged, provided however, that the same rules apply, by mutual agreement of the parties, to all appointees, in full transparency and without hidden or overt discriminations. In conclusion, any lack of independence due to cultural hurdles, conceivable in principle, should be proven in each individual instance.

* * *

5. Duties of the Arbitrator: Further Examples Touching on Independence

5.1. As pointed out above, equal treatment of the parties may be cited as the quintessence of the arbitrators' impartiality and independence. It must therefore be assured with top priority throughout the arbitral proceedings. In real terms it may sometimes become difficult for the arbitrators to strike a balance between the respect for equal treatment and the exigency not to restrict and condition unduly the parties' right of defence. Allusion is made, *inter alia*, to the postponement of existing deadlines unilaterally requested by one party, the admission of evidence requested by one party and opposed by the other, the reduction of the number of witnesses and/or hearings requested by one party and opposed by the other. Any such decisions fall within the ambit of the arbitrators' prudent discretion. Prudent justice, especially in arbitration wherein the arbitrators have no power of coercion, may seemingly encourage procedural leniency, with a view *inter alia* to avoiding procedural disputes which may bring about setting aside actions. Any test of procedural fairness should be ultimately patterned upon the need to preserve impartiality. Procedural leniency may help in the search for the truth but nonetheless unduly upset the scale of impartiality. The repercussions on independence stemming from the occurrence of any such event are indicated hereinbelow, Sub-para. 5.2.

5.2. I have already underlined, as the "leit motiv" of this report, that independence is the correct behavioural consequence of the requirements of neutrality and impartiality. These requirements must be deemed the prerequisites of the arbitrators' state of mind and propensity for action. Lacking such prerequisites the arbitrator should decline the appointment as sole arbitrator, president of the arbitral panel, or co-arbitrator. The ethical rule, as pointed out above, is the same, whatever the function of the arbitrator, unless the parties have agreed to the appointment of non-neutral arbitrators. When dealing with neutrality and impartiality, the matrices of independence, physiology rather than pathology have been privileged. In other words, greater consideration was given to the hypotheses by which an arbitrator may objectively lack neutrality or impartiality in a subjective status of good faith, or, at most, because of an excusable breach of diligence. The identification of the grounds under which neutrality and impartiality may be thus breached, with ensuing prejudice to independence, would bring about numerous cases involving different factual circumstances. A tentative series of examples is indicated hereinbelow.

5.2.1. One may lack independence because of the existence of personal, affective or financial interests and ties with one party, directly or indirectly interwoven. Attention should thus be focussed on professional, family and social relations likely to curtail the arbitrators' independence or even allow the impression that such independence is endangered. The mere negative appearance may also be harmful as the arbitrators' independence is deemed a guarantee for the correct and orderly implementation of the arbitral proceedings. The sole subjective conviction of an arbitrator that a given circumstance is not going to alter his/her independence is not sufficient. All the parties as well as the co-arbitrators must agree. The final decision exceeds the bounds of the arbitrators' own conscience and the atmosphere must be cleared beyond reasonable doubt *inter alia* to avoid possible retaliations likely to bring about deterioration of mores on which complaints are being raised with increasing frequency.

5.2.2. Without pretences to being exhaustive, the following situations are indicative of a regime likely to ignite an explosion of unwelcome misunderstandings.

5.2.2.1. The arbitrator who has rendered a prior opinion should decline an appointment whenever issues likely to be debated in the arbitration are covered by the opinion in question.

5.2.2.2. The same caveat applies in a different chronological setting. It is advisable for an arbitrator to refrain from publishing any opinions which may be related to the subject-matter of an arbitration in which he/she is engaged. I concede that the above conclusion may be debatable if envisaged in radical terms. It is hardly conceivable that an arbitrator be prevented from indulging in legal writings. It would also be harassing to request that a jurist engaged in legal publications refrain from exercising the arbitral function concerning disputes which fall within the ambit of his/her specialized knowledge. As usual the truth lies somewhere in the middle, such middle to be established following an analysis of each individual case. If prior opinions are expressed by the prospective arbitrator on specific points, without possible variables concerning special factual details or circumstances, and such points are clearly the object of the award to be rendered, it is proper that the designated arbitrator decline the appointment. Pending the proceedings the appointed arbitrator shall have to refrain from expressing opinions on issues which are before him/her for decision.

* * *

6. When Independence Is Carried Too Far

6.1. At least until the time when arbitrations are implemented through teleconferences, the physical presence of the arbitrators is required. Putting together busy arbitrators is no minor endeavour. Difficulties increase if the personal convenience of the protagonists is pushed too far. In this connection, the practice indicates the coming into being of what one may define as a sort of "dolus bonus" of certain arbitrators. By this expression allusion is made to the tendency of unduly privileging the arbitrators' personal convenience in setting dates and establishing other procedural requirements. In addition, in many a situation one tends to ignore the exigencies of other participants (parties and co-arbitrators) in the proceedings, often causing harassment and undue delay. One is thus witnessing the birth of a new specimen, i.e., the so called arbitrator-dictator. This person, when entrusted with decision-making powers, tends to act alone without any prior consultation with the parties, and, sometimes, even with the co-arbitrators. More often than not, by so doing, he/she goes beyond the bound of professional discourtesy by adversely affecting the equal treatment of the parties, with ensuing grave violations of the most elementary canons of impartiality. Once again the truth lies in the middle. It is understandable that a presiding arbitrator should not spend all his/her time chasing the co-arbitrators and the parties before organizing a hearing or a meeting. On the other hand, the most elementary duty of impartiality demands that all arbitrators and all parties enjoy the same concrete opportunity to participate in all procedural activities. This obviously implies a minimum of prior consultation and agreement. The circumstances described above indicate the metamorphosis of independence into sheer license.

7. Neutrality, Impartiality and Independence in the Relations Among Arbitrators

7.1.   I already anticipated that no arbitrator should entertain direct relations with the parties. Written communications should be sent in copy to all arbitrators who should also be privy to any oral exchanges between the arbitrator(s) and the party/parties. Neutrality and impartiality represent an important chapter in the relations among the arbitrators themselves, which should be guided by criteria of transparency and fairness. As a rule, i.e. without the delegation of special powers, the presiding arbitrator is to be deemed a "primus inter pares". Though entrusted with the institutional task of conducting the proceedings, the presiding arbitrator must, therefore, consult with the co-arbitrators in order to ensure the overall independence of the panel as a whole. I am aware that in the light of certain systems, there seem to exist rules (or habits) whereby the presiding arbitrator is institutionally endowed with wider power. However, in order to avoid misunderstandings and difficulties it is proper that the parties and the arbitration agree beforehand as regards the sphere of prerogatives that the presiding arbitrator is entitled to exercise alone.

7.2.   The need for impartiality and independence reaches its peak at the moment of decision. It is the culmination of the function entrusted to the arbitrators wherein these requirements are called to play their conclusive role. The arbitrators should resist any and all pressures from external sources. They should discuss the case openly and freely and always remain fully equidistant as far as the concrete interest of the parties is concerned. Before the award is handed down the decision should remain secret and no indiscretion should emerge outside of the hypothesis in which dissenting opinions are admitted. Also the rules concerning dissenting opinions should be punctually complied with as dissenting implies no less independence and impartiality than assenting. Independence and impartiality will also be affected if one arbitrator, whether dissenting or not in formal terms, slows down the decision by adopting dilatory tactics within the arbitral panel and by attempting to prevent the issuance of the award. Not to speak of the case, to be severely stigmatized, where an arbitrator, through direct contacts with one party, conspires to frustrate the award by revealing details of the arbitrators' discussions "in camera" and by helping the said party in the preparation of a setting aside action.

* * *

9. Neutral Versus Non-neutral Arbitrators

9.1.   The system that I depicted is based on the assumption that the parties are most inclined to appoint neutral arbitrators. This is not necessarily true in all instances, especially when the parties themselves are public entities or the State itself. In such a situation other considerations may lead to the decision of appointing functionaries or other subjects who, in one way or another, are not neutral and therefore may not be expected to remain totally impartial and independent of the appointing party.

9.2. A discussion on the pros and cons of neutral versus non-neutral arbitrators exceeds the bounds of this report. Be that as it may and whatever the system adopted, the rules of the game should be disclosed beforehand and remain the same for both parties. If a subject, including a State or a public entity, chooses an arbitrator without expecting the same to be neutral, it should inform the other party. One would thus be faced with another type of arbitral logic, clearly defined from the very beginning. It should be equally clear, however, that lack of neutrality is not meant to include a licence to kill. Even a non-neutral arbitrator must be guided by standards of reasonable fairness and honesty.

9.3. The issue of the arbitrators' independence is the same in both administered and *ad hoc* arbitration. May I only point out that in administered arbitration the requirements of neutrality, impartiality and independence are generally included, and sometimes exhaustively defined, in the rules, and their implementation is effectively checked by the administering body throughout the proceedings.

9.4. As a closing remark may I be permitted to reiterate that the strength of arbitration lies in the freedom of the parties to set the rules of the game. The parties' autonomy is the governing criterion. If the parties elect not to depart from the classic criteria of neutrality and impartiality the arbitrators are strictly duty-bound to comply with this choice and remain fully independent. I personally believe that compliance with said criteria still represents the best system. If upon the parties' agreement the arbitrators are allowed to dispense with neutrality and impartiality, it is up to them to probe their conscience before accepting the appointment. As already anticipated, there are definite limits of fairness and honesty that even non-neutral arbitrators should never trespass. All the above has an obvious bearing upon independence. It is my firm belief that in no circumstances should an arbitrator relinquish his/her independence to the point of becoming the mere agent of the appointing party.

9.5. To conclude, it is up to the arbitrators themselves to assert the dignity of their function in the light of the circumstances prevailing in each case. They must keep in mind, however, that an arbitrator shall never tolerate being turned into the servant of the appointing party. If it were not so, one would fall outside of the realm of arbitration, as traditionally known, by making recourse to a different system wherein the dispute is settled through a direct confrontation of the parties reserving no role whatsoever to any third subjects acting in a quasi-judicial fashion.

Andreas F. Lowenfeld, THE PARTY–APPOINTED ARBITRATOR IN INTERNATIONAL CONTROVERSIES: SOME REFLECTIONS

30 Tex. Int'l L. J. 59 (1995).*

I. SELECTING ONE'S ARBITRATORS

Some years ago, my then dean called me up to inform me that he had been contacted by the senior partner of a prominent law firm, who was looking for an arbitrator for a major international arbitration. Apparently I had been suggested as a possible arbitrator, and the lawyer was checking with his friend the dean. "I told him," the dean said, "that you were very smart, very hard-working, very experienced, well-known abroad, and with a good sense of procedure and a good feel for the elements of a commercial transaction. If you have a good case, you couldn't do better than appointing Professor Lowenfeld." I never heard from the firm. The last sentence, while flattering to me, was the kiss of death. The dean did not say, "Whether your case is good or bad, Professor Lowenfeld will be in there, fighting for your side."

The story highlights a critical question about the selection of party-appointed arbitrators, and about their role once they are selected. Was the dean's friend right to reject someone he could not count on to support him, come what may? I do not think so, on two quite separate levels. On one level, easy to state in the abstract, an arbitrator is a judge, not a member of a party's team. While he or she is expected to be receptive to the position of the party that appointed him or her, an arbitrator is not supposed to approach a controversy with mind made up. I can state that while I have had suspicions now and then that a party-appointed arbitrator approached the case with a sense of mission, I have only once had the experience, in a case in which I was chairman, where, when my fellow arbitrators said "we," it was not clear whether they meant "we, the tribunal" or "my client and I."

On another level, I have had the experience a number of times where my opposite number as party-appointed arbitrator seemed too zealous in defense of the party that nominated him, and thus lost credibility with the chairman, whereas the chairman believed that I was trying to sort out the facts and the law fairly and came to rely on my analysis and advice. In contrast, when both party-appointed arbitrators evidently see their role as that of judge and not advocate, arbitrators come to function as a unit, examining different aspects of the dispute or writing different parts of the award—say, one focusing on the procedural issues, another on the evidence, and the third on the legal issues, according to the particular skills and experience each brings to the process. I have heard it said—to me directly and in panel discussions— "What you say is all very well, and if everyone had your attitude, Professor, it would be a better world. But we know the kind of person

* Reprinted by permission of Texas International Law Journal.

the other side will appoint (or has appointed), and the playing field won't be level if he is unfair and you insist on being wholly fair...." Quite apart from moral or ethical considerations or the applicable rules, I reject the suggestion that if one side or one arbitrator bends the code, the other side or the other arbitrator should do so as well or wind up disadvantaged. My experience, over more than two decades, is all the other way.

Some years ago, at a conference on international arbitration, an eminent lawyer with great experience both as arbitrator and as counsel in major cases, said from the podium that counsel should never nominate an arbitrator without interviewing him or her first. I raised my hand from the floor to object. "If you are considering me for your next case, you may call my secretary for my resume or ask your librarian for a list of my publications, but I will not be interviewed." My reasoning was that an arbitrator should not seem to be applying for a job, and in particular should not try to sell himself to the lawyer who, if the interview were successful, would be appearing before him as advocate. I was not reassured by the speaker's response about the grave responsibility counsel had to his client.

Not long thereafter, I received a call from Paris from a lawyer I know telling me of an important arbitration in which he had just been retained and asking if I would be available to serve as arbitrator. He had thought of me because the case might involve issues of conflict of laws, a field in which he knew I had taught and written. I replied that in principle I would be available, that I had no conflict of interest, but that it would depend on how much time the case would take and when it would be heard. A few days later, the Paris lawyer called again, to say that he had passed my name on to his client, but that Mr. X, inside counsel for the client, was coming to New York and would like to meet with me before making a decision. I thought back to my intervention at the conference a few weeks earlier, swallowed hard, and said, "All right, have Mr. X call me when he arrives." Was I, then, a pompous hypocrite, sanctimonious in public, breaking my own rule the first time it counted? The question continues to trouble me.

When Mr. X arrived—in my office, not at a fancy club or restaurant—the conversation was at first like any two persons meeting for the first time—where we had studied, where we had worked, did he know A, did I know B, and so on. Soon it turned to the industry in which his company was engaged, though not the particular controversy. I cannot say the topics were inappropriate; if one accepts the propriety of the interview at all, Mr. X had a right to find out for himself whether I was quick or dull, realistic or dreamy, a scholar mired in books or someone who understood or could be made to understand the ways of business. I was not uncomfortable when he asked me what other arbitrations I had been involved in, and who the counsel and the other arbitrators had been. But how should I react to a question inquiring whether I believed in literal interpretation of a contract, as contrasted with doing equity between the parties? I did not answer; if I had given the obvious response that the question was too abstract, I suspect that I would have heard a thinly disguised hypothetical, and before I knew it we would be talking about the dispute to be arbitrated. Altogether, the interview went fairly well; neither of us went over the line, though perhaps we came close. I have no idea whether Mr. X interviewed other potential arbitrators as well. When I was eventually nominated, I was able to advise the administering institution that I was fully independent. I did not bend over forward or backward in addressing the parties or issues in the case. I was almost ready to concede (at least to myself) that it was my remarks at the conference that had been in error, not the interview.

* * *

II. SELECTING A PRESIDING ARBITRATOR

Once the party-appointed arbitrators are chosen, and (where provided by the rules) their appointment is confirmed by the administering authority, it is common that their first task is to choose the presiding arbitrator. It is rare in my experience that counsel attempt to instruct "their arbitrators" in this process. Nominations for chairman are in the first instance for the party-appointed arbitrators, and indeed, their acquaintance with potential chairmen may well be one of the reasons that they were chosen.

There seems to be an unwritten rule, however, that if the agreement to arbitrate provides that the two arbitrators nominated by the parties shall choose the presiding arbitrator, it is expected that the candidates being considered be cleared with counsel.[6] In some instances counsel have complete authority, in other instances they are required to check with the client. Sometimes this process works well; each party-appointed arbitrator draws up a list, the two arbitrators compare the lists and make up an agreed list, possibly ranking the candidates. The list, or the name of the favorite, is communicated to the respective counsel who say, "Anyone you choose is acceptable to us," or more commonly, "We don't know candidate C, but we'll call you back in twenty-four hours."

At other times the process works badly. Sometimes the two arbitrators cannot agree. I had one experience in an arbitration between a European company and an African country in which I suggested as chairman L, a Swiss professor and former official with an excellent reputation. I had met him once or twice in conferences but had no personal relationship with him. My counterpart rejected Mr. L at once. When I asked politely what was the objection to Mr. L, the answer was that I had suggested him. Possibly I should have waited for my opposite number to come up with his suggestion, but I concluded that the process would not get anywhere, and advised the administering authority that it should take over the task of choosing a chairman, since the arbitrators could not agree. I have also had the reverse experience, where my

6. *Contra* Code of Ethics for Vancouver Maritime Arbitrators Ass'n Rule 10, *reprinted in* William O. Forbes, *Rules of Ethics for Arbitrators and Their Application*, J. Int'l Arb., Sept. 1992, at 5, app. at 25–26 ("No arbitrator shall confer with the party or counsel appointing him regarding the selection of a third arbitrator.").

counterpart suggested Mr. *P*, an arbitrator I did not know at the time but was willing to accept on the basis of his reputation. Counsel who had appointed me rejected Mr. *P*, on the ground that the suggestion had come from the other side. I believe that if I had known and previously worked with Mr. *P*, as I did some years later, I could have persuaded counsel to accept him, but I am not sure, unless I could have certified that Mr. *P* was on my initial list as well as on the list of my counterpart.

In still another case, the other party-appointed arbitrator and I, who knew and respected one another, agreed several times on a presiding arbitrator subject to clearance, but clearance was always withheld by one side or the other. Even when counsel were prepared to accept a candidate, one client or another said no, on grounds that reminded me of nothing so much as jury selection in a big-city trial. The dispute concerned a contract between a U.S. corporation and a developing country or one of its agencies, the details of which I never learned. One candidate for the presiding arbitrator, an eminent European professor with substantial experience as an arbitrator, was vetoed because he had written about economic development, and thus might be "too sympathetic" to the developing country. Another was Swiss, in my judgment a very fair and conscientious arbitrator with whom I had worked in several other cases; he, too, was vetoed because "the Swiss are too favorable to multinational corporations." Still another candidate was vetoed because, while both my counterpart and I knew him, one of us (I forget which of us) was deemed closer to him than the other. Having first asked for an extension of the time within which to make our selection because we were confident that we could reach agreement, we finally gave up and requested the appointing authority to select a chairman. Eventually the case was settled, and the arbitration never took place.

I think some consultation between counsel and arbitrator concerning a prospective chairman is unobjectionable, so long as it is limited in time and in subject matter. But two dangers should be guarded against. Both parties to such consultations should be alert to the temptation to talk about the case, in the guise of asking, "How would candidate *T* react to an argument along the following lines ...?" More important, such consultation should not become a habit carried over to the time when the tribunal is fully formed and the actual arbitration is under way. No doubt counsel who have appointed an arbitrator do not think about contacts with him or her in the same way they would think about contacts with a judge hearing their case. Correspondingly, it is not easy for an arbitrator to just hang up on counsel who has appointed him or her and who has been on the phone regularly during the period when the presiding arbitrator was being chosen. Perhaps it would be helpful if the various rule-making authorities would provide expressly (i) that contacts concerning selection of a chairman are permissible; and (ii) that contacts after the tribunal is finally constituted are not permissible except as directed by the presiding arbitrator.[7] Proposals along these lines have

7. The exception is designed to take care of issues of scheduling, presiding over

been made before,[8] but I have not seen any such provisions in any of the rules with which I have worked.[9]

III. THE ROLE OF THE PARTY-APPOINTED ARBITRATOR

If the party-appointed arbitrator is not supposed to be a member of the appointing party's team, and is supposed to communicate with counsel only within a very limited area, what is the role, and what is the use, of a party-appointed arbitrator? It is a fair question, and some arbitral institutions have provided that if the parties do not insist on party-appointed arbitrators, some other method, typically appointment from a list, is to be used.[10] There is a perceived need, however, for party-appointed arbitrators in international arbitration, and the predominant practice, as reflected in the most widely used rules, is to presume, or even to require, that if three arbitrators are to be appointed, each party shall appoint or nominate one of the three.[11] As I see it, party-appointed arbitrators in international controversies perform two principal and overlapping functions.

First, I think the presence of a party-appointed arbitrator gives some confidence to counsel who appointed him or her, and through counsel to the party-disputant. At least one of the persons who will decide the case will listen carefully—even sympathetically—to the pre-

---

discovery in the territory of one of the arbitrators, or similar communications initiated by the arbitrator for the convenience of the tribunal.

8. Footnote *omitted*

9. *Cf.* Smith, *supra* note 2, at 331–34 (comparing impartiality provisions of leading arbitration rules); *see also* Craig, Park & Paulsson, *supra* note 3, at 240–41 ("The ICC Court of Arbitration has no doubt been reticent to publish a code of conduct (for party-appointed arbitrators) that it cannot be confident of enforcing.").

10. *Compare* American Arbitration Ass'n, Commercial Arbitration Rules Rule 13 (1991) (providing for appointment from panel) *with* American Ass'n, Int'l Arbitration Rules art. 6.3 (1993) ("If . . . all of the parties have not mutually agreed on a procedure for appointing the arbitrator(s) or have not mutually agreed on the designation of the arbitrator(s), the administrator shall, at the written request of any party, appoint the arbitrator(s) and designate the presiding arbitrator.").

11. *See, e.g.*, U.N. Comm'n on Int'l Trade Law, UNCITRAL Arbitration Rules art. 7(1), U.N. GAOR, 31st Sess., Supp. No. 17, at 34–50, U.N. Doc. A/31/17, U.N. Sales No. E77.V.6 (1976) [hereinafter UNCITRAL Rules] ("[E]ach party shall appoint one arbitrator") (emphasis added); International Chamber of Commerce, ICC Rules of Arbitration art. 2(4), ICC Pub. No. 447 (1988) ("[E]ach party shall *nominate* in the Request for Arbitration and the Answer thereto respectively one arbitrator....") (emphasis added); Arbitration Inst. of the Stockholm Chamber of Commerce, Rules of the Arbitration Inst. 5 (1988) ("[E]ach party shall appoint an equal number of arbitrators....") (emphasis added); Convention on the Settlement of Investment Disputes Between States and Nationals of Other States, Mar. 18, 1965, art. 37(2)(b), 17 U.S.T. 1270, 575 U.N.T.S. 159 ("[Unless otherwise agreed], the Tribunal *shall consist of* three arbitrators, *one arbitrator appointed by each party....*") (emphasis added).

I do not mean to discount the difference between nomination and appointment; institutions such as the London Court of International Arbitration and the Court of Arbitration of the International Chamber of Commerce do exercise a screening function and require nominees to state their independence and impartiality. This essay presumes throughout that, where such a screening function exists, the arbitrators have passed through it. Actual conflicts of interest and undisclosed relationships are of course unacceptable, but that subject is not the subject of this essay, and I use the term *party-appointed arbitrator* herein to cover both arbitrators appointed by a party and arbitrators nominated by a party and thereafter confirmed by the administering institution.

sentation, and if the arbitrator is well chosen, will study the documents with care. That fact alone is likely to spur the other arbitrators to study the documents as well, whether or not they would have done so in any case. Thus the presence of a well chosen party-appointed arbitrator goes a long way toward promising (if not assuring) a fair hearing and a considered decision.

Second, in an international case a party-appointed arbitrator serves as a translator. I do not mean just of language, though occasionally that is required as well, as even persons highly skilled in the language of the arbitration may be confused by so-called *faux amis* (false friends)—words that look the same but have different meanings in different languages. I mean rather the translation of legal culture, and not infrequently of the law itself, when matters that are self-evident to lawyers from one country are puzzling to lawyers from another.

One subject that will seem familiar to readers in the United States, and illuminating to those who have tried to explain it to persons not trained in U.S. law, concerns the relation between state and federal law and state and federal courts. Again my illustration comes from a case in which I served as arbitrator, along with two other arbitrators who were native English speakers but not U.S.-trained lawyers.

The dispute in question, between a prime contractor and a subcontractor, arose out of a large construction project in a Middle Eastern country. The parties had agreed that the contract between them was to be governed by New York law with arbitration in Switzerland. On a particular question concerning the respective obligations of the prime and the subcontractor, one side submitted several decisions of New York state courts, not all by the Court of Appeals, New York's highest court. The other side submitted a decision of the U.S. Court of Appeals for the Eighth Circuit, which seemed closest, in terms of the fact pattern, to the controversy before the arbitral tribunal. What was the authority of the federal court's decision? Was it superior, because federal courts outrank state courts? Certainly not, as American lawyers know, since the controversy arose out of a contract between private parties, and thus was subject to what we call "state-created law." Was the decision of the Eighth Circuit then irrelevant, since the federal court sitting in St. Louis, hearing an appeal from a U.S. district court in Missouri, would have applied Missouri law? Well, not quite, since the decision might well be persuasive, though not controlling, because the legal issue in question concerned interpretation of the Uniform Commercial Code, which was in effect both in New York and in Missouri. Was the tribunal free, then, to choose between the New York state courts and the federal court in Missouri? Again, not quite: insofar as the New York decision emanated from the state's highest court, they would be controlling; insofar as the New York decisions emanated from intermediate appellate courts, the arbitral tribunal could weigh them against the decision of the federal court of appeals ... and so on. I no longer remember, in the case from which this example is drawn, whether the federal or the state decisions favored the party that appointed me. The fact that an American member of the tribunal was available to explain a situation far from obvious to outsiders made it much more likely that the arbitrators would come out right, and—not incidentally—that counsel would not overreach in their submissions.

To take a quite different case, I benefited from translation by a conscientious party-appointed arbitrator in a controversy between a western company and a state agency of an Islamic country which I shall call Xandia. The contract in question called for performance of a series of services over several years, with regular payments partly in dollars and partly in local currency. As is not uncommon, the dispute settlement clause reflected a trade-off: Xandian law was to govern the contract, but disputes were to be resolved by arbitration in Switzerland, with each side to appoint one arbitrator, and the presiding arbitrator to be chosen by the appointing authority. The question arose how to handle the consequences of delay in making payments due under the contract. Some payments were clearly due, but had been withheld once the dispute arose; at least some other obligations to make payments seemed likely to be recognized by the tribunal. But what about interest? The civil code of Xandia made no mention of interest, and contained a general provision stating that any subjects not covered in the code were subject to Islamic law. The Koran, as is well known, prohibits interest.[12] The arbitrator appointed by the Xandian party explained to his colleagues, however, that it was acceptable, and indeed required under Xandian law, to award damages for nonpayment of obligations when due. Accordingly, the tribunal invited the parties to provide information about the exchange rate between the Xandian currency and dollars at stated times as compared with the current rate of exchange, and also to provide information about the cost of borrowing by the western party at stated times for conversion into Xandian currency to meet its local payroll and other local expenses. Neither of the parties had furnished this explanation, but with this translation by our Xandian colleague, the tribunal was enabled to render a rational award, not technically awarding interest, but awarding fair compensation for payments not made when due.

* * *

In each of these three cases, the same outcome might well have been achieved if an administering institution had appointed all three arbitrators, one from each country and a third country chairman, as is occasionally provided for in the agreement to arbitrate. But that practice is rare in my experience, and does not (or may not) entail the other element I have described: confidence that at least one member of the tribunal is listening, and listening sympathetically, to the submission of counsel.

It happens quite often that when the claimant has nominated A, an arbitrator from country R, respondent will nominate B, also from R. Sometimes the motivation is that the respondent does not wish the "claimant's arbitrator" to be the only one to pronounce on the law of R,

---

12. *See The Koran* ii:275–82, iii:13, iv:161, xxx:39.

if that country's law is the law to be applied; sometimes the motivation is that "*B* is someone that can stand up to *A*." Of course the two motives may well overlap. A translation function may still be present if the presiding arbitrator comes from a different country. Though my sample is small, I think it speaks well for the practice of party-appointed arbitrators in international disputes that I have never wound up with a disagreement in this situation with my fellow party-appointed arbitrator on an issue of law, even when we disagreed at the outset before studying the submissions of the parties, consulting the authorities, and working through the problem together.

* * *

STATEMENT OF INDEPENDENCE
[Arbitration Court of the Hungarian Chamber of Commerce and Industry]

(A) DECLARATION

To the Arbitration Court of the Hungarian Chamber of Commerce and Industry

I, the undersigned * * *

domiciled at: * * *

recognize my having been designated arbitrator or having been appointed presiding arbitrator of the tribunal acting in arbitration case No.: * * *

I declare that I undertake to discharge the arbitrator's duties according to the Rules of Procedure of the Arbitration Court attached to the Hungarian Chamber of Commerce and Industry.

I declare that I am independent of the parties and I am unaware of any such circumstances that would affect my impartiality and / or independence in the case.

I oblige myself to inform the Arbitration Court without delay about any such circumstances if I obtain knowledge of it at a later date in the course of the proceedings.

I declare that there are no conditions to disqualify me from being an arbitrator according to clause 12 of Law LXXI of 1994 on arbitration in the Hungarian Republic.

Hereby I accept full responsibility for the declaration given above.

(B) CLAUSE 12 OF ACT LXXI OF 1994 ON ARBITRATION IN HUNGARY

"The following may not be arbitrators:

     a) those under 24 years of age;

     b) those who have been barred from public affairs by a non-appealable court judgement;

c) those who have been non-appealably placed under curatorship by the court;

d) those who have been sentenced to imprisonment to be executed non-appealably, until they are dispensed from the disadvantages attached to a criminal record.''

Questions and Comments

1.   May an arbitrator be of the same nationality as one of the parties?

2.   In an arbitration between a Croatian party and a Serbian party could one of the arbitrators be a person of Croatian ethnic origin, born and raised in Croatia while it was part of Yugoslavia, who had moved to Switzerland and become a Swiss citizen?

Could a Turkish Cypriote arbitrate a dispute between a Greek and a Turkish party?

Would a Turkish Cypriote born and raised on Cyprus, who had moved to the U.S. and become a U.S. citizen be acceptable?

3.   In a dispute between an Israeli company and an Egyptian company, could an American of Jewish background be an arbitrator? An American of Arab background?

4.   What about an American of Catholic persuasion in a dispute between Irish and Swedish companies? What if an arbitrator is from the same law school and law class as one of the lawyers?

To sum up all the above questions, would you support a legislative act or arbitration rule screening out persons on the ground of group affiliation?

5.   A case brought before the Paris Tribunal de grande instance[7] may have foreshadowed future concerns. The ICC Court of Arbitration appointed a Greek arbitrator as a neutral third arbitrator. The Moroccan party challenged this appointment, arguing that the third arbitrator was not neutral, because both the opposing parties (companies from Germany and from Spain) and the Greek third arbitrator were from the European Union. Is this relevant? If not, will this become relevant after the introduction of a uniform currency and further integration? (The Paris court refused jurisdiction, and did not consider the challenge.) A few years after the Paris decision this problem was addressed in Article 6.3 of the 1998 London Court of International Arbitration Rules. (See the Documents Supplement.)

6.   In another case which came before the Paris Tribunal de grande instance in 1990[8], one party alleged that the arbitrator designated by the opposing party was the lover of the manager of the opposing company between 1957 and 1965. The court rejected the challenge on the ground that it was submitted late. Had the objection been lodged in time, would you consider it justified?

[7]. Société chérifienne de pétroles v. Société Mannesmann Industria Iberica, decided on January 18, 1991, reported in 1996 Revue de l'arbitrage 503.

[8]. Unpublished, cited in Ph. Fouchard, Le statut de l'arbitre dans la jurisprudence française, 1996 Revue de l'arbitrage 325, 342–343.

7. Would you distinguish between party appointed arbitrators and sole (or third) arbitrators?

8. In Italy, the Genoa Court came to the conclusion that a party-appointed arbitrator should not be disqualified for having acted as a lawyer of the appointing party in an earlier unrelated case. The court held: *"The role of attorney of the party that the arbitrator played in previous or different disputes does not match any of the cases for disqualification under Article 51 of the Code of Civil Procedure."* (Tribunale di Genoa, March 22, 1995, Corriere giuridico 12/1997, 1450; Commented by T. Tampieri, "International Arbitration and Impartiality of Arbitrators", 18 Journal of International Arbitration, 2001, 449).

Do you agree with the Genoa Court?

9. Lowenfeld stresses that the party appointed arbitrator also serves as a "translator," interpreting and transposing legal and cultural concepts. Do you see this as a useful function?

Would you mandate the presence of arbitrators who were familiar with the legal systems and cultures involved?

10. Before nominating a party appointed arbitrator, an attorney for that party is likely to want to interview the prospective arbitrator. If you were that prospective arbitrator, would you agree to be interviewed? Would you agree to go to the attorney's office for the interview? How would you respond to the following types of questions the attorney might put to you: i) What other arbitrations have you been involved in and who were the counsel and other arbitrators? ii) Do you believe in literal interpretation of a contract, or would you be inclined to rely on equity between the parties? iii) Do you believe in a strict or a loose doctrine of force majeure? iv) Do you believe an arbitrator would ever be justified in applying the mandatory law of a third country, in contrast to the law chosen by the parties? v) Have you ever decided a case against the party who appointed you?

11. As an attorney seeking to nominate a party-appointed arbitrator, would you be willing to appoint an arbitrator who refused to answer some of these questions? Would you reappoint an arbitrator who, as your party-appointed arbitrator, had ruled against you on an important point in a prior proceeding?

12. According to the WIPO Arbitration Rules *"No party or anyone acting on its behalf shall have any ex parte communication with any candidate for appointment as an arbitrator, except to discuss the candidate's qualifications, availability or independence in relation to the parties."* Is this the right standard?

13. The standard form declaration of independence proposed by the Court of Arbitration at the Hungarian Chamber of Commerce includes a promise by the arbitrators to inform the Court of Arbitration of supervening events or supervening information which may have a bearing on independence. Consider a romanesque hypothetical: Suppose that after the end of the oral hearing and during the deliberations, one arbitrator learns that the attorney for one of the parties is actually his cousin (the son of an aunt who sailed to the other side of the ocean 50 years ago, and who did not keep in

touch with the rest of the family). What should be the consequences of this late revelation?

What if the arbitrator decides "not to complicate matters", and fails to share this information with the Court of Arbitration, the deliberations continue, and the arbitrators wind up with a unanimous award in favor of the party represented by the cousin?

14. Do you agree with clause 12(a) of the Hungarian Act on Arbitration which fixes a special minimum age for arbitrators? (There is no specific minimum age for judges, although it is practically impossible to become a judge before 24, given the required education and training.)

If you agree that a specific minimum age should apply to arbitrators, would you draw the line at 24?

15. Returning to the issue of nationality of the arbitrators, are Article 9(5) of the ICC Rules and Article 6 of the LCIA Rules compatible with Article 11(1) of the UNCITRAL Model Law?

III.1.d.   *How to Get (or Not to Get) the Right Arbitrator*

Lord David Hacking: WELL, DID YOU GET THE RIGHT ARBITRATOR?*

15 Mealey's Int'l Arb. Rep. 32 (Issue No. 6; June 2000).

* * *

Broadly, in international arbitrations, arbitrators are either appointed by the parties or by one of the international arbitration institutions, for example, by the Court of International Arbitration of the International Chamber of Commerce in Paris ("ICC"), the London Court of International Arbitration in London ("LCIA") or the American Arbitration Association in New York ("AAA").

Each of these institutions has different processes under which arbitrators are appointed but all share certain common features. The foremost is the dominant safeguard of independent and neutral arbitrators. The same safeguard can be found in appointments by other international arbitration institutions: viz the Arbitration Institute of the Stockholm Chamber of Commerce, the Netherlands Arbitration Institute, the Hongkong Arbitration Centre—to name a few of the well respected international arbitration institutions.

Thus it is that arbitration institutions, throughout the world, when appointing arbitrators, go through a similar logical process on the lines of:

- Is the appointee for the arbitration neutral and independent of the parties?

- Does he or she have the right linguistic skills?

* Reprinted with kind permission of Lord David Hacking

- Does he or she have the right legal knowledge for applying the governing law of the arbitration?

- Does he or she have the right professional expertise ... in construction law ... intellectual property ... or for what ever is the subject matter of the arbitration?

Moreover almost all arbitration institutions also stipulate that the appointee should be "suitable" for being appointed the arbitrator in the arbitration in question. Under Article 9.1 of the ICC Rules of Arbitration[5] it is stipulated that the ICC Court of Arbitration "shall consider the prospective arbitrators' nationality, residence, and other relationships with the countries of which the parties or the other arbitrators are nationals and the prospective arbitrator's availability and ability to conduct the arbitration ..." (emphasis added). In Article 6.4 of the AAA International Arbitration Rules we find that, in making arbitral appointments, the AAA administrator "... after inviting consultation with the parties, shall endeavour to select suitable arbitrators".[6] Similarly in Article 5.5 of the LCIA Rules[7] the LCIA Court is under a duty when "selecting arbitrators [to give] consideration ... to the nature of the transaction, the nature and circumstances of the dispute, the nationality, location and languages of the parties...". Importantly, however, this Article is buttressed in Article 7.1 of the LCIA Rules, by giving power to the LCIA Court, when an arbitrator has been nominated by one of the parties, "to refuse to appoint any such nominee if it determines that he is not suitable or independent or impartial".

Given all of that why is there any dissatisfaction in the appointment of arbitrators by arbitration institutions? There are, I believe, several reasons. The first is that while the arbitration institutions may know more than the parties about the arbitrators, which it appoints, it does not know as much as the parties about the dispute. This may not be its fault. At the time of the appointment insufficient information may have been disclosed to it by the parties. Thus the institution may not know, for example, that the resolution of the dispute hangs upon technical points which would be best understood and resolved by arbitrators with expertise in (say) mechanical engineering or that a whole lot of procedural points will be taken in the arbitration which would be best understood and resolved by a lawyer trained in the procedural law governing the procedural issues in the arbitration.

Second, there is insufficient information known about the availability of the arbitrators for conducting the arbitration on a reasonable timetable. This is not simply a question of knowing whether one arbitrator is busy or not but whether, with a three person arbitral tribunal,

---

5. The International Chamber of Commerce Rules of Arbitration in force as from January 1, 1998.

6. The International Arbitration Rules of the American Arbitration Association as amended and effective April 1, 1997. [Au-

thor's note: This rule is unchanged in the 2001 AAA Intl Arb. Rules.]

7. The Arbitration Rules of the London Court of International Arbitration effective 1 January 1998.

each of the arbitrators can find common dates in their diaries to enable the arbitration to be conducted reasonably expeditiously.

Third there is a lack of knowledge, or a lack of acting on the knowledge, about the personal qualities of the prospective arbitrator.

- Does he or she have good management skills?
- Is he or she decisive or do arbitrations "run away" from this arbitrator?
- Is he or she good on procedural issues or is he or she just a bit of a fudger?
- Is he or she sound in judgment or profoundly lacking in it? What is known about the quality of awards of the prospective arbitrator, and are they well reasoned?
- And most fundamentally of all, is he or she up to the job of being arbitrator in this arbitration?

Some of the difficulties arise out of the different ways institutions select the arbitrators whom they appoint. For example the ICC works through National Committees. So when a French arbitrator is requested, the ICC National Committee of France makes the recommendation. The same applies for recommendations for appointments by other ICC National Committees. Some of these National Committees are very good in recommending arbitrators who have all the right qualities for the appointment in question. Others are not so good. There is a particular tendency, for example, in some European National Committees for the members to be dominated by academia. While there are in Europe those, holding academic appointments, who make brilliant arbitrators, there are also some academics—out of the cut and thrust of practical life—who make very poor arbitrators.

The AAA makes its arbitral appointments in a different way. The Secretariat of the AAA, having consulted the parties on the qualities for which they are seeking in the arbitrator, provide, from the appropriate AAA panel of arbitrators, a list to the parties of arbitrators from which they are invited to select their preferences. If the AAA is appointing a sole arbitrator the AAA Secretariat produces a list of ten persons for the parties' selection and if the AAA is setting up a three person arbitral panel then its Secretariat lists 15 persons for selection by the parties. In the former each party is then given an opportunity to "strike out", without giving reasons, three persons on the list and in the latter the right to "strike out", without reasons, five persons on the list. This can somewhat narrow the selection process because if each party "strikes out" a different three persons on the list of ten, there will only be four persons left in this list. Similarly, if the parties each challenge five different persons out of a list of 15, there will only be five potential arbitrators left in the list.

When this process has been completed the parties are invited to select in order of preference their preferred arbitrators by marking their first preference "1", their second preference "2" etc. Thus the arbitrators with the lowest "count" become the chosen arbitrators for the arbitration in question. Operating properly each party should be listing its preferences for the arbitrator by putting, in its judgment, the best first, and the worst last. It does not, however, always work out that way because, as with the selection of a jury, there is the temptation for a party, with a poor case, not to prefer arbitrators who are likely to spot the weaknesses in their case and find against them. I believe, therefore, the basic drawback in the AAA selection system, is that rather than selecting arbitrators on the basis of the "highest common denominator" it can end up, at worst, by selecting them on the basis of the "lowest common denominator".

There is also a "lacuna" in the AAA International Arbitration Rules when the parties are choosing ("designating") the arbitrators. This is done under Articles 6.1 and 6.2 of the AAA International Arbitration Rules. However, unlike under the ICC and LCIA Rules, the AAA Secretariat has no power to refuse to make the appointment of the "party-chosen" arbitrator when it knows from previous experience of that arbitrator, that he or she is a lousy arbitrator or otherwise thoroughly unsuitable for the arbitral appointment in question. It is, of course, possible for the AAA Secretariat to make it known to the parties its reservations about the proposed appointment but, if they do so, they could find themselves in an awkward position, and even litigation, with the party "designated" arbitrator when, as a result of the representations made by the AAA Secretariat, that "designated arbitrator" is not appointed!

The LCIA runs its selection process of arbitrators on a consultation process in which its Secretariat proposes to its Board its preferred choice for the arbitral appointment. The LCIA Board then decides whether to make that appointment or not. Inevitably there is a conservatism in this process. It is very important for the LCIA, as for any arbitral body, to appoint arbitrators with established records. This makes it hard for new younger, and more innovative, arbitrators to be put forward and selected.

* * *

The same problem prevails when the parties are seeking to appoint a sole arbitrator and, to some extent, when the parties are involved in the appointment of the third arbitrator or Chairman of the tribunal. The great emphasis is on finding in this arbitrator someone who is, and can be seen to be, totally neutral of the parties and the issues in dispute. It is true that, when faced with recommendations for arbitral appointments of persons unknown to the parties or their advisers, there are a few ways of finding out more about the proposed arbitrator. For example, a telephone call to the ICC Secretariat can, on an informal basis, provide useful information. There is, however, (in European Union parlance) insufficient "transparency"! The basic problem is that the more "neutral" is the candidate for arbitrator, the more the candidate is likely to be "unknown" to the parties and their advisers. Unlike judges, arbitrators do not operate in an open forum where they can be seen at work and where the products of their work, in the form of awards, are open to public inspection. What, therefore, can be done?

I believe the arbitral community, particularly the international arbitral community, can do more to assist. For example all potential arbitrators should be willing to be interviewed by the parties wanting to make the arbitral appointment. Of course a party, wanting to make an arbitral appointment, cannot argue the merits of its case to the arbitrator being interviewed but it can set out the basic facts and ascertain whether that arbitrator has the necessary experience and skills to act as arbitrator in that case. Of course these meetings should take place in a neutral venue, for example the arbitrator's office or chambers (not over a meal, with good food and wine, in a smart restaurant!) and it is prudent for the arbitrator, after the interview, to make a note of it and, if appointed, disclose it to his fellow arbitrators.

Next, parties can ask to see examples of awards written by the arbitrator who is being considered for appointment. Again there have to be safeguards. An arbitrator should not show an award, given in another arbitration, without the consent of the parties to that arbitration and usually without removing their names and other points of identification from the award. But these are not insuperable difficulties. In the annual ICCA Yearbook there are a number of international arbitration awards (suitably pruned) published.

I also see no reason also why parties should not ask a potential arbitrator for references or to ask a potential arbitrator if they can speak to an arbitration institution which has knowledge of this arbitrator's performance in the conduct of arbitrations. I am aware that the argument that the loser will not have a good word for the arbitrator who finds against him. For myself I think that is a puerile argument—if not also insulting to the parties and their advisers. Everybody, in an arbitration, knows when they are working with a good competent arbitrator and when they are not. I see no reason, therefore, why the taking of references from losing parties, as well as the successful ones, would blight the selection process.

Finally there are always the written works of an arbitrator being considered for appointment. Those who have experience in arbitration regularly attend arbitration conferences and give papers at them. They also regularly write in the many arbitration journals, which are in the public forum. In my view, therefore, a party should not make an appointment without looking at the written works of a person being considered for appointment.

I suggest, therefore, the basic problem is that there is not enough information available to the parties, and their advisers, in the arbitral appointment process. Yes, there are some directories, which list those who are holding themselves out for arbitral appointment. You can also obtain the resumes of potential arbitrators, for example in the AAA appointment system, although other institutions are more guarded about giving access to their lists of arbitrators and the resumes, which they have upon them. With a well run institution this is valuable property! Another course of action is to ask around among those who have knowledge of the personal qualities of the arbitrators in their region or professional discipline. All such enquiries should be made. But I believe the community of arbitrators themselves can provide more help. Would it not be very convenient if there was a website in the internet in which arbitrators listed their professional qualifications, the areas of their expertise, their experience as arbitrators, the names and contact points for referees and gave access (suitably tailored) to awards which they have previously published and listed their available dates for the conduct of arbitrations!

I believe too that the provision of more information on arbitrators should also be seen as part of the exercise of opening up the ranks of arbitrators so that "a new generation of resolute arbitrators"[8] may become available to tackle the new problems in the conduct of international arbitrations. As the learned authors Redfern and Hunter rightly argue.[9] "There must always be a new generation [of arbitrators] in prospect, otherwise there will only be a diminishing group of ever-more-elderly people suitable for appointment."

Dr. K.V.S.K. Nathan: WELL, WHY DID YOU NOT GET THE RIGHT ARBITRATOR?*

15 Mealey's Int'l Arb. Report 24 (July 2000).

An observer from planet Mars may well observe that the international arbitral establishment on Earth is white, male and English speaking and is controlled by institutions based in the United States, England and mainland European Union. For the most part, arbitrators and counsel appearing actively in international arbitral proceedings originate from these countries. The majority in a multi-member international arbitral tribunal is always white. The red alien from Mars will be puzzled in his own way because the majority of the published disputes before international arbitral tribunals involve parties from the developing countries and nearly three-quarters of the people on Earth live in those countries and are not white and more than half the total population are women.

Reading the Commentary by Lord David Hacking in the June issue, it is easy to conclude that arbitrators from the developing countries and women simply do not or cannot satisfy the selection criteria articulated and applied by him and others who play pivotal roles in arbitration

---

8. See Redfern and Hunter: Law and Practice of International Commercial Arbitration (Third Edition) 1999 Introduction page vi.

9. Ibid. Chapter 4 paragraph 4–44 page 208.

* Reprinted with the kind permission of Dr. K.V.S.K. Nathan of the Middle Temple,

Barrister/Arbitrator in International Practice. Dr Nathan is the author of the book "ICSID Convention: The Law of the International Centre for Settlement of Investment Disputes" published by Juris Publishing Inc. New York, 2000.

institutions. On the other hand, since the arbitral institutions named in his Commentary make or confirm most of the international arbitral appointments, one might observe that there is possibly some misapplication of the selection criteria by these institutions resulting in disproportionately few active women arbitrators and arbitrators from the developing countries. One might even challenge the validity of the criteria on the grounds that they are vague and ill defined and highly subjective and, worst of all, geared to prevent any change in the current establishment. English institutions like most European institutions are notorious for preserving the status quo and have to be dragged kicking and screaming into the modern competitive world.

I have great respect for Pierre Lalive and Martin and Hunter is my favorite book of reference. Undeniably, the most important first step in starting the ball rolling in arbitral proceedings is the selection of the arbitrators but what is the measure of a successful arbitration?: that the arbitration proceedings and deliberations went smoothly because the arbitrators were all from the same club and were good buddies or were clones (a possibility since "Dolly") or that justice was done although the tribunal deliberations were rough and bumpy and several egos were ruffled. There are so many representatives of various arbitral and professional institutions going round the ex-colonies telling the administrators, lawyers and professionals there how to select arbitrators. There was even one conference last year in Sri Lanka on invitation only behind closed doors.

Lord Hacking left out bias as a factor in the determination as to whether a nominee as arbitrator is suitable or not. One can be neutral and independent of the parties to a dispute in an objective sense and still be grossly biased. The person or persons responsible for selection or confirmation on behalf of the arbitral institutions may themselves be biased because the nominee does not originate from their own culture or club or alumni or class or ethnic group or does not share common aspirations or does not subscribe to the arbitral institution concerned. Other institutions in England face the same charges. The Society of Labour [Party] Lawyers in England recently described the judiciary there "as being dominated by white, middle-class, Oxbridge-educated males"[1] and they demand change. Every one is biased one way or another even at the highest levels of power in government, professional institutions and the society in general including the media. Lord Hacking may have a point in advertently or inadvertently not referring to bias in his detailed Commentary. The objective in institutional activity should be to eliminate the impact of individual biased behaviour through operating within an appropriate regulatory and procedural framework.

* * *

Most arbitrators from the developing countries speak several languages including fluency in more than one European language. What are

---

1. The Independent on Sunday, 9 July 2000 p. 2. I read the Times also.

then the right linguistic skills to qualify as an arbitrator? I wish Lord Hacking had elaborated on this. He probably means the ability to address orally with clarity and precision and in perfect grammar but one should not confuse advocacy skills with judicial skills. Judges seldom question the witnesses except to draw attention of the witnesses to specific details, mostly procedural, for their own benefit and most certainly judges do not cross examine witnesses. They adjourn to prepare instructions to the court. They write their judgments in their own time in the privacy of their chambers or homes or offices. Besides, arbitrators do not address a jury. Listening, observing and writing skills are far more important to a judge or arbitrator than oral skills.

By the nature of their functions too, good advocates are not necessarily the best judges. Advocates have an instinct to pursue tenaciously their Client's will and over time they develop a skill and expertise to argue for or against a particular legal or factual stance. One is a good defense lawyer or a good prosecution lawyer. Advocates tend to specialize in being one or the other and, mentally, they are suited to advance or show empathy to one cause or the other rather than to judge as between competing interests. Many lawyers spend their entire lives in their own chambers specializing in particular aspects of a narrow subject of law and when appointed as arbitrators are bound to be influenced by their concentrated experience in that narrow field of law to the point that they take the law for granted and as settled when the facts of a particular case may demand a special scrutiny.

While, therefore, agreeing with Lord Hacking that arbitrators should have some knowledge of the subject matter of the arbitration, a life entirely immersed in a field of law such as construction law or intellectual property may be a good qualification for an advocate but not for a judge or an arbitrator who should have an open mind also as to the law. His or her past experience should not be a factor in judging a particular Case as often is the case with arbitrators who have professional expertise. Engineers who practice as arbitrators should have a much broader training in the law than the present courses offered to them by arbitral and other institutions.

In a sense, arbitrators from Academia are probably better qualified to be arbitrators as exemplified by the quality of their Awards in general and they are more likely to be neutral and independent. Leading lawyers and other experienced professionals tend to make "rule of thumb" or "sniff and tell" decisions partly because they are too busy to properly study and analyse the Case and partly because they have seen it all before. Sometimes they are right but they can also be very wrong.

Not only the governing law of arbitration but the governing or applicable law to the contract or other transaction between the parties in dispute can present difficult problems to counsel and arbitrators alike. The arbitration laws of most countries have common features in respect to key matters and, in any case, they are supplemented by the rules of the administering arbitral institutions and provide for the incorporation of international conventions such as the New York Convention. The laws of arbitration in practice pose less of a problem to a watchful arbitrator than the substantive law. Counsel practising in the governing law is usually available although, where the applicable law is the law of a developing country, the arguments are often presented by European Counsel because of their right linguistic skills and sensitivities of some arbitrators.

On the other hand, arbitrators must have the intellectual and analytical skills to interpret and apply the governing law particularly in regard to the substantive aspects of the contract or other transaction. Where the laws of ex-colonies in Africa or Asia are involved, it is regrettable that many arbitrators are influenced by the law of the colonizing power and some Cases have had to be overturned on appeal for applying the wrong law. My own experience is that arbitrators will go to any length to avoid discussing the local law and if they can conveniently invoke the rule of English or French law they will do so.

In the appointment of arbitrators, party autonomy is usually respected by the arbitral institutions referred to by Lord Hacking, namely, ICC, AAA and LCIA. The fact that the institutions under their arbitration rules must find a nominee suitable and have powers to refuse to confirm a nominee by a party is possibly a deterrent to poor judgment on the part of the parties and their respective counsels. Unfortunately, it can also have the effect of persuading parties to nominate well known and entrenched names in the arbitration field to the exclusion of others more qualified. Poor judgment by the parties in dispute is exaggerated by the institutions. The fact that disruption of the arbitral proceedings inevitably results in increased costs should encourage most parties, except perhaps those rare parties with an agenda other than the resolution of the dispute they are involved in, to nominate arbitrators with the integrity to respect the arbitral process.[3]

* * *

It is obvious that ICC also is alarmed at possible intrusions into the lucrative international arbitration practice by all and sundry. The ability of the nominee to conduct an arbitration would depend on his or her qualifications and experience and, hopefully, not on secret informal exchanges of personal information by interested parties. Nonetheless, the power of these judicial institutions to find a nominee not suitable without giving an opportunity to contest their view is undeniably a travesty of the principles of fairness and justice which they purport to stand for and throws in doubt the integrity of these institutions. To be fair and honest, the ICC Court must interview the nominees concerned before taking a decision.

3. K.V.S.K. Nathan, The Selection of Arbitrators: Point of View of a Realist, Ami- cus Curiae, May 1999 at p. 16.

An example of their predisposition to prejudice is the fact that while they refuse to recognize titles of counsel and arbitrators from developing countries bestowed on them by their governments and professional bodies, they allow the use of titles by English arbitrators and counsel such as Lord, Sir, QC, MBE etc. The ICC will refuse to address a Sri Lankan President's Counsel as a PC but it will ensure that it addresses an English Queen's Counsel as a QC. A Nigerian Chief will not be honored as such by the ICC but an English Lord is a different matter. As to availability, the matter is a joke and European arbitrators dictate the pace of any arbitration to suit their busy schedules.

I believe that titles should not be used at all in an international arbitral context because the recognition of these titles places both counsel and arbitrators from developing countries in a disadvantaged position vis a vis the arbitral institutions in competition for work for which they are otherwise well qualified. I some times think that, if an English QC says $2 + 2 = 5$, one would be damned if he tries to refute it.

Having been an engineer and having been in charge of government departments and large projects with a hundred engineers and technicians at any time and having led World Bank Missions to developing countries consisting of a variety of professionals, I was amused by Lord Hacking's proposition that an arbitrator should have good management skills. He or she collaborates usually with two people in a three-member tribunal of equals. Even the president of a tribunal cannot be said to manage the panel. Rather, he or she administers the arbitral proceedings including the trial and liaises with the arbitral institution but an arbitrator should preferably have good inter-personal skills for his or her sake because it makes life easier and less stressful. Unfortunately, arbitrators with strong egos do not have a sense of humour. Lawyers working solely and independently, such as barristers in chambers in England, do not usually acquire any kind of management experience during their entire life time. In any case, arbitral tribunals are not corporations or foot ball teams. They consist of equal, neutral and independent men and women inter-acting for the purpose of finding the truth and dispensing justice.

I agree with Lord Hacking that arbitrators must be good on procedural issues and that the quality of previous awards of a sole arbitrator and the published works of an arbitrator can be a good indicator of his or her reasoning skills. Often, however, in the case of a multi-member tribunal the quality of the award is dependent on the quality of the president and majority of the tribunal. As to the other personal qualities they are largely subjective and a matter of appearances and depends on secret testimonials, often unsolicited, by people in power who are driven by their own interests or those of the club, class, group, alumni, religion or ethnicity to which they belong. This is the real world.

The appointment of the arbitrators by the arbitral institutions themselves pose even harder obstacles for arbitrators from the developing countries and women except in the case of international arbitral institutions such as the ICC until perhaps now. With the amended Article 9.1 of the ICC Rules, we have still to see how it plays out in the interests of women and non-white arbitrators and parties from developing countries. National arbitral institutions and national professional bodies maintain their own panels of arbitrators and often parties in dispute select their nominees out of those listed in these panels. Unfortunately, many outstanding arbitrators are not on these panels. However, relinquishing the power to nominate arbitrators entirely to the arbitral institutions is not advisable because much is at stake only for the party in dispute.

The suggestion that there is a "lacuna" in the AAA Rules is an unwarranted presumption by Lord Hacking. The AAA simply recognizes that people in power are not perfect and that since arbitration is a creation of the parties in dispute who pay lucrative fees for all involved in the arbitral process it would be unconscionable to take away their right as to who should judge the outcome of their dispute. I hope that the AAA does not forget July 4, 1776.

It is incredible that in this age of respect for civil and human rights and call for transparency in matters of public interest that affect people's lives, Lord Hacking should labor in his Commentary to encourage arbitral institutions to assume absolute power over the appointment of arbitrators and base their decisions on informal secret communications of interested parties on the personal qualities of a nominee by a party in dispute. I like to know what ICC has on me! Surely, Lord Hacking does not want us to go back to the times of the Gestapo. I recommend to my clients institutional arbitrations in preference to ad hoc arbitrations not because they guarantee the quality of the arbitrators but rather because they can relieve the arbitrators of the tedious task of overall administration of the arbitration.

Questions and Comments

1. Lord Hacking views the selection process in an institutional setting. In ad hoc arbitration methods of appointment may be different, but the qualities and characteristics that make an arbitrator acceptable are essentially the same.

2. Dr. Nathan suggests that "[a]rbitrators from developing countries and women simply do not and cannot satisfy the selection criteria" articulated and applied by Lord Hacking "and others".

It can hardly be denied that arbitrators from developing countries and women are underrepresented. This is a point that has often been raised— sometimes with much fervor. The issue deserves attention, but it is not easy to find the right focus. The question arises as to whether the Hacking– Nathan debate provides the right setting. In other words, one may ask whether the Hacking criteria would have a meaningful impact on the imbalance. If you see a problem here, does the problem lie in the articulated criteria, or rather in the absence of some other criteria?

3. In Hacking's opinion, more information on arbitrators could open the ranks of arbitrators. Would this be a possible way of including more women and developing-country arbitrators?

4. Hacking raises the point that arbitral institutions may not know enough about the nature of the dispute at the time of appointment to select the best suited arbitrator. Can this be remedied? Should the arbitral institution seek detailed information from the parties before making the appointment? Or would such an approach just cause delay?

5. Staying with institutional appointment, should the institution be entitled to reject a party appointed arbitrator because he or she is "a lousy arbitrator" in the opinion of the institution? Is there a lacuna in Articles 6.1 and 6.2 of the AAA Rules—which are unchanged in the 2001 edition of the AAA Rules—or does the AAA simply recognize that "people in power [in arbitral institutions] are not perfect"?

6. Everyone agrees that language skills are essential. The Hacking–Nathan debate raises the issue of what should actually be understood by "language skills". Hacking does not focus on details. Nathan is critical of one of the possible understandings and advocates another one. What is your understanding? Do language skills entail the ability to read several (or all) possibly relevant languages (the language of the proceedings, the language in which some of the documents were written, the language of the countries whose laws are (or may be) applicable)? Or do language skills rather involve the ability to communicate "orally with clarity", or "perfect grammar", in the language of the proceedings? If your first answer is "all of these", how would you set priorities if the ideal candidate is not available?

7. What is your understanding of the term "suitable". Does the notion of "suitability" allow the appointers to consider group affiliation? Do you agree with Nathan that Hacking "left out bias as a factor"?

III.1.e. Codes of Ethics

AAA/ABA CODE OF ETHICS FOR ARBITRATORS IN COMMERCIAL DISPUTES (1977)CH2

[See Documents Supplement.]

* * *

THE IBA RULES OF ETHICS FOR INTERNATIONAL ARBITRATORS*

Adopted by International Bar Association in 1986.

Introductory Note

International arbitrators should be impartial, independent, competent, diligent and discreet. These rules seek to establish the manner in which these abstract qualities may be assessed in practice. Rather than

---

* The IBA Rules of Ethics for International Arbitrators, reprinted with kind permission from the International Bar Association. All rights reserved.

rigid rules, they reflect internationally acceptable guidelines developed by practising lawyers from all continents. They will attain their objectives only if they are applied in good faith. The rules cannot be directly binding either on arbitrators, or on the parties themselves, unless they are adopted by agreement. Whilst the International Bar Association hopes that they will be taken into account in the context of challenges to arbitrators, it is emphasised that these guidelines are not intended to create grounds for the setting aside of awards by national courts.

If parties wish to adopt the rules they may add the following to their arbitration clause or arbitration agreement:

"The parties agree that the rules of Ethics for International Arbitrators established by the International Bar Association, in force at the date of the commencement of any arbitration under this clause, shall be applicable to the arbitrators appointed in respect of such arbitration."

The International Bar Association takes the position that (whatever may be the case in domestic arbitration) international arbitrators should in principle be granted immunity from suit under national laws, except in extreme cases of wilful or reckless disregard of their legal obligations. Accordingly, the International Bar Association wishes to make it clear that it is not the intention of these rules to create opportunities for aggrieved parties to sue international arbitrators in national courts. The normal sanction for breach of an ethical duty is removal from office, with consequent loss of entitlement to remuneration. The International Bar Association also emphasizes that these rules do not affect, and are intended to be consistent with, the International Code of Ethics for lawyers, adopted at Oslo on 25th July 1956, and amended by the General Meeting of the International Bar Association at Mexico City on 24th July 1964.

* * *

[See the text of the Code in the Documents Supplement.]

Robert Coulson,* AN AMERICAN CRITIQUE OF THE IBA'S ETHICS FOR INTERNATIONAL ARBITRATORS

J. Int'l Arb'n, June 1987 (Vol. 4, No. 2), at 103.**

The rules governing the ethics of international arbitrators recently issued by Committee D of the Section on Business Law of the International Bar Association state that they reflect "internationally acceptable guidelines developed by practicing lawyers from all continents." The drafting group included well known lawyers specializing in international arbitration: J.M.H. Hunter (England), J.A.S. Paulsson (France) and Dr. A.J. van den Berg (Holland).

---

* [Then] President of the American Arbitration Association.

** Reproduced with permission of Kluwer Law International.

Since I respect the draftsmen, I trust that they will endure this critique in good spirits. Many of their rules are in harmony with U.S. practice, but in one important respect there is a difference of perception on this side of the Atlantic. Except for maritime arbitrations, often held under the rules of the Society of Maritime Arbitrators, U.S. parties tend to be skeptical about the impartiality of party-appointed arbitrators. In domestic cases, party-appointed arbitrators seem ambiguous, likely to be friendly to the interests of the party that appointed them. In this regard, the IBA rules and the Code of Ethics for Arbitrators in Commercial Disputes developed jointly by the American Arbitration Association and the American Bar Association in 1977, appear to be in conflict.

It is interesting to compare the nine IBA rules with the provisions of the AAA–ABA Code. For example, the definition of bias is similar, covering situations where an arbitrator favors one of the parties, or is prejudiced as to the issues, or has relationships with one of the parties or "someone closely connected with one of the parties" such as to create a "dependence" upon that person.

IBA Rule 4 imposes a duty upon all arbitrators to disclose any facts or circumstances that may give rise to justifiable doubts as to impartiality or independence.

The AAA–ABA Code contains more concise language in Cannon II; "An arbitrator should disclose any interest or relationship likely to affect impartiality or which might create an appearance of partiality or bias." An introductory note describes various kinds of information that should be disclosed, citing the leading United States Supreme Court case, *Commonwealth Coatings Corp. v. Continental Casualty Co.*, 393 US 145 (1968). In that case, the neutral arbitrator, selected by the party-appointed arbitrators, failed to tell the petitioner that he had occasionally consulted for the respondent. Although no actual bias was shown, the court vacated the award on the basis of an appearance of bias.

So far so good: neutral arbitrators should be independent and impartial. Facts that might lead to reasonable doubts about their impartiality should be disclosed. The IBA rules require disclosures about past or present business relationships with a party or with "potentially important" witnesses. The AAA–ABA code goes further, including "existing or past financial, business, professional, family or social relationships which are likely to affect impartiality or which might reasonably create an appearance of practicality or bias." The AAA–ABA code extends to relationships with any party's "*lawyer*, or with any individual whom they have been told will be a witness" (emphasis added).

Except for the specific reference to lawyers, the difference seems slight. Perhaps the IBA draftsmen felt that "family or social relationships" were too trivial to mention. In the United States, however, courts have been asked to rule on family relationships and common memberships in organizations in motions to vacate arbitration awards. The IBA's prohibition against "continuous substantial social or professional relationships" probably covers family connections.

The AAA–ABA code states that when all parties request an arbitrator to resign, the arbitrator should do so. Where one party makes such a request, the arbitrator should withdraw, unless the parties' agreement contains a procedure for determining challenges, as would be the case under most administrative systems, or the arbitrator decides that the "reason for the challenge is not substantial" and that "withdrawal would cause unfair delay or expense to another party and would be contrary to the ends of justice."

The IBA rules contain no such procedures, seemingly leaving such an arbitrator in an uncomfortable quandary.

The "party-nominated" arbitrator seems particularly at risk under the IBA rules. Many international contracts specify that each party will "nominate" or "appoint" an arbitrator, the two arbitrators to agree upon a "presiding" arbitrator. When a prospective party-nominated arbitrator is approached by one of the parties, the IBA rules instruct such a candidate to "make sufficient enquiries in order to inform himself whether there may be any justifiable doubts regarding his impartiality or independence; whether he is competent to determine the issues in the dispute;...." He may also "respond to enquiries from those approaching him, ... provided that the merits of the case are not discussed."

But would not such a conversation oblige the prospective arbitrator to discuss the merits of the case? How can a potential arbitrator determine impartiality or competence without discussing the issue? Indeed, the candidate is directed by the rules to enquire about the "issues in the dispute."

This initial interview is not the only time that party-appointed arbitrators must communicate directly with the party that nominated them. If required to participate in the selection of the presiding arbitrator, as is generally the case, a party-appointed arbitrator is authorized by the rules to obtain the views of the appointing party as to the acceptability of candidates being considered. Can such a conversation be held without mentioning the issues in dispute?

The party-appointed arbitrator is instructed to avoid unilateral communications about the case with parties or their representatives. If such a communication should occur, the arbitrator is to inform the other parties and arbitrators of its substance.

If an arbitrator learns that a fellow arbitrator has violated the rule against unilateral communications, "normally, the appropriate initial course of action is for the offending arbitrator to be requested to refrain from making any further improper communications with the party." If unilateral communications continue, the remaining arbitrators may inform the "innocent party".

How often in international arbitration does that happen? Is the IBA vision of the behavior of party-appointed arbitrators an accurate picture of current practice? * * * How many party-appointed arbitrators have resigned because of unilateral communications? How many have been challenged and disqualified by administrative agencies?

The AAA–ABA code reflects a more pragmatic approach. It is known that in the United States some party-appointed arbitrators are expected to favor their appointing party's point of view. They are not strictly neutral. Their party appointed them because of a prior relationship, or because they came from a familiar branch of the industry, or because of their reputation, nationality or whatever. In *Vantage S.S. Corp. v. Commerce Tankers Corp.*, 342 NYS2d 281 (1973), the party-appointed arbitrator was an attorney for the party, a stockbroker for the party, related to the president of the corporation and had advised on the contract. However, the court held that there was no misconduct and upheld the arbitrators' award. Some systems of arbitration in the United States assume that party-appointed arbitrators serve as advocates during the arbitrators' deliberations, making certain that their party's point of view is fairly understood by the neutral arbitrator.

The AAA–ABA code does impose certain minimum obligations upon non-neutral arbitrators. A party-appointed arbitrator can be predisposed towards a party, but is obliged to act in good faith, with integrity and fairness. The party-appointed arbitrator's disclosures need be sufficient only to describe "the general nature and scope of any interest or relationship". Party-appointed arbitrators can consult with their appointing party about the acceptability of a candidate for neutral arbitrator and can communicate with their party about "any other aspect of the case, providing they first inform the other arbitrators and the parties that they intend to do so."

The AAA–ABA code recognizes that various degrees of neutrality are imposed upon party-appointed arbitrators. It encourages the parties to discuss their mutual understanding of the relationship. The AAA–ABA code explains the choices available to parties who elect the tripartite model, but want to protect themselves against having an arbitrator who is more "neutral" than their adversary's, or against an arbitrator who might indulge in delaying tactics or other unfair procedures.

Whereas the IBA rules state that no unilateral arrangements should be made for arbitrators' fees or expenses, the AAA–ABA code allows party-appointed arbitrators to negotiate compensation with their party. Arrangements for compensation may include the establishment of a *per diem* rate, the currency in which the fee will be paid, and whether payment will be made to the individual arbitrator, to a corporate account or to a professional firm. These questions arise in other personal service contracts. Why do the IBA rules require that they be discussed with the other arbitrators and with the non-appointing party? The parties may agree to share equally in compensating all members of the panel. But is that always the case? The time spent by each arbitrator may vary, particularly in international arbitration where arbitrators must come to the hearing from countries with different economic systems. Uniform rates and conditions of payment can have unfortunate tax consequences.

Another difference between the IBA rules and the AAA–ABA code concerns arbitrators' participation in settlement discussions. The IBA rules say that when the parties request such participation from the arbitrators, the tribunal or the presiding arbitrator may make "proposals for settlement" to both parties, "preferably in the presence of each other." The rules indicate, however, that an arbitrator who discusses settlement terms unilaterally with a party should "normally" be disqualified from any future participation in the arbitration. This, presumably, also applies to party-appointed arbitrators.

The AAA–ABA code, on the other hand, directs arbitrators not to suggest involvement in such discussions. An arbitrator should not exert pressure on parties to settle, or participate in settlement discussions. Only if requested to do so, should an arbitrator act as a mediator or conciliator.

What is the difference? A neutral arbitrator under the AAA–ABA code should not initiate proposals for settlement, discuss settlement with one party in the absence of another, but may act as a mediator or conciliator if asked to do so by the parties. Party-appointed arbitrators, on the other hand, are free to discuss possible settlements with their party, unless the parties agree otherwise.

In the United States, a party-appointed arbitrator may initiate settlement discussions. As arbitration hearings ripen towards a conclusion, a party-appointed arbitrator may point out opportunities for settlement. This practice can produce advantageous settlements. The IBA rules, where party-nominated arbitrators are forbidden to discuss the case with their parties, would inhibit such compromise settlements.

Here, the contrast between the IBA rules and AAA–ABA approach is laid bare. The IBA rules would force party-appointed arbitrators to act as neutrals, with minor exceptions. The AAA–ABA code leaves that issue to the parties. Do they want their party-appointed arbitrators to be neutral, or do they want them to serve a more partisan role? If there is a "worldwide consensus" that party-appointed arbitrators in international arbitration should be impartial, detached from the party who selected them, this aspect of the IBA rules may be realistic. But is there such a consensus? Is the "neutral" party-appointed arbitrator an unreliable myth? Further research may be necessary.

The IBA rules omit other provisions found in the AAA–ABA code. Only the draftsmen can say whether such omissions were intentional. For example, the rules do not define an arbitrator's loyalty to the process of arbitration or to the public. The AAA–ABA code instructs arbitrators not to be swayed "by outside pressure, by public clamor, by fear of criticism or by self interest."

The AAA–ABA code tells arbitrators to be "patient and courteous to the parties, to their lawyers and to the witnesses", a provision not found in the IBA rules. Perhaps international arbitrators are so uniformly polite that such a provision was thought unnecessary. Nor do specific provisions deal with the parties' right to be represented by counsel, their right to appear in person at hearings or their right to have reasonable advance notice of hearings.

The AAA–ABA code in Canon V requires arbitrators to make decisions in "a just, independent and deliberate manner," explaining in some detail what that involves. In contrast, the IBA rules say nothing about the arbitrators' decision. The AAA–ABA code, for example, warns arbitrators not to "delegate the duty to decide to any other person." Surely this is an important point.

Both the IBA rules and the AAA–ABA code impose a duty of confidentiality upon the arbitrators, during and after the arbitration. The AAA–ABA code cautions arbitrators not to use confidential information acquired during the arbitration to gain personal advantage for themselves or for others.

Arbitrators are directed not to assist in post-arbitration proceedings. The IBA rules put that prohibition in terms of giving information "in any proceedings to consider the award." Situations where one of the arbitrators has engaged in misconduct or fraud are excepted, whereas the AAA–ABA code excludes situations where the arbitrator's involvement is "required by law." The difference in practice may be minor.

One additional comment relates to style. The draftsmen of the IBA rules have chosen to inject gratuitously the male gender into their work, 36 times by my count. Rule 2.1 for example, states that "a prospective arbitrator shall accept an appointment only if *he* is fully satisfied that *he* is able to discharge *his* duties without bias." Having recently reviewed a book which did exactly the opposite, consistently assigning *she* and *her* to unidentified individuals, my sensitivity about gratuitous gendering may be unique.

This critique is not intended to detract from the importance of Committee D's contribution. These rules will encourage practitioners to think about ethical questions. Questions of disclosure, fairness and acceptable behavior are dealt with in clear, definitive terms.

Will these rules encourage litigation against arbitrators? The IBA, in its introduction, confirms the generally held view that arbitrators should be immune from suit under national laws, except where they act in "willful or reckless disregard of their legal obligations," going on to say that "the normal sanction for breach of an ethical duty is removal from office, with consequent loss of entitlement to remuneration." Removal by whom? Must one of the parties go to a domestic court? Are the agencies that provide international case administration prepared to remove arbitrators who violate the IBA rules? What obligations do international arbitrators owe to such agencies? How will the rules be enforced?

The questions raised by this paper will be answered only through experience. It will be interesting to observe whether the "fiction" that party-appointed arbitrators are totally impartial will survive in practice: a few nasty experiences with partisan party-appointed arbitrators may lead to increased skepticism. Will additional provisions be added to the IBA rules as experience accumulates?

Robert Lutz E., PARTISAN ARBITRATORS AND THE CASE AGAINST BIAS IN INTERNATIONAL ARBITRATION

International Lawyers' Newsletter vol. XII., no. 2, pp. 14–17, March/April 2000.

* * *

THE OLD ABA CODE OF CONDUCT v. THE NEWLY PROPOSED CODE

The Code of Ethics for Arbitrators, promulgated in 1977 by a joint committee of the American Arbitration Association (AAA) and the American Bar Association (ABA), currently provides for neutral and non-neutral party-appointed arbitrators. It states a general presumption of non-neutrality for party-appointed arbitrators unless otherwise specified:

"Party-appointed arbitrators should be considered non-neutrals unless both parties inform the arbitrators that all three arbitrators are to be neutral, or unless the contract, the applicable arbitration rules, or any governing law requires that all three arbitrators are to be neutral."

Currently, the AAA and the ABA Section of Dispute Resolution are proposing a revision to the 1977 ethical code. This revision—still in draft form—effectively addresses most critical categories of arbitrator conduct, but unfortunately recognizes and allows the existence of non-neutral party-appointed arbitrators in commercial arbitration.

Simply put, the continued sanctioning of non-neutral arbitrators by this new Code creates both practical and ethical problems that the arbitral process can ill-afford if it is to be a mainstream dispute resolution process deserving of consumer confidence. First, allowing an arbitrator to act as an advocate for the party that appoints him or her has adverse practical implications. It does not acknowledge and directly conflicts with the international trend against bias in commercial arbitration. Many countries and institutions internationally make no distinction between party-appointed and non-party-appointed arbitrators and require all arbitrators to be impartial and independent. This approach is followed by the International Chamber of Commerce Court of Arbitration and the UNCITRAL Model Arbitration Law, among others. Holding all arbitrators to the same standard of neutrality helps to ensure the fairness of the process and at the validity of arbitral awards, and enhances confidence in the system. Establishing ethical standards domestically that contradict international norms would create confusion and puts the US at odds with the rest of the world—a position made all the more precarious as globalization reaches into all aspects of commercial activity.

Additionally, the proposed revision would create different standards for arbitrators in domestic commercial arbitration than for those in international ones. This distinction is unnecessary and frequently would be impractical. In modern times, the difference between a clearly domestic matter and an international one is often blurred by the increasingly global nature of our economy and the transaction of e-commerce. Consequently, individuals chosen as arbitrators may be uncertain as to their respective powers and responsibilities, as will prospective parties to a dispute. This dubiety could have a deterrent effect on those looking for alternate ways to solve their differences.

Secondly, permitting party-appointed arbitrators to act as non-neutral advocates for one side is contrary to established and respected ethical norms of fair and impartial decision making. All persons presiding over arbitration proceedings, whether for a domestic or international dispute, and whether appointed by a party or by the appointees, should be held to the same ethical standards. Accordingly, any ethical code should provide clear, practical guidelines for arbitrators to follow and sound moral principles to which they may adhere. Allowing partisan arbitrators would tend to legitimize bias in arbitral decision making, which in turn could discredit the process and panels' awards.

* * *

Questions and Comments

1. Do you agree with Canon II(E) of the AAA/ABA Code of Ethics, mandating a withdrawal of the arbitrator if both parties so wish? Should the arbitrator at least warn the parties of the consequences? (Suppose withdrawal is suggested in an advanced stage of the arbitration process, should the arbitrator caution the parties on the dangers of considerable delay?)

What if the arbitrator believes that he or she is a victim of false rumors. What is more ethical, to withdraw if both parties request withdrawal, or to insist on challenge procedures?

(The IBA Rules do not contain a rule corresponding to Canon II(E), "seemingly leaving such an arbitrator in an uncomfortable quandary"—in the words of Coulson.)

2. Canon VII(A)(1) of the AAA/ABA Code states that, "Non-neutral arbitrators may be predisposed toward the party who appointed them but in all other respects are obligated to act in good faith and with integrity and fairness." What do you understand the term "predisposed" to mean in this context?

Note that the IBA Rules do not refer to arbitrators, whether party appointed or not, as "non-neutral" or "neutral". Does this difference reflect a difference in expectations about arbitrators' behavior?

In the 1996 American Arbitration Association Commercial Arbitration Rules for domestic cases, Article 15 is entitled "Appointment of Neutral Arbitrator by Party–Appointed Arbitrators". In the 2001 AAA International Arbitration Rules, however, no distinction is made between "neutral" and "non-neutral" arbitrators (the terms are not used). Why the difference in terminology? Under the AAA Rules are arbitrators expected to act differently, depending on whether the arbitration is domestic or international?

3. In ad hoc arbitration, would you allow a separate fee arrangement between a party and that party's appointed arbitrator?

(The other option is the following: fee arrangements are to be made between the parties and the arbitration panel, and fees are to be divided among the arbitrators according to an agreement the arbitrators make among themselves.)

4. Suppose an arbitrator is on a plane with one of the parties. Should the arbitrator sit in a seat adjacent to the party, or to one of the lawyers? Should an arbitrator sit at the same breakfast table with a party (or a lawyer) if they are in the same hotel? In trying to answer these questions do you find any guidance in the codes of ethics?

5. Consult Canon VI of the AAA/ABA Code. Suppose after the award is rendered an attorney for one of the parties asks an arbitrator what was really decisive in the panel's deliberations. The attorney wants to know whether any evidence or arguments were particularly persuasive and whether any missed the mark entirely. Can the arbitrator answer? Would your opinion be affected by whether the arbitrator was party appointed?

6. The ABA Code of Judicial Conduct Canon 3(B)(7) and associated commentary read as follows:

(7) A judge shall accord to every person who has a legal interest in a proceeding, or that person's lawyer, the right to be heard according to law. A judge shall not initiate, permit, or consider ex parte communications, or consider other communications made to the judge outside the presence of the parties concerning a pending or impending proceeding * * *.

Commentary

The proscription against communications concerning a proceeding includes communications from lawyers, law teachers, and other persons who are not participants in the proceeding, * * *.

Would you favor such a rule for arbitrators?

7. Lutz argues that in an age of e-commerce the difference between domestic and international disputes becomes blurred and that hence there should be no distinction between international and domestic arbitration. (Or at least not with respect to the issue of non-neutral arbitrators). Do you agree?

8. According to Section 1 of the Code of Ethics for Arbitrators of the Milan Chamber of National and International Arbitration:

An arbitrator accepting a mandate in an arbitration administered by the Chamber of National and International Arbitration of Milan shall act according to the Chamber's National and International Rules and this Code of Ethics.

This is a rather rare example of making the canons of a code of ethics binding. A sanction is also provided in Section 15, which states:

The arbitrator who does not comply with the provisions of this Code may be replaced. Where it is not appropriate to replace the arbitrator in order not to cause useless delay in the arbitral proceedings, the Arbitral

Council may sanction the behavior of the arbitrator, also after the conclusion of the arbitral proceedings, by refusing to confirm him in subsequent arbitral proceedings.

Is this an advisable approach? Should rules of codes of ethics be binding rules subject to sanctioning? If you support sanctioning (including removal), would you make this contingent on party motion?

9. Do you support the drafting of codes of ethics for arbitrators?

III.1.f. Rights and Responsibilities of the Arbitrators

Philippe Fouchard, RELATIONSHIPS BETWEEN THE ARBITRATOR AND THE PARTIES AND THE ARBITRAL INSTITUTION*

ICC ICArb. Bull. 12–23 (Supp. 1995).

I—THE RELATIONSHIP BETWEEN THE ARBITRATOR AND THE PARTIES

8. Although the arbitrator is a judge, he is only a judge by virtue of a contract, whereby he has promised the parties (and possibly the arbitration institution) that he will carry out a clearly defined task, that is usually remunerated. Hence, his status is contractual in origin. Today, the existence of such a contract is no longer seriously disputed (A), even if the precise consequences of this analysis still give rise to certain areas of uncertainty (B).

* * *

20. In fact, the particularities of this contract between the arbitrator (all the arbitrators) and the parties (all the parties) can only result from a practical analysis of its contents, which will show the importance of the contractual component of the status of the arbitrator.

B—THE EFFECTS OF THIS RELATIONSHIP

21. This afternoon, a number of speakers will stress that arbitrators should benefit from * * *protection * * * [similar to] that accorded to judges. This protection is all the more necessary nowadays as litigious combat has intensified, and certain parties seek to destabilise the arbitrator by a variety of means, particularly in the course of the arbitration.

However, we must not let this socio-psychological background prevent us from singling out the elements of a balanced contractual status, which spares the arbitrator from being subjected to any type of harassment in relation to his obligations, while at the same time reminding him what these fundamental duties are.

* The Status of the Arbitrator. Special Supplement of the ICC International Court of Arbitration Bulletin. ICC Publication No. 564—ISBN 92.842.1218.9(E). Published in its official English version by the International Chamber of Commerce Copyright 8 1995—International Chamber of Commerce (ICC), Paris. Available from: ICC Publishing SA, 38 cours Albert 1er, 75008, Paris, France. (www.iccbooks.com) Reprinted with permission from ICC.

The subject remains haphazard, for up till now international arbitration practice has been wary of offering full and balanced models of this contractual relationship between the parties and the arbitrator. The said elements are to be found in instructions to the arbitrator, in the usages of arbitration centres and in a number of provisions of their rules. More interesting are the Codes of Conduct or rules of ethical practice that the Bars or Bar Associations have adopted in relation to arbitrators' duties and rights.[22]

1) The arbitrator's obligations towards the parties

22. In the first place, it goes without saying that any arbitrator is bound to behave equitably and impartially, and to treat the parties on an equal footing throughout the whole duration of the procedure. He must also ensure that they are given every opportunity to assert their pleas. Such duties stem first of all from his status as a private judge, but they also represent precise contractual obligations that he is bound by as a direct result of accepting his task.

A number of arbitration rules mention this obligation,[23] as do various codes of ethics.[24] But such stipulations are not even necessary, because such behaviour is already imposed on arbitrators by international conventions, laws, and the national courts.

23. The second set of obligations on the arbitrator, though still relating to the conduct of the procedure, has a more direct impact on his contractual status: the arbitrator must fulfil his task within the legal or contractual time limits laid down for him.

In addition, and in any case, in accepting his task, he undertakes to fulfil it with due diligence. This rule is also a definite one, although it is seldom expressed in this form. It echoes the expression "reasonable time limit" imposed by the international conventions and declarations relating to human rights in the field of justice.

An arbitrator who is a member of an arbitral tribunal is also failing in his duty of due diligence if he refrains from taking part in the hearings or in the deliberations. If he were to seek to use this as a means of paralysing the procedure, particularly if this was in the interest of the party who nominated him, it would constitute a deliberate wrongful act.

24. The third set of obligations is complementary to the foregoing. However it is often stipulated expressly in arbitration laws or rules: the arbitrator must carry out his task until its completion, in other words until the final award is rendered. In consequence, from the moment that he accepts his task, in principle, he can no longer divest himself of it—in other words resign—at least, not without good reason.

---

22. For example the *Rules of Ethics for international arbitrators of the International Bar Association*, 1987.

23. UNCITRAL Rules, Art. 15; Italian Arbitration Association Rules, Art. 21;

Rules of the Arbitration Institute of the Stockholm Chamber of Commerce, Art. 16.

24. IBA Rules, Art. 1.

Many legal systems have clearly adopted this view, in particular the following laws: French (Art. 1462 New Code of Civil Procedure), Italian (Art. 813 Code of Civil Procedure), Belgian (Art. 1689 Judicial Code), Dutch (Art. 1029.2 Code of Civil Procedure). Hence any arbitrator who comes to find the burden and length of his duties wearisome can be accused of irresponsibility or capriciousness. But the main aim of the rule is to combat a tendency towards delay which is not uncommon; an arbitrator feeling that he is in the minority in the tribunal resigns in the aim of preventing it from delivering an award that is unfavourable to the party who nominated him. It is for this reason that the Dutch Code and the UNCITRAL Model law (Art. 14) specify that any resignation must be accepted, either by both parties, or by a predetermined third party, or by the supervising authority.[25] The Swiss federal law does not cover this question, however academic writers consider that in accordance with the "general law of arbitration" (expressed by the Belgian and French texts cited above) *"an arbitrator who has accepted his task must in principle conduct it until it is completed"* and that *"he can only divest himself of it for legitimate reasons."*[26] As another Swiss author has underlined, this view is perhaps too optimistic[27] since a recent federal appeal court judgment[28] has held that an award rendered by the two remaining arbitrators, in a case where the ICC had refused the third arbitrator's resignation, was irregular.

We shall see this afternoon that there are a variety of means whereby such conduct can be rendered ineffective. For the moment it is sufficient to point out that several sets of arbitration rules prohibit the arbitrator from untimely resignation.[29] The most restrictive rules are certainly the Rules of the Irano–American dispute settlement tribunal, Article 13 '5 of which significantly limits the arbitrator's right of resignation: he must remain a member of the tribunal in all the cases in which he has already taken part in a hearing on the substantive issues.

Naturally, provided he has legitimate reasons for resigning, for example if he is unable to continue his task, or if, through no fault of his own, a circumstance of a kind that would affect his independence vis-à-vis the parties arises, the arbitrator may resign, with or without the authority of the arbitration centre or his colleagues.

25. The arbitrator's fourth contractual obligation is his duty to respect the confidentiality of the arbitration. It is seldom stated express-

---

25. E. Gaillard *"Les manoeuvres dilatoires des parties et des arbitres dans l'arbitrage commercial international"*, *Rev. arb.* 1990, p. 759.

26. P. Lalive, JBF. Poudret, Cl. Reymond, [Le droit de l'arbitrage interne et international en Suisse 333 (1989)].

27. F. Knoepfler, comment under Trib. féd. suisse, 30 April 1991, *Rev. suisse. dr. intern. dr. eur.*, 1993, p. 197, esp. p. 192.

28. Cited in the preceding note, and also published, *ATF 117 1 at p. 166*, JT 1992 I p. 313, *Bull. ASA*, 1992, p. 259.

29. In this sense, the following rules: ICSID, *Art. 8*, which entrust the arbitral tribunal with the task as to whether or not to accept the resignation of the arbitrator acting for the party; *ICC, Art. 2.10* which provides that the arbitrator's resignation must be accepted by the Court; *CEPANI, Art. 18.4*, which provides that the arbitrator's departure must be "duly accepted."

ly and in general terms. However, we should like to cite Article 35 of the AAA International Rules of Arbitration:

> "*Confidential information disclosed during the proceedings by the parties or by witnesses shall not be divulged by an arbitrator or by the administrator. Unless otherwise agreed by the parties, or required by applicable law, the members of the tribunal and the administrator shall keep confidential all matters relating to the arbitration or the award.*"

Like the AAA, the ICC also refers to the confidential nature of arbitration, but in its internal rules it only refers to it in relation to the work of the International Court of Arbitration, that is to say its permanent administrative body (Internal Rules of the Court of Arbitration, Art. 2).

The reticence of the various texts is of little importance. One of the fundamental principles—and one of the most definite advantages—of international arbitration is its confidential character. This is so true that it is imposed on the parties as well.[30]

2) The parties' obligations towards the arbitrator

26. First of all they are pecuniary.

Indeed, in order to carry out the services he has promised, the arbitrator will incur a variety of expenses, which he can obviously ask to have reimbursed, in all circumstances. And above all, as he rarely carries out his task free of charge, he is entitled to ask the parties who request him to settle their dispute, for remuneration—in other words—fees.

It is unnecessary to describe here the modalities for the reimbursement of expenses, calls for advances on costs, and the determination and payment of fees, which are mainly matters of practice.

Certain national laws settle these questions, such as the Italian Code of Civil Procedure (Art. 814). It firstly points out that the arbitrators are entitled to the reimbursement of their costs and to fees for the work carried out, unless they have waived them. It then goes on to specify that the parties are jointly bound to pay them, without prejudice to their rights of recourse one against the other. Lastly it adds that, if the parties do not agree to the calculation of the costs and fees that the arbitrators have carried out directly, the amount will be determined by the court.

Such principles are also liable to be applied outside the Italian legal context, and rules of arbitration, which lay down the most relevant provisions in this connection, generally take them into consideration.

Most institutional rules of arbitration lay down a scale of fees, which takes into account the commercial amount in dispute, and, possibly, the difficulty of the case and the time spent by the arbitrators in deciding

---

30. J. Paulsson & N. Rawding, "The Trouble with Confidentiality," *ICC ICA Bull., May 1994, p. 48.*

it.[31] Such scales, as well as the decisions taken for applying them by the centres' administrative structures, are obviously contractual in character.

Impliedly, such payments lay down a fundamental principle, that is essential for safeguarding the independence of all arbitrators: prohibition of any unilateral financial arrangement between an arbitrator and the party who nominated him.[32]

It is less certain whether, if the parties so requested, a national judge could check and, where applicable, reduce the amount of the arbitrator's fees, if he considered they were excessive. It is true that several legal systems afford the courts such power in relation to remuneration fixed unilaterally by agents or contractors. But if the amount of the arbitrator's fees stems from the application of a scale, the parties are deemed to have known it and to have accepted it. Hence, in order to win their case they would have to maintain that the preestablished provisions of the standard form contract in question were imposed on them by an abuse of economic power. The argument has little chance of being convincing if they are international commercial operators, with long experience in the field of arbitration.

On the other hand, the arbitrator's fees may be reduced or refunded, in whole or in part, if he committed errors in the course of performing his duties. This is a consequence of the bilateral contractual nature of the arbitration agreement, and several French[33] and Italian[34] decisions have stated this expressly.

The final responsibility for the fees is decided by the arbitrator in his award. Most arbitration rules provide as follows:[35] an order to pay all or part of the costs and fees of the arbitration is one of the usual heads of the award, which the arbitrators decide on the basis of the respective success and conduct of the parties to the arbitration.

However, the arbitrator may not only decide which of the parties shall bear the payment of his fees; he may also determine the amount of these fees in his award. The question that then arises is whether he can in this way award himself a right to recover any remuneration which he has not yet received, or, owing to *res judicata* authority and subsequent enforceability of the award, prohibit any subsequent challenge by a party of the amount thereof. The French courts have replied in the negative, holding that the arbitrator cannot be both judge and party at one and the same time.[36]

31. ICC Internal Rules, Art. 18, and scale of fees; UNCITRAL Rules, Art. 39, which in the absence of a scale, specifies that the amount of the fees must be reasonable; AAA internal rules, Art. 33 *et seq.*

32. In this sense, expressly, the IBA Rules of Ethics (cited above).

33. TGI Paris, 9 Dec. 1992, *Société Annahold B.V.* and TGI Paris, 12 May 1992,

Société Raoul Duval, Gaz. Pal. 1993, Summary, p. 578.

34. Italian Arbitration Association, Art. 12 & 3; Milan Chamber of Arbitration, Art. 22 & 6.

35. UNCITRAL, Art. 40; ICC, Art. 20.1.

36. Cass. civ. II, 28 Oct. 1987, *Rev. arb.*, 1988, p. 149. note Ch. Jarrosson; Cass. civ. II, 10 Oct. 1990, *Bull. civ.* II, No. 187, p. 95;

27. The parties have other obligations, of a moral character, towards the arbitrator. This service provider is in fact charged with rendering justice; he has to comply with the arbitration agreement and the applicable procedural rules, he is not subordinate to the parties in the conduct of the arbitration proceedings. Because of the judicial nature of his task, he holds appropriate prerogatives for conducting the procedure.

Correspondingly, the arbitrator has the right to meet with faithful and cooperative behaviour from the parties throughout the whole of the arbitration procedure. This principle goes without saying, even if it is not generally referred to in rules of arbitral procedure. This is regrettable, especially at a time when certain excesses are occurring.

Likewise, the arbitrator has the right to continue his task until it is completed. He may only be dismissed with the unanimous agreement of the parties.[37] It is true that if they agree to terminate the arbitration, the arbitrator cannot oppose this. On the other hand, he may not be a plaything at the whim of one party alone, and in particular may not be dismissed unilaterally by the party who nominated him. This role is essential for safeguarding the arbitrator's authority and independence in relation to that party.

II—The Relationship Between The Arbitrator And The Arbitral Institution

28. When a permanent arbitration centre has been chosen to administer the procedure, the contractual relationship existing between the litigants and the arbitrator becomes triangular.[38]

29. As we have seen, a contract already exists between the litigants and the centre, whereby the former acknowledge that the arbitration institution has certain prerogatives, whilst the institution is bound to carry out certain actions in relation to the parties.

We also know that in principle, arbitration centres do not themselves act as arbitrators; they solely provide what French case law calls, the "policing of the arbitration procedure,"[39] or, what Swiss case law refers to as "the administration of the procedure."[40]

This contract between the parties and the administrative centre resembles an agency, since the centre is charged with carrying out a certain number of legal acts,[41] in the name of the litigants. It is also a

Journ not. av., 1991, p. 729, note P. Laroche de Roussane.

37. According to the wording of Article 1463.2 French NCPC.

38. In this sense, see G. Mirabelli, ["*Contratti nell" arbitrato (con l'arbitrato; con l'instituzione arbitrale*, "*Rassegna dell" arbitro*, 1990 (1B2), p. 3 and the references]; A. Ditchev, [*Le "contrat d'arbitrage" Cessai sur le contrat ayant pour ob-*

ject la mission d'arbitre, 1981 Revue de l'arbitrage 395].

39. TGI Paris, 28 March 1984, *Raffineries d'Homs, Rev. arb.*, 1985.141, TGI Paris, 28 Jan. 1987, *République de Guinée Rev. arb.*, 1987, p. 371, 3rd decision.

40. Zurich *Obergericht*, 26 Jan. 1987, *ASA Bull.* 1987, p. 6.

41. Included among such legal acts are, the payment to the arbitrator of his costs

contract for the hire of services, since the centre undertakes to perform various material and intellectual services listed in its rules. The said institutional functions are accepted by the parties when they choose the arbitration institution in their arbitration clause, thereby referring to the said rules, impliedly at least.[42]

30.   We will now deal with the other relationship, the one binding the arbitration centre and the arbitrator. It is more difficult to define than the two others. By endeavouring to remove a little of its mystery and its subtlety, I will seek above all to provoke future discussion.

31.   Firstly, one type of situation that should not be overlooked is the case where the arbitration centre has confined itself to drawing up a list of people who may be appointed as arbitrators in application of its rules. Registration on such a list of arbitrators does not create any right for any individual featuring on it, nor any obligation for the institution to actually appoint him as an arbitrator one day or another. And none of these individuals is bound to accept his appointment, should he be proposed.

32.   It is only from the moment of his acceptance that the prospective arbitrator and the institution actually enter into relations. They then have certain rights and obligations one towards the other, which continues throughout the whole of the arbitration procedure that is set in place. It is difficult to dispute the existence of such rights and obligations (A). On the other hand, it is less clear whether this relationship between the arbitrator and the institution is contractual in character (B).

A—Content Of The Reciprocal Rights And Obligations Of The Arbitrator And The Arbitration Centre

33.   As regards the centre's obligations towards the arbitrator, the former is bound to carry out its functions of organisation, administration and supervision of the arbitral procedure as defined by the arbitration rules laid down by the centre itself.

In addition, from the moment when the arbitration institution recognises that a person acts in the capacity of an arbitrator within the terms of its rules, it must treat him as such and respect the arbitrator's distinctive powers: power to rule on his own jurisdiction, to determine the rules of the procedure and to conduct it, etc. . . .

The institution is also bound to reimburse the arbitrator's expenses and pay him fees, in respect of which it has collected advances from the parties, naturally, in accordance with the provisions of its rules.

and fees, with a view to which the parties have remitted advances to the centre; as the said remittance did not have as its principal aim the conservation of the said sums but rather the performance of the said task, we do not view the said operation as a separate contract of deposit. The definition of agency will be retained: in this sense Cass. com., 1 June 1993, *Bull civ.*, IV, No. 221, p. 158: *Gaz. Pal.*, 29 Aug. 1995, Summary, comments p. 15, obs. B. Moisson de Vaux.

42.   Paris, 4 May 1988 and TGI Paris, 23 June 1988, *République de Guinée, Rev. arb.*, 1988, p. 657, note Ph. Fouchard.

More generally, and even where there is no special provision in the arbitration rules, it has to be acknowledged that the arbitration centre has the duty to provide the arbitrator with its administrative and technical assistance so as to facilitate completion of his task. If the arbitrator has little experience of the conduct of the institutional arbitration concerned he will sometimes need information or advice. As a general rule, the centre will provide assistance in the material organisation of the hearings, seeking the help of interpreters, and possibly secretarial tasks, etc. . . .

34. So far as the arbitrator is concerned, in accepting his task, he agrees to carry it out under the auspices of and in compliance with the centre's rules. He guarantees his independence of mind and his availability to the centre as well as to the parties. He consents to the centre exercising the functions resulting from its rules (power of confirmation, challenge, dismissal . . .). He also consents to the duration of his task being determined and extended by the centre, to the proceedings themselves being "supervised" by the centre's relevant departments and, in the case of the ICC, for example, to his draft award being scrutinised and approved by the institution.

He also agrees that the reimbursement of his expenses, the amount of his fees and the modalities relating to their payment will be decided and fixed by the centre, in accordance with the powers accorded to the centre by the rules of arbitration.

35. Hence there is little doubt that the arbitration centre and the arbitrator are bound by certain obligations one towards the other, and that each of them can demand of the other that certain rights be respected.

All that remains is to determine the legal nature of this relationship.

B—Nature Of The Relationship Linking The Arbitrator And The Arbitration Centre

36. Is it a contractual one?

37. This question has given rise to doubts. It is noted in fact that the powers of the centre are those that the litigants have conferred on it, and that it acts basically in their name, in the capacity of an agent, without personally entering into a contract. Indeed, an agent does not become a party to a contract that binds his principal to a third party.

38. This analysis is correct in the case where the litigants have only charged the arbitration centre with the tasks of appointment (or confirmation) and possibly the challenge or replacement of the arbitrator. This is the case, for example, when the AAA or the ICC act as appointing authority in the context of the UNCITRAL rules of arbitration.[43]

---

43. AAA, *Procedures for cases under the UNCITRAL Arbitration Rules*; ICC, *The ICC as appointing authority under the UN-* *CITRAL arbitration Rules*, ICC publication No. 409, 1983.

In such a case no contract is concluded between the institution and the arbitrator that it appoints. The task of acting as a pre-constituted third party is a simple mandate conferred on the centre in question by the litigants. The centre is only their representative (their joint agent) in its functions of appointment or challenge; it does not enter into any personal obligation towards the arbitrator, nor does the arbitrator have to render account to it in any way. In the conduct of the procedure, the arbitrator's only relationship is with the litigants.

39.   But this is not the commonest case. Generally, as has been pointed out, the arbitration institution carries out an ongoing task of administration and supervision of the arbitration procedure, during which it has constant dealings with the arbitrator.[44] These are functions that are peculiar to the centre and, if the litigants have agreed to entrust these tasks to it, the arbitrator has also consented to their being exercised by this institution. Moreover, certain of these powers could not be exercised by the litigants: you only have to think, for example, of the institution's scrutiny and approval of the draft award![45] The modalities for exercising these prerogatives, laid down in the arbitration rules, are generally discretionary. And when American case law extends the immunity enjoyed by arbitrators to arbitration institutions,[46] the quasi-judicial powers that it thus confers upon them can only be the powers that are peculiar to the said institution.

40.   Accordingly the relationship between the arbitrator and the arbitration centre clearly seems to be based on a contract,[47] even if it is a contract that is not clearly defined and less "characterised" than those previously analysed.

41.   This contract results from the expression of a twofold consent: the consent of the centre which appoints or confirms the arbitrator and, by sending him a copy of its rules, informs him of the functions he will carry out in the course of the said procedure; the consent of the arbitrator when he reads the said rules and agrees to fulfil his task in this context and under the centre's auspices.

42.   It is an innominate contract, in which each party, separately, undertakes to provide and does provide the other with intellectual services. Each also cooperates with the other to ensure that the arbitration the litigants have asked them to conduct progresses to a successful conclusion. Basically, it is in the interest of the litigants that the arbitrator and the centre exercise their procedural functions and are led to cooperate.

44. See, however, disputing—in our view wrongly—this "power of action" of the arbitration centre after the setting up of the arbitral tribunal: Paris, 18 Nov. 1987 and 4 May 1988, *République de Guinée, Rev. arb.*, 1988, p. 657, note Ph. Fouchard.

45. ICC Rules of arbitration, Art. 21.

46. Latterly, *Thiele v. RML Realty Partners, 18 Cal. Rptr. 2d 416 (Cal.Ct.App.*

1993); Boraks v. AAA, 517 N.W.2d 771 (Mich.Ct.App.1994).

47. This was the virtually unanimous view of the Working Party referred to above: see [Philippe Fouchard, *Final Report on the Status of the Arbitrator: ICC Commission on International Arbitration*, ICC Int'l Ct. Arb'n Bull., May 1996, at 27, 29].

43. In any case, the first step in assessing whether the arbitrator and the centre have performed their respective obligations satisfactorily is to refer to the applicable arbitration rules, which define the roles of the arbitrator and the centre.

44. One final comment, ending in a wish.

Without here emphasizing the arbitrator's claim to immunity and—insofar as it is recognised—that of the arbitration institution, it must not be forgotten that the arbitrator's task is judicial in character and that the purpose of the arbitration centre's activity is to encourage its satisfactory completion. In such an area, the assessments of each, in the conduct and administration of the arbitral procedure, are or should remain both cautious and final; there is very little room for internal quarrels and even less for recourse to claims for liability. Fortunately, there are very few examples of these in present day court proceedings, and I hope that our discussions today will not disappoint this optimism.

K/S NORJARL A/S v. HYUNDAI HEAVY INDUSTRIES CO., LTD.

Queen's Bench Division (Commercial Court), 1990.
1 Lloyd's Law Rep. 260 (1991).*

[Hyundai, Korean shipbuilders, entered into a contract with Norjarl, a Norwegian limited partnership, to build a drilling rig for Norjarl. Norjarl rejected the rig and the parties submitted the ensuing dispute to arbitration.

This case is focused on a commitment fee requested by the arbitrators. The arbitral tribunal consisted of Mr. Barclay, appointed by Hyundai, Mr. Boyd, appointed by Norjarl, and Mr. Steel, appointed as a third arbitrator. The arbitrators accepted their appointments without any reference to fees.

The parties requested that the arbitrators reserve a period of twelve weeks, beginning on April 28, 1992, for the hearing. By letter of March 1, 1990, the arbitrators expressed their willingness to do so, provided that they were paid a portion of their fees on advance as a commitment fee. This advance fee was to guarantee them some remuneration even if the dispute was settled before the hearing.

Hyundai began this action to remove the arbitrators pursuant to section 23(1) of the Arbitration Act of 1950 on the ground that the circumstances in which the arbitrators proposed the commitment fee arrangement constituted "technical misconduct". Norjarl opposed dismissal of the arbitrators. They sought a declaration to the effect that if Hyundai was unwilling to accept the commitment/fee arrangement, the arbitrators were free without impropriety or imputation of bias to conclude the fee agreement with Norjarl alone.]

JUDGMENT

PHILLIPS, J.:

* * *

THE ISSUES

These summonses raise two separate, albeit interrelated issues: (1) In seeking to persuade the parties to agree to a commitment fee have the arbitrators committed misconduct? If so, is it appropriate for the Court to remove them? (2) If the arbitrators conclude an agreement for a commitment fee with Norjarl alone, will this constitute misconduct?

HYUNDAI'S SUBMISSIONS

Mr. Beloff, QC, for Hyundai, made submissions which I can summarise as follows:

(1) Once Mr. Boyd and Mr. Steel had accepted their appointments as arbitrators, a trilateral contract was concluded between each of them and both the parties to the arbitration. That contract is still in force.

(2) Under that contract each arbitrator is obliged to exercise due diligence to perform his functions as arbitrator.

(3) Under that contract the parties are jointly and severally liable to pay the arbitrators reasonable remuneration for their services.

(4) The arbitrators right to reasonable remuneration does not entitle them to a commitment fee.

(5) The arbitrators have sought to exact a commitment fee by making this a pre-condition to continuing with the reference. This constitutes misconduct.

(6) If the arbitrators conclude a bilateral contract with Norjarl for payment of a commitment fee this will render the arbitrators subject to the imputation of bias and will constitute misconduct, albeit that actual bias is not alleged.

NORJARL'S SUBMISSIONS

Mr. Sumption, QC, did not challenge the first three submissions made by Mr. Beloff. He went on to contend, however:

(1) The arbitrators' obligation of due diligence does not extend to making a firm commitment to hold available a 60 day period two years in the future.

(2) It is reasonable for the arbitrators to require a commitment fee in consideration of making a commitment of that nature. That is all that the arbitrators have sought to do and this does not amount to misconduct.

(3) It is always open to one party to make a bilateral agreement with an arbitrator as to the amount of his fees. Such an agreement will

not bind the other party and will not constitute misconduct on the part of the arbitrator.

(4) There can be no objection to Norjarl entering into a bilateral agreement to pay Mr. Boyd and Mr. Steel a commitment fee in consideration of their agreeing to hold themselves available for the 60 day hearing period. This will constitute a contract collateral to the trilateral contract concluded between the two parties and the arbitrators when the latter accepted their appointments.

(5) The proposed agreement carries no imputation of bias. In any event it is not open to Hyundai to advance an objection of imputed bias while expressly eschewing any averment of actual bias.

Have The Arbitrators Been Guilty Of Misconduct?

Both Mr. Beloff and Mr. Sumption took as the starting point for their submissions the analysis of the relationship of arbitrators and parties to an arbitration of Mr. Justice Hobhouse, Cie Europeene de Cereals v. Tradax Export SA, [1986] 2 Lloyd's Rep 310 at p 306.

> ... since the decision of Heyman v. Darwins Ltd., [1942] 72 Ll L Rep 65; [1942] AC 356, it has been recognised that the arbitration clause is a self-contained contract collateral or ancillary to the commercial contract of which it forms part (see Lord Diplock [1981] 1 Lloyd's Rep. 253; [1981] AC 909 at p. 259 and 980). It is the arbitration contract that the arbitrators become parties to by accepting appointments under it. All parties to the arbitration are as a matter of contract (subject always to the various statutory provisions) bound by the terms of the arbitration contract. A party has a right to apply to the Court for an injunction to restrain a breach of the arbitration contract by the other parties just as with any other breach of contract.

The editors of Mustill and Boyd 2nd ed. at pp. 222–3 suggest that it may not be appropriate to treat the relationship of arbitrators and the parties to an arbitration as subject to all the incidents of a normal contract and express the hope that the Courts:

> Will not try to force the relationship between the arbitrator and party into an uncongenial theoretical framework, but will proceed directly to a consideration of what rights and duties ought, in the public interest to be regarded as attaching to the status of arbitrator.

In the present case I do not find the contractual framework an uncongenial one within which to consider the position of the arbitrators and shall proceed upon the premise, common to both parties, that contractual principles should be applied.

The basic rights and obligation of the arbitrators can be simply stated. By accepting their appointments Mr. Boyd and Mr. Steel undertook, in the words of § 13(3) of the Arbitration Act 1950, "to use all reasonable despatch in entering on the proceedings with the reference"—a due diligence obligation. Having accepted appointments as arbitrators Mr. Boyd and Mr. Steel have become entitled to reasonable remuneration for their services.

These are conventional features of a contract to provide services. Less conventional is the term, which must clearly be implied, that the parties may, at any stage, withdraw their request for the arbitrators' services as a result, for instance, of settling their dispute. Such an eventuality may expose the arbitrators to loss if it leaves them idle. Are they entitled to claim compensation for such loss?

Case precedent does not supply an answer to this question and I do not need or propose to answer it. Suffice it to say that it is not easy to find a basis for such a claim within the law of contract. It may well be reasonable that arbitrators should receive compensation in such circumstances, but that is an inadequate basis for implying a contractual term entitling them to it.

What is, in my view, quite clear is that the acceptance of appointment as arbitrator does not carry with it any right to a commitment fee which is payable regardless of whether or not loss is suffered by the arbitrator as a consequence of the withdrawal of the demand for his services. The evidence before me suggests that such a commitment fee is now quite a common feature of the terms under which Counsel accept instructions in a substantial case—at least at the Commercial Bar. While payment of a commitment fee may be a perfectly proper and reasonable term of a contract under which a professional man agrees to hold himself available to perform services over a specific period, there is no basis upon which entitlement to such a fee can arise as an implied term of a contract to provide such services.

For an arbitrator who has accepted an appointment without reservation subsequently to insist upon payment of a commitment fee as a condition of continuing to perform his services will, in my judgment, constitute misconduct. Whether such misconduct justifies removal of the arbitrator under § 23(1) of the 1950 Act will depend upon the particular circumstances.

Mr. Beloff contends that in this case the arbitrators have improperly insisted upon agreement to pay a commitment fee as a condition of continuing to perform the duties that they undertook when they accepted their appointments. Mr. Sumption challenges this analysis. He points out that the arbitrators' request for a commitment fee was a response to the parties' request that they commit themselves to hold available for the parties a period of 60 days in the middle of 1992. This undertaking is, he submits, more than the arbitrators can properly be required to give pursuant to their obligation to proceed with the reference with all reasonable despatch. What has occurred is that both the parties and the arbitrators have reciprocally sought to negotiate a degree of commitment that goes beyond that implicit in the original appointment of the arbitrators.

I accept Mr. Sumption's submission on this point. I do not consider that Mr. Boyd and Mr. Steel's duties as arbitrators required them, at the request of the parties, to hold available a 60 day period some two years ahead. Parties who appoint busy professional men as arbitrators must accept the possibility that they may have other commitments which do not permit them to accommodate the wishes of the parties as to hearing dates.

There is scope for debate as to what hearing facilities the arbitrators might have been required to offer in order to satisfy their duty to proceed with all reasonable despatch, but I am satisfied that the commitment that the parties were seeking went beyond the duty of the arbitrators. In those circumstances it does not seem to me that it was improper for the arbitrators to respond to the parties' request for such a commitment with a proposal that they should, in return, be granted a commitment fee, albeit that neither party was under any obligation to agree to this proposal. It certainly cannot be said that the arbitrators' conduct in so doing was misconduct rendering them unfit to continue as arbitrators, so that the Court should remove them under '23(1) of the 1950 Act. Mr. Boyd and Mr. Steel remain fit and proper persons to act as arbitrators in the dispute to which Norjarl and Hyundai are party.

CAN THE ARBITRATORS PROPERLY CONCLUDE AN AGREEMENT FOR A COMMITMENT FEE WITH NORJARL ALONE?

The object of the first declaration sought by Mr. Sumption is to obtain an affirmative answer to this question. Norjarl hope that such an answer will cause the arbitrators to withdraw the resignations they have tendered, conclude the proposed agreement and continue with the reference. The declaration sought focuses upon the question of bias, which is a very relevant consideration in relation to the broader question that I have posed, but not the only consideration.

Both Mr. Beloff and his clients have expressly stated that they do not suggest that the arbitrators are actually biased against them, nor that they will be so biased if they conclude the proposed agreement with Norjarl. The objection that they take to the proposed agreement is one of principle. They contend that the arbitrators have no right to require a commitment fee, that the terms proposed are not reasonable and that it is inappropriate for agreements of the nature proposed to be made between the arbitrators and only one of the parties, in the light of the general principle that arbitrators must be seen to be impartial. In argument Mr. Beloff made it plain that while no contention of actual bias was advanced Hyundai did contend that the agreement proposed would render the arbitrators susceptible to the imputation of bias.

Mr. Sumption submitted that the proposed agreement was reasonable, that it would not prejudice Hyundai as they would not be party to or bound by it. He pointed out that § 19(2) of the Arbitration Act, 1950 expressly envisages that a party may enter into a written agreement with an arbitrator in relation to his fees and submitted that there was nothing inherently objectionable in such an agreement. Nor could there be objection to one party bearing the full burden of securing fees or costs—art. 9.2 of the ICC Rules of Arbitration specifically provided for this possibility. The only possible objection to the proposed agreement was that it might give rise to bias, but such a suggestion in this case was absurd. In any event Hyundai were not averring actual bias and could not, in those circumstances, seek to rely on imputed bias—see Bremer Handelsgesellschaft mbH v. Ets Soules et Cie, [1985] 1 Lloyd's Rep. 160; [1985] 2 Lloyd's Rep. 199.

SOME GENERAL COMMENTS

Before turning to the particular facts of this case I propose to make some general observations about the agreement of the arbitrators' remuneration.

The scale and complexity of many arbitrations today are such as to render desirable a more detailed agreement between the arbitrators and the parties than one which merely requires the arbitrators to conduct the reference with due diligence in exchange for reasonable remuneration for their services. The parties are likely to wish to have a firm fixture for a continuous hearing, so that they can make appropriate arrangements for witnesses and for legal representation. They may have specific requirements in relation to venue or other matters. The arbitrators, for their part, may be reluctant to commit themselves to refusing other offers of employment for a lengthy period in which, if the arbitration settles, they may find themselves idle. They may accordingly, wish to specify precisely the terms on which they are to be remunerated and, in particular, to be compensated for the risk of idle time.

As this case demonstrates, it is highly desirable that any negotiations between the arbitrators and the parties as to the services that the arbitrators are to render and the terms upon which they are to render them should take place at the time of the appointment of the arbitrators. At that stage it will be open to the parties to appoint other arbitrators if they are not content with the terms proposed. Once arbitrators have accepted appointment it does not accord happily with their status to become involved in negotiations with the parties about fees or any other matter in which they have a personal interest. Unexpected developments may, of course, make such negotiations inevitable, but in that event the arbitrators will wish to conduct those negotiations with the greatest discretion.

Section 19(2) of the Arbitration Act, 1950 appears to envisage the possibility that the arbitrator may have agreed his fees with one party, but not with the other. It does not follow that this is a desirable state of affairs. In my judgment it is not. If an arbitrator wishes to stipulate the amount and basis of his remuneration as a condition of acceptance of his appointment it is desirable that he should, if possible, ensure that these are accepted by both parties. If one party, in apparent good faith, objects to the terms proposed by the arbitrator on the ground that they are unreasonable, he should hesitate before accepting appointment on the basis of an agreement reached with the other party alone.

Once the arbitrator has accepted his appointment, it is even less desirable for him to conclude an agreement about fees or any other matter that affects him personally with one party if the other party is not prepared to join in that agreement. Exceptionally this may be a proper thing to do if the other party confirms that no objection is taken to the proposed agreement. If, however, the other party objects I find it hard to conceive of any circumstance in which it will be appropriate for the arbitrator to conclude the agreement.

The reasons for these observations are, I hope obvious. It is important that the arbitrators are seen by the parties to be acting impartially, even-handedly and with rectitude. If an arbitrator agrees with one party that he will receive fees on a scale, or on terms, that the other party does not consider reasonable, there will be danger that the arbitrator may, at some stage, be suspected of being more favourably disposed to the party with whom the agreement has been made. In short there will be a risk that the arbitrator may lay himself open to the imputations of bias.

THE PRESENT CASE

Mr. Steel and Mr. Boyd acted properly, and in accordance with the observations that I have just made, in declining to conclude an agreement with Norjarl for a commitment fee unless assured that Hyundai had no objection to their doing so. Mr. Sumption submits that they have been over-scrupulous; that having regard to their standing no-one could suspect them of bias as a result of concluding the proposed agreement with his clients. He submits that, as Hyundai have stated that they do not suggest that there is any likelihood of actual bias, it is not open to them to contend that the agreement would give rise to imputed bias.

It may well be that if Mr. Steel and Mr. Boyd and [sic] concluded the agreement with Norjarl, and Hyundai were now seeking to have them removed for imputed bias, Hyundai would be unsuccessful. But the question that I have to consider is whether I should make a declaration which is designed to encourage the arbitrators to conclude that agreement in circumstances where, for the reasons I have given, it is not appropriate that they should do so. The answer to that question is obvious and, accordingly, I shall not grant Norjarl the declaration they seek.

DISPOSITION:

Judgment accordingly

VIENNA INTERNATIONAL ARBITRATION CENTRE ARBITRATOR'S CONTRACT

I _____ agree to act as Sole Arbitrator Chairman in the proceedings between _____ in accordance with the provisions of the Rules of Arbitration and Conciliation of the International Arbitral Centre of the

Austrian Federal Economic Chamber dated 3 July 1991 and submit to the provisions of those Rules of Arbitration and Conciliation.

No circumstances are known to me that would justify a challenge under Article 11 of those Rules of Arbitration and Conciliation.

I undertake to keep the Secretariat of the International Arbitral Centre informed of the progress of the proceedings by the continuous transmission of copies of orders issued by me in conducting the proceedings and to make available to it for safe keeping a complete set of all documents and decisions concerning the proceedings.

I note that determination of the advance against costs and fixing of the fees of the arbitrators and the other costs of the proceedings shall be undertaken exclusively by the Secretariat of the International Arbitral Centre in accordance with Articles 23 and 24 of the Rules of Arbitration and Conciliation and I acknowledge its decision as binding on me.

I shall not order any measures, such as the assignment of experts, etc., that have financial implications before receipt of the communication from the Secretariat of the Arbitral Centre that the necessary cover is available.

_____, _____
Place and date   Signature

A NOTE ON ARBITRATORS' FEES

(This Note relies in part on: Tibor Varady, Remuneration of Arbitrators as a Threshold Issue: Economic Sense and Procedural Realities, in "Corporations, Capital Markets and Business in the Law" Liber Amicorum Richard M. Buxbaum, Kluwer 2000, 585 et seq.)

The issue of remuneration

In a typical arbitration case the issue of fees remains discreetly in the background. Remuneration is a foundation stone of the arbitration process, otherwise it would not make economic sense for those who are providing the service. But foundation stones are rarely above the surface. Parties know, of course, that they have to pay, and arbitrators are very well aware that they are working for money; yet the issue is usually not discussed between the parties and the arbitrators. In an institutional setting, fees are calculated on the basis of a fee scale, and the secretariat of the institution will take practical steps to ensure that the parties pay the institution and the institution, the arbitrators. In *ad hoc* arbitration, more often than not, arbitrators will set a reasonable fee, and the parties will accept this without negotiation. Everybody has an interest in not burdening the process with another issue—and nobody wants to project an image of himself (or herself) as a person who is primarily interested in the issue of remuneration.

But typical cases are not the only cases. Sometimes there is no agreement on the amount of remuneration, at times there are misunderstandings, and there are also cases in which fees are simply not paid.

The question also arises as to what type of remuneration is best suited and in line with the interest of a speedy and efficient arbitration process. It also happens that the issue of fees becomes a **threshold issue** in the sense that it determines the very existence of the arbitration process; in other words, fees become a matter upon which the viability of the arbitration agreement hinges.

Arbitrator's Fees and the Viability of the Arbitration Agreement

Respect for arbitration agreements means deference towards valid and viable arbitration agreements. Fees certainly have an impact on the arrangement made for the settlement of disputes by arbitration. Options regarding modes of payment (ad valorem method, hourly fees, combination of the two, fixed fee method, etc.) are guided, among other considerations, by the desire to encourage efficient work. Special bonuses for timely awards, or penalties for late awards, have also been considered. In certain cases the issue of fees may also influence the viability of the arbitration agreement. One such instance occurs when the parties and the arbitrators cannot reach an agreement on the amount of the fees. The question arises whether such a failure renders the arbitration agreement "inoperative or incapable of being performed" (one of the grounds under Article II of the New York Convention for a court to disregard an arbitration agreement).

Lack of agreement on the amount of arbitrator's fees or on the modalities of payment

Fee issues might bring into play the "incapable of being performed" escape device when—in an *ad hoc* setting in particular—the parties and the arbitrators cannot agree on the amount of remuneration. The question is whether such a lack of agreement might effectively frustrate the original intention to arbitrate, or whether there is any fall-back mechanism available that would allow the performance of the arbitration agreement. The contract between the parties and the arbitrators is rarely formalized or spelled out. In the case of institutional arbitration, the rules of the institution may provide the necessary specifications, including the amount of fees by application of a fee-scale. (The rules of the institution are deemed to be accepted by the parties who submit their dispute to the institution, and by the arbitrators, as well, when they accept their appointment by the parties or by the institution.) Without institutional rules—and without agreement between the parties and the arbitrators on fees—can the contract between the parties and the arbitrators be deemed invalid for indefiniteness? Moreover, would the lack of a valid and perfected *receptum arbitri* render the arbitration agreement "incapable of being performed"?

In more practical terms, if the arbitrators are duly chosen, they propose a certain remuneration, the parties or one of them does not accept it, and further proposals are also turned down, is the arbitration agreement still viable?

Today, the UNCITRAL Rules are the prevailing framework for *ad hoc* arbitration. These Rules do not contain fee-scales. Instead, the Rules set some (rather general) guidelines. According to Article 39(1): *"The fees of the arbitral tribunal shall be reasonable in amount, taking into account the amount in dispute, the complexity of the subject-matter, the time spent by the arbitrators, and other relevant factors."* This is helpful, but certainly much less instructive than fee schedules. In typical cases reason and reasonableness are sufficient guidelines for both the parties and the arbitrators. But what happens if the arbitrators state their fees and request a corresponding advance payment that is not accepted by the parties (or by one of them)? If both parties refuse to make the advance payment because they believe it is unreasonably high, and no compromise is reached, it is difficult to see how arbitration could continue. Analytically, it is important, of course, whether this impasse occurs before or after the arbitrators accept their appointment. More often than not, the arbitrators will not negotiate their fees before accepting their nomination, expecting that there will be no dispute concerning the fees. In such a case, should a dispute and impasse nevertheless emerge, one could argue that the arbitrators are obliged to proceed, leaving the determination of their fees to a court. Counter arguments, however, may also be raised. First, even if there was an offer and acceptance, one could argue that the *receptum arbitri* has not become a binding agreement because it is indefinite. Secondly, even if there were a binding agreement under the applicable law, the arbitrators might be reluctant to perform their role, as long as the amount of their remuneration and the modalities of payment were left completely open. Seeking specific performance to oblige the arbitrators to go forward would not be a realistic option. The parties, however, might still opt for other arbitrators.

A further complication might ensue if a negotiation stance during bargaining over fees gives rise to conflicting interpretations. In Guardian Royal Assurance Group v. Phillips (Queen's Bench Division, Decision of July 30, 1993) the arbitrator asked for a commitment fee, and after one of the parties failed to respond, his clerk wrote: *"Without the commitment from the parties that I sought Mr. Burton is no longer retained for the hearing and there is no point in sending further documentation."* Guardian contended that this was, indeed, a resignation. Phillips and the arbitrator thought it was not. The court held that it was not a resignation, but only "forceful negotiation". It was a close case, and had the opposite result prevailed, the lack of agreement on the arbitrator's fees would have undermined the arbitration agreement itself.

Another difficult situation emerges when only one of the parties refuses to acquiesce in the fee payment plan set by the arbitrators. Within this scenario, two variations are conceivable. If the reluctant party does not contest the amount of the fees, but simply refuses to pay, then one might assume that the *receptum arbitri* is not contested *per se,* it is simply not performed by one of the parties. In this case, the other party is free to go ahead and deposit the entire advance payment. The arbitrators can proceed, and at the end of the process apportion the fees and other costs in the final award. Another option is termination of the arbitration agreement by the non-defaulting party.

The situation is more delicate when the reluctant party explicitly contests the amount of the fees or the amount of the deposit set. Assuming the fees were set within reason, this is unlikely to happen when both parties are expecting at least some partial success and both have a vested interest in making a good impression. There are parties, however, whose only interest is in blocking and delaying the process, and a never-ending dispute about the amount of arbitrator's remuneration might very well serve this purpose. In this case, the *receptum arbitri* has arguably not been perfected, and this may have an impact on the operativeness of the arbitration agreement.

The arbitrators could possibly rescue the threatened agreement. For example, they might decide to proceed without a full deposit, leaving the issue of the fees open, possibly subject to determination by a court. If the arbitrators do not choose this course of action, however, the viability of the arbitration agreement may be cast in doubt. If the fees are contested between a party and the arbitrators, the fees cannot be finally determined in the award, since the arbitrators only have a mandate to settle disputes between the parties. They do not and cannot have a mandate to settle disputes between themselves and the parties. (See the decision of the French *Cour de cassation, 2e Chambre Civ. In S.A.R.L. Bureau Qualitas at Conte c. Viet et Boudy* of 28 October 1987, in Revue de l'Arbitrage, 1988, 149, Note A. Chapelle. See also Ph. Fouchard, Le statut de l'arbitre dans la jurisprudence française, Revue de l'Arbitrage, 1996, 325, at pp. 365–369.)

The Norjarl v. Hyundai case is a good illustration of the difficulties that may emerge if the amount of fees is disputed between the arbitrators and the parties (or between some of the arbitrators and one of the parties).

The role of courts in setting or adjusting arbitrator's fees

The question also arises whether a court decision might replace a missing agreement between the parties and the arbitrators on fees. Under English law, a solution is offered in the 1996 Act. Section 28(1) states: "[t]*he parties are jointly and severally liable to pay to the arbitrators such reasonable fees and expenses (if any) as are appropriate in the circumstances.*" Section 28(2) also states that courts may adjust arbitrator's fees upon party motion. Article 814 of the Italian Arbitration Act (Book IV Title VIII of the Code of Civil Procedure as amended in 1994) takes the same position.

In Mexico, the possible scope of court intervention is more limited: the arbitrators are free to set their fees, but "when a party so requests and the court consents to perform the function, the arbitral tribunal shall fix its fees only after consultation with the court". (Article 1454(3) of the Mexican Commercial Code, Book V, Title IV on Commercial

Arbitration–1993). In Romania—to take another example—arbitrators can make provisional assessments of fees and may order deposits, but at the request of any party the court may reinvestigate such assessments and establish the amount of the arbitrators' fees itself, as well as the manner in which the deposit, advance payment or final payment shall be made. (Article 359 of the Romanian Code of Civil Procedure, including the 1993 amendments.)

If remuneration is set by a court, what yardstick should the court use? In an interesting decision of the Supreme Court of Argentina, a dispute concerning fees arose after the conclusion of the arbitration proceeding. The Supreme Court of Argentina decided to use the ICC fee-scale (Corte Suprema de Justicia, Decision of November 11, 1997–reported in Yearbook Comm. Arb'n 2000, p. 445).

Although explicit rules are sometimes lacking, in most legal systems the absence of an agreement between the parties and the arbitrators on fees would probably provide a basis for court action to set fees. Similarly, most systems would probably authorize court adjustment of fees set provisionally by the arbitrators themselves.

What is to be done, however, if the arbitrators want more certainty and do not want to wait until the end of court proceedings to learn when they will be paid and what the amount will be? In such a case, new arbitrators may be appointed, but the party who wants to block arbitration might again refuse to agree on remuneration, and it will again be up to the arbitrators to decide whether they will take chances. The threat of an impasse would be very much diminished if the arbitrators were allowed to set their fees without the consent of the parties (even if subject to possible *ex post* adjustment by a court).

This course of action would be workable and more appealing to the arbitrators on two assumptions: first, if advance payment by one party (of its share of the fees set by the arbitrators themselves) is not considered an illicit unilateral arrangement—otherwise, the arbitrators would still have to wait for payment until the court confirms the set fees—and secondly, if the fees set by the arbitrators are deemed valid until they are successfully challenged by a party before a competent court. The two assumptions appear to be logically interlinked, but the 1994 Italian Act (which happens to be one of the few legislative acts devoting explicit attention to this issue) nevertheless divorces them … According to Article 814/2 "[w]*here the arbitrators themselves fix the amount of the expenses and of the fee, their decision shall not be binding upon the parties if they do not accept it. In this case, the amount of the expenses and of the fee shall be determined, upon the arbitrator's petition and after hearing the parties, by an order of the president of the Court (tribunale) specified in Article 810 paragraph 2, against which there shall be no recourse.*" This solution deprives the arbitrators of the benefit of a (rebuttable) presumption, and forces **them** to go to court, instead of placing the burden of taking the initiative on the party who is contesting the fees set. It appears, however, that Article 814/2 would still allow one of the parties to accept the fees as set—and to pay in advance accordingly—without risking a later court determination that such action amounted to an "unlawful unilateral arrangement".

Lack of agreement on arbitrator's fees need not be a fatal defect. Remedies do exist. But obstinacy of the parties (or of the arbitrators) as well as blocking tactics can turn the question of fees into a threshold issue that jeopardizes the viability of the arbitration agreement.

Questions and Comments

1. Fouchard explains that the arbitrators cannot award themselves fees in the award, because the arbitrator cannot be both a judge and a party at the same time. How then can arbitrators be sure to receive their fees?

2. In *Somes v. de Saint–Rapt* the French Court of Appeal of Aix denied the request of the arbitrator for payment of the full amount of fees, holding that the arbitrator did not fulfill his mandate, because the arbitrator did not respect the arbitration agreement regarding the composition of the arbitral tribunal and rendered a decision which was *ultra petita*. (As a result of these errors, the award was vacated.) The Court of Appeal classified the agreement between the arbitrator and the party as an agency agreement (*mandat*), and reasoned that under Article 1999 of the Code Civil the agent cannot claim compensation if failure is due to his error. The Cour de cassation disagreed, holding that the relationship between the arbitrator and the party cannot be equated with agency.

Would you award fees to the arbitrator?

3. It has been said that the relationship between the arbitral institution and the arbitrator is based on contract. If the arbitrator is not paid, could he or she sue the arbitral institution, or the parties, or both?

4. Setting costs is less complex in institutional than in ad hoc arbitration. Institutions typically rely on their fee schedules which are known to the parties who accept their jurisdiction. Quite often, ad hoc arbitrators tend to assess (and justify) their fees relying on the fee schedules of well known institutions. In the majority of cases the fees set are simply accepted rather than negotiated, and thus the contractual relationship between the parties and their arbitrators is rarely in the foreground. Yet, even if dormant, this contract is undeniably relevant. The *Norjarl v. Hyundai* decision (which was confirmed by the Court of Appeal, Civil Division on February 21, 1991[9]) had to deal with the contract between parties and arbitrators. Do you agree with the court's conclusions?

If Hyundai persistently blocks any commitment fee, can the arbitration proceed?

5. Were the arbitrators in *Norjarl v. Hyundai* obliged to accept the proposition that hearings should last 12 weeks from April 1992?

6. In cases in which the arbitral institution (or the arbitrators) require a deposit of costs, sometimes one of the parties (typically Respondent) refuses to pay its share. Arbitrators then ask Claimant to deposit the whole amount, on the understanding that the final award would decide on the final

[9]. [1992] 1 QB 863, [1991] 3 All ER   211, [1991] 1 Lloyd's Law Rep. 524.

distribution of costs. Is this arrangement in conflict with the position taken by the English Court in *Norjarl v. Hyundai*?

7.   In order to avoid a distorted image of the amount of arbitrators' fees, note the closing paragraph of the Court of Appeal decision in *Norjarl v. Hyunday*[10] (by Nicolas Browne–Wilkinson):

> Finally, in case the scale of fees being demanded in this case should give rise to comment, in fairness to the rest of the Bar I should point out that they are not typical of the Bar as a whole. Many practitioners in specialist fields now demand and secure fees which to some (including myself) appear to be excessive. For most members of the Bar fees are very much lower and produce annual earnings commensurate with what could be obtained from people of similar skill working in non-legal fields. I hope that the figures mentioned in this case will not be taken as typical of the Bar as a whole.

8.   In general, fee scales established by an arbitral institution are probably the dominant solution. (According to these fee scales the amount of the remuneration depends on the amount of the dispute.) There are, however, other approaches and other considerations. One common issue is whether arbitrators in the same case should receive the same remuneration. It is widely accepted that the remuneration of the presiding arbitrator may be higher based on added responsibility and duties. Could (should) the fees of the two other arbitrators differ? (See Article 32 of the AAA Rules and Section 4(a) of the LCIA fee schedule.)

9.   Hourly fees are also an option. Here the 1995 Regulations for Arbitrator's Remuneration of the Japan Commercial Arbitration Association provide an interesting solution. Fees are set by an hourly rate, but—according to Article 4 of these Regulations—the hourly rate is to be reduced by 10% for every fifty hours in excess of the initial sixty hours. In other words, beginning at the 61st hour, arbitrators will receive 90% of their hourly fee; at the 111th hour, 80%. The Regulations also state that in no case can the reduction exceed 50%.

Do you prefer hourly rates, or fixed fees set by a fee scale (dependent on the amount in dispute). If you were to adopt hourly rates, would you choose the Japanese solution?

10.   Would you agree to arbitrate without an arrangement on fees—leaving it to a later court order to settle the issue?

11.   Do you favor statutory rules that allow courts to adjust arbitrators' fees? Or would you prefer the Mexican solution, according to which "when a party so requests and the court consents to perform the function, the arbitral tribunal shall fix its fees only after consultation with the court"?

12.   The 1996 English Arbitration Act is one of the few that deal explicitly with the issue of the responsibility of the arbitrators. The basic rule is contained in Section 29 entitled "Immunity of arbitrator." According to Section 29(1) and (2):

[10].   [1991] 1 Lloyd's Law Rep. 524.

(1) An arbitrator is not liable for anything done or omitted in the discharge or purported discharge of his functions as arbitrator unless the act or omission is shown to have been in bad faith.

(2) Subsection (1) applies to an employee or agent of an arbitrator as it applies to the arbitrator himself.

As a legislator, would you choose the same standard? (One should note that subsection (3) of Section 29 states explicitly that the rules of subsections (1) and (2) do not affect any liability incurred by an arbitrator by reason of his resigning.)

13. The Vienna International Arbitration Centre has standard arbitrator contracts for both sole arbitrators (presiding arbitrators) and for members of the panel of arbitrators. The two models are very similar. The Arbitrator's Contract for sole arbitrators (or presiding arbitrators) reproduced above specifies the duties of the sole arbitrator (presiding arbitrator of the panel) to the arbitral institution.

What are (or what should be) the consequences of an arbitrator's failure to comply with these duties? Will this (should this) affect the regularity of the arbitral proceedings?

What are the duties of the Vienna Arbitral Centre?

14. The 1998 ICC Rules have introduced a new provision according to which, "Neither the arbitrators, nor the Court and its members, nor the ICC and its employees, nor the ICC National Committees shall be liable to any person for any act or omission in connection with the arbitration."

Is this exclusion of liability conclusive? What are its effects?

Do you expect this provision to affect the number of cases submitted to the ICC?

III.1.g. *Rights and Responsibilities of the Arbitral Institution*

CUBIC DEFENSE SYSTEMS INC. v. ICC

Court of Appeal of Paris, First Chamber, section A, Judgment of September 15, 1998, corrected by a "Judgment on Rectification of Material Errors Discovered by the Court" of October 7, 1998 Mealey's International Arbitration Report, Document #05–990426–109*

COURT OF APPEAL OF PARIS

* * *

On 23 October 1977, the American Company CUBIC DEFENSE SYSTEM Inc. (hereinafter called "CUBIC") entered into two contracts with the Iranian government's delegated war ministry for the supply of arms:

* Mealey's International Arbitration Report Reprinted with the permission of Lex- isNexis, a division of Reed Elsevier Inc.

— an agreement for the sale of an ACMR system,

— a services Agreement,

in which the same arbitration clause appeared: *"any contentious matter or dispute or any claim arising under this Agreement or appertaining thereto or any breach of this Agreement shall be resolved by arbitration which will take place in the city of Zurich, Switzerland, under the laws of the State of Iran in force on the date of this Agreement"*.

At the commencement of the year of 1979, by reason of events that occurred in Iran, the performance of the agreements was at that time interrupted.

On 25 September 1991, the International Chamber of Commerce (hereinafter called the "ICC") received, under that clause, a request for arbitration from the Ministry of Defence and of Support for the Armed Forces of the Islamic Republic of Iran (hereinafter called "the Iranian party") against CUBIC.

By letter of 3 October 1991, the secretariat of the International Court of Arbitration (hereinafter called "ICA"), an emanation of the ICC, informed CUBIC of the request for arbitration submitted by the Iranian government and also informed it that under Article 4(1) of the ICC rules CUBIC had a period of 30 days within which to reply to that request.

With that letter were enclosed the ICC's Conciliation and Arbitration Rules, and the new rules and usages on costs and payment for an ICC arbitration.

By fax, a member of the firm of advocates ARENT FOX McGARRAHAN and HEARD, acting on behalf of CUBIC, confirmed a telephone conversation of 10 October 1991, whereby the ICC had been informed of the appointment as CUBIC's representative, and requested an extension of 45 days within which to reply, which period the secretariat of the ICA granted to him by letter of 6 November 1991.

After the appointment of the Arbitrators, the president of the Arbitration Tribunal, Dr. Wenger, having been appointed by the ICA * * * [because] the parties had failed to agree * * * [on the presiding arbitrator] the terms of reference were signed on 14 July 1993. On 11 August 1993, the President of the Arbitration Tribunal notified to the parties an Order establishing, in particular, the time-schedule for the proceedings.

On 6 April 1995, the Arbitration Tribunal delivered Order No. 6 in the case on the question as to whether the proceedings were barred by lapse of time. That decision was described as provisional and as remaining to be confirmed by a formal judgment stating the reasons on which it was based. The said Order mentioned the dissenting opinion of one of the Arbitrators.

On 17 April 1995, CUBIC sent to the General Secretariat of the ICA a letter criticizing that decision and containing the following passage:

"the decision of the Tribunal makes a mockery of these proceedings and of the time and money that Cubic has been forced to spend to defend itself against a claim 15 years old and barred by lapse of time.

"It is no exaggeration for Cubic to say that the Decision and the Order of 6 April, which is objectively inadequate, fails to state the reasons on which it is based, and goes beyond the matters pleaded by the parties, could gravely jeopardize the credibility of the Court of the ICC within the commercial and legal community of the United States."

In that letter, Cubic demanded that Doctors WENGER and SEIFI (the latter being the Arbitrator appointed by Iran) be replaced. On 17 May 1995, the ICA decided not to go ahead with the replacement procedure.

A number of Orders were then made:

— Order No. 8 in the case of 27 September 1995, rejecting the motion lodged by CUBIC with a view to excluding fresh arguments put forward by the Iranian party;

— Order No. 9 in the case of 12 October 1995 organizing the Hearing set down for 7 November 1995;

— Order No. 10 in the case of 1 December 1995 whereby additional Pleadings were requested.

Before the Arbitration Tribunal had even delivered, on 5 May 1997, the final Judgment [Award] holding that CUBIC had to pay the Islamic Republic of Iran US $2,808,519, CUBIC, by Summons of 15 January 1997, brought this action, * * * against the ICC, requesting the Regional Court of Paris:

— to rule that the contractual relationship between CUBIC and the ICC was not based on any cause or purpose, and to declare it void;

— in consequence to return to CUBIC the exchange value in French Francs on the date of the claim of the sum of US $185,000;

— also to Order the ICC to pay it the exchange value in French Francs on the date of the claim the sum of US $1,815,975, subject to correction, by way of damages and interest in indemnification of the tangible loss suffered by it;

alternatively,

— to rule that the ICC had not carried out the essential obligations that it allegedly had contracted with CUBIC, and that its failures to act were manifestly attributable to it;

— to rule that the contractual relationship between CUBIC and the ICC be terminated;

— to order the ICC to return the exchange value in French Francs on the date of the claim of the sum of US $185,000;

— also to Order the ICC to pay it the exchange value in French Francs on the date of the claim the sum of US $1,815,975, subject to correction, by way of damages and interest in indemnification of tangible loss suffered by it;

in the further alternative,

— to rule that the ICC has not carried out the essential obligations that it allegedly has contracted with CUBIC, and that its failures to act are manifestly attributable to it;

— to rule that the contractual relationship between CUBIC and the ICC be terminated;

— also to order the ICC to pay it the exchange value in French Francs on the date of the claim of the sum of US $2,000,975.56, subject to correction, by way of damages and interests in indemnification of tangible loss suffered by it;

in the yet further alternative,

— to rule that the ICC had not carried out the essential obligations that it allegedly * * * contracted with CUBIC, and that its failures to act were manifestly attributable to it;

— also to order the ICC to pay to it the exchange value in French Francs on the date of the claim of the sum of US $2,000,975.56, subject to correction, by way of damages and interest in indemnification of tangible loss thus caused;

— to prohibit the ICC from intervening in any manner whatsoever in the organization of the Arbitration between CUBIC and the Republic of Iran, upon pain of a penalty of 5,000 Francs per day of delay in complying with the said obligation to abstain with effect from the first day following the notification of the Judgment.

By Judgment of 21 May 1997, the Court of First Instance of Paris, after having found that French law was applicable to the action, dismissed the submission raised by the ICC to the effect that the action was * * * time [barred], held that it could not be said that the ICC had failed to comply with its obligations, and dismissed CUBIC's claims.

CUBIC has appealed against that decision. It repeats before the Court of Appeal the claims put forward at the first instance.

After having said that it has not brought any direct appeal for the overruling of the Arbitration Award of 5 May 1997 before any Swiss Court, and that it reserves the possibility of opposing any Order for the enforcement of the arbitration award in the United States, it argues:

(1) As to the formation of the Contract

— the complex system to which it had adhered did not impose any real obligation on the other contracting party, namely the ICC, such that the Contract lacked any purpose. In consequence, the obligation to which it had consented are not based on any cause;

— the Court reasoned as if it was not in the presence of a Contract that was absolutely void that could not be confirmed since it lacked a purpose and hence was not based on any cause, but was in the presence of a Contract that was voidable by reason of an error on the substance of the matter concerned;

— if one studies the Arbitration Rules of the ICC, which form the very * * * [essence] of the Contract, it results that the subject-matter of the obligations accepted by the ICC under Article 1108, 1126 at seq. of the Civil Code, essentially consists of services provided exclusively by the ICA;

— Moreover the obligations which would appear to bind the ICA under the Arbitration Rules are not legally binding on it such that the ICA escapes all control whatsoever as regards the implementation of its duties. The services promised in reality remain at the discretion of the ICC. Thus the person having an obligation has only contracted an obligation lacking any purpose, contrary to the provisions of Article 1126 of the Civil Code; or, which comes to the same thing, an obligation subject to a condition that the party bound is entirely free to implement or not, which is void under the provisions of Article 1174 of the said Code. [*Translator's note: According to Article 1126 of the French Civil Code, "Every Contract has as its purpose a thing that a party binds himself to give or that party binds himself to do or not to do." Article 1174 of the Code states: "Every obligation is void where it is contracted subject to the condition that the party bound is free to implement it or not".*]

(2) On the arbitration system

— The Arbitration Tribunal has adopted as its own the pernicious concept of institutional arbitration that inspires the Arbitration Rules of the ICC. For in fact the system contradicts a fundamental principle which requires the separation of the judicial functions allocated to the Arbitrators on the basis of an Arbitration Clause from the organizational tasks that an * * *[institution] such as the ICC can be instructed to carry out under a mere contract for the providing of services.

— This principle * * * [of] separation of functions is given effect in Article 1451 and 1455 of the New Code of Civil Procedure and it directly inspires French case law;

— Notwithstanding the provisions of Article 2(1) of the Arbitration Rules according to which "the Arbitration Court does not itself settle disputes", the Arbitration Rules in fact disregard the fundamental principle, which is a matter of public policy, according to which the judicial functions must be kept separate from the organizational tasks. For example the power given to the ICA to deliver decisions on requests for the rejection or replacement of arbitrators and the possibility of reviewing awards tend towards encroaching upon the role of the arbitrators;

— In any event, that power, which is exercised in secret, without any respect for the principle that all of the parties be heard, suffices, under Article 6 of the Civil Code, to render a contract which provides for such a power absolutely void, such that any such contract is, through that very fact, struck down as defective, forthwith upon its formation.

* * *

(3) Responsibility of the ICC

— Supposing that the Arbitration Agreement were not * * * void, the ICA of the ICC did not show any sense of urgency at all as to the duration of the Arbitration which went on for more than five years. It refused, upon * * * [reviewing] the nature of Order No. 6 in the case, to commence the procedure for the replacement of the arbitrators. It thus rendered itself contractually liable, and the failures of performance that have arisen constitute good grounds for ruling that the Contract be terminated and that the damages requested be granted under Article 1142 and 1184 of the Civil Code.

— The said damages can also be granted to CUBIC without its being necessary to declare the termination of the Contract at issue.

* * *

The International Chamber of Commerce Replies:

(1) On the admissibility of the action for a ruling that the contract is void

* * *

(2) The ICC system

* * *

The ICA does not carry on any judicial function. The matters that it adopts only consist of participating in the administering of the arbitration proceedings. Those measures are therefore not subject to any control as such for the said measures appertain to the implementation, in accordance with the Rules governing it, of the function allocated to it.

The Court of Arbitration, which does not itself settle disputes, (Article 2 of the Rules) and does not, therefore, have any judicial function, which is the case with most arbitration institutions, has thus been designed as an autonomous and independent entity such that it can fulfill the function that is allocated to it.

The decisions, of their nature, are not final decisions, and in so far as they contribute to the Arbitration Award to be delivered, the validity thereof can be examined upon the possible review of the award or of the performance of it by the State courts. The arbitration system established by the ICC does not run counter to the separation of judicial functions from organizational tasks and does not limit the procedural guarantee in favor of the parties that the Arbitrators shall be independent and impartial.

Decisions of the ICA delivered in respect of application for the rejection or replacement of Arbitrators fall within the establishing of the Arbitration Tribunal and consist of administrative tasks in respect of the arbitration. The only purpose of the review by the ICA of draft Arbitration Awards, under Article 21 of the Rules, is to ensure that the Award delivered will be the more effective.

* * *

The purpose of the contract made with the ICC is the providing of a set of Rules whereby an arbitration can be organized. The ICC is thereby required to produce all means available to it to have the said Rules respected by the parties and by the Arbitrators, without, however, meddling with the process of settling the dispute being arbitrated. Therefore the Rules impose strict obligations on the ICA. One could in principle, complain * * * that it lacks independence or lacks initiative contrary to the best interest of an arbitration.

The ICC is responsible for measures adopted by the ICA and would be liable for those measures if they were not adopted in conformity with the Rules. Therefore there is no question of an obligation lacking a purpose or of an obligation subject to the condition that the person bound is free to implement it or not.

CUBIC's observations on the duration of the arbitration are not relevant. The ICA duly extended the period of the arbitration every time that it came to an end without any reason why it should not have done so having been given.

Moreover it cannot properly be complained that the ICA refused to review Order No. 6 * * * which constituted an award subject to Article 21 of the Rules. The ICC has no capacity for substituting itself for the Arbitrators or for the courts so as to express its own view of decisions taken wholly independently.

The refusal to commence the procedure for the replacement of the Arbitrators was a mere administrative decision involved in the arbitration, provided for as such by the Rules and the intention of the parties.

* * *

JUDGMENT OF THE COURT

The right course is to note that in this Appeal the parties are in agreement in accepting that French law applies to this dispute.

On nullity by reason of lack of cause

* * *

On nullity by reason of illegal nature

* * *

Although it is true that the ICA must in all circumstances show itself to be particularly prudent as to act with fairness in the performance of its task, it has not been shown that it failed to meet that obligation. Moreover, it should be noted that the reason for submitting the draft Arbitration Award to the ICA is to bring about * * * [an efficient] Arbitration and to give effect to their desire that an Award capable of being implemented be delivered to them. This does not involve any interference in the task of the Arbitrator nor any alteration of his Award but consists primarily in the providing of drafting advice.

* * *

In these circumstances, the Court of First Instance correctly held that the Arbitration Agreement was valid.

On failure in the performance of the Contract

Any party to an agreement, even if it be an association responsible for organizing an arbitration, is liable if it fails to meet its contractual obligations. In the present case, no clause providing for exemption from liability is relied upon by the ICC. For the exemption clause which appears in its new Rules, drawn up after the making of the agreement here considered, supposing that clause to be valid is not applicable to this case.

CUBIC complains firstly that the ICC did not show any promptness at all in respect of the duration of the arbitration which extended over more than five years, secondly that it did not * * * [review] the nature of Order No. 6, and finally that it refused to commence the procedure for the replacement of the arbitrators.

As to the first complaint, it is not sufficient to render the ICC liable for CUBIC to regret that the arbitration expected to last six months, took more than five years. It is up to CUBIC to show that the ICA of the ICC, in granting, as the Rules provide, * * * any particular extension of time, failed to carry out the obligations contracted for by the ICC. Since CUBIC does not put forward a specific criticism on this matter, its complaint in this regard must be dismissed. Such is all the more the case in that it emerges from the documents disclosed in the case that the extensions of time granted, some of them at the request of CUBIC itself, were justified by the complexity of the case and by the desire that all arguments be heard.

As to the second complaint, on the manner [in] which Order No. 6 is to be classified, CUBIC does not state the text allegedly giving the ICA the power to classify that Order delivered by the Arbitrators. Here it is to be borne in mind that neither the provisions of Article 21 of the Arbitration Rules, nor the provisions of Article 17 of the Internal Rules, authorized the ICA to substitute its own judgment for the judgment of the Arbitration Tribunal. Therefore the ICA could only invite the Arbitrators, as it did on 19 June 1995, to * * *[review] whether the Order was to be considered as an award under the law applicable.

As regards the third complaint, it is not denied that the ICA refused to commence the procedure for replacing arbitrators. CUBIC has not shown what it was about that refusal of the ICA that was in breach of its obligations given that the common intention of the parties to the arbitration, in adhering to the statutes of the ICC, was that the ICA was to adopt its decision on such request, as it did on 17 May 1995, having regard exclusively to the written explanations of the parties to the arbitration, without any Appeal (Article 2.13) being available, and without the reasons for its decision being given.

On the tortuous liability of the ICC

* * *

ON THOSE GROUNDS

THE COURT

Confirms all of the provisions of the Judgment appealed against except the provision thereof dismissing the [time-bar]argument * * * raised by the ICC:

Overruling that Judgment in that regard,

Declares that the action brought by CUBIC to the effect that the contract should be held to be void for lack of cause and of purpose is inadmissible:

Adding thereto,

Orders CUBIC to pay to the International Chamber of Commerce (ICC) the sum of 20,000 Francs under Article 700 of the New Code of Civil procedure,

Orders Cubic to bear the costs of [the] appeal, which shall be obtainable in conformity with the provisions laid down in Article 699 of the New Code of Civil Procedure.

Questions and Comments

1. The Cubic Defense Systems (Cubic) case has many ramifications. The most pertinent facts are the following. On May 5, 1997 an ICC Tribunal issued an award which obliged Cubic to pay $2,808,510 with interest to Iran. (Iran demanded $5,403,651.) Within the three-member panel there were two dissenting opinions. Arbitrator Richard Mosk (nominated by Cubic) dissented from the award; arbitrator Seyed–Jamal Seifi (nominated by Iran) also dissented on the ground that Iran was entitled to more relief. The award was rendered by arbitrator Werner Wenger, the presiding arbitrator of the tribunal. (Read Article 25(1) of the ICC Rules and consider whether awards

can be rendered by one member only of a three-member tribunal. Article 25(1) of the present 1998 Rules is worded the same as Article 19 of the 1988 Rules. The latter rules applied to the Cubic arbitration.)

Cubic contested the award. It opposed (without success) recognition and enforcement in the U.S. (See the December 7, 1998 decision of the U.S. District Court, S.D. California, 29 F.Supp.2d 1168). Cubic also contested the proceedings and submitted arbitrator challenges **before** the award was rendered. In the case reproduced above, in January 1997, Cubic sued the International Chamber of Commerce seeking annulment of the contract between Cubic and the ICC.

2.   The decision of the Paris Court of Appeal reproduced above was confirmed by the French Cour de cassation on February 20, 2001. In his commentary on the decision of the Cour de cassation (Revue de l'arbitrage, 2001, 513), Thomas Clay states that the contract with the arbitral institution (*contrat d'organisation d'arbitrage*) is a contract between the two parties (claimant and respondent) on one side, and the arbitral institution on the other side. If one accepts this characterization, the question arises whether one of the parties on one side of the contract can sue the other contracting party (the arbitral institution)?

3.   Suppose the *contrat d'organisation d'arbitrage* were annulled. What would be the consequences? Would (should) such an annulment mean that the award rendered in the meantime by the tribunal organized by the institution must be considered null and void? Consider this issue from the opposite angle. Suppose the parties do not pay the institution the sum owed by the *contrat d'organisation d'arbitrage*. Could the institution seek termination of the contract, and if the contract were terminated, would this entail nullity of the award? If not, why not?

4.   Cubic criticized the ICC arbitration system, stating:

"The Arbitration Tribunal adopted as its own the pernicious system of institutional arbitration that inspires the Arbitration Rules of the ICC. For in fact the system contradicts a fundamental principle which requires the separation of the judicial functions allocated to the Arbitrators on the basis of an Arbitration Clause from the organisational tasks that an * * * [institution] such as the ICC can be instructed to carry out under a * * * contract for the providing of services."

Review Article 27 of the ICC Rules. The basic idea is simple: the judicial (decision-making) function is exercised by the arbitrators, while the Court of Arbitration (in spite of its name) is a mere administrative entity. Are the powers bestowed on the Court by Article 27 compatible with this basic idea?

5.   Cubic argued further that "the power given to the ICA to deliver decisions on requests for the rejection and replacement of arbitrators" also blurs the line between judicial and organizational functions. Do you agree?

6.   Cubic asserted that the established system does not "impose any real obligation on the other contracting party, namely the ICC". In other words, it contended that the ICC's obligations carry no sanctions, and cannot be enforced. The Court of Appeal mentions in this context the "exemption clause" that was adopted in Article 34 of the 1998 Rules. The Court of Appeal stresses that the exemption clause of the new Rules was "drawn up

after the making of the agreement here considered", and points out that the ICC did not rely on any exemption clause. Suppose Article 34 of the 1998 Rules had been applicable, and the ICC had relied on it; would this reinforce or weaken Cubic's argument?

7. Cubic also objected to inordinate delays. In his comment in the *Revue de l'arbitrage,* Clay states:

"Everybody knows that in practice the extension of deadlines is often for the benefit of the arbitrators rather than for the benefit of the parties, and arbitration centers should nevertheless remember that arbitration is made for the parties rather than for the arbitrators."

Even if Cubic were right, such a finding would probably not result in nullity, but would merely show improper performance of the *contrat d'organisation d'arbitrage.* What should be the remedy?

8. Regarding the alleged failure of the ICC to perform its part of the bargain because the proceedings were inordinately delayed, the Court of Appeal states that an expression of "regret" that arbitration lasted much longer than expected is not sufficient: "It is up to CUBIC to show that the ICA of the ICC, in granting, as the Rules provide, * * * any particular extension of time, failed to carry out the obligation contracted for by the ICC." How can this be demonstrated?

9. Staying with the issue of delay, the *Tribunal de grande instance* found that

"[T]he signature of the * * * [terms of reference] and the implementation of this arbitration were delayed, not by the effect of a failure imputable to the ICA, but by reason of difficulties provoked by IRAN and CUBIC during designation of the arbitrators, demands for extension of the period granted to pronounce upon this designation or the replacement of chosen arbitrators..."

Assuming delays were caused by party requests and behavior, does this mean that the ICC—whose tasks are to organize and administer–cannot be liable?

III.1.h. Can the Arbitrators Abandon Their Function? (Truncated Tribunals)

Stephen M. Schwebel, THE VALIDITY OF
AN ARBITRAL AWARD RENDERED
BY A TRUNCATED TRIBUNAL

ICC Int'l Ct. Arb'n Bull. (November 1995)*

* * *

II—The Milutinovic Case

In *Ivan Milutinovic PIM* v. *Deutsche Babcock AG,* an arbitration held under the Rules of the International Chamber of Commerce, the

* *The ICC International Court of Arbitration Bulletin.* Vol. 6/No. 2CISSN 1017–284X. Published in its official English version by the International Chamber of Commerce. Copyright 8 1995—ICC International Court of Arbitration. Available from: ICC Publishing SA, 38 cours Albert 1er, 75008 Paris, France. (*www.iccbooks.com*) Reprinted with permission from ICC.

three-man Tribunal was composed of Professor Eugene Bucher, chairman, and Professors Vladimir Jovanovic and Karl–Heinz Böckstiegel, arbitrators.[14] It concerned a monetary dispute between members of a construction consortium which had contracted to build a power station in Homs, Libya. The Consortium Agreement provided that the place of the arbitration would be Zurich. The Terms of Reference agreed upon by the parties recorded that the Rules of the ICC Court of Arbitration and the Code of Civil Procedure of the Canton of Zurich governed the procedure of the arbitration. It was further provided that the Tribunal might deviate from the non-mandatory provisions of the Zurich Code.

The parties exchanged three sets of written briefs and additional written submissions. Two sessions of oral hearings were held at which witnesses were examined. At the latter set of hearings, at the end of the examination of witnesses, claimant's counsel called for the re-examination of some witnesses and the hearing of additional witnesses, which defendant's counsel opposed. The Arbitral Tribunal, after *"great internal deliberation ... by majority and against the explicit opposition of the arbitrator proposed by claimant, took the decision to reject claimant's request and not to allow additional evidence to be presented ..."*[15] The next day, upon the chairman's communication of this decision to the parties, Professor Jovanovic announced his resignation because *"he disagreed with the decision of the Arbitral Tribunal."*[16] Claimant's counsel thereupon refused to present its final pleadings.

Claimant's counsel then moved in the ICC Court of Arbitration to replace Chairman Bucher and Professor Böckstiegel. The ICC Court of Arbitration, by a decision of January 29, 1987, rejected the challenge of Professors Bucher and Böckstiegel and *"refused to accept the resignation of Mr. Jovanovic not failing to underscore that in the absence of any justification of his withdrawal, Mr. Jovanovic was obliged to continue to act as arbitrator."*[17] The chairman then invited the co-arbitrators to an internal meeting of the Tribunal, which Professor Jovanovic did not attend; rather, he confirmed his resignation. A Partial Award in the arbitration was agreed upon in his absence by Professors Bucher and Böckstiegel, which Professor Jovanovic was invited to sign, and which was submitted to the ICC Court of Arbitration pursuant to its Rules and accepted by it.

14. *Ivan Milutinovic PIM* v. *Deutsche Babcock AG*, International Chamber of Commerce (ICC) No. 5017, Partial Award of November 8, 1987. I wish to thank the Secretary–General of the Court of International Arbitration of the ICC, Eric Schwartz, for his assistance in securing the consent of the parties to the publication of the Award in this paper, and for providing the texts of the judgements of Swiss courts discussed below.

15. Partial Award typescript provided by the ICC, p. 13.

16. *Ibid.*

17. *Ibid.*

The Partial Award records that the Tribunal earlier had decided that the parties were to have a last and final possibility to present requests for the taking of evidence and that, upon the hearing of agreed additional witnesses, the final pleadings would be made. All witnesses accordingly proposed at that time by the claimant were admitted. *"The request for additional evidence presented by claimant is belated and the tardiness is not excused ... Claimant did not indicate which facts ... should be evidenced by the newly proposed witnesses ..."*[18] The claimant had earlier opposed additional examination of defendant's witnesses while proposing the examination of no further witnesses called by it. *"Given the clear decision of the Arbitral Tribunal and its approval by the parties ... the Arbitral Tribunal could not accept claimant's request presented at the end of the taking of evidence ..."*[19] The Award then continues:

> *"The present award can be rendered notwithstanding the declaration of Professor Jovanovic to 'resign' as arbitrator and notwithstanding his not participating at the arbitrators' meeting of February 7, 1987. Both under the Zurich procedural law and the ICC rules for arbitration the withdrawal of Professor Jovanovic, not justified by any legitimate and lawful cause, is ineffective and therefore the present Arbitral Tribunal continues to be correctly constituted. It is settled under Zurich procedural law that the arbitrator cannot withdraw at his free will ..."*

> *"In accordance with the given situation under Zurich law, the ICC Court of Arbitration on January 29, 1987, decided 'not to accept the resignation tendered by the co-arbitrator, Professor V. Jovanovic on November 12th, 1986' and, after admonition of Professor Jovanovic, expressed the confidence 'that the arbitral tribunal as it is presently constituted will conclude its task in the instant case and that the arbitral tribunal will fully accept the decision rendered by the ICC Court of Arbitration.'*

> *"The determination of the chairman and of one co-arbitrator to take a decision in the absence of the other co-arbitrator seems to be justified by the given circumstances and is in accordance with the provisions of ZPO/ZH [Zurich Code of Civil Procedure], even if the latter do not include an explicit rule with respect to the present situation. Not only a decision by majority is valid, but § 254 ZPO makes clear that a refusal of a dissenting arbitrator to sign the award cannot question the validity of the award signed by the majority only; the signing 'durch deren Mehrheit unter Anmerkung der Weigerung der Minderheit' is explicitly admitted. If a refusal of an arbitrator to sign does not exclude the validity of the award, the result cannot be different if the minority-arbitrator does refuse to participate in the internal deliberations until their end. The rule that the finding of the final award must be performed with the partic-*

---

18. *Ibid.*, p. 16.   **19.** *Ibid.*, p. 18.

ipation of all arbitrators ... intends to deal with different problems: An arbitrator deceased before the decision of the Arbitral Tribunal must be replaced by a successor and likewise an arbitrator who by an admissible and therefore valid withdrawal has ceased to hold office; the majority of an arbitral tribunal is not allowed to exclude a minority from the further deliberations; an arbitral tribunal is not allowed to depart from oral deliberations inter praesentes *without the consent of every member ... These (and other) problems justify the provision of § 254 cited above which stipulates positive obligations with respect to the question how to proceed in finding the award but does not exclude its validity if one arbitrator refuses to observe these obligations by not participating in the final stage of deliberations. The latter situation is in all relevant respects identical to that of an arbitrator refusing to sign. A position concurring with this conclusion has been taken by the Zurich authorities ... ('The renunciation to an oral [internal] deliberation [of the arbitral tribunal] is furthermore justified if an arbitrator tries to delay or to prevent the taking of the final decision by abusive shirking from the oral deliberation, a risk not existing with ordinary courts'.) This* obiter dictum *precisely foresees the circumstances realized in the present arbitration. The decision of the Swiss Federal Tribunal (SFT) of October 3, 1985 ... setting aside an arbitral award does not provide an argument against the position exposed above, as all relevant facts are different: In the case decided by the SFT the decision of the arbitrators was not taken during oral deliberations of the arbitrators but by exchange of writings, and the not-signing arbitrator never gave his consent to this way of procedure (even a majority decision to that end does not seem to exist). By way of contrast in the present case the decision of the arbitral tribunal was taken during oral deliberations to which all arbitrators (including Professor Jovanovic) were invited. Professor Jovanovic had no objective cause preventing him from participating in the last part of these oral deliberations which took place at the meeting on February 7. The SFT decision, as it does not refer to an arbitrator refusing without justification to participate in internal oral deliberations, is therefore no precedent to the present case. Nevertheless, it may be added that it is based on the 'Concordat,' the Swiss intercantonal arbitration convention, while the present arbitral proceedings are governed by the Zurich law of Civil Procedure. Furthermore and consequently, the present decision applying, it is not submitted to the control of the SFT if not under the general aspect of the Swiss Federal Constitution (arbitrariness; art. 4).*

"Again it must be said that under the rules of the Zurich ZPO as well as under the rules of the ICC, Professor Jovanovic is considered to be an arbitrator, even if refusing to effectively cooperate ... It is correct that both under the Zurich ZPO (§ 254) and the ICC rules (art. 2.8) Professor Jovanovic could be removed and replaced. However, no procedure for his removal had even been started before the *final decision of the arbitral tribunal on this partial award, much less has a refusal taken effect. Both parties refrained from presenting such a request, either before the competent authorities in Zurich or the ICC Court of Arbitration. The other members of the Arbitral Tribunal cannot recognize a duty to present such request ex officio, if the parties choose to renounce to request Professor Jovanovic's removal and replacement. Claimant, who presented a request for removal of the other two arbitrators, by not including Professor Jovanovic in the request for removal, evidences his willingness to accept the given situation, i.e., the arbitrator proposed by claimant not participating in the further proceedings; claimant has no title to reproach the arbitrators for not presenting a request for Professor Jovanovic's removal, as he did not himself present such a request. The rendering of the present award is the consequence of the Arbitral Tribunal not doing so.*

"Obviously, the possibility to continue the proceedings without all arbitrators cooperating is strictly limited. Taking of evidence or accepting oral pleadings in the absence of an arbitrator would seem to be, except perhaps in exceptional circumstances, generally inadmissible. But this issue is not at stake here, since in the present case Professor Jovanovic declared his intention to resign after the conclusion of the taking of evidence only. The final pleadings were not presented orally but in writing ... Professor Jovanovic therefore was not absent in any of the tribunal's activities requiring his presence. He also participated in all internal deliberations up to the moment of his declaration on October 28, 1986. Obviously, the internal deliberations in which he was involved also concerned the merits of the case. This is especially true for the deliberations on the evening of October 27, 1986, concerning the taking of additional evidence.

"A decision of the Arbitral Tribunal to the contrary, i.e., to present a request for the removal of Professor Jovanovic (either in Zurich or in Paris) and to re-start the proceedings with the eventual successor of Professor Jovanovic, would be contrary to the requirements of orderly and correct arbitration, providing to an arbitrator (or a party influencing him) the means to sabotage the correct coming to an end of an arbitral procedure and to extort from the tribunal and the opposed party the reopening of the proceedings. Such a possibility would neglect the demands of the solution of international commercial disputes and question the credibility of the arbitration both as offered by ICC and as performed in Zurich or Switzerland. The present Arbitral Tribunal is even less allowed to depart from a speedy settling of the main issue of the present arbitration by rendering an award (not only requested by defendant, but, up to and including the telex of October 13, 1986, also by claimant), as it is a view more and more accepted that in international commercial arbitration the possibility of delaying tactics is a serious concern and the elimination of these effects a primary task of all involved ...

"By a possible request of a party, the present award can be subject to the annulment procedure provided by the Zurich Code of Civil Procedure; the Obergericht of the Canton of Zurich ... is competent. In the present context it may be pointed out that an eventual annulment of the present award by the Zurich Obergericht would neither stop the competence of the arbitral tribunal as installed by the ICC nor terminate the effectiveness of the arbitration clause. § 256 ZPO/ZH implicitly presupposes that the arbitral tribunal, whose award was set aside, has again to decide on the issue. Should the same arbitral tribunal not be in the position to act, under said rule a new arbitral tribunal would have to be constituted in conformity with the arbitration clause and would be competent to render an award."[20]

I have quoted from the Partial Award in the *Milutinovic* case at such length because it is the fullest analysis of the authority of a truncated tribunal known to have been made in an international commercial arbitral award; because of the cogency of that analysis; because of the distinction of the arbitrators—Professors Bucher and Böckstiegel—who are the authors of the Award; and because the Award hitherto has not been published. I agree with the Tribunal that a contrary decision would have been incompatible with *"the requirements of orderly and correct arbitration, providing an arbitrator (or a party influencing him) with the means to sabotage the correct coming to an end of an arbitral procedure and to extort from the tribunal and the opposing party the reopening of the proceedings. Such a possibility would neglect the demands of the solution of international commercial disputes and question the credibility of the arbitration both as offered by the ICC and as performed in Zurich or Switzerland."*[21]

Prior to the rendering of the Partial Award which has been so substantially quoted, the plaintiff in the proceedings, Milutinovic, brought an action before the Administrative Commission of the Supreme Court of the Canton of Zurich requesting that the Tribunal accept Professor Jovanovic's withdrawal as legally operative and maintaining that continuation of proceedings by two arbitrators gave rise to presumption of prejudice on their part. The Administrative Commission rejected the challenge, holding that continuation of the arbitral proceedings by the two arbitrators in the unusual situation that had arisen was justifiable and did not warrant a presumption of bias.[22]

On appeal to the Court of Cassation of the Canton of Zurich, the foregoing judgement was reversed. It was held that, while the ICC Rules governed the proceedings of the Arbitral Tribunal, they did not contemplate unilateral resignation of an arbitrator. Under the Zurich Code of Civil Procedure, no party in an arbitration could be accorded a preferen-

20. *Ibid.*, pp. 20–26.

21. *Ibid.*, p. 25.

22. *Obergericht des Kantons Zürich, Verwaltungskommission, Beschluss vom 2. Juni 1987, Verw.-Komm. Nr. 431/87.* I wish to thank the Librarian of the International Court of Justice, Arthur Eyffinger for providing a translation from the German of this judgement as well as for the customary support of the Court's Library.

tial position. Equality of the parties was the essential, imperative principle. In accordance with that principle, it was absolutely prohibited that a three-member arbitral tribunal could, in the person of its chairman and one member, deliberate and take a decision which ought to have been taken collegially. While the refusal of an arbitrator to sign the award is of no legal consequence, this in no way implies that a party-appointed arbitrator and the chairman may deliberate in the absence of another legally designated arbitrator and reach a decision that must be taken collectively. Professors Bucher and Böckstiegel could have requested dismissal of Professor Jovanovic on the ground of his refusal to fulfil his functions; that would have been the lawful procedure to have been followed in this case. Whether Professor Jovanovic's resignation was right or wrong is irrelevant. Violation of the principle of non-discrimination between the parties and according one party preferential treatment was not only unlawful, it seriously compromised confidence in the tribunal, creating as it did a presumption of partiality. Accordingly, the decision of the Administrative Commission was annulled and the case was remanded to the Administrative Commission.[23] The Commission, finding that Professors Bucher and Böckstiegel did in fact discuss and draw up the Partial Award without the participation of Professor Jovanovic, and being bound by the foregoing judgement of the Cantonal Supreme Court, required Professors Bucher and Böckstiegel to retire from the arbitration.[24] Subsequently, the Court of Cassation declined to consider annulment of that decision on the ground that the application to annul was not filed within ten days of the decision's service.[25]

On appeal to the Swiss Federal Tribunal it was held, by a judgement of December 20, 1989, that the criticized actions of Professors Bucher and Böckstiegel were insufficient in the themselves to create an appearance of bias. Accordingly, the judgement of the Administrative Commission divesting Professors Bucher and Böckstiegel of their positions as arbitrators in the case was vacated.[26] Thus the Administrative Commission of the Zurich Court of Appeals definitely dismissed the challenge to the arbitral status of Professors Bucher and Böckstiegel.[27]

However, Milutinovic also submitted a request to the Court of Appeals of the Canton of Zurich for nullification of the Partial Award, arguing that it violated the Code of Civil Procedure of Zurich as well as

23. *Das Kassationsgericht des Kantons Zürich, 10. Februar 1988, Kass.-Nr. 219/87.* I have drawn my rendering of this case from the French translation provided by the ICC, and from an English translation of the French provided by the Registry of the Court, for which I thank Mr. E. Didier and his colleagues.

24. Appeal Court of the Canton of Zürich, Administrative Commission, Postal Decision of 25 April 1968, VK No. 183/1988, English translation provided by the ICC.

25. *Das Kassationsgericht des Kantons Zürich, 9. Dezember 1988, Kass–Nr. 207/88.*

I have relied on the French translation provided by the ICC, and an English translation of the French provided by the Registry of the Court.

26. *Urteil des Schweizerischen Bundesgerichts, 20. Dezember 1989. 4P.110/1988/bm.* I have relied on the French translation provided by the ICC, and an English translation from the French provided by the Registry of the Court.

27. By decision of 19 May 1990, as recounted in the judgement of the Swiss Federal Tribunal of 30 April 1991 discussed below.

Article 6 of the European Convention on Human Rights. The Court of Appeals dismissed the nullification request by decision of July 4, 1990. Milutinovic's argument that, irrespective of whether Professor Jovanovic had serious reasons justifying his withdrawal, after his withdrawal a properly constituted tribunal no longer existed, was unsubstantiated. An arbitrator is obliged to serve until the conclusion of the arbitral proceedings, and withdrawal is excluded in the absence of cause. Professor Jovanic had justified his resignation solely by reason of the fact that the two other arbitrators had declined to admit further testimony at that stage of the proceedings. But the fact that the arbitrators differed in that regard manifestly did not furnish a serious reason justifying withdrawal of the outvoted arbitrator. Accordingly, his resignation did not vacate the functions of Professor Jovanovic. Thus the tribunal could be treated as properly composed. In the circumstances, there was no transgression of Articles 4 and 58 of the Swiss Federal Constitution or Article 6 of the European Convention on Human Rights. It was uncontested that Professor Jovanovic had, without providing justification, failed to take up an invitation to a session of the Tribunal. It was equally uncontested that he had received a draft of the Partial Award but did not sign it. His refusal to take part in the Tribunal's deliberations may be equated with a refusal to sign. It is true that by the terms of Article 254 of the Code of Civil Procedure, an award must be given with the participation of all the arbitrators. That does not mean that all arbitrators must actually meet; a written exchange may suffice, provided that no arbitrator is deprived of the opportunity to participate in the hearing. The fact that Professor Jovanovic justified his refusal to take part solely as he did is uncontested. That refusal was abusive; that it lacked cause, moreover, was made clear to him by the ICC. Milutinovic had chosen to identify itself with that abuse by not requesting the removal of its delinquent arbitrator. If it has therefore been "penalized", it can only blame itself. In any event, the remaining arbitrators and the other party may not be held to have acted irregularly. There is no ground in the circumstances for maintaining that the principle of the equality of the parties has been impinged upon by the remaining arbitrators rendering an award, when Milutinovic alone is responsible for any lack of opportunity to participate.[28]

Finally, after this multiplicity of conflicting judgements, the Swiss Federal Tribunal set aside the foregoing judgement of the Zurich Court of Appeals and upheld the nullification appeal submitted by Milutinovic. The guarantees of the Federal Constitution and of the European Convention on Human Rights, it held, embrace not only state courts but private arbitral tribunals. They must assure the independent administration of justice. This applies, in particular, to the right to a proper composition of the tribunal. Under the governing Code of Civil Procedure of the Canton of Zurich, the final award must be made with the

---

28. *Cour d'Appel du Canton de Zurich, Arrêt rendu le 4 juillet 1990, ZN87439U/IIIe Chambre Civile.* I have drawn my rendering from the French text provided by the ICC, and from a translation from the original German into English by Maurizio Brunetti of the staff of the Iran–United States Claims Tribunal.

participation of all arbitrators. That is a fundamental principle of procedure. The case was to be distinguished from the practice cited by the Court of Appeals, because here a member of the tribunal had resigned from his function and refused to participate further in the proceedings; therefore he did not simply withdraw from an oral deliberation with an intent to delay the proceedings. It was not a question of an arbitrator simply refusing to sign the decision; such a case would have to be considered differently. Whether an arbitrator may withdraw at any time is an open question. If it is accepted that an arbitrator may withdraw only for cause, then the question immediately arises as to who must decide whether a withdrawal is legitimate. That the remaining arbitrators may decide is out of the question. The only proper solution appears to be referral of this decision to the competence of a regular judge. The judge must either establish that the mandate to arbitrate is terminated or, if there are no substantial reasons justifying withdrawal, require the withdrawing arbitrator to continue to participate. An unjustified withdrawal does not simply lead to continuation of the proceedings in the absence of the withdrawing arbitrator and without appointing a new one. This could be argued only if the arbitration agreement so provides. Absent such a provision, the arbitral tribunal will again be properly composed either when the withdrawing arbitrator, if need be, pursuant to court order—reconsiders his withdrawal or when he has been replaced. The result of illegitimate withdrawal is limited to the arbitrator's possible liability for damages and disciplinary measures. If the remaining members of the arbitral tribunal continue with the proceedings despite the withdrawal of an arbitrator, without having been authorized to so do by the parties, then the arbitral tribunal is not properly composed. The contrary view expressed by the Court of Appeals is inconsistent with the fundamental right of the parties to a proper composition of the tribunal and thus violates both Article 58 of the Federal Constitution and Article 6 of the European Convention on Human Rights. The parties referred the dispute to an arbitral tribunal consisting of three arbitrators; the Partial Award was rendered by two arbitrators only. The Code of Civil Procedure of the Canton of Zurich was violated and the Court of Appeals acted arbitrarily when it failed to nullify the Partial Award on this ground as well.[29]

The ultimate consequence has been that the Partial Award rendered by the truncated tribunal composed of Professors Bucher and Böckstiegel was effectively quashed. In the circumstances, a new arbitral tribunal has been established under ICC auspices which, it is understood, is as of this writing in the course of adjudicating the dispute-which initially was brought to arbitration as long ago as 1984.

The result is deplorable, and not only because it has given rise to an arbitral process extending more than ten years. The judgement of the

---

29. Swiss Federal Tribunal, First Civil Section, 30 April 1991, BGE 117 la 166. I wish to thank Mr. Brunetti for his translation of the Tribunal's judgement from German into English, on which I have drawn, and for his analysis of the Tribunal's judgement.

Swiss Federal Tribunal is inconsonant with the general principle of law that a party may not invoke its own wrong (or a wrong that it adopts) to deprive another party of its rights. It runs counter to the predominant practice of international arbitration. It places the Swiss Federal Tribunal in conflict with the Court of Arbitration of the International Chamber of Commerce: whereas the ICC, by refusing to accept the purported resignation of Professor Jovanovic or the challenge to the status of the remaining arbitrators, and by approving their Partial Award, in authoritative interpretation of its own Rules authorized the truncated arbitral tribunal to proceed and ratified its holding when it did proceed, the Swiss Federal Tribunal held that, despite those ICC positions—to which it hardly refers, still less defers—the Award was null. If, indeed, the judgement of the Swiss Federal Tribunal were today still the law of Switzerland, there might be reason to question—as did the arbitral tribunal—the suitability of the Canton of Zurich, and Switzerland itself, as optimal sites for the pursuit of international commercial arbitration. The practical effect of the judgement conduces to obstruction if not subversion of the international arbitral process.

One hesitates to gainsay holdings of the Swiss Federal Tribunal about the Constitution of Switzerland and Swiss law. Being uninformed about the exegesis of the Swiss Constitution, little more will be said than that, on its face, the provision of the Constitution invoked by the Swiss Federal Tribunal does not appear to be dispositive.[30] Article 58 provides:

> *"No one may be deprived of his constitutional judge; therefore no exceptional courts of law may be set up." ("Nul ne peu être distrait de son juge naturel. En conséquence, il ne pourra être établi de tribunaux extraordinaires.")*[31]

Presumably the Swiss Federal Tribunal invoked Article 58 because it concluded that Professor Jovanovic's "resignation" deprived Milutinovic of its constitutional judge; if so, the question arises whether the deprivation was not self-induced or adopted (as the Zurich Court of Appeals held that it was). Or perhaps the Swiss Federal Tribunal, in passing upon lower court judgements, reasoned that the failure of Professors Bucher and Böckstiegel, or the ICC, to move to replace Professor Jovanovic (a motion which it might be thought rather rested with Milutinovic) deprived Milutinovic of its constitutional judge; if so, that is a singular

---

30. Albert P. Blaustein & Gisbert H. Flanz, eds., *Constitutions of the Countries of the World* (1982), "Switzerland", p. 4, Articles 4 and 58.

Article 4 provides:

"All Swiss citizens are equal before the law. In Switzerland, there shall be no subject, nor privileges of place, birth, person or family."

Any pertinence of Article 4—which the Swiss Federal Tribunal did not expressly invoke—to arbitral proceedings between two foreign parties is unclear. It is under-

stood that Swiss jurisprudence derives from Article 4 a prohibition of arbitrary judicial action but that hardly answers the question of whether a lower court acted arbitrarily in sustaining the decision of the arbitral tribunal in the *Milutinovic case*. It may be that what the Swiss Federal Tribunal meant was that the failure of lower courts to apply mandatory provisions of the Zurich Code was arbitrary and hence a violation of Article 4.

31. *Ibid.*, pp. 50–51.

interpretation of the facts. It may be observed that the Constitutional holdings of the Swiss Federal Tribunal were not shared by some other Swiss courts.

In any event, if the reliance of the Swiss Federal Tribunal on Article 6 of the European Convention of Human Rights is an indicator of the strength of its reasoning, its position is strikingly unpersuasive. Only paragraph 1 of Article 6 concerns civil suits and it provides:

> "*In the determination of his civil rights and obligations ... everyone is entitled to a fair and public hearing within a reasonable time by an independent and impartial tribunal established by law.*"[32]

Assuming, *arguendo*, that this provision embraces *in camera* arbitral proceedings, the implicit reasoning of the Swiss Federal Tribunal appears to be that the proceedings of the truncated arbitral tribunal in the *Milutinovic* case could not have been "fair", that the tribunal could not have been "independent and impartial" by reason of the fact that one party-appointed arbitrator absented himself during some of the tribunal's deliberations and in the preparation of the Award. It is not easy to reconcile the sense of such a judgement of the Swiss Federal Tribunal with its own judgement of December 20, 1989, rejecting the challenge to Professors Bucher and Böckstiegel.

The implication of any such holding is worrisome, for it strikes against a fundamental assumption of international commercial arbitration, namely, that all members of the tribunal are independent, whether or not they are party-appointed. If Professor Jovanovic acted independently, why should it be assumed that his absence from the tribunal cut against the interests of Milutinovic? Why should it be assumed that the tribunal was any less fair, independent and impartial in the absence of Professor Jovanovic than in his presence? The ICC and Zurich Court of Appeal made no such assumption. They rather appear to have acted on the presumption that, if party-appointed arbitrators are to act not as advocates but arbitrators, they are independent; their independence and impartiality is not prejudiced by the walkout of one of them; and, in circumstances in which the tribunal had had the benefit of extensive written pleadings and oral argument, heard the witnesses agreed upon, and embarked upon its deliberations, it had every capacity to render a fair and impartial award. There is nothing in the Partial Award actually rendered which suggests otherwise.

It should be noted that the tribunal was initially constituted in precise conformity with the will of the parties and the ICC Rules. It was the walkout of one party-appointed arbitrator at an advanced stage of the proceedings which prejudiced not the constitution but the continued effective composition of the tribunal. The distinction, as the International Court of Justice has observed, is fundamental.[33] It follows that an

---

32. European Convention on Human Rights, reproduced in Ian Brownlie, *Basic Documents on Human Rights* (1992), pp. 326, 329.

33. See *Interpretation of Peace Treaties with Bulgaria, Hungary and Romania (Sec-*

unjustified withdrawal should not be treated as vitiating the authority of a tribunal which initially was duly constituted.

The various judgements of Swiss courts in the *Milutinovic* case were based on provisions of law, some of which have been superseded by the arbitral provisions of the Swiss Private International Act of December 18, 1987. Article 179 of that Act provides:

> *"(1) The arbitrators shall be appointed, removed or replaced in accordance with the agreement of the parties.*
>
> *"(2) In the absence of such an agreement, it shall be possible for applications to be brought before the seat of the arbitral tribunal; the court shall apply the provisions of cantonal law regarding the appointment, removal or replacement of arbitrators."*

Article 189 provides:

> *"(1) The arbitral award shall be rendered in accordance with the procedure and in the form agreed upon by the parties."*[34]

A leading Swiss arbitrator and counsel, Dr. Marc Blessing, has been reported to have maintained that, in view of the latter provision, a Swiss court applying current law would not annul an award rendered in the circumstances of the *Milutinovic* case.[35] The parties are free to agree upon the procedure governing the arbitration. It consequently may be concluded that, if they have provided for the governance of ICC procedures, ICC Rules and the ICC's interpretation of those Rules should be dispositive.[36]

It is unclear why such reasoning was not applied by the Swiss Federal Tribunal in the *Milutinovic* case even taking the governing Swiss law as it then was. The Swiss Federal Tribunal found that it was obliged to apply the Zurich Code of Civil Procedure, which required that all the arbitrators must participate in all the deliberations and decisions of the arbitral tribunal (as equally did Article 31 of the Intercantonal Arbitration Convention of 1969, the "Concordat", which was not applicable in this case.) But that provision could have been read as satisfied by offering the absent arbitrator the opportunity to participate in the deliberations and in the adoption of the decision, offers in fact made in

---

ond Phase), *I.C.J. Reports 1950*, pp. 221, 229.

34. International Council on Commercial Arbitration, *International Handbook on Commercial Arbitration*, general eds., Albert Jan van den Berg and Pieter Sanders. Vol. III. "Switzerland", by Robert Briner, Annex II (containing a translation of the Act into English), at pp. 2, 4.

35. See, *International Council for Commercial Arbitration*, Congress Series No. 5, "*Preventing delay and disruption of arbitration ...*", general ed. Albert Jan van den Berg (1991), at p. 273.

36. See also to this effect Briner in the work cited in footnote 34, who notes that, under the Act now in force, "*the Swiss judge at the seat of the arbitral tribunal is competent to make the decision regarding a challenge unless the parties have agreed on any specific applicable rules. If the parties have agreed that, e.g., the Rules of the ICC Court of International Arbitration ... are to apply, the decision of the ICC Court ... is final (Art. 180(3) Act)*". (At p. 14) See also Judge Briner's analysis of the Act, and the previously applicable Concordat, on points pertinent to this paper, at pp. 15, 17, 22, 29, 30, 31, 32, 33, 34, 35.

the *Milutinovic* case; or by treating the parties as having adopted the governing ICC Rule as authoritatively interpreted by the ICC;[37] or on other grounds on which the Zurich Court of Appeals relied, including abusive conduct by Professor Jovanovic and the adoption of that conduct by Milutinovic. In any event, as will be shown shortly, the rules of arbitral institutions in addition to the ICC may be interpreted or applied to sustain the authority of a truncated arbitral tribunal to act when a member arbitrarily withdraws.

Questions and Comments

1. The fortunate thing about the *Milutinovic* case is that such difficulties occur rarely.

One of the authors of this book had an opportunity to discuss this case with Professor Jovanovic. He explained that during presentation of evidence new light was shed on the case, which suggested a different outcome, favorable to the Yugoslav side. To substantiate this new perspective it was necessary to recall some witnesses, and to review new evidence. Professor Jovanovic was quite passionate in presenting his views. He thought that the other arbitrators simply sacrificed truth for the sake of simplicity. He resigned in belief that the road towards truth was blocked. His fellow arbitrators and the ICC Court of Arbitration thought differently.

Should the validity of the award be contingent on whether Professor Jovanovic did or did not have a sound (or at least plausible) reason to resign?

If this is relevant, who then decides on the appropriateness of the resignation?

(In reflecting on these questions you need not restrict yourself to the given procedural setting: ICC Rules plus Zurich Code of Civil Procedure.)

2. If you accept the reasoning of Judge Schwebel and of the ICC Court of Arbitration, would you allow the two remaining arbitrators to continue after an unjustified resignation of the third arbitrator at any point in the proceedings?

3. The Swiss Federal Tribunal states that an unjustified withdrawal does not lead to continuation of the arbitral proceedings in the absence of the withdrawing arbitrator, unless the arbitration agreement so provides. One may assume that if the parties agree to submit their dispute to an institutional tribunal, they also accept the rules of the institution selected. The 1998 ICC Rules Article 12(1) states: "An arbitrator shall be replaced upon his death, upon the acceptance by the Court of the arbitrator's resignation, upon acceptance by the Court of a challenge or upon the request of all the parties."

Does this provision help you in deciding whether two remaining arbitrators can continue when the Court does not accept the third arbitrator's resignation (but this arbitrator nevertheless refuses to perform his functions)?

37. The problem with this approach is that the pertinent provisions of the Zurich Code were mandatory and were held to be so.

4.   Suppose the remaining two arbitrators continue but are unable to agree on an award. What result?

5.   Professor Jovanovic was an arbitrator appointed by one of the parties. Would the case be different if the third neutral arbitrator, the chairman of the panel, were to resign?

6.   The Swiss Federal Tribunal was clearly guided by considerations of due process, but it did not articulate a rule that would prevent abuses. Suppose a court finds that the resignation is unjustified and invites the arbitrator to continue, but the arbitrator refuses to do so. What result? Does the reasoning of the Federal Tribunal allow two arbitrators to continue in such circumstances?

7.   Suppose a new arbitrator is nominated and he also resigns after hearing the evidence and before the closing arguments of the parties. Clearly, there should be some remedy. What would it be?

Would you deprive the party of his right to nominate a replacement arbitrator because the first arbitrator nominated by him resigned without justification?

8.   Intending to create possible recourse against a resigning arbitrator, the 1996 English Arbitration Act provides as follows in Section 25:

(1) The parties are free to agree with an arbitrator as to the consequences of his resignation as regards

(a) his entitlement (if any) to fees and expenses, and

(b) any liability thereby incurred by him.

(2) If or to the extent that there is no such agreement, the following provisions apply.

(3) An arbitrator who resigns his appointment may (upon notice to the parties) apply to the court—

(a) to grant him relief from any liability thereby incurred by him, and

(b) to make such order as it thinks fit with respect to his entitlement (if any) to fees and expenses, or the repayment of any fees or expenses already paid.

(4) If the court is satisfied that in all the circumstances it was reasonable for the arbitrator to resign, it may grant such relief as is mentioned in subsection (3)(a) on such terms as it thinks fit.

(5) The leave of the court is required for any appeal from a decision of the court under this section.

If these rules had applied to the Jovanovic resignation, what result?

Assuming you are convinced that Professor Jovanovic really believed that it became impossible to establish the truth without the evidence his colleagues refused to admit, and assuming you are not convinced he was right, could you relieve him under Section 25? What is the relevance of the opinion of the ICC Court of Arbitration?

Suppose that in our hypothetical case the English court does not grant Professor Jovanovic relief from liability, but he insists on resigning nevertheless, and returns to Belgrade. What happens to the arbitration proceedings?

9. As stated before, according to the 1998 ICC Arbitration Rules: "Neither the arbitrators, nor the Court and its members, nor the ICC or its employees, nor the ICC national Committees shall be liable to any person for any act or omission in connection with the arbitration."

Does this preclude liability of arbitrators who abandon their function without justification? (Assume that arbitration is held in London under the 1998 ICC Rules.)

10. After the case of Professor Jovanovic, a number of arbitral institutions included in their rules provisions on truncated tribunals (e.g. Article 12 of the 1998 LCIA Rules, or Section 19 of the 1998 DIS /German Institute of Arbitration/ Rules).

Legislative attention has also been devoted to this issue. Section 30 of the new (1999) Swedish Arbitration Act deals explicitly and thoroughly with the issue of truncated tribunals. Section 30 states:

> "Where an arbitrator fails, without valid cause, to participate in the determination of an issue by the arbitral tribunal, such failure will not prevent the other arbitrators from ruling on the matter. Unless the parties have decided otherwise, the opinion agreed upon by the majority of the arbitrators participating in the determination shall prevail. If no majority is attained for any opinion, the opinion of the chairman shall prevail."

The Swedish solution clearly tries to shield arbitration from disruption. A lot depends, of course, on the interpretation of "valid cause". Who should interpret the term? The arbitral institution? (This is a sensible solution, but what should happen in ad hoc arbitration? One might also raise the question whether arbitral institutions should deal with issues beyond the realm of administration. Is this an administrative matter?)

One of the problems with decision-making by truncated tribunals is that the votes may be evenly split. (This is not a very likely outcome, however, because—as in the Jovanovic case—walking out is probably meant to be a protest against the other two arbitrators and their opinion.) In any event, Section 30 of the Swedish Act provides a solution. The vote of the presiding arbitrator will prevail. But what happens if the presiding arbitrator is the one who walks out?

III.2. APPOINTMENT AND APPOINTING AUTHORITIES

III.2.a. *Note—Options in Appointment of Arbitrators*

Tibor Varady, ON APPOINTING AUTHORITIES IN INTERNATIONAL COMMERCIAL ARBITRATION

2 Emory J. Int'l. Dispute Res. 311, 311–28 (1988)*

I. BETWEEN IMPERFECTION AND LEGAL NON-EXISTENCE

A distinctive characteristic of courts is that their organization allows a party with a grievance to unilaterally set their mechanisms into motion. As far as arbitration is concerned, the machinery for settling disputes is created by the parties; and this is often not accomplished by the execution of an arbitration agreement. In most cases, the arbitration agreement itself does not provide a mechanism which can subsequently be set into motion by one party alone. This is particularly true with respect to ad hoc arbitration. An arbitration clause providing that all disputes arising out of or related to a given contract shall be settled by three arbitrators in city A (let us say Atlanta) has vested dispute settling powers in an institution not yet in existence, and therefore not yet available to the party seeking remedy. The creation of a self-sufficient dispute settling mechanism is dependent upon either further cooperation of the parties or on outside help. The appointment of arbitrators is the most frequent problem which keeps the arbitration agreement at a certain distance from an established tribunal which would render justice. In their arbitration agreement, parties will rarely nominate specific persons as arbitrators. This is particularly true with respect to compromisory clauses which are much more frequent in practice, and thereby more important, than the *compromis*.[1] (One has to add that even an agreement on the choice of one or more arbitrators may fall short of creating a viable mechanism, because the persons chosen may refuse to accept their nomination.) The question may be asked, what level of perfection should an arbitration clause achieve in order to represent a valid agreement capable of "ousting" the jurisdiction of courts? Considering the same problem from another angle, what imperfections of the arbitration clause would lead us to the conclusion that assistance in the constitution of the tribunal would be improper and undeserved, because no coherent and valid arbitration agreement has actually come into being?

The line between imperfection and legal non-existence shifts depending on the available remedies and on the recognition of these remedies in municipal laws or international law. One may distinguish

---

* Reprinted by permission of Emory Journal of International Dispute Resolution, Emory University School of Law.

1. On the history of the distinction between "compromis" and "clause compromissoire" in French law, *see* von Mehren, *International Commercial Arbitration: The*

Contribution of the French Jurisprudence, 46 La. L. Rev. 1045 (1986); Carbonneau, *The Elaboration of a French Court Doctrine on International Commercial Arbitration: A Study in Liberal Civilian Judicial Creativity*, 55 Tul. L. Rev. 1 (1980).

four possible ways to bring to perfection an agreement to arbitrate: 1) arbitrators may be nominated by an arbitral institution; 2) the parties themselves may complete their agreement and nominate the arbitrators directly; 3) assistance may be rendered by courts; 4) the parties may create a special appointing authority in their arbitration agreement.

* * *

A. Implementation of the Agreement to Arbitrate by an Arbitral Institution

If the parties entrusted their dispute to an institutional arbitration tribunal, the lack of their further cooperation with respect to the nomination of arbitrators, and the absence of detailed provisions in the arbitration agreement, would not normally render the arbitration agreement inoperative. By choosing an institution, the parties have placed their arbitration clause against a normative background which provides solutions. Problems may arise, however, if the parties included in their arbitration agreement provisions on nomination of arbitrators which are not compatible with the rules of the chosen arbitral institution, or if the agreement confers jurisdiction over certain issues to another institution.[2] There may also be dilemmas regarding the competence of courts to reexamine nominations made by an arbitral institution.[3]

B. Further Cooperation of the Parties

The parties may, of course, cooperate in establishing a viable dispute-settling mechanism, and it is not rare for them to do so. Yet the expected cooperation of the other party is a rather precarious ground to rely upon. Once a difference has arisen which cannot be settled amicably, initiatives may be hampered by mistrust, and one of the parties may also be tempted to exploit the imperfections of the arbitration clause and obstruct the composition of the arbitration panel, or the choice of the sole arbitrator. It may also happen that the party seeking arbitration, finds himself under pressure to agree to the nomination of a person whom he does not consider suitable, if the alternative is to lose the chance to get an arbitration panel at all.

In principle, if it may be inferred from the arbitration clause that the party who refused to cooperate was under an obligation to do so, a claim for damages because of a breach of contract, or even a request for specific performance, may conceivably be pursued. Yet, such an attempt would encounter too many difficulties. First of all, it is difficult to see how a court could compel the reticent party to nominate an arbitrator.

---

2. *See* the Preliminary Award Made in International Chamber of Commerce [I.C.C.] Case No. 2321 (1974), in 1976 Y. B. Com. Arb. 133; *See also* Judgment of Apr. 16, 1984, Swiss Fed. Trib. discussed in Klein, *Zur Ernennung von Schiedsrichtern durch im voraus bezeichnete Dritte,* Praxis des Internationalen Privat-und Verfahrensrechts [IPRax] 53 (1986). * * *

3. *See* the decision of the Swiss Federal Tribunal in Westland Helicopters Ltd. v. The Arab Organization for Industrialization, United Arab Emirates, Saudi Arabia, Quatar, Egypt, Arab British Helicopter Company. Judgment of May 16, 1983, Swiss Fed. Trib., *reported in* Bulletin d'Association Suisse d'Arbitrage 203 (1984).

This remedy is rarely mentioned as a possibility,[4] and it is unlikely that it would yield positive results. Damages could more easily be awarded, but the basic aim of settling the dispute by arbitration would not be achieved. Furthermore, the amount of damages awarded would probably be reduced to extra procedural costs, since a refusal to cooperate in the constitution of the arbitration panel does not amount to a total blocking of the plaintiff to present his claim.[5] Also it would be difficult to make a proper assessment of damages before the merits of the claim were actually litigated before an arbitration tribunal or a court. The position of the party seeking damages may, however, be strengthened by a clause in the original agreement stipulating liquidated damages—a possibility which is explicitly foreseen by article 1911 of the Peruvian Civil Code of 1984.[6]

C. *Assistance Rendered by Courts Pursuant to Municipal Procedural Norms*

* * *

The perspective from which the relationship between courts and arbitration tribunals is most often viewed is determined by the endeavors of international commercial arbitration to gain "independence" and to establish itself as a parallel means of adjudication with a standing equal to that enjoyed by courts. The development of international commercial arbitration is sometimes equated with a process of gradual elimination of possible instances of court interference. This line of thinking is not unjustified, but it loses sight of the fact that the establishment of international commercial arbitration as a viable alternative mechanism of dispute resolution, and the growth of its importance, are also marked by increased availability of judicial assistance in the pre-arbitral and post-arbitral phases.

Today, in most countries, statutory or other municipal rules provide for court assistance in the constitution of the arbitration panel or in the choice of a single arbitrator, and also in filling vacancies which could emerge after the constitution of the tribunal. This has been foreseen in the United Nations Commission on International Trade Law (UNCITRAL) Model Law on International Commercial Arbitration[7] and in numerous statutes including those in effect in the United States,[8]

---

4. Arbitration in Sweden is one of the rare examples to be noted. *See,* Stockholm Chamber of Commerce, Arbitration in Sweden 75 (1977).

5. The arbitration tribunal may still be constituted with some outside help, or the claim may be presented before a court. In the latter case, when the arbitration agreement does not bring about a mechanism which is capable of replacing courts, it should be considered invalid. Otherwise, it may still retain its power to exclude courts, without having the power to replace them.

6. Civil Code art. 1911 (Peru); *see also* Samtleben, *Schiedsklauseln in Peru and Venezuela.* Recht der Internationalen Wirtschaft [R.I.W.] 20 (1987).

7. UNCITRAL Model Law on International Commercial Arbitration *adopted by* UNCITRAL on June 21, 1985. U.N. Doc. A/40/17 at arts. 6, 11 (1985) [hereinafter UNCITRAL Model Law]. The UNCITRAL Model Law received its first implementation in the Canadian Arbitration Act, 1986.

8. 9 U.S.C. 392, & 1, *enacted on* July 30, 1947.

Yugoslavia,[9] the Netherlands,[10] Canada,[11] France,[12] Italy,[13] Austria,[14] the Federal Republic of Germany,[15] the United Kingdom,[16] Sweden,[17] Switzerland,[18] and Czechoslovakia.[19]

* * *

There are essentially two possible threats to the viability of arbitration agreements which invite judicial assistance. One is the inherent imperfection of an arbitration agreement which lacks efficient instruments for its self-implementation (the constitution of an arbitral tribunal); the other is drafting imperfections which may give rise to a dramatic increase of the difficulties in commencing arbitration. Not all imperfections are met with benevolent understanding, and there are considerable differences between particular countries as to the degree of availability of judicial intervention. National procedural norms also vary with respect to the measure of interference with the arbitration process-

9. Code on Civil Litigation art. 475 (Yugoslavia), *enacted on* Dec. 24, 1976. *See Sluzbeni SFRJ* (Official Gazette of Yugoslavia) 212 (1977).

10. Netherlands Arbitration Act. arts. 1027, 1028, 1073. *See* the English text of the Netherlands Arbitration Act, 1986, *in* Arbitration & the Law 141 (1986) with a comment by Sanders, *Id.* at 162; *see also* Duintjer Tebbens, *A Facelift for Dutch Arbitration Law*, Neth. Int'l L.R. 141 (1987).

11. Canadian Arbitration Act, 1986, arts. 1, 6, 11, *in* 26 I.L.M. 714 (1987).

12. Code of Civil Procedure, 1980 arts. 1457, 1493 (France), *enacted* in accordance with the Decree of May 14, 1980 (published in Journal Officiel, May 18, 1980), and Decree of May 12, 1981 (published in Journal Officiel, May 14, 1981). English translations appear in 1982 Y.B. Com. Arb. 271; and 20 I.L.M. 917 (1982).

13. Code of Civil Procedure, art. 810 (Italy). An English translation incorporating the changes effected by Act. No. 28 of Feb. 9, 1983, is contained in 1984 Y.B. Com. Arb. 309.

14. Code of Civil Procedure, arts. 482, 583, 585 (Austria). An English text incorporating the changes effected by Federal Law of Feb. 2, 1983, appears in 1984 Y.B. Com. Arb. 301. *See also* Melis, *La réforme autrichienne de l'arbitrage*, Revue de l'Arbitrage [Rev. Arb.] 415 (1987).

15. Code of Civil Procedure, arts. 1029, 1031 (F.R.G.). *See* the English text of the relevant rules of the Code of Civil Procedure (Zivilprozessordnung) in Glossner, Commercial Arbitration in the Federal Republic of Germany 35–48 (1984). On July 25, 1986, amendments to the Code were enacted as 1986 Bundesgesetzblatt [BGB1] arts. 1039, 1041, 1044–45 (F.R.G.).

16. United Kingdom Arbitration Act § 6 (a) (1979). *See* 1980 Y.B. Com. Arb. 239, and a comment by Schmitthoff, *Id.* at 231. The 1979 Act has rejected the position taken in National Enterprise Ltd. v. Racal Communications Ltd, 2 W.L.R. 222 (1975), in which it was held that the refusal of an appointing authority to make the nomination extinguishes the arbitration agreement.

17. Swedish Arbitration Act, art. 26, *See* Arbitration in Sweden, *supra* note 4, at 192–201; for the 1982 amendments, *see* 1982 Y.B. Com. Arb. 68. The effect of this law is that as of Jan. 1, 1982, the authority rendering assistance is no longer the Överexecutor but rather the district courts (Tingsratten).

18. Intercantonal Arbitration Convention, approved by the Federal Council of Switzerland Aug. 27, 1969, commonly referred to as the "Concordat" [hereinafter, Swiss Concordat] has been adopted by 22 out of the 26 Swiss cantons. Among the cantons adhering to the Concordat are all those which are frequently the site of international commercial arbitration including Geneva, Vaud, Zurich, Bern, and Basel. *See also* Swiss Federal Act on Private International Law, art. 179 (1987), contained in 27 I.L.M. 37 (1988) [hereinafter Swiss Federal Act]. The Federal Act will enter into force in the second half of 1988, after the referendum period expires; its relation to cantonal law (and the Concordat) is regulated in art. 176.

19. Act 98, Relating to Arbitration in International Trade and to Enforcement of Awards. 1963. § 7 (Czechoslovakia). The English text of this act appears in 21 Bulletin of Czechoslovakia Law 269 (1963).

falling on both sides of the fine line between desired assistance and unwanted tutorship. It is also of particular importance whether courts which assist in the composition of the arbitral tribunal are required to examine the validity of the arbitration agreement, or whether such examination is discretionary or even forbidden.

* * *

An arbitration agreement which is inoperative because it does not by its own terms ensure the establishment of the arbitration tribunal need not be considered legally non-existent. The validity of the arbitration agreement does not necessarily suppose the possibility to arbitrate, but rather the possibility to request arbitration under the applicable law (in the same way that the validity and operation of a contract does not mean that the contract itself provides for performance, but rather, that it is a proper basis for requesting performance under the applicable law). The remaining problem is, of course, that the arbitration agreement, just as any contract, must meet some minimum standards of coherence and operativeness in order to qualify for outside assistance. These standards vary under different national laws. Under some national laws—and here the analogy with contracts in general stops—no outside assistance is available whatsoever. Serious difficulties might also be encountered in ascertaining the national law under which judicial assistance may be sought.

The arbitration agreement, in order to qualify for judicial assistance, must possess some essential coherence and clarity which would place beyond doubt the fact that the parties did envisage settlement of their dispute by arbitration and that this has been provided for in a feasible way. Courts will nominate an arbitrator when one party does not make this nomination despite the fact that the arbitration agreement obliges him to do so. Courts will also step in if, according to the arbitration agreement, two arbitrators are supposed to agree on the third arbitrator but they fail to do so. A dilemma appears, however, if the parties delegate the choice of one or more arbitrators to an appointing authority which refuses to make the appointment. According to Swedish law, in such a case the arbitration clause loses its validity (unless the parties would agree otherwise).[23] The same attitude was adopted in German court practice. In a 1958 decision, the Higher Court (Oberlandesgericht) in Karlsruhe found that the arbitration agreement loses its validity if the appointing authority chosen by the parties fails to make the appointment.[24] In the opinion of the Higher Court, by choosing an appointing authority the parties excluded the court which may otherwise act as appointing authority by virtue of article 1029 of the Code of Civil Procedure. The failure of the appointing authority (in this case a chamber of industry and commerce) to make the appointment rendered

23. Swedish Arbitration Act, § 8/2; *see also* Arbitration in Sweden, *supra* note 4, at 75–76.

24. Judgment of Apr. 4, 1958, Oberlandesgericht, Karlsruhe (F.R.G.) *reported in* 30 Neue Juristische Wochenschrift [N.J.W.] 1148 (1958).

the arbitration clause invalid under article 1033 of the same Code.[25] This approach, however, represents an exception rather than a rule. The UNCITRAL Model Law, and a considerable number of national statutes, provide explicitly for judicial assistance in case the appointing authority established in the arbitration agreement fails to appoint an arbitrator.[26] In other countries—like the United States[27] and France[28]—the relevant legislative provisions clearly appear to be broad enough to encompass this situation as well.

* * *

D.   Appointing Authorities Established by the Parties

Appointing authorities chosen by the parties may improve considerably the effectiveness of arbitration agreements aiming at the establishment of ad hoc tribunals. Such appointing authorities are in practice the only remedy for the failure of the parties to cooperate, if the arbitration is governed by a national law which does not permit judicial assistance in the constitution of ad hoc tribunals. Also, an appointing authority chosen by the parties wards off difficulties in finding and establishing the competent court and the applicable *lex arbitri*.

* * *

In the words of a Swiss author, *"On ne doit donc pas confondre la désignation par un tiers et la désignation judiciaire."*[50]

The essential difference is actually not in the person of those who would make the appointment, but rather in the source of their power. The president of a given court may be chosen by the parties as their appointing authority, but he may also have distinct competences under his national law to act as an appointing authority. His responsibilities, his powers, and the nature of his decisions would not be the same in these two situations. Speaking about the powers and responsibilities of the President of the International Court of Justice in acting as an appointing authority chosen by the parties, Mann says:

> With the greatest respect for the eminent office which the President holds, it is suggested that, when he appoints an arbitrator, he acts in no other capacity than the Secretary of the National Association of Fishmongers who is called upon to perform the same task.[51]

25. *See* K.H. Schwab, Schiedsgerichtsbarkeit 53 (1959); Stein–Jonas & Schlosser, Kommentar zur Zivilprozessordnung, & 1029 Rz. 7 (1980).

26. UNCITRAL Model Law, U.N. Doc. A/40/17, *supra* note 7, at art. 11; Code of Civil Procedure, art. 810 (Italy); UK Arbitration Act. '6(4). *See also* arts. 7 and 8 of the Uniform Law made in pursuance of the Council of Europe Convention Providing a Uniform Law on Arbitration, Jan. 20, 1966. Europ. T.S. No. 56.

27. 9 U.S.C. § 5 (1947).

28. Code of Civil Procedure, art. 1493 (France).

50. "One should not confuse appointment by a third party with judicial appointment." S. Contini, Contribution à L'étude de L'arbitrage en Procedure Civile Vaudoise (1957).

51. Mann, [*State Contracts in International Arbitration*, 1967 Brit. Y.B. Int'l L.], at 22.

Although presidents of courts are chosen as appointing authorities with a somewhat greater frequency than the Secretary of the National Association of Fishmongers, it is true that as long as the source of their competence is the agreement of the parties, their action is not channelled by official procedure, just as their right to refuse the request is not restrained by the existence of official duties.

The establishment of a third party as appointing authority, of a *tiers préconstitué*, may be understood as a further step towards the establishment of a self-sufficient, alternative dispute-settling mechanism and a step towards strengthening the independence of arbitration tribunals from courts. At the same time, however, an ad hoc structuring of important functions outside the shield of institutionalized patterns is a difficult task, and imperfections * * * [can lead to] considerable dangers.

* * *

III.2.b. *Appointment by Courts*

Tibor Varady, ON APPOINTING AUTHORITIES IN INTERNATIONAL COMMERCIAL ARBITRATION

2 Emory J. Int'l. Dispute Res. 311, 321–26 (1988).*

3. *The relevance of the validity of the arbitration agreement*

One of the most important questions concerning judicial assistance in the constitution of the arbitration tribunal is that of the powers of the court to investigate the validity of the arbitration agreement itself. This is also the point at which the borderline between assistance and interference becomes disputed, given that one of the most important prerogatives of the arbitrators is that of deciding upon their own competence, i.e., upon the validity of the arbitration agreement which represents the source of their competence.

In the opinion of F.A. Mann, it is not open to a court or other body to refuse to appoint an arbitrator on the ground that there may be doubt about the continued validity of the arbitration clause.[39] I believe that such a conclusion is probably unavoidable if the appointing authority derives its powers from the agreement of the parties. However, other solutions are conceivable if the appointing authority is a court which proceeds on the basis of a national procedural law. According to the Swiss Federal Act of Private International Law, a judge charged with appointment will not proceed if a *summary examination* shows that no arbitration agreement exists between the parties.[40] A similar position is advocated by Phillippe Fouchard, who believes that "it would be reason-

* Reprinted by permission of Emory Journal of International Dispute Resolution, Emory University School of Law.

39. Mann, *State Contracts in International Arbitration*, 1967 BRIT. Y.B. INT'L L. 1, 25.

40. *See* Swiss Federal Act, art. 179 '3 (1987).

able" to permit the competent French authority to refuse the nomination of an arbitrator if the authority concludes that the arbitration clause is manifestly void.[41]

It certainly appears to be reasonable to refrain from assisting in the creation of an arbitral mechanism which may be costly, time consuming, and which is doomed to failure because of the obvious lack of a valid arbitration agreement. Yet the dividing line between manifest and non-manifest nullity, and between summary and ordinary examination, is an extraordinarily sensitive one, and one which often defies definition. On the other hand, the practical significance of this problem is considerably reduced by the fact that in most cases courts will have an opportunity to investigate the existence and the validity of the arbitration clause by deciding upon their own jurisdiction and upon the law applicable to the appointment of the tribunal. The majority of national laws on the subject give courts the jurisdiction to render assistance in naming an arbitration tribunal only if the *lex arbitri* is the law of the forum, or if the seat of the arbitration tribunal is in the forum state.[42] These facts are normally established by reference to a coherent arbitration clause. There can be no indication as to the site of arbitration without some arbitration agreement; the parties' choice of the procedural law applicable to arbitration cannot be ascertained except by an examination of the arbitration agreement (and such a choice cannot be valid without a valid arbitration agreement); the applicability of a certain national law as *lex arbitri* on grounds other than an express choice made by the parties is in most cases based on some elements of the arbitration agreement. For example, in a 1985 French case[43] the arbitration agreement read:

> If any disputes arise between the General Contractor and the Designer in connection with this contract, it shall be referred to the arbitration and final decision of the Chambre de Commerce International de La Haye.[44]

The French designation of the (non-existent) institution in The Hague, Netherlands, did not prove to be sufficient to provide for the assistance of the *Tribunal de grande instance de Paris*. The Court, after investigating the arbitration clause, refused to appoint arbitrators on the grounds that it had no jurisdiction to do so because the arbitration clause neither provided for French law to be applied, nor established the site of arbitration in France. Thus the court did review the arbitration agreement; not to address head-on the issue of its validity, but to establish

---

41. Fouchard, Note, REV. ARB. 191, 194 (1987).

42. This has been explicitly stated in the French Code of Civil Procedure, art. 1493, and in the Swiss Concordat, arts. 3, 12. The same position has been adopted in the Netherlands Arbitration Act as well. Netherlands Arbitration Act, 1986, art. 1073. The Dutch Act, however, makes one exception: Dutch courts may also act when

the domicile or the actual residence of one of the parties is in the Netherlands.

43. Société Europe Etudes Gecti c. Sociétés E.T.P.O., L.T.P.A. et Al Ashram Contracting & Co., Judgment of June 3, 1985, Trib. gr. inst. Paris, *reported in* REV. ARB. 179 (1987).

44. *Id.*

whether it furnishes points of contact which would enable a French court to render assistance in the given case.

Under the new 1986 Dutch Arbitration Act,[45] however, this malformed arbitration clause might still have had a chance. Article 1027 of this Act contains a most radical and most explicit denial of the competence of the court regarding the preliminary verification of the existence of a valid arbitration agreement. In the first sentence of article 1027, section 4 it is emphasized that "[t]he President [of the District Court] or the third person shall appoint the arbitrator or arbitrators without regard to the question whether or not there is a valid arbitration agreement". In his comment on the new Dutch Arbitration Act, Pieter Sanders has stated: "The issue of whether a valid arbitration agreement exists was banned from the appointment stage."[46] It is interesting to add that under the Dutch Act, an indirect examination of the existence and of the validity of the arbitration agreement (on the occasion of an examination of the jurisdiction of the court) may also be foreclosed. According to article 1073 of the law, a Dutch court may appoint arbitrators either on the ground that the place of arbitration is situated within the Netherlands, or on the ground that one of the parties has its domicile or residence in the Netherlands. The latter ground may be established without any reference to an arbitration agreement, i.e., without offering an opportunity for indirect scrutiny of the arbitration clause.

The wording of the Dutch statute might conceivably permit the appointment of an arbitrator even without any arbitration agreement— it remains to be seen what attitudes will be developed in practice.

Before appointment takes place, the problem of whether a court should pass judgment upon the validity of the arbitration agreement presents itself. A further ramification of the same problem appears if the court refuses to assist in the appointment of the arbitral tribunal. In the event that a court does refuse, the question arises whether such a refusal should (or may) be accompanied by a declaration that the arbitration agreement as a whole is invalid. There are several reasons for a negative answer. A full-scale investigation into the validity of the arbitration agreement would be contrary to the principle that the arbitrators themselves are competent to decide upon their own competence. It might also turn judicial assistance to the arbitrators in performing their functions into an impediment to the very same performance of functions. On the other hand, a summary or indirect examination of the arbitration agreement may justify a refusal to render assistance, but it is less than a proper basis for a judgment on the validity of the arbitration agreement. One has to add that in some countries, like the Netherlands, no exami-

---

45. Netherlands Arbitration Act (1986).

46. *See* Sanders, *supra* note [10] [see supra p. 346] at 166.

nation of the existence of a valid arbitration agreement is possible whatsoever at the appointment stage.[47] I shall also mention that in German court practice it is established that nomination of arbitrators by state courts does not imply a decision on the existence of a valid arbitration agreement.[48] From this position one might reasonably infer that the refusal by a court to nominate an arbitrator need not have to be accompanied by, and does not imply, such a decision either.

One might perhaps argue that the refusal of a court to make the appointment without declaring the arbitration agreement invalid could only aggravate the position of the moving party, because this may threaten his right to bring the case before a court instead of an arbitration tribunal. It does happen, though not frequently, that the defendant, after successfully opposing arbitration, will go on to oppose the jurisdiction of the court, in which the plaintiff subsequently brings his claim as well, arguing this time that the jurisdiction of the court was ousted by the arbitration agreement.[49] In such a situation a refusal of the appointment which stops short of declaring the invalidity of the arbitration agreement, and the continued doubts about the legal existence of an agreement which proved to be imperfect, represents a burden rather than an additional opportunity to find a proper forum for the settlement of the dispute. Nevertheless, the possibility that such situations may arise and the ensuing problems cannot outweigh the disadvantages of a contrary solution. In other words, possible abuses of a decision denying judicial assistance without declaring the arbitration agreement invalid, do not amount to sufficient reason for asking courts to declare the invalidity of the arbitration agreement whenever they refuse to appoint an arbitrator. First of all, such declarations may not prevent abuses, because they may not be binding on courts in other countries. Against a party who would first refuse to observe the arbitration agreement, and later oppose the jurisdiction of a court referring to the same arbitration agreement, a reliance on estoppel, or on the principle of *venire contra factum proprium*, might offer more efficient protection. Furthermore, I would like to repeat that the position of courts versus arbitration tribunals, and the procedural requirements with respect to appointment (or the refusal of the same), do not justify a judgment on the validity of the arbitration agreement at the appointment stage.

---

47. *See* Netherlands Arbitration Act, art. 1027 § 4 (1986).

48. Judgment of Feb. 27, 1969, [Bundesgerichtshof, F.R.G., in K. Straatman & Ulmer, I Handelsrechtliche Schiedsgerichtspraxis Sammlung von Schiedssprüchen unter Einschluss von Urteilen und Texten zur Schiedsgerichtsbarkeit] A(2), case No. 3 (1975) * * *.

49. An example of such tactics (which did not bring final success though) appeared in a case between a Czech party and a Yugoslav party, *see* Varady, *Zastarelost i autonomija volje u medjunarodnom privatnom pravu (Statute of Limitations and Party Autonomy in Private International Law)*, 8 Prinosi za Poredbeno Prouèavanje Prava i Medjunarodno Privatno Pravo 3 (1975).

SWITZERLAND
SWISS PRIVATE INTERNATIONAL LAW ACT (1987)
ARTICLE 179 OF CHAPTER 12: INTERNATIONAL ARBITRATION.

IV. ARBITRAL TRIBUNAL

1. Constitution

Article 179

1. The arbitrators shall be appointed, removed or replaced in accordance with the agreement of the parties.

2. In the absence of such an agreement, the matter may be referred to the court where the arbitral tribunal has its seat; the court shall apply by analogy the provisions of cantonal law concerning the appointment, removal or replacement of arbitrators.

3. When a judge has been designated as the authority for appointing an arbitrator, he shall make the appointment unless a summary examination shows that no arbitration agreement exists between the parties.

CZECH REPUBLIC
AN ACT OF 1 NOVEMBER 1994 ON ARBITRAL PROCEEDINGS AND ENFORCEMENT OF ARBITRAL AWARDS

* * *

Article 9

(1) If the party having to appoint an arbitrator fails so to do within thirty (30) days upon receipt of the invitation of the other party so to do, or if the appointed arbitrators are unable to agree on the person of the president then, unless a provision to the contrary is found in the arbitration agreement, the Court of law shall appoint such arbitrator or the president of the arbitral tribunal, as the case may be. Any party or any of the already appointed arbitrators shall be at liberty to apply to the said Court of law for such nomination.

(2) Unless otherwise agreed by the parties, the Court of law, acting upon application of any party or of an arbitrator, shall appoint a new arbitrator in case the already appointed arbitrator resigns his function or is not in a position to exercise the function.

* * *

TUNISIA

ANNEX 1: Arbitration Code, promulgated by Law No. 93–42 of 26 April 1993

Article 47

2. With the exception of Arts. 53, 54, 80, 81 and 82 of this Code, the provisions of this law apply only if the place of arbitration is in the territory of Tunisia, or only if either the parties or the arbitral tribunal have chosen these provisions.

Article 56

1. No person shall be precluded by reason of his nationality from acting as an arbitrator, unless otherwise agreed by the parties.

2. The parties are free to agree on a procedure of appointing the arbitrator or arbitrators, subject to the provisions of paragraphs 4 and 5 of this article.

3. Failing such agreement.

a) in an arbitration with three arbitrators, each party shall appoint one arbitrator, and the two arbitrators thus appointed shall appoint the third arbitrator. If a party fails to appoint the arbitrator within thirty days of receipt of a request to do so from the other party, or if the two arbitrators fail to agree on the third arbitrator within thirty days of their appointment, the appointment shall be made, upon request of a party, by the First President of the Court of Appeal of Tunis in summary proceedings.

b) in an arbitration with a sole arbitrator and if the parties are unable to agree on the arbitrator, he shall be appointed upon request of a party, by the First President of the Court of Appeal of Tunis in summary proceedings.

In appointing an arbitrator the judge shall take into account the qualifications prescribed in paragraph 1 of Article 10 of this Code.

4. If the parties agreed on a procedure to appoint the arbitrators but did not foresee other provisions in their agreement for securing the appointment, any party may request the First President of the Court of Appeal of Tunis to take the necessary measures, in one of the following cases:

a) If a party fails to act as required under such procedure.

b) If the parties, or the two arbitrators, are unable to reach an agreement in accordance with such procedure.

c) If an authority, including an institution, fails to perform any function entrusted to it under such procedure.

5. The decisions on matters entrusted by paragraph 3 or 4 of this article to the First President of the Court of Appeal of Tunis shall not be subject to any appeal.

PORTUGAL

LAW NO. 31/86 OF 29 AUGUST 1986
(in force 29 November 1986).

VOLUNTARY ARBITRATION

Article 11. Constitution of the tribunal

1. The party wishing to refer a dispute to the arbitral tribunal shall notify that fact to the other party.

2.   The notice shall be made by registered mail with acknowledgment of receipt.

3.   The notice shall refer to the arbitration agreement and specify the subject matter of the dispute, if it has not yet been specified in the arbitration agreement.

4.   If the parties may appoint one or more arbitrators, the notice shall include the appointment of the arbitrator or arbitrators by the party wishing to commence the arbitral proceedings, as well as an invitation addressed to the other party to appoint the arbitrator or arbitrators whom that party may appoint.

5.   If a sole arbitrator is to be appointed by both parties, the notice shall indicate the proposed arbitrator and an invitation addressed to the other party to accept him.

6.   If one or more arbitrators are to be appointed by a third person, that person shall be notified to make such appointment if it has not yet done so, and to inform the parties.

Article 12.   Appointment of the arbitrators and specification of the subject matter of the dispute by the court

1.   Whenever an arbitrator or arbitrators have not been appointed according to the provisions of the previous articles, such appointment shall be made by the president of the Court of Appeal at the place of arbitration or, if that place has not been established, at the domicile of the applicant.

2.   In the cases mentioned in Article 11(4) and (5), the appointment may be requested one month after the notification mentioned in Article 11(1), or in the case mentioned in Article 7(2), within the month subsequent to the last appointment of the arbitrators who have been empowered to make such choice.

3.   The appointments made in accordance with the provisions of the previous paragraphs may not be challenged.

4.   If, within the time limit mentioned in paragraph 2, the parties do not reach an agreement regarding the specification of the subject matter of the dispute, the court shall decide. This decision may be appealed.

5.   If the arbitration agreement is manifestly void, the court shall declare that the appointment of the arbitrators and the specification of the subject matter of the dispute shall not take place.

* * *

RUSSIAN FEDERATION

LAW OF THE RUSSIAN FEDERATION ON INTERNATIONAL COMMERCIAL ARBITRATION

(in force 14 August 1993).

* * *

CHAPTER 1. GENERAL PROVISIONS

Article 1.   Scope of Application

1.   The present Law applies to international commercial arbitration if the place of arbitration is in the territory of the Russian Federation. However, the provisions of articles 8, 9, 35 and 36 apply also if the place of arbitration is abroad.

* * *

Article 6.   Authority for Certain Functions of Arbitration Assistance and Control

1.   The functions referred to in articles 11(3), 11(4), 13(3) and 14 shall be performed by the President of the Chamber of Commerce and Industry of the Russian Federation.

* * *

Article 11.   Appointment of Arbitrators

1.   No person shall be precluded by reason of his nationality from acting as an arbitrator, unless otherwise agreed by the parties.

2.   The parties are free to agree on a procedure of appointing the arbitrator or arbitrators, subject to the provisions of paragraphs 4 and 5 of this article.

3.   Failing such agreement.

— in an arbitration with three arbitrators, each party shall appoint one arbitrator, and the two arbitrators thus appointed shall appoint the third arbitrator: if a party fails to appoint the arbitrator within 30 days of receipt of a request to do so from the other party, or if the two arbitrators fail to agree on the third arbitrator within 30 days of their appointment, the appointment shall be made, upon request of a party, by the authority specified in article 6(1):

— in an arbitration with a sole arbitrator, if the parties are unable to agree on the arbitrator, he shall be appointed, upon request of a party, by the authority specified in article 6(1).

4.   Where, under an appointment procedure agreed upon by the parties.

— a party fails to act as required under such procedure, or

— the parties, or two arbitrators, are unable to reach an agreement expected of them under such procedure; or

— a third party, including an institution, fails to perform any function entrusted to it under such procedure,

any party may request the authority specified in article 6(1) to take the necessary measures, unless the agreement on the appointment procedure provides other means for securing the appointment.

5. A decision on any matter entrusted by paragraph 3 or 4 of this article to the authority specified in article 6(1) shall be subject to no appeal. The authority, in appointing an arbitrator, shall have due regard to any qualifications required of the arbitrator by the agreement of the parties and to such considerations as are likely to secure the appointment of an independent and impartial arbitrator and, in the case of a sole or third arbitrator, shall take into account as well the advisability of appointing an arbitrator of a nationality other than those of the parties.

* * *

BELGIUM

BELGIAN JUDICIAL CODE, SIXTH PART: ARBITRATION

(adopted July 4, 1972, as amended through May 19, 1998).

Article 1678

1. An arbitration agreement shall not be valid if it gives one of the parties thereto a privileged position with regard to the appointment of the arbitrator or arbitrators.

* * *

Questions and Comments

1. P. Sanders's conclusion is that the Dutch Act excludes the issue of the arbitration agreement's validity from the appointment stage. Do you support such an exclusion?

2. Among the five arbitration acts quoted, only the Swiss and the Portuguese acts contain an explicit provision regarding the nature of court scrutiny of the arbitration agreement. The Swiss Act opts for a "summary examination." Similarly, the Portuguese Act states that appointment shall not take place if the arbitration agreement is "manifestly void." What kind of examination would you recommend, if any?

3. If you ask a court to appoint an arbitrator, and the court refuses, would you want the court (a) to give reasons, and (b) to rule on the validity of the arbitration agreement?

4. Typically, courts at the seat of the arbitral tribunal have jurisdiction to make a default appointment. Should jurisdiction over appointment be based as well on grounds other than the place of the arbitration? (Consider at least the legislation excerpted above.)

5.   A case decided by the Paris Cour d'appel (Court of Appeal) on March 29, 2001 (Reported in Revue de l'arbitrage, 2001 p. 609) tested the limits of court jurisdiction regarding appointment. The question arose whether French courts may intervene to appoint an arbitrator even if the arbitration does not take place in France and French lex arbitri is not applicable. In the Court of Appeal case, the National Iranian Oil Company (NIOC) asked the President of the Paris Tribunal de grande instance to appoint an arbitrator where the respondent (the State of Israel) had failed to do so. The arbitration clause provided for an appointing authority (the President of the ICC), but only with respect to the third arbitrator. Since the problem arose in connection with nominating the second arbitrator, there was no institutional appointing authority. NIOC first sought a remedy in Israel, but the Israeli court refused to make an appointment. Default appointment by Iranian courts was not a viable option. The question therefore arose whether under these circumstances the Paris court had competence to make the default appointment of the second arbitrator.

Article 1493 of the French Code of Civil Procedure provides for court intervention "if any difficulty arises in the constitution of the arbitral tribunal"—a condition that was clearly met. It is also important, however, that court intervention is only justified if the case has some relevant connection with the court (with the country to which the court belongs). The connection required in the French Code is either "arbitration taking place in France", or arbitration "in regard to which the parties have agreed that French procedural law should apply". Neither of these two conditions was met in the given case.

The French court decided nevertheless that it could make the appointment, stating that a judge may also intervene in a case where a denial of justice has taken place in another country, assuming that the case has some ties with France. The Paris Court of Appeal stated that the right of the parties to an arbitration agreement to submit their dispute to arbitration is a matter of public policy. It also held that since the parties designated the ICC as appointing authority (for the third arbitrator)—and the ICC is a legal person constituted under French law with its seat in Paris—a link with France was established. The Court of Appeal decided to invite the State of Israel to nominate its arbitrator within a given time period and stated that the Court would make the substitute appointment if Israel failed to do so.

Is this a good solution? The authors believe that the case's link to France (through the ICC as appointing authority for the third arbitrator) clearly did not satisfy the requirements of Article 1493. It also seems clear that the arbitration agreement would have been frustrated without appointment of the second arbitrator. Would this have constituted a denial of justice? Assuming the answer is yes, is denial of justice a sufficient ground to depart from the Code's jurisdictional requirements?

Could the ICC have made the default appointment?

6.   The Russian Act entrusts the President of the Russian Chamber of Commerce and Industry with the task of appointing arbitrators, if the mechanism designed by the parties fails. Typically, chambers of commerce and their presidents have such power of appointment only if the arbitration

agreement so provides. In the Russian case, their appointment power derives from a legislative act.

Do you see merit in this solution?

7. The Belgian Code is one of the rare statutes that impose explicit conditions on the **substantive validity** (as well as the formal validity) of the arbitration agreement. If one of the parties has a "privileged position" in the appointment process, the arbitration agreement is invalid.

The 1997 Rules of the Foreign Trade Court of Arbitration at the Yugoslav Chamber of Economy contained the following provision in Article 5(4):

> "A foreign party may choose as arbitrator a foreign citizen who is not on the List of Arbitrators, and the domestic party may choose as arbitrator a foreign citizen only if he is on the List of Arbitrators. In such a case, a Yugoslav citizen who is on the List of Arbitrators shall be appointed chairman of the arbitral tribunal."

(This provision is no longer in force after the 2001 amendments to the Yugoslav Rules.)

Suppose a Yugoslav and a Belgian party execute an arbitration agreement in which they submit their dispute to the Yugoslav Court of Arbitration and choose the 1997 Yugoslav Rules. Would this arbitration agreement be null and void under Belgian law?

III.2.c. *Appointing Authorities Chosen by the Parties*

III.2.c.i.   The Nature of the Decision of the Appointing Authority

SAPPHIRE INTERNATIONAL PETROLEUMS LTD. v. NATIONAL IRANIAN OIL COMPANY

35 Int'l L. Rep. 136 (1967).
Arbitral Award, March 15, 1963.*

CAVIN, SOLE ARBITRATOR.[1]

* * *

The Arbitrator then gave the following account of the procedure followed by the parties:

"PROCEDURE"

"1. By a letter of September 28, 1960, Sapphire Petroleums Ltd. notified NIOC that, in view of the dispute between the parties, they considered it futile to resort to the optional conciliation procedure laid down in Article 39 of the agreement. They requested an immediate arbitration, and appointed as their arbitrator the Denver lawyer, Mr.

---

* Reprinted by permission of International Law Reports, Cambridge University Press.

1. M. Pierre Cavin, Federal Judge, Lausanne, Switzerland.

Tippit, and invited NIOC to appoint their arbitrator in accordance with Article 41 of the agreement.

"By a letter of November 21, 1960, NIOC refused to do this, on the pretext *inter alia*, that Sapphire Petroleums Ltd. had assigned their rights to Sapphire International Petroleums Ltd. and only this latter company, and not Sapphire Petroleums Ltd., was qualified to take advantage of the contract and in particular of the arbitral clause.

"By letter of January 10, 1961, Sapphire International requested the President of the Swiss Federal Court to apply Article 41 of the agreement, and to appoint a sole arbitrator to settle the dispute between them and NIOC.

"2. By an order dated January 12, 1961, the President of the Swiss Federal Court made the following decision:

"In accordance with Article 41, letter 2, of the agreement of the parties of June 16, 1958, Federal Judge Pierre Cavin, of Lausanne, is hereby chosen as sole arbitrator." (Translation.)

"This order, of which a copy is attached to the original of the present arbitral award, states in its conclusions that the conditions required by Article 41 of the agreement for the appointment of a sole arbitrator were satisfied.

"The chosen arbitrator accepted his appointment in a letter of January 12, 1961.

"3. By a decision given on March 17, 1961, the President of the Swiss Federal Court rejected a request by NIOC that the order made on January 12, 1961, be revoked and Sapphire International's request for the appointment of a sole arbitrator be rejected. This decision, which is also attached to the original of the present arbitral award, rejects the arguments invoked by the petitioner and in particular the argument that it is Sapphire and not Sapphire International who sent NIOC the letter of September 28, 1960.

* * *

"5. The parties failed to inform the arbitrator, within the time-limit given to them, of any agreement fixing the place of the arbitration and the arbitral procedure. The arbitrator therefore applied Article 41(7) of the contract, and by order of June 13, 1961:

— fixed the place of the arbitration in Lausanne, Canton de Vaud, Switzerland; and

— decided upon the rules to be applied to the proceedings before the arbitrator. A copy of this order is attached to the original of the arbitral award.

"6. An order made by the arbitrator on June 13, 1961, was sent to the parties. By a letter of August 2, 1961, NIOC sent the arbitrator an acknowledgment of its receipt, but said that they disputed the jurisdiction of the arbitrator, whose appointment they regarded as tainted with nullity.

"7. On October 11, 1961, in accordance with the time-limit given by the arbitrator, Sapphire International lodged the plaintiff's memorial, entitled 'Memorial Number 3', together with 78 documents and a request for the hearing of witnesses; in the memorial the claims made against NIOC were as follows:

"1. To decide that the encashment by NIOC of the contractual penalty of $350,000 was unauthorized in law and to sentence them to restore this sum to Sapphire with interest at 5 per cent from January 24, 1961.

"2. To sentence NIOC to indemnify Sapphire for all other damage suffered by them and to refund to them with interest at 5 per cent from the date of the institution of the present proceedings, namely September 28, 1960—

(a) The expenses incurred in making the agreement of June 16, 1958, amounting to $165,175

(b) The expenses of registering the Canadian Companies in the Companies Register at Teheran, amounting to $3,500

(c) The sum of $5,000, which was subscribed by Sapphire to the capital of the Iran Canada Oil Company

(d) The cost of all the work done by Sapphire in performance of the agreement of June 16, 1958, from the start of the agreement, on July 23, 1958, until January 24, 1961, the day when the letter of guarantee was cashed by NIOC, amounting to $1,018,932 ($1,027,-432 less $3,500 and $5,000 mentioned above under (b) and (c))

(e) The amount of the loss of profit estimated at $5,000,000.

'3. To sentence NIOC to pay the whole amount of the fees and costs of the arbitration, including the lawyers' fees, the expert witnesses' fees and every other expense concerning the settlement of the dispute. (Translation.)'

"8. A copy of this memorial was sent to NIOC, giving them a time-limit expiring on January 31, 1962, in which to lodge a defence memorial.

"By letter of November 1, 1961, NIOC acknowledged the receipt of the memorial, but stated that they refused to accept the document, which they did not, however, return to the arbitrator. They maintained this attitude in a letter of December 5, 1961, in which they once more claimed that the appointment of the arbitrator was a nullity. They produced no defence memorial within the time-limit fixed.

"9. At the request of the plaintiff, a time-limit was fixed for both parties to lodge an additional memorial. On receiving notice of this, the defendant informed that arbitrator, in a letter of February 24, 1962, that they considered his appointment as null.

* * *

"10. * * *

"By letters of August 13 and 28, 1962, NIOC once more alleged the nullity of the arbitrator's appointment by the President of the Federal Court, and again refused to consider the arbitrator's communications, which they returned to him."

* * *

Held: that the arbitrator had jurisdiction in accordance with the agreement, and that he was competent to lay down rules of procedure to govern the arbitration. In general, the arbitration was governed by the law of procedure of the Canton of Vaud. The substantive law applicable to the interpretation and performance of the concession agreement was the principles of law generally recognized by civilized nations.

On the merits, the arbitrator found that NIOC had deliberately failed to carry out certain of its obligations under the agreement, and that this failure was a breach of contract of a nature which released Sapphire from the obligation of further performance. Sapphire was entitled to damages for this termination of the contract as a result of breach by NIOC, and to the refund of the sum paid by it under the penalty clause. Sapphire was also entitled to compensation for loss of profit, the amount being established *ex aequo et bono*. NIOC was ordered to pay the costs of the arbitration, and the costs and expenses of Sapphire in the arbitration.

After setting out the facts as quoted above, the arbitrator said:

"THE QUESTION AT ISSUE"

* * *

"The question at issue then is the following:

"1. Should NIOC be sentenced to refund to Sapphire the amount of the penalty clause of $350,000 which they had cashed with interest at 5 per cent. from January 24, 1961, by declaring that the said encashment was unauthorized in law?

"2. Should NIOC be sentenced to indemnify Sapphire for all other damage suffered by them and to refund to them, with interest at 5 per cent. from the date of the institution of the present proceedings, namely from September 28, 1960 * * * [the expenses listed supra].

* * *

"3. Should NIOC be sentenced to pay the costs of the arbitration?

"IN LAW"

"A. *Jurisdiction of the Arbitrator*

"1. The jurisdiction of the undersigned arbitrator is based on Article 39 and 41 of the agreement made on June 16, 1958, between NIOC and Sapphire, an agreement whose rights and obligations had been taken over by Sapphire International from Sapphire.

"According to these provisions, the parties have agreed, in default of the optional conciliation under Article 39, para. 1, to resort to arbitration as the sole means of settling any difference which might arise between them concerning the interpretation and performance of the said agreement. According to Article 49, para. 9, the arbitrator has power to award damages.

"The validity and extent of this arbitration clause, as well as the fact that it is an arbitration clause, are neither open to question nor in dispute. Furthermore, it is not open to question nor in dispute that the present dispute concerns the interpretation and performance of the agreement and that it is a proper occasion for arbitration in accordance with Article 39 of the agreement. Finally, Sapphire International are qualified to take advantage of the arbitral clause, since they have succeeded to all the rights and obligations of Sapphire, with the express agreement of NIOC and in accordance with Article 36 of the agreement.

"All this was impliedly recognized by NIOC in its request of February 5, 1961, to the President of the Federal Court, in which it made known that it had already appointed its arbitrator on January 10, 1961. In addition, in a letter to Sapphire International dated March 27, 1961, NIOC expressly declared that it had agreed to arbitration, and chose its arbitrator. By alleging to the President of the Federal Court that Sapphire International were alone qualified to take advantage of the arbitral clause and by informing the latter company that they had chosen their arbitrator, NIOC have expressly recognized that the transfer of the agreement to Sapphire International included also the transfer of the arbitral clause.

"2. What NIOC disputed, on the other hand, was the correctness of the decision by which the President of the Federal Court had appointed the undersigned as sole arbitrator. On the ground that the notice of September 28, 1960, came from Sapphire and not from Sapphire International, they maintained that the time-limit of two months laid down by Article 41, para. 2, of the agreement could not be said to start running as a result of this notice, since Sapphire International alone were qualified to send such a notice and to take advantage of the arbitral clause.

"But the decision given on January 12, 1961, by the President of the Federal Court, in his capacity as such, is a judicial decision. According to the case-law, such a decision is a final judgment (Cantonal Court of Vaud, in *Journal des Tribunaux*, Lausanne, 1928, III, p. 48). The jurisdiction of this Judge results from an extension of his forum agreed upon by the parties and accepted by the Swiss Federal jurisdiction (*cf.* decision of the President of the Federal Court published in *Recueil Officiel of* Federal Court Decisions, vol. 88, 1962, 1, p. 104). By entrusting a judicial authority with the responsibility of choosing a sole arbitrator under conditions determined by their agreement, the parties necessarily clothed this authority with the power to make a preliminary examination and decision as to whether the conditions laid down for this appointment had been satisfied. It is an established rule in practice that the judge with jurisdiction to appoint arbitrators is also competent to examine first of all whether the conditions for an appointment have been satisfied (Cantonal Court of Vaud, *Journal des Tribunaux*, 1926, III, p. 63; above-cited decision of the President of the Federal Court; Stein–Jonas *Kommentar zur Zivilprozessordnung*, 17th ed. (Tübingen 1956), vol. II, No. 3, *ad* para. 1029). The decision thus reached is a judicial decision, or a judgment, and has the full force of *res judicata*, unless the law allows an appeal to a superior jurisdiction which is not the case here (Stein–Jonas, *op. cit.*; Von Staff, *Das Schiedsgerichtsverfahren nach dem heutigen deutschen Recht* (Berlin 1926), p. 138; Baumbach–Schwaab, *Schiedsgerichtsbarkeit*, 2nd ed. (Munich and Berlin, 1960), p. 110).

"While it is generally accepted in doctrine and case-law that the arbitrator can decide his own jurisdiction in matters concerning the validity of the arbitration deed and the extent of his judicial knowledge, provided these questions have not been previously settled in the law courts, there is no authority for saying that he can revise a judicial decision which has the force of *res judicata*, concerning the appointment of an arbitrator.

"Therefore the undersigned arbitrator has no power to review the order given on January 12, 1961, by the President of the Federal Court. This order concerning the appointment of a sole arbitrator has the force of *res judicata*.

"This is in accordance with the wishes of the parties, who charged a judicial authority with the appointment, under certain conditions, of a sole arbitrator. Since this authority has given a decision which has the force of *res judicata*, the defendant is bound to fail in his claim to re-open this decision and by contesting its validity to maintain that the appointment of the arbitrator is null.

"The President of the Federal Court was acting in conformity with these rules, and in accordance with the established practice, when in his decisions of January 12, and March 17, 1961, he made a preliminary investigation to see whether the conditions laid down by Article 41 of the contract for the appointment of a sole arbitrator had been satisfied.

"In addition, it was not to the arbitrator that NIOC made their application of February 5, claiming exemption from his jurisdiction by a declinatory plea under the arbitral procedure; it was to the President of the Federal Court that they applied, claiming a reconsideration by a plea of 'revision' of the Order of January 12, in order to annul it, and setting out the grounds on which they considered that the conditions required for the appointment of a sole arbitrator had not been fulfilled.

"3. Thus, the undersigned arbitrator has received his authority as a result of a binding judicial decision, whose correctness it is not for him to question, and since he is bound by the acceptance of his appointment which he gave, he is also bound to decide the merits of the plaintiff's claim."

ELF AQUITAINE IRAN (FRANCE) v. NATIONAL IRANIAN OIL CO. (IRAN)[b]

11 Yearbk. Comm. Arb'n 97 (1986).[*]

Prof. Dr. Jur. Bernhard Gomard, *Sole Arbitrator*

Facts

On 27 August 1966, the National Iranian Oil Company ("NIOC") signed in Tehran an exploration and production contracting agreement with the Entreprise de Recherches et d'Activités Pétrolières ("ERAP"), a French State agency, and the French company Société Française de Pétroles d'Iran (Sofiran). The agreement contained in Art. 41 a comprehensive arbitration clause.

Sofiran was to explore for oil within certain designated areas of Iran, and to supply the technical services to exploit the oil fields discovered. ERAP was to contribute the initial funds for financing the exploration operations and, if oil fields were discovered, carry out the exploitation, until the cash flow, accruing to NIOC as a result of the operations, would enable NIOC to provide the financing. NIOC was liable for the repayment of the funds advanced by ERAP, but only if oil fields were discovered and commercial production of oil (regular export of at least 100,000 cubic metres of oil) had commenced. NIOC also undertook to sell to ERAP a certain percentage of the crude oil extracted from the discovered fields, at a preferential price.

Under the agreement, ERAP had the right to associate its affiliate, Société Nationale des Pétroles de Aquitaine ("SNPA"), with its activities, and ERAP and SNPA had a right to transfer their interests in the rights acquired and the obligations undertaken by them under the agreement to companies controlled by either ERAP or SNPA. During the period from 1967 to 1977 ERAP assigned all its interests to its subsidiary, Elf Iran; SNPA assigned all its interests in the agreement to Aquitaine Iran. Thereafter, Elf Iran and Aquitaine Iran merged into Elf Aquitaine Iran ("ELF"), which, therefore, became a party to the agreement. ELF is the claimant in the present arbitration.

Two oil fields were discovered, and their commercial exploitation commenced in the month of December 1978. Notwithstanding its con-

---

b. Published in French translation in 1984 Revue de l'arbitrage 401.

[*] Reprinted with permission of Yearbook Commercial Arbitration, International Council for Commercial Arbitration.

tractual obligations, NIOC did not refund the exploration and development loans received from ERAP, and refused to sell oil at the preferential price provided for in the agreement.

On 8 January 1980, the Islamic Republic Revolution Council of Iran passed an Act establishing a Special Committee to review oil agreements (the "Single Article Act"). The text of the Single Article Act reads:

> "All the Oil Agreements, which at the discretion of the Special Committee to be convened by the Ministry of Oil, may be found to be at variance with the provisions of the Act on Nationalization of the Oil Industry of Iran, shall be declared null and void, and all the claims arising from entering into and performance of such agreements, shall be settled according to the resolution of such Committee. Such Committee shall be held with participation of the Representative of the Ministry of Foreign Affairs."

By a letter of 11 August 1980, ELF was informed by NIOC that the Special Committee had declared null and void the agreement of 27 August 1966. Thereupon, ELF resorted to arbitration according to the arbitration clause in the 1966 agreement. According to this clause, each party was to appoint an arbitrator, and the two arbitrators were to appoint an umpire. If the parties did not appoint their arbitrator, or the arbitrators failed to agree on an umpire, the President of the Danish Supreme Court was to appoint a sole arbitrator in the first case, or an umpire in the second.

When NIOC refused to appoint its arbitrator, the President of the Danish Supreme Court appointed * * * a sole arbitrator, Prof. Bernhard Gomard. * * * NIOC objected on various grounds to the sole arbitrator's competence. In a preliminary award * * * the arbitrator rejected NIOC's objections and declared [himself] to have competence.

* * *

[Authors' note: One of NIOC's objections was that the arbitration agreement was no longer in force and that it had become void by virtue of Iranian legislation enacted after its conclusion. The President of the Court, Mogens Hvidt took the view that this objection (whether well founded or not) did not prevent him from acting as an appointing authority. In a letter to the NIOC, Hvidt stressed:

> * * * *It is not for me to determine whether the arbitration agreement became void with respect to the French company, or what were the consequences of* [the Iranian legislation]. *These questions should be resolved by the arbitration tribunal, the constitution of which is requested by the French company * * *]*[c]

Questions and Comments

1. Arbitrator Cavin's characterization of the decisions rendered by appointing authorities has some support in scholarly writings. In one well-

---

c. See 1984 Revue de l'arbitrage 399 (authors' translation).

known Swiss work on private international law,[11] it is suggested that the decision of the President of the Swiss Federal Tribunal is "indiscutablement" (indisputably) a judicial act. Essentially the same opinion has been expressed by Pierre Lalive.[12] A contrary opinion has, however, received more backing. Referring to appointing authorities chosen by the parties, F. A. Mann stresses that:

> * * * such a person or body does not in any circumstances perform any judicial function in exercising the power. By making the appointment it renders no decision in the dispute between the parties, expresses no opinion on a procedural aspect or on the merits of the case nor precludes the arbitrators (or any competent court) from reviewing the validity and the effect of the appointment that is made.[13]

In an article devoted to the *Sapphire* case, David Suratgar also criticizes the position taken by arbitrator Cavin, arguing that the President of the Federal Tribunal did not act in his official function but rather as a private person.[14] Suratgar relies on Sylvain Contini[15] and agrees with him that dilemmas with respect to the capacity of the appointing authority who occupies a judicial post may only emerge, "where the parties agree to have as their third party selector the very judge who would be competent to decide the case, or the judge competent under the law to appoint the arbitrators in the absence of such an agreement."[16]

In *Sapphire*, the President of the Swiss Federal Tribunal would have had no power to act without the authorization given by the parties. In the opinion of Pierre Jolidon, the decisions and acts of a designated third party should be equated with those of the parties themselves.[17]

Do you agree with arbitrator Cavin or with those who have criticized his views on the nature of the appointment made by the President of the Swiss Federal Tribunal?

2. In *Sapphire*, the President of the Swiss Federal Tribunal had no authority to make the appointment other than that he derived from having been chosen by the parties as the appointing authority. Suppose the parties chose a court that already had a statutory basis for making the appointment (a court of the site of arbitration or a court at the defendant's domicile). Would this affect the nature of the act of appointment?

[11]. Dutoit, Knoepfler, Lalive & Mercier, Répértoire de Droit international privé Suisse, 152 (1982).

[12]. P. Lalive, *De la désignation par un tiers de l'arbitre international*, Festgabe Schönenberger, 373, 380–81 (1968).

[13]. F.A. Mann, *State Contracts in International Arbitration*, 1967 Brit. Y.B.Int'l L.1, 20.

[14]. Suratgar, *The Sapphire Arbitration Award, the Procedural Aspects: A Report and a Critique*, 3 Colum.J. Transnat'l L. 152, 191 (1964).

[15]. S. Contini, Contribution a l'étude de l'arbitrage en procédure civil vaudoise (1957).

[16]. Suratgar, loc. cit. 191.

[17]. P. Jolidon, Commentaire du Concordat Suisse sur l'Arbitrage, 206 (1984).

3. Assuming the decision of the President of the Federal Tribunal is subject to reinvestigation, what would be the focus of this new scrutiny and who should make it? The key clause in the Concession agreement read:

Article 41.2

If one of the parties does not appoint its arbitrator or does not advise the other Party of the appointment made by it within two months of the institution of the proceedings, the other party shall have the right to apply to the President of the Swiss Federal Tribunal to appoint a sole arbitrator.

4. Did NIOC contest the validity of the arbitration agreement?

5. On January 10, 1961, NIOC nominated as arbitrator Charles Carabiber, a well known French professor, while Sapphire nominated on September 28, 1960 Mr. Tippit, an attorney from Denver, who later testified as a witness for Sapphire. Both these nominations became moot, but on different grounds. What were these grounds?

6. It has been argued that an appointing authority need not undertake a full scrutiny of the arbitration agreement. But should it verify the conditions to its own mission?

7. If you were the President of the Swiss Federal Tribunal, what would you check and verify before proceeding to make the appointment?

8. In *Elf Aquitaine v. NIOC,* Justice Hvidt decided to proceed with the appointment without facing the issue of the continued validity of the arbitration agreement.

Do you agree with this position?

What other options did he have?

9. In what respect did the problem the President of the Swiss Federal Tribunal had to face in the *Sapphire* case and the problem that was presented to the President of the Supreme Court of Denmark differ?

III.2.c.ii.   An Appointing Authority Not Relied Upon

PHILIPS HONG KONG, LTD. (HONG KONG) v. HYUNDAI ELECTRONICS INDUSTRIES CO. LTD. (HONG KONG)

Supreme Court of Hong Kong, 1993.
1 Hong Kong Law Reports 263 (1993).

FACTS

[Philips Hong Kong Limited trading as Eastern Electronics Company (Philips) requested the court to appoint an arbitrator pursuant to Sect. 12 of the Hong Kong Arbitration Ordinance which regulates the domestic regime. The Arbitration Clause in the contract between the parties provided as follows:

"All disputes, differences or questions ... arising between the parties ... shall be referred to the arbitration of a single arbitrator, who shall be agreed between the parties or who failing such agreement shall be appointed at the request of either party by the Chairman of the Hong Kong General Chamber of Commerce, or in accordance with the Rules of Conciliation and Arbitration then obtaining of the International Chamber of Commerce.

The arbitration shall be in accordance with the Arbitration Ordinance...."

The Hong Kong General Chamber of Commerce were invited to appoint, but declined to do so and at the time of these proceedings, the ICC had not been approached.][d]

KAPLAN, J.:

* * *

Mr. Horace Wong who appears for the plaintiffs, who wish an arbitrator to be appointed, takes two basic points. His first point relates to the construction of § 12 of the Ordinance and his second point relates to the Arbitration Clause itself and the rules of the International Chamber of Commerce (ICC).

Section 12 of the Arbitration Ordinance provides as follows:—

"Power of Court in certain cases to appoint an arbitrator or umpire

(1) In any of the following cases—

(a) where an arbitration agreement provides that the reference shall be to a single arbitrator, and all the parties do not, after disputes have arisen, concur in the appointment of an arbitrator;

(b) * * *;

(c) where a party or an arbitrator is required or is at liberty to appoint, or concur in the appointment of, an umpire or an arbitrator and does not do so;

(d) * * *;

any party may serve the other parties or the arbitrators, as the case may be, with a written notice to appoint, or, as the case may be, concur in appointing, an arbitrator, umpire or third arbitrator, and if the appointment is not made within 7 clear days after the service of the notice, the Court or a judge thereof may, on application by the party who gave the notice, appoint an arbitrator, umpire or third arbitrator * * *

(2) In any case where—

(a) an arbitration agreement provides for the appointment of an arbitrator or umpire by a person who is neither one of the parties nor an existing arbitrator (whether the provision applies

d. Summary of facts taken from 17 Yearbk. Comm. Arb'n 209 (1994).

directly or in default of agreement by the parties or otherwise); and

    (b) that person refuses to make the appointment or does not make it within the time specified in the agreement or, if no time is so specified, within a reasonable time,

any party to the agreement may serve the person in question with a written notice to appoint an arbitrator or umpire and, if the appointment is not made within 7 clear days after the service of the notice, the Court or a judge thereof may, on the application of the party who gave the notice, appoint an arbitrator or umpire * * * "

Mr. Wong's first point is that he contends that he can bring this application within the terms of § 12(1). He submits that:

    (1) the agreement provides for a single arbitrator; and

    (2) disputes have arisen; and

    (3) after disputes have arisen the parties have not concurred in the appointment of an arbitrator; and

    (4) the defendants have failed to concur after written notice has been served upon them.

Because these pre-conditions have been met, Mr. Wong submits that it is competent for the plaintiffs to apply to the court and for the court to exercise its discretion to appoint an arbitrator.

Miss Hazledine of Allen and Overy who appears for the defendants submits that this construction of § 12(1) cannot be correct because it ignores the provisions of § 12(2) which deal expressly with the situation where a third party named in the arbitration clause as the appointor refuses or fails to do so.

The facts relevant to this agreement are as follows. The Hong Kong General Chamber of Commerce were invited to appoint but declined to do so on the grounds that for some time they had not appointed arbitrators but had instead transferred their appointing functions to the Chairman of the Hong Kong International Arbitration Centre * * *

    It is also common ground that the ICC have not been approached. * * *

    It is therefore submitted that this application should fall to be considered under § 12(2) and as the second appointing authority has not yet refused or failed to make an appointment this application is premature and should be dismissed.

* * *

I am quite satisfied as a matter of construction of § 12 as a whole that, subject to Mr. Wong's argument about the inappropriateness of the ICC as an appointing authority in this case, his construction of § 12(1) cannot be correct.

It seems to me that § 12(1) deals with cases where there is no provision for appointment by a third party where the parties have failed to concur. If the parties cannot agree then the court steps in to prevent the arbitral process from being rendered nugatory. I accept the submission of Mr. Wong, based on observations at p. 178 in Mustill and Boyd on *Commercial Arbitration* (2nd Edition) that it is not necessary under § 12(1) for the parties to have attempted to agree first because the wording refers to the parties not concurring in the appointment of an arbitrator as opposed to having failed to agree.

However, § 12(2) clearly posits a situation where the parties have provided for either simple appointment by a third party or a default provision for appointment by a third party if they cannot or do not concur in an appointment themselves.

It is true that § 12(2) does not refer in terms to a default procedure, i.e., only if the parties do not concur. Some clauses provide simply that the appointment shall be by a third party such as the President of an Institution. Other clauses, such as the present, provide for agreement between the parties but failing that appointment by a third party.

If I were to read § 12(1) as Mr. Wong suggests, I would be ignoring the provisions of § 12(2) and further would be ignoring the clear agreement of these parties that if they could not agree on the appointment of an arbitrator either of the two named default appointers should appoint. As a matter of construction it seems clear to me that § 12(2) governs the present position because the arbitration agreement does in fact provide 'for the appointment of an arbitrator by a person who is neither one of the parties ...' It does not cease to so provide merely because it sensibly provides that initially the parties should attempt to agree.

Mr. Wong's second line of attack is to submit that the reference to appointment by the ICC is surplusage and should be ignored and that in those circumstances I should appoint. This argument stems from the words "in accordance with the Rules of Conciliation and Arbitration then obtaining of the International Chamber of Commerce".

Mr. Wong submits that if appointment is made in accordance with those rules then the whole panoply of an ICC arbitration would come into play and this would conflict with the parties' express agreement that the arbitration should be considered in accordance with the Arbitration Ordinance.

Mr. Wong has pointed to a number of ICC rules which he says would be quite inapplicable to an arbitration conducted under the Arbitration Ordinance. He refers, inter alia, to provisions about deposits for costs, arbitrator's fees, security for costs, approval of the award by the ICC court and the time limit for rendering an award. One can, of course, think of many examples of how an ICC administered arbitration would differ to an arbitration conducted under the Arbitration Ordinance.

However, it is necessary to refer to Appendix III para. 4 of the ICC Rules which provides as follows:

"A registration fee of US$1,000 is payable by the requesting party in respect of each request made to the ICC to appoint an arbitrator for any arbitration not conducted under the ICC Rules of Arbitration. No request for appointment of an arbitrator will be entertained unless accompanied by the said fee, which is not recoverable and becomes the property of the ICC."

There is thus specific provision in the ICC Rules for appointment to be made under the ICC in an arbitration not conducted or administered by the ICC Rules. This must have been what the parties intended and I do not propose to allow the plaintiffs to deviate from that expressed intention by semantic arguments about what precisely is meant by the phrase "in accordance with the rules". Appendix III para. 4 is part of the rules referred to and that deals with ICC appointments simpliciter. It ill behooves the plaintiffs, who freely entered into this arbitration agreement, now to attempt to circumvent its clear provisions by semantic argument.

The simple fact of the matter is that the ICC has never been asked to appoint. Even if there had been no para. 4 of Appendix III, I would still have considered that the ICC should have been asked to appoint on the basis that it was not to be a full ICC arbitration. Had they refused to do so, then the court's default power could have been properly invoked.

As there is express provision in the ICC rules dealing with appointment only, I can see no reason why the ICC should not be invited to exercise that power. If they should decline or if they should, for some reason, insist that they will only do so in relation to an ICC administered arbitration, then this can be taken as a refusal.

* * *

I therefore conclude that as a matter of law this application to the court for the appointment of an arbitrator is premature because the plaintiffs have not exhausted the contractual mechanism for appointment and I do not consider that they can rely on § 12(1). Regardless of my view of the legal position I would have refused to exercise my discretion to appoint unless and until some approach had been made to the ICC and their reaction discovered.

* * *

Questions and Comments

1. In *Philips v. Hyundai*, the Hong Kong Court obviously undertook some scrutiny before refusing to make the requested appointment. What did the court scrutinize? Did it verify the validity of the arbitration agreement?

2. The Hong Kong Arbitration Ordinance states in Section 12(2)(b) that the appointing authority must make appointments within the time specified by the parties, or within a reasonable time if no time was specified.

Can you suggest guidelines and considerations for the interpretation of this standard?

Is this a good solution, or should the legislator instead set a specific number of days?

3. Suppose the parties try but fail to agree on a sole arbitrator, and thereafter one party addresses the Chairman of the Hong Kong General Chamber of Commerce, while the other party addresses the ICC. Both appointing authorities respond positively, and both appoint a sole arbitrator. What result?

4. Suppose Philips Hong Kong had requested that the ICC nominate an arbitrator, but that the ICC had refused to make the nomination. Could the Hong Kong court still refuse to make a nomination?

Assume the same facts but assume also that the reason the ICC did not make the nomination was that Philips Hong Kong did not advance the appropriate fee. What result?

(The 1998 ICC Arbitration Rules Appendix III, Article 3 provides:

"A registration fee normally not exceeding US $2500 is payable by the requesting party in respect of each request made to the ICC to appoint an arbitrator for any arbitration not conducted under the Rules. No request for appointment of an arbitrator will be considered unless accompanied by the said fee, which is not recoverable and becomes the property of the ICC.")

III.2.c.iii.   An Appointing Authority That Ceased to Exist

GATOIL INTERNATIONAL, INC. (PANAMA) v. NATIONAL IRANIAN OIL CO. (IRAN)

England, High Court of Justice, Queen's Bench Division, 1988.
17 Yearbk. Comm. Arb'n 587 (1992).*

FACTS

On 17 April 1982, the parties entered into a written contract for the purchase by Gatoil International Inc. (Gatoil) from National Iranian Oil Company (NIOC) of a quantity of oil during the period between 1 April and 31 December 1982. Sect. 8 of the contract provided for arbitration as follows:

"Any dispute between the parties arising out of this Contract shall be settled by arbitration in accordance with the laws of Iran. The party who wants to submit such a dispute to arbitration shall advise the other party in writing, stating therein its claim and nominating its arbitrator. The other party shall nominate a second arbitrator within 30 days after receiving the said advice.

The two arbitrators thus appointed shall appoint a third arbitrator who shall be the president of the board of arbitration. Should

* Reprinted with permission of Yearbook Commercial Arbitration, International Council for Commercial Arbitration.

the other party fail to appoint and nominate the second arbitrator or should the two arbitrators fail to agree on the appointment of the third arbitrator within 30 days, the interested party may request the President of the Appeal Court of Tehran, Iran, to appoint the second arbitrator or the third arbitrator as the case may be.

The arbitrators appointed as per above provisions shall have broad experience with respect to the petroleum industry practices and oil marketing and be reasonably fluent in written and spoken English.

The arbitration award may be issued by majority and shall be binding on both parties.

The seat of arbitration shall be in Tehran, unless otherwise agreed by the parties.''

Sect. 10 of the contract provided that it would be governed and construed according to the laws of Iran.

A dispute arose between the parties regarding the delivery of oil and on 17 March 1987, Gatoil served a writ on NIOC. Gatoil did not wish to arbitrate in Tehran. NIOC was not willing to have the dispute litigated and was only prepared to arbitrate in Tehran. NIOC applied for a mandatory stay under Sect. 1(1) of the Arbitration Act 1975, which implements the New York Convention in the United Kingdom,[e] alternatively, for an order that the action be dismissed or stayed pursuant to the inherent jurisdiction of the Court on the ground of *forum non conveniens*.

The Court (*per* Mr. Justice Gatehouse) granted the stay as it was not convinced that the arbitration clause was null and void, inoperative, or incapable of being performed.

EXTRACT

[1] "The clause in question is, of course, a non-domestic arbitration clause and the defendant is entitled, as of right, to a stay of the action under Sect. 1(1) of the 1975 Act, unless the Court is satisfied that the arbitration agreement is null and void, inoperative or incapable of being performed.

(. . . .)

[2] "The first argument relied upon by the plaintiff was directed to the description of the default appointer in the arbitration clause, namely

---

e. Sect. 1(1) of the Arbitration Act 1975 reads:

"(1) If any party to an arbitration agreement to which this section applies, or any person claiming through or under him, commences any legal proceedings in any court against any other party to the agreement, or any person claiming through or under him, in respect of any matter agreed to be referred, any party to the proceedings may at any time after appearance, and be-

fore delivering any pleadings or taking any other steps in the proceedings, apply to the court to stay the proceedings, and the court, unless satisfied that the arbitration agreement is null and void, inoperative or incapable of being performed or that there is not in fact any dispute between the parties with regard to the matter agreed to be referred, shall make an order staying the proceedings."

the President of the Appeal Court of Tehran. No such person has existed since the revolution. By the post-revolutionary law, which abolished the Appeal Court, that Court's functions were transferred to the Municipal Court of Tehran, and the function of appointing an arbitrator where the parties are unable to agree is now exercisable by a Judge of that Municipal Court. The experts are also now agreed that if such an appointment had to be made, Art. 644(2) of the Civil Code of Procedure provides that it would have to be from amongst those residing or domiciled within the jurisdiction of that Court, a restriction which would not have applied if the President of the Court of Appeal had been the default appointer.

[3] "Mr. Sabi, the Iranian lawyer engaged by the plaintiff, in his first affidavit pointed to Art. 232 of the Iranian Civil Code, which provides that in regard to contracts:

"the following conditions are of no effect, though they do not nullify the contract itself:—

I.   Conditions which are impossible to fulfil."

Mr. Sabi also relies upon Art. 190 of the Iranian Civil Code, which provides:

"For validity of a contract, the following conditions are essential:

I.   The intention and mutual consent of both parties,"

Mr. Sabi says that Art. 8, the arbitration clause, is a condition of the contract and that it lacks two vital elements necessary if it is to be capable of being performed, namely: (a) it is impossible to enforce the provisions relating to the appointment of the second and third arbitrators; and (b) the parties did not intend to constitute the Municipal Court, or a Judge thereof, as the default appointer.

[4] "I prefer the opinions expressed by Dr. Movahed and Professor Safai to the effect that Art. 8 is not a condition of the contract but a collateral contract consisting of a number of different conditions or terms. If, as contended by the plaintiff, the condition relating to the default appointer is void, that does not nullify the rest of Art. 8. The parties entered into this contract some two and a half years after the enactment of the Iranian law abolishing the pre-revolutionary Appeal Court and replacing it and its functions with the Municipal Court of Tehran. But as Art. 8 itself is not nullified, and as the parties' mutual intention is to arbitrate further disputes, should they arise, in Tehran, according to the substantive and curial laws of Tehran, it seems to me that they must both be bound by the provisions of law as to the substitute default appointer.

[5] "... The plaintiff has not appointed its own arbitrator as required by the opening paragraphs of Art. 8, because it is obviously the claimant in the dispute.... The defendant is therefore not yet in a position when it is called upon to appoint its own arbitrator. If and when that arises, it seems obvious that it will do so because failure to co-operate would present the plaintiff with a virtually irrefutable argument

that Art. 8 is incapable of being performed. It would then fall to the two appointed arbitrators to agree upon the appointment of the third. Only if they failed to agree upon the third appointment would a Judge of the Municipal Court be called upon to exercise his default function. I do not think that I should assume at this stage that the two appointees will not be able to agree upon the third arbitrator.

[6] "The plaintiff suggests that the defendant's appointee will be likely to be obstructive in the knowledge that this must result in the Municipal Court being called upon to exercise its default function, and thus appoint a third arbitrator from within the restricted class, because this would be the defendant's wish, and the defendant is likely to be consulted by, and would be able to dictate the actions of, its own arbitrator. I am not prepared to assume in advance that the defendant's arbitrator will so abnegate his duty to act independently in agreeing an acceptable third arbitrator.

[7] "Even if, in the event, agreement as to the third arbitrator proves impossible and a Municipal Court Judge is called upon to exercise the default function, it is not inevitable that such appointee will have some connection with the defendant, as suggested in * * * Mr. Sabi's first affidavit, though the field of potential candidates will no doubt be more limited than the field which would theoretically have been available to the President of the Court of Appeal. I am not, therefore, prepared to hold that the arbitration clause is inoperative or incapable of being performed on this ground.

* * *

[11] "The third alternative ground relied upon by the plaintiff is that, practically speaking, it is impossible for them to find a qualified arbitrator who is willing to go to Tehran. There are exhibited ... four replies from potential arbitrators who were approached in late 1986 and the early months of 1987. Each refused, and there is an unparticularised allegation that a number of other candidates have been approached and have refused. I am asked to infer that the result will be the same, whomsoever is approached and that the arbitration clause is incapable of being performed for that reason.

[12] "Of the four replies in evidence it would seem that two were not in any case properly qualified candidates. What can be said by the plaintiff is that despite the cease fire in the Iran/Iraq war, the evidence of Mr. Sabi shows that Tehran remains an uncomfortable venue and that there are many reasons, good or supposed, which will deter many potential arbitrators from accepting appointment as the plaintiff's nominee. * * * It would be totally unrealistic to expect any plaintiff to show that it had exhausted the possible field. There must come a point far short of this where the Court can be satisfied on balance of probabilities that a corporation such as the plaintiff is unable, as a practical reality, to find an appointee of its choice who is willing to sit as an arbitrator in Tehran. But I am not satisfied that that point has been reached on the evidence before me.

[13] "The required qualifications of the arbitrators are that they should have broad experience of petroleum industry practice and be reasonably fluent in spoken and written English. There is no requirement that they should be legally qualified, though no doubt that would be desirable. Since English is, broadly speaking, the lingua franca of the oil industry worldwide, the potential field is enormous. I think that I am entitled to take judicial notice of the fact that there are likely to be English-speaking people, lawyers and/or oil company executives, all over the world, including of course the important areas of the Third World, who would be acceptable to the plaintiff as arbitrator, and who would not necessarily be deterred from sitting in Tehran."

[The court considered the *forum non conveniens* issue premature. The requested stay was granted, since it was not established that Section 8 was null and void, or inoperative, or incapable of being performed.]

Questions and Comments

1. The court notes that the parties agreed to arbitration in 1982 after the Iranian Revolution, and after the reorganization of the Iranian court system. The parties appear to have contracted on the assumption that the pre-Revolution court structure continued to exist; thus they nominated an appointing authority which ceased to exist before the parties referred to it. Accepting this premise, three interpretations are possible:

(a) the whole arbitration clause is invalid;

(b) the provision on appointment is invalid;

(c) the arbitration clause (including provisions on appointment) is valid, and the reference to the President of the Appeal Court of Tehran should be interpreted as reference to the legal successor of this court, which is the Municipal Court of Tehran.

Which would you choose?

2. Would your conclusions be different had the parties concluded their arrangement after the Iranian revolution, but while the Appeal Court of Tehran was still functioning?

3. Suppose the arbitration agreement had been executed in 1978, before the Iranian Revolution. Would that have affected the outcome of the case?

4. As a matter of general principle, are the powers of an appointing authority "inheritable"? (Can they pass to the legal successor of an institution, or to the heirs of a natural person?)

5. What if any weight would you attribute to the argument of Gatoil that "it is impossible to find a qualified arbitrator who is willing to go to Tehran"?

6. If you were counsel to Gatoil after this decision, would you advise Gatoil to cooperate in the appointment of arbitrators?

III.2.d. *Multi–Party Arbitration and Selection of Arbitrators*

Although the classic arbitration agreement envisions two parties, many international transactions are more complex. A construction project or a joint-venture, for example, can involve multiple parties and they may all enter the same contractual arrangement and provide in their contract for arbitration of all disputes. If a dispute arises between only two of the parties, arbitration can proceed in the classic pattern. But what if more than two parties are involved in the dispute and two (or more) of them have some convergent and some divergent interests? For example, suppose a project owner brings a claim against two co-contractors. The two contractors have a joint interest in proving that the work was done properly and, at the same time, in showing that if there were any inadequacy in the work it was the fault of the other co-contractor. What if the agreement calls for three arbitrators, one chosen by each of the parties and the third by the first two so chosen? Is it fair to treat the two co-contractors as one party and to force them to agree upon an arbitrator? Though the facts are different, this is the general situation that arose in the *Dutco* case immediately below.

SIEMENS AG AND BKMI INDUSTRIEANLANGEN GMBH v. DUTCO CONSTRUCTION CO., LTD.

Cour de cassation (Supreme Court of France) Civ. I, 7 January, 1992.
Bull. Civ. I no. 2r.

7 Mealey's International Arbitration Report
B–3 (1992) (English translation)*

THE COURT, * * *

Combines Appeals No. 89–28.708 Y and No. 89–18.726 T, the grounds of which are similar;

On the two first sections of the single grounds of each of the appeals, combined:

In view of articles 1502, section 2, and 1504 of the New Code of Civil Procedure, and of article 6 of the Civil Code;

Whereas the principle of the equality of the parties in the designation of the arbitrators is a concern of public order; which can only be renounced after the beginning of the litigation;

Whereas, on 26 March 1981, a consortium agreement was concluded between Dutco Construcion company of Dubai, and the two German companies, BKMI and Siemens, the aim of which was to construct a cement factory in Oman; it was stipulated therein that all differences would be resolved according to the arbitration regulations of the International Chamber of Commerce, by three arbitrators named in accordance with these regulations; upon the single request for arbitration presented by Dutco against its two co-contractants, separately, for distinct credits concerning the two firms, an arbitration tribunal of three arbitrators was appointed, one designated jointly by the two respondents with

* Mealey's International Arbitration Report. Reprinted with the permission of Lexis–Nexis, a division of Reed Elsevier Inc.

protestations and reservations; the tribunal determined that it had been regularly constituted, and that the arbitration proceedings should go forward in a multiparty form against the two respondents;

Whereas, by rejecting the appeals for annulment filed by Siemens and BKMI against the arbitration decision, the contested ruling holds that the arbitration clause integrated in the agreement linking the three firms expresses unambiguously the common desire of the parties for a similar contract to submit all differences resulting from their agreement to three arbitrators, thus it is necessarily deducted from the multiparty nature of the contract itself, with the foreseeable eventuality of differences between the three partners, that the parties have admitted the possibility of a single tribunal composed of three arbitrators to decide upon a dispute between the three partners, with the arrangements arising from such a situation;

Whereas ruling thus, the court of appeals violated the aforementioned texts;

FOR THESE REASONS, without it being necessary to rule on the other complaints of the appeals:

OVERTURNS AND ANNULS the ruling by the Paris Court of Appeals on 5 May 1989, in all its dispositions for the parties; as a result, returns the matter and the parties to the state in which they found themselves before the said ruling, and in order to effect justice, sends them back before the Versailles Court of Appeals;

Condemns Dutco Construction to the costs of the two appeals and to the expenses for the execution of the present ruling;

Orders that, by the diligence of the Prosecutor General at the Supreme Court, the present ruling be transmitted for transcription in the registers of the Paris Court of Appeals, in the margins of or following the annulled ruling;

Thus done and determined by the Supreme Court, First Civil Chamber, pronounced by the President in public session on 7 January 1992.

Questions and Comments

1. Do you agree with the Dutco case outcome? The parties agreed to the arbitration clause, as written, didn't they? Should the Cour de cassation have given more weight to this consideration?

2. Was it a mistake for Siemens and BKMI to proceed with the arbitration under protest? Or was it a mistake on Dutco's part to bring a claim against both Siemens and BKMI? Why didn't the three disputants agree to have each party appoint an arbitrator? Could Dutco have sought court assistance at the stage of choosing arbitrators? What court? When? and What assistance? How should a court have responded?

3. In the wake of the Dutco case, a number of arbitral institutions amended their rules. Read in the documents supplement, for example, ICC Rules Art. 10; London Court of International Arbitration Rules Art. 8; and

AAA International Rules Art. 6(5). Which of these institutional approaches do you prefer?

4. Suppose the parties prefer ad hoc arbitration, would the UNCITRAL rules be adequate? If not, how would you advise the parties? Would it be a solution to choose UNCITRAL rules and a sole arbitrator? But what if the parties prefer three arbitrators? For a discussion of drafting arbitration clauses for multi-party arbitration, see Paul D. Friedland, ARBITRATION CLAUSES FOR INTERNATIONAL CONTRACTS (2000).

III.3. CHALLENGES

III.3.a. *Introduction*

Albert Jan van den Berg,[f] REPORT ON
THE CHALLENGE PROCEDURE

The Arbitral Process and the Independence of Arbitrators
87–93 (ICC ed., 1991)*

INTRODUCTION

1. There is no doubt that the impartiality and independence of arbitrators are fundamental requirements of the arbitral process. It is not within the scope of my presentation to discuss the circumstances in which an arbitrator can be deemed not to meet these requirements. This question is the subject of the previous session concerning the standards of behaviour of arbitrators.

2. My view on this question is that we should be rather strict in interpreting and applying the requirements: any arbitrator—whether appointed by a party or a third person—should be absolutely impartial and independent. In case of any objective doubt as to impartiality, he or she should not act.

AVOIDANCE OF CHALLENGE

3. A preliminary observation regarding the subject of my presentation on the challenge procedure concerns the avoidance of challenge. At the outset, a prospective arbitrator can avoid a challenge at two stages.

4. First, if, when he is approached by a party or a third person with the invitation to act as arbitrator, he believes that there will probably be objective doubts in the eyes of any of the parties about his independence or impartiality, he should decline the invitation forthwith. The flattery of the invitation should not cause him to take lightly circumstances which may affect his impartiality or independence.

5. Second, if the prospective arbitrator does not decline and accepts the invitation, but there are circumstances which might give rise to

---

f. Partner, Hanotiau & van den Berg, Brussels, Belgium.

The Arbitral Process and the Independence of Arbitrators. ICC Publication No. 472CISBN 92.842.0093.8 (EF). Published in its official English version by the International Chamber of Commerce. Copyright 8 1991—International Chamber of Commerce (ICC), Paris. Reprinted with permission from ICC.

doubt about his impartiality or independence, he should disclose them in writing to both parties and, if an arbitral institution is involved, to the latter as well. The duty to disclose is a requirement of most modern arbitration cases and arbitration rules.[1] If a party then objects on serious grounds, he should resign, without a formal challenge procedure being necessary. If no party promptly objects, the right to challenge the arbitrator will in most cases be forfeited.

Possible Reasons for the Recent Increase of Challenge Procedures

6. Having regard to the foregoing, one may wonder why the number of formal challenge procedures in international arbitration has increased so dramatically.[2] As I see it, there are four probable reasons for this increase. Considering the limitations of my presentation, [I] will merely mention them.

7. A first reason may be that the interpretation as to what constitutes impartiality and independence has become stricter.

8. A second reason may be that parties from certain countries who previously did not use or scarcely used international arbitration misconceive the requirements of impartiality or independence of the arbitrator whom they have to appoint.

9. A third reason may be that challenge of an arbitrator can be a powerful delaying tactic. A challenge may also be thought to have a psychological effect on the challenged arbitrator. Even if the challenge is rejected, some parties think that the challenge has the effect that the challenged arbitrator will be more impartial and independent towards them than towards the other party. A variation on the * * * [third] reason is that a party deliberately appoints an arbitrator who lacks impartiality and independence in an attempt to frustrate the arbitral process.

10. And a fourth reason may be that the increase in the challenge proceedings is just one aspect of the general tendency which we witness in our times that international arbitration has become more litigious in procedural respects.

The Two Issues Concerning Challenge Procedures

11. I may now turn to the subject of my presentation: the challenge procedures. For these procedures, one has to look first at the law applicable to the arbitration. Any rules of a mandatory nature regarding the challenge of arbitrators in that law must be deemed to prevail over provisions on the same subject in arbitration rules.

---

1. *See, e.g.,* UNCITRAL Model Law on International Commercial Arbitration of 1985, Art. (12)1; Netherlands Arbitration Act 1986, Art. 1034. However, the French (1981) and Swiss (1987) International Arbitration Law do not contain provisions concerning disclosure. With respect to arbitration rules, *see, e.g.,* ICC Rules (1988), Art. 2(7); UNCITRAL Arbitration Rules (1976), Art. 9 ; NAI Rules (1986) Art. 11.

2. For example, the number of challenges brought before the ICC Court of Arbitration was 11 in 1986 and 22 in 1987.

12. With the purpose of not complicating my presentation unduly, it is assumed that the arbitration law of the place of arbitration governs international arbitration since this principle is applied in most cases in practice.

13. Certain countries, such as France and Switzerland, make a distinction between domestic and international arbitration. Similarly, the UNCITRAL Model Law is limited to international commercial arbitration. This distinction does not affect the principle that the arbitration law of the place of arbitration governs international arbitration : in these countries one has to consult the special law on international arbitration if the arbitration in that country can be qualified as international under that law.

14. The exception to the above principle is ICSID arbitration which is outside the reach of national arbitration laws and is solely governed by the Washington Convention of 1965 and the Rules and Regulations issued thereunder.[3]

15. Every arbitration law requires either expressly or implicitly that an arbitrator be impartial and independent. Every arbitration law also provides that compliance with this requirement is subject to court supervision. The manner in which this is done, however, varies from country to country. Here we come to the first issue which I would like to consider: at what moment can court control be exercised?

16. Arbitral institutions frequently have their own procedure for challenging arbitrators appointed by them or under their auspices. The concurrent existence of such institutional procedure and the challenge procedure provided in the applicable arbitration law raises the second issue which I would like to consider: to what extent are institutional challenge procedures compatible with the applicable arbitration law?

17. Both issues involve a balancing of various considerations, which are not always easy to reconcile:

(a) the arbitration should take place with due dispatch and the possibility of delaying tactics should be reduced to a minimum;

(b) it should be avoided that, when completed, an arbitration turns out to have been a waste of time and money because the award cannot be enforced on account of some irregularity in the arbitral tribunal;

(c) a serious complaint about an arbitrator's impartiality or independence should be honoured;

(d) a satisfactory degree of international uniformity in the interpretation and application of the grounds for challenging an arbitrator should be attained.

3. The procedure for disqualification of an arbitrator is provided in Arts. 57 and 58 of the Washington Convention and in Rule 9 of the Arbitration Rules.

A. Court Control

18.　Most arbitration laws provide that a party can challenge an arbitrator during the arbitration before a court.[4] The advantage of this system is that a question about the arbitrator's impartiality or independence can be decided forthwith. Once the court has rendered a decision, it is unlikely that the question will arise thereafter in the arbitration proceedings or during enforcement and/or setting aside proceedings relating to the award.

19.　The system of challenge in court during the arbitration has the disadvantage that it can be used as a delaying tactic. An average challenge procedure in court takes one to six months. This disadvantage will be aggravated if the court decision is open to appeal and even recourse to the Supreme Court. Modern arbitration laws therefore provide that the court decision on the challenge is not subject to appeal.[5]

20.　The arbitration laws of some countries provide that during the arbitration a party may bring a challenge before the arbitral tribunal itself and that if the arbitral tribunal rejects the challenge, the impartiality or independence of the arbitrator can be questioned before a court *only after the award is made*, either in enforcement proceedings or in proceedings relating to the setting aside of the award. I understand that this system, for example, prevails in Sweden.[6]

21.　The advantage of this system is that a delay in the arbitration proceedings is minimized. Furthermore, if the arbitral tribunal accepts the challenge, no subsequent arbitration proceedings will take place which may turn out to have been a nullity.

22.　A disadvantage is that if the arbitral tribunal rejects the challenge, a court may have a different view, resulting in a refusal to enforce or a setting aside of the award.

23.　Another disadvantage can be that a direct discussion between a party and the arbitral tribunal occurs about the impartiality or independence of one or more of the latter's members. Such a discussion may have an impact on the further conduct of the arbitration proceedings if the arbitral tribunal rejects the challenge. In my view, it seems preferable that such a direct confrontation does not take place but rather that a

---

4.　*Although the U.S. Federal Arbitration Act does not contain any provision on challenging an arbitrator, U.S. courts do allow the challenge of an arbitrator during the arbitral proceedings under their inherent power to remove an arbitrator. See H. Holtzmann, National Report United States, in the International Handbook on Commercial Arbitration, p. 14.* [Authors' note: Holtzmann has more recently commented, concerning U.S. practice: "Courts generally do not remove arbitrators before or during the arbitration proceeding, although they have an inherent power to do so. In practice, judicial review of the qualifications of arbitrators usually occurs after an award has been rendered, when one party seeks to set aside the award on the ground that the arbitrators should have been disqualified for being partial." Id., Supplm. 13, at 17 (1992).]

5.　*See, e.g.,* UNCITRAL Model Law on International Commercial Arbitration of 1985, Art. 13(3), text quoted at n. 14 *infra;* Netherlands Arbitration Act 1986, Arts. 1035 and 1070.

6.　U. Holmbäck, National Report Sweden, in The International Handbook on Commercial Arbitration, p. 7.

third party (court or arbitral institution) is entrusted with the judging of the question whether an arbitrator lacks impartiality or independence.[7]

24. Before moving to the second issue, it should be noted that court control over the impartiality or independence of an arbitrator is not confined to the courts of the country where the arbitration takes or has taken place. Court control can also be exercised in foreign countries where enforcement of the award is sought under the New York Convention on the Recognition and Enforcement of Foreign Arbitral Awards of 1958. According to Art. V(2)(b), the enforcement court may, on its own motion, refuse enforcement of the award if it violates the public policy of its country. It is generally accepted that this ground for refusal of enforcement encompasses the lack of impartiality or independence of an arbitrator.[8]

25. In practice, however, this court control appears to be rather theoretical. In none of the more than 330 court decisions from 23 Contracting States reported in the Yearbook Commercial Arbitration to date, has a court refused enforcement on account of a lack of independence or impartiality of an arbitrator. In this connection, the courts frequently apply the narrow criterion of international public policy.

B. INSTITUTIONAL CHALLENGE PROCEDURES

26. As observed, most arbitral institutions provide for a challenge procedure within the framework of the institution.

An example is the Court of Arbitration of the International Chamber of Commerce whose Rules (in effect as of 1 January 1988) contain an improved challenge procedure to be brought before, and to be decided by, the Court of Arbitration.[9]

27. Institutional challenge procedure should, however, be compatible with the applicable arbitration law which, as explained before, can be deemed in most cases to be the arbitration law of the place of arbitration. The issue is whether, and if so to what extent, an arbitral institution can provide its own challenge proceedings. Basically, three systems can be said to exist in this respect.

(i) Challenge to be decided exclusively by a court

28. Arbitration acts of certain countries provide that a court has exclusive jurisdiction to decide on the challenge of an arbitrator. I understand this to be the case, for example, under the Swiss Concordat

---

7. The procedure discussed in the text, which involves a decision by an arbitral tribunal on a challenge, is to be distinguished from the case—which can be found in many arbitration acts—where a challenge is to be notified to the arbitrator and only if the arbitrator does not resign upon receipt of the notification, the challenge can be brought before the court. The latter case does as a rule not include a direct discussion between the challenging party and the arbitral tribunal.

8. See the author of this contribution, The New York Arbitration Convention of 1958 (Deventer 1981) p. 377; see also the same author, Commentary Court decisions New York Convention 1958, Article V sub ground 2 '2, which appears annually in Part V of the Yearbook Commercial Arbitration.

9. The challenge provisions are contained in Art. 2(8)–(9) of the ICC Rules.

on Arbitration of 1969.[10] It means that provisions in arbitration rules pursuant to which the arbitral institution rules on a challenge cannot be applied if the place of arbitration is located in such country.

29. The advantage of this system is that in case of institutional arbitration the arbitral proceedings will not be delayed by proceedings in two instances, i.e., first, the arbitral institution and, second, the court.

30. A disadvantage of this system in the context of international arbitration is that a court may have views on the impartiality or independence of an arbitrator which differ from the views of courts in other countries and, in particular, from those of the international arbitral institution concerned. An arbitral institution will have an interest in having a uniform concept of impartiality and independence which can be applied to all arbitrations administered by it, irrespective of the place of arbitration. Such uniformity will be lost if courts in various countries interpret differently the requirements of impartiality and independence.

(ii) Challenge to be decided exclusively by arbitral institution

31. The system whereby the arbitral institution decides exclusively on a challenge without court interference, is implied in the French law on international arbitration of 1981.[11] This system means, for example, for ICC arbitration that the ICC Court of Arbitration is the sole judge for challenges brought against ICC arbitrators if the place of arbitration is situated in France.[12]

32. The advantage of this system is that it limits the challenge procedure to one instance and that, as a consequence, the delay in the arbitral proceedings can be minimized (provided that the arbitral institution can act with due dispatch on a challenge brought before it). The advantage of having a uniform concept of impartiality and independence was mentioned above. That advantage, however, can be attained only if a fairly large number of countries accept an exclusive competence of an institutional decision on a challenge. At present, this is not the case since very few countries appear to be prepared to adopt this approach.

33. A disadvantage of this system can be that the legal status of the institution's decision on the challenge may be uncertain. This gives rise to the question whether a court is bound by such decision, in

10. R. Briner, National Report Switzerland, in the International Handbook on Commercial Arbitration, p. 8. The Swiss International Arbitration Law of 1987 provides in Article 180(3):

"To the extent that the parties have not made a provision for this challenge procedure, the judge at the seat of the arbitral tribunal shall make the final decision."

According to M. Blessing, The New International Arbitration Law in Switzerland, 5 Journal of International Arbitration (1988) p. 9 at 40, this provision has the effect that

"In respect of the challenge procedure the agreement by the parties has priority. This means that, in the case of ICC arbitration, the ICC's exclusive competence to rule on a challenge is now fully recognized."

11. Y. Derains, National Report France, in International Handbook on Commercial Arbitration p. 11.

12. The same principle seems to prevail under the Swiss International Arbitration Law of 1987. See n. 10 supra.

particular in proceedings after the award is made. Perhaps, a French court may not be allowed to review in enforcement or setting aside proceedings relating to the arbitral award a decision of the ICC Court of Arbitration rejecting a challenge. But would a foreign court be obliged to give a binding effect to such decision in enforcement proceedings under the New York Convention of 1958?

34. A different question of a more fundamental nature is whether a court control over an institutional decision on an arbitrator's challenge is necessary at all. With due respect to those arbitral institutions which carry out their functions with great diligence on the basis of longstanding experience, they are nevertheless composed of private individuals. The principle still remains that the trial of disputes is a prerogative of State courts. That prerogative can be attributed to private mechanisms of doing justice by national legislators. In the international context, the same can be achieved by international conventions amongst States (e.g., the Washington Convention of 1965) but not otherwise.

35. It would, in my opinion, be wishful thinking to consider that at present an international arbitration system can effectively exist outside the reach of national legislation and/or international conventions. Since the impartiality and independence are the cornerstones of arbitration, a State court should have the last word thereon, whether during the arbitration or after the award is made.

(iii) Challenge to be decided by arbitral institution with a possibility of recourse to a court against the institutional decision on the challenge

36. Most arbitration acts provide a system by which the parties may agree on a challenge procedure, which includes a third person (usually an arbitral institution) who decides on the challenge. The challenge can, however, subsequently be brought before the court, since recourse to the court cannot be excluded by agreement of the parties.[13]

37. This system can, for example, be found in Art. 13 of the UNCITRAL Model Law on International Commercial Arbitration of 1985:

> "1. The parties are free to agree on a procedure for challenging an arbitrator, subject to the provision of paragraph (3) of this article.
>
> "2. Failing such agreement, a party who intends to challenge an arbitrator shall, within fifteen days after becoming aware of the constitution of the arbitral tribunal or after becoming aware of any

---

13. This system can be deemed to prevail under the Netherlands Arbitration Act 1986 as well. Although the text of Art. 1035 of the Act does not provide expressly for a challenge procedure agreed to by the parties, it is assumed that such procedure is to be followed before a challenge can be brought to the President of the District Court. It is also assumed that the President will generally follow the institution's decision on the challenge. If the time limit for bringing the challenge before the President will expire before the institution has taken a decision on the challenge, the request for a challenge should be filed pro forma with the President with the request to suspend the proceedings until the institution has given a decision. See P. Sanders and A.J. van den Berg, The Netherlands Arbitration Act 1986, [___, n.31 (1987)].

circumstance referred to in Art. 12(2), send a written statement of the reasons for the challenge to the arbitral tribunal. Unless the challenged arbitrator withdraws from his office or the other party agrees to the challenge, the arbitral tribunal shall decide on the challenge.[14]

"3. If a challenge under any procedure agreed upon by the parties or under the procedure of paragraph (2) of this article is not successful, the challenging party may request, within thirty days after having received notice of the decision rejecting the challenge, the court or other authority specified in Art. 6 to decide on the challenge, which decision shall be subject to no appeal; while such a request is pending, the arbitral tribunal, including the challenged arbitrator, may continue the arbitral proceedings and make an award."

38.   The advantage of this system is that an arbitral institution has the opportunity to decide on the challenge. In case of respectable arbitral institutions, it is likely that a court will follow the institution's decision. This advantage promotes the desired degree of uniformity in the concept of impartiality and independence in international institutional arbitration. It also has the advantage that a court can exercise a certain control over arbitral institutions which take their functioning less seriously. Furthermore, once the court has decided on the challenge, the question of impartiality or independence is not likely to arise any more during the arbitration and after the award is made (unless other circumstances affecting the impartiality or independence come up).

39.   A disadvantage of this system is that it may delay the arbitral proceedings since two instances—the arbitral institution and the court—can be called upon to decide on the challenge.

40.   A question for the above system is whether the court should examine the question of impartiality and independence *de novo* or should limit itself to a marginal review of the institution's decision on the challenge. Under the former method, the court may take into account the institution's decision as persuasive authority but nevertheless engage in its own examination of the circumstances giving rise to the doubts as to the arbitrator's impartiality or independence. This type of examination seems to prevail in virtually all countries which adhere to the above system. Under the marginal control method, the court would limit its review to whether a reasonable arbitral institution could have come to the decision.

41.   In my view, the method of an examination *de novo* is to be preferred since, although the court is likely to reach the same conclusion as the arbitral institution, it alleviates any doubt about the correctness of the institution's decision. Such a clear situation is beneficial for the remainder of the arbitral proceedings. Moreover, the question then is less likely to be raised successfully again after the award is made, than

---

14. I consider it rather unfortunate that the arbitral tribunal is to decide on the challenge under the UNCITRAL Model Law. See text accompanying no. 7 supra.

could be done if the court's review were marginal only. The method of an examination *de novo* would also be more in line with the court's control over this fundamental aspect of the arbitral process.

SOME OTHER PROCEDURAL ASPECTS

42. Besides the differing statutory systems for the challenge procedure, some other differences merit brief mention.

(a) Time limits

43. Certain arbitration acts contain a time limit for bringing a challenge against an arbitrator. For example, the Swiss Statute on International Arbitration of 1987 provides in Art. 180(2) that "The ground for challenge must be notified to the arbitral tribunal and the other party without delay". Other Acts do not contain such time limits and leave the question of the time limit to the agreement of the parties (which is usually embodied by arbitration rules). An example of the latter is the French law on international arbitration of 1981.

* * *

(b) Challenge of a party-appointed arbitrator

46. Most arbitration acts provide that a party may not challenge an arbitrator whom he has appointed, except on a ground which came to that party's attention after such appointment. This is, for example, the case for the Swiss Statute on international arbitration of 1987 (Art. 180(2)) and the Netherlands Arbitration Act 1986 (Art. 1033(2)). Other Acts, such as the French law on international arbitration, are silent in this respect.

47. The ICC Rules do not contain a provision regarding the challenge of a party-appointed arbitrator either. Consequently, if an ICC arbitration takes place in a country where the arbitration act does not impose limitations on the party's right to challenge the arbitrator appointed by him, this may open the door to a delaying tactic by that party—enabling him to appoint and subsequently challenge a biased arbitrator.

(c) Suspension of arbitral proceedings

48. The UNCITRAL Model Law of 1985 and the Netherlands Arbitration Act 1986 contain express provisions on the question of the effect of the bringing of a challenge on the arbitral proceedings. Art. 13(3) of the Model law provides in pertinent part: "While such a request (for a challenge) is pending (before the court), the arbitral tribunal, including the challenged arbitrator, may continue the arbitral proceedings and make an award". Art 1035(1) of the Dutch Act provides: "The arbitral tribunal may suspend the arbitral proceedings as of the day of receipt of the notification (of the challenge)". Thus, the tribunal has a discretionary power to suspend the proceedings in the case of a challenge. It may decide to continue the proceedings notwithstanding the challenge, for example, if the challenge appears prima facie unjustified.

49. The Rules of the Netherlands Arbitration Institute contain a similar rule on suspension of proceedings pending a challenge.[16] On the other hand, the ICC Rules and UNCITRAL Rules are silent in this respect. ICSID Arbitration Rules provide for an automatic suspension of the proceedings until a decision has been taken on the proposal for disqualification of an arbitrator.[17]

CONCLUSIONS

50. Court control over the impartiality and independence of an arbitrator is indispensable. This principle is not different for international arbitration unless another control mechanism is provided on the basis of an international convention such as the Washington Convention of 1965.

51. The procedure for bringing a challenge is provided to a differing degree of detail in the various arbitration acts. Furthermore, the arbitration acts differ as to whether, and if so to what extent, a challenge procedure can be entrusted to an arbitral institution. In the international context, it emphasizes the need for a careful choice of the place of arbitration.

52. The provisions in the challenge procedure in the various arbitration rules also vary. Some are rather succinct, thereby creating uncertainties; others are more detailed.

53. It seems to me that a fairly large number of arbitral institutions should review the challenge proceedings provided in their rules. The better the institutional challenge procedures are regulated, the more likely it is that courts will follow an institution's decision on a challenge. This attitude of the courts will be beneficial to international arbitral institutions in the sense that they can establish an internationally uniform interpretation and application of the grounds for challenging arbitrators and that it may deter challenging parties from bringing unmeritorious challenges before a court.

Questions and Comments

1. Assume the UNCITRAL Model Law applies. Suppose the parties choose ad hoc arbitration and do not choose any arbitral rules. Who decides on a challenge to an arbitrator? Does the challenged arbitrator participate in the decision? If the parties, still in ad hoc arbitration, had chosen UNCITRAL Rules, how would this have affected the challenge procedure?

2. At what point in the arbitration process are courts competent to decide a challenge to an arbitrator? In New York Convention countries can the issue be raised on enforcement of the award? Under what provision of the Convention? If a challenge has previously been decided by the arbitrators themselves or by an arbitral institution, how much deference to that decision should a court give in enforcement proceedings? Should courts be authorized to decide on challenges before or during arbitral proceedings?

---

16. NAI Rules, ART. 19(5).   **17.** ICSID Arbitration Rules, Rule 9(6).

III.3.b.   *Challenges and Court Control*

REFINERIES OF HOMS AND BANIAS (SYRIA) v. INTERNATIONAL CHAMBER OF COMMERCE[g]

Tribunal de grande instance of Paris, March 28, 1984; Court of Appeal, Paris, May 15, 1985. Mealey's Int'l Arb'n Rep. 502 (1986).*

TRIBUNAL DE GRANDE INSTANCE OF PARIS, MARCH 28, 1984—SUMMARY AND EXTRACTS.

In this arbitration between a Syrian party and a Yugoslav party, the Court of Arbitration granted a request for the recusation of the arbitrator nominated by the Syrian party, in conformity with the Rules. The Syrian party sought the annulation of the Court of Arbitration's decision to remove the arbitrator. Subsidiarily it sought damages from the ICC in the amount of one franc. The Tribunal de Grande Instance first recalled that the arbitrator's power to settle a dispute stems from the common will of the parties involved in this dispute:

"Whereas the choice of an arbitrator—judge and not agent of the party who appointed him—must see his power of jurisdiction to stem from a single and common act of will of both parties to the arbitration, even if, in a first stage, he was appointed on the initiative of one party only;

Whereas once such an appointment is made, and the arbitration regularly started, the maintenance of an arbitrator within an arbitral tribunal can be imposed only insofar as it is authorized by the common will of the parties."

The Tribunal then held that the parties may vest any third party with the power of taking the measures necessary for ensuring the fair development of the arbitral process until the arbitrators render their final award. The Tribunal deduced from the reference to the ICC Rules of Arbitration in the arbitration clause that both parties had intended to entrust the ICC Court of Arbitration with the power to decide all disputes relating to the nomination, the confirmation, the challenge or the replacement of the arbitrators. This was further confirmed by the correspondence between the ICC and the Refineries, their counsel and the arbitrator appointed by them.

The Tribunal found that the arbitrator had been removed in conformity with the ICC Rules of Arbitration. As to the necessary content and the nature of the ICC Court decision, the Tribunal answered the arguments of the Refineries as follows:

"Whereas it suffices that the explanations of the parties and their respective grievances and arguments have been requested and re-

g. 1985 Revue de l'arbitrage 140.   * Mealey's International Arbitration Report. Reprinted with the permission of LexisNexis, a division of Reed Elsevier Inc.

ceived by the General Secretariat of the Court of Arbitration in order that there should be recognized a sufficient binding effect to an administrative decision in the arbitral proceeding, and it does not matter that the legal, factual or policy * * * [reasons] motivating this decision have not been communicated to the parties, since the parties have expressly wished it thus, and since in addition, a decision on an incidental plea for the challenge or replacement of an arbitrator does not involve the exercise of the power to judge and to decide a dispute and is not subject to the same mandatory rules."

The Tribunal further considered that the ICC Court of Arbitration could not be held to have caused a tort since the arbitrator initially appointed by the Refineries had been challenged in conformity with the rules chosen by the parties. The Tribunal thus rejected the claims presented by the Refineries.

COURT OF APPEAL OF PARIS, MAY 15, 1985—SUMMARY AND EXTRACTS.

The Court of Appeal declared inadmissible both the action for annulment and the claim in tort instituted by the Refineries. With respect to the action for annulment, the Court held that all the arguments relied upon by the Refineries were "inoperative in the context of an international arbitration of an entirely contractual nature". The Court of Appeal stated that the complainant had not shown in what ways the Rules of the ICC, which it had agreed were applicable, had been violated. Moreover, the Court of Appeal found that in any event the documents produced showed that the Court of Arbitration had respected its own rules, and that while the ICC Court decision did not state the reasons on which its decision was based, in any event such reasons had been previously communicated to the removed arbitrator. It dismissed the claim in tort on the ground that "the alleged tort committed by the defendant can be judged only in the context of a regulation, the violation of which was never asserted."[h]

STATE OF QATAR v. CREIGHTON LTD (CAYMAN ISLANDS)

25 Yearbk Comm. Arb'n 451*
Cour de Cassation [Supreme Court of France] 16 March 1999.

FACTS

In 1982 the Government of Qatar entered into a contract with Creighton Limited (Creighton), as the main contractor, to build a new hospital in Doha, the Qatari capital. The contract provided for the

---

h. [[*Mealey Report*] *Author's Comment.* The French courts continue to be supportive of the ICC Court of Arbitration's role in administering and supervising arbitrations and are reluctant to intervene in this process. For further comment, see Craig, "International Ambition and National Restraints in ICC Arbitration," 1 Arbitration International 49 (1985), and J.Y. Art, "Challenge of Arbitrators: Is An Institutional Decision Final," 2 Arbitration International 261 (1986) * * *.]

* Reprinted with permission of Yearbook Commercial Arbitration, International Council for Commercial Arbitration.

application of Qatari law and for the final settlement of all disputes by ICC arbitration.

In 1986, Qatar expelled Creighton from the construction site for unsatisfactory performance; one year later, in 1987, Creighton commenced ICC arbitration as agreed upon in the contract.

The ICC arbitrators issued three awards in favour of Creighton, directing Qatar to pay Creighton a sum exceeding US $8 million in damages, interest and attorneys' fees.

Creighton sought enforcement of the awards in France and in the United States. In France, the Paris Court of Appeal held that the Qatari assets in France were immune from attachment under French law. In its decision of 6 July 2000, the French Supreme Court held that by agreeing to ICC arbitration, Qatar had waived its immunity from execution. In the United States, the US District Court for the District of Columbia held that it lacked personal jurisdiction over Qatar because Qatar did not have sufficient contact with the United States to make it amenable to suit there. The US Court of Appeal for the District of Columbia Circuit affirmed this decision on 2 July 1999.

In its turn, Qatar sought to have the awards set aside in France. On 12 January 1996, the Paris Court of Appeal denied the request, dismissing Qatar's ground for annulment based on the alleged lack of impartiality and independence of the arbitrator appointed by Creighton. By the present decision the Supreme Court affirmed the lower court's decision.

EXCERPT

[1] "The State of Qatar attacks the lower court decision (Court of Appeal, Paris, 12 January 1996) for its dismissal of Qatar's request for annulment of three arbitral awards rendered in Paris in Qatar's dispute with the American company Creighton Limited concerning the execution of a building contract for a hospital in Doha (Qatar). Qatar maintains that the Court of Appeal did not legally justify its decision on the need for arbitrators to be independent and impartial, by refusing to take into account the dissimulations and lies of the arbitrator designated by [Creighton] concerning his connection to Creighton before, during and after the arbitration, and by refusing to examine whether that arbitrator's participation in another arbitration in the same case did not prejudice the State of Qatar.

[2] "However, it pertains to the court deciding on the validity of the arbitral award to ascertain the independence and impartiality of the arbitrator, by examining any circumstance that may affect the arbitrators judgment and raise a reasonable doubt in the mind of the parties, as to the arbitrator's [independence and impartiality], which are essential characteristics of the arbitral function.

[3] "In this respect the Court of Appeal found that Mr. X, the arbitrator appointed by Creighton, had assisted Creighton in finding a lawyer before the arbitral proceedings, but that nothing showed that he

was materially or intellectually connected to Creighton, which subsequently appointed him as its arbitrator. Also, [the Court of Appeal found that] the arbitrator's behaviour during the proceedings did not reflect any such connection, and [that] his participation as an arbitrator in proceedings opposing Creighton to one of its sub-contractors did not affect his impartiality, since this latter dispute did not concern the relationship between Creighton and the State of Qatar.

[4] "By its findings, which pertain to its sovereign power of evaluation, the Court of Appeal legally justified its decision on this issue.

[5] "Qatar further attacks the decision [of the Court of Appeal] for failing to ascertain whether the parties had been informed that arbitrator X had obtained information on [Qatari] law during the evidence-gathering phase of the arbitration, in conformity with the principle of contradictory proceedings and the right to defend oneself, and for failing to examine, in the light of the above principle and of the principle of a fair process, the decision of the arbitral tribunal to set a time limit for the intervention of experts without inviting the parties to discuss it.

[6] "However, the Court of Appeal found that the arbitral tribunal did not rely in its final award on the result of the personal inquiries of arbitrator X, and that the arbitral tribunal in its final decision only drew conclusions from elements that had all been previously submitted and discussed, thereby complying with the principle of contradictory proceedings and the right to defend oneself. The attacked judgment is legally justified also on this point."

Questions and Comments

1. Van den Berg states that in French law a party-chosen arbitral institution, such as the ICC in Paris, has exclusive jurisdiction to decide on challenges. Does the *Syrian Refineries* case support his conclusion? Does it matter whether the institution upholds or denies the challenge?

2. Assisting a party to find a lawyer in the very same case may be perceived as helping one of the parties in the case. In Qatar v. Creighton, the Cour de cassation found that this was not a sufficient ground for challenge. What do you think?

3. Some parties often appoint the same person as arbitrator in various cases. Is this just good practice, or does such a practice create a link between the arbitrator and the party that gives an appearance of bias?

ANDROS COMPANIA MARITIMA v. MARC RICH & CO., A.G.

United States Court of Appeals, Second Circuit, 1978.
579 F.2d 691.

* * *

I

The controversy arises out of a charter party, dated at London, July 30, 1974, between Andros as "disponent owner" of the tanker Kissavos[1]

---

1. A "disponent owner" does not hold legal title to a vessel, but for purposes of the charter party acts as if he does.

and Marc Rich, under which the latter chartered the tanker to carry a cargo of crude oil from West Africa to two ports on the Peruvian coast. Marc Rich agreed to pay demurrage (charges for excessive time used by the charterer in loading and discharging cargo) at a rate of $5,606.25 per day for all time expended in excess of allowed laytime of 72 hours. In accordance with instructions, the vessel carried the cargo to Peru, but was kept at the two ports well beyond the allowed laytime. Because of the delay, Andros claimed $116,037.70 in demurrage against Marc Rich, which made partial payment but disputed its liability for the balance, some $90,000. In early 1975, under the arbitration clause of the charter,[2] Andros appointed Mr. Philip Moyles and Marc Rich named Captain George Stam as arbitrators. They, in turn, selected Mr. Manfred Arnold, manager of the Maritime Division, National Bank of North America, as the chairman of the arbitration panel. Captain Stam died before the arbitration commenced, and Marc Rich selected Mr. Jack Berg in his place.

* * *

At the arbitration hearings, we are told, Andros produced two witnesses and submitted 67 exhibits; Marc Rich produced no witnesses and 15 exhibits. The principal focus of the controversy was whether the conceded delay in unloading the tanker had been caused by a deficiency in the ship's discharge pumps or by other causes for which the ship could not be held responsible. In an award dated September 30, 1977, Arbitrators Arnold and Moyles found in favor of Andros for the entire balance due ($88,178.97 plus $20,849.43 interest) for a total of $109,028.40. Arbitrator Berg dissented in part.[5]

In October 1977, Andros petitioned the district court for an order confirming the arbitration award. Shortly thereafter, without making a motion to vacate or challenge the award, Marc Rich noticed depositions of all three arbitrators, to be held eight days later in the office of counsel for Marc Rich. The notices did not indicate why the arbitrators were being summoned for examination, except that the notice to Arnold warned that Marc Rich intended to subpoena the following:

2. The portion of the arbitration clause relevant to this appeal provides:

ARBITRATION. Any and all differences and disputes of whatsoever nature arising out of this Charter shall be put to arbitration in the City of New York or in the City of London whichever place is specified in Part I of this charter pursuant to the laws relating to arbitration there in force, before a board of three persons, consisting of one arbitrator to be appointed by the Owner, one by the Charterer, and one by the two so chosen. The decision of any two of the three on any point or points shall be final.

The charter specified New York City as the place of arbitration.

5. Mr. Berg construed the evidence before the panel to demonstrate that the Kissavos was "deficient in her pumping capacity," with the result that "it necessarily follows that the delay or time lost from this deficiency should properly be deducted from used laytime" as part of the demurrage calculation.

> All documents in [Mr. Arnold's] possession, custody or control, evidencing or reflecting business dealings and social relationships between [Mr. Arnold] or his employer, National Bank of North America, and Orion & Global Chartering Co., Inc., and any of its affiliated companies or Lloyd C. Nelson.

At the time, Lloyd C. Nelson was president of Orion & Global Chartering Co., Inc., the New York brokers and agents for Andros, which in turn was the managing agent for the registered owners of the Kissavos.[6]

The matter was assigned to Judge Brieant, and with commendable dispatch the judge called the attorneys before him to cut through a potentially complicated procedural tangle. The subpoenas were quashed, and Marc Rich was directed to move to vacate the arbitration award. The judge advised the parties that if the papers revealed "a legitimate disputed factual issue" concerning the adequacy of disclosure, Mr. Arnold would be called to testify in court under the judge's "direct supervision and control and briefly and quickly. . . ."

In short order, Marc Rich did move to vacate. On the issue of disclosure, it submitted affidavits of its lawyers, one from George L. Graff, who did not participate in the arbitration proceeding, and the other from Robert Thomajan, who represented Marc Rich at the arbitration. The Graff affidavit alleged that

> we have recently learned that Mr. Arnold has had a close personal and professional relationship with Lloyd C. Nelson, one of the principals of Orion & Global, the firm which actually operates the vessel.

The Thomajan affidavit alleged:

> I discussed the [arbitration] decision, after it came down, with our client and with members of the maritime community. In the course of the inquiry, I learned that Mr. Nelson and Mr. Arnold were close friends and served together on many panels. That relationship was never disclosed nor hinted at in the course of the arbitration proceeding.

Only the Graff affidavit purported to disclose any concrete basis for the claims that Arnold and Nelson "were close friends" or had "a close personal and professional relationship":

> Following [the arbitration award], we undertook an exhaustive review of approximately 1200 published awards of the Society of Maritime Arbitrators.
>
> Our review of those awards indicated that Mr. Arnold has sat as the neutral arbitrator on 19 panels since 1975. In 12 of those cases, one of the arbitrators who selected him was Lloyd C. Nelson. Of the remaining cases, one involved Andros—the same owner as in this case—and, in another, Healy & Baillie also represented the owner and the charterer defaulted.

---

6. Cf. note 1 supra.

In all but one of the cases in which Mr. Arnold was chairman and Mr. Nelson a member (the exception being a case in which the owner admitted liability), Mr. Arnold cast his vote, and carried the panel for the party who nominated Mr. Nelson. Indeed, in each of the 19 occasions when they have sat together on the same panel, Mr. Nelson and Mr. Arnold have voted together.

Needless to say, it would be impossible—and unnecessary—to establish that Mr. Arnold's vote in the instances in which Mr. Nelson was involved was influenced by Mr. Nelson. Yet, an adversary party of Mr. Nelson's would certainly want to know of such a relationship before submitting his case to Mr. Arnold as the neutral chairman.

We have no desire, nor do we, accuse Mr. Arnold of bias or improper conduct. It is precisely to avoid the need to consider such unseemly questions that the Supreme Court has established the *Commonwealth Coatings* requirement for complete disclosure before the arbitration takes place.

In reply, Andros submitted affidavits of its counsel, Raymond A. Connell, and of Lloyd C. Nelson, president of Orion. These affidavits stated—and it now seems conceded—that Orion is the agent for Andros in the United States and has been for more than 20 years;[7] that Nelson has no equity interest in Orion but has been in its employ for over 28 years, and is currently its president; that Orion appointed the local port agents for the Kissavos in Peru; and that Orion's involvement with Andros was apparent in the papers submitted at the arbitration. More significantly, Nelson swore:

> Over the course of more than twenty years I have served as arbitrator in scores of New York maritime arbitrations, and I have been a member of the Society of Maritime Arbitrators for more than 13 years. In my capacity as arbitrator I must have sat on panels with most members of the New York maritime community who are willing to serve as arbitrator and who are chosen to serve by those involved in a maritime dispute. Insofar as the KISSAVOS panel is concerned, both Mr. Jack Berg and Mr. Manfred Arnold are members of the Society of Maritime Arbitrators and I have served on many panels with both of those arbitrators, and, on occasion, all three of us have sat on the same panel.
>
> I first met Mr. Arnold in or about August of 1973 when we happened to be members of the same arbitration panel, and since then there have been other panels on which we have served together. Insofar as my contact with Mr. Arnold is concerned, it is limited to those instances where we happen to be members of the same panel and to occasions associated with our memberships in the Society of the Maritime Arbitrators. Neither Mr. Arnold nor his employer, National Bank of North America, have any business or

---

7. This period incorporates services performed by Orion's predecessor company.

financial relationship of whatsoever nature with either Orion or Andros, and insofar as I am aware there is no reasonable potential for such a relationship developing in the future. Moreover, there is no social relationship at all. I have never been to Mr. Arnold's home and he has never been to mine; our wives have never met save for one chance meeting at an affair hosted by the Maritime Law Association two years ago; my calendar indicates that aside from actual arbitration hearings and deliberations, I have had lunch with Mr Arnold on nine occasions since January 1st of this year and all nine occasions were either, for the purpose of discussing our Society's work or to deliberate on a decision on an arbitration, and on an almost all of these occasions other people were present. In sum, all of my contacts with Mr. Arnold are strictly limited to activity as members of the Society of Maritime Arbitrators, and in this regard I should also note that this is the same contact I have had with Mr. Jack Berg, the arbitrator appointed by Marc Rich, except that I have known Mr. Berg since 1957 and we have sat on arbitration panels together over a much longer period of time than I have done with Mr. Arnold.

On these papers, Judge Brieant found that Marc Rich had failed to raise a genuine factual issue requiring an evidentiary hearing. The judge denied the motion of Marc Rich to vacate the arbitration award and granted that of Andros to confirm it. Marc Rich appealed, claiming, inter alia, that it should have been allowed to depose the arbitrators and that it was entitled to an evidentiary hearing to demonstrate that Arnold's disclosure had been inadequate.[8]

II

The disclosure issue posed by appellant generates a somewhat unusual request for relief. Marc Rich argues not that it has demonstrated that the arbitration award should be set aside, but only that it was denied a chance to show why this should be done. At first blush, such an approach seems reasonable, particularly in light of the broad discovery usually allowed in the federal courts. We conclude, nevertheless, that the rulings of the district court were correct.

The starting point in any discussion of the issues before us must be *Commonwealth Coatings Corp. v. Continental Casualty Co.*, 393 U.S. 145, 89 S.Ct. 337, 21 L.Ed.2d 301 (1968), where the Supreme Court for the first time addressed itself to the "requirements of impartiality" in an arbitration proceeding and held that arbitrators must "disclose to the parties any dealings that might create an impression of possible bias." 393 U.S. at 145, 149, 89 S.Ct. at 339. In that case there had been a relationship between the third—and "supposedly neutral"—arbitrator and the successful party in the arbitration: the former had been engaged by the latter "as an engineering consultant" for "fees of about $12,000

---

8. Marc Rich has not pressed a claim, made in the papers submitted to the district court, that Moyles's disclosure was also inadequate.

over a period of four or five years and the relationship even went so far as to include the rendering of services on the very projects involved in [the arbitration]." 393 U.S. at 146, 89 S.Ct. at 338. The Court held that the arbitrator's failure to disclose these facts justified vacation of the arbitration award.

There was an obvious tension, however, between the plurality opinion of Justice Black[9] and the concurring opinion of Justice White, joined by Justice Marshall. The former relied heavily on the similarity of function linking arbitrators, judges and juries:

> We have no doubt that if a litigant could show that a foreman of a jury or a judge in a court of justice had, unknown to the litigant, any such relationship, the judgment would be subject to challenge. This is shown beyond doubt by *Tumey v. Ohio*, 273 U.S. 510, [47 S.Ct. 437, 71 L.Ed. 749] (1927), where this Court held that a conviction could not stand because a small part of the judge's income consisted of court fees collected from convicted defendants.

393 U.S. at 148, 89 S.Ct. at 339. Justice Black added that

> It is true that arbitrators cannot sever all their ties with the business world, since they are not expected to get all their income from their work deciding cases, but we should, if anything, be even more scrupulous to safeguard the impartiality of arbitrators than judges, since the former have completely free rein to decide the law as well as the facts and are not subject to appellate review.

Id. at 148–49, 89 S.Ct. at 339.

Justice White's concurring opinion, however, took pains to state at the outset:

> The Court does not decide today that arbitrators are to be held to the standards of judicial decorum of Article III judges, or indeed of any judges. It is often because they are men of affairs, not apart from but of the marketplace, that they are effective in their adjudicatory function. . . . This does not mean the judiciary must overlook outright chicanery in giving effect to their awards; that would be an abdication of our responsibility. But it does mean that arbitrators are not automatically disqualified by a business relationship with the parties before them if both parties are informed of the relationship in advance, or if they are unaware of the facts but the relationship is trivial. I see no reason automatically to disqualify the best informed and most capable potential arbitrators.

393 U.S. at 150, 89 S.Ct. at 340. The concurring opinion continued:

> And it is far better that the relationship be disclosed at the outset, when the parties are free to reject the arbitrator or accept him with

---

9. Nominally, Justice Black's opinion represented the views of six justices, since Justice White's concurrence, joined by Justice Marshall, stated that the author was "glad to join my brother Black's opinion," 393 U.S. at 150. However, as explained infra, the two texts cannot be entirely reconciled. Only four justices subscribed without reservation to Justice Black's opinion.

knowledge of the relationship and continuing faith in his objectivity, than to have the relationship come to light after the arbitration, when a suspicious or disgruntled party can seize on it as a pretext for invalidating the award. The judiciary should minimize its role in arbitration as judge of the arbitrator's impartiality. That role is best consigned to the parties who are the architects of their own arbitration process, and are far better informed of the prevailing ethical standards and reputations within their business.

Of course, an arbitrator's business relationships may be diverse indeed, involving more or less remote commercial connections with great numbers of people. He cannot be expected to provide the parties with his complete and unexpurgated business biography. But it is enough for present purposes to hold, as the Court does, that where the arbitrator has a substantial interest in a firm which has done more than trivial business with a party, that fact must be disclosed. If arbitrators err on the side of disclosure, as they should, it will not be difficult for courts to identify those undisclosed relationships which are too insubstantial to warrant vacating an award.

393 U.S. at 151–52, 89 S.Ct. at 340.

The dissenting opinion of Justice Fortas, joined by Justices Harlan and Stewart, criticized the Court for announcing

a *per se* rule that ... has no basis in the applicable statute or jurisprudential principles: that, regardless of the agreement between parties, if an arbitrator has any prior business relationship with one of the parties of which he fails to inform the other party, however innocently, the arbitration award is always subject to being set aside. This is so even where the award is unanimous; where there is no suggestion that the non-disclosure indicates partiality or bias; and where it is conceded that there was in fact no irregularity, unfairness, bias, or partiality.

393 U.S. at 153, 89 S.Ct. at 341. The dissent continued:

I agree that failure of an arbitrator to volunteer information about business dealings with one party will, prima facie, support a claim of partiality or bias. But where there is no suggestion that the nondisclosure was calculated, and where the complaining party disclaims any imputation of partiality, bias, or misconduct, the presumption clearly is overcome.

. . .

Arbitration is essentially consensual and practical. The United States Arbitration Act is obviously designed to protect the integrity of the process with a minimum of insistence upon set formulae and rules. The Court applies to this process rules applicable to judges and not to a system characterized by dealing on faith and reputation for reliability.

393 U.S. at 154–55, 89 S.Ct. at 342.

[1, 2] The diverse views expressed in these opinions pose difficulties in applying the teachings of *Commonwealth Coatings*. It is certainly true, as Justice White's concurrence emphasizes, that the Court did not decide that "the standards of judicial decorum" apply equally to arbitrators. The latter are usually recompensed for their services by the parties, a custom which would be inappropriate for judges. Also, the very practice required of arbitrators in *Commonwealth Coatings* is not now permitted to federal judges under a recent statute. Generally, a federal judge may not state for the record possible disqualifying circumstances and ask the parties to decide whether they want him to continue.[10] More fundamentally, the parties in a judicial proceeding do not choose their judges, as they do in arbitration. Nevertheless, one common feature of both the plurality and concurring opinions in *Commonwealth Coatings* is clear. Disclosure by arbitrators should be encouraged; failure to make appropriate disclosure will justify setting aside an award.[11]

* * *

10. See 28 U.S.C. §§ 455(b), (e). Cf. Frank, Commentary on Disqualification of Judges—Canon 3C, 1972 Utah L. Rev. 377, 387–88 (comparing such disclosure to "a velvet black jack"). In 1975, the Judicial Conference of the United States amended the Code of Judicial Conduct for United States Judges to strike Canon 3D, which had provided for waiver of disqualification by the parties following judicial disclosure under certain circumstances. See Reports of the Proceedings of the Judicial Conference of the United States 13 (1975). This action was taken to bring the Code "into conformity with the new Judicial Disqualification Statute," cited above. See id. at 12.

11. *Commonwealth Coatings* involved review of an arbitration award pursuant to 9 U.S.C. § 10, which sets out certain preconditions for judicial refusals to confirm awards. Among these is "evident partiality or corruption in the arbitrators, or either of them." Id. § 10(b). The parties in the instant case dispute whether review of their award is governed by that section or by Chapter 2 of the Arbitration Act, 9 U.S.C. § 201–208, the so-called Convention on the Recognition and Enforcement of Foreign Arbitral Awards. Article 1 of the Convention renders it applicable to awards "not considered as domestic awards in the State where their recognition and enforcement are sought." Marc Rich argues that, although this case involves two foreign parties, the award at issue was rendered in New York and should be considered domestic, removing it from the reach of the Convention and placing it within the ambit of 9 U.S.C. § 10 for our purposes. Andros dis-

agrees citing 9 U.S.C. § 202 (which broadly restates the scope of the Convention) and *Antco Shipping Co. v. Sidermar S.p.A.*, 417 F.Supp. 207 (S.D.N.Y.1976), aff'd in open court by oral opinion, 553 F.2d 94 (2d Cir. 1977) (holding Convention applicable to arbitration agreement between two foreign corporations, although the arbitration was to take place in New York). Our affirmance of *Sidermar* was pursuant to Local Rule § 0.23, and is without precedential effect.

We find this controversy intriguing, but we need not resolve it here. If the Convention applies, a request for confirmation of an arbitral award must be granted unless one of the Convention's grounds for "refusal or deferral of recognition or enforcement of the award" appears. 9 U.S.C. § 207. The only such ground conceivably pertinent to this case is found in Article V, section 2(b): "The recognition or enforcement of the award would be contrary to the public policy of [the forum state]." We have held that this provision "is to be construed narrowly to be applied only where enforcement would violate the forum state's most basic notions of morality and justice." *Fotochrome, Inc. v. Copal Co.*, 517 F.2d 512 (2d Cir.1975); *Parsons & Whittemore Overseas Co. v. Societe Generale de L'Industrie du Papier (RAKTA)*, 508 F.2d 969, 974 (2d Cir.1974). Certainly the Convention is no more liberal than 9 U.S.C. § 10 on the matter of vacating awards, and since—for reasons developed infra—we find none of appellant's contentions adequate under section 10, resort to the Convention would not alter the result. Cf. *Parsons & Whittemore Overseas Co.*, supra, 508 F.2d at 977 (declining to

[3, 4] * * * There is an obvious possibility, alluded to by Justice White in *Commonwealth Coatings* that "a suspicious or disgruntled party can seize" upon an undisclosed relationship "as a pretext for invalidating the award." 393 U.S. at 151, 89 S.Ct. at 340. Courts are usually reluctant to impugn the decisions of a jury because of claims of subsequently discovered bias, see *King v. United States,* (2d Cir. 1978) (citing cases), and challenges to a judge's impartiality are typically ruled untimely when the complaining party delays an objection past the point at which he is deemed on notice of potentially disqualifying circumstances. Surely, even greater caution is justified when the decision to be set aside is the product of the theoretically informal, speedy, and inexpensive process of arbitration, freely chosen by the parties. Moreover, a principal attraction of arbitration is the expertise of those who decide the controversy. Expertise in an industry is accompanied by exposure, in ways large and small, to those engaged in it, and the dividing line between innocuous and suspect relationships is not always easy to draw. But as Justice White recognized, an arbitrator "cannot be expected to provide the parties with his complete and unexpurgated business biography." 393 U.S. at 151, 89 S.Ct. at 340. The very intimacy of the group from which specialized arbitrators are chosen suggests that the parties can justifiably be held to know at least some kinds of basic information about an arbitrator's personal and business contacts.

[5] With these precedents and observations in mind, we turn to the record before us. Marc Rich alleged in the district court that Arnold had a "close personal and professional relationship" with Nelson, who was president of a firm (Orion) that allegedly operated the Kissavos, the vessel involved in the arbitration.[13] The primary basis of the claimed close relationship was that Arnold and Nelson had "served together" on 19 arbitration panels and that in 12 of these, one of the arbitrators who selected Arnold was Nelson. Marc Rich furnished no other concrete support for its characterization of Arnold and Nelson as "close personal friends," and Nelson swore that his contact with Arnold was "limited to those instances where we happen to be members of the same panel and to occasions associated with our membership in the Society of the Maritime Arbitrators." Nelson also swore that neither Arnold nor his employer, National Bank of North America, had any business relationship with either Orion or with Andros, the winning party in the arbitration, and that there was no social relationship between Arnold and Nelson; the two men had never so much as visited each other's homes. Nelson also pointed out that his contacts with Arnold were similar to those he had with Berg, the arbitrator appointed by Marc Rich, except that he had known Berg since 1957, while he had known Arnold only since 1973.

---

decide whether a 9 U.S.C. § 10 ground for vacating arbitral awards, arbitrator's "manifest disregard" of applicable law, is subsumed in the Convention's "public policy" reservation, since result would be the same regardless).

13. For purposes of analysis, we put to one side whether this description of Orion's role was accurate. Andros claims that Orion's involvement was minor and ministerial.

We believe that on this record Judge Brieant was justified in denying both discovery and an evidentiary hearing, and in refusing to vacate the award. From the papers presented, it can fairly be concluded that the relationship between Arnold and Nelson was a professional one, growing out of their service as arbitrators. There was no "business relationship" in the ordinary sense between them or between their employers. Whatever Orion's duties were with respect to the Kissavos, Orion had no direct financial stake in the outcome of the arbitration, and Nelson's interest was even more attenuated. Marc Rich argues that Arnold and Nelson had a relationship that should have been disclosed because allegedly "(a) most of Mr. Arnold's appointments as Chairman of arbitration panels (and the fees which resulted) were attributable to Mr. Nelson, and (b) Mr. Arnold consistently voted for Mr. Nelson's side in those disputes." But appellant's own affidavits recognized that when Arnold was appointed chairman of an arbitration panel that included Nelson, the third arbitrator, as well as Nelson, chose the chairman. And Andros points out that in all but one of those arbitrations, the award was unanimous. We simply do not regard this as the sort of information an arbitrator would reasonably regard as creating an impression of possible bias. It is worth noting that Marc Rich's own arbitrator, Jack Berg, did not think it important to disclose that he had known Nelson since 1957 and had sat with him on at least 15 panels, with Arnold on at least 10 panels, and with both Arnold and Nelson on at least three.[14]

Obviously, Arnold knew Nelson as a fellow arbitrator and perhaps in that capacity knew him well. But their service together on arbitration panels was no secret. Marc Rich based its claim of Arnold's inadequate disclosure upon "an exhaustive review of approximately 1200 published awards of the Society of Maritime Arbitrators," which it conducted after the award was handed down. It could have made such a review just as easily before or during the arbitration rather than after it lost its case. Indeed, it is not at all uncommon for parties to check the past decisions of arbitrators before an arbitration begins. Nor is it an adequate response that Marc Rich had no reason to scrutinize Arnold's prior service with Nelson because it had no way of knowing that Nelson had any "interest" in the proceeding. Whatever connection Orion had with the Kissavos was made clear from the documents submitted by Andros at the arbitration, and the name of its president was easily ascertainable. Finally, we note that Marc Rich was not at all concerned over Arnold's disclosure that he had been appointed as an arbitrator in the past by Andros, the opposing party in this arbitration, and that his employer "might have had [some business] dealings" with Andros. Nor was Marc Rich interested in Berg's disclosure that there may have been "business dealings" between his employer and Andros in the past. Judge Brieant obviously regarded Marc Rich's petition as a classic example of a losing party seizing upon "a pretext for invalidating the [arbitration] award." *Commonwealth Coatings*, supra, 393 U.S. at 151, 89 S.Ct. at 340 (White,

---

14. These statistics appear in appellee's brief and, we are told, were obtained by examining the published awards of the Society of Maritime Arbitrators.

J., concurring). We believe that the judge properly denied discovery on this issue and was justified in refusing to explore it further.

* * *

* * * [I]n the special context of what are in effect post hoc efforts to induce arbitrators to undermine the finality of their own awards, we agree with the district court that any questioning of arbitrators should be handled pursuant to judicial supervision and limited to situations where clear evidence of impropriety has been presented.

* * *

Questions and Comments

1. What connections to the parties, direct or indirect, must a proposed arbitrator disclose? Suppose a dispute between Coca–Cola and its exclusive distributor in China is brought to arbitration. Must the proposed neutral arbitrator disclose that he or she once acted as counsel for Pepsi Cola in China? Suppose Pepsi Cola is still a client of the proposed neutral arbitrator?

2. What connections to the other arbitrators must a proposed neutral arbitrator disclose? Arbitrators, especially in specialized areas like maritime arbitration, often know one another and will have sat together on previous occasions. Must all these occasions and other social contacts be disclosed? To whom, the parties or the other arbitrators?

3. May two judges who sit on a judicial panel together be friends? What if they become friends after being appointed judges? How is this different from arbitration?

4. On the basis of the *Andros Compania Maritima* case, would you say that courts are likely to be better than arbitral institutions at setting standards for disclosure and for valid challenges of arbitrators?

5. Does *Andros Compania Maritima* cause you to favor those systems that allow judicial intervention in challenge procedures before the arbitrators hand down an award, or those systems that delay judicial scrutiny until after an award is rendered?

AT&T CORPORATION AND ANOTHER
v. SAUDI CABLE COMPANY

Queen's Bench Division (Commercial Court).
QBD (Comm. Ct) 1 Lloyd's Rep. 22 (2000)*
Oct. 13, 1999.

The applicants (AT&T) were among seven international telecommunications companies, who in 1992 were invited by the Saudi Arabian Ministry of Post Telephone and Telegraph (MOPTT) to submit bids for the Saudi Kingdom's sixth telecommunications expansion project ("TEP–6"). One of the requirements of the bid was that cable required for TEP–6 should be acquired from Saudi Cable Co. (SCC) (the respondents). In 1993 SCC approached each of the bidders with a view to reaching agreement for the supply of cable for TEP–6 in the event that the bidder

---

* Reprinted with permission of Lloyd's Law Reports.

was ultimately successful in obtaining the TEP–6 contract, and on Aug. 10, 1993 concluded a Pre–Bid Agreement (PBA) with AT&T. Paragraph 6 of that agreement provided that upon award of any cable related contract to AT&T the parties would meet promptly and negotiate in good faith mutually satisfactory agreements. The PBA also contained an arbitration clause submitting disputes to the International Chamber of Commerce, the place of arbitration being London. English law was thus the proper law of the arbitration agreement (the curial law).

In May, 1994 it became clear that AT&T was going to be awarded the contract and the TEP–6 contract was concluded between AT&T and MOPTT on Aug. 13, 1994. One of the disappointed bidders was a competitor company Northern Telecom Ltd. (Nortel) a substantial Canadian company.

AT&T and SCC began negotiating pursuant to the PBA. These negotiations come to nothing and AT&T terminated the PBA on Dec. 10, 1994. On Feb. 3, 1995 AT&T filed a request for arbitration with the ICC claiming a declaration that the PBA had been correctly terminated. SCC filed its answer claiming that the contract had not been validly terminated and asking for an order that AT&T comply with the agreement and negotiate in good faith.

Each party nominated their arbitrator and the arbitrators then had discussions to see if they could agree on the appointment of a chairman of the tribunal.

In the event Mr. L. Yves Fortier, Q.C., who practised in Montreal was confirmed as chairman. Unfortunately the fact that Mr. Fortier was a non-executive director of Nortel was not disclosed.

The tribunal made two awards, one in September, 1996 and the other in 1997, both in favour of SCC.

In November, 1998, while further hearings about the appropriate sum payable to SCC by AT&T were being conducted it was discovered that Mr. Fortier was a non-executive director of Nortel. AT&T filed a challenge to Mr. Fortier with ICC. That challenge was rejected and on Sept. 16, 1999 the arbitrators produced their third award which assessed the damages payable by AT&T to SCC.

AT&T applied for the removal of Mr. Fortier and for the awards to be set aside on the grounds of bias in that Mr. Fortier was a non-executive director of Nortel which was a competitor company that had been unsuccessful in the bid for the TEB–6 project.

SCC sought to rely on the ICC finality clause which provided inter alia:

Decisions of the [ICC] Court as to the appointment, confirmation, challenge ... of an arbitrator shall be final.

* * *

JUDGMENT

MR. JUSTICE LONGMORE:

The question in this case is whether it is right to order removal of an arbitrator and to set aside three awards to which he has been a party on the grounds of bias when one of the parties to the dispute was at relevant times unaware that the arbitrator was a non-executive director of a competitor company which was not merely a commercial rival of that party in the field of telecommunications but was also a disappointed bidder for the very contract that formed the background to the dispute submitted to arbitration.

* * *

ICC rules permit each party to a dispute to nominate its own arbitrator subject to confirmation by the ICC; AT&T nominated Maitre Michael Schneider, a German lawyer practising in Geneva and SCC nominated Mr. Robert Von Mehren, a partner in a New York law firm. They were, in due course, confirmed. As is customary, the parties and their arbitrators had discussions to see if they could agree on a chairman of the tribunal. If the parties are able to reach agreement, ICC will usually be content to confirm such person as chairman; in the absence of agreement ICC will make the appointment. A number of names were canvassed and rejected. One name that commanded some assent was that of Mr. L. Yves Fortier, Q.C. who practised in Montreal. Inter-party negotiations about the appointment of the chairman took place, at any rate mainly, between Mr. John Beechey of Clifford Chance in London solicitors acting on behalf of AT & T, and Mr. Rayner Hamilton of White & Case in New York, attorneys acting on behalf of SCC. On Mar. 17, Mr. Beechey faxed Mr. Fortier's office in Montreal asking him if he would be available to act as chairman of an arbitration tribunal, telling him a little about the dispute and requesting him to forward a curriculum vitae (C.V.). On Mar. 20, 1995 Mr. Beechey while having various meetings in Paris received a telephone call from Mr. Fortier who happened to be in Oxford. A certain amount of discussion took place. Mr. Fortier says that he mentioned he was a director of Nortel; Mr. Beechey does not recollect this and Mr. Fortier accepts that he did not mention it in the context of making any disclosure but probably just to indicate that he had some experience of the telecommunications industry. He said his C.V. would be forthcoming and when Mr. Beechey returned to London he found a copy of that C.V. waiting for him dated Mar. 20, 1995.

By what is now agreed to be a most unfortunate secretarial error, no mention was made in this C.V. of Mr. Fortier's directorship of Nortel although a number of other directorships were mentioned. ICC had on record a copy of an earlier version of Mr. Fortier's C.V. which did record his directorship of Nortel. Contrary to their usual practice ICC did not forward their own copy of the C.V. of a proposed tribunal chairman to the parties. It so happens that on the same day (Mar. 20, 1995) as Mr. Fortier caused his C.V. to be sent to Clifford Chance, he had a reason to send his C.V. to Mr. V. V. Veeder, Q.C. of Essex Court Chambers in London for an unrelated purpose. That recorded his directorship of Nortel. The explanation for all this is that Mr. Fortier had an administrative assistant and a secretary. One C.V. must have been sent from the computer file operated by the word processor of one of those ladies and one must have been sent from the word processor operated by the other; why the C.V.s were not the same is a mystery but the probability is that, as can happen in the best regulated offices, one copy of the C.V. held on one computer file came to have part of it omitted in the course of an updating operation while the other copy held on the other computer file did not carry the same omission. The detail of the matter is set out on pp. 8–9 of Mr. Fortier's letter to ICC of Feb. 5, 1999. As I say, it is now accepted (though at one time it was not) that the omission was due to a secretarial error and that the omission was not, in any way, intentional.

* * *

Article 2 of the ICC rules makes provision about the constitution of arbitral tribunals; arts. 2.7, 2.8 and 2.9, provide as follows:

> 7.   Every arbitrator appointed or confirmed by the Court must be and remain independent of the parties involved in the arbitration.

> 8.   Before appointment or confirmation by the Court, a prospective arbitrator shall disclose in writing to the Secretary General of the Court any facts or circumstances which might be of such a nature as to call into question the arbitrator's independence in the eyes of the parties. Upon receipt of such information, the Secretary General of the Court shall provide it to the parties in writing and fix a time-limit for any comments from them.

> 9.   An arbitrator shall immediately disclose in writing to the Secretary General of the Court and the parties any facts or circumstances of a similar nature which may arise between the arbitrator's appointment or confirmation by the Court and the notification of the final award.

* * *

The parties did agree on Mr. Fortier as the chairman of the tribunal and ICC asked Mr. Fortier (as well as the other arbitrators) to sign a statement of independence on a printed form in which, having declared to the ICC his willingness to act as an arbitrator, he was required to check one of two boxes as follows:

> I am independent of each of the parties and intend to remain so; to the best of my knowledge, there are no facts or circumstances, past or present, that need be disclosed because they might be of such nature as to call into question my independence in the eyes of any of the parties.

> I am independent of each of the parties and intend to remain so; however, in consideration of Article 2, paragraph 7 of the ICC Rules of Arbitration, I wish to call your attention to the following facts or circumstances which I hereafter disclose because I consider that they might be of such a nature as to call into question my indepen-

dence in the eyes of any of the parties. (Use separate sheet if necessary.)

Mr. Fortier put a cross in the first box and signed the document on Mar. 28. He was thereupon confirmed by ICC as the third arbitrator and chairman of the tribunal. I am satisfied that when he signed the document Mr. Fortier considered himself to be independent of the parties, that he intended to remain so and that it did not occur to him that his non-executive directorship of Nortel could call into question his independence in the eyes of either of the parties.

It has emerged in the course of these proceedings that Mr. Fortier had at the time of appointment 300 "common" shares in AT&T. Sir Sydney Kentridge, Q.C. for AT&T submitted that Mr. Fortier's failure to disclose that small shareholding in the statement of independence showed that his attitude to disclosure was casual in the extreme. It has also emerged that Mr. Fortier has a practice of acquiring a shareholding in the corporations on whose boards he sits and that in March, 1995 he held 474 "common" shares in Nortel. This is, at most, a cumulative point; AT&T have always maintained that it is really his directorship which gives rise to the question of bias.

* * *

While the ICC challenge was in progress, the arbitrators ceased working on what was to become their third award; once the ICC had rejected the challenge, they resumed work and on Sept. 16, 1999 produced their third award which assessed damages payable by AT&T to SCC. In the course of the hearing I granted AT&T leave to amend their application to include an application to set aside this third award.

Sir Sydney Kentridge for AT&T expressly disclaimed any assertion that there had been any actual bias against AT&T on the part of Mr. Fortier but submitted:

> (1) that Mr. Fortier's failure to disclose his non-executive director-ship of Nortel constituted a breach of both his obligations under the ICC rules and the common law of England and Wales;

> (2) that such breach was misconduct requiring the awards to be set aside and his appointment to be revoked pursuant to ss. 1 and 23 of the Arbitration Act, 1950;

> (3) that, in any event, there was an appearance of bias and that when an arbitrator's award was infected by the appearance of bias it should be set aside. This was for one of two reasons: (i) Mr. Fortier was effectively a judge in his own cause and was thus automatically disqualified as an arbitrator because he was a director of a direct competitor of a party to the suit; (ii) even if he was not automatically disqualified by reason of his position, the awards should nevertheless be set aside because arbitrators were in a different position from judicial officers (whom the parties did not choose for the resolution of their disputes); the appropriate test to apply was, therefore, (a) a reasonable appre-

hension of bias by AT&T; or (b) an objectively reasonable apprehension of bias, rather than the test of real danger of bias laid down in R. v. Gough, [1993] A.C. 646.

(4) Whatever test was adopted, the awards should not be allowed to stand.

* * *

Breach of any obligation of disclosure

Having concluded that any question of breach of that part of Mr. Fortier's contract with the parties which is governed by ICC terms has been finally determined by ICC and cannot now be revisited by AT&T, I think I should resist the temptation to say whether, in my view, Mr. Fortier was in breach of the ICC obligations of disclosure. I will only say that the facts and matters put forward by Mr. Fortier in his letter to the ICC of Feb. 5, 1999 and, indeed, the considerations put forward by his co-arbitrators in their response of the same date would need most careful consideration.

I should, however, deal with Sir Sydney's further argument that any failure to disclose in breach of ICC rules, if established, was misconduct which must inevitably result in all three awards being set aside and the revocation of Mr. Fortier's authority to determine the dispute. That submission I reject; it must, to my mind, depend (as Mr. Pollock contended) whether the awards are affected by the rules of assumed bias, whatever those rules are as applied to arbitrators. It cannot be the case that any breach of the obligation to disclose however venial must lead to an award being set aside. One must ask whether the arbitrator was (or must in law be presumed to have been) biased; if he was not biased in this sense, it would be contrary to good sense to send the parties back to the drawing board; if, however, he was biased, the awards ought not to stand. One is therefore sent back to the critical question: should the awards be set aside by reason of bias on common law principles?

Bias at common law—General

No suggestion is made that Mr. Fortier was consciously biased. AT&T claim that there was an appearance of bias or that there was a risk that Mr. Fortier was unconsciously biased against them. The present state of English law in relation to apparent or assumed bias, as it applies to Judges and inferior tribunals, is that there is an automatic disqualification for any Judge who has a direct pecuniary interest (such as owning shares) in one of the parties or is otherwise so closely connected with a party that he can truly be said to be judge in his own cause; apart from that, if an allegation of apparent or unconscious bias is made, it is for the Court to determine whether there is a real danger of bias in the sense that the Judge might have unfairly regarded with favour or disfavour the case of a party under consideration by him or, in other words, might be pre-disposed or prejudiced against one party's case for reasons unconnected with the merits of the issue. These propositions are settled by R.

v. Gough, [1993] A.C. 646 at p. 670 per Lord Goff of Chieveley, R. v. Inner West London Counsel ex parte Dallaglio, [1994] 4 All E.R. 139 at p. 151 per Lord Justice Simon Brown and R. v. Bow Street Metropolitan Stipendiary Magistrate ex parte Pinochet (No. 2), [1999] 2 W.L.R. 272 at pp. 281–282 per Lord Browne–Wilkinson.

* * *

(2) Unconscious bias

Sir Sydney's main argument on this aspect of the case was that arbitrators are different from Judges and that, by reason of the consensual nature of arbitration, a more stringent rule should apply to arbitrators than to Judges. This rule he formulated as being that an arbitrator's award should be set aside if a reasonable party to the arbitration would have reasonably apprehended that the arbitrator might be biased.

* * *

The fact that arbitration is a consensual process in the sense that the parties choose their arbitrators in a way that they cannot choose their jurors or their Judges does not, in any event, lead to a conclusion that the test for bias should be any different.

* * *

Application to the facts

The question, therefore, is whether the Court is satisfied on the evidence that there was a real danger of unconscious bias in the sense of Mr. Fortier being pre-disposed or prejudiced against AT&T's case for reasons unconnected with the merits of the case.

I am satisfied that there was no such danger for the following reasons:

(1) Mr. Fortier's position as a non-executive director of Nortel was more of an incidental than a vital part of his professional life; he was independent of management and did not sit on the executive committee of the board; as a member of the Bar and international arbitrator he had neither time nor inclination to involve himself in the day to day commercial decisions of Nortel.

(2) His shareholding of 474 common shares in Nortel is sufficiently small to be of no consequence. It seems that Mr. Fortier did not consider his investment portfolio when he accepted nomination as chairman of the tribunal. I have already said that Sir Sydney castigated that as extremely casual; it certainly gives rise to potential difficulties in as much as if, Mr. Fortier had held shares (however few) in either of the parties in front of him that would, in the present state of English law, mean that he was automatically disqualified at the suit of the other party. (Australian law may be more flexible in this respect, see Clenae v. Australia and New Zealand Banking, [1999] V.S.C.A. 35.) But I am not concerned to decide whether Mr. Fortier was casual; I am concerned to ask whether there was a real danger of Mr. Fortier being pre-disposed

against AT&T; in my view, it is as absurd to think of Mr. Fortier being pre-disposed against AT&T by reason of his non-executive directorship or his shareholding in Nortel as it would be to think he might be pre-disposed against SCC because he owned 300 shares in AT&T.

* * *

(4) One of the main reasons why parties to arbitration proceedings select as arbitrators experienced lawyers (let alone Queen's Counsel of such evident distinction as Mr. Fortier) is that such lawyers are trained from their earliest days to decide cases on the evidence before them and the submissions made to them and to put aside all extraneous matters. It is axiomatic to any experienced lawyer that he must and will decide cases without fear or favour, affection or ill will. Judges in England take an oath to that effect but no one supposes they would act differently if no oath were sworn. The same applies to experienced legal arbitrators. Another reason for selecting arbitration rather than the Courts is that the parties may actually prefer men of the world to what some may perceive as the cloistered calm of judicial life. It cannot be in the least surprising that an experienced arbitrator will have some interest in business affairs and he may be all the better equipped to arbitrate if he has.

(5) The actual evidence of unconscious bias in this case is no more than Mr. Fortier's non-executive directorship of and small shareholding in Nortel. Nothing that Mr. Fortier has said or done in the arbitration proceedings has shown any bias of any kind. Sir Sydney submitted that, even if there was no ground of complaint in relation to the first partial award in which it was decided that the parties were obliged to negotiate, he should have raised the matter of his directorship of Nortel (and presumably have recused himself on request) when confidential information was ordered to be disclosed for the purpose of substantiating AT&T's case about the amount of their profits. The implication of this submission is that there was some danger of Mr. Fortier, in breach of his duty as arbitrator, disclosing to the board of directors of Nortel this confidential information so that Nortel could gain some competitive advantage. There is no evidence whatever of any such danger and, in the absence of any such evidence, it advances AT&T's case of unconscious bias nowhere even in relation to the second and third partial awards.

* * *

AT&T's applications will be dismissed.

* * *

The above decision of the Commercial Court was confirmed by a May 15, 2000 decision of the Court of Appeal—2 Lloyd's Rep. 127 (2000).

Questions and Comments

1. The challenge raised in the AT&T case relies on two alleged irregularities: i) lack of full disclosure, and ii) connection with a party, who—

although not a party to the dispute—has an interest in the outcome of the dispute.

   2.   As far as disclosure is concerned, consider the following issues:

   —   What can and cannot be omitted? (one of the basic issues in *Commonwealth Coatings*.) Justice Longmore found that arbitrator Fortier's position in Nortel "was more of an incidental than a vital part of his professional life" and that this alleviated his failure to disclose it. Is this point decisive?

   —   Suppose Fortier had been a non-executive director of one of the parties. This may have been an equally "incidental part of his professional life". Would the situation be the same?

   3.   The Court found that non-disclosure (or rather incomplete disclosure) was the result of a secretarial error. Is this relevant? Suppose Mr. Fortier typed his C.V. himself and forgot to mention his position with Nortel. Or, suppose he did not forget, but came to the conclusion that it need not be mentioned because it was irrelevant. Would this make a difference?

   4.   Did the Court give any weight to the fact that Mr. Fortier was the chairman of the tribunal? Should this matter?

   5.   At about the time the *AT&T* case was decided, the issue of "real danger of bias" also emerged in a high profile case decided by another English court. In the *Pinochet Extradition* case, the decision of Lord Hoffmann was set aside by the House of Lords because of Hoffman's connections with Amnesty International. (House of Lords in Regina v. Bow Street Metropolitan Stipendiary Magistrate and others, Ex parte Pinochet Ugarte, 1999 WL 250051). Amnesty International obtained leave to intervene in the appeal, and was represented by counsel in the proceedings arguing for a particular result. Lord Hoffmann was chairman and director of Amnesty International Charity Ltd., a registered charity set up to oversee charitable aspects of Amnesty International's work. The House of Lords held that "the principle that a man cannot be judge in his own cause is not limited to automatic disqualification of a judge who had a pecuniary interest in the outcome of the case but is equally applicable if the judge's decision would lead to the promotion of a cause in which he was involved together with one of the parties".

   Actual bias was not alleged in either the *AT&T* or the *Pinochet* case. How would you distinguish the two cases? One of the two was an arbitration case, the other was a court case. Is this difference significant? Justice Longmore mentions that parties need experienced arbitrators, and experienced arbitrators typically have some interest in business affairs. Would this circumstance justify a lower standard? Was the standard applied in the *AT&T* case a lower standard?

   In which of the two cases do you perceive a greater danger of bias?

Chapter IV

FOCAL POINTS IN THE ARBITRATION PROCESS

IV.1. SELECTED ELEMENTS OF PROCEDURE BEFORE ARBITRATION TRIBUNALS

IV.1.a. Note

"Informal and speedy procedure" are probably the most often mentioned characteristics of international commercial arbitration. Informality responds to the aspirations of businessmen and the search for an alternative to lengthy and complicated court proceedings. During the infancy of modern commercial arbitration, the effort to find an informal alternative method of dispute resolution was essentially made by parties who remained on good terms and who sought—and were capable of agreeing upon—a more amicable form of dispute settlement. As arbitration became the dominant method of settling international disputes, it had to face the task of resolving a wide variety of disputes, including conflicts in which deep mistrust prevents procedural cooperation. In these circumstances, arbitration must find a proper mix of flexibility and procedural safeguards.

The governing principle of arbitral procedure is party autonomy. The principal expression of this autonomy is usually not direct drafting of procedural norms. Much more often, party choice is made through the designation of a pre-established set of norms—the rules of an arbitral institution—or, in case of *ad hoc* arbitration, a set of rules established independently of particular institutions. (Among these latter norms, the most prominent are undoubtedly the UNCITRAL Rules.) In practice institutional rules thus establish the essential procedural framework of arbitration. Guidance is also provided by Article V of the New York Convention, which sets out the procedural deficiencies on the basis of which recognition of a foreign award may be denied. These grounds correspond to typical grounds for setting aside contained in municipal procedural laws. Obviously, international commercial arbitration and proceedings must seek to avoid procedural deficiencies on the basis of which the award rendered can be set aside or denied recognition and enforcement.

In addition to institutional rules, procedural norms of the municipal law governing arbitration (the *lex arbitri*) are relevant. They occupy a prominent position within the hierarchy of rules that govern the arbitration procedure; however, practical steps within the arbitration process are today predominantly molded by party autonomy and institutional norms, rather than by the *lex arbitri*.

In this subsection we shall first investigate the meaning and scope of the *lex arbitri* and consider the relative significance, place, and order of various procedural rules. Turning to the actual conduct of arbitral proceedings, attention is first given to a checklist of matters that deserve consideration in organizing arbitral proceedings. Thereafter, selected issues, principles and techniques are scrutinized: the observance of due process within a procedure driven by parties and arbitrators; the conduct of hearings; presentation of the case before the arbitrators; representation by counsel; privacy and confidentiality; time limits; and related matters.

IV.1.b. *The Scope and the Relative Importance of the Lex Arbitri*

UNION OF INDIA v. MCDONNELL DOUGLAS CORPORATION

Queen's Bench Division (Commercial Court), 22 December 1992.
[1993] 2 Lloyd's Law Rep. 48.*

* * *

[This was an action by the plaintiffs (the Union of India) against the defendants (McDonnell Douglas Corporation) for decision of the question whether the arbitration between the parties was to be governed by the laws of India or the laws of England.]

JUDGEMENT:

SAVILLE J.: By a written agreement dated July 30, 1987 the plaintiffs contracted with the defendants for the latter to undertake services for the former in and about the launch of a space satellite. Article 11 of the agreement provided that the agreement was to be governed by, interpreted and construed in accordance with the laws of India. The agreement also contained an arbitration clause (art. 8) in the following terms:

> In the event of a dispute or difference arising out of or in connection with this Agreement, which cannot be resolved by amicable settlement, the same shall be referred to an Arbitration Tribunal consisting of three members. Either Party shall give notice to the other regarding its decision to refer the matter to arbitration. Within 30 days of such notice, one Arbitrator shall be nominated by

---

* Reprinted by permission of Lloyd's Law   Reports, LLP Limited.

each Party and the third Arbitrator shall be nominated by agreement between the Parties to this Agreement. If no such agreement is reached within 60 days of the mentioned notice, the President of the International Chamber of Commerce shall be requested to nominate the third Arbitrator.

The third Arbitrator shall not be a citizen of the country of either Party to this Agreement. The arbitration shall be conducted in accordance with the procedure provided in the Indian Arbitration Act of 1940 or any re-enactment or modification thereof. The arbitration shall be conducted in the English language. The award of the Arbitrators shall be made by majority decision and shall be final and binding on the Parties hereto. The seat of the arbitration proceedings shall be London, United Kingdom. Each Party shall bear its own cost of preparing and presenting cases. The cost of arbitration including the fees payable to Arbitrators, shall be shared equally by the Parties to this Agreement.

Work under this Agreement shall continue during arbitration proceedings and no payment due or payable by DOS [Department of Space] shall be withheld. If, after consultation with MDC [McDonnell Douglas Corporation], DOS determines that the lack of resolution of a matter in dispute will adversely affect the Schedule Launch Date or will adversely impact the timely preparation of the launch and associated services, MDC shall perform the matter in dispute in the manner determined by DOS, within the framework of this Agreement and without prejudice to the final resolution of the matter in dispute.

It is common ground that a dispute or difference arising out of or in connection with this agreement exists between the parties. This dispute or difference has been referred to arbitration under the provisions of art. 8. The hearing before the arbitrators is presently fixed to begin in London on Jan. 11, 1993. The question before me is as to the law governing the arbitration proceedings. The parties are, as I understand it, agreed that this Court should decide this question, and should do so on the basis that there is no difference on this issue between English and Indian law.

In essence the plaintiffs contend that the words:

> ... The arbitration shall be conducted in accordance with the procedure provided in the Indian Arbitration Act 1940 ...

make clear that the parties have chosen Indian law, or at least those parts of Indian law found in the 1940 Act, to govern any arbitration proceedings arising under art. 8. The defendants, on the other hand, contend that by stipulating London as the "seat" of any arbitration proceedings under art. 8, the parties have made clear not merely that any arbitration will take place in London, but that English law will govern the arbitration proceedings.

An arbitration clause in a commercial contract like the present one is an agreement inside an agreement. The parties make their commercial bargain, i.e., exchange promises in relation to the subject matter of the transaction, but in addition agree on a private tribunal to resolve any issues that may arise between them. The parties may make an express choice of the law to govern their commercial bargain and that choice may also be made of the law to govern their agreement to arbitrate. In the present case it is my view that by art. 11 the parties have chosen the law of India not only to govern the rights and obligations arising out of their commercial bargain but also the rights and obligations arising out of their agreement to arbitrate. In legal terms, therefore, the proper law of both the commercial bargain and the arbitration agreement is the law of India.

The fact that the law of India is the proper law of the arbitration agreement does not, however, necessarily entail that the law governing the arbitration proceedings themselves is also the law of India, unless there is in that agreement some effective express or implied term to that effect. In other words, it is, subject to one proviso, open to the parties to agree that their agreement to arbitrate disputes will be governed by one law, but that the procedures to be adopted in any arbitration under that agreement will be governed by another law: see James Miller & Partners v. Whitworth Street Estates (Manchester) Ltd., [1970] 1 Lloyd's Rep. 269; [1970] AC 583. * * * [Thus], in an international bargain of the present kind, the parties, subject to the proviso mentioned (to which I shall return below) may make a choice of a law to govern their commercial bargain, of a law to govern their arbitration agreement, and of a law to govern the procedures in any arbitration held under that agreement. In theory at least (and subject to the proviso) the parties could chose a different law for each of these purposes.

If the parties do not make an express choice of procedural law to govern their arbitration, then the Court will consider whether they have made an implicit choice. In this circumstance the fact that the parties have agreed to a place for the arbitration is a very strong pointer that implicitly they must have chosen the laws of that place to govern the procedures of the arbitration. The reason for this is essentially one of common sense. By choosing a country in which to arbitrate the parties have, ex hypothesi, created a close connection between the arbitration and that country and it is reasonable to assume from their choice that they attached some importance to the relevant laws of that country, i.e., those laws which would be relevant to an arbitration conducted in that country. Indeed, English law at least has turned its face against the notion that it is possible to have arbitral procedures that are wholly unconnected with any national system of law at all: see, for example, Bank Mellat v. Helliniki Techniki SA, [1984] 1 QB 291 at p. 301.

In the present case, Mr. Veeder, QC for the defendants places great stress on the fact that the parties have expressly selected London as the "seat" and not just the place of the arbitration. The word "seat", he suggests, is a legal term of art, meaning the legal place of the arbitration proceedings. By choosing the legal place of the arbitration proceedings the parties ipso facto choose the laws of that place to govern their arbitration proceedings. Indeed, although the choice of a "seat" also indicates the geographical place for the arbitration, this does not mean that the parties have limited themselves to that place. As is pointed out by Redfern and Hunter in The Law and Practice of International Commercial Arbitration 2nd ed. at p. 93, in a passage approved by the Court of Appeal in Naviera Amazonica Peruana v. Cie Internacional de Seguros del Peru, [1988] 1 Lloyd's Rep. 116 at p. 121, it may often be convenient to hold meetings or even hearings in other countries. This does not mean that the "seat" of the arbitration changes with each change of country. The legal place of the arbitration remains the same even if the physical place changes from time to time, unless of course the parties agree to change it. In short, Mr. Veeder suggested that the word "seat" carried with it much more clearly the meaning conveyed by the French word "siege" than the English word "place" though his submission was that this word too in an arbitration agreement would be primarily concerned with the legal rather than the physical place of the arbitration.

Mr. Colman, QC (as he then was) accepted that in the absence of agreement to the contrary, the choice of a "seat" would carry with it the choice of the law of that place as the law governing the arbitration proceedings, though he categorized that result as arising from implication rather than from the meaning of the word "seat" itself. In the present case, however, his submission was that the parties, by stipulating that the arbitration should be conducted in accordance with the procedure provided in the Indian Arbitration Act, had made an express choice of Indian law to govern the arbitration proceedings and that this choice must, on ordinary principles, prevail over anything inconsistent that might otherwise be implied.

These arguments are nicely balanced. It is clear from the authorities cited above that English law does admit of at least the theoretical possibility that the parties are free to choose to hold their arbitration in one country but subject to the procedural laws of another, but against this is the undoubted fact that such an agreement is calculated to give rise to great difficulties and complexities, as Lord Justice Kerr observed in the Amazonica decision. For example (and this is the proviso to which I referred earlier in this judgment) it seems to me that the jurisdiction of the English Court under the Arbitration Acts over an arbitration in this country cannot be excluded by an agreement between the parties to apply the laws of another country, or indeed by any other means unless such is sanctioned by those Acts themselves. Thus, to my mind, there can be no question in this case that the English Courts would be deprived of all jurisdiction over the arbitration. However, much of that jurisdiction is discretionary in character so that if the Court were convinced that the parties had chosen the procedural law of another country, then it might well be slow to interfere with the arbitral process. Again, for the sake of avoiding parallel Court proceedings, the Court might be minded to regard the choice of a foreign legal procedure as amounting to an exclusion agreement within the meaning of s. 3 of the Arbitration Act, 1979.[a] Be that as it may, the choice of a procedural law different from the law of the place of the arbitration will, at least where that place is this country, necessarily mean that the parties have actually chosen to have their arbitral proceedings at least potentially governed both by their express choice and by the laws of this country.

Such a state of affairs is clearly highly unsatisfactory: indeed in Black Clawson International Ltd. v. Papierwerke Waldhof–Aschaffenburg AG [1981] 2 Lloyd's Rep. 446 at p. 453, Mr. Justice Mustill (as he then was) described the converse situation (i.e., a foreign arbitration suggested to be governed by English procedural law) as producing an absurd result.

In the end, therefore, the question is whether the parties have agreed to such a potentially unsatisfactory method of regulating their arbitration procedures. In my judgment, they have not because, as Mr. Veeder submitted, there is a way of reconciling the phrase relied upon by Mr. Colman with the choice of London as the seat of the arbitration, namely by reading that phrase as referring to the internal conduct of the arbitration as opposed to the external supervision of the arbitration by the Courts. The word used in the phrase relied upon by Mr. Colman is "conducted" which I agree with Mr. Veeder is more apt to describe the way in which the parties and the tribunal are to carry on their proceedings than the supervision of those proceedings by the Indian courts, for example through the Special Case provisions of the Indian Act. It is true, as Mr. Colman pointed out, that this would mean that only s. 3 and Schedule 1 of the Indian Act would be applicable (though many of the other provisions are still to be found in the English statutes and so would be applicable in the English Courts) but the construction for which he contends would, to my mind, not only have the unsatisfactory and possibly absurd results to which I have referred, but would also necessarily give the word "seat" a meaning which excluded any choice of London as the legal place for the arbitration. In my view, such a change from the ordinary meaning to be given to that word in an international arbitration agreement (the ordinary meaning being that submitted by Mr. Veeder) cannot be accepted, unless the other provisions of the agreement show·clearly that this is what the parties intended. I am not persuaded that that is the case here. On the contrary, for the reasons given, it seems to me that by their agreement the parties have chosen English law as the law to govern their arbitration proceedings, while contractually importing from the Indian Act those provisions of that Act which are concerned with the internal conduct of their arbitration and

a. Authors' note: Section 3 of the 1979 Arbitration Act (England) provides for appeal to the High Court with respect to a question of law arising out of an award or in the course of an arbitration, unless "the parties to the reference in question have entered into an agreement in writing (in this section referred to as an 'exclusion agreement') which excludes * * * [such] right of appeal * * *." For the current provisions on "stating a case" in English arbitration law, see section 45 of the 1996 English Arbitration Act in the Documents Supplement.

which are not inconsistent with the choice of English arbitral procedural law.

The question posed in the amended summons before me is whether upon the proper construction of art. 8 of the Launch Agreement the pending arbitration between the parties and any award made by the arbitral tribunal is subject to the supervisory jurisdiction of the Indian Courts or the English Courts. For the reasons given my answer to this question is that it is the latter.

Judgment accordingly.

ENGLAND

ARBITRATION ACT 1996[b]

* * *

The arbitral proceedings

33.—(1) The tribunal shall—

    (a) act fairly and impartially as between the parties, giving each party a reasonable opportunity of putting his case and dealing with that of his opponent, and

    (b) adopt procedures suitable to the circumstances of the particular case, avoiding unnecessary delay or expense, so as to provide a fair means for the resolution of the matters falling to be determined.

    (2) The tribunal shall comply with that general duty in conducting the arbitral proceedings, in its decisions on matters of procedure and evidence and in the exercise of all other powers conferred on it.

34.—(1) It shall be for the tribunal to decide all procedural and evidential matters, subject to the right of the parties to agree any matter.

    (2) Procedural and evidential matters include—

    (a) when and where any part of the proceedings is to be held;

    (b) the language or languages to be used in the proceedings and whether translations of any relevant documents are to be supplied;

    (c) whether any and if so what form of written statements of claim and defence are to be used, when these should be supplied and the extent to which such statements can be later amended;

    (d) whether any and if so which documents or classes of documents should be disclosed between and produced by the parties and at what stage;

    (e) whether any and if so what questions should be put to and answered by the respective parties and when and in what form this should be done;

b. 36 I.L.M. 155, 172 (1997).

(f) whether to apply strict rules of evidence (or any other rules) as to the admissibility, relevance or weight of any material (oral, written or other) sought to be tendered on any matters of fact or opinion, and the time, manner and form in which such material should be exchanged and presented;

(g) whether and to what extent the tribunal should itself take the initiative in ascertaining the facts and the law;

(h) whether and to what extent there should be oral or written evidence or submissions.

(3) The tribunal may fix the time within which any directions given by it are to be complied with, and may if it thinks fit extend the time so fixed (whether or not it has expired).

* * *

INDIA

THE ARBITRATION AND CONCILIATION ORDINANCE 1996.

* * *

Determination of rules of procedure

19. (1) The arbitral tribunal shall not be bound by the Code of Civil Procedure, 1908 or the Indian Evidence Act, 1872.

(2) Subject to this Part, the parties are free to agree on the procedure to be followed by the arbitral tribunal in conducting its proceedings.

(3) Failing any agreement referred to in sub-section (2), the arbitral tribunal may, subject to this Part, conduct the proceedings in the manner it considers appropriate.

(4) The power of the arbitral tribunal under sub-section (3) includes the power to determine the admissibility, relevance, materiality and weight of any evidence.

* * *

Howard M. Holtzmann & Joseph E. Neuhaus, A GUIDE TO THE UNCITRAL MODEL LAW ON INTERNATIONAL COMMERCIAL ARBITRATION: LEGISLATIVE HISTORY AND COMMENTARY

550; 564–68 (1989).*

ARTICLE 18. EQUAL TREATMENT OF PARTIES

The parties shall be treated with equality and each party shall be given a full opportunity of presenting his case.

* * *

ARTICLE 19.   DETERMINATION OF RULES OF PROCEDURE

(1) Subject to the provisions of this Law, the parties are free to agree on the procedure to be followed by the arbitral tribunal in conducting the proceedings.

(2) Failing such agreement, the arbitral tribunal may, subject to the provisions of this Law, conduct the arbitration in such manner as it considers appropriate. The power conferred upon the arbitral tribunal includes the power to determine the admissibility, relevance, materiality and weight of any evidence.

COMMENTARY

The UNCITRAL Secretariat observed that Article 19, along with Article 18, was the "Magna Carta of Arbitral Procedure" and said that these Articles might be regarded as "the most important provision[s] of the model law." Article 19 establishes the principle of the autonomy of the parties and the arbitrators in governing the procedural conduct of the arbitration. The autonomy principle is critical to an effective system of commercial arbitration for international cases because in such cases there is a special need to be free of unfamiliar local standards.[2] Moreover, this principle is at the heart of modern systems of arbitration; it expresses a profound confidence in the ability of parties and arbitrators to conduct the arbitration in a fair and orderly manner so as to arrive at a just resolution of a dispute. At the same time, however, Article 18 places fundamental restrictions on this principle.

Article 19 contains three rules: (1) the parties are free to agree on the arbitral procedure to be followed, subject to the mandatory provisions of the Model Law;[4] (2) absent such an agreement, the arbitral tribunal may conduct the arbitration as it considers appropriate, subject to both the mandatory and nonmandatory provisions of the Law; and (3) the arbitral tribunal's power includes the power to determine the admissibility, relevance materiality, and weight of evidence (unless the parties have agreed otherwise).

The Secretariat's commentary on Article 19 noted that as to each of these points the agreement of the parties that is referred to may include agreements to apply a set of rules (such as the UNCITRAL Arbitration rules) or even to apply the procedural code of a given legal system, as long as its provisions do not conflict with the mandatory provisions of the Model Law.[5] On the other hand, it was noted that the parties also

2. For examples of how parties from various legal traditions might usefully take advantage of the autonomy provided by Article 19, see the Seventh Secretariat Note, A/CN.9/264, Art. 19, para. 6, p. 584 *infra*. For a comparative study of arbitral practice in various parts of the world, see "Working Group I—Comparative Arbitration Practice," in *Comparative Arbitration Practice* and *Public Policy in Arbitration* 17–174

(ICCA Congress Series No. 3, P. Sanders ed. 1987).

4. For a list of mandatory provisions concerning the conduct of the arbitral proceedings and the making of the award, *see* Seventh Secretariat Note, A/CN.9/264, Art. 19, para. 3, p. 583 *infra*.

5. Seventh   Secretariat   Note, A/CN.9/264, Art. 19, para. 2, p. 583 *infra*. In the latter case, though, the chosen law

have the power to agree on particular points of special concern to them rather than adopting a comprehensive system of rules to govern the conduct of the arbitration. On all agreed points, their agreement will be given effect under paragraph 1 (as long as it does not conflict with the mandatory provisions of the law); on other matters, the arbitrators will have discretion under paragraph 2 to conduct the arbitration as they consider appropriate.

Similarly, where the parties have adopted a set of rules that does not touch on a particular point at issue, the arbitrators, retain the power to determine the procedure to be followed on that point. The Secretariat offered language that would have explicitly granted such a gap-filling power, but the Working Group declined to adopt the proposal.[7] It appears, however, that the Working Group simply thought that the proposed language was unnecessary. This was the view of the Secretariat, which noted in its commentary on the Working Group's final draft that the arbitral tribunal's power to conduct the arbitration in such * * * [manner] as it considered appropriate existed "[w]here the parties have not agreed ... on the procedure (*i.e. at least not on the particular matter at issue*)."

One matter that was considered at some length during the drafting of Article 19 was whether there should be a limitation on when the parties could agree on a procedural point. The Secretariat suggested that the Working Group amend draft Article 19 so as to require that any agreement on the arbitral procedure be reached before the first or sole arbitrator was appointed. The rationale for the proposal was that the rules of procedure should be clear from the outset and that any arbitrator should know from the beginning the rules under which he or she is expected to perform his or her functions.[10] The Working Group rejected this idea, finding instead that the freedom of the parties to agree on a procedure "should be a continuing one"; the Working Group interpreted paragraph 1 to provide for such a continuing freedom. The matter was raised again before the Commission, where conflicting proposals were offered, one that the Working Group's understanding be made explicit

---

would be applicable by virtue of the parties having exercised their right of choice under Article 19 and not by virtue of the chosen code's status as law. *Id. See also* the commentary on Article 1, paragraph 2, pp. 35B36 *supra*, which discusses a proposal whereby the parties could choose to have their arbitration be governed by the arbitration law of a State other than the place of arbitration, and that law would apply as a matter of law rather than merely as an agreement of the parties. Note also that under Article 2(e) of the Law, the parties' power to agree on a subject includes the power to choose arbitration rules to govern that subject. *See also* Summary Record, A/CN.9/SR.330 paras. 52B54, p. 588 *infra*.

7. *See* Fourth Working Group Report, A/CN.9/245, para. 75, pp. 577–78 *infra*. The proposal was that the second paragraph of Article 19 begin with the words, "Failing such agreement on the respective point at issue, ..." *See* Second Draft, A/CN.9/WG.II/WP.40, Art. XV(2), p. 577 *infra*.

10. *Id.* The Secretariat noted that such a rule had been adopted with respect to the parties' power to bar the arbitral tribunal from appointing an expert under Article 26(1). That time limitation was subsequently eliminated. *See* Fifth Working Group Report, A/CN.9/246, para. 87, appearing in the section on Article 26, pp. 727–28 *infra*.

and the other that it be reconsidered.[13] After extended discussion, the Commission decided not to change the Working Group's draft. There was some sentiment in favor of each proposal, but it was noted that in any case the arbitrators could not be forced to accept any procedures with which they disagreed, since they could always resign rather than carry out the unwanted procedural stipulations. Moreover, if the matter was of strong concern, the timing of any agreement on procedure could be regulated by agreement between the parties and the arbitrators.

The provision regarding evidence in Article 19(2) was modeled on Article 25(6) of the UNCITRAL Arbitration Rules. It is placed in the second paragraph of the Article and should be taken to be nonmandatory. That is, the term "the power conferred upon the arbitral tribunal" should be taken to mean the power conferred directly by the Model Law in the first sentence of paragraph 2, and not the "power" conferred by the parties' agreement under paragraph 1. As a result, if the parties agree that certain evidence should be inadmissible, or that a certain kind of document be the exclusive evidence, that agreement should be respected. Similarly, if they agree on procedural rules that contain or incorporate rules of evidence,[19] the arbitral tribunal should abide by that choice. This was the clear intent of the drafters: the Working Group's initial instructions on the point were that "the model law should empower the arbitral tribunal to adopt its own rules of evidence *subject to contrary stipulation by the parties*; this view was never contradicted; and it was the Secretariat's understanding of the provision."

On the other hand, where the parties have not adopted a comprehensive set of evidentiary rules, it is clearly within the power of the arbitral tribunal to do so. Thus, although the Working Group deleted language that would have expressly granted the power to adopt rules of evidence, it did so because the point was thought to be expressed with sufficient clarity already.

During the Commission's deliberations on Article 19, it was pointed out that that Article might be thought to conflict with Article 28, which allows the parties, or, failing that, the arbitral tribunal, to choose the substantive law that will govern the dispute. Under some legal systems, the admissibility, relevance, materiality, and weight of evidence are considered questions of substantive law. Suppose, for example, that the substantive law of Italy is to govern the resolution of the merits of a dispute, either as a matter of party choice or tribunal determination. Suppose also that under Italian law certain rules limiting the admissibili-

---

13. *See* Summary Record, A/CN.9/SR.316, para. 52, pp. 584–85 *infra*; Sixth Secretariat Note (Government Comments), A/CN.9/263, Art. 19, para. 2, p. 580 *infra*. This proposal was to allow the parties to agree on a procedural point after the arbitrators have accepted their duties only if the arbitrators also agree.

19. For example, a number of sets of arbitration rules empower parties to pres-

ent evidence in the form of written statements, such as affidavits. *E.g.,* UNCITRAL Arbitration Rules, Art. 25(5); American Arbitration Assn. Commercial Arbitration Rules, Rule 32; Rules of the London Court of International Arbitration, Art. 11.4. One can also imagine a case in which parties agreed on application of the hearsay rules of the common law or a particular national code of evidence.

ty of testimony of parties are considered substantive. Would the arbitral tribunal be bound to follow those rules or could it decide the admissibility of such testimony under different rules it chose pursuant to Article 19(2)? The Commission determined that the discretion accorded to the arbitrators by Article 19(2) (in the absence of a choice by the parties) should not be affected by the choice of law applicable to the substance of the dispute under Article 28.[25] This result is sound. As a matter of interpretation, the specific provision in Article 19(2) should prevail over the general one in Article 28. As a matter of policy, it is desirable for arbitration to avoid the application of technical rules of evidence where possible.

The Commission refused to adopt two further provisions touching on evidentiary matters. First, it was proposed that the Model Law should provide, as does Article 25(5) of the UNCITRAL Arbitration rules, that the parties may present evidence of witnesses in the form of signed written statements. The Commission did not consider it necessary to include such a provision in the Model Law, preferring to leave this point of detail to the agreement of the parties or the discretion of the arbitrators.

Second, several representatives proposed that the Model Law make clear that each party was to have the burden of proving the facts relied on to support its claim or defense. Such a provision appears in Article 24(1) of the UNCITRAL Arbitration Rules. The Commission noted that it was "a generally recognized principle" that reliance by a party on a fact required the party to prove that fact, but it felt that such a provision might interfere with the choice of substantive law under Article 28 and the broad freedom in the conduct of the arbitration granted by Article 19. Therefore, the matter is not regulated by the Model Law.

RULES OF THE ICC INTERNATIONAL COURT OF ARBITRATION

(in force from 1 January 1998).

* * *

Article 15

Rules Governing the Proceedings

1. The proceedings before the Arbitral Tribunal shall be governed by these Rules and, where these Rules are silent, any rules which the parties or, failing them, the Arbitral Tribunal may settle, whether or not reference is thereby made to the rules of procedure of a national law to be applied to the arbitration.

---

25. Commission Report, A/40/17, para. 174, p. 590 *infra*; *see* Summary Record, A/CN.9/SR.316, para. 70, p. 587 *infra*. The Commission declined to adopt a proposal that would have had the opposite effect, that is, that would have made the exercise of the power conferred in Article 19(2) subject to the choice of law made under Article 28. Summary Record, A/CN.9/SR.330, paras. 55–60, pp. 588–89 *infra*.

2. In all cases, the Arbitral Tribunal shall act fairly and impartially and ensure that each party has a reasonable opportunity to present its case.

* * *

WORLD INTELLECTUAL PROPERTY ORGANIZATION ARBITRATION RULES

(effective from October 1, 1994).

* * *

Laws Applicable to the Substance of the Dispute, the Arbitration and the Arbitration Agreement

Article 59

* * *

(b) The law applicable to the arbitration shall be the arbitration law of the place of arbitration, unless the parties have expressly agreed on the application of another arbitration law and such agreement is permitted by the law of the place of arbitration.

* * *

Questions and Comments

1. Do you agree with Judge Saville's argument that the choice of a *lex arbitri* different from the law of the place of arbitration results in a "highly unsatisfactory state of affairs"?

2. What issues or questions are usually decided by the *lex arbitri*? (See infra section IV.3.a. fn. [20]).

3. May the parties freely choose the *lex arbitri* to be applied?

4. The arbitration clause agreed upon between Mc Donnell Douglas and the Union of India stated: "The arbitration shall be conducted in accordance with the procedure provided by the Indian Arbitration Act of 1940 or any re-enactment or modification thereof." What is your reading of this provision?

5. Mr. Veeder Q.C. argued that the choice of the term "seat" instead of "place" had a great significance in this case. Do you agree? Is it likely that the parties made a conscious and deliberate choice between these terms?

Assuming the parties used the word "place" would you reach a different decision?

6. Since the decision of the Queen's Bench in 1992, both India and England have passed new arbitration acts. Take Judge Saville's place, and assume articles 33 and 34 of the 1996 English Act, and Section 19 of the 1996 Indian Act were applicable. Would you come to the same conclusion, or to a different one?

7. Alter the *McDonnell Douglas* facts by assuming that England had adopted the UNCITRAL Model Law. In the light of this assumption would Article 19 suggest a different result from the one reached by Judge Saville?

(After the adoption of the Model Law in particular countries, ***"this Law"*** becomes, of course, an act of the adopting country—and, in the hypo, this is England.)

8. What is your understanding of the reference to "the law applicable to arbitration" in the WIPO Rules in the light of Judge Saville's distinction between internal conduct and external supervision of arbitration?

(The WIPO Rules certainly assume their own applicability to arbitration proceedings. The question is what role remains for the "law applicable to arbitration".)

9. Article 15 of the 1998 ICC Rules mentions procedural rules of national laws only as one of the options among which the arbitrators (or the parties) are free to choose. Does this envisage (or can this mean) arbitration possibly free of the procedural control of any municipal law?

10. Article 3 of the Inter–American (Panama) Convention on Arbitration contains a provision on arbitration rules to be applied in the absence of party agreement. According to Article 3:

> "In the absence of an express agreement between the parties, the arbitration shall be conducted in accordance with the rules of procedure of the Inter–American Commercial Arbitration Commission."

The Panama Convention thus mandates default institutional rules, which is not a common solution—but might be a helpful one.

In Bancol et al. v. Bancolombia et al. , 123 F.Supp.2d 771 (S.D.N.Y.2000) (decision of December 18, 2000), the question arose whether a party is entitled to court enforcement of Article 3. After it was established that the case was arbitrable—and before the arbitrators were selected—plaintiffs asked the U.S. federal district court to apply Article 3 and order that arbitration proceed under the Rules of the IACAC (Inter–American Commercial Arbitration Commission). The court held instead:

> "Even though an order compelling arbitration does not divest a district court of jurisdiction over the underlying case, the court's authority to direct or oversee that arbitration is narrowly confined. In particular, it has little or no power to afford interlocutory review of procedural matters, let alone to determine at the outset what procedural rules are to be applied. Rather, '[o]nce it is determined...that the parties are obligated to submit the subject matter of a dispute to arbitration, "procedural" questions which grow out of the dispute and bear on its final disposition should be left to the arbitrator' ". (References omitted)

The court concluded:

> "Accordingly, plaintiffs' application is denied and the parties are ordered to proceed immediately with the selection of arbitrators under Clause Seventeenth of the Contract.... Any further delay would raise obvious questions of good faith."

One may assume that the Panama Convention (including its Article 3) has become part of the lex arbitri in countries that are parties to the

Convention. The question is when can this rule of the lex arbitri be enforced. Under the district court's logic, the arbitrators should establish the applicable rules of procedure. This does not necessarily exclude later court scrutiny focusing on whether Article 3 of the Panama Convention was duly observed.

Suppose the arbitrators do not apply the Rules of the IACAC, but opt, say, for the UNCITRAL Rules. Could a party to the dispute contest recognition of the award under Article V of the New York Convention? Under which provision(s) of Article V?

If one accepts that the court's authority to direct or oversee the arbitration process is "narrowly confined", and if these matters should be left to the arbitrators, can the court order the parties "to proceed immediately with the selection of the arbitrators"?

IV.1.c. *Organizing Arbitral Proceedings*

UNCITRAL NOTES ON ORGANIZING ARBITRAL PROCEEDINGS

United Nations, Vienna, 1996.

[See Documents Supplement; read in particular the introduction, the "List of matters for possible consideration in organizing arbitral proceedings", and item 9 (Arrangements for the exchange of written submissions).]

Questions and Comments

1. The UNCITRAL Notes on Organizing Arbitral Proceedings start with a checklist ("list of matters for possible consideration") and continue with **annotations** outlining and explaining possible options regarding the items on the checklist.

This initiative—while supported by representatives of the member states—has given rise to some doubts and criticism. One of the most prominent critics is the French author Fouchard, who commented on the "Notes" while they were still in draft form. Fouchard—who has been a strong supporter of other UNCITRAL actions in the domain of arbitration—has called the Notes a "questionable initiative",[1] Ph. Fouchard, Une initiative contestable de la CNUDCI, 1994 Revue de l'arbitrage 461. and voiced concern that they might adversely affect the flexibility and subtlety of the arbitration process by bringing about preliminary conferences even where they are not needed, pushing the parties to "foresee the unforeseeable", and an atmosphere of mistrust. Hostilities could emerge prematurely; and given the prestige of UNCITRAL, its recommendations might in practice turn soft law into firm rules lacking sufficient flexibility.

Comments such as Fouchard's resulted in the rather cautious wording of the final text of the Notes adopted at the 29th Session of the UNCITRAL in New York between May 28th and June 14th 1996. See in the Documents

[1]. Ph. Fouchard, Une initiative contestable de la CNUDCI, 1994 Revue de l'arbitrage 461.

Supplement the Introduction to the Notes, the checklist, and item 9 (Arrangements for the exchange of written submissions).

2. Do the Notes provide welcome assistance to parties and arbitrators or threaten the flexibility and subtlety of the arbitration process?

3. Are consecutive, or simultaneous, written submissions preferable? As an arbitrator, would you allow written submissions after the hearing?

IV.1.d. Party Discretion, Discretion of the Arbitrators, and Due Process

ABATI LEGNAMI (ITALY) v. FRITZ HÄUPL

Corte di Cassazione [Italian Supreme Court], 3 April 1987.
17 Yearbk. Comm. Arb'n 529 (1992).*

FACTS

An arbitral award in favour of Häupl was rendered by the Arbitration Court at the Vienna Commodity Exchange.

Häupl sought enforcement of the award in Italy before the Court of Appeal of Milan. The Court of Appeal granted enforcement, whereupon Abati appealed to the Supreme Court.

The Supreme Court reversed the lower court's decision on the following grounds and remanded the case before a different section of the Court of Appeal of Milan.

* * *

[13] "As to [Abati's contention] that the Court of Appeal violated Art. V(1)(b) [of the New York Convention] …, we hold that the petitioner correctly contends that the reasons given by the Court of Appeal of Milan for its decision were insufficient and illogical on this issue."

[14] Abati was summoned on 11 August 1981 to appear before the Vienna arbitral tribunal. The date scheduled for Abati's appearance was 8 September 1981. The Court of Appeal held that this notice period was sufficient and reasoned inter alia that commercial activities cannot be unilaterally suspended because one of the two States involved habitually concentrates vacations in the month of August. The Supreme Court accepted the Court of Appeal's reasoning but noted that there are legal provisions concerning this issue. Particularly, the Supreme Court noted that the Italian legal notice period is ninety days and that all time limits for proceedings before Italian courts are suspended between 1 August and 15 September, with certain exceptions (Law no. 742 of 7 October 1969). The Supreme Court held that this provision leads to a "thinning out" of all juridical activities, so that Abati's opportunity of defending itself may have been affected.

---

* Reprinted with permission of Yearbook Commercial Arbitration, International Council for Commercial Arbitration.

[15]   Hence, the Supreme Court remanded the case to the Court of Appeal of Milan, requesting that it determine whether Abati's opportunity of defending itself had been affected.

FIRM P (U.S.A.) v. FIRM F (F.R.G.)

Oberlandesgericht [Court of Appeal] Hamburg, 3 April 1975.
2 Yearbk. Comm. Arb'n 241 (1977).*

Extract

The German firm F and the U.S. firm P had referred their dispute to arbitration under the Rules of the American Arbitration Association (AAA). The single arbitrator decided on the basis of the documents, not permitting oral hearings. The U.S. firm P submitted a letter, which the arbitrator did not forward to the German firm F, which had consequently no knowledge of its existence. On the other hand, the German firm F submitted a letter of a German Ministry, which contradicted the letter of the U.S. firm P. The arbitrator did not, however, take account of this letter. The award was made in favour of the U.S. firm P. The District Court of Oregon (U.S.A.) declared the award to be enforceable.

The German Court of first instance (Landgericht) granted enforcement. On appeal, the Court of Appeal (Oberlandesgericht) refused to enforce the award.

The Court of Appeal first observed that the German–American Treaty of Friendship, Commerce and Navigation of 1954 (Art. VI) had still to be applied to the present case, because the U.S.A. had only ratified the New York Convention in 1970 after the parties had concluded their contract.

With respect to the defence of the German firm F that it had not been able to present its case (*audi et alteram partem*), the Court of Appeal referred to a leading decision of the Supreme Court of 21 October 1971 which draws a distinction between domestic and international public policy with respect to the recognition and enforcement of foreign arbitral awards. Reference was made to the same trend in France and Switzerland where the same distinction, in the case of foreign arbitral awards, is made.

It was held, however, that in the case of a foreign award, not every infringement of the mandatory provisions of German law constitutes a violation of German public policy. Only in extreme cases, where a party had not been able to present his case in an arbitration abroad, would the basic principles of the German legal order be violated.

The Court of Appeal deemed that such an extreme case was present. The arbitrator and the A.A.A. had not only violated the principle of a fair hearing, but the award was made without giving an opportunity to the

* Reprinted with permission of Yearbook Commercial Arbitration, International   Council for Commercial Arbitration.

German firm F to obtain knowledge of the letter the other party had submitted. Moreover, the arbitrator had not paid any attention to the letter of the German Ministry, which was submitted by the German firm F.

The Court observed that the German Firm F had rightly remarked that the A.A.A. Rules make little allowance for foreign parties. On the other hand it referred to Section 31, para. 2, last sentence, of the A.A.A. Rules, which states that all parties shall be afforded opportunity to examine documents.

The violation could not be cured by the fact that the arbitral decision would not have been otherwise if there had been a fair trial. The Court of Appeal stated that a violation is present as soon as it cannot be excluded that a hearing (of the German firm F) could have led to a more favourable decision (for the German firm F).

Roger K. Ward, THE FLEXIBILITY OF EVIDENTIARY RULES IN INTERNATIONAL TRADE DISPUTE ARBITRATION: PROBLEMS POSED TO AMERICAN-TRAINED LAWYERS

J. Int'l Arb'n, Sept. 1996, at 5, 15–17.*

* * *

V.   PROBLEMS POSED TO AMERICAN-TRAINED LAWYERS

As stated briefly in the introduction to this article, the use of civilian procedures in the admission of evidence in international trade dispute arbitration is problematic to most American-trained lawyers who lack experience in such proceedings.[79] With the exception of law schools in Louisiana, most American law students do not receive adequate training in civil law. As a result, they are usually bewildered when, upon their initial exposure to an international trade dispute arbitration, they are unable to utilize the "objection!" skills they learned in law school to exclude hearsay, impeach the witness via cross-examination, and bar the admission of certain prejudicial evidence. Introduction to international trade dispute arbitration is a learning experience. The American-trained lawyer is bound to feel as though he has been "thrown to the lions".[81]

There are many reasons why the American-trained lawyer will find the evidentiary procedures of this type of arbitration troublesome. One reason will certainly be the inquisitorial nature of the proceedings. American-trained lawyers are trained to be adversarial and aggressive. These learned behaviors become useless in an arbitration proceeding

---

* Reprinted with permission from Kluwer Law International.

79. Throughout this article, I have referred to a lawyer trained in a common law school as an "American-trained" lawyer. This is due, in part, to my natural affinity toward this country. For clarification, it should be noted that such lawyers are also trained in common law in other countries such as Great Britain, Canada, Australia, New Zealand and other "children of the common mother" (England).

81. The Roman (civilian) lions, that is.

that relies upon inquisition of the parties. The American-trained lawyer will find it odd that the judge is not passive, but rather an active participant in the proceedings.

The relative absence of discovery, which has long been touted as an advantage to arbitration as opposed to litigation, will be unfamiliar to the American-trained lawyer. Discovery is a uniquely American mechanism. American-trained lawyers are taught to make generous use of discovery devices such as interrogatories and depositions to narrow the issues in the case and to prevent unfair surprise to the other party. Discovery even results in settlement of many cases when adverse parties learn the strengths, weaknesses and misconceptions of their own or their adversary's position. Limited discovery means limited need for an attorney. For a common-law lawyer trained in a notoriously litigious country like the United States, limited discovery threatens one's livelihood.

* * *

In order to overcome the difficulties that civil-law evidentiary procedures will pose, an American-trained lawyer should avoid relying on common-law rules of evidence because they have virtually no application in the international arbitration setting. Over-reliance on the common-law system will become an albatross that will not easily disappear.[86] Instead, an American-trained lawyer should become familiar with the civilian tradition and how it differs from the common-law tradition. Further, a review of the evidentiary procedures in a civil-law jurisdiction will be helpful.[87] Finally, American-trained lawyers should keep an open mind when appraising the evidentiary procedures used in international trade dispute resolution. Although not to the same degree as the British, Americans are somewhat hesitant to alter tradition and custom, especially in matters involving the sacred cow that is the legal procedure. Acceptance of the differences between the two systems is necessary if American-trained attorneys wish to operate effectively in the global market-place.

Questions and Comments

1.   Arbitral institutions and arbitration rules typically do not provide for fixed time limits. Dates for hearings and deadlines for submissions result either from party agreement or from an exercise of the arbitrators' discretion.

86. Reference to *The Rime of the Ancient Mariner* by Samuel Taylor Coleridge.

87. Unfortunately, Louisiana's Code of Evidence has many provisions that are grounded in the Federal Rules of Evidence, which in turn are modeled after common-law rules of evidence. Therefore, an English-speaking American attorney will be disappointed that the great bastion of civilian tradition in the United States utilizes an evidentiary scheme that is more like common law than civil law. However, some of the procedural codes of non-English speaking civil-law countries have been translated into English. [For a general discussion of German civil procedure that can serve as a model for continental European civil procedure in general, see A. von Mehren and J. Gordley, The Civil Law System 150–208 (2d ed. 1977).]

2.   In *Abati v. Häupl* arbitrators sitting in Vienna sent a notice on August 11 for a hearing on September 8. Should whether Abati "was not given proper notice * * * of the arbitration proceedings or was otherwise unable to present his case" turn on what the Italian legal notice period is or that the legal notice period in Italy is suspended between August 1 and September 15? Did the arbitrators need to comply with the legal notice periods of either Austria or Italy?

3.   Should the Italian party have anticipated the notice and made arrangements for someone to open or forward mail?

4.   Suppose the Italian party received the arbitrators' summons but was unable to find any competent Italian lawyer willing to appear in Vienna on September 8. Would these circumstances justify the Italian court in refusing to enforce the award? Would a due process problem be presented?

5.   Suppose in a case in which Respondent is from an Orthodox, while Claimant from a Catholic, country, the arbitrators set the hearing for January 7th, the Orthodox Christmas. The Respondent objects and requests a more convenient date. The arbitrators refuse to reschedule the hearing, explaining that they all have very crowded schedules and simply cannot find another date in the foreseeable future which would suit all. Respondent does not appear and contests the award on ground of violation of due process. What result?

(Experienced arbitrators will typically respect religious and cultural customs and differences, which is certainly advisable. The question is whether a less broad-minded attitude would affect the validity of the arbitration process-and of the award.)

6.   Suppose the arbitrators in a given case are businessmen and engineers, not lawyers, and—in order to expedite the process—they establish a rule that the parties may be advised by lawyers during the hearing but that the lawyers will not be allowed to cross-examine witnesses, to raise questions, or to make arguments to the arbitrators. Would the award be valid?

7.   Are the procedural problems in the case decided by the OLG Hamburg between the U.S. Claimant and German Respondent more or less serious than those in the *Abati v. Häupl* case?

8.   How could the losing German firm have known that "the arbitrator had not paid any attention to the letter of the German Ministry, which was submitted by the German firm, F"? Do you have a theory?

9.   The principle is clear: There should be no unilateral communication. Whatever is submitted by the parties or by the arbitrators, must reach both parties and all arbitrators.

But how broadly does it reach? Suppose the arbitrators inform both parties that the respondent is accorded 30 days to submit its statement of defence. An extension is sought but denied. The arbitrators fail to communicate to claimant the respondent's letter seeking extension, nor do they inform claimant of the tribunal's response. Is due process violated?

10.   In international commercial arbitration the parties have very broad powers to control the way in which the case is to be presented. The choices made have traditionally been influenced by such factors as the type of issues

raised and the procedural styles to which the parties, their lawyers, and the arbitrators are accustomed. When these persons represent a single procedural tradition, that tradition's practices respecting such matters as the examination of witnesses and the roles of lawyers and of adjudicators have often been followed, though typically in a more relaxed and less formal manner than would be found in a court proceeding. When different procedural traditions are represented in an arbitration, the arbitral proceeding may well utilize a mixed procedure. In recent years, moreover, a style and tradition proper to international commercial arbitration has emerged. One cannot speak of unification, but there is a noticeable trend towards harmonization. Within this trend, adversarial presentation of evidence is loosing ground.

11.   The Ward article points out that American approaches to the gathering and presentation of evidence differ from the dominant pattern in international commercial arbitration. Compromises are possible given the party-driven nature of arbitration, yet cases in which the parties agree on American-style presentation of evidence are relatively scarce. What are the reasons behind this development? The absence of juries in arbitration? Striving for speed?

Another explanation is that the American approach to the gathering and presentation of evidence is more recondite and, accordingly, requires more specialized learning than does the Continental European approach. Consequently, it is easier for an American-trained lawyer to adapt to the European approach than *vice versa*.

12.   Arbitrators have rather wide powers in handling evidence. According to Article 24(6) of the UNCITRAL Rules, *"The arbitral tribunal shall determine the admissibility, relevance, materiality, and weight of the evidence offered."* Rights and discretionary power carry with them responsibilities. Does the duty of the arbitrator to evaluate evidence cease at the point where an allegation or an item of evidence is not contradicted by the other party?

Suppose the following: a manufacturer in Russia regularly receives shipments of parts from a supplier in Latvia on the first of each month; the Russian party asks the Latvian party to ship one-half of the March 1 shipment early, on February 15, and the remainder on March 1, which the Latvian party does; the parties later go to arbitration on a number of issues, including the Latvian party's claim for the extra shipping cost incurred by the February 15 shipment. Assume that the shipping cost is normally calculated as a fixed cost per kilometer traveled (for shipment by truck) and that the Latvian party's written claim states the truck-route distance between the relevant locations in Latvia and Russia (which cannot be determined simply by looking at a map) is 550 kilometers, whereas the sole arbitrator knows from personal experience that the distance is about 200 kilometers. When the arbitrator asks the lawyer for the Latvian claimant about the distance, he responds that the distance was given to him by his client and he stands by the claim. The lawyer for the Russian defendant does not challenge the claim. What should the arbitrator do?

IV.1.e.   *What Belongs to Arbitration Proceedings?*

Note: It is beyond doubt that due process encompasses the right of the parties to equal treatment during the arbitral proceedings. It is also uncontested that both parties must be given equal opportunity to appear at hearings. The question arises, however, as to what really belongs to "arbitral proceedings" or to a "hearing". If an expert appointed by the arbitral tribunal undertakes an inspection in the factory of one of the parties, should the other party be invited? Is this a part of the arbitral proceedings? Can the presiding arbitrator of the tribunal attend an on site visit by experts without inviting the co-arbitrators? These are exactly the questions that arose in a recent Hong Kong case, Hebei Import & Export Corp. v. Polytek Engineering Comp. Ltd., 1 Hong Kong Law Reports 287 (Hong Kong Ct. App., 1998), reversed, 1 Hong Kong Law Reports 665 (Hong Kong Ct. Final App., 1999).

In this case, Polytek of Hong Kong agreed to sell Hebei equipment for the production of rubber powder. In May 1995 Hebei claimed that the equipment failed, and initiated arbitration proceedings before the CIETAC (China International Economic and Trade Arbitration Commission). In May 1997, the CIETAC found in favor of Hebei and awarded HK$14 million. Polytek initiated proceedings in Hong Kong challenging the award, but did not succeed with its challenge in the trial court. On appeal, the Court of Appeal in its judgment of January 16, 1998 set aside the leave to enforce the award. Regarding the issue of inspection the Court of Appeal held:

> "It would seem that such an inspection was very much part of the arbitration proceedings during which both parties should be present. In our view, the defendant should have been notified and allowed to be present at the inspection."

The Court of Appeal's decision was overruled by a Judgment of February 9, 1999, of the Court of Final Appeal of the Hong Kong Special Administrative Region. The Court of Final Appeal reinstated the leave to enforce the award.

Below we reproduce first a summary of facts, as stated in the 1998 Judgment of the Court of Appeal. Then we follow with excerpts from the 1999 Judgment of the Court of Final Appeal (including a somewhat different statement of facts).

HEBEI IMPORT & EXPORT CORP. v. POLYTEK ENGINEERING CO. LTD.

HONG KONG COURT OF APPEAL OPINION, 1998.

1 Hong Kong Law Reports 287.

* * *

THE ISSUES IN THIS APPEAL

In the present appeal, the defendant [seller] seeks to rely on three main grounds to show that the judge was wrong. First, the defendant was not given proper notice of an inspection which took place in the plaintiff's factory and was attended by the Chief Arbitrator and three experts in the presence of the plaintiff's representatives but in the absence of the defendant's representatives. It is submitted that the defendant was deprived of an opportunity to properly present its case to the arbitrators.

Second, the award was tainted with apparent bias in that there were communications by the plaintiff's staff to the Chief Arbitrator in the absence of the defendant. It is submitted that it would be contrary to public policy if the award is to be enforced. Third, the award should not be enforced without regard to the plaintiff's corresponding obligation under the award to return the equipment in an acceptable condition.

The plaintiff contends that the defendant is estopped from raising in the Hong Kong courts points which had or could have been raised in proceedings in another court, namely the Beijing No.2 Intermediate People's Court.

THE FACTS

The defendant's complaints are based on certain alleged facts relating to the conduct of the arbitration proceedings. It is submitted that what happened gives rise to legitimate grounds for the Hong Kong courts to refuse enforcement of the award under s. 44 of the Arbitration Ordinance.

Some of the facts are not in dispute. It transpired that at the defendant's request, the Arbitration Tribunal appointed three experts to inspect and examine the equipment in question. The Chief Arbitrator and the experts went to the plaintiff's factory with a representative of VETAC (the body which arranged the appointment of the experts) and a representative of CIETAC for the inspection, which lasted a whole day. During the inspection, two of the plaintiff's technicians were present. However, the defendant was not informed of the inspection and was therefore absent.

The facts which are in dispute centre around two matters. First, whether the Tribunal had promised that the inspection would be conducted in the presence of both parties, but had breached such promise by failing to inform the defendant. Second, whether during the inspection, the plaintiff's technicians were merely assisting in the testing and examination of the equipment and only showing records of previous testings to the Chief Arbitrator and the experts, or whether they had also been briefed by the technicians or staff of the plaintiff.

On the first matter, according to the defendant, at the hearing of the arbitration on 10th October 1995, the evidence was not completed. The Tribunal adjourned for the purpose of appointing its own experts and inspecting the equipment and promised that the parties could attend such inspection. But the defendant was never notified of the date of the inspection and was therefore not able to attend or to brief its own experts. Hence, it had no opportunity to call the manufacturer of the equipment to give evidence or to comment on the experts' report. It is also alleged that the defendant was wrongly refused a second hearing.

On the other hand, the plaintiff alleges that the Tribunal never undertook to invite the parties to be present at the inspection and that the parties had agreed to make written submissions to the Tribunal. The defendant had indeed made its supplemental written submission on 24th November 1995. After obtaining the experts' report, the Tribunal invited the parties to make further supplemental submissions on the report. This the defendant did on 20th January 1996. Its request to call the manufacturer either to give evidence or to comment on the report was refused by the Tribunal. A deadline was set at 16th February 1996 for the parties to make further submissions. The defendant made a second further supplemental submission on 14th February 1996. In that submission, the defendant asked for the Tribunal to postpone its decision since it was still waiting for the comments of the US manufacturer. This was not granted since the matter had been delayed for a long time. There was no request for a second hearing.

As to the second matter, the defendant alleges that the documentation showed that the Chief Arbitrator and the experts had been given "seminars" by the plaintiff's technicians and staff on the equipment. But there was no independent record of what went on at the inspection and the defendant was kept ignorant of what happened. The plaintiff denies that its technicians and staff had briefed the Chief Arbitrator and the experts. It is said that they just assisted in the testing of the equipment and showing records of previous testings to the Chief Arbitrator.

* * *

COURT OF FINAL APPEAL OPINION, 1999

1 Hong Kong Law Reports 665 (1999).

CHIEF JUSTICE LI:

* * *

THE FACTS

It is an admitted fact that the seller [defendant] received a copy of the experts' report in mid-December 1995. * * * [Chief Justice Li refers here to a "letter of 4 January 1996 from the tribunal to the seller, where the Chief Arbitrator's presence at the inspection was disclosed".] There were further submissions thereafter from the seller, in the course of which the seller asked that the American manufacturer of the equipment, Jacobson Inc., be made a party to the arbitration proceedings or be called as a witness to explain the defects in the equipment. Not surprisingly this was declined by the tribunal. In its reply dated 25 January 1996 the tribunal went on to say:

> "If you have any opinion on the contents of the expert assessment report, please submit the same in writing to the Tribunal before 16 February 1996."

The seller responded on 14 February 1996 with lengthy submissions and ended up by saying:

> "The equipment has up to now failed to attain the targets pre- scribed in the Agreement. Although this was not caused by the deliberate act of ... the seller, and [the seller] was in fact a victim, [the seller] is willing to assume its own responsibility of compensa- tion if the equipment is repairable...."

There was then an admission of liability to the tune of US$55,994.38 and RMB 77309.39. This was followed by a request that the tribunal should postpone making an award for two months. Not surprisingly, this was not accepted by the tribunal which then published its detailed award on 29 March 1996.

On the facts I conclude that the seller comes nowhere near establishing a case for intervention by the court on public policy grounds. As I read the Court of Appeal's judgment, it was led astray by the notion that, at the inspection at the end-user's factory, there was some process of assess- ment of the state of the equipment by the Chief Arbitrator in the presence of the experts, but in the absence of the other two arbitrators, and of the seller. Whether such a process, had it occurred, might have brought the case within s. 44(3) is beside the point. There is no evidence that this had occurred. On the evidence, the Chief Arbitrator was there to ensure propriety of conduct on the part of the experts; he was not there to form any kind of judgment on the state of the equipment, nor whether modification of its design was possible. The arbitral tribunal ultimately based its award on the report of the experts, not on the Chief Arbitrator's evaluation of the state of the equipment. As to the contents of the experts' report, the seller had ample opportunity to comment and to challenge its conclusions.

The Court of Appeal, in my judgment, made far too much of the so-called briefing by the technicians on the history of the equipment, when the experts attended at the end-user's factory, accompanied by the Chief Arbitrator. On the evidence, this was the first view of the equipment by the experts. They had been appointed by the tribunal at the seller's request, and their initial task was to see whether, as the seller contend- ed, the equipment might be modified so as to perform to the contract specification. That was the focus of the "briefing". On these facts, it was not open to the Court of Appeal to conclude that the seller, being absent at the inspection, had been prevented from presenting its side of the case. The inspection at the factory was not a "hearing" nor was it an occasion for either party to present its case.

* * *

MR. JUSTICE BOKHARY PJ:

This appeal is concerned with the enforcement in Hong Kong of a Convention award, i.e. an award made in pursuance of an arbitration agreement in a State or territory, other than Hong Kong, which is a party to the New York Convention. * * * I * * * wish only to emphasise the following matters.

In the Court of Appeal's judgment delivered by the Chief Judge, two crucial statements as to the facts are made. The first is that "the award ... was apparently based on the condition of the equipment as assessed by the experts and the Chief Arbitrator during the inspection". And the second one, immediately following the first, is that: "How far they were influenced by the briefing of the [appellant buyer's] staff in the absence of the [respondent seller] is unknown". The implication is that the experts and the Chief Arbitrator were—and therefore the award itself was—so influenced to some extent.

If I had felt able wholly to share the Court of Appeal's view of the facts, I might have been disposed to affirm the result which it reached, which was to refuse enforcement of the award. It might be mentioned that if the facts were indeed as the Court of Appeal saw them, the seller may, for all we know, have succeeded in its application to the court in the supervisory jurisdiction, the Beijing No. 2 Intermediate Court, for the setting aside of the award. But the evidence does not support the Court of Appeal's view of the facts. According to the Arbitration Tribunal, the Chief Arbitrator accompanied the experts merely to see that they went about their work properly. There is no evidence that he made any assessment of the condition of the equipment during the inspection. Nor is there any evidence that anybody briefed him during the inspection.

What the evidence suggests is as follows. Two technicians, who were in the end-user's employ but acted as agents for the buyer, assisted the experts to the extent necessary for them to carry out the inspection. (It was of course the seller itself which had wanted an inspection done.) Probably the technicians did tell the experts, in the Chief Arbitrator's hearing, what had gone wrong in the past. But that would have been of limited importance since the experts were not there to consider what the equipment had failed to do. They were concerned to discover what the equipment could be made to do through modification.

Inability to present case?

True it is that the seller did not attend the inspection because it had not been notified of it. And I think that this lack of notice did provide the seller with some cause for complaint. But in all the circumstances, including the seller's inaction after discovering the existence of this cause for complaint, I do not think that the complaint can legitimately be taken so far as to say that the seller had been unable to present its case.

* * *

Questions and Comments

1. The Court of Appeal states that the inspection was "very much part of the arbitration proceedings", and thus both parties should have been

present. In the opinion of the Court of Final Appeal, the inspection was not a hearing, "nor was it an occasion for either party to be present".

"Proceedings" and "hearing" are, of course, not synonyms. The hearing is only one segment of the arbitral proceedings. Do you agree with the position of the Court of Appeal, which seems to suggest that both parties should be present (or at least, entitled to be present) throughout the arbitral proceedings?

2.   In the *Polytek v. Hebei* case, the problem is not only that one of the parties was not present during the inspection undertaken by the experts, but also that the other party was there (because inspection was undertaken in that party's factory). Invitations were not sent to either of the parties, but one party was bound to be there anyway. Is this, in itself, a violation of due process requirements?

3.   According to Article 38(2) of the CIETAC Rules:

"When investigating and collecting evidence by itself, the arbitration tribunal shall promptly inform the parties to be present, if it considers it necessary. Should one party or both parties fail to appear, the investigation and collection of evidence shall not be affected."

(There is no difference of any substance between the 1995 and the 2000 CIETAC Rules concerning this provision.) Do you support the granting of such discretionary powers to the arbitrators? Do you see the need for a special provision for cases in which the investigation is conducted at the premises of one of the parties?

4.   The Court of Final Appeal states that under the circumstances of the case, the party absent from the inspection was not prevented from presenting its side of the case. Is this the critical dividing line?

5.   Suppose a witness is not accessible to the tribunal, and the arbitral tribunal asks a national court to examine the witness. Suppose this takes place by way of court assistance. Should the court invite the parties to the arbitration proceedings to attend the taking of the testimony? Should the arbitral tribunal inform the parties?

IV.1.f.   Terms of Reference

ICC RULES OF ARBITRATION

(in force from 1 January 1998).

* * *

Article 18

Terms of Reference; Procedural Timetable

1.   As soon as it has received the file from the Secretariat, the Arbitral Tribunal shall draw up, on the basis of documents or in the presence of the parties and in the light of their most recent submissions, a document defining its Terms of Reference. This document shall include the following particulars:

a) the full names and descriptions of the parties;

b) the addresses of the parties to which notifications and communications arising in the course of the arbitration may be made;

c) a summary of the parties' respective claims and of the relief sought by each party, with an indication to the extent possible of the amounts claimed or counterclaimed;

d) unless the Arbitral Tribunal considers it inappropriate, a list of issues to be determined;

e) the full names, descriptions and addresses of the arbitrators;

f) the place of the arbitration; and

g) particulars of the applicable procedural rules and, if such is the case, reference to the power conferred upon the Arbitral Tribunal to act as amiable compositeur or to decide *ex aequo et bono*.

2.   The Terms of Reference shall be signed by the parties and the Arbitral Tribunal. Within two months of the date on which the file has been transmitted to it, the Arbitral Tribunal shall transmit to the Court the Terms of Reference signed by it and by the parties. The Court may extend this time limit pursuant to a reasoned request from the Arbitral Tribunal or on its own initiative if it decides it is necessary to do so.

3.   If any of the parties refuses to take part in the drawing up of the Terms of Reference or to sign the same, they shall be submitted to the Court for approval. When the Terms of Reference are signed in accordance with Article 18(2) or approved by the Court, the arbitration shall proceed.

4.   When drawing up the Terms of Reference, or as soon as possible thereafter, the Arbitral Tribunal, after having consulted the parties, shall establish in a separate document a provisional timetable that it intends to follow for the conduct of the arbitration and shall communicate it to the Court and the parties. Any subsequent modifications of the provisional timetable shall be communicated to the Court and the parties.

Article 19

New Claims

After the Terms of Reference have been signed or approved by the Court, no party shall make new claims or counterclaims which fall outside the limits of the Terms of Reference unless it has been authorized to do so by the Arbitral Tribunal, which shall consider the nature of such new claims or counterclaims, the stage of the arbitration and other relevant circumstances.

* * *

ICC RULES OF ARBITRATION

(in force from 1 January 1988).

Article 13

Terms of reference

1.   Before proceeding with the preparation of the case, the arbitrator shall draw up, on the basis of the documents or in the presence of the parties and in the light of their most recent submissions, a document defining his Terms of Reference. This document shall include the following particulars:

a) the full names and description of the parties,

b) the addresses of the parties to which notifications or communications arising in the course of the arbitration may validly be made,

c) a summary of the parties' respective claims,

d) definition of the issues to be determined,

e) the arbitrator's full name, description and address,

f) the place of arbitration,

g) particulars of the applicable procedural rules and, if such is the case, reference to the power conferred upon the arbitrator to act as amiable compositeur,

h) such other particulars as may be required to make the arbitral award enforceable in law, or may be regarded as helpful by the Court of Arbitration or the arbitrator.

2.   The document mentioned in paragraph 1 of this Article shall be signed by the parties and the arbitrator. Within two months of the date when the file has been transmitted to him, the arbitrator shall transmit to the Court the said document signed by himself and by the parties. The Court may, pursuant to a reasoned request from the arbitrator or if need be on its own initiative, extend this time-limit if it decides it is necessary to do so.

Should one of the parties refuse to take part in the drawing up of the said document or to sign the same, the Court, if it is satisfied that the case is one of those mentioned in paragraphs 2 and 3 of Article 8, shall take such action as is necessary for its approval. Thereafter the Court shall set a time limit for the signature of the statement by the defaulting party and on expiry of that time limit the arbitration shall proceed and the award shall be made.

3.   The parties shall be free to determine the law to be applied by the arbitrator to the merits of the dispute. In the absence of any indication by the parties as to the applicable law, the arbitrator shall apply the law designated as the proper law by the rule of conflict which he deems appropriate.

4. The arbitrator shall assume the powers of an amiable compositeur if the parties are agreed to give him such powers.

5. In all cases the arbitrator shall take account of the provisions of the contract and the relevant trade usages.

* * *

Article 16

The parties may make new claims or counter-claims before the arbitrator on condition that these remain within the limits fixed by the Terms of Reference provided for in Article 13 or that they are specified in a rider to that document, signed by the parties and communicated to the Court.

* * *

J. Gillis Wetter,[c] THE PRESENT STATUS OF THE INTERNATIONAL COURT OF ARBITRATION OF THE ICC: AN APPRAISAL

1 Am. Rev. Int'l Arb'n 91, 101–2 (1990)*

3. *Terms of Reference.* One of the most controversial and antiquated relics in the [1988] ICC Rules is the requirement that the arbitrators and the parties must agree on a definition of the dispute at their first meeting. This was prompted by the rule obtaining in France when the Rules were [originally] promulgated that an arbitration agreement entered into before a dispute arose was invalid-a notion that unfortunately still persists in some jurisdictions, notably in South America. Although this reason has long since disappeared in France, the ICC Court still regards terms of reference as indispensable for the purpose of establishing bases for (i) fixing deposits in relation to stated monetary claims (the Secretariat denies that this is a rationale), and (ii) reviewing the award for compliance with the stipulations in the document concerning claims and issues to be decided.

The terms of reference should indicate with precision the issues in dispute, but this is not always possible. A former first president of France's highest court wisely remarked at an ICC Conference in Paris some years ago that he had never decided a case in which the issues could be defined before argument was closed. Two additional rationales for retaining the present system are often cited: it is useful for the parties and the tribunal to meet at an early point (an objective which evidently can be achieved anyway), and the process of negotiating terms of reference sometimes leads to settlement (which is correct).

A troubling aspect of the practice is the time and thus the expense that the exercise entails, mostly without producing tangible results toward advancing a resolution of the case. * * *

c. Solicitor–Royal (Sweden), Member of the Stockholm Bar.

* Reprinted by permission of American Review of International Arbitration.

It is said that terms of reference have many supporters, even among common law lawyers. However, the fact that no other arbitral institution, no other arbitration rules, and, to the writer's knowledge, no ad hoc tribunals require terms of reference is sufficient proof that the notion is ill-conceived and that the requirement should be abolished in the interest of both economy and justice. A useful substitute would be rules on pre-trial meetings, modeled, e.g., on note 4 to article 15 of the UNCITRAL Arbitration Rules adopted by the Iran–United States Claims Tribunal, which provide that "[t]he arbitral tribunal may make an order directing the arbitrating parties to appear for a pre-hearing conference."[19]

Stephen R. Bond,[d] THE PRESENT STATUS OF THE INTERNATIONAL COURT OF ARBITRATION OF THE ICC: A COMMENT ON AN APPRAISAL
1 Am. Rev. Int'l Arb'n 108, 116–118 (1990).

E.   TERMS OF REFERENCE

Terms of Reference (TOR) must be viewed in the context of international commercial arbitration, which generally involves parties and arbitrators of several nationalities with differing legal training and backgrounds, who are compelled to deal with inherently difficult subjects under legal systems with which they are not all equally familiar. Thus, while this feature of ICC arbitration most often raises questions by those whose arbitration experience tends to be in the domestic sphere, we generally hear praise for the utility of TOR for a number of reasons.[13]

---

19. Final Tribunal Rules of Procedure, 3 May 1983, 2 Iran–U.S. C.T.R. 419. The Internal Guidelines of the Tribunal suggest that the following matters may be on the agenda of a pre-trial meeting:

The following list is illustrative of the matters which may be considered at the pre-hearing conference held pursuant to Note 4 to Article 15 of the Tribunal Rules, and the arbitral tribunal may in its discretion determine to consider additional, or fewer, matters at the pre-hearing conference:

(a) clarification of the issues presented and the relief sought;

(b) identification of any issues to be considered as preliminary questions;

(c) status of and settlement discussions;

(d) whether any further written statements, including any reply or rejoinder, is requested by the arbitrating parties or required by the arbitral tribunal (see Tribunal Rules, Article 22);

(e) fixing a schedule for submission by each arbitrating party of a summary of the documents or lists of witnesses or other evidence it intends to present (see Tribunal Rules, Article 24 (2));

(f) fixing a schedule for submission of any documents, exhibits or other evidence with the [sic] arbitral tribunal may then require (see Tribunal Rules, Article 24(3));

(g) whether voluminous and complicated data should be presented through summaries, tabulations, charts, graphs or extracts in order to save time and costs;

(h) desirability of appointing an expert by the arbitral tribunal, and if so the expert's qualifications and terms of reference; whether the arbitrating parties intend to present experts, and, if so, the qualifications of and the areas of expertise to be covered by any such expert;

(i) determining what documentary evidence will require translation;

(j) fixing a schedule of hearings;

(k) other appropriate matters.

1 Iran–U.S. C.T.R. 98 (1981–82).

d. Secretary General, International Court of Arbitration.

13. The multiple advantages of Terms of Reference include the following:

Deemed by Dr. Wetter to be "an antiquated relic" which should be "abolished" (p. 101), he states that:

The ICC Court still regards terms of reference as indispensable for the purpose of establishing bases for (i) fixing deposits in relation to stated monetary claims (the Secretariat denies that this is a

a. *Technical Advantages*

i.   The Terms of Reference provide a means to bring order to what is often an incoherent and incomplete set of initial pleadings, permitting the arbitral tribunal to establish a rational structure and organization for the future path of the entire arbitration. Terms of Reference, for example, result in pulling together complex claims and counterclaims into a single document, making it easier for all concerned to deal with the issues. Where all of the parties sign the Terms of Reference, the document can also be used to record definitively agreement by the parties on such matters as applicable law, the language of the arbitration, the extent that discovery and cross-examination of witnesses will be permitted, and a variety of other procedural matters.

ii.   The signature of Terms of Reference marks the end of the period during which the initial claims and counterclaims can be introduced, thus preventing defendants from raising "new" claims as a dilatory tactic. Thereafter, the Terms of Reference may be amended only with the agreement of all parties.

iii.   Examination of the Terms of Reference helps the ICC Court to ensure that the arbitration will be conducted in accordance with the ICC Arbitration Rules.

iv.   Terms of Reference make clear to the arbitral tribunal on what issues it must render a decision. A comparison of the Terms of Reference with the draft award helps the arbitrator to determine not only whether he has ruled on all of the issues raised by the parties, but also whether he has ruled only on those issues. Should the arbitral tribunal go beyond its mandate and determine issues *ultra petita*, the award could well be subject to annulment before a national court. The Terms of Reference also make it easier to assess whether additional claims made by a party after an award has been rendered are to be considered as having already been covered by the award or are indeed new claims to be resolved in a new arbitration.

v.   Terms of Reference assist the ICC Court in scrutinizing the award pursuant to Article 21 to make sure that the tribunal has rendered a decision on all points submitted to it and did not go beyond the mandate accorded to it by the parties.

b. *Psychological Advantages*

i.   The process of establishing the Terms of Reference and the meeting of the arbitral tribunal and the counsel/parties that generally is held for this purpose is often similar in effect to a "pre-trial conference" or even a "mini-trial," permitting the parties to assess as objectively as possible the strengths and weaknesses of their case. It has been found that the process of establishing Terms of Reference frequently leads to agreement on subsidiary issues or points and sometimes to settlement of the entire case. Indeed, many of the amicable settlements reached in ICC cases occur around the establishment of the Terms of Reference.

ii.   Even where no settlement is reached, the process of establishing the Terms of Reference serves an important *educational function* when parties are from diverse legal and national backgrounds, permitting counsel and arbitrators to have a common understanding of the claims and issues at stake.

c. *Legal Advantages*

i.   Many Arab or Latin American countries still do not accept the validity of a clause agreeing to submit a future dispute to arbitration. Unless there is a specific reservation on the point, signature of the Terms of Reference by all of the parties can constitute a *compromis* whereby the parties agree to have an existing dispute submitted to arbitration: this helps protect an arbitral award which must be enforced in such countries against annulment on the grounds of failure to agree to arbitrate the dispute. In other cases, signature of the Terms of Reference can cure possible jurisdictional defects in the original arbitration clause.

ii.   Signature of Terms of Reference has also been cited by a U.S. District Court as an element proving the participation of a foreign governmental entity in a foreign arbitration. It was held that under the U.S. Foreign Sovereign Immunities Act the entity had waived its immunity from suit in the U.S. even though the entity had not appeared in the arbitration which followed signature of the Terms of Reference.

rationale) and (ii) reviewing the award for compliance with the stipulations in the document concerning claims and issues to be decided.

Dr. Wetter was closer to getting it right in 1985 when he wrote:

> The reason why [Terms of Reference] have been kept is not the fact that they may facilitate enforcement in some cases, nor even the need to affirmatively determine the amounts in dispute which are so important for purposes of fixing deposits and fees but primarily the desirability in many cases to bring order to an incoherent, incomplete and bewildering set of initial pleadings and allow the tribunal, preferably with the concurrence of both parties, to structure the subsequent proceedings in a rational manner. The necessity for the tribunal and the parties to meet for the purpose of drawing up the terms of reference also brings indirect benefits not the least of which is an opportunity for the parties to seriously consider a settlement.[14]

It would be useful here to correct a misunderstanding sometimes encountered about amending TOR. It is sometimes said that TOR are too restrictive because claims incorporated into them cannot thereafter be amended. However, Article 16 of the ICC Rules makes it clear that the agreement of the parties is needed only for the addition of new claims or counterclaims that are not already within the limits fixed by the TOR. Thus, an increase or decrease in an amount already claimed does *not* require the agreement of the parties, nor does the addition of new "issues to be decided" so long as they relate to claims already contained in the TOR.

The abolition of TOR, in this author's view, would be a serious error, given its many benefits.[15] Still, the relevant rules might be redrafted in a way that would set out more clearly what TOR should contain and what their legal nature is. The Secretariat is now preparing, as a part of a *Handbook for Arbitrators*, several model TORs so as to better illustrate to arbitrators how to utilize TOR to their full advantage.

CARTE BLANCHE (SINGAPORE) PTE. LTD. v. CARTE BLANCHE INTERNATIONAL, LTD.

United States District Court, Southern District of New York, 1988.
683 F.Supp. 945.

OPINION & ORDER

LEISURE, DISTRICT JUDGE:

Petitioner Carte Blanche (Singapore) PTE. Ltd. ("CBS") seeks confirmation of an arbitration award in its favor against respondent Carte

---

14. Wetter, [*The Conduct of Arbitration*, 2 J. Int'l Arb'n 7 (No. 2, 1985)] at 22.

15. For a recent example of a case where the signature by a party of Terms of Reference was decisive in having a U.S. court confirm and enforce an ICC award against a Pakistani government enterprise, *see* American Construction Machinery & Equipment Corp. Ltd. v. Mechanised Construction of Pakistan Ltd., 659 F. Supp. 426 (S.D.N.Y.1987). *aff'd* 828 F.2d 117 (2d Cir. 1987).

Blanche International ("CBI"). CBI has cross-moved to vacate the arbitration award, or, in the alternative, to modify the award.

FACTUAL BACKGROUND

CBS is a corporation organized and existing under the laws of Singapore and having its principal place of business in Singapore. CBI is a corporation organized and existing under the laws of the State of Delaware and having its principal place of business in the State of New York.

* * *

On or about May 30, 1986, CBS filed an Amended Demand for Arbitration. By this amendment, CBS sought specific damages in the amount of $4,945,000 for the value of stock, $697,000 for reimbursement of certain loans, and loss of earnings on the foregoing amounts, estimated to be in excess of $1,000,000.

On April 29, 1986, the ICC duly confirmed the appointments of William Piel, Esq., Professor Hans Smit, and Theodore Sorenson, Esq., as arbitrators for the arbitration to take place in New York City. The panel held hearings for eleven days during June, July and August of 1986 in the Southern District of New York.

On February 18, 1987, a majority of the panel consisting of Mr. Piel and Professor Smit found for CBS on all claims and handed down an Interim Award, from which Mr. Sorensen dissented. The majority held that "[d]amages should therefore be awarded to CBS for the value of a promised business opportunity destroyed or gravely impaired...." Mr. Sorenson's dissent expressed his view that CBI did not breach the Franchise Agreement, that the agreement terminated by its own terms in March of 1985, and that no damages could be awarded for the period after March 31, 1985.

After the interim award, CBS sought leave to amend its pleading and the Terms of Reference to assert a claim for $3.5 million in consequential damages. CBI expressed its objection to such an amendment, and no formal amendment was ever made. Chairman Piel suggested that CBS could proceed with a claim for consequential damages without amending its pleadings or the Terms of Reference. Nine days of further hearings were conducted on the issue of an appropriate remedy. In these hearings, CBS sought a total of $16,745,994 in damages, costs and fees. CBI argued that CBS failed to mitigate damages and urged that the interim award be withdrawn based on CBS's concealment of its plan to convert the CBS business to a MasterCard business.

On January 25, 1988, the arbitrators made a written Final Award. Final Award (hereinafter "FA"), * * *. CBS was awarded damages and costs in the following amounts:

fair and reasonable value of CBS,

including reasonable prospects for future profitability: $4,300,000.00

consequential damages (operating losses and expenses):   5,116,477.00

costs: 312,161.20

Subtotal   9,728,638.20

Less: credit for CBI's transfer to CBS of rights in cardholder's accounts   735,000.00

TOTAL   8,993,638.20

* * *

CBS was also awarded interest and injunctive relief. The award was delivered[2] to the parties by Chairman Piel on January 28, 1988, and this action was commenced on February 1, 1988, by the filing of the Petition and Affidavit of Sheldon Elsen, Esq. On February 1, 1988, the Court ordered respondent to show cause on February 9, 1988, why an order should not be made confirming the award of the arbitrators.

* * *

On February 9, 1988, the parties appeared before the Court, and, after some discussion of the issues, the Court instructed petitioner to submit answering papers to respondent's cross-motion. The Court now decides that the award made by the arbitrators should be confirmed for the reasons stated below.

* * *

7.   Consequential Damages. Finally, CBI contends that the award of $5.1 million in consequential damages exceeded the power of the arbitrators. CBI asserts that the original pleading in the case sought total damages of approximately $6.7 million, and that the original pleading was not amended to allow so large a claim for consequential damages. After the Interim Award was handed down, CBS sought leave to amend its pleading and the Terms of Reference to assert a claim for $3.5 million in consequential damages. CBS ultimately sought a total of $16,745,994 in damages. Chairman Piel allowed CBS to proceed with its claim for consequential damages without a formal amendment to the pleadings or Terms of Reference, over CBI's objection. CBI maintains that this was beyond the power of the arbitrators, and in violation of ICC Rules of Arbitration, and that vacatur of the award is therefore required.

CBI has submitted the Declaration of Yves Derains ("Derains"), in support of its petition to vacate the award. * * * Declaration of Yves Derains, dated February 15, 1988 (hereinafter "Derains Decl."). Derains declared that he had examined the arbitration demands made by the parties, CBS's amended demand for arbitration, the Interim Award, the

2. The initial delivery of the award was made by Chairman Piel on January 28, 1988. The effective date of the Final Award is addressed below.

Final Award, portions of CBS and CBI's motion papers, and the Terms of Reference. On the basis of the information provided to him, Derains concluded that at least four ICC Rules of Arbitration had been violated.

* * *

Specifically, Derains maintains that Articles 6, 16, 21 and 23 of the ICC Rules of Arbitration were violated. Article 16 limits new claims to those made within the Terms of Reference.[8] According to Derains, a claim presented after the execution of the Terms of Reference may be permitted by the arbitrators only if it is within the original Terms of Reference. Otherwise, a rider must be signed by the parties and communicated to the Court. Derains asserts that such a rider was essential in this case for the claim for consequential damages to be before the arbitrators.

Derains pointed out that even if a claim is not new, it may require an amendment to the Terms of Reference if a substantial increase in the amount of damages sought under a particular claim is asserted. Derains stated that CBS's claim for consequential damages required a rider to the Terms of Reference because it was an entirely new claim, and, even if not new, was for significantly more than any prior claims made. If one party did not consent to the rider, the ICC Court would not allow the claim to be heard, but would require the party pressing the claim to commence a separate arbitration. Because Derains concluded that the arbitrators were not authorized to permit new claims in this case, "the provisions of Article 16 of the ICC Rules have been grossly violated."

* * *

CBS raises other reasons for rejecting the Derains Declaration. CBS maintains that to the extent that ICC rules are relevant here in this proceeding, they should have been taken into account by the arbitrators and the ICC Court, not raised by an expert on arbitration law in this proceeding. Counsel for CBI replied that "[e]xpert testimony is, of course, the normal way for evidence as to interpretation of foreign law to be brought before a court." Rule 44.1 of the Federal Rules of Civil Procedure provides for the determination of foreign law:

> A party who intends to raise an issue concerning the law of a foreign country shall give notice by pleadings or other reasonable written notice. The court, in determining foreign law, may consider any relevant material or source, including testimony, whether or not submitted by a party or admissible under the Federal Rules of Evidence. The court's determination shall be treated as a ruling on a question of law.

8. Article 16 of the ICC Rules of Arbitration provides:

The parties may make new claims or counterclaims before the arbitrator on condition that these remain within the limits fixed by the Terms of Reference provided for in Article 13 or that they are specified in a rider to that document, signed by the parties and communicated to the Court.

Fed.R.Civ.P. 44.1. The language of the rule and the Advisory Committee Note make it clear that the rule applies to determination of the law of a foreign country. No foreign country is involved here. Indeed, the Court finds that although the governing body of the ICC Court is located in Paris, and that it has its own procedural rules, this Court is able to understand those rules as well as the rules of other arbitration associations located in this country. Thus, it is not clear that this Court should consider the declaration submitted by Derains as expert testimony. As most of the arguments in the Derains Declaration are incorporated in the Reply Memorandum of CBI, the Court will consider those arguments as it would in deciding an issue of law.

Counsel for CBS contends that if the losing party in an arbitration proceeding could raise issues on procedural rulings of the arbitrators, proceedings to confirm arbitration awards would lose their summary nature, and courts would be plunged into an examination of the entire record of the arbitration proceeding to determine whether all procedural rules were complied with. A major purpose of the Federal Arbitration Act is to avoid delay and unnecessary expense to the parties, see, e.g., Prima Paint Corp. v. Flood & Conklin Mfg. Co., 388 U.S. 395, 404, 87 S.Ct. 1801, 1806, 18 L.Ed.2d 1270 (1967); Dean Witter Reynolds Inc. v. Byrd, 470 U.S. 213, 220, 105 S.Ct. 1238, 1242, 84 L.Ed.2d 158 (1985), and the delay that would result from reviewing procedural rulings of the arbitrators would be substantial.

But to hold that a district court may not review any procedural rulings of the arbitration panel, as counsel for CBS suggests, would result in judicial abdication in reviewing arbitration awards. Although the Arbitration Act requires restraint in reviewing arbitration awards, it does not call for total abdication of reviewing power. See Newark Morning Ledger Co. v. Newark Typographical Union Local 103, 797 F.2d 162, 165–66 n. 3 (3d Cir.1986) (quoting Summers, Judicial Review of Labor Arbitration, 2 Buffalo L.Rev. 1, 21–22, 24 (1952)). Thus, a district court may consider procedural irregularities insofar as they rise to the level of requiring vacatur or modification of the award pursuant to sections 10 and 11 of the Arbitration Act. To hold otherwise would not serve the purposes of the Act.

Considering the assertions in the Derains Declaration and in the Morril Reply Affidavit that numerous rules of the ICC Court were violated, this Court finds those assertions unpersuasive. First and foremost, the Terms of Reference explicitly state under "The Issues to be Determined" the following issue: "Has CBS established a claim for damages, and, if so, in what amount?" No limitation on the amount of damages is present in this section of the Terms of Reference.[12] Only in the Rules of Procedure, part VI of the Terms of Reference, are damages stated with any specificity. RP11 states: "Counsel for CBS having advised of the intention of CBS to include a claim for damages of from

---

12. Moreover, there is no requirement that the Terms of Reference include the amount of damages claimed. Article 13(1) of the ICC Rules of Arbitration deals with the Terms of Reference * * * [reproduced supra at 425].

US $5,000,000 to US $10,000,000, leave is hereby granted to the parties to present any amendments of their pleadings at least 15 days before the commencement of the evidentiary hearings, or at a later time in the discretion of the Arbitrators.''

Derains points to the first Rule of Procedure contained in the Terms of Reference as requiring consistency with the ICC Rules. But that Rule of Procedure also vests the arbitrators with substantial discretion:

> All proceedings in this arbitration shall be governed by Paragraph 7.09 of the Franchise Agreement, by the Rules for the ICC Court of Arbitration, and, to the extent consistent with the ICC Rules, by the following Rules of Procedure ("RP"), reserving to the Arbitrators, however, the authority in their discretion, on application of a party or on their own initiative, to modify or suspend any of these Rules of Procedure.

TR, at 5. The arbitrators thus had the power to suspend the Rules of Procedure, in which the only limitations on damages were contained.

The ICC Court did indeed confirm the award, and when it did so, it had before it the Final Award. It also had before it the dissent filed by Mr. Sorenson alleging that the award of damages was unconscionably high and unsupported by the evidence. The fact of the matter is that the ICC Court nevertheless confirmed the award. Article 21 of the ICC Rules for Arbitration requires scrutiny of any award by the ICC Court before it is signed. See supra n. 10. The ICC Court is the best judge of whether its procedural rules have been satisfied, and when it certified the award as final, it certified that the procedural rules had been complied with to its satisfaction. No violation of those rules constitutes a basis for vacatur of the award pursuant to section 10 of the Arbitration Act.

CBI asserts that vacatur is required because the award of consequential damages exceeded the arbitrators' power under the reasoning of Totem Marine Tug & Barge, Inc. v. North American Towing, Inc., 607 F.2d 649 (5th Cir.1979). Respondent's Memo at 31–32. In Totem Marine, the Court of Appeals for the Fifth Circuit found that

> [t]he arbitration panel exceeded its powers by awarding damages for charter hire to North American. Not only did North American fail to list charter hire in its itemized statement of damages submitted to Totem, but in its brief submitted to the arbitration panel, North American conceded that charter hire was not an issue in the arbitration.

* * *

> It is anomalous for the arbitration panel to award an unrequested item of damages three times larger than any item claimed by North American and then to hear the panel action supported with an argument that the awarded item was naturally intertwined within the scope of the arbitration.

Id. at 651. Totem Marine is distinguishable on several grounds. CBI knew from the outset that CBS was asserting a claim for consequential damages. At no time did CBS deny that it was making such a claim. CBI was on notice that the arbitrators were considering the full amount of damages claimed by CBS, even though the pleadings and Terms of Reference were not amended. Moreover, unlike Totem Marine, in which the arbitrators decided an issue that was not submitted to them at all, the claim for damages in the instant case was within the Terms of Reference. The Court therefore declines to vacate the award on the basis that the award of consequential damages exceeded the arbitrators' powers.

* * *

Questions and Comments

1.   In Article 18, which replaces Article 13 of the 1988 Rules, the 1998 ICC Rules seek to encourage planning and structuring in advance of the arbitration process by changing the provisions on the Terms of Reference and by requiring a **Procedural Timetable**. Do you support this line of development?

2.   A novel feature of the 1998 Rules is increased discretionary power given to the arbitration tribunal. Unlike Article 16 of the 1988 Rules, Article 19 of the 1998 Rules allows the arbitrators to accept claims that fall outside the limits of the Terms of Reference even if one of the parties who signed the Terms of Reference objects. What arguments could you advance in favor of- or against-this solution? Once we have Terms of Reference, should they be binding?

3.   If the Terms of Reference adopt a broader formulation of the scope of the dispute submitted to arbitration than the wording of the arbitration agreement, is this conclusive? (Do the Terms of Reference in such cases supersede the arbitration agreement?)

What are the consequences if the Terms of Reference contain a more restrictive description than the arbitration agreement of the controversy submitted to arbitration?

4.   One of the recurring problems in connection with the Terms of Reference is the issue of their preclusive force.[2] Once formulated, do the Terms of Reference preclude any claim or argument that does not fall within the Terms of Reference wording?

In the *Carte Blanche* case it appears that one of the reasons for avoiding a formal amendment of the Terms of Reference, was to avoid extra fees. Suppose CBS moved formally to amend the Terms of Reference to include consequential damages, and CBI explicitly opposed this. Could the arbitrators still award consequential damages?

5.   Does the *Carte Blanche* case help you in choosing between the positions urged by Mr. Wetter and Mr. Bond respectively?

[2]. See O. Sandrock, Die "Terms of Reference" und die Grenzen ihrer Präklu- sionswirkungen, Recht der internationalen Wirtschaft, 1987, 649.

6.   Do you find the ICC review of the award argument persuasive?

IV.1.g.   Records and Minutes of the Hearing

ICC COMPARATIVE ARBITRATION PRACTICE AND PUBLIC POLICY IN ARBITRATION
137–40 (Pieter Sanders ed., 1987).*

HYPOTHETICAL CASE [STEELCO v. HIGHTECH]

The [UNCITRAL] rules provide that the arbitral tribunal is free to make arrangements for a "record of the hearing" if it considers that necessary in the circumstances of the case, but it is not required to do so. Nor is there any explanation in the Rules concerning the form of "record" that might be made. (Art. 25(3)).

QUESTION 56

Is it customary for the arbitral tribunal to make arrangements for a record of the hearing in a case such as this? If so, are stenographic transcripts used or tape recordings?

ANSWER TO QUESTION 56

MR. HOELLERING [USA]

In arbitration cases such as our hypothetical case, arrangements for a record of the hearing are invariably made, either at the request of the parties or of the arbitral tribunal. Usually, a stenographic record is taken by a certified court stenographer. Tape recordings are rarely used, because they are not deemed fully reliable and may be subject to damage or abuse.

MR. HUNTER [England]

This is mainly a question of expense relative to the size of the case and the other costs of the arbitration. The cost of a full "daily" transcript of the oral proceedings in England would (in 1985) be approximately ,500 per day. ("Daily" means that the parties have the transcript for a particular day in their hands on the evening of the day in question, or at the latest early the following morning.) The cost of a transcript produced subsequent to the hearing is somewhat less, but it is still expensive. In the case of the size of *Steelco v. Hightech*, it is probable that the *evidence* would be transcribed, but not the arguments. In cases where there are three-member tribunals, which are clearly going to involve deliberations which may take place sometime after the conclusion of the hearings, arbitrators find it helpful to have an accurate record of the evidence that has been given.

Where a verbatim record is being transcribed, it is not usual to rely solely on tape recordings. Experience shows that these are very difficult to transcribe accurately, and it is often difficult to identify precisely who

* Reprinted with permission from Kluwer Law International.

is speaking at any given time. Normally, a stenographic service is used, but most firms of stenographers now use tape recordings as a "back up" to their own shorthand or mechanically taken notes.

MR. JARVIN [ICC]

No, in the majority of cases; but probably yes in a case of a certain complexity like this. If a record of the hearing is arranged, it would be done by stenographic transcripts more often than by tape recordings, and would record the evidence but not parties' arguments.

If the arbitrator does not make arrangements on his own initiative for a record of the hearing, a party may ask him to do so and the arbitrator would adhere to such a request.

PROF. LEBEDEV [Russia]

In the light of customary practice in the country of arbitration, verbatim records (most often by stenography) of the oral hearings in the course of the proceedings of the case are made only when both parties request it (see also Art. 25(3) of the UNCITRAL Rules).

DR. SZURSKI [Poland]

It is not customary to use stenographic transcripts or tape recordings in arbitrations in Poland. However, on request of the parties, stenographic transcriptions can be arranged.

On the other hand, it is customary to prepare minutes of each hearing session. Minutes are normally made by the recording-secretary of the arbitral tribunal. First of all, statements by the representatives of the parties which are important for the evaluation of the case, as well as for the conduct of the proceedings are recorded in the minutes. The minutes also reflect all decisions of the arbitral tribunal made during the hearing.

Very often the most important statements which are to be recorded in the minutes are dictated by the presiding arbitrator so as to avoid any mistake in the formulation.

When important statements are recorded in the minutes they are read aloud by the recording-secretary of the tribunal for their confirmation by the party who made the statement.

The minutes are normally signed by the recording-secretary and all members of the arbitral tribunal.

In case the minutes reflect a settlement agreement made at the hearing, they are signed also by the representatives of the parties.

* * *

QUESTION 57

Is it customary for the Chairman or secretary to prepare minutes of each session? What is included in the minutes and how detailed are they? Do they summarize evidence and arguments? Are they submitted to the parties for comment? Are they signed? If so, by whom?

ANSWER TO QUESTION 57

MR. HOELLERING [USA]

It is not customary for minutes of each hearing session to be prepared. Where a stenographic record of the proceedings is taken, copies of the record are provided to the tribunal and all parties, and can be delivered within a short time after the hearings, if desired. Such records, except for off-the-record discussions, are verbatim transcripts and contain all evidentiary references and arguments. The parties always have an opportunity to correct any errors in the stenographic record.

In AAA administered cases, a brief record of [the] hearing is completed by the tribunal chairman or tribunal administrator. It includes the case docket number, the identity of the parties, the names of the arbitrators, the time when the hearing commenced, a listing of each documentary exhibit, the name and address of each witness, and a note as to any special stipulations and arrangements, such as filing of briefs or additional evidence. The record of hearing is signed either by the presiding arbitrator or by the AAA administrator. These records do not summarize evidence and arguments and are not submitted to parties for comment. Rather, they constitute a part of the arbitration case file.

A similar record may be kept by the presiding arbitrator in non-AAA cases.

MR. HUNTER [England]

A minute would normally be prepared by the Chairman (or registrar or secretary) recording procedural rulings or decisions of the tribunal, unless they are in any event going to be reproduced in a verbatim transcript. The Chairman will normally be responsible for producing a record of the administrative decisions taken at preliminary meetings. This record might be submitted to the parties in draft form for comment, depending on whether the tribunal considered it necessary. The record would normally be signed by all the arbitrators, although sometimes the parties or the arbitrators themselves might authorize the Chairman to sign them alone. This rather depends on the status and importance of the matters recorded in the minutes.

It would not be normal practice for minutes to be taken of the substantive hearings, summarizing arguments or evidence. If there is no verbatim transcript of the evidence, the arbitrators would be expected to make their own personal notes for use in the deliberations of the tribunal at a later stage.

MR. JARVIN [ICC]

First question: Yes.

Second question: Not extensive, they would merely record * * * [procedural] events and rulings by the arbitrators.

Third question: No, the minutes would not contain arguments or evidence.

Fourth question: No, they are not submitted to the parties for comment.

Fifth question: Yes, they are signed, always by the Chairman, most often also by the co-arbitrators in addition to the Chairman, and sometimes also by the parties.

It is customary in ICC arbitration that the award contains a description of the procedure, indicating when and where hearings were held, who was present, what witnesses were heard, when notifications were posted and received, etc. The minutes from each session are of great help in establishing this history of the proceedings and offer a means of proof of what took place; the minutes sometimes will be indispensable as proof in a setting aside action against the arbitration award.

PROF. LEBEDEV [Russia]

It may be considered customary practice in the country of arbitration to prepare minutes, where legal and factual arguments of the parties, including testimony of the witnesses, expert-witnesses, experts, appointed by the arbitral tribunal, etc., are briefly noted. As a rule, minutes are prepared by the secretary (see Question 5) and then are checked and signed by all arbitrators. When there is proper request, minutes may be given to the parties, who, of course, may comment on them.

CAIRO REGIONAL CENTRE FOR INTERNATIONAL COMMERCIAL ARBITRATION

CASE NO. 20/90

_____ a SINGAPORE COMPANY, Claimant

v.

EGYPT, Respondent

MINUTES

of the oral hearing held in the premises of the Cairo Regional Centre for International Commercial Arbitration, 3 Abu El Feda, Zamalek, Cairo, on November 26, 1991 at 11:00 a.m.

Present:

Arbitrators:

_____, Chairman

_____

_____

For the Claimant: *For Respondent*:

_____   _____

_____   _____

_____   _____

For the Cairo Regional Centre for International Commercial Arbitration:

_____

Having heard the suggestions of all three arbitrators presented by the Chairman, both parties agreed to the following:

All hearings will be tape recorded and a complete tape will be given to both parties. In addition, minutes will be taken in a summarized form, and the Chairman will dictate the summarized minutes giving always an opportunity to the fellow arbitrators and the parties to suggest amendments.

The oral hearing was adjourned at 4:30 p.m., to be continued on November 27th, 1991 at 10:00 a.m.

The arbitrators: For Claimant:

_____   _____

_____   For Respondent

_____   _____

Recording Secretary:

_____

Questions and Comments

1. In a transcultural venture such as international commercial arbitration, actors within the process will soon learn that very few obvious things remain obvious. Transcripts and minutes are among the examples.

The excerpt from the ICCA publication edited by P. Sanders gives a survey of answers of real experts to the ramifications of a hypothetical case. Mr. Hoellering represents the AAA, Mr. Hunter gives an account of the English experience, Mr. Jarvin is from the ICC, Mr. Lebedev and Mr. Szurszki represent Russian and Polish viewpoints, respectively. These rapporteurs were asked to answer questions on the basis of customary practice in their systems.

Of course, different cases may justify different methods of recording. The observations made in the above excerpt were made with respect to a given hypothetical. Still, the alternatives outlined give a basically good picture of the range of available options.

2. Would you prefer a verbatim record of the oral hearing, or minutes summarizing what was said? Who should sign the record (minutes)?

3. Would you recommend the compromise reached in the *Cairo* case?

4. Mr. Hunter suggests that **evidence** should be transcribed, but not the **arguments**. Do you agree? It has been noted that it is difficult to transcribe a verbatim record accurately. If corrections are needed, who should be entitled to make them? The arbitrators? The parties?

5. Arbitration rules typically do not devote direct attention to the issue of the minutes, but there are exceptions. For example, Article 21 of the Rules

of the Court of Arbitration at the Estonian Chamber of Commerce and Industry (as modified on Sept. 30, 1999) states under the heading "Minutes of the Hearing":

> "Minutes of the hearing of the Arbitration Court shall be taken including:
>
>   1) Name of the Arbitration Court,
>
>   2) The time and place of the hearing,
>
>   3) The names of the parties,
>
>   4) The names of the arbitrators, representatives of the parties, witnesses and experts,
>
>   5) A brief description of the hearing
>
> The arbitrator or arbitrators who reviewed the claim shall sign the minutes."

Section 29 of the 1998 DIS (German Institution of Arbitration) Rules state under the heading "Records of Oral Proceedings":

> " A record shall be made of all hearings. The record shall be signed by the chairman. The parties shall each receive a copy of the record."

The Estonian Rules have opted for a summary. The term "record" used in the German Rules ("Protokoll" in German) is ambiguous. It may refer to a full transcript or less than a full transcript. Would you suggest changes or additions to these rules?

IV.1.h.   *Presentation of the Case*

IV.1.h.i.   Problems With Discovery

IN RE APPLICATION OF TECHNOSTROYEXPORT, A FOREIGN ECONOMIC ASSOCIATION ORGANIZED UNDER LAWS OF RUSSIAN FEDERATION, PETITIONER

United States District Court, Southern District of New York, 1994.
853 F.Supp. 695.

Russian seller filed a petition seeking discovery in aid of a Swedish arbitration proceeding commenced by a New York corporation that bought minerals. The buyer sought to quash subpoenas and to dismiss. The District Court, Griesa, Chief Judge, held that, under Russian or Swedish law, parties to an arbitration proceeding could not bypass the arbitrators and go directly to court for a decision on a discovery question that had not been presented to arbitrators.

Order and subpoenas vacated.

* * *

GRIESA, CHIEF JUDGE.

This is a petition to obtain discovery in aid of arbitration proceedings now pending in Moscow and Stockholm. Petitioner Technostroyexport ("Technostroy") is a foreign economic association organized under the laws of the Russian Federation. Technostroy has initiated an arbitration in Moscow against International Development and Trade Services, Inc. ("IDTS"). IDTS has brought an arbitration proceeding against Technostroy in Stockholm.

IDTS is a New York corporation. Its president is Edith Reich. Brigitte R. Jossem–Kumpf is a director and sole shareholder of IDTS. Both of these persons maintain residences and offices in New York.

The present petition seeks to obtain documents from IDTS and to obtain the deposition testimony of Reich and Jossem–Kumpf for use in the arbitration proceedings. On January 6, 1994, based on the ex parte application of Technostroy, Judge Mukasey, sitting in Part I of this court, signed an order permitting the issuance of a subpoena duces tecum to IDTS and deposition subpoenas to Reich and Jossem–Kumpf. The subpoenas were duly served.

On February 18, 1994 respondents IDTS, Reich and Jossem–Kumpf filed a motion seeking to have the court vacate the January 6 order, quash the subpoenas, dismiss the petition, and refer the parties to the pending arbitration proceedings. Technostroy has moved to compel compliance with the document subpoena, taking the position that it is not required to affirmatively move to enforce the testimony subpoenas. In any event, Technostroy seeks to enforce the January 6 order and all the subpoenas. Hearings were held on March 8 and March 15 before Judge Griesa, who was then the Part I judge and is ruling on the pending motions.

The court grants the motion of IDTS and denies Technostroy's motion.

Facts

The problems involved in the arbitration proceedings involve certain contracts by the Russian association to sell minerals to IDTS. Also involved is an agreement by the Russian association appointing IDTS and another company as agent for the sale of minerals. The Russian association will be referred to in this opinion as Technostroy, although a different name may have been used in at least some of the contracts, and it may be that there is some question about whether Technostroy is actually the successor to that contracting Russian entity. However, this issue is not involved in the present motions. The arbitration proceedings are between Technostroy and IDTS.

In the Moscow arbitration Technostroy claims that IDTS has purchased large amounts of minerals from Technostroy and has refused to pay for them. Technostroy bases its claims on seven written sales contracts, and asserts that IDTS owes approximately $172 million. It appears that one crucial issue is whether the written contracts were amended orally to reduce the total price. Another issue is whether IDTS has made payment of some $58 million. All seven of the sales contracts provide for arbitration in Russia. The agency contract provides for arbitration in Stockholm. The latter circumstance has resulted in IDTS bringing an arbitration proceeding in Stockholm and asserting claims against Technostroy under the agency agreement and two of the sales contracts. Technostroy has raised jurisdictional objections in the Stockholm arbitration.

THE ISSUES

In the petition to this court, Technostroy asserts that the nature of the issues in the arbitration proceedings make it imperative to obtain discovery from respondents IDTS, Reich and Jossem–Kumpf. In addition to the need for obtaining relevant documents, there is the need, according to Technostroy, to obtain the testimony of Reich and Jossem–Kumpf, who were both intimately involved in the relevant transactions and negotiations.

Respondents have a number of arguments as to why this court cannot properly order discovery in aid of the foreign arbitrations. Basically, respondents argue that the parties should be relegated to applying to the arbitration tribunals for permission to take discovery.

Both Technostroy and respondents have submitted sworn statements from experts on Russian and Swedish law. Respondents' experts concede that, under certain circumstances, discovery may be available in arbitration proceedings in those countries. But they assert that application must be made to the arbitrators, and that court intervention can occur only in the Russian and Swedish courts, and then only to enforce the ruling of the arbitrators. Technostroy's experts, on the other hand, assert that the provisions relied upon by respondents' experts apply only to situations where the discovery is sought in Russia or in Sweden and do not touch the question of discovery sought in foreign countries. Therefore, according to Technostroy's experts, there is no bar under Russian or Swedish law preventing Technostroy from going directly to a United States court and obtaining an order for discovery in the United States.

Technostroy relies upon 28 U.S.C. § 1782(a), which gives a Federal District Court the authority to obtain testimony or document production "for use in a proceeding in a foreign ... tribunal." Respondents deny that '1782 is applicable.

At the hearing of March 8, the court attempted to have the discovery dispute resolved by agreement. While never conceding that this court has the power to order discovery, respondents referred to the practical problem, that if there is to be discovery it should be two-way, and there is no assurance that respondents can obtain discovery of Technostroy in Moscow.

On March 15 Technostroy stated to the court that it would consent to submit to appropriate discovery in Russia. Technostroy asserted that there was no bar to such voluntary discovery under Russian law.

Despite the assurances by Technostroy, respondents refused to agree to discovery, and maintained their legal argument that the court could not require them to submit to discovery.

DISCUSSION

28 U.S.C. § 1782(a), on which Technostroy relies, provides in pertinent part:

> The district court of the district in which a person resides or is found may order him to give his testimony or statement or to produce a document or other thing for use in a proceeding in a foreign or international tribunal. The order may be made pursuant to a letter rogatory issued, or request made, by a foreign or international tribunal or upon the application of any interested person....

Technostroy argues that an arbitrator or an arbitration panel is a "foreign ... tribunal" within the meaning of § 1782(a) and that the plain language of the statute empowers a Federal District court to order discovery in the United States for use in connection with foreign arbitration proceedings. Technostroy relies on a recent Second Circuit decision holding that § 1782 empowers a court to obtain discovery even where the rules of the foreign tribunal do not provide for such discovery. Application of Aldunate, 3 F.3d 54 (2d Cir.1993). Also, it has been held that § 1782 does not require prior resort to the foreign tribunal. In Re Malev Hungarian Airlines, 964 F.2d 97 (2d Cir.1992).

[1] The court is of the view that an arbitrator or arbitration panel is a "tribunal" under § 1782. The court further believes that, if Technostroy had obtained a ruling from a foreign arbitrator that discovery should take place, the court would be empowered under § 1782 to enforce that ruling in the United States. However, Technostroy has made no effort to obtain any ruling from the arbitrators. It has come directly to the Federal District Court. The court concludes that, under these circumstances, it would be improper to order the discovery requested.

[2] It appears to be generally accepted that the rules and procedures in arbitration are intended to be radically different from the rules and procedures in the courts. Arbitrators govern their own proceedings, generally without assistance or intervention by a court. Whether or not there is to be pre-hearing discovery is a matter governed by the applicable arbitration rules (as distinct from court rules) and by what the arbitrators decide. It has been expressly held that a Federal District Court has no power to order discovery under court rules where the matter is being litigated in an arbitration. Commercial Solvents Corp. v. Louisiana Liquid Fertilizer Co., 20 F.R.D. 359 (S.D.N.Y.1957). See also Penn Tanker Co. of Delaware v. C.H.Z. Rolimpex Warszawa, 199 F.Supp. 716 (S.D.N.Y.1961). However, there is authority that a court can enforce a discovery ruling of an arbitrator. Western Employers Ins. Co. v. Merit Ins. Co., 492 F.Supp. 53 (N.D.Ill.1979).

[3]   The applicable provisions of Russian and Swedish law make it clear that questions about the obtaining of evidence in arbitration proceedings are to be determined by the arbitrators.

Rule 30 of the Rules of the Arbitration at the USSR Chamber of Commerce and Industry provides in part:

> The parties must prove circumstances relied on by them in support of their demands or objections. The arbitral tribunal may require the parties to present other evidence. It also may, at its own discretion, direct that expert examination be conducted and obtain evidence from third parties as well as summon and hear witnesses.

Although the USSR no longer exists, it appears that Rule 30 applies under current Russian law. In addition, the Law of the Russian Federation on International Commercial Arbitration contains the following provisions:

Article 5. Extent of Court Intervention

In matters governed by this Law, no court intervention shall take place except where so provided in this law.

Article 27. Court Assistance in Taking Evidence

The arbitral tribunal or a party with the approval of the arbitral tribunal may request from a competent court of the Russian Federation assistance in taking evidence. The court may execute the request within its competence and according to its rules on taking evidence, including court orders.

As to the Swedish arbitration, Section 15 of the Swedish Arbitration Act provides:

> Unless the parties otherwise provide, the arbitrators may take steps in order to promote the investigation of the matter, such as summoning a party or an expert or any other person to attend for examination, or call upon a party or any other person in possession of a written document or other object, which may be assumed to have importance as evidence, to produce the document or object. The arbitrators may not make orders on penalty of a fine, nor use other means of constraint, nor may they administer oaths or truth affirmations.

> If a party wishes that a witness or an expert should be heard in court or that a party should be examined there on truth affirmation or that an order should be made for a party or any other person to produce as evidence a written document or an object on penalty of a fine, he shall apply to the District Court in whose area the person is present who is to be heard or otherwise affected. If the arbitrators have considered the procedure necessary, and if the requisite information is made available, the court shall arrange for the examination or issue an order on penalty of a fine, provided that there is no legal obstacle to such procedure. The rules on evidence taken

otherwise than at the trial in an ordinary action shall, to the extent relevant, apply to the procedures referred to above.

These provisions do not literally refer to "discovery." They refer broadly to the obtaining of evidence. However, both Technostroy and respondents agree that arbitrators in both Russia and Sweden have the power to order pre-hearing discovery. It is clear that, once an arbitration panel has ruled that there should be discovery, a Russian or Swedish court can enforce that ruling if necessary.

There is, of course, no provision for resort to a foreign court. Technostroy argues that this circumstance enables Technostroy to come directly to a court in the United States to obtain discovery, without any prior resort to the arbitrators in Russia or Sweden.

The court disagrees. The Russian and Swedish provisions of law just quoted make it clear that in those countries it is the arbitrators, and not the courts, who are to decide the question of what discovery is to be obtained in arbitration proceedings. Although courts in Russia and Sweden are able to enforce the rulings of the arbitrators, parties to arbitrations in those countries cannot bypass the arbitrators and go directly to court.

This basic principle of law, which is consistent with United States law, should be honored in determining the applicability of 28 U.S.C. § 1782. There is nothing in the wording of § 1782 which prevents this. Indeed, the statute states that a District Court "may" act. Application of § 1782 is a matter left to the sound discretion of the court. Aldunate, 3 F.3d at 59. For these reasons, the court concludes that the ex parte order of January 6, 1994 and the subpoenas issued thereunder must be vacated. This ruling is without prejudice to a future application based on the ruling of Russian or Swedish arbitrators.

SO ORDERED.

Elizabeth A. Fuerstman & Peter C. Thomas, THE IMPLICATIONS OF THE TECHNOSTROY– EXPORT DECISION

22 Int'l Bus. Law. 364, 365 (1994).*

Although *Technostroyexport* appears to expand the possibilities for US discovery in aid of an international arbitration by holding [for the first time] that an arbitral panel is a "tribunal" within the meaning of Section 1782, a tension exists between the decision and * * * [In re Malev Hungarian Airlines, 964 F.2d 97 (2d Cir.1992)]. First, the court's suggestion that it lacked any power under Section 1782 to order discovery unless a prior application had been made to a foreign arbitral tribunal appears to present a clear conflict with *Malev* and with the

* Published by and reprinted with permission from the International Bar Association.

plain language of the statute that omits any exhaustion requirement. Second, while the court addressed only the laws of Sweden and Russia, the laws governing arbitrations in many centres of international commerce empower arbitrators, not the courts, to decide what discovery, if any, might be ordered in an arbitration. Thus, the practical effect of the decision is to impose an exhaustion requirement in all (or most) cases where the foreign "tribunal" is an arbitration panel, notwithstanding the fact that the *Malev* court seemingly rejected an exhaustion requirement under Section 1782, 963 F.2d at 100.

On the other hand, *Technostroyexport* might be harmonised with *Malev* insofar as the court's decision can be said to rest on the exercise of its discretion under either Section 1782 or the Federal Rules of Civil Procedure. Indeed, the *Malev* court specifically approved the possibility of a US court requiring an applicant, under Rule 26 of the Federal Rules, to present a "discovery plan" to the foreign tribunal for a determination as to relevance before coming to the US district court for a discovery order. *Malev*, 963 F 2d at 102. According to the *Malev* court, however, the purpose of this requirement would be to limit any burden on US courts of supervising discovery. This was not the reason given by the court in *Technostroyexport* for imposing a quasi-exhaustion rule for discovery in aid of international arbitrations.

Finally, while not expressly recognised by the *Technostroyexport* court, there is another ground that might support the court's decision. Broad discovery is typically not available in international arbitrations and, indeed, may be one of the reasons why parties choose arbitration over traditional court litigation. Moreover, in choosing arbitration rules that empower arbitrators, not courts, to make discovery decisions, parties arguably obligate themselves to seek permission from arbitrators before applying to US courts for relief under Section 1782. Thus, a requirement that parties make a discovery request to the arbitral tribunal in the first instance may better accord with the principle of party autonomy and the parties' contractual expectations in choosing to resolve their disputes through arbitration. This possible ground for decision, however, is at best implicit in the *Technostroyexport* court's opinion.

Questions and Comments

1. For a number of reasons, discovery is to a certain extent at odds with the arbitration process. First of all, parties often choose arbitration over court litigation in order to avoid broad discovery procedures. Also, arbitrators are ill-equipped to mandate sufficient cooperation of the parties, because they largely lack coercive power. At the same time, court assistance in gathering evidence is clearly needed in some cases. The question is, who can apply for such assistance.

2. The *Technostroyexport* case focuses on court-administered discovery, but in connection with the arbitration process (and on the understanding that the decision on the merits remains in the hands of the arbitrators). The key issue is whether a party seeking discovery under Section 1782 must first

obtain a formal request for discovery from the foreign tribunal. *Technostroyexport* says that it must. In *Re Malev Hungarian Airlines*, the Second Circuit held that it need not. In *Malev*, the "foreign tribunal" was a Hungarian **court**; in *Technostroyexport*, the "foreign tribunal" was an **arbitration tribunal**. Can this difference explain the opposite holdings?

3. One of the arguments raised by respondents in *Technostroyexport* is that they could not obtain from Technostroyexport in Moscow the same discovery as the one to which they were subject in New York. As a matter of fact, U.S. rules on discovery are broader than corresponding rules in European countries. Is this a valid reason for denying U.S. style discovery where the arbitral tribunal requests it in support of the arbitration process? Where a party, without permission of the arbitral tribunal, makes the request?

IV.1.h.ii.   Experts

International Council for Commercial Arbitration, COMPARATIVE ARBITRATION PRACTICE AND PUBLIC POLICY IN ARBITRATION

107–111 (Pieter Sanders, ed., 1987).*

* * *

I. Experts

HYPOTHETICAL CASE

The decision of several aspects of the case between *Steelco* and *Hightech* will require specialized technical evidence. For example: (i) Was the failure of the System to perform due to failures of design or manufacture by *Hightech*, or to burnouts caused by improper air conditioning? (ii) Were the correct air-conditioning specifications provided by Hightech, and were they as complete as industry custom required? (iii) Did the course of training provided by Hightech to Steelco's employees meet the standards generally recognized in the industry? (iv) What financial valuation principles should be applied in determining the amount of profits lost by Steelco because the System was not available on time? If the arbitral tribunal decides to hear the issues of patent validity and infringement, other highly technical questions will be involved.

QUESTION 38

Would the arbitral tribunal appoint its own experts, or rely on experts presented by the parties?

ANSWERS TO QUESTION 38

MR. HOELLERING [USA]

It is customary for arbitral tribunals to rely on experts presented by the parties. In a case such as the hypothetical case, both Hightech and

---

* Reprinted with kind permission from Kluwer Law International.

Steelco will want to present their own experts to testify on their behalf. Opposing counsel, in turn, would want an opportunity to cross-examine the other party's expert, so as to impeach his testimony and rebut any negative inference which may be drawn from any expert report. Should the parties' expert testimony prove inconclusive or confusing to the arbitrators, the tribunal may appoint its own experts, if so authorized by the applicable rules or by agreement of the parties.[75] This "neutral" expert would then either assist the tribunal with a report on outstanding technical matters, or give testimony thereon. Both parties thereafter would be given the opportunity to interrogate the expert with regard to his findings at the hearing.[76]

When arbitration is conducted under its auspices, the AAA will assist the arbitrators and the parties in the appointment of neutral experts. One possible approach is for the parties to submit a list of mutually agreeable experts to the AAA for transmission to the arbitral tribunal. The arbitral tribunal would then make a selection from that list. A second method is for the AAA to submit a list of proposed experts drawn from its panel. The tribunal would then make its selection from the AAA list. A third way would be for the arbitrators, who themselves know the field, to pick an expert on their own. Whatever the way, the tribunal normally will seek the parties' concurrence to the selection and role of the neutral expert.

MR. HUNTER [England]

It could be either, or both. In general, English arbitrators prefer the adversarial approach; that is to say, they would listen to the evidence of experts presented by the parties, which is subject to questioning by the members of the tribunal and cross-examination.

There is, however, a growing appreciation that an arbitrator who has little or no expertise in the subject matter of a dispute involving complex technical issues can get little assistance even from skilled cross-examinations of opposing technical experts of high standing.

Where a tribunal takes this view, it will appoint an expert to assist. It has this power under the general law of England, and it is given expressly by Article 27 of the UNCITRAL Rules. The UNCITRAL Rules (Art. 27(4)) also reflect the general position in English arbitration law that, even where the tribunal invokes the assistance of an expert, the parties themselves may still present expert witnesses to testify on the points at issue.

75. The tribunal is expressly granted such authority under Art. 27 of the UNCITRAL Rules. Under AAA Commercial Arbitration Rules sect. 31, such power, while not expressly stated, is implied. As a practical matter, however, use of experts appointed by the tribunal is not customary. This may be due to the high level of expertise typical of panel members in international arbitrations conducted under AAA auspices.

76. Stein and Wotman, *International Commercial Arbitration in the 1980's*, [38 Bus. Law. 1685 (1983)] at 1716–17.

MR. JARVIN [ICC]

It would appoint its own experts.[77] As regards experts, all the civil law countries I have examined permit the arbitrator to appoint an expert on his own initiative and for his own information.[78] The expert's opinion must be made available to the parties and the expert prepared to answer questions from the parties.

However, since the costs of an expert are borne by the parties, there are limits to what an arbitrator can order. If, therefore, the parties refuse to pay the advance required for an expertise, the arbitrator will draw his conclusions from such behavior.

On the other hand, if the parties want to present their own experts, the arbitrator would accept this. In complex cases, there may be experts appointed by the party and the arbitrator. The expert appointed by the arbitrator may be of great assistance to evaluate the statements of the party-appointed experts.

PROF. LEBEDEV [Russia]

It is submitted that in accordance with the usual practice in the country of arbitration, at least the presiding arbitrator will be inclined to call for the report of expert(s) appointed by the arbitral tribunal itself in accordance with Article 27 of the UNCITRAL Rules, especially on technical questions.

PROF. ELBHAKIM [Syria]

Under Egyptian and Syrian laws on evidence (Arts. 136 and 139 respectively) the tribunal must confirm the appointment of the experts agreed on by the parties. Failing such agreement, it is up to the arbitrators to appoint one or three experts.

PROF. MICHIDA [Japan]

In Japanese practice, arbitral tribunals usually rely on experts presented by the parties. By doing so, the amicable nature of dispute settlement is preserved. However, in maritime cases, where special problems affecting highly technical issues have been involved and qualified experts on these issues were well known to the arbitrators, tribunals have appointed their own experts.

DR. SZURSKI [Poland]

The arbitral tribunal will generally be inclined to appoint an expert whom both parties will recognize as impartial and properly qualified to evaluate the technical questions of the dispute. It is only in case of lack of agreement between the parties in this respect that the arbitral tribunal will not hesitate to appoint an expert based exclusively on the tribunal's own choice.

---

77. ICC Court of Arbitration Rules, Art. 14(2) stipulates: "The arbitrator may appoint one or more experts, define their Terms of Reference, receive their reports and/or hear them in person."

78. *Switzerland*, Yearbook Commercial Arbitration, Vol. III, 1978, p. 193; *France*, Yearbook 1981, p. 14; *Germany*, Yearbook 1979, p. 70; *Sweden*, Yearbook 1978, p. 170; *Austria*, Yearbook 1979, p. 32.

Also while preparing the questions to be answered by the expert, the arbitral tribunal will normally take into consideration the suggestions made by the parties. It may even be expected that any suggestion of a party in this respect will be taken into consideration by the arbitral tribunal, unless the tribunal finds the suggestion completely irrelevant.

* * *

QUESTION 39

If the arbitral tribunal were to appoint its own experts, would it request the parties to submit suggestions for the experts' terms of reference? Would the arbitral tribunal submit its proposed terms of reference to the parties for comment before giving them to the experts? Would it solicit comments on the names of experts before appointing them?

ANSWERS TO QUESTION 39

MR. HOELLERING [USA]

As noted above, if the arbitrators consider it necessary to appoint an expert, it is customary for them to seek the agreement of the parties with regard to the precise functions of such experts. Under the UNCITRAL Rules, the costs of such experts are allocable in the award, and thus will be borne by the parties.[79] Whether the tribunal would first request the parties to submit suggestions, or would take the initiative to propose its own terms of reference will depend on the preference of the tribunal in the context of the arbitral proceedings. In either case, the tribunal will consult the parties regarding the scope of the role and testimony to be provided by the neutral expert.

MR. HUNTER [England]

The way in which a particular tribunal would proceed would vary according to the circumstances. However, under Article 27(1) of the UNCITRAL Rules, the tribunal must determine the "specific issues" on which the expert is to submit his report.

In practice, the present Rapporteur considers that the tribunal would first ask the parties to submit suggestions for the terms of reference of the expert; then draw up terms of reference in draft form, taking into account its own requirements as well as the views of the parties; and then submit those terms of reference to the parties in draft form for their comments.

There is no general practice as to the method of selection of an expert. The present Rapporteur doubts that many English arbitrators would consult the parties *before* making the appointment. However, they would certainly listen carefully to any objection that might be made subsequently.

79. *See* Art. 38(c).

MR. JARVIN [ICC]

Answer to the first two questions: Yes.

Answer to the third: Probably yes, but no practice can be established.

PROF. LEBEDEV [Russia]

It is quite possible that, taking into account the complexity of technical questions, the arbitral tribunal would first ask the parties to give their views concerning the terms of reference for the expert and, very likely, offer them an opportunity to prepare the draft of such terms themselves.

Likewise, the arbitral tribunal most probably will ask the parties to give their opinion in regard of its own draft of the terms of reference, prepared on the basis of the parties' suggestions, including the joint ones (since in the end an expert should present a report on specific issues "to be determined by the tribunal"—Art. 27(1) of the UNCITRAL Rules). Such procedure has undoubted advantages. Certainly, the time factor should be taken into regard when following it; however, this factor may not be of practical importance if the question of terms of reference can be settled—subject to sufficient preliminary preparations—in the course of pre-hearing conference (Sect. E) or in the course of the first hearing of the case.

The tribunal may wish to discuss the names of experts with the parties. It would hardly appoint an expert to whom both parties objected.

ENGLAND

ARBITRATION ACT 1996[e]

* * *

Power to appoint experts, legal advisers or assessors.

37.—(1) Unless otherwise agreed by the parties—

(a) the tribunal may—

(i) appoint experts or legal advisers to report to it and the parties, or

(ii) appoint assessors to assist it on technical matters,

and may allow any such expert, legal adviser or assessor to attend the proceedings; and

(b) the parties shall be given a reasonable opportunity to comment on any information, opinion or advice offered by any such person.

(2) The fees and expenses of an expert, legal adviser or assessor appointed by the tribunal for which the arbitrators are liable are expenses of the arbitrators for the purposes of this Part.

* * *

e.   36 I.L.M. 155, 173 (1997).

INDIA

THE ARBITRATION AND CONCILIATION ORDINANCE, 1996

* * *

Expert appointed by arbitral tribunal

26.   (1) Unless otherwise agreed by the parties, the arbitral tribunal may—

> (a) appoint one or more experts to report to it on specific issues to be determined by the arbitral tribunal, and

> (b) require a party to give the expert any relevant information or to produce, or to provide access to, any relevant documents, goods or other property for his inspection.

(2) Unless otherwise agreed by the parties, if a party so requests or if the arbitral tribunal considers it necessary, the expert shall, after delivery of his written or oral report, participate in an oral hearing where the parties have the opportunity to put questions to him and to present expert witnesses in order to testify on the points at issue.

(3) Unless otherwise agreed by the parties, the expert shall, on the request of a party, make available to that party for examination all documents, goods or other property in the possession of the expert with which he was provided in order to prepare his report.

* * *

MEXICO

DECREE 22 JULY 1993 CONTAINING AMENDMENTS AND DIVERSE ADDITIONAL PROVISIONS MADE TO THE COMMERCIAL CODE AND THE FEDERAL CODE OF CIVIL PROCEDURE

COMMERCIAL CODE, TITLE IV (OF BOOK V)

Commercial Arbitration

* * *

Article 1442

Unless otherwise agreed by the parties, the arbitral tribunal may appoint one or more experts to report to it on specific issues and may require a party to give the expert any relevant documents, goods or other property for his inspection.

Article 1443

Unless otherwise agreed by the parties, if a party so requests or if the arbitral tribunal considers it necessary, the expert shall, after delivery of his written or oral report, participate in a hearing where the parties have the opportunity to put questions to him and to present expert witnesses in order to testify on the points at issue.

* * *

THE GREEK 1999 ACT ON INTERNATIONAL COMMERCIAL ARBITRATION

(Act No. 2735/1999).

ARTICLE 26.　EXPERT APPOINTED BY ARBITRAL TRIBUNAL

1. Unless otherwise agreed by the parties, the arbitral tribunal

   a. may appoint one or more experts charged with the duty to report to it on specific issues to be determined by the arbitral tribunal;

   b. may require a party to give the expert any relevant information or to produce, or proved access to, any relevant documents, goods or other property for his inspection.

   2. Unless otherwise agreed by the parties, if a party so requests or if the arbitral tribunal considers it necessary, the expert shall, after delivery of his written or oral report, participate in a hearing, at which hearing the parties have the opportunity to put questions to him and to present expert witnesses.

* * *

PAKLITO INVESTMENT LTD. v. KLÖCKNER EAST ASIA LTD.

United Kingdom, High Court of Hong Kong, 1993.
1993 (Vol. 2) Hong Kong Law Reports 40.

KAPLAN J.:

On 15th November 1990 the China International Economic and Trade Arbitration Commission (CIETAC) rendered an arbitral award in favour of the Plaintiffs in the sum of approximately US$800,000.

On 12th August 1991 Master Cannon granted the Plaintiffs ex parte leave to enforce this award as a judgment of this court. This was done under the provisions of s. 44 of the Arbitration Ordinance (*Cap.* 341) which is the means by which the New York Convention of 1958, to which Hong Kong and China are both parties, is given statutory effect in Hong Kong. The application was also made under Order 73 of The Rules of The Supreme Court.

On 11th February 1992 Master Cannon, after an inter partes hearing, set aside her order dated 12th August 1991 and I have before me an appeal from that decision. I should add that the appeal was listed before me on 1st April 1992 but was adjourned at the request of both parties in order to obtain from CIETAC a recording or a transcript of the hearing before them held on 25th April 1990.

PROCEDURE

* * *

FACTS

The point at issue in this appeal goes to the very heart of the arbitral process and in order for it to be fully appreciated a recitation of the basic facts of this matter is essential.

By a contract in writing made between the parties on the 17th August 1988 the defendants agreed to sell to the plaintiffs and the defendants agreed to buy 2500 MT of hot dip galvanised steel in coil at a total price of US$1,944,000 C & F to be delivered in November 1988. The port of loading was Istanbul, Turkey and the port of destination was Huangpu, China.

Between 10th October and 19th November 1988 the goods were inspected at the manufacturer's plant by Vitsan S.A. The inspection confirmed that the goods were in good order.

On 20th December 1988, the steel coils were loaded on board m.v. "Kornat" at Istanbul. They arrived in Huangpu, China on 19th January 1989. The goods were then transhipped to Haikou, China, leaving Huangpu on 25th January and were unloaded in Haikou on 2nd February 1989.

On arrival at Haikou, the goods were examined by the Hainan Import and Export Inspection Bureau and on 14th February 1989 they were moved to storage outside a warehouse in Haikou.

When the examination certificates were published, they revealed certain defects in the steel. The Weight Inspection Certificate was issued on 20th March, showing the steel to be 9.190 tons under weight. On 14th April the Quality Inspection Certificate was issued, concluding that the goods did not comply with the quality requirements. Some white rust had formed and certain parts of the steel coils had not been galvanized.

On 19th April 1989, claims were made by a series of sub-purchasers and by the Plaintiff against the defendant for defective goods. The contract contained an arbitration clause providing for arbitration in China. Pursuant to this the plaintiffs submitted to CIETAC their written application for arbitration on 10th August 1989.

THE HEARING

On the morning of 25th April 1990 an oral hearing was held by the arbitration tribunal. The plaintiff maintains that this was a full hearing with detailed submissions on the evidence and issues, whereas the defendant says the hearing was merely a preliminary hearing.

The defendant also says that at the hearing they made a request for a further oral hearing to consider the causes of the formation of white rust. It appears that the defendant has since requested a copy of the recording of or transcript of the hearing but CIETAC has refused to release a transcript or to allow the defendant to listen to the original tape.

CIETAC gave a direction at the hearing allowing the submission of further evidence within one month from that date. The defendant submitted their defence on 10th May 1990 and the plaintiff submitted certain exhibits on 19th May.

On 31st July 1990 CIETAC notified the defendant of its decision to appoint its own experts to carry out investigations. The Rules of Arbitration of CIETAC allow an arbitral tribunal to take this course of action. The relevant articles of the Rules state:

> "26. The parties shall give evidences for the facts on which the claims or defences are based. The arbitration tribunal, in case of deeming necessities, may make investigations and collect evidences on its own." (*sic*)

> "28. The arbitration tribunal may consult specialists for special problems arising from the cases or appoint appraisers for appraisals, Specialists or appraisers may be the institutes or citizens of the PRC or foreign countries." (*sic*)

On 11th August the defendant wrote to the Commission objecting to this appointment on the ground that such an investigation would be useless having regard to the almost one and a half years that had elapsed since the goods were delivered in Haikou. The defendant also stated that they would not accept the results of any such investigation.

On 12th September 1990 the experts employed by the arbitral tribunal made their inspection and took away samples of the five specifications of steel coils. The report, issued on 31st October, concluded that there were deficiencies in the galvanized layer on the samples, including ungalvanised patches, and that the rate of corrosion of the galvanised layers was twice that expected "except for industrial areas in the tropics". That the report was intended to conclude whether the defects were of manufacture or storage is made clear at the commencement of the Report where it was stated the purpose of the inspection was:

> "... in order to rule out the responsibility for the quality of the galvanized layer of the galvanized sheet being attributed to the time *after* the goods had left the factory ..."

(emphasis added)

The report was received by the defendant's lawyer on 8th November. It is common ground that the Tribunal were informed orally that the defendant wished to comment after considering the report. On 12th November the defendant wrote to CIETAC stating their intention to submit a further defence in answer to the report and questions arising from it.

On 15th November 1990 the Arbitration Tribunal rendered its award in favour of the plaintiff. The letter from the defendant was received by CIETAC on 20th November. On 8th January the defendant wrote to the Commission outlining their expectation of having an opportunity to adduce further evidence at an oral hearing. No reply was ever received from CIETAC.

Procedure Before Cietac

There is some question both as to exactly what occurred at the CIETAC hearing in the present case and as to the procedure normally followed at a CIETAC arbitration tribunal. As regards the latter question, the plaintiffs contend that there is no right to cross-examination either under Chinese law or under CIETAC's Arbitration Rules.

In support of this the Plaintiffs filed an affidavit from Mr. Xi Xiao Tam, the PRC lawyer who represented them at the hearing of 25th April 1990, and a letter from the Secretariat of CIETAC. The Defendants answer this with an opinion from Professor An Chen, Professor of International Economic Law and Dean of the School of Law and Politics at Xiamen University, who is also a member and arbitrator of CIETAC, and an affirmation from Mr. Anthony Neoh, QC, who is a member of CIETAC's panel of arbitrators and has been an active arbitrator for the past three years.

As I feel this issue is both very relevant to the present case and of general importance, I propose to consider this evidence in some detail.

Mr. Xi states that the Chinese system is an inquisitional one and that the common law notion of cross-examination of witnesses is "totally absent". He says that in Chinese arbitration proceedings the Tribunal may conduct its own enquiries to verify evidence submitted by the parties, deciding the extent of its enquiries and whether to accept the evidence so obtained, and may engage experts if it thinks fit. The parties are not allowed to challenge evidence obtained in such a manner unless the Tribunal invites them to make submission on it. There is thus, he states, no right to cross-examine the Tribunal's own witnesses and no right of cross-examination at all in China.

In a letter of 15th February 1992 the Secretariat of the Arbitration Commission affirms this view. The Secretariat states "any party in the proceedings cannot raise any objection to the expert report prepared by the independent expert employed by the Arbitration Tribunal. This is because the expert report is compiled by an independent and impartial third person. It is a practical and scientific report and is authoritative."

Professor An Chen was asked by the defendant to give his opinion on whether these two views were in accordance with the true position in China. The following is a summary of his evidence.

Professor An Chen says that the most important purpose of PRC Civil Procedure Law is "to protect the exercise by the parties of their procedural rights". The proper ascertaining of the facts is regarded as the basis for the correct application of the law. Further provisions of the Civil Procedure Law state, inter alia, that all evidence, including expert conclusions, must be collected and examined "comprehensively and objectively". Such provisions aim to ascertain the true facts, verify the annexures and help ensure the court does not listen only to one party.

The Professor affirms that there is in the trial procedures in China the right to comment, raise objection and refute the evidence of witnesses, including producing new evidence. The Civil Procedure Law allows the questioning of witnesses with the approval of the court. In fact, the court will always approve a proper request and even encourages such requests because, as the Professor says, "these greatly assist the clarification of facts and the ascertainment of the truth".

The litigant may present new evidence in court, including evidence that refutes that of the appraisers. A new provision makes this even clearer by stating that "evidence shall be presented in court and examined by the parties." Examination means cross-examination. It is thus wrong to say that there is no system of cross-examination in China.

The Professor confirms that the same principles should be observed by CIETAC in arbitration proceedings. Under the 1988 Rules of Arbitration of CIETAC there are no specific provisions allowing the parties to raise objections or refute reports of experts engaged by the tribunal but neither are there specific provisions denying any such right, as the plaintiff asserts.

Three reasons are given for the absence of such provisions. Firstly, the rules are very brief. Secondly, it is well known that the Civil Procedure Law provides the basic principles, in particular "to guarantee parties to a law suit equal exercise of their litigation rights". Thirdly, the principles relevant to hearing arbitrations involving foreign interests can be found in other legislation and in international conventions.

A June 1988 State Council document clearly directed that the new CIETAC rules cannot be read to breach either China's laws regarding fundamental legal principles, including standards of conduct during trial, or international treaties to which the PRC has acceded.

Under Article 142 of the 1986 General Principles of Civil Law, the provisions of international treaties to which China has acceded apply in preference to the provisions of Chinese law where the two differ.

Article 238 of the 1991 Civil Procedure Law, repeating Article 189 of the earlier, 1982 version, provides for the application of the stipulations found in international treaties where they differ from those of Chinese law.

In the light of the above, the CIETAC rules must not be in breach of international treaties, including the New York Convention. In recognition of this, the Civil Procedure Law as amended in 1991 contained provisions allowing the People's Court to deny execution of the award of CIETAC "if the person against whom the application was made was not requested to appoint an arbitrator or take part in the arbitration proceedings or was unable to state his opinions due to reasons for which he was not responsible."

The conclusion drawn from all this is that if the CIETAC award was based on the appraisals of experts and the party against whom the application was made did not have any opportunity to plead its own case, raise objection, refute the evidence or provide new evidence, this will amount to a situation where he was unable to state his opinions. This would be contrary to the Civil Procedure Law and the New York Convention and the party can therefore apply to the People's Court for the award not to be enforced temporarily, until the tribunal listens to the evidence or objection and a new, enforceable award is made.

In this case the Professor concluded that the expert reports "were delivered too late, and the award was issued too soon".

The defendants also engaged Mr. Anthony Neoh, Q.C. to give an opinion on the same matter. His view is summarised as follows.

The 1988 amendments to the CIETAC Arbitration Rules were adopted pursuant to an approval of the State Council given in June 1988, which stated that the Rules shall be "in accordance with China's laws and international treaties concluded or acceded to by China and with reference to international practice". By this stage, China had already acceded to the New York Convention.

In April 1987, the Supreme People's Court issued a circular on enforcement under the New York Convention, instructing the People's Courts to study the Convention and to handle matters in accordance with it. Furthermore, the circular instructed the courts to make orders refusing the recognition and enforcement of an award where the conditions under article 5 of the Convention are present. Article 5, para. 1(b) provides for such refusal where "the Party against whom the award was made ... was ... unable to present his case".

CIETAC arbitrators therefore regard the procedural standards of the New York Convention as fundamentally governing their actions. The Rules are to be seen against this background. In particular, arbitrators are conscious of the need to give the parties every opportunity to present their case "including affording an opportunity to both parties to comment or present further evidence if necessary on any expert report produced by experts appointed by the tribunal".

The Arbitration Rules do not specifically allow or disallow cross-examination or give the parties the right to challenge the evidence of experts appointed by the Tribunal. The general practice adopted by CIETAC is more instructive.

Mr. Neoh states that at the hearing, the proceedings are generally divided into two stages, an initial, fact-finding stage and a second stage involving debate on the merits of the case and on the law applicable. Article 22 requires the tribunal to hold a hearing unless the parties agree otherwise.

Thus the tribunal will, during the first stage, generally allow the parties to ask questions of witnesses, who are not bound to answer but adverse inferences maybe drawn if they refuse. Expert evidence, usually provided in reports, is also commented on, both as to the qualification of the expert and as to the detail of the reports. A party may also dispute a report by bringing their own expert report either at the hearing or at an adjourned hearing if needed. If the tribunal feels that further investigation is needed, it may adjourn the hearing for investigations or for the submission of further evidence.

At the second stage, an offer to conciliate will be made by CIETAC. If the hearing proceeds, submissions are made on the merits of the case. If further evidence is needed, the parties may choose to reserve their positions until after they have seen this evidence, and may later request a further hearing. Finally, hearings are adjourned pending publication of the award.

This procedure is similar to that used in the People's Courts, as provided for in articles 103 to 111 of the Civil Procedure Law. Mr. Neoh went on, "The underlying principle in the Law is that each party will have the opportunity to challenge evidence collected by the Tribunal (including expert evidence) before a judgment is rendered."

Thus whereas there is indeed no right to cross-examination in a Common Law sense, both CIETAC Arbitration Rules and PRC Civil Law give the parties opportunity to challenge expert evidence collected by the Tribunal.

Mr. Neoh concluded as follows:

"I cannot agree with the opinion expressed by the Secretariat that no-one has the right to disagree with the findings of the tribunal's experts. As I have already stated hereinabove, the Rules are to be interpreted against the background of the New York Convention in the light of the State Council's direction that the CCPIT shall enact rules in accordance with international treaties and practice. To comply with the New York Convention, it is necessary in my view that any finding that is adverse to any party must be given to that party to allow that party to answer the case against him/her/it. Perhaps that accounts for the fact that the expert reports were sent to and received by the defendant's legal representatives in the PRC, otherwise, if the defendant had no right to comment on the expert reports, there would have been no point in sending them at all."

Having carefully considered all the opinions expressed above, I am particularly impressed by those of Professor An Chen and Mr. Neoh. I do not accept the plaintiff's submissions that Chinese law and arbitral practice does not allow cross-examination either in general or in relation to experts engaged by the Tribunal. In the light of the above, I think the defendants did have the right to expect they would be able to comment on the reports of the Tribunal appointed experts. This is such a basic right that I cannot conceive that the position would be otherwise. The conclusion at which I have arrived certainly accords with what I have seen during the course of enforcing over forty CIETAC awards.

There are in effect two issues, either of which is sufficient to have the appeal dismissed. The first issue is whether the hearing of 25th April 1990 was a substantive hearing on the merits of the case or a preliminary one, dealing only with procedural matters and entitling the defendant to expect a further hearing.

The second issue is whether the defendants were unable to present their case because they were given no opportunity to deal with the expert's reports.

As the second of these issues in itself is sufficient to dispose of this case, I propose to deal with this matter first.

NO OPPORTUNITY TO DEAL WITH EXPERT'S REPORTS

Sections 44(1), (2) & (3) of the Arbitration Ordinance provide:

"(1) Enforcement of a Convention award shall not be refused except in the cases mentioned in this section.

(2) Enforcement of a Convention award maybe refused if the person against whom it is invoked proves—

(a) . . .

(b) . . .

(c) that he was not given proper notice of the appointment of the arbitrator or of the arbitration proceedings or was otherwise unable to present his case; or

(3) Enforcement of a Convention award may also be refused if the award is in respect of a matter which is not capable of settlement by arbitration, or if it would be contrary to public policy to enforce this award."

I have little doubt that if these facts arose in the context of a domestic arbitration in Hong Kong either a successful application would have been made for the removal of the arbitrators on the ground of misconduct or else enforcement under s. 2H of the Arbitration Ordinance would have been refused in the exercise of the court's discretion.

I hasten to add that the term "misconduct" implies no impropriety on the part of the arbitrators but refers to situations where there has been a serious procedural irregularity.

I must of course take into account that these parties agreed on a CIETAC arbitration and that therefore they must be deemed to take Chinese arbitral practices and procedures as they find them.

I must also take into account that when applying the terms of s.44 which give rise to Hong Kong's New York Convention obligations I am also to have regard to the principles of due process in Hong Kong.

I have no doubt whatsoever that a serious procedural irregularity occurred and that on reflection the arbitral tribunal would recognise it as such. The defendants had taken the stand throughout that inspection reports made many months after delivery were of no assistance in ascertaining whether at the time of delivery the goods were defective. They took a policy decision to confess and avoid the inspection reports. I can therefore well understand their concern when, contrary to their submissions, the Tribunal decided to instruct experts who then went further by preparing a report which indicated that the white rust seen was not caused by post-delivery storage but was more likely than not present at the time of delivery. This was a very different case which confronted them and I can well understand their desire to challenge this view and to adduce evidence to the contrary. (I have seen the evidence which the defendants would like to adduce and it raises serious questions as to the methodology of the Tribunal appointed experts.)

It is clear that the Tribunal relied on these reports and that the defendants were given no chance to deal with this very different case which suddenly presented itself. The Defendants should have been given an opportunity to deal with this new evidence. They asked for such an opportunity but the award came too soon and they never received an answer to their request.

Taking all the matters canvassed by both sides into account I have come to the very clear conclusion that the defendants were prevented from presenting their case and they have thus made out the grounds set out in s. 44(2)(c) of the Arbitration Ordinance. The defendants were denied a fair and equal opportunity of being heard.

Mr. Chan, Q.C. attempted to argue that both sides had in fact been given an equal opportunity of presenting their cases because both had been prevented from commenting upon or adducing evidence to contradict the evidence of the tribunal's experts. I reject this argument. The plaintiffs were perfectly happy for the tribunal to rule on the basis of this unseen evidence. What is required is equal and *fair* treatment and this most unfortunately did not happen (see *Hong Kong Arbitration Cases and Materials*, Butterworths p. 201).

I go further. On the basis of Professor An Chen's report and the affidavit of Mr. Anthony Neoh, Q.C., both of which I accept, I am satisfied that the procedural irregularity which I have found to have occurred would also have been found by a Chinese court had they been invited to consider the matter. I am satisfied on the evidence placed before me that questions are permitted of court or tribunal appointed witnesses and that a party is entitled to adduce evidence to rebut the view of the court appointed expert.

Conclusion

I therefore come to the same conclusion as the learned Master and dismiss this appeal. I will make a costs order nisi in favour of the defendants together with a certificate for two counsel.

I cannot leave this judgment without making the following observation. In the three years 1990–1992 this court has enforced approximately 40 CIETAC awards. Some of these applications were opposed but this is the first time that enforcement has been refused. This is a creditable record and I would not like it thought that problems such as occurred in this case are commonplace in CIETAC arbitrations. Judges and arbitrators in all jurisdictions occasionally and unwittingly fall into error and it is in serious cases involving arbitral awards that the enforcing court refuses enforcement to prevent injustice. It has been my experience that in all other cases that I have considered from CIETAC the due process requirements have been fairly met.

I would like to thank both counsel for their helpful and most interesting written and oral arguments which I have found of the greatest possible assistance.

Application dismissed.

Questions and Comments

1. The panel of rapporteurs encountered in connection with the question of recording hearings, is here enlarged by professors El–Hakim and Michida, representing two important regions: the Arab countries and Japan. The key issue regarding experts stems from one of the major differences which exist between the consistently adversarial system adopted in the U.S. and some other (typically common-law) countries on one hand, and the less adversarial approach which characterizes legal systems in Continental Europe. Once again, we face the dilemma of the relative merits of neutrality and balance.

International commercial arbitration has been setting its own standards; these have become increasingly harmonized and do not necessarily mirror the practice prevailing in the country of the site of arbitration.

In light of the remarks of these rapporteurs, how would you describe the emerging international standard? Is it tilting towards party experts, or neutral experts?

2. What arguments could one advance in favor of party-appointed experts in the context of international commercial arbitration? For experts appointed by the arbitrators?

3. It appears that even in countries with a common-law tradition, in recent legislation, neutral experts appointed by the arbitrators have become the **presumed** solution.

On the other hand, recent legislative acts in civil-law countries (Mexico being one of many examples), while providing for experts to be appointed by the arbitrators, specify that this applies subject to a contrary agreement of the parties.

4. The Indian Act in Article 26(2), following the wording of the UNCITRAL Model Law, gives some maneuvering room for party-appointed experts (expert witnesses) in addition to neutral experts appointed by the arbitrators. The same solution was adopted in Article 26(2) of the 1999 Greek Act. What role do expert witnesses play in this context?

5. *Paklito v. Klöckner* shows that the real problem lies not, in principle, in the choice between neutral and party-appointed expert witnesses, but in due process regardless of the approach taken.

How would you define the due-process standards infringed in the *Paklito* case? In other words, what act or omission of the arbitrators was critical: the appointment of an expert in spite of strong objections of one of the parties? Failing to give the parties an opportunity to comment on the findings of the expert? Lack of cross examination? Unequal treatment of the parties?

6. Suppose the arbitrators find the report of the expert unpersuasive. Can they disregard it on their own motion?

7. Suppose the arbitrators in *Paklito v. Klöckner* decided not to give credit to the findings of the expert. Could Claimant raise a due process argument relying on the fact that he had no opportunity to comment on the expert opinion?

Would the argument be persuasive that the arbitrators rejected the expert opinion because of a misunderstanding which Claimant could have contributed towards removing had it had a chance to state its views?

8. According to the 2000 CIETAC Rules, Article 39, experts are appointed by the arbitration tribunal. Article 40 of the Rules also states that:

''The expert's report and the appraiser's report shall be copied to the parties so that the parties may have the opportunity to give opinions thereon. At the request of any party to the case and with the approval of the arbitration tribunal, the expert and appraiser may be present at the hearing and, if considered necessary and appropriate by the arbitration tribunal, be required to give explanations of their reports''.

Did the CIETAC proceedings in *Paklito* meet this standard?

Has Article 40 introduced cross-examination of experts into CIETAC proceedings?

IV.1.h.iii. Language Issues

Howard M. Holtzmann & Joseph E. Neuhaus, A GUIDE TO THE UNCITRAL MODEL LAW ON INTERNATIONAL COMMERCIAL ARBITRATION: LEGISLATIVE HISTORY AND COMMENTARY

628–30 (1989).*

ARTICLE 22. LANGUAGE

(1) The parties are free to agree on the language or languages to be used in the arbitral proceedings. Failing such agreement, the arbitral tribunal shall determine the language or languages to be used in the proceedings. This agreement or determination, unless otherwise specified therein, shall apply to any written statement by a party, any hearing and any award, decision or other communication by the arbitral tribunal.

(2) The arbitral tribunal may order that any documentary evidence shall be accompanied by a translation into the language or languages agreed upon by the parties or determined by the arbitral tribunal.

* Reprinted with permission from Kluwer Law International.

COMMENTARY

The determination of the language to be used in an arbitration is a subject that is not commonly addressed in national arbitration laws. It is nonetheless a question of considerable importance to the cost, efficiency, and fairness of the arbitration, and the Working Group thought it advisable to state explicitly that the matter is controlled by the discretion of the parties and the arbitral tribunal and not, for example, by the statutes designating the official language at the place of arbitration. Article 22 is modeled on Article 17 of the UNCITRAL Arbitration Rules and adopts much of the wording of that provision.

Paragraph 1. The first sentence of the Article—stating that the parties are free to agree on the language or languages to be used—was agreed on at the outset and was not subsequently discussed. It must, of course, be read in conjunction with the third sentence and with the second paragraph, which define the presumptive scope of the parties' agreement. Thus, "unless otherwise specified therein," the agreement applies to written statements by a party, to hearings, and to communications by the arbitral tribunal. The agreement presumably will not apply to documentary evidence, which, under the terms of paragraph 2, is left to the discretion of the tribunal. In the light of the suggestion in paragraph 1 that parties may stipulate the scope of the agreement, paragraph 2 should probably be read as nonmandatory. That is, if the parties specifically agree that documentary evidence should—or should not—be translated, the arbitrators should presumably be deemed to lack discretion on the point. A contrary reading would make little sense: because the parties clearly can control whether written statements are translated, there is no reason they should not be able to do so as to documentary evidence.[5]

Article 22 does not state at what point in the proceedings the parties must agree on, or the arbitral tribunal must determine, the language to be used. The Secretariat Note that first discussed the proposed Article suggested that the parties should be free to agree "either in the arbitral agreement or at some time before or even after the commencement of arbitral proceedings." In Article 17 of the UNCITRAL Arbitration Rules, the arbitral tribunal is instructed to decide on language "promptly after its appointment." This concept is not explicitly incorporated into Article 22, and, except for the Secretariat's comment, the question is not discussed in the legislative history. The exigencies of arbitral procedure would suggest, however, that any agreement or determination should be made early.

---

5. In this connection, it may be noted that the Working Group elsewhere cautioned that, while "it was desirable to express the nonmandatory character in all provisions of the final text which were intended to be nonmandatory," it was understood that the decision to express the nonmandatory nature of certain articles "did not mean that all those provisions of the model law which did not express their nonmandatory character were necessarily of a mandatory nature." Fifth Working Group Report, A/CN.9/246, para. 177, appearing in the section on Matters Not Addressed in the Final Text, pp.1152–53 *infra*.

The bulk of the discussion during the Commission's consideration of Article 22 focused on the second sentence of paragraph 1, which provides for the arbitral tribunal to choose the language to be used when the parties have not reached an agreement on the point. The primary concern was that the arbitral tribunal might choose the language of one of the parties but not of the other. One proposal was to require that all the languages of the parties be used where the parties had not either come to a different agreement or expressly asked the tribunal to choose the language. Another suggestion was to require that a party always be permitted to present its own case in its own language, with the costs of translation and interpretation into the language of the tribunal included in the costs of arbitration (which, it was noted, are commonly borne by the losing party). A third proposal would have made clear that a party could always express its view in its own language and arrange for translation of proceedings at its own expense. In Reply to these proposals, it was said that Article 18 which requires the arbitral tribunal to treat the parties with equality and give each party a full opportunity of presenting its case, sufficiently guaranteed the fairness of the choice. It was also felt that the proposal to require use of all the parties' languages was too rigid. Ultimately, none of the proposals was incorporated into the text of the law, but it was in this context that the Commission decided to move the former Article 19(3) into a new Article 18, in order to emphasize its importance and the fact that it applied to all aspects of the arbitral proceedings. The Commission also observed that it was not necessary to stipulate that a party could provide for translation from and to its own language, since there was no intention of preventing a party from doing so.

Paragraph 2. Paragraph 2 of Article 22 occasioned little discussion during the legislative history. One point raised during the Commission's deliberations was a proposal to make it clear that, in arbitrations being conducted in more than one language, the arbitral tribunal could, if it seemed appropriate, accept documentary evidence in only one of the languages of the arbitration. The concern was that the phrase "the language or languages agreed upon" in paragraph 2 might be interpreted to require translation into all of the chosen languages, whereas it might be sufficient in some circumstances to accept various documents in only one language.[15] The Commission accepted this principle and asked the Drafting Group to decide whether it was expressed by the existing language of Article 22. The Drafting Group did not change the applicable language.[17]

One final point noted in the legislative history was that there is no requirement of certification for translations submitted to the arbitral

15. The Secretariat also noted that some documentary evidence can be voluminous and may be relevant only in part. Seventh Secretariat Note, A/CN.9/264, Art. 22, para. 5, p. 639 *infra.*

17. *Compare* Fifth Draft, A/CN.9/246 (Annex), Art. 22(2), p. 636 *infra, with* Arti-

cle 22(2) in the final text. In its commentary on the Fifth Draft, the Secretariat had interpreted the draft Article as already providing this discretion. *See* Seventh Secretariat Note, A/CN.9/264, Art. 22, para. 5, p. 639 *infra.*

tribunal under Article 22. Although Article 35(2) contains such a requirement for submission of the award to a court for enforcement, the Commission considered that requiring certification before the arbitral tribunal might unnecessarily add to the costs of proceedings.[18]

N.Z. (NO NATIONALITY) v. I. (ROMANIA)

Appellationsgericht [Court of Appeal], Basel–Stadt, 1989.
17 Yearbk. Comm. Arb'n 581 (1992).*

FACTS

On 5 December 1988 the lower court in Basel (Switzerland) granted leave to enforce an arbitral award rendered in Romania. The Court of Appeal (*Appellationsgericht*) confirmed the lower court's decision on the following grounds.

EXCERPT

[1]   "The arbitral award of 11 February 1988 of the Arbitration Committee of the Chamber of Commerce and Industry of the Socialist Republic of Romania, which is the subject of the appealed judgment, orders the appellant to pay * * * a sum of money. The enforcement of this award in Switzerland is governed by the [1958 New York Convention], to which both Switzerland and Romania adhered. The Convention rules prevail over cantonal law of civil procedure. Sect. 258 of the Code of Civil Procedure (ZPO), which by the way expressly provides for the prevalence [sic] of international treaties, is therefore not applicable here."

* * *

[3]   "The appellant does object, however, to the lower court's resorting to oral proceedings instead of the regular procedure under Sect. 258 ZPO. Such objection is unfounded. Art. III *in fine* of the [1958 New York Convention] provides that there shall not be imposed substantially higher fees or charges or substantially stricter rules of procedure on the recognition or enforcement of arbitral awards to which the Convention applies than are imposed on the recognition or enforcement of domestic arbitral awards. Issues of enforceability of domestic awards are decided by one or three judges in oral proceedings. The appellee's application therefore rightly was dealt with that way."

* * *

[5]   "The appellant further argues that the first invitation to participate in the arbitration proceedings was in Romanian. He allegedly received an invitation in a 'comprehensible' language only 4 to 5 days

---

18. Commission Report, A/40/17. para. 192, p. 645 *infra*; Summary Record, A/CN.9/SR.322, paras. 15–17, pp. 642–43 *infra*. This presumably does not prevent the arbitral tribunal from requiring certified translations in appropriate cases, however.

before the start of the proceedings. Art. V of the [1958 New York Convention] enumerates the grounds for refusal of enforcement or recognition of an award. The fact that an invitation to arbitration proceedings was drafted in the language of the seat of the arbitration-a language that one of the parties did not understand-is not part of that enumeration. It rather follows from the Convention that certain decisive documents, such as the award itself, merely have to be translated for enforcement purposes (Cf. Art. IV (2) of the 1958 New York Convention)."

[6]   The appellant's objection was thus held to be unfounded.

[7]   "Besides, the Romanian arbitral tribunal's way of proceeding did not cause any substantial disadvantage to the appellant who stated before the lower court that he did not want to go to Romania to recover the goods since one never knows what will happen there. One therefore may assume that a speedier invitation in English or German would not have had any effect."

* * *

SELLER (DENMARK) v. BUYER (GERMANY)

Oberlandesgericht [Court of Appeal], Cologne, 16 December 1992.
21 Yearbk. Comm. Arb'n 535 (1996).*

* * *

EXCERPT

[1]   "The award of the ICC sole arbitrator ... should have been held enforceable under Art. 1044 ZPO[1] in conjunction with Arts. IV, V, and VII of the [1958 New York Convention], Art. I(2)(a) of the [European Convention of 1961] and Sect. 1027(2) ZPO."[2]

* * *

[15]   "Defendant—on which * * * [rests] the burden of allegation and proof under Art. V of the Convention—invokes to no avail violation of public policy or its right to due process. Defendant wrongly alleges that this is the case in particular because, notwithstanding its objections,

---

* Reprinted with permission of Yearbook Commercial Arbitration, International Council for Commercial Arbitration.

1.   Art. 1044 of the German Code of Civil Procedure (*Zivilprozessordnung*) regulates the enforcement of foreign arbitral awards and largely reproduces Art. V of the New York Convention.

2.   Art. 1027 of the German Code of Civil Procedure reads:

"1.   The arbitration agreement must be concluded expressly and in writing; the instrument must not contain any agreements other than those referring to the arbitration procedure. Admission to the arbitral

discussions on the substance of the case overrides any faults in form.

"2.   The above provision does not apply, if the arbitration agreement is a business matter for the two parties and if either of the two parties belongs to the trading professions set out in Sect. 4 of the Commercial Code.

"3.   Insofar as, in accordance with para. 2, the arbitration agreement does not have to be laid down in writing, each party may require a written instrument concerning the agreement."

English was chosen as the language of the proceedings, and the arbitrator did not obtain evidence on defendant's allegations."

[16] "The arbitrator's choice of English as the language of the proceedings does not constitute a violation of due process for defendant. We do not need to establish whether defendant accepted the determination of the language of the proceedings by signing the Terms of Reference. In any case, it was possible under point 5.3 of the Terms to file pleadings in German, a possibility of which defendant has made use. Consequently, there were two languages of the proceedings, as allowed by Art. 15(3) of the ICC Rules. Also, defendant has not been able to indicate in concreto on which occasions it could not follow the arbitration because of comprehension or communication difficulties. This is reason enough not to deal with the issue why the arbitrator chose English as the language of the proceedings although the contract concluded between the parties was drawn in German and, according to Art. 15(3) of the ICC Rules, the language of the contract must in principle be decisive for the choice of language of the proceedings. After all, it cannot be ignored that by doing so the arbitrator chose a neutral language, as the mother tongue of the claimant is Danish, and by choosing only German as the language of the proceedings defendant would have been unilaterally privileged."

[17] "Defendant's fear not to have been correctly understood by the arbitrator is a mere supposition—defendant itself uses this term. There are no reasons to deduce this from the arbitral award. In particular, we may not deduce that the arbitrator did not understand the literal meaning of the memo of 27 June 1986. The fact that he did not give to it the value and meaning alleged by defendant is a legal evaluation which has nothing to do with the choice of the language of the proceedings."

* * *

Questions and Comments

1. The Model Law has made an important step by clarifying the scope—and the effects that flow from—party agreements and tribunal decisions respecting the language of the arbitration. Article 22 is important not only for the rule contained in its second sentence, but also because it heightens awareness of problems that are often overlooked.

It is not unusual for the correspondence between two firms to be conducted in more than one language; contracts are concluded in one language and then amended in another. For example, executives of an Austrian and a Rumanian firm write to each other in German as long as the Rumanian firm has a German speaking correspondent: after he (she) retires, they switch to English. If the language of the arbitration is English, the question arises, whether all relevant German correspondence has to be translated into English. This is of course possible (and may be necessary as well), but it is certainly very costly and time-consuming. Also, translations have never ceased to be a source of misunderstandings and errors. Therefore—assuming all the arbitrators can at least read German—it would be expedient to allow the presentation of all written communications in their original form. But this has to be specified. Accordingly, it is important to bear in mind all forms of communication and to reach agreement regarding the language—or languages—in which written statements, minutes or transcripts of the hearing, notices, evidence presented, the award, and so on are to be communicated to the parties and the tribunal.

2.   In the Swiss–Rumanian case the respondent actually received notice in a language it could understand four or five days before the start of the proceedings. Suppose the respondent had not received such notice until after the proceedings had concluded. Should the result in the case be the same?

3.   Should all arbitral institutions send notice of a proceeding in the language of the recipient, or should the parties be responsible for regulating this language issue; or should all communications be submitted in the language or languages chosen by the arbitrators or, conceivably, in the language of the seat of arbitration?

If the parties choose an arbitral institution, but not a language, what should be the language of communication before the tribunal is constituted? In what language, for example, should claimant address the arbitral institution? In what language should the institution invite respondent to choose its arbitrator?

4.   Suppose the parties (or the arbitrators) agree that one language covers all communications and presentations. Documents are translated into the language of arbitration by a sworn court translator, but one of the parties contests the accuracy of the translation. How should the arbitrators proceed?

5.   For practical reasons it is quite important for the parties to agree on the language of the arbitration process before the constitution of the tribunal. (Command of the language of the proceedings is clearly one of the important considerations in choosing arbitrators.) Suppose the parties, after the arbitrators are chosen, agree on a language which is understood by only two of the three arbitrators. What happens?

6.   A somewhat similar problem can arise if the arbitrators choose a language that is not spoken by the attorney of one of the parties. That party will then face the option of appointing another attorney, of adding an attorney who has an adequate command of the chosen language, or of taking the risk of relying on translation.

These dilemmas and inconveniences can best be handled if the language of the proceedings is chosen before the start of the arbitration process so that both sides' strategic choices can take the language question into account.

7.   The language agreed upon by parties is sometimes a language not spoken by one or both parties (or their attorneys). In this situation, parties sometimes choose to present their oral pleadings through a translator of their choice.[3]

[3].   This is, incidentally, a solution we would not recommend. Translations are often done by linguists not trained in law, and, consequently, legal terms are not infrequently improperly translated. As a result, legal nuances may be lost or distorted.

Suppose a party (or the parties) decides to communicate through a translator, and the ensuing award is based on a mistranslated party pleading. Is there any remedy?

Would the situation be different if the translator were hired by the arbitration tribunal?

8. In the case decided by the OLG Köln, the defendant was unable "to indicate in concreto on which occasions it could not follow the arbitration because of comprehension or communication difficulties". Suppose defendant had demonstrated that he **did** have difficulties in presenting his case, because of his less than satisfactory command of English (the language chosen by the arbitrators), and suppose this handicap may have had an influence on the outcome. What result?

9. In Gemtel Partnership v. Société La Belle Créole,[4] a challenge against an arbitrator was lodged before the Paris Tribunal de grande instance, alleging that he did not have a sufficient command of English technical expressions in the field of construction. The Paris court took the position that "the appreciation of the competence and of the linguistic aptitude of an arbitrator is outside the tasks of the President of the Tribunal de grande instance". The Court added that it was up to the conscience of the arbitrator to accept or not to accept the assignment offered to him.

Do you agree?

10. In a "real" 1997 contract concluded between a U.K. and a Hungarian party, the last section has the heading "Arbitration", and the following somewhat baffling text: *"Legal disputes shall be settled by the chosen court accepted by the Hungarian Chamber of Commerce."*

Is this a valid arbitration clause? Let us add that the Hungarian term for arbitration is "választottbíróság"—and in literal translation this means "chosen court". In all probability, the original of the contract was drafted in Hungarian, and it was translated by someone who was not a lawyer, and who came up with the grammatically correct—but rather misleading—translation: "chosen court".

11. In a 1991 decision of the Cour d'appel de Paris (Court of Appeal of Paris) (published in Revue de l'arbitrage, 1991, 97) the language issue appeared along with the question of ex parte communication. The language of arbitration was English, but the Spanish party sent copies of his pleadings in Spanish to the two Spanish-speaking arbitrators. An award was rendered, and it was challenged before the Paris court. The party challenging the award asserted that this was improper communication, because it provided to one of the parties preferential access to certain members of the tribunal. The court rejected the challenge, stating that the content of the pleadings submitted in Spanish was not different from the content of the same pleadings submitted in English.

Commenting on this case Lazareff notes:

It is preferable to hire an attorney who can communicate directly. This attorney would act instead of, or in collaboration with, the attorney who does not speak the language in which the oral hearings are conducted.

[4]. Tribunal de grande instance, Decision of September 21, 1989, Reported in 1990 Revue de l'arbitrage at 176 with comments of Ph.Kahn at 189.

"This decision can be criticized since, whatever one might say about it, such procedure infringes the equality between the parties and, in fact, authorizes arbitrators not to work in the language of the proceedings and to create an imbalance within the Arbitral Tribunal." (S. Lazareff, The Language of Institutional Arbitration, the ICC International Court of Arbitration Bulletin, May 1997, 18, at p. 25).

Do you agree with the Paris court, or with Lazareff?

12. The 2001 Rules of the Vienna Arbitral Centre of the Austrian Federal Economic Chamber have added a new provision on "languages of correspondence" (Article 4(a)). According to this provision: "Correspondence by the Parties with the Board and the Secretary shall be conducted in German or English." This provision implies a distinction between the language of the arbitration process and the "language of correspondence" between the arbitral institution (the administration) and the parties. A consequence of this rule is that the language agreed upon by the parties need not be recognized as the "language of correspondence". Do you agree with this solution?

Article 4(a) gives discretion to the Board (or more typically the Secretary) to choose between German and English. In a dispute between, for example, a U.S. and an English firm, the Vienna Arbitral Centre has discretion whether to choose English as the language of correspondence. (It will probably choose English, as a matter of good practice.) Do you see any other solution? (For example, should the administration respond in the language in which it receives a communication; or should it respond in the language in which it receives a communication as long as this is German or English?)

IV.1.i.　*Representation in the Proceedings; Is Local Counsel Required?*

Michael Polkinghorne, THE RIGHT
OF REPRESENTATION IN A
FOREIGN VENUE

4 Arb'n Int'l 333 (1988).*

"WITH exceedingly insignificant exceptions . . . the whole world has accepted the right for parties in international arbitrations to be represented by advocates without subjecting them to any formal or material requirements as to their competence . . . In legal systems permeated by the monopoly of lawyers, this is nothing but a quiet revolution."[1]

Ideally, international arbitration is a moveable feast which provides the same nourishment wherever the table is set. Accordingly, much has been written about the trend toward internationalisation of legal norms applied by arbitrators[2] and, indeed, of awards themselves.[3] This theoreti-

---

* Reprinted with permission from Kluwer Law International.

1. J. Gillis Wetter, Review of W.L. Craig, W.W. Park, & J. Paulsson. *ICC Arbitration*, 1984 *Scensk juristtiduing* 156, at 160.

2. *See e.g.* Lord Justice Mustill's recent study, "The New Lex Mercatoria," 4 *Arb Int* 86 (1988).

cal evolution has been accompanied by similar developments in practice, in particular the removal of idiosyncratic traps for the unwary contained in provisions of national laws affecting international arbitrations,[4] and the increased acceptance of arbitration by parties outside the traditional mainstream of commerce.[5] There is, however, a more prosaic development supportive of these trends which has not received the attention it perhaps requires. That is the internationalisation of the corps of advocates who represent parties in arbitration. This corps of arbitration experts is internationalised, at least in part because of the general lack of national obstacles to their participation as advocates in arbitration proceedings, wherever they occur. The members of such a corps have, as one commentator noted "shared values and viewpoints, which in turn promotes the growth of a new unitary international law of arbitration."[6]

Yet one should not be entirely sanguine about an internationally-accepted unobstructed right to be represented by such advocates. A poignant illustration of the proposition that all may not be well is that of *In the matter of an Arbitration between Builders Federal (Hong Kong) Limited and Joseph Gartner & Co, and Turner (East Asia) Pte Ltd* (No. 90 of 1987)[7] ("the Turner Case"), in which the High Court of Singapore, on 30 March 1988, may have undone all the good that was achieved toward making Singapore attractive as an international arbitration venue by the Arbitration (Amendment) Act 1980.[8]

In a case involving parties based in three different countries, Judicial Commissioner Chan Sek Keong ruled that the (foreign) respondents could not have the (foreign) counsel of their choice, in that the provisions of Singapore's Legal Profession Act operated, in effect, to bar foreign lawyers from representing their clients in international arbitrations in that country.

* * *

Whilst the *Turner* decision evidently cannot augur well for Singapore's development as a centre for international arbitration,[12] there is,

---

3. *See e.g.* J. Paulsson, "Arbitration Unbound," 30 *Int Comp. L.Q.* 358 (1981).

4. *See e.g.* Section 34 of the Malaysian Arbitration Act (added in 1980) quoted in VI *Yearbook Commercial Arbitration* 194 (1981); the 1984 International Arbitration Code of the Republic of Djibouti, reprinted in 1984 *Revue de l'arbitrage* at 533; G. Hermann, UNCITRAL Adopts Model Law on International Commercial Arbitration, 2 *Arb Int.* 2 (1986). F. Chiasson & M. Labonde, "Recent Canadian Legislation on Arbitration" 2 *Arb. Int.* 370 (1986); P. Sanders, "The New Dutch Arbitration Act," 3 *Arb Int.* 194 (1987); P. Lalive, "The New Swiss Law on International Arbitration," 4 *Arb Int.* 2 (1988); not to mention the well-documented reforms around the turn of the present decade in England, France, Austria and Italy.

5. See e.g. J. Paulsson, "Third World Participation in International Investment Arbitration," 1987 *ICSID Review* 19.

6. Wetter, *supra* note 1.

7. Reported in the Malaysian Law Journal at (1988) 2 MLJ 280.

8. This amendment was "to a large extent a re-enactment of changes introduced in England by the 1979 Arbitration Act." P. Kimbrough, "National Report, Singapore," XI *Yearbook Commercial Arbitration* 29 (1986).

12. A letter from the Chairman of a Working Party on the Proposed International Arbitration Centre appeared in the *Straits Times* on 22 April 1988, arguing that the decision must necessarily be restricted to those cases involving Singapore

further, the depressing possibility that it might have ramifications in other jurisdictions where the question has not been judicially considered. Will we now see a rash of similar applications for injunctions brought by other parties wishing to take advantage of this new found restriction?

This issue is far from moot. In Japan, for example, the Code of Civil Procedure (Law No. 29 of 1890) makes no provision for representation and legal assistance in an arbitration, although Article 72 of the Bengo-shi (or "Lawyers") Law (Law No. 205 of 1949) makes it a crime for a non-bengoshi to engage "in the unauthorised practice of law". Prof. Teruo Doi, Professor of Law at Waseda University considered the point fleetingly in a 1979 commentary, concluding only that it was "an open question whether a foreign party to an arbitration of international nature, which is to be held in Japan, may hire a non-Japanese attorney to represent him in the arbitration proceedings."[13] It has not been unknown, however, for local Japanese lawyers to threaten foreign counsel engaged there, with proceedings based on Article 72. The *Turner* decision must give such parties more ammunition, and, if that is so, one might surmise that similar applications would be brought in other jurisdictions.

Despite the obvious attraction the decision holds for parties interested in raising such arguments, it is suggested that *Turner* may not represent the thin end of the wedge. There remain other factors to consider before international lawyers and clients alike start scouring the local legal directories of countries chosen as potential arbitral fora. One initial practical factor is that a party wishing to obtain the necessary injunction faces in many jurisdictions a significant procedural hurdle. Generally, the party needs to show some real likelihood that its rights have been, or will be, infringed before injunctive relief will be granted. This could be difficult to establish in those cases where the act complained of is simply that the other party wishes to enlist (foreign) counsel of its choice.[14]

At the same time, the absence of many decisions on this question suggests that public authorities, responsible for taking action in the public interest, are themselves neither particularly interested in mounting a challenge nor persuaded that such action would be successful. In 1983, a director of the Ministry of Justice of Japan, for example, expressed the view that foreign lawyers *could* come into the country and handle matters on behalf of Japanese or overseas clients without breach-

---

law. Whilst this interpretation/limitation arises as a matter of logic, it does not *necessarily* follow from a reading of either the judgment or the Act itself. (*Compare* the earlier article in the 31 March 1988 edition of the same newspaper "Foreign lawyers in arbitration cases here must be admitted to bar," where no such distinction was drawn.)

13. "Japan" in IV *Yearbook Commercial Arbitration* 115 at 129, (1979). This point is also discussed by Toshio Sawada in "Practice of Arbitral Institutions in Japan," 4 *Arb Int* 120 at 125. No firm conclusion is reached.

14. The requirement of demonstrating a likelihood of infringement of rights was waived in the *Turner* case.

ing that country's laws of practice.[15] This view obviously runs counter to the threats and representations of local lawyers in the past, and may explain why the question has never come before that country's courts.[16]

The question has, moreover been judicially considered in another jurisdiction where a decision contrary to *Turner* has been rendered. The High Court of Barbados in 1983,[17] in deciding that a party was entitled to enlist foreign counsel to argue on its behalf, ruled that the Legal Profession Act (Cap 370 A) of Barbados did not derogate from the established "common law right of everyone who is *sui juris* to appoint an agent for any purpose."[18] The judgment stressed the essentially private nature of arbitration, and the right of the arbitrator to be the master of the arbitral proceedings. It referred to other local legislation under which parties could appoint "non-qualified" persons to appear on their behalf, and read the provisions of the Legal Profession Act in the light of that other legislation. Having interpreted the Act to avoid the apparent inconsistency between such legislation and the mandates of the Legal Profession Act, the Court had little difficulty in finding no intention on the part of the legislature to impinge upon the (otherwise "inconsistent") rights of parties going to arbitration.[19]

Many of these problems will not be encountered in jurisdictions where the legislature has already considered the matter. Hong Kong, for example, dealt with one aspect of this problem in its 1982 law reforms. By virtue of section 20(2A) of the Hong Kong Arbitration Ordinance (1963–1982),[20] it became possible for the first time for a winning party to recover its legal costs, notwithstanding its use of lawyers not qualified to practise there.[21] While England and Wales have no mandatory rules governing the way in which arbitrations are conducted,[22] there has been

15. *See* Hideo Chigusa, then Director of the Legal System and Research Division, "Background and Problem Points of the Foreign Lawyers Problem," *Rule of Law*, Spring 1983 issue (No. 54). (Pages 54 and 55 contain the relevant passage in English.)

16. Further evidence of a more relaxed attitude on the part of the Japanese can also be seen in that country's enactment of the "Special Measures Law Concerning the Handling of Legal Business by Foreign Lawyers," (No. 66 of 1986) pursuant to which, since March 17, 1987, foreign lawyers wishing to practise foreign law in Japan can apply for qualifications as "gaikokuho-jimu-bengoshi" ("foreign legal consultants").

17. *In the matter of an Arbitration between Lawyers: Matusky and Skelly, Engineers and the Attorney General of Barbados*, (No. 320 of 1981), August 22, 1983.

18. Section 12 of that Act provides:

"12(1) Subject to this Act, if a person whose name is not registered on the Roll—

(a) practises law,

(b) willfully pretends to be an attorney-at-law; or

(c) makes use of any name, title or description implying that he is entitled to be recognised or to act as an attorney-at-law, he is guilty of an offence and liable on summary conviction to a fine of five thousand dollars or to imprisonment for one year or both.

(2) A person who, not being entitled to act as an attorney-at-law, acts in any respect as an attorney-at-law in any action or matter or in any court in the name or through the agency of an attorney-at-law entitled so to act, is guilty of an offence and liable on summary conviction to a fine of five thousand dollars or to imprisonment for one year or to both."

19. As a corollary, the judgment also endorsed the arbitrator's ruling that the party's (foreign) counsel be assisted by a local lawyer on matters of local law.

20. Cap. 341 of the Laws of Hong Kong.

21. *See*, further, B.E.D. deSpeville, "Arbitration in Hong Kong: The Arbitration Ordinance 1963–1982." I *Arb. Int.* 109 (1985).

22. *See*, for instance, Mr. Justice Steyn's article "Arbitration in England: The Current Issues," in *International Business Lawyers* (Nov. 1987) at 432.

recent legislation reflecting the essentially different nature, not only of arbitration itself, but of *international* arbitration as a whole.[23] In addition, the view has been expressed that, in this context "[there] is no requirement to employ the English legal profession and no restriction or prohibition against overseas representation . . . in international arbitrations conducted in [that jurisdiction]."[24]

It has even been recognised there that there may be cases in which it is quite appropriate that *no* lawyers appear. It has long been accepted, in England for example, that it is not contrary to public policy to stipulate in an arbitration agreement that neither counsel nor solicitor be engaged by the parties to an arbitration, and that an arbitrator can accordingly refuse leave for the parties to be so represented.[25] Notions of Judge Chan's "protection of the public" seem far removed from this context.

If Singapore is to retain any aspirations as a major Asian centre for commercial arbitration, it must itself hope for either legislative intervention, or, perhaps more simply, reversal of the position articulated by the High Court of Singapore.[26] On an international level, it is to be hoped and expected that the *Turner* decision remains the anomaly it now appears to be. For if the laws of any venue of an international arbitration are interpreted to preclude the participation of one party's habitual legal adviser, it may not only result in severe unfairness in the particular case, as well as naturally causing that lawyer (and others) to oppose arbitration in that venue. More generally, it cannot but have a deleterious effect on unifying developments presently witnessed in international arbitration.

GOVERNMENT OF MALAYSIA v. ZUBLIN–MUHIBBAH JOINT VENTURE (GERMANY; MALAYSIA)

High Court, Kuala Lumpur, 19 June 1989.
16 Yearbk. Comm. Arb'n 166 (1991).*

* * *

FACTS

On 24 September 1981, Zublin and the Government of Malaysia entered into a contract under which Zublin was to construct three berths at Johor Port.

---

23. *Note* recent changes in the Rules of the English bar (Overseas Practice Rules, paragraph 1(d) Annex 14 to the Code of Conduct of the Bar of England and Wales, as amended by Annual Statement 1985–1986, page 65), whereby foreign attorneys gained, for the first time, the right of direct access to English barristers in "international arbitration proceedings."

24. *See* booklet "Arbitration in London," The London International Arbitration Trust Limited, at 18 (1983).

25. *Henry Bath & Son Ltd. v. Birgby Products* (1962) 1 Lloyd's Rp 389; see also Goff, "La présentation de la preuve en droit anglais," 1974 *Revue de l'arbitrage* at 123–127.

26. This will not occur in the context of the *Turner* case. An appeal lodged by the respondents was never heard as the dispute subsequently was settled.

* Reprinted with permission of Yearbook Commercial Arbitration, International Council for Commercial Arbitration.

A dispute arose between the parties and was referred to arbitration in Malaysia.

Zublin retained a Malaysian firm of advocates and solicitors to represent it in the arbitral proceedings. Counsel for Zublin required the assistance of an American attorney, Mr. Mahir Jalili, to cross-examine witnesses because of his "wide experience in international arbitration matters involving engineering contracts." Counsel for the Government of Malaysia objected to Mr. Jalili's presence on the ground that he was not an advocate and solicitor under the Malaysian Legal Profession Act 1976. The arbitrator, being a non-legal man, required the parties to sort out this objection.

On application by Zublin, the High Court of Kuala Lumpur rejected the objection to Mr. Jalili's presence in the arbitration on 19 June 1989. The Government of Malaysia filed an appeal with the Supreme Court, which dismissed the appeal without comment. The reasoning of the High Court in its decision of 19 June 1989 is reproduced herebelow.

Excerpt

Decision of the High Court, Kuala Lumpur, 19 June 1989

[1] "Having heard submissions from both parties, and Dato Peter Mooney from the Bar Council, I gave a decision on 20 April 1989 that a person representing a party in an arbitration proceeding need not be an advocate and solicitor within the meaning of the Legal Profession Act 1976; and that the said Act has no application to an arbitration proceeding in West Malaysia."

[2] "The declarations sought by [Zublin] are

(a) Foreign lawyers who are not advocates and solicitors within the meaning of the Legal Profession Act, 1976, are not prohibited by the said Act from representing parties to arbitration proceedings in West Malaysia;

(b) the said Act has no application to arbitration proceedings in West Malaysia."

[3] "The main objection by the learned [Counsel for Government] is that Mr. Jalili has not been admitted as an advocate and solicitor of the High Court Malaya and since he is an unauthorized person within the meaning of Sect. 36(1) of the Legal Profession Act 1976 (Act 166), he is precluded to act for any party under Sect. 37 of that Act, and that even if he had acted, he is precluded from recovering any costs by the provision of Sect. 40 of the Act."

[4] "As regards the question of cost in an arbitration proceedings it is to be governed by the provision of Sects. 19 to 21 of the Arbitration Act 1952 (Act 93)."

[5]   "For the purpose of this judgment it is necessary to quote here the relevant provisions of Sects. 35(1), 36(1), 37(1), and 40 of the Legal Profession Act."

"35.   *Right of Advocate and Solicitor*"

(1) Any advocate and solicitor shall, subject to this Act and any other written law, have the exclusive right to appear and plead in all Courts of Justice in Malaysia according to the law in force in those Courts; and as between themselves shall have the same rights and privileges without differentiation.

["36] *Advocate and solicitor to have name on the Roll before practice.*"

(1) Subject to this section, no person shall practise as an advocate and solicitor or do any act as an advocate and solicitor unless his name is on the Roll and he has a valid practising certificate authorising him to do the act; a person who is not so qualified is in this Act referred to as an "unauthorised person".

"37.   *No unauthorised person to act as advocate and solicitor.*"

(1) Any unauthorized person who:

(a) acts as an advocate and solicitor or an agent for any party to proceedings or in any capacity, other than as a party to an action in which he is himself a party, sues out any writ, summons or process, or commences, carries on, solicits or defends any action, suit or other proceedings in the name of any other person in any of the Courts in Malaysia or draws or prepares any instrument relating to any proceedings in any such Courts; or

(b) willfully or falsely pretends to be, or takes or uses any name, title, addition or description implying that he is duly qualified or authorized to act as an advocate and solicitor, or that he is recognised by law [as] so qualified or authorised, shall be guilty of an offence and shall on conviction be liable to a fine not exceeding two thousand five hundred ringgit or to imprisonment for a term not exceeding six months or to both.

"40.   *No cost payable to unauthorized person.*"

(1) No costs in respect of anything done by an unauthorised person as an advocate and solicitor or in respect of any act which is an offence under Sect. 37 or 39 shall be recoverable by any person in any action, suit or matter.

(2) Any payment to an unauthorised person for anything done which is an offence under Sect. 37 or 39 may be recovered in a Court of competent jurisdiction by the person who has paid the money."

[6] "An advocate and solicitor who is a qualified person under Sect. 36(1) is given exclusive right by the law to appear and plead in all Courts of Justice in Malaysia. This Sect. 36(1) does not give exclusive right to him, nor prohibit him from appearing in other tribunals which are not Courts of Justice in this country. An unauthorised person is prohibited under pain of penalty from performing any of the acts mentioned in Sect. 37 of the Act. However, Sect. 37 of the Act is specific in the sense that those acts to be performed must be done in the Courts of Malaysia, or relating to any proceedings in any Court in Malaysia.

[7] "An arbitration is not a Court of Justice in Malaysia as envisaged by the Legal Profession Act, 1976. It is a private tribunal. Subject to Sect. 12 of the Arbitration Act 1952, the arbitrator is appointed by the parties to an arbitration agreement to adjudicate on certain specific facts before him, and ultimately to settle the disputes between the contracting parties arising out of their contract. The parties who may appear before the arbitrator are those provided for by the arbitration agreement, or if the agreement does not so provide, then the provisions of Sect. 13 of the Arbitration Act shall apply. Any person who assists a party in presenting his case may also attend, e.g. a shorthand writer, an assessor, an engineer, an architect, and such parties should not be excluded without good ground when their presence are desired by a party or the award of the arbitrator may be set aside. Thus in *Haigh v. Haigh* (1861) 31 L.J. Ch. 420, where one of the parties desired to have his son present because the son was versed in the accounts of the business, and the arbitrator excluded the son and also a shorthand writer, the award was set aside."

[8] "In the case before me, [Zublin's] learned counsel desires the presence of Mr. Jalili whose engineering qualifications and experience would place him in a more advantageous position to assist [counsel] to conduct the cross-examination of technical witnesses because there are many engineering issues which arise from the pleadings. Following *Haigh v. Haigh*, Mr. Jalili who is an American Attorney and Chemical Engineer, ought not to be excluded from appearing in the arbitration proceedings. Even if Mr. Jalili might have taken actions or performed the duties which normally are done by an advocate and solicitor in this country, he had done so not in or relating to a Court in Malaysia, but only in or relating to an arbitration proceeding. His actions therefore did not offend Sect. 37 of the Legal Profession Act, 1976."

[9] "I also find that the law governing arbitration proceedings in Malaysia is the Arbitration Act 1952 (revised 1972) (Act 93) which came into force in Sarawak on 17 June 1952, and in other States on 1 November 1972, and that the Legal Profession Act 1976 has no application to arbitration proceedings in West Malaysia."

[10] "The learned [counsel for the Government] in the course of his submission also challenged this application as being improperly brought to this Court. He submitted that the arbitrator should have taken action under Sect. 22 of the Arbitration Act, which states:

"22(1) An arbitrator or umpire may, and shall if so directed by the High Court, state

(a) any question of law arising in the course of the reference; or

(b) an award or any part of an award, in the form of a special case for the decision of the High Court.

(2) A special case with respect to an interim award or with respect to a question of law arising in the course of a reference may be stated, or may be directed by the High Court to be stated, notwithstanding that proceedings under the reference are still pending.

(3) A decision of the High Court under this section shall be deemed to be a judgment of the High Court within the meaning of Sect. 67 of the Courts of Judicature Act, 1964 (which relates to the jurisdiction of the Federal Court to hear and determine appeals from any judgment of the High Court), but no appeal shall lie from the decision of the High Court on any case stated under subsection (1)(a) without the leave of the High Court or of the Federal Court."

[11] "It is to be borne in mind that the arbitrator here is a non-legally qualified person. There is nothing to stop the claimant or the respondent in the arbitration proceedings to apply to the High Court for an order directing the arbitrator to state a special case for the decision of the Court. The respondent in the arbitration proceedings should initiate that application since the respondent is the one objecting to Mr. Jalili's assisting the claimant's solicitors in that arbitration proceedings. Further, for the arbitrator to state a case under Sect. 22 of the Act, he may need the services of a solicitor to assist him to do so. I, therefore, am of the view that I should not direct the arbitrator to state a case to the High Court but to proceed with his application before me and give a decision notwithstanding that my decision may be appealed against to the Supreme Court without leave required, as would have been the case if this matter had come to me under Sect. 22(3) of the Act."

Questions and Comments

1. What rational reasons may lie behind the rules prohibiting foreign lawyers to appear before domestic courts?

Do these reasons apply to arbitration as well?

2. The *Zublin* case made it clear that foreign counsel may assist parties in arbitration in Malaysia (although he/she cannot appear before Malaysian courts). Does this mean that the winning party may recover from the losing party fees paid to the foreign counsel? To a foreign attorney? To a foreign counsel who is not a trained lawyer?

3. Is there any reason to allow foreigners to be arbitrators and to disallow at the same time foreigners to act as attorneys in the arbitration process?

4. In June 1996, the Japanese Diet passed new legislation which clarified the issue of representation by foreign counsel in arbitration proceedings.[5] According to the new amendments of the Act on Attorneys and of the Act on Special Measures for the Handling of Legal Matters by Foreign Attorneys, "non-bengoshies" are now clearly allowed to represent clients before arbitration tribunals.

5. What do you see as the relative advantages and disadvantages of hiring a foreign instead of a local attorney?

IV.1.j.   *Privacy and Confidentiality*

HASSNEH INSURANCE CO. OF ISRAEL AND OTHERS v. STUART J. MEW

Queen's Bench Division (Commercial Court), 22 December 1992.
2 Lloyd's Law Rep. 243 (1993).*

[The plaintiffs, Hassneh Insurance Co. of Israel and others, seek an injunction to restrain disclosures by the defendant, reassured Mr. Steuart J. Mew, of certain documents produced in an earlier arbitration between the plaintiffs and the defendant. The plaintiffs had reinsured the defendant under various reinsurance contracts executed between 1979 and 1984. The placing brokers were C.E. Heath and Co. (Heath). The defendant sought to recover on these reinsurance contracts, or alternatively against Heath for negligence in negotiating inadequate reinsurance contracts and for misrepresentations to the re-insurers that allowed them to avoid certain coverage. There was an arbitration clause in the reinsurance contracts, but none in the agreement between defendant and Heath. Defendant and Heath therefore agreed to a standstill of their dispute until arbitration of defendant's claim against the reinsurers had been completed.

The arbitral tribunal rendered an interim award including reasons in which the defendant was substantially unsuccessful and therefore the defendant wanted to continue its claim against Heath. For that purpose defendant wanted initially to disclose to Heath the interim award and the reasons. Defendant also contemplated wanting to disclose later in the proceedings transcripts of witness statements, pleadings, and other documents from the arbitration.

The plaintiffs were willing to have the defendant disclose to Heath the award and the reasons referred to in the award. They objected, however, to disclosure of the whole of the reasons or of any other documents produced in the arbitration. They sought an injunction to restrain such disclosure on the ground that this would be a breach of confidence by the defendant. They claimed that specific documents

---

[5]. See *Developments in Arbitration from Around the World During 1996* (prepared by the White & Case International Dispute Resolution Group) Martindale–Hubbell, International Arbitration and Dispute Resolution Directory 1997, 31, at pp. 35–36

* Reprinted by permission of Lloyd's Law Reports, LLP Limited.

should be produced only if the court so ordered at each specific request during the discovery phase of the defendant's action against Heath.

The defendant counterclaimed for permission to disclose, arguing that there was only a qualified duty of confidence in arbitration so that documents could be disclosed to a third party if to do so was reasonably necessary for protection of the defendant's own interests.]

JUDGEMENT

MR. JUSTICE COLMAN:

[This is a claim by the plaintiffs Hassneh Insurance Co. of Israel and others for an injunction to restrain disclosures by the reinsured defendant, Mr. Steuart J. Mew, and other members of Lloyd's Syndicate 342 of certain documents submitted or generated in the course of an arbitration between the plaintiffs and the defendant.]

* * *

The starting point for any consideration of this subject must be to investigate the nature and scope of the duty of confidence which applies in relation to arbitrations and the documents in them. Surprisingly, there is little authority on this point, at least in English law.

* * *

It is to be observed that Lord Justice Parker identifies an "implied obligation" as the basis for the confidentiality attaching to documents used in or engendered in the course of an arbitration. Such an obligation can exist only because it is implied in the agreement to arbitrate and like any other implied term must be capable of reasonably precise definition. The implication of the term must be based on custom or business efficacy. If the parties to an English law contract refer their disputes to arbitration they are entitled to assume at the least that the hearing will be conducted in private. That assumption arises from a practice which has been universal in London for hundreds of years and, I believe, undisputed. It is a practice which represents an important advantage of arbitration over the Courts as a means of dispute resolution. The informality attaching to a hearing held in private and the candour to which it may give rise is an essential ingredient of arbitration, so essential that if privacy were denied by an officious bystander, I have no doubt that, in the case of practically every arbitration agreement, both the parties would object.

If it be correct that there is at least an implied term in every agreement to arbitrate that the hearing shall be held in private, the requirement of privacy must in principle extend to documents which are created for the purpose of that hearing. The most obvious example is a note or transcript of the evidence. The disclosure to a third party of such documents would be almost equivalent to opening the door of the arbitration room to that third party. Similarly witness statements, being so closely related to the hearing, must be within the obligation of confidentiality. So also must outline submissions tendered to the arbitrator. If outline submissions, then so must pleadings be included.

Then one comes to a somewhat wider group of documents: those documents which are disclosed as produced by one party to another by reason of the application to the arbitrator of the English rules of discovery of documents. In the context of litigation there is an implied "undertaking" by each party not to use any document disclosed in that litigation for any purpose, save in relation to the litigation in which the document was disclosed: see *Distillers Co. (Bio-chemicals) Ltd. v. Times Newspapers Ltd.*, [1975] Q.B. 613 and *Riddick v. Thames Board Mills*, [1977] Q.B. 881. Such undertaking arises regardless of whether there is a pre-existing contract between the parties to the litigation. In as much as the parties to an English law arbitration impliedly agree to use English discovery procedure, or at least to submit to the possibility that such procedure will apply, it must by implication be their mutual obligation to accord to documents disclosed for the purposes of the arbitration the same confidentiality which would attach to those documents if they were litigating their disputes as distinct from arbitrating them. The fact that the proceedings are in private lends weight to the necessity for that implication.

Then one comes to the award itself, which in this case incorporated reasons, a practice which in English commercial arbitration is usual, if not invariable, in accordance with the provisions of the Arbitration Act, 1979. There are important distinctions between the reasoned award and the other documents which I have already considered.

First, the reasoned award, containing the arbitrator's determination of the issues between the parties which have been referred, identifies the rights and duties of the parties inter se in relation to which they have been in dispute. In so far as it awards that one party shall pay, or do something for the benefit of the other, it gives rise to an independent contractual obligation to perform the award. (*Bremer Oeltransport GmbH v. Drewry*, (1933) 45 Ll. L. Rep. 133; [1933] KB 753). In as much as it contains the arbitrator's reasons it explains how that obligation arises.

Second, the award by reason of the Arbitration Acts, 1950 and 1979 is subject to the supervisory jurisdiction of the English Courts. It can be set aside or remitted to the arbitrator, for example, for misconduct. It can be the subject of an appeal on a point of law. For these purposes the award may have to be brought into open Court and the consequence of that will usually be that its contents are reproduced in the judgment which will be public and may well be published in the law reports. If one obliterated from the law reports all those cases where a substantial part of an arbitration award had been published for all to read one would be deprived of a massive part of the development of English commercial law, particularly in the fields of carriage of goods by sea and commodity sales contracts.

Thirdly, awards can be enforced in the English Courts by the summary procedure provided for by s. 26 of the Arbitration Act 1950 or by an action on the award. If the latter course is adopted the award will be opened to the Court in open Court and may therefore, be the subject of a law report which anybody can read.

Accordingly these three factors invest an award with two characteristics not associated with the other documents. First, an award is an identification of the parties' respective rights and obligations and secondly it is at least potentially a public document for the purposes of supervision by the Courts or enforcement in them.

It follows, in my judgment, that any definition of the scope of the duty of confidence which attaches to an arbitration award—and I include the reasons—which omitted to take account of such significant characteristics would be defective. Since the duty of confidence must be based on an implied term of the agreement to arbitrate, that term must have regard to the purposes for which awards may be expected to be used in the ordinary course of commerce and in the ordinary application of English arbitration law.

I consider first the ordinary course of commerce. There are many circumstances where one party to an arbitration may require to establish against a third party that the arbitrating party is or has been under an obligation to satisfy an award. One example is where an insurer must establish his liability to the primary assured for the purpose of claiming on his reinsurers. Another in the context of the insurance market is where an assured under a professional indemnity policy has to establish that he has become liable for breach of his professional duty and needs to place before the insurer an award which has been made against him to this effect. In the quite different field of ship-chartering a head charterer may be able to make good his claim against the shipowner only by reference to an arbitration award made against the head charterer in favour of a sub-charterer. A closely analogous position might also arise as between the parties to commodity trade contracts whereby goods were sold and purchased down a line of buyers and sellers, but where there was no applicable string contract provision enabling disputes to be resolved in one arbitration between the first seller and the last buyer. In all these cases the arbitrating party may require for the purposes of establishing his legal rights against the third party to produce the award against him to that third party. The suggestion by an officious bystander of a duty of confidentiality which precluded the use of arbitration awards for the establishment by arbitrating parties of their rights against third parties, unless the leave of a Court were first obtained, would be unlikely to be enthusiastically received by the commercial community.

* * *

Implicit in all these formulations of the scope of the duty of confidence is that the bank should be able to disclose the information if to withhold it would or might prejudice the bank in the establishment or protection of its own legal rights vis-à-vis the customer or third parties.

The essence of the matter is that it might need to disclose the information either as the foundation of a defence to a claim by a third party, or as the basis for a cause of action against a third party.

In my judgment a similar qualification must be implied as a matter of business efficacy in the duty of confidence arising under an agreement to arbitrate. If it is reasonably necessary for the establishment or protection of an arbitrating party's legal rights vis-a-vis a third party, in the sense which I have described, that the award should be disclosed to that third party in order to found a defence or as the basis for a cause of action, so to disclose it would not be a breach of the duty of confidence.

Is there any justification for treating the reasons differently from the formal parts of the award? After all, the reasons may contain references to the pleadings, the submissions and the evidence, all of which material would in the ordinary way be subject to the duty of confidence. On the other hand, the bald conclusion reached by the formal award will in many cases be insufficiently explicit for the purpose of the protection of the arbitrating party's rights against the third party. It is not merely that the award may not be fully comprehensible without reference to the reasons, but that the process of reasoning leading to the arbitrator's conclusion may be the particular feature of the award which gives rise to the right against the third party. Moreover, if there were confidentiality in the reasons save where the arbitrating party could satisfy the other party or, failing that, a Court, that disclosure was reasonably necessary for the protection of its rights against a third party, that would potentially involve the parties to the arbitration in an investigation, perhaps by the Court, and perhaps at no little expense, of the claims of one of them against a third party which had nothing to do with the other party to the arbitration, merely to see whether all the reasons ought to be disclosed or only some of them. Given the prevalence of reasoned awards, the implication of such a cumbersome fetter on the exception to confidentiality would seem highly improbable. Accordingly, I conclude that the exception to the duty of confidentiality which I have held to apply by implication to arbitration awards applies equally to the reasons, if it is reasonably necessary for the protection of an arbitrating party's rights vis-a-vis a third party that the award should be disclosed to that third party, so to disclose it, including its reasons, would not be a breach of the duty of confidence. That Counsel has advised the arbitrating party of such reasonable necessity should in practice normally be conclusive of the matter.

Similarly, it is an exception to the duty of confidence that one arbitrating party may bring the award and reasons into Court for the purpose of invoking the supervisory jurisdiction of the Court over arbitration awards and for the purpose of enforcement of the award itself.

* * *

Therefore, I conclude in the present case that if, as asserted, it is reasonably necessary for the establishment by the defendant of his causes of action against Heath that he should disclose or in his pleadings quote from the arbitration award, including the reasons, of Mar. 12, 1992, he should be entitled to do so, without editing either the award or the reasons and without having to apply to the Court for leave to do so.

* * *

As I have said, the defendant does not propose in the immediate future to disclose any other arbitration documents to Heath. However, the issues of principle relating to such disclosure have had to be fully argued and, no doubt with regard to whether it is necessary for the defendant to give an undertaking not to disclose such documents without an order of the Court, I have been asked to consider the appropriate principle applicable to them. This I shall now briefly do. I refer to pleadings, witness statements, disclosed documents in the arbitration and transcripts.

It is reasonably clear that, as I have held, such documents are subject to a duty of confidence. They are merely the materials which were used to give rise to the award which defined the rights and obligations of the parties to the arbitration. Accordingly, that qualification to the duty of confidentiality based on the reasonable necessity for the protection of an arbitrating party's rights against a third party cannot be expected to apply to them. It is the final determination of rights expressed in the award which is pertinent as against third parties, not the raw materials for that determination. The relevant exception in the case of such documents is an order or leave of the Court. This is the conclusion arrived at by the Court of Appeal in *Dollin–Baker v. Merrett.*

Subject to what I have already held, the documents engendered by or in the course of an arbitration to which an obligation of confidence attaches, cannot in principle have any different status from any other documents which are the subject of a duty of confidence. Accordingly, the approach adopted to such documents by the House of Lords in *Scientific Research Council v. Nasse,* [1980] A.C. 1028 must equally apply to arbitration documents.

* * *

There is, therefore, in my judgment nothing to justify the voluntary disclosure to a third party of such arbitration documents, other than the award, in anticipation of the commencement of proceedings by or against that third party. To disclose such documents without the consent of the other arbitrating party would be a breach of the obligation of confidence. In the absence of such consent the arbitrating party should proceed to discovery in proceedings by or against the third party, list the document, if relevant, and then decline to permit inspection except upon an order by the Court. It is ordinarily not appropriate that the Court should be invited at any earlier stage to perform the task of resolving the conflicting interests of protection of confidence and disclosure. There may, however, be exceptional cases where earlier disclosure might be justified and where therefore an earlier determination of the issue would be applied.

Accordingly if it were in issue whether the defendant might now disclose such documents to Heath it would be appropriate for them to be enjoined from so doing in the absence of an undertaking not to do so prior to obtaining the plaintiffs' consent or an order for inspection under O. 24 r. 11 being made upon Heath's application in future proceedings. This is subject always to this being one of the very exceptional cases to which I have previously referred.

I have not seen the documents in question and I express no view as to their relevance or the necessity for their production in such future proceedings as the defendant may pursue.

* * * There is of course in place the ex parte injunction which will continue to protect confidentiality of all the documents in question, * * *.

* * * [I]n so far as the injunction currently applies to the whole of the reasons as well as the award the order should to that extent be discharged.

DISPOSITION: Judgment accordingly.

ESSO AUSTRALIA RESOURCES LTD. & ORS v. THE HONORABLE SIDNEY JAMES PLOWMAN (THE MINISTER FOR ENERGY AND MINERALS) & ORS

Supreme Court of Victoria, Appeal Division, 1993.
Mealey's Int'l Arb'n Rep., June 1993 (Vol. 8, Issue 6), at D1–D36.*

[The Minister for Manufacturing and Industry Development brought in the Supreme Court of Victoria an action in June, 1992 against two producers of natural gas—Esso and BHP Petroleum—and two utility companies. The Minister sought declarations concerning whether information disclosed by Esso and BHP in the course of their respective arbitrations with the two utilities was "subject to an obligation of confidence."

The court of first instance concluded that "the litigation process, arbitral or curial, is sufficiently protected by an understanding of the legal principles in terms of misuse. The Court is able to protect a party (even to an arbitration) against misuse (in the present context) not only in its supervisory role over discovery but by reason of its power to make restraining orders against misuse in an appropriate case...." *Plowman v. Esso Australia Resources Ltd. et al.*, Supreme Court of Victoria, 1992, reported in 8 Mealey, International Arbitration Report no. 1 (January 1993) H1B27, at H26. The court decided "that the law does not provide

* Mealey's International Arbitration Report. Reprinted with the permission of Lex- isNexis, a division of Reed Elsevier Inc.

that disclosure of information arising in an arbitration is restricted in the broad terms claimed on behalf of Esso/BHP."

The decision was appealed by Esso and BHP. They asked that the following declarations be made:

"That it is an implied term of each arbitration agreement that each arbitration is to be conducted in private in the sense that strangers are to be excluded from the hearing and the conduct of the arbitration.

That it is an implied term of each arbitration that GFC and SECV [the utility companies arbitrating with Esso and BHP] may not use for a purpose other than the arbitration information disclosed to them by the appellants for the purpose of the arbitration."

In a long and learned opinion, Judge Brooking remarked that:]

If I were to be persuaded to uphold any such principle of confidentiality in arbitrations as that for which the appellants contend, I should almost certainly wish to see it cut down by exceptions to cover cases of disclosure under compulsion of law, disclosure where the interests of the party require it and (unless this be regarded as excluded by the statement of the general rule or treated as an instance of the second exception just mentioned) disclosure for the purposes of legal proceedings concerning the award of the arbitration. True it is that the apparent inability of the members of the Court of Appeal in *Tournier's* case to agree on exceptions did not prevent their Lordships from accepting the banker's duty of secrecy. But one of the great obstacles to the adoption of the principle of confidentiality now put forward lies in identifying and stating the exceptions which will prove the rule, particularly that permitting disclosure where the interests of the party require it. I could not accept a general rule which was not subject to some such exception, having regard to what I believe occurs in practice and to what I believe to be "equitable". But in what terms is the exception to be expressed? If one adapts the language of Bankes, L.J. in *Tournier's* case and says, "where the interests of the party require disclosure", then what is comprehended by "interests" and what is meant by "require"? Must disclosure be necessary or is it enough that it be reasonable? These difficulties cannot be met by saying that whether a given case falls within the exception may be a question of fact and degree. I suppose most of the acts of a person in a commercial matter are motivated by what he conceives to be his interests and his view of how those interests may be served. If a major customer of a party to an arbitration has some commercial reason for wanting to know what is going on in the arbitration (not being a reason related to the standing or the position of the party) and asks the party what is going on, and threatens to withdraw his custom if the question is not answered, may the interests of the party be said to require disclosure? Is the exception confined to legitimate interests and, if so, what does "legitimate" mean?

One thing to be borne in mind is that the suggested implied term can bind only the parties to the arbitration agreement. No doubt it would be said that each party was under a duty to cause its servants and agents to keep information confidential, but a servant or agent who disclosed information to a third person would presumably commit no wrong as against the opposite party, and presumably he would not even commit a wrong towards his employer unless he had as servant received or as agent received and accepted an instruction from the employer prohibiting disclosure. Moreover, it is difficult to see how a witness who was not a party or a servant or agent of a party would commit a wrong to any person merely by virtue of the fact (without regard to the nature of the information) that he disclosed to a third person information about the arbitration. And whatever argument might be constructed with regard to what a mere witness heard in the course of the arbitration, it is very difficult to see how he could be said to commit a wrong merely by reason of the fact that he told an outsider that he had given evidence and what that evidence was. To say that proceedings before arbitrators are heard in camera (*Redfern and Hunter, Law and Practice of International Commercial Arbitration*, 2nd Ed., p. 345) is to go too far if it is meant to convey that duties arise the same as or similar to those which arise when a court of justice sits in camera.

The argument in favour of the implied term of confidentiality is essentially this: Privacy is innate in the notion of an arbitration and so it is an incident of all arbitrations not only that the hearing shall be in private but also that the parties shall keep confidential what takes place in the course of the arbitration. I accept the first conclusion—the private hearing—but not the second. The first implied term can be rested on "the custom of the country"; it can be precisely formulated; it is supported by judicial dicta uttered over many years and the opinions of text-writers; there are no practices and no judicial dicta which conflict with the term; it is an "equitable" one; and it derives support from the consideration that the room for the hearing is private in the sense that the parties provide it either directly or through their arbitrator.

The second implied term cannot be rested on "the custom of the country": I am not satisfied that it is reflected in any uniform course of conduct in Victoria or for that matter any other common law jurisdiction. Despite the long history of arbitration, this suggested term was not until very recently supported by any judicial decision or dictum of any text. The supposed term is not recognised in the United States of America. The difficulty in formulating both the general rule and the exceptions (for one cannot consider the one without the other) tells against its recognition.

To return yet again to the speech of Viscount Simonds, I am not persuaded that it is "a necessary condition" of the relation between parties who have agreed to arbitrate that confidentiality in some suitably defined sense exists. I have not arrived at "an assured certainty" about the term which the law is said to import. In a decision cited earlier, *Castlemaine Tooheys Ltd. v. Carlton & United Breweries Ltd.* (1987) 10 N.S.W.L.R. 468, the Court of Appeal of New South Wales discussed the test to be applied in determining whether a term should be implied as an incident of a particular class of contract. I am persuaded that a term that the proceedings shall be private, in the sense already indicated, is required by the nature of the agreement for arbitration but I am not persuaded that the suggested term for confidentiality is required by the nature of the contract.

What was said on the point by the Court of Appeal in the *Dolling-Baker* case was by way of obiter dictum in an extempore decision in which the matter received only brief consideration. What was there said does not persuade me that the suggested incident of arbitrations should be recognised in Victoria.

* * *

His Honour granted declarations that the utilities were not restricted from disclosing to the Minister and third parties information provided to them by Esso/BHP pursuant to their obligation under the clauses. These declarations should in my respectful opinion not in any event have been made. They were necessarily in general terms, which had no regard to the nature of the information that might be provided or the person to whom or purpose for which disclosure might be made. The reasons for decision show that His Honour accepted that information supplied pursuant to clauses 12.8 and 19.5 might be confidential in the sense that equity would, in the exercise of its exclusive jurisdiction, protect against misuse. In view of this His Honour cannot have intended that the declarations should prevent Esso/BHP from arguing that an obligation not to disclose arose in equity in relation to information supplied pursuant to the clauses. Yet the declarations as drawn may well have that effect.

* * *

[The court allowed the appeal, stayed—pending further orders—the proceedings "commenced by GFC and SEC[V] respectively against Esso/BHP for an order for the provision of details pursuant to * * * the respective sales agreements", and set aside, in part, the orders made below.]

BULGARIAN FOREIGN TRADE BANK
v. A.I. TRADE FINANCE INC.
Supreme Court of Sweden, October 27, 2000.
Mealey's Int. Arb. Court Documents–Doc. No. 05–001127–101*

The Supreme Court confirms the final judgment of the Court of Appeal.

* * *

REASONS FOR DECISION

The background to the decision is that AIT called for arbitration proceedings in relation to BUL Bank pursuant to an arbitration clause in a

* Mealey's International Arbitration Report. Reprinted with the permission of Lex-   isNexis, a division of Reed Elsevier Inc.

loan contract between Bulbank and an Austrian credit provider. Bulbank initially objected in the arbitration proceedings stating that the arbitration clause was not binding for Bulbank in relation to AIT. The arbitration panel issued a separate decision on that matter and considered in that connection that the panel was competent in the case and that the proceedings should continue regarding the substantive issue.

Sometime after the decision of the arbitration panel, the decision was published in the journal Mealey's International Arbitration Report which is published in the USA. The decision was provided to the journal by representatives of AIT.

When Bulbank noticed the publication, Bulbank wrote to the AIT and the arbitration panel and, referring to the publicizing, declared that * * * on the grounds of gross breach of contract [it] revoked the arbitration agreement with immediate effect and also requested that the arbitration panel declare the arbitration agreement invalid on this ground.

The arbitration panel dismissed the application by a separate decision and thereafter issued an arbitral award regarding the substantive issue.

Bulbank subsequently appealed against the arbitral award requesting that it should be declared invalid or alternatively be revoked.

The issue in the case now is whether Bulbank can succeed in its action on the ground that Bulbank revoked the arbitral agreement * * * [for] breach of contract and that therefore there was no valid arbitration agreement in existence when the arbitral award was issued.

* * *

A precondition for Bulbank being able to succeed with its action is that AIT as a consequence of the agreement was subject to a duty of confidentiality. It is undisputed between the parties that the arbitration agreement does not cover this issue explicitly. Nor are there any provisions concerning a duty of confidentiality in the applicable Arbitration Act of 1929. It may be added that the issue is not covered by the new Arbitration Act, which now has replaced the 1929 Act.

As support for AIT being subject to a duty of confidentiality, Bulbank has referred to Article 29 in the ECE–Rules where it is stated that "the proceedings shall be held *in camera* unless both parties request that they be held in public". * * * [According to Bulbank, even if the wording applies strictly only to the hearing, this provision should be interpreted as imposing an obligation of secrecy covering the entire arbitration proceedings, including a preliminary determination.] However, the provision as such, even when it is read in conjunction with the ECE–Rules generally, cannot lead to any other conclusion than that an oral hearing should be held *in camera* if the parties do not agree that a hearing should be public. The issue of the parties' duty of confidentiality is not expressly dealt with in the ECE–Rules, and nothing has transpired in the case that * * * [justifies interpreting the ECE–Rules to imply] a duty of confidentiality to the extent that Bulbank now claims.

Bulbank has otherwise claimed that secrecy regarding arbitration proceedings applies between the parties as a part of the arbitration agreement, in which connection secrecy follows due to general principles and the nature of the arbitration proceedings.

Information * * * concerning arbitration proceedings may relate to various circumstances, * * * [to the circumstance] that arbitration proceedings are pending (or have taken place) between certain specific parties relating to a particular dispute, contained in the arbitral award issued or a decision that has been issued during the proceedings and [to] circumstances of various kinds that arose during the process of the dispute. Bulbank has not claimed any difference between various circumstances but has claimed that the duty of confidentiality applies generally irrespective of what the information concerns.

When assessing the issue whether there is a duty of confidentiality on the grounds alleged by Bulbank, there is in principle no support for * * * [distinguishing] between various kinds of information. In this connection there is cause to mention that according to Section 6 of the Act on the Protection of Trade Secrets (1990:409), it is a rule that a person who intentionally or by carelessness discloses a business secret * * * that he has received in confidence in conjunction with a business relationship * * * shall compensate the loss that arises through his conduct. In the event that these preconditions are satisfied regarding anything that occurred in arbitration proceedings, there is thus an obligation based on statute not to disclose the information on pain of liability to pay damages * * *.

A general starting point for assessing the issue of the duty of confidentiality is that the arbitration proceedings are based on a contract. * * * This consequently means that the proceedings are of a private nature, something that is not altered because the proceedings are in certain respects governed by statute. The statutory rules are rather aimed at ensuring that arbitration proceedings have a certain status and quality and are required in order that the arbitration agreement and arbitral award should be acknowledged to have legal effect* * *.

From the private nature of the arbitration proceedings, it follows that outsiders are not entitled to attend the hearings during the proceedings or [to] have access to the written submission[s] in the dispute. There should also probably be in principle a unanimous view that arbitrators on the grounds of the assignment with which they have been entrusted must observe discretion in the arbitration proceedings; this also applies even if an arbitrator has been appointed by a Court. Counsel for a party should probably be regarded as having a similar obligation to his principal based on the assignment given. However, no conclusion can be drawn from the[s]e circumstances regarding the issue of a legally sanctioned duty of confidentiality applying * * * [to] a party, * * * [concerning which issue] completely different views are held.

One of the advantages with having a dispute considered by arbitration proceedings in comparison with judicial proceedings, and which to a great extent results in enterprises choosing arbitration proceedings, is considered to be the secrecy that is connected to arbitration proceedings. This is often expressed * * * [by saying that arbitration proceedings are shielded from public view]. A large part of the literature that Bulbank adduced refers to this aspect. However, this advantage does not mean that it is a precondition that a duty of confidentiality prevails for the parties. [The] real meaning of this, compared with judicial proceedings, is instead obviously that the proceedings are not public, i.e. that the public does not have any right * * * to attend the hearings or * * * [have] access to documents in the matter. There is no contradiction in the parties simultaneously being entitled to disclose information to outsiders concerning the arbitration proceedings.

Both parties in arbitration proceedings should in the majority of cases have an interest in the dispute and what occurs during the proceedings not becoming known to outsiders. However, this is not always the case. A party who, for example, occupies a subordinate position in relation to a strong opposing party that he considers to be * * * [acting irresponsibly] may decide to put pressure on him by publicizing. A party can also for other reasons be interested and even obliged to inform a third party about pending arbitration proceedings and about determinations issued within them.

That a party in arbitration proceedings in general is anxious to ensure that information concerning the dispute is not disclosed and assumes that the opposing party has the same approach, and also that the parties often in fact actually probably observe discretion, is however, something quite different * * * [from] there being a legal obligation to observe confidentiality on pain of sanction—* * * [i.e.] liability to pay damages—in connection with a violation of the duty of confidentiality.

It is clear that parties, who themselves resolve a dispute by negotiations or arrange an assessment in another manner than by arbitration proceedings, are not subject to a duty of confidentiality without a special undertaking. The question is then what would comprise a ground for a duty of confidentiality when a dispute is being considered in * * * arbitration proceedings. * * * [The court refers here to its previous reasoning.] That remaining is mostly the issue of whether * * * [there has] developed in the field a generally broad view that a duty of confidentiality applies for both of the parties in relation to the other party, based on the nature of the arbitration proceedings. In this connection the views that have been expressed in the *travaux preparatoires* and [by] learned writers are also of interest.

Of the investigation that has been presented in this respect it does not appear that any general view concerning a duty of confidentiality for parties * * * [prevails] in the circles mentioned. The generally prevailing view among attorneys and arbitrators appears rather to be that the duty of confidentiality does not apply without a separate agreement thereon.

The fact that such an extensive circumstance as a duty of confidentiality for a party has not been expressly governed by statutory rules, * * * even in the new Arbitration Act, comprises strong support for no such obligation existing. The Arbitration Commission has also in its report *Näringslivet tvistlösning* [Resolving Commercial Disputes] (Official Government Report–SOU 1995:65 page 186) stated that the confidential nature of arbitration proceedings rests upon a rather weak legal foundation and that a party who for some reason wishes to publicise a dispute is unimpeded in doing so.

On the other hand there are certain statements made by learned writers in support of a duty of confidentiality. In Jarvin, *Sekretess i Svenska och internationella skiljedomsförfaranden* [Secrecy in Swedish and International Arbitration Proceedings] contained in *Juridisk Tidskrift* 1996–97 page 149 ff [translator's note: a renowned Swedish legal journal], gives the impression that some secrecy applies but that it appears unclear what this would in detail mean as regards Swedish law. In Cars, *Lagen om skiljeförfarande* [The Arbitration Act] (1999) page 103, it is state[d] that it may be assumed that secrecy applies to arbitration proceedings, unless otherwise agreed between the parties, and that this means, *inter alia*, that the parties may not disclose anything concerning the proceedings * * * [to] outsiders. This is justified * * * [on the ground] that one reason for parties choosing arbitration proceedings instead of judicial proceedings is normally that arbitration proceedings are exempted from public insight, a justification which in the forgoing has not been considered sustainable. Even Heuman *Skiljemansrätt* [Arbitration Law] (1999), expresses that a party has a duty of confidentiality, in any event to some extent (page 30 ff). It is thus expressed there, *inter alia*, that it is generally expected that the arbitration proceedings are secret and also that * * * parties [w]ho enter into an arbitration agreement may be deemed to have entered into an agreement about the proceedings being confidential (page 32 f).

There is thus no clear and well founded view by learned writers and the *travaux preparatoires* concerning a duty of confidentiality for the parties.

As regards foreign law, the investigation to which the Supreme Court has had access does not allow any other secure conclusion than that there exist * * * [in] some countries various principles on the matter. In English law the general opinion appears to be that parties have a duty of confidentiality (see for example Ali Shipping corp. v. Shipyard Trogir [1998] 2 All E.R. 136). One determination in 1986 of a French Court of Appeal (G.Aïta c. A. Ojjeh, reviewed in *Revue de l'Arbitrage* 1986, No 4, p. 584), appears to rest upon a duty of confidentiality in principle based on the nature of the arbitration proceedings. However, in one noticeable case observed from 1995 (Esso Australia Resources Ltd v. Plowman, 183 C.L.R. 10), the High Court of Australia adopted a contrary position. * * * [It] follows that there is no clear position in other countries * * *.

Against the background of that stated, the Supreme Court considers that a party in arbitration proceedings cannot be deemed to be bound by a duty of confidentiality, unless the parties have concluded an agreement concerning this.

It consequently follows that AIT has not committed a breach of contract by allowing the publication of the decision that the arbitration panel issued during the proceedings. Therefore, Bulbank did not have grounds for revoking the arbitration agreement and Bulbank's application for a declaration of invalidity of the arbitral award can therefore not be granted.

Questions and Comments

1.   According to Article 25(4) of the UNCITRAL Rules, hearings shall be held **in camera** unless the parties agree otherwise.

Do you agree that the presumption should be in favor of a closed hearing?

2.   Who is (or who should be) bound by confidentiality: the parties? arbitrators? witnesses? experts? recording secretaries? employees of the arbitral institutions?

3.   What (if anything) should be the object of confidentiality: the award? written submissions of the parties? testimony of witnesses and experts?

Judge Colman in *Hassneh v. Mew* took a position on these issues. Do you agree with his conclusions?

4.   The International Bar Association's Rules of Ethics for International Arbitrators, reproduced above in Chapter III.1 at pp. 301–305, provides in Rule 9 on Confidentiality of the Deliberations:

> The deliberations of the arbitral tribunal, and the contents of the award itself, remain confidential in perpetuity unless the parties release the arbitrators from this obligation. An arbitrator should not participate in, or give any information for the purpose of assistance in, any proceedings to consider the award unless, exceptionally, he considers it his duty to disclose any material misconduct or fraud on the part of his fellow arbitrators.

Suppose an award is rendered without a statement of reasons, as provided for in the arbitration agreement. Suppose further that the losing party had claimed a defense under the U.S. antitrust law and as a part of its opposition to enforcement of the award in the U.S. wants the presiding arbitrator of the arbitral tribunal to testify that the tribunal did not consider the U.S. antitrust law applicable. Should the tribunal chair be allowed to testify, over the objection of the winning party? Should the losing party be allowed to compel the presiding arbitrator's testimony? (Note that Canon VI of the AAA/ABA Code of Ethics for Arbitrators provides: "After an arbitration award has been made, it is not proper for an arbitrator to assist in any post-arbitration proceedings, except as may be required by law." Supra, Chapter III.1 at page 297.)

5.   In another English Case (Ali Shipping Corporation v. Shipyard Trogir, decided on December 17, 1997 by the Court of Appeal, Civil Division),[6] the issue before the Court of Appeal was whether the defendants, Shipyard Trogir (the Yard), should be restrained from submitting in arbitra-

---

[6].   [1998] 1 Lloyd's Rep. 643.

tions against three Liberian companies certain materials generated in the course of an earlier arbitration between the plaintiffs (Ali) and the defendants (the Yard). Both the current and the previous arbitrations involved shipbuilding contracts for shipowning companies (Ali and the Liberian companies) that were linked through common beneficial ownership. In the first arbitration the arbitrator was satisfied that the Liberian companies were in breach of contract by failing to make certain payments. Rejecting the Yard's attempt to pierce the corporate veil, however, he would not allow the Yard to set off against Ali the valid claims the Yard had against the Liberian companies.

In the instant litigation, the Yard argued that it would be convenient, efficient and reasonable to allow some of the evidence from the previous arbitration to be used in the current arbitration, especially because Ali and the Liberian companies were linked by common beneficial ownership. The Yard also argued that disclosure of the materials from the first arbitration was necessary, because the Liberian companies might seek to dismiss the Yard's claim on the ground that the Yard's delay in prosecution (presumably to await the outcome of the first arbitration) had prejudiced their defense— that is, because witnesses' memories would be diminished. Finally, the Yard argued that the Liberian companies would in all probability rely on the same witnesses who testified in the first case, and that inconsistent testimony should not be allowed. The court ruled against the Yard, holding that the Yard should be restrained from using the materials from the previous arbitration, subject to certain qualifications. Excerpts from the opinion follow.

> Are there good reasons why * * * [the principle of confidentiality] should not apply or, put another way, should a further exception be created to the confidentiality rule, simply because the parties to whom disclosure is contemplated are in the same beneficial ownership and management as the complaining party? I do not think so. I say that for two particular reasons. First, whatever the position in this case, it is possible to envisage a situation where, despite the feature of common beneficial ownership between them, one entity may wish to keep private from another the details of materials generated in an earlier arbitration. Second, where the problem arises in relation to disclosure in later proceedings, to propound such an exception is to leave out of account that (as appears to be the position in this case) the real interest of the objecting party is to withhold disclosure of such materials from the subsequent decision maker. In this context the latter is the "third party stranger" in respect of disclosure to whom the objecting party seeks protection. While such motives may not be "worthy" in the broad sense, and certainly do not assist the course of justice, they may yet be a permissible tactic in advancing or protecting the interests of the objecting party. The fact that the arbitrator in the subsequent proceedings will in turn be bound by duties of confidentiality is no cure for the damage which the objecting party perceives may be caused to his interests from an adverse decision resulting from, or influenced by, the disclosure sought to be made. * * *

* * *

* * * [T]he materials sought to be relied on were generated in the course of an arbitration with a third party who is unwilling to waive confidentiality. That being so, the ability of the Yard to make use of those materials must be governed by the principle of confidentiality already discussed. That principle seems to me to preclude disclosure of the transcripts, at least at this stage of the proceedings.

* * *

[Elaborating on the proviso just stated, the opinion continued.]

* * * [T]he Yard may well be justified in disclosing and relying upon their evidence in the First Arbitration, in order to rebut any suggestion of evidential prejudice by reason of delay. If it were asserted that the memory of witnesses had dimmed, the quality, nature and substance of their evidence upon the issues raised in the Hull 202–204 Arbitrations would be highly relevant. In those circumstances therefore, it seems to me that the Yard would be likely to succeed in establishing that disclosure was reasonably necessary in protection of its litigation interests.

Turning briefly to the Yard's * * * [further arguments]. If it appears that * * * [the Liberian companies] will be seeking to rely upon evidence which is significantly at odds or inconsistent with the evidence of witnesses in the First Arbitration, then it would indeed be contrary to the interests of justice to allow Ali to seek to suppress that earlier evidence. However, that is not a position which has been reached or, in my view, ought to be assumed at this stage. Finally, for the reasons already stated, I do not think it right to say that Ali has no "legitimate interest" in seeking to restrain the disclosure * * *. While, in broad terms, the position of Ali appears to be more tactical than meritorious, it is based upon an assertion of principle which, in my view, entitles Ali to relief.

Is this postponement of a possible lifting of the duty to observe confidentiality consistent with purposeful arbitration proceedings and preserving arbitration as a fair and efficient dispute settlement process?

6. The *Esso v. Plowman* case failed to endorse the concept of an **implied term** of the arbitration agreement obliging the parties not to reveal outside the arbitration process information disclosed during arbitration. Suppose the arbitration agreement contains an explicit undertaking to the effect that the parties will hold in confidence what transpires in the arbitration proceedings. Could such an undertaking validly restrict the maneuvering room of the parties even in court proceedings concerning setting aside or recognition and enforcement of a given award?

7. Suppose that in a country like England (which adheres to the concept of an implied term on confidentiality) a party to an earlier arbitration submits as evidence in a later arbitration proceeding both the full award and the minutes of the oral hearing in the first proceeding, including the testimony of witnesses. The other party objects, but the arbitrators choose to disregard this objection. What recourse is available to the aggrieved party?

8. The two English cases as well as the Australian case deal with confidentiality in the context of subsequent proceedings. In the *Bulbank* case

the issue arose as to whether publication of the award constituted a breach of the duty of confidentiality, and if it did, what consequences should follow. The Australian courts (the Supreme Court of Victoria, and the High Court of Australia confirming the decision of the Supreme Court of Victoria) had ruled against the proposition of an implied term (providing for confidentiality), and the Swedish Supreme Court reached the same conclusion. In the words of H. Bagner, a Swedish commentator, *"The myth about the duty of confidentiality in arbitration, fatally wounded in 1995 by the Australian High Court, has now been laid to rest, at least in Sweden."* (Bagner, Confidentiality—A Fundamental Principle in International Commercial Arbitration? 18 Journal of International Arbitration /2001/ 243, at 248.)

Do you have sympathies for the wounded (and now deceased) confidentiality? (What we are talking about is, of course, only confidentiality on the ground of "an implied term", and not every country has made its position clear.)

Note that the *Bulbank* award dealt only with jurisdiction, and thus—at least in principle—was less likely to reveal sensitive information. Do you think that this circumstance had (or should have had) an impact?

9. Suppose the Swedish Court had held that there **was** an implied commitment not to publish the award. Would the breach of this commitment constitute a breach of the arbitration agreement, and if it would, what consequences would follow? Nullity of the award? Article 34 of the Model Law states grounds for annulment that are incorporated in many arbitration statutes worldwide. Which of these grounds (if any) could be brought into play if an award is published in breach of confidentiality?

10. Suppose an explicit party agreement on confidentiality prohibits publication of the award. Should an infringement of this prohibition give rise to annulment? What if publication is caused by the arbitral tribunal itself, rather than by one of the parties?

11. If annulment is not the correct remedy, what remedy is there?

12. A specific provision on confidentiality regarding publication of the award is contained in the 2001 Rules of the Arbitration Court at the Hungarian Chamber of Commerce. According to Article 15:

"(1) The Arbitration Court may not give any information on its decisions or their contents.

(2) The decision of the Arbitration Court may be published in legal journals or special publications only upon the permission of the President of the Arbitration Court and only in such a way that the interests of the parties will suffer no harm; furthermore, the names of the parties, their countries of residence, the nature and counter-value of the services rendered, or any one of these particulars can only be included in a publication with the express consent of both parties."

Is this a good solution? And again, what happens if a party publishes an award without following the Article 15 guidelines?

IV.1.k. Time Limits for Accomplishing the Mission of the Arbitrators

M. Tod, INTERNATIONAL ARBITRATION AMONGST THE GREEKS

310–12 (1913).*

The court, constituted in the way we have described, set about the fulfilment of its task as speedily as possible. The Magnesian arbitrators in their report pride themselves upon the promptness of their decision: no sooner had they been elected judges than "straightaway ... we heard the statements of the contending parties." The alacrity of this beginning was matched by the extraordinary rapidity with which the case was heard. "We gave them", the report continues, "not only the available time of the day, but also the greater part of the night." So it would seem that this complicated and important suit was disposed of within twenty-four hours! It must be remembered, however, that this was the second occasion within a very few years on which the Magnesians were appointed as arbitrators in this dispute, so that at least the outlines of the case were probably already well known to most, if not to all, of the judges, and also that the representatives of the two contending states had already reached Magnesia, and brought with them all the witnesses and documents to which they intended to appeal. Moreover, the precise question to be decided was formulated in a Roman SC.; the arbitrators were asked to settle a point not of law but of fact, and were instructed to give their award in favour of that state which had been in possession of the land and the island in dispute on the eve of the Cretan war which had led to the dispatch of Servius Sulpicius Galba and his fellow legati to Crete. Thus the task of the Magnesians was greatly simplified, and it is possible that their award, although so rapidly reached, was neither hasty nor ill-considered.

But such promptitude is quite exceptional. Ordinarily time had to be allowed sufficient for the collection of the evidence, for a visit of the tribunal to the territory in dispute, if that was thought advisable, and for the proper preparation of the case. Sometimes the actual hearing occupied several days, as we learn from a Magnesian decree passed in honour of the Mylasian judges who gave an award in favour of Magnesia after devoting several days to hearing the evidence. The possibility of a long delay is suggested by phrases which appear in several arbitration decrees or treaties. Thus the agreement under which Maco of Larisa is requested to act as arbitrator fixes the month in which the inquiry is to take place, and similarly the Roman praetor, in directing the Mylasians to hear a case for the Senate, determines the date on which the trial is to commence and that on which the verdict must be given. Again, the arbitration-treaty between Lates and Olus contains the stipulation that judgement shall be given within ten months, while the second treaty at

* Marcus Niebuhr Tod, M.A., International Arbitration Amongst the Greeks 1913.   Reprinted by permission of Oxford University Press.

first allows only six months, but subsequently extends the time by another twelve months. Indeed, it must sometimes have been the case that no limit was prescribed to the period within which the award must be given. The pseudo-Plutarch explains the proverbial saying "Bunas judges" by the story that Bunas was an Athenian arbitrator who, knowing that the states which appealed to him had pledged themselves to suspend hostilities until his verdict should be pronounced, kept on postponing the delivery of his award until he died,—a tale which, though it may lack historical warrant, is at least suggestive. The court was doubtless usually free to determine when and how to go to work, though sometimes it received instructions regarding these points, embodied in a decree of the state which it represented. An example of such a decree has survived, regulating the conduct of the suit brought by Cos against Calymna, and, as it prescribes the exact day on which the depositions of those witnesses who cannot be present are to be taken and the time within which these must be sent to Cnidus, there can be little doubt that the initial portion of the decree, now lost, contained a clause enacting that the trial should begin on a stated day.

* * *

ENGLAND

ARBITRATION ACT 1996[f]

* * *

50.C(1) Where the time for making an award is limited by or in pursuance of the arbitration agreement, then, unless otherwise agreed by the parties, the court may in accordance with the following provisions by order extend that time.

(2) An application for an order under this section may be made—

(a) by the tribunal (upon notice to the parties), or

(b) by any party to the proceedings (upon notice to the tribunal and the other parties), but only after exhausting any available arbitral process for obtaining an extension of time.

(3) The court shall only make an order if satisfied that a substantial injustice would otherwise be done.

(4) The court may extend the time for such period and on such terms as it thinks fit, and may do so whether or not the time previously fixed (by or under the agreement or by a previous order) has expired.

(5) The leave of the court is required for any appeal from a decision of the court under this section.

* * *

f. I.L.M. 155, 176 (1997).

PERU

DECREE LAW NO. 25935[g]

(in force 10 December 1992).

* * *

Award

Article 42

Unless otherwise provided in the agreement or in the rules for the proceedings, the award must be issued within a term of twenty business days after the stage of presentation of proof has been completed, or once the steps referred to in Article 28 item (2), have been completed, if there are no facts to be proven.

* * *

ROMANIA
BOOK IV, CODE OF CIVIL PROCEDURE, ARTS. 340–370 ON ARBITRATION

(as amended by Law No. 59 of 23 July 1993).

* * *

Article 353

If not otherwise provided by the parties, the arbitral tribunal shall make its award within not more than five months after the date of its constitution.

The terms shall be suspended for the period during which a challenge petition or any other incident petition submitted to the court specified in Article 342 is being decided.

The parties may consent in writing to an extension of the arbitration term.

Likewise, the arbitral tribunal may, for good reasons, provide for an extension of the term by two months at the most.

The term shall be extended *de facto* by two months in the case provided under Article 360, as well as in the case of the death of one of the parties.

The passage of the term provided under the present article may not constitute a ground for the termination of the arbitration, except in the case in which one of the parties has informed the other party and the arbitral tribunal up to the first term of appearance before the first hearing of its intention to invoke the termination.

* * *

g. I.L.M. 155, 176 (1997).

THAILAND

ARBITRATION ACT

BE 2530 (1987).

* * *

Section 21

The award must be rendered within a period of 180 days from the date of the rightful appointment of the last arbitrator or umpire, unless otherwise agreed by the parties.

The time limit of 180 days or the time limit agreed on by the parties pursuant to paragraph 1 may be extended subject to the mutual consent of all parties. If the parties are unable to agree on the extension, any party, arbitrator or the umpire may apply to the competent court which is empowered to extend the time limit as appropriate.

The parties are not allowed to raise the arbitrator's or umpire's failure to render an award within the time limit under paragraphs 1 and 2 as a ground to challenge the enforceability of the award, unless the challenge is made in writing to the arbitrator or umpire within fifteen days of the expiration of the time limit and before a copy of the award is delivered to each respective party.

After the award has been made, the arbitrator or umpire shall have a copy of the award delivered to all parties involved in the dispute.

* * *

RULES OF THE ICC INTERNATIONAL
COURT OF ARBITRATION

(in force from 1 January 1998).

* * *

Article 24

Time-limit for the Award

1.   The time-limit within which the Arbitral Tribunal must render its final award is six months. Such time-limit shall start to run from the date of the last signature by the Arbitral Tribunal or of the parties of the Terms of Reference, or, in the case of application of Article 18(3), the date of the notification to the Arbitral Tribunal by the Secretariat of the approval of the Terms of Reference by the Court.

2.   The Court may extend this time-limit, pursuant to a reasoned request from the Arbitral Tribunal or on its own initiative, if it decides it is necessary to do so.

* * *

Questions and Comments

1. A glimpse into Ancient Greece shows that some things never really change. There are still arbitrators, who (like those from Magnesia) work day and night; others take their time. Of course, cases are different; some need more time, others can (or could) yield an award sooner. Some parties endeavor to set time limits for the rendering of the award. The second treaty between Latos and Olus set 6 months, the same time limit as the one set by the 1998 ICC Rules.

As the Bunas legend shows, in given circumstances, not speed, but protraction may be a virtue. (Assuming, of course, that litigants are civil enough to suspend all hostilities while the arbitrators are pondering their dispute.)

A modern Bunas is not likely to be remembered, however, as a hero in the field of international commercial arbitration.

2. In Dubois et Vanderwalle v. Boots Frites BV[7] the Paris Cour d'appel decided upon recognition of a Dutch award. The party opposing recognition claimed, inter alia, that the award was not rendered within the time limit set by the parties. The arbitration agreement contained the following provision: "The tribunal shall have to render the award within a period of three months from the date of its constitution." It was common ground that the award was rendered a few weeks after this deadline had passed.

Boots Frites, the party requesting recognition, argued that this provision was a mere instruction and that Dutch law—which was the *lex arbitri*—allows the arbitrators to determine themselves when the award would be rendered.[8]

The Paris court held that the observance of a time limit set by the parties themselves was a matter of public policy (*ordre public international*). Given the contractual nature of arbitration, such a provision of the parties' agreement cannot be changed by the arbitrators. Recognition and enforcement were denied.

Do you agree with the result?

Does party agreement take precedence over the rule established by the *lex arbitri*?

3. What can Boots Frites do now that recognition has been denied?

Can they re-start arbitration?

4. Suppose the *lex arbitri* is the present (1996) English Arbitration Act. Could Boots Frites prevail?

5. Article 25(3) of the 1998 ICC Rules (like Article 22 of the 1988 Rules) states that "*The award shall be deemed to be made at the place of the arbitration and on the date stated therein.*" Suppose the arbitrators actually

---

[7]. Decision of the Paris Cour d'appel of September 22, 1995, Reported in 1996 Revue de l'arbitrage 100.

[8]. According to Article 1048 of the Dutch Act:

"*The arbitral tribunal is free to determine the time when the award shall be made.*"

rendered the award beyond the time limit, and backdated the award. The party opposing recognition insists on the actual date; the party seeking recognition argues that by accepting the ICC Rules, the parties implicitly agreed not to contest the date stated by the arbitrators. What result?

Article 31 of the Model Law, after stressing that *"The award shall state its date and the place of arbitration,"* goes on to state that *"The award shall be deemed to have been made at that place,"* but does not say that the award shall be deemed to have been made on the date indicated in the award. Would you reach under Article 31 the same result as under Article 25(3) of the ICC Rules?

6.   The Peruvian statute sets a relatively short deadline that begins to run from the moment the presentation of proof is completed. The Romanian and the Thai rules pose a more generous deadline that runs from the date of the constitution of the tribunal.

Which approach do you prefer?

7.   The English, Romanian, and Thai statutes have endeavored to make the time limits less rigid by giving some opportunities to extend (or to disregard) the deadline. Please identify and evaluate these opportunities.

8.   Finally, if you were a party in arbitration proceedings, would you feel better (and safer) having a time limit set for the award?

IV.2.   THE AWARD

IV.2.a.   *Form and Content of the Award*

IV.2.a.i.   *Statutory and Institutional Rules*

Howard M. Holtzmann & Joseph E. Neuhaus, A GUIDE TO THE UNCITRAL MODEL LAW ON INTERNATIONAL COMMERCIAL ARBITRATION: LEGISLATIVE HISTORY AND COMMENTARY

836–39 (1989).*

* * *

ARTICLE 31. FORM AND CONTENTS OF AWARD

(1) The award shall be made in writing and shall be signed by the arbitrator or arbitrators. In arbitral proceedings with more than one arbitrator, the signatures of the majority of all members of the arbitral tribunal shall suffice, provided that the reason for any omitted signature is stated.

(2) The award shall state the reasons upon which it is based, unless the parties have agreed that no reasons are to be given or the award is an award on agreed terms under article 30.

(3) The award shall state its date and the place of arbitration as determined in accordance with article 20(1). The award shall be deemed to have been made at that place.

* Reprinted with permission from Kluwer Law International.

(4) After the award is made, a copy signed by the arbitrators in accordance with paragraph (1) of this article shall be delivered to each party.

COMMENTARY

Article 31 establishes the minimum formal requirements for all awards issued under the Model Law. Most of these standards—such as the requirement that the award be in writing, that it be signed, that it state the place and date of making, and that it be delivered to the parties—were relatively noncontroversial. In addition, the Working Group agreed early that, like the New York Convention, the Model Law should not require that the parties deposit the award with any government or other registry in order to make it binding.[1] There was some difference of opinion, however, on other points, in particular, whether the arbitrators should be permitted to sign the award at a date and place other than that stated in the award, whether dissenting opinions should be permitted, and whether the Model Law should state the precise point when an award becomes binding. On the last point the disagreement prevented the inclusion of any provision whatsoever. All of these matters are discussed in the commentary that follows.[2]

Paragraph 1. Both the requirement that an award be in writing and that it be signed were considered "obvious" by the Secretariat and, it appears, by the Working Group. There was also little disagreement over the method of dealing with cases in which not all arbitrators signed an award. This might happen, for example, if an arbitrator died, became incapacitated, or refused to sign the award. The Working Group adopted the solution found in Article 32(4) of the UNCITRAL Arbitration Rules and in a number of national laws, pursuant to which a majority of the arbitrators is required to sign the award and the reasons for the missing signature must be stated. This corresponds with the rule in Article 29 that decisions be made by a majority of the arbitrators. Unlike Article 29, however, the signature requirement apparently is not waivable: it does not provide that the parties may agree otherwise. The Secretariat suggested that the signature requirement of Article 31 be fully aligned with Article 29 and made nonmandatory, but the Commission did not act on the suggestion.[5]

1. *See* First Working Group Report. A/CN.9216. para. 101. p. 848 *infra*. The question of a requirement that awards be deposited is discussed further below under the heading "Paragraph 4."

2. The question of the date and place of making the award is discussed under the heading "Paragraph 3"; the question of the rights of dissenting arbitrators is discussed under the heading "Paragraph 1"; the question of when the award becomes binding is discussed under the heading "Paragraph 4."

The Working Group and the Commission considered—but did not adopt—a definition of the term "award." These materials appear in the section on Article 2, *supra*.

5. *See* Seventh Secretariat Note, A/CN.9/264, para. 1, n. 83, p. 855 *infra; see also* Sixth Secretariat Note (Government Comments), A/CN.9/263/Add.1, Art. 29, para. 3, pp. 817–18 *supra* (suggesting that Article 31 requires majority to sign award even if the parties have agreed under Article 29 that the presiding arbitrator is to make the decision). It may be argued that Article 31 is nonmandatory even though it

One further point that was raised in connection with the requirement that an award be in writing was whether the Model Law should address the rights of dissenting arbitrators to have the arbitral tribunal issue dissenting opinions. In their comments on the Working Group's final draft of Article 31, two delegations addressed the question, reflecting very different national traditions on the question: the Norwegian delegation urged that the Law state explicitly that a dissenting arbitrator is entitled to state the reasons for his dissent; the delegation of the Sudan proposed that it state that the award could not include any "dissenting judgement." The Secretariat suggested that the Commission take up the question of whether dissenting opinions would be permitted; the Secretariat added that under the Working Group's final draft—which is the same as the final text on this point—the question would presumably be governed by Article 19, which regulates the conduct of the arbitral proceedings.[8] The Commission did not address the question.

Paragraph 2. The arguments for and against requiring awards to state the reasons upon which they were based were summarized by the Working Group in its first report on the Model Law. In favor of the requirement it was noted that many national arbitration laws required reasons and that this requirement was thought to improve the quality of the arbitral decision. Against the requirement it was suggested that awards that did not state reasons could be issued more speedily and were less subject to challenge, and that certain kinds of arbitrations, such as those to determine whether the quality of goods met industry or contractual standards, were generally conducted without giving reasons. The Working Group decided to adopt the solution contained in Article 32(3) of the UNCITRAL Arbitration Rules, which is to require reasons but to permit the parties to waive the requirement. Both the Working Group, and the Secretariat in its commentary on the final draft of the Law, emphasized that the parties' waiver did not have to be explicit, but could be inferred from the fact that the type of arbitration envisioned does not usually result in an award with reasons.[10]

Paragraph 3. The debate on the third paragraph of Article 31 reveals two somewhat conflicting principles. On the one hand, it was recognized at the outset that the award would have to state the place at

does not state that the parties may agree otherwise. In connection with the drafting of a proposed Article that would have listed the mandatory provisions of the Law, the Working Group cautioned that the fact that some Articles were stated to be nonmandatory did not mean that all other Articles were necessarily intended to be mandatory. *See* Fifth Working Group Report, A/CN.9/246, para. 177, appearing in the section on Matters Not Addressed in the Final Text, pp. 1152–53 *infra.*

8. Seventh Secretariat Note, A/CN.9/264, Art. 31, para. 2, pp. 855B56 *infra.* The Secretariat's discussion was presumably limited to the question of whether

a dissenting opinion will be issued by the arbitral tribunal. It is submitted that the Model Law does not address the quite different question of whether a dissenting arbitrator might issue his or her dissenting opinion separately if the arbitral tribunal does not issue it.

10. *See id.;* Seventh Secretariat Note, A/CN.9/264, Art. 31, para. 3, p. 856 *infra.* The Secretariat noted that the same could be said of a submission to arbitration that contemplated that the statement of reasons would be contained in a separate, confidential document. *Id.*

which it was made because that would determine the law under which the award could be set aside and under which it would be judged for certain purposes in enforcement proceedings. On the other hand, it was repeatedly noted that, particularly in international arbitrations, the arbitrators often found it inconvenient to perform the physical task of signing the award in the country whose law was intended to govern it. They might, for example, reside in other countries or, by the time the award was ready for signing, be engaged in business elsewhere. The First Draft of Article 31 thus provided, on the one hand, that the award had to be made at the place of arbitration, but, on the other hand, included as a suggested alternative a provision that the award would be *deemed* to be made at the place stated therein. The Working Group was somewhat torn between these two approaches at its next session. There was some reluctance to "imply that the arbitral tribunal ha[d] a right to state a fictitious place of making the award," but it was nevertheless agreed that as a basis for further discussions the draft Article would provide that the award would be deemed to be made at the place of arbitration stated therein.

The discussion continued at the next session at which the Article was discussed, and this "deeming" approach ultimately prevailed. As the proponents of this view argued, "[T]he making of the award was a legal act which in practice was not necessarily one factual act but, for example, done in deliberations at various places, by telephone conversation or correspondence." The provision remained unchanged in subsequent deliberations. It is thus clear that while the award must state the place of arbitration[16] and that place should be treated as the place of making for all purposes, the actual deliberations, agreement, and signing may take place elsewhere.

Paragraph 3 does not, however, apply the same presumption to the *date* of making. The initial drafts of the provision did provide that the award would be deemed made at the place and date stated therein, but the reference to the date was deleted by the Working Group without explanation in the Reports. The omission was raised during the Commission's deliberations, but the Commission decided to retain the text as drafted. The reason for applying an irrebuttable presumption to the place of making the award but not to the date is nowhere completely stated, but the legislative history does point to a basic difference between the significance of the place and that of the date of the award. Since it was widely agreed that the arbitral proceedings may take place elsewhere than at the place of arbitration, the actual place at which the award was signed is essentially irrelevant. In other words, the signifi-

---

16. The Working Group stated at the outset that the award should not be declared invalid for failure to comply with this requirement. First Working Group Report, A/CN.9/216, para. 79, pp. 847–48 *infra*. To implement this proposal, the Secretariat drafted a provision that if the place where the award had been made was not stated, the award would be deemed to have been made at the place of arbitration. First Draft, A/CN.9/WG.II/WP.38, Art. 27(2) & n. 9, p. 849 *infra*. This provision was not specifically discussed later and was not included in subsequent drafts or the final text of Article 31.

cance of the place stated in the award is purely legal—it identifies the procedural law governing the arbitration—so the stated place may appropriately be made a legal fiction. The date of making an award, on the other hand, should not be divorced from the actual date the award was made, because in certain cases—such as when new evidence is discovered or when the arbitrators fail to meet a time limit set for the rendering of the award—it might be important to show that the award was not in fact made on the date stated in the award, but at an earlier or later date.[20]

THE NETHERLANDS

ARBITRATION ACT

(1 December 1986).

CODE OF CIVIL PROCEDURE
BOOK FOUR: ARBITRATION

* * *

Article 1057—majority decision; refusal of minority to sign: form and contents of award

1. Unless the parties have agreed otherwise, if the arbitral tribunal is composed of more than one arbitrator, it shall decide by a majority of votes.

2. The award shall be in writing and signed by the arbitrator or arbitrators.

3. If a minority of the arbitrators refuses to sign, the other arbitrators shall make mention thereof beneath the award signed by them. This statement shall be signed by them. A similar statement shall be made if a minority is incapable of signing and it is unlikely that this impediment will cease to exist within a reasonable time.

4. In addition to the decision, the award shall contain in any case:

(a) the names and addresses of the arbitrator or arbitrators;

(b) the names and addresses of the parties;

(c) the date on which the award is made;

(d) the place where the award is made;

(e) the reasons for the decision, unless the award concerns merely the determination only of the quality or condition of goods as

---

20. This distinction is suggested by several comments recorded in the Summary Record, *see* Summary Record, A/CN.9/SR.328, paras, 32, 39, pp. 857–58 *infra*; and by the Commission Report's somewhat cryptic discussion of the question: "The former [the presumption regarding the place stated in the award] is an irrebuttable presumption to assure the territorial link between the award and the place of arbitration. The latter [regarding the date stated in the award] must be rebuttable, since the arbitrations, as well as the parties, might have reasons for stating the date of the award to be earlier or later than the date it was actually rendered," A/40/17, para. 254, p. 864 *infra*.

provided in article 1020(4)(a) or the recording of a settlement as provided in article 1069.

* * *

UNCITRAL ARBITRATION RULES

* * *

Form and Effect of the Award

Article 32

1. In addition to making a final award, the arbitral tribunal shall be entitled to make interim, interlocutory, or partial awards.

2. The award shall be made in writing and shall be final and binding on the parties. The parties undertake to carry out the award without delay.

3. The arbitral tribunal shall state the reasons upon which the award is based, unless the parties have agreed that no reasons are to be given.

4. An award shall be signed by the arbitrators and it shall contain the date on which and the place where the award was made. Where there are three arbitrators and one of them fails to sign, the award shall state the reason for the absence of the signature.

5. The award may be made public only with the consent of both parties.

6. Copies of the award signed by the arbitrators shall be communicated to the parties by the arbitral tribunal.

7. If the arbitration law of the country where the award is made requires that the award be filed or registered by the arbitral tribunal, the tribunal shall comply with this requirement within the period of time required by law.

* * *

Settlement or Other Grounds For Termination

Article 34

1. If, before the award is made, the parties agree on a settlement of the dispute, the arbitral tribunal shall either issue an order for the termination of the arbitral proceedings or, if requested by both parties and accepted by the tribunal, record the settlement in the form of an arbitral award on agreed terms. The arbitral tribunal is not obliged to give reasons for such an award.

2. If, before the award is made, the continuation of the arbitral proceedings becomes unnecessary or impossible for any reason not mentioned in paragraph 1, the arbitral tribunal shall inform the parties of its intention to issue an order for the termination of the proceedings.

The arbitral tribunal shall have the power to issue such an order unless a party raises justifiable grounds for objection.

3. Copies of the order for termination of the arbitral proceedings or of the arbitral award on agreed terms, signed by the arbitrators, shall be communicated by the arbitral tribunal to the parties. Where an arbitral award on agreed terms is made, the provisions of article 32, paragraphs 2 and 4 to 7, shall apply.

* * *

AMERICAN ARBITRATION ASSOCIATION INTERNATIONAL ARBITRATION RULES

(As amended and effective on November 1, 2001).

* * *

Form and Effect of the Award

Article 27

1. Awards shall be made in writing, promptly by the tribunal, and shall be final and binding on the parties. The parties undertake to carry out any such award without delay.

2. The tribunal shall state the reasons upon which the award is based, unless the parties have agreed that no reasons need be given.

3. The award shall contain the date and the place where the award was made, which shall be the place designated pursuant to Article 13.

4. An award may be made public only with the consent of all parties or as required by law.

5. Copies of the award shall be communicated to the parties by the administrator.

6. If the arbitration law of the country where the award is made requires the award to be filed or registered, the tribunal shall comply with such requirement.

7. In addition to making a final award, the tribunal may make interim, interlocutory, or partial orders and awards.

Settlement or Other Reasons for Termination

Article 29

1. If the parties settle the dispute before an award is made, the tribunal shall terminate the arbitration and, if requested by all parties, may record the settlement in the form of an award on agreed terms. The tribunal is not obliged to give reasons for such an award.

2. If the continuation of the proceedings becomes unnecessary or impossible for any other reason, the tribunal shall inform the parties of its intention to terminate the proceedings. The tribunal shall thereafter

issue an order terminating the arbitration, unless a party raises justifiable grounds for objection.

* * *

CHINA INTERNATIONAL ECONOMIC AND TRADE ARBITRATION COMMISSION [CIETAC] ARBITRATION RULES

(Revised and Adopted by China Council for the Promotion of International Trade/China Chamber of Commerce on September 5, 2000. Effective as from October 1, 2000).

* * *

Article 54 Where a case is heard by an arbitration tribunal composed of three arbitrators, the arbitral award shall be decided by the majority of the arbitrators and the minority may be recorded and placed on file.

When the arbitration tribunal cannot attain a majority opinion, the arbitral award shall be decided in accordance with the presiding arbitrator's opinion.

Article 55 The arbitration tribunal shall state in the tribunal award the claims, the facts of the dispute, the reasons on which the arbitral award is based, the result of the arbitral award, the allocation of the arbitration costs, the date on which and the place at which the arbitral award is made. The facts of the dispute and the reasons on which the arbitral award is based may not be stated in the arbitral award if the parties have agreed not to state them in the arbitral award, or the arbitral award is made in accordance with the contents of the settlement agreement reached between the parties.

Article 56 Unless the arbitral award is made in accordance with the opinion of the presiding arbitrator or the sole arbitrator, the arbitral award shall be signed by a majority of arbitrators. An arbitrator who has a dissenting opinion may sign or not sign his name on the arbitral award.

The arbitrators shall submit the draft arbitral award to the Arbitration Commission before signing the award. The Arbitration Commission may remind the arbitrators of any issue related to the form of the arbitral award on condition that the arbitrators' independence of decision is not affected.

The Arbitration Commission's stamp shall be affixed to the arbitral award.

The date on which the arbitral award is made is the date on which the arbitral award comes into legal effect.

Article 57 An interlocutory award or partial award may be made on any issue of the case at any time in the course of arbitration before the final award is made if considered necessary by the arbitration tribunal, or if the parties make such a proposal and it is agreed to by the arbitration tribunal. Either party's failure to perform the interlocutory award will not affect the continuation of the arbitration proceedings, nor will it prevent the arbitration tribunal from making a final award.

* * *

Questions and Comments

1.   Often arbitrators agree on the basic content of the award after the final oral hearing, leaving to the chairman of the tribunal the task of preparing a written draft. Thereafter, the arbitrators who do not reside at the place of arbitration return to their home countries. The final text of the award is settled by correspondence.

Given that the arbitrators may sign the award after they have returned to their home countries, what would be considered the place of the award? Is the place of the award important?

2.   What if the parties reach a settlement during the arbitral proceedings? Does the settlement constitute an award? Why might this be an important issue?

3.   Should a dissenting arbitrator be entitled to write a dissenting opinion?

4.   According to the prevailing trend, arbitral awards have to be motivated, unless the parties provide otherwise. This is a rather clear cut solution, but the question remains how detailed and how scrupulous need a statement of reasons of the award be, for it to be "motivated".

In *Government of Guinea v. MINE (Maritime International Nominees Establishment from Liechtenstein)*, an appeal to an ICSID Ad Hoc Committee (which provides a limited measure of appellate review within the International Centre for Settlement of Investment Disputes), the party seeking annulment argued that the award lacked an adequate statement of reasons regarding several issues and, accordingly, should be set aside under Article 52 of the ICSID Convention because it "failed to state the reasons on which it is based". The Ad Hoc Committee explained the failure-to-state-reasons standard as follows:

> The Committee is of the opinion that the requirement that an award has to be motivated implies that it must enable the reader to follow the reasoning of the Tribunal on points of fact and law. It implies that, and only that. The adequacy of the reasoning is not an appropriate standard of review under paragraph (1)(e), because it almost inevitably draws an *ad hoc* Committee into an examination of the substance of the tribunal's decision, in disregard of the exclusion of the remedy of appeal by Article 53 of the Convention. A Committee might be tempted to annul an award because that examination disclosed a manifestly incorrect application of the law, which, however, is not a ground for annulment.

> In the Committee's view, the requirement to state reasons is satisfied as long as the award enables one to follow how the tribunal proceeded from Point A. to Point B. and eventually to its conclusion,

even if it made an error of fact or of law. This minimum requirement is in particular not satisfied by either contradictory or frivolous reasons. (5 ICSID Rev. 95, 105 (1990) (Ad Hoc Committee decision, 1988).)

5.   The Dutch Act (Art. 1057), the AAA Rules (Art.29), the CIETAC Rules (Art. 55)—and other rules as well—state that awards based on a settlement do not have to be motivated. Why?

6.   Suppose one party publishes an AAA award in clear contravention of Article 27(4) of the AAA Rules. What result?

7.   The CIETAC Rules state in Article 54/2 that the presiding arbitrator's opinion will prevail if no majority can be attained. Can you describe a situation in which the president's vote will carry?

Who will sign such an award?

8.   Statutory and institutional rules refer to several types of awards: final, partial, interim, and interlocutory ones. Clear distinctions and definitions are, unfortunately, lacking, and arbitral practice in this area is still unclear. We here suggest some criteria that have been used with some frequency, and that are—we believe—logical as well. In doing so, we stress again that firmly established normative distinctions are still lacking.

Final awards are those awards which finally settle all claims submitted to the arbitrators and by which the mission of the tribunal is completed.[9] **Partial** awards yield a final settlement of some of the claims submitted to arbitration, and they typically have a direct monetary impact. (We shall return to the distinction between final and partial awards in Chapter V.3.b.iii, in the context of recognition and enforcement.) **Interim** awards can also conclusively settle some of the claims presented to the arbitrators. The terms "partial award" and "interim award" are often used interchangeably. They might, however, be distinguished on the following grounds: Partial awards typically yield a final and enforceable settlement of a claim. (E.g. claimant seeks a certain amount as direct damages, and another amount as consequential damages. If the arbitrators decide to render first an award regarding direct damages, this will be a **partial** award.) Interim awards may also represent a final word on the merits but usually regarding a claim that can be recognized but does not require affirmative enforcement. (E.g., respondent contests both its liability, and the amount of possible damages. If the tribunal issues an award that establishes the respondent's liability but does not decide damages, it is an **interim** award. On the other hand, if the tribunal finds that the respondent is not liable, the award is **final**.) **Interlocutory** awards are not directed to the merits; they deal with such issues as jurisdiction, and the determination of the applicable law.

9.   In its "interim award" No. 6560 of 1990, 17 Yearbk. Comm. Arb'n 226 (1992), an ICC tribunal decided one issue: the substantive law applicable in the dispute between the seller from the Netherlands Antilles and the buyer from France. After a careful analysis of various points of contact, the arbitrators concluded that French rather than English law was the proper law of the contract.

---

[9].   Final awards may, however, be subject to interpretation and corrections. See below IV.2.b.ii.

Leaving terminological debates aside, can this "interim award" be recognized? Enforced?

Is such an award useful?

IV.2.a.ii.   An Award Written by Someone Else

SACHERI (ITALY) v. ROBOTTO (ITALY)

Italy Corte di Cassazione [Supreme Court], 7 June 1989.
16 Yearbk. Comm. Arb'n 156 (1991).*

FACTS

An arbitral award was rendered in formal arbitration (*arbitrato rituale*)[1] between the parties following a dispute concerning certain construction works. The arbitrators, who were not legally trained, delegated a lawyer—who had been appointed as expert [*consulente tecnico*]—to draw up the award.

Sacheri initiated court proceedings before the Court of Appeal of Genova seeking annulment of the award on the ground that the arbitrators did not fulfill an essential part of their task. On 13 June 1985, the Court of Appeal of Genova held that the award was valid.

The Supreme Court reversed the lower court's decision, reasoning as follows.

EXCERPT

[1]   "[Sacheri] contends that the task entrusted to [the expert] was not limited materially to drawing up the award. Due to the arbitrators' professed incapacity to decide issues other than technical construction problems, it amounted to delegating a third person to formulate the final decision, which the arbitrators were not able to conceive and which they could not critically examine once it had been drafted. Hence, the arbitrators totally abdicated their jurisdictional powers.

[2]   "Two principles were thereby violated: the principle according to which the decision must be rendered by a legally constituted judge, and the personal character of the arbitral mission, which the parties confer upon the arbitrators *intuitu personae*. [Sacheri] further contends that the expert's activity violated due process.

(. . . .)

---

* Reprinted with permission of Yearbook Commercial Arbitration, International Council for Commercial Arbitration.

1.   *Editor's note.* In Italy, there exist two principal types of arbitration. The first is known as *arbitrato rituale* (formal or procedural arbitration) and is governed by the Italian Law on Arbitration set forth in the Code of Civil Procedure. The second is *arbitrato irrituale* (informal or contractual arbitration) which is entirely based on contract law and is not governed by the provisions of the Law on Arbitration. The main difference between the two is that the decision rendered in an *arbitrato irrituale* cannot be enforced as an arbitral award but only by means of a contract action. See G. Bernini, *National Report Italy* in [2 International Handbook on Commercial Arbitration, at tab Italy, p.1 (Pieter Sanders & Albert Jan van den Berg eds., supp. 3 (1985)].

[3]   "The issue is whether Italian procedural law allows arbitrators in *arbitrato rituale* to delegate an expert (*consulente tecnico*), to decide legal issues which are essential to the decision-making process.

[4]   "This question must be answered in the negative. First of all, there is a difference within the framework of the *arbitrato rituale* between arbitrators who decide according to rules of law and arbitrators called upon to decide *ex aequo et bono*. Under Italian procedural law it does not seem possible to allow the former to delegate a third person to assess the legal issues which are relevant for the decision-making process.

[5]   "This is possible, however, in one case only, i.e., when the parties have waived their right to file a recourse against the award (last paragraph of Art. 829 CCP).[2] In that case, there can be no action for setting aside the award on the ground of errors of law (with the exception of the violation of public policy). *A fortiori*, the arbitrators may dispose in a limited way of the *res judicanda*, i.e., delegate a third person to propose a solution for the legal issues of the case."

[6]   "The Court stressed that this is the only exception to the rule that arbitrators deciding according to the law may not delegate a third party to solve the legal issues of the dispute.

[7]   "Hence, the Court of Appeal's holding that the parties referred their dispute to the arbitrators and therefore could not deny them the faculty to seek the legal advice of an expert, is erroneous. On the contrary, in the absence of a contractual clause authorizing the arbitrators to decide *ex aequo et bono*, or excluding all means of recourse against the award (last paragraph of Art. 829 CCP), the position of an arbitrator deciding according to the law does not differ from the position of a judge.

[8]   "It is not relevant that the contract between the parties contained a clause which provided that the law must be followed 'if and insofar possible.' The above-mentioned principle is a structural element of the [Italian] legal system and cannot be derogated from contractually by the parties who require from the arbitrators a decision according to the law, and even less by the arbitrators."

Questions and Comments

1.   Court decisions are sometimes written by a clerk, and then signed by the judge, who—let us hope—reads it carefully, before signing. What is the difference between this situation, and the *Sacheri v. Robotto* pattern? Is it crucial that in the Italian case the arbitrators "could not critically examine" the award after it was drafted?

2.   Suppose the arbitrator is a good lawyer, who has had no experience, however, in the field of international commercial arbitration. He faces a

2.   Art. 829, last paragraph, of the Italian Code of Civil Procedure reads:

"One may also make recourse on the ground of nullity where the arbitrators, when making their decisions, have not observed the rules of law, unless the parties have authorized them to decide according to equity or unless they have declared that there may be no recourse against the award."

complicated jurisdictional issue, calls his former professor whom he trusts, and decides the way the professor suggested. Is this a valid award in light of the analysis of the **Corte di Cassazione**?

3.   Given that arbitrators are sometimes business or trade experts, not trained in law, how should they proceed when it comes to rendering a decision or drafting an award involving significant legal questions?

IV.2.b.   *Interventions After the Award Is Written*

IV.2.b.i.   *Institutional Scrutiny*

The award may be subject to *institutional control*. The most prominent example of such scrutiny can be found in ICC arbitration. According to Article 27 of the 1998 Rules:

"Before signing any award, the Arbitral Tribunal shall submit it in draft form to the [International] Court [of Arbitration]. The Court may lay down modifications as to the form of the award and, without affecting the Arbitral Tribunal's liberty of decision, may also draw its attention to points of substance. No award shall be rendered by the Arbitral Tribunal until it has been approved by the Court as to its form."

This is certainly a procedural step that goes beyond the arbitrators' agreement among themselves on the text of the award.

Further institutional control is introduced through Article 28.(1) of the Rules, which state that *"Once an award has been made, the Secretariat shall notify to the parties the text signed by the Arbitral Tribunal; provided always that the costs of arbitration have been fully paid to the ICC by the parties or by one of them"*.

The institutional scrutiny set in Article 27 of the ICC Rules[10] inspired the drafters of the 1995 CIETAC Rules. The same type of institutional control (although in a somewhat more restrained form) is provided in Article 56 para. 2 of the Chinese Rules. In addition to para. 2, we reproduce here also para. 3 and 4, of Article 56; they are also relevant in interpreting the range of the CIETAC institutional control:

"The arbitrator shall submit his draft arbitral award to the Arbitration Commission before signing the award. The Arbitration Commission may remind the arbitrator of any issue related to the form of the arbitral award on condition that the arbitrator's independence of decision is not affected.

The Arbitration Commission's stamp shall be affixed to the arbitral award.

The date on which the arbitral award is made is the date on which the arbitral award comes into legal effect."

[10].   Article 27 of the 1998 Rules is not an innovation. It rather confirms a stance adopted in earlier versions of the Rules. There is practically no difference between the wording of Article 27 of the 1998 Rules and the drafting of Article 21 of the 1988 Rules.

The institutional control provided by the ICC is at the far end of the spectrum of possible options. This may have brought about the inclusion in Article 27 of a rather unusual, almost apologetic explanation stating that review by the International Court of Arbitration is not "affecting the arbitrator's liberty of decision".

A more modest (and more typical) approach to institutional control is seen in Article 18(2) of the 1991 Rules of Arbitration and Conciliation of the International Arbitration Centre of the Federal Economic Chamber in Vienna (Vienna Rules), which states:

"Awards are confirmed on all the necessary copies by the signature of the Secretary and the stamp of the Centre and served on to the parties."

Questions and Comments

1.   The question may be asked whether an award would be binding if ICC arbitrators were to bypass Article 27 by rendering their award and issuing it to the parties. Could this represent a ground for refusal of recognition in the light of Article V(1)(d) of the New York Convention, which permits refusal of recognition if "the arbitral procedure was not in accordance with the agreement of the parties"?

Suppose CIETAC arbitrators fail to submit their award to the Arbitration Commission. Instead they sign it, ask the clerk of the Arbitration Commission to put the Commission's seal on it, which the clerk does, and send it to the parties. Will the award be legally effective? If so, would it be if the seal is not affixed?

2.   Suppose that an ICC award was sent to the parties by the personal secretary of the chairman of the arbitration panel, rather than by the ICC Secretariat; would the award be binding?

If it turned out that the costs had not been fully paid after all, would this affect the award's legal status?

IV.2.b.ii.   Correction, Interpretation, and Additional Award

WINTERSHALL A.G. (F.R. GERMANY) ET AL v. GOVERNMENT OF QATAR

15 Yearbk. Comm. Arb'n 30 (1990).*

Partial award of 5 February 1988

Final award of 31 May 1988

Arbitrators: John R. Stevenson (US, chairman); Ian Brownlie (UK); Bernardo Cremades (Spain)

FACTS

Parties entered into an "Exploration and Production Sharing Agreement—Qatar Offshore" (EPSA) on 10 April 1976 whereby the Govern-

* Reprinted with permission of Yearbook Commercial Arbitration, International Council for Commercial Arbitration.

ment of Qatar granted to the claimants "the exclusive right to explore for, drill for and produce petroleum in a defined area offshore of Qatar (the 'Contract Area') and the right to store, to transport and sell petroleum for use in Qatar or for export, and to export or otherwise dispose of petroleum" (Arts. I and II EPSA). Petroleum was defined in Art. I EPSA to include liquid crude oil, gas and all other hydrocarbon substances in the Contract Area.

The "Effective Date" of the EPSA was 18 June 1973 * * * and it was to run for a term of 30 years (Art. IV). It also contained the following relevant time periods:

— five years after the Effective Date, claimants were required to relinquish to respondent 50% of the Contract Area, but could continue to exploit the remaining 50% for a further three years (Art. XI EPSA);

— eight years after the Effective Date, claimants were required to relinquish to respondent an additional 20% of the Contract Area (Art. XI EPSA). If during that eight year period claimants did not discover in the Contract Area "crude oil in commercial quantities" or "economically utilizable non-associated natural gas" respondent was entitled to terminate the EPSA (Art. XXXV);

— twelve years after the Effective Date, Claimants were entitled to retain only the producing areas (Art. XI).

If claimants discovered crude oil in the Contract Area, they were entitled to produce it in accordance with the EPSA; if they discovered non-associated natural gas, they were entitled to produce it either pursuant to further contractual arrangements to be mutually agreed by parties, or pursuant to the principles specified in Art. XV.3(3) EPSA.

Crude oil in commercial quantities was not discovered. Due to a boundary dispute with Bahrain, respondent did not permit claimants to drill in the "Structure A" area, which the claimants regarded as most likely to contain crude oil. The Emir of Qatar, in a meeting on 20 May 1978, instructed claimants not to drill on Structure A and advised claimants that an extension of the exploration period would be studied by respondent.

Claimants relinquished 50% of the Contract Area in 1978 as provided for in the EPSA. Respondent did not require any further relinquishment. Claimants did not offer any further relinquishment, nor did they relinquish their rights to the Structure A area.

By letter of 3 April 1980, claimants informed respondents that they had discovered non-associated natural gas in substantial quantities in the Contract Area and respondent requested them to provide them with all the relevant studies. Following this, parties considered several projects for the utilization of non-associated natural gas in the Contract Area or an adjacent area in which the petroleum rights were held by the Qatar General Petroleum Corporation (QGPC), a corporation wholly owned by respondent.

On 19 June 1985, respondents telexed claimants informing them that "the term of this Agreement [the EPSA] expired on the 18th day of

June 1985. Accordingly, this agreement is terminated with effect from this date." Notwithstanding this, claimants paid the annual rental fee which respondent accepted and neither party treated the EPSA as expired or terminated.

The discussions concerning projects for the utilization of natural gas ended unsuccessfully and claimants, by letter of 10 March 1986 to the Minister of Finance of Qatar, referred the dispute to arbitration. The arbitral tribunal, in an Order of 18 March 1987, provided that the arbitration procedure would be governed by UNCITRAL Arbitration Rules,[1] as agreed by the parties in their Agreement of 22 October 1986 and in accordance with Art. 16 of the UNCITRAL Rules fixed the place of arbitration in the Hague, the Netherlands.[2]

The arbitral tribunal issued its *Partial Award on Liability* on 5 February 1988. The Partial Award contained a "Statement by Dr. Cremades" (see infra under D) and had appended to it a "Separate Opinion by Prof. Brownlie" and a "Comment by the Honorable John R. Stevenson and Dr. Bernardo M. Cremades on Separate Opinion of Professor Ian Brownlie, QC" (see infra). The Partial Award held that the EPSA remained in force and that the parties' obligations thereunder continued. It extended the time period for relinquishment under the EPSA. The arbitral tribunal offered the parties several options including the valuation and relinquishment of the rights of the claimants under the Partial Award. The respondent did not elect the valuation and relinquishment under the Partial Award and claimant requested the arbitral tribunal to confirm its holdings with respect to relinquishment.

On 31 May 1988, the arbitral tribunal issued its *Final Award* confirming the Partial Award. It incorporated into its Final Award its interpretation of the Partial Award and/or its additional award of the same date as the Final Award.

EXCERPT

I. Partial Award on Liability

A. *Applicable Law*

(a) *Arbitral law*

[1] "By ... its Order of 18 March 1987, the Tribunal provided that the procedure of the arbitration shall be governed by the UNCITRAL

---

1. The UNCITRAL Arbitration Rules are reproduced in Yearbook II (1977) pp. 161–171.

2. Art. 16 of the UNCITRAL Arbitration Rules reads:

1. Unless the parties have agreed upon the place where the arbitration is to be held, such place shall be determined by the arbitral tribunal, having regard to the circumstances of the arbitration.

2. The arbitral tribunal may determine the locale of the arbitration within the country agreed upon by the parties. It may hear witnesses and hold meetings for consultation among its members at any place it deems appropriate, having regard to the circumstances of the arbitration.

3. The arbitral tribunal may meet at any place it deems appropriate for inspection of goods, other property or documents. The parties shall be given sufficient notice to enable them to be present at such inspection.

4. The award shall be made at the place of arbitration.

Arbitration Rules, as agreed by the parties in the Agreement of 22 October 1986, subject to any mandatory provisions of the Netherlands Arbitration Law, which, in the event of conflict with any of the UNCI-TRAL Rules, shall prevail. The Tribunal has concluded that its Partial Award on Liability, determining the substance of the claims on both jurisdiction and the merits, and proposed Final Award [see infra] are consistent with the UNCITRAL Arbitration Rules and in no respect in conflict with any of the mandatory provisions of the Netherlands Arbitration Law."

* * *

J.   *Final Award*

[58] "The Tribunal will issue a final award sixty days after the effective date of this Partial Award on Liability, either confirming the Partial Award; or, if the claimants and respondents both elect, ten days in advance of such date for the issuance of the Final Award, the valuation and relinquishment of the rights of the claimants under the Partial Award on Liability, the Tribunal will schedule hearings (not later than one hundred and twenty days after the election of this election by the claimants and respondent) on the sole question of the value (i.e., the market value between a willing seller and a willing buyer) of the claimants' rights under the EPSA as declared in the Partial Award on Liability, with a Final Award to be made as soon thereafter as practical, providing for payment by the respondent to the claimants of the value so determined and the relinquishment by claimants of these rights. (To the extent this involves an amendment or modification of the EPSA, it is authorized by Art. XXXIII of the EPSA).

[59] "The claimants and respondent may elect, if both so elect, rather than the relinquishment by claimants of all their rights declared in the Partial Award, to value only, and provide for the claimants' relinquishment of only their rights, in respect of the Structure A area and retain their rights in respect of their exercise of the 'go it alone' option under the third paragraph of Art. XV.3 of the EPSA. Alternatively, the claimants and respondent may elect, if both so elect, to retain only claimants' rights under the Structure A area, as declared in the Partial Award on Liability, and to value and relinquish their other rights in respect of the exercise of the option under the third paragraph of Art. XV.3 of the EPSA, as determined in the Partial Award on Liability."

* * *

II.   Final Award

A.   *Possibility of Interpretation of Award*

[81] "The Tribunal hereby issues its Final Award pursuant to ... its Partial Award on Liability signed 5 February 1988 (the 'Partial Award'), confirming the Partial Award. The Tribunal notes that the respondent has not elected under the Partial Award valuation and relinquishment of the rights of the claimants (...). Claimants have

asked the Tribunal to confirm its holdings with respect to relinquishment. Accordingly, the Tribunal wishes to confirm that ... the relinquishment rights of the claimants are as follows:

"A. The claimants are not required to relinquish their rights to exercise their option under the third paragraph of Art. XV.3 of the EPSA in any part of the 50% of the Contract Area still held by the claimants, if not in production, until eight years from the date of this Final Award.

"B. The term for the application of the EPSA Art. XI relinquishment provisions to the Structure A area begins on the date the respondent permits claimants to develop Structure A under the EPSA.

"C. With respect to the terms for performance stipulated in other provisions of EPSA, the Tribunal hereby confirms the extension of the performance periods required to make meaningful the relinquishment rights above provided...."

[82] "The Tribunal recognizes, as pointed out in ... the Further Observations of 16 May 1988 that the Netherlands Arbitration Act 1986 does not provide for an interpretation of an award and that the Minister of Justice's report referred to in ... the Further Observations indicates that the Minister of Justice does not propose to insert in the Act the possibility of an interpretation of an award by the Tribunal. However, the parties by their agreement of 22 October 1986, signed by duly authorized representatives of the parties, adopted as procedural rules the UNCITRAL Rules adopted by the United Nations General Assembly on 15 December 1976, and Art. 35 of these Rules provides for an interpretation of the award and Art. 37 for an additional award, subject to certain notice provisions which have been fully satisfied in this case. It is the Tribunal's view that this agreement governs the arbitration since the UNCITRAL Arbitration Rules are not in conflict with any provisions of the Netherlands law from which the parties cannot derogate (Arts. 1–2 of the UNCITRAL Arbitration Rules) and Art. 1036 of the Netherlands Arbitration Act 1986, providing that 'Subject to the provisions of this Title, the arbitral proceedings shall be conducted in such manner as agreed between the parties ...'. There is no provision in the Netherlands Arbitration Act 1986, expressly excluding the parties from agreeing to an interpretation and their agreement under UNCITRAL Art. 35 is, in the Tribunal's opinion, controlling.

[83] "It is the further view of the Tribunal that Art. 1059 of the Netherlands Arbitration Act 1986[11] providing for the *res judicata* effect

---

11. Art. 1059 of the Netherlands Arbitration Act 1986 reads:

"Res judicata of the award

"1. Only a final or partial final arbitral award is capable of acquiring the force of *res judicata*. The award shall have such force from the day on which it is made.

"2. If, however, an appeal to a second arbitral tribunal is provided for, the final or partial final award shall have the force of *res judicata* from the day on which the time limit for lodging the appeal has lapsed or, if the appeal has been lodged, the day on which a decision is rendered on appeal, if

of a partial final award in no sense deprives the parties of the ability to agree to an interpretation of a partial award under Art. 35 of the UNCITRAL Rules. The Tribunal agrees with the claimants that the 'principle of *res judicata* prevents the re-opening of necessarily decided points. It does not prevent the clarification of a decision nor the giving of a decision on points which an award has left undecided'.

[84] "The Tribunal has also noted that in his preface to the Netherlands Arbitration Act 1986, the Minister of Justice of the Netherlands, F. Korthals Altes, referred to the new Act duly taking into account the Model Law on International Commercial Arbitration, adopted in 1985 by the United Nations Commission on International Trade Law (UNCITRAL), which expressly provides in Art. 33 for an interpretation of an award if so agreed by the parties (Art. 33(1)(b)).[12]

[85] "Finally, while in no sense controlling, the respondent by recognizing in its letter of 28 April ... that Art. 40(4) of the UNCITRAL Rules prohibits the charging of additional fees in respect of an interpretation, in effect recognizes that Art. 35 is applicable.[13]

[86] "Nonetheless, in view of the contention by the respondent that the Tribunal is without authority under Netherlands law to interpret its award, the Tribunal has determined whether the substance of the attached interpretation could be included in an additional award under Art. 37 of the UNCITRAL Rules and Art. 1061[14] of the Nether-

and to the extent that the award rendered at first instance is affirmed on appeal."

Art. 33(1)(b) of the UNCITRAL Model Law on International Commercial Arbitration reads:

"1. . . .

"(a) . . .

"(b) if so agreed by the parties, a party, with notice to the other party may request the arbitral tribunal to give an interpretation of a specific point or part of the award."

12. Art. 33(1)(b) of the UNCITRAL Model Law on International Commercial Arbitration reads:

"1. . . .

"(a) . . .

"(b) if so agreed by the parties, a party, with notice to the other party may request the arbitral tribunal to give an interpretation of a specific point or part of the award."

13. Art. 40(4) of the UNCITRAL Arbitration Rules reads:

"No additional fees may be charged by an arbitral tribunal for interpretation or correction or completion of its award under Arts. 35 to 37."

14. Art. 1061 of the Netherlands Arbitration Act 1986 reads:

"Additional award

"(1) If the arbitral tribunal has failed to decide on one or more matters which have been submitted to it, either party may, not later than thirty days after the date of deposit of the award with the Registry of the District Court, request the arbitral tribunal to render an additional award.

"(2) A copy of the request shall be communicated by the arbitral tribunal to the other party.

"(3) The arbitral tribunal shall give the parties an opportunity to be heard before deciding on the request.

"(4) An additional award shall be regarded as an arbitral award to which the provisions of Section Three to Five inclusive of this Title shall be applicable.

"(5) If the arbitral tribunal rejects a request for an additional award, it shall inform the parties accordingly in writing. A copy of this notification, signed by an arbitrator or the secretary of the arbitral tribunal, shall be deposited with the Registry of the District Court, in accordance with the provisions of Art. 1058(1).

"(6) If an appeal to a second arbitral tribunal has been agreed, the arbitral

lands Arbitration Act 1986, and, as required by Art. 1061(3) of the Netherlands Arbitration Act 1986, the Tribunal has given to the parties an opportunity to be heard on this question, in particular, the view of the claimants ... that 'the inevitable and logical consequence of the respondent's counterclaim is that claims and matters related to Art. XV.3, Third Alternative, were before the Tribunal for decision'. These included clarification how the cost recovery and production sharing principles of Art. XIII of the EPSA apply to a non-associated Natural Gas project under the third paragraph of Art. XV.3.

[87] "It is the determination of the Tribunal that the substance of the attached interpretation could be included in an additional award under Art. 37 of the UNCITRAL Rules and/or Art. 1061 of the Netherlands Arbitration Act 1986.

[88] "The Tribunal hereby incorporates into and makes a part of this Final Award its interpretation of the Partial Award and/or additional award, issued today's date."

B. Interpretation by Tribunal of its Partial Award on Liability Pursuant to Application of Claimants[15]

[89] "The tribunal has decided that it will interpret its Partial Award on Liability signed on 5 February 1988 (the 'Partial Award'), pursuant to claimants' Application of 16 March 1988 (the 'Application'), and Art. 35 of the UNCITRAL Arbitration Rules.

[90] "The Partial Award did not become a Final Award on 17 April 1988, since the Tribunal has determined to interpret its Partial Award and is considering the submissions of the parties pursuant to Arts. 15 and 23 of the UNCITRAL Arbitration Rules,[16] and has also afforded the

---

award rendered at first instance may only be supplemented on appeal. Any request for supplementation shall be made within the period of time applicable to the lodging of the appeal."

15. The arbitrators added in a footnote:

"For the reasons set forth in the Final Award, the Tribunal holds that it has authority to interpret its Partial Award. If the respondent does not put this question to a Netherlands Court, or if the respondent puts this question to a Netherlands Court and a Netherlands Court agrees, the Tribunal's determination on its authority to issue an additional award is moot. However, if the Court finds the Tribunal does not have authority to grant this interpretation, then the question of whether or not the Tribunal can, under UNCITRAL Rule 37 and Art. 1061 of the Netherlands Arbitration Act 1986, issue an additional award, containing the substance of this interpretation, is not moot. The parties have been given, pursuant to Art. 1061(3) of the Netherlands Arbitration Act 1986, an opportunity to be heard on the claimants' alternative request

for an additional award, and the Tribunal has decided that the Tribunal can issue such an additional award, including the substance of this interpretation."

16. Arts. 15 and 23 of the UNCITRAL Arbitration Rules read:

"*15. General Provisions*

"1. Subject to these Rules, the arbitral tribunal may conduct the arbitration in such manner as it considers appropriate, provided that the parties are treated with equality and that at any stage of the proceedings each party is given a full opportunity of presenting his case.

"2. If either party so requests at any stage of the proceedings, the arbitral tribunal shall hold hearings for the presentation of evidence by witnesses, including expert witnesses, or for oral argument. In the absence of such a request, the arbitral tribunal shall decide whether to hold such hearings or whether the proceedings shall be conducted on the basis of documents and other materials.

"3. All documents or information supplied to the arbitral tribunal by one party

parties the opportunity to be heard on the claimants' alternative request under Art. 37 and/or Art. 1061 of the Netherlands Arbitration Act of 1986 ... and has determined that this alternative request is valid.

(. . . .)

[91] "The Tribunal agrees with the respondent, in ... Respondents Observations of 31 March 1988 (the 'Observations'), that the Tribunal in its Partial Award did not undertake to interpret the relevant provisions of EPSA ... but rather gave its reasons for regarding the third option under Art. XV.3 of the EPSA as a joint venture. However, in the claimants' Application, the Tribunal is being asked to interpret certain provisions of the EPSA. This constitutes an interpretation or clarification of the Partial Award since, in the Tribunal's view, the meaning of such Partial Award depends on the meaning of the cited provisions of EPSA.

AMERICAN ARBITRATION ASSOCIATION INTERNATIONAL ARBITRATION RULES

(As amended and effective on November 1, 2001).

* * *

Interpretation or Correction of the Award

Article 30

1. Within thirty days after the receipt of an award, any party, with notice to the other parties, may request the tribunal to interpret the award or correct any clerical, typographical or computation errors or make an additional award as to claims presented but omitted from the award.

2. If the tribunal considers such a request justified, after considering the contentions of the parties, it shall comply with such a request within thirty days after the request.

* * *

shall at the same time be communicated by that party to the other party."

"*23. Periods of Time*

"The periods of time fixed by the arbitral tribunal for the communication of written statements (including the statement of claim and statement of defense) should not exceed 45 days. However, the arbitral tribunal may extend the time limits if it concludes that an extension is justified."

CHINA INTERNATIONAL ECONOMIC AND TRADE ARBITRATION COMMISSION (CIETAC) ARBITRATION RULES

(Revised and Adopted by China Council for the Promotion of International
Trade/China Chamber of Commerce on September 5, 2000. Effective
as from October 1, 2000).

* * *

Article 61 Either party may request in writing that a correction be made to any writing, typing, calculating errors or any errors of a similar nature contained in the arbitral award within 30 days from the date of receipt of the arbitral award; if there is really an error in the arbitral award, the arbitration tribunal shall make a correction in writing within 30 days from the date of the receipt of the written request for correction. The arbitration tribunal may likewise correct any errors in writing on its own initiative within 30 days from the date on which the arbitral award is issued. The correction in writing forms a part of the arbitral award.

Article 62 If anything claimed or counterclaimed is found to have been omitted in the arbitral award, either of the parties may make a request in writing to the arbitration tribunal for an additional award within 30 days from the date on which the arbitral award is received. If there is really something omitted, the arbitration tribunal shall make an additional award within 30 days from the date on which the arbitral award is issued. The additional award forms a part of the arbitral award previously issued.

* * *

Questions and Comments

1. Should the UNCITRAL rule providing for the possibility of interpretation of the award supersede the Dutch *lex arbitri* (which only provides for correction and additional awards)? The arbitrators in *Wintershall v. Qatar* took a cautious approach and characterized their intervention as either an interpretation or an additional award. Can you be more definite?

2. Is the "partial award" issued by the arbitrators on February 5, 1988, a partial award in the sense that it finally resolves one segment, i.e. one part, of the dispute?

Should it (or could it) have had **res judicata** effects?

3. The February 5 "**partial award on liability**" contains a section (Section "J") which sets the parameters of a future final award, and offers the parties certain options.

Who was entitled to exercise these options?

What practical considerations would support or justify the rendering of an award with options?

4. Suppose the parties choose the valuation and relinquishment option. How will their agreement become enforceable?

5.   Suppose an award rendered in China under the CIETAC Rules fails to state the date on which the award was made.

Could rectification be obtained under Article 61 of the CIETAC Rules? Perhaps in light of Article 62?

If rectification is not effected, is the award invalid?

6.   Article 30 of the AAA Rules provides two time limits, one in section (1), the other in section (2). In both cases the Rules have set thirty days. What are the consequences if one or the other time limit is not kept?

7.   A U.K. case, In the Matter of Two Arbitration Applications Gannet Shipping Ltd v. Eastrade Commodities Inc., (Queen's Bench Div. (Comm. Ct.)) 2001 WL 1476272 (December, 2001), involved an arbitration in London between shipowners and charterers under the London Maritime Arbitrators Association (L.M.A.A.) Terms (1997). The umpire issued an award in favor of the owners for $35,330 in demurrage charges and for all costs. The umpire based his award on written submissions only. In his reasons the umpire included a sum of $21,858 for demurrage at a certain point in the voyage. The umpire used this figure because "he misread some manuscript amendments made in the laytime calculations". The actual text of the documents in the record agreed to by the owners and charterers valued the particular demurrage in question at only $860. After the charterers received the award, they pointed out the discrepancy to the umpire, and this was acknowledged by the owners. The umpire stated that he had made a mistake and issued a new award entitled "Correction to Final Award". In the "Correction to Final Award" the umpire valued the owners claim at $15,119 (a reduction of over $20,000), and also altered the award of costs. In the corrected award the charterers were required to pay their own costs and one-half of the owners' costs (instead of all of the owners' costs). The umpire explained that he changed the cost allocation because the lowered award meant that the owners had not succeeded quite to the extent that he had originally thought.

How would you rule in a U.K. court if the owners sought to set aside the "Correction Award" as beyond the umpire's authority? Would you accept both the lowered award and the change in the allocation of costs?

8.   The parties had not expressly agreed on the tribunal's power to correct an award. In such a case the English Arbitration Act of 1996 provides as follows:

Section 57(3)

"(a) The tribunal may on its own initiative or on the application of a party correct an award so as to remove any clerical mistake or error arising from an accidental slip or omission or remove any ambiguity in the award,"

Rule 26(A) of the L.M.A.A. Terms (1997) provides:

"In addition to the powers set out in Section 57 of the Act, the tribunal shall have the following powers to correct an award or to make an additional award:

(i) The tribunal may on its own initiative or on the application of a party correct any accidental mistake omission or error of calculation in its award . . ."

Explaining his corrected award, Umpire Burbidge stated that "[t]he kernel of the matter is that a clerical or arithmetical error has been made", and he added that "[w]hen the arbitrator's decision on a particular point, in this case liability for costs, is based on an admitted mistake, then surely as a matter of common sense the arbitrator must have power to review his decision in the light of that mistake." Does this "common sense" have sufficient support in Article 57 of the English Act?

9.   In the *Eastrade* case, the U.K. High Court upheld both aspects of the Correction to Final Award. The court distinguished between "clerical mistake" and "accidental slip". Justice Langley stated:

"Although Mr. Ashcroft, for the Owners, submitted that the error in the amount of the Award was a 'clerical mistake', and not 'an accidental slip or omission', and Mr. Burbidge himself described it as 'a clerical error', I do not agree. Mr. Burbidge wrote what he intended to write but he was mistaken in the substance of what he wrote. Even if that could be described as a 'clerical mistake' it was, I think, in common parlance, an accidental slip or at least also an accidental slip. It was a slip because it was wrong. It was accidental because he did not mean to use the wrong figure and he misread some manuscript amendments made in the laytime calculations submitted by the Charterers. . . ."

Do you see a difference between "clerical error" and "accidental slip"?

10.   Suppose the charterers had submitted a set-off claim based on an unjust enrichment theory, but that the umpire's award had rejected the claim on the ground that the unjust enrichment theory was not supported by any respectable juridical opinion. Suppose the charterers call the umpire's attention to one of their written submissions in which Judge Devlin, a famous and respected British judge, supported the unjust enrichment theory they urged on the umpire. Suppose the umpire thereafter issues a "Corrected Award" in which he accepts the unjust enrichment theory and lowers the ship owners award: a) because he had read the submitted documents too quickly and had not realized that there was a document in the submissions explaining Judge Devlin's views on unjust enrichment; or b) because he had read the Devlin submission too quickly and had not realized that Judge Devlin's view actually supported the charterers' position. As a judge in a set-aside proceeding, would you uphold the Corrected Award? As to both variant (a) and (b)?

11.   Comparing the *Eastrade* decision and the (a) and (b) hypos immediately above, would you say that some involve a "clerical mistake" while others do not? Or would you say that they all involve "errors" or "accidental slips", and therefore all can be corrected in a new award? If so, what kind of reconsideration by an arbitrator would be considered impermissible, if any? Is correction of an error or second guessing more problematic in arbitration than in litigation? How would you compare the two?

12.   In a case between claimant Entreprise Industrielle S.A., against respondents Philipp Holzmann A.G. and Nord France SA, an arbitral tribunal rendered its award deciding on both the claim and on the counterclaim. On March 15, 2000, the arbitrators awarded FFR 6.2 million to claimant "with interest", and FFR 1.7 million to respondents "with interest". More than two months after the award was rendered, on May 25, 2000 the

tribunal issued another award changing the original decision with respect to the interest awarded. The new award stated that respondents owe "compound interest" under the terms of the relevant French statutory rules. Respondents filed an action to set aside the second award on the ground that the tribunal was functus officio after the first award. The case reached the Swiss Supreme Court (ATF 126 III 524). The Supreme Court qualified the second award as a **correction.** It held that arbitrators may correct the award under the applicable Swiss law, although the pertinent Swiss statute (Chapter 12 of the Act on Private International Law) is silent on this question. The Court relied on the fact that the tribunal actually explained in its statement of reasons that respondents should pay compound interest— but this was omitted from the "dispositif" (final order) of the award.

Had the statement of reasons not mentioned compound interest, would you come to the same conclusion?

Since the Swiss statute is silent on the matter, it has no provision regarding the time within which a correction can be made. Should there be a time limit? Would you consider 70 days (the time elapsed between the rendering of the award and the issuance of the correction) to be within an appropriate time limit?

IV.2.c.   *Deposit, Authentication, Certification*

Deposit

The moment from which an award is binding may be delayed by the requirement of *deposit*. In some countries it is still necessary to deposit the award with a court at the place of arbitration. Other terms for essentially the same institution are: "registration", "filing", or "homologizing". A similar institution serving essentially the same purpose is *notarization* of the award by a notary public (rather than by courts).

Deposit can more easily be likened to authentication than to control, and in most legislative acts deposit is optional. For example, Article 193 of the Swiss Private International Law Act provides that:

1.   Each party may at its own expense deposit a copy of the award with the Swiss court of the seat of the arbitral tribunal.

2.   At the request of a party, the court shall certify the enforceability of the award.

3.   At the request of a party, the arbitral tribunal shall certify that the award has been rendered in conformity to this Act; such certificate has the same effect as the deposit of the award.

Swiss commentators consider deposit an institution which has no bearing on the validity of the award; it rather serves the purpose of keeping the award safe.[11] A declaration of enforceability (art. 193/2) entails more than a mere deposit, it assumes a certain scrutiny of the award.[12]

---

[11]. See Siehr, in *IPRG Kommentar,*   **[12].** Id., 1616–1617.
Schultess Verlag Zürich 1993, 1615.

The concept of deposit has been accepted in a considerable number of countries. For example:

Article 1702 of the Judicial Code of Belgium (Part VI: Arbitration, as amended through May 19, 1998) provides:

1.   The chairman of the arbitral tribunal shall give notice of the award to each party by sending it a copy thereof, signed in accordance with paragraph 4 of Article 1701.

2.   The chairman of the arbitral tribunal shall deposit the original of the award with the registry of the Court of First Instance; he shall notify the parties of the deposit.

3.   The arbitrator's function ends when the award terminating the litigation has been notified and deposited according to the preceding provisions.

The Dutch rules adopt the same approach as the Belgian code. Deposit shall be made by the arbitration tribunal itself, and it is specified in Article 1058/1/b that deposit shall be made *"with the registry of the District Court within whose district the place of arbitration is located"*. Failure to deposit the award is not mentioned among grounds for setting aside (Article 1965), and the award has **res judicata** effects from the day it was made (article 1959). It is interesting that, according to Article 1064/3, the time limit for requesting setting aside is three months *"after the date of deposit of the award with the Registry of the District Court"*.

According to Article 47 of the new (1994) Arbitration Act of Egypt:[13]

The party in whose favor the arbitral award has been made shall deposit, at the secretariat of the court referred to in Article 9 of this Law, the original award or a copy thereof in the language in which it was rendered, or an Arabic translation thereof authenticated by a competent authority if it was rendered in a foreign language. The court's secretary shall evidence such deposit in a **procès-verbal**, and each of the two parties to arbitration may request a copy of the said **procès-verbal**.

Failure to make the deposit is not mentioned among grounds for annulment (Article 53); however, there is a sentence in Article 55 which may conceivably provide a foothold for denying **res judicata** effects to awards which were not deposited. According to Article 55:

"Arbitral awards rendered in accordance with the provisions of the present Law have the authority of **res judicata** and shall be enforceable in conformity with the provisions of this Law."

Should deposit be considered a step within the process of "rendering the award"?

[13]. Law No. 27/1994 Promulgating   and Commercial Matters.
the Law Concerning Arbitration in Civil

In Yugoslavia (Serbia and Montenegro, where the 1977 Code of Civil Procedure of the former Yugoslavia applies), and in Croatia (which essentially accepted the rules of the Code of Civil Procedure of the former Yugoslavia as part of the new Croatian legislation[14]), a distinction is made between institutional and ad hoc arbitration. According to Article 483(2) of both acts:

> At the request of a party, the court referred to in Article 475(3) of this law shall put a clause in the award confirming its finality and enforceability. Permanent arbitration courts shall confirm themselves the finality and enforceability of their awards.

In Spain, registration in the form of notarization (**"protocolización"**) is required. The significance of this confirming clause was considered in a 1994 decision of the Supreme Court of Spain.[15] The party moving for annulment of an ICC award (rendered in Madrid, under Spanish law) asserted—among other grounds—that the award was not notarized as required under Spanish law, and that therefore it should be set aside. Other grounds advanced by the moving party were not accepted by the Spanish court, but annulment was granted on ground of lack of notarization. Notarization was held to be a formal requirement which is **ad solemnitatem**; therefore the award was not valid without notarization. This decision was under the 1953 Arbitration Act because the arbitration was initiated in September 1988, before the adoption in December of the 1988 Act. The new Act also contains a rule on notarization (Article 33(2)):

> "The award shall be notarized and the parties shall be notified of the award in a reliable manner."

It has not been tested yet whether the omission of **"protocolización"** would constitute a ground of nullity under the 1988 Act.

Deposit and similar forms of filing may still figure in the legislation of a considerable number of countries, yet the trend is to abandon deposit as a requisite or to make it optional. United States law does not require deposit or notarization. An important watershed is the UNCITRAL Model Law in which—after a thorough debate—the idea of deposit was abandoned without much opposition.[16] What is particularly important is that deposit is not specifically required by the New York Convention.

[14]. On October 8, 1991, the Yugoslav Code of Civil procedure was adopted with very slight modifications in Croatia, and published in the Croatian Official Gazette (**Narodne novine**) No. 53/1991.

[15]. ABC v. C. Espanola SA, decided on March 28, 1994, reported in French in 1994 Revue de l'arbitrage 748–751, with comments of F. Montilla–Serrano on pp. 752–756.

[16]. See Article 31 of the Model law; see also H. Holtzman & J. Neuhaus, A Guide to the UNCITRAL Model Law on International Commercial Arbitration: Legislative History and Commentary, 854–65, (1989). Holtzman reports that in the working group there was some support for requiring deposit or registration, arguing that this would "ensure the continued availability of the award" (p. 1009). This argument did not prevail, "The Working Group agreed early that, like in the New York Convention, the Model Law should not require that the parties deposit the award with any government or other registry in order to make it binding" (p. 836).

Authentication, Certification

Article IV of the New York Convention, speaking of the formal requirements applicable to the submission of a demand for recognition and enforcement states that the applicant has to supply *"the duly authenticated original award, or a duly certified copy thereof"*. This is not the same thing as deposit, and it has no bearing on the binding character and preclusive effects of the award. The requirement of authentication is in essence a rule of evidence in the process of granting leave to enforce. The two institutions are, however, linked in that deposit (or notarization) may be accepted by the recognizing court as authentication (or certification).

Explaining the terms of Article IV, van den Berg states:

"The authentication of a document is the formality by which the signature thereon is attested to be genuine. The certification of a copy is the formality by which the copy is attested to be a true copy of the original."[17]

The Convention does not specify the authority that is to issue the attestation or the law that governs authentication or certification. A 1969 decision of the Supreme Court of Austria reached the conclusion that authentication is satisfactory if it complies with either the law of the country in which (or under the law of which) the award was made, or the law of the country in which recognition is being sought. The Supreme Court (Oberster Gerichtshof) added that "in order to avoid difficulties it is recommended to have the copies certified by the foreign mission of the country whose courts will be requested to recognize or enforce the arbitral award ... but this is not obligatory."[18]

In a more recent decision, the High Court of Tokyo held that authentication by the consul of the country in which the decision was rendered (rather than of the country in which enforcement was requested) was also adequate. (An award of the China International Economic and Trade Arbitration Commission was authenticated by the consul of the PR of China in Japan.[19]) A clear choice was made in the 1996 Indian Ordinance on Arbitration and Conciliation. According to Article 47(1)a, a foreign award has to be authenticated *"in the manner required by the law of the country in which it was made"*; Article 47(2) requires that a translation of a foreign award into English has to be certified *"by a diplomatic or consular agent of the country to which that party belongs or certified as correct in such other manner as may be sufficient according to the law in force in India"*.

[17]. A. van den Berg, The New York Arbitration Convention of 1958, 251, (1981).

[18]. Oberster Gerichtshof, June 11, 1969, reported in 2 Yearbk. Comm. Arb'n 232 (1977).

[19]. The decision was reported in 20 Yearbk. Comm. Arb'n 742 (1995).

SOCIETÀ DISTILLERIE MERIDIONALI (ITALY)
v. SCHUURMANS & VAN GINNEKEN BV
(THE NETHERLANDS)

Italy, Corte di Cassazione [Supreme Court], 14 March 1995.
21 Yearbk. Comm. Arb'n 607 (1996).*

FACTS

On 19 July 1991, an award was rendered in London between
SODIME—Società Distillerie Meridionali (SODIME) and Schuurmans &
Van Ginneken BV (Schuurmans). The three arbitrators directed SO-
DIME to pay Schuurmans US$251,168.23 for non-performance of a
contract of 5 February 1986 for the sale of sugar cane syrup.

On 11 November 1991, Schuurmans sought enforcement of the
English award before the Court of Appeal of Naples. On 19 June 1993,
the Court of Appeal granted enforcement.

Upon appeal by SODIME, the Supreme Court reversed the lower
court's decision, finding that the award submitted by Schuurmans when
requesting enforcement was not duly certified under Art. IV of the
Convention and Italian law, as only two of the three signatures of the
arbitrators had been authenticated.

EXCERPT

[1]   "[SODIME] objects that . . . only two of the three signatures of
the arbitrators are authenticated in the arbitral award submitted by
[Schuurmans], and alleges that the award should not have been deemed
duly certified according to Art. IV(1)(a) of the [New York Convention], as
the original award contained three signatures and the copy, in order to
be valid, should equally have contained three authenticated signatures.
It also observes that, as this objection can be raised *ex officio*, it is
irrelevant that it was not raised in [SODIME's] first statement after the
award had been submitted.

(. . .)

[2]   "This ground for appeal is founded. Art. IV(1) of the [New York
Convention] provides that: '. . . the party applying for recognition and
enforcement shall, at the time of the application, supply: (a) the duly
authenticated original award or a duly certified copy thereof; . . .'. The
judgment [of the Court of Appeal of Naples] held that this requirement
is met; it found that, according to the law of the place where recognition
and enforcement of the arbitral award are sought, any question concerning the authenticity [of the award], as provided for in Art. III of the
Convention, must be solved according to [Italian law] and it concluded
that, in casu, the authenticity of the [award] resulted from the fact that
the interested party had not objected to it in a timely manner, as it
should have done in the first hearing or in its first statement after the
award had been submitted. [The Court] added that, in the practice of the

* Reprinted with permission of Yearbook
Commercial   Arbitration,   International
Council for Commercial Arbitration.

English legal system, the authentication of the signatures of the two
English arbitrators only suffices for the submitted [award] to be authentic, and that any reference to the Italian notary public law as to the
authentification of the signatures in the original foreign award is irrelevant.

[3]   "The reasoning of the [Court of Appeal] cannot be shared....
[A]ccording to Art. III of the Convention, each State shall recognize an
arbitral award and enforce it 'in accordance with the rules of procedure
of the territory where the award is relied upon ...'. Hence, the existence
of the required conditions for authenticity must be ascertained according
to the procedural law of the State seized.[1] This results in the applicability of Italian law, ... which requires that all signatures, not only some of
those appearing on the act, be authenticated for an act to be authentic,
and in the inapplicability of the Anglo–Saxon practice (which is different
from Italian law), which the Court of Appeal summarily deemed applicable on the basis of a generic reference made to it by [Schuurmans].

(...)

[4]   "The [Court of Appeal] failed to consider that, in the context of
the Convention, submission of the original award or a certified copy
thereof affects the possibility to commence enforcement proceedings and
must be ascertained *ex officio*, independent of the statements and objections of the party, and that, in this light, the fact that the submitted
document was not * * * objected to according to Italian law was in any
case of no procedural relevance with respect to an act signed by third
parties, to which act apply, under Art. III of the Convention, the
authentication formalities provided for by the law of the court of
enforcement.

[5]   "The fact that the 'duly authenticated' [award] requested by
Art. IV(1)(a) of the said Convention was not submitted together with the
request for enforcement should thus have prevented the Court deciding
on the merits from hearing the request for enforcement in the Italian
legal system."

APPELLANT R. SA v. APPELLEE A. LTD.

Cour de Justice (Court of Appeal) Geneva, April 15, 1999.
ASA Bulletin No. 4/2000, pp. 786–792; Semaine Judiciaire, 2000/I
p. 310 (Summarized and translated by the authors).

[On January 28, 1999, a Swiss court of first instance (*Tribunal de
première instance –hereinafter "Tribunal"*) granted recognition and enforcement to a Chinese (CIETAC) award. Under this award, R. SA was
obliged to pay SF 918,772 with interest to A. Ltd. R. SA appealed,
alleging a violation of Article IV of the New York Convention. Seeking
recognition and enforcement, the Appellee (A. Ltd) submitted the following documents:

1. The Supreme Court referred to its
own decision of 26 May 1987, no. 4706
(*Jassica SA v. Ditta Gioacchino Polojaz*),
reported in Yearbook XVII (1992) pp. 525–
528 (Italy no. 109).

— a non-authenticated English version of the contract (including the arbitration clause);

— a copy of the original of the award in Chinese; and

— a full French translation of the Chinese award. The first and the last page of this translation were certified by an employee of the Swiss Embassy in Beijing. The first page contained the designation of the arbitral institution, the names and addresses of the parties, while the last page contained the actual decision, the "*dispositif*" of the award, and the names of the three arbitrators.

— The Tribunal granted recognition and enforcement. R. SA appealed to the Geneva *Cour de Justice*—hereinafter the "Court"), which rendered the following decision]:

"R. SA objects that the Tribunal granted '*exequatur*" even though it established in its judgment that A. Ltd did not submit the documents prescribed in Article IV of the New York Convention, and accordingly, did not fulfill the conditions for recognition and enforcement of foreign arbitral awards established by the Convention."

[In its statement of legal reasons the Geneva *Cour de Justice,* acting as an appellate court, first established that the New York Convention was applicable, and then gave a short survey of the drafting history of the Convention, stressing that the principal difference between the New York Convention on one hand, and earlier texts on the other hand, is "a significant improvement of the position of the party seeking recognition". The Court stated that Article IV has to be interpreted in the same spirit. It added that the Convention "does not further describe the contents and the nature of the formal obligations it creates, nor does it indicate how their violation is sanctioned".]

"As far as the submitted documents are concerned, one has to agree with Van den Berg in that the applicant must supply at least, a copy of the arbitration agreement and of the award. If these are lacking, the competent authority must dismiss the request for enforcement. The court must, however, show flexibility ('*souplesse'*) when evaluating the manner in which these documents were supplied whether as authenticated originals or as certified copies. * * * Regarding the translation of these documents into one of the official languages of the country of recognition, some authors even take the position that the party seeking recognition need not supply translations if the court is deemed to know the original language."

[The Court here analyzes earlier Swiss court practice and concludes that Swiss courts have interpreted Article IV with considerable flexibility.]

"Taking into account the arguments stated above, the Court considers that the Tribunal was correct in recognizing and declaring enforceable the award rendered by the Chinese arbitration commission, in spite of the established violations of Article IV of the Convention.

The objection was raised that the party seeking recognition submitted the original of the award without authentication. The Court notes that appellant admits that the award submitted was indeed the original award, and that it did not contest that the award is stamped on its last page with the official stamp of the CIETAC. The only objection advanced by the appellant regarding this document is that it lacks authentication as prescribed by Article IV(1)(a) of the Convention. This objection is purely formal, since appellant does not contest the authenticity of the award, and hence [this objection] was rightly dismissed by the Tribunal, avoiding thereby excessive formalism.

Appellee submitted a French translation of the award, of which translation only the first and the last page was certified by a diplomatic agent of the Swiss Embassy in Beijing. The Court concludes—just as the Tribunal did—that the two pages at issue are the most important ones, because they identify the parties, contain the *"dispositif"*, and confirm that the award is final. Moreover, the Court confirms that this objection is also of a purely formal nature, since the appellant does not contest the conformity of the translation with the original. Accordingly, the appeal is denied.

The decision [of the Tribunal] is thus confirmed."

Questions and Comments

1. What arguments can you advance in favor of or against the institution of deposit?

2. Once deposit is required, what should be the legal consequences of this requirement?

3. Do you see a reason for distinguishing between awards of institutional and ad hoc tribunals respectively, as has been done by the Yugoslav and by the Croatian rules?

4. According to the Belgian rules, the person who has to deposit the award is **the president of the arbitration panel**. According to Dutch law, deposit is made by **the arbitration panel**; Swiss rules foresee deposit by **the parties**; while Egyptian norms envisage deposit by **the winning party**. Do you see practical consequences behind these options?

5. It is stressed in some rules that the arbitrator's office does not end before deposit has been made. Is this important?

6. The Italian Supreme Court (Corte di Cassazione) took a more restrictive position than Austrian and Japanese Courts did. The Italian Court relies on Article III of the New York Convention. Do you agree that Article III mandates authentication according to the rules of the country of recognition?

7. If you had powers to legislate, what law would you designate as applicable to authentication of arbitral awards?

8. Is authentication (or lack of authentication) a matter the court should have to investigate ex officio?

9. Deciding on recognition of the Chinese award, the Geneva Court dealt with two objections:

— that the award was not duly authenticated—as required by Article IV(1((a), and

— that the translation was not properly certified—as required by Article IV(2).

The Court admitted that there was a violation of Article IV, but recognized the award nevertheless, arguing that authenticity was actually not contested and that a denial of recognition under the given circumstances would represent "excessive formalism".

Do you see a violation of both Article IV(1)(a) and Article IV(2)?

If there was indeed, a violation, can the award nevertheless be recognized?

10. The Geneva Court—endeavoring to find a flexible solution and to avoid refusal of recognition in a case in which the authenticity of the award is not challenged and there are no other grounds for refusal of recognition—states that the New York Convention "does not further describe the contents and nature of the formal obligations it creates" in Article IV, "nor does it indicate how their violation is sanctioned".

Isn't the sanction implied in Article IV(1), which stresses that in order "to obtain the recognition and enforcement" the party applying for recognition and enforcement shall, at the time of application supply the requisite documents (duly authenticated original or certified copy and—if needed—certified translation)? And yet, does it make sense to refuse recognition on the ground of lack of authentication, if the authenticity of the award is not disputed? Does Article IV protect any interests beyond those of the party opposing recognition?

11. In the opinion of the Geneva Court imperfect certification (certification of the first and last page only) does not represent a sufficient ground for refusing recognition, if the authenticity of the award (or the accuracy of the translation) are not challenged. Suppose no page of the translation of the CIETAC award had been certified, but authenticity was not challenged. If one follows the logic of the Geneva Court, would the award nevertheless be recognized?

IV.3. CHOICE OF LAW ISSUES BEFORE THE ARBITRATORS

IV.3.a. Note

The choice of arbitration simplifies some of the problems of conflict of laws (private international law) that arise in disputes before courts. For example, the issue of jurisdiction over the parties is resolved by party consent, as reflected in the arbitration agreement. The problems of recognition and enforcement of the award—the topic of Chapter V—are defined and limited by the provisions of the New York Convention.

At the same time, the choice of law problem is at least theoretically more complicated in arbitration. Difficulties arise because of the autonomous, anational character of international arbitration—that is to say, because of the absence of a forum. In proceedings before a court, the forum's procedural law, including its body of choice of law rules, automatically applies. How is the choice of law problem resolved in international arbitration?

As far as procedure is concerned, as we have seen in the opening sections of this chapter, most problems are solved through party autonomy and a tendency of arbitrators to favor pragmatic and flexible solutions. If the parties choose institutional arbitration, the institution's rules will provide a basic procedural framework. If they choose ad hoc arbitration and do not mention any body of procedural rules, the arbitrators will function flexibly and pragmatically, perhaps guided or assisted by the *lex arbitri*, the supervisory law applicable to the procedural aspects of the arbitration. We shall return to the *lex arbitri* issue later in this note.

These party procedural arrangements are subject generally to the basic standards of due process, enforced either through the *lex arbitri* just mentioned, or in any event, brought into play at the point of enforcement of the award through the provisions of Article V of the New York Convention. There is a tendency to allow the parties considerable maneuvering room; moreover, the standards imposed by national *lex arbitri* are in conformity to a significant extent with the basic rules of the New York Convention.

Turning to the law governing the arbitration agreement, the choice-of-law problem also yields in most respects to party autonomy, though with lingering difficulties. One difficulty arises if the arbitration agreement itself is attacked as invalid. What law should decide this question? The issue can arise before a court or before the arbitrators. Before a court, the forum's choice-of-law rules will apply, limited, however, in most countries by the binding provisions of the New York Convention. In Chapter II we have already examined the most important validity issues, namely formal validity and nonarbitrability. That examination concerned mostly the effects of the New York Convention and how courts have dealt with the issues.

Before arbitrators the validity issue is more complicated, because party autonomy, at least as a matter of logic, is a less compelling guide if the parties' agreement itself is under attack. The New York Convention does not, moreover, speak directly to arbitrators. Nevertheless, even on this issue party autonomy and a certain preference for validating law tend to prevail, and logic is to some extent ignored.

It is noteworthy that the New York Convention encourages this solution; Article V(1)(a) authorizes a contracting state to refuse to enforce an award if the arbitration agreement: " * * * is not valid under the law to which the parties have subjected it or, failing any indication thereon, under the law of the country where the award was made * * * ." (Where the award is made is of course generally determined, directly or indirectly, by party autonomy.) Although the New York Convention does not apply to arbitrators, it would be difficult to quarrel with an approach in harmony with the requirements for enforceability of the award in most countries. (For an example of an arbitrator's reliance on Article V(1)(a) of the New York Convention to uphold the validity of an arbitration agreement, see the interim award in the *Seller (Korea) v. Buyer (Jordan)* case, reproduced below below in section IV.3.e.)

On the issue of what law the arbitrators should apply to the merits of the dispute, the answer is again dominated by party autonomy. Just as party choice of institutional rules or the UNCITRAL Rules resolves most of the basic procedural questions, it also resolves basic choice of law issues because these rules normally include provisions on choice of law. As we shall see, they uniformly favor party autonomy. We examine in particular the provisions of the UNCITRAL Model Law, the UNCITRAL Rules, and the 1998 ICC Rules.

The Role of the *Lex Arbitri*. In addition to a basic reliance on party autonomy arbitrators are also generally conscious of the supervisory and facilitating role played by what may be called variously the *lex arbitri*, the curial law, or the law governing the arbitration. The concept here is of a national law that facilitates and supervises to a certain extent the arbitration proceedings. For example, if the parties choose ad hoc arbitration but no appointing authority or procedure, the *lex arbitri* will generally be consulted to decide how arbitrators are chosen. (The courts of the country whose *lex arbitri* applies will normally be considered to have jurisdiction for this purpose.) Or, once an award is given, what law will decide whether the award should be set aside? This is normally the *lex arbitri*. (Again, the courts of the country whose *lex arbitri* applies will usually have jurisdiction.)[20]

The issue of how the *lex arbitri* is to be chosen can pose problems, as we saw in the *McDonnell Douglas* case in section IV.1.b. As a theoretical matter, most courts and scholars agree that the parties are free to choose the *lex arbitri*. Nevertheless, the parties are rarely explicit about such a choice; thus, in the vast majority of cases courts and arbitrators apply the *lex arbitri* of the place of arbitration. This is probably a vestige of the jurisdictional theory of international arbitration that generally prevailed before World War II. In the first half of the nineteenth century, before the autonomous or anational character of international arbitration

---

[20]. One writer lists the following issues as generally governed by the *lex arbitri* (though differences exist in various countries): " * * * (a) the parties' autonomy to agree on substantive and procedural issues in the arbitration; (b) procedural issues (such as type of hearings, administration of oaths, discovery, evidentiary matters, and the like); (c) appointment and removal of arbitrators; (d) extent of judicial supervision of, or interference in, the arbitration proceedings (such as ordering provisional relief or discovery in aid of arbitration); (e) arbitrators' liability and ethical standards; and (f) form and making of the award. In addition, and less clearly, the * * * [*lex* *arbitri*] sometimes governs; (g) the interpretation and enforceability of the parties' arbitration agreement (including issues of non-arbitrability); (h) conflict of law rules applicable to the substance of the dispute; and (i) quasi-substantive issues, such as rules concerning interest and attorneys' fees." G. Born, International Commercial Arbitration in the United States: Commentary & Materials 162 (1994). Born also notes that Article V(1)(e) of the New York Convention permits a contracting party to refuse to recognize or enforce an award set aside by courts of the country "under the law of which, * * * [the] award was made"—that law being the *lex arbitri*. Id.

gained in acceptance, arbitration proceedings were considered subject to the sovereignty of the country in which they took place, and, therefore, to the law of that country. The continued role of the *lex arbitri* as a supervisory law is implicitly recognized by Article V(1)(e) of the New York Convention, which provides that an award need not be recognized or enforced if: "The award * * * has been set aside or suspended by a competent authority of the country in which, or under the law of which, that award was made." It would seem that the phrase "under the law of which" recognizes the possible role of party autonomy.

The materials below examine the role courts and arbitrators ascribe to the *lex arbitri* and how it is determined. The question remains, however, whether any such concept is necessary.

The Problem of Mandatory Law. Finally, at the end of this choice of law section, the materials turn to the perplexing problem of mandatory law. This issue arose obliquely earlier in the materials in connection with the problem of nonarbitrability taken up in Chapter II. One issue raised there, for example, was whether arbitrators would be justified in applying the antitrust law (mandatory law) of country A, even if the arbitration agreement explicitly subjects all disputes to the law of country B. If arbitrators derive their authority and legitimacy from the arbitration agreement and if that agreement is explicit about the applicable law, how can arbitrators—who are not public servants or officials of any sovereign—justify applying the mandatory law of a country not chosen by the parties? The materials raise both theoretical and practical considerations that inform the debate surrounding this difficult issue.

IV.3.b. *Applicable Substantive Law—The Prevailing Concept: Party Choice or Choice by the Arbitrators*

We reproduce below the 1961 Geneva Convention on International Commercial Arbitration, Article VII, the 1998 ICC Rules of Arbitration Article 17, and Article 28 of the UNCITRAL Model Law with commentary on that article by Howard Holzmann and Joseph Neuhaus. The basic provisions of Article 28 of the Model Law are also contained in the UNCITRAL Rules, Article 33. These rules represent the prevailing concept regarding the applicable substantive law in international commercial arbitration.

1961 EUROPEAN (GENEVA) CONVENTION ON INTERNATIONAL COMMERCIAL ARBITRATION, ARTICLE VII

Applicable Law

1.   The parties shall be free to determine, by agreement, the law to be applied by the arbitrators to the substance of the dispute. Failing any indication by the parties as to the applicable law, the arbitrators shall apply the proper law under the rule of conflict that the arbitrators deem

applicable. In both cases the arbitrators shall take account of the terms of the contract and trade usages.

2. The arbitrators shall act as *amiables compositeurs* if the parties so decide and if they may do so under the law applicable to the arbitration.

1998 INTERNATIONAL CHAMBER OF COMMERCE RULES OF ARBITRATION,

ARTICLE 17

1. The parties shall be free to agree upon the rules of law to be applied by the Arbitral Tribunal to the merits of the dispute. In the absence of any such agreement, the Arbitral Tribunal shall apply the rules of law which it determines to be appropriate.

2. In all cases the Arbitral Tribunal shall take account of the provisions of the contract and the relevant trade usages.

3. The Arbitral Tribunal shall assume the powers of an amiable compositeur or decide ex aequo et bono only if the parties have agreed to give it such powers.

Howard M. Holtzmann & Joseph E. Neuhaus, A GUIDE TO THE UNCITRAL MODEL LAW ON INTERNATIONAL COMMERCIAL ARBITRATION

764–72 (1989).*

ARTICLE 28. RULES APPLICABLE TO SUBSTANCE OF DISPUTE

(1) The arbitral tribunal shall decide the dispute in accordance with such rules of law as are chosen by the parties as applicable to the substance of the dispute. Any designation of the law or legal system of a given State shall be construed, unless otherwise expressed, as directly referring to the substantive law of that state and not to its conflict of laws rules.

(2) Failing any designation by the parties, the arbitral tribunal shall apply the law determined by the conflict of laws rules which it considers applicable.

(3) The arbitral tribunal shall decide *ex aequo et bono* or as *amiable compositeur* only if the parties have expressly authorized it to do so.

(4) In all cases, the arbitral tribunal shall decide in accordance with the terms of the contract and shall take into account the usages of the trade applicable to the transaction.

COMMENTARY

At least as a matter of theory, the problem of selecting the rules applicable to the substance of the dispute is more complicated in interna-

---

* Reprinted with permission from Kluwer Law International.

tional commercial arbitration than it is for a domestic court or for an arbitral tribunal in a purely domestic arbitration. In courts and in domestic arbitration, there is generally a single set of choice of law rules that govern the choice. For a court, this set will be the binding choice of law rules promulgated by the legislature of the State in which the court sits. In a domestic arbitration, the situation is often similar: the arbitral tribunal will either, like a domestic judge, employ the domestic conflicts rules of the place of arbitration, or it will almost automatically apply the substantive law of the State in which the parties reside, the contract was to be performed, and the arbitration takes place.[1] There will in any event not usually be a choice of several potentially applicable rules to govern the selection of the applicable law.

In international commercial arbitration, on the other hand, the tribunal is not bound to apply the conflicts rules of the place of arbitration, and no single body of substantive law or rules will necessarily be the obvious and unquestioned choice. The element that makes the arbitration international—be it the place of arbitration, the place of performance, or the state of residence of one party—will generally introduce a potentially different rule of private international law.

National arbitral laws rarely address the question of choice of law.[2] They are generally designed primarily for arbitrations connected solely with the enacting State, and in such noninternational arbitration there is rarely a serious choice of law question. In order fully to meet the needs of international arbitration, therefore, the Model Law, like international conventions on arbitration[4] and some rules designed for international arbitration,[5] provides guidelines on this subject. As the Commission report noted, there was wide support for the view "that the model law would be incomplete without a provision on rules applicable to the substance of disputes, particularly in view of the fact that the model law

---

1. The problem is a bit more complicated in federal systems, because each state, province, canton, or district may well have differing provisions of both substantive law and conflicts rules. Still, a federal rule for choosing among those provision will frequently apply.

2. See Y. Derains, Possible Conflict of Laws Rules and the Rules Applicable to the Substance of the Dispute in UNCITRAL's *Project for a Model Law on International Commercial Arbitration* 169, 174 (ICCA Congress Series No. 2. P. Saunders ed. 1984). This author notes only two recent laws that address the topic, and each of these provides a special regime designed for international arbitration. *Id.* These are the French Code of Civil Procedure of 1981, in its Article 1496, and the Djiboutian Code on international arbitration adopted in 1984, in its Article 12.

The French provision states (in translation): "The arbitrator shall decide the dispute according to the rules of law chosen by the parties; in the absence of such a choice, he shall decide according to the rules he deems appropriate. In all cases he shall take into account trade usages." *Id.* The Djiboutian provision is essentially to the same effect. *Id.*

4. *E.g.*, European Convention on International Commercial Arbitration. Art. VII, 484 U.N.T.S. 349 (Geneva 1961); Convention on the Settlement of Investment Disputes between States and Nationals of Other States. Art. 42 575 U.N.T.S. 159 (Washington 1965).

5. *E.g.*, UNCITRAL Arbitration Rules. Art. 33 (1976); ICC Rules of Arbitration. Art. 13(3) (1988); Rules of the London Court of International Arbitration. Art. 13.1(a) (1985).

dealt with international commercial arbitration where a lack of rules on that issue would give rise to uncertainty."

The Model Law attempts to provide rules that are in line with generally accepted modern theory and practice. There was little disagreement on the main points of policy: first, that the parties should have complete autonomy to choose any rules to govern the substance of the dispute, even if those rules are territorially unconnected with the contract or the dispute; second, that in the absence of a choice by the parties the choice should be made by the arbitral tribunal; third, that the Model Law should recognize an agreement by the parties to have the arbitral tribunal decide the dispute *ex aequo et bono* or as *amiable compositeur*.

Nevertheless, there was a divergence of opinion and lengthy discussion as to some of the details of these policies, in particular, as to the precise scope of both the parties' power to agree on, and the arbitral tribunal's power to choose, the applicable rules governing the substance of the dispute.

Paragraph 1. Paragraph 1 permits the parties to make a binding choice of law to govern the dispute and provides a rule of construction for interpreting whether that choice includes the chosen law's conflict of law rules. The primary issue here was whether the parties could choose not only the body of law in force in a particular jurisdiction but also parts of other legal codes or part or all of sets of rules not in force as such anywhere. For example, the parties might wish their dispute to be decided in accordance with an international convention or uniform law that is not yet in force, or they may wish a decision based on parts of the law of various States. In favor of this latter approach, it was noted that allowing the parties to choose such rules was not essentially different from recognizing their freedom to choose a national law that was unconnected with the dispute—a freedom that was widely accepted.

The Working Group adopted this view. The First Draft specifically mentioned the possibility of the parties' choosing "even if not yet in force, a pertinent international convention or uniform law." This specific approach was thought to raise problems, however.[10] A broader and less explicit rule was suggested:

> [I]t was ... suggested that the statement as to the autonomy of the parties might be broadened in this article to enable the parties implicitly to designate parts of different systems of law as applicable to the substance of their dispute. It was suggested that the autonomy of the parties could be broadened implicitly by a rule according to which "the tribunal shall decide a dispute in accordance with such rules of law as may be agreed by the parties."

10. "It was felt that the designation of an international convention or uniform law which was not yet in force in any State would cause difficulties in determining the relationship between the text and the other national law applicable to the substance of the dispute." Second Working Group Report, A/CN.9/232, para. 162, p. 779 *infra*. As noted below, though, the view of those who prevailed on these issues in the Commission appears to have been that the text finally adopted would permit choosing legal texts not yet in force.

This approach, with its crucial phrase "rules of law," was preferred by the Working Group and ultimately incorporated into the law. The Working Group stated that it was intended to allow the parties to choose, for example, "rules of more than one legal system, including rules of law which had been elaborated on the international level." There were limits on the choice, however: "While some representatives would have preferred an even wider interpretation or an even broader formula, to include, for example, general legal principles or case law developed in arbitration awards, the Working Group, after deliberation, was agreed that this was too far-reaching to be acceptable to many States, at least for the time being."

During the consideration of the provision by the full Commission, a number of delegations expressed reservations about the phrase "rules of law," both in written comments and in oral interventions. It was thought, on the one hand, that this approach was novel and ambiguous, and would create considerable difficulties in practice, that it might lead to "extravagant choices" by the parties, and that it might encourage dividing up the contract into innumerable parts, each governed by a separate set of rules. On the other hand, some thought the provision unnecessary, on the ground that most legal systems already recognized the right to select different laws for different parts of the relationship, a practice known as *dépeçage*, and that the parties could always incorporate the provisions of international conventions and the like into their agreements as contractual terms.

The Commission initially decided to replace the term "rules of law" with the more traditional expression "law." It agreed, however, that this expression should be interpreted to be essentially as broad as "rules of law": it would allow both *dépeçage* and selection of international conventions not yet in force. The Commission later reversed itself and reinstated the term "rules of law." This decision was connected with a similar debate that arose during the discussion of paragraph 2 of Article 28, which deals with the choice of law by the arbitral tribunal rather than by the parties. There, the question was whether the arbitral tribunal was to choose the applicable substantive law directly or only via the more traditional route of choosing a particular set of choice of law rules, which then would refer the tribunal to a body of substantive law. A similar division of opinion surfaced. In such circumstances, where no consensus for a change emerged, the Commission pursued a general policy of retaining the text drafted over several years by the Working Group, and this was the course followed in this instance.

What, then, does the phrase "rules of law" mean? What rules may the parties choose to govern the substance of their dispute? The Commission Report is reasonably clear that the parties may choose the national law of any State and that they may choose the national laws of different States to govern various aspects of their relationship (that is, *dépeçage*). Similarly, they can probably agree to have a given national law apply but exclude the provisions on a specific topic. For example, it was said that there have been occasions when parties to international contracts have chosen Swiss law except for the rules governing judicially ordered set-offs, which are viewed by some as providing too much authority to the court. Another analogous example is the common contract provision stipulating application of a law as it was worded at a particular time, excluding subsequent amendments. Finally, as noted above, there was also a clear indication that the chosen provision need not be "law" as such; the Commission Report notes that it was stated in support of the term "rules of law" that it would allow parties to "choose the rules embodied in a convention or similar legal text elaborated on the international level, even if not yet in force."

In addition, a few examples appear elsewhere in the legislative history. On the one hand, several governments expressed their understanding that the term could include trade usages and "the rules of businessmen and business associations." On the other hand, as noted above, the Working Group decided at an early stage that the term did not extend to "general legal principles" or law developed in arbitration awards.

The rationale for placing any limits on the parties' choice is probably that the rules chosen should be reasonably ascertainable by the arbitral tribunal. Beyond this, however, it is submitted that there is little reason for limiting the parties. If they are empowered to authorize decisions *ex aequo et bono*—that is, based on equity and divorced from strict legal standards-and if they may incorporate as a contractual term virtually any rule they wish, they should likewise be empowered to choose virtually any set of rules to govern the dispute (subject to the limits imposed by public policy and substantive law).

The parties' freedom to choose rules applicable to the dispute must be interpreted in the light of two other important sections of the Model Law. First, under Article 2(d), the parties may not empower a third party, such as an arbitral institution, to choose the applicable law. It must be accomplished by agreement of the parties, or else the arbitral tribunal will do it. Second, Article 19 of the Model Law confers on the arbitral tribunal the power to determine the admissibility, relevance, materiality, and weight of any evidence, unless the parties have agreed to the contrary. In some States, such questions are matters of substantive law, not procedure. Nevertheless, the Commission agreed that the discretion of the arbitral tribunal conferred by Article 19(2) would not be affected by the choice of law applicable to the substance of the dispute selected under Article 28. This interpretation-which is merely an application of the maxim that the specific rule controls the general-means that the parties' choice of the substantive law of a particular State will not include the rules of evidence of the designated State, unless the parties specifically refer to those rules.

Paragraph 2. As noted above, a debate like that over the wording of paragraph 1 arose in connection with paragraph 2 of Article 28, which deals with the arbitral tribunal's power to choose the applicable law in the absence of a designation by the parties. The question with respect to paragraph 1 was the extent of the parties' freedom to choose the rules applicable to the substance of the dispute. With respect to paragraph 2 there were two primary issues. One was whether the tribunal might be empowered to choose the applicable substantive law directly or only via the conflict of law rules that it considered to be applicable. The second, related issue was whether the arbitral tribunal could choose "rules of law," and not only the "law" of any given national State, just as the parties were permitted to do under paragraph 1.

The discussions of paragraphs 1 and 2 were inevitably linked. It was argued by some that the two provisions should be in harmony, that is, that the arbitral tribunal's power under paragraph 2 should be the same as the parties' freedom under paragraph 1. The proponents of this view argued that in the absence of designation by the parties the arbitral tribunal should be directed simply to "apply the rules of law it considers appropriate," which would free the tribunal from both a particular set of conflict rules and any particular "law." They argued, *inter alia*, that this would accord better with present practices in international commercial arbitration, in which the tribunal frequently did not first decide on conflict of law rules but rather chose the substantive law by more direct means.

Others disagreed, stating that the broader freedom conferred by paragraph 1 was appropriate in a provision directed at the parties but less so in one like paragraph 2 aimed at the arbitral tribunal. They said that the narrower freedom given the arbitral tribunal would provide greater predictability and certainty and would help to ensure that the arbitral tribunal gave reasons for its choice of law.

The Working Group and the Commission favored the latter approach and adopted the more restrictive language requiring recourse to conflict of law rules (which would in turn require application of a "law" to the substance of the dispute). This "more cautious approach" was viewed as advisable in view of the "rather progressive step" taken in paragraph 1.

In the end, though, it was widely recognized that the practical result would generally be the same regardless of which formulation were chosen, particularly with respect to whether reference to conflict of law rules was required. It was said that the reasons invoked by arbitral tribunals when they select the governing law directly, without separate reference to conflicts rules, are often similar to the connecting factors used in such rules.[36]

36. *See* Commission Report, A/40/17, para. 237, p. 806 *infra*; Second Working Group Report, A/CN.9/232, para. 163, p. 780 *infra*. *Cf.* Y. Derains, *supra* n. 2. p. 192. The author of the last-cited work suggests that the requirement that the arbitral tribunal refer to "conflict of laws rules" is merely a requirement that the tribunal indicate the reasons for its choice, because it does not require reference to a "conflict system" of any given State, but merely to "rules." In view of the Working Group's evident belief that paragraph 2 as drafted provided to the arbitral tribunal a narrower "scope" than paragraph 1 did to the parties, *see, e.g.,* Fourth Working Group Report, A/CN.9/245, para. 97, p. 782 *infra*, one

Paragraph 3. Paragraph 3 gives effect to the parties' agreement to have the arbitral tribunal decide *ex aequo et bono* or as *amiable compositeur*.

Both terms are used because some systems use one term and some the other, and because it was thought that some systems might distinguish between them. The Secretariat commented that though this type of arbitration is not known in all legal systems, the provision seemed appropriate in the Model Law for several reasons: first, on the ground that the Law should not bar established features and practices of arbitration used in certain legal systems; second, because it was consistent with the general policy of reducing the importance of the place of arbitration in international commercial arbitration, insofar as it recognized practices unknown in domestic arbitration at that place; and third, because there was no risk of misleading an unwary party since the provision requires express authorization of the parties.

During the drafting of paragraph 3, three kinds of limitations or guidelines were proposed for tribunals acting *ex aequo et bono* or as *amiable compositeurs*, only one of which was actually incorporated into Article 28. That one is contained in paragraph 4 and instructs the tribunal in all cases to decide the case in accordance with the terms of the contract and to take into account usages of the trade applicable to the transaction.[39] One feature that was proposed but not included in the law was a requirement that arbitrators, even when acting *ex aequo et bono* or as *amiable compositeurs*, should strive to ensure the enforceability of the decision in States with which the dispute has a significant connection. Similarly, the Secretariat suggested that tribunals acting *ex aequo et bono* or as *amiable compositeurs* be required to "observe those mandatory provisions of law regarded in the respective country as ensuring its (international) *ordre public*." These proposals were not adopted primarily because of the difficulty of developing a comprehensive definition of the mandate of arbitrators authorized to decide *ex aequo et bono* or as *amiable compositeurs*.

Paragraph 4. The First Draft of Article 28 contained two proposals for a paragraph on the importance of trade usage and the terms of the contract. The first was based on article 33(3) of the UNCITRAL Arbitration Rules and was similar to the provision in the final text. The second was based on Article 9 of the United Nations Convention on Contracts for the International Sale of Goods (Vienna 1980). This approach attempted to define the term "trade usage." It stated that the arbitral tribunal

> [. . . shall apply any usage to which the parties have agreed; the parties are considered, unless otherwise agreed, to have impliedly

may question whether this suggestion reflects the intent of the drafters.

39. *See* First Secretariat Note, A/CN.9/207, para. 90, p. 774 *infra*. The Working Group at first specifically decided not to apply such a provision to *amiable composition*, noting that this seemed consistent with an earlier decision not to define the mandate of an *amiable* Commission when it added paragraph 4 of article 28. Commission Report, A/40/17, para. 241, p. 807 *infra*.

made applicable to their contract or its formation a usage of which they know or ought to have known and which in international trade is widely known to, and regularly observed by, parties to contracts of the type involved in the particular trade concerned.][43]

The Working Group deleted this longer definition because it had been designed primarily in respect of contracts for the sale of goods and was felt to be inapplicable to some other types of contracts that might give rise to disputes subject to the Model Law, such as investment contracts.

Later, reservations were raised in the Working Group about the appropriateness of having any provision along the lines of paragraph 4. First, it was said that the reference to contract terms might be misleading where those terms conflicted with mandatory provisions of law or "did not express the true intent of the parties." Second, the reference to trade usage was considered both redundant—since reference to trade usage frequently was required by the national law applicable to the dispute—and dangerous—since "their legal effect and qualification was not uniform in all legal systems." As a result, the provision was deleted by the Working Group.

The Commission reinstated the provision. It was suggested that such a provision was well known and appears in both the UNCITRAL Arbitration Rules and the European Convention on International Commercial Arbitration. Moreover, the provision was said to ensure that the parties' expectations were fulfilled, on the ground that parties choose arbitration in part because they expect that arbitrators "will above all base their decisions on the wording and history of the contract and the usages of trade."

Questions and Comments

1. What differences are there in the provisions on applicable law one finds in the 1961 Geneva Convention, in Article 17 of the ICC Rules, and in Article 28 of the UNCITRAL Model Law. Which version do you prefer?

2. Refer to the UNCITRAL Model Law and Arbitral Rules.

a. Suppose in the arbitration clause the parties provide: "the law of Switzerland shall govern this agreement". Should the arbitrators apply Swiss law on substantive issues, on procedural issues, on conflict of laws issues?

b. May the parties choose to apply the provisions of an international convention that has never come into force? If the parties fail to include a choice-of-law clause, may the arbitrators choose as applicable law the provisions of an international convention that has never come into force?

c. Suppose the parties specifically provide for the application of an early version of the U.N. Convention on the International Sale of Goods (Vienna Sales Convention), a version that never was adopted and never

---

43. First Draft, A/CN.9/WG.11/WP.36. Art. 31(3), p. 778 *infra*. The use of square brackets in the draft indicates wording that was offered as an alternative or that was otherwise still under consideration. The Vienna Sales Convention may be found at A/Conf.97/18 (Annex I).

became law. Would the arbitrators still be free to choose a national law to govern substantive issues? Would they be required to do so? If so, how should they choose this law? Could the law they choose actually invalidate provisions of the Vienna Sales Convention chosen by the parties?

3.   Article 17 of the 1998 ICC Rules would apply if the parties specifically choose ICC arbitration. The UNCITRAL Rules would function in the same way. The Model Law, on the other hand, was intended for adoption as national law in countries seeking a modern law supportive of international arbitration, and it has in fact been adopted by a number of countries. If arbitration is anational and has no forum, how would the Model Law (or the nationally enacted equivalent) ever become applicable? Return to this question after considering the materials immediately below.

IV.3.c. *Interpreting Choice of Law Clauses and the Role of the Lex Arbitri*

UNION OF INDIA v. MCDONNELL DOUGLAS CORPORATION

Queen's Bench Division (Commercial Court) 22 December 1992.
[1993] 2 Lloyd's Law Rep. 48.

[This case is reproduced earlier in the chapter in section IV.1.b.]

CLAIMANT: BUYER (MOZAMBIQUE) v. DEFENDANT: SELLER (THE NETHERLANDS)

Preliminary Award in ICC case no. 5505 of 1987.
Place of Arbitration: Lausanne, Switzerland 13 Yearbk. Comm. Arb'n 110 (1988).*

GEORGES MULLER, ARBITRATOR

FACTS

The contract for the sale of seed potatoes between the Dutch seller and the Mozambique buyer contained the following clause contained in an Annex II:

"*Arbitration*:

"Both parties undertake to fulfill this contract in good faith. Any dispute arising in consequence thereof, or in connection therewith, should be settled through an amicable negotiation. Should no agreement be arrived at, they must finally undertake to submit the matter according to the regulation for agreement and arbitration of the International Chamber of Commerce to one or more arbitrators as per the said laws. The arbitration will take place in Switzerland, the law applicable is that known in England."

* Reprinted with permission of Yearbook   Council for Commercial Arbitration.
Commercial   Arbitration,   International

The parties disputed the meaning and effect of the words "the law applicable is that known in England" as appearing in the last sentence of the above quoted clause. The arbitrator held that the words meant a valid choice in favor of English substantive law for the following reasons.[1]

E x c e r p t

A. *Introduction*

[1] "The claimants assert that English substantive law applies to the dispute. Their position is based on the clause 'Arbitration' of Annex II to the contract executed by the parties. They consider this provision as embodying a valid choice in favor of English substantive law.

"The defendants hold that the arbitrator should apply Dutch substantive law to resolve the dispute. Their contention is based on several arguments regarding the interpretation, the validity, and the effects of the provisions contained in Annex II.

[2] "There is no dispute that the arbitration clause contained in Annex II has been agreed upon by the parties and that it should govern these arbitration proceedings.

"(. . . .)

"Further, it is not disputed that the parties have agreed to have any dispute among them settled in accordance with the rules of conciliation and arbitration of the ICC Court of Arbitration.

"Finally, the parties have chosen Switzerland as a place of arbitration.

"The sole issue to be determined by the arbitrator at this stage relates to the substantive law which he should apply to resolve the dispute.

[3] "In this respect, the arbitrator must first consider the ICC Rules which the parties have adopted.

" * * * Art. 13(3) of the ICC Rules [provides]:[i]

> 'The parties shall be free to determine the law to be applied by the arbitrator to the merits of the dispute. In the absence of any indication by the parties as to the applicable law, the arbitrator shall apply the law designated as the proper law by the rule of conflict which he deems appropriate.'

"The parties to an agreement are free, under the ICC Rules, to adopt the substantive law which should govern their agreement and an arbitral tribunal has to apply the law so adopted. It is only if there is no designation by the parties of the applicable law that the arbitral tribunal shall resort to a rule of conflict of laws. An arbitral tribunal should

---

1. *Note General Editor.* After issuance of the preliminary award, the parties reached a settlement.

i. Authors' note: The current version of this provision, as modified, is found in Article 17(1) of the 1998 ICC Rules.

probably also deviate from the law chosen by the parties if it would appear that such a choice, if applied by the arbitral tribunal, could prevent that the award be implemented (Art. 26 of the ICC Rules;[2] L. Craig, W. Park, J. Paulsson, *International Chamber of Commerce Arbitration*, Part III, p. 88, Paris 1984).

[4] "In the present instance, the parties are in conflict as to whether or not they have made an election in the contract for a substantive law to apply.

"Therefore, the arbitrator shall first make a decision upon the meaning of the words 'the law applicable is that known in England'. Does it or does it not represent a choice of substantive law?

"If the decision is that it does * * * represent such a choice, then the arbitrator will have to consider whether it is a valid choice of laws and whether there are clear indications that the application of English law to resolve the dispute could obstruct the implementation of the award either in the Mozambique or in the Netherlands."

B.   Rules of construction

[5]   "In making that decision, one has first to select which system or principles of law one has to apply.

"One could construe the disputed sentence by applying English law as being the law presumably chosen by the parties, or by applying Swiss law as the *'lex fori'*, or by resorting to principles of law generally admitted (among others: L. Craig, W. Park, J. Paulsson, *International Chamber of Commerce Arbitration*, Part II, p. 17, Part III, p. 67 et seq., Paris 1984; P. Fouchard, *L'arbitrage commercial international*, p. 62 et seq., 319 et seq., 362 et seq., Paris 1965; E. Bucher," Arbitration under the ICC Rules in Switzerland and the Concordat, "*Recuel de Travaux suisses sur l'arbitrage international*, p. 134–135, Zurich 1984; J. Robert, *L'arbitrage*, 5th ed., p. 231 et seq., 269 et seq., 279 et seq., Paris 1983; P. Lalive," Les règles de conflit de lois appliquées au fond du litige par l'arbitre international siégeant en Suisse:, in *L'arbitrage international privé et la Suisse*, p. 67 et seq., Geneva 1977; O. Lando, "The law applicable to the merits of the dispute, contemporary problems" in *International Arbitration*, p. 104 et seq., London 1986).

"It does not seem adequate to apply English law to determine the issue as it could lead to preempting the solution. Therefore, the arbitrator will be guided by Swiss law and general principles of law (P. Jolindon, *Commentaire du Concordat suisse sur l'arbitrage*, p. 455, Bern 1984).

"It has to be noted that in the present instance there is no absolute need to resort to a specific system of law to construe the said sentence.

---

2. Art. 26 of the ICC Rules [Art. 35 of the 1998 ICC Rules] provides:

"In all matters not expressly provided for in these Rules, the Court of Arbitration and the arbitrator shall act in the spirit of these Rules and shall make every effort to make sure that the award is enforceable at law."

[6] "Under Swiss law, the wording of contracts forms the basis of their construction, but Swiss judges also look at all the circumstances which seem appropriate to establish the common intention of the parties (ATF 99 II 285).

"The statements of a party must be construed as the other party had to understand them *bona fide*, i.e., as an honest and reasonable person would have understood them under the same circumstances (ATF 101 I a 43). If the real intention of the parties cannot be proven, the judge will look at the objective meaning of the contract, defined in accordance with the general experience of life and the principle of good faith (ATF 95 II 437).

"Generally, the judge may assume that the words of the agreement have been used in their common meaning (ATF 82 II 452) or, in contracts between specialists, in their technical meaning (ATF 100 II 145). If the text of a contract is clear, it should not be altered on an interpretation based on extrinsic evidence (ATF 99 II 285). Swiss law further accepts the principle according to which the terms of a contract are to be construed more strongly against the maker of the contract (ATF 100 II 153). However, this principle applies only in cases of ambiguity, and not if both parties have taken part in the making of the contract.

"In the present case, there are no facts known to the arbitrator which could help establishing the common intention of the parties as regards the disputed sentence. Nor did the parties bring any extrinsic evidence in their memorials.

"(. . . .)

"The construction of the disputed sentence shall therefore rest on its terms."

C. *Possible meanings*

[7] "The arbitrator is of the opinion that the parties to the contract did not include inadvertently the said sentence into Annex II, but that they were rather willing to give to that sentence a definite meaning in the context of the arbitration clause.

"In the said context, one may elaborate four possible meanings, that is,

— a choice of substantive law

— a choice of procedural law

— a choice of a rule of conflict of laws

— a choice of a law to determine the validity and effect of the arbitration clause.

"The arbitrator will review whether the disputed sentence may be regarded as a choice of procedural law, or a choice of a rule of conflict of laws, or a choice of a law to determine the validity and effect of the arbitration clause, or a choice of substantive law. In this connection, the arbitrator will address the argument made by the defendants that clauses which embody a choice of substantive law have to be clear, specific and unambiguous.

"In reviewing the possible meanings of the disputed sentence, the arbitrator will apply the following test: How could that sentence be understood in good faith by a reasonable man active in the international trade."

D. The word "law"

[8] "Beforehand, the arbitrator notes that the word 'law' appears twice in the arbitration clause of Annex II.

"The first reference is to 'as per said laws'. The 'said laws' obviously refer to the Rules of Conciliation and Arbitration of the ICC. Another construction is not reasonable and the parties do not pretend to the contrary.

"The second reference to the word 'law' appears in the disputed sentence, in connection with the word 'applicable'. The defendants allege that 'the law applicable' could refer to 'as per said laws'. This does not seem, however, to be a valid construction of these words.

"The word 'law' has several meanings and there is no reason why it should not have been used under two imports. As far as the form is concerned, it is difficult if not impossible to connect the 'law' and the 'said laws'. As regards the substance, it makes no sense to do that kind of reference.

"Therefore, one shall admit that the 'law applicable' does not refer to the 'said laws'."

E. Does the "law applicable" indicate a choice of procedural law?

[9] "It is quite uncommon to find in an arbitration clause an indication of the law which shall govern the procedure under which the arbitration shall take place (among others, see P. Fouchard, *L'arbitrage commercial international*, p. 304, Paris 1965).

"Parties adopting an arbitration clause expect mostly to escape procedural particularities of local courts; the designation of a municipal law is most often contrary to the advantages sought in an arbitration clause (L. Craig, W. Park, J. Paulsson, *International Chamber of Commerce Arbitration*, Part III, p. 68, Paris 1984).

"In this case, the choice of the ICC Rules was well sufficient to settle the problems of procedure (Art. 11 of the Rules for the ICC Court of Arbitration[j]).[3] The choice of Switzerland as the place of arbitration

---

j. Art. 11 of the ICC Rules [Art. 15(1) of the 1998 ICC Rules] provides:

"The Rules governing the proceedings before the arbitrator shall be those resulting from these Rules and where these Rules are silent, any rules which the parties (or, fail-ing them, the arbitrator) may settle, and whether or not reference is thereby made to a municipal procedural law to be applied to the arbitration."

3. Art. 11 of the ICC Rules [Art. 15(1) of the 1998 ICC Rules] provides:

implied in any case the application of the Swiss mandatory provisions. Nothing indicates that the parties could have reasons to avoid the application of Swiss procedural law and to choose specifically English procedural law. Moreover, such a choice could bring with it numerous difficulties.

"Therefore, quite clearly, if the parties intended a reference to procedural law, they would have made it plain and would not have used the words 'the law applicable' which designate ordinarily the substantive law (see thereafter).

"Further, one cannot understand why the parties would have chosen such an extraordinary law of procedure under the circumstances, but not a substantive law.

"The arbitrator is therefore of the opinion that a reasonable man active in the international trade could not have understood the disputed sentence as a reference to a choice of procedural law."

F. Does the "law applicable" indicate a choice of a rule of conflict of laws?

[10] "It seems unlikely that parties to an international contract choose a rule of conflict of laws, but not the substantive law: it is hard to understand how the parties cannot agree to a proper law, but can agree to the rules of conflict that determine the proper law. This may sometimes happen, but for certain reasons (L. Craig, W. Park, J. Paulsson, *International Chamber of Commerce Arbitration*, Part II, p. 67, Paris 1984).

"In this case, there is no evidence of any reason of that kind.

"Further, one may assume that, if the parties had in mind to refer to a rule of conflict of laws, as opposed to a substantive law, they would have made it clear.

* * *

"The arbitrator is therefore of the opinion that a reasonable man active in the international trade could not have understood the disputed sentence as a reference to a rule of conflict of laws."

G. Does the "law applicable" indicate a choice of a law to determine the validity and effect of the arbitration clause?

[11] "Parties may submit an arbitration agreement to a law which is not the substantive law of the main contract. But in that case, they almost always designate the law governing the arbitration agreement *and* the law applying to the contract.[k] If not, they indicate that the selected law applies specifically to the arbitration agreement. Obviously,

"The Rules governing the proceedings before the arbitrator shall be those resulting from these Rules and where these Rules are silent, any rules which the parties (or, failing them, the arbitrator) may settle, and whether or not reference is thereby made to a municipal procedural law to be applied to the arbitration."

k. Authors' note: See, for example, the *Pepsico* case supra in section II.1.b

the parties to an international contract are likely to have in mind the problems of jurisdiction or arbitration, possibly of substantive law, but not of the law governing the arbitration clause itself, which is mostly thought to be governed either by the selected law or by the 'lex fori' (the law of the place of arbitration).

"In this case, there is no evidence that the parties might have intended or at least had reasons to submit the arbitration clause to a specific law.

"The arbitrator is therefore of the opinion that a reasonable man active in the international trade could not have understood the disputed sentence as a reference to a law that would have determined the validity and effect of the arbitration clause."

H. Does the "law applicable" indicate a choice of substantive law?

[12] "Universally, the words 'the law applicable' or 'the law which applies' are used in the context of the determination of the substantive law governing private international relationships (example: Art. 13(3) of the Rules of the ICC Court of Arbitration [quoted above under [3]]; G. Delaume, *Transnational Contracts, Applicable Law and Settlement of Disputes, Law and Practice*, Part II, Conflict issues, chapter VII, Party autonomy and express stipulations of applicable law; P. Sanders, "The Netherlands", in *Yearbook Commercial Arbitration* VI (1981), p. 75).

"In contracts containing no arbitration clause, the choice of the 'applicable law' unambiguously refers to the substantive law, the procedure being in any case governed by the 'lex fori'. The word 'substantive' therefore never or very rarely appears in connection with the expression 'the law applicable', although always implied. This usage certainly extends to contracts containing an arbitration clause.

"Whereas the reference to the law known in England cannot be construed as a designation of the procedural law, or of the rule of conflict of laws, or of the law governing the arbitration clause, there are clear indications which speak in favor of the designation of a substantive law.

"The parties had valid reasons to refer to the substantive law known in England. English law is neutral; its provisions are adapted to the needs of international commerce; it is fairly well accessible and known to lawyers of other countries, such as Switzerland, Mozambique and the Netherlands; English is far more common than Dutch, Portuguese or even French.

"The parties could thus consider the application of English law as perfectly acceptable and the presence of a choice of substantive law clause under the title 'Arbitration' was in nothing peculiar.

"The arbitrator is therefore of the opinion that a reasonable man active in the international trade should have understood the disputed sentence as a reference to a substantive law.

[13] "Although somewhat unusual, the expression 'the law known in England' is not ambiguous. It is wide enough to include, as appropri-

ate, international rules and usages recognized in England. However, this expression cannot reasonably imply a reference to a national law other than the English. The parties cannot have intended to designate all the laws of the world. Considering the plain meaning of the words, the arbitrator finds that the use of the expression 'the laws known in England' does not affect the validity of the clause.

[14] "The argument has been made by the defendants that a clause of choice of substantive law should be clear and unambiguous.

"Under Swiss law, the choice of the applicable law is considered as the result of a contract between the parties, which is separate from the main contract (F. Fischer, *Internationales Vertragsrecht*, p. 66 et seq., Bern 1962; ATF 91 II 248; ATF 102 II 143). This 'choice of law' is not subject to any formality and can be express or implied (TC VD, 8 February 1980, Marks).

"Whereas implied choice of law has to result clearly and unambiguously from the terms of the contract or the circumstances, express choice of law clauses do not have to be drafted with such a degree of clarity that they should not be construed. It does not seem that any decision of a Swiss Court has ever set particular requirements as to the form, wording or precision of clauses mentioning expressly the 'law applicable'. The draft of the Swiss Statute on International Private Law does not either require any form for express choice of law clauses, as it states that 'the choice of law must be express *or* result with certainty from the provisions of the contract or from the circumstances of the case' (Art. 113(2)).[1]

* * *

"In this case, the arbitrator finds that the express election in favor of English law is sufficiently clear to be regarded.

"As a preliminary conclusion, the arbitrator decides that the contract between the parties contains an express choice of substantive law in favor of the English law."

I.   *The validity of the choice of English law*

[15] "The defendants allege that the parties were not free to choose English law as the law applicable to their contract, * * * there being no connection between the matter and English law.

"Whether English law is a valid choice of law has to be scrutinized both under Swiss law and English law (B. Dutoit, F. Knoepfler, P. Lalive, P. Mercier, *Répertoire de droit international privé suisse*, Vol. 1, p. 31,

---

1. Art. 113(3) of the draft Swiss Statute on International Private Law (the equivalent of Art. 116 in the final version) provides:

"1. The agreement is governed by the law chosen by the parties.

"2. The choice of law must be express or result in a clear fashion from the provisions of the agreement or from the circumstances surrounding the case; furthermore, the choice of law is governed by the substantive law chosen by the parties.

"3. The choice of law may be made or modified at any time. If it is subsequent to the conclusion of the agreement, it has retroactive effects as from the conclusion of the agreement, subject to the right of third parties."

Bern 1982; M. Keller, K. Siehr, *Allgemeine Lehren des internationalen Privatrechts*, p. 376, Zurich 1986; also Art. 113(3) of the draft of the Swiss Statute on International Private Law).

[16] "Under Swiss law, the freedom of the parties as to their choice of the applicable law has not been finally settled. Swiss courts do not require the existence of a 'natural connection between the matter and the chosen law' and recognize the validity of a choice of law in each case where the parties have a reasonable interest in the application of the chosen law (ATF 91 II 44.51; ATF 102 II 143). Such an interest exists for example when the chosen law contains a regulation of the matter which seems appropriate, when the parties are willing to submit their relationship to certain usages assuming the application of the chosen law or when the contract is in connection with another business submitted to the chosen law. It does not seem that any decision of a Swiss court has ever denied the existence of a reasonable interest of the parties in the application of a chosen law (B. Dutoit, F. Knoepfler, P. Lalive, P. Mercier, *Répertoire de droit international privé suisse*, Vol. 1, p. 30, Bern 1982). The draft of the Swiss Statute on Private International Law of 10 November 1982 does not limit the choice of the parties with any requirement regarding the connection with a chosen law. The Federal Council regards the criterion of the 'reasonable interest of the parties' as inappropriate and useless. It has limited the choice of the applicable law only for the types of contracts in which a party needs special protection (*Message du Conseil Fédéral concernant une loi fédérale sur le droit international privé*, 10 November 1982, p. 141–142).

[17] "Under English law, the question of the connection between the matter and the chosen law seems to be somewhat controversial. There seems to be no reported case in which an English court refused to give effect to an express choice of law because of the deficient connection between the contract and the chosen law (Dicey and Morris, *The Conflict of Laws*, 10th ed., vol. 2, p. 755, London 1980). In *Vita Food Products Inc. v. Unus Shipping Co. Ltd.* (1939, AC 277 (PC)), it was stated that 'a connection with English law is not, as a matter of principle, essential'. In this decision, the judge mentioned in particular the importance of English law in international commercial relationships, even unconnected with England. He considered reasonable for the parties to commercial contracts to submit their transaction to English law, although that law might have nothing to do with the facts of the particular case.

"Swiss and English laws largely reflect the international practice. 'In most countries, the parties to transnational contracts enjoy a large degree of autonomy in selecting the proper law of their contract. Except in those situations in which compliance with mandatory rules is required, the parties are generally free to choose by way of express stipulation the law applicable to their relationship. In the overwhelming majority of cases, the law stipulated applicable is the domestic law of a specific country to which the contract bears some connection or the law of a "third" country selected for reason of expertise (such as English law in regard to maritime matters) or of "neutrality" (such as Swedish,

Swiss or French law) ...' (G. Delaume, *Transnational Contracts, Applicable Law and Settlements of Disputes, Law and Practice*, Part II, Conflict issues, Chapter VII, Party Autonomy and Express Stipulations of Applicable Laws, p. 2; also, M. Keller, K. Siehr, *Allgemeine Lehren des internationalen Privatrechts*, p. 384, Zurich 1986).

[18] "In this case, the arbitrator finds that the parties have a reasonable interest in the application of English law. The choice of English substantive law cannot be held * * * invalid for there being no connection between the matter and English law.

"There is further no indication that the choice of English substantive law was made to escape some mandatory provisions of the laws of the Netherlands or Mozambique.

"Nor is there any indication that an award which would be based in English substantive law would not be enforceable in the Netherlands (see also *New York Convention of 10 June 1958)* or in the Mozambique.

[19] "Therefore, the arbitrator considers that the parties have made a valid choice in favor of English substantive law. In accordance with Art. 13(3) of the Rules for the ICC Court of Arbitration, the arbitrator shall apply English substantive law."

A. von Mehren & E. Jiménez de Aréchaga, FINAL REPORT ON ARBITRATION BETWEEN STATES AND FOREIGN ENTERPRISES

63–II Annuaire de l'Institut de Droit International 193–96 (1989).*

* * *

7. Arbitral tribunals are in a predicament that national courts do not face. In order to decide in a principled way, an adjudicator requires what can be called a *lex fori*, that is to say, an explanation of the source of his power and a method of establishing the rules and principles in terms of which the tribunal will adjudicate. At least as a practical matter, these are not perplexing issues for national courts. A court is a creature of its legal order which confers on the court authority to adjudicate and supplies in various ways the authoritative rules and principles in terms of which the judge is to discharge his responsibility.

2. Jurisdictional theory: Its inadequacies.

8. Unless arbitral tribunals are treated as a special kind of national court, the arbitrator's situation with regard to a *lex fori* is difficult and complex. Much of the attraction of the so-called jurisdictional theory of arbitration doubtless lies in its ability, once accepted, to provide the arbitrator with a *lex fori*. When embraced, the theory provides a coherent explanation of the source and content of the arbitrator's authority.

* Reprinted by permission of Annuaire de l'Institut de Droit International volume 63–I, PEDONE Publishing House, Paris.

9.   However, the jurisdictional theory faces in the contemporary world practical as well as theoretical difficulties such that the theory no longer provides an acceptable explanation of how an arbitral tribunal establishes its *lex fori*. The practical difficulty is, on the one hand, that many widely accepted contemporary practices in international arbitration are inconsistent with the theory and, on the other, that arbitration—unlike national-court adjudication—is a dispute resolution process whose venue is contingent and transitory so that the place of arbitration neither represents nor establishes a permanent geographical or governmental relationship with a given national legal system. Among widely accepted arbitration practices that are inconsistent with a meaningful jurisdictional theory are the very broad powers that the parties exercise with respect as well to the rules and principles regulating the underlying controversy as to those regulating the arbitral process. The days when national legal systems intervened, as England did through the case-stated system, with on-going arbitrations are largely past; arbitrations will simply not be conducted on the territory of States that seek to give real meaning to the jurisdictional theory by interfering with ongoing arbitrations.

10.   Imposition on the arbitral tribunal of the *lex fori* that obtains for the national courts of the territory in which the tribunal is sitting involves the practical difficulty that arbitrary results will follow and the arbitration process will lose much of its efficacy. The place of arbitration is typically selected because it is convenient for the parties and their counsels, because needed facilities are available, and because the legal climate is supportive of arbitration. The selection may very well be made without considering at all the local court's *lex fori*. The procedural and choice-of-law considerations that play so large a role in a plaintiff's selection among available judicial forums or party stipulations for a judicial forum, typically play no role in the parties' selection of the place of arbitration. Accordingly, party choice of a location in which to arbitrate should not—unless the parties intend otherwise—affect the outcome decisively by imposing on the arbitration the local judicial *lex fori*; it is capricious to thwart party intention where well advised parties could have chosen another location that would have allowed them full control over the procedural and substantive rules governing the arbitration.

11.   The contemporary reality is that arbitral proceedings are ambulatory in a way that judicial proceedings are not. No particular sovereign controls the arbitral adjudicatory process; as a consequence, until the enforcement stage is reached, sovereignty usually has relatively little importance—at least where the parties are well advised—for arbitration. It follows that local-court intrusion on the on-going arbitration process will simply lead to the flight of international arbitrations. In practice, international arbitration will not be carried on in jurisdictions that do not permit the parties to control the tribunal's *lex fori*.

3. *Other theories.*

12.   The empirical fact of international arbitration and the problem of how adjudicatory authority can exist when it is not an emanation of a sovereign can be understood in various ways. One can posit an international order that has emerged through consensus and which accords to participants in international intercourse the right to establish a dispute resolution process and a body of substantive rules and principles that will have an existence independent of national legal orders. The concepts of a *lex mercatoria* and of an autonomous theory of arbitration rest, at least in part, on a vision of such an international legal order.

13.   Yet another explanation is to suggest that adjudicatory authority need not emanate from any discrete sovereign. Constraints and pressures that flow from economic or social groupings—the merchant community of international commerce, for example—can give reality to an adjudicatory process even where no political authority is prepared to lend its aid. Furthermore, these constraints or pressures may, in the case of arbitration, be reinforced by enlisting the aid of one or more national legal systems. As the controversies involve international transactions and international actors, in many situations more than one national jurisdiction will be in a position to put pressure on the recalcitrant party. One is back at the level of sovereignty but several sovereigns are now in the picture. Accordingly, no single, discrete sovereign controls the effectiveness of the arbitral process and arbitration largely escapes Austinian logic.

Questions and Comments

1.   The parties in *Seed Potatoes* included an express choice of law clause: " * * * the law applicable is that known in England." Arbitrator Muller lists four possible meanings of "the law applicable": i) substantive law; ii) procedural law; iii) choice of law rules; iv) law to determine the validity and effect of the arbitration clause. This is a helpful catalogue of choice-of-law issues that can arise in international arbitration. Is it complete? Could "procedural law" have more than one meaning? What do you understand the *McDonnell Douglas* case to say on this point? Do you agree with the *McDonnell Douglas* court's interpretation of the choice of law clause at issue in that case? ("The arbitration shall be conducted in accordance with the procedure provided in the Indian Arbitration Act of 1940 * * * .") With the arbitrator's interpretation of the relevant clause in *Seed Potatoes*?

2.   Obviously an arbitrator must interpret the arbitration agreement, including the choice-of-law clause. What law or laws does Arbitrator Muller turn to for this purpose in *Seed Potatoes*? Why? What is the choice of law rule he seems to be using? In the end, is it really important what body of law governs interpretation of the arbitration clause?

3.   Does Arbitrator Muller scrutinize the validity of the choice of law provision? Why is this an issue? What law does he apply for this purpose? Is this a role for the *lex arbitri*? Do you agree with the need to scrutinize the validity of the choice of law provision?

4.   How should an arbitrator decide what country's *lex arbitri* applies?

5.   Given that the large majority of international contracts contain an express choice of law clause, would you conclude that choice of law rules are relatively unimportant in international commercial arbitration?

6.   The excerpt from von Mehren & Jiménez de Aréchaga expresses a preference for an anational, delocalized conception of international commercial arbitration. Do you agree? Would their approach lead to a different outcome in *Seed Potatoes* or *McDonnell Douglas*? To different reasoning?

IV.3.d.   *The Role of Lex Mercatoria*

NORSOLOR S.A. (FRANCE) v. PABALK TICARET SIRKETI S.A. (TURKEY)

Tribunal de grande instance of Paris, March 4 1981.[m]
Cour d'appel of Paris, December 15, 1981 and November
19, 1982.[n] Cour de cassation, October 9, 1984.[o]

TRIBUNAL DE GRANDE INSTANCE, MARCH 4, 1981—SUMMARY AND EXTRACTS

After Norsolor, a French corporation, terminated an agency agreement with Pabalk, its Turkish agent, Pabalk initiated arbitration against Norsolor in Vienna under the ICC Arbitration Rules and won an award for damages. Instead of applying the law of a particular country, the arbitrators based their award on international *lex mercatoria;* moreover, they relied on equity to decide on liability and to assess damages in a lump sum. Thereafter, on February 5, 1980, the President of the Tribunal de grande instance granted Pabalk leave to enforce the Austrian award in France. Norsolor challenged this decision before the Tribunal de grande instance, arguing that the arbitrators had violated Article 13 of the ICC Arbitration Rules by acting as "amiables compositeurs" without having been authorized to do so in the arbitration agreement.

The Tribunal noted that principles such as good faith and commercial reasonableness were part of *lex mercatoria* and that the arbitrators had assessed the parties' actions in the light of these general principles; the arbitrators had asked whether the breakdown in the contractual relationship was attributable to the actions of one of the parties and whether those actions had caused unjustified prejudice to the other party. The Tribunal concluded:

> * * * [I]t is undeniable that in accordance with Article 13 of * * * [the ICC Rules of Arbitration], the arbitrators have applied *the law* designated by the conflict of laws rule which they deemed appropriate, namely, the general principles of obligations generally applicable

m.   1983 Revue de l'arbitrage 465; see also B. Goldman, "Une bataille judiciaire autour de la lex mercatoria: l'affaire Norsolor", 1983 Revue de l'arbitrage 379.

n.   1983 Revue de l'arbitrage 465, 470–76.

o.   24 Int'l Legal Materials 360 (1985). For the judgment in French, see Recueil Dalloz Sirey (Jurisprudence) 1985 at 104.

to international commerce.[p] It was of no importance that they twice used in their reasoning the rather ambiguous word 'equity' because they defined the content of the rule [they applied], which rule was also able to satisfy equity.

* * *

[T]herefore the arbitrators did not, either in fact, or in law, decide as amiables compositeurs; they thus stayed within the terms of the arbitration agreement.

The Tribunal rejected Norsolor's claim.

Court Of Appeal Of Paris, December 15, 1981 And November 19, 1982—Summary And Extracts

Norsolor appealed the Tribunal's decision and also sought a stay of the French proceedings pending the outcome of the decision of the Court of Appeal of Vienna, where Norsolor had instituted a parallel proceeding to set the award aside. On December 15, 1981, the Court granted Norsolor's request for a stay on the ground that "if the award were annulled by the Court in Vienna, the action for leave to enforce would be deprived of its purpose." Thereafter the Court of Appeal of Vienna set aside the arbitral award rendered in Vienna.[q]

Subsequently, on November 19, 1982, the Court of Appeal of Paris held that it was compelled, by virtue of Article V(1)(e) of the New York Convention, to rescind the order for leave to enforce the award granted on February 5, 1980 by the President of the Tribunal de Grande Instance because this order concerned an award that had been annulled by the Court of Appeal of Vienna.

Cour De Cassation, October 9, 1984—Summary And Extracts[r]

The Cour de cassation (Supreme Court) annulled the November 19, 1982 decision of the Court of Appeal of Paris, holding that Article VII of the New York Convention of 1958 and the French New Code of Civil Procedure Article 12, taken together, compelled the Court of Appeal "to determine, even *sua sponte*, whether French law would allow Pabalk to avail itself of the award at stake." It thus rejected the decision of the Court of Appeal of Paris because the latter had referred exclusively to Article V(1)(e) of the New York Convention to deny leave to enforce the award.

Questions and Comments

1. Why was it arguable that the arbitrators acted as "amiables compositeurs"? If the French court of first instance had found this characterization

---

p. 24 Int'l Legal Materials 360 (1985). For the judgment in French, see Recueil Dalloz Sirey (Jurisprudence) 1985 at 104.

q. 24 Int'l Legal Materials 360, 361 (1985). On November 18, 1982, the Austrian Supreme Court reversed the Court of Appeal of Vienna and reinstated the award. Id.

r. The Cour de cassation decision is reproduced and examined more fully infra in section V.3.c.v.

correct, would it have been fatal to the award's enforcement in France? If so, what provision of the New York Convention would have justified nonenforcement? Would nonenforcement have been required?

2. Article 13 of the version of the ICC Arbitration Rules in effect at the time of the *Norsolor* decision provided in part as follows:

> " * * *

> 3. The parties shall be free to determine the law to be applied by the arbitrator to the merits of the dispute. In the absence of any indication by the parties as to the applicable law, the arbitrator shall apply the law designated as proper by the rule of conflict which he deems appropriate.

> 4. The arbitrator shall assume the powers of an amiable compositeur if the parties are agreed to give him such powers.

> 5. In all cases the arbitrator shall take account of the provisions of the contract and the relevant trade usages."

If the arbitrators did not act as "amiables compositeurs", what "law" did they apply? What choice of law rules were they guided by?

3. Once the Vienna court set aside the award, why did this not determine the matter for the French courts. Would not Article V(1)(e) of the New York Convention provide a ground for nonenforcement of the award? Why would French courts be willing to enforce an award that had been set aside by the courts of the country where the award had been rendered? (We take up these issues more completely in Chapter V at section V.3.c.v.)

4. Consider the inverse of the *Norsolor* case. Suppose the arbitration agreement expressly grants the arbitrators the power to decide as amiables compositeurs, but they instead expressly find the contract governed by a specific national law and apply that law to decide the case with no further reasoning, should the award be set aside? What if the arbitrators merely apply the specific clauses of the contract to justify their result, with no further reasoning? French courts have held that awards in both such cases should be set aside. Arbitrators expressly given the power to decide as amiables compositeurs must base their decision on equity, and if they decide solely on the basis of national law or contract clauses, without re-examining these results in the light of equity—either expressly in the award, or at least impliedly—their award will be set aside. See Halbout et société Matenec HG v. Epous Hanin, Cour de cassation (2d Ch. Civ., Feb. 15, 2001), 2001 Revue de l'arbitrage 136–137; Société Eurovia et autres v. SARL Grenobloise d'investissements, Cour d'appel de Grenoble (Ch. Com., Dec. 15, 1999) (two separate decisions), Id. at 137–141.

Do you agree with the position taken by the French courts?

IV.3.e.   Applicable Law in the Absence of Party Choice

SELLER (KOREA) v. BUYER (JORDAN)

Interim Award in ICC Case No. 6149 of 1990.
20 Yearbk. Comm. Arb'n 41 (1995).*

[The claimant, a Korean seller, entered into three contracts with the defendant, a Jordanian buyer, for the sale of 1,200,000 units of a good to be delivered in installments. The Jordanian buyer had entered into a previous contract to deliver these same goods to a buyer in Iraq. All three contracts between the Korean seller and Jordanian buyer contained the identical arbitration clause, numbered clause 11:

> Any dispute with regards to this contract will be solved cordially; otherwise by two arbitrators appointed by each side. In an eventual non agreement it will be governed by the laws and regulations of the International Chamber of Commerce in Paris whose ruling should be final.

After delays in delivery, the parties negotiated new delivery dates and then fell into dispute over whether the final installments were shipped in due time. The claimant appointed an arbitrator, and when the defendant refused to appoint its arbitrator, the claimant initiated arbitration proceedings with the ICC in Paris, which selected an arbitral tribunal. The validity of the arbitration clauses was challenged before the tribunal on the ground of Section 2 of Jordanian Law no. 35 of 1983 which reads:

> Regardless of whatever is contained in any other law, any agreement, or stipulation which bars the Jordanian courts from * * * [hearing] disputes relating to bills of lading or carriage of goods is null and void.

The arbitral tribunal issued an interim award in which it first decided that Section 2 of Jordanian Law no. 35 of 1983 did not apply to the agreements and that hence they were valid. The tribunal also decided that the agreement covered the disputes at issue. The interim award then turned to the question of what law governed the merits of the dispute and chose Korean law.]

EXCERPT

* * *

A.   *The Non-applicability of Sect. 2 of the Jordanian Law no. 35 of 1983 * * **

* * *

[2]   " * * * [In response to the defendant's argument that the arbitration agreements were invalid by virtue of Sec. 2 of Jordanian Law

* Reprinted with permission of Yearbook Commercial Arbitration, International   Council for Commercial Arbitration.

no. 35 of 1983, the tribunal concluded that the Jordanian law did not apply for the following reasons.]

"1) Sect. 2 of the Jordanian Law no. 35 of 1983 is based upon motivations of Jordanian public policy. Its obvious purpose is to prevent Jordanian courts from being ousted of their jurisdiction as far as certain matters are concerned, considered to be of primordial importance for the Jordanian public interest. The effect of the said Sect. 2 therefore is to deny *arbitrability* to all matters defined by it. Non-arbitrability means that a matter is not capable of settlement by arbitration (cp. Art. II(1) of the [1958 New York Convention]). Sect. 2 of the said law thus removes arbitrability from 'all disputes relating to bills of lading or carriage of goods'.

[3]   "2) National provisions on non-arbitrability of disputes are constituent parts of the public policy provisions of the issuing state. The question of whether at all and, if so, to what extent an international arbitral tribunal has to apply national provisions on the non-arbitrability of certain matters, therefore has to be answered on the basis of the doctrines dealing with the *validity of international arbitration agreements under national public policy provisions*. The present arbitral tribunal thus is called upon to apply the general rules of conflict of laws on the validity, under national public provisions, of international arbitration agreements.

[4]   "3) Such validity of international arbitration agreements depends upon the proper law by which they are governed. It may be disputed whether an arbitration agreement, as a matter of principle, is subject to the same proper law by which also the main contract is governed so that both, arbitration agreement and main contract, share the same proper law, or whether the proper law of the arbitration agreement has to be determined upon its own, i.e., irrespectively of the proper law of the main contract. This controversy does not need to be decided within the present context. For both doctrines lead to the same result in the present dispute, i.e., to the non-applicability of the afore-mentioned Jordanian Law no. 35 of 1983.

[5]   "If the arbitral tribunal would follow the first doctrine and assume the proper law of the arbitration agreement to be identical with the proper law of the main contract, the validity of the three arbitration agreements here under consideration would hinge upon the proper law of the three sales contracts. It will be seen in the following section of this interim award * * * that the said three sales contracts are certainly *not* governed by Jordanian law. Thus, under the afore-mentioned first doctrine, an application of the Jordanian Law no. 35 of 1983 would be excluded.

[6]   "The same conclusion would have to be drawn if the arbitral tribunal would follow the afore-mentioned second, alternative doctrine by which the proper law of an arbitration agreement would have to be determined upon its own, i.e., without having regard to the proper law of the main contract. Pursuant to Art. 13(3) of the ICC Rules of Concilia-

tion and Arbitration, failing any indication by the parties as to the applicable law, the arbitrator shall apply the law designated as the proper law by the rule of conflict which he deems appropriate. If, according to the second doctrine, the proper law of the three arbitration agreements could not necessarily be derived from the proper law of the three sales contracts themselves, the only other rule of conflicts of laws whose application would seem appropriate in the sense of the above-mentioned Art. 13(3), would be the application of the law where the arbitration takes place and where the award is rendered.

[7] "This conclusion would be supported also by Art. V(1)(a) of the above-mentioned [1958 New York Convention] (a Convention which has been ratified by the Republic of Korea, Jordan, France and Iraq). According to the said Art. V, the validity of the arbitration agreement has to be determined 'under the law of the country where the award was made'. In the case here under consideration, the above-mentioned second doctrine therefore would lead to the application of French law, i.e., of Arts. 1493–1495, 1442–1446 of the *Nouveau Code de Procédure Civile*.[4] Under these French provisions, the three arbitration agreements would be valid and binding. In other words: the application of Sect. 2 of the Jordanian Law no. 35 of 1983 would again be excluded.

[8] "4) The non-applicability of that provision may be based upon * * * [an additional consideration:] There can be no doubt that, if Jordanian courts would have to decide on the present subject-matter, such courts would have to apply Sect. 2 of the Jordanian Law no. 35 of 1983. But when the parties to the three sales contracts, in exercising their rights of autonomy to choose an appropriate forum or arbitral tribunal for their eventual disputes, agreed upon the jurisdiction of the ICC International Court of Arbitration in Paris, they obviously had the *intention to withdraw any jurisdiction from Korean, Jordanian and Iraqi state courts* and to subject all disputes resulting from their three sales contracts exclusively to the jurisdiction of the ICC International Court of Arbitration. Such court, being an international arbitration body sitting in a state other than Jordan, is not necessarily bound by considerations of Jordanian domestic public policy at least insofar as Jordanian law is not applicable to the subject-matter. It would therefore run counter to the common intention of the parties at the time when they entered into the three sales contracts, if the arbitral tribunal would apply a public policy provision of Jordanian law while there had been a clear intention of the parties to remove this subject-matter from Jordanian domestic jurisdiction.

* * *

B. *Determination of the Proper Law of Contract*

[38] "Art. 13(3) of the [1988] ICC Rules of Conciliation and Arbitration provides that, where the parties have failed to indicate the proper

---

4. Arts. 1493–1495 and 1442–1446 of the French New Code of Civil Procedure provide the formal and substantive rules for the validity of the arbitration agreement in international arbitration.

law, the arbitral tribunal shall apply the law designated as the proper law by the rule of conflict which it deems appropriate. The arbitral tribunal decides that two different sets of conflict of law rules are 'the appropriate law' in the sense of the above-mentioned Art. 13(3). One of these sets is composed of the conflict of law rules of the states most closely connected with the three sales contracts, such conflict of laws rules being in harmony with each other. The other set of conflict of law rules regarded to be 'appropriate' in the sense of the said Article, materializes in the general principle of conflicts of law that the substantive law most closely connected with the contract should be applied and that the 'home law' of the seller is such substantive law.

[39]   "The arbitral tribunal, therefore comes to the conclusion that it has to apply Korean substantive law to the subject-matter of this arbitration.

[40]   "*A comparison of the conflict of law rules of the states most closely connected with the subject-matter of the present arbitration* shows that they all are in harmony with each other and that they therefore have to determine the proper law of contract.[9]

[41]   "The three sales contracts are most closely connected with the Republic of Korea (seat of seller; place of contracting); with Jordan (seat of buyer); with Iraq (final place of delivery of goods sold); and with France (place of arbitration). The arbitral tribunal therefore has consulted the conflict of law rules of these four states.

[42]   "According to *Art. 9, sentence 2 as well as to Art. 11 of the Korean Conflict of Laws Act* of 15 January 1962 the law in effect at the place where a contract has been entered into, shall govern such contract if the parties did not choose the proper law. The three sales contracts were consummated in Korea. They would be governed, therefore, by Korean substantive law if the arbitral tribunal would apply Korean conflict of law rules.

[43]   "*Art 20(1) of the Jordanian Civil Code* provides that, in the absence of any choice of law by the parties and of a common residence of them, a contract is governed by the substantive law of the place where the parties entered into it. Thus the application of the Jordanian conflict of law rules would also lead to Korean substantive law as the proper law by which the sales contracts would be governed.

[44]   "In essence, *Art. 25 of the Iraqi Civil Code of 1951* is identical with Art. 20(1) of the Jordanian Civil Code: Failing any contrary

---

9. The arbitral tribunal referred to further references: "W.L. Craig/W.W. Park/J. Paulsson, *International Chamber of Commerce Arbitration*, Paris 1984, Sect. 17.01 p. 75: 'The principal method used by ICC arbitrators to choose an appropriate conflict of laws rule is the cumulative application of the different rules of conflict of the countries having a relation to the dispute'; Y. Derains, 'Determination de la lex contractus', in: Chambre de Commerce International, Institut du Droit des Affaires Internationales (ed.), *L'apport de la jurisprudence arbitrale*, Paris 1986, p. 7, 14 et seq.: '*application cumulative des systèmes de conflit de lois intéressées au litige*' (English translation: 'cumulative application of the systems of conflict of laws interested in the dispute')."

common intention of the parties or any common residence of them, the local law in effect at the place where the contract was concluded, is the proper law of contract. (It may be mentioned in parenthesis that the conflict of law rules of many other Arabian states adhere to the same principle (see e.g., Art 20(1) of the Syrian Civil Code of 1949 and Art. 19(1) of the Egyptian Civil Code of 1948), the application of the law of the place of contracting thus being a general principle recognized by many important Arabian states).

[45] "Finally, the same result would be obtained if the arbitral tribunal would apply *French conflict of law rules*.[10]

[46] "A comparison of the conflict of law rules of the jurisdictions most closely connected with the present dispute therefore leads to the result that those rules are essentially in conformity with each other, the application of the law where the contract was made being their common core. Hence the application of this common core of conflict of law rules seems 'appropriate' in the sense of Art. 13(3) of the ICC Rules of Conciliation and Arbitration. The arbitral tribunal thus determines Korean substantive law to be the proper law of the three sales contracts.

[47] "This decision is further supported by some other *general principles prevalent in modern conflict of laws*. One of those principles is enunciated by *Art. 3(1), first sentence of the Hague Convention of 15 June 1955 on the Law relating to International Sales of Corporeal Movable Property* which provides that, if the parties have not chosen the applicable law, the contract shall be governed by the domestic law of the country where the seller has his habitual residence at the date of receipt of the order. It is thus the home law of the seller which takes precedence over the home law of the buyer. The above-mentioned Hague Convention [at the time of the initiation of the arbitration] had been signed by 12 states and ratified by 9 states. In the case here under consideration, Art. 3 of the said Convention would lead to the application of substantive Korean law to the three sales contracts.

[48] "Another general principle of conflict of laws would bring about the same result, i.e., that Korean substantive law would have to be regarded as the proper law of contract. This principle is embodied in *Art. 4 of the before-mentioned Convention on the Law Applicable to Contractual Obligations* signed by the then member states of the European Community on 18 June 1980. Said Art. 4 provides:

> '... it shall be presumed that the contract is most closely connected with the country where the party who is to effect the performance which is characteristic of the contract has, at the time of conclusion of the contract, his habitual residence, or, in the case of a body corporate or unincorporate, its central administration.'

---

10. The arbitral tribunal referred to "the report on French conflict of laws by H. Batiffol/P. Lagarde, op. cit., no. 580, p. 253, 254". [Authors' note: The Rome Convention on choice of law for contract issues is currently the law in France and came into effect on April 1, 1991—after the award in the *Seller (Korea) v. Buyer (Jordan)* case was rendered. Under the Rome Convention the approach to contract choice-of-law issues is different from that stated by the arbitrator to be the French approach.]

In a contract of sale, it is the seller who, in the absence of special circumstances pointing to the contrary, renders the performance most characteristic of the contract. Under the rule enunciated above, contracts of sale are therefore in general governed by the domestic law of the seller. In the case here under consideration, this rule would thus also lead to the application of Korean law as the proper law of the three sales contracts.

[49] "Art 3(1), first sentence of the Hague Convention of 15 June 1955 on the Law relating to International Sales of Corporeal Movable Property as well as Art. 4 of the Convention on the Law Applicable to Contractual Obligations of 18 June 1980 are grounded upon the assumption that, in general, the 'home law' of the seller is the law most closely connected with the contract, i.e., that a contract of sale normally has its center of gravity at the residence or central administration of the seller.

[50] "In summary, then the arbitral tribunal states: It is immaterial whether it would apply to the subject-matter of the present arbitration the conflict of law rules of Korea, of Jordan, of Iraq or of France. In any case, the three sales contracts would be governed by Korean substantive law. It would likewise be irrelevant if the arbitral tribunal would assume the modern principles of conflict of laws to be controlling, such principles having been enunciated in the two Conventions of 1955 and 1980 and prescribing that a contract of sale, in general, is subject to the 'home law' of the seller. These principles alike would lead to the application of one and the same law to the three sales contracts, namely of Korean substantive law. The arbitral tribunal therefore decides that all claims introduced by claimant into the present arbitration proceedings are governed by the substantive law of the Republic of Korea."

[51] Claimant had argued that the application of Korean law would be impracticable and that the arbitrators should therefore directly choose the law to be applied to the contract. Such choice, according to the claimant, should lead to the application of the so-called *lex mercatoria* which, in its turn, would essentially mean the application of the Vienna Convention on the International Sale of Goods of 11 April 1980; and that, where said Convention would be silent, French law subsidiarily would have to be applied as the law in effect at the seat of the arbitration.

[52] "The arbitral tribunal is, on the other hand, not persuaded that the application of the so-called *lex mercatoria* would be feasible under the circumstances of the case here under consideration.

[53] "Apart from the fact that it is highly disputed whether such theory is viable and whether it would withstand the scrutiny by a state court eventually reviewing this interim award, the application of the so-called *lex mercatoria* would not solve all conflict of law problems possibly arising in the present arbitration proceedings. Claimant points out that the application of the *lex mercatoria* would be tantamount to the application of the Vienna Convention, i.e., the United Nations Convention on Contracts for the International Sale of Goods of 11 April 1980.

This is certainly true. But it might be that the arbitral tribunal, in the present arbitration proceedings, would have to decide on claims based upon an unjust enrichment of the buyer and/or upon the limitation of any claim introduced by claimant into this arbitration.

[54] "There are no provisions, in the Vienna Convention, covering claims for the restitution of an unjust enrichment or the limitation of claims. In order to be able to decide on these issues, the arbitral tribunal therefore would have to recur to the determination, by another rule of conflict of laws, of a national law as the proper law of contract and the arbitral tribunal would have to apply insofar such national law to the subject-matter of the present arbitration. If the arbitral tribunal therefore would follow claimant's argument and decide that the *lex mercatoria* would be the proper law of the three sales contracts, probably only one part of its arbitral duties would have been accomplished. The arbitral tribunal still would eventually have to determine the law by which a claim for the restitution of an unjust enrichment and the limitation of claims would be governed.

[55] "In the preceding section of this interim award, the arbitral tribunal has decided that all claims introduced into the present arbitration proceedings are governed by one and the same proper law of contract and that a concurrent application of different national laws does not take place. It is therefore consequential for the arbitral tribunal to discard the *lex mercatoria* (besides Korean law) as the proper law of contract. The Vienna Convention could only become the proper law of the three sales contracts if the parties, by an agreement, would stipulate its application (while Korean substantive law would govern the issues not covered by the Convention). Such agreement has not come about."

(. . . .)

Questions and Comments

1.   Article 13(3) of the 1988 ICC Arbitration Rules, which was applied in *Interim Award No. 6149*, was amended in the 1998 ICC Rules. The new provision, Article 17(1) of the 1998 Rules, reads:

> The parties shall be free to agree upon the rules of law to be applied by the Arbitral Tribunal to the merits of the dispute. In the absence of any such agreement, the Arbitral Tribunal shall apply the rules of law which it determines to be appropriate.

Do you favor the applicable law provision of the new or the old ICC Rules?

2.   Should the tribunal have applied the *lex mercatoria* or the Vienna Convention on the International Sale of Goods? Could such a choice have been justified under Article 13(3) of the 1988 ICC Arbitration Rules? Under Article 17(1) of the 1998 ICC Rules?

3.   For the first half of the twentieth century arbitrators frequently applied the choice-of-law rules of the seat of arbitration—France in the case of *Interim Award No. 6149*—in order to select a governing law. Would you favor that approach? Would it be reasonable to conclude that by choosing

arbitration in Paris, the parties expected the choice-of-law rules of France to apply, as they would in a French court? Or would it be more reasonable to conclude that the parties expected the substantive law of France to apply? Or would it be more reasonable still to conclude that the parties' choice of Paris as the seat of the arbitration says nothing about their expectations concerning applicable law?

4.   The UNCITRAL Model Law in Article 28 contains a provision similar to that of the 1988 ICC Rules concerning the applicable law:

(1) The arbitral tribunal shall decide the dispute in accordance with such rules of law as are chosen by the parties as applicable to the substance of the dispute. Any designation of the law or legal system of a given State shall be construed, unless otherwise expressed, as directly referring to the substantive law of that State and not to its conflict of laws rules.

(2) Failing any designation by the parties, the arbitral tribunal shall apply the law determined by the conflict of laws rules which it considers applicable.

* * *

Under what circumstances would the Model Law provision apply? Would it apply to arbitrations with their seat in the country enacting the Model Law? Would the theory of application be the same as that of the traditional approach mentioned above in question 2? (Article 33 of the UNCITRAL Arbitration Rules is similar to the provisions of the Model Law just quoted. The arbitration rules, as distinct from the Model Law, come into play of course only if the parties expressly choose them.)

5.   The choice-of-law methodology in *Interim Award No. 6149* is sometimes called the cumulative approach. What should the arbitrators do if the choice-of-law rules do not happily coalesce to reveal a single choice-of-law approach?

6.   Do you agree with the tribunal's conclusion that Sec. 2 of Jordanian Law No. 35 of 1983, a mandatory provision of Jordanian Law, was not applicable? Suppose each of the three sales contracts had included a separate choice of law clause which stated: "Jordanian law will be applicable". Should that have caused the tribunal to apply Sec. 2 of the 1983 Jordanian Law? Recall the *Egyptian Local Authority* case mentioned in Chapter II.2.d., question and comment 5, p. 265 There, on the issue of arbitrability, the arbitral tribunal applied the law of the seat of arbitration (Switzerland), instead of Egyptian law, although the contract said: "Egyptian laws will be applicable". (Under Swiss law the dispute was arbitrable; under Egyptian law it was not.) Should it matter if the phrase, "Jordanian law will be applicable", is included in the arbitration clause itself?

7.   Should arbitrators ever apply the mandatory law of a country other than that of the proper law of the contract? Should they do so if the proper law of the contract is determined by an express choice of law clause? We turn to these issues in the next section of the materials.

IV.3.f.　The Problem of Mandatory Law

PRINCIPAL (ITALY) v. DISTRIBUTOR (BELGIUM)

Final Award in ICC case no. 6379 of 1990.
Place of Arbitration: Cologne, Germany, 17 Yearbk. Comm. Arb'n 212 (1992).*

FACTS

By a contract made in 1981, defendant became the exclusive distributor for claimant's products in a certain territory.

Clause 29 of the contract:

"JURISDICTION

All disputes which may arise under the present contract shall be finally decided according to the Rules of Conciliation and Arbitration of the International Chamber of Commerce, Paris, by one or more arbitrators appointed according to the said Rules; recourse to court is hereby excluded."

The contract also provided for the application of Italian law.

Some seven years after the conclusion of the contract, claimant gave notice of termination of the contract to defendant. Notice was given three months before termination, as provided for in Clause 20 of the contract. Defendant objected that mandatory Belgian law provisions provided for a notice of at least 36 months and indemnification.

In the year following the termination notice, defendant initiated court proceedings against claimant before a Belgian court. The court action was still pending at the time of rendition of the present award. In the court proceedings, claimant in the arbitration objected to the Belgian courts' jurisdiction and did not defend itself on the merits of the case.

Later in the same year, claimant filed a Request for Arbitration with the ICC; defendant filed a counterclaim for indemnification.

The Terms of Reference were signed in Cologne in 1989 by the parties and the sole arbitrator.

The sole arbitrator found that Italian law applied to the contract at issue and that he should disregard mandatory Belgian law provisions. On the merits, the sole arbitrator found that the distributorship contract had been validly terminated and that the three months notice was in line with Italian law reasoning as follows.

EXCERPT

[1] "The arbitrator must ascertain as a preliminarily matter whether the Arbitral Tribunal has jurisdiction over the dispute and whether the law applicable to the substance of the dispute is Italian or Belgian law. . . .

* Reprinted with permission of Yearbook Commercial Arbitration, International Council for Commercial Arbitration.

[2] "By Clause 27(1) of the Contract, the parties have provided that the contract is governed by the law in force at the seat of the manufacturer.... Hence, the intention of the parties at the moment of signing the Contract was that Italian law apply to the substance of any dispute between them.

[3] "Further, the Contract not only provides that all disputes shall be definitively settled by [ICC] arbitration, but it also rules out any recourse to the courts (Clause 29). The parties also declared in the Contract, below the date and signatures, that they have taken cognizance of and approve in particular Clause 29 on jurisdiction. This stipulation has been separately dated and signed by both parties.

[4] "The letter of these clauses is clear; their juridical relevance however, must first be examined.

[5] "These clauses express the common intention of the parties when entering into the Contract. The common intention of the parties to an international contract cannot be disregarded unless in exceptional cases, according to the principle of the parties' contractual autonomy. As it was said in ICC award no. 1512,[1] few principles are more universally recognized in private international law than the principle 'according to which the law of the contract is the law chosen by the parties' (see S. Jarvin, Y. Derains, *Recueil des sentences arbitrales de la CCI*, 1990, p. 210).

[6] "The present dispute is characterized by the fact that the parties are legal entities having—at the moment of conclusion of the arbitral clause—their seat in Italy and Belgium, respectively, i.e., in two Contracting States other than the Contracting State in the territory of which the arbitral award shall be made, and that the dispute arises under a legal relationship qualified as commercial in both Italian and Belgian law. The arbitral award shall be based on an arbitration clause valid between the parties. Hence, all requirements of Art. I of the New York Convention of 1958 and Art. I of the Geneva Convention of 1961 for the Conventions to apply, are met in this case.

[7] "The contractual autonomy of the parties to determine the law applicable to the substance of their disputes is recognized by Art. V(1)(a) of the [New York Convention] (see A.J. van den Berg, *The New York Arbitration Convention of 1958*, The Hague 1981, p. 267) and by Art. VII(1) of the [Geneva Convention]. Belgium adhered to the former Convention on 16 November 1975 and to the latter on 7 January 1976; for Italy, the corresponding dates are 1 May 1969 and 1 November 1970.

[8] "The common intention of the parties, expressed in Clause 27 of the Contract, was to choose Italian law as the law applicable to the substance of any dispute; it cannot be disregarded in the present case. Defendant maintains that claimant, which was in a stronger bargaining

---

1. Two preliminary awards in ICC case   (1980) pp. 171–177.
no. 1512 are published in Yearbook Vol. V

position, forced it to accept these contractual provisions. However, defendant does not show in which way these provisions bring about an imbalance. Claimant shows that—according to defendant's own data—the distributorship at issue represented in 1987, i.e., after six years, only approximately 10% of defendant's turnover.

[9]   "At the moment of entering into the Contract, the parties were free to decide as they did.

[10]   "We hold that the Contract is governed by Italian law. Hence, the validity of the arbitral clause must be ascertained according to Italian law (Art. VI(2) of the Geneva Convention of 1961; P. Bernardini, *L'arbitrato internazionale*, 1987, p. 55).

[11]   "According to the Italian Supreme Court, the provisions on jurisdiction of the New York convention of 1958 prevail over national law in the Italian legal system. Hence, the validity of a clause for foreign arbitration must be ascertained according to Art. II of the New York Convention (Rivista di diritto internazionale privato e processuale 1981, 176, 177). This reasoning applies by analogy to the Geneva Convention of 1961.

[12]   "The requirements of Arts. I and II(1) and (2) of the New York Convention and of Art. I of the Geneva Convention are undoubtedly met in the present case; hence, the arbitral clause is valid under Italian law.

[13]   "Defendant objects to the jurisdiction of the Arbitral Tribunal and maintains that Art. II(3) of the New York Convention does not compel the Belgian court to refer the parties to arbitration.

[14]   "Defendant recognizes in principle that the parties have chosen Italian law to apply to their contract. However, it invokes in casu Arts. 4 and 6 of the Belgian Law of 27 July 1961, as modified by the Law of 13 April 1971 'Law of 1961/1971', contending that these provisions are 'provisions of mandatory application' and relying on the mandatory nature of provisions concerning the modalities and consequences of the termination of a distributorship contract for reasons other than gross negligence. The above-mentioned Articles read:

> "*Art. 4*
>
> The agent who has suffered damages as a result of the termination of a distributorship contract having effect in the whole or part of the Belgian territory, may always initiate court proceedings in Belgium against the principal, either before the court of his own domicile, or before the court of the domicile or seat of the principal.
>
> When the dispute is brought before a Belgian court, this court shall only apply Belgian law.
>
> *Art. 6*
>
> The provisions of this Law apply notwithstanding any agreement to the contrary stipulated before the end of the distributorship contract.

They apply to distributorship contracts made before the entry into force of this Law."

[15] "Defendant mentions in this context Art. 7 of the Rome Convention of 19 June 1980 on the law applicable to contractual obligations. Art. 7 provides that

"When applying under this Convention the law of a country, effect may be given to the mandatory rules of the law of another country with which the situation has a close connection, if and in so far as, under the law of the latter country, those rules must be applied whatever the law applicable to the contract. In considering whether to give effect to these mandatory rules, regard shall be had to their nature and purpose and to the consequences of their application or non-application."

Defendant alleges that, under Art. 7 above-mentioned, Clause 29 of the Contract is null and void, inoperative or incapable of being performed, in the sense of Art. II(3) of the New York Convention of 10 June 1958. These arguments shall be examined *infra*.

[16] "The Rome Convention of 19 June 1980 has not entered into force.[8] Arbitral clauses are expressly excluded from its scope of application (Art. I(2)(d)).[9] Hence, the Rome Convention cannot be applied. From Art. 1(2)(d) it also ensues that, if the Convention shall ever come into force, it shall not affect arbitration clauses.

[17] "The concept of provisions of mandatory application (*'règles d'application immédiate (ou impérative')*) was introduced by G. Sperduti (see G. Sperduti, 'Les lois d'application nécessaire en tant que lois d'ordre public', Revue critique de droit international public, 1977, 257, 258). Sperduti underlines that 'a provision of mandatory application is *such only in its legal system of origin*; its nature does not in itself hinder the application of the law of another State' (Sperduti, op. cit., p. 265; emphasis added by the arbitrator).

[18] "It clearly results from the works of Gothot and Sperduti ... that Sperduti's theory has been broadly discussed by various authors in various countries and that it has many partisans, but also many opponents. It is far from clear what are the exact contents of this concept or which provisions fall within its scope. P. Gothot ... speaks of a 'rather confused discussion'. It is a very interesting concept, but it is not a universally accepted norm of Italian law, which should be applied by the arbitrator in the present case.

---

8. *Note General Editor*. The Rome Convention entered into force on 1 April 1991.

9. Art. I(1) and (2)(d) of the Rome Convention reads:

"1. The rules of this Convention shall apply to contractual obligations in any situation involving a choice between the laws of different countries.

2. They shall not apply to:

(. . . .)

(d) arbitration agreements and agreements on the choice of court;

(. . . .)"

[19] "The Geneva Convention of 1961, which has become part of the Italian legal system and which prevails over internal provisions, allows the parties to agree on the law applicable to their contract (Art. VII). It provides that the validity of the arbitral clause must be ascertained according to the law chosen by the parties (Art. 6(2)), i.e., in the present case, according to Italian law. The Geneva Convention makes no exception for foreign provisions of mandatory application.

[20] "According to Italian law, the Belgian Law of 1961/1971 does not prevail over Italian law and, therefore, does not prevail either on the contractual provisions freely agreed upon by the parties. Hence, the arbitration clause in the Contract is not null and void, inoperative or incapable of being performed.

[21] "Further considerations confirm this outcome. In international arbitration, an Arbitral Tribunal is not an institution under the legal system of a State. M. Bogdan writes: 'An arbitral tribunal is not an instrumentality of any particular State' (Some Arbitration–Related Problems of Swedish Private International Law, in: *Swedish and International Arbitration* 1990, pp. 70, 76). J. Lew says: '. . . an international arbitration tribunal is a non-national institution; it owes no allegiance to any sovereign State; it has no *lex fori* in the conventional sense' (*Applicable Law in International Commercial Arbitration*, 1978, p. 535).

[22] "In conformity with these principles, the Law of 1961/1971 does not aim at binding the international arbitrator, as made clear in Art. 4(2): 'When the dispute is brought before a *Belgian court, this court* shall only apply Belgian law'. (Emphasis added).

[23] "Further, the said Law does not compel the distributor to bring his dispute before a Belgian court; rather, it gives him the possibility to do so ('The distributor . . . may . . .'). Belgian doctrine and case law support this conclusion. Thus, R. Prioux writes: 'Contrary to courts, international arbitrators are in principle not bound to follow the conflict-of-laws rules of a certain State rather than those of another State'; '. . . in international arbitration there is neither lex fori, nor foreign law'; 'Certain authors go so far as to say that no foreign mandatory law provisions bind arbitrators . . .'. (R. Prioux, RDCB, 1988, 251, 267 . . .).

[24] "The same author shows that Belgian case law is divided on the issue whether Belgian mandatory provisions have effect outside the Belgian territory (R. Prioux, op. cit., pp. 290, 291 and notes 153 through 158).

[25] "The Court of Appeal of Brussels, in a decision of 4 October 1985,[10] examined the validity of an arbitral clause referring to Swiss law as the law applicable to an exclusive distributor contract having effect in the Belgian territory. The Court considered the Law of 1961/1971, relied upon the New York Convention of 1958 and held: 'In order to ascertain

---

10. Reported in Yearbook XIV (1989) pp. 618–620 (Belgium no. 6). [The case is included in the materials supra, Chapter II.2.d. at p. 262].

the validity of an arbitration clause contained in an exclusive distributor contract having its effect in Belgium, we must not apply the *lex fori* but the law of autonomy. . . . The *lex fori* of the court seized with the dispute must be applied to the issue of the validity of the arbitral clause, only when the court hears a request for recognition or enforcement of the arbitral award'; '. . . it is therefore the law of autonomy that answers the question of arbitrability'; '. . . the arbitrator . . . must first of all determine which law applies to the arbitral clause and later ascertain whether, according to this law, the case at hand may be settled by arbitration'. (Journal des Tribunaux 1986, p. 93).

[26] "Hence, the Court of Appeal of Brussels reversed the lower court's decision, which held that the arbitral clause was null and void, inoperative or incapable of being performed; it further held that the *Tribunal de Commerce* of Brussels had no jurisdiction over the dispute and, therefore, referred the parties to arbitration, as provided for in the contract between them.

[27] "In the present case, it is not contested that the parties agreed in the Contract that their contractual relationship would be governed by Italian law. Nor is it contested, and it also appears from the documents submitted by claimant, that Italian law allows the dispute between the parties to be settled by arbitration. The Belgian Law of 1961/1971 does not affect this situation.

[28] "In conclusion, the arbitration clause agreed upon by the parties is valid and the Arbitral Tribunal has jurisdiction to hear and decide the case, applying Italian law as the law applicable to substance."

[29] [On the merits of the case the sole arbitrator held:] "The applicable law to the Contract is Italian law. Italian law recognizes party autonomy as a general principle that is not limited to the right of the parties mutually to determine the applicable substantive law. . . ."

[30] "As the Rome Convention is not yet in force and the theory according to which a foreign mandatory law is to be respected is not recognized in Italian law as applicable to the present case which concerns an exclusive distributorship, there is no mandatory provision or public policy provision in Italian law that imposes a longer notification period between the producer and the distributor. On the contrary, the contractually agreed upon period should be respected. . . . Consequently, the provisions of Belgian law providing for a longer notification period for the distributor shall not be applied by the arbitrator."

[31] The arbitrator followed the same reasoning when denying defendant's counterclaim for indemnification.

* * *

Questions and Comments

1. Note that the arbitrator relied on party autonomy—the choice of Italian law in the distribution contract—to decide the validity of the arbitration clause. Is this logical? Is it a bootstrap theory? Note that the arbitrator

also relied on Article VII of the 1961 European (Geneva) Convention on International Commercial Arbitration (reproduced supra at page 530 and in the Documents Supplement). The 1961 Geneva Convention was part of Italian law, but how does one get to Italian law in the first place? Moreover, is it clear that Article VII applies to the issue of the arbitration agreement's validity? Is there a better approach to the law applicable to the validity of the arbitration agreement? As arbitrator in this case, would you have found the arbitration clause valid?

2. Note that the Belgian distributor had begun an action against the Italian manufacturer in a Belgian court. Under the New York Convention rules, should the Belgian court retain or dismiss the case? Under the New York Convention rules, is a Belgian court obligated to give res judicata effect to the arbitral award?

3. The arbitrator says in paragraph [7]: "The contractual autonomy of the parties to determine the law applicable to the substance of their disputes is recognized by Art. V(1)(a) of the [New York Convention]." Do you agree?

4. The Rome Convention provides a body of choice of law rules for contract issues. It entered into force on April 1, 1991; all members of the European Union, including Italy, are parties. The Belgian distributor sought to rely on Article 7 of the Rome Convention to establish that articles 4 and 6 of the Belgian law of 1961/1971 should apply as mandatory law and thus that the arbitration agreement was invalid. In paragraph [16] the arbitrator rejected this argument on two grounds: first, that the Rome Convention was not in force at the time of this arbitration; and second, that the Rome Convention expressly provides that it does not apply to "arbitration agreements" (Art. I(2)(d) of the Rome Convention). The Belgian distributor returned to the Rome Convention in arguing for Belgian law to apply to the merits of the dispute, namely concerning the notification period required for termination of a distribution agreement and the distributor's claim for indemnification. This time, in paragraph [30], the arbitrator relied only on the first ground (the Convention's not having entered into force) in rejecting the argument. Had the dispute arisen after April 1, 1991, when the Rome Convention became operative, should the arbitrator have applied the Convention to reach Belgian law on the merits? Is the Rome Convention a part of Italian substantive law or choice of law rules?

5. As arbitrator in this case, would you have applied the Belgian mandatory law on the notice period and indemnification? If so, how would you explain the arbitrator's authority to do so, given that arbitrators derive their authority from the will of the parties?

6. Suppose a French firm, negotiating to sell technology for producing fans to a Chinese firm, wants to include a clause prohibiting the Chinese firm from exporting the fans, but learns that mandatory Chinese law forbids such an export restraint. Suppose Chinese law also provides that, to be valid, a contract for the sale of technology (a licensing agreement) must be approved by officials in the Technology Licensing Administration of China. The parties enter a licensing agreement without the restrictive clause but include a separate annex to the agreement in which they provide that if the Chinese firm exports the fans, it must pay a penalty to the French licensor of seven times the normal royalty fee. The parties include a clause in the

agreement providing for arbitration in Geneva under ICC rules and choosing Swiss law as the law to govern all disputes under the contract. They submit the contract to the appropriate Chinese officials for approval, but do not include the annex. The contract—minus the annex—is approved. Later the Chinese firm ships fans to Sweden, and the French firm initiates arbitration in Geneva claiming seven times the normal royalty fee on the fans shipped to Sweden. As arbitrator would you rule the agreement invalid or award seven times the normal royalty fee?

Yves Derains, PUBLIC POLICY AND THE LAW APPLICABLE TO THE DISPUTE IN INTERNATIONAL ARBITRATION

International Council for Commercial Arbitration, Comparative Arbitration Practice and Public Policy in Arbitration 242– 254 (Pieter Sanders, ed., 1986).*

* * *

IV.   Mandatory Rules

37.   Can we not purely and simply state that the international arbitrator does not have to concern himself with the public policy of laws that are foreign to the *lex contractus*? It is tempting to reply in the affirmative, at least when the problems faced by the arbitrator are contractual in nature, that is to say connected with the interpretation, performance, termination, or validity of the contract, etc. * * *

Although this approach has the merit of simplicity, it would not, however, take sufficient account of the existence, in addition to public policy in the domestic law sense of the term, of mandatory rules which are too important in the interests of a given national society to enter into competition with foreign laws and whose "field of application is consequently determined basically with regard to their objective".

38.   Two * * * examples * * * illustrate the claim of such laws to intervene despite the fact that they do not belong to the *lex contractus*:

First example

A Swiss bank granted a loan in U.S. dollars to a Portuguese company. The loan agreement was subject to English law and provided for arbitration in Zurich.

The Portuguese company did not repay the funds lent to it, claiming that it had not obtained the necessary authorization for transfer from the Portuguese exchange control authorities.

Second example

Two firms, one Italian, the other German, concluded a contract subject to Swiss law and fixing Geneva as the place of arbitration. This contract was contrary to the competition law provisions under the

* Reprinted with permission from Kluwer Law International.

Treaty of Rome, which are mandatory rules in both German and Italian law.

In both the above examples, laws foreign to the *lex contractus* claim to affect the contract. Indeed, the field of application of the Portuguese exchange control regulations and the European competition rules does not depend on the choice of the law applicable to a contract. As mandatory rules, their very aim is to disallow parties from excluding them by making their contract subject to a law foreign to the legal system from which they stem, or a judge or arbitrator preventing them from coming into effect by deciding to apply such a foreign law to the contract.

39.   When faced with difficulties like this, the national judge has to distinguish between mandatory rules "of the forum" and foreign mandatory rules. The mandatory rules of the forum have a natural priority which the judge has to apply, whatever the proper law of the contract. Therefore, a Portuguese judge would give effect to the Portuguese exchange control regulations, and a German or Italian judge to the rules of the Treaty of Rome. The mandatory rules of the forum by their very existence preclude the operation of the applicable law by virtue of the conflict of laws rule of the *lex fori*.

The question of foreign mandatory rules is more complicated. Should the judge apply them only when they fall within the legal system that its conflict of law rules designate as having jurisdiction, subject to the intervention of overriding international public policy? Does the judge, on the contrary, have to require foreign mandatory rules to be observed in all cases where he considers this is necessary if they are to achieve their objective? To date these questions have not been answered definitively, although the Rome Convention of 19 June 1980 provides useful guidance on this.

40.   Since there is no *lex fori* and accompanying distinction between the respective national and foreign laws, the international arbitrator does not go into the question of the application of mandatory rules in the same way as the judge. He takes no account of the distinction between mandatory rules of the forum and foreign mandatory rules. He can only take account of the distinction between mandatory rules of the *lex contractus* (1) and mandatory rules of another legal system (2).

1.   *Mandatory Rules of the* Lex Contractus

41.   Arbitrators seem to approach the problem of the intervention of mandatory rules of the *lex contractus* differently depending on whether the parties have chosen this law (a.), or whether it is up to the arbitrator to determine it (b.).

a.   *The* lex contractus *has been chosen by the parties*

* * *

[Derains reasons that if parties choose a *lex contractus*, normally their choice will be understood to include mandatory rules as well. He then turns to the question of the parties' freedom to choose a particular *lex contractus* but with the proviso that certain mandatory rules of the *lex contractus* are not to be applied. For illustration he returns to the second example above (an Italian and a German firm enter a contract contrary to the competition law of the European Union but choose Swiss law and arbitration in Geneva, Switzerland).]

43.   * * * Let us suppose that instead of having chosen Swiss law * * * [as] the *lex contractus* the parties had chosen German law and specified that their agreement was not subject to European competition law. Would the arbitrator then be able to take the view that he does not have to apply these rules on the grounds that the parties have made their choice of German law only partial by excluding some of its mandatory rules.

The answer is in the negative since the claim of mandatory rules to affect a contractual operation, unlike domestic public policy, is not necessarily dependent on the choice of the *lex contractus*. In the example given above, the European competition law rules are intended to be applied to the contract whether the *lex contractus* chosen by the parties is German law shorn of its policy laws or Swiss law.

The problem thus leads to the question whether the arbitrator has to apply the mandatory rules of a law other than the *lex contractus* when that law was chosen so as to preclude the operation of the mandatory rules in question * * * [see infra para. 50].

b.   *The* lex contractus *is determined by the arbitrator*

44.   Unlike the national judge, the arbitrator is not affected by the concept of a particular law with jurisdiction over the contract. Consequently, unless the parties have chosen the *lex contractus* all laws that claim to affect the contract have *a priori* equal right to be applied. Therefore it is not surprising to find that arbitrators decide on the applicability of the mandatory rules directly without asking whether they belong to the *lex contractus*.

An award rendered in ICC Case No. 4132 in 1983 illustrates this type of process.[38] The arbitrator was dealing with a dispute regarding a contract that had to be performed by a party in Korea and another party in the EEC. He considered the question of the application to the contract of Korean mandatory rules and EEC competition law before determining the law applicable to the contract.

* * *

[In the excerpt from the award in ICC Case No. 4123 quoted by Derains, the arbitrator first noted that the contract was to be performed in part in Korea and thus was "likely to affect the domain of Korean (public) law", namely Korean antitrust law. The arbitrator concluded, however, that the defendant had not shown that the contract involved an illegal tie-in under Korean antitrust law. Because the contract was also

---

38.   *Cf.* Yearbook, Vol. X (1985) p. 49.

to be performed partly in Italy, the arbitrator also scrutinized the agreement under the European Union antitrust law. Thereafter the arbitrator declared that Korean law was applicable to the contract.]

* * *

2. *Mandatory Rules Foreign to the* Lex Contractus

46. With regard to mandatory rules foreign to the *lex contractus*, the two examples set out above * * * [in para. 38] enable us to distinguish between two different cases:

　　a.　The taking into consideration of mandatory rules.

　　b.　The application of mandatory rules.

47. a. In the first example, the Portuguese debtor who claimed that a refusal of authorization for the transfer by the Portuguese exchange control authorities was grounds for his non-payment did not ask the arbitrator to apply the Portuguese mandatory rules that caused this refusal. He merely wanted it to be "taken into consideration"[40] although English law was applicable to the loan agreement. Moreover, it must be admitted that, in any case, the arbitrator would not be able to apply the Portuguese regulations in question by reason of their very nature. All that he has to do is to take its operation into consideration so as to draw legal conclusions under English law, the proper law of the contract.

Situations of this type can be found in decisions in arbitration cases: refusal of the exchange control authorities of the buyer's country to allow the performance of a contract for the sale of oil subject to the law of the seller's country;[41] refusal of consent by the authorities of the place of performance of the contract which was subject to another law.[42] In these examples, it is clear that arbitrators would have had no jurisdiction to apply the public law provisions underlying the administrative measures whose effects on the performance of the contract they had to evaluate. The question of the applicability of these mandatory rules is not discussed. The effects engendered by them are noted and taken into account in accordance with the *lex contractus*.

47. b. The first example only needs to be slightly amended to take us away from the question of the taking into consideration of the mandatory rules of the *lex contractus* into the field of their applicability. For example, if we were to assume that the Portuguese debtor was no longer claiming that it was impossible to transfer the funds as a result of refusal of authorization by the exchange control authorities, but rather that the loan agreement was void for lack of authorization by the same authorities prior to the loan; the arbitrator would then have to decide whether he could declare a contract subject to English law was void by the application of a Portuguese mandatory rule.

40. On the distinction between application and taking into consideration, *cf.* P.Mayer "Les lois de police étrangères", Clunet (1981) p. 307 *et seq.*

41. ICC Case No. 2216, Clunet (1975) p. 917; Jurisprudencia arbitral p. 105.

42. ICC Case No. 1782, Clunet (1975) p. 923; Jurisprudencia arbitral, p. 111.

Yet again, the question raised by the second example is the applicability of a mandatory rule foreign to the *lex contractus*. Can a contract subject to Swiss law be declared void by an international arbitrator by virtue of the EEC competition rules?

The ICC award rendered in Case No. 4132 * * * (see above para. 44) is an actual example of this type of problem. It seems that the question has to be asked in different terms depending whether the parties have or have not chosen the *lex contractus* (*a.* and *b.*).

a. *The parties have chosen the* lex contractus

48. The principle whereby arbitrators are bound to apply the law chosen by the parties * * * is sometimes all that is needed for them to set aside a mandatory rule foreign to that law. An example of this is the decision by the Court of Arbitration of the Chamber of Foreign Trade of the German Democratic Republic.[43] The arbitrators were called to rule on the validity of a licence agreement concluded between a firm in the GDR [East Germany] and another firm in the GFR [West Germany]. The second firm considered, *inter alia*, that the contract was void as being contrary to the competition law provisions of its own country and to Article 85 of the Treaty of Rome. Stressing that the parties had made the contract subject to the law of the GDR, the arbitrators put forward the following argument:

> "The validity of the agreement must be judged under the law of the GDR designated in the arbitral clause as the law applicable to the agreement.
>
> . . . .
>
> The invalidity of the licence agreement cannot result from Sect. 20 of the Law on Restrictive Trade Practices of the FRG and Sects. 85 *et seq.* of the EEC Treaty. In determining the validity of the licence agreement under GDR law, these provisions must be taken into account only if they would render the performance of the agreement effectively impossible and the invalidity of the agreement would have to be accepted pursuant to Sect. 306 Civil Code (GDR). Such factual impediments for performance have not been proven by the respondent."

49. However, arbitrators are not usually satisfied with indicating that a mandatory rule is foreign to the *lex contractus* as a reason for not applying it. Indeed, the designation of the *lex contractus* does not necessarily imply that the parties had intended all mandatory rules liable to affect the contract to be excluded. And arbitrators prefer to explain that there are no serious grounds for applying the mandatory rules in question * * *.

* * *

43. *Cf.* Yearbook, Vol. IV (1979) p. 197,   award of 27 June 1976.

In this connection an award rendered in ICC Case No. 1512 in 1971[46] appears * * * significant:

This dispute arose from the non-performance by a Pakistani bank of a guarantee issued in favor of an Indian company which was made expressly subject to Indian law. *Inter alia*, the arbitrator was faced with the question of deciding whether the bank was discharged from its obligations as a result of Pakistani decrees declaring any payment to an Indian party illegal—passed because of hostilities between India and Pakistan which had broken out after the guarantee had been issued. After noting that the question of the extinguishment of the contractual obligations was subject to the proper law the arbitrator added:

> "The question might however be raised of the possible effect, in this respect, of the law of the place of performance (*lex loci solutionis*). It might be raised owing to the reference made by one of the parties, or by both of them, to English and other cases on this point.

> "Sitting in Geneva as an international arbitrator acting under the ICC Rules chosen by the Parties, I do not feel bound by these cases as an English judge or arbitrator would feel, however great the respect with which I consider these decisions. Were I sitting in England, moreover, I would be reluctant to decide that illegality supervening under the (foreign *lex loci solutionis*) as such, has any effect when the proper law is a foreign law.

> "The prevailing trend of opinion, however, in the absence of any direct authority on this point, seems clearly to favour the negative answer, i.e., that determines the question whether the debtor is discharged by law of his contractual obligation.

> "While it may be uncertain whether the foreign law of the place of performance (foreign in relation to the forum) determines this question, on one point, at least, there appears to exist unanimity: where the contract is valid under its proper law and such law is the law of the place of performance.... In the present case, the guarantee indicated that the payment should take place in India. The arbitrator is of the opinion that Pakistani law, the law of the place of the debtor's residence, should not intervene."

It should be noted that the arbitrator did not ground his decision on the fundamental inapplicability of the mandatory rule foreign to the *lex contractus* chosen by the parties. He felt it was important to demonstrate that it had no serious right to be applied in view of the nature of the transaction that gave rise to the dispute.

* * *

50. The question remains as to the answer that arbitrators ought to reserve for a mandatory rule foreign to the *lex contractus* chosen by the parties when there are serious grounds for applying that law. [T]he arbitrators might by analyzing the parties' intentions conclude that their

---

46. [5 Yearbk. Comm. Arb'n 174 (1980).]

choice of law did not exclude the operation of mandatory rules of other legal systems. But would the same rule apply if the parties had expressly stated that this choice was exclusive or if it appeared that by choosing a given law the parties had deliberately decided to take themselves outside the field of operation of certain mandatory rules, e.g., those of the place of performance of the contract?

The second of the examples put forward * * * [para. 38 above] might possibly be used to illustrate a situation of this type.

Indeed, we have to take as a possibility the fact that the German and Italian parties had stipulated that a contract contrary to EEC competition rules was subject to Swiss law with the sole intention of avoiding being penalized for infringing a mandatory rule of the place of performance. They had recourse to arbitration, seeking by this means to reinforce the guarantee apparently given to the choice of the law of a country outside the EEC.

From a theoretical point of view, this question is presented in the same terms as that of the express exclusion by the parties of a mandatory rule of the lex contractus chosen by them * * * [see para. 43 above]. In both cases the question is whether an international arbitrator is mandatorily bound to respect the will of the parties as to the choice of rules applying to their contract even at the expense of a deliberate fraud against a national law.

It seems that the only way of resolving this question is by recourse to the theory of "truly international public policy". First of all, it goes without saying that if the mandatory law excluded was considered to be contrary to truly international public policy by virtue of its content, an arbitrator would have to give effect to the parties' intention of excluding its application (e.g., a law establishing a racial discrimination). Likewise, if the object of that law is to guarantee the respect of principles considered by the arbitrator as forming part of truly international public policy, the arbitrator would have to make that law, or at least its principles, prevail over the will of the parties. But situations as clear-cut as this are seldom met with in practice.

In fact, once it is admitted that in exceptional cases an arbitrator can in the name of a concept of truly international public policy refuse to give effect to certain agreements by parties—such as cases of corruption—one is led to the conclusion that in the same way an arbitrator should not agree to be an accomplice in a deliberate fraud on a mandatory rule that the arbitrator considers has an undisputed right to be applied.

Like every case of overriding international public policy, it is all a question of sensitivity. It seems, however, that if he wishes to avoid abuse of office, the international arbitrator has to guarantee as a minimum the respect of the mandatory rules of the place of performance of the contract, which the arbitrators consider to apply as a matter of course when the parties have not chosen a lex contractus * * * [see para. 53 infra].

b. *The* lex contractus *is determined by the arbitrator.*

52. As we mentioned above, * * * [see para. 44] in the absence of the concept of competent law, all national or a-national laws have the same weight so long as the arbitrator has not decided that one or more of them are to be applied. Consequently, there is nothing to prevent the application of a mandatory law foreign to the law designated by the arbitrator as the *lex contractus*. In fact, in such a case the arbitrator will decide to restrict the field of application of the *lex contractus* by excluding from its operation those questions he considers should be subject to one or other mandatory law which in his view has a serious right to be applied.

* * *

[Here, Derains discusses several more ICC awards.]

56. It would, therefore, appear that there is no unanimous viewpoint among arbitrators as to the applicability of mandatory rules foreign to the *lex contractus* when this law has not been chosen by the parties. The majority seem to tend towards favoring the application of mandatory rules of the place of performance of the contract. It is clear that opinions are much more divided on the question of mandatory rules of the parties' respective countries.

As a matter of fact, I have taken the view[52] that here too it was the concern to respond to the legitimate expectations of the parties that guided the arbitrators when they had to make a ruling on the applicability of mandatory rules foreign to the *lex contractus*. This is why in the vast majority of cases the arbitrator will apply mandatory rules of the place of performance of the contract, or more precisely, of the contractual obligation whose performance is in question. International practice is in fact to respect the mandatory rules of the states in which a contract is being performed. These laws come within the domain of the contract.

If there is no stipulation to the contrary in the contract, the parties are entitled to legitimately expect the arbitrator to presume that their agreement did indeed accord with that practice.

Thus, it is only if a mandatory rule of the place of performance is incompatible with truly international public policy that an arbitrator can exclude its application.

The same rule apparently does not apply in cases where mandatory rules of the country of one or other of the parties are concerned and the contract is not performed in that country.

52. Cf. Y. Derains, "Les normes d'application immédiate dans la jurisprudence arbitrale internationale", in Études offertes à B. Goldman, p. 45.

Ole Lando, CONFLICT–OF–LAWS RULES FOR ARBITRATORS, IN FESTSCHRIFT FÜR KONRAD ZWEIGERT 157, 172–74
(H. Bernstein, U. Drobnig & H. Kötz eds., 1981).*

* * *

For the arbitrator and especially the "stateless" arbitrator, the situation is sometimes different from that of the national judge. He has no forum whose rules he must apply. He cannot apply every national law, which might claim application to the issue. These laws may be conflicting. On the other hand, he should not disregard them all. He should not do so even when the chances are very small that the authorities of any of the interested countries might be able to interfere. The arbitrator will have to consider not only the interests of the parties but also those of international commercial arbitration considered as an institution. Today arbitration still enjoys the prestige which has induced the liberality shown to it by most Western countries. If it becomes known that arbitration is being used as a device for evading the public policy of states which have a governmental interest in regulating certain business transactions, its reputation may suffer.

Arbitration can only survive as long as it is tolerated by the states. It is in the interests of the business community that arbitration should be kept as free as possible from government intervention.

The question then is, when should the arbitrator apply the laws referred to? This has to be left to his discretion. As mentioned above, he should apply those laws which can reasonably claim application to the issue.

In accordance with these considerations, the Group has in * * * [art. 9] made an attempt to formulate a rule governing these questions. The Members of the Group which support art. 9, first alternative, also refer to art. 26 *in fine* of the ICC Rules of Arbitration, which provides "In all matters not expressly provided for in these Rules, the Court of Arbitration and the Arbitrator ... shall make efforts to make sure that the award is enforceable at law."[s] This rule may be interpreted as a *caveat* to the arbitrator not to render arbitral awards which violate the public policy or the directly applicable rules of the country in which enforcement, if any, of an award is likely to be requested, and not to violate the public policy rules laid down in the International Conventions on Arbitration, such as art. V1(a) and art. V2(a) and (b) of the New York Convention of June 10, 1958, in cases where the arbitration is covered by these conventions.

Some members, again, are reluctant to introduce a rule similar to the one in art. 7 of the EC Convention[t] and would favour a rule which

---

* Reprinted by permission of Ole Lando.

s. Authors' note: This provision is now found in Article 35 of the 1998 ICC Rules.

t. Authors' note: Article 7(1) of the European Community Convention on the Law Applicable to Contractual Obligations (1980) was quoted in the Belgian distributor case (ICC no. 6379) supra. It reads:

"When applying under this convention the law of a country, effect may be given to the mandatory rules of the law of another country with which the situation has a close connection, if and in so far as, under law of the latter country, those rules must be applied whatever the law applicable to the contract. In considering whether to give

underlines what should be the main concern of the arbitrator, namely the enforcement of the award. They have proposed the second alternative, which is also bracketed.

Appendix

Draft Recommendations on the Law Applicable to International Contracts[u]

The International Chamber of Commerce

wishing to promote arbitration as a means of solving disputes among parties to international commercial relationships considering that such disputes often give rise to questions concerning the law applicable to contracts that under art. 13(3)[v] of the International Chamber of Commerce Rules of Arbitration the parties shall be free to determine the law to be applied by the arbitrator to the merits of the dispute. In the absence of any indication by the parties as to the applicable law the arbitrator shall apply the law designated as the proper law by the rule of conflict which he deems applicable that art. 13(5)[w] of the rules provides that in all cases the arbitrator shall take account of the provisions of the contract and the relevant trade usages that arbitrators may wish to pursue a policy of uniformity in the choice of the rule of conflict which they deem applicable has found it appropriate to recommend arbitrators to consider the following conflict of law rules for cases where the law applicable to contracts is in issue

Art. 1—Choice of Law by the Parties

(1) The Law chosen by the parties shall govern the contract. This choice of law may be made at the time of the conclusion of the contract or later.

(2) The choice of law must be express or must appear clearly from any indications in the contract or from the behaviour of the parties.

Art. 2—Law Governing in the Absence of Choice of Law by the Parties

(1) In the absence of a choice of law by the parties, [and except as provided in paragraph (2)] the law with which the contract has its most significant connection shall govern.
The connecting factors to be taken into consideration in the determination of that law include:
— the place of business of the parties
— the place of performance
— the location of immovable or movable property which is the subject matter of the contract

effect to these mandatory rules, regard shall be had to their nature and purpose and to the consequences of their application or non-application."

u. Authors' note: The Draft Recommendations were never adopted.

v. Authors' note: Now Article 17(1) of the 1998 ICC Rules.

w. Authors' note: Now Article 17(2) of the 1998 ICC Rules.

— the place where the contract was negotiated or concluded
— the use by the parties of a standard form contract or general conditions drafted with regard to a certain legal system
— the connection of the contract with another contract governed by a certain legal system
— the selection by the parties of the place of arbitration.

[(2) In selecting the law applicable to the contract in the absence of a choice of law by the parties the arbitrators may also take into consideration the conflict-of-law rules of two or more of those legal systems which have a significant connection with the contract where they lead to the application of the substantive rules of the same legal system.]

Art. 3—Law of the Party Who is to Effect the Characteristic Performance

(1) Except as provided in paragraph (3) and in art. 4–7 [dealing with specialized contracts concerning publishing, employment, labor and work, and immovables] it is to be presumed that a contract has its most significant connection with the law of the country where the party who is to effect the performance which is characteristic of the contract has, at the time of the conclusion of the contract, his place of business.

(2) Hence, the sale of movable goods is presumed to [be] most closely connected with the law of the country where the seller has his place of business,

— the leasing of movable goods with the law of the country where the lessor has his place of business,
— the licence contract with the law of the country where the licensor has his place of business,
— the distributorship contract, except for the seller-buyer relationship, with the law of the country where the distributor has his place of business,
— the agency contract with the law of the country where the agent has his place of business,
— the contract for services rendered by a member of the professions by the law of the country where the professional has his place of business.

(3) The presumptions provided for in paragraphs 1 and 2 do not apply when the characteristic performance of a contract cannot be determined, or if it appears from the circumstances that the contract has its most significant connection with the law of another country.

[Art. 9   Mandatory Rules

Alternative 1

Even when the arbitrator does not apply the law of a certain country as the law governing the contract he may nevertheless give effect to mandatory rules of the law of that country if the contract or the parties have a close contact to that country and if and insofar as under its law those rules must be applied whatever be the law applicable to the contract. On considering whether to give effect to these mandatory rules, regard shall be had to their nature and purpose and to the consequences of their application or non-application.

Alternative 2

Even when the arbitrator does not apply the law of a certain country as the law applicable to the contract he may nevertheless give effect to the mandatory rules of the law of that country if the contract or the parties have a close contact to the country in question especially when the arbitral award is likely to be enforced there, and if and insofar as under the law of that country those rules must be applied whatever be the law applicable to the contract.]

Questions and Comments

1. In paragraph [43] Derains seems to conclude that an arbitrator should not follow the parties' will if the parties expressly choose, for example, German law minus the rules of European competition law. In part he rests this conclusion on the observation that "the claim of mandatory rules to affect a contractual operation" does not depend on the law chosen by the parties! He also notes that in the example given "the European competition rules are intended to be applied to the contract" irrespective of the parties' choice of law. Does this explain why the arbitrator, who is not an official of any sovereign, should respect the "claim of mandatory rules" or the intent of the legislator who promulgated them? Do you agree with Derains?

2. Derains says in paragraph [50]:

" * * * [A]n arbitrator should not agree to be an accomplice in a deliberate fraud on a mandatory rule that the arbitrator considers has an undisputed right to be applied.

* * *

" * * * [I]f he wishes to avoid abuse of office, the international arbitrator has to guarantee as a minimum the respect of the mandatory rules of the place of performance of the contract, which the arbitrators consider to apply as a matter of course when the parties have not chosen a *lex contractus*."

Do you agree? Take the case Derains expressly raises: the parties enter into a contract to be performed in a European Union country whose antitrust law would invalidate the contract; they nevertheless provide in the contract for the application of Swiss law and expressly forbid the application of the antitrust law of the place of performance. Should an arbitrator invalidate the contract under the mandatory law of the place of performance or enforce the contract under Swiss law? Derains, it seems, would apply the mandatory antitrust law. Do you agree?

3. Review the Ole Lando excerpt and the Draft Recommendations on the Law Applicable to International Contracts prepared by the ICC Working Group. If a similar effort were undertaken today to draft recommendations

to arbitrators on the law applicable in arbitration, would you favor including one of the versions of Article 9?

4. Article 19 of the Swiss Private International Law Act is similar in basic content to Ole Lando's proposed Article 9.[21] However, unlike Lando's proposed Article 9, which is addressed to arbitrators, Article 19 is a general Swiss choice-of-law provision addressed to Swiss judges and applicable in Swiss courts.[22] It reads as follows:

> "1. A mandatory provision of a foreign country other than that to which the provisions of this Act refer may be given effect, provided that legitimate and manifestly preponderant interests (of one party) according to the Swiss conception of law so requires, and provided that the case has a close connection with that system of law.
>
> 2. In order to establish whether such a provision shall be given effect its policy and the consequences of its application shall be taken into account, in order that a satisfactory decision according to the Swiss conception of law may be reached."

An ICC arbitral tribunal applied this provision in a case involving two construction companies, one American and the other Turkish. The two companies formed a joint venture to complete a construction project in Turkey. In the agreement they specified that Swiss law would apply and that disputes would be settled through ICC arbitration in Geneva, Switzerland. In the award the arbitrators relied on PILA Article 19 to justify applying Turkish mandatory law (concerning the allowed beneficiaries of certain Turkish tax privileges).[23] See Final Award in ICC Case #8528 of 1996, 25 Yearbook Comm. Arb. 341 (2000). Do you agree with this approach? Given that many legal systems contain choice of law provisions similar to Swiss PILA Article 19, is the *ICC Case #8528* approach likely to be applicable in most arbitrations—even in the absence of party-chosen institutional rules containing a version of Lando's Article 9?

In *ICC Case #8528*, why exactly is it appropriate for the arbitrators to apply Article 19 of the Swiss PILA in the first place? The award does not really clarify this point. Would you consider it crucial, or irrelevant, that the parties chose Swiss law? Or, alternatively, does the award seem to resurrect the early twentieth century practice of applying the choice of law rules of the place of arbitration?

5. Both Derains (see paras. 43 and 50) and Lando conclude that in certain situations arbitrators must ignore the instructions given them by the

---

[21]. Article 7 of the Rome Convention on the Law Applicable to Contractual Obligations also has a similar content.

[22]. The provisions of the Swiss PILA addressed to arbitrators and to international arbitration—i.e., the lex arbitri of Switzerland—are found in chapter 12 (see the documents supplement). Article 19 is not in chapter 12.

[23]. Whether the arbitrators applied the Turkish mandatory law correctly may be debatable. The dispute concerned the Turkish joint venturer's desire to keep all the benefits from certain tax privileges for itself—despite a profit sharing provision in the joint venture agreement. Although the arbitrators found, as a technical matter, that mandatory Turkish law disallowed the transference to non-Turkish entities of certain tax privileges, at the same time they concluded that nothing prevented a non-Turkish entity from participating—by agreement with a Turkish entity—in the monetary benefits deriving from such tax privileges.

parties with respect to the applicable law in order to apply rules of law that must, in light of *l'ordre public international*, be considered mandatory. In practice, arbitrators certainly do their best to avoid facing the dilemma that such situations pose. But, if there is no intellectually principled and respectable way to avoid this dilemma, is the appropriate solution for the arbitrator simply to disregard the parties' instructions? Would it not be more fitting for the arbitrator to resign? Or is the arbitrator required to commit "a fraud on the parties" in order to prevent a fraud *a l'ordre public international*?

6. Between 1992 and 1995 the United Nations mandated an embargo on all sales to Yugoslavia (Serbia and Montenegro). Germany implemented the U.N. embargo so that transactions violating the embargo were declared invalid and exposed the parties to criminal penalties. Suppose in Germany during the period of the embargo the parties negotiate a sales contract for a shipment from the seller in Germany to the buyer in Belgrade, Yugoslavia. The contract chooses Yugoslavian law (under which the contract is valid) and arbitration under the ICC rules in Geneva. The contract provides for liquidated damages, even in the event of force majeure, a provision that is valid and enforceable under Yugoslavian law. The seller fails to perform, and the Yugoslav buyer initiates arbitration. As the arbitrator, would you enforce the contract and award damages, if it involved the following shipments in violation of the embargo:

     a) Books to a university in Belgrade?

     b) Arms likely to be transhipped to the Bosnian Serbian forces?

7. Assume the facts immediately above in question 5. How would it affect your conclusion or analysis if the contract provided for ad hoc arbitration in Geneva under the UNCITRAL Arbitration Rules? (The UNCITRAL Rules have no provision similar to Article 35 of the 1998 ICC Rules (Article 26 of the 1988 ICC Rules).)

Chapter V

THE EFFECTS AND LIMITS OF AWARDS RENDERED IN INTERNATIONAL COMMERCIAL ARBITRATION

V.1. CONFIRMATION, MERGER INTO JUDGMENT, CONCURRENT AND CONSECUTIVE PROCEEDINGS

V.1.a. Note

Self-contained finality, one of the important goals of the arbitration process, would be attained if, as soon as the arbitration proceeding is completed and the award is given to the parties, the award (1) could in principle be enforced and (2) could not be set aside or refused enforcement by any court. The present international status of arbitral awards has come very close to satisfying the first requirement for self-contained finality. In principle, arbitral awards have effects from the moment they are rendered. The 1986 Dutch Arbitration Act (Book IV of the Code of Civil Procedure) in Article 1059(1) states that the award shall have res judicata effects *"from the day on which it is made."* Article 190(1) of the 1987 Swiss Private International Law Act takes a slightly different approach: *"The award is final from the moment of its communication."*

The second requirement is, however, not generally satisfied. It must also be kept in mind that an award that is final and not subject to being set aside can still be denied recognition and enforcement by national courts. In this respect, arbitral awards can be compared with foreign court judgments.

Institutional control or requirements such as *notarization* or *deposit* may delay an award's taking effect.[1] A failure to observe requirements of institutional control may undermine the award in almost all countries, since control by the chosen institutional tribunal may be perceived as part of the procedure set by the parties, and therefore non-observance of such control may amount to a ground for refusal of recognition under

[1]. See on institutional control, notarization, and deposit, section IV.2.c.

Article V(1)(d) of the New York Convention ("procedure not in accordance with the agreement of the parties"). Non-observance of notarization or deposit may, however, have more limited effects outside an award's home country.

We should clarify that we mean by an award's "home country" the country within which the award is considered domestic. An award's "home country" would thus be the country whose courts would take jurisdiction to decide whether the award should be set aside. So defined, an award's home country is not necessarily the country where the arbitral tribunal hands down the award. Many countries will indeed take jurisdiction to set aside an award only if the award is handed down within their own borders.[2] However, in some countries—the United States, for example—even an award rendered within its borders may not be considered domestic if it has various foreign elements. In these countries such an award would be "foreign" and hence subject to recognition and enforcement under the New York Convention, not to setting aside under domestic arbitration law. (Such an award might thus have no home country.) A country may also consider an award domestic if the *lex arbitri* of that country governs the arbitration, even though the award is handed down beyond its borders. (Germany was such a country before the most recent amendment of German arbitration law.)[3] Thus it is possible for an award to have two home countries, one where the award was handed down and the other, under whose *lex arbitri* the award was rendered—or no home country at all.

V.1.b.   *Confirmation, Leave to Enforce*

Assuming that an award's home country does not require deposit or notarization—or assuming that in the given country there is such a requirement and it has been complied with—the question arises whether the award has full (or any) effects in the absence of court scrutiny. (Deposit itself cannot be classified as scrutiny, since it does not entail any reinvestigation and does not entail either adversary or inquisitory proceedings.)

In analyzing this question, it is important to consider the country in which the award is relied upon. If the winning party is trying to enforce the award in a country where the award is not considered domestic, recognition and enforcement proceedings are conducted there. Enforcement does not require confirmation or any other scrutiny by the country of origin; the New York Convention (Article V) does not allow refusal of recognition and enforcement on the ground that such scrutiny is absent. Thus the New York Convention does away with the former requirement of double-scrutiny (double exequatur). Recognition and enforcement can take place in all contracting states without prior confirmation in the country of origin; however, the convention does not bestow effects on an award until recognition or leave to enforce is granted by the court addressed.

---

[2].   See section V.2.a.   **[3].**   Id.

The position of the award in its country of origin depends on local procedural law. The possible options are:

(a) the award must be confirmed by domestic courts

(i) to be enforceable and

(ii) to have preclusive effects;

(b) the award must be confirmed to be enforceable, but it has preclusive effects without court scrutiny

(i) after it is rendered,

(ii) after it is communicated,

(iii) after the time limit for beginning a set-aside proceeding has expired without action;

(c) the award is enforceable and has preclusive effects without court scrutiny.

Most modern statutes have adopted a variation of solution (b). Where confirmation (entry of judgment) is needed, the *lex arbitri* may pose a time-limit within which it can be sought. Assuming that without confirmation the award has preclusive effects but it is not enforceable, one may wonder about the options available to a plaintiff who did not apply for confirmation within the stated time limit. In Protocom Devices Inc. v. Antonio Figueroa[4] it was held that in these circumstances arbitration proceedings cannot be restarted. The memorandum decision states:

> The IAS court properly determined that the prior arbitration award in favor of the respondent, which was not confirmed within one year pursuant to CPLR Section 7510, nevertheless warranted a stay of the subsequent arbitration proceeding initiated by the respondent, premised upon the same claim. Contrary to respondent's assertions, an arbitration award "rendered in compliance with all legal requirements is a complete, final and binding determination of a controversy which may not be disturbed, unless the statutory grounds for doing so exist."

The position of the holder of an unconfirmed (and due to the time elapsed, unconfirmable) award is even more tantalizing in the light of William Katz, a/k/a Zev Zvi Katz v. Pincus Kar,[5] where the preclusive effects of an unconfirmed award thwarted subsequent court proceedings in the same matter:

> We find that the plaintiff's action is barred pursuant to CPLR 3211(a)(5), which states that a cause of action cannot be maintained where there has been a prior "arbitration and award" on the same claim. The plaintiff and defendant herein voluntarily submitted to the Beth Din. At the conclusion of the hearing, the Beth Din awarded the plaintiff the full value of the diamonds. Accordingly,

---

[4]. 173 A.D.2d 177, 569 N.Y.S.2d 80 (App.Div.1991).

[5]. 192 A.D.2d 695, 597 N.Y.S.2d 135 (App.Div.1993).

since there has been an arbitration and award in this matter, the plaintiff is precluded from bringing a separate action based on the same claim.

(Neither of these cases involved *international commercial* arbitration.)

A number of interesting issues have also arisen with regard to the legal effects of confirmation or entry of judgment upon an award. The principal question is whether the award maintains (or loses) its identity after a confirmation judgment is rendered: does confirmation result in conversion (merger of the award into a judgment)?

V.1.c.   *Confirmation and Conversion*

COSID, INC. (U.S.) v. STEEL AUTHORITY OF INDIA, LTD. (INDIA)

India, High Court of Delhi, 1985.
11 Yearbk. Comm. Arb'n 502 (1985).*

FACTS

By an exchange of letters in August–September 1977, the Steel Authority of India Ltd. (SAIL), a "Government company",[1] agreed to supply COSID with 25,000 tons of hot rolled steel sheet coils. SAIL's letter to COSID, dated 10 August 1977, mentioned Terms and Conditions to which reference was made. Condition 15 read:

* * *

"15. Any dispute arising in connection with this agreement shall, unless amicably settled between the parties hereto, be referred to arbitration and shall be settled under the Rules of Conciliation and Arbitration of the International Chamber of Commerce by one or more arbitrators appointed in accordance with the said Rules. The venue of the arbitration proceedings shall be London, England."

Supplies were to be effected in two installments. SAIL had delivered only half of the quantity of coils agreed upon, when the Indian Government imposed a ban on the export of hot rolled steel sheet coils.

COSID resorted to ICC arbitration in London, according to Condition 12 of the Terms and Conditions. On 1 March 1981, an award was rendered in favour of COSID, directing SAIL to pay US $1,647,495.90 as damages for the failure of supplying the remaining half of the coils, as well as interest thereon and costs.

---

* Reprinted with permission of Yearbook Commercial Arbitration, International Council for Commercial Arbitration.

1.   The decision reads in relevant part:

"SAIL is a Government company as defined in Sect. 617 of the Companies Act,
1956. Under this Section Government Company means a company in which not less than fifty per cent of the paid up share capital is held by the Central Government."

On 30 May 1981, COSID obtained from the High Court of Justice, Queen's Bench Division, in London, an order pursuant to Sect. 26 of the English Arbitration Act 1950.[2] The Court ordered that COSID be at liberty to enforce the award in the same manner as a judgment or order to the same effect. * * *

[Enforcement was then sought before the High Court of Delhi. Enforcement was refused because the Court found that the export ban bound SAIL and hence to enforce would violate Indian public policy. The extracts below do not deal with this issue.]

Extract

* * *

Foreign award

3. The Court secondly dealt with the question whether the award at issue could be considered a foreign award within the meaning of the 1961 Act. According to Sect. 2 of the Act,

> "Foreign award means an award on differences between persons arising out of legal relationship in pursuance of an agreement in writing for arbitration to which the Convention on the recognition and enforcement of foreign arbitral award applies."

The Court stated:

> "The Convention applies to the recognition and enforcement of arbitral awards made in the territory of a State other than the State where the recognition and enforcement of such awards are sought. It also applies to arbitral awards not considered as domestic awards in the State where their recognition and enforcement are sought. The term 'arbitral awards' includes not only awards made by arbitrators appointed for each case but also those made by the permanent arbitral bodies to which the parties have submitted (Art. I). Under Art. II(1) each Contracting State recognises an agreement in writing under which the parties undertake to submit to arbitration all or any differences which have arisen between them and (2) the term 'agreement in writing' includes an arbitral clause in a contract or an arbitration agreement signed by the parties or contained in an exchange of letters or telegrams.

> "It would thus appear that conditions stipulated in the Convention would apply in the present case and the award in question would be a foreign award within the meaning of Sect. 2 of the Act. The provisions of the Act, which is a complete Code in itself in respect of foreign awards, would apply.

2. Sect. 26 of the English Arbitration Act 1950 reads:

"(1) An award on an arbitration agreement may, by leave of the High Court or judge thereof, be enforced in the same manner as a judgment or order to the same effect, and where leave is so given, judgment may be entered in terms of the award."

4.   "The Convention applies to the recognition and enforcement of an arbitral award made in London, U.K., and the recognition and enforcement of this award is being sought in New Delhi in India."

Merger of award in judgment

5.   On this issue, the Court stated:

"It was submitted that COSID having invoked the provisions of Sect. 26 of the English Arbitration Act 1950, resulting in the award being enforced as a judgment and order, the award thus became merged into an order and decree of the court and was no more actionable as an award and no enforcement and recognition thereof could be sought."

* * *

"COSID submitted that plea of merger could not be allowed to be raised at this stage and that it had filed a copy of the order of the English court merely to show that the award in question had become final in the country where it was made and that this document could not be used by SAIL for raising a new plea not contained in the pleadings of the parties and in respect of which no issue had been framed. I do not think that COSID is quite correct."

* * *

"Filing of the order of the English court cannot be limited only to show that the award had become final. But, then I am not quite satisfied that plea of merger could be raised in the present case. For one thing doctrine of merger as contended, is no bar to the enforcement of the foreign award. The foreign award cannot be enforced if it has yet not become binding on the parties or has been set aside or suspended by a competent authority of the country in which or under the law of which that award was made. * * * Secondly, as held by Anand J. in *Mls Copal Singh Hira Singh v. Punjab National Bank* (AIR 1976 Delhi 115), * * * a foreign judgment only creates a new obligation to pay but does not extinguish the original cause of action for the debt, and * * * a foreign judgment involves no merger of the original cause of action and creditor who obtained a foreign judgment has two remedies open to him: either to bring an action in the domestic tribunal on the foreign judgment or to bring an action in the domestic tribunal on the original cause of action. * * * According to COSID, [the] original cause of action in this case has been the award in question."

* * *

6.   "Reference was made by COSID to a well known commentary on *The New York Arbitration Convention of 1958 (Towards a Uniform Judicial Interpretation)* by Albert Jan van den Berg (1981 edition) wherein the learned author dealt with the question of merger of award into judgment (p. 346). The learned author has referred to a decision of

the Court of Appeal of Hamburg in respect of an award made in London, on which award the High Court in London had given a judgment in terms of the award pursuant to Sect. 26 of the English Arbitration Act. The argument of the respondent was that the award could not be enforced under the Convention because it had been merged into the judgment of the English High Court. The Court rejecting the defence observed that although it can be assumed that under English law the award merges into the judgment, in view of Art. V(1)(e) of the Convention which requires the award to be 'binding', and which Convention has the purpose of facilitating enforcement of foreign awards, in Germany the award must be considered as not having been absorbed by the English judgment. The Court also held that the effects of the merger were limited to English jurisdiction only and observed that English courts do not apply the merger doctrine to foreign awards declared enforceable by judgment in the country of origin either. The learned author, therefore, answered the question as to whether the merger of the award into the judgment in the country of origin has an extra-territorial effect, in the negative. Thus, according to the learned author 'the award can, therefore, be deemed to remain a cause of action for enforcement in other countries'. I have already observed above that the merger of the foreign award into judgment under Sect. 26 of the English Arbitration Act would be no bar to the enforcement of the same in the present case. This is not one of the conditions on the basis of which a foreign award may not be enforced under the Act."

FRATELLI DAMIANO (ITALY) v. AUGUST TOPFER & CO. (GERMANY)

Italy, Corte di Cassazione [Supreme Court], 1991.
17 Yearbk. Comm. Arb'n 559 (1992).*

Facts[a]

* * *

Topfer and Damiano entered into a contract for the sale of sugar. The contract contained a clause referring all disputes to arbitration before the Arbitration Board of the Refined Sugar Association, London.

A dispute arose when Damiano refused to take delivery of a shipment of 4,000 tons of sugar, and an arbitral award was eventually rendered in London on 18 August 1976 by the Arbitration Board of the Refined Sugar Association. The award, which did not give reasons, directed Damiano to pay Topfer the difference between the contract price and the price of sale to third parties, being DM 304,000.

On 24 April 1977, Topfer sought enforcement of the award before

---

* Reprinted with permission of Yearbook Commercial Arbitration, International Council for Commercial Arbitration.

a. Authors' note: The facts of this case are reported in more detail in 9 Yearbk. Comm. Arb'n 418–21 (1984) (Italy no. 57).

the Court of Appeal of Messina. Enforcement was granted but the lower court's decision was subsequently reversed by the Supreme Court on 8 February 1982 (this decision is reported under Italy no. 57).[b]

The case was remanded before the Court of Appeal of Catania which, on 12 June 1984, refused Topfer's request for enforcement.

In the meantime, on 16 August 1982, Topfer initiated court proceedings in England, seeking a declaratory judgment confirming the award. On 9 April 1984, the High Court of Justice issued a judgment confirming the contents of the arbitral award rendered between the parties.

On 16 March 1985, Topfer sought enforcement of the English High Court judgment before the Court of Appeal of Messina. The Court of Appeal held that the judgment concerned a dispute other than the dispute underlying the arbitral award rendered between the parties. Hence, enforcement was not barred on grounds of *res judicata*.

Damiano appealed from this decision. The Supreme Court reversed the lower court's decision and remanded the case to the Court of Appeal of Catania.

Excerpt

[1] "Damiano's ground for appeal is founded. The Court of Appeal of Messina, when examining the request for enforcement of the High Court judgment granting 'enforcement by action' [in English in the original text] to the English arbitral award—the enforcement of which has been refused in Italy—should have ascertained * * * [what] relation existed between the two decisions...."

[2] "The enforcement court totally relied on a judgment of this Supreme Court.[1] The decision of the Court of Appeal of Messina is clearly based on an incorrect reading of the * * * case law.... The Supreme Court firstly mentioned in its decision no. 1273 of 1979 that the nature of the foreign decision for which enforcement is sought must be ascertained according to the law of the place of rendition, in order to ascertain whether, independent of the name given to it in the foreign legal system, the decision meets the requirements considered by the [Italian] system as essential to that type of decision.... This examination concerns the facts, i.e., it aims at determining the contents of the decision, and the law, i.e., it aims

b. [Authors' note: The Corte di Cassazione (Supreme Court) held that because the two parties were domiciled in countries (Germany and Italy) party to the 1961 European [Geneva] Convention on International Commercial Arbitration, the provisions of that Convention should in effect be read into their agreement. The European [Geneva] Convention states in Article I that it applies to arbitration agreements between parties having their habitual residence or their seat in different contracting states. Article VIII of the European [Geneva] Convention provides in effect that reasons for an award must be given if either party so requests. During the arbitral proceedings Damiano had requested that reasons be given. See 9 Yearbk. Comm. Arb'n 418 (1984).]

1. The Court referred to its own decision of 27 February 1979, no. 1273, *Oleificio Bestetti v. X Can Grain*, reported in Yearbook VII (1982) pp. 333–337 (Italy no. 41).

at determining the essential elements of the decision according to the law of the place where it was rendered and to [Italian] law. The former examination falls exclusively within the competence of the court deciding on the merits ...; the latter falls within the competence of the Supreme Court...."

[3] The Supreme Court stressed that in the case of 1979, enforcement of the award had not been requested either in Italy or in England.

[4] "The Court of Appeal of Messina, in relying upon the said Supreme Court decision, clearly mistook the in abstracto admissibility of a request for enforcement of a High Court judgment confirming an arbitral award (which is beyond doubt in the case at issue) for the in concreto admissibility of such a request when the contents of the High Court decision are at odds with one of the requirements of [Italian law]. Particularly, the Court of Appeal of Messina failed to examine the contents of the decision for which enforcement is sought, i.e., to make the examination of the facts which falls within its exclusive competence, and held that the decision, being a judgment, was by definition enforceable in Italy. It then ruled that the arbitral award did not violate Italian public policy, because it played no autonomous role within the High Court decision. Using the wording of the Supreme Court decision no. 1273 of 1979, ... the Court of Appeal held that the arbitral award was merely the basis on which the High Court judgment was founded.

[5] "However, the Supreme Court words only aimed at ruling out the possibility ... that the fact that the award had not been autonomously enforced may result in the refusal to enforce the High Court decision incorporating the award."

[6] "The situation in this case is totally different. Enforcement of the arbitral award was sought and denied in Italy, and the judgment denying enforcement has become final. The Court of Appeal of Messina should have examined the contents and scope of the High Court judgment with respect to the arbitral award of the Arbitration Board of the Refined Sugar Association of London, in order to ascertain whether the High Court had rendered a totally new and autonomous decision with respect to the award—a decision, therefore, the enforcement of which was not barred on *res judicata* grounds—or whether it had merely founded its enforcement declaration on the arbitral award...."

[7] "These issues should have been decided by the court competent to decide on the merits, as mentioned above, as they concern the merits of the High Court decision. The judgment of the Court of Appeal of Messina does not give reasons on this issue and must, therefore, be reversed...."

SEETRANSPORT WIKING TRADER SCHIF-
FAHRTSGESELLSCHAFT MBH & CO. v.
NAVIMPEX CENTRALA NAVALA

United States Court of Appeals, Second Circuit, 1994.
29 F.3d 79.

JON O. NEWMAN, CHIEF JUDGE:

This appeal concerns the enforceability under New York Law of a ruling by a French court made with respect to a French arbitration award. Under the New York Uniform Foreign Money–Judgments Recognition Act, which is Article 53 of the Civil Practice Law and Rules, New York law permits enforcement of a "foreign country judgment which is final, conclusive and enforceable where rendered...." The precise issue in this case is whether a ruling of the Paris Court of Appeals conferring "exequatur" upon an arbitration award is within the category of judgments comprehended by Article 53. The issue arises on an appeal by two Romanian companies, Navimpex Centrala Navala ("Navimpex") and Uzinexportimport, from a judgment of the District Court for the Southern District of New York (Charles L. Brieant, Judge) awarding Seetransport Wiking Trader Schiffahrtsgesellschaft MBH & Co., Kommanditgesellschaft ("Seetransport") the sums awarded by an arbitration panel in France. *Seetransport Wiking Trader Schiffa[h]rt[s]gesellschaft MBH & Co. v. Navimpex Centrala Navala*, 837 F.Supp. 79 (S.D.N.Y.1993).[1]

On an earlier appeal, we held that Seetransport's action to enforce the arbitral award under the Convention on the Recognition and Enforcement of Arbitral Awards (the "Convention") was time-barred. The pending appeal presents Seetransport's alternative action to enforce the ruling of the Paris Court of Appeals as a foreign judgment recognized under New York law. We affirm.

Background

We set forth the background only briefly as it is more fully developed in our decision in the earlier appeal. Seetransport is a German corporation which owns and operates ships. Navimpex was a Romanian government trading company engaged in the business of shipbuilding. In 1980, Navimpex contracted to build four ships for Seetransport, but disputes arose and the ships were never built. The parties arbitrated their disputes before the Court of Arbitration of the International Chamber of Commerce in Paris. On March 26, 1984, the arbitral tribunal rendered an award in favor of Seetransport, ordering Navimpex to pay six million deutsche marks, plus interest at the rate of eight percent per year from January 1, 1981. The award also required Navimpex to pay Seetransport $72,000 as reimbursement for Navimpex's

---

1. It appears that Seetransport's full name has been spelled variously throughout these proceedings. This opinion uses the German spelling "Schiffahrtsgesellschaft," which has been translated as "shipping company." *See* Peter Terrell *et al.*, Collins *German–English English–German Dictionary* 571 (1981).

unpaid share of the cost of the arbitration. Navimpex sought to annul the award in the Court of Appeals in Paris, but the Court dismissed the application on March 4, 1986.

By the time that Seetransport sued Navimpex in the United States in 1988 to collect on the arbitral award, the statute of limitations to enforce an award under the Convention had run.[2] This was our holding in the prior appeal, in which we reversed a grant of summary judgment in favor of Seetransport on its action to enforce the arbitral award under the Convention. *See Seetransport I*, 989 F.2d at 581. However, Seetransport had sued not only to enforce the arbitral award, but also to enforce, under New York's Article 53, what it believed to be a French judgment confirming the award. We accordingly remanded to the District Court to consider whether Seetransport could succeed on its New York cause of action. We directed the Court to allow the parties to supplement the record on the issue of "whether the decision of the Court of Appeals of Paris is enforceable in France and thus should be enforced by the district court." After accepting supplemental affidavits on this issue, the District Court ruled that the Paris Court of Appeals' dismissal of Navimpex's application had conferred *exequatur* on the award, making it enforceable in France. It then reinstated the judgment in favor of Seetransport that the District Court had originally granted before the prior appeal. Navimpex and Uzinexportimport appeal.

Discussion

Appellants first challenge the District Court's assertion of subject matter jurisdiction over the action to enforce a foreign judgment. As instrumentalities of the Romanian state, Navimpex and Uzinexportimport are entitled to foreign sovereign immunity unless one of the exceptions to immunity, such as waiver, applies. We have already ruled on the earlier appeal that there is jurisdiction. We held that, by signing the Convention and proceeding to arbitration, Romania waived its immunity to an action to enforce a foreign money judgment under Article 53. Appellants attempt to distinguish our earlier ruling by arguing that the instant action does not involve an attempt to enforce a foreign money judgment, but rather a foreign arbitral award. Because, as we explain later, we believe that New York would recognize a French decree conferring *exequatur* on an arbitral award as the functional equivalent of a foreign money judgment, appellants' jurisdictional challenge is squarely foreclosed by our earlier opinion.

The central dispute on this appeal is over the significance of the decision of the Paris Court of Appeals dismissing Navimpex's application to annul the award. According to Seetransport, this dismissal conferred *exequatur* on the award. Seetransport further contends that the decree conferring *exequatur* constituted a French judgment awarding the sums specified in the award. New York will enforce a foreign decree under

---

2. Also by the time Seetransport sued, Romania had dissolved Navimpex, transferring all of its assets and liabilities to Uzi-nexportimport, which has been joined as a party in this case.

Article 53 only if that decree is a "foreign country judgment which is final, conclusive and enforceable where rendered...." Appellants contend that even if the Paris Court of Appeals' ruling conferred *exequatur* on the arbitral award, that action did not create a French "judgment." Thus, appellants reason, there is no foreign country judgment that can be enforced under Article 53.

Because questions of foreign law are treated as questions of law under Fed.R.Civ.P. 44.1, we subject the District Court's determinations on the foreign law issues to *de novo* review.

Preliminarily, we agree with the District Court that the Court of Appeals' decision conferred *exequatur* on the arbitral award. Article 1490 of the French New Code of Civil Procedure provides that "[r]ejection of an appeal or a motion to set aside confers *exequatur* on the arbitral award, or on such of its dispositions as are not censored by the Court of Appeal." This provision applies to international arbitrations by operation of Article 1507 of the French code. Seetransport's French law expert, Judge Simone Rozes, who retired in 1988 from her position as the Chief Judge of the *Cour de Cassation*, the highest judicial tribunal in France, testified through her affidavits that the Court of Appeals' rejection of Navimpex's challenge to the award conferred *exequatur*. She cited two cases in which French Courts of Appeals concluded that declaring *exequatur* on an arbitral award at the request of a successful party to an arbitration was unnecessary because the earlier rejection of a challenge to the award by the losing party had automatically conferred *exequatur* by operation of Article 1490.

The issue is whether the ruling conferring *exequatur* merely made the arbitration award enforceable or was itself an enforceable judgment within the meaning of Article 53. We agree with the District Court that, for purposes of Article 53, the decree conferring *exequatur* on the award was the functional equivalent of a French judgment awarding the sums specified in the award. French courts use the device of *exequatur* to make a decision of an outside tribunal enforceable in France. The New York Court of Appeals has offered the following understanding of the device: "[I]n France an exequatur is regarded as nothing more than an execution of a judgment rendered in a foreign jurisdiction." *In re James' Will*, 248 N.Y. 1, 4–5, 161 N.E. 201, 202 (1928). A legal dictionary provides a similar definition:

Exequatur: Let it be executed.

. . . . .

In French practice, this term is subscribed by judicial authority upon a transcript of a judgment from a foreign country, or from another part of France, and *authorizes the execution of the judgment* within the jurisdiction where it is so indorsed.

Black's Law Dictionary 513 (5th ed. 1979) (emphasis added). *Exequatur* thus seems to presuppose the existence of a "judgment" that can be rendered executable. However, while we do not believe that New York would recognize the arbitral award-without-*exequatur* as a judgment in and of itself,[4] we think that it would recognize as a judgment the decree that confers *exequatur* on the arbitral award. New York is "relatively generous" in recognizing foreign judgments. In *Fotochrome, Inc. v. Copal Co.*, 517 F.2d 512 (2d Cir.1975), we considered whether an arbitral award rendered in Japan was enforceable as a foreign judgment under Article 53 on the ground that Japanese law treated arbitral awards as having the same effect as judgments. We held that the arbitral award could not be deemed a Japanese judgment because there had been no opportunity to challenge the award under the few grounds set forth in the Convention: "Since under our procedure the losing party may object to confirmation on limited grounds that are specified in the Convention, we cannot treat the Japanese arbitral award as equivalent to a final judgment barring such recourse by the losing party when enforcement is sought." Id. at 519. By contrast, the process of obtaining exequatur in France allows the losing party in an arbitration to challenge the award on the bases enumerated in the Convention. Indeed, Navimpex did challenge the award on Convention grounds before the Paris Court of Appeals. Thus, the policy consideration that motivated our decision in *Fotochrome* to refuse to treat the arbitral award as a foreign judgment does not apply here. Instead, the instant case is closer to *Island Territory of Curacao v. Solitron Devices, Inc.*, 489 F.2d 1313 (2d Cir.1973), *cert. denied*, 416 U.S. 986, 94 S.Ct. 2389, 40 L.Ed.2d 763 (1974), in which we enforced as a foreign judgment a foreign court decree confirming an arbitral award. There a Curacaoan court had issued a "writ of execution" on an arbitral award issued in that territory and the losing party in the arbitration had failed to exercise its right to challenge the award on grounds akin to those available in the United States under 9 U.S.C. § 10 (which in turn presents grounds similar to those available under the Convention). Because the losing party had failed to challenge the award in Curacaoan courts, we held that the local court's issuance of a writ of execution had confirmed the award and functioned as a final judgment under Curacaoan law. Likewise, Navimpex's unsuccessful challenge to the award in the French courts made the award-with-*exequatur* enforceable under French law, and the decree accomplishing that result is to be regarded as a judgment enforceable under Article 53.

* * *

The judgment of the District Court is affirmed.

---

4. Professor David Siegel, however, suggests that there may be some situations where the arbitral award can be enforced without any judicial intervention:

The statute does not expressly require that the judgment be shown to be that of a court, although courts are referred to elsewhere in the article. There is room to include such equivalent tribunals as an arbitral panel and an administrative-type agency, if their determinations otherwise satisfy the criteria set forth in Article 53. It may be that the determination emerges from such a foreign tribunal with the same status there as a judicial judgment has, and without having to be converted into such a judgment. If that is so, it should not be indispensable that such a conversion occur before New York recognizes the judgment.

N.Y.Civ.Prac.L. & R. 5301 at 487–88 (McKinney 1978) (practice commentary).

ORIENTAL COMMERCIAL & SHIPPING CO. (UK), ORIENTAL COMMERCIAL & SHIPPING CO. (SAUDI ARABIA), ABDUL HAMID BOKHARI v. ROSSEEL, N.V.

United States District Court, Southern District of New York, 1991.
769 F.Supp. 514.

Opinion

SWEET, DISTRICT JUDGE.

Defendant Rosseel, N.V. ("Rosseel") has moved pursuant to Rule 12(b)(6), Fed.R.Civ.P., to dismiss the complaint of plaintiffs Oriental Commercial & Shipping Co. (U.K.), Ltd. ("OC & S–UK"), Oriental Commercial & Shipping Co., Ltd., ("OC & S") and Abdul Hamid Bokhari ("Bokhari") (collectively, "Oriental"), or in the alternative, for summary judgment under Rule 56. For the following reasons, the motion for summary judgment is granted and the complaint is dismissed.

The Parties

OC & S is a Saudi Arabian corporation engaged in the petroleum business. OC & S–UK is an English corporation affiliated with OC & S. Bokhari is a citizen and resident of Saudi Arabia and is the principal owner of both OC & S and OC & S–UK. Rosseel is a Belgian corporation also engaged in the petroleum business.

The Facts

In 1984, OC & S–UK and Rosseel entered into a contract for the sale of oil. When the transaction was not completed as planned, Rosseel sought arbitration in New York pursuant to an arbitration clause in the contract. In support of this goal, Rosseel applied to the Honorable Peter K. Leisure of this district for an order compelling OC & S–UK to submit to arbitration. OC & S–UK resisted this application on the grounds that the arbitration clause was unenforceable. After Judge Leisure granted Rosseel's request, Rosseel sought to join OC & S and Bokhari as parties to the arbitration, asserting that they were principals of OC & S–UK. Oriental thereupon sought a further stay of the arbitration on the grounds that * * * OC & S and Bokhari were not subject to the terms of the contract. After an evidentiary hearing on the issue, Judge Leisure denied the request for the stay on December 19, 1988. *Oriental Commercial & Shipping Co. v. Rosseel, N.V.*, 702 F.Supp. 1005 (S.D.N.Y.1988) ("the December Opinion").

Oriental filed a timely notice of appeal of the December Opinion. However, during a pre-argument conference in connection with the appeal the Staff Counsel for the Second Circuit suggested that the Circuit Court lacked jurisdiction over the appeal and Oriental agreed to withdraw it. However, in order to preserve its rights for future resolution, Oriental insisted on the addition of a stipulation to the standard

Second Circuit form for withdrawing an appeal. The language agreed upon read as follows:

> The parties agree that any proceedings to confirm or vacate the arbitration award will be brought in the U.S.D.C., S.D.N.Y. In any appeal therefrom, the issues sought to be raised here can be raised at that time.

("the Stipulation"). After both parties had signed the form, it was filed with the Clerk of the Circuit Court and marked "SO ORDERED" by the clerk on May 15, 1989.

On May 11, 1989, Judge Leisure filed an order dismissing the case in light of the December Opinion, Oriental filed a second appeal from this order, but again agreed to withdraw it on the same terms, by means of a second stipulation identical to the one entered on May 15.[1]

The arbitration between Rosseel and OC & S–UK, OC & S and Bokhari took place in January and May, 1990, and in June the arbitrators awarded Rosseel over $4 million. An amended award was issued on August 16, 1990 ("the Award").

Thereafter,[2] Rosseel initiated proceedings before the High Court of Justice in London ("the London Action") seeking to enforce the Award under the provisions of the New York Convention on the Recognition and Enforcement of Foreign Arbitral Awards ("the Convention"). Oriental argued that this action was barred by the Stipulation, which required Rosseel to seek confirmation of the award in the Southern District of New York before attempting to enforce it abroad. After reviewing the language of the Stipulation and the other evidence presented and arguments raised by Oriental, the High Court ruled that Stipulation did not bar Rosseel's action and proceeded to grant the application to enforce the award. *Rosseel, N.V. v. Oriental Commercial & Shipping Co.*, 1990 Folio No. 1623 (Q.B. decided Oct. 5, 1990) ("the London Judgment").

During the pendency of the London action, Oriental filed the present complaint, seeking declaratory judgment that the London Action was barred by the Stipulation, that Rosseel was required to seek confirmation of the Award in this jurisdiction and that the Award was not binding on the parties until such confirmation was granted. Oriental's stated goal in this proceeding is to preclude Rosseel from recovering on the Award until Oriental obtains appellate review of Judge Leisure's rulings enforcing the arbitration clause and extending its reach to OC & S and Bokhari. Oriental did not move to vacate the Award and its time to do so has expired.

---

1. As discussed below, Oriental's initial appeal of the order compelling arbitration was untimely in light of 9 U.S.C. § 16. It is not at all clear that the same conclusion would have applied to the appeal from the judgment dismissing the case. See 9 U.S.C. § 16(a)(3) (permitting appeal from "a final decision with respect to an arbitration that is subject to this title").

2. It is not clear from the record whether the London action was filed before or after the arbitrators issued the amended award in August.

Rosseel filed the present motion on January 29, 1991, and it was argued and fully submitted on March 8, 1991.

Discussion

Rosseel's motion seeks dismissal of the complaint or summary judgment. Because both sides have submitted affidavits and have relied on materials outside of the pleadings, the motion will be treated as one for summary judgment.

The standards for summary judgment are well-known. The court is not "to weigh the evidence and determine the truth of the matter but to determine whether there is a genuine issue for trial." *Anderson v. Liberty Lobby, Inc.*, 477 U.S. 242, 249, 106 S.Ct. 2505, 2511, 91 L.Ed.2d 202 (1986). Summary judgment is warranted only if "the evidence is such that a reasonable jury could not return a verdict for the nonmoving party." *Id.* at 248, 106 S.Ct. at 2510.

1. Arbitration Terminology and Procedure.

Of primary importance in this case is the distinction between confirming an arbitral award and enforcing one. As the High Court explained, before the Convention was adopted a party seeking to enforce an arbitration award rendered in one jurisdiction against a defendant in a second jurisdiction was generally required to seek leave to enforce the award in both the rendering jurisdiction and the enforcing jurisdiction. Under the Convention, it is no longer necessary to seek leave to enforce in the rendering jurisdiction: the party seeking to enforce an award may proceed directly to the jurisdiction in which it wishes to enforce the award and may apply directly to that jurisdiction's court for an order of enforcement.[3]

Thus, with the advent of the Convention, a party to an American arbitration which seeks to enforce the award abroad need not seek any order from an American court. Therefore, confirmation proceedings in federal court are now usually filed only where the prevailing party seeks to enforce the award in this country, when the Convention procedures would be of no assistance.

The Second Circuit has explained the difference between an action to enforce a foreign arbitral award under the Convention and one to enforce a foreign judgment confirming an arbitral award, which must proceed according to the normal rules for the enforcement of foreign judgments. *See Island Territory of Curacao v. Solitron Devices, Inc.*, 489 F.2d 1313, 1319 (2d Cir.1973); *Victrix Steamship Co. v. Salen Dry Cargo A.B.*, 825 F.2d 709, 713–14 nn. 2 & 3 (2d Cir.1987); *Waterside Ocean Navigation Co. v. International Navigation, Ltd.*, 737 F.2d 150, 154 (2d Cir.1984). In both of the latter two cases, the court specifically commented that even after an award had been confirmed in the foreign

---

3. In addition, a party may often avoid relying on the Convention by applying in the rendering jurisdiction for an order confirming the award, which converts the award into a judgment which may be enforced abroad under the appropriate procedures for enforcement of foreign judgments.

jurisdiction—making it enforceable as a foreign judgment—it was still enforceable as a foreign award under the Convention; the foreign confirmation had simply increased the options available to the enforcing party. It is not clear whether such a broad approach to enforcement would be adopted by the United Kingdom. During oral argument, Rosseel suggested that it would not be, that confirmation here would have irrevocably converted the Award to a judgment and made it impossible to enforce it as an award under the Convention, although it has cited no authority in support of this contention.

Thus in the absence of the Stipulation there would be no question as to the propriety of Rosseel's action in refraining from further proceedings in this jurisdiction and instituting the London Action to enforce its award. The only remaining question is whether the Stipulation altered this conclusion.

2. The Stipulation is Not Ambiguous.

Oriental's primary argument is that the language of the Stipulation is ambiguous, and that the parties specifically agreed that there would be post-award proceedings in this district. Rosseel contends that the Stipulation is unequivocal, albeit somewhat open-ended, and that the choice not to seek confirmation before applying for enforcement in London was not a violation of the agreement between the parties.

Rosseel argues that the Stipulation simply specifies that if Rosseel elected to confirm the Award then the action would be brought in this district. Oriental concedes, as it must, that the Stipulation is at least susceptible to this interpretation, but asserts that other interpretations are also possible, and that the inherent ambiguity entitles it to introduce parol evidence to support its proposed construction.

Oriental argues that the first sentence of the Stipulation—"any proceedings to confirm or vacate the arbitration award will be brought in the U.S.D.C., S.D.N.Y."—can and should be interpreted to compel Rosseel to seek confirmation in this jurisdiction. In the absence of some specific language indicating that the parties intended by their agreement to create a condition that further proceedings would necessarily take place, the first sentence is most naturally understood as identifying the proper forum for any actions for confirmation or vacation of the Award which either party elected to bring, with no requirement that any such action be brought at all.[4]

---

4. Under Oriental's suggested interpretation, it would seem that the Stipulation also required Oriental to seek to vacate the Award, a step which it elected not to take. Oriental claims that it could not have filed an action to vacate because, aside from objecting to Judge Leisure's order compelling OC & S and Bokhari to participate in the arbitration it could find no fault with the conduct of the arbitration itself. Therefore, it claims, an action to vacate would have been frivolous and would have subjected it to sanctions under Rule 11, Fed.R.Civ.P. Rule 11 of the Federal Rules of Civil Procedure reads in pertinent part:

Signing of Pleadings, Motions, and Other Papers; Sanctions

Every pleading, motion, and other paper of a party represented by an attorney shall be signed by at least one attorney of record in the attorney's individual name, whose address shall be stated. A party who is not represented by an attorney shall sign the

In further support of its position, Oriental asserts that it believed at the time it signed the Stipulation that the agreement did require a post-award proceeding to be brought in this court, and that to read the language as narrowly as Rosseel does would render the Stipulation virtually meaningless. However, where the language of a contract is itself unambiguous, neither the intention of the parties nor the possibly unintended and unfortunate consequences of enforcing the agreement according to its terms offers a basis for modifying those terms. Because the Stipulation cannot be considered ambiguous, this evidence is irrelevant and therefore summary judgment in Rosseel's favor is appropriate.

3. *Oriental's Evidence Does Not Support Its Interpretation of the Stipulation.*

Even if, contrary to the preceding determination, it were found that the language of the Stipulation was ambiguous, Oriental has not adduced evidence which would establish that its interpretation should apply. With respect to the parties' intention at the time the Stipulation was signed, there is evidence that prior to the signing of the second Stipulation, Oriental's counsel had been put on notice of the alleged ambiguity. In the London Action, Oriental's New York counsel submitted an affidavit in which he stated that Counsel for Rosseel had, prior to the arbitration, suggested that Rosseel might seek enforcement of any award in London rather than confirmation in New York:

> One of the grounds which I put forward then was the agreement contained in the Joint Stipulation and I went on to say that I could see no justification in the light of the Joint Stipulation for Rosseel to apply to the English Court to confirm *or give effect to an award* in its favour, such application falling [sic] to be taken in the District Court. I made that point well before Rosseel obtained its arbitration award, and indeed *before the second Joint Stipulation was entered into.*

Thus even before it signed the Stipulation withdrawing its second appeal, Oriental had been placed on notice that Rosseel believed that it could seek to "give effect to an award," abroad without seeking confirmation in this jurisdiction. In these circumstances, Oriental should have sought to clarify or amend the language of the second Stipulation if it believed that such an action was barred by the parties' agreement. Its

---

party's pleading, motion, or other paper and state the party's address ... The signature of an attorney or party constitutes a certificate by the signer that the signer has read the pleading, motion, or other paper; that to the best of the signer's knowledge, information, and belief formed after reasonable inquiry it is well grounded in fact and is warranted by existing law or a good faith argument for the extension, modification, or reversal of existing law, and that is not interposed for any improper purpose, such as to harass or to cause unnecessary delay or needless increase in the cost of litigation ... If a pleading, motion, or other paper is signed in violation of this rule, the court, upon motion or upon its own initiative, shall impose upon the person who signed it, a represented party, or both, an appropriate sanction, which may include an order to pay to the other party or parties the amount of the reasonable expenses incurred because of the filing of the pleading, motion, or other paper, including a reasonable attorney's fee.

failure to do so belies its assertion that it intended such an interpretation when it entered the Stipulation.

Oriental's second argument in support of its construction of the Stipulation is that under Rosseel's interpretation the Stipulation is virtually meaningless. Because the only real connection between any of the parties and the United States was the location of the arbitration in New York, Oriental asserts that even without the Stipulation any proceedings to confirm or vacate would naturally take place in this forum. Therefore, Oriental claims, the Stipulation must have had a purpose beyond identifying the proper forum, and that purpose was to require that an action to confirm or vacate would be filed.

While it is true that under Rosseel's interpretation the Stipulation may have little meaning,[5] this fact does not offer much support to Oriental. In order to interpret the Stipulation it is necessary to consider each party's position at the time the agreement was signed. As mentioned above, Oriental was informed after filing its notice of appeal that there was no appellate jurisdiction over the orders compelling it to submit to arbitration. Oriental claims that this jurisdictional defect was the result of the then-recent enactment of 9 U.S.C. § 16 (originally enacted as § 15),[6] and in fact specifically represented to the High Court of Justice that prior to the November, 1988 enactment of this statute, "the Circuit Court would undoubtedly have had jurisdiction over such an appeal." This assertion is incorrect. Section 16 was enacted to codify the law which already existed in this Circuit, under which there was no appeal from an order compelling arbitration.

Thus in "agreeing" to withdraw its appeal Oriental gave up nothing to which it was legally entitled. That being the case, there is no reason to believe that Rosseel would have consented to a requirement binding it to take some post-award action in this forum, as it would have nothing to gain by such a move. This is the same conclusion reached by the High Court in the London Action. In discussing Oriental's proposed interpretation of the Stipulation, the court commented that

> [That interpretation] would be an extraordinary one. It [would involve Rosseel] giving up valuable rights under an otherwise binding award for no consideration of substance. From [Rosseel's] point of view there was no commercial justification for such a stipulation.

---

5. Of course, Oriental's argument does not even consider the effect of the second sentence of the Stipulation, which guaranteed that if any post-award action were brought in this court then Oriental would be permitted to raise its objections to Judge Leisure's orders on an appeal from that action.

6. Appeals

(b) Except as otherwise provided in section 1292(b) of title 28, an appeal may not be taken from an interlocutory order—

(1) granting a stay of any action under section 3 of this title;

(2) directing arbitration to proceed under section 4 of this title;

(3) compelling arbitration under section 206 of this title; or

(4) refusing to enjoin an arbitration that is subject to this title.

Therefore, even if the Stipulation were found to be ambiguous, Oriental's evidence as to the party's intentions in signing the Stipulation would not be sufficient to establish that the agreement was intended to require a post-award action to be brought in this district, and therefore summary judgment is appropriate.[7]

Conclusion

Oriental's error in this case was in not filing a timely motion to vacate the Award. Particularly when it became clear that Rosseel did not intend to seek confirmation in this jurisdiction, a motion to vacate would have been the proper vehicle for reopening the prior proceedings and for obtaining appellate review of the prior orders of Judge Leisure compelling OC & S and Bokhari to participate in the arbitration. Although a motion to vacate is not generally to be encouraged where the losing party disclaims any basis for the motion, given the context of this case and the course of prior proceedings it would not have been improper for Oriental to have made such a motion, which would have obviated the problem here.

For all of the foregoing reasons, Oriental has failed to present evidence sufficient to establish that the Stipulation required Rosseel to bring a confirmation action in this district or that the Award was not intended to be binding until such a proceeding had been brought. Therefore, Rosseel's motion for summary judgment dismissing the complaint is granted.

It is so ordered.

Questions and Comments

1.   Confirmation (or leave to enforce) makes the award enforceable in the confirming state. The French equivalent is the concept of exequatur, which was characterized by the New York Court of Appeals in *Seetransport Wiking* as follows: "the decree conferring exequatur on the award was the functional equivalent of a French judgment awarding the sums specified in the award." Since we are dealing with a judicial verification rendered in the form of a judgment, the question arises whether that judgment replaces the award.

Suppose that in the country of Eurostan on August 31, 1996, an award is rendered obliging Finex to pay Belgimp $100,000. The award receives confirmation (leave to enforce) in the form of a judgment of the competent court of Eurostan, and becomes thereby enforceable in Eurostan. What are the legal consequences of this proceeding? There are three ways of conceiving the consequences of confirmation.

a)   One may reason that the award merges into the judgment (which has the same holding), so that, after confirmation, only the judgment exists, while the award vanishes.

---

7.   As Rosseel's motion to dismiss Oriental's complaint on the merits is granted, it is not necessary to consider whether the London Judgment and its consideration of the arguments raised here by Oriental might constitute res judicata or might collaterally estop Oriental from relitigating the issues in this case.

b) Another possibility is that confirmation creates a parallel entitlement.

c) A third view is that confirmation yields a judgment with a distinct (and very limited) holding. In other words, if the award of August 31, 1996 holds that Finex should pay Belgimp $100,000, confirmation in Eurostan does not result in a holding whose content is identical with that of the award. Instead the confirmation simply holds that the award of August 13, 1996 is enforceable in Eurostan. If one adopts this understanding, it would be meaningless to seek recognition of the judgment outside Eurostan. Although the winning party would have clear incentive to seek recognition and enforcement of the award in any country where Finex has assets against which the award could be enforced, it would not benefit Finex at all to seek recognition and enforcement of the confirmation judgment outside Eurostan since it says only that "the award is enforceable in Eurostan."

2.   Which of the three possible understandings of confirmation was adopted in *COSID v. Steel Authority of India*?

(One should bear in mind that the different conceptualizations of confirmation become particularly important when enforcement is sought in a state other than that of the confirmation, and when the question arises whether the award, the judgment, or both are entitled to recognition and enforcement.)

In R. Schreter v. Gasmac Inc.[6] recognition and enforcement were sought for an award rendered in Atlanta, which was confirmed by the competent Georgia court. The party opposing recognition claimed that the award merged into the Georgia judgment, and therefore only the judgment was available for enforcement, not the award. The Ontario court did not accept this reasoning, and enforced the award, stating that under the UNCITRAL Model Law, enacted as the International Commercial Arbitration Act in Ontario,[7] an arbitral award does not merge into the judgment which confirms it.

3.   In *Oriental v. Rosseel*, Oriental objected to the trial court's ruling that certain parties were included in the arbitration agreement and were required to join the arbitration proceedings. At the end of the day, Rosseel will be able to enforce the award in the U.K. without Oriental having ever appealed the contested ruling that joined these parties. Oriental claims that it entered the disputed stipulation in order to preserve its rights to litigate this point further. If Oriental had wanted to litigate the point, what should it have done?

4.   How does Oriental explain its failure to seek to set aside the award? Is its explanation convincing? (See footnote 4 for its explanation that such an effort would have been frivolous. Is this persuasive?)

5.   Suppose countries A and B are both parties to the New York Convention and have also entered into another international agreement under which they agreed to enforce each other's judicial judgments despite "public policy" objections to enforcement. Suppose an arbitral award is rendered in A and the winning party obtains a judgment in the courts of A

[6].   7 O.R.3d 608 (Can.).

[7].   International Commercial Arbitration Act, R.S.O. ch.1.9 (1990) (Can.).

confirming the award. Suppose the award itself would be subject to a public-policy defense if the winning party were to seek enforcement in B. May the winning party avoid this defense by seeking enforcement in B of the court judgment in A confirming the award? *Seetransport Wiking* suggests an affirmative answer; but is the situation distinguishable from this hypothetical? Is the *Seetransport Wiking* holding reconcilable with *Damiano*?

The reverse situation, which may actually be more common, can also arise: the rules governing recognition of the award are more favorable than those governing recognition of the judgment. One might also imagine a situation in which it is difficult to assess in advance which rules are more favorable, those applicable to recognition of foreign judgments, or to recognition of foreign awards. Would it be possible to rely on both? Is the holding in the *Damiano* case relevant to this question? If so, what answer would it require? (If the winning party chooses to seek enforcement in B of the award and loses on public policy grounds, *Damiano* would say that the party could not turn around and seek enforcement of the judgment, because the issue is res judicata. It is essentially the same claim, even though different legal arguments would apply to the judgment as compared to the award.) But if *Damiano* does not allow two attempts, does it allow a free choice between submitting the award, or the judgment to the recognizing court?

In *Seetransport Wiking* the winning party brought both the award and the judgment to the B courts at the same time asking for enforcement of one or the other. This strategy avoided splitting a cause of action, because in one proceeding the claimant brought all of his legal theories for redress. Does it explain the success of the winning party?

6.   Note the following language from the *Oriental v. Rosseel* case which supports the view that the award and the judgment by which it is confirmed exist independently of each other:

"... the court specifically commented that even after an award had been confirmed in the foreign jurisdiction—making it enforceable as a foreign judgment—it was still enforceable as a foreign award under the Convention; the foreign confirmation had simply increased the options available to the enforcing party." 769 F.Supp. 514 at 516.

If one accepts this view, could one even envisage a possible double enforcement? (Enforcing the award and the judgment, and thus forcing the losing party to pay twice.) This result would obviously be senseless, but on what ground could you prevent it?

V.1.d.   *Concurrent and Consecutive Proceedings*

Parallel proceedings in the same case are always a cause for concern. If the proceedings in question are court proceedings, and if they take place within the same legal system, the solution is relatively simple. The objection of lis pendens will (or at least should) terminate, or at least stay, one of the two competing proceedings (normally the one which was started later). More serious difficulties are presented when lawsuits are initiated in two or more different legal systems. In this case, principles of consistency and expedience may conflict with concepts of sovereignty,

and a search for balance may have to rely on such traditionally controversial notions as comity and reciprocity.

As the elements of the puzzle become more heterogeneous, the
problem grows even more complex; now the proceedings in question are
separated not only by sovereign boundaries, but also by their nature. To
take a simple case, do arbitral proceedings under way in country "A",
halt (or suspend) court proceedings in the same matter in country "B".
The current respectability of international commercial arbitration—
buttressed and encouraged by international conventions and recent pro-
arbitration development in national statutes and case law—could allow
courts to accord lis pendens effects to ongoing arbitral proceedings.[8]
Article VI(3) of the 1961 European (Geneva) Convention on International Commercial Arbitration explicitly adopts such a solution (although
with qualifications):

> "Where either party to an arbitration agreement has initiated
> arbitration proceedings before any resort is had to a court, courts of
> Contracting States subsequently asked to deal with the same sub-
> ject-matter between the same parties or with the question whether
> the arbitration agreement was non-existent or null and void or had
> lapsed, shall stay their ruling on the arbitrator's jurisdiction until
> the award is made, unless they have good and substantial reasons to
> the contrary."

The argument for deferring to a pending arbitration process is
actually stronger than that for deference to a parallel court proceeding.
The added leverage derives from the existence of an arbitration agreement, and the treaty-based duty to refer the parties to arbitration if
there is a valid arbitration agreement.[9] Article II of the New York
Convention and similar enactments establish "negative effects of the
arbitration agreement"[10] which impose a duty on courts to decline
competence in the face of an arbitration agreement. If the internationally binding force of an arbitration agreement means that at the beginning
of a dispute a court must refer the parties to arbitration, a fortiori a
court is obligated to defer to arbitration proceedings that are already
under way.

When an arbitral proceeding has ripened into an award, the reasons
for judicial deference are even more compelling. The French Code of
Civil Procedure rule on this point is admirably straightforward: "The
award has, from the moment it is rendered, res judicata effect with
respect to the dispute it decides." (Article 1476). Numerous problems

---

[8]. The exact moment at which an arbitration becomes lis pendens varies in different national legal systems. This may be
important for various reasons, including the
issue of when an applicable statute of limitation ceases to run. Under the UNCITRAL
Model Law, for example, arbitration proceedings "commence" at the moment the
respondent receives from the claimant a
request for arbitration (Art. 21). *See* Ber-
ger, INTERNATIONAL ECONOMIC ARBITRATION
375–80 (1993).

[9]. This duty is clearly set out in Article II of the New York Convention and in
most national statutes.

[10]. R. Fouchard et al., Traité de l'arbitrage commercial international [Treatise
of International Commercial Arbitration]
416–430 (1996).

occur, however, in connection with the res judicata effect of arbitral awards—as the following pages will illustrate.

The further question arises whether an arbitral award has collateral-estoppel (issue-preclusion) effects in countries that accord such effects to court judgments; here views differ. Since collateral estoppel yields fact-finding finality,[11] arguably differences in the fact-finding standards of courts and arbitral tribunals preclude courts giving such effects to arbitral decisions. Collateral estoppel is more common in countries belonging to the common-law tradition than in other countries. An interesting exception is found in Article 370(3) of the 1993 Romanian Code of Civil Procedure (Book IV on Arbitration): "Foreign arbitration awards, made by a competent arbitral tribunal, shall have the force of evidence before courts in Romania with regard to facts which have been established."

V.1.e.   Concurrent Proceedings

SUMITOMO CORPORATION, OSHIMA SHIPBUILDING CO. v. PARAKOPI COMPANIA MARITIMA

United States District Court, Southern District of New York, 1979.
477 F.Supp. 737.

WERKER, DISTRICT JUDGE.

Opinion

Petitioners Sumitomo Corporation ("Sumitomo") and Oshima Shipbuilding Co., Ltd. ("Oshima") commenced this action against respondent Parakopi Compania Maritima, S.A. ("Parakopi") for an order compelling Parakopi to proceed to arbitration and appointing a third arbitrator.

Background

The principal facts are not in dispute.

Sumitomo and Oshima are corporations organized and existing under the laws of Japan. Sumitomo has its principal place of business in Tokyo, Japan, and Oshima has its principal place of business in Nagasaki, Japan. Parakopi is incorporated in Panama, and has its principal place of business in Piraeus, Greece.

In September 1975, Sumitomo and Parakopi entered into a contract whereby Sumitomo agreed to construct for and sell to Parakopi a bulk carrier.[1] Oshima, as the builder, agreed to be bound by all the terms and conditions of the contract applicable to it.

---

[11]. See R. Shell, *Res Judicata and Collateral Estoppel Effects of Commercial Arbitration*, 35 UCLA L. Rev. 623 (1988); R. Hulbert, *Arbitral Procedure and the Preclusive Effects of Awards in International Com-* *mercial Arbitration*, 7 Int'l Tax & Bus. Law., 155 (1989).

1. The contract was negotiated in New York and executed in Greece.

Section 1 of Article XIV of the purchase agreement provides for the resolution of all non-technical disputes by arbitration in New York:

> Should any dispute arise between the parties in regard to the construction of the VESSEL, her engines and/or materials or to any other technical matters, such dispute shall forthwith be referred to the Principal Surveyor of the Classification Society in Japan, whose opinion shall be final and binding upon both parties hereto. Any other dispute arising under or by virtue of this Contract or any difference of opinion between the parties hereto concerning their rights and obligations under this Contract ... shall be settled by arbitration in New York, New York in accordance with the rules of the United States Arbitration Act.

Under section 2 of Article XIV, a party seeking arbitration must serve a written demand for arbitration on the other side and designate an arbitrator. The other party is obligated, within 20 days after receiving the written demand, to designate its arbitrator. The two arbitrators are then to select a third arbitrator, and the three arbitrators will constitute the arbitration panel.

The vessel was completed in 1977 and was delivered to and accepted by Parakopi in June of that year. Under the terms of the contract, the purchase price of the vessel was fixed in terms of Japanese yen. Some 70 per cent of the purchase price was to be paid over a seven-year period in 14 semi-annual installments. Although Parakopi has been paying the installments due to date, it commenced an action in Greece in January 1979 seeking to be relieved of its obligations under the contract on the basis of unforeseeable circumstances, *i. e.*, the sharp rise in value of the yen against the dollar,[3] and on the ground of fraud, *i. e.*, the petitioners' alleged fraudulent concealment from Parakopi of knowledge that the yen would increase in value.[4]

Petitioners served a demand for arbitration of the matter in controversy on Parakopi in April 1979 and designated an arbitrator pursuant to section 2 of Article XIV of the contract. Although Parakopi did subsequently select an arbitrator, its arbitrator refused to proceed with the selection of a third arbitrator. Thereafter, it became apparent that Parakopi was not going to voluntarily proceed to arbitration, and petitioners commenced this action.

Parakopi's opposition to the petition is predicated on four arguments: (1) that the parties entered into a stipulation which precludes the

---

3. According to Parakopi's calculations, the vessel's value in U. S. dollars at the time the contract was entered into was $10,197,000, computed at a rate of 304 yen per dollar. By January 1979, the exchange rate had apparently changed to 180 yen per dollar. Hence, the contract price in U. S. dollars had apparently increased to $17,222,000, even though the contract price in terms of Japanese yen remained the same.

4. Parakopi's charge of fraudulent concealment rests on its assertion that the petitioners assured it that it had "nothing to fear from the payment of the debt in yen" when they knew that the value of the yen would rise through their close relationship with the Export–Import Bank of Japan.

petitioners from taking any action to proceed to arbitration until October 19, 1979; (2) that the Court lacks subject matter jurisdiction; (3) that the petitioners' proper remedy is to seek a stay of the suit in Greece from a Greek court; and (4) that even assuming this Court has jurisdiction, it should defer to the Greek litigation for reasons of comity.

Discussion

A.   *Preclusion by Stipulation*

[The court found there was no stipulation barring Sumitomo and Oshima from commencing arbitration.]

* * *

B.   *Subject Matter Jurisdiction*

Petitioners commenced this action under the Convention on the Recognition and Enforcement of Foreign Arbitration Awards (the "Convention"), 21 U.S.T. 2517, T.I.A.S. No. 8052. Subject matter jurisdiction is claimed under 9 U.S.C. s 203, which provides:

> An action or proceeding under the Convention shall be deemed to arise under the laws and treaties of the United States. The district courts of the United States ... shall have original jurisdiction over such an action or proceeding, regardless of the amount in controversy.

In contending that this Court lacks subject matter jurisdiction over the instant petition, Parakopi relies on 9 U.S.C. ss. 1 and 202. Section 202 provides than an arbitration agreement or arbitral award falls under the Convention if it "aris(es) out of a legal relationship, whether contractual or not, which is considered as commercial...." Section 1 of Title 9 defines "commerce" as follows:

> "commerce", as herein defined, means commerce among the several States or with foreign nations, or in any Territory of the United States or in the District of Columbia, or between any such Territory and any State or foreign nation....

Citing cases holding that "commerce" as defined by 9 U.S.C. s 1 does not include commerce involving only foreign parties,[6] Parakopi argues that "commercial" disputes involving only foreign entities should also be excluded from coverage under 9 U.S.C. ss. 202 and 203. I disagree.

The language of the relevant sections of the statute does not support Parakopi's assertion that the definition of "commerce" in section 1 controls the scope of section 202. First of all, section 202 does not use the term "commerce" at all, but utilizes the term "commercial." Secondly, section 202 uses "commercial" in a substantive rather than geographical sense, while section 1 does not substantively define "commerce" at all, defining it only in geographical terms. Section 202 refers to "a legal

---

6. *The Volsinio,* 32 F.2d 357 (E.D.N.Y. 1929); *Petroleum Cargo Carriers, Ltd. v. Unitas, Inc.,* 31 Misc.2d 222, 220 N.Y.S.2d 724 (Sup.Ct.N.Y.Co.1961), *aff'd,* 15 App. Div.2d 735, 224 N.Y.S.2d 654 (1st Dep't 1962).

relationship ... which is considered as commercial," while section 1 provides that " 'commerce' ... means commerce among the several States or with foreign nations...." Moreover, in limiting the application of the Convention to "commercial" disputes, the United States did not make reference to 9 U.S.C. s. 1; instead it referred to "legal relationships ... which are considered as commercial under the national law of the United States." Convention, n. 29. While 9 U.S.C. s. 1 is certainly part of the national law of the United States, it does not constitute all of the national law of the United States. In delineating the coverage of the Convention, Congress explicitly excluded purely domestic transactions. 9 U.S.C. s. 202. Had Congress also intended to exclude purely foreign transactions, it undoubtedly would have done so explicitly as well.

The fact that 9 U.S.C. s. 1 is part of Chapter 1 of the Arbitration Act while 9 U.S.C. s. 202 is part of Chapter 2 is also an indication that section 1 does not control section 202. Chapter 1 existed prior to the United States' accession to the Convention, and indeed was not designated as "Chapter 1" until the provisions implementing the convention were added to Title 9 as Chapter 2. See Act of July 31, 1970, Pub.L. No. 91–368, 84 Stat. 692. The provisions of Chapter 1 apply to proceedings brought under Chapter 2 only to the extent that they do not conflict with the provisions of Chapter 2 or the Convention. 9 U.S.C. s. 208.

Concluding that the Court has subject matter jurisdiction over this matter would certainly further the policies underlying the Convention. The Supreme Court has noted that:

> The goal of the Convention, and the principal purpose underlying American adoption and implementation of it, was to encourage the recognition and enforcement of commercial arbitration agreements in international contracts and to unify the standards by which agreements to arbitrate are observed and arbitral awards are enforced in the signatory countries.

Scherk v. Alberto–Culver Co., 417 U.S. 506, 520 n. 15, 94 S.Ct. 2449, 2457, 41 L.Ed.2d 270 (1974). To hold that subject matter jurisdiction is lacking where the parties involved are all foreign entities would certainly undermine the goal of encouraging the recognition and enforcement of arbitration agreements in international contracts.

Finally, although the issue of whether the scope of Chapter 2 is limited by the definition of "commerce" in Chapter 1 has not been previously addressed, American courts have applied the Convention to situations involving only foreign entities. *Beromun Aktiengesellschaft v. Societa Industriale Agricola "Tresse,"* 471 F.Supp. 1163 (S.D.N.Y.1979); *Ipitrade International, S.A. v. Federal Republic of Nigeria*, 465 F.Supp. 824 (D.D.C.1978); *Matter of Ferrara S.p.A., United Grain Growers, Ltd.*, 441 F.Supp. 778 (S.D.N.Y.1977), *aff'd mem.*, 580 F.2d 1044 (2d Cir. 1978); *Antco Shipping Co. v. Sidermar S.p.A.*, 417 F.Supp. 207 (S.D.N.Y. 1976), *aff'd mem.*, 553 F.2d 93 (2d Cir. 1977).

Accordingly, the request for dismissal of the petition for lack of subject matter jurisdiction is denied.

C. Propriety of the Petition

Parakopi's third defense is that the petitioners' proper remedy is to apply to the Greek court for a stay of the Greek proceedings. Parakopi contends that the petitioners do not have an arbitrable claim because they "cannot claim that (it) has breached the contract" and because "it has fully performed all of its contractual obligations." These claims, however clearly go to the merits of the underlying dispute and thus do not constitute grounds for dismissing the petition.

D. Comity

Parakopi's fourth and final defense is premised on principles of international comity. Parakopi contends that this Court should stay or dismiss the instant proceeding in deference to the pending litigation in Greece. For the reasons which follow, this contention is rejected.

Comity is "the recognition which one nation allows within its territory to the legislative, executive, or judicial acts of another nation, having due regard both to international duty and convenience...." *Hilton v. Guyot*, 159 U.S. 113, 164, 16 S.Ct. 139, 143, 40 L.Ed. 95 (1895). In deciding whether to accord comity to a decision of a foreign court, a forum court must determine whether the foreign court is one of competent jurisdiction and whether recognizing the foreign court's decision would violate the laws and policies of the forum nation or state. *Id.* at 202–03, 16 S.Ct. 139; *Clarkson Co. v. Shaheen*, 544 F.2d 624, 629 (2d Cir.1976); *Cornfeld v. Investors Overseas Services, Ltd.*, 471 F.Supp. 1255, 1259 (S.D.N.Y.1979).

In the instant case, no legislative, executive or judicial act of another nation is involved. Although litigation is pending in Greece, all that has transpired is the filing of a complaint. The petitioners have not yet put in answers, and the Greek courts have not yet had to review the merits of the dispute herein in issue. Hence, compelling Parakopi to arbitration at this juncture would not in any way waste or duplicate the efforts of the Greek courts.

In interstate situations, federal courts have refused to permit a party to a contract to circumvent an arbitration clause by commencing litigation in a state court. *Commonwealth Edison Co. v. Gulf Oil Corp., 400 F.Supp. 888, 890 (N.D.Ill.1975), aff'd, 541 F.2d 1263 (7th Cir.1976); Burger Chef Systems, Inc. v. Baldwin, Inc.*, 365 F.Supp. 1229, 1233–34 (S.D.N.Y.1973); *Network Cinema Corp. v. Glassburn*, 357 F.Supp. 169, 172 (S.D.N.Y.1973). The principles espoused in these cases apply with equal force to an international situation such as the instant one. The parties herein clearly contracted to arbitrate all non-technical disputes arising from the contract in New York. The parties further agreed that New York law would apply. Both Greece and the United States are signatories to the Convention, and the Convention is clearly intended to foster "recognition and enforcement of commercial arbitration agreements in international contracts and to unify the standards by which agreements to arbitrate are observed ... in the signatory countries."

Scherk v. Alberto–Culver Co., 417 U.S. 506, 520 n. 15, 94 S.Ct. 2449, 2457, 41 L.Ed.2d 270 (1974). In implementing the Convention, Congress clearly adopted the Convention's goals. These goals and the strong federal and New York policy in favor of arbitration would not in any way be furthered by recognizing and deferring to litigation pending in Greece which seeks to avoid arbitration. Accordingly, the comity defense must be rejected.

Conclusion

In accordance with the above, the petition to compel arbitration and for the appointment of a third arbitrator is granted. The respondent is hereby ordered to submit to arbitration in New York, New York and the Hon. Samuel C. Coleman, of Two West 89th Street, New York, New York 10024, is hereby appointed as the third arbitrator.

SO ORDERED.

RENUSAGAR POWER CO. (INDIA) v. GENERAL ELECTRIC CO. (U.S.)

India, High Court of Bombay, 1989.
16 Yearbk. Comm. Arb'n 553 (1991).*

Facts

The facts of this case are reported in more detail in Yearbook X (1985) pp. 431–449 (India no. 10), Yearbook XIV (1989) pp. 663–672 (India no. 17) and Yearbook XV (1990) pp. 465–492 (India no. 18).

On 24 August 1964, GEC and Renusagar entered into a contract for the sale of equipment for a thermal electric generating plant to be erected at Renukoot, India. The contract contained an ICC arbitration clause. The law applicable to the contract was the law of the State of New York.

A dispute arose between the parties and on 2 March 1982, GEC initiated ICC arbitration proceedings. On 16 September 1986, a majority award was rendered in Paris in favour of GEC. The award was enforced in India by a single Judge of the High Court of Bombay, on 21 October 1988. This decision is reported in Yearbook XV, India no. 18.

In the meantime, several court decisions were rendered in India between the parties. On 11 June 1982, Renusagar sought a declaration in the Bombay High Court, that the claims referred to ICC arbitration were beyond the scope of the arbitration clause in the contract. On 11 August 1982, GEC requested the Court to stay proceedings pending arbitration. GEC's request was granted and eventually upheld by the Supreme Court on 16 August 1984 (Yearbook X, India no. 10).

* Reprinted with permission of Yearbook Commercial Arbitration, International Council for Commercial Arbitration.

On 19 August 1982, GEC filed suit in the Calcutta High Court against the United Commercial Bank to enforce a bank guarantee. On 25 November 1982, Renusagar in its turn requested the Court of Civil Judge at Mirzapur to issue a declaration that the bank guarantee was unenforceable. On 4 April 1985, GEC applied to stay court proceedings pending arbitration. The Mirzapur Court rejected the application, holding that GEC had not filed its request before taking any steps in the proceedings and had, therefore, accepted the jurisdiction of the Court. This decision was affirmed by the Allahabad High Court but was reversed on 11 August 1987 by the Supreme Court, which ordered a stay of the proceedings before the Mirzapur Court (Yearbook XIV, India no. 17). Prior to the Supreme Court's decision, Renusagar had asked the ICC arbitrators to stay the arbitration proceedings in view of the rejection of GEC's application for a stay of the court suit. By an award dated 1 October 1985, a majority of the arbitrators held that they had not become *functus officio* and proceeded with the arbitration which resulted in the award of 16 September 1986 mentioned above.

The present judgment affirms the single Judge's decision granting enforcement in India to the ICC award of 16 September 1986 (Yearbook XV, India no. 18).

* * *

II. Are Arbitrators Functus Officio?

"The arbitration award was given during the pendency of the suit before the Civil Court at Mirzapur which allegedly covered substantially the same matters which were referred to arbitration. The arbitration award was given on 16 September 1986 much before the Supreme Court passed an order on 11 August 1987 staying the suit before the Mirzapur court. The appellants contend that the award, pronounced when the court proceedings were not stayed, is a nullity. As the suit was pending, the arbitrators had become *functus officio*."

"The contention is without merit. In the first place, the Supreme Court set aside the orders of the lower courts refusing stay. The Supreme Court held that the provisions of Sect. 3 of the Foreign Awards (Recognition and Enforcement) Act 1961 were attracted. Sect. 3 of the Foreign Awards (Recognition and Enforcement) Act 1961 is as follows:

"3. Stay of proceedings in respect of matters to be referred to arbitration. Notwithstanding anything contained in the Arbitration Act 1940, or in the Code of Civil Procedure 1908, if any party to an agreement to which Art. II of the Convention set forth in the Schedule applies, or any person claiming through or under him commences any legal proceedings in any court against any other party to the agreement or any person claiming through or under him in respect of any matter agreed to be referred to arbitration in such agreement, any party to such legal proceedings may, at any time after appearance and before filing a written statement or taking any other step in the proceedings, apply to the Court to stay the proceedings and the Court, unless satisfied that the agreement is null and void, inoperative or incapable of being performed, or that there is not, in fact, any dispute between the parties with regard to the matter agreed to be referred, shall make an order staying the proceedings."

"Under this section a stay of the suit is mandatory if requirements set out in that section are fulfilled. These requirements were admittedly fulfilled in the present case. Hence, under the order of the Supreme Court, the previous orders of the Allahabad High Court as well as of the Mirzapur Court were set aside. Moreover, during the pendency of proceedings before it, the Supreme Court did not prevent the arbitrators from proceeding with the reference. It merely took an undertaking from GEC that in case an award was made GEC should not take steps to enforce it. Ultimately the Supreme Court set aside the earlier orders and stayed the suit. The orders which have been so set aside cannot now be looked at in order to render the arbitration award, which has been given in the interregnum, a nullity. (. . .) Therefore, a wrongful refusal to stay the suit in the teeth of Sect. 3 of the Foreign Awards (Recognition and Enforcement) Act 1961 which has been set aside by the Supreme Court cannot render an arbitration unlawful."

"Secondly, there is no provision in the Foreign Awards (Recognition and Enforcement) Act 1961 which renders a foreign award made by a foreign tribunal during the pendency of a legal proceeding (on the same subject matter) in a local court invalid. The appellants say that the principle of Sect. 35 of the Arbitration Act 1940 should be extended, by analogy, to the Foreign Awards (Recognition and Enforcement) Act for invalidating such an arbitration. But the scheme of Foreign Arbitration (Recognition and Enforcement) Act is quite different from that of the Arbitration Act. Sects. 34 and 35 of the Arbitration Act are designed to avoid a conflict between a local court and a local private tribunal. The latter gives way to the former. In cases such as the present, the conflict is between a local court and a foreign private tribunal which is beyond the jurisdiction of the local court. A local court may face difficulties in superseding a foreign tribunal. The principles of the Arbitration Act cannot, therefore, be easily applied to foreign arbitrations.

"Under Sect. 34 of the Arbitration Act, if a party to an arbitration agreement commences any legal proceedings regarding subject matter of the agreement, the court may stay the legal proceedings, if prescribed requirements of Sect. 34 are met. *If such stay is not granted* then under Sect. 35, upon notice to the arbitrators, all further proceedings in a pending reference become invalid (provided the legal proceedings cover the entire subject matter of the reference). It is difficult to extend this principle of Sect. 35 to arbitration proceedings pending before a foreign tribunal. Hence, unlike Sect. 34 of the Arbitration Act, Sect. 3 of the Foreign Awards (Recognition and Enforcement) Act provides for a mandatory stay of legal proceedings in a local court. When stay of legal proceedings is mandatory, there is no question of applying Sect. 35 which comes into operation only if stay is not granted. Sect. 3 of the

Foreign Awards (Recognition and Enforcement) Act clearly gives precedence to the forum chosen by the parties rather than to a Civil Court.

* * *

"In the present case Sect. 3 applies to the legal proceedings instituted in the civil court at Mirzapur. In view of its express provision for a mandatory stay of the suit, there can be no question of invoking the principles of Sect. 35 of the Arbitration Act 1940."

* * *

Questions and Comments

1. The *lis pendens* problem can arise with respect to parallel proceedings in a single legal order or two or more different legal orders. Our concern is with the latter situation; here many legal systems assign priority—often on the basis of which was first filed—to one of such multiple proceedings. Should that principle have been followed in the *Parakopi* case? What principle did the New York court follow in deciding not to defer to the Greek court proceeding?

The court said it was not deferring to the Greek proceeding because it had hardly begun. Should deference be given where a proceeding has progressed some considerable distance? Does first filing provide a better test? What other possibilities are worth considering?

2. Very little is said in the District Court's decision about Parakopi's third defense that the petitioner's proper remedy is to apply to the Greek court for a stay of the Greek proceeding. Why was this argument ignored? Why did Sumitomo choose to seek in New York, rather than in Greece, a stay of the Greek court proceeding and to compel arbitration?

In the circumstances of the given case, it cannot be said that Sumitomo simply failed to invoke the arbitration clause before the Greek court. Sumitomo sought adjournment, and may have raised the issue later; the arbitration agreement was also relied upon in the procedural deal struck by the parties. But suppose a party is simply silent about the arbitration clause, enters into litigation, and then remembers the arbitration agreement when the litigation takes a bad turn. Should the arbitration agreement now be honored by a) the court before which the litigation is pending, or b) by the courts of another country?

3. Should the arbitration proceeding always be given priority? If so, on what grounds?

4. Was Sumitomo's motion to compel arbitration really necessary? What would be the effect of simply seeking to have the third arbitrator nominated?

5. If the Greek court had already rendered a judgment on the merits in favor of the Greek party, should the New York court dismiss the proceedings before it?

The answer to this question depends, first of all, on the rules for recognizing or enforcing foreign judgments. New York has adopted the Uniform Foreign Money–Judgments Recognition Act, Uniform Laws Annotated: Civil Procedural and Remedial Laws 276 (1975) and Supp. (1979) at 68, which permits a court to refuse to enforce a foreign judgment if it were given contrary to "an agreement between the parties under which the dispute in question was to be settled otherwise than by proceedings in that court ..." § 4(b)(5). If the parties had fully litigated the question of the validity of the arbitration clause before the Greek court and the court had expressly found the arbitration clause invalid, would then the issue of the clause's validity be res judicata in the New York court?

6. Suppose you are an arbitrator in the *Renusagar v. G.E.* case. When you learn that the Indian court (Mirzapur Court) has refused to stay proceedings before it, covering essentially the same issues as were submitted to arbitration, would you vote to continue the arbitration during the pendency of court proceedings? Why or why not?

7. Section 5 of the 1996 Indian Arbitration and Conciliation Ordinance states that: "Notwithstanding anything contained in any other law for the time being in force, in matters covered by this Part, no judicial authority shall intervene except where so provided in this Part." (The "Part" referred to is Part I devoted to arbitration. Part II deals with enforcement under the New York and the European (Geneva) Conventions. Part III deals with conciliation.) Should courts have a right to stop arbitration proceedings, or should judicial relief be available only after the award has been rendered?

8. In Tai Ping Insurance Co. v. M/V Warschau, the U.S. District Court for the Eastern District of Louisiana stayed arbitration proceedings in London, referring to the "inherent equitable power of a federal court to control its docket"[12] and arguing that by the stay "the possibility of inconsistent fact-finding between the arbiter and the court would be prevented."[13] The party opposing the stay argued on appeal that "the stay of arbitration contravened the language and intent of the Federal Arbitration Act."[14] The U.S. Court of Appeals for the Fifth Circuit held that an order to stay arbitration proceedings is within the powers of the district court, referring to Texaco v. American Trading Transport Co.,[15] in which such a stay was ordered since the dispute was not covered by the arbitration clause. It also held, however, that the *doctrine of intertwining* (relating to cases in which a party asserts several causes of action, at least one of which falls within the exclusive jurisdiction of federal courts) is **not** applicable, because it only applies to cases which involve inherently non-arbitrable issues.[16] The Court of Appeals concluded that in the given case, the district court abused its discretion when it ordered a stay of arbitration, because "only the most exceptional circumstances will justify an action on the part of a federal court that serves to impede arbitration of an arbitrable dispute. Duplication of

[12]. 556 F.Supp. 187, 190 (E.D.La. 1983).

[13]. Id. at 190.

[14]. 731 F.2d 1141, 1143 (5th Cir. 1984).

[15]. 644 F.2d 1152 (5th Cir.1981).

[16]. The doctrine of intertwining can be summarized as follows: when arbitrable and non-arbitrable claims arise out of the same transaction, and are sufficiently in-terrelated factually and legally, the court may, in its discretion, deny arbitration even to arbitrable claims, and try all claims together in federal court. In Dean Witter Reynolds v. Byrd, 470 U.S. 213 (1985), the Supreme Court held that the Federal Arbitration Act precluded federal courts from trying claims within the scope of a valid arbitration clause.

effort does not constitute such a circumstance; nor does piecemeal resolution of the dispute."[17]

Let us return to questions already posed in the light of this case: Should a court have the right to stop arbitration proceedings or should the only target of remedies be the award itself? Does it matter whether the arbitration is pending in the forum state or abroad? Does it matter whether a stay is requested on the ground of an alleged absence of a valid arbitration agreement or on some other ground?

9. Concerning the difficulties to which parallel proceedings may lead, we present here the facts of an unpublished case, based on the recollections of one of the authors. The parties agreed to arbitration in Belgrade using an arbitration clause which was much less than clear. The claimant sued before a German court. The German court stayed court proceedings in deference to the agreement calling for arbitration in Belgrade. After this, the claimant sued before the Belgrade court of arbitration. The arbitrators found, however, that the arbitration clause was invalid and therefore that they had no jurisdiction. What should the German court do if the parties return to it? Is the matter res judicata?

Here one of the basic issues tackled in Chapter II—that of the nature of the act of referring the parties to arbitration—arises in a different guise. Is this a binding decision establishing that the arbitration agreement is valid? Or does "referring the matter to arbitration" actually mean that the decision regarding the existence and the validity of the arbitration agreement is left—either until the proceedings are concluded or definitively—to the arbitrators?

Suppose the claimant first addressed the Belgrade Court of Arbitration, which then refused jurisdiction. Would (and should) this influence the German court, or should the German court rely exclusively on its own assessment of the arbitration agreement's validity?

V.1.f. *Effects of a Partial Award*

MEXICAN CONSTRUCTION CO. v. BELGIAN CO.

Arbitral Award (International Chamber of Commerce) 1984.
12 Yearbk. Comm. Arb'n 87 (1987).*

Facts

This arbitration [which took place in Switzerland] was the subject of a partial award rendered 14 June 1979, and reported in *Yearbook*, Vol. VII (1982), pp. 96–106. A related dispute between the claimant and the bank which issued a "risk exposure guarantee" in its favor was decided by an award made 23 October 1979, Case No. 3316 (published in *Yearbook,* Vol. VII (1982) pp. 106–116).

The dispute related to a construction contract entered into in June 1976 between a Saudi Arabian government entity and a Belgian consor-

[17]. 731 F.2d 1141, 1146 (5th Cir. 1984).

* Reprinted with permission of Yearbook Commercial Arbitration, International Council for Commercial Arbitration.

tium of which the defendant was a member. In January 1977, the defendant subcontracted part of the project to claimant.

The subcontract required claimant to post the standard performance bonds, and also an Advance Payment Guarantee in an amount equal to the entire amount of the advance payment made by defendant to claimant. Claimant pledged to the issuing bank the advance payment as collateral for the Advance Payment Guarantee.

In consideration, defendant caused a "Risk Exposure Guarantee" to be issued in favor of claimant. This guarantee provided for payments to claimant in the event of termination by defendant, in graduated amounts at different phases of completion of the contract.

Difficulties arose in the first few months of performance under the contract. Claimant was unable to meet various milestones, and the defendant made deductions from the sixth and seventh installment payments. On 17 November, claimant gave notice terminating the contract, and on 18 November defendant gave claimant notice.

Claimant thereupon initiated the arbitration. The partial award made 14 June 1979 found in favor of claimant on a certain number of points. It held that claimant's termination of the contract was legitimate, on account of defendant's withholding of certain sums due under the contract. Defendant objected that the amount payable to claimant under the Risk Exposure Guarantee (in excess of $18 million) was excessive, in the nature of a penalty, and should be reviewed by the arbitral tribunal. The arbitral tribunal ruled, however, that such amount was a legitimate liquidated damage amount, which, pursuant to the contract, could be claimed as an alternative to actual damages. Such a contractual term is acceptable under various legal systems and is also a general practice in the construction industry.

As regards the Advance Payment Guarantee and Performance Bonds, the arbitral tribunal held that they should remain in force pending the final award on the merits.

Subsequent to this partial award, there were a number of significant procedural developments. Defendant entered bankruptcy, and its case was thereafter conducted by its trustees in bankruptcy. Defendant initiated criminal proceedings in Belgium against claimant, and sought a review of the partial award pursuant to Art. 41 of the Swiss Concordat. This request, as well as a request for a stay of execution of the partial award, was rejected by the Supreme Court of Justice of Geneva. Furthermore, the claimant proved unable, as a practical matter, to obtain payment of amounts due under the Risk Exposure Guarantee, on account of court actions in Switzerland and Belgium initiated by defendant. After extensive negotiations, amounts due to claimant under the Risk Exposure Guarantee, and to defendant under the various performance guarantees, were deposited into various escrow accounts, and held subject to the final disposition of the case by the arbitral tribunal.

Extract

1. *Effect of Prior Partial Award*

The arbitrators first considered the effect of the partial award on issues remaining to be decided:

"The fundamental issue in this arbitration was to decide which of the two notices of termination of the contract was effective, claimant's or defendant's. This issue was decided in favour of claimant in the first award. Such award, which was not challenged at the time by defendant as open to it under Swiss law (Art. 36 of the Swiss Concordat sur l'Arbitrage),[1] is now *res judicata* between the parties and binding upon this arbitral tribunal, all the more so that defendant's later petition for review was dismissed by the Geneva Court of Justice.

"This arbitral tribunal is further of the opinion that the binding effect of its first award is not limited to the contents of the order thereof adjudicating or dismissing certain claims, but that it extends to the legal reasons that were necessary for such order, i.e., to the *ratio decidendi* of such award. Irrespective from the academic views that may be entertained on the extent of the principle of *res judicata* on the reasons of a decision, it would be unfair to both parties to depart in a final award from the views held in the previous award, to the extent they were necessary for the disposition of certain issues. By contrast, the arbitral tribunal made clear in other parts of its first award that the views expressed therein on certain other aspects of the case were of a preliminary nature only and without prejudice to its final decision. On such aspects, the arbitral tribunal holds itself entirely free to adopt other views with the benefit of further evidence and investigations."

* * *

1. Swiss Intercantonal Arbitration Convention, Art. 36 provides:

"An action for annulment of the arbitral award may be brought before the judicial authority provided for in Article 3, where it is alleged that:

a. the arbitral tribunal was not properly constituted;

b. that the arbitral tribunal erroneously declared itself to have or not to have jurisdiction;

c. that it pronounced on points not submitted to it or, subject to Article 32, failed to make a determination on one of the items in the claim;

d. that there was a breach of one of the mandatory procedural rules referred to in Article 25;

e. that the arbitral tribunal awarded to one of the parties something more or other than claimed, without being authorised to do so by a provision of the law;

f. that the award is arbitrary in that it was based on findings which were manifestly contrary to the facts appearing on the file, or in that it constitutes a clear violation of law or equity * * * "

[Authors' note: The Swiss Intercantonal Arbitration Convention continues to apply only to domestic arbitration in Switzerland. From January 1, 1989 arbitration in Switzerland deemed international (at the time of signing the arbitration agreement at least one party had its domicile, habitual residence, or seat outside of Switzerland) is governed by the Swiss Private International Law Act of 1987. See Documents Supplement. The parties may agree in writing, however, to apply the cantonal law instead of the Private International Law Act.]

Questions and Comments

1. There are cases in which the arbitrators issue more than one award. In the dispute between the Mexican and the Belgian Company, the ICC panel of arbitrators issued first a partial award. This was followed by a final award. If one assumes that a partial award is a "real" final award covering a limited number of issues, it follows that the holding of a partial award is res judicata. The arbitrators in the *Mexican Construction Co.* case went one step beyond this. They suggested that the binding effect of the first (partial) award "is not limited to the contents of the order thereof adjudicating or dismissing certain claims, but it extends to the legal reasons that were necessary for such order." 12 Yearbk. Comm. Arb'n 87, 87 (1987).

Is observance of the ratio decidendi a legal obligation of the arbitrators, or rather a matter of expediency or, perhaps, of pride? Should this question be answered differently if the second award is not rendered by the arbitrators that gave the first (partial) award?

2. Suppose Claimant raises two claims, each depending on whether a notice protesting a nonconforming delivery was sent in time. The arbitrators come to the conclusion that the notice was timely, and render a partial award regarding the first claim, ordering Respondent to pay $100,000. When the second claim is argued, Respondent hires a better lawyer who convinces the arbitrators that the notice was not timely. What can (and should) the arbitrators do?

If they were to decide in their final (second) award that the notice was sent too late, what consequences—if any—would follow for the $100,000 award?

3. In a case decided by the Cairo Regional Centre for International Commercial Arbitration, a partial award was rendered on April 22, 1992, and the final award was made on April 22, 1993. The arbitrators rendered the partial award, because one of the claims presented (request for payment of the purchase price) was ripe for decision, while another claim (for damages after a guarantee was called) depended on the outcome of a lawsuit pending before a court, seeking to stop the guarantee-payment. In these circumstances, the claim concerning damages appeared premature, and since the issues were separable, the arbitrators decided to render a partial award on payment of the purchase price. After the partial award was made, Claimant asked the arbitrators to award damages against the party that called the guarantee on the ground that it acted improperly in calling the guarantee. Respondent argued that the partial award was final, since it had decided on costs; the authority of the arbitrators had, therefore, lapsed and they were not entitled to decide any further issues respecting the first claim. The arbitrators held:

> "Respondent in its submissions dated June 4, 1992, and September 22, 1992, took the position that the Partial Award is a final award, because a final award, not a partial award, decides on costs and fees of an arbitration. The Tribunal rejects this contention. UNCITRAL Rule 38 provides that the arbitral tribunal shall fix the costs of arbitration in its award. The Tribunal interprets this as meaning that it may fix the costs of arbitration in any award it makes, whether partial or final. It is logical and fair that in an arbitration where earlier stages may be

completed by the issuance of a partial award, an arbitration tribunal may fix costs in a partial award prior to the completion of all stages and the rendering of the final award."

Article 32 sections 1 and 2 of the UNCITRAL Rules read:

"1.　In addition to making a final award, the arbitral tribunal shall be entitled to make interim, interlocutory, or partial awards.

2.　The award shall be made in writing and shall be final and binding on the parties. The parties undertake to carry out the award without delay."

According to the first sentence of Article 38:

"The arbitral tribunal shall fix the costs of arbitration in its award."

Do you agree with the position taken by the Cairo Tribunal? Should the preclusive-effect issue that the partial award raises, turn on whether the costs related to that part of the proceeding are set out in the award or later?

V.2.　JUDICIAL CONTROL OVER THE AWARD: SETTING ASIDE

V.2.a.　Note—Judicial Control in the Country Where the Award Is Considered to Be Domestic

Global convergence and harmonization in international commercial arbitration are particularly evident in the area of judicial control of the award. In most countries today, judicial control over the award occurs in just two settings: (i) opposition to recognition and enforcement, and (ii) the claim for setting aside. There is also a developing world-wide consensus on the appropriate grounds for challenging awards in these two proceedings.

The grounds for challenge in recognition and enforcement proceedings are specified in the New York Convention. Parties to the convention are obligated not to refuse recognition and enforcement on grounds other than those stated in Article V. Given the success of the New York Convention (and also the strong influence Article V has had on national legislators), one could say that the standards of Article V have practically become world law.

With respect to the grounds for setting aside (annulment, recours en annulation, Aufhebung), no international treaty exists that mandates harmonization. There is, however, a very strong trend toward convergence anchored in the UNCITRAL Model Law. Moreover, and this is very important, the grounds for setting aside stated in the Model Law, and adopted in most modern arbitration statutes, are basically the same as the grounds for refusing recognition and enforcement set out in Article V of the New York Convention.

According to Article 34 of the Model Law:

(1) Recourse to a court against an arbitral award may be made only by an application for setting aside in accordance with paragraphs (2) and (3) of this article.

(2) An arbitral award may be set aside by the court specified in article 6 only if:

    (a) the party making the application furnishes proof that:

        (i) a party to the arbitration agreement referred to in article 7 was under some incapacity; or the said agreement is not valid under the law to which the parties have subjected it or, failing any indication thereon, under the law of this State; or

        (ii) the party making the application was not given proper notice of the appointment of an arbitrator or of the arbitral proceedings or was otherwise unable to present his case; or

        (iii) the award deals with a dispute not contemplated by or not falling within the terms of the submission to arbitration, or contains decisions on matters beyond the scope of the submission to arbitration, provided that, if the decisions on matters submitted to arbitration can be separated from those not so submitted, only that part of the award which contains decisions on matters not submitted to arbitration may be set aside; or

        (iv) the composition of the arbitral tribunal or the arbitral procedure was not in accordance with the agreement of the parties, unless such agreement was in conflict with a provision of this Law from which the parties cannot derogate, or, failing such agreement, was not in accordance with this Law; or

    (b) the court finds that:

        (i) the subject-matter of the dispute is not capable of settlement by arbitration under the law of this State; or

        (ii) the award is in conflict with the public policy of this State.

(3) An application for setting aside may not be made after three months have elapsed from the date on which the party making that application had received the award or, if a request had been made under article 33, from the date on which that request had been disposed of by the arbitral tribunal.

(4) The court, when asked to set aside an award, may, where appropriate and so requested by a party, suspend the setting aside proceedings for a period of time determined by it in order to give the arbitral tribunal an opportunity to resume the arbitral proceedings or to take such other action as in the arbitral tribunal's opinion will eliminate the grounds for setting aside.

There are thus essentially two ways to obtain judicial review of an arbitral award: a) one may attack the award with a claim for setting aside in a country in which the award was made or that considers the award to be domestic, b) one may oppose recognition and enforcement in a country in which the winner chooses to rely on the award. Although the grounds for setting aside are regulated by the New York Convention but by the forum's general law, in practice the grounds that may be advanced in each type of proceeding are very similar in most legal systems, and in the Model Law they are practically identical.

We turn now to a number of basic issues pertaining to setting aside.

1. Which awards are domestic awards (and can therefore be set aside by domestic courts)? One need not invest hours of research to discover that the decision of an Atlanta court (whether state or federal) is a U.S. judgment, and will be considered a domestic decision in the United States. Likewise, a court decision rendered in Buenos Aires is an Argentinean judgment, and will be considered domestic in Argentina. But what about an arbitral award rendered in a dispute between a Mexican buyer and a French seller; where one of the arbitrators is Mexican, another, French, and the third, Hungarian; where the oral hearing takes place in Geneva, Switzerland; and where the award is made in Budapest, Hungary? (These facts are neither fictitious nor completely uncommon.) The provisions of Article V of the New York Convention that limit the extent of judicial scrutiny of arbitral awards apply to "awards not considered as domestic awards in the state where their recognition and enforcement are sought." Art. I(1). Where then is an award domestic?

The New York Convention only indirectly indicates the relevant criteria for determining "domesticity". According to Article V(1)(e), recognition and enforcement may be refused, if the award has been set aside by a competent authority "of the country in which, or under the law of which" the award was made. It follows that a distinction has been drawn between countries whose competence for setting aside is internationally recognized, and all other countries. Setting aside may be accepted and given force in a member-state of the New York Convention if it was effected in the country in which the award was rendered, or in the country under the law of which the award was rendered. This means that if setting aside is granted by a court which assumes jurisdiction on a ground other than that of the place of the award or of the law under which it was rendered—for example, the domicile of the defendant—the setting aside judgment would not be relevant in other countries party to the New York Convention. The criteria set out by Article V(1)(e) are therefore clearly influential and important, but they cannot and do not mandate a rule stating which awards can—and which cannot—be annulled by national courts.

A further problem with the New York Convention criteria is their lack of clarity. In which country exactly is the award made (the country where arbitration takes place, or where the award is written, or maybe where the last signature is added if the text is circulated for signatures)? Another dilemma is whether the "under the law of which" phrase refers to substantive or procedural law, or perhaps to the law applicable to the arbitration agreement.

The Model Law opts for the territorial criterion, stating in Article 1 (which defines the scope of application) that most provisions of the Law, including those on setting aside, apply "only if the place of arbitration is in the territory of this State." Most countries that have adopted the Model Law have accepted verbatim this formulation, or have chosen very similar language (such as Paragraph 1 of the 1994 Hungarian Arbitration Act, which states that the Act applies if "the arbitration has its place (or seat) in Hungary").

The 1987 Swiss Private International Law Act also opted for the seat-of-arbitration concept: "The provisions of this chapter apply to all arbitrations if the seat of the arbitration tribunal is situated in Switzerland and if, at the time when the arbitration agreement was concluded, at least one of the parties had neither its domicile nor its habitual residence in Switzerland."

To cite another example, according to Article 1504 of the 1981 French Code of Civil Procedure: "An arbitral award rendered in France in international arbitral proceedings is subject to an action to set aside on grounds set forth in Article 1502." (The French formulation is closer to the New York Convention criteria because it selects the place in which the award was made, rather than the place of arbitration, or the seat of the tribunal.)

It is important to mention here the new 1998 German Arbitration Act (new Book X of the German Code of Civil Procedure) which brings Germany into line with other countries by allowing German courts to take jurisdiction for setting aside purposes only if the place of arbitration is Germany. (See section 1025 of the new German act.) Under the previous law German courts took jurisdiction whenever German *lex arbitri* applied.

2. What decisions may be subject to setting aside? The Model Law speaks of setting aside "arbitral awards," without distinguishing between "final," "partial," "interim," "interlocutory," or other awards (or without drawing a distinction between other terms covering essentially the same form of decision). Distinctions have, however, been imposed in practice.[18]

By its nature, setting aside applies to awards with respect to which the arbitration process has been completed. Therefore, if an appellate level exists within the arbitration structure agreed upon by the parties, decisions of the first arbitration instance should not be subject to setting aside. In a case decided on July 7, 1995 by the Cour d'appel de Paris[19] the parties submitted their dispute to arbitration under the auspices of the Chambre arbitrale maritime de Paris, the rules of which provide for an appellate level if the disputed amount exceeds 100,000 FF. On November 15, 1993 the arbitrators of the first instance awarded US $81,290 to Corelf (which sum is considerably higher than FF 100,000), and Worldwide moved to set aside. The Paris court held that if "arbitration implies two levels, setting aside may only be requested with regard to the sentence rendered on the second level."

---

[18]. *See* A. Carrier, *Challenges to Interim Jurisdictional Awards in Local Courts: The Power of Arbitral Tribunals Over the Proceedings*, 4 Am. Rev. Int'l Arb'n 66 (1993).

[19]. Société Corelf v. Société Worldwide, CA Paris, 1e ch., reported in 1996 Revue de l'arbitrage 270, with comments by E. Loquin.

Setting aside of partial awards has usually been held admissible, which is logical if partial awards are understood as final, although not exhaustive. More complicated is the issue of interim awards that settle a preliminary question, such as that of jurisdiction. Article 1064(4) of the 1986 Dutch Arbitration Act takes an explicit position on this issue: "An application to set aside an interim arbitral award may be made only in conjunction with an application for setting aside a final or partial award."

Article 827 of the Italian Code of Civil Procedure (as amended in 1994) adopted essentially the same position:

> The award partially deciding on the merits of the dispute may be challenged immediately, whereas the award which decides some of the issues without resolving the dispute submitted to arbitration may be challenged only together with the final award.

The Swiss 1987 Private International Law Act has attempted a compromise, allowing setting aside of interim (preliminary) awards, but only on limited grounds: "As regards preliminary awards, setting aside proceedings can only be initiated on the grounds of the above paras. 2(a) and 2(b);" (Article 190/3).[20]

3. The issue of standard of review. Setting aside, as it is structured today in most states, implies a limited review. In most arbitration laws, the award is subject to a scrutiny restricted essentially to a listed number of procedural issues. It is clear that, in the course of this scrutiny, some findings of the arbitrators may be reinvestigated. If the arbitrators decide that they are competent, this does not bind the court in every respect; otherwise the judicial scrutiny of jurisdiction would be meaningless. Where the award may be vacated in a case in which the party making the application was not given proper notice of the arbitral proceedings, the last word as to whether proper notice was given belongs to the court. The question is whether the court owes any deference to the findings of the arbitrators, to conclusions they reached after adversary proceedings; in other words, the issue is whether a court is free to substitute its own view of the facts—and of the law—for those of the arbitrators. For example, if respondent misses the deadline for a submission and claims that he was not put on notice, and, after hearing the postman, the neighbors, and the respondent himself, the arbitrators conclude that the notice was indeed served, is the court bound by this finding of fact, or is it free (or even obliged) to reach an independent assessment?

4. Is the right to seek setting aside waivable? In principle, before the award is rendered, parties cannot waive their right to seek setting aside. In some countries, however, such an option nevertheless

---

[20]. [2(a): "where the sole arbitrator has been incorrectly appointed or where the arbitral tribunal has been incorrectly constituted;"

2(b): "where the arbitral tribunal has wrongly declared itself to have or not to have jurisdiction;"]

exists. Consider the following provisions of the Swiss Private International Law Act, Article 192:

> 1. Where none of the parties has its domicile, its habitual residence, or a business establishment in Switzerland, they may, by an express statement in the arbitration agreement or by a subsequent agreement in writing, exclude all setting aside proceedings, or they may limit such proceedings to one or several of the grounds listed in Art. 190, para. 2.

> 2. Where the parties have excluded all setting aside proceedings and where the awards are to be enforced in Switzerland, the New York Convention of 10 June 1958 on the recognition and Enforcement of Foreign Arbitral Awards shall apply by analogy.

This approach was greeted with mixed responses, and commentators have suggested a cautious and restrained interpretation.[21]

Recent Tunisian legislation follows the Swiss approach. Article 78(6) of the 1993 Arbitration Code states: "The parties who have neither domicile, principal residence nor a business establishment in Tunisia, may expressly exclude totally or partially all recourse against an arbitral award."

Reflecting the difficulty of the issue, the Belgian legislature first adopted one position, and then another. The 1985 Belgian Arbitration Act (Part of the Judicial Code—*Code judiciaire*) took a radical position. It provided:

> Courts of Belgium may hear a request for annulment only if at least one of the parties to the dispute decided by the award is either a physical person having Belgian nationality or residence, or a legal entity created in Belgium or having a Belgian branch or other seat of operation. (Article 1717)

This meant of course an *ex lege* exclusion of recourse if none of the parties had personal ties to Belgium (Belgian nationality, residence or seat). If one believes that some degree of judicial scrutiny of arbitral awards actually encourages parties to submit to arbitration, the 1985 Belgian provisions would have discouraged foreign parties from choosing Belgium as a seat of arbitration.

In any event, in the May 19, 1998 modifications of the Belgian Judicial Code, Belgium reverted to the Swiss solution. The only variance from the Swiss solution is that Article 1717(4) of the Belgian Code only allows the parties to waive the action for annulment, it does not allow them to restrict review to certain grounds.[22]

[21]. *See* K. Siehr, Op. cit. 1612.

[22]. Article 1717(4) of the Belgian Judicial Code provides:

"By an express provision in an arbitration agreement or by subsequent agreement, the parties may exclude all recourse to setting aside proceedings if neither party is a natural person with Belgian nationality or residence or a legal entity having its principal place of business or a branch in Belgium."

Sweden is the most recent country to adopt the Swiss approach. Section 51 of the Swedish Arbitration Act of 1999, which contains the relevant Swedish rules, also spells out: "An award which is subject to such an agreement [one excluding a set aside proceeding in Sweden] shall be recognized and enforced in Sweden in accordance with the rules applicable to a foreign award." Without such an explicit provision, one might wonder whether the award could be subjected to recognition and enforcement in Sweden under the New York Convention, because such an award—having its seat in Sweden—would not be considered a foreign award. The Swiss statute takes the same approach in Article 192(2).

The Swiss, Tunisian, Belgian, and Swedish solutions rest on considerations of expediency and efficiency. The question is whether they sacrifice minimum safety and control. The issue is particularly sensitive with regard to awards denying the relief sought. In this situation, opposition to recognition and enforcement does not offer a last opportunity for judicial control (as it does if relief is granted, and enforcement is pending); the winning party is satisfied with the res judicata effect and does not have to seek recognition and enforcement, while the losing party has no procedure available for challenging the award.[23]

5. Is the right to seek setting aside expandable? Regarding the mandatory or non-mandatory character of rules pertaining to setting aside, the opposite perspective also deserves attention. The question may be raised whether the parties are allowed to broaden (rather than to limit or exclude) options of recourse. In a case that reached the French Cour de cassation,[24] the parties stipulated forms of recourse that are available in connection with domestic arbitration for a case which was international under French standards. The Cour de cassation held that such a stipulation is without effect, and that the only available recourse in international arbitration is setting aside (recours en annulation). In another case decided by the Cour d'appel de Paris,[25] the parties inserted into their arbitration clause a provision stating that they retained the right to lodge an appeal against the arbitral award before the court of appeal. In this case, the outcome was rather drastic. It was held that the parties cannot create a recourse outside the one fixed in the Code of Civil Procedure, and that therefore the arbitration agreement containing such

---

[23]. One possibility would be for the claimant (the losing party in arbitration) to present the original claim to a court in a country other than the country where the award was rendered. Respondent (winner in the arbitration case) would claim res judicata, and the court would then face an issue of recognition of the award under the New York Convention. Presumably such a procedure would not be available in the place of arbitration, since most countries would consider such an award to be domestic and not subject to the New York Convention. Since the Swiss, Tunisian, and Belgian solutions depend upon neither party's having any important connection to the place of arbitration, however, it is unlikely that the location of the respondent's assets (and certainly not its domicile) would force the claimant to bring the action in the place of arbitration.

[24]. Société Buzichelli v. Hennion et autre, Cour de cassation, 1e ch., April 6, 1994, reported in 1995 Revue de l'arbitrage 263, comment by P. Level.

[25]. Société de Diseno v. Société Mendes, CA Paris, 1e ch., October 27, 1994, reported in 1995 Revue de l'arbitrage 265.

a provision was invalid. The award was annulled on the ground of lack of a valid arbitration agreement.

We take up the American approach to this issue in a major case, Lapine Technology Corp. v. Kyocera Corp., 130 F.3d 884 (9th Cir.1997), reproduced below in section V.2.d.ii.

6. The consequences of setting aside. If an award is set aside, it has no effects in the country where it was vacated. If setting aside occurs in a country in which, or under the law of which the award was made, such setting aside may serve as a ground under the New York Convention for other countries refusing to recognize and enforce the award; however, the New York Convention does not require this result.[26]

We explore this issue more fully infra in section V.3.c.v, which deals with the relevance of setting aside for recognition proceedings.

Another important question is whether the arbitrators are *functus officio* after setting aside is pronounced; or do they retain jurisdiction to rehear the case.

The U.S. Arbitration Act (Section 10) provides: "(e) Where an award is vacated and the time within which the agreement required the award to be made has not expired the court may, in its discretion, direct a rehearing by the arbitrators."

The 1986 Dutch Arbitration Act takes a different position. According to Article 1076: "Unless the parties have agreed otherwise, as soon as the award has become final, the jurisdiction of the court shall revive."

A 1970 decision of the Supreme Court of Poland offers a further refinement.[27] The Polish Supreme Court held that after annulment the arbitration agreement remains in force, unless the award was annulled because the arbitration agreement was deemed to be void or expired.

7. Are there relevant procedural standards superior to those of national courts? Standards of due process have become an essential element of the catalogue of human rights, and have found

---

[26]. Concerning this point, it is interesting to note that there is a difference between the English and the French wording of the Convention. According to the English text "Recognition and enforcement of the award may be refused ... only if ..." (if one of the grounds set out in Article V is evidenced); while according to the French text "La reconnaissance et l'exécution de la sentence ne seront refusées ... que ..." (meaning that recognition and enforcement of the award will not be refused ... unless ...) It appears that the French wording is closer to a mandated refusal, yet court decisions which grant recognition in spite of annulment in the relevant country, are abundant precisely in the French practice. (See e.g.: Pabalk v. Norso-

lor, Cour de cassation, 1e ch. civ., Oct. 9, 1984, reported in 1985 Revue de l'arbitrage 431; Hilmarton v. OTV, Cour de cassation 1e ch. civ., March 23, 1994, reported in 1994 Revue de l'arbitrage 327, English text in 20 Yearbk. Comm. Arb'n 663 (1995); See also Fouchard, Gaillard, Goldman, op. cit. 928–929. [Authors' note: Several in a series of French decisions in the *Hilmarton* matter are reproduced infra in section V. 3. c. vi.]) On the other hand, the French practice is based on New York Convention Article VII, which would support the French outcome even if V(1)(e) were mandatory.

[27]. Decision of the Supreme Court of October 5, 1970, SN III CZP 63/70 (OSNCP 1971, No. 5, poz. 78).

expression, for example, in Article 6 of the European Convention for the Protection of Human Rights and in Article 14 of the International Covenant on Civil and Political Rights. In rare cases, courts have invoked the norms embodied in human rights conventions in connection with arbitration proceedings.[28] A case set out below in section V.2.e. illustrates this problem. There the party dissatisfied with a setting-aside judgment tried to reverse it before the European Court of Human Rights.

V.2.b. *Domestic and Foreign Awards*

INTERNATIONAL STANDARD ELECTRIC CORP. v. BRIDAS SOCIEDAD ANONIMA PETROLERA

United States District Court, Southern District of New York, 1990.
745 F.Supp. 172.

OPINION AND ORDER

CONBOY, DISTRICT JUDGE:

In this action, the parties seek, on the one side, to vacate a foreign arbitration award, and, on the other, to enforce that award pursuant to an international convention. This case, then, requires us to evaluate and apply the relevant standards for vacatur and enforcement of an award made under the aegis of the International Chamber of Commerce Court of Arbitration in Paris.

Background

* * *

On December 20, 1989, the Panel, in accordance with the rules which require the advance review and approval by the ICC International Court of Arbitration, signed the final Award, which was released and issued to the parties on January 16, 1990.

The Arbitral Award ("Award") found unanimously by the Panel, concluded that Bridas had not established that ISEC had made misrepresentations or committed fraud in connection with the sale of certain stock to Bridas in 1979; that Bridas had not established that ISEC had unlawfully mismanaged CSEA; that Bridas had established that in July of 1984 ISEC breached its fiduciary obligations to Bridas in connection with a 1984 recapitalization of CSEA; and that Bridas had established that in March of 1985 ISEC breached its contractual and fiduciary obligations to Bridas by selling, over Bridas' objection, its 97% interest in CSEA to Siemens, the German multinational corporation and a major competitor of Bridas in Argentina. The Panel also concluded that ISEC

---

[28]. See e.g. three decisions of the Paris Tribunal de grande instance rendered in the controversy between the Republic of Guinea and the Chambre arbitrale de Paris. 1987 Revue de l'arbitrage 371; See also T. Varady, *On Appointing Authorities in International Commercial Arbitration*, 2 Emory Journal of International Dispute Resolution 309, at 355 (1988).

had failed to "comply with the norms of good faith demanded of a fiduciary" by not giving Bridas adequate notice of the proposed sale and its terms. Though describing these findings against ISEC as erroneous, ISEC concedes that they are beyond this Court's review. The Panel awarded Bridas damages of $6,793,000 with interest at 12%, compounded annually, from March 14, 1985. Bridas was also granted $1 million in legal fees and expenses plus $400,000 for the costs of the arbitration.

On February 2, 1990, ISEC filed a petition in this Court to vacate and refuse recognition and enforcement of the Award. Respondent Bridas has cross-petitioned to dismiss ISEC's petition to vacate on the grounds that this Court lacks subject matter jurisdiction to grant such relief under the Convention, and for failure to state a claim pursuant to Fed.R.Civ.P. 12(b)(1) and (6). Bridas further cross-petitions to enforce the Award pursuant to Article III of the Convention.

Analysis

We will first address the question of whether, under the binding terms of the New York Convention, we lack subject matter jurisdiction to vacate a foreign arbitral award. The situs of the Award in this case was Mexico City, a location chosen by the ICC Court of Arbitration pursuant to rules of procedure explicitly agreed to by the parties. Since the parties here are an American Company and an Argentine Company, it is not difficult to understand why the Mexican capital was selected as the place to conduct the arbitration.

Bridas argues that, under the New York Convention, only the courts of the place of arbitration, in this case the Courts of Mexico, have jurisdiction to vacate or set aside an arbitral award. ISEC argues that under the Convention both the courts of the place of arbitration and the courts of the place whose substantive law has been applied, in this case the courts of the United States, have jurisdiction to vacate or set aside an arbitral award.

Under Article V(1)(e) of the Convention, "an application for the setting aside or suspension of the award" can be made only to the courts or the "competent authority of the country in which, or under the law of which, that award was made." ISEC argues that "the competent authority of the country ... under the law of which [the] award was made," refers to the country the substantive law of which, as opposed to the procedural law of which, was applied by the arbitrators. Hence, ISEC insists that since the arbitrators applied substantive New York law, we have jurisdiction to vacate the award.

ISEC cites only one case to support this expansive reading of the Convention, Laminoirs–Trefileries–Cableries de Lens v. Southwire Co., 484 F.Supp. 1063 (N.D.Ga.1980). That case, however, did not involve a foreign award under the Convention, and did not implicate the jurisdictional question here raised, since there the parties' substantive and procedural choice of law, and the situs of the arbitration were both New York. It seems plain that the Convention does not address, contemplate or encompass a challenge to [such] an award in the courts of the state where the award was rendered, since the relation of th[es]e courts to the arbitral proceedings is not an international, but a wholly domestic one, at least insofar as the Convention is concerned. Whether such an arbitration would be considered international because of the parties' nationalities under the Federal Arbitration Act, is irrelevant. See A. Van den Berg, The New York Arbitration Convention of 1958 19–20, 349–50 (Kluwer 1981).

Bridas has cited a case decided by our colleague Judge Keenan, American Construction Machinery & Equipment Corp. v. Mechanised Construction of Pakistan Ltd., 659 F.Supp. 426 (S.D.N.Y.), aff'd, 828 F.2d 117 (2d Cir.1987), cert. denied, 484 U.S. 1064, 108 S.Ct. 1024, 98 L.Ed.2d 988 (1988), as authority against the ISEC position. This case involved a dispute between a Cayman Islands Company and a Pakistani company, arguably controlled by Pakistani substantive law and arbitrated in Geneva. Judge Keenan was asked to decline enforcement of the award on the ground that a challenge to it was pending in the courts of Pakistan. He ruled that "[t]he law under which this award was made was Swiss law because the award was rendered in Geneva pursuant to Geneva procedural law" 659 F.Supp. at 429. This analysis was expressly affirmed in the Court of Appeals, and the Supreme Court declined to review it.

Our Circuit has set forth a brief history of the Convention in an enforcement, as distinguished from a jurisdictional, case under the Convention in Parsons & Whittemore Overseas Co., Inc., v. Societe Generale De L'Industrie Du Papier (RAKTA), 508 F.2d 969, 973 (2d Cir.1974), and in general terms has recognized that the basic thrust of the convention was to limit the broad attacks on foreign arbitral awards that had been authorized by the predecessor Geneva Convention of 1927, 92 League of Nations Treaty Ser. 2302.

The New York Court of Appeals, in an opinion by its Chief Judge, in a jurisdictional case involving pre-arbitration attachment under the Convention, asserted that the policy underlying the Convention, the avoidance of "the vagaries of foreign law for international traders" would be defeated by the allowance of multiple suits (there in New York, the home of one of the parties), where the parties have agreed, by contract, to place their dispute in the hands of an international arbitral panel in a neutral legal forum, (there Switzerland). Cooper v. Ateliers de la Motobecane, S.A., 57 N.Y.2d 408, 410, 456 N.Y.S.2d 728, 729, 442 N.E.2d 1239, 1240 (1982).

In Bergesen v. Joseph Muller Corp., 710 F.2d 928 (2d Cir.1983), the Court interpreted certain terms of the Convention in a case involving an award arising from an arbitration held in New York between two foreign entities. The court construed the United States position in the draft proceedings leading to the adoption of the Convention as urging adoption of a territorial criterion on jurisdiction, this is, that the situs of the award, without regard to such factors as the nationality of the parties, the subject of the dispute and the rules of arbitral procedure, would determine if the award was "foreign" under the Convention. France and Germany, the Court pointed out, had on the other hand, urged that the nationality (that is, is the award foreign and therefore within the Convention, or domestic and therefore outside the Convention) of an award should be determined "by the law governing the procedure," 710 F.2d at 931. The Court noted that although an effort at compromise was made to restrict the territorial concept, the "final action by the convention appears to have had the opposite result, i.e., except as provided in paragraph 3, the first paragraph of Article I means that the convention applies to all arbitral awards rendered in the country other than the state of enforcement, whether or not such awards may be regarded as domestic in that state. . . ." Id.

We conclude that the phrase in the Convention "[the country] under the laws of which that award was made" undoubtedly referenced the complex thicket of the procedural law of arbitration obtaining in the numerous and diverse jurisdictions of the dozens of nations in attendance at the time the Convention was being debated. Even today, over three decades after these debates were conducted, there are broad variations in the international community on how arbitrations are to be conducted and under what customs, rules, statutes or court decisions, that is, under what "competent authority." Indeed, some signatory nations have highly specialized arbitration procedures, as is the case with the United States, while many others have nothing beyond generalized civil practice to govern arbitration. See Lowenfeld, The Two–Way Mirror: International Arbitration as Comparative Procedure, 7 Mich. Y.B.Int'l Legal Studies 163, 166–70 (1985), reprinted in 2 Craig, Park and Paulsson, International Chamber of Commerce Arbitration, App. VII at 187 (1986).

This view is confirmed by Professor van den Berg to the effect that the language in dispute reflects the delegates' practical insight that parties to an international arbitration might prefer to equalize travel distance and costs to witnesses by selecting as a situs forum A, midpoint between two cities or two continents, and submit themselves to a different procedural law by selecting the arbitration procedure of forum B.

> The "competent authority" as mentioned in Article V(1)(e) for entertaining the action of setting aside the award is virtually always the court of the country in which the award was made. The phrase "or under the law of which" the award was made refers to the theoretical case that on the basis of an agreement of the parties the award is governed by an arbitration law which is different from the arbitration law of the country in which the award was made.

A. van den Berg, The New York Arbitration Convention of 1958 350 (1981). This view is consistent with a commentary on the circumstances under which the Soviet delegate offered the amendment embracing the language in issue. See United Nations Conference on International Commercial Arbitration, Summary Record of the 23rd Meeting, 9 June 1958, E/CONF. 26/SR.23 at 12 (12 Sept. 1958), reprinted in G. Gaja, International Commercial Arbitration: New York Convention III C. 213 (Oceana Pub.1978).

It is clear, we believe, that any suggestion that a Court has jurisdiction to set aside a foreign award based upon the use of its domestic, substantive law in the foreign arbitration defies the logic both of the Convention debates and of the final text, and ignores the nature of the international arbitral system. This is demonstrated overwhelmingly by review of cases in foreign jurisdictions that have considered the question before us.

Decisions of foreign courts deciding cases under the Convention uniformly support the view that the clause in question means procedural and not substantive (i.e., in most cases contract) law. [citing decisions in India, Belgium, France, Germany, Spain, and South Africa]

Finally, we should observe that the core of petitioner's argument, that a generalized supervisory interest of a state in the application of its domestic substantive law (in most arbitrations the law of contract) in a foreign proceeding, is wholly out of step with the universal concept of arbitration in all nations. The whole point of arbitration is that the merits of the dispute will not be reviewed in the courts, wherever they be located. Indeed, this principle is so deeply imbedded in American, and specifically, federal jurisprudence, that no further elaboration of the case law is necessary. That this was the animating principle of the Convention, that the Courts should review arbitrations for procedural regularity but resist inquiry into the substantive merits of awards, is clear from the notes on this subject by the Secretary–General of the United Nations.

Accordingly, we hold that the contested language in Article V(1)(e) of the Convention, "... the competent authority of the country under the law of which, [the] award was made" refers exclusively to procedural and not substantive law, and more precisely, to the regimen or scheme of arbitral procedural law under which the arbitration was conducted, and not the substantive law of contract which was applied in the case.

In this case, the parties subjected themselves to the procedural law of Mexico. Hence, since the situs, or forum of the arbitration is Mexico, and the governing procedural law is that of Mexico, only the courts of Mexico have jurisdiction under the Convention to vacate the award. ISEC's petition to vacate the award is therefore dismissed.

* * *

CROATIAN COMPANY v. SWISS COMPANY

Croatia, High Commercial Court, 1986.
2 Croatian Arb'n Yearbk. 205 (1995).*c

Facts of the case:

"In the proceedings before the Commercial County Court in Split No. P–2352/84, the plaintiff, a Croatian company, applied for setting aside the arbitral award made by an arbitral tribunal of the International Court of Arbitration at the International Chamber of Commerce (ICC), No. 4151/AS of May 18, 1984. This award, favorable to the other party, which was a foreign company, was made in Switzerland, and therefore it had to be considered a Swiss arbitral award. By a court order of October 11, 1985, the Commercial County Court rejected the application for the lack of international jurisdiction. The High Commercial Court of Croatia in Zagreb confirmed the decision made in the first instance (court order Pz–186/86 of March 18, 1986). Both decisions are grounded on the opinion that domestic courts do not have jurisdiction to decide upon applications for setting aside foreign arbitral awards. The High Commercial Court of Croatia accepted the opinion that the applications for setting aside have to be submitted to the court of the country in which the arbitral award had been made already in 1977, because such award belonged to the legal system of the place of arbitration (court order No. SL–2457/76 of March 23, 1977)."

From the reasoning of the decision:

"The Commercial County Court in Split (. . .) declared itself incompetent to decide on this issue, annulled all acts undertaken in the proceedings, and rejected the suit. The essential reasons for such decision were the following: the plaintiff requested setting aside of an arbitral award made in Switzerland by the International Court of Arbitration at the International Chamber of Commerce in Paris (. . .); such award pursuant to Art. 97 of the CLA has to be considered foreign; the same award was made in the proceedings in which domestic procedural law was not applied (. . .), instead it was made pursuant to the procedural law of a foreign state (Switzerland); therefore, setting aside is not within the jurisdiction of domestic courts, * * *."

The appellant argues in his appeal the following:

That the Court incorrectly invokes provisions of the (* * *) CLA, because in this case the provisions of the Law on ratification of the New York Convention on Recognition and Enforcement of Foreign Arbitral Awards (NYC) of June 10, 1958 (* * *) should have been applied instead. That pursuant to this Convention, under Art. V, (1)(e), domestic

* Reprinted with permission of Yearbook Commercial Arbitration, International Council for Commercial Arbitration.

c. Arbitral Jurisprudence Compiled by: Prof. Dr. Mihajilo Dika. Translated and Prepared by: Allan Uzelac.

courts have jurisdiction for setting aside this arbitral award, because the substantive domestic law was applied in the case. * * *

The appeal has to be rejected.

The appellant incorrectly assumes that setting aside of this foreign arbitral award falls within jurisdiction of the domestic courts pursuant to the provisions of NYC. Namely, the provision of Art. V, (1)(e) reads that "... the award has not yet become binding on the parties, or has been set aside or suspended by a competent authority of the country in which, or under the law of which, that award was made". According to the opinion of this Court, from this provision and from the fact that domestic substantive law was applied in the award, we could not draw the conclusion that domestic courts have jurisdiction to set aside this award. On the contrary, this court concluded that, pursuant to the cited provision, competent courts for setting aside are the courts of the country (state) in which the award was made. The same conclusion may follow from the provisions of the Geneva Protocol on Arbitration Clauses (* * *) and Geneva Convention on the Execution of Foreign Arbitral Awards—Art. 1 and 2 (* * *), as well as from the provision of Art. IX of the European Convention on International Commercial Arbitration (* * *).

Considering the indisputable fact that the procedural law of a foreign state—the state in which award was made—was applied in the award, this Court holds the decision of the Court in the first instance to declare itself (internationally) incompetent and reject the claim as correct. * * *

OIL & NATURAL GAS COMMISSION v. WESTERN CO. OF NORTH AMERICA

India, Supreme Court of India, 1986.
74 All India Rep. S.C. 674 (1987).*

THAKKAR, J.:—Was the High Court "right" in granting the restraint order earlier, and "wrong" in vacating the said order later?

2. By the order in question the Respondent, Western Company of North America (Western Company), was restrained from proceeding further with an action instituted by it in a USA Court against the appellant, Oil and Natural Gas Commission (ONGC). The said action was targeted at seeking a judgment from the concerned Court in U.S.A. on the basis of an arbitral award rendered by an Umpire in arbitration proceedings held in London but governed by the Indian Arbitration Act, 1940, which was the law of choice of the parties as per the arbitration clause contained in the drilling contract entered into between the parties. The Western Company has moved the USA Court for a judgment in terms of the award notwithstanding the fact that:—

* Reprinted with permission of All India
Reporter Pvt. Ltd.

1) ONGC had already initiated proceedings in an Indian Court to set aside the award and the said proceeding was as yet pending in the Indian Court.

2) The said award was not as yet enforceable in India as a domestic award inasmuch as a judgment in accordance with the Indian law had yet to be procured in an Indian Court, by the Western Company.

3.　　The events culminating in the order under appeal may be briefly and broadly recounted. The appellant, ONGC, and the Respondent Western Company, had entered into a drilling contract. The contract provided for any differences arising out of the agreement being referred to arbitration. The arbitration proceedings were to be governed by the Indian Arbitration Act 1940 read with the relevant rules. A dispute had arisen between the parties. It was referred to two Arbitrators and an Umpire was also appointed. The Arbitrators entered on the reference in London which was the agreed venue for hearing as per the Arbitration Clause contained in the contract. On October 1, 1985 the Arbitrators informed the Umpire that they were unable to agree on the matters outstanding in the reference. Consequently the Umpire entered upon the arbitration, and straightway proceeded to declare the interim award of October 17, 1985. Thereafter on November 5, 1985, the Respondent, Western Company, requested the Umpire to authorise one Shri D.C. Singhania to file the award dated October 17, 1985 in the appropriate Court in India. The Umpire accordingly authorised the said Shri Singhania in this behalf. And pursuant to the said authority the award rendered by the Umpire was lodged in the Bombay High Court on November 22, 1985. Subsequently, on November 28, 1985 the Umpire rendered a supplementary award relating to costs which has been termed as "final" award. About a month after the lodging of the award in the High Court of Bombay by the Umpire at the instance of the Respondent, Western Company, the latter lodged a plaint in the U.S. District Court, inter alia, seeking an order (1) confirming the two awards dated October 17, 1985 and November 28, 1985 rendered by the Umpire; (2) a Judgment against the ONGC, (Appellant herein) in the amount of $256,815.45 by way of interest until the date of the Judgment and costs etc.

4.　　On January 20, 1986, appellant ONGC on its part instituted an Arbitration Petition (Petition No. 10 of 1986), under Sections 30 and 33 of the Indian Arbitration Act 1940 for setting aside the awards rendered by the Umpire. * * * The appellant, ONGC, also prayed for an interim order restraining the Western Company from proceeding further with the action instituted in the U.S. Court. The learned single Judge granted an ex parte interim restraint order (On January 20, 1986) but vacated the same after hearing the parties by his impugned order (Interim Order No. 11 of 1986 passed on April 3, 1986 in Arbitration Petition No. 10 of 1986), giving rise to the present appeal by Special Leave.

5. In order to confine the dialogue strictly within the brackets of the scope of the problem, four points deserve to be made at the outset before adverting to the impugned order rendered by the High Court.

* * *

3) We are not concerned with the question as to how an arbitral award which is not a domestic award in India can be enforced in a Court in India in the context of the Indian legislation enacted in that behalf namely the Foreign Awards (Recognition and Enforcement) Act, 1961. The said Act was enacted in order to give effect to an international convention known as New York Convention to which India has acceded. The provisions of the said Act would be attracted only if a foreign award is sought to be enforced in an Indian Court. We are not concerned with such a situation. The award which is the subject-matter of controversy in the present case is admittedly a domestic award for the purposes of the Indian Courts, governed by the provisions of the Indian Arbitration Act of 1940. When the Western Company seeks to enforce the award in question in the US Court they do so on the premise that it is a foreign award in the US Court. In considering the question as regards the proceeding initiated by the Western Company in the US Court, there is no occasion to invoke the provisions of the aforesaid Act. The provisions of the said Act can be invoked only when an award which is not a domestic award in India is sought to be enforced in India. Such is not the situation in the present case. We are therefore not at all concerned with the provisions of the said Act.

* * *

9. The situation which emerges is somewhat an incongruous one. The arbitral award rendered by the Umpire may itself be set aside and become non-existent if the ONGC is able to successfully assail it in the petition under Section 30/33 for setting aside the award in question in India. The High Court does not hold that the petition is prima facie liable to fail. We do not wish to express any opinion on the merits of the petition as in our opinion it would be improper to do so and might occasion prejudice one way or the other. We are however not prepared to assume for the purpose of the present discussion that the petition is liable to fail. The question is wide open. The final decision of the Court cannot and need not be anticipated.

10. In the light of the foregoing discussion, the following submissions, pressed into service by the appellant, ONGC, require to be examined.

(1) The award sought to be enforced in the USA Court may itself be set aside by the Indian Court and in that event, an anomalous situation would be created.

(2) Since the validity of the award in question and its enforceability have to be determined by an Indian Court, which alone has

jurisdiction under the Indian Arbitration Act of 1940, the American Court would have no jurisdiction in this behalf.

(3) The enforceability of the award must be determined in the context of the Indian Law as the arbitration proceedings are admittedly subject to the Indian Law and are governed by the Indian Arbitration Act of 1940.

(4) If the award in question is permitted to be enforced in USA without its being affirmed by a Court in India or a USA Court, it would not be in conformity with law, justice or equity.

* * *

13. The submission that while the validity of the award is required to be tested in the context of the Indian law if the Western Company is permitted to pursue the matter in the American Court, the matter would be decided under a law other than the Indian law, by the American Court. Admittedly, Western Company has prayed for confirmation of the award. The American Court may still proceed to confirm the award.

* * *

It is essential to emphasise at this juncture and in this context, that under the Indian law, an arbitral award is unenforceable until it is made a rule of the Court and a judgment and consequential decree are passed in terms of the award. Till an award is transformed into a judgment and decree under Section 17 of the Arbitration Act, it is altogether lifeless from the point of view of its enforceability. Life is infused into the award in the sense of its becoming enforceable only after it is made a rule of the Court upon the judgment and decree in terms of the award being passed. The American Court would have therefore enforced an award which is a lifeless award in the country of its origin, and under the law of the country of its origin which law governs the award by choice and consent.

* * *

In these premises it was argued that for the purposes of the Convention the award should be considered as binding if no further recourse to another arbitral tribunal was open and that the possibility of recourse to a Court of law should not prevent the award from being binding. On the other hand it was contended on behalf of ONGC that an award should be treated as binding only when it has become enforceable in the country of origin. It was argued that the word "binding" was used in the sense of an award from which the parties could not wriggle out. So far as the present matter is concerned it is unnecessary to examine this aspect at length or in depth for we are not resting our decision on the question as to whether the American Court is likely to refuse enforcement or not. * * *

* * *

17. It was next contended on behalf of Western Company that in the five cases decided under the New York Convention involving parallel proceedings, in no case did a Court decide that an injunction such as sought by ONGC was necessary. * * *

We are afraid that this argument loses sight of the fact that in the present matter we are not concerned with the question as to whether a foreign Court should adjourn the decision on the enforcement of the award under Article VI. We are not enforcing any foreign award and the question is not whether or not a decision on enforcement should be adjourned. It is the American Court which will have to address itself to that question if an occasion arises.

* * *

18. In the result we are of the opinion that the facts of this case are eminently suitable for granting a restraint order as prayed by ONGC. It is no doubt true that this Court sparingly exercises the jurisdiction to restrain a party from proceeding further with an action in a foreign Court. We have the utmost respect for the American Court. The question however is whether on the facts and circumstances of this case it would not be unjust and unreasonable not to restrain the Western Company from proceeding further with the action in the American Court in the facts and circumstances outlined earlier. We would be extremely slow to grant such a restraint order but in the facts and circumstances of this matter we are convinced that this is one of those rare cases where we would be failing in our duty if we hesitate in granting the restraint order, for, to oblige the ONGC to face the aforesaid proceedings in the American Court would be oppressive in the facts and circumstances discussed earlier. * * * And in such a situation the Courts have undoubted jurisdiction to grant such a restraint order whenever the circumstances of the case make it necessary or expedient to do so or the ends of justice so require. The following passage extracted from paragraph 1039 of Halsbury's Laws of England Vol. 24 at page 579 supports this point of view:

> With regard to foreign proceedings the Court will restrain a person within its jurisdiction from instituting or prosecuting proceedings in a foreign Court whenever the circumstances of the case make such an interposition necessary or expedient. In a proper case the Court in this country may restrain person who has actually recovered judgment in a foreign Court from proceeding to enforce that judgment. The jurisdiction is discretionary and the Court will give credit to foreign Courts for doing justice in their own jurisdiction. * * *

* * *

21. And now we come to the conclusion. While we are inclined to grant the restraint order as prayed, we are of the opinion that fairness demands that we do not make it unconditional but make it conditional to the extent indicated hereafter. There are good and valid reasons for making the restraint order conditional in the sense that ONGC should be required to pay the charges payable in respect of the user of the rig belonging to the Western Company at the undisputed rate regardless of the outcome of the petition instituted by the ONGC in the High Court for setting aside the award rendered by the Umpire. India has acceded to the New York Convention. One of the objects of the New York Convention was to evolve consensus amongst the covenanting nations in regard to the execution of foreign arbitral awards in the concerned Nations. The necessity for such a consensus was presumably felt with the end in view to facilitate international trade and commerce by removing technical and legal bottlenecks which directly or indirectly impede the smooth flow of the river of international commerce. Since India has acceded to this Convention it would be reasonable to assume that India also subscribes to the philosophy and ideology of the New York Convention as regards the necessity for evolving a suitable formula to overcome this problem. The Court dealing with the matters arising out of arbitration agreements of the nature envisioned by the New York Convention must therefore adopt an approach informed by the spirit underlying the Convention. It is no doubt true that if the arbitral award is set aside by the Indian Court, no amount would be recoverable under the said award. That however does not mean that the liability to pay the undisputed amount which has already been incurred by ONGC disappears. It would not be fair on the part of ONGC to withhold the amount which in any case is admittedly due and payable. The Western Company can accept the amount without prejudice to its rights and contentions to claim a larger amount. No prejudice will be occasioned to ONGC by making the payment of the admitted amount regardless of the fact that the Western Company is claiming a larger amount. And in any case, ONGC which seeks an equitable relief cannot be heard to say that it is not prepared to act in a just and equitable manner regardless of the niceties and nuances of legal arguments. These are the reasons which make us take the view that the restraint order deserves to be made conditional on the ONGC paying the undisputed dues at an early date subject to final adjustments in the light of final determination of the dispute.

22.   We accordingly allow this appeal and, direct as under:

I

The appeal is allowed. The order passed by the Bombay High Court on April 3, 1986 is set aside. The order passed by the Bombay High Court on January 20, 1986 is restored subject to the conditions engrafted hereafter.

II

The appellant ONGC shall pay to the Respondent Western Company, in the manner indicated hereinafter, the amount payable at the undisputed rate of $18,500 per day for the period as computed by the Umpire in his award amounting to $2,528,339 along with interest at 12% till the date of payment.

* * *

Appeal allowed.

NATIONAL THERMAL POWER CORPORATION
v. THE SINGER COMPANY

India, Supreme Court of India, 1992.
80 All India Rep. S.C. 998 (1993).*

THOMMEN, J.:—Leave granted.

2. The National Thermal Power Corporation ("NTPC") appeals from the judgment of the Delhi High Court ... dismissing the NTPC's application to set aside an interim award made at London by a tribunal constituted by the International Court of Arbitration of the International Chamber of Commerce ("ICC Court") in terms of the contract made at New Delhi between the NTPC and the respondent—the Singer Company ("Singer")—for the supply of equipment, erection and commissioning of certain works in India. The High Court held that the award was not governed by the [Indian] Arbitration Act, 1940; the arbitration agreement on which the award was made was not governed by the law of India; the award fell within the ambit of the Foreign Awards (Recognition and Enforcement) Act, 1961 (Act 45 of 1961) (the Foreign Awards Act); [and] London being the seat of arbitration, English Courts alone had jurisdiction to set aside the award; * * *

3. The NTPC and the Singer entered into two formal agreements dated 17–8–1982 at New Delhi. The General Terms and Conditions of Contract dated 14–2–81 (the "General Terms") are expressly incorporated in the agreements and they state:

"the laws applicable to this Contract shall be the laws in force in India. The Courts of Delhi shall have exclusive jurisdiction in all matters arising under this Contract." (7.2).

The General Terms deal with the special responsibilities of foreign contractors * * *

4. * * * [Clause 27(7) provides:]

"27.7. In the event of foreign Contractor, the arbitration shall be conducted by three arbitrators, one each to be nominated by the Owner and the Contractor and the third to be named by the President of the International Chamber of Commerce, Paris. Save as above all Rules of Conciliation and Arbitration of the International Chamber of Commerce shall apply to such arbitrations. The arbitration shall be conducted at such places as the arbitrators may determine."

In respect of an Indian Contractor, sub-clauses 6.2 of clause 27 says that the arbitration shall be conducted at New Delhi in accordance with the provisions of the Arbitration Act, 1940. It reads:

* Reprinted with permission of All India Reporter Pvt. Ltd.

"27.6.2. The arbitration shall be conducted in accordance with the provisions of the Indian Arbitration Act, 1940 or any statutory modification thereof. The venue of arbitration shall be New Delhi, India."

The General Terms further provide:

"the Contract shall in all respects be construed and governed according to Indian laws." (32.3).

The formal agreements which the parties executed on 17–8–82 contain a specific provision for settlement of disputes. Article 4.1 provides:

"4.1. Settlement of Disputes: It is specifically agreed by and between the parties that all the differences or disputes arising out of the contract or touching the subject matter of the contract, shall be decided by process of settlement and arbitration as specified in clause 26.0 and 27.0 excluding 27.6.1 and 27.6.2, of the General Conditions of the Contract."

5.   * * * [T]he dispute which arose between the parties was referred to an Arbitral Tribunal constituted in terms of the rules of arbitration of the ICC Court ("ICC Rules"). In accordance with Article 12 of those Rules, the ICC Court chose London to be the place of arbitration.

* * *

8.   The award was made in London as an interim award in an arbitration between the NTPC and a foreign contractor on a contract governed by the law of India and made in India for its performance solely in India. The fundamental question is whether the arbitration agreement contained in the contract is governed by the law of India so as to save it from the ambit of the Foreign Awards Act[d] and attract the provisions of the Arbitration Act, 1940. Which is the law which governs the agreement on which the award has been made?

* * *

21.   As regards the governing law of arbitration, Dicey says:

"Rule 58.—(1) The validity, effect and interpretation of an arbitration agreement are governed by its proper law.

(2) The law governing arbitration proceedings is the law chosen by the parties, or, in the absence of agreement, the law of the country in which the arbitration is held." (Vol. I, Pages 534–535)

22.   The principle in Rule 58, as formulated by Dicey, has two aspects—(a) the law governing the arbitration agreement, namely, its proper law; and (b) the law governing the conduct of the arbitration, namely, its procedural law.

---

d.   Authors' note: India implemented the New York Convention through the Indian "Foreign Awards Act"; however, Section 9 of that act excludes from the act's coverage "any award made on an arbitration agreement governed by the law of India."

23. The proper law of the arbitration agreement is normally the same as the proper law of the contract. It is only in exceptional cases that it is not so even where the proper law of the contract is expressly chosen by the parties. Where, however, there is no express choice of the law governing the contract as a whole, or the arbitration agreement as such, a presumption may arise that the law of the country where the arbitration is agreed to be held is the proper law of the arbitration agreement. But that is only a rebuttable presumption. See Dicey, Vol. 1, p. 539; *Whitworth Street Estates (Manchester) Ltd. v. James Miller & Partners Ltd.*, 1970 AC 583, 607, 612 and 616.

24. The validity, effect, and interpretation of the arbitration agreement are governed by its proper law. Such law will decide whether the arbitration clause is wide enough to cover the dispute between the parties. Such law will also ordinarily decide whether the arbitration clause binds the parties even when one of them alleges that the contract is void, or voidable or illegal or that such contract has been discharged by breach or frustration. The proper law of arbitration will also decide whether the arbitration clause would equally apply to a different contract between the same parties or between one of those parties and a third party.

25. The parties have the freedom to choose the law governing an international commercial arbitration agreement * * * as well as the procedural law governing the conduct of the arbitration. * * * Where there is no express choice of the law governing the contract as a whole, or the arbitration agreement in particular, there is, in the absence of any contrary indication, a presumption that the parties have intended that the proper law of the contract as well as the law governing the arbitration agreement are the same as the law of the country in which the arbitration is agreed to be held. On the other hand, where the proper law of the contract is expressly chosen by the parties, as in the present case, such law must, in the absence of an unmistakable intention to the contrary, govern the arbitration agreement which, though collateral or ancillary to the main contract, is nevertheless a part of such contract.

26. Whereas, as stated above, the proper law of arbitration (i.e., the substantive law governing arbitration) determines the validity, effect, and interpretation of the arbitration agreement, the arbitration proceedings are conducted, in the absence of any agreement to the contrary, in accordance with the law of the country in which the arbitration is held. On the other hand, if the parties have specifically chosen the law governing the conduct and procedure of arbitration, the arbitration proceedings will be conducted in accordance with that law so long as it is not contrary to the public policy or the mandatory requirements of the law of the country in which the arbitration is held. If no such choice has been made by the parties, expressly or by necessary implication, the procedural aspect of the conduct of arbitration (as distinguished from the substantive agreement to arbitrate) will be determined by the law of the place or seat of arbitration. Where, however, the parties have, as in the instant case, stipulated that the arbitration between them will be conducted in accordance with the ICC Rules, those rules, being in many respects self-contained or self-regulating and constituting a contractual code of procedure, will govern the conduct of the arbitration, except insofar as they conflict with the mandatory requirements of the proper law of arbitration, or of the procedural law of the seat of arbitration. See the observation of Kerr, LJ, in Bank Mellat v. Helliniki Techniki SA, (1983) 3 All ER 428. To such an extent the appropriate courts of the seat of arbitration, which in the present case are the competent English courts, will have jurisdiction in respect of procedural matters concerning the conduct of arbitration. But the overriding principle is that the Courts of the country whose substantive laws govern the arbitration agreement are the competent Courts in respect of all matters arising under the arbitration agreement, and the jurisdiction exercised by the Courts of the seat of arbitration is merely concurrent and not exclusive and strictly limited to matters of procedure. All other matters in respect of the arbitration agreements fall within the exclusive competence of the Courts of the country whose laws govern the arbitration agreement. * * *

27. The proper law of the contract in the present case being expressly stipulated to be the laws in force in India and the exclusive jurisdiction of the Courts in Delhi in all matters arising under the contract having been specifically accepted, and the parties not having chosen expressly or by implication a law different from the Indian law in regard to the agreement contained in the arbitration clause, the proper law governing the arbitration agreement is indeed the law in force in India, and the competent Courts of this country must necessarily have jurisdiction over all matters concerning arbitration. Neither the rules of procedure for the conduct of arbitration contractually chosen by the parties (the ICC Rules) nor the mandatory requirements of the procedure followed in the Courts of the country in which the arbitration is held can in any manner supersede the overriding jurisdiction and control of the Indian law and the Indian courts.

28. This means, questions such as the jurisdiction of the arbitrator to decide a particular issue or the continuance of an arbitration or the frustration of the arbitration agreement, its validity, effect, and interpretation are determined exclusively by the proper law of the arbitration agreement, which, in the present case, is Indian law. The procedural powers and duties of the arbitrators, as for example, whether they must hear oral evidence, whether the evidence of one party should be recorded necessarily in the presence of the other party, whether there is a right of cross-examination of witnesses, the special requirements of notice, the remedies available to a party in respect of security for costs or for discovery etc. are matters regulated in accordance with the rules chosen by the parties to the extent that those rules are applicable and sufficient and are not repugnant to the requirements of the procedural law and practice of the seat of arbitration. The concept of party autonomy in international contracts is respected by all systems of law so far as it is not incompatible with the proper law of the contract or the mandatory procedural rules of the place where the arbitration is agreed to be conducted or any overriding public policy.

* * *

33. * * * An award rendered in the territory of a foreign State may be regarded as a domestic award in India where it is sought to be enforced by reason of Indian law being the proper law governing the arbitration agreement in terms of which the award was made. The Foreign Awards Act, incorporating the New York Convention, leaves no room for doubt on the point.

* * *

37. A "foreign award", as defined under the Foreign Awards Act, 1961 means an award made on or after 11–10–1960 on differences arising between person(s) out of legal relationships, whether contractual or not, which are considered to be commercial under the law in force in India. To qualify as a foreign award under the Act, the award should have been made in pursuance of an agreement in writing for arbitration to be governed by the New York Convention on the Recognition and Enforcement of Foreign Arbitral Awards, 1958, and not to be governed by the law of India. Furthermore, such an award should have been made outside India in the territory of a foreign State notified by the Government of India as having made reciprocal provisions for enforcement of the Convention. These are the conditions which must be satisfied to qualify an award as a "foreign award" (S.2 read with S.9).

38. An award is "foreign" not merely because it is made in the territory of a foreign State, but because it is made in such a territory on an arbitration agreement not governed by the law of India. An award made on an arbitration agreement governed by the law of India, though rendered outside India, is attracted by the saving clause in S.9 of the Foreign Awards Act and is, therefore, not treated in India as a "foreign award".

39. A "foreign award" is (subject to S.7) recognised and enforceable in India "as if it were an award made on a matter referred to arbitration in India" (S.4) * * *

40. Section 7 of the Foreign Awards Act, in consonance with Art. V of the New York Convention which is scheduled to the Act, specifies the conditions under which recognition and enforcement of a foreign award will be refused at the request of a party against whom it is invoked.

41. A foreign award will not be enforced in India if it is proved by the party against whom it is sought to be enforced that * * * [one of the exceptions in Article V of the New York Convention applies.]

42. The Foreign Awards Act contains a specific provision to exclude its operation to what may be regarded as a "domestic award" in the sense of the award having been made on an arbitration agreement governed by the law of India, although the dispute was with a foreigner and the arbitration was held and the award was made in a foreign State.

* * * Such an award necessarily falls under the Arbitration Act, 1940, and is amenable to the jurisdiction of the Indian Courts and controlled by the Indian system of law just as in the case of any other domestic award, except that the proceedings held abroad and leading to the award were in certain respects amenable to be controlled by the public policy and the mandatory requirements of the law of the place of arbitration and the competent Courts of that place.

* * *

45. Significantly, London was chosen as the place of arbitration by reason of Article 12 of the ICC Rules which reads:

> "The place of arbitration shall be fixed by the International Court of Arbitration, unless agreed upon by the parties."

The parties had never expressed their intention to choose London as the arbitral forum, but, in the absence of any agreement on the question, London was chosen by the ICC Court as the place of arbitration. London has no significant connection with the contract or the parties except that it is a neutral place and the Chairman of the Arbitral Tribunal is a resident there, the other two members being nationals of the United States and India respectively.

* * *

49. The arbitration clause must be considered together with the rest of the contract and the relevant surrounding circumstances. In the present case, as seen above, the choice of the place of arbitration was, as far as the parties are concerned, merely accidental in so far as they had not expressed any intention in regard to it and the choice was made by the ICC Court for reasons totally unconnected with either party to the contract. On the other hand, apart from the expressly stated intention of the parties, the contract itself, including the arbitration agreement contained in one of its clauses, is redolent of India and matters Indian. The disputes between the parties under the contract have no connection with anything English, and they have the closest connection with Indian laws, rules and regulations. In the circumstances, the mere fact that the venue chosen by the ICC Court for the conduct of arbitration is London does not support the case of Singer on the point. Any attempt to exclude the jurisdiction of the competent Courts and the laws in force in India is totally inconsistent with the agreement between the parties.

50. In sum, it may be stated that the law expressly chosen by the parties in respect of all matters arising under their contract, which must necessarily include the agreement contained in the arbitration clause, being Indian law and the exclusive jurisdiction of the courts in Delhi having been expressly recognised by the parties to the contract in all matters arising under it, and the contract being most intimately associated with India, the proper law of arbitration and the competent Courts are both exclusively Indian, while matters of procedure connected with the conduct of arbitration are left to be regulated by the contractually chosen rules of the ICC to the extent that such rules are not in conflict with the public policy and the mandatory requirements of the proper law and of the law of the place of arbitration. The Foreign Awards Act, 1961 has no application to the award in question which has been made on an arbitration agreement governed by the law of India.

51. The Tribunal has rightly held that the "substantive law of the contract is Indian law". The Tribunal has further held "the laws of England govern procedural matters in the arbitration".

52. All substantive rights arising under the agreement including that which is contained in the arbitration clause are, in our view, governed by the laws of India. In respect of the actual conduct of arbitration, the procedural law of England may be applicable to the extent that the ICC Rules are insufficient or repugnant to the public policy or other mandatory provisions of the laws in force in England. Nevertheless, the jurisdiction exercisable by the English Courts and the applicability of the laws of that country in procedural matters must be viewed as concurrent and consistent with the jurisdiction of the competent Indian Courts and the operation of Indian laws in all matters concerning arbitration in so far as the main contract as well as that which is contained in the arbitration clause are governed by the laws of India.

53. The Delhi High Court was wrong in treating the award in question as a foreign award. The Foreign Awards Act has no application to the award by reason of the specific exclusion contained in S.9 of that Act. The award is governed by the laws in force in India, including the Arbitration Act, 1940. Accordingly, we set aside the impugned judgment of the Delhi High Court and direct that Court to consider the appellant's application on the merits in regard to which we express no views whatsoever. * * *

Jan Paulsson,[e] COMMENT, THE NEW YORK CONVENTION'S MISADVENTURES IN INDIA

Mealey's Int'l Arb'n Rep., June 1992 (Vol. 7, Issue 6), at 18–21*

In two salient recent cases involving arbitral awards rendered in London, the courts of India have revealed an alarming propensity to exercise authority in a manner contrary to the legitimate expectations of the international community.

In Oil & Natural Gas Commission v. Western Company of North America, 1987 All India Reports SC 674, excerpted in XIII Yearbook Commercial Arbitration 473 (1988), the Supreme Court held not only that the Indian courts had jurisdiction to hear an action brought by the losing Indian party to set aside the award, but upheld an Indian court's

e. (Mr. Paulsson is a partner at the firm of Freshfields, Paris; Vice–President, London Court of International Arbitration; Co–Author, ICC Arbitration [2nd Ed. 1990].

The author had no involvement in the cases discussed.)

* Reprinted by permission of Jan Paulsson.

order that the winning American party desist from enforcement actions in the United States pending the Indian action.[1] The basis for the Court's decision was that Indian law applied to the arbitration agreement, and that the courts of the country whose law governs the arbitration agreement must have jurisdiction to deal with the subsequent award in the same way that it might deal with domestic awards.

In National Thermal Power Corporation v The Singer Corp. et al. * * * the same Court on 7 May 1992 similarly decided that the Indian courts had jurisdiction to hear an action to set aside a partial award rendered in London. The award had held that while Indian law was the proper law of the contract, English law governed matters of procedure; that the arbitration was not prevented by contractual time bars; and that neither the claims nor the counterclaim were barred by time limitations under Indian law. Again, the Court focused on the fact that Indian law was substantively applicable, and that this applicability extended to the arbitration clause itself.

The Court writes, at paragraph 23: "The proper law of the arbitration agreement is normally the same as the proper law of the contract." This is unremarkable. But after embroidering on this theme, the judgment suddenly makes a quantum leap in paragraph 26:

"... the overriding principle is that the courts of the country whose substantive laws govern the arbitration agreement are the competent courts in respect of all matters arising under the arbitration agreement, and the jurisdiction exercised by the courts of the seat of arbitration is merely concurrent and not exclusive and strictly limited to matters of procedure. All other matters in respect of the arbitration agreement fall within the exclusive competence of the courts of the country whose laws govern the arbitration agreement."

This, it is submitted, is simply untrue. At the end of the just-quoted passage, the Court cites four well-known English treatises: Mustill and Boyd, Redfern and Hunter, Russell on Arbitration, and Cheshire & North. But it does so *without referring to specific pages*. The fact is that none of these authorities support the radical thesis propagated by the Indian court. The scholarly references are, to put it charitably, window dressing.

Under Article V(1)(a) of the New York Convention, it would be open to a losing party to argue *before the enforcement court* that the arbitration agreement was invalid "under the law to which [the parties] have subjected it." That might mean that evidence of Indian law would be relevant to an enforcement court in, say, New York. It does not mean that Indian courts have competence by virtue of some "overriding principle."

---

1. See the vigorous criticism of M. Tupman, "Staying Enforcement of Arbitral Awards under the New York Convention," 1987 Arbitration International 209; and a rebuttal by V.S. Deshpande, "Jurisdiction Over 'Foreign' and 'Domestic' Awards in the New York Convention," 1991 Arbitration International 123.

The earlier *ONGC* decision had held that the New York Convention was irrelevant, since the Indian courts had not been asked to enforce a foreign award. They had been asked to entertain an application to set aside an award which, although it had been rendered in London, was governed by Indian law; so the only question was whether as a matter of Indian law they had jurisdiction to do so.

The *Singer* decision took an entirely different course, stating in paragraph 8 that the "fundamental question" was whether the Foreign Awards Act 1961 (which implemented the New York Convention in India) was applicable. The Court considered that the award was not "foreign" for the purposes of the New York Convention, and that therefore the Convention did not apply—thus opening the door to whatever panoply of remedies might be available under local law.

It is submitted that these two Indian decisions misunderstand the New York Convention in a dangerous fashion, *ONGC* in subverting general principles of the post-award process which have emerged as international consensus over the course of the last 30 years and *Singer* in disregarding the text of the Convention. These are examples of parochial overreaching by a national legal system. It is to be hoped that the trend will be reversed in India, and not copied elsewhere. For now, India stands alone in this respect; no other legal system has adopted such an aggressively nationalistic posture. The position elsewhere is illustrated by the French Minister of Justice's Report to Parliament introducing what was to become the 1981 Decree on international arbitration, where it is flatly stated:

> "the possibility to bring before a French judge an action for annulment against an award made abroad is excluded." (Quoted in J.L. Delvolve, Arbitration in France, at 96 (1982)).

In *Singer*, the Court's reasoning is long on affirmation (one might be tempted to say repetition) and short on textual analysis. There are numerous citations to English authorities relating to the concept of the proper law, but the New York Convention is never quoted at all.

In fact, one need look no further than Article I(1) of the Convention to find the following relevant provision:

> "This Convention shall apply to the recognition and enforcement of arbitral awards made in the territory of the State other than the State where the recognition and enforcement of such awards are sought, and arising out of differences between persons, whether physical or legal. It shall also apply to arbitral awards not considered as domestic awards in the State where their recognition and enforcement are sought."

This language would clearly cover an award rendered abroad, even if—as was the case in *Singer*—the applicable substantive law was that of the enforcement jurisdiction. There is apparently a current of thinking in the Indian legal community which would want to change two words in the last sentence: to delete the word "also" and to move the word "not" so that the sentence would read:

"It shall *not* apply to arbitral awards * * * considered as domestic awards in the State where their recognition and enforcement are sought."

In the *Singer* judgment, the only semblance of rebuttal of the true text of Article I(1) appears in paras. 37 and 38, where the Court writes:

To qualify as a foreign award under the Act, the award should have been made in pursuance of an agreement in writing for arbitration to be governed by the New York Convention on the Recognition and Enforcement of Foreign Arbitral Awards, 1958, and not to be governed by the law of India * * *

An award is 'foreign' not merely because it is made in the territory of a foreign State, but because it is made in such a territory on an arbitration agreement not governed by the law of India. An award made on an arbitration agreement governed by the law of India, though rendered outside India, is attracted by the saving clause in S.9 of the Foreign Awards Act and is, therefore, not treated in India as a 'foreign award'.

The crucial middle sentence of this passage has no foundation in the New York Convention. But apparently Section 9 of the Indian Foreign Awards Act 1961 provides that:

Nothing in this Act shall

* * *

(b) apply to any award made on an arbitration agreement governed by the law of India.

If the effect of this Indian Act is to oblige Indian courts to rewrite Article I(1) of the New York Convention in the manner just described, then perhaps the Indian courts are correctly applying Indian law, but with a graver implication: India is in violation of its international obligations as a signatory of the New York Convention.

The unfortunate potential consequences of these two decisions can hardly be exaggerated. They could lead to dangerous and doubtless escalating rivalry between competing legal systems. * * * [T]hey would result in "concurrent" jurisdiction between the court of the place of arbitration and those of the country whose law governs the arbitration agreement. Doubtless such a conception of the international arbitral process would ultimately lead some arbitrators not to confront the issue of applicable law until they have decided the merits of the case, and then to exercise their imagination to find that the law applicable to the arbitration agreement was *not* that of the losing party—so as to protect the award from attacks in that party's home courts. That would regrettably put expedience before principle. Furthermore, it could provoke courts into disregarding arbitrators' findings of applicable law. The result would be a grave erosion of the authority of arbitrators. Much of the international acceptance of arbitration, achieved by painstaking efforts since 1958, would be imperilled.

These kinds of reactions would likely be but the beginning of a spiral of one-upmanship, irreversibly damaging the valuable mechanisms of the international arbitral process.

It would be an unfortunate mistake to view this as a matter of favouring "Western" arbitration over Third World court systems. Rather, what is at stake is the reliability of *neutral* mechanisms for the resolution of international commercial disputes. That such mechanisms can be made to work in the interest of parties from developing countries should be beyond cavil. (See J. Paulsson, "Third World Participation in International Investment Arbitration," 1988 *ICSID Review—Foreign Investment Law Journal* 19.) To the extent that reliance on these mechanisms is shaken by attitudes like that shown in the *Singer* decision, parties will be more hesitant to venture into the international arena, and will insist on terms that compensate for the legal risk. There would be a disincentive to any long-term transactions (particularly investments) and to entrepreneurial cooperation.

Looking again at the *Singer* decision, one notes that, in addition to the arbitration clause, the relevant contract provided that:

> the laws applicable to this contract shall be the laws in force in India. The Courts of Delhi shall have exclusive jurisdiction in all matters arising under this Contract.

Furthermore, the contract did not specify a place of arbitration, but simply referred to the arbitration rules of the ICC. Under its rules, the ICC was thus to select the venue. It could have chosen Delhi (which would have been somewhat coherent with the just-quoted reference to the "exclusive jurisdiction" of the courts of that city), but it preferred London (doubtless justified by the weightier competing consideration of neutrality).

Under these circumstances, it would have been preferable for the Indian courts, if they were dead set on asserting jurisdiction, to have done so on the basis of the contractual reference to the courts of Delhi. That would still leave a contradiction with the New York Convention, but a more palatable one, since (1) the parties could be said to bear the responsibility for having brought the contradiction down upon themselves by drafting such a clause, and (2) this approach would allow one to view the *Singer* case as one of limited application. Although Article V(1)(e) of the New York Convention allows non-recognition of awards set aside by "a competent authority of the country in which, *or under the law of which*, that award was made," there are few illustrations in practice of international contracts that contemplate arbitration in country A all the while providing that the law of country B shall govern the conduct of the arbitration and that its courts shall have "exclusive jurisdiction".

The six just underlined words in Article V(1)(e) do not *grant* jurisdiction to the courts of the country whose laws govern the arbitration.[2] Jurisdiction would have to be *asserted* by those courts. The thrust of this commentary is that it would be grievously wrong for them to do so in the absence of an unusual contractual stipulation giving them such authority.

Unfortunately, while it is true that the Supreme Court in *Singer* repeatedly quotes the parties' contractual reference to the courts of Delhi, its purpose in so doing is not to act on the contractual stipulation of exclusive Indian *jurisdiction*, but simply to buttress the rather uncontroversial finding (already made by the arbitrators) that the *applicable law* was that of India. That in turn led it to the deeply regrettable conclusion that the Indian courts had jurisdiction because Indian law was applicable. Accordingly, *Singer* (like its predecessor *ONGC*) puts a cloud over all awards against Indian parties rendered outside India where Indian law may have some claim of substantive application.

It is to be hoped that the Indian legal system will find a way to reverse this deleterious holding and to reassure the international legal community of its intent to apply the New York Convention faithfully. Meanwhile, practitioners must be advised to attempt by all means, if they wish to ensure that contractual disputes may be resolved by arbitral awards enforceable anywhere under the New York Convention, to avoid subjecting their contracts to Indian law—or more specifically to subject the arbitration agreement to another law. Such is the practical effect of the *ONGC* and *Singer* decisions. Whether this evolution is in India's national interest would seem a fit subject of serious debate within its legal community.

Questions and Comments

1. The agreement under which ISEC sold to Bridas a 25% interest in Compania Standard Electric Argentina (CSEA) provided that it would be "governed by and construed under and in accordance with the laws of the State of New York." To authorize New York courts to assume jurisdiction to vacate, ISEC urged that the language "under the law of which, that award was made" in New York Convention Article V(1)(e) should be interpreted to mean "under the law governing the merits of the dispute." ISEC noted that this would ensure that the reviewing court was thoroughly familiar with the law governing the dispute. Is this argument convincing?

2. In rejecting ISEC's argument the court says: "(t)he whole point of arbitration is that the merits of the dispute will not be reviewed in the courts, wherever they be located." The court adds: "[t]hat this was the animating principle of the Convention, that the Courts should review arbitrations for procedural regularity but resist inquiry into the substantive

---

2. N.b. that Article V(1)(e) does not recognize any role for the courts of the country whose law governs the arbitration *agreement* (usually the same as that which governs the contract in general). What is contemplated here is a stipulation to the effect that the *arbitration* shall be conducted in accordance with the law of country X. Article V(1)(e) thus accommodates the rare cases where such a stipulation refers to a law other than the one of the place of arbitration.

merits of awards, is clear from the notes on this subject by the Secretary–General of the United Nations." Do you agree that the New York Convention's restrictive grounds for court review of awards is relevant to ISEC's argument?

3. In the Croatian case, appellant and the High Commercial Court differ in their interpretation of Article V of the New York Convention. The arguments rely, however, on the assumption that the New York Convention is relevant to a proceeding to set aside pending in a Croatian court. Is this assumption justified?

4. Although the New York Convention and the Model Law both use a territorial criterion, they formulate it differently. The Model law stresses the "place of arbitration," whereas the New York Convention refers to the "country in which the award was made." The country where arbitration takes place and the country where the award is made need not be the same. This is an added source of difficulty.

In Hiscox v. Outhwaite[29] the House of Lords drew a distinction between the "curial seat of arbitration", which was England (because the arbitration hearings were held there and English curial law applied), and the place where the award was made, which was Paris. In fact two of the arbitrators signed in London; but the third signed in Paris, stated that the award was done in Paris, and dispatched the award. The House of Lords concluded:

> A document is made when and where it is perfected. An award is perfected when it is signed, at any rate in the absence of something in the arbitration agreement or the rules under which the arbitration is conducted, requiring some further formality before the award becomes effective.[30]

On these grounds, the award was held to be a foreign award and hence subject to recognition and enforcement.[31]

The decision of the High Court—which was overturned by the House of Lords—had followed a different line of reasoning:

> * * * an arbitration which from its inception through to its penultimate stage has been rooted entirely in one country will be capriciously transferred to another territory simply and solely as a result of the fortuitous circumstance of the place of the signature of the award. Such a result would be highly unreasonable, and would cause great uncertainty, since the parties would not know the territory of the award until they knew where it had been signed.[32]

In a similar case, a French court reached a conclusion opposite to that of the House of Lords. In *Chimimportexport*[33] the parties agreed that the place

---

[29]. 3 All ER 641 (H.L.1991).

[30]. *Id.* at 646.

[31]. Adding to the confusion, the decision deemed English courts to be competent not only for recognition, but also for setting aside, thus treating the same court as "two separate courts with the judges wearing two different hats." *Id.* at. 647, 649. How can this result be explained?

[32]. *Hiscox v. Outhwaite*, L.R. 1991 Q.B.D. ___ (The Times 7 March 1991).

[33]. Versailles, filed Jan. 14, 1987 (unpublished). Cited in R. Fouchard/E. Gaillard/B. Goldman, Traité de l'arbitrage commercial international [Treatise of International Commercial Arbitration] 785, 923 (1996).

of arbitration was Paris, but on the award it was stated "done in Brussels" (*fait à Bruxelles*). The French court held that it was nevertheless a French award, and therefore a proceeding which would lie against a French award could be lodged.

How would you deal with the situation described in *Hiscox* and in *Chimimportexport*:

> — a) as a judge;
>
> — b) as legal advisor at the time when the arbitration clause is drafted?

5. In Spector v. Torenberg, reproduced infra in the next section (V.2.c), the U.S. District Court for the Southern District of New York (852 F.Supp. 201 (1994)), held that because the award involved foreign parties (although it was rendered in New York), the party relying on the award had a "choice of methods," and could seek either recognition or confirmation. At the same time, although Torenberg sought enforcement under the New York Convention, the District Court decided to consider Spector's motion to set aside. Do you agree with this approach?

6. In *Oil & Natural Gas Commission v. Western Co. of N. America*, the Indian Supreme Court reasoned: "If the award in question is permitted to be enforced in USA without its being affirmed by a Court in India or a USA Court, it would not be in conformity with law, justice or equity."[34] Do you agree?

7. The Indian Supreme Court also asserted: " * * * Western Company is seeking to violate the very arbitration clause on the basis of which the award has been obtained by seeking confirmation of the award in the New York Court under the American Law." Do you agree with this view?

8. The Court emphasized that: "Life is infused into the award in the sense of its becoming enforceable only after it is made a rule of the Court upon the judgment and decree in terms of the award being passed. The American Court would have therefore enforced an award which is a lifeless award in the country of its origin, and under the law of the country of its origin * * *." Should a "lifeless award" have another chance outside the country of its origin?

9. Assuming it had jurisdiction to set aside the award, was the Indian Supreme Court justified in enjoining Western from proceeding with its action in New York?

10. In *National Thermal Power Corporation v. The Singer Company*, the Supreme Court of India asserted:

> "The fundamental question is whether the arbitration agreement contained in the contract is governed by the law of India so as to * * * attract the provisions of the Arbitration Act, 1940." Later it reasoned: " * * * [W]here the proper law of contract is expressly chosen by the parties, as in the present case, such law must, in the absence of an unmistakable intention to the contrary, govern the arbitration agreement * * * ." Since the Court did not find any "unmistakable intention to the contrary," it held that Indian law governs the arbitration agree-

---

[34]. 74 All India Rep. S.C. 674, at 680 (1987).

ment, and therefore the award may be considered as domestic in India. Is this understanding in conflict with the New York Convention?

11. The Court emphasized that the choice of London as the seat of arbitration was made by the ICC Court of Arbitration and not by the parties themselves. It thus concluded that the choice of London as the seat of arbitration was "merely accidental" and not an expression of the parties' intent and thus should not influence the issue of which forum should have jurisdiction (and what law should apply) to decide an action to set aside the award. Do you agree?

12. Paulsson argues that: "these two Indian decisions [*Western* and *Singer*] misunderstand the New York Convention in a dangerous fashion. * * *" He adds: "These are examples of parochial overreaching by a national legal system." Do you concur? If you see overreaching, do you see it in both cases?

13. In *Western*, two actions of the Indian Court may conceivably be qualified as "overreaching": a) treating the award as an Indian award, and b) enjoining Western from proceeding in a New York court. What is your assessment of these actions?

14. Paulsson says:

The unfortunate potential consequences of these two decisions can hardly be exaggerated. They could lead to dangerous and doubtless escalating rivalry between competing legal systems. * * * [T]hey would result in 'concurrent' jurisdiction between the courts of the place of arbitration and those of the country whose law governs the arbitration agreement.

If this is true, does the fault lie in the two Indian decisions, the ambiguity of the Indian Act, or the wording of the New York Convention?

Questions and Comments on the Two Indian Decisions in Light of the New 1996 Indian Arbitration and Conciliation Act

[See the selected provisions of the 1996 Indian Arbitration and Conciliation Act included in the Documents Supplement and consider the two Indian decisions, *Western* and *Singer*, in the light of these provisions.]

1. Will the decision of the Supreme Court of India in *National Thermal Power Corp. v. The Singer Company* that "an award rendered in the territory of a foreign state may be regarded as a domestic award in India where it is sought to be enforced by reason of Indian law being the proper law governing the arbitration agreement in terms of which the award was made" continue to be good law under the Arbitration and Conciliation Act, 1996 ("1996 Act")?

Section 2(2) of the 1996 Act states that Part I of the 1996 Act applies if the situs of arbitration is India. This is so even in an international commercial arbitration when the laws applicable to the substance of the dispute are foreign. This conclusion follows from Section 2(2) and Section 28(b). This means that such an award can be set aside in India on the grounds enumerated in Part I of the 1996 Act. The grounds follow those enumerated in Article V of the New York Convention. See Section 34 of the 1996 Act.

2. In *Singer* the place of arbitration was foreign; accordingly Part I of the 1996 Act does not apply to *Singer*, at least not by virtue of Section 2(2).

Part II Chapter 1 Section 44 of the 1996 Act describes "foreign awards" as those to which the New York Convention applies. Article I of the New York Convention provides that the Convention applies to an award made in a State other than the State where enforcement is sought. The *Singer* award was made in London and enforcement was being sought in New Delhi. Hence the New York Convention would apply to an action in India to recognize and enforce the *Singer* award.

3. In *Singer*, however, the action in India was to set aside the award, not to recognize and enforce it. The National Thermal Power Corporation argued that the parties had chosen Indian law as the lex arbitri and that hence India had jurisdiction to set aside the award. Note that Section 2(2) of the 1996 Act states that Part I (which contains the setting aside provisions in Section 34) applies "where the place of arbitration is in India". It does not say "**only** where the place of arbitration is in India." Note that the UNCITRAL Model Law, which was the model for the 1996 Act (see the Preamble to the 1996 Act, first "Whereas"), provides in Article 1(2) that certain provisions of the Act—including the setting aside provisions—apply "***only*** if the place of arbitration is in the territory of this State." (emphasis added) Thus, the Indian Act varies from the Model Law by omitting the word "only".

4. Under the 1996 Act is an Indian court precluded from applying the *Singer* analysis? The Foreign Awards Act, 1961 stands repealed by the 1996 Act and so does its saving clause, Section 9(b). On the other hand, since Section 2(2) of the Act does not say that the setting aside provisions apply "only" if the place of arbitration is in India, could an Indian court interpret the Indian setting aside provisions to apply where the parties expressly choose Indian lex arbitri, even where the place of arbitration is in a country other than India? This is of course the *Singer* case, at least as interpreted by the Indian Supreme Court. What would you expect the result to be if the *Singer* fact pattern arises again before Indian courts?

V.2.c. Public Policy, Fraud, and Evident Partiality as Grounds for Setting Aside

SPECTOR v. TORENBERG

United States District Court, Southern District of New York, 1994.
852 F.Supp. 201.

LEISURE, DISTRICT JUDGE:

Background

On January 19, 1989, David Spector, the president of Specurity Industrial Ltd. ("Specurity"), an Israeli corporation, entered into a shareholders agreement (the "Shareholders Agreement") with respondents Dov Torenberg, an American citizen, Ximena Florez, a resident American alien, Nicolas Fucci, an American citizen, and TRS Computers, Ltd., a New York corporation. The Shareholders Agreement provided for the distribution of one-third of the shares of stock of Microguard, Inc. ("Microguard"), a New York corporation, to each of the following: (1) Spector and his wife; (2) Torenberg and Florez, and (3) Fucci and TRS.

Microguard was created for the purpose of importing and marketing PC–Guard, a device manufactured by Specurity which is designed to protect the security of personal computers. Accordingly, on January 30, 1989, Specurity entered into an exclusive distribution agreement (the "Distribution Agreement") with Microguard, which established minimum annual purchases of PC–Guard over a four year period. Both the Shareholders Agreement and the Distribution Agreement contain arbitration clauses and choice of law clauses specifying New York law.

Specurity made its first shipment of PC–Guard on July 27, 1989. Microguard made a 25% downpayment but failed to pay the balance. On January 9, 1990, Torenberg wrote Spector a letter indicating that Microguard would not fulfill the remaining terms of the contract. Then, on March 19, 1990, Microguard, Torenberg and Florez made a demand for arbitration proceedings claiming that Spector had "made false statements * * * about the performance and success" of PC–Guard, which was in fact "defective and unmerchantable." They further asserted that in reliance upon these representations, they had contributed money, time, and energy to founding and running Microguard, and had entered into both the Distribution and Shareholders Agreements. Respondents sought the following relief: (1) rescission of both agreements; (2) restitution of monies paid to Spector and Specurity; (3) compensatory damages; and (4) a declaratory judgment that termination of the Distribution Agreement was Specurity's sole remedy for Microguard's alleged failure to purchase further units of PC–Guard as set forth in the Distribution Agreement. On May 11, 1990, Spector and Specurity filed a counter-demand for Arbitration, alleging breach of contract, and seeking damages, declaratory relief, specific relief and reasonable attorney's fees.

Arbitration took place in the Southern District of New York over a period of three years. By a partial final award signed on May 20, 21, and 28, 1993 (the "May Award"), the arbitrators (1) found Spector and Specurity jointly and severally liable in the amount of $25,772.00 plus interest to Microguard, (2) found Spector and Specurity jointly and severally liable in the amount of $34,205.00 plus interest and $21,650 in arbitral costs to Microguard, Torenberg and Florez, and (3) dismissed petitioners' claim with prejudice. By an award signed August 9 and 16, 1993 (the "August Award"), the arbitrators found Spector and Specurity jointly and severally liable for the attorney's fees of Microguard, Torenberg, and Florez in the amount of $5,000.00, and of Fucci and TRS in the amount of $33,092.50.

Four days later, on August 20, 1993, Spector and Specurity brought the instant petition to vacate or modify the August Award, contending that the arbitrators had no authority to award attorney's fees and that the award was the result of evident partiality and misconduct by the arbitrators. Petitioners also claimed the award was irrational and contradictory because it awarded damages to Microguard, which either no longer existed or, if it did exist, was not [sic] wholly owned by Spector because Florez and Torenberg had ceded their interest in Microguard to him in a letter dated January 9, 1990.

On September 2, 1993, respondents Torenberg and Florez wrote to the arbitration panel requesting a modification of the August Award to address petitioners' claim that the award was irrational because damages were awarded in part to Microguard. The arbitrators responded by issuing a modification, dated October 14, 19, and 20, 1993 (the "October Award"). In it, Spector and Specurity were directed to pay Torenberg and Florez the amounts previously awarded Microguard.

Discussion

I. Standard of Review

An arbitral award may be enforced under the Convention on the Recognition and Enforcement of Foreign Arbitral Awards (the "Convention") if it was "pronounced in accordance with foreign law or involv[es] parties domiciled or having their principal place of business outside the enforcing jurisdiction." Bergesen v. Joseph Muller Corp., 710 F.2d 928, 932 (2d Cir.1983).[3] An award fitting this description is enforceable under the Convention even if it is also enforceable under the Federal Arbitration Act (the "FAA"). This "overlapping coverage" provides a party with a choice of methods by which to enforce an award in its favor, a choice that in Bergesen permitted the party seeking enforcement to benefit from the longer statute of limitations applicable to enforcement actions under the Convention.

In the instant case, respondents have exercised their right to seek confirmation of their award under the Convention pursuant to 9 U.S.C. § 207 since the award involves foreign parties. Respondents mistakenly contend, however, that petitioners are therefore foreclosed from seeking to vacate the award under the FAA. Section 10 of the FAA provides that "[t]he United States court in and for the district wherein the award was made may make an order vacating the award upon the application of any party to the arbitration." 9 U.S.C. § 10. This provision clearly vests the Court with the authority to vacate the award at issue herein. The question, then, is whether the Convention negates this authority, which it does not.

The Convention provides that the enforcement of an award may be refused when "the award ... has been set aside or suspended by a competent authority of the country in which, or under the law of which, that award was made." See Convention, Art. V(1)(e). Since the award at issue in this case was made in the United States, this Court is plainly a competent authority within the meaning of Article V(1)(e). See generally International Standard Elec. Corp. v. Bridas Sociedad Anonima, 745

---

3. Such an award is one "not considered as domestic" within the meaning of Article I of the Convention. Id. at 932 n.2.

F.Supp. 172, 178 (S.D.N.Y.1990) (holding that only a court of the country in which the award was made may vacate the award). Accordingly, rather than foreclosing this Court from vacating the award, the Convention explicitly acknowledges the authority of this Court to do so.[4]

The bases upon which an award may be vacated under the FAA are set forth in Section 10 thereof as follows:

(a) Where the award was procured by corruption, fraud, or undue means.

(b) Where there was evident partiality or corruption in the arbitrators, or either of them.

(c) Where the arbitrators were guilty of misconduct in refusing to postpone the hearing, upon sufficient cause shown, or in refusing to hear evidence pertinent and material to the controversy; or of any other misbehavior by which the rights of any party have been prejudiced.

(d) Where the arbitrators exceeded their powers, or so imperfectly executed them that a mutual, final, and definite award upon the subject matter submitted was not made.

9 U.S.C. § 10.

In addition to these statutory grounds, it is well settled that a court may vacate an award when the arbitrators manifestly disregarded the law in reaching their decision. Folkways Music Publishers, Inc. v. Weiss, 989 F.2d 108, 111–12 (2d Cir.1993). Manifest disregard will be found where an "arbitrator 'understood and correctly stated the law but proceeded to ignore it,' " Siegel v. Titan Industrial Corp., 779 F.2d 891, 893 (2d Cir.1985) (citation omitted), or where "error must have been obvious and capable of being readily and instantly perceived by the average person qualified to serve as an arbitrator." Merrill Lynch, Pierce, Fenner & Smith, Inc. v. Bobker, 808 F.2d 930, 933–34 (2d Cir.1986).

A party moving to vacate an arbitration award has the burden of proof, and the showing required to avoid confirmation is very high. This limited judicial review reflects the desire to "avoid undermining the twin goals of arbitration, namely, settling disputes efficiently and avoiding long and expensive litigation." Folkways, 989 F.2d at 111. As the Court of Appeals for the Second Circuit has observed, "[a]rbitration cannot achieve the savings in time and money for which it is justly renowned if it becomes merely the first step in lengthy litigation." National Bulk

---

4. It may also be observed that 9 U.S.C. § 207 does not restrict this Court's authority for it does no more than reaffirm the principles of the Convention. 9 U.S.C. § 207 provides that the Court shall "confirm the award unless it finds one of the grounds for refusal or deferral of recognition or enforcement of the award specified in the said Convention." Since the Convention permits the Court to refuse enforcement of an award that the Court has vacated, the Court may therefore deny confirmation of the award under 9 U.S.C. § 207 upon this basis.

Carriers, Inc. v. Princess Management Co., 597 F.2d 819, 825 (2d Cir.1979).

* * *

IV. Evident Partiality and Misconduct

Petitioners' third basis for seeking vacatur of the award is that the award was a product of "evident partiality" and "misconduct" within the meaning of 9 U.S.C. § 10(b) and (c).

In general, courts have been reluctant to set aside awards based on a claim of evident partiality. An award should only be set aside on this basis when "a reasonable person would have to conclude that an arbitrator was partial to one party to the arbitration." Morelite Constr. Corp. v. New York City Dist. Council Carpenters Ben. Funds, 748 F.2d 79, 84 (2d Cir.1984).

Petitioners claim that the partiality of one of the arbitrators, Lawrence N. Weiss, was demonstrated by his conduct during the arbitration proceedings. Petitioners contend that early in the proceedings, Mr. Weiss discussed the authority of the panel to impose sanctions on petitioners for frivolous litigation, thus suggesting that he had prejudged the case. In addition, petitioners contend that Mr. Weiss allegedly coached respondents' witnesses. Finally, petitioners contend that a comment by Mr. Weiss during the hearings suggests he had an anti-Israeli bias that worked to the disadvantage of Spector, who is Israeli. In substance, Mr. Weiss allegedly commented that Israel's policy of preventing money from leaving the country to go the United States was ridiculous in light of the United States' financial support of Israel.[6]

Considering these allegations in their entirety, the Court finds no evident partiality. With respect to Mr. Weiss's comments on sanctions, an arbitrator is not precluded from developing views regarding the merits of a dispute early in the proceedings, and an award will not be vacated because he expresses those views. In addition, what petitioners characterize as the coaching of witnesses, this Court views as in keeping with the relative informality of arbitral proceedings.[7] See generally id. Finally, with respect to Mr. Weiss's alleged anti-Israeli comment, respondents note that Torenberg also has Israeli connections, as he was born in Israel, served in the Israeli army, and worked for the Israeli airline.

---

6. No transcript of the hearings was made on the day Mr. Weiss made his comment, so the precise language of this comment is unavailable.

7. The following, for example is an exchange to which petitioners object:

Q. You don't know of any bugs in the DOS No. 4 and why the marketing of this DOS was stopped?

A. I have no personal knowledge on that.

Weiss: I don't know that the marketing of DOS 4 was stopped. The manufacturers never made a serious attempt to market DOS 4.0 as a replacement for 3.3. Am I right about that, Mr. Torenberg?

A. That's right.

Affidavit of Michael A. Roth, sworn to on August 19, 1993, at & 39.

Even were this not true, Mr. Weiss's comments do not suggest a degree of animus sufficient to call his objectivity into question.

Petitioners also contend that Mr. Weiss engaged in misconduct by having an ex parte communication with Torenberg. This conversation, of which petitioners caught the tail-end, took place during a break in the hearings with a stenographer present[8] and concerned a computer problem that Mr. Weiss had once had. In order to vacate an award based on an ex parte conversation, a party must show that this conversation deprived him of a fair hearing and influenced the outcome of the arbitration. Generally, the subject matter of the conversation must have gone to the heart of the dispute's merits, and an award will therefore not be vacated if the conversation concerned a merely peripheral matter.[9] * * * see Metropolitan Property & Cas. Ins. Co. v. J.C. Penney Cas. Ins. Co., 780 F.Supp. 885, 893 (D.Conn.1991) (enjoining the participation of arbitrator who had discussed merits of case before hearing). In the instant case, petitioners have failed to make a showing sufficient to vacate the award. The subject matter of the conversation between Mr. Weiss and Mr. Torenberg was not directly related to the merits of the dispute being arbitrated.[10] Moreover, the circumstances of their conversation do not evince any attempt at secrecy that might provoke deeper concerns regarding their purposes.

Accordingly, the Court does not find that there is a sufficient basis to vacate the award based on evident partiality or misconduct.

* * *

Conclusion

For the reasons stated above, the Court hereby denies the petition to vacate or modify the arbitration award and grants the petition to confirm the award. Respondents' motion for attorney's fees incurred in this enforcement action is denied. Respondents are directed to prepare and submit a form of judgment consistent with this Order, to be entered by this Court, no later than June 3, 1994.

SO ORDERED.

8. Petitioners do not deny that the stenographer was present during the conversation. See Petitioners' Reply Memorandum at 11.

9. The Court recognizes, however, that the burden may shift to the party seeking confirmation to demonstrate the absence of prejudice if the party seeking vacatur makes a preliminary showing that the ex parte contacts were carried out in secretive or conspiratorial manner.

10. Thus, this case is distinguishable from Goldfinger v. Lisker, 68 N.Y.2d 225, 508 N.Y.S.2d 159, 500 N.E.2d 857 (1986), cited by petitioners. In that case, the arbitrators's communication "was deliberate in nature and designed clearly to enable [the arbitrator] to resolve in his own mind any doubt he may have had as to [the witness's] credibility or the validity of the claim itself." Id., 68 N.Y.2d at 234, 508 N.Y.S.2d at 163, 500 N.E.2d at 861.

United Nations Commission on International Trade
Case Law on Uncitral Texts (Clout)

A/CN.9/SER.C/ABSTRACTS/10

16 August 1996

ORIGINAL: ENGLISH

* * *

Cases Relating to the Uncitral Model Arbitration Law (Mal)

MAL 146: 18, 34(2)

Russian Federation: Moscow City Court

10 November 1994

Original in Russian

Unpublished

The plaintiff, whose claim in arbitration proceedings had been dismissed, filed an application to have the award set aside on the grounds that in the course of the arbitration proceedings article 18 of the Russian Federation Act on "international commercial arbitration" (corresponding to art. 18 MAL) had been violated in that the parties had not been treated with equality and the award was in conflict with public policy.

The plaintiff argued that the decision to dismiss the claim had been made despite the fact that the defendant partially acknowledged the claim brought against it. In that regard, the court held that such acknowledgment did not constitute grounds for setting aside the award since, in making the award, the arbitrators were not bound by an acknowledgment of the claim.

Since the plaintiff failed to establish that the award was in conflict with public policy, its claim in that respect was found to be unjustified. At the same time, the court noted that a procedural infringement in the arbitral proceedings had no relevance to the notion of "public policy".

On the basis of the facts presented, the court dismissed the plaintiff's application to set aside the arbitral award.

* * *

EUROPEAN GAS TURBINES SA (FRANCE)
v. WESTMAN INTERNATIONAL LTD.
(UNITED KINGDOM)

France, Cour d'appel [Court of Appeal], 1993.
20 Yearbk. Comm. Arb'n 198 (1995).*

Facts

On 11 December 1985, Alsthom Turbines à Gaz SA (Alsthom)—the predecessor of European Gas Turbines SA (EGT)—and Westman International Ltd. (Westman) concluded a contract under which Westman

---

* Reprinted with permission of Yearbook Commercial Arbitration, International Council for Commercial Arbitration.

undertook to assist Alsthom in obtaining first the "pre-qualification" and then the contract for the supply of gas turbines for a petrochemical project at Arak, Iran. The pre-qualification was a first selection by the main contractor, the National Petrochemical Company of Iran (NPC), aiming at limiting the number of companies which could submit an offer.

The contract read (from the French translation of the English original):

"Westman shall have the role of promoting Alsthom's gas turbines in order to have Alsthom specially pre-qualified for the project.

In case of special pre-qualification, Westman shall transmit to Alsthom all possible information and communicate its suggestions for supporting Alsthom's offer.

During the negotiations, Westman shall give Alsthom all advice which may be useful in order to obtain the contract under the best possible conditions.

After the contract has been signed, Westman shall give Alsthom all assistance which can be reasonably expected for the good execution of the present contract."

The contract was concluded for three years and provided for a commission fee covering "the expenses of all nature borne by Westman in order to perform its task"; the amount of the commission was to be "determined by mutual agreement before Alsthom submits its offer" (Art. 4). Further, "Westman shall not be entitled to any indemnity of any kind" if Alsthom "does not receive an order for the project during the [contract's] period of validity" (Art. 6). Art. 6 also provided, however, that "if Alsthom is pre-qualified for the project within ... two years and it obtains the contract within six months after the present agreement has expired, Alsthom shall pay to Westman half the fee provided for in Art. 4 above".

The contract provided for the application of French law and for ICC arbitration.

By a letter of 9 July 1987, NPC requested Alsthom to communicate whether it was interested in the Arak petrochemical project and, if it was, to send all "useful" information for "the evaluation of your company".

By a letter of 2 September 1987, Westman informed Alsthom that the latter had been pre-qualified for the Arak project together with other three companies and, on 11 July 1988, it requested "confirmation of the percentage of the commission which shall be paid ... by Alsthom upon being granted the contract".

By letters of 18 July and 16 September 1988, Westman, alleging "considerable expenses", requested Alsthom to agree to a negotiation to determine the amount of the commission.

By a letter of 1 March 1989, Alsthom informed Westman that it did not intend to renew the contract of 11 December 1985, which had expired on 11 December 1988. On 12 March 1989, Alsthom and NPC signed the supply contract for gas turbines.

By a letter of 23 May 1989, Westman suggested that the commission be determined at "3% of all the sums received by [Alsthom] for supplying gas turbines for the Arak project." When Alsthom turned down the suggestion, Westman initiated ICC arbitration as provided for in the contract. Arbitration took place in Paris.

On 2 July 1991, the arbitral tribunal re-opened the arbitral proceedings in order to request Westman to submit a detailed report of its expenses for the Arak project. On 9 July 1991, Westman submitted a list of expenses for a total amount of 7,104,983.00 Swiss francs, including personnel's salaries and the rent of an office in Teheran.

An arbitral award in favour of Westman was rendered on 21 March 1992. The award read (French original):

> "[The arbitral tribunal] holds that there is a contract between the parties, aiming at obtaining a contract to supply gas turbines to National Petrochemical Company in the context of the petrochemical project at Arak, Iran;
>
> It qualifies the contract as a *sui generis* contract combining a brokerage contract (*contrat de courtage)* and a contract for work (*contrat d'entreprise*);
>
> It holds that the contract is valid;
>
> It holds that Westman has proven that it performed its obligation to obtain Alsthom's pre-qualification;
>
> It holds that Westman was prevented by Alsthom from performing its obligations after Alsthom's pre-qualification;
>
> It holds that Alsthom is bound to pay a commission of 4% of the amount of the contract granted by NPC;
>
> It directs Alsthom to pay Westman 5,712,240 Swiss francs, augmented, if applicable, by the effect of the commission on the delay interest which NPC may have to pay to Alsthom . . . ."

Alsthom, which had by then changed its company name to European Gas Turbines SA (EGT), sought annulment of the award before the Court of Appeal of Paris, alleging that the award's enforcement would violate public policy on two grounds: first, because the award gave effect to a contract which was null and void as its real object was traffic in influence and bribery; second, because it was based on a fraudulent report of expenses submitted by Westman in the arbitration. An expert report by an accounting firm, submitted by EGT in the annulment proceedings, showed that Westman had not paid any rent or salaries for the Arak pre-qualification.

The Court of Appeal dismissed EGT's first ground for annulment, finding that there was no proof of the fact that the 1985 contract was an illicit contract of traffic in influence. However, it found that the second ground for annulment was partially well-founded, and that some parts of the arbitral award were affected by the fraud committed by Westman in the arbitration. It therefore annulled the award insofar as it was based on Westman's fraudulent accounts, applying the general principle of law *fraus omnia corrumpit*, with the exception of the arbitrators' finding that a valid *sui generis* contract (combining a brokerage contract and a contract for work) had been concluded by the parties.

Excerpt

I. Contract Is Illicit

[1] "First ground for annulment: the arbitral award violates French public policy and international public policy as its enforcement in France would give effect to an illicit contract the aim and object of which being traffic in influence or the payment of bribes."

[2] "EGT maintains that it considered it advisable to conclude the contract of 11 December 1985 because 'it did not want ... to run the risk of excluding Westman, as it did not know how much [Westman] could influence the persons granting the contract [EGT] sought to obtain' ..., and then essentially relies upon the following arguments:

— The conclusion of "a contract of traffic in influence or payment of bribes' ..., which, according to French law ... is null and void because [the contract's] aim or object are immoral or illicit, violates French public policy as well as 'morality in international commerce, so much so that this prohibition is considered a general principle of law";

— The arbitral tribunal's findings and evaluations do not bind the Court, which may examine all legal and factual elements of the ground for annulment;

— The real nature of the contract of 11 December 1985 can only be determined by an "accumulation" of indications (*indices*). Those submitted to the arbitrators ... (the uselessness of the intervention of an intermediary in "an adjudication procedure on a tender", the "evasive" character of the contractual provisions as to Westman's "performance", the expressions used in the "internal memos" addressed by Westman's Teheran "office" to its London headquarters, the absence of contacts between Alsthom and the main contractor established by Westman, the absence of an activity report, of "working documents" for the main contractor's information and of a mail exchange between Westman and the latter, the conditions for the payment of the commission and the manner of calculation of the same, the payment of the commission in a "numbered account in Switzerland") all show in [EGT's] opinion a "real and evident" absence of [any activity on the part of] Westman;

— he documents concerning Westman's activity, drawn up by Touche and Ross, chartered accountants, on the basis of the Companies House of London's register, and submitted in the present annulment proceedings equally reveal Westman's "total inactivity";

— The total absence of any activity on the part of Westman proves the "necessarily illicit character of the performance intended by [Westman], as not corresponding to any real and evident activity", and, therefore, the real nature of the contract, which is a "contract of traffic in influence and payment of bribes";

— The drawing up and submission before the arbitral tribunal of the detailed report of expenses and its annexes, which are "'false certifications" aimed at "proving before the arbitral tribunal a fictitious activity which conceals a traffic in influence for which [Westman] sought to be paid".

[3] "Westman essentially relies upon the arbitrators' reasons for finding that the contract of 11 December 1985 was valid.... In a later statement, [Westman] maintains that the expenses mentioned in the report of expenses and its annexes, submitted to the arbitral tribunal, do not appear in its 'accounts' filed with the London commercial register because these expenses 'have been borne directly by (its) shareholders,' to whom they will be reimbursed after 'recovery' of the amount of the commission, so that said expenses, incurred 'by third persons on its behalf ... have not been registered as a debt of the company'".

* * *

[4] "Corruption is sanctioned in French law (with the exception of tax law, where it is somewhat tolerated in international commercial relations for reasons typical to this subject matter), both in criminal law (be it active or passive ...) and in civil law, where contracts aiming at corruption or traffic in influence are null and void because their aim or object is immoral or illicit (Art. 1133 of the Civil Code),[1] if the immoral or illicit aim is known to the parties, on the basis of the adage *nemo auditur propriam turpitudinem allegans.*

[5] "The parties' awareness of the immoral or illicit aim of the contract, required by jurisprudence, is not meant (whatever its actual consequences may be) to lessen the rigor of the sanction of nullity; on the contrary, it aims at reinforcing it by protecting the contracting party who has nothing to reproach himself with as to the conclusion of the contract; the application of the above-mentioned adage aims at preventing performance of an immoral or illicit contract by depriving the party which first executes it of all protection.

[6] "A contract having as its aim and object a traffic in influence through the payment of bribes is, consequently, contrary to French international public policy as well as to the ethics of international commerce as understood by the large majority of States in the international community.

[7] "The power, granted to the arbitrator in international arbitration, to ascertain whether a contract is licit in the light of the rules of international public policy, and to sanction its being illicit by holding that it is null and void implies, in annulment proceedings based on the

---

1. Art. 1133 of the French Civil Code reads: "A *causa* is illicit when it is prohibited by law, or when it is contrary to morality or public policy."

allegation that the recognition or enforcement of the arbitral award would be contrary to international public policy (Art. 1502(5) of the New Code of Civil Procedure),[2] a review of the award by the annulment court. This review concerns all legal and factual elements justifying (or not) the application of the international public policy rule, and in former case, the evaluation of the validity of the contract according to this rule. A different conclusion would deprive the court's control of all efficacy and, therefore, of its *raison d'être*.

[8] "The arbitral tribunal rightly held that it does not result from the intrinsic analysis of the provisions of the contract of 11 December 1985 that Westman 'undertook to exercise an influence over NPC (the main contractor) in order to obtain the pre-qualification' ..., a statement which is not in any way contested by the parties.

[9] "The indications of this aim relied upon by EGT in the arbitral proceedings do not lead to the certain inference that there was no activity on the part of Westman and, even less, that the contract of 11 December 1985 was illicit because its aim or object was a traffic in influence or the payment of bribes.

[10] "In fact, particularly if we take into account [Westman's] alleged knowledge of the local customs for a 'pre-qualification', aimed at selecting, according to criteria apparently not precisely defined, the enterprises admitted to the tender, the task of broker (*courtier*) entrusted to Westman by the contractual provisions and, in the light of the importance and complexity of the contract, its task of advisor for the submission of the offer and of technical assistant for the execution of the contract cannot be regarded as being totally useless.

[11] "The allegedly 'evasive' character of the contractual provisions defining 'Westman's activity for Alsthom's pre-qualification' ('promoting Alsthom's gas turbines') cannot be considered an expression of [Westman's] intention to conceal a contract of traffic in influence or payment of bribes, since, according to the uncontested findings of the arbitrators * * *, Alsthom itself drew up the contract of 11 December 1985 (apart from 'three minor modifications').

[12] "The 'internal memos' * * *—the authenticity of which is, however, contested by EGT—do not reveal, in the absence of [further] details, any actual activities which can be qualified as traffic in influence.

[13] "The arbitral tribunal also rightly noted that in the context of the task of promoting Alsthom for the 'pre-qualification', the contract of 11 December 1985 'did not provide that Westman had to report to Alsthom' * * * that [NPC]'s letter of 9 July 1987 to Alsthom regarding the above-mentioned purpose shows that there was 'a rapprochement' between these companies in view of the 'pre-qualification' of Alsthom

---

2. Art. 1502 of the New French Code of Civil Procedure reads in relevant part:

"An appeal against a decision granting recognition or enforcement may be brought only in the following cases:

. . .

5. If the recognition or enforcement is contrary to international public policy."

* * *; and that Alsthom made no reproaches to Westman as far as its performance as a broker for the 'pre-qualification' was concerned * * *

[14] "The stipulation of a performance fee conditioned on the performance's success does not in itself characterize a 'contract of traffic in influence or payment of bribes', since it is not proven nor even alleged that this stipulation does not correspond to a current usage in the field of international brokerage contracts.

[15] "The existence of a bank account in Switzerland in which Westman asked that the commission be paid * * * does not as such establish that the aim and object of the contract are illicit.

[16] "Furthermore, the contractual provisions which subordinate Westman's right to a commission covering 'the expenses of all nature' incurred in order to accomplish its task to obtain the pre-qualification of Alsthom are hardly compatible with [Westman's] alleged intention to conceal a bribery contract under a brokerage contract for the 'pre-qualification' as provided for in the contract, since in that case, if [Alsthom] were not granted the pre-qualification, [Westman] would not have obtained reimbursement of the bribes paid.

[17] "However, the documents submitted in the present annulment proceedings ... reveal that [Westman] did not sustain any of the expenses that it certified it made and, therefore, that it did not perform in any way under the contract of 11 December 1985.

[18] "Furthermore, Westman has proven at present neither that it has undertaken to reimburse the expenses which its shareholders allegedly bore under the contract of 11 December 1985, nor even that these expenses were made by the shareholders.

[19] "However, the non-performance by Westman of its contractual obligation to promote the gas turbines in view of 'Alsthom's pre-qualification' (as it results from the documents in the file) and its concealing of this lack of activity through the submission of a fallacious report of expenses in the arbitral proceedings do not necessarily imply that, under cover of a brokerage contract and a contract for work, the contract of 11 December 1985 was in reality, according to the common will of the parties or in the intention of one of them, Westman, a contract having as its aim and object a traffic in influence or the payment of bribes.

[20] "Hence, on the one hand, the arbitral tribunal, after having examined the contractual provisions and the indications relied upon by EGT in the arbitral proceedings, correctly held that the contract could not be qualified as such and, on the other hand, the documents filed in the present annulment proceedings are not such as to affect this finding.

[21] "The ground for nullity of the award based on its being contrary to international public policy, because of the fact that the contract of 11 December 1985 is a contract for traffic in influence and payment of bribes and therefore illicit, must be rejected."

II. *Fraud in the Arbitral Proceedings*

[22] "Second ground for nullity: the award is contrary to international public policy as its enforcement would lead to sanctioning a fraud committed by Westman during the arbitral proceedings.

[23] "EGT maintains that Westman committed a fraud by submitting to the arbitral tribunal a detailed report of expenses, certifying that they were incurred in order to perform its task, whereas it did not bear any of these expenses. [EGT also maintains] that this fraud 'necessarily affected' the decision of the arbitral tribunal, not only as to the latter's evaluation of the amount of the commission but also as to its understanding of Westman's real activity, since, 'in the absence of any expense, the arbitral tribunal would have necessarily concluded that the contract at issue could only be a contract for the payment of bribes'. . . .

[24] "Westman denies that it 'sought to mislead' the arbitral tribunal, noting that its expenses report contains the following words: 'the amount of the commission for this kind of activity is speculative and is not calculated or determined on the basis of the expenses borne' and also denies, in any case, that the alleged fraud influenced the decision of the arbitral tribunal, since the latter evaluated 'the performance under the contract * * * on the basis of the whole of the documents submitted by the parties and their exchange of statements in the proceedings' and held that 'since Alsthom has been pre-qualified, Westman is presumed to have fulfilled its obligations as to the promotion of the gas turbines of Alsthom in view of [Alsthom's] pre-qualification'.

[25] "By reopening the discussion phase of the proceedings in order to request Westman to submit an expenses report—although that document, which originates with one of the parties, has in itself no probative force—the arbitral tribunal showed that it considered [this aspect] particularly important.

[26] "Under these circumstances, Westman's drawing up and submitting an erroneous report to create the false impression that it had borne high expenses for performing its task under the contract of 11 December 1985 is a fraud and not a sleight of hand (*habileté*).

[27] "If, in the absence * * * of other sufficiently probative elements, such fraud does not lead in itself to concluding with certainty that there was a contract for traffic in influence or payment of bribes, it results however from the arbitral award itself ('taking into account the accounts submitted by Westman * * * ') that the arbitral tribunal took the voluntarily erroneous report of expenses into consideration, in order to determine the commission which it held was due to Westman.

[28] "Further, this fraud—which also reveals that Westman did not bear any of the expenses on which it relied to prove the performance of its contractual obligation to promote Alsthom for the 'pre-qualification', and its right to the payment of a commission—is such as to set aside the simple presumption of performance of the contract which the arbitral tribunal derived from 'Alsthom's pre-qualification' * * * and

even to deprive Westman of its right to request reimbursement, ex Art. 4 of the contract, of the considerable expenses which it has not borne. The fraud committed by Westman in the arbitral proceedings, which influenced the arbitrators' evaluation of the commission, is also such as to affect [Westman's] right to payment of the commission.

[29] "Hence, with the exception of its finding that there was 'a contract between the parties, aiming at obtaining a contract to supply gas turbines to National Petrochemical Company in the context of the petrochemical project at Arak, Iran', that this contract is a *'sui generis* contract combining a brokerage contract and a contract for work', and that it is valid, the dispositions of the arbitral award are affected by the fraud committed by Westman in the arbitral proceedings.

[30] "In application of the general principle of law according to which fraud is an exception to all rules *(fraus omnia corrumpit)*, these dispositions are contrary to French international public policy and must therefore be annulled."

* * *

III.   Conclusion

[31] "[The Court] rejects the request for annulment insofar as it is based on [the allegation that] the enforcement in France of the arbitral award would be contrary to international public policy, as [the award] gives effect to a contract having as its aim and object a traffic in influence or the payment of bribes.

[32] "As to the request for annulment [based on the allegation that] the enforcement in France of the arbitral award would be contrary to international public policy, as [the award] consecrates a fraud committed by Westman in the arbitral proceedings, [the Court] holds that the request is partially well-founded and consequently partially annuls the arbitral award insofar as the arbitral tribunal held:

— that Westman proved that "it performed its obligation to obtain Alsthom's pre-qualification";

— that Westman was "prevented by Alsthom from performing its obligations after Alsthom's pre-qualification";

— that Alsthom was "bound to pay a commission of 4% of the price of the contract granted by NPC" * * *

Questions and Comments

1. The U.S. Federal Arbitration Act [9 U.S.C. § 10(a),(b), and (c)] states explicitly as grounds for setting aside "corruption," "fraud," "evident partiality or corruption in the arbitration," and "misconduct of the arbitrators." These vices are not mentioned as bases for setting aside in the Model Law. Does this mean that awards cannot be set aside on the ground of fraud, corruption, or partiality in countries that have adopted the Model Law, or in countries that have limited the grounds for annulment essentially to those enumerated in the Model Law?

(Note that the 1986 Dutch Arbitration Act, in Article 1965, limits the grounds for setting aside essentially to those enumerated in Article 34 of the Model Law, but in Article 1068 it also provides a further recourse: Revocation of the award in case of fraud, forgery, or new documents).

2. The Moscow City Court decision stated that procedural infringements in the arbitral proceedings have no relevance to the notion of public policy. Do you agree? (The Russian Federation enacted its present Law on International Commercial Arbitration based largely on the Model law. The new Act has been in force since August 14, 1993. The grounds for setting aside are stated in article 34 and are essentially identical to those for refusing recognition set out in Article V of the New York Convention. The question confronting the Russian court was whether procedural reasons for setting aside are limited to those stated in Article 34(2)(a), thus relegating the public policy ground in Article 34(2)(b) exclusively to control of the merits).

3. Partiality can mean biased decision making or creating an appearance of bias. In the latter case the appearance of bias suggests a higher probability of actual biased arbitration. Does it make sense to consider appearance of bias, or likelihood of biased arbitration, after the award has been rendered? Should one restrict the partiality exception in setting aside proceedings to cases in which it is established that there was actual tampering with the outcome on the merits? What arguments could you raise pro and con?

4. In Commonwealth Coatings Corp. v. Continental Casualty Co.[35] the Supreme Court of the United States held that an appearance of bias may be a sufficient ground for setting aside an award. In *Commonwealth Coatings*, the key facts supporting an appearance of bias finding were (former) business ties of one of the arbitrators with the party prevailing in arbitration and the failure of the arbitrator to disclose these ties.[36] If you accept this line of reasoning in *Commonwealth Coatings*, would you also allow setting aside on the ground of potential bias evidenced by a negative attitude toward the losing party in arbitration? Could a negative attitude toward the larger community to which the losing party belongs also be relevant?

Would you classify the grounds which purported to substantiate evident partiality in the *Spector* case as allegations of appearance of bias (potential bias) or as allegations of actual tampering with the decision on the merits?

5. Suppose that arbitrator Weiss made a statement that was much more anti-Israeli than disagreeing with "Israel's policy of preventing money from leaving the country to go to the United States."[37] Suppose that Mr. Weiss (or some other arbitrator) said that "Israel does not deserve to be a state," or that "Israel is conducting racist policies toward Arabs." Would this be a ground for setting aside?

Would it matter whether the award was unanimous? Would it matter whether the arbitrator made these derogatory statements during a public lecture on the eve of the arbitration hearings, or whether the statements

[35]. 393 U.S. 145, 150 (1968).

[36]. Id. at 146.

[37]. Spector v. Torenberg at 209.

were made on the day of the hearing, during a coffee break with fellow arbitrators?

Is the nature of the dispute submitted to arbitration relevant?

6. In the *European Gas Turbines* case, a distinction was drawn between fraud, and "sleight of hand." What is your understanding of this difference?

The decision was confirmed by the Cour de cassation on December 19, 1995.[38] The Cour de cassation stressed that the fraud in question was "procedural fraud." Do you agree that what Westman did was fraud? Was it "procedural fraud?" How does fraud become relevant within the French system of limited grounds for setting aside?

According to Article 1504 of the French Code of Civil Procedure, an award rendered in international arbitral proceedings may only be set aside on one of the grounds which justify refusal of recognition and enforcement, and which are stated in Article 1502.

According to Article 1502:

"An appeal against a decision granting recognition and enforcement may be brought only in the following cases:

1. If the arbitrator decided in the absence of an arbitration agreement, or on the basis of a void or expired agreement;

2. If the arbitral tribunal was irregularly composed or the sole arbitrator irregularly appointed;

3. If the arbitrator decided in a manner incompatible with the mission conferred upon him;

4. Whenever due process has not been respected;

5. If the recognition or enforcement is contrary to international public policy."

V.2.d. Standard of Review

V.2.d.i. Judicial Deference—or Lack Thereof—to Arbitrator Discretion

TRANSPORT EN HANDELSMAATSCHAPPIJ "VEKOMA" B.V. (NETHERLANDS) v. MARAN COAL CORP. (U.S.A.)

Switzerland, Bundesgericht [Federal Court], 1995, unpublished.[f]

1. The Dispute

The parties' dispute in *Maran/Vekoma* concerned a cargo of coke breeze (a coal product used in the steel industry) delivered by Vekoma to

---

[38]. Reported in 1996 Revue de l'arbitrage 49.

f. Paul Friedland, attorney for the winning party in arbitration (the losing party in the court case) published a comment on the decision in 13 Journal of International Arbitration, March, 1996, at 111 (The Swiss Supreme Court Sets Aside an ICC Award).

The excerpts reproduced here are translated from the German original of the Bundesgericht decision, and in part they are taken from the Friedland article. To the extent that they are from the Friedland article, reprinting is with permission of Kluwer Law International.

Maran in 1991. The buyer contended that the cargo was so inter-mixed with coal that it could not be resold as coke breeze for the ordinary purpose for which coke breeze is used.

The seller denied that the cargo was defective and argued *inter alia* that the contract's penalty clause precluded recovery of the damages claimed. The seller also raised several threshold defenses, including the defense that the buyer's claim in arbitration was time-barred because the buyer had not filed its request for arbitration within the thirty-day deadline provided in the parties' contract. The contract was subject to Swiss law, and provided for ICC arbitration in Geneva.

The buyer filed its request for arbitration with the ICC on May 11, 1992.

In an award dated August 22, 1994, the ICC Tribunal found in favor of the buyer, and required the seller to pay US $657,442 (plus interest), plus costs and attorneys' fees of US $270,000.

The seller petitioned the Swiss Federal Court to set aside the award on the grounds that:

> (i) the arbitration was time-barred because the buyer had not met the thirty-day contractual deadline for resorting to arbitration—and therefore the arbitrators acted without having jurisdiction;

> (ii) the arbitrator appointed by the buyer allegedly lacked independence; and

> (iii) the seller had allegedly been denied its right to be heard when the ICC Tribunal declined the seller's post-hearing request that the Tribunal use Swiss court procedures to obtain certain evidence located outside Switzerland.

The seller cited Article 190, section 2, subsections a, b, and d of the 1987 Private International Law Act, as support for these arguments.

The critical issue in the case—and the one we shall focus on—is the seller's lack of jurisdiction claim based on Article 190(2)(b).

2. The Icc Tribunal's Ruling Regarding Jurisdiction

The arbitration clause in the parties' contract provided as follows:

Any dispute of whatever nature arising out of or in any way relating to the Contract or to its construction or fulfillment may be referred to arbitration; such arbitration shall take place in Geneva (Switzerland) and shall proceed in accordance with the rules of the International Chamber of Commerce. The said difference or dispute shall [be] so referred by either party within thirty days after it was agreed that the difference or dispute cannot be resolved by negotiation.

The ICC Tribunal found that, by using the phrase "may be referred to arbitration," the parties had provided for arbitration only as an option, rather than as a mandatory dispute resolution mechanism. The buyer in any event had opted for arbitration, and the clause indisputably required that the party choosing arbitration comply with the thirty-day requirement. The seller contended that that requirement had not been met, and that the buyer was therefore deprived of its arbitration option.

The key issue before the ICC Tribunal was what was contemplated by the parties when they provided that the thirty-day limitation period would be triggered when "it was agreed that the difference or dispute cannot be resolved by negotiation." The essential issue was when the parties had effectively "agreed that the difference or dispute cannot be resolved by negotiation." The arbitration award recites the following facts relevant to that issue.

In October 1991, the buyer notified the seller of the apparent non-conformity of the cargo and requested the seller's comments. The seller answered , expressing its willingness to investigate, and the parties then met twice to discuss the matter, but did not achieve any resolution.

On January 9, 1992, the buyer submitted a written claim to the seller, appending a schedule of costs, and ended its fax with the following statement:

> If you have any questions, we are, of course, prepared to answer them for you. In the meantime, we should like to have your reply as quickly as possible and no later than 17 January. If, by that time, you are not prepared to settle the claim, we shall most regrettably have to apply for arbitration under the terms of our contract.

The seller did not respond to the buyer's January 9th fax. Three months passed. On April 3, 1992, the buyer wrote: "We continue to await a response to the settlement proposal set forth in our [fax] to you dated 9 January 1992." On April 13, 1992, the seller answered that it: "had assumed that the subject was closed" and that it believed that it had "no outstanding obligations in respect of our contract".

On the basis of the foregoing, the seller argued to the ICC Tribunal that, when it did not comply with the buyer's January 17th deadline for responding to the buyer's January 9th settlement proposal, it became, or should have become, obvious that the seller had rejected the buyer's negotiation efforts. As of January 17th then, the seller argued, the parties must be deemed to have "agreed" that their dispute could not be resolved by negotiation, and hence the buyer had until February 17, 1992, to commence an arbitration. By failing to commence the arbitration until May 11, 1992, the buyer lost its right to resort to arbitration.

The ICC Tribunal rejected the seller's argument. The Tribunal first ruled that the parties' contract required an unequivocal agreement, whether express or implied, between the parties that negotiations had failed before the thirty-day period could be triggered.

The Tribunal then found, on the basis of disputed oral testimony, that the seller had, in late 1991, invited the buyer to submit a statement of its claim with substantiation, thereby signalling the seller's willingness to settle. The buyer's faxed proposal of January 9, 1992, constituted its response. Although the seller's silence after January 9th communicated its unwillingness to settle on terms advanced by the buyer, the Tribunal found that:

> (i) under the circumstances such silence was not an unequivocal statement that negotiations had definitely failed;

> (ii) the seller's silence was deliberate and not in good faith, and the seller could not be permitted to benefit from conduct incompatible with the principle of good faith; and

> (iii) the seller's final written communication (of April 13, 1992) showed that the seller had, in the interim, examined the matter in depth, thus indicating that its final decision had not been made as of January 17, 1992.

On the basis of these considerations, the ICC Tribunal concluded that the trigger date was not January 17th, but rather April 13, 1992, the date of the seller's final fax, and therefore the request for arbitration of May 11, 1992, was within the thirty-day contractual limitations period and timely.

3. The Swiss Supreme Court's Ruling Regarding Jurisdiction

The Swiss Supreme Court endeavored to set the framework and the limits of its scrutiny:

> A decision pertaining to jurisdiction in international commercial arbitration may be reinvestigated freely by the Bundesgericht (BG) from a legal point of view, while with respect to facts review is only possible within the limits of substantiated objections which claim that factual findings result from non-observance of procedural guarantees set by law (i.e. those set in Article 190/2/d and 182/3 of the Private International Law Act), or that they are incompatible with procedural ordre public. No party claimed that the factual findings of the contested award would result from an infringement of these guarantees. For these reasons the BG had to rely on facts established by the court of arbitration, and it had to examine whether the jurisdiction of the court of arbitration can be confirmed on ground of these facts.

Having set out this position, the BG continued:

> The jurisdiction of the court of arbitration is established on ground of the content of the arbitration clause ascertained by way of contract interpretation. The ICC arbitration tribunal in Geneva did not ascertain the meaning of the contract in an empirical, but rather in a normative manner (*nicht empirisch, sondern normativ ermittelt*). This is why the BG is allowed to exercise free legal control (*freie Rechtskontrolle*) within the framework of the principle of acting only upon motion (*im Rahmen des Rügeprinzips*).

The Swiss Supreme Court found that:

The thirty-day time-limit for initiating the arbitration starts running as soon as it becomes obvious to the parties, from an objective or normative point of view, that no amicable settlement can be reached.

Applying this standard, the Court then ruled that the seller's silence in response to the buyer's imposition of a January 17th deadline in its January 9th fax had to be interpreted by the buyer "as a dismissal of its offer and as a disagreement triggering the thirty-day period ..."

The BG also argues that if one would interpret the wording as requiring an explicit consent to trigger the 30 days period, any of the parties could have easily escaped arbitration by withholding such consent. It was held that this cannot be the right meaning of the agreement.

The Court further ruled that the seller's motivations for not responding to the buyer's January 9th fax were irrelevant, and that the buyer was obliged to accept the consequences of its unilateral imposition of a date by which the seller was supposed to respond.

On these grounds, the Court set aside the ICC award.

ARAB REPUBLIC OF EGYPT v. SOUTHERN PACIFIC PROPERTIES, LTD & SOUTHERN PACIFIC PROPERTIES (MIDDLE EAST), LTD.

France, Paris Court of Appeals, (1984).
23 Int'l Legal Materials 1048 (1984).*

Introductory Note[g]

In recent years, arbitrators have often been tempted to enlarge the scope of their own jurisdiction. This phenomenon occurs in regard to affiliated corporations when arbitrators assume jurisdiction over a parent company where only a subsidiary has signed the arbitration agreement and in regard to states when a state is subjected to arbitration solely by virtue of an arbitration clause entered into by a public entity under the state's authority or by virtue of its administrative approval of such contract. The decision reported below demonstrates the intention of the Court of Appeals of Paris to adhere to the parties' initial agreement in determining the scope of arbitration. As is stated in the decision, the rule that arbitrators have jurisdiction to rule on their own jurisdiction (competenz-competenz) does not bar judicial review of whether an arbitration clause is binding on all the parties.

As a result of the decree of May 12, 1981 [20 I.L.M. 917 (1981)], which erased the uncertainties of the previous case law [20 I.L.M. 883

---

g. Prepared by Emmanuel Gaillard, then Professor of International Law at the University of Lille, France. Currently, Professor, University of Paris XII; Managing Partner, Shearman & Sterling, Paris.

(1981)], French law grants such power of review over all awards rendered in France as well as over awards whose enforcement is sought in France. In both cases, the review, somewhat more limited than that permitted by the New York Convention, is restricted to the following grounds: (1) The arbitrator decided in the absence of an arbitration agreement or on the basis of a void or expired agreement; (2) The tribunal was irregularly composed or the sole arbitrator irregularly appointed; (3) The arbitrator decided in a manner incompatible with the mission conferred upon him; (4) Due process was not respected; (5) Recognition or enforcement would be contrary to international public policy (Article 1502 the new Code of Civil Procedure).

Pursuant to Article 1502(1), the Court set aside the ICC Award rendered in the case SPP and SPP (ME) v. The Arab Republic of Egypt and EGOTH [22 I.L.M. 752 (1983)], which held that the Egyptian State was bound by the arbitration clause in a contract between SPP and EGOTH when the Minister of Tourism affixed his signature on the bottom of the agreement after the words, "approved, agreed and ratified" and when there were no arbitration clauses in related contracts to which the government was undoubtedly a party. Contrary to the arbitrator's decision, the Court of Appeals ruled that this ratification did not constitute an agreement to enter into the contract but was only the approval given by the minister in his capacity as EGOTH's supervisory authority and that, therefore, there was no arbitration agreement binding on the State.

The decision, which was the first to set aside an award since the 1981 decree, should have a two-fold effect on arbitration in France. It provides greater security to the parties by ensuring that their initial legal arrangements will be respected. Also, by indicating the seriousness of the review exercised by the French Courts in the five instances of Article 1502, it should further the aims of the New York and Geneva Conventions, to which France is a party, in facilitating enforcement abroad of awards rendered in France, since foreign jurisdictions should not find it necessary to strengthen their own control mechanisms at the enforcement stage.

* * *

THE COURT: Concerning the Ground Based on Article 1502– 1 of the New Code of Civil Procedure, As for the A.R.E.'s Signature of the Terms of Reference:

———

WHEREAS it is a fact that the A.R.E., in accordance with the provisions of the I.C.C. Court of Arbitration Rules, responded to the Court's communications and signed the terms of reference as provided under Article 13;

WHEREAS it is however true that the appellant unceasingly contested the jurisdiction of the Arbitral Tribunal and that upon being informed of the claim of SPP and SPP–ME, alleged both the non-existence of any arbitration clause by which it might be bound as well as the State's sovereign immunity; that during the course of the proceedings, it persisted in denying that it was a party to the contract of December 12, 1974 and had signed no agreement containing an "I.C.C. arbitration clause";

WHEREAS appellees wrongfully assert that the terms of reference signed by the parties on May 3, 1980 constitute an arbitration agreement and that the A.R.E. is bound by the arbitrators' assessment of the facts and agreements submitted for their review, especially those concerning their own jurisdiction;

WHEREAS, in this case, the arbitration agreement consists only of the December 12, 1979 arbitration clause, on the grounds of which a request for arbitration was submitted by SPP and SPP–ME to the I.C.C. Court of Arbitration; the arbitrators were appointed in accordance with the Rules. Furthermore these Rules make a clear distinction between the arbitration agreement, as contemplated in Articles 7 and 8, and the terms of reference, whose main purpose is to define the issues to be determined and the arbitrators' mandate.

WHEREAS furthermore it would not be possible to explain how the terms of reference, in which the A.R.E. claims immunity from jurisdiction and maintains, before any argument on the merits, that there was no arbitration agreement, could replace such an agreement;

WHEREAS the fact of defending a case on the merits before a court after having raised its lack of jurisdiction cannot imply waiver of the jurisdictional defense;

WHEREAS the Egyptian State had legitimate reasons for defending the case on the merits, even before arbitrators whom it deemed to lack jurisdiction, in order to attempt to mitigate the prejudice which might result from an award against it;

WHEREAS it is also important to note that since the Arbitral Tribunal is the judge of its own jurisdiction, in fact the A.R.E. had to appear before it to manifest its opposition to its opponents' claims. This again underlines the difference between terms of reference, signed by a party anxious not to default, and an arbitration agreement characterized by the freely-expressed will of the parties to grant the arbitrators jurisdiction;

WHEREAS SPP and SPP–ME, which refuse to take into account the numerous and continuous reservations expressed by the A.R.E., are not entitled to allege that the A.R.E., in signing the terms of reference, expressed its will to see the dispute settled in accordance with the I.C.C. Rules; rather the Egyptian State always clearly manifested its intent not to be judged by the arbitration panel set up under the auspices of that body;

WHEREAS, moreover, it is an error to maintain that the arbitral tribunal had the power without being subject to review to rule on its jurisdiction and that the Court of Appeals can uphold the arbitrators' interpretation of the parties' intent, as inferred from the various elements argued before it; whereas if the arbitrators, whose jurisdiction is challenged, have the power to rule on the existence or validity of the arbitration agreement, it is no less certain that their ruling is subject to review by the Judge competent to set aside the award as provided for in Article 1504 of the New Code of Civil Procedure, such remedy being available "if there is no valid arbitration agreement or the arbitrator ruled on the basis of a void or expired agreement" (Article 1502 & First);

WHEREAS, if followed, appellees' reasoning would have the paradoxical effect of completely eliminating one of the recognized unrestricted powers of the Court and which is only the counterpart of the jurisdiction granted to arbitrators to rule on their own jurisdiction;

WHEREAS it should be noted that Article 24 of the ICC Rules contemplate the parties' waiver of their right to any form of appeal insofar as such waiver can validly be made—which is obviously not the case with the action now before this Court;

* * *

Concerning The Contract Of December 12, 1974

WHEREAS the Egyptian State did not appear among the persons having the capacity of parties to the transaction and, consequently, was not bound by it;

WHEREAS the approval of the Minister of Tourism as described above does not imply the will of the State to become a party to the contract by waiving its immunity from jurisdiction;

WHEREAS the notation "approved, agreed and ratified" must by understood in accordance with Egyptian law, which confers supervision of tourist sites upon the Ministry of Tourism (Statute no. 2–73) and grants him the power to approve the creation of economic complexes (Statute no. 60–71) as well as the creation, operation and management of tourist and hotel establishments (Statute no. 1–73);

WHEREAS these statutes, the latter two of which are cited in Article 21 of the agreement, convincingly account for the intervention by this minister, apart from any will to become a party to this contract, thus waiving the State's immunity from jurisdiction;

WHEREAS, furthermore, the three aforementioned words must also be construed in the context of the statement signed by the "contracting parties—EGOTH and SPP", which thereby agreed that the obligations placed the same day upon EGOTH would be "subject to the approval of the competent governmental authorities";

WHEREAS, in this regard, SPP and SPP–ME cannot claim, without contradicting themselves, that on the one hand, the signature affixed by the Ministry of Tourism manifests "the permanency of the State's commitment", and, on the other, that the joint Statement only concerns "various and routine administrative authorizations", which could have constituted an obstacle to the performance of the contract if not obtained;

WHEREAS, in reality, given the words employed, their location at the end of the document and the connection which must be made with the attached statement, it appears that the ratification which follows the signatures of SPP and EGOTH constitutes, not a solemn commitment by the State to enter into the contract, but specifically the material manifestation of approval by the supervising authority mentioned in the Statement;

WHEREAS the existence of said Statement thus provides clear confirmation that, even though the Minister of Tourism did indeed grant his approval, the Egyptian State was not itself a party to the contract;

WHEREAS, the arbitrators deemed the authorization of the Minister of Tourism, as supervising authority, to be redundant, even peculiar, and that its absence would not have affected the validity of the agreement;

WHEREAS such reasoning cannot be adopted since both SPP and EGOTH were entitled to consider it appropriate to specify that the obligations placed upon the latter were subordinate to such an agreement, which in addition is necessary as a matter of the Egyptian administrative practice that was to govern performance of the project;

WHEREAS it should also be noted that the second attachment to the contract—the confidential report—bore a manuscript notation indicated that it was the document "referred to in Article 4 of the contract signed December 12, 1974 between EGOTH and SPP" and that that notation is followed by the signatures of the representatives of EGOTH and SPP, who thereby again designate themselves as the only two parties bound by the agreement;

WHEREAS no decisive or even serious inference can be drawn from the fact that the last page of the contract was re-typed because Mr. Gilmour, unhappy with the simple notation "approving", had demanded some expression which would commit the Egyptian Government;

WHEREAS it suffices to observe that on the one hand, this circumstance has not been demonstrated, since Mr. Gilmour's statements constitute unsatisfactory evidence, and on the other hand, none of the terms used signifies a personal commitment by the Minister to assume responsibility for EGOTH's contractual obligations;

WHEREAS it is useful to note that the use here of the title "Minister of Tourism", whereas in the initial contract and the intervening draft it was "Minister of Tourism, representing the Government of the A.R.E.", which alone would have been unequivocal proof of the participation of the State in EGOTH's contractual commitments;

WHEREAS, even if it is not common for a supervisory authority to affix his authorization directly on the document submitted for his supervision, the exceptional nature of the negotiations in question could be sufficient to explain this circumstance;

WHEREAS, on the contrary, it should be emphasized that the parties carefully separated their signatures and that the Minister's signature was affixed separately and clearly placed at the end of the contract;

WHEREAS, in contrast to the Heads of Agreement of September 23, 1974 and to the ensuing Draft, the Agreement of December 12 contains only obligations upon SPP and EGOTH relating *inter alia* to their obligation to incorporate ETDC; whereas it is correct to believe that its wording would have been different if the Egyptian State had been considered a party to the document and whereas several of EGOTH's commitments would not have been set down in the form of best efforts obligations;

* * *

WHEREAS on December 12, 1974, Mr. Gilmour wrote to the A.R.E.'s Minister of Housing and Reconstruction to "confirm" that an agreement had been signed that day between EGOTH and SPP for the incorporation of ETDC and to discuss the infrastructures of each of the sites;

WHEREAS in that correspondence, Mr. Gilmour also alludes to the Agreement of September 25, 1974 between SPP, EGOTH and the Minister of Tourism, thereby making a clear distinction between the two documents; whereas in particular, although the latter agreement also deals with infrastructure, he refers uniquely in his relations with the Government to the initial Agreement;

WHEREAS, by another letter also of December 12, the recipient Minister responded by acknowledging the existence of the agreement between SPP and EGOTH and by guaranteeing that the contract of September 23, 1974 would be respected;

WHEREAS the necessity for accounting for the apportionment of authority among the ministers—as explained by appellees, cannot justify such an exchange of correspondence which once again demonstrates that at the very time the December 12 Contract and its attachments were signed, there was no doubt for the Egyptian Government or SPP's representatives as to the fact that those documents were binding only on SPP and EGOTH;

* * *

For These Reasons

SETS ASIDE award no. 3493, given on February 16, 1983 by the arbitration court set up under the auspices of the International Chamber of Commerce;

Orders Southern Pacific Properties, Ltd. ("S.P.P.") and Southern Pacific Properties (Middle East), Ltd. (S.P.P.–ME) to pay costs;

* * *

Questions and Comments

1. Concerning the *Maran Coal* decision, Paul Friedland had the following to say:

> [T]he conclusion is inescapable that the Supreme Court substituted its judgement for that of the ICC Tribunal with respect to what circumstances must have made it obvious to the parties that no settlement could be achieved. While professing to accept the factual findings made by the ICC Tribunal, the Supreme Court, in truth, simply found that the seller's silence in response to the buyer's 9 January fax communicated to the buyer something different than the ICC Tribunal had found it did. A determination as to what one party's act or omission communicated to the other party requires an appreciation of the factual context. The ICC Tribunal heard testimony (and had the benefit of a complete record) regarding that context. The Swiss Supreme Court did not, yet nevertheless arrogated to itself the power to disagree with the arbitrators and to set aside the arbitral award on the basis of its disagreement.[39]

Do you agree with this assessment?

How would you define the standard of review applied by the Swiss Supreme Court? Did it really revisit the facts?

2. According to Article 190(2) of the Swiss Private International Law Act:

"Action for setting aside the award may only be initiated:

(a) where the sole arbitrator has been incorrectly appointed, or where the arbitral tribunal has been incorrectly constituted;

(b) where the tribunal has wrongly declared itself to have or not to have jurisdiction;

(c) where the award has gone beyond the claims submitted to the arbitral tribunal, or failed to decide one of the claims;

(d) where the principle of equal treatment of the parties or their right to be heard in adversarial procedure has not been observed,

(e) where the award is incompatible with public policy."

Did the Swiss Federal Tribunal duly observe these standards?

Compare the standards for judicial review of a Swiss domestic award where all parties are domiciled in Switzerland. In such a case, the Swiss Intercantonal Arbitration Convention would apply. Article 36 of that Convention provides:

---

[39]. P. Friedland, *The Swiss Supreme Court Sets Aside an ICC Award*, 13 J. Intl.   Arb. 111, 114–115 (March, 1996).

"An action for annulment of the arbitration award may be brought * * *, where it is alleged that:

(a) the arbitral tribunal was not properly constituted;

(b) that the arbitral tribunal erroneously declared itself to have or not to have jurisdiction;

(c) that it pronounced on points not submitted to it * * *;

(d) that there was a breach of one of the mandatory procedural rules * * *;

(e) that the arbitral tribunal awarded to one of the parties something more or other than claimed, without being authorised to do so by a provision of the law;

(f) that the award is arbitrary in that it was based on findings which were manifestly contrary to the facts appearing on the file, or in that it constitutes a clear violation of law or equity. * * *"

Which set of Swiss standards involves more intrusive judicial review?

3. Should the standard of review be less deferential if the issue at hand pertains to jurisdiction?

4. Criticizing the *Maran Coal* decision, Friedland remarks:

Parties choosing Switzerland as a *situs* for international arbitration are henceforth on notice of the risk (or benefits, as the case may be) of this kind of second-guessing by Swiss courts. If contracting parties are not Swiss (and do not do business in Switzerland) and wish to avoid judicial review by Swiss courts, they should use the opportunity granted by Article 192 of the Swiss PIL, by excluding in writing the grounds for setting aside awards otherwise available under the Swiss PIL.[40]

Do you agree?

5. Would you recommend to your clients an arbitration clause stating "The said difference or dispute shall be referred by either party to arbitration within thirty days after it was agreed that the difference or dispute cannot be resolved by negotiation." If you would not recommend this specific wording, would you recommend setting a deadline within which arbitration may be commenced?

6. In *Arab Republic of Egypt v. Southern Pacific Properties* the Court of Appeal of Paris does not seem to show any deference whatsoever to the arbitrators' decision pertaining to their jurisdiction. Should it have shown some deference? How much? If it had shown deference, would that have affected the outcome?

7. In his Introductory Note to the case in International Legal Materials, Gaillard praises the decision of the Paris Court of Appeals, stating that such decisions provide "greater security to the parties by ensuring that their initial legal arrangements will be respected." Do you agree? Would greater deference be in the interest of the arbitrators themselves, or of the parties, or would it be in the interest of the arbitration process?

[40]. Id. at 116.

8. The scrutiny of the Paris Court appears to be virtually de novo regarding the significance of the Terms of Reference, and with respect to the consequences of the fact that the Contract was "approved, agreed and ratified" by the Ministry of Tourism.

The issue is, of course, whether the Egyptian State was a party to an existing arbitration agreement. In that context, would you say that the proper standard of review should be influenced by the fact that the arbitrators are potentially biased? Arguably, they have a personal interest both to find a valid arbitration agreement and to hold the State a party thereto, so that they will have authority to decide all aspects of the case. How strong is the argument that only if the parties actually entered into an arbitration agreement should a court defer to the arbitrators' decision since the justification for such deference is that this is what the parties agreed?

9. What is the meaning of "*Kompetenz-Kompetenz*" (the principle according to which the arbitrators are competent to decide upon their own competence) if their findings are subject to de novo court review?

According to the Paris Court, appellee's reasoning that the decision of the arbitral tribunal on its own jurisdiction should not be subject to review "would have the paradoxical effect of completely eliminating one of the recognized unrestricted powers of the Court, and which is only the counterpart of the jurisdiction granted to arbitrators to rule on their own jurisdiction." Do you agree?

V.2.d.ii.   Can the Parties Provide for Heightened Judicial Scrutiny of Arbitral Awards?

LAPINE TECHNOLOGY CORP. v. KYOCERA CORPORATION

United States Court of Appeals, Ninth Circuit, 1997.
130 F.3d 884.

Before: KOZINSKI, MAYER, and FERNANDEZ, * * *.

FERNANDEZ, CIRCUIT JUDGE:

Kyocera Corporation appeals the district court's judgment in favor of LaPine Technology Corporation, LaPine Holding Company, Inc. and Prudential–Bache Trade Services, Inc.[1] The district court determined that it could not review an arbitration award under a substantial evidence and error of law standard, even though that standard was part of the arbitration agreement made by the parties. The court, therefore, confirmed the arbitration award against Kyocera by using the much more deferential standard authorized in the Federal Arbitration Act ("FAA").

BACKGROUND

In 1984, Kyocera, LaPine, and Prudential–Bache began a venture to manufacture and market computer disk drives. LaPine had a drive

---

1. We refer to LaPine Technology and LaPine Holding collectively as "LaPine." We refer to LaPine and Prudential–Bache collectively as "Claimants" and use their own names when referring to them individually.

design, which it licensed to the manufacturer, Kyocera. Prudential–Bache provided financing for the venture: it would purchase Kyocera's entire output of drives and sell those drives to LaPine, which would then market them to its customers. However, that arrangement lasted for a relatively short time because LaPine's fortunes took a downward turn in 1986. The change in LaPine's financial condition set off a series of events that culminate in our decision today.

In late 1986, the parties began to negotiate a restructuring of their venture and reached an agreement in principle. On November 13, 1986, they memorialized their deal in a Definitive Agreement ("DA"). A revised DA, circulated on November 14, included as an exhibit the Amended Trading Agreement ("ATA"). The ATA eliminated Prudential–Bache's role as middleman, thus requiring Kyocera to sell drives directly to LaPine. Kyocera objected to that provision some time after the ATA was circulated. When Kyocera refused to comply with the ATA, LaPine gave notice of its claim of breach and then began the instant proceedings in the district court.

[1] The district court granted Kyocera's motion to compel arbitration pursuant to § 8.10(d) of the DA. That arbitration clause provided as follows:

> (d) Manner. A party desiring to submit a matter to arbitration shall give written notice to the other parties hereto.... The arbitrators shall decide the matters submitted based upon the evidence presented, the terms of this Agreement, the Agreement in Principle and the laws of the State of California. The arbitrators shall issue a written award which shall state the bases of the award and include detailed findings of fact and conclusions of law. The United States District Court for the Northern District of California may enter judgment upon any award, either by confirming the award or by vacating, modifying or correcting the award. The Court shall vacate, modify or correct any award: (i) based upon any of the grounds referred to in the Federal Arbitration Act, (ii) where the arbitrators' findings of fact are not supported by substantial evidence, or (iii) where the arbitrators' conclusions of law are erroneous.

The dispute was submitted to a panel of three arbitrators (the "Tribunal") for decision in accordance with a document entitled "Terms of Reference." That document provided, inter alia, that,

> The decisions and awards of the Tribunal may be enforced by the judgment of the Court or may be vacated, modified or corrected by the Court (a) based upon any grounds referred to in the Act, or (b) where the Tribunal's findings of fact are not supported by substantial evidence, or (c) where the Tribunal's conclusions of law are erroneous.

The Tribunal issued its final decision on August 24, 1994 and on November 23, 1994, Kyocera made a Motion to Vacate, Modify and Correct the Arbitral Award. Kyocera based its motion on claims that: (1) the Tribunal's findings of fact were not supported by substantial evidence, (2) the Tribunal had made errors of law, and (3) there existed various statutory grounds for vacatur or modification under the FAA.

The district court denied Kyocera's motion to vacate. In doing so, the court held that it would not review the arbitration award for errors of law or fact as provided in the DA and Terms of Reference. Rather, it considered only the statutory grounds for vacatur and found none of them applicable in this case. Thus, the court denied vacatur, granted Claimants' motion to confirm, and subsequently entered judgment. * * *.

JURISDICTION AND STANDARD OF REVIEW

[2] The district court had diversity jurisdiction pursuant to 28 U.S.C. § 1332 and we have jurisdiction under 28 U.S.C. § 1291. We review de novo the district court's decision to deny vacatur and to confirm the arbitration award.

DISCUSSION

[3] This appeal boils down to one major issue: Is federal court review of an arbitration agreement necessarily limited to the grounds set forth in the FAA or can the court apply greater scrutiny, if the parties have so agreed? The district court answered "yes" to the first part of the question and "no" to the second. It said: "This court is satisfied that the parties may not by agreement alter by expansion the provisions for judicial review contained in the Federal Arbitration Act." We do not agree with its answers.

[4] It is beyond peradventure that in the absence of any contractual terms regarding judicial review, a federal court may vacate or modify an arbitration award only if that award is "completely irrational," exhibits a "manifest disregard of law," or otherwise falls within one of the grounds set forth in 9 U.S.C. §§ 10 or 11. The instant case does not, however, fall neatly within the contours of the usual rule. That is because the parties indisputably contracted for heightened judicial scrutiny of the arbitrators' award when they agreed that review would be for errors of fact or law.

[5] We hold that we must honor that agreement. We must not disregard it by limiting our review to the FAA grounds. To locate the principle that animates our holding, one need not look very much further than the Supreme Court's decisions applying and interpreting the FAA. Those decisions make it clear that the primary purpose of the FAA is to ensure enforcement of private agreements to arbitrate, in accordance with the agreements' terms. As the Supreme Court said in Volt Info. Sciences v. Board of Trustees, 489 U.S. 468, 478–79, 109 S.Ct. 1248, 1255–56, 103 L.Ed.2d 488 (1989) (citations omitted):

> In recognition of Congress' principal purpose of ensuring that private arbitration agreements are enforced according to their terms, we have held that the FAA preempts state laws which "require a judicial forum for the resolution of claims which the contracting

parties agreed to resolve by arbitration." But it does not follow that the FAA prevents the enforcement of agreements to arbitrate under different rules than those set forth in the Act itself. Indeed, such a result would be quite inimical to the FAA's primary purpose of ensuring that private agreements to arbitrate are enforced according to their terms. Arbitration under the Act is a matter of consent, not coercion, and parties are generally free to structure their arbitration agreements as they see fit. Just as they may limit by contract the issues which they will arbitrate, so too may they specify by contract the rules under which that arbitration will be conducted.

That declaration recognized Congress's design " 'to overrule the judiciary's longstanding refusal to enforce agreements to arbitrate,' " id. at 474, 109 S.Ct. at 1253, and acknowledged that "[t]here is no federal policy favoring arbitration under a certain set of procedural rules; the federal policy is simply to ensure the enforceability, *according to their terms*, of private agreements to arbitrate." Id. at 476, 109 S.Ct. at 1254 (emphasis added).

[6], [7] In keeping with those principles, the Court has enforced contract terms that have called for arbitration under rules other than those established by the FAA itself, see id. at 478, 109 S.Ct. at 1255; under agreements to arbitrate punitive damages despite contrary state law, see Mastrobuono v. Shearson Lehman Hutton, Inc., 514 U.S. 52, 55, 115 S.Ct. 1212, 1216, 131 L.Ed.2d 76 (1995); and under agreements limiting the scope of the issues submitted to arbitration. See First Options of Chicago, Inc. v. Kaplan, 514 U.S. 938, 942, 115 S.Ct. 1920, 1923, 131 L.Ed.2d 985 (1995); Mitsubishi Motors Corp. v. Soler Chrysler–Plymouth, Inc., 473 U.S. 614, 628, 105 S.Ct. 3346, 3354–55, 87 L.Ed.2d 444 (1985). In short, "arbitration is simply a matter of contract between the parties." First Options, 514 U.S. at 943, 115 S.Ct. at 1924. The FAA's purpose was to make arbitration agreements just as enforceable as other contracts; not less so, "not more so." Prima Paint Corp. v. Flood & Conklin Mfg. Co., 388 U.S. 395, 404 n. 12, 87 S.Ct. 1801, 1806 n. 12, 18 L.Ed.2d 1270 (1967).

Following this guidance from the Supreme Court, the Fifth Circuit has held that federal courts have the authority, and, indeed, the obligation, to conduct heightened judicial review of an arbitration award in accordance with the parties' agreement. See Gateway Techs., Inc. v. MCI Telecomm. Corp., 64 F.3d 993, 996–97 (5th Cir.1995). As it wisely put it:

> Because these parties contractually agreed to expand judicial review, their contractual provision supplements the FAA's default standard of review and allows for de novo review of issues of law embodied in the arbitration award.

> The district court accordingly erred when it refused to review the "errors of law" de novo, opting instead to apply its specially crafted "harmless error standard." This choice apparently reflected the district court's unwillingness to enforce the parties' contract because "the parties have sacrificed the simplicity, informality, and expedi-

tion of arbitration on the altar of appellate review." Prudent or not, the contract expressly and unambiguously provides for review of "errors of law"; to interpret this phrase short of de novo review would render the language meaningless and would frustrate the mutual intent of the parties. When, as here, the parties agree contractually to subject an arbitration award to expanded judicial review, federal arbitration policy demands that the court conduct its review according to the terms of the arbitration contract.

Id. at 997 (footnote and citation omitted). And if substantial evidence and error of law review seems less efficient than the normal scope of arbitration review, that should not cause much pause because:

> it nevertheless reduces the burden on the Court below that which would exist in the absence of any provision for arbitration. Whereas in an ordinary commercial litigation the Court would be required to decide all aspects of the dispute, here the Court is being asked only to review the arbitrators' findings for substantial evidence and legal validity. This is clearly a far less searching and time-consuming inquiry than a full trial.

Fils et Cables d'Acier de Lens v. Midland Metals Corp., 584 F.Supp. 240, 244 (S.D.N.Y.1984). Of course, an arbitration issue would not be in the federal courts at all were it not for the fact that they would have jurisdiction over and the obligation to decide the whole matter in the absence of arbitration. See Moses H. Cone Mem'l Hosp. v. Mercury Constr. Corp., 460 U.S. 1, 25 n. 32, 103 S.Ct. 927, 942 n. 32, 74 L.Ed.2d 765 (1983) (the FAA does not create an independent source of federal jurisdiction).[h] We recognize that agreeing to the scope of review by a court is not precisely the same as agreeing to the scope of the arbitration itself. Nevertheless, the standards against which the work of the arbitrator will be measured are inexorably intertwined with the arbitration's scope, affect its whole structure, and may even encourage the arbitrator to adhere to a high standard of decision making. Perhaps an arbitrator need not be a Rhadamanthus, neither need he be a Panjandrum. We perceive no sufficient reason to pay less respect to the review provision than we pay to the myriad of other agreements which the parties have been pleased to make.

[8] Thus, we fully agree with the Fifth Circuit. Federal courts can expand their review of an arbitration award beyond the FAA's grounds, when (but only to the extent that) the parties have so agreed. To do otherwise would make hostility to arbitration agreements erumpent under the guise of deference to the arbitration concept. Historically, courts rather doubted that arbitral " 'tribunals possess adequate means of giving redress.' " Red Cross Line v. Atlantic Fruit Co., 264 U.S. 109,

h. [Author's note: This statement is correct for an action under Chapter 1 of the FAA seeking to confirm or set aside an arbitral award. *Kyocera* involves such a case. If an action falls under Chapter 2 of the FAA, seeking to recognize or enforce, or deny recognition or enforcement to, an arbitral award under the New York Convention, the FAA provides an independent ground for jurisdiction (federal question jurisdiction) in U.S. federal courts. See FAA section 203.]

121 & n. 1, 44 S.Ct. 274, 276 & n. 1, 68 L.Ed. 582 (1924) (citation omitted). Therefore, they jealously guarded their own jurisdiction to decide cases. That led them to refuse to enforce parties' agreements to arbitrate, and the FAA was designed to end that resistance. Now courts are again asked to refuse to enforce parties' agreements, but this time they are asked to do so by jealously eschewing their own jurisdiction. That would turn the FAA on its head. It was enacted to ensure enforcement of arbitration in accordance with parties' agreements. By confirming an award without the searching review that the parties have earlier agreed to, a court goes against the parties' wishes and does the opposite of what Congress intended. That is a result the Supreme Court has spurned, see First Options, 514 U.S. at 943, 115 S.Ct. at 1924; so too must we.

[9]   We recognize that a Seventh Circuit decision contains language which suggests that, if faced with the question we answer today, that court might reach a different result. In Chicago Typographical Union v. Chicago Sun–Times, Inc., 935 F.2d 1501, 1505 (7th Cir.1991), the court stated, "If the parties want, they can contract for an appellate arbitration panel to review the arbitrator's award. But they cannot contract for judicial review of that award; federal jurisdiction cannot be created by contract." The court, however, did not explain what had evoked that pronouncement, nor did it further explain the reasoning behind it. The opinion does not indicate that the parties attempted to confer appellate jurisdiction on the court, nor does it even indicate that the parties had asked for some exotic standard of review. If the court intended to refer to the FAA as a jurisdictional statute, it would have been negating the established principle that the FAA is a regulation of commerce rather than a limitation on or conferral of federal court jurisdiction. Thus, it seems that the court's cryptic assertion about jurisdiction is dicta. If it is not, we simply do not agree with the holding. On the contrary, we hold that the district court erred when it decided that it could not expand judicial review of an arbitration award beyond the grounds set forth in the FAA to the more generous review for substantial evidence and errors of law agreed to by the parties.

[10], [11] We are also unpersuaded by Claimants' alternate argument that by agreeing in the DA to arbitrate in accordance with the Rules of International Chamber of Commerce, Kyocera gave up any right to judicial review. It is true that Article 24 of the Rules of Conciliation of the International Chamber of Commerce, to which Kyocera agreed in the DA, provides for finality of the arbitration award and waiver of judicial review. However, that article notwithstanding, the Terms of Reference, to which the Claimants, Kyocera, and the Tribunal all agreed and pursuant to which the arbitration was conducted, provided for judicial review in accordance with the terms of the DA. To the extent that they conflict with Article 24, the Terms of Reference control. See Western Employers Ins. Co. v. Jefferies & Co., Inc., 958 F.2d 258, (9th Cir.1992) (arbitration procedure must comply with submission agreement). At any

rate, the specific judicial review provisions override the general ICC provisions.

In fine, when Kyocera and LaPine agreed to submit disputes to arbitration, they did so on the condition that the federal district court would review the arbitrators' decisions for errors of fact and law. They did not agree to abide by an arbitral tribunal's erroneous decisions. The FAA does not prohibit that kind of agreement; it encourages it. When the district court refused to abide by the terms of the agreement and then confirmed the results of the arbitration, it violated the purposes of the FAA and denied Kyocera the benefit of its bargain.

CONCLUSION

When parties are able to scry the possibility of future disputes, they may allow those to be resolved through the normal litigation process in court, or they may agree to remove them from that forum and resort to the use of an arbitral tribunal. When they do the latter, they may leave in place the limited court review provided by §§ 10 and 11 of the FAA, or they may agree to remove that insulation and subject the result to a more searching court review of the arbitral tribunal's decision, for example a review for substantial evidence and errors of law. In short, the FAA is not an apotropaion designed to avert overburdened court dockets; it is designed to avert interference with the contractual rights of the parties.

Therefore, we must reverse the district court's determination that it could not review the arbitral tribunal's decision on the standard agreed to by the parties, and remand this case for review of the decision by use of the agreed to standard.

AFFIRMED in part, REVERSED and REMANDED in part. Kyocera shall recover its costs on appeal.

KOZINSKI, CIRCUIT JUDGE, concurring.

While I join Judge Fernandez's opinion, I find the question presented closer than most. The Supreme Court cases on which the opinion relies are helpful, but they don't get us all the way there. As Judge Mayer points out, they say that parties may set the time, place and manner of arbitration; none says that private parties may tell the federal courts how to conduct their business. In general, I do not believe parties may impose on the federal courts burdens and functions that Congress has withheld. A partial answer is that any case properly in district court under the Federal Arbitration Act must have an independent jurisdictional basis. See Garrett v. Merrill Lynch, Pierce, Fenner & Smith, Inc., 7 F.3d 882, 883 (9th Cir.1993). Thus, enforcing the arbitration agreement—even with enhanced judicial review—will consume far fewer judicial resources than if the case were given plenary adjudication. The rub is that the work the district court must perform under this arbitration clause is not a subset of what it would be doing if the case were brought directly under diversity or federal question jurisdiction. It's not just less work, it is different work. Nowhere has Congress authorized courts to review arbitral awards under the standard the parties here adopted.

Nevertheless, I conclude that we must enforce the arbitration agreement according to its terms. The review to which the parties have agreed is no different from that performed by the district courts in appeals from administrative agencies and bankruptcy courts, or on habeas corpus. I would call the case differently if the agreement provided that the district judge would review the award by flipping a coin or studying the entrails of a dead fowl. Given the strong policy of party empowerment embodied in the Arbitration Act, I see no reason why Congress would object to enforcement of this agreement. This is not quite an express congressional authorization but, given the Arbitration Act's policy, it's probably enough.

MAYER, CIRCUIT JUDGE, Dissenting:

Whether to arbitrate, what to arbitrate, how to arbitrate, and when to arbitrate are matters that parties may specify contractually. See Volt Info. Sciences v. Board of Trustees, 489 U.S. 468, 478–479, 109 S.Ct. 1248, 1255–1256, 103 L.Ed.2d 488 (1989). However, Kyocera cites no authority explicitly empowering litigants to dictate how an Article III court must review an arbitration decision. Absent this, they may not. Should parties desire more scrutiny than the Federal Arbitration Act, 9 U.S.C. §§ 10–11 (1994), authorizes courts to apply, "they can contract for an appellate arbitration panel to review the arbitrator's award[;] they cannot contract for judicial review of that award." Chicago Typographical Union v. Chicago Sun–Times, 935 F.2d 1501, 1505 (7th Cir.1991). I would affirm the district court's self-restraint.

Questions and Comments

1. In today's world, as we have seen repeatedly, courts and commentators alike tend to be pro-arbitration. In *Kyocera* which solution is proarbitration, Judge Fernandez's majority opinion or Judge Mayer's dissent? Return to this question after considering some of the issues raised in the questions that follow.

2. In *Kyocera* Judge Ingram in the district court, with whom dissenting Judge Mayer in the 9th Circuit agrees, refused to enforce the provisions of the arbitration agreement expanding the standards for judicial review of the award. Judge Ingram summarized his position as follows:

> "It appears to this court that the contractual provisions existing in this case wherein the parties choose and specify the scope of judicial review to pertain in their arbitration is offensive to the public policy which supports arbitration and those aspects of arbitration which are beneficial to the parties as well as to the courts whose responsibilities are eased by alternative forms of dispute resolution." [Lapine Technology Corp. v. Kyocera Corp., 909 F.Supp. 697, 705 (N.D.Cal.1995)].

Do you agree? Is the Ingram/Mayer position in *Kyocera* more pro-arbitration than that of the 9th Circuit majority (Fernandez/Kozinski)?

3.   If the Ingram/Mayer position had prevailed, would the award have been unenforceable because the arbitration agreement was invalid? Judge Ingram in the district court found the offending language in the arbitration agreement to be separable because it dealt with review of the arbitration procedure conducted by the court, whereas the rest of the arbitration agreement was devoted to the arbitration procedure conducted by the arbitrators. He therefore found the arbitration agreement, shorn of the offending provisions, to be valid. Do you agree?

Recall that in a similar case the Cour d'appel de Paris (Court of Appeal of Paris) found the arbitration agreement invalid and nullified the award. [Société de Diseno v. Société Mendes, CA Paris, 1e ch., October 27, 1994, reported in 1995 Revue de l'arbitrage 265. Discussed in the text above at V.2.a. (4).] How would you respond to an argument by Kyocera that it had agreed to arbitration only on condition that the award would be subject to a heightened standard of judicial review? Should one give more weight to the parties' intention to arbitrate or to the mistrust they expressed toward arbitration without strict judicial supervision? Will it encourage arbitration— or discourage it—if parties know that courts will enforce an arbitration agreement even when some of its carefully negotiated provisions are held invalid and not applied?

4.   If the district court position had prevailed and an award had been rendered that was not subject to the heightened judicial review provided for by the written arbitration agreement, could Kyocera have successfully defeated recognition and enforcement of the award outside the U.S. on the ground of New York Convention V(1)(d): "the arbitral procedure was not in accordance with the agreement of the parties * * * "? Is the post-award standard of judicial review in a set aside proceeding part of the arbitral procedure?

5.   On remand in the *Kyocera* case, the district court applied the heightened standard of review detailed in the arbitration agreement, but upheld the award against all challenges. 2000 WL 765556 (N.D.Cal.2000). This was a happy result for arbitration. Consider other possible variations.

The arbitration agreement reads: "The United States District Court for the Northern District of California may enter judgment upon any award, either by confirming the award or by ***vacating, modifying or correcting the award***. * * * " (emphasis added). Suppose the district court had modified the arbitral award and held: (1) that Kyocera owes LaPine, let us say, $165 million from the moment of the ICC award (instead of $257 million as awarded by the ICC arbitrators) because the evidence supporting the higher award did not meet the "substantial evidence" test; and (2) that LaPine owes Kyocera $35 million from the moment of the district court judgment because the arbitral panel had reached an erroneous legal conclusion in rejecting a Kyocera counterclaim. How should one characterize this result? Is it still an arbitral award within the purview of the New York Convention, or is it simply a court judgment? Suppose LaPine sought to enforce the award under the New York Convention in Japan. Is it entitled to $257 million as originally awarded by the ICC arbitrators, $165 million, because of the court determined factual error, or $130 million, because of the court determined error in law in addition to the factual error?

Note that New York Convention Article I(2) defines an arbitral award as follows:

> 2. The term "arbitral awards" shall include not only awards made by arbitrators appointed for each case but also those made by permanent arbitral bodies to which the parties have submitted.

Note further that Article I(2) speaks of awards rendered by arbitrators, whether appointed for the particular case or sitting as a permanent arbitral body. Which way does this definition cut?

6. Article V(1)(e) of the New York Convention provides that an award may be refused recognition and enforcement if it "has not yet become binding on the parties * * *." An award rendered by the arbitrators and delivered to the parties would be considered as binding on the parties, even though one of the parties had initiated annulment proceedings. On the other hand, if the parties have provided for an appellate arbitral body to review an original panel's award, presumably the award is not binding on the parties until the appellate process has run its course. How would you characterize the appellate process in *Kyocera*? Had the ICC panel's award become binding on the parties?

7. The parties in the *Kyocera* transaction were sophisticated business entities. At least one of them must have had reasons for wanting expanded judicial review after the award was rendered. What might some of those reasons have been? How would you advise a client who has similar reasons for wanting to include such provisions in an arbitration clause? (Full speed ahead? Caution? or No way?)

8. Although both the French and American legal systems are strongly pro-arbitration, as noted above in the text at V.2.a (subparagraph 5), French law does not accept the *Kyocera* result. Agreements seeking to expand the grounds for judicial review would be rejected in France as against public policy. See Laurence Franc, *Contractual Modification of Judicial Review of Arbitral Awards: The French Position*, 10 Am. Rev. Int'l Arb. 215 (1999). (Indeed, not all U.S. decisions agree with *Kyocera*. See, e.g., Bowen v. Amoco Pipeline Co., 254 F.3d 925 (10th Cir.2001) (refusing to enforce an agreement to expand judicial review of an award rendered in domestic arbitration).)

Consider the result under the UNCITRAL Model Law. Article 34(1) reads:

> Recourse to a court against an arbitral award may be made only by an application for setting aside in accordance with paragraphs (2) and (3) of this article [listing the grounds for setting aside].

How would the *Kyocera* issue be resolved under a national arbitration statute based on the UNCITRAL Model Law?

9. In his separate opinion, Judge Kozinski accepts the parties' power to provide for expanded judicial review, but only within certain limits:

> "I would call the case differently if the agreement provided that the district judge would review the award by flipping a coin or studying the entrails of a dead fowl."

His examples are of course fanciful. What if the arbitration agreement said that the reviewing court should conduct a de novo trial of any fact challenged by one of the parties? What if it said that the reviewing court should decide "ex aequo et bono"? Or according to "lex mercatoria"?

10.   For a full discussion of the issues raised by the *Kyocera* case, see T. Varady, *On the Option of a Contractual Extension of Judicial Review of Arbitral Awards—What Is Actually Pro–Arbitration?* (accepted for publication in Liber Amicorum for Sinisa Triva, Zagreb.)

V.2.e.   *Due Process in Setting Aside as an Issue of Human Rights*

STRAN GREEK REFINERIES & STRATIS ANDREADIS v. GREECE

European Court of Human Rights, 1994.
Revised opinion at 301–B Eur. Ct. H.R. (ser. A).*

* * *

Procedure

1.   The case was referred to the Court by the European Commission of Human Rights ("the Commission") on 12 July 1993, within the three-month period laid down by Article 32 § 1 and Article 47 of the Convention. It originated in an application (no. 13427/87) against the Hellenic Republic lodged with the Commission under Article 25 by a Greek private limited company, Stran Greek Refineries, and the latter's sole shareholder, Mr Stratis Andreadis, on 20 November 1987. The second applicant died in 1989 and his son and heir, Mr Petros Andreadis, expressed the wish to continue with the application.

The Commission's request referred to Articles 44 and 48 and to the declaration whereby Greece recognised the compulsory jurisdiction of the Court (Article 46). The object of the request was to obtain a decision as to whether the facts of the case disclosed a breach by the respondent State of its obligations under Article 6 of the Convention and Article 1 of Protocol No. 1.

* * *

A.   *The background to the case*

7.   Under the terms of a contract concluded on 22 July 1972 with the Greek State, which at the time was governed by a military junta, Mr Andreadis undertook to construct a crude oil refinery in the Megara region, near Athens. The refinery was to be built, at an estimated cost of 76,000,000 US dollars, by a company which it was proposed to form, Stran Greek Refineries, of which the second applicant was to be the sole owner. All the latter's rights and obligations were to be automatically transferred to the company upon its incorporation.

The Government ratified the contract by Legislative Decree no. 1211/1972, published in the Official Gazette of 26 July 1972. Under

* Reprinted by permission of Carl Hey-   manns Verlag KG.

Article 21 of the contract, the State undertook to purchase, not later than 31 December 1972, a plot of land in Megara suitable for the construction of the refinery. On 27 July 1972, by a Royal Decree (no. 450), issued pursuant to Legislative Decree no. 2687/1953 on "the Investment and Protection of Capital Funds from Abroad", the State authorised Mr Andreadis to import 58 million US dollars to finance the scheme.

8. However, the project stagnated because the State failed to fulfil its obligation. On 28 November 1973 the Ministers of Industry and Agriculture announced at a press conference in Megara the Government's decision to return to the proprietors the land which had already been expropriated in accordance with Article 21 of the contract. The following day the Megara police ordered that the work should cease.

In December 1973 Stran protested to the relevant authorities and sought permission to proceed with the work. On 27 February 1974 it even issued an extra-judicial summons inviting the State to ratify the purchase of the land in question, but the State refused to revoke the police order prohibiting the continuation of the work.

9. Once democracy had been restored, the Government took the view that the contract and Decree no. 450 were prejudicial to the national economy; they relied on Article 2 § 5 of Law no. 141/1975 on the termination of preferential contracts (*kharistikes svmvasseis*) concluded under the military regime (1967–1974). This Law, which was enacted by special authorisation under the 1975 Constitution (Article 107—see paragraph 24 below), possessed superior force.

The applicants did not respond to a proposal addressed to them by the Minister for Co-ordination on 19 November 1975 inviting them to enter negotiations for the revision or termination of the contract. Accordingly, a ministerial committee on the economy terminated the contract on 14 October 1977. The applicants did not challenge this decision in the courts.

B. The proceedings in the Athens Court of First Instance

10. Prior to the termination of the contract, Stran had incurred expenditure in connection with the scheme. In particular, it had concluded contracts for the supply of goods and services with foreign and Greek undertakings and had taken out loans.

A dispute then arose between Stran and the State. On 10 November 1978 Stran brought an action (*anagnoristiki agogi*) in the Athens Court of First Instance for a declaration that the State should pay it compensation in the amounts of 251,113,978 drachmas, 22,799,782 US dollars and 877,466 French francs. It argued that the State had been in breach of its obligations during the period of validity of the contract, in particular in so far as it had, since 27 November 1973, prohibited the continuation of work on the construction of the refinery at Megara and had not, since 9 February 1974, taken any steps to expropriate the land required for that construction. It also sought the return of a cheque for 240 million drachmas which it had lodged with the Ministry of the National Economy as security for the proper performance of the contract; it further claimed reimbursement of the commission and the fiscal stamp fee paid to the Commercial Bank of Greece.

The State challenged the jurisdiction of the court. It contended that the dispute should be referred to arbitration. In accordance with Article 27 of the contract, the relevant paragraphs of which were worded as follows:

> 1.   Any difference, dispute or disagreement arising between the State and the Concessionaire as to the application of this Agreement and relative to the interpretation of the terms and conditions thereof and the extent of the rights and obligations deriving thereof and the extent of the rights and obligations deriving therefrom shall be resolved exclusively by arbitration by three arbitrators according to the following procedure, no other arbitration agreement being required.

* * *

> 9.   The arbitration award shall be definite, final and irrevocable, and shall constitute an enforceable instrument requiring no further action for enforcement or any other formality. It shall be liable to no ordinary or extraordinary judicial remedies, nor shall it be subject to cancellation or suspension before ordinary courts of justice. The party failing to comply with the provisions of the arbitration award shall be obligated to make good any and all damage (*damnum emergens* or *lucrum cessans*) caused to the other party.

11.   In a preliminary decision (no. 13910/1979) of 29 September 1979, the Athens Court of First Instance rejected the State's main submission. It held that the arbitration clause concerned solely the settlement of disputes arising from the performance of the contract and not the failure of one of the parties to perform the contract. It found further that the ministerial committee on the economy had terminated the contract in issue in its entirety (see paragraph 9 above) which had the effect of rendering the arbitration clause void as it was not an autonomous provision. In addition, the court dismissed the State's argument that two of the conditions subsequent contained in the contract, namely the lodging of a cheque as security and the payment of the second part of the minimum capital, had not been satisfied. Finally, the court ordered additional investigative measures, including the hearing of five witnesses, in order to determine the existence and extent of the damage alleged by Stran.

C.   The arbitration proceedings

12.   On 12 June 1980 the State filed an arbitration petition and appointed an arbitrator. It requested the arbitration court to declare that all the claims for compensation against the Greek State lodged by

Stran in the Athens Court of First Instance (see paragraph 10 above) were unfounded.

In its memorial of 28 June 1980 Stran—which had appointed a professor of law at Athens University as arbitrator—maintained primarily that the arbitration court lacked jurisdiction and requested that the arbitration be stayed until the proceedings instituted on 10 November 1978 had been concluded; in the alternative and in order to rebut the State's arguments on the merits, it referred the arbitrators to its pleadings in the Athens Court of First Instance.

13. The arbitration court was constituted on 3 July 1980; its president was chosen jointly by the two other arbitrators (Article 27 § 3 of the contract). It made its award on 27 February 1984.

It found that it had jurisdiction in that, in its view, the disputes arising from the total failure to perform the contract were also subject to arbitration, which was not restricted to those deriving from non-performance of individual clauses as had been argued by the State. The wording of the arbitration clause in Article 27 (see paragraph 10 above) was sufficiently general and clear to rule out such distinctions.

On the merits, the arbitration court relied on the evidence adduced by the parties before the Athens Court of First Instance on 10 November 1978 (see paragraph 10 above). It found that responsibility for the losses sustained by Stran was shared—70% for the State and 30% for the company. The latter had commenced work on land which had been the subject of a contested expropriation order and without first obtaining the necessary planning permission. It therefore held Stran's claims to be well-founded in an amount not exceeding 116,273,442 drachmas, 16,054,-165 US dollars and 614,627 French francs, plus interest at 6% from 10 November 1978; however, this reference to interest did not appear in the operative part of the decision. Finally, the court declared that the State was unlawfully retaining the cheque lodged as security (see paragraph 10 above).

14. On 24 July 1984 the applicant company sought an order from the Athens Court of First Instance requiring the State to return the security, but the court stayed the proceedings pending the conclusion of those instituted on 10 November 1978 (see paragraph 10 above).

D. The appeals against the arbitration award of 27 February 1984

1. In the Athens Court of First Instance

15. On 2 May 1984 the State had asked the Athens Court of First Instance to set aside the arbitration award of 27 February 1984.

It argued that the arbitration court had lacked jurisdiction to hear disputes arising from the contract in issue and Stran's financial claims against the State. In the alternative, it affirmed that the contracting parties had intended to limit the jurisdiction of the arbitration court to disputes concerning the performance and interpretation of the clauses of the contract and the scope of the rights and duties deriving therefrom;

its jurisdiction could not therefore extend to disputes relating to the total failure to perform the contract. It followed that the dispute in question was a matter for the ordinary civil courts, as the Athens Court of First Instance had recognised in its judgment no. 13910/1979. In the further alternative, the State argued that the arbitration court's lack of jurisdiction was confirmed by the fact that Stran's claims against it had become statute-barred following the termination of the contract. Finally, it stressed the declaratory nature of the action brought by Stran on 10 November 1978 (see paragraph 10 above).

16. In a judgment (no. 5526/1985) of 21 April 1985 the Athens court dismissed the State's application, holding that the decision terminating the contract had not rendered the arbitration clause void. That clause continued to produce its effects in relation to disputes which had arisen during the period of validity of the contract.

17. On 19 December 1986 the applicant company withdrew its first action in the Athens Court of First Instance (see paragraph 9 above), but sought to pursue its action for the return of the cheque lodged as security (see paragraph 14 above).

When this action was heard in the Athens Court of First Instance, on 6 February 1987, the State, relying on Article 294 of the Code of Civil Procedure, opposed the discontinuance of the first action. It maintained that the latter action would have resulted in a finding unfavourable to Stran and that the State thus had a legitimate interest in seeking a final decision.

However, the court again stayed the proceedings (decision no. 2877/1987) on account of the appeal on points of law which was pending (see paragraph 19 below).

2. *In the Athens Court of Appeal*

18. In a judgment (no. 9336/1986) of 4 November 1986, the Athens Court of Appeal, basing its decision on the same grounds, upheld the judgment of 21 April 1985.

It ruled, *inter alia*:

"In modern Greek legislation the principle of the autonomy of an arbitration clause in relation to the contract prevails. The termination of the contract, for whatever reason, does not bring an end to the power of the arbitrators designated to hear disputes which have arisen during the period of validity of the contract ... The decision of the ministerial committee on the economy did not annul the arbitration clause contained in Article 27 of the contract and, accordingly, it does not preclude the arbitrators from examining the merits of the dispute."

3. *In the Court of Cassation*

19. On 15 December 1986 the State appealed to the Court of Cassation.

The hearing was initially set down for 4 May 1987, but on that date it was postponed to 1 June 1987 at the State's request, on the ground that a draft law concerning the case in question was before Parliament.

In reply to a question put by the European Court at the hearing on 19 April 1994, the applicants' lawyer maintained that the Court of Cassation's judge-rapporteur had sent his opinion, which had been favourable to the applicants' arguments, to the parties before 4 May and this affirmation was not disputed by the Government.

20.　On 22 May 1987 Parliament enacted Law no. 1701/1987 on "the compulsory participation of the State in private undertakings ... and the redemption of shares", which entered into force upon its publication in the Official Gazette of 25 May 1987. This Law dealt principally with the renegotiation of a concession for the prospecting for and extraction of oil and natural gas in an area of the Sea of Thrace. However, Article 12 of the Law was worded as follows:

1.　The true and lawful meaning of the provisions of Article 2 § 1 of Law no. 141/1975 concerning the termination of contracts entered into between 21 April 1967 and 24 July 1974 is that, upon the termination of these contracts, all their terms, conditions and clauses, including the arbitration clause, are *ipso jure* repealed and the arbitration tribunal no longer has jurisdiction.

2.　Arbitration awards covered by paragraph 1 shall no longer be valid or enforceable.

3.　Any principal or ancillary claims against the Greek State, expressed either in foreign or local currency, which arise out of the contracts entered into between 21 April 1967 and 24 July 1974, ratified by statute and terminated by virtue of Law no. 141/1975, are now proclaimed time-barred.

4.　Any court proceedings at whatever level pending at the time of the enactment of this statute, in respect of claims within the meaning of the preceding paragraph, are declared void.

21.　On 10 July 1987, after hearing the opinion of the judge-rapporteur calling for the appeal to be dismissed, the First Division of the Court of Cassation delivered its judgment (no. 1387/1987). It held that Article 12 was unconstitutional on the following grounds:

"...

Not only does [Article 107] of the Constitution confer superior force on Law no. 141/1975, but it also prohibits subsequent amendments or additions thereto, or even authoritative interpretation thereof, in the form of ordinary legislation. The purpose of that superior force and of the provision in the Constitution requiring that a single law be enacted once and for all within three months of the entry into force of the Constitution was to ensure legislative stability and international confidence for investments in Greece. This opinion is based on the only possible meaning to be attributed to the expression 'single law to be enacted once and for all' and on the ease with which the said provision would be flouted if amendments, additions or authoritative interpretation of that law were allowed. * * *

It follows that * * * the provision of Article 12 of Law no. 1701/1987 which purport to provide an authoritative interpretation of and to amend and supplement Article 2 § 1 of Law no. 141/1975 and which were enacted after the expiry of the time-limit laid down in Article 107 § 2 of the Constitution are contrary to that instrument. In accordance with Article 93 § 4 of the Constitution the court is therefore precluded from applying them. The Division refuses to apply unconstitutional provisions and, pursuant to Article 563 § 2 of the Code of Civil Procedure, holds that it is bound to refer the case to the Court of Cassation sitting in plenary session. . . ."

22. The hearing in the Court of Cassation sitting in plenary session opened on 19 November 1987, but as a result of the death of one of its members Stran sought a new hearing, which was held on 25 February 1988.

The Court of Cassation delivered its judgment (no. 4/1989) on 16 March 1989. It observed, *inter alia*:

" * * * [The Constitution] provides for the enactment of 'a single law to be enacted once and for all' which by definition possesses superior force inasmuch as it may be neither supplemented nor amended by ordinary legislation. * * * However, the prohibition on supplementing or modifying the content of [such] laws does not mean that they may never be interpreted. The fact that they are *sui generis*, which gives them precedence over ordinary legislation, * * * does not preclude their interpretation where the circumstances so require. The purpose of such interpretation is not to amend the substance of the law interpreted, but to clarify its original meaning and to resolve disputes that have arisen in connection with its application or which may do so in the future. [The need for such interpretation] will ultimately be determined by the court which will have to ascertain whether the meaning of the law interpreted actually gave rise to doubts justifying the intervention of the legislature * * * Accordingly, the interpretation of Law no. 141/1975 is not contrary to the Constitution merely because it is a law of superior rank. It must nevertheless be determined, on the one hand, whether the interpretation was necessary in the specific case and, on the other, whether the non-interpretative provisions of this Law, which have a bearing on the solution of the case in issue, are contrary to the Constitution. * * * The wording [of Article 2 § 5 of Law no. 141/1975] lacks clarity and creates doubt as to whether the arbitration clause survives the termination of the contract * * * and as to the jurisdiction of the arbitration court. In the instant case doubt first arose in the course of the proceedings brought by [the applicants] in the ordinary civil court and again—following the preliminary decision of the Athens Court of First Instance—when those proceedings had been discontinued and recourse was had to arbitration, where diametrically opposed arguments were put forward. * * * Irrespective of those doubts, the main issue is the acceptance or rejection of the principle of the autonomous character of the arbitration clause and of its scope. For a long time this matter has been the subject of significant differences of opinion in international case-law and among legal writers. In some countries the principle of the survival of the clause to resolve disputes arising prior to the termination of contracts * * * prevails. In other countries the dominant view is that termination of the contract entails the annulment of the clause and therefore the referral of all the disputes to the ordinary courts. In other countries again, the accepted view is that the autonomous character of the arbitration clause operates only in respect of certain types of dispute. It was therefore necessary to provide an interpretation of Law no. 141/1975 and that interpretation resolved the problem for the purposes of Greek law by opting for the annulment of arbitration clauses * * * and the removal of jurisdiction from the arbitration court. The fact that the intervention of the legislature occurred * * * five days before the hearing in the First Division of this Court and following a previous adjournment does not mean that it was not necessary and does not render it contrary to Article 26 §§ 1 and 3 and Articles 77 and 87 of the Constitution. The dispute in question provided the opportunity to resolve a problem which had already arisen. Consequently, it cannot be concluded that, in giving such an interpretation in this case, the legislature interfered with the jurisdiction of the ordinary courts and usurped that jurisdiction. It follows that, contrary to the finding of the First Division, Article 12 § 1 of Law no. 1701/1987 is not in breach of the Constitution * * * "

The Court of Cassation took the view that paragraph 2 of Article 12 was not unconstitutional as it essentially supplemented paragraph 1 and sought to deprive of effect any arbitration awards that were made after the termination of contracts and that would not have been made if the meaning of Law no. 141/1975 had been clarified in time. In addition, the court refused to examine the constitutionality of paragraph 3, finding that it had no bearing on the case before it. Finally, it held that the adoption of paragraph 4 shortly before the hearing purported to remove from the courts the possibility of determining the validity of the contested awards. That provision therefore violated the principle of the separation of powers.

23.　The Court of Cassation remitted the case to the First Division which, on 11 April 1990, quashed the Court of Appeal's judgment of 4 November 1986 (see paragraph 18 above) and declared void the arbitration award of 27 February 1984 (see paragraph 13 above).

* * *

B. *Compliance with Article 6 § 1*

1. *Fair trial*

42. The applicants claimed that they had been deprived of a fair trial and even of their right of access to a court. They relied in particular on the Golder v. the United Kingdom judgment of 21 February 1975 (Series A no. 18).

By enacting and applying in respect of the applicants Article 12 of Law no. 1701/1987, the State had effectively removed jurisdiction from the courts called upon to determine the validity of the arbitration award and prevented any proper judicial investigation of the subject of the dispute. Such an interference was, in the words of the Golder judgment, "indissociable from a danger of arbitrary power" and repugnant to the general principles of international law and the notion of the rule of law inherent in the Convention. The State had determined by legislative action a case in which it was a party. "Legislative legerdemain" had resulted in wholesale inequality of arms in the proceedings in issue.

43. The Government contested this view. Parliament, the source of all power, was fully justified in interpreting authoritatively the laws which it enacted where they were ambiguous. Moreover, the power to do this was expressly conferred on it by Article 77 of the Constitution. Clearly such an interpretation applied to all existing cases, irrespective of whether they were pending before the courts, because it did not introduce new rules and did not amend the provision in question, but merely clarified its true meaning.

Such intervention by the legislature could not be regarded as unlawful interference with the power of the judiciary especially where the latter had at its disposal the means necessary to ensure that there was no arbitrariness. That was the position in the Greek legal system. Article 93 of the Constitution prohibited the courts from applying laws whose content was contrary to that instrument. In the present case, when Article 12 of Law no. 1701/1987 came into force, the dispute concerning the validity of the arbitration award was still pending in the Court of Cassation. That court could therefore ascertain whether the conditions justifying the authoritative interpretation by the legislature of Law no. 141/1975 obtained and whether that interpretation infringed the principle of the separation of powers.

44. The Court takes the view that the proceedings subsequent to the entry into force of Law no. 1701/1987, when the case was pending in the Court of Cassation, are of decisive importance for the purposes of its investigation. However, in order to assess whether the applicants had a fair trial in that court, it is necessary to take account of the earlier proceedings, what was at stake in those proceedings and the attitude of the parties.

The dispute, which was brought before the Athens Court of First Instance by the applicants on 10 November 1978 (see paragraph 10 above), concerned their claim that they were entitled to compensation since the State had already been in breach of its obligations under the contract before its termination. It was referred to the arbitration court on the initiative of the State, which had maintained that the arbitration clause was still valid and had challenged the jurisdiction of the ordinary courts on that basis (see paragraph 10 above).

The applicants, albeit in the alternative, accepted the jurisdiction of the arbitration court and, when the latter court had partly allowed their claim, clearly showed that they intended to abide by its decision (see paragraph 17 above). The State, however, then changed course by bringing the dispute before the ordinary civil courts, before which it contested on this occasion the validity of the arbitration clause and, consequently, that of the award (see paragraphs 15 and 18 above).

The enactment by Parliament of Law no. 1701/1987 indisputably represented a turning-point in the proceedings, which up to that point had gone against the State.

45.   The Government contended that it had been necessary to enact the Law in question on account of the differing opinions of eminent professors of law, contradictory judicial decisions, the formulation of dissenting opinions by judges and the attitude of the parties, who had changed their stances on the validity of the arbitration clause alternately. The growing debate and public policy reasons had thus made it necessary to clarify the intention of the legislature on this question by providing an authoritative interpretation—even twelve years on—of Law no. 141/1975. The democratic legislature had been under a duty to eradicate from public life the residual traces of measures taken by the military regime. Mr Andreadis had been a giant of the economy and the scheme that he had envisaged had at the time been on a huge scale for a country the size of Greece. Moreover, the announcement of the scheme had led, before the fall of the military regime, to one of the largest anti-dictatorship demonstrations.

46.   The Court does not question the Government's intention to act in response to the Greek people's concern that democratic legality be re-established.

However, by rejoining the Council of Europe on 28 November 1974 and by ratifying the Convention, Greece undertook to respect the principle of the rule of law. This principle, which is enshrined in Article 3 of the Statute of the Council of Europe, finds expression, *inter alia*, in Article 6 of the Convention. That provision secures in particular the right to a fair trial and sets out in detail the essential guarantees inherent in this notion as applied to criminal proceedings. As regards disputes concerning civil rights and obligations, the Court has laid down in its case-law the requirement of equality of arms in the sense of a fair balance between the parties. In litigation involving opposing private interests, that equality implies that each party must be afforded a reasonable opportunity to present his case—under conditions that do not place him at a substantial disadvantage *vis-à-vis* his opponent (see the

Dombo Beheer B.V. v. the Netherlands judgment of 27 October 1993, Series A no. 274, p. 19 § 33).

47. In this connection, the Court has had regard to both the timing and manner of the adoption of Article 12 of Law no. 1701/1987. Shortly before the hearing in the Court of Cassation, which had initially been set down for 4 May 1987, and after the parties had received the opinion of the judge-rapporteur recommending the dismissal of the State's appeal, the State sought the adjournment of the hearing on the ground that a draft law concerning the case was before Parliament (see paragraph 19 above).

This draft law was adopted on 22 May 1987 and entered into force on 25 May after its publication in the Official Gazette (see paragraph 20 above). The hearing was held on 1 June (see paragraph 19 above). Moreover, while Law no. 1701/1987 was principally concerned with the renegotiation of the terms of a contract relating to the prospecting for and extraction of oil and gas—likewise concluded during the dictatorship between the State and companies other than Stran—, Article 12 was an additional provision to that law and was in reality aimed at the applicant company—although the latter was not mentioned by name (see paragraph 20 above).

The Court is fully aware that in order to meet the pressing needs of urgent legislation and to avoid the delays of the legislative machinery, legislatures nowadays often deal with similar matters in the same law.

It is nevertheless an inescapable fact that the legislature's intervention in the present case took place at a time when judicial proceedings in which the State was a party were pending.

48. The Government sought to play down the effect of this intervention. In the first place the applicants could have requested a further adjournment of the hearing to give them more time to prepare their case. Secondly, paragraph 2 of Article 12 was not an autonomous provision and did not in itself render the arbitration award void, because it presupposed judicial examination of the nullity provided for in paragraph 1. Finally, the applicants had had the opportunity to put forward their arguments before the First Division of the Court of Cassation, which had heard the case on its merits in the light of the decision of the plenary court.

49. The Court is not persuaded by this reasoning. The requirement of fairness applies to proceedings in their entirety; it is not confined to hearings *inter partes*. There can be no doubt that in the instant case the appearances of justice were preserved, and indeed the applicants did not complain that they had been deprived of the facilities necessary for the preparation of their case.

The principle of the rule of law and the notion of fair trial enshrined in Article 6 preclude any interference by the legislature with the administration of justice designed to influence the judicial determination of the dispute. The wording of paragraphs 1 and 2 of Article 12 taken together effectively excluded any meaningful examination of the case by the First Division of the Court of Cassation. Once the constitutionality of those paragraphs had been upheld by the Court of Cassation in plenary session, the First Division's decision became inevitable.

50. In conclusion, the State infringed the applicants' rights under Article 6 § 1 by intervening in a manner which was decisive to ensure that the—imminent—outcome of proceedings in which it was a party was favourable to it. There has therefore been a violation of that Article.

* * *

Questions and Comments

1. Article 6.1 of the European Convention on Human Rights and Fundamental Freedoms (Nov. 4, 1950, 213 U.N.T.S. 222) reads as follows:

Article 6

1) In the determination of his civil rights and obligations or of any criminal charge against him, everyone is entitled to a fair and public hearing within a reasonable time by an independent and impartial tribunal established by law. Judgement shall be pronounced publicly but the press and public may be excluded from all or part of the trial in the interest of morals, public order or national security in a democratic society, where the interests of juveniles or the protection of the private life of the parties so require, or to the extent strictly necessary in the opinion of the court in special circumstances where publicity would prejudice the interests of justice.

* * *

How would you define the meaning of "civil rights and obligations" implied in the Strasbourg decision? If "civil rights and obligations" are in fact rights and obligations of civil (private) character, does this mean that recourse to the Strasbourg Court is possible in practically any commercial case (assuming that a violation of due process is alleged)?

2. In a case decided by the Paris Tribunal de grande instance, the Republic of Guinea sued the Paris Chamber of Commerce,[41] stating that the Paris Chamber of Commerce assumed jurisdiction in three related cases, only two of which were submitted to it (the third was submitted to the I.C.C.). The Republic of Guinea also alleged that the Paris Chamber of Commerce disregarded party stipulations regarding the appointment of arbitrators. The Republic of Guinea asked the Paris court to revoke the arbitration clauses conferring jurisdiction on the Paris Chamber of Commerce because the actions of this institution were so erroneous as to preclude the institution from enjoying the confidence of the parties in the cases submitted. Faced with rather obvious errors committed by the Paris Chamber of Commerce, yet lacking clear procedural standards of conduct against which these mistakes could be measured, the Paris court decided to rely on standards of due process formulated in documents on human rights. Referring to Article 6 of the European Convention for the Protection of Human Rights, and to Article 14 of the 1966 International Covenant on Civil and Political Rights, the court voided the conferral of authority to the Paris

[41]. *République de Guinée v. Chambre arbitrale de Paris*, judgments of May 30, 1986, Oct. 30, 1986, Jan. 28, 1987, reported in 1987 Revue de l'arbitrage 371.

Chamber of Commerce, and held that, with respect to the two contracts concerned, ad hoc arbitration should be instituted.[42]

Does *Stran Refineries v. Greece*, while widening the scope for recourse against court decisions in which arbitration is treated unfairly, also widen the scope for recourse against arbitration awards that have (in the opinion of the moving party) infringed the due process principles set by human rights conventions?

3. A number of scholarly writings have been devoted to the relationship between arbitration and the human rights documents, particularly by French authors.[43] In an article inspired by the *Stran* decision, A. Bencheneb writes:

> The issue in the Stran Refineries case was the annihilation of an arbitration clause by way of legislation. In disregard of a contractual undertaking signed by a state. In disregard of the autonomy of this clause. In disregard of the principle of prohibition against contradicting oneself at the expense of others, since the Greek state itself relied on the clause in order to compel the refinery to arbitrate.[44]

Do you agree?

How important is it that the Greek State relied—at an earlier stage in the proceedings—on the arbitration clause?

4. Is the time sequence critical? Would the outcome be the same if Law No. 1701/1987, providing "authoritative interpretation" regarding the validity of the arbitration clause was enacted, let us say, after the award was rendered, but before annulment was sought? Before the arbitration was initiated?

What if the 1987 provision declaring that the arbitration clause was invalid had been part of the original 1975 Act on the Termination of Preferential Contracts?

5. Should those who have sympathy for arbitration be pleased or apprehensive after *Stran Refineries*?

V.2.f. Penalizing a Party for a Frivolous Challenge to an Award

FLEXIBLE MANUFACTURING SYSTEMS PTY. LTD. v. SUPER PRODUCTS CORPORATION

United States Court of Appeals, Seventh Circuit, 1996.
86 F.3d 96.

Before POSNER, CHIEF JUDGE, and BAUER and DIANE P. WOOD, CIRCUIT JUDGES.

DIANE P. WOOD, CIRCUIT JUDGE.

In this appeal, Super Products Corp. seeks to persuade this Court that an arbitration award in a commercial arbitration should be vacated

---

[42]. See *République de Guinée v. Chambre arbitrale de Paris*, judgment of January 28, 1987, *id.* at 380.

[43]. See e.g. Charles Jarosson, L'arbitrage et la Convention européenne des droits de l'homme, 1989 Revue de l'arbitrage 576.

[44]. A. Bencheneb, La contrariété à la Convention européenne des droits de l'homme d'une loi anéantissant une sentence arbitrale? 1996 Revue de l'arbitrage 181, at 185.

because the arbitrators failed to enforce the agreement reached by the parties and manifestly disregarded the applicable law. We find that there was a valid arbitration agreement, and that Super Products has not carried its burden of showing the invalidity of the award by clear and convincing evidence. See Wis. Stat. § 788.10(1)(d), DeBaker v. Shah, 194 Wis.2d 104, 533 N.W.2d 464, 468 (1995). We therefore affirm.

The underlying facts are straightforward. On March 5, 1988, Super Products (a Wisconsin corporation) entered into a licensing agreement to provide Flexible Manufacturing Systems (an Australian company) with drawings and technical information for manufacturing industrial vacuum loading equipment. Shortly after the execution of the agreement, Flexible began to complain that Super Products was not providing the technology required by the agreement. The relationship degenerated on all sides, and on August 24, 1989 Flexible filed the underlying suit in this case in federal court, asserting diversity jurisdiction and claiming breach of contract and fraud in the inducement. On October 17, 1989, Super Products retaliated by sending Flexible notice of its intent to terminate the agreement.

Section 11 of the License Agreement contained a standard commercial arbitration clause. It provided as follows:

> In the event of there arising any difference of opinion between the parties or other dispute as to any of the matters provided for herein, the parties shall endeavor to settle the differences or dispute in an amicable manner through mutual consultation.

> In the event of such difference or dispute being incapable of resolution by such consultation, such dispute or difference shall be referred to and determined by the Commercial Arbitration Association in the United States and the governing law should be of the state of Wisconsin, or elsewhere as the parties may agree under the Commercial Arbitration Association of the U.S.A.

On February 11, 1991, the district court entered an order granting Super Products' motion to compel arbitration pursuant to Section 11. The order bifurcated the dispute into two parts: the breach of contract claims, which were to be submitted to arbitration, and the fraud in the inducement claims, which the court held in abeyance pending the outcome of the arbitration. (Because there is no entity known as the Commercial Arbitration Association in the United States, the court ordered the parties to arbitrate before the American Arbitration Association (AAA).)

On November 9, 1992, Flexible commenced arbitration before the AAA by filing a demand that set forth the breach of contract claims. Super Products responded with a counterclaim. The arbitration went forward before a three-person panel, which held a seventeen day evidentiary hearing. The panel heard testimony from sixteen witnesses, received over 400 exhibits, and heard full argument from both parties. On March 7, 1994, the panel issued an award of $2,000,000 to Flexible on its claim, $20,395 to Super Products, and costs to Flexible of $28,000. The panel was split two-to-one, but no written opinions were issued.

Following the entry of the arbitrator's award, Super Products returned to the district court with a motion to vacate the award. The district court, in a careful opinion, concluded that the award was valid and enforceable, denied Super Products' motion, and entered an order confirming the award and entering judgment for Flexible.[1] The court began by considering the applicable arbitration law for the dispute (as opposed to the law governing the underlying dispute). After evaluating both the Federal Arbitration Act (FAA), 9 U.S.C. § 1 et seq., and the Wisconsin Arbitration Act, Wis.Stats. § 788.01 et seq., the court concluded that both laws provided for essentially the same type of review of arbitral awards. Both listed very limited and specific grounds upon which a court can vacate an award. The court concluded that the Wisconsin Arbitration Act was not preempted by the FAA, that FAA precedents were persuasive authority for the Wisconsin statute, and that Wisconsin law applied to the case.

On the merits, the court stressed the extremely narrow grounds recognized by the Wisconsin Supreme Court for overturning an arbitration award. In City of Madison v. Madison Professional Police Officers Association, 144 Wis.2d 576, 425 N.W.2d 8 (1988), the Wisconsin Supreme Court said that it would "not overturn the arbitrator's decision for mere errors of law or fact, but only when 'perverse misconstruction or positive misconduct [is] plainly established, or if there is a manifest disregard of the law or if the award itself is illegal or violates strong public policy.'" 425 N.W.2d at 11 (quoting Milwaukee Board of School Directors v. Milwaukee Teachers' Education Association, 93 Wis.2d 415, 287 N.W.2d 131 (1980)). The district court might have added that the Supreme Court of the United States takes an identical approach to the scope of judicial review under the FAA. Paperworkers Union v. Misco, Inc., 484 U.S. 29, 36–38, 108 S.Ct. 364, 369–71, 98 L.Ed.2d 286 (1987); Wilko v. Swan, 346 U.S. 427, 436–37, 74 S.Ct. 182, 187–88, 98 L.Ed. 168 (1953), overruled on other grounds, Rodriguez de Quijas v. Shearson/American Express, Inc., 490 U.S. 477, 109 S.Ct. 1917, 104 L.Ed.2d 526 (1989).

* * *

1. On January 31, 1995, Flexible, having won on the breach of contract claim and not desiring the expense and delay of future litigation, moved for a voluntary dismissal of its remaining claims. The district court granted Flexible's motion in the same order that it denied Super Products' request for modification of the court's order denying Super Products' motion to vacate the arbitration award.

This Court has had numerous occasions on which to address the proper approach to review of an arbitral award at the enforcement stage. If there is an agreement to arbitrate, and the issues presented to the arbitrator fell within that agreement, courts may overturn the arbitrator's award only on very narrow grounds. The list in the FAA, § 10, includes the following: (1) the award was procured by corruption, fraud, or undue means; (2) there was evident partiality or corruption in the arbitrator(s); (3) the arbitrators were guilty of certain kinds of procedural misconduct; and (4) "the arbitrators exceeded their powers, or so imperfectly executed them that a mutual, final, and definite award" was not made. 9 U.S.C. § 10. The language of Wis.Stats. § 788.10, as the district court recognized, is virtually identical. Judge Bauer, writing for this Court recently in Gingiss International, Inc. v. Bormet, 58 F.3d 328 (7th Cir.1995), summarized the principles that govern review of an arbitrator's award. "Thinly veiled attempts to obtain appellate review of an arbitrator's decision," he held, are not permitted under the FAA. Id. at 333. "Factual or legal errors by arbitrators—even clear or gross errors—do not authorize courts to annul awards.... [I]nsufficiency of the evidence is not a ground for setting aside an arbitration award under the FAA." Id. (internal citations omitted).

We faced a similar challenge to an arbitral award in Widell v. Wolf, 43 F.3d 1150 (7th Cir.1994), in which we once again held that parties are not entitled to reargue their claims in a proceeding to vacate an arbitral award, citing Paperworkers Union v. Misco, Inc., supra. This Court noted that litigation like this defeats the goal of arbitration to provide a quick and cheap decision. 43 F.3d at 1151. See also National Wrecking Co. v. IBT, Local 731, 990 F.2d 957, 960 (7th Cir.1993); Health Services Management Corp. v. Hughes, 975 F.2d 1253, 1267 (7th Cir.1992); Chicago Typographical Union v. Chicago Sun–Times, 935 F.2d 1501, 1505 (7th Cir.1991).

In the case before us, Super Products rested its hopes on the statutory authority of a court to vacate an arbitrator's award "where the arbitrators exceeded their powers, or so imperfectly executed them that a mutual, final, and definite award on the subject matter submitted was not made." Wis.Stats. § 788.10(1)(d). The district court found, however, that Super Products failed to overcome, with clear and convincing evidence, the presumption of validity that an arbitral award enjoys. It rejected outright Super Products' principal argument, which was that Super Products' own termination of the License Agreement rendered invalid the arbitrator's award of future lost profits for time periods following termination. It was for the arbitrator to decide who breached the agreement first, and what damages were recoverable as a consequence. The panel did so, and that was the end of it.

We agree. If courts were to undertake the kind of searching review of arbitral awards that Super Products invites here, arbitration would be transformed from a commercially useful alternative method of dispute resolution into a burdensome additional step on the march through the court system. This is why courts will not overturn an arbitration decision for mere errors of judgment as to law or fact, as the Wisconsin Supreme Court noted in Madison Professional Police Officers. The fact that an arbitrator makes a mistake, by erroneously rejecting a valid, or even a dispositive legal defense, does not provide grounds for vacating an award unless the arbitrator deliberately disregarded what she knew to be the law. See Eljer Mfg. Inc. v. Kowin Development Corp., 14 F.3d 1250, 1255 (7th Cir.), cert. denied, ___ U.S. ___, 114 S.Ct. 2675, 129 L.Ed.2d 810 (1994) (interpreting the FAA's counterpart to Wis.Stat. § 788.10(1)(d)).

The arguments Super Products tries to raise here all go to its purported termination of the agreement, the legal consequences of that termination, and the amount of damages. These were the points that the arbitration panel was charged with deciding. Super Products itself, it is worth recalling, both entered into a License Agreement that contained an arbitration clause and took the initiative to invoke the arbitral procedure before the district court. This is therefore not a case in which there may not be an agreement to arbitrate between the parties, like First Option. This case falls instead into the mainstream of commercial arbitration agreements, which exist precisely because deals or relationships sometimes fall apart and disputes must be resolved somehow. It is worth noting that arbitration is especially useful in international transactions, like this one between an Australian company and an American one, where both sides have the assurance ex ante that dispute resolution can take place away from potentially unfamiliar courts and legal systems. See generally Mitsubishi v. Soler Chrysler–Plymouth, 473 U.S. 614, 629–31, 105 S.Ct. 3346, 3355–56, 87 L.Ed.2d 444 (1985); Scherk v. Alberto–Culver, 417 U.S. 506, 516–17, 94 S.Ct. 2449, 2455–56, 41 L.Ed.2d 270 (1974). The district court correctly applied the law governing review of arbitral awards, and correctly entered judgment on this one.

Last, Flexible has moved for an order finding that this appeal is frivolous and awarding double costs and other damages, pursuant to Fed.R.App.P. 27 and 38. Rule 38 provides that if this Court determines that an appeal is frivolous, this Court "may award just damages and single or double costs to the appellee." Fed.R.App.P. 38. An appeal is frivolous within the meaning of Rule 38, when it "was prosecuted with no reasonable expectation of altering the district court's judgment and for purposes of delay or harassment or out of sheer obstinacy." Rosenburg v. Lincoln American Life Insurance Co., 883 F.2d 1328, 1340 (7th Cir.1989) (quoting Reid v. United States, 715 F.2d 1148, 1155 (7th Cir.1983)). This Court has awarded Rule 38 sanctions in other frivolous appeals seeking to overturn arbitral awards. Widell, 43 F.3d at 1152; Chicago Typographical Union, 935 F.2d at 1506–07; Hill v. Norfolk & Western Ry., 814 F.2d 1192, 1203 (7th Cir.1987). "The promise of arbitration is spoiled if parties disappointed by its results can delay the conclusion of the proceeding by groundless litigation in the district court followed by groundless appeal to this court; we have said repeatedly that we would punish such tactics and we mean it." Hill, 814 F.2d at 1203.

Super Products' appeal had absolutely no prospect of success and has served only to tax the resources of this Court, the district court, and the defendants. Super Products' tactics have cost Flexible more than two years of delay in collecting its arbitration award. We therefore conclude that this is an appropriate case in which to grant Flexible's Rule 38 motion. Flexible shall have fifteen days within which to submit to the Clerk of this Court proper documentation of its expenses in defending this appeal and damages resulting from the delayed receipt of the arbitration award.

The judgment below is AFFIRMED.

Questions and Comments

1. Penalizing the party whose motion to set aside is judged frivolous will certainly limit judicial scrutiny of the arbitration process. Do you agree with the policy behind the decision of the U.S. Court of Appeals?

2. Should frivolous challenges against an arbitration award be treated differently than frivolous challenges against a court decision?

3. Would you say that any motion aiming at a de novo review of the merits is a frivolous challenge?

4. Suppose Super Products challenged the award on the ground that the arbitration clause did not yield a valid arbitration agreement, because it was unclear (it contained reference to a non-existing institution, and it also included unorthodox grammar here and there). Would you consider this to be a frivolous challenge?

5. Suppose the challenge was based on ambiguities in the arbitration clause, and suppose that it was not Super Products, but Flexible, who moved to compel arbitration. What result?

V.3. JUDICIAL CONTROL OVER THE AWARD: RECOGNITION AND ENFORCEMENT

V.3.a. Awards Subject to the New York Convention

An arbitral award that will not be recognized (for res judicata purposes) or enforced in national courts does not have much practical value. A major purpose of the New York Convention was to ensure the efficacy of awards by limiting the grounds upon which a national court could refuse to recognize or enforce an award. In sections V.3.b-e, below, we shall turn to a careful examination of the grounds listed in Article V for refusing recognition or enforcement. In this section we examine the preliminary issue of the type of award to which the New York Convention, and hence Article V, applies.

Some of the questions relevant to this issue have already been examined in connection with the problem of enforcing agreements to arbitrate. The question there was which arbitration agreements are governed by the New York Convention. The question now is which awards are so governed. The convention provisions relevant to its coverage are contained mostly in Article I. Under that article the

Convention applies to two major categories of awards: (1) those "made in the territory of a State other than the State where the recognition and enforcement of such awards are sought" and (2) those "not considered as domestic awards in the State where their recognition and enforcement are sought". We have examined above how one localizes an award in a particular territory. Once an award is so localized, it is relatively easy to decide whether an award falls into the first category.[45] In this subsection we examine the decisive issue of the second category: when is an award not considered a domestic award?

V.3.a.i.   *An Award Rendered in the State Where Recognition or Enforcement is Sought*

SIGVAL BERGESEN v. JOSEPH MULLER CORPORATION

United States Court of Appeals, Second Circuit, 1983.
710 F.2d 928.

CARDAMONE, CIRCUIT JUDGE:

The question before us on this appeal is whether the 1958 Convention on the Recognition and Enforcement of Foreign Arbitral Awards is applicable to an award arising from an arbitration held in New York between two foreign entities. Responding to the rapid expansion of international trade following World War II, the Convention reflects the efforts of businessmen involved in such trade to provide a workable mechanism for the swift resolution of their day-to-day disputes. International merchants often prefer arbitration over litigation because it is faster, less expensive and more flexible. But previous international agreements had not proved effective in securing enforcement of arbitral awards; nor had private arbitration through the American Arbitration Association, the International Chamber of Commerce, the London Court of Arbitration and the like been completely satisfactory because of problems in enforcing awards.

In 1958, a convention was called to deal with these problems. The United States attended and participated in the conference but did not sign the Convention. Ten years later, in 1968, the Senate gave its consent, but accession was delayed until 1970 in order for Congress to enact the necessary implementing legislation. * * *

In resolving the question presented on this appeal, we are faced with the difficult task of construing the Convention. The family of nations has endlessly—some say since the Tower of Babel—sought to breach the barrier of language. As illustrated by the proceedings at this conference, the delegates had to comprehend concepts familiar in one state that had no counterpart in others and to compromise entrenched and differing

[45]. Recall that New York Convention Article I(3) allows an adhering State to limit applicability of the convention to (i) awards made in the territory of another contracting State and (ii) those concerning disputes arising out of relationships considered "commercial under the national laws of the State making * * * [this] declaration."

national commercial interests. Concededly, 45 nations cannot be expected to produce a document with the clear precision of a mathematical formula. Faced with the formidable obstacles to agreement, the wonder is that there is a Convention at all, much less one that is serviceable and enforceable. Yet, the proposals agreed upon in the Convention have not raised the kinds of legal questions that a commentator reported one of the delegates feared would be the joy of jurists, but the bane of plaintiffs,

I

The facts are undisputed and may be briefly stated. Sigval Bergesen, a Norwegian shipowner, and Joseph Muller Corporation, a Swiss company, entered into three charter parties in 1969, 1970 and 1971. The 1969 and 1970 charters provided for the transportation of chemicals from the United States to Europe. The 1971 charter concerned the transportation of propylene from the Netherlands to Puerto Rico. Each charter party contained an arbitration clause providing for arbitration in New York, and the Chairman of the American Arbitration Association was given authority to resolve disputes in connection with the appointment of arbitrators.

In 1972, after disputes had arisen during the course of performing the 1970 and 1971 charters, Bergesen made a demand for arbitration of its claims for demurrage and shifting and port expenses. Muller denied liability and asserted counterclaims. The initial panel of arbitrators chosen by the parties was dissolved because of Muller's objections and a second panel was selected through the offices of the American Arbitration Association. This panel held hearings in 1976 and 1977 and rendered a written decision on December 14, 1978. It decided in favor of Bergesen, rejecting all of Muller's counterclaims save one. The net award to Bergesen was $61,406.09 with interest.

Bergesen then sought enforcement of its award in Switzerland where Muller was based. For over two years Muller successfully resisted enforcement. On December 10, 1981, shortly before the expiration of the three-year limitations period provided in 9 U.S.C. § 207, Bergesen filed a petition in the United States District Court for the Southern District of New York to confirm the arbitration award. In a decision dated October 7, 1982 and reported at 548 F.Supp. 650 (S.D.N.Y.1982), District Judge Charles S. Haight, Jr. confirmed Bergesen's award, holding that the Convention applied to arbitration awards rendered in the United States involving foreign interests. Judgment was entered awarding Bergesen $61,406.09, plus interest of $18,762.01. Additionally, Bergesen received $8,462.00 for Muller's share of arbitrators' fees and expenses which it had previously paid, together with interest of $2,253.63 on that amount.

On appeal from this $90,883.73 judgment, Muller contends that the Convention does not cover enforcement of the arbitration award made in the United States because it was neither territorially a "foreign" award nor an award "not considered as domestic" within the meaning of the Convention. Muller also claims that the reservations adopted by the

United States in its accession to the Convention narrowed the scope of its application so as to exclude enforcement of this award in United States courts, that the statute implementing the treaty was not intended to cover awards rendered within the United States, and finally, that Bergesen's petition to obtain enforcement was technically insufficient under the applicable requirements of the Convention.

II

Whether the Convention applies to a commercial arbitration award rendered in the United States is a question previously posed but left unresolved in this Court. The two district courts that have addressed the issue have reached opposite conclusions, with little in the way of analysis. Compare Transmarine Seaways Corp. of Monrovia v. Marc Rich & Co., A.G., 480 F.Supp. 352, 353 (S.D.N.Y.) (Haight, J.) (finding the Convention applicable), aff'd mem., 614 F.2d 1291 (2d Cir.1979), cert. denied, 445 U.S. 930, 100 S.Ct. 1318, 63 L.Ed.2d 763 (1980) with Diapulse Corporation of America v. Carba, Ltd., No. 78 Civ. 3263 (S.D.N.Y. June 28, 1979) (Broderick, J.) (Convention did not apply "by its terms"), remanded on other grounds, 626 F.2d 1108 (2d Cir.1980). The facts of the instant case make it necessary to resolve what this Court earlier termed an "intriguing" issue, see Andros Compania Maritima, S.A., 579 F.2d at 699 n. 11.

To resolve that issue we turn first to the Convention's history. Under the auspices of the United Nations, the Convention on the Recognition and Enforcement of Foreign Arbitral Awards was convened in New York City in 1958 to resolve difficulties created by two earlier treaties—the 1923 Geneva Protocol on Arbitration Clauses, 27 L.N.T.S. 157 (1924), and the 1927 Geneva Convention on the Execution of Foreign Arbitral Awards, 92 L.N.T.S. 301 (1929). Because of the legal and practical difficulties which arose from application of these earlier treaties,[1] one commentator wrote, "The formidable amount of highly qualified labor which went into their preparation has not been rewarded by any perceptible progress in international commercial arbitration." Nussbaum, Treaties on Commercial Arbitration—A Test of International Private–Law Legislation, 56 Harv.L.Rev. 219, 236 (1942).

A proposed draft of the 1958 Convention which was to govern the enforcement of foreign arbitral awards stated that it was to apply to arbitration awards rendered in a country other than the state where enforcement was sought. This proposal was controversial because the delegates were divided on whether it defined adequately what constituted a foreign award. On one side were ranged the countries of western Europe accustomed to civil law concepts; on the other side were the eastern European states and the common law nations. For example, several countries, including France, Italy and West Germany, objected to

---

1. For a discussion of the exact nature of the problems see Contini, International Commercial Arbitration, 8 Am.J.Comp.L. 283, 288–90 (1959); Quigley, Accession by the United States to the United Nations Convention on the Recognition and Enforcement of Foreign Arbitral Awards, 70 Yale L.J. 1049, 1055 (1961).

the proposal on the ground that a territorial criterion was not adequate to establish whether an award was foreign or domestic. These nations believed that the nationality of the parties, the subject of the dispute and the rules of arbitral procedure were factors to be taken into account in determining whether an award was foreign. In both France and West Germany, for example, the nationality of an award was determined by the law governing the procedure. Thus, an award rendered in London under German law was considered domestic when enforcement was attempted in Germany, and an award rendered in Paris under foreign law was considered foreign when enforcement was sought in France. As an alternative to the territorial concept, eight European nations proposed that the Convention "apply to the recognition and enforcement of arbitral awards other than those considered as domestic in the country in which they are relied upon." Eight other countries, including the United States, objected to this proposal, arguing that common law nations would not understand the distinction between foreign and domestic awards. These latter countries urged the delegates to adopt only the territorial criterion.

A working party composed of representatives from ten states to which the matter was referred recommended that both criteria be included. Thus, the Convention was to apply to awards made in a country other than the state where enforcement was sought as well as to awards not considered domestic in that state. The members of the Working Party representing the western European group agreed to this recommendation, provided that each nation would be allowed to exclude certain categories of awards rendered abroad. At the conclusion of the conference this exclusion was omitted, so that the text originally proposed by the Working Party was adopted as Article I of the Convention. A commentator noted that the Working Party's intent was to find a compromise formula which would restrict the territorial concept. The final action taken by the Convention appears to have had the opposite result, i.e., except as provided in paragraph 3, the first paragraph of Article I means that the Convention applies to all arbitral awards rendered in a country other than the state of enforcement, whether or not such awards may be regarded as domestic in that state; "it also applies to all awards not considered as domestic in the state of enforcement, whether or not any of such awards may have been rendered in the territory of that state."

To assure accession to the Convention by a substantial number of nations, two reservations were included. They are set forth in Article I(3). The first provides that any nation "may on the basis of reciprocity declare that it will apply the Convention" only to those awards made in the territory of another contracting state. The second states that the Convention will apply only to differences arising out of legal relationships "considered as commercial under the national law" of the state declaring such a reservation. These reservations were included as a necessary recognition of the variety and diversity of the interests represented at the conference, as demonstrated, for example, by the statement of the delegate from Belgium that without any right of reservation his country would not accede.

III

With this background in mind, we turn to Muller's contentions regarding the scope of the Convention. The relevant portion of the Convention, Article I, is set forth in the margin.[2] The territorial concept expressed in the first sentence of Article I(1) presents little difficulty. Muller correctly urges that since the arbitral award in this case was made in New York and enforcement was sought in the United States, the award does not meet the territorial criterion. Simply put, it is not a foreign award as defined in Article I(1) because it was not rendered outside the nation where enforcement is sought.

Muller next contends that the award may not be considered a foreign award within the purview of the second sentence of Article I(1) because it fails to qualify as an award "not considered as domestic." Muller claims that the purpose of the "not considered as domestic" test was to provide for the enforcement of what it terms "stateless awards," i.e., those rendered in the territory where enforcement is sought but considered unenforceable because of some foreign component. This argument is unpersuasive since some countries favoring the provision desired it so as to preclude the enforcement of certain awards rendered abroad, not to enhance enforcement of awards rendered domestically.

Additionally, Muller urges a narrow reading of the Convention contrary to its intended purpose. The Convention did not define non-domestic awards. The definition appears to have been left out deliberately in order to cover as wide a variety of eligible awards as possible, while permitting the enforcing authority to supply its own definition of "non-domestic" in conformity with its own national law. Omitting the definition made it easier for those states championing the territorial concept to ratify the Convention while at the same time making the Convention more palatable in those states which espoused the view that the nationality of the award was to be determined by the law governing the arbitral procedure. We adopt the view that awards "not considered as domestic" denotes awards which are subject to the Convention not because made abroad, but because made within the legal framework of another country, e.g., pronounced in accordance with foreign law or involving parties domiciled or having their principal place of business outside the enforcing jurisdiction. We prefer this broader construction because it is more in line with the intended purpose of the treaty, which was entered into to encourage the recognition and enforcement of international arbitration awards. Applying that purpose to this case

2. This Convention shall apply to the recognition and enforcement of arbitral awards made in the territory of a State other than the State where the recognition and enforcement of such awards are sought, and arising out of differences between persons, whether physical or legal. It shall also apply to arbitral awards not considered as domestic awards in the State where their recognition and enforcement are sought.

involving two foreign entities leads to the conclusion that this award is not domestic.

IV

Muller also urges us to interpret the Convention narrowly based on the fact that, as stated in a Presidential Proclamation dated September 1, 1970, 21 U.S.T. 2517, T.I.A.S. No. 6997, the 1970 accession by the United States to the Convention adopted both reservations of Article I(3). The fact that the United States acceded to the Convention with a declaration of reservations provides little reason for us to construe the accession in narrow terms. Had the United States acceded to the Convention without these two reservations, the scope of the Convention doubtless would have had wider impact. Nonetheless, the treaty language should be interpreted broadly to effectuate its recognition and enforcement purposes.

V

We now turn to the argument that the implementing statute was not intended to cover awards rendered within the United States. Section 202 of Title 9 of the United States Code which is entitled "Agreement or award falling under the Convention," provides in relevant part:

> An agreement or award arising out of such a relationship which is entirely between citizens of the United States shall be deemed not to fall under the Convention unless that relationship involves property located abroad, envisages performance or enforcement abroad, or has some other reasonable relation with one or more foreign states.

The legislative history of this provision indicates that it was intended to ensure that "an agreement or award arising out of a legal relationship exclusively between citizens of the United States is not enforceable under the Convention in [United States] courts unless it has a reasonable relation with a foreign state." H.R.Rep. No. 91–1181, 91st Cong., 2d Sess. 2, reprinted in 1970 U.S.Code Cong. & Ad.News 3601, 3602. Inasmuch as it was apparently left to each state to define which awards were to be considered nondomestic, Congress spelled out its definition of that concept in section 202. Had Congress desired to exclude arbitral awards involving two foreign parties rendered within the United States from enforcement by our courts it could readily have done so. It did not.
* * *

Additional support for the view that awards rendered in the United States may qualify for enforcement under the Convention is found in the remaining sections of the implementing statute. It has been held that section 203 of the statute provides jurisdiction for disputes involving two aliens. Section 204 supplies venue for such an action and section 206 states that "[a] court having jurisdiction under this chapter may direct that arbitration be held … at any place therein provided for, whether that place is within or without the United States" (emphasis supplied). It would be anomalous to hold that a district court could direct two aliens to arbitration within the United States under the statute, but that it could not enforce the resulting award under legislation which, in large part, was enacted for just that purpose.

Muller's further contention that it could not have been the aim of Congress to apply the Convention to this transaction because it would remove too broad a class of awards from enforcement under the Federal Arbitration Act, 9 U.S.C. §§ 1–13, is unpersuasive. That this particular award might also have been enforced under the Federal Arbitration Act is not significant. There is no reason to assume that Congress did not intend to provide overlapping coverage between the Convention and the Federal Arbitration Act. Similarly, Muller's argument that Bergesen only sought enforcement under the terms of the Convention because it has a longer statute of limitations than other laws under which Bergesen could have sued is irrelevant. Since the statutes overlap in this case Bergesen has more than one remedy available and may choose the most advantageous.

VI

Finally, Muller asserts that Bergesen's petition for enforcement was technically insufficient and did not meet the requirements of the Convention. Bergesen submitted the affidavit of Harry Constas, chairman of the arbitration panel, certifying the award and the charter parties on which it was based. Under Article IV(1) of the Convention

> [t]o obtain the recognition and enforcement mentioned in the preceding article, the party applying for recognition and enforcement shall, at the time of the application supply:
>
> (a) The duly authenticated original award or a duly certified copy thereof;
>
> (b) The original agreement referred to in article II or a duly certified copy thereof.

Muller would have us read this provision as requiring either a duly authenticated original or a duly certified copy of a duly authenticated original. Such an interpretation is unnecessarily restrictive and at odds with a common sense reading of the provision. Copies of the award and the agreement which have been certified by a member of the arbitration panel provide a sufficient basis upon which to enforce the award and such were supplied in this case.

The judgment is affirmed.

Questions and Comments

1. As the *Bergesen* opinion explains, several European civil law countries considered awards made abroad, but under their own *lex arbitri*, to be domestic awards. They thus proposed that the Convention "apply to the recognition and enforcement of arbitral awards other than those considered as domestic in the country in which they are relied upon." In the end the Convention was amended to include the last sentence of Article I(1): "It [the

Convention] shall also apply to arbitral awards not considered as domestic awards in the State where their recognition and enforcement are sought."

In what sense did the European civil law countries gain, if at all, by the addition of this language? Is an award made in a foreign country, but under the *lex arbitri* of the state asked to enforce it, governed by the Convention? Can that award be set aside by that state without regard to New York Convention standards?

2. Suppose the arbitration law (*lex arbitri*) of Europa allows Europa's courts to set aside an award if the court finds the facts the arbitrators relied upon are not supported by substantial evidence introduced in the arbitral proceedings. If an award made in Switzerland under the *lex arbitri* of Europa is brought to Europa for enforcement, presumably Europa could not refuse Article V enforcement on the ground of lack of substantial evidence, because this is not a ground recognized by that article. Instead, may a Europa court set aside the award on the ground of lack of substantial evidence to support the award?

3. To decide whether the award in *Bergesen*, though made in the U.S., is not a domestic U.S. award, the *Bergesen* court relies on section 202 of the Federal Arbitration Act (the U.S. statute implementing the New York Convention):

> An agreement or award arising out of * * * [a commercial] relationship which is entirely between citizens of the United States shall be deemed not to fall under the Convention unless that relationship involves property located abroad, envisages performance or enforcement abroad, or has some other reasonable relation with one or more foreign states.

Under this statutory language, does the award in *Bergesen* fall under the Convention? In view of the Convention's legislative history recounted in *Bergesen*, did the U.S. implementing statute capture the intent of Article I(1)? Does the U.S. implementing language do violence to the purpose of Article I(1)?

4. In Brier v. Northstar Marine, Inc. (1992 WL 350292 [D.N.J. April 28, 1992]), a U.S. federal district court refused to enforce an agreement to arbitrate in London between two American parties, the owner of a yacht and the salvage company that refloated the yacht after she ran aground in New Jersey waters. The court applied the U.S. implementing statute language cited above to find that the parties' relationship was not reasonably related to a foreign state (the U.K.) and refused to order arbitration in London. If an award had been rendered in London in this case, would a U.S. court have been entitled to consider the award not subject to the New York Convention?

V.3.a.ii.   *Binding Awards and Awards Producing Only "Obligatory Effects"*

DECISION OF 8 OCTOBER 1981

Bundesgerichtshof (Supreme Court).

Recht der Internationalen Wirtschaft [RIW], 210 (1982).*[i]

[An action was brought in the German courts under the UN Convention on the Recognition and Enforcement of Foreign Arbitral Awards

---

* Reprinted by permission of Recht der Internationalen Wirtschaft, Verlag Recht und Wirtschaft GmbH.

i. Authors' translation.

to enforce an award rendered in Italy in an *arbitrato irrituale*. The court of first instance's judgment denying recognition was reversed by the court of appeals. The matter was then taken to the Bundesgerichtshof which reinstated the judgment in first instance on the ground that an award rendered in an *arbitrato irrituale* was not an "arbitral award" for the purposes the UN Convention.]

The UN Convention is, as a multilateral agreement, to be interpreted on the basis of its text ... with special attention being given to the language used, the sense and purpose of the Convention's provisions, and its drafting history.

The Chinese, English, French, Russian, and Spanish texts of the UN Convention are equally authentic. The term "arbitration" utilized in the English text and the French word "arbitrage" have ... the meaning of a proceeding in which the arbitrator is charged with deciding a legal controversy in the place of a national court.... The language of the Convention thus supports not applying its provisions to proceedings that, though similar to arbitration, produce only the effects of an obligation. The *lodo irrituale* of Italian law is such a procedure; it establishes the performance that is due but with only contractual effect (*schuldrechtlicher Wirkung*) and cannot be executed as a judgment (*keine Urteilswirkung*).

It follows that to apply the UN Convention to an *irrituale* award would go against the Convention's sense and purpose. Among other things, the UN Convention seeks to treat equally arbitral awards with effects in other Contracting States and thus to unify the law. But uniformity would be jeopardized if, as a consequence of the Convention, arbitral awards engendered different legal effects in the various Contracting States. Applying the UN Convention to an *irrituale* award would—even if limited (as the court of appeals did) to recognition—have this result. In Germany and in other non-Italian Contracting States the *irrituale* award would be recognized under the provisions of the UN Convention while, in Italy, the rules of the national Italian law would apply, under which the *irrituale* award engenders only obligational effects.

Moreover, the *irrituale* award would thus be given abroad a broader effect than under the law of its Italian home without there being in the UN Convention any basis for such a significant legal consequence. The UN Convention is only intended to extend to other Contracting States the effects of arbitral awards that are capable of execution under their domestic law, but not to go beyond the national laws and create additional arbitral awards that are capable of execution.

Nor does the drafting history of the UN Convention speak for the Convention's applicability to *irrituale* awards. The *irrituale* award was apparently not discussed during the drafting of the Convention. Even if, as the petitioner argued, the Italian delegation after the conclusion of the negotiations proceeded on the premise that the Convention covered *irrituale* awards, no corresponding view is found among the other delegations at the time of the signing of the Convention.

In so far as writers take the position that the UN Convention applies fully to *irrituale* awards ... or is, in all events, at least applicable in that an *irrituale* award can be recognized ..., the considerations advanced are not persuasive.

Broggini seeks to derive the applicability of the Convention from Art. V(1)(e) of the Convention.... Under this provision, the recognition and enforcement of an arbitral award can be denied if, *inter alia*, ... the award has not yet become binding for the parties. This formula does not, however, have the meaning that an obligational bond (*schuldrechtliche Bindung*) suffices.... The drafting history ... reveals a quite different meaning. Previously the Geneva Convention on Enforcement of Foreign Arbitral Awards of 26 September 1927 ..., through the requirement that the arbitral award must be final, had made a double *exequatur* necessary for enforcing an award abroad. In order to avoid this result, the UN Convention chose the term "binding"; but this language did not give up the requirement that the award be capable of execution....

Schlosser would apply the UN Convention to *irrituale* awards because they have practical importance in international commerce. Schlosser thus sees the Convention as encompassing all the forms, characteristic for international commerce, by which—outside of state-administered justice—disputes over reciprocal rights and duties are resolved by binding decisions of third parties.

This conception finds no support in the language of the UN Convention. Concerns respecting legal security also stand in the way of accepting this position....

Questions and Comments

1. In its Decision No. 3150 of October 1, 1969, the Supreme Court of Italy (*Corte di Cassazione*) described the difference between *arbitrato rituale* and *arbitrato irrituale* as follows:

> The distinction between arbitrato rituale and irrituale must be traced back to the intent of the parties. In the first case, such intent is aimed at attributing to the arbitrators a jurisdictional function in order to secure from them a decision susceptible of acquiring efficacy similar to that of a judicial decision. In the second case, the parties attribute to the arbitrator the function of giving birth to a negozio di accertamento, which must be referred exclusively to the intent of the parties themselves, and has the same value as that of a contract executed by such parties.

Arbitrato irrituale was and remained outside the Italian Code of Civil procedure. This has not been changed by its 1994 Amendments either. Underlining the difference between *arbitrato irrituale* and binding adjudication, Italian courts have even held that courts cannot grant interim measures in connection with a case which is pending before "irrituale" arbitration.[46] At the same time, *arbitrato irrituale* has never ceased to be relevant and important in Italy. Do you have an explanation?

2. The decision of the Bundesgerichtshof, set out above, set aside a decision of the Higher Court (Oberlandesgericht) of Hamburg of February 7, 1980,[47] holding that an "irrituale" award is an award within the meaning of Article I(1) of the New York Convention and that it was recognizable (although not enforceable). The Bundesgerichtshof[48] (German Supreme Court) reversed the decision of the OLG Hamburg, and held that a decision resulting from an *arbitrato irrituale* can neither be enforced nor recognized under the New York Convention. It is interesting to mention that on September 18, 1978[49], the Italian Supreme Court (*Corte di Cassazione*) came to the conclusion that *irrituale* awards do fall under the New York Convention (the award in question was not an Italian award, but a decision rendered under the rules of the London Corn Trade Association). Recognition was not accorded, however, because the *Corte di Cassazione* found that the arbitration clause did not comply with the formal requirements posited by Article II. of the New York Convention. In Martin Spier v. Calzaturificio Tecnica[50], a U.S. court was faced with the issue as to whether awards rendered in *irrituale* arbitration (*lodo irrituale*) fall under the New York Convention. The question was avoided, however, since annulment proceedings were pending in Italy, and the U.S. court decided—relying on Article VI of the New York Convention—to suspend its own proceedings pending the Italian courts' decision.

If you were the judge in *Spier*, and if you could not avoid facing the issue head on, how would you rule?

Is the "recognizable but not enforceable" option consistent with logic?

3. Could one argue that *arbitrato irrituale* falls under the New York Convention only for the purpose of requiring a contracting State to enforce the agreement to arbitrate, i.e. to refer the parties to arbitration under Article II of the Convention?

4. If one considers *arbitrato irrituale* to be within the scope of the Convention (having in view Article II(3)), then Art. V(1)(e), which speaks of the need for a "binding" award, would still serve as a ground for not recognizing and not enforcing the award if "binding" in the New York Convention denotes a "judgment-effect" (Urteilswirkung) rather than just a "contractual effect" (schuldrechtlicher Wirkung).

5. Do you agree with the argument of the Bundesgerichtshof that recognition can never accord broader effects than those acquired in the country of origin?

[46]. Pian del Sole s.p.a. v. s.r.l. Immobiliare La Fonte Cass. No. 6567 of June 17, 1993, reported in a digested form in European Current Law, April 1994, 80.

[47]. Reported in 2 IPRax 147 (1982).

[48]. See IPRax 1982, 143–146; English excerpts in 8 Yearbk. Comm. Arb'n 366–70 (1983).

[49]. Reported in English in 4 Yearbk. Comm. Arb'n 296–300 (1979).

[50]. 663 F.Supp. 871 (S.D.N.Y.1987).

V.3.a.iii.   Partial Awards

In the *Star Lines* case that follows the action is not one for recognizing or enforcing an award under the New York Convention, but rather an action to confirm a domestic U.S. award. Under the Federal Arbitration Act, section 9, a domestic award may be "vacated", that is, set aside, if the arbitrators "so imperfectly executed . . . [their powers] that a mutual, *final*, and *definite* award . . . was not made." (emphasis added). Thus the precise issue in the case is whether the partial award rendered by the arbitrators was a "final" or "definite" award. Similar "finality" language under the 1927 Geneva Convention had been interpreted by courts in countries party to that convention to mean the winning party had to obtain judicial confirmation of the award to prove its "finality". This resulted in a "double exequatur" procedure. The drafters of the New York Convention wanted to eliminate this "double exequatur" requirement and for that reason omitted any reference to an award's being "final". See A. van den Berg, The New York Convention of 1958 pp. 333–37 (1981). If the *Star Lines* case were to arise as a recognition and enforcement action under the New York Convention, would the partial award be an "award" under the Convention?

PUERTO RICO MARITIME SHIPPING AUTHORITY v. STAR LINES LTD.

United States District Court, Southern District of New York, 1978.
454 F.Supp. 368.

[Prior to 1977 Star Lines was responsible for servicing and booking cargo for the S.S. Puerto Rico, owned by Puerto Rico Maritime Shipping Authority (PRMSA). In February, 1977 PRMSA terminated the agency relationship with Star Lines. Thereafter the parties fell into dispute over their respective obligations under the previous agency contract. Each party made claims against the other. Each denied most of the opponent's claims and contested the amount due on other claims, with respect to which it admitted liability. The parties submitted these claims to arbitration. The present action relates to only one of PRMSA's claims against Star Lines. In the course of the arbitration, the arbitrators gave a partial award in PRMSA's favor, and PRMSA filed an action in federal district court to confirm the partial award.]

Robert L. Carter, District Judge

* * *

It is the general rule with regard to the confirmability of arbitration awards that, in order to be "final" and "definite," the award must both resolve all the issues submitted to arbitration, and determine each issue fully so that no further litigation is necessary to finalize the obligations of the parties under the award. *See, e. g., Cofinco, Inc. v. Bakrie & Bros., N. V.*, 395 F.Supp. 613, 616 (S.D.N.Y.1975) (Frankel, J.); *Mobil Oil Indonesia v. Asamera Oil (Indonesia)*, 43 N.Y.2d 276, 401 N.Y.S.2d 186 (1977); *Herbst v. Hagenaers*, 137 N.Y. 290 (1893); *Jones v. Welwood*, 71

N.Y. 208 (1877); *Wolff & Munier, Inc. v. Diesel Construction Co.*, 41 A.D.2d 618, 340 N.Y.S.2d 455 (1st Dep't.1973), *appeal after remand*, 44 A.D.2d 530, 353 N.Y.S.2d 22 (1st Dep't.1974), *aff'd*, 36 N.Y.2d 750, 368 N.Y.S.2d 828 (1975); *Hoffman v. Harry Greenberg Co.*, 109 Misc. 170, 178 N.Y.S. 398 (1st Dep't.1919); 5 Am.Jur.2d Arbitration & Award §§ 136, 141, 142.[6] There is, however, an exception to this rule: if an award is valid in part and invalid in part, and the valid portion concerns claims that are "separable" from and "non-dependent" on claims covered by the invalid portion, the valid portion of the award is confirmable, notwithstanding the absence of an award that finally disposes of all the claims that were submitted to arbitration. *Moyer v. Van–Dye–Way Corp.*, 126 F.2d 339 (3d Cir.1942). *See also, Herbst v. Hagenaers, supra*, 137 N.Y. at 296; *Jones v. Welwood, supra*, 71 N.Y. at 216. While there is little case law which illuminates the precise contours of the separability doctrine outlined in these cases, it would appear that PRMSA's claim regarding the freight monies is "separable" from the other claims at issue between the parties within the meaning of that doctrine. Consequently, if the award before the court had resolved the entirety of PRMSA's freight monies claim, it would probably have been confirmed. See *Moyer v. Van–Dye–Way Corp., supra*.

But, as is apparent from the award itself, the arbitrators did not do that. Rather, the arbitrators granted PRMSA a quantified award only to the extent that Star Lines admitted liability on PRMSA's claim, and with regard to the rest of PRMSA's claim, merely ordered Star Lines to "pay over ... such other freight monies as are or may come into its possession." This latter part of the freight monies award is, quite simply, an insufficient and unconfirmable resolution of the freight monies dispute. *See Herbst v. Hagenaers, supra*. "The goal of the proceeding was, and remains, a money award," *Cofinco, Inc. v. Bakrie & Bros., N. V., supra*, 395 F.Supp. at 616, and a declaration of liability which leaves the question of the amount of money owing unanswered and the possibility of further disputes between the parties open does not achieve this objective. For these reasons, an award with a defect similar to that in the award in this case was held unconfirmable in *Herbst v. Hagenaers, supra*.

Because of the insufficiency of the portion of the award concerning the disputed part of the freight monies claim, the interim award fails to dispose of the claim it deals with. Although the award decides in PRMSA's favor on part of PRMSA's claim, it rules for neither party on the rest of the claim, aside from the mere determination of liability. An award that fails to lay any one issue to rest is contrary to the general principles of arbitration law, as discussed above, and is not "final"

---

6. Because "[t]he federal Arbitration Act is the same or almost the same as the arbitration law in New York ... 'the state practice may be regarded as highly persuasive, even if not controlling'." *Island Territory of Curacao v. Solitron Devices, Inc.*, 356 F. Supp. 1, 11–12 (S.D.N.Y.) (Wyatt, J.), aff'd, 489 F.2d 1313 (2d Cir.1973), quoting *The Hartbridge*, 57 F.2d 672, 673 (2d Cir. 1932). It is thus appropriate to look to New York State cases for illumination on the meaning of the "finality" and "definiteness" requirements of the federal statute which governs here.

within the meaning of the federal Arbitration Act. *See, e. g., Herbst v. Hagenaers, supra. See also, Jones v. Welwood, supra,* 71 N.Y. at 216 (partial award vacated on grounds "that it does not dispose of any one controversy"); *Cf. Cofinco, Inc. v. Bakrie & Bros., N. V., supra,* 395 F.Supp. at 616 (award disapproved because it directed the payment of an unspecified amount of "accrued expenses" and "interest"). Nor can it be persuasively argued that the two portions of the freight monies award or claim are "separable;" if a confirmable partial award could issue from arbitration solely because liability for a portion of a claim or for a part of the award was admitted or easy to determine, the separability exception would swallow the rule.

WTB (GERMANY) v. CREI (ITALY)

Italy, Corte di Appello [Court of Appeal], Bologna, 1993.
21 Yearbk. Comm. Arb'n 590 (1996).*j

Facts

Costruire Società Cooperativa a responsabilità limitata (CREI), as main contractor, and WTB, as subcontractor, concluded a contract for certain construction works in the Milan area. The contract contained an ICC arbitration clause.

On 6 December 1983, CREI sent notice of termination to WTB and thereafter initiated ICC arbitration, seeking termination for WTB's breach of contract and damages.

On 27 June 1988, the arbitral tribunal issued a partial award deciding on the an debeatur, and found CREI liable of wrongfully terminating the contract. On 4 August 1989, a final award was rendered on the quantum debeatur, directing CREI to pay WTB DM 110,033.03.

WTB sought enforcement of the final award of 1989 before the Court of Appeal of Bologna, which denied the petition, holding that enforcement of a final award must be sought together with the enforcement of the connected partial award, when these awards are to be considered, formally and substantially, as a whole. In casu, the Court found that the requirement of Art. IV had not been met, as the partial award had not been submitted by WTB at the time of requesting enforcement, and this omission could not be cured by CREI's submitting a non-certified copy of the partial award in the proceedings.

"In its final statement, defendant has raised the objection that the request for enforcement of the final award of 4 August 1989, concerning the quantum debeatur, is inadmissible since all the issues concerning the an debeatur have been decided by the partial award rendered on 27 June 1988. The latter is thus a step in the formation of the whole arbitral decision as well as the premise on which the final award is based. Hence, as the two awards are necessarily connected and interdependent, they

---

* Reprinted with permission of Yearbook Commercial Arbitration, International Council for Commercial Arbitration.

j. Also published in 4 Rivista dell'arbitrato (1994, no. 2) p. 303–305, with note by G.F. Borio, p. 305–310.

must be considered as a whole also from the point of view of the requirement for enforcement provided for in Art. IV of the New York Convention of 1958.

"Defendant's objection, which could also have been raised *ex officio*,[1] concerning the compliance with the said provision of the Convention, is well-founded.

"It appears from the documents submitted by the parties that CREI initiated arbitration, seeking termination of the construction (sub-)contract between the parties for breach of contract by (sub-)contractor WTB, and damages. In the proceedings, [WTB] opposed the request and filed a counterclaim to obtain payment of various sums.

"In the course of the proceedings the parties requested the arbitral tribunal to render a partial award on the merits of the dispute and their liability as to the termination of the construction contract, brought about on 6 December 1983 by a notice of termination. By a partial award of 27 June 1988, the arbitral tribunal dismissed CREI's request to terminate the contract, considering [CREI's] notice of termination unjustified and deciding on the issues of an debeatur, and reserved 'any decision as to the quantum and the costs of the proceedings'. The definitions of the quantum and the parties' mutual debts were given in the final award of 4 August 1989.

"By the present petition, WTB seeks enforcement of said final award, the original of which it submitted when formally appearing in the proceedings, without (requesting enforcement of and) submitting the partial award as well. A non-certified photocopy of this latter award has been submitted by defendant during the proceedings, in order to support its further objections raised in the statement of defence.

"As defendant rightly maintains, the final award without the partial award does not provide any basis for defendant's liability and its obligation to pay under the award, as it only contains in its paras. 7.3 to 7.5 an extremely succinct summary of the first award. The reasons of the partial award of 27 June 1988 are referred to several times—but not copied—in the final award. In para. 6.8 we read that: 'CREI requested the arbitral tribunal to try and obtain directly from the Municipality of Milan certain information regarding the level of the watertable in 1983. This request in the evidence-gathering phase gave rise to a discussion which was described separately among the reasons of the partial award. The Arbitral Tribunal dismissed it, see the reasons of the partial award.' In para. 11.1 we read: 'Defendant criticized it (the partial award) because it did not take into consideration the behaviour of the parties after 6 December 1983, which behaviour the Tribunal ignored in order to settle the issue of [an debeatur]. The Tribunal cannot in any case re-examine the partial award, which is res judicata.' When determining in concreto the parties' mutual debts and deciding that CREI pay WTB the

---

1. The Court of Appeal referred to the Supreme Court's decision of 12 February 1987, no. 1526 (Jassica SA v. Ditta Gioac- chino Polojaz), reported in Yearbook XVII (1992) pp. 525–528 (Italy no. 109).

sum of DM 110,033.03 (and accessories), the arbitral tribunal, by majority, based these decisions on the decision in the partial award as to the liability of CREI, as it clearly appears from the final award.

"From the above summary considerations it derives that the final award on the quantum is closely connected to the partial award and cannot be considered as 'autonomous' from the latter, also as far as the obligation to give reasons is concerned (which is expressly provided for by Art. 14.2(c) of the contract mentioned in para. 4.1 of the final award). The Pubblico Ministero apparently thought the same, since he based his conclusions in favour of the enforcement of the final award on the reasons in the partial award.

"Only the joint examination of the partial award and the final award can allow to ascertain whether the decision of the arbitrators is final, certain, consistent and decides all the claims and issues filed by the parties. The two awards are thus inseparably united and must be considered as a whole, also from the formal point of view.

"Claimant's omission to seek enforcement of the partial award and submit the original or certified copy of the same at the time of initiating this action makes the request for enforcement of the final award inadmissible under Art. IV of the New York Convention. According to this provision, the party seeking recognition and enforcement of the foreign award must submit 'at the time of the application' the original or certified copy of the award and the written agreement (arbitral clause or arbitration agreement).

"The timely submission of the award—in casu, of the arbitral awards being an inseparable whole—in the prescribed form is a condition for enforcement and non-compliance with this condition makes exequatur impossible;[2] it is irrelevant that a non-certified copy of the partial award was submitted by defendant.

"WTB's application is therefore inadmissible; all other issues raised by defendant in its statement of defence do not need to be examined."

Questions and Comments

1. Fouchard suggests that "in order to avoid confusion", partial awards should be contrasted with "global" awards, rather than with final (*définitive*) awards.[51] This understanding has been confirmed in a number of court decisions. The same position was taken regarding *interim awards* in Fidelitas Shipping v. Exportchleb,[52] where the English court held that interim awards are final as to the matters they decide.

2. In Puerto Rico Maritime Shipping v. Star Lines, 454 F.Supp. 368 (S.D.N.Y.1978), respondent claimed that what the arbitrators called a partial award was actually not an award and could not be confirmed. The court held

2. The Court of Appeal referred to the Supreme Court's decision mentioned in fn. 1 and to the decision of the same Court in the same case, dated 26 May 1987, no. 4706 (*Jassica SA v. Ditta Gioacchino Polojaz*); both decisions are reported in Yearbook XVII (1992) pp. 525–528 (Italy no. 109).

[51]. Fouchard, Gaillard, Goldman, Op. cit. 754.

[52]. 1966 QB 630 (CA).

that a partial award cannot be issued solely because "liability for a portion of the claim or for a part of the award was admitted or easy to determine". How would you define the instances in which arbitrators may issue a confirmable partial award?

3. In *WTB v. CREI* the relationship between two awards is again at issue. The Italian Court held that the *quantum debeatur* award cannot be independently recognized without the *an debeatur* award.

Which award is then final, the "partial" or the "final" award? Or none of them independently?

4. Would you recognize the partial (*an debeatur*) award if submitted without the *quantum debeatur* award?

5. Is the *WTB v. CREI* decision reconcilable with the holding of the *Puerto Rico* case?

6. Did the Italian court stay within the boundaries of the New York Convention when it stated that "Only the joint examination of the partial award and the final award can allow to ascertain whether the decision of the arbitrators is final, certain, consistent and decides all the claims and issues filed by the parties."

In other words, does the position taken by the Italian court, and its insistence on "consistency", and "certainty", imply a reexamination of the merits?

V.3.b.　Grounds Under the Convention for Refusing Recognition and Enforcement—An Introductory Case

PARSONS AND WHITTEMORE OVERSEAS CO. v. SOCIETE GENERALE DE L'INDUSTRIE DU PAPIER (RAKTA)

United States Court of Appeals. Second Circuit, 1974.
508 F.2d 969.

[Plaintiff American corporation appealed from an order of the United States District Court for the Southern District of New York, granting to defendant Egyptian corporation a summary judgment confirming a foreign arbitral award holding plaintiff liable to defendant for breach of contract. Defendant appealed from the Court's concurrent order declaring that the award had not met the documentation requirements of a letter of credit issued in defendant's favor at plaintiff's request. The Court of Appeals, held that (1) the lower court's confirmation of the award would be affirmed, notwithstanding plaintiff's arguments that enforcement of the award would violate United States public policy, that the award represented an arbitration of matters not appropriately decided by arbitration, that the arbitration tribunal denied plaintiff an adequate opportunity to present its case, that the award was predicated on a resolution of issues outside the scope of the contractual agreement to submit to arbitration, and that the award was in manifest disregard of law; (2) since the affirmance rendered academic the validity of the court's disposition of defendant's letter of credit claim, no ruling would be made thereon; (3) the court's computation of plaintiff's liability to defendant was not erroneous; and (4) plaintiff was not liable for damages and double costs on the ground of bringing an allegedly frivolous appeal.]

Before SMITH, HAYS and MANSFIELD, CIRCUIT JUDGES.

J. JOSEPH SMITH, CIRCUIT JUDGE:

Parsons & Whittemore Overseas Co., Inc., (Overseas), an American corporation, appeals from the entry of summary judgment on February 25, 1974, by Judge Lloyd F. MacMahon of the Southern District of New York on the counter-claim by Societe Generale de L'Industrie du Papier (RAKTA), an Egyptian corporation, to confirm a foreign arbitral award holding Overseas liable to RAKTA for breach of contract. RAKTA in turn challenges the court's concurrent order granting summary judgment on Overseas' complaint, which sought a declaratory judgment denying RAKTA's entitlement to recover the amount of a letter of credit issued by Bank of America in RAKTA's favor at Overseas' request. Jurisdiction is based on 9 U.S.C. 203, which empowers federal district courts to hear cases to recognize and enforce foreign arbitral awards, and 9 U.S.C. 205, which authorizes the removal of such cases from state courts, as was accomplished in this instance.[2] We affirm the district court's confirmation of the foreign award. Since it has been established that RAKTA can fully satisfy the award out of a supersedeas bond posted by Overseas, we need not and do not rule on RAKTA's appeal from the adjudication of its letter of credit claim.

In November 1962, Overseas consented by written agreement with RAKTA to construct, start up and, for one year, manage and supervise a paperboard mill in Alexandria, Egypt. The Agency for International Development (AID), a branch of the United States State Department, would finance the project by supplying RAKTA with funds with which to purchase letters of credit in Overseas' favor. Among the contract's terms was an arbitration clause, which provided a means to settle differences arising in the course of performance, and a "force majeure" clause, which excused delay in performance due to causes beyond Overseas' reasonable capacity to control.

Work proceeded as planned until May, 1967. Then, with the Arab–Israeli Six Day War on the horizon, recurrent expressions of Egyptian hostility to Americans—nationals of the principal ally of the Israeli enemy—caused the majority of the Overseas work crew to leave Egypt. On June 6, the Egyptian government broke diplomatic ties with the United States and ordered all Americans expelled from Egypt except those who would apply and qualify for a special visa.

Having abandoned the project for the present with the construction phase near completion, Overseas notified RAKTA that it regarded this

---

2. Overseas initiated suit in New York Supreme Court and the case was removed   to federal court on RAKTA's petition.

postponement as excused by the force majeure clause. RAKTA disagreed and sought damages for breach of contract. Overseas refused to settle and RAKTA, already at work on completing the performance promised by Overseas, invoked the arbitration clause. Overseas responded by calling into play the clause's option to bring a dispute directly to a three-man arbitral board governed by the rules of the International Chamber of Commerce. After several sessions in 1970, the tribunal issued a preliminary award, which recognized Overseas' force majeure defense as good only during the period from May 28 to June 30, 1967. In so limiting Overseas' defense, the arbitration court emphasized that Overseas had made no more than a perfunctory effort to secure special visas and that AID's notification that it was withdrawing financial backing did not justify Overseas' unilateral decision to abandon the project.[3] After further hearings in 1972, the tribunal made its final award in March, 1973: Overseas was held liable to RAKTA for $312,507.45 in damages for breach of contract and $30,000 for RAKTA's costs; additionally, the arbitrators' compensation was set at $49,000, with Overseas responsible for three-fourths of the sum.

Subsequent to the final award, Overseas in the action here under review sought a declaratory judgment to prevent RAKTA from collecting the award out of a letter of credit issued in RAKTA's favor by Bank of America at Overseas' request. The letter was drawn to satisfy any "penalties" which an arbitral tribunal might assess against Overseas in the future for breach of contract. RAKTA contended that the arbitral award for damages met the letter's requirement of "penalties" and counter-claimed to confirm and enter judgment upon the foreign arbitral award. Overseas' defenses to this counterclaim, all rejected by the district court, form the principal issues for review on this appeal. Four of these defenses are derived from the express language of the applicable United Nations Convention on the Recognition and Enforcement of Foreign Arbitral Awards (Convention), 330 U.N.Treaty Ser. 38, and a fifth is arguably implicit in the Convention. These include: enforcement of the award would violate the public policy of the United States, the award represents an arbitration of matters not appropriately decided by arbitration; the tribunal denied Overseas an adequate opportunity to present its case; the award is predicated upon a resolution of issues outside the scope of contractual agreement to submit to arbitration; and the award is in manifest disregard of law. In addition to disputing the district court's rejection of its position on the letter of credit, RAKTA seeks on appeal modification of the court's order to correct for an arithmetical error in the sum entered for judgment, as well as an assessment of damages and double costs against Overseas for pursuing a frivolous appeal.

3. RAKTA represented to the tribunal that it was prepared to finance the project without AID's assistance.

I. Overseas' Defenses Against Enforcement

In 1958 the Convention was adopted by 26 of the 45 states participating in the United Nations Conference on Commercial Arbitration held in New York. For the signatory state, the New York Convention superseded the Geneva Convention of 1927, 92 League of Nations Treaty Ser. 302. The 1958 Convention's basic thrust was to liberalize procedures for enforcing foreign arbitral awards: While the Geneva Convention placed the burden of proof on the party seeking enforcement of a foreign arbitral award and did not circumscribe the range of available defenses to those enumerated in the convention, the 1958 Convention clearly shifted the burden of proof to the party defending against enforcement and limited his defenses to seven set forth in Article V. *See* Contini, International Commercial Arbitration, 8 Am.J.Comp.L. 283, 299 (1959). Not a signatory to any prior multilateral agreement on enforcement of arbitral awards, the United States declined to sign the 1958 Convention at the outset. The United States ultimately acceded to the Convention, however, in 1970, (1970) 3 U.S.T. 2517, T.I.A.S. No. 6997, and implemented its accession with 9 U.S.C. 201–208. Under 9 U.S.C. 208, the existing Federal Arbitration Act, 9 U.S.C. 1–14, applies to the enforcement of foreign awards except to the extent to which the latter may conflict with the Convention. *See generally*, Comment, International Commercial Arbitration under the United Nations Convention and the Amended Federal Arbitration Statute, 47 Wash.L.Rev. 441 (1972).

A. *Public Policy*

Article V(2)(b) of the Convention allows the court in which enforcement of a foreign arbitral award is sought to refuse enforcement, on the defendant's motion or *sua sponte*, if 'enforcement of the award would be contrary to the public policy of (the forum) country.' The legislative history of the provision offers no certain guidelines to its construction. Its precursors in the Geneva Convention and the 1958 Convention's ad hoc committee draft extended the public policy exception to, respectively, awards contrary to 'principles of the law' and awards violative of 'fundamental principles of the law.' In one commentator's view, the Convention's failure to include similar language signifies a narrowing of the defense. Contini, *supra*, 8 Am.J.Comp.L. 283 at 304. On the other hand, another noted authority in the field has seized upon this omission as indicative of an intention to broaden the defense. Quigley, Accession by the United States to the United Nations Convention on the Recognition and Enforcement of Foreign Arbitral Awards, 70 Yale L.J. 1049, 1070–71 (1961).

Perhaps more probative, however, are the inferences to be drawn from the history of the Convention as a whole. The general pro-enforcement bias informing the Convention and explaining its supersession of the Geneva Convention points toward a narrow reading of the public policy defense. An expansive construction of this defense would vitiate the Convention's basic effort to remove preexisting obstacles to enforcement. Additionally, considerations of reciprocity—considerations given express recognition in the Convention itself[4]—counsel courts to invoke the public policy defense with caution lest foreign courts frequently accept it as a defense to enforcement of arbitral awards rendered in the United States.

We conclude, therefore, that the Convention's public policy defense should be construed narrowly. Enforcement of foreign arbitral awards may be denied on this basis only where enforcement would violate the forum state's most basic notions of morality and justice.

Under this view of the public policy provision in the Convention, Overseas' public policy defense may easily be dismissed. Overseas argues that various actions by United States officials subsequent to the severance of American–Egyptian relations—most particularly, AID's withdrawal of financial support for the Overseas–RAKTA contract—required Overseas, as a loyal American citizen, to abandon the project. Enforcement of an award predicated on the feasibility of Overseas' returning to work in defiance of these expressions of national policy would therefore allegedly contravene United States public policy. In equating "national" policy with United States "public" policy, the appellant quite plainly misses the mark. To read the public policy defense as a parochial device protective of national political interests would seriously undermine the Convention's utility. This provision was not meant to enshrine the vagaries of international politics under the rubric of "public policy." Rather, a circumscribed public policy doctrine was contemplated by the Convention's framers and every indication is that the United States, in acceding to the Convention, meant to subscribe to this supranational emphasis.[5]

To deny enforcement of this award largely because of the United States' falling out with Egypt in recent years would mean converting a defense intended to be of narrow scope into a major loophole in the Convention's mechanism for enforcement. We have little hesitation, therefore, in disallowing Overseas' proposed public policy defense.

B.   *Non–Arbitrability*

Article V(2)(a) authorizes a court to deny enforcement, on a defendant's or its own motion, of a foreign arbitral award when "the subject matter of the difference is not capable of settlement by arbitration under the law of that (the forum) country." Under this provision, a court sitting in the United States might, for example, be expected to decline enforcement of an award involving arbitration of an antitrust claim in

---

4. A Contracting State shall not be entitled to avail itself of the present Convention against other Contracting States except to the extent that it is itself bound to apply the Convention.

Article XIV. *Cf.* Comment, *supra,* 47 Wash. L.Rev. 441 at 486–87:

[I]n a system based upon reciprocity any tendency to take an overly narrow view of foreign arbitral awards will be balanced by a desire to obtain the widest acceptance of America's awards among the courts of other signatory states, which also have the public policy loophole available to them.

5. Moreover, the facts here fail to demonstrate that considered government policy forbids completion of the contract itself by a private party.

view of domestic arbitration cases which have held that antitrust matters are entrusted to the exclusive competence of the judiciary. *See, e.g.,* American Safety Equipment Corp. v. J.P. Maguire & Co., 391 F.2d 821 (2d Cir.1968). On the other hand, it may well be that the special considerations and policies underlying a "truly international agreement," Scherk v. Alberto–Culver Co., *supra,* 417 U.S. 506 at 515, 94 S.Ct. 2449, call for a narrower view of non-arbitrability in the international than the domestic context. *Compare id. with* Wilko v. Swan, 346 U.S. 427, 74 S.Ct. 182, 98 L.Ed. 168 (1953) (enforcement of international but not domestic, agreement to arbitrate claim based on alleged Securities Act violations.)

Resolution of Overseas' non-arbitrability argument, however, does not require us to reach such difficult distinctions between domestic and foreign awards. For Overseas' argument, that "United States foreign policy issues can hardly be placed at the mercy of foreign arbitrators 'who are charged with the execution of no public trust' and whose loyalties are to foreign interests," plainly fails to raise so substantial an issue of arbitrability. The mere fact that an issue of national interest may incidentally figure into the resolution of a breach of contract claim does not make the dispute not arbitrable. Rather, certain *categories* of claims may be non-arbitrable because of the special national interest vested in their resolution. *Cf.* American Safety Equipment Corp., *supra,* 391 F.2d 821 at 826–827. Furthermore, even were the test for non-arbitrability of an ad hoc nature, Overseas' situation would almost certainly not meet the standard, for Overseas grossly exaggerates the magnitude of the national interest involved in the resolution of its particular claim. Simply because acts of the United States are somehow implicated in a case one cannot conclude that the United States is vitally interested in its outcome. Finally, the Supreme Court's decision in favor of arbitrability in a case far more prominently displaying public features than the instant one, Scherk v. Alberto–Culver Co., *supra,* compels by analogy the conclusion that the foreign award against Overseas dealt with a subject arbitrable under United States law.

The court below was correct in denying relief to Overseas under the Convention's non-arbitrability defense to enforcement of foreign arbitral awards. There is no special national interest in judicial, rather than arbitral, resolution of the breach of contract claim underlying the award in this case.

C. Inadequate Opportunity to Present Defense

Under Article V(1)(b) of the Convention, enforcement of a foreign arbitral award may be denied if the defendant can prove that he was "not given proper notice ... or was otherwise unable to present his case." This provision essentially sanctions the application of the forum state's standards of due process.

Overseas seeks relief under this provision for the arbitration court's refusal to delay proceedings in order to accommodate the speaking schedule of one of Overseas' witnesses, David Nes, the United States Charge d'Affairs in Egypt at the time of the Six Day War. This attempt to state a due process claim fails for several reasons. First, inability to produce one's witnesses before an arbitral tribunal is a risk inherent in an agreement to submit to arbitration. By agreeing to submit disputes to arbitration, a party relinquishes his courtroom rights—including that to subpoena witnesses—in favor of arbitration "with all of its well known advantages and drawbacks." Washington–Baltimore Newspaper Guild, Local 35 v. The Washington Post Co., 143 U.S.App.D.C. 210, 442 F.2d 1234, 1238 (1971). Secondly, the logistical problems of scheduling hearing dates convenient to parties, counsel and arbitrators scattered about the globe argues against deviating from an initially mutually agreeable time plan unless a scheduling change is truly unavoidable. In this instance, Overseas' allegedly key witness was kept from attending the hearing due to a prior commitment to lecture at an American university—hardly the type of obstacle to his presence which would require the arbitral tribunal to postpone the hearing as a matter of fundamental fairness to Overseas. Finally, Overseas cannot complain that the tribunal decided the case without considering evidence critical to its defense and within only Mr. Nes' ability to produce. In fact, the tribunal did have before it an affidavit by Mr. Nes in which he furnished, by his own account, "a good deal of the information to which I would have testified." Moreover, had Mr. Nes wished to furnish all the information to which he would have testified, there is every reason to believe that the arbitration tribunal would have considered that as well.

The arbitration tribunal acted within its discretion in declining to reschedule a hearing for the convenience of an Overseas witness. Overseas' due process rights under American law, rights entitled to full force under the Convention as a defense to enforcement, were in no way infringed by the tribunal's decision.

D. Arbitration in Excess of Jurisdiction

Under Article V(1)(c), one defending against enforcement of an arbitral award may prevail by proving that:

> The award deals with a difference not contemplated by or not falling within the terms of the submission to arbitration, or it contains decisions on matters beyond the scope of the submission to arbitration. . . .

This provision tracks in more detailed form 10(d) of the Federal Arbitration Act, 9 U.S.C. 10(d), which authorizes vacating an award "where the arbitrators exceeded their powers." Both provisions basically allow a party to attack an award predicated upon arbitration of a subject matter not within the agreement to submit to arbitration. This defense to enforcement of a foreign award, like the others already discussed, should be construed narrowly. Once again a narrow construction would comport with the enforcement-facilitating thrust of the Convention. In addition, the case law under the similar provision of the Federal Arbitration Act strongly supports a strict reading.

In making this defense as to three components of the award, Overseas must therefore overcome a powerful presumption that the arbitral body acted within its powers. Overseas principally directs its challenge at the $185,000 awarded for loss of production. Its jurisdictional claim focuses on the provision of the contract reciting that "neither party shall have any liability for loss of production." The tribunal cannot properly be charged, however, with simply ignoring this alleged limitation on the subject matter over which its decision-making powers extended. Rather, the arbitration court interpreted the provision not to preclude jurisdiction on this matter. As in United Steelworkers of America v. Enterprise Wheel & Car Corp., *supra*, the court may be satisfied that the arbitrator premised the award on a construction of the contract and that it is "not apparent," 363 U.S. 593 at 598, 80 S.Ct. 1358, that the scope of the submission to arbitration has been exceeded.

The appellant's attack on the $60,000 awarded for start-up expenses and $30,000 in costs cannot withstand the most cursory scrutiny. In characterizing the $60,000 as "consequential damages" (and thus proscribed by the arbitration agreement), Overseas is again attempting to secure a reconstruction in this court of the contract—an activity wholly inconsistent with the deference due arbitral decisions on law and fact. The $30,000 in costs is equally unassailable, for the appellant's contention that this portion of the award is inconsistent with guidelines set by the International Chamber of Commerce is twice removed from reality. First of all, contrary to Overseas' representations, these guidelines (contained in the Guide to ICC Arbitration and reproduced in relevant part in Appendix to Brief of Appellant at 408a) do not require, as a precondition to an award of expenses, express authority for such an award in the arbitration clause. The arbitration agreement's silence on this matter, therefore, is not determinative in the case under review. Secondly, since the parties in fact complied with the *Guide's* advice to reach agreement on this matter prior to arbitration—i.e., the request by each for such an award for expenses amounts to tacit agreement on this point—any claim of fatal deviation from the *Guide* is disinguous to say the least.

Although the Convention recognizes that an award may not be enforced where predicated on a subject matter outside the arbitrator's jurisdiction, it does not sanction second-guessing the arbitrator's construction of the parties' agreement. The appellant's attempt to invoke this defense, however, calls upon the court to ignore this limitation on its decision-making powers and usurp the arbitrator's role. The district court took a proper view of its own jurisdiction in refusing to grant relief on this ground.

E. Award in "Manifest Disregard" of Law

Both the legislative history of Article V and the statute enacted to implement the United States' accession to the Convention[6] are strong authority for treating as exclusive the bases set forth in the Convention for vacating [sic] an award. On the other hand, the Federal Arbitration Act, specifically 9 U.S.C. 10, has been read to include an implied defense to enforcement where the award is in "manifest disregard" of the law. Wilko v. Swan, 346 U.S. 427, 436, 74 S.Ct. 182, 98 L.Ed. 168 (1953); Saxis Steamship Co. v. Multifacs International Traders, Inc., 375 F.2d 577, 582 (2d Cir.1967); Amicizia Societa Navegazione v. Chilean Nitrate and Iodine Sales Corp., 274 F.2d 805, 808 (2d Cir.1960).

This case does not require us to decide, however, whether this defense stemming from dictum in *Wilko, supra*, obtains in the international arbitration context. For even assuming that the "manifest disregard" defense applies under the Convention, we would have no difficulty rejecting the appellant's contention that such "manifest disregard" is in evidence here. Overseas in effect asks this court to read this defense as a license to review the record of arbitral proceedings for errors of fact or law—a role which we have emphatically declined to assume in the past and reject once again. "Extensive judicial review frustrates the basic purpose of arbitration, which is to dispose of disputes quickly and avoid the expense and delay of extended court proceedings." Saxis Steamship Co., *supra*, 375 F.2d 577 at 582.

Insofar as this defense to enforcement of awards in "manifest disregard" of law may be cognizable under the Convention, it, like the other defenses raised by the appellant, fails to provide a sound basis for vacating [sic] the foreign arbitral award. We therefore affirm the district court's confirmation of award.

* * *

Affirmed.

Questions and Comments

1. The United States became a party to the New York Convention in 1970. Thus *Parsons & Whittemore* was one of the first cases to test judicial attitudes toward the Convention in the United States and has become an important precedent. What attitude toward the Convention would you say is reflected in the case?

2. The court seems to agree that Overseas acted in accord with United States national policy in withdrawing from the Egyptian project. Why then would it not violate U.S. "public policy" under the New York Convention for an American court to enforce the arbitral award against Overseas stemming from that withdrawal? What does "public policy" under the New York Convention mean? Suppose the U.S. government had issued a direct order to Overseas forbidding its continued participation in the project, would this have affected the outcome of the case?

6. " * * * The court shall confirm the award unless it finds one of the grounds for refusal or deferral of recognition or enforcement specified in the said Convention." 9 U.S.C. 207.

3. The court's opinion seems to say that the arbitrators awarded damages for loss of production, although the contract provides: "[n]either party shall have any liability for loss of production." What ground under the New York Convention for refusing to enforce the award do these facts implicate? Do you find the court's treatment of this issue adequate?

4. "Manifest disregard of the law" is a ground under U.S. federal arbitration law for refusing to enforce an award falling under the U.S. Federal Arbitration Act. Is this also a ground for refusing to enforce a foreign award falling under the New York Convention? Suppose the arbitrators had decided as "amiables compositeurs" in this case, would that have been a ground for refusing to enforce the award? Under what provision of the New York Convention? Would deciding in "manifest disregard of the law" be equivalent to deciding as "amiables compositeurs"? Would Art. V(1)(d) provide a ground for refusing to enforce the award in the case of "manifest disregard of the law"?

V.3.c.   *Procedural Grounds Under the Convention for Refusing Recognition and Enforcement*

V.3.c.i.   *Validity of the Agreement and Standard of Review*

New York Convention Article V groups the grounds for refusing recognition and enforcement of an award into subparagraphs (1) and (2). Subparagraph 2(a) allows nonenforcement if the subject matter of the dispute "is not capable of settlement by arbitration under the law of that country"—the country in which enforcement is sought. Subparagraph 2(b) allows nonenforcement if recognition and enforcement would be "contrary to the public policy of that country"—again the country in which enforcement is sought. Given that the enforcing court is to apply its own law on these questions—regardless of the law the arbitrators applied in rendering their award—one might conclude that the enforcing court will be forced to consider these issues de novo, without deference to the arbitrators' decision. This issue of standard of review as it applies to Article V(2) grounds is explored below in Section V.3.d.

In this subsection we are concerned with "procedural grounds" under the New York Convention for refusing to enforce an award— generally those grounds listed in Article V(1). Nothing in the wording of Article V(1) supports an inference that a de novo review by the enforcing court is contemplated; the fundamental inquiry is what should be the standard of review a court should exercise in deciding whether to recognize or enforce an award when Article V(1) grounds are invoked. How much deference should be given to the arbitrators' decision? In particular, we take up that question in connection with an Article V(1)(a) claim that the arbitration agreement is invalid or nonexistent and a V(1)(c) claim that the award deals with a difference not submitted to arbitration.

AMERICAN CONSTRUCTION MACHINERY & EQUIPMENT CORP. LTD. v. MECHANISED CONSTRUCTION OF PAKISTAN LTD.

United States District Court, Southern District of New York, 1987.
659 F.Supp. 426.

KEENAN, DISTRICT JUDGE.

Background

Petitioner, American Construction Machinery & Equipment Corporation, Ltd. ("ACME"), brings this instant motion to confirm a foreign arbitration award it obtained against the respondent, Mechanised Construction of Pakistan Ltd. ("MCP"). ACME is a Cayman Islands corporation with a Westchester County office. During the relevant activities, the office was located in Tarrytown. MCP is a wholly-owned enterprise of the Pakistan government.

On January 6, 1977, the parties entered a contract that called for ACME to supply MCP with goods and services to be used in MCP's Iraq construction project. The contract included an arbitration clause which stated,

> [a]ny dispute or difference arising between the parties concerning the interpretation of any provision of this agreement or performance or any action taken there-under shall be settled in the first instance directly between the parties and if no such settlement is possible by referring to the International Chamber of Commerce [ICC] at Paris/Geneva for arbitration.

The parties entered a Supplementary Agreement dated May 22, 1978, which stated the governing law would be that of Pakistan.

Almost one year later, on May 1, 1979, ACME filed a claim with the ICC. On June 24, 1979, MCP participated in the arbitration proceedings by filing a reply and a counterclaim for $1 million. The ICC Court of Arbitration selected Geneva as the site for the arbitration and Max W. Abrahamson, Q.C., was chosen as the sole arbitrator. After designating authorized representatives, on March 19, 1980 the parties signed the Terms of Reference for the arbitration. One of the issues the parties agreed to have arbitrated was what effect, if any, the Supplementary Agreement would have on the original January 6, 1977 Agreement. A hearing was scheduled for June 1 and 2, 1981. Despite receiving proper notice of the hearing, MCP elected not to attend.

By signing the Terms of Reference, MCP had accepted the Arbitrator's jurisdiction, Geneva as the location of the arbitration, and the use of Geneva's procedural rules. MCP, however, decided to pursue another strategy. In July, 1980, MCP stated that it viewed the arbitration as invalid under the law of Pakistan. It proceeded to petition a court in Lahore, Pakistan for a declaration invalidating both the arbitration and the arbitration clause. In that action, ACME and Arbitrator Abrahamson were named as defendants. MCP's petition, which according to the Arbitrator contained "omissions and positive misstatements," was granted on January 13, 1981.

The Arbitrator reached his decision in this case on May 24, 1982. He found in favor of ACME on its claim, and against MCP on its counterclaim. In addition, he determined that even if Pakistani law were applicable, MCP's objections were meritless. New York law was found to govern the January 6, 1977 Agreement, and the Supplementary Agreement was held invalid. ACME timely filed a petition in this Court on May 17, 1985 to confirm the arbitral award pursuant to the Convention on the Recognition and Enforcement of Foreign Arbitral Awards ("Convention"), which is given the force of United States law at 9 U.S.C. § 201.

In this Court, MCP has previously moved to dismiss the petition to confirm the award on grounds of lack of personal and subject matter jurisdiction and improper venue. The Court rejected these positions, and briefs were filed on the motion to confirm the arbitration award. For the reasons set forth below, the Court confirms the award which directed MCP to pay ACME, (a) $1,402,924.00 including interest up to December 21, 1981; (b) interest at the rate of 17% on that sum from December 22, 1981 until the date of payment; (c) arbitration costs of $45,057.57; and (d) ACME's legal costs calculated at $87,500.00.

Discussion

On a motion to confirm an arbitral award entered pursuant to the Convention, a federal court "shall confirm the award unless it finds one of the grounds for refusal or deferral of recognition or enforcement of the award specified in the said Convention." 9 U.S.C. § 207. Respondent raises several of the defenses set forth in Article V of the Convention. First, it is asserted that the arbitration agreement "is not valid under the law to which the parties have subjected it." See 9 U.S.C. § 201, note, Article V, 1(a). Second, respondent argues that the award contains decisions on matters beyond the scope of the arbitration agreement. See id., Article V, 1(c). Third, respondent states that "the arbitral authority or the arbitral procedure was not in accordance with the agreement of the parties...." [See Article V, 1(d).] Finally, respondent claims that the award has been set aside "by a competent authority of the country in which, or under the law of which, that award was made." See Article V, 1(e). Two defenses not found within Article V(1) are also presented: the arbitration agreement should be vacated as contrary to United States public policy and the award was in "manifest disregard" of the applicable law. The Court rejects each of these defenses.

As a preliminary matter, the Court notes that there is a "general pro-enforcement bias" manifested in the Convention. See Parsons & Whittemore Overseas Co. v. Societe Generale de l'Industrie du Papier (RAKTA), 508 F.2d 969, 973 (2d Cir.1974). The party opposing confirmation of the award bears the burden of proof. MCP has failed to meet this burden.

MCP first argues that the award should not be confirmed because it is invalid under the laws of Pakistan. This argument is unavailing because it assumes that the laws of Pakistan were designated by the parties to apply to their agreement. While it is true that the Supplementary Agreement contained a choice of law clause selecting Pakistani law, the Arbitrator ruled that the Supplementary Agreement was invalid under both Pakistani and New York law. Thus, to accept MCP's Article V(1)(a) defense would require this Court to reverse one of the Arbitrator's express findings of law. This can only be done if the findings were made in "manifest disregard" of the law. The scope of the Court's review in this regard is extremely limited. An examination of the Arbitrator's findings shows he carefully considered the applicable Pakistani law in ruling that the Supplementary Agreement was invalid. Because his result is certainly a "colorable justification for the outcome reached," see Andros Compania Maritima, S.A. v. Marc Rich & Co., 579 F.2d 691, 704 (2d Cir.1978), MCP's Article V(1)(a) defense is rejected.

MCP's defense under Article V(1)(c) is also rejected. That defense asserts that the Arbitrator decided matters beyond his authority. Article V(1)(c) is construed narrowly to advance the "enforcement-facilitating thrust of the Convention." Parsons, 508 F.2d at 976. In this case, there is no doubt that MCP consented to arbitration of the matters ultimately decided by the Arbitrator. As was previously noted, MCP signed the Terms of Reference which set forth the issues to be arbitrated.

In its answer, MCP raises a defense under Article V(1)(d). That provision of the Convention provides a defense if, "[t]he composition of the arbitral authority or the arbitral procedure was not in accordance with the agreement of the parties, or, failing such agreement, was not in accordance with the law of the county where the arbitration took place." This is inapplicable in the instant case. MCP agreed to have the ICC Court of Arbitration select the arbitrator, see Connolly Affidavit, Exh. 1, and in the Terms of Reference accepted the arbitrator's jurisdiction and Geneva as the place of arbitration, along with its procedural rules.

Article V(1)(e) permits non-recognition of an arbitral award when it "has not yet become binding on the parties, or has been set aside or suspended by competent authority of the country in which, or under the law of which, that award was made." This provision does not assist the Respondent. The law under which this award was made was Swiss law because the award was rendered in Geneva, pursuant to Geneva procedural law. The Terms of Reference clearly spelled out that this law would apply. MCP asserts that the award was rendered under Pakistani law based on the Supplementary Agreement's choice of law provision. However, as mentioned earlier, this Court will not employ its view of the Supplemental Agreement's validity, or invalidity, and displace the view of the Arbitrator.

Respondent's contention based upon Article V(2)(b), that recognition of the award would be contrary to United States public policy is not pursuasive [sic]. This defense is very narrow and is only applicable when enforcement "would violate the forum state's most basic notions of morality and justice." See Parsons, 508 F.2d at 976. This is hardly such a case. Respondent urges that this Court conclude United States public policy would be offended by confirming an arbitral award in the face of a Pakistani judgment that the arbitration clause and proceeding were void. In fact, public policy would be violated if the Court declined to confirm the award. The Pakistani proceeding was, according to the Arbitrator, marked by MCP's "omissions and positive misstatements." Respondent had agreed to arbitrate, appeared in the proceeding, and then sought to circumvent the process. In light of this strategy, enforcing the award in no way violates this forum's notions of justice.

* * *

Conclusion

Petitioner's motion to confirm the arbitral award is granted and its request for Rule 11 sanctions against respondent is denied. Judgment shall be so entered.

SO ORDERED.

SOUTHERN PACIFIC PROPERTIES (MIDDLE EAST) LTD. v. ARAB REPUBLIC OF EGYPT

The Netherlands, District Court of Amsterdam (1984).
24 Int'l Legal Materials 1040 (1985).*

Introductory Note[k]

In a decision of July 12, 1984 / 23 I.L.M. 1048 (1984) / the Court of Appeals of Paris set aside an arbitral award made in Paris between SPP and SPP (ME) *v.* The Arab Republic of Egypt and Egoth /22 I.L.M. 752 (1983)/. The Court of Appeals held that there was no arbitration agreement binding the Egyptian State.

On exactly the same day (i.e., July 12, 1984), the President of the District Court of Amsterdam granted SPP's request for a leave of enforcement on the same award. The President reached a conclusion which was diametrically opposed to that of its [sic] French colleagues: the President held that there was an arbitration agreement binding the Egyptian State. A translation of the President's decision is reproduced below.

k. [The Introductory Note and English translation were prepared for *International Legal Materials* by Albert Jan van den Berg of the law firm Van Doorne & Sjollema, Rotterdam, attorneys for SPP in the Netherlands.]

The facts of the case are briefly the following:

On September 23, 1974, "Heads of Agreement" were executed concerning a tourist village on the Pyramids Plateau ("the Pyramids Oasis project") and a similar tourist resort at Ras–El–Hekma on the Mediterranean coast in Egypt. Parties to this Agreement were SPP, the Minister of Tourism and EGOTH (Egyptian General Organisation for Tourism and Hotels). This Agreement was followed by a second agreement on December 12, 1974, between SPP and EGOTH. However, beneath the signatures of their representatives, the words appeared "approved, agreed and ratified by the Minister of Tourism" followed by the signature of the Minister. The Heads of Agreement did not contain an arbitration clause whereas the December Agreement did, providing for ICC arbitration.

In the early part of 1978, when the works had already started, opposition to the Pyramids Oasis project developed, especially in Egypt's People's Assembly. The project was attacked on both legal and environmental grounds. In response to this criticism, both the Minister of Tourism and the Minister of Economy defended the project in the People's Assembly. Yet, at the end of May 1978, the project was stopped by various measures of the Egyptian Government.

When an amicable settlement proved to be impossible, SPP initiated ICC arbitration against both the Egyptian State and EGOTH, claiming approximately US$42,500,000 as damages. Egypt objected to the competence of the arbitrators, arguing that it was not a party to the December Agreement in which the arbitration clause was included.

OPINION (unofficial translation)

1. Petitioner has submitted duly certified copies of the arbitral award and the arbitration agreement. The aforementioned award and agreement are drawn up in the English language which language we master sufficiently to have taken full cognizance of the contents of these documents. We therefore consider that the provisions of art. IV(2), of the applicable Convention on the Recognition and Enforcement of Foreign Arbitral Awards, done at New York, June 10, 1958 (hereafter "the Convention") are complied with.

2. Respondent has, summarized briefly, requested in the first place to refuse the leave for enforcement, and in the alternative to adjourn the decision on enforcement, and in the further alternative, in case enforcement is granted, to order petitioner to provide security.

3. In the present proceedings, the merits of the case will not be reviewed but it will be examined only whether respondent is justified in invoking the grounds for refusal mentioned in art. V(1), of the Convention and whether the decision on enforcement should be adjourned in virtue of art. VI of the Convention.

4. With reference to art. V(1)(a), of the Convention, respondent contends in the first place that no valid arbitration agreement exists

because it was not a party to the agreement of December 12, 1974, in which the arbitration clause is included.

5. Respondent made the same contention in the arbitral proceedings. This issue is dealt with extensively in the arbitral award. We hold that the afore-mentioned contention of respondent is not proven, having regard to what the arbitrators have considered about the contention and in particular the fact that the following words are mentioned at the bottom of the agreement of December 12, 1974:

> "Approved, agreed and ratified by the Minister of Tourism his Excellency Mr. Ibrahim Naguib on the twelfth day of December 1974."

accompanied by the stamp and signature of this Minister.

6. Respondent contends in the second place that the arbitral award is not yet binding *casu quo* that its enforcement is suspended within the meaning of art. V(1)(*e*), of the Convention because, by writ of March 28, 1983, an action for setting aside (*recours en annulation*) the award was initiated in virtue of art. 1502 *juncto* art. 1501 of the French New Code of Civil Procedure (NCCP), which means of recourse has, in virtue of art. 1506 NCCP, suspensive effect, and the Court of Appeals of Paris has not yet rendered a decision thereon.

7. It results from both the legislative history of the Convention and the text of arts. V(1)(*e*) and VI, that the mere initiation of an action for setting aside, to which the initiated *recours en annulation* must be deemed to belong, does not have as consequence that the arbitral award must be considered as not binding. An arbitral award is not binding if it is open to appeal on the merits before a judge or an appeal arbitral tribunal. If this were otherwise, the words "has been set aside or suspended" in art. V(1)(*e*), to which reference is made in art. VI, would have no meaning. The drafters of the Convention chose the word "binding" in order to abolish the requirement of the double-exequatur which was the result of the word "final" in the Geneva Convention of 1927. Having regard to the system of arts. 1504 and 1490 NCCP, the view expounded by respondent would result in a re-introduction of the double-exequatur.

8. The second part of the ground of refusal of art. V(1)(*e*) reads:

> "The award ... has been set aside or suspended by a competent authority of the country in which or under the law of which, that award was made."

The suspension by operation of law, which is accorded in art. 1506 NCCP to the *recours en annulation*, cannot be brought under this provision. The text of the Convention is clear on this point: a judicial authority must have had the opportunity to consider the question whether a request for suspension is made for good cause. A broader interpretation deviating from the text of the grounds of refusal, which are listed limitatively, would be in violation of the system of the Convention.

9. The foregoing considerations lead to the conclusion that respondent has not succeeded in proving the existence of the grounds of refusal mentioned in art. V(1)(e) of the Convention.

10. Having regard to the purpose of the Convention to enhance the recognition and enforcement of foreign arbitral awards by subjecting the recognition and enforcement to a minimum number of conditions, the *recours en annulation* initiated by respondent is no reason for us to adjourn the decision on enforcement. This is especially so since respondent has not shown any readiness to give suitable security.

11. There is also no reason for giving of security by petitioner in the case of a granting of the leave for enforcement, leaving aside that the Convention does not offer a basis therefor.

12. Because the grounds of refusal mentioned in the second paragraph of art. V of the Convention are not applicable, the requested leave for enforcement must be granted. Respondent, being the losing party, is adjudicated to pay the costs of these proceedings.

Questions and Comments

1. In the *ACME* case, the defendant, Mechanized Construction of Pakistan, Ltd (MCP), urged Article V(1)(a) (the arbitration agreement "is not valid under the law to which the parties have subjected it") as a ground for refusing enforcement of the award. What were the court's reasons for rejecting this argument? Since the arbitrator, himself, had considered the invalidity argument (as had the Lahore court), the enforcing court had to decide what standard of review to use in re-visiting a question decided by the arbitrator. How would you characterize the standard of review the enforcing court used? Did it decide the validity question de novo or did it defer to the arbitrator (significantly or modestly)? Do you consider the court's standard of review proper?

2. In *Southern Pacific Properties (Middle East), Ltd v. The Arab Republic of Egypt* (the "Pyramids case") before the enforcing court in Amsterdam, a similar issue arose concerning the validity of the agreement. The precise question was whether the state of Egypt was a party to the December 12 contract, which provided for arbitration. The arbitrators had decided that Egypt was a party to the agreement and hence to the arbitration clause. The Amsterdam court decided to enforce the award. What standard of review did the court use concerning whether Egypt was a party to the arbitration agreement? How does this approach compare with that of the court in *ACME*? Do you think the Amsterdam court applied the correct standard of review?

3. On the very same day that the Amsterdam court handed down its decision in *Southern Pacific Properties v. The Arab Republic of Egypt*, the Court of Appeals of Paris set aside the award, which had been made in Paris. The Paris Court of Appeals decided that Egypt was not a party to the December 12 contract. Excerpts from the Paris Court of Appeals opinion are given supra at p. 678. How would you characterize the Paris Court of Appeals' standard of review? How does this approach compare with that taken by the Amsterdam court and by the U.S. federal district court in

ACME? The Paris Court of Appeals was exercising set-aside jurisdiction, which is not governed by the New York Convention. Should that make a difference?

4. When the issue is the validity (or existence) of the arbitration agreement, as it was in *ACME* and *Southern Pacific Properties*, what standard of review should an enforcing court exercise? Is it arguable that the arbitrators might have a personal stake in finding an arbitration clause valid? Should that influence the standard of review at the enforcement stage? Do any other factors argue for either an invasive or deferential standard of review?

SA X (BELGIUM) v. MR. Y (SPAIN)

Spain, Tribunal Supremo [Supreme Court], 1986.
13 Yearbk. Comm. Arb'n 512 (1988).[*][1]

Facts

The Belgian company X had maintained continuous commercial relations with Mr. Y (Spain) consisting of the supply by X to Y of a number of shipments of fruit. The documents confirming the sale and the receipts describing the goods supplied by X (standard models used by company X in all of their transactions) contained the statement "supplies delivered under the conditions of sale described on the back and the particular conditions indicated above". According to the conditions, any dispute arising between the parties was to be settled by arbitration before the Arbitration Chamber of Strasbourg.

When a dispute arose over the payment of certain shipments of fruit and notably its quality, X began arbitration proceedings before the Arbitration Chamber of Strasbourg. Mr. Y defaulted in the proceedings. The arbitral tribunal decided in favour of X who then sought enforcement of the award in Spain before the Supreme Court.

Mr. Y did not appear in the court proceedings. The Supreme Court granted leave for enforcement (exequatur) after verifying the existence of the arbitration clause (in accordance with Art. II of the New York Convention) and the arbitrability of the dispute (in accordance with Art. V(2) of said Convention).

Excerpt

1. The Supreme Court considered that in arbitration the existence of an arbitration clause is a necessary pre-condition for arbitrating the dispute and that the existence of the clause should be properly determined in accordance with Art. II of the Convention. The arbitration clause should be in writing, be precise, and without the application of the formal requirements of Spanish domestic law (e.g., the public deed requirement of the Spanish Arbitration Law of 1953). The Supreme

* Reprinted with permission of Yearbook Commercial Arbitration, International Council for Commercial Arbitration.

1. Also published in *Revista de la Corte Espanola de Arbitraje* (1986), pp. 249–253.

Court explained that such an interpretation of the Convention is derived from the special nature of international commercial relations.

2. The Supreme Court stated that according to Art. II, the signing of the arbitration clause is not necessary when an agreement is "contained in an exchange of letters or telegrams," or in "communications by teleprinter" as provided in Art. I(2)(a) of the European Convention of 1961. In this case, considering (1) that the parties maintained continuous commercial relations, (2) that Mr. Y knew the general conditions under which company X operated, and (3) that Mr. Y received, without protest, the goods described in the receipts, whose content he had acknowledged, the Supreme Court found that there existed a binding arbitration clause in the sense of Art. II.

3. The Supreme Court further considered that since Mr. Y did not appear and thus did not invoke any of the exceptions of Art. V(1) of the Convention, it therefore had to limit itself to an examination on its own motion of the grounds for refusal of enforcement listed in Art. V(2) of the Convention. The Supreme Court decided that the matter was arbitrable under Spanish law and that the award would not be contrary to Spanish public policy.

Questions and Comments

1. Note that the Belgian company, X, proceeded to arbitration in Strasbourg unilaterally and that Mr. Y, a Spanish national, defaulted. Then company X enforced the award in Spain, again without Mr. Y's participation. Did the parties agree to arbitrate this dispute? Note the reference in the case to the Spanish Arbitration Law of 1953. Apparently under that law, "if an arbitration clause exists and the public deed (compromise) is not executed, the arbitral clause is ineffective and the arbitration cannot proceed." 8 Yearbk. Comm. Arb'n. 514 (1988) (Spain No. 13, *Audiencia Territorial* [Court of Appeal, Barcelona, 11 April 1986]). It seems that under the 1953 law Spain refused to enforce an arbitration clause in a contract. Instead it was necessary for the parties to agree to submit an existing dispute to arbitration through a "compromise" agreement formalized by a public deed. This approach to arbitration was once widespread and partly accounts for the terms-of-reference procedure adopted by the ICC arbitration rules. It should be noted that on December 5, 1988, Spain adopted a new arbitration statute (Law 36/1988) which abandons the requirement of a separate and distinct agreement to submit existing disputes to arbitration.

2. Why did the Spanish Supreme Court decide not to apply the public deed requirement of the Spanish Arbitration Law of 1953? Note that the Barcelona Court of Appeals observed in the case cited in comment 1:[53] "The international provisions contained in a treaty by Spain have primacy in case of conflict or contradiction with requirements of internal law." 8 Yearbk. Comm. Arb'n. 515 (1988). What provisions of the New York Convention, if any, were applicable?

3. What standard of review did the Spanish Supreme Court use in deciding whether an agreement to arbitrate existed and was valid?

[53]. 8 Yearbk. Comm. Arb'n p. 515 (1988).

4. Why did the Spanish Supreme Court consider, on its own motion, the New York Convention Article V(2)(a) and (b) grounds for refusing recognition and enforcement but not the Article V(1) grounds?

5. Was it consistent for the court to consider, on its own motion, the existence of a valid arbitration agreement? What bearing, if any, does New York Convention Article IV have on the answer to this question?

V.3.c.ii.   Notice of Appointment of the Arbitrator and Waivability

DANISH BUYER v. GERMAN SELLER

Germany, Oberlandesgericht Köln [Court of Appeal of Cologne], 1976.
4 Yearbk. Comm. Arb. 258 (1979).*

Facts

On the basis of the arbitral clause contained in the "Copenhagan Contract" concluded between a German seller and a Danish buyer, the latter initiated arbitration at the Copenhagen Arbitration Committee for Grain and Feed Stuff Trade (*Kθbenhavns Bedθmmelses—og Voldgiftsudvalg for Korn-og Foderstofhandelen*).

Rule 4 of the Arbitration Rules[1] provides in part the following:

1. The president (of the Committee) shall have the supreme administrative management of the Committee's work. . . .

4. The president or the vice-president shall, in regard to the cases which they are to deal with, appoint the members who are to take part in the decision of the particular case, and care must be taken that the members appointed are in possession of expert knowledge of the particular case to be dealt with by them.

5. No information can be given to any of the parties involved or to anyone else as to who is dealing with any particular case.

6. A list of all the members of the Committee can be had on demand.

7. The parties interested in a case can protest against one or several members of the Committee taking part in a certain case. Should the president who is holding office consider this protest justified, these members cannot take part in the settlement of the case in question. . . .

Rule 7 provides:

1. The deliberation shall be verbal.

2. The members shall observe secrecy about the deliberation and negotiations.

* Reprinted with permission of Yearbook Commercial Arbitration, International Council for Commercial Arbitration and by permission of Carl Heymanns Verlag KG, because the case originally appeared in 91 Zeitschrift für Zivilprozess 318 (1978).

1. English translation provided by The Merchants' Guild, Copenhagen. This Guild elects the members of the Committee.

3. The Committee shall decide whether it will give grounds for its findings in the particular case.

4. In a book kept for that purpose shall be entered a summary of the case and the award made. The summary shall be signed by all the members who took part in the decision.

5. An extract of the award made, only signed by the president, shall be handed over to each party to the case.

In the present case the German seller was not informed of the names of the arbitrators; only the name of the Chairman of the arbitral tribunal was communicated to him.

On March 20, 1973, an award was rendered in favour of the Danish buyer. Thereupon the Danish buyer sought enforcement in F.R. Germany. The Court of First Instance (Landgericht) refused to enforce the award. The Court of Appeal (Oberlandesgericht) of Cologne affirmed the refusal for the reasons summarized below.

Extract

1. The Court of Appeal first stated that the present case fell under the New York Convention.[2] The New York Convention entered into force in Denmark on March 22, 1973, which was made known by the German Government on February 23, 1973, and May 24, 1973. The Court of Appeal concluded:

"F.R. Germany and Denmark therefore were Contracting States at the time at which the petitioner started the procedure for enforcement (October 4, 1973). This is sufficient for the application of the Convention."

2. The Court of Appeal found, however, that the conditions for enforcement as required by the Convention had not been complied with. In the first place, the petitioner had not supplied all documents required by Art. IV, as he had not presented the duly authenticated original of the award or a copy of which the conformity with the original was duly certified (Art. IV, para. 1 under a). The original had not been presented to the Court. Instead, a copy was presented which lacked the certification that the copy was in conformity with the original, since the official certification on the copy concerned only signatures.

3. Moreover, the copy did not reflect the complete original because it did not contain the names of the arbitrators who had participated in the decision. The Court of Appeal considered that:

Rule 7 (para. 4) of the Arbitration Rules provides that the arbitral award must be signed by all members of the Committee who took part in the decision. Their signatures are an essential element of the arbitral award and must therefore appear on the copy. This principle cannot be changed by Rule 4 (para. 5) of the Arbitration Rules which

2. The European Convention on International Commercial Arbitration, signed at Geneva, April 21, 1961, was also held applicable. This extract deals only with the New York Convention.

declares that the names of the arbitrators will not be made known. According [to] Art. IV of the New York Convention, which cannot be modified by an agreement of the parties, the copy must reflect the original in its entirety.

4. The Court of Appeal stated further that enforcement had to also be refused on the basis of Art. V, para. 1 under b, because the responding German seller was not given notice of the appointment of the arbitrator(s). The Court of Appeal considered that:

> The parties have not disputed the fact that—with the exception of the president of the arbitration tribunal—the respondent never had knowledge of the names of the persons who have decided the arbitration between the parties. The respondent is not estopped from invoking Art. V, para. 1 under b, of the New York Convention and Art. IX, para. 1 under b, of the European Convention because he could have requested by virtue of Rule 4 (para. 6) of the Arbitration Rules the list of all arbitrators from amongst whom the arbitrators for the arbitration in question were chosen.

> Apart from the fact that Art. V, para. 1 under b, implies that the affected party is informed of the appointment of the arbitrator, failing a disclosure of the arbitrators who conducted the arbitral procedure, the respondent is unable to examine whether the members of the Committee challenged by him were effectively excluded from the arbitration or whether prejudiced arbitrators participated who were not mentioned on the list transmitted to him.

5. The enforcement could also not be based on the domestic law for the enforcement of foreign arbitral awards (Sect. 1044 ZPO). In this connection the Court of Appeal considered:

> The New York Convention ... does not exclude the application of domestic law concerning recognition. In Art. VII of the New York Convention it is expressly provided that no interested party shall be deprived of the right to rely on the domestic law of the State where enforcement is sought ... The rationale of this provision is to avoid depriving a party who seeks recognition of an award of more favourable possibilities under the national law of the State where enforcement is sought. The so-called most favourable right-principle does, however, not justify combining more favourable individual provisions taken from different legal systems. On the contrary, a legal system should be applied in its entirety.

6. The Court did not consider the question whether under applicable Danish law the award had acquired binding force. The award could not be enforced as its recognition would have been against the public order of the F.R. of Germany (Sect. 1044, para. 2 no. 2 ZPO).

It is a fundamental principle of both F.R. Germany and international legal order that a judge is impartial. Since an arbitrator performs the same functions as a judge, this principle also applies to arbitration (for the impartiality of an arbitrator under German law: Sect. 1025, para. 1, and 1032 ZPO). Accordingly, sufficient guarantees of his independence and impartiality must be present.

The procedural means for the realization of the impartiality of a judge is the challenge. This applies also to arbitration, where, in particular, influences can exist that may give rise to questions concerning impartiality, such as business contacts or common economic interests between an arbitrator and a party. As the right of the parties to challenge has a fundamental meaning for a fair arbitral procedure, the exclusion of this right constitutes a violation of the German public order.

The Court of Appeal continued by considering that

the institution of challenge can be effective only if the parties have the possibility of knowing the names of the judges or arbitrators who take part in the decision of the dispute in question. Only if this condition is fulfilled, can it be investigated whether the judge or arbitrator who takes part is partial and can his participation be prevented. In international law also, great importance is attached to the disclosure of the names of arbitrators: in the New York Convention (Art. V, para. 1 under b) as well as in the European Convention (Art. IX, para. 1 under b), the lack of notification of the appointment of the arbitrators is mentioned expressly as a ground for refusal of recognition and enforcement.

The Court of Appeal declared that it did not ignore that the regulation contained in Rules 4 and 6 may strengthen the impartiality of arbitrators in a specific case as the nondisclosure of their names may serve the freedom of decision-making. However, this regulation excludes the possibility for the parties to challenge a partial arbitrator. The latter principle is more important.

The Court of Appeal reasoned also that it is not sufficient for the right to challenge that the parties may object to one or more persons on the list of arbitrators. Since the parties are not informed of the names of the arbitrators who actually take part in the arbitration, they cannot investigate whether the persons objected to have in fact been excluded. Moreover, it may be possible that persons have acted as arbitrator who were not mentioned on the list.

Furthermore, the Court of Appeal declared that it was also not sufficient that the Danish petitioner could prove that in the arbitration in question no arbitrators had participated who were employees of, or linked in another manner with, him. This does not exclude the possibility that other arbitrators, especially arbitrators not mentioned on the list of arbitrators, have acted who were not impartial.

7. The German respondent had also requested the setting aside of the arbitral award. The Court of Appeal observed that the German respondent had a justified interest in this request as he had been blacklisted by the Copenhagen Arbitration Committee. However, the Court of Appeal held that in F.R. Germany a foreign arbitral award can only be refused recognition, but that it cannot be set aside (Sect. 1044,

para. 3 ZPO). The latter decision would mean an impermissible interference with foreign arbitration.

Questions and Comments

1.   What Article V(1) ground is the respondent invoking in the *Oberlandesgericht Köln* case to prevent enforcement of the award? Is this a waivable right? Has the respondent waived its Article V rights by entering the arbitration agreement?

2.   In judicial proceedings before a court, a losing party can always waive its right to appeal by simply not filing an appeal. A pre-adjudication agreement to waive one's right to appeal would probably not be enforced in most legal systems. Should this distinction influence how you analyze the waivability issue in the *Oberlandesgericht Köln* case?

3.   Could the Danish procedure give rise to an Article V(2) claim for nonenforcement? Are Article V(2) grounds waivable?

4.   Is there a difference between a challenge to an award under Article V(1) and a challenge under Article V(2)? Does the difference relate to the waivability issue?

5.   Has New York Convention Article IV been satisfied in this case? Are its provisions waivable?

V.3.c.iii.   Scope of the Parties' Submission to Arbitration

MANAGEMENT & TECHNICAL CONSULTANTS S.A. v. PARSONS–JURDEN INTERNATIONAL

United States Court of Appeals, Ninth Circuit, 1987.
820 F.2d 1531.

Before ANDERSON, SKOPIL, and REINHARDT, CIRCUIT JUDGES.

J.   BLAINE ANDERSON, CIRCUIT JUDGE:

Parsons–Jurden International appeals two petitions by Management & Technical Consultants made in the district court to enforce a foreign arbitral award. The district court granted the petitions and Parsons–Jurden contends that the arbitrators lacked authority to make the award in that they decided subject matter not within the scope of the agreement to arbitrate. We affirm the judgment of the district court.

Management and Technical Consultants ("*MTC*") is a Liberian corporation with its principal place of business in Monrovia, Liberia. Parsons–Jurden International Corp. ("*P–J*") is a corporation organized under the laws of the State of Nevada, U.S.A., with its primary place of business in Pasadena, California, U.S.A. In December, 1972 *P–J* and *MTC* entered into an agreement whereby *MTC* was to assist *P–J* in obtaining a contract or contracts with the Government of Iran to develop mining facilities at the Sar Cheshmeh copper mines in Iran. The agreement provided that if *P–J* was awarded such a contract, *P–J* would pay *MTC* five percent of *P–J*'s "gross billings" to the Iranian Sar Cheshmeh Copper Mining Company (Sar Cheshmeh). On July 3, 1973, *P–J* entered into a contract to furnish materials for the mining operation. The amount of the contract was to be either 2.35% of the project's actual final costs or as calculated by the projected costs plus an additional fee for services rendered at the mine, at Sar Cheshmeh's option.

After the materials were furnished, Sar Cheshmeh chose the latter method of calculation and under it paid P–J $7,402,500.00. MTC was awarded a portion of this payment pursuant to the December, 1972 P–J agreement with MTC. However, by 1974 the parties disagreed over the meaning of the term "gross billings" in the December, 1972 agreement. P–J contended the term meant only the compensation for the additional fees it was paid, whereas MTC maintained the term included all payments made to P–J.

In light of this disagreement, P–J and MTC entered into a subsequent superseding letter agreement on March 22, 1974, in which P–J agreed to pay MTC an additional amount as "full settlement" of the disputed payments. The March 22 letter agreement also contained the following proviso to the "full settlement" which the parties reached:

> [P–J] hereby agree[s] that should its gross billings to [Sar Cheshmeh] exceed a gross total of [$350 million] [MTC] shall become entitled to receive from [P–J] additional compensation. In such event and at such time [P–J] will negotiate the terms and conditions of such payments to [MTC].

The letter agreement also included an arbitration clause which stated:

> This Letter of Agreement shall be governed by and construed in accordance with the laws of the Commonwealth of Bermuda. Any dispute arising between us concerning this Letter of Agreement which cannot be settled amicably, shall be resolved by arbitration to be held by a three-man arbitration panel to be appointed in accordance with the rules of arbitration of the International Chamber of Commerce of Paris. The site of the arbitration shall be in Hamilton, Bermuda.

In the years following the letter agreement, disputes over the total "gross billings" to Sar Cheshmeh continued. Finally, in 1982, MTC initiated arbitration against P–J under the arbitration clause contained in the letter agreement. MTC contended the gross billings P–J received exceeded $350 million dollars and that MTC was not receiving additional compensation as required by the agreement. P–J argued that while it agreed the arbitrators had authority to decide whether the gross billings exceeded $350 million, once that decision was made the arbitral panel lacked the authority to set the amount of additional compensation due MTC since this amount was to be determined "at such time [P–J] will negotiate the terms and conditions of such payments to [MTC]." In short, P–J argued the arbitration decision was limited to determining whether P–J had exceeded $350 million in gross billings, (thereby requiring the parties to negotiate further to set the amount owed MTC), and did not include determining what actual amount MTC was to be paid.

Proceedings with the arbiters were held in Bermuda in 1983, with *P–J* and *MTC* filing pleadings, legal memoranda and sworn witness statements on the arbitrability issue. Oral argument was also presented. On June 14, 1984, the arbiters issued an award pursuant to the 1974 letter agreement requiring *P–J* to pay *MTC* $1.85 million plus interest as the amount due for the gross billings to Sar Cheshmeh. However, the reasons for the award were not made a part of the written arbiters' decision. Later, in light of the $1.85 million award, the arbiters also awarded *MTC* $414,686.00 as costs ($402,000.00 costs plus $12,686.00 in fees) for obtaining and confirming the prior award.

In 1985, *MTC* filed in district court a "Petition and Motion for Recognition, Confirmation and Enforcement of Foreign Arbitral Award" under the Convention on the Recognition and Enforcement of Foreign Arbitral Awards, 9 U.S.C. §§ 201–208, to enforce the $1.85 million award. *P–J* opposed the petition on the ground that the arbiters exceeded their authority in making an award [concerning a matter] which was to be determined by negotiation between the parties. The district court granted the petition, affirming the $1.85 million award plus interest from the date the arbitration award was entered. Additionally, *MTC* filed a similar petition for $414,686.00 to enforce the arbitrators' award of costs. This petition was also granted.

P–J appeals both the district court's judgment to enforce the $1.85 million award and the $414,686.00 award of costs. While each was appealed separately, they have been consolidated here. Jurisdiction rested under 9 U.S.C. § 203 in the district court and rests under 28 U.S.C. § 1291 in this court.

The language at issue in the letter agreement states that "[a]ny dispute . . . which cannot be settled amicably, shall be resolved by arbitration. . . ." Since this language concerns the enforcement of an agreement to arbitrate, it is clear the letter agreement falls within the scope of the Convention on the Recognition and Enforcement of Foreign Arbitral Awards ("Convention"). *See* 9 U.S.C. § 202.[1] Under the Convention, an arbiter's award can be * * * [refused recognition and enforcement] only on the grounds specified in the Convention. *See* 9 U.S.C. § 207.[2] In interpreting the grounds specified, it is generally recognized

---

1. 9 U.S.C. § 202 provides:

An arbitration agreement or arbitral award arising out of a legal relationship, whether contractual or not, which is considered as commercial, including a transaction, contract, or agreement described in section 2 of this title, falls under the Convention. An agreement or award arising out of such a relationship which is entirely between citizens of the United States shall be deemed not to fall under the Convention unless that relationship involves property located abroad, envisages performance or enforcement abroad, or has some other reasonable relation with one or more foreign states. For the purpose of this section a corporation is a citizen of the United States if it is incorporated or has its principal place of business in the United States.

2. 9 U.S.C. § 207 provides:

Within three years after an arbitral award falling under the Convention is made, any party to the arbitration may apply to any court having jurisdiction under this chapter for an order confirming the award as against any other party to the arbitration. The court shall confirm the award unless it finds one of the grounds for refusal or deferral of recognition or enforce-

that the Convention tracks the Federal Arbitration Act, 9 U.S.C. § 1, *et seq. Compare* 9 U.S.C. § 201 with 9 U.S.C. § 1 *et seq.*

P–J argues the arbitral award was erroneous because it included a subject, i.e., the additional compensation to be paid MTC, not within the letter agreement to submit to arbitration. This ground of error is enumerated in the Convention under ARTICLE V, § 1(c) which provides:

> Recognition and enforcement of the award may be refused, at the request of the party against whom it is invoked, only if that party furnishes to the competent authority where the recognition and enforcement is sought, proof that:

> * * *

> [t]he award deals with a difference not contemplated by or not falling within the terms of the submission to arbitration, or it contains decisions on matters beyond the scope of the submission to arbitration, provided that, if the decisions on matters submitted to arbitration can be separated from those not so submitted, that part of the award which contain decisions on matters submitted to arbitration may be recognized and enforced....

9 U.S.C. § 201.

Federal arbitration law has established a presumption that an arbitral body has acted within its powers. This presumption exists to effectuate the " 'liberal federal policy favoring arbitration agreements.' " The policy favoring arbitration "applies with special force in the field of international commerce." We review de novo a contention that the subject matter of the arbitration lies outside the scope of a contract, since the arbitrability of a dispute concerns contract interpretation and only those disputes which a party has agreed to submit to arbitration may be so resolved. However, we construe arbitral authority broadly to comport with the enforcement-facilitating thrust of the Convention and the policy favoring arbitration. *Parsons & Whittemore*, 508 F.2d at 976.

Here, the parties agree the arbiters had authority to determine whether the gross billings exceeded $350 million. They disagree on whether the arbiters had the further authority to determine the amount of additional compensation due. The letter agreement indicates that "[a]ny dispute" which could not be "settled amicably" would be resolved by arbitration. We construe the word "any" broadly. *Cf. Mediterranean Enterprises*, 708 F.2d at 1463 ("any dispute" read narrowly where limiting language of "arising hereunder" immediately followed). An agreement to arbitrate "any dispute" without strong limiting or excepting language immediately following it logically includes not only the dispute, but the consequences naturally flowing from it—here, the amount of additional compensation. By agreeing to arbitrate the decision of whether there had been $350 million in sales and by using such broad

ment of the award specified in the said   Convention.

language in the letter agreement, we find the parties also conferred arbitral authority to determine the amount of additional compensation due *MTC*. *Moses H. Cone*, 460 U.S. at 24–25, 103 S.Ct. at 941 (any dispute concerning the scope of arbitral issues under the Arbitration Act should be resolved in favor of arbitration).

The second issue appealed, which concerns the award of costs, is a simple one. Since we find the arbiters' authority to reach the main decision was within the scope of the letter agreement, it follows the arbiters also had the authority to award costs and fees for obtaining the arbitral decision. *See Parsons & Whittemore*, 508 F.2d at 977 (an award for costs does not require express authority in the arbitration clause under the guidelines set by the International Chamber of Commerce).

The judgment of the district court on the petition to enforce the foreign arbitral award and the award of costs and fees is affirmed.

AFFIRMED.

FIRST OPTIONS OF CHICAGO, INC. v. KAPLAN, ET UX. AND MK INVESTMENTS, INC.

United States Supreme Court, 1995.
514 U.S. 938.

JUSTICE BREYER delivered the opinion of the Court.

In this case we consider two questions about how courts should review certain matters under the federal Arbitration Act, 9 U.S.C. § 1 *et seq.* (1988 Ed. and Supp. V): (1) how a district court should review an arbitrator's decision that the parties agreed to arbitrate a dispute, and (2) how a court of appeals should review a district court's decision confirming, or refusing to vacate, an arbitration award.

We granted certiorari to consider two questions regarding the standards that the Court of Appeals used to review the determination that the Kaplans' dispute with First Options was arbitrable. 513 U.S. 1040, 115 S.Ct. 634, 130 L.Ed.2d 539 (1994). First, the Court of Appeals said that courts "should *independently* decide whether an arbitration panel has jurisdiction over the merits of any particular dispute." 19 F.3d, at 1509 (emphasis added). First Options asked us to decide whether this is so (i.e., whether courts, in "reviewing the arbitrators' decision on arbitrability," should "apply a *de novo* standard of review or the more deferential standard applied to arbitrators' decisions on the merits") when the objecting party "submitted the issue to the arbitrators for decision." Pet. for Cert. i. Second, the Court of Appeals stated that it would review a district court's denial of a motion to vacate a commercial arbitration award (and the correlative grant of a motion to confirm it) "*de novo.*" 19 F.3d, at 1509. First Options argues that the Court of Appeals instead should have applied an "abuse of discretion" standard. See *Robbins v. Day*, 954 F.2d 679, 681–682 (C.A.11 1992).

II

The first question—the standard of review applied to an arbitrator's decision about arbitrability—is a narrow one. To understand just how narrow, consider three types of disagreement present in this case. First, the Kaplans and First Options disagree about whether the Kaplans are personally liable for MKI's debt to First Options. That disagreement makes up the *merits* of the dispute. Second, they disagree about whether they agreed to arbitrate the merits. That disagreement is about the *arbitrability* of the dispute. Third, they disagree about *who should have the primary power to decide the second matter*. Does that power belong primarily to the arbitrators (because the court reviews their arbitrability decision deferentially) or to the court (because the court makes up its mind about arbitrability independently)? We consider here only this third question.

Although the question is a narrow one, it has a certain practical importance. That is because a party who has not agreed to arbitrate will normally have a right to a court's decision about the merits of its dispute (say, as here, its obligation under a contract). But, where the party has agreed to arbitrate, he or she, in effect, has relinquished much of that right's practical value. The party still can ask a court to review the arbitrator's decision, but the court will set that decision aside only in very unusual circumstances. See, *e.g.*, 9 U.S.C. § 10 (award procured by corruption, fraud, or undue means; arbitrator exceeded his powers); *Wilko v. Swan*, 346 U.S. 427, 436–437, 74 S.Ct. 182, 187–188, 98 L.Ed. 168 (1953) (parties bound by arbitrator's decision not in "manifest disregard" of the law), overruled on other grounds, *Rodriguez de Quijas v. Shearson/American Express, Inc.*, 490 U.S. 477, 109 S.Ct. 1917, 104 L.Ed.2d 526 (1989). Hence, who—court or arbitrator—has the primary authority to decide whether a party has agreed to arbitrate can make a critical difference to a party resisting arbitration.

We believe the answer to the "who" question (*i.e.*, the standard-of-review question) is fairly simple. Just as the arbitrability of the merits of a dispute depends upon whether the parties agreed to arbitrate that dispute, see, *e.g., Mastrobuono v. Shearson Lehman Hutton, Inc.*, 514 U.S. 52, ___, 115 S.Ct. 1212, 1216, 131 L.Ed.2d 76 (1995); *Mitsubishi Motors Corp. v. Soler Chrysler–Plymouth, Inc.*, 473 U.S. 614, 626, 105 S.Ct. 3346, 3353, 87 L.Ed.2d 444 (1985), so the question "who has the primary power to decide arbitrability" turns upon what the parties agreed about *that* matter. Did the parties agree to submit the arbitrability question itself to arbitration? If so, then the court's standard for reviewing the arbitrator's decision about *that* matter should not differ from the standard courts apply when they review any other matter that parties have agreed to arbitrate. See *AT & T Technologies, Inc. v. Communications Workers*, 475 U.S. 643, 649, 106 S.Ct. 1415, 1418, 89 L.Ed.2d 648 (1986) (parties may agree to arbitrate arbitrability); *Steelworkers v. Warrior & Gulf Navigation Co.*, 363 U.S. 574, 583, n. 7, 80 S.Ct. 1347, 1353, n. 7, 4 L.Ed.2d 1409 (1960) (same). That is to say, the court should give considerable leeway to the arbitrator, setting aside his or her decision only in certain narrow circumstances. See, *e.g.*, 9 U.S.C. § 10. If, on the other hand, the parties did *not* agree to submit the arbitrability question itself to arbitration, then the court should decide that question just as it would decide any other question that the parties did not submit to arbitration, namely independently. These two answers flow inexorably from the fact that arbitration is simply a matter of contract between the parties; it is a way to resolve those disputes—but only those disputes—that the parties have agreed to submit to arbitration.

We agree with First Options, therefore, that a court must defer to an arbitrator's arbitrability decision when the parties submitted that matter to arbitration. Nevertheless, that conclusion does not help First Options win this case. That is because a fair and complete answer to the standard-of-review question requires a word about how a court should decide whether the parties have agreed to submit the arbitrability issue to arbitration. And, that word makes clear that the Kaplans did not agree to arbitrate arbitrability here.

When deciding whether the parties agreed to arbitrate a certain matter (including arbitrability), courts generally (though with a qualification we discuss below) should apply ordinary state-law principles that govern the formation of contracts. The relevant state law here, for example, would require the court to see whether the parties objectively revealed an intent to submit the arbitrability issue to arbitration.

This Court, however, has (as we just said) added an important qualification, applicable when courts decide whether a party has agreed that arbitrators should decide arbitrability: Courts should not assume that the parties agreed to arbitrate arbitrability unless there is "clea[r] and unmistakabl[e]" evidence that they did so. In this manner the law treats silence or ambiguity about the question "*who* (primarily) should decide arbitrability" differently from the way it treats silence or ambiguity about the question "*whether* a particular merits-related dispute is arbitrable because it is within the scope of a valid arbitration agreement"—for in respect to this latter question the law reverses the presumption. See *Mitsubishi Motors, supra*, at 626, 105 S.Ct., at 3353 ("'[A]ny doubts concerning the scope of arbitrable issues should be resolved in favor of arbitration'") * * *

But, this difference in treatment is understandable. The latter question arises when the parties have a contract that provides for arbitration of some issues. In such circumstances, the parties likely gave at least some thought to the scope of arbitration. And, given the law's permissive policies in respect to arbitration, see, *e.g.*, *Mitsubishi Motors, supra*, at 626, 105 S.Ct., at 3353, one can understand why the law would insist upon clarity before concluding that the parties did *not* want to arbitrate a related matter. See Domke § 12.02, p. 156 (issues will be deemed arbitrable unless "it is clear that the arbitration clause has not included" them). On the other hand, the former question—the "who (primarily) should decide arbitrability" question—is rather arcane. A party often might not focus upon that question or upon the significance of having arbitrators decide the scope of their own powers. And, given the principle that a party can be forced to arbitrate only those issues it specifically has agreed to submit to arbitration, one can understand why courts might hesitate to interpret silence or ambiguity on the "who should decide arbitrability" point as giving the arbitrators that power, for doing so might too often force unwilling parties to arbitrate a matter they reasonably would have thought a judge, not an arbitrator, would decide.

On the record before us, First Options cannot show that the Kaplans clearly agreed to have the arbitrators decide (*i.e.*, to arbitrate) the question of arbitrability. First Options relies on the Kaplans' filing with the arbitrators a written memorandum objecting to the arbitrators' jurisdiction. But merely arguing the arbitrability issue to an arbitrator does not indicate a clear willingness to arbitrate that issue, *i.e.*, a willingness to be effectively bound by the arbitrator's decision on that point. To the contrary, insofar as the Kaplans were forcefully objecting to the arbitrators deciding their dispute with First Options, one naturally would think that they did *not* want the arbitrators to have binding authority over them. This conclusion draws added support from (1) an obvious explanation for the Kaplans' presence before the arbitrators (*i.e.*, that MKI, Mr. Kaplan's wholly owned firm, was arbitrating workout agreement matters); and (2) Third Circuit law that suggested that the Kaplans might argue arbitrability to the arbitrators without losing their right to independent court review, *Teamsters v. Western Pennsylvania Motor Carriers Assn.*, 574 F.2d 783, 786–788 (1978); see 19 F.3d, at 1512, n. 13.

First Options makes several counterarguments: (1) that the Kaplans had other ways to get an independent court decision on the question of arbitrability without arguing the issue to the arbitrators (*e.g.*, by trying to enjoin the arbitration, or by refusing to participate in the arbitration and then defending against a court petition First Options would have brought to compel arbitration, see 9 U.S.C. § 4); (2) that permitting parties to argue arbitrability to an arbitrator without being bound by the result would cause delay and waste in the resolution of disputes; and (3) that the Arbitration Act therefore requires a presumption that the Kaplans agreed to be bound by the arbitrators' decision, not the contrary. The first of these points, however, while true, simply does not say anything about whether the Kaplans intended to be bound by the arbitrators' decision. The second point, too, is inconclusive, for factual circumstances vary too greatly to permit a confident conclusion about whether allowing the arbitrator to make an initial (but independently reviewable) arbitrability determination would, in general, slow down the dispute resolution process. And, the third point is legally erroneous, for there is no strong arbitration-related policy favoring First Options in respect to its particular argument here. After all, the basic objective in this area is not to resolve disputes in the quickest manner possible, no matter what the parties' wishes, but to ensure that commercial arbitration agreements, like other contracts, " 'are enforced according to their terms,' " *Mastrobuono*, 514 U.S., at ____, 115 S.Ct., at 1214 (quoting *Volt Information Sciences*, 489 U.S., at 479, 109 S.Ct., at 1256), and according to the intentions of the parties. That policy favors the Kaplans, not First Options.

We conclude that, because the Kaplans did not clearly agree to submit the question of arbitrability to arbitration, the Court of Appeals was correct in finding that the arbitrability of the Kaplan/First Options dispute was subject to independent review by the courts.

III

We turn next to the standard a court of appeals should apply when reviewing a district court decision that refuses to vacate or confirms an arbitration award. Although the Third Circuit sometimes used the words *"de novo"* to describe this standard, its opinion makes clear that it simply believes (as do all Circuits but one) that there is no *special* standard governing its review of a district court's decision in these circumstances. Rather, review of, for example, a district court decision confirming an arbitration award on the ground that the parties agreed to submit their dispute to arbitration, should proceed like review of any other district court decision finding an agreement between parties, i.e., accepting findings of fact that are not "clearly erroneous" but deciding questions of law *de novo*.

One Court of Appeals, the Eleventh Circuit, has said something different. Because of federal policy favoring arbitration, that court says that it applies a specially lenient "abuse of discretion" standard (even as to questions of law) when reviewing district court decisions that confirm (but not those that set aside) arbitration awards. See, *e.g., Robbins v. Day*, 954 F.2d, at 681–682. First Options asks us to hold that the Eleventh Circuit's view is correct.

We believe, however, that the majority of Circuits is right in saying that courts of appeals should apply ordinary, not special, standards when reviewing district court decisions upholding arbitration awards. For one thing, it is undesirable to make the law more complicated by proliferating review standards without good reasons. More importantly, the reviewing attitude that a court of appeals takes toward a district court decision should depend upon "the respective institutional advantages of trial and appellate courts," not upon what standard of review will more likely produce a particular substantive result. The law, for example, tells all courts (trial and appellate) to give administrative agencies a degree of legal leeway when they review certain interpretations of the law that those agencies have made. See, *e.g., Chevron U.S.A. Inc. v. Natural Resources Defense Council, Inc.*, 467 U.S. 837, 843–844, 104 S.Ct. 2778, 2781–2782, 81 L.Ed.2d 694 (1984). But, no one, to our knowledge, has suggested that this policy of giving leeway to agencies means that a court of appeals should give extra leeway to a district court decision that upholds an agency. Similarly, courts grant arbitrators considerable leeway when reviewing most arbitration decisions; but that fact does not mean that appellate courts should give *extra* leeway to district courts that uphold arbitrators. First Options argues that the Arbitration Act is special because the Act, in one section, allows courts of appeals to conduct interlocutory review of certain antiarbitration district court rulings (*e.g.*, orders enjoining arbitrations), but not those upholding arbitration (*e.g.*, orders refusing to enjoin arbitrations). 9 U.S.C. § 16 (1988 Ed., Supp. V). But that portion of the Act governs the timing of review; it is therefore too weak a support for the distinct claim that the court of appeals should use a different *standard* when reviewing certain district court decisions. The Act says nothing about standards of review.

We conclude that the Court of Appeals used the proper standards for reviewing the District Court's arbitrability determinations.

The judgment of the Court of Appeals is affirmed.

It is so ordered.

Questions and Comments

1. In *Parsons–Jurden* the court articulates a de novo standard of review. Do you agree with this standard and the court's justification for it? Should this be the standard concerning all Article V(1) grounds for refusing to recognize and enforce an award? Should it be the standard of any of the other Article V(1) nonenforcement grounds?

2. If the *Parsons–Jurden* court had favored a more deferential standard of review, how could it have applied such a standard to the award under review?

3. In the *First Options* case the U.S. Supreme Court addresses the issue of the appropriate standard of review concerning the scope of submission to arbitration. The Court refers to the issue as one of "arbitrability", but by that term it does not mean the issue of whether "the subject matter of the difference … is capable of settlement by arbitration"—the issue covered by New York Convention Article V(2)(a). It means what the New York Convention calls the "scope of submission" in Article V(1)c. Moreover, the *First Options* case does not arise under the New York Convention, because it concerns a domestic U.S. award, not the enforcement of a foreign award. Would you find the Court's reasoning equally applicable to the recognition and enforcement of foreign awards? If so, what would that reasoning lead you to conclude about the appropriate standard of review when a defendant invokes one of the Article V(1) grounds for refusing enforcement? Does your answer depend upon which Article V(1) ground is at issue?

V.3.c.iv.   Improper Composition of Arbitral Authority or Improper Arbitral Procedure

CHINA NANHAI OIL JOINT SERVICE CORPORATION, SHENZHEN BRANCH v. GEE TAI HOLDINGS

Supreme Court of Hong Kong, High Court, 1994.
20 Yearbk. Comm. Arb'n 671 (1995).*

[Portions of the opinion in this case dealing with the more general issue of estoppel are omitted here and reproduced later in the materials under V.3.e. The portion of the opinion reproduced here is based on an alternative ground, under which the Hong Kong High Court was prepared to enforce the award despite agreeing with the defendant's argument that the arbitral tribunal was not constituted according to the parties' agreement and that the arbitration should have taken place in Beijing, instead of Shenzhen. The facts and the court's reasoning concerning the alternative ground are reproduced immediately below.]

Facts

China Nanhai Oil Joint Service Corporation Shenzhen Branch (plaintiff) and Gee Tai Holdings Co. Ltd. (defendant) entered into a contract which, *inter alia*, provided for arbitration of disputes at the "Foreign Trade Arbitration Commission of the China Council for the Promotion of International Trade, Peking", in accordance with the Commission's Provisional Rules of Procedure. A dispute arose between the parties and plaintiff applied to the China International Economic and Trade Arbitration Commission (CIETAC), Shenzhen, for arbitration.

On 15 April 1989, in default of appointment by the defendant, CIETAC, Shenzhen appointed an arbitrator for the defendant. Plaintiff appointed its arbitrator and the Shenzhen Sub–Commission appointed a president arbitrator. In mid May 1989, Chen Jian, the defendant's Shenzhen lawyer, pointed out to CIETAC, Shenzhen, that the arbitration should be held in Beijing (Peking). CIETAC, Shenzhen, claimed to have jurisdiction, and on 17 June 1989 it stated that it accepted jurisdiction over the dispute. The award was rendered on 10 February 1990.

Plaintiff sought to have the award enforced in Hong Kong. The Hong Kong High Court, *per* Kaplan, J., granted leave to enforce the award, holding that the defendants were estopped from relying on the wrongly constituted arbitral tribunal.

* Reprinted with permission of Yearbook Commercial Arbitration, International Council for Commercial Arbitration.

Excerpt

[1] "I have before me an application to enforce an arbitration award dated 10 February 1990 rendered by the Shenzhen Sub–Commission of the China International Economic and Trade Arbitration Commission. The defendants oppose the enforcement of the award on the ground set out in Sect. 44(2)(e) of the Arbitration Ordinance Cap. 341....[1] It is clear therefore that the only grounds upon which enforcement can be refused are those specified in this section and that the burden of proving a ground is upon the defendant. Further, it is clear that even though a ground has been proved, the court retains a residual discretion."

[2] The Court noted, *inter alia*, that the CIETAC has its headquarters in Beijing and has two sub-commissions, one in Shenzhen and one in Shanghai. The same rules of arbitration apply to arbitrations conducted in Beijing, Shanghai or Shenzhen. In 1989, each sub-commission maintained its own Panel of Arbitrators.

1. Issues

[3] "*Issue 1.* In the light of the materials presented to me, I am satisfied that in 1989 the Shenzhen Sub–Commission kept its own list of arbitrators. If an arbitrator was on the Shenzhen list but not on the Beijing list, then he/she was not qualified to arbitrate in Beijing and vice versa. I believe that one of the reasons for having a unified list was to get over this very problem. I agree that the conclusion is a little strange, given that we are dealing with a single Arbitration Commission but I have to have regard to the way in which these problems are considered in China and must not impose my own method of solving this dilemma. If a Chinese Court is not prepared to hold that a clause providing for arbitration at CIETAC, Guangdong, is a sufficient reference to include CIETAC Shenzhen, then I am quite satisfied that a Chinese Court would not be impressed with a Shenzhen arbitrator dealing with a dispute in which the parties had agreed on CIETAC in Beijing and where one of the appointed arbitrators was not even on the Beijing list.

[4] "I conclude, therefore, somewhat reluctantly, that technically the arbitrators did not have jurisdiction to decide this dispute and that in all the circumstances of this case, the ground specified in the section has been made out. I say technically because the parties did agree to have a CIETAC Arbitration and that is what they got even though it was held at a place within China not specified in the contract and by arbitrators who apparently were not on the Beijing list. The promulgation of a united list as from 1 June 1994 will ensure that this problem

---

1. Sect. 44 of the Arbitration Ordinance reads in relevant part:

"(1) Enforcement of a Convention award shall not be refused except in the cases mentioned in this section.

(2) Enforcement of a Convention award may be refused if the person against whom it is invoked proves— ...

(e) that the composition of the arbitral authority or the arbitral procedure was not in accordance with the agreement of the parties or, failing such agreement, with the law of the country where the arbitration took place; ..."

does not arise again, save perhaps in respect of arbitrations commenced before the new rules and new list.

* * *

II. Discretion

[25] "As I have decided that the defendants are estopped from relying upon the wrongly constituted arbitral tribunal, it is not strictly necessary for me now to consider the question of discretion although I have discussed it briefly in the context of the doctrine of estoppel. However, just in case this matter goes further, and lest another court should disagree with my view as to estoppel, it is necessary for me to state how I should have exercised my discretion.

[26] "In *Paklito* (supra),[6] I briefly described that sort of situation where a court was satisfied that a ground had been made out but, nonetheless, proceeded to enforce the award. The example I gave is where the defendant was prevented from submitting some evidence as part of its case but where the enforcing court looked at that evidence and could see that it would not have made any difference at all to the result. However, I was not required in that case to decide whether this was the only circumstance where such view might be taken. . . .

[27] "How should I exercise my discretion in this case? The parties agreed on a CIETAC Arbitration under CIETAC Rules. They got it. CIETAC, Shenzhen, is a Sub–Commission of CIETAC in Beijing. The defendants participated in the arbitration and have raised no other grounds whatsoever which go to the procedure of the arbitration or the substance of the award. Had they won, they would not have complained.

[28] "Further, I am quite satisfied on the material placed before me that no one would be placed on the arbitration panel of the Shenzhen Sub–Commission without the approval of the Commission in Beijing. It was, after all, CIETAC which is headquartered in Beijing that set up the Shenzhen Sub–Commission at about this very time and later set up another one in Shanghai. . . .

[29] "I am quite satisfied that the defendants got what they agreed in their contract in the sense that they got an arbitration conducted by 3 Chinese arbitrators under CIETAC Rules. To exercise my discretion against enforcement on the facts of this case would be a travesty of justice. Had I thought that the defendants' rights had been violated in any material way, I would, of course, have taken a different view. However, this is an obvious case where the court can exercise its discretion to enforce the award notwithstanding a ground of opposition in the New York Convention being made out. This conclusion is, in my judgment, quite consistent with the pro enforcement bias of the Conven-

6. Reported in Yearbook xix (1994) pp. 664–674 (Hong Kong no. 6). [Authors' note: Paklito Investment Ltd. v. Klockner East Asia Ltd., 1993 (vol. 2) Hong Kong Law Reports 40 (High Court of Hong Kong), is reproduced in the materials supra in section IV.1.h.ii].

tion and the pro enforcement attitude of most enforcing courts around the world.

* * *

Questions and Comments

1. The Hong Kong High Court concluded that although the defendant had successfully shown an Article V(1)(d) ground for nonenforcement—"the composition of the arbitral authority or the arbitral procedure was not in accordance with the agreement of the parties"—the award would nevertheless be enforced. Is this consistent with the New York Convention? Do you agree with the court's reasoning?

2. Should it matter that the plaintiff was the Shenzhen branch of a Chinese company?

COMPAGNIE DES BAUXITES DE GUINEE v. HAMMERMILLS, INC.

United States District Court, District of Columbia.
1992 WL 122712.

JOHN GARRETT PENN, DISTRICT JUDGE.

* * *

I.   Facts

In evaluating a motion for summary judgment, the Court must resolve genuine disputes of material fact in favor of the non-moving party. That is, the Court may grant summary judgment in favor of a party only if facts that are undisputed—or that cannot genuinely be disputed—demonstrate that the moving party is entitled to judgment as a matter of law. In this case, there is no genuine issue as to any of the following material facts.

Petitioner CBG is a Delaware corporation with its principal place of business in the Republic of Guinea, where it operates a bauxite mining and crushing facility. Respondent Hammermills is a dissolved corporation formerly organized under the laws of Missouri, that was engaged in the manufacture of ore-crushing equipment. In 1970, CBG and Hammermills entered into a contract for the purchase and sale of ore-crushing and handling equipment for use at CBG's bauxite-crushing facility. The contract provided, inter alia, that all disputes relating to interpretation of and performance under the contract would be settled through arbitration, pursuant to the Rules of Conciliation and Arbitration of the International Chamber of Commerce ("ICC"), by either one or a panel of arbitrators designated pursuant to such rules.

In May 1985, CBG initiated arbitration proceedings against Hammermills, alleging that Hammermills had breached the contract by providing erroneous "load data" that was used to build a faulty concrete support structure at CBG's facility, and seeking some $46 million in damages. In January 1986, Hammermills filed, in the United States Bankruptcy Court for the Northern District of Illinois, a voluntary petition for reorganization pursuant to Chapter 11 of the Bankruptcy Code. As a result of the filing of this petition, the arbitration proceeding was automatically stayed pursuant to section 362(a) of the Bankruptcy Code, 11 U.S.C. § 362(a).

In March 1987, CBG and Hammermills filed a joint motion to modify the automatic stay to permit the arbitration proceeding to go forward, on the ground that Hammermills' litigation costs in that proceeding were being covered by its insurer, Argonaut–Midwest Insurance Company ("Argonaut"), and therefore the bankrupt's assets would not be diminished by allowing the arbitration action to proceed. Argonaut's duty to defend Hammermills in the arbitration proceeding had been established in a declaratory judgment action brought by CBG against Argonaut in the United States District Court for the Western District of Pennsylvania. On March 17, 1987, the Bankruptcy Court granted the parties' motion and modified the automatic stay to allow the arbitration to go forward, on the condition that Argonaut "defends and continues to defend Hammermills in the Arbitration" as well as any confirmation proceedings.

Hearings on the merits of CBG's breach-of-contract claim were held before a single ICC Arbitrator between July 18 and August 10, 1988, during which the Arbitrator heard approximately 20 days of testimony from 18 witnesses. Following the hearings, the parties submitted post-hearing briefs and reply briefs. The matter remained under advisement before the Arbitrator for some time until, on September 29, 1989, counsel received by telefax a letter from the Arbitrator requesting a statement of each party's legal costs. By letter dated October 13, 1989, counsel for CBG responded to the arbitrator's request, reporting legal expenses totalling $1,968,802.24. Counsel for Hammermills responded by letter dated October 18, 1989, stating that Hammermills had incurred legal costs totalling $1,073,220.60.[2] Counsel for CBG received its copy of Hammermills' counsel's October 18 letter on Saturday, October 21, 1989. On October 24, 1989, counsel for CBG contacted the ICC Court in Paris to inquire about the status of the Arbitrator's decision, and was advised that award had been approved by the ICC Court on October 19, 1989, and was final.

ICC Rules provide that the Arbitrator must submit a draft of his award to the ICC Court of Arbitration, which must approve the form of the draft prior to issuance of the award. Specifically, Article 21 of the ICC Rules provides:

2. Apparently, counsel for Hammermills did not immediately respond to the Arbitrator's September 29 letter, prompting a second letter from the Arbitrator dated October 17, 1989. CBG asserts strenuously in its memoranda that it was not provided with a copy of the Arbitrator's October 17 letter. The significance of this oversight, however, is never explained. It is undisputed that CBG received a copy of the Arbitrator's initial letter of September 29, as well as Hammermills' counsel's ultimate response on October 18.

Before signing an award, whether partial or definitive, the arbitrator shall submit it in draft form to the Court. The Court may lay down modifications as to the form of the award and, without affecting the arbitrator's liberty of decision, may also draw his attention to points of substance. No award shall be signed until it has been approved as to form.

Sometime prior to October 19, 1989, the Arbitrator submitted his draft award to the ICC Court for approval. The draft award denied CBG's claim against Hammermills in its entirety. On October 19, 1989, the ICC Court approved the draft award. Thereafter, the Arbitrator added to the award an assessment against CBG of Hammermills' "normal legal costs" amounting to $993,220.60,[3] in addition to the arbitration costs of $145,441.78. The arbitrator signed the award on or about October 26, 1989. On November 24, 1989, the parties were officially notified by the ICC Secretariat of the Arbitrator's decision and provided with copies of the Arbitrator's 103–page Award Sentence, dismissing CBG's claim in its entirety and assessing against CBG Hammermills' "normal legal costs" of $993,220.60 as well as the costs of arbitration.

On January 24, 1990, CBG initiated this action by filing a petition to vacate, modify or correct the arbitration award. CBG asserts that the award of Hammermills' legal fees against it cannot stand for two principal reasons. First, CBG claims that it was denied due process because it was deprived of adequate notice of the Arbitrator's intention to assess legal fees against it and had no opportunity to be heard on the issue. Second, CBG claims that the Arbitrator's addition of the fee assessment subsequent to approval by the ICC Court violated ICC procedures. CBG also claims that Hammermills is not the "real party in interest" in this litigation under Fed.R.Civ.P. 17(a).[4] Hammermills has filed a counter-petition seeking recognition and enforcement of the arbitral award.

II.   The Standard Of Review

The parties agree that this action falls within the scope of the Convention on the Recognition and Enforcement of Foreign Arbitral Awards (the "Convention"), as implemented, 9 U.S.C. §§ 201–08. The statute implementing the Convention authorizes the parties to a foreign arbitration to bring an action in federal court seeking confirmation of

---

3. The precise manner in which the costs assessment was added to the award is not entirely clear from the record. CBG asserts that the draft award submitted to the ICC Court for approval contained no mention whatsoever of the assessment of legal costs against it. Hammermills, on the other hand, believes that the draft contained a provision assessing legal costs against CBG, but with a blank space for the amount of the assessment, which the arbitrator completed after the draft was approved. CBG argues that at the very least it should be entitled to discovery on this issue.

For the reasons that follow, however, the Court does not find this issue to be material, and will assume for purposes of this opinion that CBG's version of events is what transpired.

4. CBG has raised numerous arguments in its lengthy papers, and the Court has addressed the principal contentions in this opinion. The other arguments not specifically addressed have been reviewed and considered, but deemed not to affect the ultimate result.

the award. 9 U.S.C. § 207. The statute directs that the reviewing court "shall confirm the award unless it finds one of the grounds for refusal or deferral of recognition or enforcement of the award specified in the said convention." 9 U.S.C. § 207. Thus, a reviewing court may refuse to recognize and enforce an arbitral award only if the party seeking such refusal establishes one of the grounds specified in the Convention.

The grounds for refusal to enforce an arbitral award are specified in Article V of the Convention. As pertinent to this case, Article V provides that recognition and enforcement of an award can be refused only if the party asserting such refusal furnishes proof that:

(b) The party against whom the award is invoked was not given proper notice of the appointment of the arbitrator or of the arbitration proceedings or was otherwise unable to present his case; or

* * *

(d) The composition of the arbitral authority or the arbitral procedure was not in accordance with the agreement of the parties....

Convention, Article V, §§ 1(b), (d).

* * *

III.   CBG's Due Process Argument

Under section 1(b) of Article V of the Convention, enforcement of an arbitration award may be refused if it can be shown that "the party against whom the Award is invoked was not given proper notice of ... the arbitration proceedings or was otherwise unable to present his case...." CBG claims that it did not receive proper notice of the arbitrator's intent to impose legal costs against it, and was therefore "unable to present his case" in opposition to such costs.[6]

---

6. Specifically, the "case" that CBG claims it was unable to present is the argument that Hammermills is not entitled to collect legal costs under ICC Rules because those costs were incurred not by Hammermills but rather by its insurer, Argonaut. CBG argues that ICC Rules authorize the Arbitrator to assess only "normal legal costs incurred by the parties." ICC Rules, Article 20(2). Because Hammermills' costs were paid by Argonaut, CBG's argument goes, they were not costs "incurred by [a] part[y]."

This argument appears to be dubious, at least as a matter of American law. The prevailing rule is that an insured may recover attorneys fees from a third party (where there is some duty on the part of the third party to pay such fees, such as a duty of indemnification or a litigation rule authorizing a court to assess fees) notwithstanding the fact that technically the fees have been incurred by the insurer rather than the insured. See, e.g., Manor Healthcare Corp. v. Lomelo, 929 F.2d 633, 639 (11th Cir.1991) (holding that, under Fed. R.Civ.P. 54(d), costs could be awarded to prevailing party even though those costs were paid by party's insurer; to hold otherwise, court reasoned, "would allow plaintiffs to bring lawsuits against insured defendants without incurring litigation costs after losing on the merits"); Safeway Rental & Sales Co. v. Albina Engine & Machine Works, Inc., 343 F.2d 129, 135 (10th Cir. 1965) (noting that "[i]t is difficult to find a distinction between subrogation to the right to recover the amount of the judgment which was paid by another, and subrogation of the right to recover fees"); Boiler Engineering & Supply Co. v. General Controls, Inc., 443 Pa. 44, 277 A.2d 812, 814 (1971) (overruling prior decision and noting that "weight of authority" favors allowing recov-

The few courts to address this provision of the Convention have concluded that the provision "essentially sanctions the application of the forum state's standards of due process." See Parsons & Whittemore Overseas Co., 508 F.2d at 975; Geotech Lizenz AG v. Evergreen Systems, Inc., 697 F.Supp. 1248, 1253 (E.D.N.Y.1988) (citing Parsons & Whittemore Overseas Co.). Due process requires notice "reasonably calculated, under all the circumstances, to apprise interested persons of the pendency of the action and afford them an opportunity to present their objections." Mullane v. Central Hanover Bank & Trust Co., 339 U.S. 306, 314 (1950).

The Court is convinced that CBG was afforded sufficient notice that the assessment of legal fees was an issue in the arbitration to comport with due process. First, the ICC Rules themselves expressly placed CBG on notice that the assessment of legal costs would necessarily be incident to the final disposition of the proceeding. Article 20 of the ICC Rules states in relevant part:

> 1. The Arbitrator's award shall, in addition to dealing with the merits of the case, fix the costs of the arbitration and decide which of the parties shall bear the costs or in what proportions the costs shall be borne by the parties.

> 2. The costs of the arbitration shall include the arbitrator's fees and the administrative costs fixed by the [ICC] Court ..., the expenses, if any, of the arbitrator, the fees and expenses of any experts, and the normal legal costs incurred by the parties.

Second, the "Arbitrator's Terms of Reference," the document "defin[ing] ... the issues to be determined" in the arbitration, ICC Rules, Article 13(c), which was signed by counsel for both parties, stated in part:

IV. The basic issues in this arbitration are as follows:

> 1. to decide on the claims submitted by the parties,

---

ery of fees under these circumstances); Howard P. Foley Co. v. Employers–Commercial Union, 15 Ariz.App. 350, 488 P.2d 987 (1971). As a matter of policy, the fact that Hammermills has taken the precaution of purchasing insurance should not excuse CBG from a liability for legal costs that would otherwise be assessed against it. Ultimately, of course, the costs are recovered by the insurer pursuant to its subrogation right, so there is no "windfall" to the insured. CBG, citing John F. Wanamaker, New York, Inc. v. Otis Elevator Co., 228 N.Y. 192, 126 N.E. 718 (1920), urges that under New York law (which CBG claims to control this issue) an insured cannot recover attorneys' fees from a third party where those expenses were actually incurred by the insurer and not by the insured. There is considerable authority, however, for the proposition that New York has moved away from the Wanamaker result and now allows recovery of legal costs despite insurance coverage. See Dankoff v. Bowling Proprietors Ass'n of America, Inc., 69 Misc.2d 658, 331 N.Y.S.2d 109 (1972) (citing, inter alia, Crowley's Milk Co. v. American Mutual Liab. Ins. Co., 313 F.Supp. 502, 507–08 (E.D.N.Y.1969)); see also Sassower v. Field, No. 88 Civ. 5775 (S.D.N.Y. Aug. 12, 1991) (not discussing Wanamaker, but calling "absurd" the argument that costs cannot be awarded in favor of prevailing party because the insurer actually incurred the costs); Boiler Engineering & Supply Co., 443 A.2d at 814 (noting that validity of Wanamaker decision "is open to serious question in light of several decisions of the New York courts").

2. to fix the costs of the arbitration and decide which of the parties shall bear the costs or in what proportions of the costs shall be borne by the parties.

"Costs of arbitration" is a term of art under the ICC Rules which includes the "normal legal costs incurred by the parties." ICC Rules, Article 20(2).

Third, at the conclusion of its post-hearing brief, which was filed and served on CBG in October 1988, a full year before the award was issued, Hammermills urged the Arbitrator to "enter an award in favor of Hammermills, including the costs of arbitration, such as Hammermills attorneys' fees and expert witness fees." Hammermills' Post–Hearing Brief (October 26, 1988) at 111. Finally, CBG was again put on notice that the assessment of legal costs was an issue when it received the Arbitrator's September 29, 1989 letter requesting the parties to submit their legal costs.[7] This letter, in its entirety, states:

Dear Sirs:

I would appreciate if each of you would kindly send me by fax the statement of his client's legal costs, according to art. 20(2) last part [sic] of the ICC Rules of conciliation and arbitration.

CBG responded to this letter by submitting an itemization of its own legal costs, without requesting an additional opportunity to be heard or raising any concerns regarding this issue.

Thus, despite actual notice that the Arbitration was empowered to assess legal costs in the final award, that Hammermills was seeking an award of such costs, and that the Arbitrator had solicited cost information from the parties, CBG did not once raise before the Arbitrator its argument that Hammermills was not entitled to recover its legal costs because those costs were being paid by Argonaut.[8] Under these circumstance, the Court is convinced that the notice requirements of the due process clause were satisfied.

IV. Compliance With Icc Procedures

CBG next contends that the Arbitrator violated ICC procedure by inserting into the award the amount of the legal costs to be assessed

---

7. It is important to note that CBG is not claiming that it did not have an opportunity to challenge the amount of legal costs imposed by the Arbitrator. Rather, CBG claims that it was denied the opportunity to challenge the propriety of the assessment of legal costs vel non. Thus, there is no merit to the argument that CBG was not placed on notice of this issue until October 21, 1989, when it received its copy of Hammermills' counsels' letter to the Arbitrator specifying the amount of costs Hammermills was seeking.

8. It is undisputed, of course, that CBG was aware throughout the arbitration that Hammermills' costs were being paid by Ar-

gonaut, because it was CBG itself that had secured Argonaut's duty to defend. Moreover, it is also undisputed that the Arbitrator was well aware that Hammermills' legal costs were being paid by Argonaut. After the parties secured the modification to the automatic stay that allowed the arbitration to proceed, the Arbitrator stated in a June 1987 letter to the parties:

[A]s I understand the Bankruptcy Court order of March 17th, 1987, the modification of the automatic stay of the arbitral proceedings is subject to the condition that Argonaut–Midwest defends Hammermills.

against it after the draft award had been approved by the ICC Court. CBG argues that this procedural violation gives rise to a defense to the award under section 1(d) of Article V of the Convention, which provides that recognition and enforcement may be refused if "[t]he composition of the arbitral authority or the arbitral procedure was not in accordance with the agreement of the parties...." CBG reasons that the arbitration clause in its contract with Hammermills provided for arbitration "according to the Rules of Conciliation and Arbitration of the [ICC]," and therefore any procedural violation of ICC Rules necessarily violates "the agreement of the parties" under the Convention.

The Court does not believe that section 1(d) of Article V was intended, as CBG argues, to permit reviewing courts to police every procedural ruling made by the Arbitrator and to set aside the award if any violation of ICC procedures is found. Such an interpretation would directly conflict with the "pro-enforcement" bias of the Convention and its intention to remove obstacles to confirmation of arbitral awards. Rather, the Court believes that a more appropriate standard of review would be to set aside an award based on a procedural violation only if such violation worked substantial prejudice to the complaining party. Whatever the scope of section 1(d), however, the Court concludes that it is not applicable here because CBG has not met its burden of establishing that a violation of ICC procedure occurred.

CBG's theory is that the Arbitrator's actions violated Article 21 of the ICC Rules, which provides:

> Before signing an award, whether partial or definitive, the arbitrator shall submit it in draft form to the [ICC] Court. The Court may lay down modifications as to the form of the award and, without affecting the arbitrator's liberty of decision, may also draw his attention to points of substance. No award shall be signed until it has been approved as to form.

CBG observes that Article 20(1) states that the arbitrator's award "shall ... fix the costs of the arbitration." Therefore, CBG argues, when Articles 21 and 20(1) are viewed in conjunction, they require that the draft submitted to the ICC Court for approval include the costs assessment.

The Court believes that at most the rules relied upon by CBG give rise to some ambiguity as to whether the assessment of legal costs must be included in the draft award submitted to the ICC Court. Material submitted by both parties from experts on ICC procedures, however, convinces the Court that CBG has not established that there was a violation of ICC rules in this case. After the final award was issued, the parties wrote to Benjamin Davis, Counsel at the Secretariat of the ICC, requesting that he explain, inter alia, the procedures under the ICC Rules for fixing of the costs of the arbitration and for awarding attorneys' fees. Hammermills has submitted to the Court Mr. Davis sworn response to the parties' inquiries, which includes, in question-and-answer format, the following information:

1. Please explain the procedures under the ICC Rules for the fixing of the costs of arbitration.

In an arbitration that proceeds to a final award, at the time the draft award is submitted to the [ICC Court] for scrutiny in accordance with Article 21 of the ICC Rules, in the event the Court approves the final award pursuant to this Article, it also fixes the administrative charge of the ICC and fees of the Arbitral Tribunal . . .

Pursuant to the ICC Rules (Article 20(2)[)] it is the responsibility of the Arbitral Tribunal itself to determine the "normal legal costs" incurred by the parties.

2. Please explain the procedures under the ICC Rules for awarding attorney's fees.

There are no required procedures for the awarding of normal legal costs, i.e. attorney's fees. Pursuant to Article 20(2) of the ICC Rules these amounts are not fixed by the [ICC] Court. They are, as already explained, fixed by the Arbitral Tribunal.

The substance of Mr. Davis' letter, therefore, is that while the assessment of costs of the arbitral tribunal and the administrative charge of the ICC is the responsibility of the ICC Court, the assessment of "normal legal costs", which includes legal fees, is within the "exclusive competence" of the Arbitrator, and there are no formal procedural requirements governing that assessment. This conclusion is buttressed by an affidavit, submitted by CBG itself, of William Park, co-author of a treatise on ICC arbitration, in which Professor Park states that "there is no provision of the ICC Rules which dictates a specific procedure for the arbitrator to follow in addressing the award of legal costs. . . ." Professor Park confirms Mr. Davis' statement that "[u]nlike arbitrator's fees and ICC administrative costs, which are fixed by the ICC Court, the quantum of legal costs is fixed by the arbitrator himself."

Given the undisputed proposition that there are "no required procedures" governing the assessment of legal costs, it is difficult to see how this Court could conclude that CBG has met its burden of establishing that the procedures used by the Arbitrator to assess costs in this case were in contravention of ICC Rules.

* * *

Questions and Comments

1. As the *Hammermills* court notes, Article 21 of the 1988 ICC Rules provides:

Before signing an award, whether partial or definitive, the arbitrator shall submit it in draft form to the Court. The Court may lay down modifications as to the form or the award and, and without affecting the arbitrator's liberty of decision, may also draw his attention to points of substance. No award shall be signed until it has been approved as to form.

[For the current wording, see 1998 ICC Rules, Article 27]

What do you suppose is the purpose of this procedure? Was it followed in the *Hammermills* arbitration?

2.   Were not the arbitration costs one of the basic issues submitted to the arbitrator? As the court notes, the terms of reference stated in part:

IV.   The basic issues in this arbitration are as follows:

1.   to decide on the claims submitted by the parties,

2.   to fix the costs of the arbitration and decide which of the parties shall bear the costs or in what proportions of [sic] the costs shall be borne by the parties. 1992 WL 12272 at 4.

The court explains that "costs of arbitration" is a term of art that includes the "normal legal costs incurred by the parties". Id. Should not the ICC Court of Arbitration have had an opportunity to review the arbitrator's award of costs before the award was signed? Under the ICC rules, what is the role of the ICC Court after all?

3.   Drawing on the statements of ICC Counsel Benjamin Davis, the court concludes that only the administrative charge of the ICC is the responsibility of the ICC Court and that the assessment of "normal legal costs" including "legal fees" is within the "exclusive competence" of the arbitrator. What is the relevance of this conclusion? Are not the merits also within the exclusive competence of the arbitrator? Does not the arbitrator nonetheless have to submit the award on the merits to the ICC Court for its review and to give it an opportunity to "draw his [the arbitrator's] attention to points of substance"? Should not the arbitrator have submitted the legal fees award also?

4.   What if the parties had expressly agreed on a particular expert, but the arbitrator decided to use a different expert, one the arbitrator thought was better qualified? Would that violate New York Convention Article V(1)(d)? Should the award not be enforced in such a case?

5.   Does your answer to the previous question depend on whether the procedural irregularity prejudiced the losing party? If so, who would have the burden of proof on this point? If the proof showed a reasonable possibility of the error's having affected the outcome, would that be sufficient to prevent enforcement?

6.   How would you compare the *Hammermills* court's approach with that of the Hong Kong court in the previous *Shenzhen* case? Do you believe the Hong Kong court was more honest about the Article V(1)(d) error?

7.   If you agree with the outcome but not the reasoning in *Hammermills*, what reasoning would you have used to support that outcome?

V.3.c.v.   An Award Set Aside in "the Country in Which, or Under the Law of Which, That Award Was Made"

COMPANY A (NATIONALITY NOT INDICATED) v. COMPANY B (SLOVENIA)

Austria, Oberster Gerichtshof [Supreme Court], 1993.
20 Yearbk. Comm. Arb'n 1051 (1995).*

Facts

On 7 July 1988, an arbitral award in the amount of 4 million Austrian shillings was rendered by the Foreign Trade Arbitration Court at the Yugoslav Chamber of Economy in Belgrade against B, a company having its seat in Slovenia.

On 26 September 1988, B requested the setting aside of the award from a court in the territory now forming part of Slovenia. The request for setting aside was rejected by this court and the court of appeal.

On 3 July 1992, however, the Supreme Court of the Republic of Slovenia set aside the relevant parts of the award, holding that:

> The setting aside of awards is governed by the 1961 European Convention on International Commercial Arbitration. This Convention provides that an award may be set aside if it is contrary to the public policy of the State in which the award has been made. The contract between the parties had given defendant in the arbitration proceedings [Company B], if not a monopoly, at least a privileged position in the marketplace. This contract therefore violated Art. 255 of the Constitution, then in force, of the Socialist Federal Republic of Yugoslavia[2] and thus its public policy.

A requested enforcement of the award in Austria against assets held by B in Austria. B, relying on the decision of the Slovene Supreme Court, requested the Court of First Instance of Bad Radkersburg to abstain from enforcing the award.

The Court of First Instance denied this request and granted enforcement. The Court of Appeal of Graz reversed and refused to enforce the award but allowed a further appeal to the Supreme Court.

The Supreme Court restored the decision of the Court of First Instance of Bad Radkersburg and enforced the award.

* * *

* Reprinted with permission of Yearbook Commercial Arbitration, International Council for Commercial Arbitration.

2. Art. 255 of the Constitution of the Socialist Federal Republic of Yugoslavia reads:

"An association of organizations of associated labour and every other activity and act of organizations and state organs which are directed to the prevention of the free movement and association of labour and resources and the free movement of goods and services or to creation of a monopoly position on the single Yugoslav market by which material and other benefits not based on work are acquired and by which unequal relationships in business operations are created or by which other economic and social relationships determined by the Constitution are disrupted, are prohibited."

[Where]   * * * as in the present case, an award governed by the European Convention has been set aside in a Contracting State, Art. IX of the Convention is * * * applicable. Pursuant to its para. 1, the setting aside of an award shall only constitute a ground for the refusal of recognition or enforcement in another Contracting State, if such setting aside took place in the State in which, or under the law of which the award was made, and on one of the grounds enumerated in Art. IX(1)(a)–(c).

The Supreme Court already harbours doubts as to whether the first of these conditions is met. The award was made in Yugoslavia and under Yugoslav law. Slovenia is not a successor State of Yugoslavia. However, this does not need to be decided here as, merely according to their literal interpretation, the grounds exhaustively enumerated in Art. IX(1)(a)–(c) as justifying refusal of recognition or enforcement do not include the setting aside of an award on account of violation of public policy of the State of rendition.

In particular, the argument of the Court of Appeal has to be rejected, according to which the present case could be held to fall under Art. IX(1)(c). This rule provides for the recognition of the setting aside of an award which deals with a difference not contemplated by or not falling within the terms of the submission to arbitration, or contains decisions on matters beyond the scope of the submission to arbitration. A violation of public policy has nothing to do with the submission to arbitration or with the arbitral clause. These provisions concern the admissibility of the arbitral procedure, whereas the violation of public policy concerns the material content of the award.

Moreover, Klein (ZZP 1963, 351 et seq.), relying on the drafting history of the European Convention, establishes convincingly that violation of public policy of the country of origin of the award is not one of the reasons which have to be taken into account (thus also Schlosser in *Stein/Jonas*, ZPO, 20th ed., Annotation Sect. 1044, no. 134). Klein is right in pointing out that the insertion of Art. IX(2) into the European Convention is explained by the intention that this Convention should apply to Contracting States, which are Contracting States not only to the European Convention but also to the New York Convention. It is therefore irrelevant that both Austria and Slovenia also adhere to the New York Convention, the latter pursuant to a declaration of continuity (BGB1 1992/781 as modified by BGB1 1993/290) and that the New York Convention admits broader, further reasons for the refusal to recognize or enforce an award.

Pursuant to Art. IX(2) of the European Convention, its para. 1 restricts the application of the terms of Art. V(1)(e) of the New York Convention admitting the setting aside of an award—without any restriction—as a ground for refusing its enforcement, to the grounds for such a refusal enumerated in Art. IX(1) of the European Convention. The violation of public policy of the country of origin does not figure in this enumeration.

Thus, pursuant to Art. IX of the European Convention, the setting aside of the present award is no reason to refuse its enforcement. * * *

It follows from the above that the facts relied upon by [B] do not justify a refusal to enforce the award. Thus, the Court of First Instance reached a correct result when it rejected [B]'s request to abstain from enforcing the award. Hence, the decision of the Court of First Instance must be restored.

Questions and Comments

1. A reason for seeking to set aside an award is the greater preclusive force of success in such an action as compared with success in preventing recognition and enforcement. If the lawyer succeeds in getting the award set aside, the set-aside judgment could serve as a ground for other New York Convention countries to refuse to enforce the award. It is true that, as we have seen in French court practice in particular,[54] the New York Convention does not require a Convention country to refuse to enforce an award that has been set aside, but it allows such a country to do so. By contrast, one Convention country's refusal to enforce a foreign arbitral award is not an express ground for refusing to enforce the award in another Convention country.

The 1961 European Convention on International Commercial Arbitration (concluded in Geneva) has restricted the relevance of setting aside as a ground for refusal of recognition. Since rules on setting aside are not unified by multilateral international conventions, and since these grounds vary from state to state, the European Convention endeavored to identify (and to limit) those grounds which deserve international acknowledgment. Article IX of the European Convention has named four such grounds—these are the same as grounds for refusal of recognition enumerated in the New York Convention under Article V.1.a–d. What is very important, the grounds for refusal of recognition listed in Article V.2 of the New York Convention (arbitrability, and public policy) are not among those which are recognized as internationally relevant in Article IX of the European Convention. This means that in a member state of the European Convention, recognition cannot be refused under Article V.1.e of the New York Convention if the award was set aside on ground of infringement of public policy in another member country of the European Convention. To make this point absolutely clear, Article IX.2 of the European Convention stresses:

> In relations between Contracting States that are also parties to the New York Convention on the Recognition and Enforcement of Foreign Arbitral Awards of 10th June 1958, paragraph 1 of this Article limits the application of Article V(1)(e) of the New York Convention solely to the cases *of setting aside set out under paragraph 1 above.*

2. The Austrian Supreme Court (Oberster Gerichtshof) refused to observe Slovenian annulment granted on ground of infringement of Sloveni-

---

[54]. See the introductory Note to sub-section, V.2.a, item 6: "The consequences of   setting aside".

an public policy. Does this mean that the Oberster Gerichtshof could not refuse recognition on ground of public policy?

3. According to both the European Convention and the New York Convention, setting aside is only relevant if it was effected in the "country in which, or under the law of which" the award was made.

In this case, the award was made in Belgrade, Yugoslavia, under the laws of Yugoslavia. At the time when the award was made, Slovenia was a constituent republic (federal unit) of Yugoslavia. The situation was the same when annulment was requested on September 26, 1988. Annulment was granted, however on July 3, 1992 by the Supreme court of Slovenia—and at that time, Slovenia was an independent country, rather than part of Yugoslavia. Slovenia has also become a foreign country with regard to the place of rendering the award (Belgrade, Yugoslavia). This issue is mentioned in the decision of the Oberster Gerichtshof, but not decided because the Slovenian annulment was held irrelevant on other grounds.

Do you think that in the given circumstances the Austrian courts dealt with an award set aside "by the competent authority of the country in which, or under the law of which, that award was made"?

Relevance of the Enforcing State's National Arbitration Law

A number of countries, most notably France, have found ways to bypass New York Convention article V(1)(e) so that it does not operate as a separate ground for refusing to enforce a foreign arbitral award. This result follows from the French interpretation of New York Convention Article VII and because of the content of the French arbitration law. The *Norsolor* case, immediately below, is one of the leading French decisions on the effect of New York Convention Article VII. The French statute on enforcement of foreign (or international) arbitral awards does not include the award's having been set aside in a foreign court as a ground for nonenforcement. The statute allows non-enforcement on five grounds: (1) absence or invalidity of the arbitration agreement; (2) irregularities in the appointment of the arbitrator(s); (3) the arbitrators' exceeding the authority conferred on them; (4) violation of due process; (5) where recognition or enforcement would violate international public policy (*ordre public international*). New Code of Civil Procedure art. 1502 (1981).

PABALK TICARET v. NORSOLOR[m]

France, Cour de cassation 1984.
24 I.L.M. 360 (1985).[*]

Introductory Note[n]

The decision translated below is the last episode of a long dispute about the validity and the enforceability of the award rendered in Vienna

---

m. [This case was also included supra in section IV.3.d. because of its relevance to the problem of the applicable law in arbitration.]

* Reproduced with permission from September 1985 issue of International Legal

Materials, © The American Society of International Law.

n. [The Introductory Note and English translation were prepared for *International*

on October 26, 1979 by an arbitral tribunal (B. Cremades, Chairman; J. Ghestin; R. Steiner) set up under the auspices of the ICC.

The award, which dealt with the termination of an agency agreement between the French corporation Ugilor (Norsolor) and its Turkish agent Pabalk, is notable in that it did not rely on any national legal system. After an attempt to determine the law applicable according to traditional choice of law rules, the arbitral tribunal concluded:

> Faced with the difficulty of choosing a national law the application of which is sufficiently compelling, the Tribunal considered that it was appropriate, given the international nature of the agreement, to leave aside any compelling reference to a specific legal system, be it Turkish or French, and to apply the international *lex mercatoria*.
>
> One of the principles which comprises *lex mercatoria* is that of good faith, which must be adhered to in the formation and the performance of contracts. The emphasis placed on contractual good faith is moreover one of the dominant references revealed by the convergence of national laws on the matter.

On these bases, the Tribunal found the French party to be responsible for the termination of the agency agreement and awarded damages in a lump sum based on equity. (The French text of the award appears in *Revue de l'Arbitrage* 1983, p. 525 and English extracts in *Yearbook Commercial Arbitration*, 1983, ICC award no. 3131.)

As Vienna was the place of arbitration, an action to set aside was brought by Norsolor before the Austrian Courts. Meanwhile, enforcement was sought by Pabalk in France.

I. The first question to be decided by the courts was whether the arbitrators, who were not granted the powers to rule in equity as *amiable compositeurs*, could disregard all national legal systems and rely on *lex mercatoria* only.

Pursuant to Article 595(5) and (6) of the Austrian Code of Civil Procedure (ZPO), an award rendered in Austria could be set aside, *inter alia*, "if the Arbitral Tribunal dealt with matters beyond those referred to it" and "if the award violated mandatory provisions of law". Later on, the Federal Law of February 2, 1983, which came into effect on May 1, 1983, limited the latter provision to cases in which "the award is incompatible with the basic principles of the Austrian legal system or infringes mandatory provisions of the law, the application of which cannot be derogated by a choice of law of the parties even in a case where a foreign contract according to paragraph 35 of the International Private Law Act is involved".

Legal Materials by Emmanuel Gaillard, Professor of International Law, Lille University; Visiting Professor of Law, Harvard Law School (1984–1985); Avocat à la Cour de Paris. Excerpts of the decision begin at I.L.M. page 363.]

Contrary to the decision of the Tribunal of Commerce of Vienna, which dismissed Pabalk's claim on June 29, 1981, the Vienna Court of Appeals partially set aside the award in its decision of June 29, 1982, on the ground that the Arbitral Tribunal, which had to determine the applicable law pursuant to Article 13, paragraph 3 of the ICC Rules, exceeded its powers in referring to *lex mercatoria*, which was described by the Court as a "world law of questionable validity" instead of grounding its decision in a particular national legal order.

On November 18, 1982, the Austrian Supreme Court reversed this decision on the ground that (1) in relying on the principle of good faith to determine the principal's liability for the damage caused by the termination of the agency agreement, it did not infringe any mandatory rule in force in any of the two concerned jurisdictions within the meaning of Article 595(6) ZPO and that (2) in determining the amount of damages on the basis of equity without special authorization from the parties, the Arbitral Tribunal did not transgress the limits of its competence within the meaning of Article 595(5) ZPO. (See *Yearbook Commercial Arbitration* 1984, p. 161, note W. Melis.)

Similarly, in the enforcement proceeding, the Tribunal de Grande Instance of Paris held on March 4, 1981, that in applying the principle of good faith as one of the "general principles of obligations applicable to international trade," the arbitrators did not rule as *amiables compositeurs* and, therefore, did not exceed their powers under the terms of the arbitral agreement.

On appeal, the Paris Court of Appeals did not address this issue because of the answer it gave to the second question raised in this case. However, the Cour de Cassation followed the Tribunal de Grande Instance solution in deciding the SNCT Fougerolle v. Banque du Proche Orient case on December 9, 1981. (*Clunet* 1982, p. 931, note Oppetit.)

Only the possible conflict between *lex mercatoria* and mandatory rules of a legal order with a close connection with the case remains undecided. If such a situation arose, recognition and enforcement would not be carried out in France if they were held "contrary to international public policy (ordre public)" within the meaning of Article 1502(5) of the New Code of Civil Procedure [20 I.L.M. 921 (1981)] and would not be carried out in Austria if they were held contrary to the mandatory rules "applicable even to foreign contracts" within the meaning of the new Article 595(6) ZPO.

II. The second question concerns the possible relationship between the action to set aside brought in the country where the seat of the arbitration is located and the enforcement actions initiated in other countries.

On December 15, 1981, the Paris Court of Appeals decided to stay the enforcement proceedings until the decision of the Vienna Court of Appeals on the action to set aside. On November 19, 1982, it held that the January 29, 1982 Vienna Court of Appeals' decision to set aside the award should preclude enforcement in France. Both decisions were based on Article V(1)e of the New York Convention of June 10, 1958, on the recognition and enforcement of foreign arbitral awards according to which "recognition and enforcement of the award may be refused ... if the award has not yet become binding on the parties or has been set aside or suspended by a competent authority of the country in which, or under the law of which, that award was made".

After the Austrian Supreme Court decision to recognize the validity of the award, which led the Tribunal de Grande Instance of Paris to enforce it on June 20, 1983, the decision of the Cour de Cassation on October 9, 1984, reproduced below, merely clarifies the French position.

The Cour de Cassation clearly condemns the view that the New York Convention would direct the courts in which enforcement is sought not to recognize an award set aside in the country where the seat of the arbitration is located. The solution brings the French position in harmony with the wording of Article V(1)e and of Article VII, which specifies that "the present Convention ... [does not] deprive any interested party of any right he may have to avail himself of an arbitral award in the manner and to the extent allowed by the law ... of the country where such award is sought to be relied upon."

However it is still an open question whether the vacating of an award by a court where the seat of arbitration is located could be enforced in France pursuant to the French general rules on the recognition and enforcement of arbitral awards. Now the controversy will probably focus on the meaning of Article 1498 of the New Code of Civil Procedure (Decree of May 12, 1981) which states "arbitral awards shall be recognized in France if *their existence* is proven by the parties relying thereupon and if this recognition is not manifestly contrary to international public policy" [20 I.L.M. 919 (1981)] and on the conflict between the recognition of the award and the recognition of the foreign court decision setting aside the award (see B. Goldman, "La bataille judiciaire autour de la lex mercatoria." *Revue de l'Arbitrage* 1983, p. 379). Certainly, the controversy about "delocalization" of arbitral awards will not end with the Norsolor case.

Opinion

* * *

ON THE SOLE GROUND:

Considering jointly Article VII of the Convention on the Recognition and Enforcement of Foreign Arbitral Awards, signed in New York on June 10, 1958, and Article 12 of the New Code of Civil Procedure;

Whereas, according to Article VII of the New York Convention, the Convention does not deprive any interested party of any right he may have to avail himself of an arbitral award in the manner and to the extent allowed by the law or the treaties of the country where such award is sought to be relied upon; as a result the judge cannot refuse enforcement when his own national legal system permits it, and, by virtue of Article 12 of the New Code of Civil Procedures, he should, even *sua sponte*, research the matter if such is the case;

Whereas Pabalk Ticaret Limited Sirketi (Pabalk), a Turkish company incorporated in Turkey, and Ugilor, a company incorporated in France, which has since become Norsolor, were parties to an agency agreement which contained an arbitration clause referring to the Rules for the International Chamber of Commerce (ICC) Court of Arbitration and in particular to Article 13 of these Rules prescribing that in the absence of any indication by the parties as to the applicable law, the arbitrators should apply the law designated as the proper law by the rule of conflict which they deem appropriate, it being specified that they shall take account of the provisions of the contract and the relevant trade usages;

Whereas in their award rendered on October 26, 1979, the arbitrators stated that, faced with the difficulty of choosing a national law the application of which is sufficiently compelling, it was appropriate, given the international nature of the agreement, to leave aside any compelling reference to a specific legal system, be it Turkish or French, and to apply the international *lex mercatoria*, of which one of the fundamental principles is that of good faith which must govern the formation and performance of contracts;

Whereas the arbitral tribunal found that the termination of the agreement was attributable to Ugilor and that Ugilor's conduct caused unjustified damages to Pabalk, which equity required to be compensated;

Whereas this award, in its four-point decree, ordered Norsolor to pay various sums to Pabalk;

Whereas the award was held enforceable in France by an order dated February 4, 1980, of the President of the Tribunal de Grande Instance of Paris, which Norsolor sought to attack on the basis of Article 1028 of the Code of Civil Procedure, since repealed but nonetheless applicable here, claiming that the arbitrators had acted as *amiables compositeurs* and thus had exceeded the bounds of their authority;

Whereas by judgment dated March 4, 1981, the Tribunal de Grande Instance rejected the demand that the enforcement order be retracted;

Whereas, to amend this decision and retract the order in that it granted enforcement of parts III and IV of the arbitral award, the judgment under attack applied Article V(1)(e) of the New York Convention, ratified both by Austria and France, and according to which the recognition and enforcement of an award would be refused only if the award had been set aside by a competent authority of the country in which, or under the law of which, that award was made, and the judgment under attack relied on the fact that these parts III and IV of the decree of the award had been set aside by a decision dated January 29, 1982 of the Vienna Court of Appeals on the ground that the arbitral tribunal, in violation of Article 13 of the Rules for the ICC Court of Arbitration, had not determined the national law applicable and limited themselves to refer to the international *lex mercatoria*, a "world law of questionable validity";

Whereas by ruling in this manner, where the Court of Appeals had a duty to determine, even *sua sponte*, if French law would not allow Pabalk to avail itself of the award at stake, the Court of Appeals violated the above mentioned provisions.

FOR THESE REASONS:

We reverse and set aside the decision rendered November 19, 1982, by the Court of Appeals of Paris and send the case to the Court of Appeals of Amiens . . .

Questions and Comments

1. Are you inclined to agree with the *Norsolor* court's interpretation of Article VII of the New York Convention?

2. What would happen in France if a defendant in an enforcement action sought to rely on New York Convention Article V(2)(a) (non-arbitrable subject matter)? Do Articles V(2)(a) and (b) overlap? Article V(2)(b) has a counterpart in the French statute, but V(2)(a) does not.

3. Given that the French national grounds for refusing enforcement of foreign arbitral awards are narrower than the New York Convention, would you expect New York Convention Article V to play any role in France?

4. Recall that the *Norsolor* result raises the issue of a possible conflict between the effect to be given a foreign award and the effect to be given the foreign judgment setting aside the award. Why should not the French courts treat the issue of the enforceability of the award as *res judicata*? Is it not true that the parties chose arbitration in Austria under the Austrian *lex arbitri*, and hence at least implicitly understood that set aside litigation, if there were any, would take place in Austria? The Cour de cassation did not reach this issue in its *Norsolor* ruling. The following case illustrates the approach to this question taken by an important United States decision.

CHROMALLOY AEROSERVICES, A DIVISION OF CHROMALLOY GAS TURBINE CORP. (U.S.) v. THE ARAB REPUBLIC OF EGYPT

United States District Court, District of Columbia, 1996.
939 F.Supp. 907.

Memorandum

JUNE L. GREEN, DISTRICT JUDGE.

I. Introduction

This matter is before the Court on the Petition of Chromalloy Aeroservices, Inc., ("CAS") to Confirm an Arbitral Award, and a Motion to Dismiss that Petition filed by the Arab Republic of Egypt ("Egypt"), the defendant in the arbitration. This is a case of first impression. The Court GRANTS Chromalloy Aeroservices' Petition to Recognize and

Enforce the Arbitral Award, and **DENIES** Egypt's Motion to Dismiss, because the arbitral award in question is valid, and because Egypt's arguments against enforcement are insufficient to allow this Court to disturb the award.

II. Background

This case involves a military procurement contract between a U.S. corporation, Chromalloy Aeroservices, Inc., and the Air Force of the Arab Republic of Egypt.

On June 16, 1988, Egypt and CAS entered into a contract under which CAS agreed to provide parts, maintenance, and repair for helicopters belonging to the Egyptian Air Force. On December 2, 1991, Egypt terminated the contract by notifying CAS representatives in Egypt. On December 4, 1991, Egypt notified CAS headquarters in Texas of the termination. On December 15, 1991, CAS notified Egypt that it rejected the cancellation of the contract "and commenced arbitration proceedings on the basis of the arbitration clause contained in Article XII and Appendix E of the Contract." Egypt then drew down CAS' letters of guarantee in an amount totaling some $11,475,968.

On February 23, 1992, the parties began appointing arbitrators, and shortly thereafter, commenced a lengthy arbitration. On August 24, 1994, the arbitral panel ordered Egypt to pay to CAS the sums of $272,900 plus 5 percent interest from July 15, 1991, (interest accruing until the date of payment), and $16,940,958 plus 5 percent interest from December 15, 1991, (interest accruing until the date of payment). The panel also ordered CAS to pay to Egypt the sum of 606,920 pounds sterling, plus 5 percent interest from December 15, 1991, (interest accruing until the date of payment).

On October 28, 1994, CAS applied to this Court for enforcement of the award. On November 13, 1994, Egypt filed an appeal with the Egyptian Court of Appeal, seeking nullification of the award. On March 1, 1995, Egypt filed a motion with this Court to adjourn CAS's Petition to enforce the award. On April 4, 1995, the Egyptian Court of Appeal suspended the award, and on May 5, 1995, Egypt filed a Motion in this Court to Dismiss CAS's petition to enforce the award. On December 5, 1995, Egypt's Court of Appeal at Cairo issued an order nullifying the award. This Court held a hearing in the matter on December 12, 1995.

Egypt argues that this Court should deny CAS' Petition to Recognize and Enforce the Arbitral Award out of deference to its court. CAS argues that this Court should confirm the award because Egypt "does not present any serious argument that its court's nullification decision is consistent with the New York Convention or United States arbitration law."

III. Discussion

A. Jurisdiction

[The court concluded that the U.S. Foreign Sovereign Immunities Act, 28 U.S.C. § 1330, et. Seq. (1976), provides for waiver of sovereign

immunity when a private party sues a foreign sovereign to enforce an arbitral award rendered under an agreement with the sovereign to submit disputes to arbitration.]

B. *Chromalloy's Petition for Enforcement*

A party seeking enforcement of a foreign arbitral award must apply for an order confirming the award within three years after the award is made. 9 U.S.C. § 207. The award in question was made on August 14, 1994. CAS filed a Petition to confirm the award with this Court on October 28, 1994, less than three months after the arbitral panel made the award. CAS's Petition includes a "duly certified copy" of the original award as required by Article IV(1)(a) of the Convention, translated by a duly sworn translator, as required by Article IV(2) of the Convention, as well as a duly certified copy of the original contract and arbitration clause, as required by Article IV(1)(b) of the Convention. 9 U.S.C. § 201 note. CAS's Petition is properly before this Court.

1. *The Standard under the Convention*

This Court *must* grant CAS's Petition to Recognize and Enforce the arbitral "award unless it finds one of the grounds for refusal ... of recognition or enforcement of the award specified in the ... Convention." 9 U.S.C. § 207. Under the Convention, "Recognition and enforcement of the award *may* be refused" if Egypt furnishes to this Court "proof that ... [t]he award has ... been set aside ... by a competent authority of the country in which, or under the law of which, that award was made." Convention, Article V(1) & V(1)(e) (emphasis added), 9 U.S.C. § 201 note. In the present case, the award was made in Egypt, under the laws of Egypt, and has been nullified by the court designated by Egypt to review arbitral awards. Thus, the Court *may*, at its discretion, decline to enforce the award.[2]

While Article V provides a discretionary standard, Article VII of the Convention *requires* that, "The provisions of the present Convention *shall not* ... deprive any interested party of any right he may have to avail himself of an arbitral award in the manner and to the extent allowed by the law ... of the count[r]y where such award is sought to be relied upon." 9 U.S.C. § 201 note (emphasis added). In other words, under the Convention, CAS maintains all rights to the enforcement of this Arbitral Award that it would have in the absence of the Convention. Accordingly, the Court finds that, if the Convention did not exist, the Federal Arbitration Act ("FAA") would provide CAS with a legitimate claim to enforcement of this arbitral award. *See* 9 U.S.C. §§ 1–14. Jurisdiction over Egypt in such a suit would be available under 28 U.S.C. §§ 1330 (granting jurisdiction over foreign states "as to any claim for relief in personam with respect to which the foreign state is not entitled

---

2. The French language version of the Convention, (which the Court notes is *not* the version codified by Congress), emphasizes the extraordinary nature of a refusal to recognize an award: "Recognition and enforcement of the award *will not be refused* ... unless...." (Response to Petitioner's Post–Hearing Brief, at 3) (emphasis in the original).

to immunity ... under sections 1605–1607 of this title") and 1605(a)(2) (withholding immunity of foreign states for "an act outside ... the United States in connection with a commercial activity of the foreign state elsewhere and that act causes a direct effect in the United States"). Venue for the action would lie with this Court under 28 U.S.C. § 1391(f) & (f)(4) (granting venue in civil cases against foreign governments to the United States District Court for the District of Columbia).

2. *Examination of the Award under 9 U.S.C. § 10*

Under the laws of the United States, arbitration awards are presumed to be binding, and may only be vacated by a court under very limited circumstances:

> (a) In any of the following cases the United States court in and for the district wherein the award was made may make an order vacating the award upon the application of any party to the arbitration—

>> (1) Where the award was procured by corruption, fraud, or undue means.

>> (2) Where there was evident partiality or corruption in the arbitrators, or either of them.

>> (3) Where the arbitrators were guilty of misconduct in refusing to postpone the hearing, upon sufficient cause shown, or in refusing to hear evidence pertinent and material to the controversy; or of any other misbehavior by which the rights of any party have been prejudiced.

>> (4) Where the arbitrators exceeded their powers, or so imperfectly executed them that a mutual, final, and definite award upon the subject matter submitted was not made.

9 U.S.C. § 10.[3]

An arbitral award will also be set aside if the award was made in " 'manifest disregard' of the law." *First Options of Chicago v. Kaplan*, 514 U.S. 938, ___, 115 S.Ct. 1920, 1923, 131 L.Ed.2d 985 (1995). "Manifest disregard of the law may be found if [the] arbitrator[s] understood and correctly stated the law but proceeded to ignore it." *Kanuth v. Prescott, Ball & Turben, Inc.*, 949 F.2d 1175, 1179 (D.C.Cir. 1991).

> Plainly, this non-statutory theory of vacatur cannot empower a District Court to conduct the same de novo review of questions of law that an appellate court exercises over lower court decisions. Indeed, we have in the past held that it is clear that [manifest disregard] means more than error or misunderstanding with respect to the law.

3. The Court has reviewed the voluminous submissions of the parties and finds no evidence that corruption, fraud, or undue means was used in procuring the award, or that the arbitrators exceeded their powers in any way.

Al–Harbi v. Citibank, 85 F.3d 680, 683 (D.C.Cir.1996) (internal citations omitted).

* * *

In the present case, the language of the arbitral award that Egypt complains of reads:

> The Arbitral tribunal considers that it does not need to decide the legal nature of the contract. It appears that the Parties rely principally for their claims and defences, on the interpretation of the contract itself and on the facts presented. Furthermore, the Arbitral tribunal holds that the legal issues in dispute are not affected by the characterization of the contract.

* * *[T]he arbitrators in the present case made a procedural decision that allegedly led to a misapplication of substantive law. After considering Egypt's arguments that Egyptian administrative law should govern the contract, the majority of the arbitral panel held that it did not matter which substantive law they applied—civil or administrative. At worst, this decision constitutes a mistake of law, and thus is not subject to review by this Court.

In the United States, "[W]e are well past the time when judicial suspicion of the desirability of arbitration and of the competence of arbitral tribunals inhibited the development of arbitration as an alternative means of dispute resolution." *Mitsubishi Motors Corp. v. Soler Chrysler–Plymouth, Inc.*, 473 U.S. 614, 626–27, 105 S.Ct. 3346, 3354, 87 L.Ed.2d 444 (1985). In Egypt, however, "[I]t is established that arbitration is an exceptional means for resolving disputes, requiring departure from the normal means of litigation before the courts, and the guarantees they afford." Egypt's complaint that, "[T]he Arbitral Award is null under Arbitration Law, ... because it is not properly 'grounded' under Egyptian law," reflects this suspicious view of arbitration, and is precisely the type of technical argument that U.S. courts are not to entertain when reviewing an arbitral award.

* * * The Court now considers the question of whether the decision of the Egyptian court should be recognized as a valid foreign judgment.

As the Court stated earlier, this is a case of first impression. [The Court here stresses the pro-arbitration policy of the New York Convention and quotes from the U.S. Supreme Court decision in Scherk v. Alberto–Cluver Co., 417 U.S.506, 519: " * * * courts of signatory countries * * * should not be permitted to decline enforcement of [arbitration] agreements on the basis of parochial views of their desirability or in a manner that would diminish the mutually binding nature of the agreements."] * * *

* * * The Court finds this argument [just quoted from *Scherk*] equally persuasive in the present case, where Egypt seeks to repudiate its solemn promise to abide by the results of the arbitration.[4]

C.   The Decision of Egypt's Court of Appeal

1.   The Contract

* * * Article XII of the contract requires that the parties arbitrate all disputes that arise between them under the contract. Appendix E, which defines the terms of any arbitration, forms an integral part of the contract. The contract is unitary. Appendix E to the contract defines the "Applicable Law Court of Arbitration." The clause reads, in relevant part:

> It is ... understood that both parties have irrevocably agreed to apply Egypt (sic) Laws and to choose Cairo as seat of the court of arbitration.

* * *

> The decision of the said court shall be final and binding and cannot be made subject to any appeal or other recourse.

This Court may not assume that the parties intended these two sentences to contradict one another, and must preserve the meaning of both if possible. Egypt argues that the first quoted sentence supersedes the second, and allows an appeal to an Egyptian court. Such an interpretation, however, would vitiate the second sentence, and would ignore the plain language on the face of the contract. The Court concludes that the first sentence defines choice of law and choice of forum for the hearings of the arbitral panel. The Court further concludes that the second quoted sentence indicates the clear intent of the parties that any arbitration of a dispute arising under the contract is not to be appealed to any court. This interpretation, unlike that offered by Egypt, preserves the meaning of both sentences in a manner that is consistent with the plain language of the contract. The position of the latter sentence as the seventh and final paragraph, just before the signatures, lends credence to the view that this sentence is the final word on the arbitration question. In other words, the parties agreed to apply Egyptian Law to the arbitration, but, more important, they agreed that the arbitration ends with the decision of the arbitral panel.

2.   The Decision of the Egyptian Court of Appeal

The Court has already found that the arbitral award is proper as a matter of U.S. law, and that the arbitration agreement between Egypt and CAS precluded an appeal in Egyptian courts. The Egyptian court has acted, however, and Egypt asks this Court to grant *res judicata* effect to that action.

---

4. The fact that this case concerns the enforcement of an arbitral award, rather than the enforcement of an agreement to arbitrate, makes no difference, because without the knowledge that judgment will be entered upon an award, the term "binding arbitration" becomes meaningless.

The "requirements for enforcement of a foreign judgment ... are that there be 'due citation' [*i.e.*, proper service of process] and that the original claim not violate U.S. public policy." *Tahan v. Hodgson*, 662 F.2d 862, 864 (D.C.Cir.1981) (*citing Hilton v. Guyot*, 159 U.S. 113, 202, 16 S.Ct. 139, 158, 40 L.Ed. 95 (1895)). The Court uses the term 'public policy' advisedly, with a full understanding that, "[J]udges have no license to impose their own brand of justice in determining applicable public policy." *Northwest Airlines Inc. v. Air Line Pilots Association, Int'l*, 808 F.2d 76, 78 (D.C.Cir.1987). Correctly understood, "[P]ublic policy emanates [only] from clear statutory or case law, 'not from general considerations of supposed public interest.' " *Id.* (*quoting American Postal Workers Union v. United States Postal Service*, 789 F.2d 1 (D.C.Cir.1986)).

The U.S. public policy in favor of final and binding arbitration of commercial disputes is unmistakable, and supported by treaty, by statute, and by case law. The Federal Arbitration Act "and the implementation of the Convention in the same year by amendment of the Federal Arbitration Act," demonstrate that there is an "emphatic federal policy in favor of arbitral dispute resolution," particularly "in the field of international commerce." *Mitsubishi v. Soler Chrysler–Plymouth*, 473 U.S. 614, 631, 105 S.Ct. 3346, 3356, 87 L.Ed.2d 444 (1985) (internal citation omitted); *cf. Revere Copper & Brass Inc., v. Overseas Private Investment Corporation*, 628 F.2d 81, 82 (D.C.Cir.1980) (holding that, "There is a strong public policy behind judicial enforcement of binding arbitration clauses"). A decision by this Court to recognize the decision of the Egyptian court would violate this clear U.S. public policy.

3. *International Comity*

"No nation is under an unremitting obligation to enforce foreign interests which are fundamentally prejudicial to those of the domestic forum." *Laker Airways Ltd. v. Sabena, Belgian World Airlines*, 731 F.2d 909, 937 (D.C.Cir.1984). "[C]omity never obligates a national forum to ignore 'the rights of its own citizens or of other persons who are under the protection of its laws.' " *Id.* at 942 (emphasis added) (quoting *Hilton v. Guyot*, 159 U.S. 113, 164, 16 S.Ct. 139, 143–44, 40 L.Ed. 95 (1895)). Egypt alleges that, "Comity is the chief doctrine of international law *requiring* U.S. courts to respect the decisions of competent foreign tribunals." However, comity does not and may not have the preclusive effect upon U.S. law that Egypt wishes this Court to create for it.

* * *

4. *Choice of Law*

Egypt argues that by choosing Egyptian law, and by choosing Cairo as the sight [sic] of the arbitration, CAS has for all time signed away its rights under the Convention and U.S. law. This argument is specious. When CAS agreed to the choice of law and choice of forum provisions, it waived its right to sue Egypt for breach of contract in the courts of the United States in favor of final and binding arbitration of such a dispute under the Convention. Having prevailed in the chosen forum, under the chosen law, CAS comes to this Court seeking recognition and enforcement of the award. The Convention was created for just this purpose. It is untenable to argue that by choosing arbitration under the Convention, CAS has waived rights specifically guaranteed by that same Convention.

5. Conflict between the Convention & the FAA

As a final matter, Egypt argues that, "Chromalloy's use of [A]rticle VII [to invoke the Federal Arbitration Act] contradicts the clear language of the Convention and would create an impermissible conflict under 9 U.S.C. § 208," by eliminating all consideration of Article V of the Convention. *See Vimar Seguros y Reaseguros, S.A. v. M/V Sky Reefer*, 515 U.S. 528, ___, 115 S.Ct. 2322, 2325, 132 L.Ed.2d 462 (1995) (holding that, "[W]hen two statutes are capable of coexistence ... it is the duty of the courts, absent a clearly expressed congressional intention to the contrary, to regard each as effective"). As the Court has explained, however, Article V provides a permissive standard, under which this Court *may* refuse to enforce an award. Article VII, on the other hand, mandates that this Court *must* consider CAS' claims under applicable U.S. law.

Article VII of the Convention provides that:

> The provisions of the present Convention shall not ... deprive any interested party of any right he may have to avail himself of an arbitral award in the manner and to the extent allowed by the law ... of the count[r]y where such award is sought to be relied upon.

9 U.S.C. § 201 note. Article VII does not eliminate all consideration of Article V; it merely requires that this Court protect any rights that CAS has under the domestic laws of the United States. There is no conflict between CAS' use of Article VII to invoke the FAA and the language of the Convention.

IV. Conclusion

The Court concludes that the award of the arbitral panel is valid as a matter of U.S. law. The Court further concludes that it need not grant *res judicata* effect to the decision of the Egyptian Court of Appeal at Cairo. Accordingly, the Court **GRANTS** Chromalloy Aeroservices' Petition to Recognize and Enforce the Arbitral Award, and **DENIES** Egypt's Motion to Dismiss that Petition.

Questions and Comments

1. By taking action to set the award aside in Egypt, did the government of Egypt "repudiate its solemn promise to abide by the results of the arbitration", as the *Chromalloy* court says? How do you interpret the arbitration clause language providing that the award is "final and binding and cannot be made subject to any appeal or other recourse"? Does the clause waive Egypt's right to institute a set-aside proceeding? Do the parties

have the power to waive that right? What law should decide that question? Would the case have been decided differently in the absence of that clause?

2. In *Chromalloy* the claimant, CAS, argues that the award should be enforced because Egypt "does not present any serious argument that its court's nullification decision is consistent with the New York Convention * * *." Does the New York Convention regulate the action taken by the Egyptian court? If your answer is technically no, do you think the claimant, CAS, could have made the same [or a similar point]—ie. Egypt's ground for nullification was not consistent with the N.Y. Convention grounds for refusing recognition and enforcement of an award—to argue that an enforcing court should exercise its discretion [accorded by the word "may" in V(1)] against applying V(1)(e) and in favor or enforcing the award? Refer to question 5 below.

3. The *Chromalloy* court, in line with the French *Norsolor* decision, interprets New York Convention Article VII to give the enforcing party a right to rely on the "national" law of the country of enforcement—that is, the law that would apply in that country in the absence of the New York Convention—if that law is more favorable to enforcement than is the New York Convention itself. Does this interpretation effectively read Article V(1)(e) out of the Convention?

Whereas in the absence of the New York Convention, the grounds in French law for refusing enforcement of an award would be narrower than those in the Convention, in U.S. law the grounds for refusing enforcement would be both narrower and potentially broader. They would be narrower because an award's having been set aside in the country of origin is not a ground for refusing enforcement under the Federal Arbitration Act. (Why not?) The potentially broader ground is "manifest disregard of the law". (Whether "manifest disregard" is a ground within Article V is considered infra in section V.3.d. in connection with the *Brandeis* case.) If "manifest disregard" is not a ground under Article V, then under *Chromalloy*, a set-aside judgment in the country of origin has the effect of requiring the award to meet the U.S. "manifest disregard" standard to be assured of enforcement in the U.S. (under Article VII). Assuming "manifest disregard" is not an Article V ground for rejection, if the award fails the "manifest disregard" test, will it be rejected outright in the U.S., or might it still be enforceable (because Article V(1)(e) appears discretionary)? Should a U.S. judge enforce it?

4. Do you agree with the *Chromalloy* court's reliance on New York Convention Article VII? The *Chromalloy* court analyzes the case under Chapter 1 of the FAA, but that Chapter applies to domestic U.S. awards. At least Chapter 1 seems to presume (require?) that the award was made in the U.S. For example, FAA section 9 states: "If no court is specified in the agreement of the parties, then such application [for confirmation or setting aside] may be made to the United States court in and for the district within which such award was made." In the case of an international award, at least one made outside the U.S., Chapter 2 applies, which is the chapter that incorporates the New York Convention. Could one restate the Chromalloy logic as follows: Article VII requires the U.S. to enforce a foreign award set aside in the country where rendered if the U.S. would have enforced the

award had it been a domestic U.S. award made in the U.S. Is this a correct interpretation of Article VII?

5. The common French (*Norsolor*) and United States (*Chromalloy*) interpretation of New York Convention Article VII (in relation to Article V(1)(e)) appears to be followed in a number of other jurisdictions. For the German position, see the German Supreme Court decision: BGH Feb. 26, 1991, 17 Yearbk.Comm.Arb'n 513 (1992). In the Netherlands the Arbitration Act of 1986 Article 1976 provides for the same result. See Sanders and van den Berg, The Netherlands Arbitration Act 1986 ___ (1987).

The issue cannot arise in Switzerland, because article 194 of the Swiss Law on Private International Law of 1989, 29 I.L.M. 1244 (1990), incorporates New York Convention Article V by reference. The same is true in Italy, where the provisions of Article V are substantially reproduced in article 840 of the Italian Arbitration Law of January 5, 1994. See G. Delaume, Introductory Note on *Chromalloy* in 35 I.L.M. 1359 at 1361 (1996). The same is also true in any country that adopts the UNCITRAL Model Law, because Article 36 of the Model Law repeats the New York Convention Article V provisions as grounds for refusing recognition or enforcement of an award.

Thus in Switzerland, Italy, and all Model Law countries, a judge faced with the *Chromalloy* situation must decide whether the language in New York Convention Article V(1) ("Recognition and enforcement of the award *may* be refused * * *" (emphasis added)) gives him or her discretion, and, if so, how that discretion should be exercised when recognition or enforcement is sought for an award set aside in its country of origin. As such a judge, would you conclude you had discretion? If so, how would you exercise it in the *Chromalloy* situation? Would you refuse to enforce only those awards set aside on one of the grounds listed in New York Convention Article V?

Apparently in *Chromalloy* the Egyptian court set aside the award on the basis of Egypt's 1994 Law on Arbitration Article 53(1)(d), which provides for annulment: "if the award fails to apply the law agreed by the parties to the subject matter of the dispute * * *." See J. Paulsson, *The Case for Disregarding LSAS (Local Standard Annulments)* under the New York Convention, 7 Amer. Rev. Int'l Arb'n 99, 101 (1996). How should this affect a judge's exercise of any available discretion under New York Convention Article (V)(1)(e)? Would you favor exercising that discretion along the lines required of countries party to the 1961 Geneva Convention discussed above in connection with the Austrian Supreme decision in the *Company A v. Company B (Slovenia)* case? How would you analyze the *Chromalloy* case under the provisions of the 1961 Geneva Convention–that is, had that Convention been applicable? Could one reach the same result by an exercise of V(1)(e) discretion?

6. Suppose an award rendered in the U.S. is set aside by a U.S. court on the ground of "manifest disregard of the law". Could that award be enforced in other New York Convention countries? Should it be?

7. In his book devoted to the New York Convention, Albert Jan van den Berg writes the following:

> It may be questioned whether the ground that the award has been set aside in the country of origin should be retained as a ground for

refusal of enforcement under the Convention. This question might be considered if it were decided to amend the Convention in the form of an additional Protocol or the like. The possible effect of this ground for refusal is that, as an award can be set aside in the country of origin on *all* grounds contained in the arbitration law of that country, including the public policy of that country, the grounds for refusal of enforcement under the Convention may indirectly be extended to include all kinds of particularities of the arbitration law of the country of origin. This might undermine the limitative character of the grounds for refusal listed in Article V, and possibly also the uniform rule of the written form of the arbitration agreement of Article II(2), and thus decrease the degree of uniformity existing under the Convention. Could it not be sufficient to provide that enforcement may be refused on the grounds listed in the Convention only, without the ground that the award has been set aside in the country of origin?

* * *

* * * [Such an elimination of Article V(1)(e)] would, in my opinion, be undesirable. A losing party must be afforded the right to have the validity of the award finally adjudicated in one jurisdiction. If that were not the case, in the event of a questionable award a losing party could be pursued by a claimant with enforcement actions from country to country until a court is found, if any, which grants the enforcement. A claimant would obviously refrain from doing this if the award has been set aside in a country of origin and this is a ground for refusal of enforcement in other Contracting States. A. J. van den Berg, The New York Convention of 1958, 355 (1981).

Do you agree with van den Berg? Would you exercise any discretion available under Article V(1)(e) in favor of always refusing enforcement? Return to this question after reading the *Hilmarton* case in the next subsection. Consider whether the *Hilmarton* saga encourages you to agree with van den Berg.

What about the discretion available under New York Convention Article VI ("If an application for the setting aside * * * of an award has been made to a competent authority referred to in article V(1)(e), the authority before which the award is sought to be relied upon, may, if it considers it proper, adjourn the decision on enforcement of the award * * *."). Should a judge always grant such an adjournment?

8. The *Chromalloy* court cites U.S. public policy in favor of "final and binding arbitration of commercial disputes" as its justification for refusing to recognize and give res judicata effect to the Egyptian set-aside judgment. Is this sound? On this test would it ever be possible to give res judicata effect to a foreign court judgment setting aside an arbitral award? Suppose in a fully litigated case a court in the country of origin sets an award aside on the ground that the arbitral procedure was not in accordance with the agreement of the parties. (Cf. Art. V(1)(d) of the New York Convention.) Should such a foreign judgment be given res judicata effect in the United States, or should the successful party in the arbitration be entitled to relitigate the arbitral procedure question before a U.S. court? Can you give a better justification for the *Chromalloy* court's refusal to recognize the Egyptian set-aside judgment?

9. A recent decision of the Second Circuit Court of Appeals in the U.S. refused to follow the *Chromalloy* approach. In Baker Marine (NIG.) Ltd. v. Chevron (NIG.) Ltd., 191 F.3d 194 (2d Cir.1999), Baker Marine, a Nigerian company, provided barge services to Chevron, also a Nigerian company. The agreement with Chevron and Danos, another Nigerian company involved in the transaction, provided (i) for arbitration of disputes under UNCITRAL Rules; (ii) that the arbitration "procedure (insofar as not governed by said UNCITRAL rules ...) shall be governed by the substantive laws of the Federal Republic of Nigeria"; and (iii) that the contracts "shall be interpreted in accordance with the laws of the Federal Republic of Nigeria." The agreement also provided that "judgment upon the award of the arbitrators may be entered in any court having jurisdiction thereof."

A dispute arose and an arbitral tribunal with its seat in Lagos, Nigeria awarded Baker Marine damages against Chevron and Danos. Baker Marine promptly sought enforcement in Nigeria, but the Nigerian Federal High Court set aside the awards. The court concluded that in the award against Chevron the arbitrators had "improperly awarded punitive damages, gone beyond the scope of the submissions, incorrectly admitted parole evidence, and made inconsistent awards, among other things." Id. at 196. In the Danos award the court held that the award "was unsupported by the evidence." Id. at 196.

Baker Marine then sought to enforce the awards in New York. The federal district court refused recognition and enforcement because the awards had been set aside where made (Nigeria). The Second Circuit Court of Appeals affirmed. In rejecting Baker Marine's Article VII argument (that the Nigerian set aside grounds were not available under the U.S. Federal Arbitration Act) the Second Circuit said:

> " * * * It is sufficient answer that the parties contracted in Nigeria that their disputes would be arbitrated under the laws of Nigeria. the governing agreements make no reference whatever to United States law. Nothing suggests that the parties intended United States domestic arbitral law to govern their disputes."

In a footnote the Second Circuit also cited with approval Professor van den Berg's argument given above in Question 7. Do you agree with the court's reasoning. Does the operation of Article VII depend on the agreement of the parties?

Baker Marine also urged that Article V(1)(e) of the New York Convention was discretionary. In rejecting this argument the Second Circuit said: " * * * Maker Marine has shown no adequate reason for refusing to recognize the judgments of the Nigerian court." Note that the court referred to recognizing the Nigerian judgments, not the award, but it did not appear to be making a sharp distinction between the two. Should it have?

In a footnote, the Second Circuit distinguished *Chromalloy* on several grounds:

> " * * * Unlike the petitioner in Chromalloy, Baker Marine is not a United States citizen, and it did not initially seek confirmation of the

award in the United States. Furthermore, Chevron and Danos did not violate any promise in appealing the arbitration award within Nigeria. Recognition of the Nigerian judgment in this case does not conflict with United States public policy." Id. at 197 n. 3.

Do you agree with this reasoning?

V.3.c.vi. The Limits of Deference—The Hilmarton Triangle and the Problem of Conflicting Awards

There is an anecdote told and retold in many cultures. There are two litigants (in some variations husband and wife) and they cannot agree on a question that is important (for them). So they go out to find the truth, and they find the right person to hear their arguments. One of them presents his (her) case to the chosen authority (the rabbi, the wise Georgian, the old Serb, the Rumanian grandfather, etc.) and he says "you are absolutely right". After this, the other contestant presents contrary arguments, and the verdict is once again "you are absolutely right". After this, one of the contenders (or, in some variants, a young boy who is watching) asks with incredulity: "But how can you say to both that they are right, when they are saying exactly the opposite." The wise man settles the matter by responding: "You are absolutely right too".

This is exactly what happened in the *Hilmarton* case. An ICC award was rendered in Switzerland in 1988, and it was recognized in France. The award was set aside in Switzerland, and the 1990 set aside decision of the Swiss Supreme Court (Tribunal Fédéral) was also recognized by French courts. Thirdly, after annulment, a new arbitration award was rendered in Switzerland in 1992 (with a holding contrary to that of the first award)—and this award was recognized by French courts too.[55] In the end, the French Supreme Court (Cour de cassation) stepped in a second time to secure the final victory (at least in France) for the first award on the ground of res judicata. That has not ended, however, the controversy surrounding the *Hilmarton* case. As we will see in the next subsection, for example, in the U.K. it was the second award that won the day.

In the materials below we have summarized the *Hilmarton* facts and the procedural history of the case. We have also included excerpts from the two Cour de casssation opinions in *Hilmarton* and, in the *Questions and Comments* that follow, an excerpt from the Paris Court of Appeal decision in the continuation of the *Chromalloy* saga in France—this latter, because it sheds light on an important ambiguity in the Cour de cassation *Hilmarton* opinion.

---

[55]. The conflicting decisions prompted weighty criticism by French commentators. See e.g. notes by Gaillard, *Clunet* 702–710 (1994); Jarosson, 1995 Revue de l'arbitrage, 651–56.

HILMARTON LTD. (U.K.) v. OMNIUM DE TRAITEMENT ET DE VALORISATION— OTV (FRANCE)

FIRST COUR DE CASSATION OPINION

France, Cour de cassation [Supreme Court], 1994.
20 Yearbk. Comm. Arb'n 663 (1995).*o

[Hilmarton, agreed to act as legal and tax consultant to OTV and in that capacity to assist OTV in obtaining a contract to design and construct a drainage project for the City of Algiers in Algeria. If OTV won the contract, OTV agreed to pay Hilmarton 4% of the construction contract price. An Algerian statute prohibited the intervention of a middleman in connection with any public contract or agreement within the ambit of foreign trade. The Hilmarton–OTV agreement, which violated that statute, provided, however, that Swiss law would govern the agreement and that all disputes would be submitted to ICC arbitration in Geneva, Switzerland.

OTV was awarded the Algerian contract but paid Hilmarton only 50% of the agreed consultancy fee. Hilmarton initiated ICC arbitral proceedings in Geneva, claiming payment of the outstanding fee. In a 1988 award the sole arbitrator denied Hilmarton's claim. The arbitrator found that the parties' agreement had as its purpose "traffic in influence" [but not bribery], thereby violating the Algerian statute (the law of the place of performance) and Swiss public policy.

Hilmarton then sought to have the 1988 award set aside in Switzerland. In November 1989, the Geneva Court of Appeal annulled the award, and in April 1990 the Swiss Supreme Court affirmed the annulment.[p]

In the meantime, OTV sought enforcement of the 1988 award in France. In February, 1990 the Paris Tribunal de Grande Instance (TGI) (trial court) recognized the award—despite its having been set aside in Geneva—and in December, 1991, the Paris Court of Appeal affirmed the Paris TGI decision. Hilmarton appealed again, this time to the French Supreme Court.

While that appeal was pending, the dispute was resubmitted to arbitration in Switzerland before a new arbitrator, and that arbitrator rendered a new award in April 1992. This time, the award granted

---

* Reprinted with permission of Yearbook Commercial Arbitration, International Council for Commercial Arbitration.

o. Also published in 1994 Revue de l'arbitrage 327–28.

p. Prior to January 1, 1989, when the Swiss Private International Law Act came into force, set aside of international awards rendered in Switzerland was governed by the Swiss Intercantonal Arbitration Convention, which provides in Article 36(f) as a ground for annulment: "that the award is arbitrary in that it was based on findings which were manifestly contrary to the facts appearing on the file, or in that it constitutes a clear violation of law or equity * * * ". The Geneva Court of Appeal noted that the contract was governed by Swiss law and that "traffic in influence", even if contrary to Algerian law, did not violate Swiss public policy, since it did not involve bribery (at least that was not proved before the arbitrator). The parties entered their agreement knowing its nature and status under Algerian law. The arbitrator's award was thus "arbitrary". Both Swiss court decisions are reported in Yearbook XIX (1994) at pp. 214–222.

Hilmarton's request and directed OTV to pay the outstanding consultancy fee. Hilmarton then succeeded in two actions before the TGI of Nanterre in France. In the first, in February 1993, the Nanterre TGI granted leave for enforcement of the 1992 Swiss award (the second award). In the second proceeding, in September 1993, the Nanterre TGI granted enforcement of the Swiss Supreme Court decision setting aside the 1988 award (the first award). OTV appealed both of these Nanterre TGI decisions to the Court of Appeal of Versailles, which appeals were pending when the French Supreme Court rendered the following decision in the appeal from the Paris Court of Appeal concerning the first award.]

Excerpt [From Cour De Cassation Opinion]

* * *

[2] "Hilmarton argues that the decision appealed (Paris, 19 December 1991) affirms the exequatur notwithstanding the fact that the award has been set aside. According to [Hilmarton's] present appeal, * * * the [New York Convention] * * * applies, and especially its Art. V(1)(e), according to which recognition and enforcement must be refused when the award has been set aside in the country of rendition. Further, the Court of Appeal violated Arts. 1498[q] and 1502(5) NCCP,[r] by giving effect to an award which had been set aside and therefore deprived of all legal existence.

* * *

[4] " * * * [T]he lower decision correctly held that, applying Art. VII of the [1958 New York Convention], OTV could rely upon the French law on international arbitration concerning the recognition and enforcement of international arbitration awards rendered abroad, and especially upon Art. 1502 NCCP, which does not list the ground provided for in Art. V[(1)(e)] of the 1958 Convention among the grounds for refusal of recognition and enforcement.

[5] "Lastly, the award rendered in Switzerland is an international award which is not integrated in the legal system of that State, so that it remains in existence even if set aside and its recognition in France is not contrary to international public policy."

q. Art. 1498 of the French New Code of Civil Procedure reads:

"Arbitral awards shall be recognized in France if their existence is proven by the party relying thereon and if such recognition is not manifestly contrary to international public policy (*ordre public*).

Subject to the same conditions, such awards shall be declared enforceable in France by the enforcement judge."

r. Art. 1502 of the French New Code of Civil Procedure reads:

"An appeal against a decision granting recognition or enforcement may be brought only in the following cases:

1. If the arbitrator decided in the absence of an arbitration agreement or on the basis of a void or expired agreement;

2. If the arbitral tribunal was irregularly composed or the sole arbitrator irregularly appointed;

3. If the arbitrator decided in a manner incompatible with the mission conferred upon him;

4. Whenever due process has not been respected;

5. If the recognition or enforcement is contrary to international public policy (*ordre public*)."

SECOND COUR DE CASSATION OPINION

France, Cour de cassation [Supreme Court], 1997.

[While the appeal from the Paris Court of Appeal to the French Supreme Court in the above case was pending, the dispute was resubmitted to arbitration in Switzerland before a new arbitrator, and that arbitrator rendered a new award in April 1992. This time, the award directed OTV to pay the outstanding consultancy fee.

Hilmarton then succeeded in two actions before the TGI of Nanterre in France. In the first, in February 1993, the Nanterre TGI granted leave for enforcement of the 1992 Swiss award (the second award). In the second, in September 1993, the Nanterre TGI granted enforcement of the Swiss Supreme Court decision setting aside the 1988 award (the first award). OTV appealed both Nanterre TGI decisions to the Court of Appeal of Versailles, which—in the face of the French Supreme Court decision of March 1994 (above)—affirmed them both. Thus, both the first and second arbitral awards, though completely inconsistent, were recognized by different courts in France.

Though the Versailles Court of Appeal tried to reason that the two awards did not deal with the same subject matter and that various doctrines of French law prevented res judicata principles from operating, many commentators saw the decision as a veiled challenge to the March 1994 Cour de cassation decision enforcing an annulled award. Hilmarton appealed the Versailles court's decision to the Cour de cassation.]

Excerpt from the opinion*

"Whereas in * * * [ordering the exequator of the Swiss court judgment of April 1990 and the arbitral award of 1992], [although] the existence of an irrevocable French decision on the same subject matter between the same parties prevented the recognition in France of an incompatible judicial or arbitral decision rendered abroad, the court of appeal violated * * * [article 1351 of the Civil Code[s]]."

Questions and Comments

1. The French Supreme Court (Cour de cassation) did not explain how its decision was consistent with the New York Convention. In your view, was it?

2. Is there an ambiguity in the Cour de cassation's first opinion (March 1994)? Paragraph 5 of that opinion says that the first Swiss award: "is an international award which is not integrated in the legal system of [Switzerland]". Does this mean that there could be some international awards that were so integrated, and hence that a different result would follow in those cases? Or is paragraph 5 merely additional reasoning justifying the result?

Recall the *Chromalloy* case in the immediately preceding subsection. Chromalloy sought enforcement of its award against Egypt not only in the U.S., but also in France. In January, 1997 the Paris Court of Appeal

---

* See E. Schwartz, *French Supreme Court Renders Final Judgment in the Hilmarton Case*, 1 Int'l Arb. L. Rev. 45, 46 (1997).

s. Article 1351 of the French Civil Code establishes the principle of res judicata ("l'autorité de la chose jugée").

approved granting exequatur to the award Egypt had set aside. The Paris Court of Appeal reasoned as follows:

> "Considering that the French judge may not refuse enforcement except in those limited cases enumerated in Article 1502 of the New Code of Civil Procedure that constitute national law on the matter and on which Chromalloy has relied;

> "And considering that this Article 1502 of the New Code of Civil Procedure does not include among the grounds for refusal to recognize and enforce the grounds outlined in Article V of the [New York] Convention, the application of which must be barred;

> "Considering finally that the award rendered in Egypt was an international award which by definition was not integrated into the legal order of that country such that its existence continues despite its nullification and that its recognition in France is not contrary to international public policy. * * * "[56]

Does this put all ambiguity to rest? Are international awards "floating awards" rising above the control of national law?

3. Does the possibility of a second award—inconsistent with the first but legitimate in the eyes of the home state—raise serious doubts about the wisdom of the *Hilmarton–Chromalloy* line of cases? Is it appropriate in such a case for the first award always to be given preference? Will it always be given preference in France? In the U.S.? In countries party to the 1961 Geneva Convention?

4. Is the *Hilmarton* case a reflection of national bias, since the French courts in the end recognized the award (of the two that existed) that protected the French party from liability?

Or could one reason that the *Hilmarton* rule will generally work to the disadvantage of French defendants, because they will have assets in France and will be subject to having annulled awards enforced against them in France? Or is the *Hilmarton* rule simply outcome neutral, because it favors the first award whether for or against a French defendant?

5. Could one argue persuasively that the *Hilmarton* case ignores the agreement of the parties, since by choosing arbitration in Switzerland they chose to subject themselves to Swiss *lex arbitri*. Thus, it is only the second award that is consistent with the agreement of the parties.

6. Does the country where the award was made have a greater claim to legitimacy in determining the award's fate, or the country where the award is sought to be enforced? One country has an interest because it is the seat of arbitration (which potentially engages the local bar and hotels and restaurants) and was actually chosen by the parties. The other presumably has within its territory substantial assets of the defendant. Should the final outcome rest on these considerations, or on the ground for annulling an award? Which country is more likely to be objective and neutral in reviewing

---

[56]. Translation taken from E.Gaillard, *The Enforcement of Awards Set Aside in the Country of Origin*, 14 ICSID Review Foreign Investm. L. J. 16, 25 (1999). The Gaillard article also discusses the issues raised in questions 4 through 7 that follow.

the award, the country where the award is made or the country where it is sought to be enforced?

7. Note that in France [and in the United States under *Chromalloy*] the ground on which the first award was set aside does not matter. The more-favorable-law principle of Article VII controls, so that France [and the United States under *Chromalloy*] must enforce the first award as long as it passes through the very limited filter imposed by French national arbitration law—a filter that does not ask whether an award has been annulled. [In the United States under *Chromalloy* the approach is similar, though not identical.] This leads to the *Hilmarton* problem of two awards competing for enforcement.

Should the ground on which the first award was set aside matter? Recall that the drafters of the 1961 Geneva Convention thought so. For parties to that Convention, when it applies, only awards set aside on one of the New York Convention V(1) grounds (not V(2) grounds) will be refused recognition and enforcement. This rejects idiosyncratic grounds for setting aside and also allows each country to be guided by its own notions of public policy. As we discussed above in connection with the *Chromalloy* case (see Question 5 following *Chromalloy*) some commentators favor adopting the 1961 Geneva Convention solution as a general guide for discretionary refusal to enforce an annulled award. See J. Paulsson, *The Case for Disregarding LSAS (Local Standard Annulments) under the New York Convention*, 7 Amer. Rev. Int'l Arb'n 99, 101 (1996). How would the first *Hilmarton* award have fared under this approach?

Note that under the "generalized" 1961 Geneva Convention solution, whenever a home jurisdiction annulment is not respected in another country, the two-awards dilemma of *Hilmarton* can arise. Does this mean that the "generalized" 1961 Geneva Convention solution is unwise? Or does the problem lie in idiosyncratic or intrusive set-aside laws—e.g., the pre–1989 Swiss grounds for annulling international awards?

8. Is it preferable to ensure order, predictability, and finality, by giving presumptive or conclusive priority to the award approved by the place of arbitration (the second award in *Hilmarton*)? Or to encourage arbitration by restricting the role of reviewing courts (as results from the operation of France's limited grounds for challenging an award and the more-favorable-law principle of New York Convention Article VII)—even at the expense of a having a potential two-awards problem? Or to encourage harmonization of the grounds for setting aside (as results from the 1961 Geneva Convention solution)—again at the expense of a two-awards problem? Or is there some other even better solution?

9. Although the 1997 Cour de cassation decision prevented recognition of two inconsistent awards in the same jurisdiction, the *Hilmarton–Chromalloy* approach (and that of the 1961 Geneva Convention) increases the risk of inconsistent results across jurisdictions. Two inconsistent awards can come into circulation at the same time, with one recognized in some countries and the other, in other countries. In fact, precisely this situation has arisen in the *Hilmarton* episode, since in the United Kingdom Hilmarton succeeded in having the **second** award enforced against OTV. See Omnium de Traitement et de Valorisation SA v. Hilmarton Ltd., [1999] 2 Lloyd's Rep. 222

(Queen's Bench, Comm. Ct.) reproduced below in subsection V.3.d.iii. Is the resulting unpredictability and confusion healthy for international arbitration? If not, what should be the remedy?

V.3.d.   Review of the Merits Under the Convention

V.3.d.i.   Review of the Merits Under Article V(1) Standards

FERTILIZER CORP. OF INDIA v. IDI MANAGEMENT, INC.

United States District Court, Southern District of Ohio, 1981.
517 F.Supp. 948.

[Fertilizer Corporation of India (FCI) brought an action under the New York Convention for recognition and enforcement of an arbitral award rendered in India in FCI's favor against respondent IDI Management (IDI). FCI is a wholly-owned entity of the Government of India engaged in the manufacture and sale of fertilizers. IDI is an Ohio corporation whose business includes the design, engineering and construction of complex fertilizer plants. FCI and IDI's predecessors in interest entered into a contract for construction of a nitrophosphate plant near Bombay, India. The contract provided that all disputes between the parties "shall be finally settled by arbitration in conformity with the rules of conciliation and arbitration of the International Chamber of Commerce by one or more arbitrators appointed in accordance with the rules." After the plant was built, the parties fell into dispute over the quantity of daily production from the plant, and FCI initiated arbitration through the ICC. After the arbitral tribunal rendered an award for FCI, IDI filed in an Indian court to set aside the award, and FCI brought this action in the United States for recognition and enforcement of the award. The federal district court rejected various defenses before turning to IDI's objection that the award was based on consequential damages.]

SPIEGEL, DISTRICT JUDGE.

* * *

V.   Fifth Affirmative Defense, Consequential Damages

It is IDI's position that the arbitrators exceeded their authority in awarding consequential damages and that the award is therefore unenforceable under Article V, section 1(c) of the Convention. This argument is based on the parties' contract which expressly excludes from damages any amount for lost profits.

FCI contends that Article V(1)(c) of the Convention covers only the case where a particular issue was not *submitted* to the arbitrators. Here, the question of consequential damages was included in the terms of reference, signed by both parties, which constituted the framework of the arbitration. Therefore, they argue, IDI has no defense under the Convention based on the award of consequential damages.

IDI concedes that the terms of reference included the question of consequential damages, but they maintained at oral argument that at all times they protested vigorously against awarding any damages whatsoever on the basis of lost profits. FCI counters that even if this defense is available under the Convention, the defense must fail because the law does not permit this Court to substitute its judgment for that of the arbitrators.

It is beyond dispute that the contract between these parties clearly excluded consequential damages. It is also undisputed that the arbitrators rendered a large award, based almost exclusively on consequential damages, in FCI's favor. The award is a long one and, after reviewing it carefully, the Court finds it to be a thorough and scholarly opinion, written for a unanimous panel by Lord Devlin, a well-respected jurist and former Law Lord of the English House of Lords.

The dispute, according to Lord Devlin's opinion, centered around a contract clause which guaranteed that the plant would produce a certain number of tons per day of fertilizer. There is an exhaustive account of the design and construction of the plant, of the two basic processes which were to be used, and of the problems which were encountered in bringing production up to the guarantee. In fact, the guarantee was never met while IDI's predecessors controlled the plant. At oral argument, IDI claimed that FCI took judicial possession of the plant and ejected the respondent before changes could be made to achieve the guaranteed production. The arbitrators found, however, that respondent had spent more time than the longest reasonable time allowed under the contract as interpreted by the arbitrators, without achieving the guaranteed production level. At this point, FCI "rescinded" the contract, took over complete management of the plant, and, within nine months, by using a process different from the two designated in the contract, brought the plant to a profitable level of production.

Based on these facts, the arbitrators found that, as of a certain date, IDI's predecessors "repudiated" the contract by failing to hold, within a reasonable time, tests which were to demonstrate that the plant could meet its guarantee, and that FCI "rescinded" the contract based on respondent's repudiation. Using the concept of "fundamental breach," the arbitrators found that, in such a situation, the limitation of damages clause no longer applied. They awarded to FCI damages based on profits lost between the date the contract was "repudiated" and the date when the plant became profitable. Otherwise, there would have been virtually nothing on which to base damages, even though the panel found that, as of the date representing the outside limit of reasonable time, the plant's production was significantly below that promised. The award was predicated on the theory that there must have been some quid pro quo for FCI's promise not to claim consequential damages to which they otherwise might have been entitled; that, presumably, was IDI's promise to build a plant which would produce a guaranteed quantity of fertilizer within a reasonable time. Crucial to the award was a finding by the arbitrators that the production failure was caused by a basic design flaw in the plant. The design flaw, they found, was demonstrated by the fact that the plant's "wet section" produced a material with a moisture content too high for the plant's "dry section" to deal with efficiently. Subsequently, by using a process other than the two processes recommended by IDI's predecessor and called for in the contract, FCI was able to produce a material of lower moisture content which the dry section could handle effectively.

At oral argument, IDI alleged that FCI, at a later time, duplicated exactly the plant which respondent had designed and built for them. IDI implied that this duplication proved that the original plant was properly designed. While this matter is outside the record before us, we note that, according to the arbitration award, FCI was able to make profitable use of the plant by employing a different production process than the two designated in the contract by IDI's predecessors. If so, it would not be unreasonable for FCI to have duplicated the plant, planning to use the third production process.

At oral argument, IDI also claimed that the theory of "fundamental breach" was a pet theory of Lord Devlin's which was not accepted by anyone else. The Court has, however, reviewed a very complete and well-documented commentary on the concept of fundamental breach in F. Dawson, "Fundamental Breach of Contract," 91 L.Q.Rev. 380 (1975). The Nitrophosphate Award's analysis is consistent with the explanation of fundamental breach provided by Professor Dawson. We find, therefore, that this is a viable theory of law, at least in the English system.

Without engaging in an in-depth analysis of the law of contract in the United States, we cannot say with certainty whether a breach of contract found to be material or "fundamental" would abrogate an express clause limiting damages to those other than consequential. The answer, however, is irrelevant. The standard of review of an arbitration award by an American court is extremely narrow. *General Telephone Co. of Ohio v. Communications Workers of America*, 648 F.2d 452 at 456 (6th Cir., 1981). The Convention "does not sanction second-guessing the arbitrator's construction of the parties' agreement," nor would it be proper for this Court "to usurp the arbitrator's role." *Parsons & Whittemore, supra*, 508 F.2d at 977.

We find under the Convention that the arbitrators did not exceed their authority in granting consequential damages in the Nitrophosphate Award. As the Supreme Court said years ago:

> Arbitrators are judges chosen by the parties to decide the matters submitted to them, finally and without appeal. As a mode of settling disputes, it should receive every encouragement from courts of equity. If the award is within the submission, and contains the honest decision of the arbitrators, after a full and fair hearing of the parties, a court of equity will not set it aside from error, either in law or fact. A contrary course would be a substitution of the judgment of the chancellor in place of the judges chosen by the

parties, and would make an award the commencement, not the end, of litigation.

Burchell v. Marsh, 58 U.S. (17 How.) 344, 349, 15 L.Ed. 96 (1854). In the present case the award is within the submission to the arbitrators, there were numerous hearings, and we are impressed with the thoroughness and scholarship of the arbitrators' decision.

The Court of Appeals for the Second Circuit has stated:

When arbitrators explain their conclusions ... in terms that offer even a barely colorable justification for the outcome reached, confirmation of the award cannot be prevented by litigants who merely argue, however persuasively, for a different result.

Andros Compania Maritima, supra, 579 F.2d at 704. We find at least colorable justification for the result reached in the Nitrophosphate Award.

In a case very similar to the present one, the Second Circuit affirmed a foreign arbitral award which granted damages for loss of production, though the contract excluded such liability. The Court found that Article V(1)(c) of the Convention tracked s. 10(d) of the Federal Arbitration Act, 9 U.S.C. s. 10(d), and that both sections required a narrow reading. The Court explained:

Both provisions basically allow a party to attack an award predicated upon arbitration of a subject matter not within the agreement to submit to arbitration. This defense to enforcement of a foreign award, like the others already discussed, should be construed narrowly. Once again a narrow construction would comport with the enforcement-facilitating thrust of the Convention. In addition, the case law under the similar provision of the Federal Arbitration Act strongly supports a strict reading.

Parsons & Whittemore Overseas Co., Inc., supra, 508 F.2d at 976.

* * *

We therefore agree with FCI that this Court, acting under the narrow judicial review of arbitral awards granted to American courts, may not substitute its judgment for that of the arbitrators. However, this arbitration was held in India, and, while the contract does not state specifically whose law shall govern, no party has claimed that American law should control. Since the contract was executed and was to be performed in India, and the venue of arbitration was expressly stated to be New Delhi, India, the Court concludes that the law of India governs the contract rights of the parties.

Indian courts are given broader review of arbitral awards than are American courts, when reasons for the award are given by the arbitrators. When a proposition of law is stated in the award and forms a basis of the award, that award can be set aside or remitted on the ground of error of law apparent on the face of the record, if the stated proposition of law is found by a court to be erroneous. *Chellapan v. Kerala State*

Electricity Board, A.I.R. 1975 Supreme Court 230, 235 (dictum). We interpret this to mean that an Indian court could set aside the Nitrophosphate Award if it were to find that the law of fundamental breach, upon which a substantial portion of the award is based, is erroneous under Indian law. Therefore, while we do not find under the Convention that the arbitrators exceeded their authority in awarding consequential damages, as the issue was properly submitted to them, we believe that we must consider seriously IDI's contention that we should adjourn our decision, under Article VI, pending resolution of this issue by the Indian court.

* * *

Summary

Having determined that IDI's defenses to enforcement of the Nitrophosphate Award fail, we adjourn our final decision on enforcement, pursuant to Article VI of the Convention, until the Indian courts resolve with finality pending actions relating to this award. If it is determined in India that the award is in accord with Indian law, we will enter judgement for FCI * * *.

SO ORDERED.

Questions and Comments

1. The court in the *FCI* case says the contract between the parties expressly excluded the award of consequential damages. Nevertheless the arbitrators rendered a large award based almost exclusively on consequential damages. On the basis of these facts, on what New York Convention Article V ground does the respondent rely to resist enforcement of the award? Do you agree that the asserted ground applies?

2. At one point the *FCI* opinion says that it is irrelevant whether the theory of "fundamental breach" applies in U.S. contract law because the New York Convention "does not sanction second-guessing the arbitrator's construction of the parties' agreement * * * ." Does this mean that even if the arbitrators gave no theory of contract law to justify their result, the court would still have upheld the award? What about a fanciful theory no one had ever heard of before? Would you argue that even in the latter two situations, Article V(1)(c) does not apply? If so, when would it apply?

3. How does it influence the result (if at all), that the issue of consequential damages was included in the terms of reference?

4. At another point in the opinion the *FCI* court says that there was at least a "colorable justification" for the arbitrators' award. Does this mean that in the court's view Article V(1)(c) justifies a review of the arbitrators' decision on the merits but under a highly deferential standard of review: colorable justification? Do you agree with this interpretation of Article V(1)(c)?

5. Would any other ground be available under Article V to justify a refusal to enforce the award? Would "manifest disregard of the law" be available?

6.   Suppose the arbitrators had acted as *"amiables compositeurs"*, could the award be challenged under Article V? If so, on what ground?

7.   Suppose the parties had put the exclusion of consequential damages in the arbitration clause itself, instead of in the other provisions of the contract. Would that have made a difference? What Article V ground for refusing recognition would then be implicated? Should the standard of review in these circumstances be deferential?

PABALK TICARET v. NORSOLOR

[Reconsider this decision included above in section V.3.c.v dealing with the enforcement of awards previously set aside.]

Questions and Comments

1.   In the *Norsolor* case the lower court in Austria set aside the award because the arbitration was under the ICC Rules and the court found that the arbitrators had violated Article 13 of the ICC rules by deciding as *amiables compositeurs* without having been authorized to do so. In the action to enforce the award in France, if the French courts had reached the same conclusion, what ground for not enforcing the award under the New York Convention Art. V would have been available, if any? Would this amount to judicial review of the merits of the award? Should review on the merits always be deferential?

2.   If the parties had chosen ad hoc—instead of ICC—arbitration, what grounds of review would have been available, if any?

V.3.d.ii.   Review of the Merits for Manifest Disregard of the Law

BRANDEIS INTSEL LIMITED v. CALABRIAN CHEMICALS CORP.

United States District Court, Southern District of New York, 1987.
656 F.Supp. 160.

Memorandum Opinion And Order

HAIGHT, DISTRICT JUDGE:

Petitioner Brandeis Intsel Limited ("Brandeis") moves for an order confirming an arbitration award rendered in its favor and against respondent Calabrian Chemicals Corporation ("Calabrian") following arbitration before the London Metal Exchange ("LME"), pursuant to an arbitration agreement contained in a written contract of sale pursuant to which Calabrian agreed to sell, and Brandeis agreed to purchase, a quantity of cuprous chloride. Jurisdiction in this Court is based on 9 U.S.C. § 203, which empowers federal district courts to hear cases to recognize and enforce foreign arbitral awards. 9 U.S.C. § 203 forms a part of Chapter 2 of the Federal Arbitration Act, 9 U.S.C. §§ 201–208, which implements the United Nations Convention on the Recognition and Enforcement of Foreign Arbitral Awards of June 10, 1958 (the "Convention").

Respondent Calabrian has cross-moved to * * * [deny recognition and enforcement to] the LME arbitration award.

For the reasons which follow, the motion of Brandeis to confirm the award is granted, and the cross-motion of Calabrian for * * * [refusal to recognize and enforce] is denied.

I.

Brandeis is an international trading company located in London, England. It is one of 52 member companies of the LME.

The LME was first formally established in 1877. It performs the basic functions of a commodities exchange. The LME registers daily price quotations in respect of the supply of and demand for metals; it acts as a physical market where metals can be bought or sold at any time; and it provides facilities for "hedging" and so enables all those connected with the metal trade to make off-setting purchases or sales against their firm commitments.

In early 1984, Brandeis entered into negotiations with Danubiana, a Rumanian company, which desired to purchase 60 metric tons of cuprous chloride. A representative of Brandeis "approached" (I have quoted the arbitrators' award) Calabrian as manufacturers of cuprous chloride for an offer. Calabrian referred Brandeis to AIC as Calabrian's U.K. agent. The subsequent negotiations took place between employees of Brandeis and Mr. Peter le Maistre, a director of AIC. Ultimately, AIC confirmed to Brandeis Calabrian's contract to sell 60 metric tons of cuprous chloride to Brandeis at a price of $1,700 per metric ton, C & F Rotterdam. Brandeis contracted to sell the same quantity to Danubiana at $1,798 per metric ton.

Calabrian shipped the indicated quantity on board the motor vessel TOLUCA, which sailed from Houston for Antwerp on May 9, 1984. The cuprous chloride had been packed in 1,323 plastic pails (or drums), which were placed on 48 pallets and stowed in three containers.

The TOLUCA reached Antwerp on June 5, 1984 and there discharged the three containers, from whence they were delivered by road to a Rotterdam warehouse, two arriving on June 5 and the third on June 8. Damage to the shipment was discovered when the containers were opened. A Lloyds surveyor ascribed the damage to "weak pallets and too much free space in the containers which enabled the pallets to shift." That initial survey described 35 pails as "cracked/losing contents." The other pails were in their "original state"; "repalletised"; or "loose."

These observations gave rise to further surveys, correspondence, telexes, demands, silences, rejections and refusals which the arbitrators detail in their award. Ultimately, on August 8, 1984, Brandeis advised Calabrian that it had rejected the shipment in its entirety, and requested a replacement in 30 days. On August 10, AIC passed on Calabrian's reply, which refused rejection and replacement.

Brandeis thereupon sought arbitration with Calabrian before the LME in accordance with the arbitration agreement in its contract with Calabrian. The arbitrators concluded, in summary, that Brandeis was entitled to reject the goods, and to recover from Calabrian the sum of $102,000, plus interest and related costs of coping with the goods following discharge. The award totals $115,664.40. The arbitrators further directed that Calabrian pay the arbitration costs and fees, in the total amount of £2,258.75, with the further provision that if Brandeis paid those costs to the LME, Brandeis should be reimbursed by Calabrian. It is not clear from the motion papers whether in fact such costs have been paid by Brandeis, and are now sought from Calabrian.

II.

The first point that Calabrian makes in its effort to * * * [deny recognition and enforcement to] the award is that the arbitrators acted in "manifest disregard" of the law, a phrase derived from the decision of the United States Supreme Court in *Wilko v. Swan*, 346 U.S. 427, 436, 74 S.Ct. 182, 187, 98 L.Ed. 168 (1953).

Before considering *Wilko v. Swan* and subsequent American decisions interpreting it, one must take into account the Convention, which governs the cross-motions in this case.

Chapter 2 of the Federal Arbitration Act, at 9 U.S.C. § 207, requires this Court to confirm the award "unless it finds one of the grounds for refusal or deferral of recognition or enforcement of the award specified in the . . . Convention." This implicates Article V of the Convention, which sets forth the bases upon which recognition and enforcement of a foreign arbitral award may be refused. "Foreign awards are vulnerable to attack only on the grounds expressed in other articles of the Convention, particularly Article V." *Fotochrome, Inc. v. Copal Company, Limited*, 517 F.2d 512, 518 (2d Cir.1975). *See also Ipitrade International S.A. v. Federal Republic of Nigeria*, 465 F.Supp. 824, 826 (D.D.C.1978) ("Article V of the Convention specifies the only grounds on which recognition and enforcement of a foreign arbitration award may be refused.").

The ground in Article V upon which Calabrian relies appears in Article V(2)(b), which provides:

"Recognition and enforcement of an arbitral award may also be refused if the competent authority in the country where recognition and enforcement is sought finds that: . . .

"(b) The recognition or enforcement of the award would be contrary to the public policy of that country."

In the case at bar, Calabrian's first effort to * * * [deny recognition and enforcement to] the arbitrators' award comes down to this. *Wilko v. Swan, supra,* suggests that an arbitration award is vulnerable in the federal courts for "manifest disregard" of the law. This concept should be raised to the level of "public policy" within the context of Article V of the Convention. Since, in Calabrian's submission, the English arbitrators were guilty of manifest disregard of law, American public policy requires that the award be * * * [denied recognition and enforcement].

The arbitrators, in ruling in favor of Brandeis, purported to interpret and apply the Sale of Goods Act of 1979, which Calabrian says is the "English equivalent" of the Uniform Commercial Code in this country. Calabrian makes an extended argument as to why the arbitration award flies in the face of that statute. However, in the view I take of the case I need not reach that issue.

In *Wilko v. Swan*, the Supreme Court construed Chapter 1 of the Federal Arbitration Act, within the context of the federal securities laws and a contract for purchase of securities containing an arbitration clause requiring arbitration before an American stock exchange. The Court held that the arbitration agreement was void under the federal securities statutes, notwithstanding the seemingly broad provisions of the federal arbitration statute. During the course of its opinion, the Court in *Wilko v. Swan* said this:

> "In unrestricted submissions, such as the present margin agreements envisage, the interpretations of the law by the arbitrators in contrast to manifest disregard are not subject, in the federal courts, to judicial review for error in interpretation." 346 U.S. at 436–37 (footnote omitted).

As the Second Circuit justly observed in *I/S Stavborg v. National Metal Converters, Inc.*, 500 F.2d 424, 430 n. 13 (2d Cir.1974), the quoted sentence from *Wilko* is "ungrammatical in structure" and "unnecessary to the decision." Nonetheless, succeeding generations of losing parties in arbitration have relied upon *Wilko's* "manifest disregard" phrase in efforts to vacate domestic arbitration awards.

These efforts to vacate arbitration awards have met an almost total lack of success. The Supreme Court has not again addressed the issue, or further defined the phrase. Various circuit courts of appeal recognize the existence of "manifest disregard" of law as a ground for vacating an award existing independently of the grounds specified in 9 U.S.C. § 10. However, those decisions define the phrase in the narrowest possible terms, and invariably conclude that the phrase, so defined, does not meet the facts of the particular case.

We see then that American courts are unreceptive, to say the least, to arguments that arbitral awards should be vacated for manifest disregard of law. But I conclude that, in any event, the "manifest disregard" defense is not available to Calabrian. That is because "manifest disregard" of law, whatever the phrase may mean, does not rise to the level of contravening "public policy," as *that* phrase is used in Article V of the Convention. Nor, unlike proceedings under Chapter 1 of the Federal Arbitration Act, can manifest disregard of law be urged as an independent ground for * * * [refusing to recognize or enforce] an award falling within the Convention.

* * *

In my view, the "manifest disregard" defense is not available under Article V of the Convention or otherwise to a party such as Calabrian, seeking to * * * [deny recognition and enforcement to] an award of foreign arbitrators based upon foreign law. That conclusion is itself rooted in concepts of public policy. In Scherk v. Alberto–Culver Co., 417 U.S. 506, 520 n. 15, 94 S.Ct. 2449, 2457 n. 15, 41 L.Ed.2d 270 (1974), the Supreme Court said of the Convention:

> "The goal of the Convention, and the principal purpose underlying American adoption and implementation of it, was to encourage the recognition and enforcement of commercial arbitration agreements in international contracts and to unify the standards by which agreements to arbitrate are observed and arbitral awards are enforced in the signatory countries."

That salutary goal and purpose will be better achieved by applying to proceedings brought in this country to enforce foreign arbitral awards the narrow concept of "public policy" articulated in the cases cited supra. Defining "public policy" as used in the Convention to include "manifest disregard" of law, the phrase tossed off by the Supreme Court in Wilko v. Swan, would require an American court to consider whether foreign arbitrators had disregarded governing foreign law. It is one thing to ask an American judge to hold American arbitrators guilty of a manifest disregard of American law. It is quite another to ask an American judge to determine whether foreign arbitrators manifestly disregarded the internal, substantive law of a foreign nation by which the parties agreed in their contract to be bound. That seems to me a slippery slope upon which American judges should not embark, in clear derogation of the public policy underlying the Convention.

Accordingly I hold that the "manifest disregard" defense is not available to Calabrian within the context of the Convention.

* * *

If I am wrong in concluding that Wilko's "manifest disregard" defense is not available to awards falling under the Convention, then the question arises whether the present arbitrators can be said to have acted in manifest disregard of the United Kingdom's Sale of Goods Act of 1979.

As appears from their award, the arbitrators concluded on the basis of physical evidence at the place of delivery that damage to the shipment was "initiated by the inadequate stowage" chargeable to Calabrian. In consequence, the goods were not delivered "in a merchantable condition on arrival." Brandeis was entitled by Section 34(1) of the Sales Act to take "conditional property" in the goods, and was further entitled "to reject the goods in toto on 8th August, which was reasonable time for rejection.''

Calabrian assails these conclusions. With copious references to the arbitration record, it argues, in essence, that the number of damaged pails was so small in relation to the total that rejection of the shipment was not justified; that contemporaneous declarations of Brandeis showed that in fact Brandeis had accepted the balance of the shipment outright, not just conditionally; that its ultimate rejection of the entire shipment was unreasonable and contrary to law; and that the arbitrators aided and abetted Brandeis in a wrongful thrusting upon Calabrian of Brandeis's loss when, for unknown reasons, Brandeis's customer Danubiana failed to take delivery of the shipment.

These arguments are made plausibly and with professional skill. But they do not demonstrate "manifest disregard" of controlling English sales law by the arbitrators, as American courts define that phrase. "Manifest disregard" does not confer upon the courts "a license to review the record of arbitrable proceedings for errors of fact or law," Parsons at 977. * * * I do not find it necessary or appropriate to agree or disagree with the arbitrators' conclusions. It is sufficient to say that their award reflects the arbitrators' awareness of the governing statute and efforts to apply its terms to the facts as found. The legal consequences of the quantum of damage, the effect to be given to the parties' utterances, the reasonableness of rejection of the goods: these are issues that frequently arise in sales disputes, and I am "not at liberty to set aside an arbitration panel's award because of an arguable difference regarding the meaning or applicability of laws urged upon it." Mansfield, Ct.J., in [Merrill Lynch, Pierce, Fenner & Smith, Inc. v. Bobker, 808 F.2d 930 (2d Cir.1986)] at 934.

* * *

Conclusion

The motion of Brandeis to confirm the award of arbitrators is granted.

The cross-motion of Calabrian to vacate the award is denied.

* * *

Questions and Comments

1. The *Brandeis* case decides the point left open in *Parsons & Whittemore*, namely whether "manifest disregard" of the law (generally available in the United States under the Federal Arbitration Act as a ground for refusing to enforce a domestic award) is also a ground for refusing to enforce an award under the New York Convention. Of course the Convention does not list such a ground, but could it be incorporated into the Convention under "public policy". The *Brandeis* court says no. Do you agree?

2. The *Brandeis* court accepts a very deferential interpretation of "manifest disregard": "It is sufficient to say that their award reflects the

arbitrators' awareness of the governing statute and efforts to apply its terms to the facts as found." Under such a standard, would it be necessary to know very much about foreign law to decide if the arbitrators had acted in "manifest disregard" of the law?

3. If an arbitral award did not meet the *Brandeis* test of "manifest disregard"—that is, if the award did not reflect the arbitrators' awareness of the governing statute and did not reflect efforts to apply its terms to the facts found—could the award nevertheless be consistent with public policy? Could any other ground of nonrecognition under the New York Convention be invoked for refusing to enforce the award?

V.3.d.iii. Review of the Merits Under Article V(2)(b)—the Public Policy Standard

OMNIUM DE TRAITEMENT ET DE VALORISATION SA v. HILMARTON LTD.

Queen's Bench Division (Commercial Court) 1999.
2 Lloyd's Rep 222*

JUDGMENT

TIMOTHY WALKER J:

The applicant (OTV) applies to set aside the ex parte order of Mr. Justice Tuckey (as he then was) made on Sept. 3, 1998, giving effect in England to an ICC award dated Apr. 10, 1992 in favour of Hilmarton. OTV further seeks an order that the award be refused enforcement in England under s 103 of the Arbitration Act, 1996.ᵗ * * *

It is OTV's principal case that the award should not be enforced in England because such enforcement would be contrary to public policy. That can of course only be English public policy. As Lord Justice Waller said in Soleimany v Soleimany, [1998] 3 WLR 811 at p. 824C "... enforcement here is governed by the public policy of the lex fori". I must also have in mind the precise scope of the duty of the English Court to enforce New York Convention awards. Under s. 103 of the Arbitration Act, 1996 (which is in identical terms to its predecessor s. 5 of the Arbitration Act, 1975) enforcement of a Convention award "shall not be refused" except in certain limited cases, and enforcement "may also be refused" if it would be contrary to public policy to enforce the award.

The public policy point invoked by OTV is that the agreement was unlawful in its place of performance. It is however in my judgment necessary for OTV to go further, and establish that this infects the award as well.

The first step is to evaluate the award itself * * *. [Here the court recounts the *Hilmarton* facts given above in connection with the *Hilmar-*

---

* Reprinted by permission of Lloyd's Law Reports, LLP Limited.

t. Section 103 of the English Arbitration Act of 1996 repeats the grounds for refusing recognition and enforcement of a foreign award found in New York Convention Article V(1) and (2).

ton case before the French Cour de cassation in subsection V.3.c.vi. The court notes that Hilmarton initiated arbitration in 1986 seeking the remaining installment of its consultancy fee and that the award at issue in this enforcement proceeding (the second award, after the first was annulled) was not issued until April, 1992.]

[The 1992 award] is a lengthy document. The sole arbitrator went into all the matters raised with great care. Its length is partly accounted for by the setting out in the award of the litigation history, including appeals to the Court of Justice of Geneva and the Supreme Court of Switzerland, together with an account of the proceedings before the original sole arbitrator who had heard the oral evidence, but who resigned subsequent to the reversal of his decision by the Swiss Courts. The new sole arbitrator directed himself, entirely correctly as a matter of Swiss law, that he was bound by the opinions expressed by the Court of Justice and the Supreme Court.

The only matters relevant for present purposes are the findings of the (second) sole arbitrator on OTV's contention that Hilmarton's claim should be dismissed because it was "contrary to a mandatory law of the place of performance of the contract". In summary, the arbitrator held:

(1) The work performed by Hilmarton, with OTV's agreement, consisted of approaching public servants and Algerian government officials in order to obtain the public contract. Such activity "wittingly" breached an Algerian statute which prohibits the intervention of a middleman in connection with any public contract or agreement within the ambit of foreign trade * * *.

But (2) This activity did not involve any bribery or other similar corrupt activity. Thus—

> ... No bribe was foreseen. It has not been established that the Claimant would have paid bribes, carried out "lobbyist" or "insider" acts intended to divert Public Servants or Ministers from their duties, or indulged in the trading of favours. * * *.

It would of course, be quite wrong for this Court to entertain any attempt to go behind this explicit and vital finding of fact. Nor was one made.

(3) As a matter of Swiss law (the law chosen by the parties) the agreement, albeit that it breached Algerian law, was not unlawful "from the point of view of Swiss law". It was not contra bonae mores, in the absence of bribes and other dubious activities or illicit practices * * *. The Algerian statute in question constituted a prohibited measure of a protectionist nature, to ensure that Algeria maintains a state monopoly on foreign trade; thus ethically speaking, it could not take priority over the parties' freedom of contract * * *.

Therefore Swiss law made its own evaluation of the foreign statute, and in the light of the finding of fact that no corrupt activity was involved, refused to admit any illegality or public policy defence to the claim. Indeed, the Court of Justice regarded it as "absolutely shocking" that OTV, which had regularly paid the amounts due until the public contract was awarded, then refused to comply fully with its contractual obligations * * *.

Thus the very point which OTV now puts forward as a reason for refusal of enforcement in England was (1) ruled upon on the face of the award, and (2) rejected by the application of the law chosen by the parties, (3) on the basis of a finding of fact that no corrupt practices were involved.

It may well be that an English arbitral tribunal, chosen by the parties, and applying English law as chosen by the parties, would have reached a different result. It may well be that such a tribunal would have dismissed Hilmarton's claim, applying the full rigour of the principle stated by Viscount Simonds in Regazzoni v KC Sethia (1944) Ltd, [1957] 2 Lloyd's Rep. 289 at p. 294, col. 2; [1958] AC 301 at p. 317 thus:

> ... whether or not the proper law of the contract is English law, an English Court will not enforce a contract, or award damages for its breach if its performance will involve the doing of an act in a foreign and friendly State which violates the law of that State.

I should add that in applying this principle it is immaterial whether the contract itself is governed by English or foreign law.

But I am not adjudicating upon the underlying contract. I am deciding whether or not an arbitration award should be enforced in England. In this context it seems to me that (absent a finding of fact of corrupt practices which would give rise to obvious public policy considerations) the fact that English law would or might have arrived at a different result is nothing to the point. Indeed, the reason for the different result is that Swiss law is different from English law, and the parties chose Swiss law and Swiss arbitration. If anything, this consideration dictates (as a matter of policy of the upholding of international arbitral awards) that the award should be enforced.

* * *

Finally, OTV's reliance on Soleimany v Soleimany, [1998] 3 WLR 811, where in a judgment delivered by Lord Justice Waller * * * the Court of Appeal declined to permit enforcement of an arbitral award, was in my view misplaced. In that case it was apparent from the face of the award that the arbitrator was dealing with an illicit enterprise for smuggling carpets out of Iran. It was quite simply a smuggling contract. The case thus clearly fell into the category of cases where as a matter of public policy no award would be enforced by an English Court, and the whole of the judgment of the Court of Appeal has to be read in that context. The element of corruption or illicit practice was present which, on the arbitrator's unchallengeable finding of fact in this case, was not present here.

In my judgment there are no public policy grounds on which the enforcement of this award could be refused. Thus the case never gets within s. 103(3) of the Arbitration Act, 1996. It would be artificial to go further and say that in any event on these facts I would have exercised my discretion in favour of the enforcement of this award.

* * *

In the result the arbitration application fails on all points and is dismissed.

Questions and Comments

1.   The Queen's Bench Commercial Court says that in a case originating before English courts, even if the parties had expressly chosen English law, an English court would have applied Algerian law to strike down the OTV–Hilmarton fee agreement as illegal and unenforceable. Would this result be based on English public policy? Yet at the same time the Commercial Court refuses to rely on section 103 of the English Arbitration Act of 1996 (incorporating the public policy standard of New York Convention V(2)(b)) to reject the second arbitrator's award enforcing the fee agreement. Are there two different types of public policy operating here? How would you describe the difference between them?

2.   Suppose Hilmarton's "services" had included smuggling certain building materials into Algeria to avoid paying high customs duties. Would the Queen's Bench Commercial Court have enforced a fee award? If not, why not? The Queen's Bench gives the following as one of the arbitrator's findings: "The Algerian statute in question constituted a prohibited measure of a protectionist nature, to ensure that Algeria maintains a state monopoly on foreign trade; thus ethically speaking, it could not take priority over the parties' freedom of contract * * *." Aren't customs duties a form of protectionism in foreign trade? Is it only smuggling of completely prohibited items that would "infect" an award, or all smuggling, even where the purpose is to avoid protectionist duties?

3.   What if the arbitrator had explicitly found that Hilmarton made small payments to certain Algerian officials to "facilitate" the transaction (small "greese" payments) and that these were a common way of doing business in Algeria and as a practical matter were never penalized by the state (even though technically illegal). If Swiss law allowed enforcement of Hilmarton's fee claim and the arbitrator so held, would the Queen's Bench have enforced the award? Suppose there was outright bribery, but Swiss law still allowed collection of the fee and the arbitrator enforced the agreement? What result in the U.K.?

4.   Does the Queen's Bench decision reflect the extreme reluctance of courts to review the merits of arbitral awards, at least under the New York Convention? To consider this point from another angle, compare the outcome (or likely outcome) of the first arbitral award in Hilmarton under two different Swiss standards of review—that of the Swiss Intercantonal Arbitration Convention and that of the New York Convention. We know the outcome under the former, because in the original Hilmarton litigation in Switzerland, the Swiss courts annulled the award. They reviewed the merits and concluded that the arbitrator's award (refusing to enforce the consultancy fee) was "arbitrary", in part because the arbitrator misunderstood Swiss

law as requiring a public-policy-based refusal to enforce the fee agreement.[57] Consider how Swiss courts would have reacted to the first arbitral award, had the parties agreed to dispense with Swiss set aside jurisdiction (after January 1, 1989). In that case, under the Swiss Private International Law Act of 1987—which came into force on January 1, 1989—the award would have been reviewable in Switzerland only under the standards of the New York Convention. Would the award have been upheld in this situation?

5. Despite the reluctance of courts to do so, they will nevertheless review the merits of an award when public policy considerations are particularly weighty. Eco Swiss China Time Ltd v Benetton International NV, Case C–126/97, 1998 ECR I–4493 (June 01, 1999), is a good example. (See supra Question 6 after the *Mitsubishi* case in subsection II.2.c.i.) Recall that there the Court of Justice of the European Communities (ECJ) required a Dutch court to annul a Dutch award if the award was based on a licensing agreement that was void under European Union antitrust law (now Article 81 of the EC Treaty). In the *Benetton* case, neither the parties nor the arbitrators had raised antitrust issues during the arbitral proceedings. The ECJ did not limit its holding to set-aside cases, but also included recognition and enforcement proceedings under the New York Convention:

> "32 It is to be noted * * * that, where questions of Community law are raised in an arbitration resorted to by agreement, the ordinary courts [of the member states] may have to examine those questions, in particular during review of the arbitration award, which may be more or less extensive depending on the circumstances and which they are obliged to carry out in the event of an appeal, for setting aside, for leave to enforce an award or upon any other form of action or review available under the relevant national legislation * * *.

> * * *

> "39 For the reasons stated in paragraph 36 above [stressing the importance of antitrust enforcement in EU law], the provisions of Article 85 of the Treaty [now Article 81] may be regarded as a matter of public policy within the meaning of the New York Convention."

Presumably the ECJ would have reached the same conclusion had the arbitrators incorrectly applied EU antitrust law, at least if the error were obvious on the face of the award. It remains unclear to what extent the ECJ would require a reviewing court to relitigate findings of fact and conclusions of law to ensure correct application of EU antitrust law. The same uncertainty prevails in U.S. law following the U.S. Supreme Court *Mitsubishi* decision.

Recall that in *Benetton* the Dutch courts had concluded that violation of Dutch antitrust law (as opposed to EU antitrust law) would not have required annulment of the Dutch award. Thus, we again see two different types of public policy operating. French commentators speak of the standard

---

[57]. Recall that at the time of the *Hilmarton* case awards made in Switzerland were reviewed in Swiss courts under the Swiss Intercantonal Arbitration Convention, which provides in Article 36(f) as a ground for annulment: "that the award is arbitrary in that it was based on findings which were manifestly contrary to the facts appearing on the file, or in that it constitutes a clear violation of law or equity * * *."

under New York Convention Article V(2)(b) as requiring a violation of **international** public policy. Recall that in *Parsons and Whittemore* (supra subsection V.3.b.) the court explained that the Article V(2)(b) public policy concept required a violation of "the forum state's most basic notions of morality and justice."

V.3.e. *Estoppel*

CHINA NANHAI OIL JOINT SERVICE CORPORATION SHENZHEN BRANCH (PR CHINA) v. GEE TAI HOLDINGS CO. (NATIONALITY NOT INDICATED)

Hong Kong, Supreme Court of Hong Kong, [High Court] 1994.
20 Yearbk. Comm. Arb'n 673 (1995).*

JUDGE KAPLAN.

[The facts of the following Hong Kong High Court case are reproduced above in section V.3.c.iv.]

* * *

[5] *Second Issue.* As to the second issue, Mr. Reyes submitted that the defendants were able to participate in the arbitration and, if they lost, they could challenge the composition of the tribunal at the enforcement stage. He seeks to rely upon certain passages in my judgment in *Paklito Investment Ltd. v. Klöckner (East Asia) Ltd.* [1993] 2 HKLR 39.[2]

[6] In that case, I was dealing with an argument made, that even if I was satisfied that the ground of opposition has been established, nevertheless, I should exercise my discretion in favour of enforcement. Counsel making that submission relied strongly upon the fact that the defendant in that case had taken no steps to set aside the award in China and that I should take that fact into account. That was a case where the defendant voluntarily appeared before a properly constituted tribunal but as a result of the way in which the arbitration was conducted they were, most unfortunately, unable to present their case. They did not apply to a Chinese court to have the award set aside but they waited until the award was brought to Hong Kong for enforcement under the New York Convention and then they raised the appropriate ground. All I said in that case was:

> There is nothing in s. 44 nor in the New York Convention which specifies that a Defendant is obliged to apply to set aside an award in the country where it was made as a condition of opposing enforcement elsewhere. In my judgment, the defendants were entitled to take this stance. . . .

* Reprinted with permission of Yearbook Commercial Arbitration, International Council for Commercial Arbitration.

2. Reported in Yearbook XIX (1994) pp. 664–674 (Hong Kong no. 6). [Authors' note: *Paklito* is reproduced in the materials supra section IV.1.h.ii.].

[7]   The present case is somewhat different. The defendant's lawyer was alerted at the earliest possible opportunity to the point that this arbitration should have been heard in Beijing. She raised it somewhat informally, so it appears to me, before one of the appointed arbitrators. He opined that there was jurisdiction. She appears to have done nothing else. She did not raise it with the tribunal and make it part of her submissions. She did not apply to a Chinese court for an order declaring that the tribunal had no authority. Perhaps what is more important, she did not take the basic precaution of writing, phoning or faxing CIETAC, Beijing and point out to them that the Shenzhen Sub–Commission was taking on a case which should have been heard in Beijing. She did none of these things and took part in the arbitration and I am sure did her very best to succeed on behalf of her clients.

[8]   The award went against her clients and now at this stage, it is being suggested that there was no jurisdiction and that the composition of the arbitral authority was different to that specified in the contract. This is not an attractive proposition. Under most systems of law, parties are obliged to put forward their arguments at an early stage and not wait and see how the case turns out and then, and only then, if they lose take jurisdictional points. Nevertheless, this is a serious point and I have to consider whether in the context of an enforcement action under the New York Convention, there is any scope whatsoever for the doctrine of estoppel.

[9]   Estoppel has certainly been considered in relation to Art. II of the New York Convention. The first part of Art. II obliges each contracting state to recognise an agreement in writing under which parties have agreed to submit to arbitration their differences concerning a subject matter capable of settlement by arbitration. The second part of Art. II attempts to define the term "agreement in writing" and the third part of Art. II obliges a court of a contracting state to refer cases submitted to it when there is an arbitration clause to arbitration unless it finds that the agreement is null and void, inoperative or incapable of being performed.

[10]   The question has arisen in cases where there has been an arbitration and an award rendered and enforcement steps taken. At that stage a respondent takes a point on the absence of sufficient written form to comply with Art. II. . . . This specific point is raised by Dr. Albert Jan van den Berg in his book, *The New York Arbitration Convention of 1958*, Kluwer, 1981. At p. 182 he poses the following question:

> There is, however, one case in which this may be questioned: if a party has acted specifically in respect of the arbitration agreement without objection, thereby implying that he considers it valid, is he then subsequently estopped from invoking the lack of compliance of the agreement with the written form as required by Article II(2)? This case may, for instance, come up where a party has co-operated in the appointment of the arbitrator(s), has participated in the arbitration, or has invoked the arbitration agreement for objecting to the competence of a court to try the merits of the dispute.

The question forms part of a more general question whether a party can be estopped from invoking any of the provisions of the Convention.

[11]   Dr. van den Berg then goes on to point out that courts appear to be somewhat divided on the question of estoppel and Art. II(2). He refers to decisions in Germany and Italy which he concluded are not wholly satisfactory. At p. 184, he makes reference to an observation of the President of a Dutch court of first instance, which rejected the invocation of the formal invalidity of the arbitration agreement.

> The judge observed that from the minutes of the hearing before the arbitrators, at which the respondent was assisted by a lawyer, it appeared that neither the respondent nor his lawyer, had objected to the formal contents of the arbitration agreement. The judge held that "... at present ... more that 2 years after the hearing ... the respondent is estopped from his right to question the validity of the arbitration agreement...."

[12]   I should point out in passing that the award in this case was made by the CIETAC arbitrators on 10 February 1990 and as far as I am aware the first time at which this point was taken was in the affidavit of Chen Jian dated 25 September 1992.

[13]   Dr. van den Berg then discusses 3 possible solutions to the question of estoppel from invoking the non-compliance with the written form of the arbitration agreement as required by Art. II(2) but I believe his observations are equally apposite in relation to other parts of the Convention.

[14]   His first solution is to follow the views of the Italian and German court and conclude that the written form prescribed by Art. II(2) was a condition for the enforcement of the agreement and award which must be complied with under all circumstances. On this basis, there could be no scope for the doctrine of estoppel.

[15]   The second solution is to approach the matter on the basis of municipal law and not as one being regulated by the Convention. He suggests that the municipal law relevant will be the law of the forum. He goes on:

> Under this solution, the Convention remains applicable to the enforcement, whilst the estoppel from invoking the non-compliance with Article II(2) is to be decided according to municipal law. Thus, under this solution it may happen that the enforcement can be pursued on the basis of the Convention although the written form of Article II(2) is not met, because under the law of the forum a party is deemed to be estopped from invoking the non-compliance.

[16]   Under this second solution, he points out that more modern arbitration statutes tend towards an acceptance of estoppel and he points to the European Uniform Law of 1966 as an example. A similar view is discernable from the Model Law. Art. 16 requires parties to raise a plea that the arbitral tribunal does not have jurisdiction not later than the

submission of a statement of defence. The tribunal may admit a later plea if it considers the delay justified but, if not, then clearly the party is estopped from raising the point. Similarly, under Art. 16(3) if the tribunal rules that it has jurisdiction any party may request within 30 days, the court to decide the matter. It seems to follow from this that if you do not seek the view of the court, then you cannot raise the matter subsequently at enforcement stage.

[17]   Dr. van den Berg's third solution is set out on p. 185, where he says:

> The third solution is to regard the question of estoppel as a fundamental principle of good faith, which principle overrides the formalities required by Article II(2). Under this solution the Convention would also remain applicable, differing from the second solution in that it does not depend on the diverse municipal laws. The principle of good faith may be deemed enshrined in the Convention's provisions. The legal basis would be that Article V(1) provides that a court *may* refuse enforcement if the respondent proves one of the grounds for refusal of enforcement listed in that Article. The permissive language can be taken as a basis for those cases where a party asserts a ground for refusal contrary to good faith.

> It is submitted that the third solution is, in principle, to be preferred. It would, for example, exclude the unsatisfactory result of the aforementioned decision of the Italian Supreme Court. It would also correspond with the trend in the more modern arbitration laws. And, finally, it has the advantage that the question would not depend on municipal law as will be the case if the second solution was adopted. Although the Court of Appeal of Hamburg and the Dutch Court of First Instance have not expressly held so, it can be said that they implicitly favour the third solution.

[18]   I am quite satisfied that Dr. van den Berg's third solution is the correct one for me to apply. If the doctrine of estoppel can apply to arguments over the written form of the arbitration agreement under Art. II(2), then I fail to see why it cannot also apply to the grounds of opposition set out in Art. V. It strikes me as quite unfair for a party to appreciate that there might be something wrong with the composition of the tribunal yet not make any formal submission whatsoever to the tribunal about its own jurisdiction, or to the arbitration commission which constituted the tribunal and then to proceed to fight the case on the merits and then 2 years after the award attempt to nullify the whole proceedings on the grounds that the arbitrators were chosen from the wrong CIETAC list.

[19]   I think there is much force in Dr. van den Berg's point that even if a ground of opposition is proved, there is still a residual discretion left in the enforcing court to enforce nonetheless. This shows that the grounds of opposition are not to be inflexibly applied. The residual discretion enables the enforcing court to achieve a just result in all the circumstances although I accept that in many cases where a

ground of opposition is established, the discretion is unlikely to be exercised in favour of enforcement.

[20]   If the enforcing court was obliged to refuse enforcement in the event of the establishing of a ground of opposition, I believe that it would be far harder to import the doctrine of estoppel. But there is, and I for myself am prepared to hold that on a true construction of the Convention there is indeed a duty of good faith which in the circumstances of this case required the defendant to bring to the notice of the full tribunal or the CIETAC Commission in Beijing its objections to the formation of this particular arbitral tribunal. Its failure to do so and its obvious policy of keeping this point up its sleeve to be pulled out only if the arbitration was lost, is not one that I find consistent with the obligation of good faith nor with any notions of justice and fair play.

[21]   I am encouraged to note that other enforcing courts have taken a similar attitude. The Swiss Federal Supreme Court had a case where enforcement was opposed on the grounds that the tribunal consulted an expert in the absence of the parties. The court declined to get involved in arguments about Art. V(1)(b) because the respondent had failed to object when it was informed by the president of the tribunal shortly after the consultation had taken place. According to the Court the raising of this objection at the enforcement stage only manifested bad faith and constituted an abuse of rights.

[22]   Similarly the Spanish Supreme Court held that a respondent was barred from objecting to the competence of arbitrators at the enforcement stage because they should have done so during the arbitral proceedings.

[23]   The Court of Appeal of Athens took the view that arguments about the lack of written form of the agreement to arbitrate and the authorization to conclude the agreement cannot be raised at the enforcement stage if that party participated in the arbitration proceedings without reservation. The Court arrived at this conclusion both on the basis of German law (law of situs) and Greek arbitration law.

[24]   It is for these reasons, therefore, that I am quite satisfied that I am entitled to apply the doctrine of estoppel to the conduct of the defendants in this case and to find that, even though technically, the arbitration tribunal was wrongly constituted, nevertheless, this is not in all the circumstances of this case a point which they are now entitled to take.

* * *

Questions and Comments

1.   The Hong Kong High Court discusses three approaches to the estoppel issue. Do you agree with the court's choice of the third approach?

2.   Concerning the elements needed to make out a case of estoppel, note that the defendant's lawyer apparently did object to arbitration in Shenzhen instead of Beijing:

She raised it somewhat informally, so it appears to me, before one of the appointed arbitrators. He opined that there was jurisdiction. She appears to have done nothing else. She did not raise it with the tribunal and make it part of her submissions. She did not apply to a Chinese court for an order declaring that the tribunal had no authority. Perhaps what is more important, she did not take the basic precaution of writing, phoning or faxing CIETAC, Beijing and point out to them that the Shenzhen Sub–Commission was taking on a case which should have been heard in Beijing. She did none of these things and took part in the arbitration....

Were all of the steps necessary to prevent an estoppel? Suppose the defendant's lawyer had raised the objection informally with all the arbitrators; or suppose she had done so formally, but without contacting CIETAC, Beijing, would there have been an estoppel?

3. Should estoppel operate on all Article V(1) grounds for refusing recognition and enforcement? On all Article V(2) grounds?

INDEX

References are to Pages

AD HOC ARBITRATION
Arbitrators conduct, requirements for, 262.
Comparison to institutional arbitration, 27–35.
UNCITRAL rules, 27–35, 62–64.

AMERICAN ARBITRATION ASSOCIATION (AAA)
Arbitrators, Code of Ethics, 284.
Form and effect of awards, 524–525.
Interpretation and correction of award, 538.
Non-neutral arbitrators, 291–292.
Rules governing arbitral proceedings, 62–66, 68–71, 426–428.

ANTI-TRUST
See also Arbitrability.
Non–Arbitrability of claims 208, 221–235.

APPEAL
See Review.

APPOINTMENT
See also Arbitrators, Selection.
Mediators, 12–14.

ARBITRABILITY
Generally, 207–210.
Anti-trust, 208, 221–235.
Applicable law, 247–251.
Arbitrating arbitrability, See Kompetenz–Kompetenz.
Cargo damage (COGSA) claims, 219, 235–246.
Contract-based tort claims, 94–95, 168–172.
Court determination of arbitrability, 99–101.
Domestic policy limitations on, 207–210, 592–599.
Mandatory Rules, 208–210, 236–246.
New York Convention, 207–217, 226.
Presumption of arbitrability, 91–99, 196.
Statutory definitions of, 210–221.
UNCITRAL Model Law, 221.

ARBITRAL INSTITUTIONS
Rights and responsibilities of arbitral institutions, 317–327.

ARBITRAL PROCEEDINGS
Concurrent proceedings, 627–639, 817–823.

ARBITRAL PROCEEDINGS—Cont'd
Constituents of, 431–437.
Counsel, , 428–431, 486–495.
Delay tactics, 102–109, , 381.
ICC Rules of Arbitration, 422–423.
ICC Terms of Reference, 437–450.
Institutional norms, 68–71, 412–425.
Language issues, 478–486.
Lex arbitri, role of, 411–425.
Party autonomy, 42–48, 411–425.
Privacy and confidentiality, 495–512.
Records and minutes, 450–455.
Time limits, 513–518.
UNCITRAL
    Model Law, equal treatment of parties, 418.
    Model Law, determination of rules of procedure, 419–422.
    Model Law, language issues, 478–486.
    Notes on Organizing Arbitral Proceedings, 425–426.
WIPO Rules of Arbitration, 423.

ARBITRATION
Controlling norms, 62–67.

ARBITRATION ACTS
Dutch Arbitration Act, 350–351.
English Arbitration Act of 1950, 73–83.
English Arbitration Act of 1996, 134, 340, 417–418.
Federal Arbitration Act, 183–187.
    Vacating awards, 678–683, 692–694.
French Arbitration Act, 387.
German Arbitration Act, 646.
Indian Arbitration Act, 412–418, 657–669.
Netherlands Arbitration Act, 522–523.
Spanish Arbitration Act, 109.
Swiss Arbitration Act, 351–352.

ARBITRATION AGREEMENTS
    See also, Enforcement of Awards; Compelling Arbitration.
Generally, 84–91.
Battle of forms, 151–154.
Enforcement, compelling arbitration, 48–54, 84–85, 339–341.
Form and drafting, 29–30, 136–154.
Formal requirements, 88–90.
Scope, 90, 168–183.

ARBITRATION AGREEMENTS—Cont'd
Scope—Cont'd
    Settlements, 168–180.
    Renewals, 180–183.
Separability of arbitral clauses, 86–88, 109–136.
    No contest provisions, 172–177.
Split arbitration clauses, 193–203.
Unconscionability, 96–98.
Validity, 86–88, 109–136, 344–351.
    See also Arbitrability.
Variations, 84.
Waiver of form requirements, 139–141, 185.

ARBITRATION PROCEEDINGS
Advantages and disadvantages compared to litigation, 24–26.

ARBITRATORS
    See also Arbitration Agreements, Jurisdiction.
    Generally, 252–284.
Ad hoc arbitration, conduct requirements, 262.
Affidavit of independence, 270.
Codes of ethics, 284–294.
    AAA, ABA Code of Ethics, 284.
    IBA Rules of Ethics for Arbitrators, 284–285.
Criticism of appointing criteria, 278–279.
Disclosure of bias, , 284–294, 389–410.
Delegation of duty to render an award, 528–530.
Fees, 30–31, 288, 297–317.
    Remuneration, related issues, 310–315.
Kompetenz-Kompetenz, 109–118.
Misconduct, consequences of, 678–694.
    See also Setting Aside Awards, Grounds for.
Neutrality and independence, 256–262.
Resignation of, 295–296, 327–341.
Rights and responsibilities of, 258–260, 294–317.
Selection of, 30–31, 71–83, 273–284, 342–348.
    Appointment by courts, 348–358.
    Appointment, causes of dissatisfaction, 273–278.
    Appointing authorities
        Chosen by the parties, 300–301, 347–348, 358–376.
        International arbitral institutions and municipal appointing authorities, 343–347.
        Nature of their decision, 358–367.
    Appointing authorities when refuse to appoint, 68–71.
    Appointing authorities not relied on, 367–372.
    Appointing authorities that have ceased to exist, 372–376.
    Background, 280–281.
    Chairmen and umpires, 263–270.
    Challenges to appointment, 389–410.

ARBITRATORS—Cont'd
Selection of—Cont'd
    Conflict between party stipulation and lex arbitri, 73–83.
    Counsel, role of, 263–270.
    Multiparty arbitration, 376–379.
    Neutral and non-neutral arbitrators, 256–273,.
    Party refuses to co-operate, 71–73.
Unilateral communications, 258–270, 284–294.
UNCITRAL model law, articles 5, 6, and 11, 252–255.

ATTORNEYS
See Arbitral Proceedings, Counsel.

AWARDS
    See also Enforcement of Awards; Setting Aside Awards.
Awards producing only obligatory effects, 741–744.
Confidentiality of, 495–501.
Deposit, authentication, certification of, 518–519, 542–550.
Dissenting opinions, 518–520.
Domestic awards, 643–678, 734–741.
Foreign awards, 651–662.
Form and content of, 518–530.
Heightened Judicial Scrutiny, 706–716.
Interim awards, 646–647, 749–750.
Interlocutory awards, 646–647.
Interventions after writing, 530–542.
Judicial deference or the lack of, 694–706.
Partial awards, 639–643, 745–750.
Rendered by third party, 528–530.
Res Judicata, 542–544, 606–609, 628, 639–643, 815–821.
Validity of, 542–550.

BANKRUPTCY
    See also Arbitrability.
Non-arbitrability of claims, 207–210.

BIAS
See Arbitrators, generally.

CHALLENGES
See Arbitrators, Selection, Challenges to appointment.
Challenge procedure, 379–388.

CHINA INTERNATIONAL TRADE ARBITRATION COMMISSION (CIETAC),
Experts, 468–478.
Correction of the award, 539.
Form and effect of award, 525–526.

CHOICE OF LAW
    Generally, 550–553.
Arbitrability, 247–251.
Arbitrators, role in, 599–605.
Express choice of law, 553–562, 412–417.
Lex arbitri, 411–425, 552–553, 562–574, 606–609.
Lex mercatoria, 574–576.

CHOICE OF LAW—Cont'd
Mandatory law, 553, 585–605.
Party autonomy, 42–48, 553–562, 577–584.
Procedural law, 64–66, 411–425.
Tacit choice of law, 412–417.
UNCITRAL Model Law.
    Determination of rules governing proce-
        dure, 419–422.
    Law governing the substance of a dis-
        pute, 421–422, 554–562.
Validity of the arbitration agreement, role
    of, 574–592.

COMITY
See Arbitral Proceedings, Concurrent Pro-
    ceedings; Awards, Concurrent. Pro-
    ceedings.

COMMUNICATIONS
See Arbitrators, Codes of Ethics; Arbitra-
    tors, Unilateral Communications.

COMPELLING ARBITRATION
    Generally, 48–54, 84–109, 339–341.
Appointing arbitrators, 342–348.
French Code of Civil Procedure, 87.
International Chamber of Commerce,
    99–101.
New York Convention, 84–85, 148–149.
UNCITRAL Model Law, 87–88.
Waiver of right to compel, 102–109.

COMPETENCE
See Jurisdiction.

CONCILIATION
    See also Settlement.

CONFIDENTIALITY
See Arbitrators, Codes of ethics; Discovery;
    Documents.

CONFLICT OF LAWS
See Choice of Law; Jurisdiction.

CONTRACTS
    See Also Arbitration Agreements, Arbi-
        trators.
Adaptation of (in contrast of arbitration),
    18–23.

CONTROL MECHANISMS
See Enforcement of Awards; Setting awards
    aside.

CONVENTIONS
    See also New York Convention.
Brussels Convention, 143, 235–246.
Geneva Convention
    Applicable law, 553–554.
    Concurrent proceedings, 627–628.
    Refusing enforcement, 795–798.
(New York) Convention on the Recognition
    and Enforcement of Foreign Arbitral
    Awards, 72, 102–109.

CONVENTIONS—Cont'd
United Nations Convention on Carriage of
    Goods by the Sea, 138–139.

CORRECTION
See Awards, Intervention after writing.

COUNTRIES
Appointment of neutral expert witnesses,
    comparative policies on, 462–468.
Arbitrability, comparative statutory defini-
    tions of, 210–211.
Arbitration, comparative policies on, 54–62.
Court scrutiny of arbitration agreements,
    comparative standards for, 350–356.
Right to counsel in arbitral proceedings,
    comparative policies on, 486–490.
Time limits, comparative policies on,
    514–516.

COUNSEL
See Arbitral Proceedings, Counsel.

DAMAGES
    See also Awards.
Costs, 480, 542–643.

DECISIONS
See Awards.

DEFAULT
    Generally, 34.
    See also Awards.
Delay tactics and refusal to arbitrate,
    102–109,.

DEFENSES
    See also Enforcement of Awards; Setting
        Aside Awards,
Changed circumstances, 203–207.

DISCOVERY
    See also Witnesses.
    Generally, 428–429.
Disclosure, 495–501.
Misuse, 501–504.
Problems, 455–462.
DISPUTE RESOLUTION
Unilateral and Bilateral approaches to dis-
    pute resolution, 2–8.

DOCUMENTS
    See also Arbitral Proceedings; Discovery;
        Evidence.
Confidentiality, 495–512.
Language issues, 478–481.

DUE PROCESS
Notice and opportunity to be heard,
    426–431, 647.
Notice of inspection by experts, 432–436.

ENFORCEMENT OF AWARDS
    See also Awards,
    Generally, 207–210, 606–609.
Arbitrating enforceability, 102–109.

ENFORCEMENT OF AWARDS—Cont'd

Awards producing only obligatory effects, 741–744.

Concurrent proceedings, 627–639.

Confirmation and conversion, 609–627.

Confirmation, leave to enforce, 607–609.

Consecutive proceedings, 627–628.

Convention on the Recognition and Enforcement of Foreign Arbitral Awards, 72–73, 102–109,.

Estoppel, 837–842.

Merger into judgment, 625–627.

New York Convention

 Awards subject to, 669–678, 733–750.

 Form requirements for enforceability, 165.

Partial Awards, 745–750.

Refusing enforcement, grounds for, 80–83, 643–651, 750–759.

 Award previously set aside, 552–553, 575–576, 795–815.

 Improper composition of arbitral authority, 73–79, 783–794.

 Improper procedure, 759–769, 783–794.

 Inarbitrability, 754–755.

 Insufficient notice or opportunity to be heard, 755–756, 769–773.

 Invalidity of the arbitration agreement, 191–193, 759–769.

 Outside scope of submission, 756–757, 773–782.

 Public policy, 753–754.

EQUITY

See Choice of Law, Lex mercatoria.

ESTOPPEL

See Jurisdiction; Enforcement of Awards.

ETHICS

See Arbitrators.

EVIDENCE

 See also Arbitral Proceedings, Discovery; Documents, Witnesses.

Generally, 428–431.

Recording presentation of, 450–453.

UNCITRAL Model Law, 419.

EXPEDITED ARBITRATION

Generally, 36–41.

Stockholm Rules for Expedited Arbitration, 40–41.

EXPENSES

 See also Arbitrators, Fees.

EXPERT TESTIMONY

See Witnesses.

FORUM SELECTION

See Arbitration Agreements

FRAUD

FRAUD—Cont'd

See Arbitration Agreements; Setting Aside Awards.

FRENCH CODE OF CIVIL PROCEDURE

Compelling arbitration 87.

HISTORY OF ARBITRATION

 Generally, 41–48.

Arbitration, change in attitude towards it, 48–54

Jurisdictional theory, 552–553, 571–573.

Standing of arbitration within the legal system, a comparative historical look, 54–62.

IMPARTIALITY

See Arbitrators; Setting Aside.

IMPLIED TERMS

See Arbitration Agreements.

INDEPENDENCE

See Arbitration Agreements, Separability of arbitral clauses.

INSTITUTIONAL ARBITRATION

 Generally, 27–35, 62–64.

Advantages, 29–34.

Arbitrators, 299–303.

INTERNAL REVIEW

See Review.

INTERNATIONAL CHAMBER OF COMMERCE (ICC)

 Generally, 27–35.

Adaptation of contracts, 22–23.

Choice of law, 554.

Default award, 34.

Expedited arbitration,36–40.

Fees, 35.

Institutional appointment of arbitrators, 68–69.

Language issues, 483.

Records and minutes, 450–455.

Terms of reference, 437–450.

 1998 rules, 437–438.

 1988 rules, 439–440.

Time limits, 516.

INTERPRETATION OF AWARDS

See Awards, Interventions after writing.

JUDGMENTS

See Enforcement of Awards, Conformation.

JURISDICTION

 See also Arbitration Agreements, Separability of arbitral clauses.

Courts,

 Judging threshold disputes over arbitrability, 99–101.

 New York Convention, declining jurisdiction, 628.

 Pending arbitral proceeding, effect of, 627–629.

JURISDICTION—Cont'd
Courts—Cont'd
Requirement of validity of the arbitration agreement, 348–351.
Jurisdiction by tacit submission or estoppel, 154–166.
Kompetenz–Kompetenz, 90–91, 109–136, 647, 698–699.

LANGUAGE
Generally, 478–486.

LAWYERS
See Arbitral Proceedings, Counsel.

LEX ARBITRI
See also Choice of Law.
Arbitral procedure, 411–425.
Conflict between party agreement and state norms, 80–83.

LEX MERCATORIA
See Choice of Law

LIS PENDENS
See Arbitral Proceedings, Concurrent proceedings

LITIGATION
Compared to arbitration, 23–27.

MANDATORY RULES OF LAW
See also Arbitrability; Choice of Law.
Generally, 236–246.
Arbitrability, 208–210.

MEDIATION
Generally, 8–16
WIPO Mediation, 11–15

MINI-TRIALS
Zurich Chamber of Commerce Rules for, 17

NEUTRALITY
See Arbitrators, Generally.

NEW YORK CONVENTION
Arbitrability, 207–217, 247–251.
Domestic policy limitations on, 207–217, 226.
Arbitration Agreements
Formal requirements, 88–90, 139–147, 159–166, 190, 545.
Validity, 191–193, 212–217.
Awards covered by the convention, 669–678, 733–734.
Compelling arbitration, 84–85.
Courts, Declining Jurisdiction, 628.
Recognition of Awards, 149–151, 551, 574–592.
Formal requirements, 545, 770–771.
Refusing enforcement, grounds for, 80–83, 643–651, 750–759.
Award previously set aside, 552–553, 575–576, 795–815.
Improper composition of arbitral authority, 73–79, 783–794.

NEW YORK CONVENTION—Cont'd
Refusing enforcement—Cont'd
Improper procedure, 759–769, 783–794.
Inarbitrability, 754–755.
Insufficient notice or opportunity to be heard, 755–756, 769–773.
Invalidity of the arbitration agreement, 191–193, 759–769.
Outside scope of submission, 756–757, 773–782.
Public policy, 753–754.
Review of the merits, 821–837.
Under article V(1) standards of NY Convention, 821–826,
For manifest disregard of law, 826–832.
Under article V(2)(b) standard of NY Convention, 832–837.

OBJECTIONS
Generally, 428–431.

PARTIALITY
See Arbitrators, Misconduct; Setting Aside Awards, Grounds for.

PARTIES
See also Arbitration Agreements; Arbitrators, Selection; Choice of law; Party autonomy.
Non-signatories to the arbitration agreement, 183–193.
Obligations towards arbitrators, 297–317.

PARTY AUTONOMY
See also Arbitrability, Arbitrators, Selection; Choice of Law.
Generally, 62.
Arbitrability, 209.
Choice of arbitrators, 68–71.
Party stipulation vs. institutional rules, 68–71.
Party stipulation vs. state norms, 71–83.
Prunier rule, 42–48.

POLICY
See Arbitrability; Enforcement of Awards; Setting Awards Aside.

PRELIMINARY DECISIONS
Validity of arbitration agreements, court determination of, 348–351.

RECOGNITION
See Enforcement of Awards.

RES JUDICATA
See Awards

REVIEW
See also Awards, Interventions after writing; Enforcement of Awards; Setting Aside Awards.
Generally, 643–651.
Merits, New York Convention, 821–837.
Under article V(1) standards of NY Convention, 821–826,

REVIEW—Cont'd
Merits—Cont'd
    For manifest disregard of law, 826–832.
    Under article V(2)(b) standard of NY
        Convention, 832–837.

SECRECY
    See also Arbitrators, Codes of Ethics.
Awards, prior to writing, 261.

SETTING ASIDE AWARDS
    Generally, 643–733.
Consequences of, 650.
Domestic and foreign awards, 643–678.
Due process and human rights, 716–728.
Expansion of the right to set aside,
    649–650.
Frivolous challenges, penalties for, 728–733.
Grounds for, 678–694.
Standard of review, 647, 694–716.
Waiver of right to set aside, 647–649.
UNCITRAL Model Law, 643–651.

SETTLEMENT
Arbitrators, role in, 289–291.

SEVERABILITY
See Arbitration Agreements, Separability of
    the arbitral clause.

SIGNATORIES
See Parties.

SITUS
    See also Choice of Law; Lex Arbitri.

STAY
See Enforcement of Awards.

STIPULATION
Party stipulation vs. institutional rules,
    68–71.
Party stipulation vs. state norms, 71–83.

TECHNICAL EXPERTISE
ICC rules, 18.

TESTIMONY
See Witnesses.

TRIBUNALS

TRIBUNALS—Cont'd
See Arbitral Proceedings; Arbitrators.

UNCITRAL Model Law
Arbitrators,
    Appointment of, 252–255.
    Appointment of sole arbitrator, 253–255.
    Challenges to appointment of, 385–388.
    Equal treatment of the parties, 418–422.
    Resignation of, 295–296.
Arbitration agreements,
    Enforcement, compelling arbitration,
        86–88, 221.
    Form requirements for arbitration
        agreements, 91, 136–154,
        154–161, 163–168.
    Waiver of form requirements,154–161.
Costs, 642–643.
Choice of law, 558.
    Choice of procedural law, 419–422.
    Rules applicable to the substance of dis-
        putes, 421–422, 554–562.
Dissenting opinions, 518–520.
Draft amendment to 'Article 7', 166–168.
Enforcement of awards,
    Effects of awards, 523.
    Form and contents of award, 518–522.
    Refusal of enforcement on grounds of
        non-arbitrability, 221.
Ex aequo et bono, amiable compositeur,
    560.
Jurisdiction and Kompetenz–Kompetenz
    90–91, 109–136.
Language issues, 478–486.
Setting Awards aside,
    Procedural deficiencies, 411.
    Set aside on grounds of non-arbitrabili-
        ty, 221, 643–651.

VENUE
See Arbitration Agreements; Arbitral Pro-
    ceedings; Situs.

WITNESSES
    See also Discovery; Evidence.
Experts, 462–478.
    UNCITRAL Rules, appointment of ex-
        perts, 463.

WRITING REQUIREMENT
See Arbitration Agreements, Form and
    drafting.

†